Twentieth-Century Literary Criticism

Guide to Gale Literary Criticism Series

For criticism on	Consult these Gale series
Authors now living or who died after December 31, 1999	*CONTEMPORARY LITERARY CRITICISM (CLC)*
Authors who died between 1900 and 1999	*TWENTIETH-CENTURY LITERARY CRITICISM (TCLC)*
Authors who died between 1800 and 1899	*NINETEENTH-CENTURY LITERATURE CRITICISM (NCLC)*
Authors who died between 1400 and 1799	*LITERATURE CRITICISM FROM 1400 TO 1800 (LC)* *SHAKESPEAREAN CRITICISM (SC)*
Authors who died before 1400	*CLASSICAL AND MEDIEVAL LITERATURE CRITICISM (CMLC)*
Authors of books for children and young adults	*CHILDREN'S LITERATURE REVIEW (CLR)*
Dramatists	*DRAMA CRITICISM (DC)*
Poets	*POETRY CRITICISM (PC)*
Short story writers	*SHORT STORY CRITICISM (SSC)*
Literary topics and movements	*HARLEM RENAISSANCE: A GALE CRITICAL COMPANION (HR)* *THE BEAT GENERATION: A GALE CRITICAL COMPANION (BG)* *FEMINISM IN LITERATURE: A GALE CRITICAL COMPANION (FL)* *GOTHIC LITERATURE: A GALE CRITICAL COMPANION (GL)*
Asian American writers of the last two hundred years	*ASIAN AMERICAN LITERATURE (AAL)*
Black writers of the past two hundred years	*BLACK LITERATURE CRITICISM (BLC-1)* *BLACK LITERATURE CRITICISM SUPPLEMENT (BLCS)* *BLACK LITERATURE CRITICISM: CLASSIC AND EMERGING AUTHORS SINCE 1950 (BLC-2)*
Hispanic writers of the late nineteenth and twentieth centuries	*HISPANIC LITERATURE CRITICISM (HLC)* *HISPANIC LITERATURE CRITICISM SUPPLEMENT (HLCS)*
Native North American writers and orators of the eighteenth, nineteenth, and twentieth centuries	*NATIVE NORTH AMERICAN LITERATURE (NNAL)*
Major authors from the Renaissance to the present	*WORLD LITERATURE CRITICISM, 1500 TO THE PRESENT (WLC)* *WORLD LITERATURE CRITICISM SUPPLEMENT (WLCS)*

ISSN 0276-8178

Volume 244

Twentieth-Century Literary Criticism

**Criticism of the
Works of Novelists, Poets, Playwrights,
Short Story Writers, and Other Creative Writers
Who Lived between 1900 and 1999,
from the First Published Critical
Appraisals to Current Evaluations**

Lawrence J. Trudeau
Project Editor

GALE
CENGAGE Learning

Detroit • New York • San Francisco • New Haven, Conn • Waterville, Maine • London

GALE
CENGAGE Learning

Twentieth-Century Literary Criticism, Vol. 244

Project Editor: Lawrence J. Trudeau

Dana Barnes, Sara Constantakis, Kathy D. Darrow, Matthew Derda, Kristen Dorsch, Dana Ferguson, Jeffrey W. Hunter, Michelle Kazensky, Jelena O. Krstović, Michelle Lee, Marie Toft, Jonathan Vereecke

Content Conversion: Katrina D. Coach, Gwen Tucker

Indexing Services: Laurie Andriot

Rights and Acquisitions: Margaret Chamberlain-Gaston, Kelly Quin, Tracie Richardson

Composition and Electronic Capture: Gary Leach

Manufacturing: Cynde Lentz

Product Manager: Janet Witalec

For product information and technology assistance, contact us at
Gale Customer Support, 1-800-877-4253.
For permission to use material from this text or product,
submit all requests online at **www.cengage.com/permissions.**
Further permissions questions can be emailed to
permissionrequest@cengage.com

Gale
27500 Drake Rd.
Farmington Hills, MI, 48331-3535

LIBRARY OF CONGRESS CATALOG CARD NUMBER 76-46132

ISBN-13: 978-1-4144-7024-5
ISBN-10: 1-4144-7024-X

ISSN 0276-8178

Printed in the United States of America
1 2 3 4 5 6 7 14 13 12 11 10

Contents

Preface

Since its inception *Twentieth-Century Literary Criticism* (*TCLC*) has been purchased and used by some 10,000 school, public, and college or university libraries. *TCLC* has covered more than 1000 authors, representing over 60 nationalities and nearly 50,000 titles. No other reference source has surveyed the critical response to twentieth-century authors and literature as thoroughly as *TCLC*. In the words of one reviewer, "there is nothing comparable available." *TCLC* "is a gold mine of information—dates, pseudonyms, biographical information, and criticism from books and periodicals—which many librarians would have difficulty assembling on their own."

Scope of the Series

TCLC is designed to serve as an introduction to authors who died between 1900 and 1999 and to the most significant interpretations of these author's works. Volumes published from 1978 through 1999 included authors who died between 1900 and 1960. The great poets, novelists, short story writers, playwrights, and philosophers of the period are frequently studied in high school and college literature courses. In organizing and reprinting the vast amount of critical material written on these authors, *TCLC* helps students develop valuable insight into literary history, promotes a better understanding of the texts, and sparks ideas for papers and assignments. Each entry in *TCLC* presents a comprehensive survey on an author's career or an individual work of literature and provides the user with a multiplicity of interpretations and assessments. Such variety allows students to pursue their own interests; furthermore, it fosters an awareness that literature is dynamic and responsive to many different opinions.

Every fourth volume of *TCLC* is devoted to literary topics. These topics widen the focus of the series from the individual authors to such broader subjects as literary movements, prominent themes in twentieth-century literature, literary reaction to political and historical events, significant eras in literary history, prominent literary anniversaries, and the literatures of cultures that are often overlooked by English-speaking readers.

TCLC is designed as a companion series to Gale's *Contemporary Literary Criticism,* (*CLC*) which reprints commentary on authors who died after 1999. Because of the different time periods under consideration, there is no duplication of material between *CLC* and *TCLC*.

Organization of the Book

A *TCLC* entry consists of the following elements:

- The **Author Heading** cites the name under which the author most commonly wrote, followed by birth and death dates. Also located here are any name variations under which an author wrote, including transliterated forms for authors whose native languages use nonroman alphabets. If the author wrote consistently under a pseudonym, the pseudonym is listed in the author heading and the author's actual name is given in parenthesis on the first line of the biographical and critical information. Uncertain birth or death dates are indicated by question marks. Single-work entries are preceded by a heading that consists of the most common form of the title in English translation (if applicable) and the name of its author.

- The **Introduction** contains background information that introduces the reader to the author, work, or topic that is the subject of the entry.

- The list of **Principal Works** is ordered chronologically by date of first publication and lists the most important works by the author. The genre and publication date of each work is given. In the case of foreign authors whose works have been translated into English, the English-language version of the title follows in brackets. Unless otherwise indicated, dramas are dated by first performance, not first publication. Lists of **Representative Works** by different authors appear with topic entries.

- Reprinted **Criticism** is arranged chronologically in each entry to provide a useful perspective on changes in critical evaluation over time. The critic's name and the date of composition or publication of the critical work are given at the beginning of each piece of criticism. Unsigned criticism is preceded by the title of the source in which it originally appeared. All titles by the author featured in the text are printed in boldface type. Footnotes are reprinted at the end of each essay or excerpt. In the case of excerpted criticism, only those footnotes that pertain to the excerpted texts are included. Criticism in topic entries is arranged chronologically under a variety of subheadings to facilitate the study of different aspects of the topic.

- A complete **Bibliographical Citation** of the original essay or book precedes each piece of criticism. Source citations in the Literary Criticism Series follow University of Chicago Press style, as outlined in *The Chicago Manual of Style,* 15th ed. (Chicago: The University of Chicago Press, 2003).

- Critical essays are prefaced by brief **Annotations** explicating each piece.

- An annotated bibliography of **Further Reading** appears at the end of each entry and suggests resources for additional study. In some cases, significant essays for which the editors could not obtain reprint rights are included here. Boxed material following the further reading list provides references to other biographical and critical sources on the author in series published by Gale.

Indexes

A **Cumulative Author Index** lists all of the authors that appear in a wide variety of reference sources published by Gale, including *TCLC*. A complete list of these sources is found facing the first page of the Author Index. The index also includes birth and death dates and cross references between pseudonyms and actual names.

A **Cumulative Topic Index** lists the literary themes and topics treated in *TCLC* as well as other Literature Criticism series.

A **Cumulative Nationality Index** lists all authors featured in *TCLC* by nationality, followed by the numbers of the *TCLC* volumes in which their entries appear.

An alphabetical **Title Index** accompanies each volume of *TCLC*. Listings of titles by authors covered in the given volume are followed by the author's name and the corresponding page numbers where the titles are discussed. English translations of foreign titles and variations of titles are cross-referenced to the title under which a work was originally published. Titles of novels, dramas, nonfiction books, and poetry, short story, or essay collections are printed in italics, while individual poems, short stories, and essays are printed in roman type within quotation marks.

In response to numerous suggestions from librarians, Gale also produces a paperbound edition of the *TCLC* cumulative title index. This annual cumulation, which alphabetically lists all titles reviewed in the series, is available to all customers. Additional copies of this index are available upon request. Librarians and patrons will welcome this separate index; it saves shelf space, is easy to use, and is recyclable upon receipt of the next edition.

Citing *Twentieth-Century Literary Criticism*

When citing criticism reprinted in the Literary Criticism Series, students should provide complete bibliographic information so that the cited essay can be located in the original print or electronic source. Students who quote directly from reprinted criticism may use any accepted bibliographic format, such as University of Chicago Press style or Modern Language Association (MLA) style. Both the MLA and the University of Chicago formats are acceptable and recognized as being the current standards for citations. It is important, however, to choose one format for all citations; do not mix the two formats within a list of citations.

The examples below follow recommendations for preparing a bibliography set forth in *The Chicago Manual of Style,* 15th ed. (Chicago: The University of Chicago Press, (2003); the first example pertains to material drawn from periodicals, the second to material reprinted from books:

Cardone, Resha. "Reappearing Acts: Effigies and the Resurrection of Chilean Collective Memory in Marco Antonio de la Parra's *La tierra insomne o La puta madre.*" *Hispania* 88, no. 2 (May 2005): 284-93. Reprinted in *Twentieth-Century Literary Criticism.* Vol. 206, edited by Thomas J. Schoenberg and Lawrence J. Trudeau, 356-65. Detroit: Gale, 2008.

Kuester, Martin. "Myth and Postmodernist Turn in Canadian Short Fiction: Sheila Watson, 'Antigone' (1959)." In *The Canadian Short Story: Interpretations,* edited by Reginald M. Nischik, pp. 163-74. Rochester, N.Y.: Camden House, 2007. Reprinted in *Twentieth-Century Literary Criticism.* Vol. 206, edited by Thomas J. Schoenberg and Lawrence J. Trudeau, 227-32. Detroit: Gale, 2008. The examples below follow recommendations for preparing a works cited list set forth in the Modern Language Association of America's MLA Handbook for Writers of Research Papers, 7th ed. (New York: MLA, 2009. Print); the first example pertains to material drawn from periodicals, the second to material reprinted from books:

Cardone, Resha. "Reappearing Acts: Effigies and the Resurrection of Chilean Collective Memory in Marco Antonio de la Parra's *La tierra insomne o La puta madre.*" *Hispania* 88.2 (May 2005): 284-93. Rpt. in *Twentieth-Century Literary Criticism.* Eds. Thomas J. Schoenberg and Lawrence J. Trudeau. Vol. 206. Detroit: Gale, 2008. 356-65. Print.

Kuester, Martin. "Myth and Postmodernist Turn in Canadian Short Fiction: Sheila Watson, 'Antigone' (1959)." *The Canadian Short Story: Interpretations.* Ed. Reginald M. Nischik. Rochester, N.Y.: Camden House, 2007. 163-74. Rpt. in *Twentieth-Century Literary Criticism.* Eds. Thomas J. Schoenberg and Lawrence J. Trudeau. Vol. 206. Detroit: Gale, 2008. 227-32. Print.

Suggestions are Welcome

Readers who wish to suggest new features, topics, or authors to appear in future volumes, or who have other suggestions or comments are cordially invited to call, write, or fax the Associate Product Manager:

Product Manager, Literary Criticism Series

Gale

27500 Drake Road

Farmington Hills, MI 48331-3535

1-800-347-4253 (GALE)

Fax: 248-699-8884

Acknowledgments

The editors wish to thank the copyright holders of the criticism included in this volume and the permissions managers of many book and magazine publishing companies for assisting us in securing reproduction rights. Following is a list of the copyright holders who have granted us permission to reproduce material in this volume of *TCLC*. Every effort has been made to trace copyright, but if omissions have been made, please let us know.

COPYRIGHTED MATERIAL IN *TCLC*, VOLUME 244, WAS REPRODUCED FROM THE FOLLOWING PERIODICALS:

Contemporary Literature, v. 14, summer, 1973. Copyright © 1973 by the Board of Regents of the University of Wisconsin System. Reproduced by permission.—*The Critical Review,* 1991. Reproduced by permission.—*Hartford Studies in Literature,* v. 2, 1970. Copyright © 1970 by the University of Hartford. Reproduced by permission.—*The Hudson Review,* v. 20, winter, 1967-1968. Copyright © 1967-1968 by The Hudson Review, Inc., translated by John Simon. Reproduced by permission.—*Italiana, v. 8, 1999.* Copyright © 1999, The Authors & The Editors. All rights reserved. Reproduced by permission.—*Journal of European Studies,* v. 36, September, 2006. Copyright © 2006 by SAGE Publications Ltd. Reproduced by permission of SAGE Publications.—*MLN,* v. 102, January, 1987. Copyright © 1987 by The Johns Hopkins University Press. Reproduced by permission.—*Modern Fiction Studies,* v. 18, spring, 1972. Copyright © 1972 by Purdue Research Foundation, West Lafayette, IN 47907. All rights reserved. Reproduced by permission of The Johns Hopkins University.—*The New Republic,* 1955. Copyright 1955 by The New Republic, Inc. Copyright 1955, renewed 1984 The New Republic, Inc. Reproduced by permission of *The New Republic.*—*Southerly,* v. 52, March, 1992 for "'This Is Not Understanding': Christina Stead's *For Love Alone*" by Nick Mansfield; v. 53, December, 1993 for "Re-reading Christina Stead" by Susan Sheridan; v. 61, 2001 for "'A Monster of Indecision': Abortion, Choice and Commodity Culture in Christina Stead's *The Beauties and Furies*" by Nicole Moore. All reproduced by permission of the authors.—*Studies in the Novel,* v. 11, summer, 1979. Copyright © 1979 by the University of North Texas. Reproduced by permission.—*World Literature Written in English,* v. 32, spring, 1992. Copyright © 1992 *World Literature Written in English.* Reproduced by permission.

COPYRIGHTED MATERIAL IN *TCLC,* VOLUME 244, WAS REPRODUCED FROM THE FOLLOWING BOOKS:

Blake, Ann. From "A Political Sense of Place," in *Christina Stead's Politics of Place.* University of Western Australia Press, 1999. Copyright © Ann Blake 1999. Reproduced by permission of the author.—Geering, R. G. From *Christina Stead.* Twayne Publishers, Inc., 1969. Copyright © 1969 by Twayne Publishers, Inc. All rights reserved. Reproduced by permission of Gale, a part of Cengage Learning.—Gribble, Jennifer. From *Christina Stead.* Oxford University Press, 1994. Copyright © Jennifer Gribble 1994. Reproduced by permission of the author.—Herr, Christopher J. From *Clifford Odets and American Political Theatre.* Praeger, 2003. Copyright © 2003 by Christopher J. Herr. All rights reserved. Reproduced with permission of ABC-CLIO, LLC, Santa Barbara, CA.—Kiernan, Brian. From *Images of Society and Nature: Seven Essays on Australian Novels.* Oxford University Press, 1971. Copyright © Oxford University Press 1971. Reproduced by permission of the author.—Lancaster, Rosemary. From *Je Suis Australienne: Remarkable Women in France, 1880-1945.* University of Western Australia Press, 2008. Copyright © 2008 Rosemary Lancaster. Reproduced by permission.—Mendelsohn, Michael J. From "The Early Plays: Written in Anger," in *Clifford Odets: Humane Dramatist.* Everett/Edwards, Inc., 1969. Copyright 1969 by Michael J. Mendelsohn. All rights reserved. Reproduced by permission of the author.—Miller, Gabriel. From *Clifford Odets.* Frederick Ungar, 1989. Copyright © 1989 by Gabriel Miller. All rights reserved. Republished with permission of The Continuum International Publishing Company, conveyed through Copyright Clearance Center, Inc.—Minghelli, Giuliana. From *In the Shadow of the Mammoth: Italo Svevo and the Emergence of Modernism.* University of Toronto Press, 2002. Copyright © University of Toronto Press, Incorporated 2002. Reproduced by permission.—Morrison, Fiona. From "A 'Cruel Book': Menippean Satire and the Female Satirist in *I'm Dying Laughing,*" in *The Magic Phrase: Critical Essays on Christina Stead.* Edited by Margaret Harris. University of Queensland Press, 2000. Compilation, introductory essay and bibliography © Margaret Harris 2000. Copyright in the individual essays remains with the authors. Reproduced by permission.—Murray, Edward. From *Clifford Odets: The Thirties and After.* Frederick Ungar Publishing Co., 1968. Copyright © 1968 by Frederick Ungar Publishing Co., Inc. Republished with permission of The Continuum International Publishing Company, conveyed through Copyright Clearance Center, Inc.—Puppa,

Gale Literature Product Advisory Board

The members of the Gale Literature Product Advisory Board—reference librarians from public and academic library systems—represent a cross-section of our customer base and offer a variety of informed perspectives on both the presentation and content of our literature products. Advisory board members assess and define such quality issues as the relevance, currency, and usefulness of the author coverage, critical content, and literary topics included in our series; evaluate the layout, presentation, and general quality of our printed volumes; provide feedback on the criteria used for selecting authors and topics covered in our series; provide suggestions for potential enhancements to our series; identify any gaps in our coverage of authors or literary topics, recommending authors or topics for inclusion; analyze the appropriateness of our content and presentation for various user audiences, such as high school students, undergraduates, graduate students, librarians, and educators; and offer feedback on any proposed changes/enhancements to our series. We wish to thank the following advisors for their advice throughout the year.

Clifford Odets
1906-1963

American playwright and screenwriter.

The following entry provides an overview of Odets's life and works. For additional information on his career, see *CLC*, Volumes 2, 28, and 98.

INTRODUCTION

Clifford Odets is remembered as one of the foremost American playwrights of the 1930s. With the production of his best-known dramatic works, including *Awake and Sing!* (1935), *Till the Day I Die* (1935), and *Waiting for Lefty* (1935), Odets established a reputation as an advocate of the proletariat and a champion of leftist political ideals. In these early plays the author depicted the plight of working-class Americans, particularly Jewish-Americans, as they struggled against corruption and materialism within Depression-era society. Critics have also praised Odets for his innovative staging techniques and for introducing a ground-breaking dramatic style that combined grand aesthetic ideals with the raw vernacular of American street culture. In later works Odets drifted away from the social and political activism that characterized his early successes, focusing instead on psychological and personal themes, including familial and marital discord, sexual relations, guilt, and redemption. He also moved in and out of Hollywood throughout his career and devoted much of his time to writing screenplays. As a result, his reputation as an idealist and activist playwright waned during the final decades of his life, and he never recaptured the critical acclaim he enjoyed during the 1930s. Nevertheless, Odets remains a figure of historical significance in American theater, who is generally recognized as a stylistic innovator and a keen spokesman of his times.

BIOGRAPHICAL INFORMATION

Odets was born July 18, 1906, in Philadelphia, to Louis and Pearl Geisinger Odets, who were recent Jewish immigrants from Eastern Europe. The family moved several times to facilitate Louis Odets's various business ventures in advertising and printing. As a result, the author's childhood years were spent alternately between Philadelphia and the fledgling middle-class Jewish neighborhoods in New York's Bronx region. In his youth Odets read avidly, particularly the novels of Vic-

tor Hugo, and became interested in acting and performing, participating in school theater and local amateur productions. His grades were poor, however, and at the age of seventeen he dropped out of high school. He found small acting jobs during this time and wrote his first dramatic works, two one-act plays, one of which was broadcast on WFBH in New York in 1926.

Odets continued to pursue an acting career in New York, and by the time the stock market crashed in 1929, he had landed several small roles on Broadway. He performed frequently with the Theatre Guild, an elite organization that featured the work of important playwrights, including Eugene O'Neill, and he later joined the Group Theatre, founded by former Guild members Harold Clurman, Cheryl Crawford, and Lee Strasberg. During the early 1930s Odets began writing longer and more ambitious plays, and in 1933 he completed his first full-length drama, initially titled "I Got the Blues," but later renamed *Awake and Sing!* when it was produced on Broadway in 1935. In 1934 Odets joined the Communist Party, which he left a few months later, and completed his next play, *Waiting for Lefty,* which reflected his growing leftist sentiments. The drama won the New League Theatre-*New Masses* playwriting contest in 1934 and premiered on Broadway a year later, on a double-bill with *Till the Day I Die.*

In 1936 Odets accepted an offer to write screenplays in Hollywood and was paid twenty-five hundred dollars a week for his adaptation of Charles G. Booth's novel *The General Died at Dawn,* which starred Gary Cooper. Odets continued to write for the Group Theatre in New York and moved back to the city to work on the Group's production of his next play, *The Silent Partner.* But in January 1937 the company temporarily disbanded and *The Silent Partner* remained unrealized. Odets returned to Hollywood shortly thereafter to work on the screenplay for a Civil War movie, called *Gettysburg,* which was never filmed.

Severely criticized by the New York press for abandoning the theater and selling out to Hollywood, Odets was determined to produce another successful play. In the summer of 1937 he returned to New York to revive the Group Theatre and produce *Golden Boy,* a work he had partially completed in Hollywood. Eventually staged in November of that year, the play enjoyed a successful run on Broadway and later toured the United States and Europe. During the next year Odets divided his time between Hollywood and New York, and in November of 1938 produced his next major play, *Rocket to the Moon.* He followed this success with his first comedy, *Night Music* (1940), which failed to win audiences and ultimately marked the decline of the Group Theatre.

During the 1940s Odets's affiliation with the Group Theatre dwindled, and in 1942 he made a permanent move to Los Angeles. In Hollywood he contributed to several successful films, including Frank Capra's *It's a Wonderful Life,* and wrote and directed *None but the Lonely Heart* (1944), based on the novel by Richard Llewellyn and featuring Cary Grant and Ethel Barrymore, who won an Oscar for her performance. During the late 1940s Odets was placed on a list of suspected communists and sympathizers working in Hollywood. Increasingly disillusioned with the commercialism of the movie industry, he began writing a new play for the stage and contemplated a move back to New York. He returned to Broadway in 1949, with the production of *The Big Knife,* which he followed with *The Country Girl* in 1950.

In 1951 Odets was once again targeted for his previous affiliation with the Communist Party and finally cooperated with the House Un-American Activities Committee by naming communist members in the Group Theatre. The decision brought scorn and ridicule from both his colleagues and the media, and his literary reputation suffered significantly. In 1954 he produced his last completed stage play, the critically successful *The Flowering Peach.* Odets returned to Hollywood soon after and over the next few years worked on various movie scripts and, later, wrote for a television series. In the final year of his life he adapted his former work, *Golden Boy,* into a musical for Sammy Davis, Jr. On August 14, 1963, Odets died of stomach cancer at the age of fifty-seven.

MAJOR WORKS

During the early years of his literary career Odets was primarily concerned with social and political issues, and his dramatic works often demonstrate a sympathy with the struggles of the working class. In *Awake and Sing!* the author exposes the banalities and tensions of life for the Bergers, a modern Jewish and middle-class family living in the Bronx. Bessie, the materialistic matriarch of the family, rules over her meek husband, Myron, as well as her two grown children, Hennie and Ralph. As a result of Bessie's overbearing nature and interference, Hennie is forced into an arranged marriage to cover up a pregnancy, while Ralph hides his romantic attachments from his mother. Bessie's father, Jacob, a passionate Jewish immigrant, also lives with the family and serves as a mentor for Ralph, schooling him in such diverse topics as opera, religious mysticism, and

radical socialism. Encouraging Ralph to eschew his mother's materialism and remake the world according to his own ideals, Jacob ultimately sacrifices his life to provide insurance money so that his grandson can assert his independence. Meanwhile, Hennie abandons her infant and leaves her loveless marriage to start a new life with Moe, a World War I amputee. In addition to offering a critique of materialism and the American capitalist system, Odets also challenges middle-class values in the play and explores themes related to individual freedom.

In another significant early work, *Waiting for Lefty,* which was inspired by a violent strike of New York taxi-drivers in 1934, Odets confronts the exploitation of American workers and the hypocrisies of their union leaders. The play consists of a series of scenes, in which the striking workers act out their own stories at a meeting, while they wait for their leader, Lefty, who will serve as their negotiator with the company and the union bosses. Fatt, the foreman, and other union bosses preside over the meeting, and along with armed gunman attempt to persuade the workers to settle. One by one the strikers come on stage and enact the struggles of their daily lives, as they face injustice or racial discrimination, fight corruption, and attempt to support their families with meager wages. At the end of the play, when someone announces that Lefty has been murdered, the workers reject the idea of compromise and demand another strike. Odets has been credited with using innovative staging techniques in *Waiting for Lefty* and introducing a bold new vernacular to the American stage.

Till the Day I Die, a one-act play that premiered with *Waiting for Lefty,* explores themes related to political persecution, strength in the face of adversity, and self-sacrifice. Inspired by the persecution of German communists and Jews under rule of the Nazis, the play consists of seven scenes and features Ernst, the protagonist, and an underground cell of agitators, who are being pursued by the Gestapo for their subversive activities. As the play progresses Ernst is arrested by the Gestapo and eventually tortured when he refuses to provide information on his comrades. The Nazis release him, however, in hopes that he will lead them to his group, which includes Ernst's brother, Carl, and his girlfriend, Tilly. Realizing the probable motivation for Ernst's release, the group subsequently cuts off all contact with him. After being arrested and released again under surveillance, Ernst decides that the only way to free his comrades of danger is to commit suicide.

With *Rocket to the Moon,* Odets began to turn away from the political and social themes that characterized his earlier dramatic works. In this play he explores psychological themes, focusing on such issues as marital discord and sexuality. The protagonist, Ben Stark, a dentist, is an average man, crippled by his own indecision, spiritual impotence, and inability to act. Suffering through both financial strain and the tensions associated with an unhappy marriage, Stark pursues an affair with his young secretary, Cleo, who attracts the attention of numerous suitors. Stark is ultimately unable to choose between Cleo and his wife, however, and eventually Cleo leaves all of her suitors, including Stark, to pursue her freedom and a more meaningful romantic relationship. After Cleo departs, Stark is finally able to appreciate his wife and the vows they have made to one another.

Corruption and the corrosive effects of American commercialism are the major themes of *The Big Knife,* one of Odets's last major plays. In this work the protagonist, Charlie Castle, is a Philadelphia-born actor turned movie star, who, at the height of his acting career, faces the deterioration of his personal life. Estranged from his wife, Marion, and having lost his artistic passion, Charlie is also haunted by the death of a young boy he killed in a car accident, a crime for which his loyal publicist took the blame. Meanwhile, Charlie's mistress, Dixie, an aspiring actress, is a witness to the crime and threatens to blackmail him. The situation is further complicated when Hollywood studio representatives suggest that Dixie can be "gotten rid of." Marion, realizing that her husband's ideals have been lost to the materialism of Hollywood, finally leaves Charlie. At the end of the play the protagonist chooses suicide as an act of redemption, in an effort to reclaim his lost integrity.

CRITICAL RECEPTION

Odets first drew attention as a playwright with the production of *Waiting for Lefty,* which, though written after *Awake and Sing!,* debuted first, in January of 1935. Audiences responded favorably to the play's focus on the stories of everyday working individuals, and its unapologetic use of American slang. Theater reviewers also praised the play but were ambivalent over Odets's leftist political message in the work, leading some to label him a radical propagandist. The recognition Odets achieved as a result of *Waiting for Lefty* facilitated the production on Broadway of *Awake and Sing!,* also in 1935, which reinforced his reputation as an innovative and idealistic new playwright on the American stage.

His next play, *Paradise Lost,* which premiered in December of 1935, was less successful, in part because of its more poetic, less plot-driven focus, and closed after only a few weeks. After a brief hiatus in Hollywood Odets returned to the New York stage with *Golden Boy* in 1937, which was hailed as a triumphant return for the author, as well as the Group Theatre company. *Rocket to the Moon,* which appeared the following year,

was also favorably received, particularly for its exploration of emotional and psychological themes, as opposed to political ideas, which some critics perceived as an indication of the playwright's growing maturity.

While Odets was consistently regarded as one of the most promising new playwrights during the latter half of the 1930s, his reputation waned after 1940, a change resulting, in part, from the commercial failure of such works as *Night Music* and *Clash by Night* (1941). As some scholars have noted, however, the playwright's tumultuous personal life overshadowed his literary achievements during this time and influenced popular and critical reactions to his work. Odets received some recognition for his final plays, *The Big Knife, The Country Girl,* and *The Flowering Peach,* which was shortlisted for the Pulitzer Prize in 1955, but he never fully overcame the perception that he sold out his ideals for commercial success and money in Hollywood and failed to develop as an artist. At the time of his death in 1963, Odets was generally considered a playwright of great promise who had never fully lived up to his potential.

In the decades following his death Odets's contributions as a playwright and screenwriter received ambivalent reactions from scholars of American drama. Most continued to maintain that his best works were those written earliest in his career, during the socially turbulent period of the Great Depression. While some critics, such as Malcolm Goldstein, criticized the repetitive nature of his work and claimed that Odets failed to evolve beyond the materialist themes of his early plays, other commentators, such as Robert J. Griffin, Edward Murray, and Michael J. Mendelsohn, emphasized the author's formal and stylistic achievements as a young playwright. Griffin characterized Odets as an "imaginative spokesman" of his times and argued that his "humanitarian" focus and vivid characterizations elevated his work above the category of agitprop drama. Murray lauded Odets's dramaturgical achievements, including his "complex construction, his rich characterizations," and "his unforgettable dialogue," and described the author as "one of the finest writers we have produced in the American theater."

In more recent years scholars such as Gabriel Miller, Michael Woolf, and Christopher J. Herr, have revisited lesser-known works in the playwright's canon and reassessed his importance within the greater scope of American theater. While Miller has explored Odets's use of symbol and allegory in later plays, such as *The Big Knife* and *Golden Boy,* Herr has examined the author's treatment of popular culture in his late works, stating that Odets attempted to show "how popular forms both embodied the American Dream and betrayed it." Woolf, however, has reconsidered several presumptions regarding Odets's "complex career," refuting the generally accepted ideas that his work should be relegated to the category of proletarian literature, and that his creative ability suffered as a result of his involvement with Hollywood.

Despite the commonly held opinion that Odets remains a marginal figure of twentieth-century American literature, critics have increasingly acknowledged the artistry of his writing and the innovations he brought to the theater in the 1930s and later. Woolf has asserted that "the tendency to categorize Odets as a writer contained and bounded by the 1930s distorts the real value of the work which encompasses the emotional signs of those nightmarish times but goes beyond them," adding that he should be regarded as "a playwright whose work sought to address broad issues of human behaviour, passion and inspiration," and not just political themes. Woolf concludes that Odets's "considerable talent was to encompass" the complexities of his times, "and express them in forms that were passionate, articulate, and, at times, profound."

PRINCIPAL WORKS

Awake and Sing! (play) 1935

Paradise Lost (play) 1935

Till the Day I Die (play) 1935

Waiting for Lefty (play) 1935

The General Died at Dawn [adaptor; from the novel by Charles G. Booth] (screenplay) 1936

Golden Boy (play) 1937

Rocket to the Moon (play) 1938

Night Music (play) 1940

Clash by Night (play) 1941

The Russian People [adaptor; from the play by Konstantin Simonov] (play) 1942

None but the Lonely Heart [adaptor; from the novel by Richard Llewellyn] (screenplay) 1944

Deadline at Dawn [adaptor; from the novel by William Irish] (screenplay) 1946

Humoresque [adaptor, with Zachary Gold; from the short story by Fannie Hurst] (screenplay) 1946

The Big Knife (play) 1949

The Country Girl (play) 1950

The Flowering Peach (play) 1954

Sweet Smell of Success [adaptor, with Ernest Lehman; from the novella *Tell Me About It Tomorrow* by Lehman] (screenplay) 1957

The Story on Page One (screenplay) 1960

Wild in the Country [adaptor; from the novel *The Lost Country* by I. R. Salamanca] (screenplay) 1961

CRITICISM

R. Baird Shuman (essay date 1962)

SOURCE: Shuman, R. Baird. "The Locust and the Peach." In *Clifford Odets*, pp. 119-45. New York: Twayne Publishers, Inc., 1962.

[*In the following essay, Shuman critiques Odets's three late plays,* The Big Knife, The Country Girl, *and* The Flowering Peach, *maintaining that while these works "mark a redirection of the author's interests," and show him "grappling with new techniques and with new social problems," they nonetheless give evidence of his ongoing concern with "the effect of mendacity on a broad social situation."*]

> "There is idealism
> in just survival."
>
> (From *The Flowering Peach*)

Clifford Odets spent the years following **Clash by Night** writing motion picture scenarios in Hollywood. He was not to produce another stage play until 1948, when he finished working on **A Winter Journey**; renamed **The Big Knife,** it reached Broadway early in 1949. This play was followed in 1950 by **The Country Girl,** and in 1954 by **The Flowering Peach.**

Odets' years in the film industry had brought about very noticeable changes in him. If **Waiting for Lefty** and **Till the Day I Die** had reflected the vigorous anger of his youth, and if **Rocket to the Moon** and **Clash by Night** had revealed a cynicism not evident in the younger Odets, then surely **The Big Knife** gave evidence, first, of an Odets who had grown immeasurably in dramatic technique and, second, of an Odets who was proving himself sufficiently versatile to write with as much feeling about problems of the well-to-do as, fifteen years earlier, he had written of the problems of those who were oppressed through poverty. **The Country Girl** represented, in many respects, a continuation of the promise found in **The Big Knife.** The play dealt superficially with theatrical life, but more deeply with the effects of alcoholism and insecurity. The hero, Frank Elgin, is grappling with the problems of conquering his alcoholism so that he may make a comeback as an actor. The play is basically concerned with the deep and complicated insecurities which face him and over which he must gain control.

When it appeared that Odets had settled into a pattern of writing plays about show business and the people in it, he surprised his public and the critics. At the same time, he gave further evidence of his versatility with the presentation of **The Flowering Peach,** a warm and humorous allegory based on the biblical account of Noah and the flood. This play reached Broadway in December, 1954, and ran for some four months.

Odets is presently hopeful that he will be able to produce alternately film plays and stage plays. He recently was quoted by the *New York Herald Tribune* as saying with assurance and genuine conviction, "My best plays are ahead."

I. *The Big Knife*

In a statement to the press in 1938, Mr. Odets said that ". . . acting is a whorish thing." What he meant becomes fully clear in *The Big Knife*, a play which chronicles the events in the life of a highly successful actor who ultimately commits suicide. This actor, Charlie Castle, is one of the leading cinema idols in the country and, as such, is worth millions of dollars to the studio which holds his contract. Marcus Hoff, a motion-picture tycoon, is determined that Charlie shall sign with his studio and has had an unprecedented contract drawn up offering the actor nearly four million dollars for his services during the next fourteen years and offering him, also, the right to reject any scripts which he does not deem worthy of his talents.

But Charlie does not wish to sign such a contract because his wife Marion, who is now living apart from him, vows that she will not return if he makes such a commitment. However, a simple refusal to sign is not possible; for Marcus Hoff is blackmailing Charlie, threatening that if he does not accept the contract, he will make public the fact that Charlie is responsible for a hit-and-run death for which his publicity man, Buddy Bliss, out of friendship for Charlie, took the responsibility and subsequently served time in prison. Because of his fear of this revelation Charlie finally signs the contract; but, having signed it, he cannot live with himself. He comes to realize that he is little more than a chattel. His self-respect has been sold for a price, and without self-respect Charlie cannot face himself. He does the only thing left for him to do; he slashes his wrists and dies.

Odets' identification with Charlie Castle is very obvious in many instances throughout the play. Castle, like Odets, had read Victor Hugo and, in the play, he states that ". . . Hugo's the one who helped me nibble my way through billions of polly seeds. Sounds grandiose, but Hugo said to me: 'Be a good boy, Charlie. Love people, do good, help the lost and fallen, make the world happy, if you can!'" (*The Big Knife*, Random House Edition, p. 9. All subsequent references to the play shall be to this edition.) Stated with simplicity, this was the ideal by which Charlie Castle desired to live; it was his awareness of the gap between his ideal and the reality of his life which caused him to be essentially a weakling and an escapist—a man who, in his mid-thirties, could look forward to very little except the forgetfulness which he found in an overindulgence in liquor.

Actually, Charlie had accepted fame in exchange for his manhood. He had become an object to be haggled over, to be lent out, to be subdivided, just as Joe Bonaparte had become such an object in *Golden Boy*. His loss of identity, first engineered by the studio, which made him change his name from Cass to Castle, increases with the action of the play. His recognition of this loss of identity is fully realized when, in conversation with a neighbor, Charlie says, "I'll bet you don't know why we all wear these beautiful, expensive ties in Hollywood. . . . It's a military tactic—we hope you won't notice our faces" (106).

Charlie, at the acme of success in his profession, has reached his nadir as a man; he is not in control of his own destiny. He can never act naturally, never speak frankly, because someone is always watching and listening; someone is always eager to help lead the great man to his downfall. He tells his wife that "free speech is the highest-priced luxury in this country today" (16). Charlie must, in this atmosphere, have his thoughts shaped for him and must yield his ideals utterly to the forces which have brought about his success. He has no choice but to make an amoeba-like adaptation to the sort of life which is now inevitable for him. He must pay heed to the words of Marcus Hoff's toady, Smiley Coy, who advises him, "Don't study life—get used to it" (81). It is in such casual statements as this that one finds Odets' most cutting, most subjective criticism of the film industry.

Only in *Till the Day I Die* and in *Golden Boy* has Odets produced such a clearly defined and fully delineated central character as Charlie Castle. In *Waiting for Lefty* there was no single central character; rather, the working class emerged as hero. In *Awake and Sing!* and in *Paradise Lost,* the emergent character was a composite family character. In the plays dealing with love, the emphasis was not on a single character. However, *The Big Knife* revolves around Charlie Castle, who, peculiarly enough, is probably the weakest character in the play. The only thing which makes him central is that he can make money for his studio. Marcus Hoff can use Charlie as a means towards making millions. Buddy Bliss and Dixie Evans are both attracted to Charlie because of the position which Hoff has given him. Charlie, as an individual, does not assume any overwhelming proportions in the play, hence it can be only a false Hollywood glamor, contrived by the studio, which draws people to him. Even the kindly Nat Danziger has no deep intrinsic feeling for Charlie. He is, of necessity, involved with him in business dealings, and his nature is so obviously outgoing and humanitarian that he does all in his power to give Charlie the kindly counsel of which he stands in need; however, Odets does not give the reader cause to suppose that Nat could have become Charlie's friend through any natural affinity.

Marion Castle's relationship to her husband also boils down essentially to a matter of economics. Marion, the daughter of a noted history professor, has always known security and been socially above Charlie, whose background is sketched in at the beginning of the play when, in telling about his uncle, he says, "He merely raised me when my parents died. . . . They were awfully poor, my aunt and uncle. I made money too late to be able to help them. I regret that" (9). The cultural gap between the two is re-emphasized throughout the play in various incidental ways, as when Marion asks Charlie, "Why do you keep using words like 'ain't'?" (60).

Marion, because of her inborn security, something which Charlie will never be able to attain, is essentially a fearless person. Audacious enough to tell Patty Benedict, the gossip columnist, to mind her own business, she also stands her ground with Marcus Hoff, one of the most powerful men in Hollywood, when she says, "Mr. Hoff, can't you stop talking about yourself?" (124). To Charlie, who is very much in love with her, she represents all that is not Hollywood. Hank Teagle characterized the relationship between them very well when he said to Charlie, "I know that Marion stands in your life for idealism . . . and that you've wounded her and it" (109). Charlie cannot deny this. It is clear to him that, just as their expected child has been killed by an abortion, so has his idealism been annihilated by the false and destructive values which he had to accept as the price of success in Hollywood.

Odets' most direct criticism of Hollywood is found in *The Big Knife*. Hollywood is depicted as the place of "sin" which Odets had called it some years earlier. Even as the play opens, the venomous Patty Benedict gives a vivid insight into Hollywood's social attitudes:

PATTY:

I like the airiness of this room. . . . French paintings, dear one?

CHARLIE:

Yeah.

PATTY:

Don't you buy American any more?

CHARLIE:

. . . I don't know one painter from another. . . . I wouldn't want my fans to say I've gone arty, would I?

(6)

Because Patty is a widely read columnist, and because she is basically so warped and unwholesome, every question she asks must be answered with extreme caution. She is to be fenced with rather than talked to. Her question—"Don't you buy American any more?"—is an irrelevant and unfair one. Charlie's answer, while a safe one, is also characteristic: the implication is obviously that the buyers of paintings are more prestige-conscious than artistically aware. Finally Charlie admits in this bit of dialogue that he must live and act constantly in the shadow of what his fans are likely to think of him; for him to admit a proclivity towards one of the finer aspects of human endeavor would be damaging to him professionally.

There seems in this situation to be an echo of the central conflict of *Golden Boy*; but the deeper conflict is the one within the author who is faced with the problems of writing what is within him, or of producing popular films which he knows to be of limited artistic value. Down to the present time, Odets has not completely solved the problem of merging his artistic integrity with practical necessity, and the question of how to meet both the artistic and practical needs in his life is still one of his major personal problems. Marion speaks directly of this conflict when she tells Charlie that "Your sin is living against your own nature. You're denatured—that's your sin!" (62). But by this time Charlie is so far removed from his real nature that he can no longer be said to have one. He has lost his personality; life has eroded his ideals to such a point that the only thing that remains of him is his likeness on a kiosk. His life is one of constant retreat.

The insincerity of Hollywood is a major factor in bringing about Charlie's disillusionment. The film magnates who stoop to blackmailing him are the very people who profess adoration of him. Charlie, disgusted after having been forced into signing his fourteen-year contract, very tellingly says, "The free giving of hearts out here begins to freeze my blood" (47). His eyes are open to the real Hollywood: the Hollywood which can pay a man a thousand dollars a week for four years and not even ". . . remember his name or what he wrote" (114); the Hollywood which can ponder over how a man is able to live so well ". . . on four thousand a week" (36-37).

In writing a critique of life in Hollywood, Odets has not departed so far from his original interests and ideals as many of his critics would have one believe. One must remember Odets' statement: "All of my plays . . . deal with one subject; the struggle not to have life nullified by circumstances, false values, anything." All of Odets' plays have been concerned with the problems brought about by the effect of mendacity on a broad social situation. In *The Big Knife* he has chosen to write of a level of society with which he had not previously concerned himself, and many critics viewed this as a weakness, as a retreat from the social problems which were at the heart of the earlier Odets plays. But who is to limit the playwright in this way? It must be remembered that Charlie Cass came from the same sort of background which Odets had been writing about in his earlier plays and from which Odets himself had come. The play is concerned with the effect of a notably false society upon a person who, by circumstances, is forced into it. Odets is able to write of this problem with feeling and conviction because of his intimate personal association with it.

Charlie ultimately is forced into committing suicide because his life has ceased to have any meaning. Hollywood has nullified all of the challenge which his life had held during the early days of his marriage when he and Marion had struggled to eke out an existence in New York. In addressing Hank Teagle, Charlie makes his desperation quite clear:

> And do you say in your book it isn't even easy to go to hell today? That there's nothing left to sin against? . . . Correction! There's health left to sin against! Health—the last, nervous conviction of the time! We're sick at heart, but we'll increase the life span! What for? Nobody knows! . . . You're right, Hank. Your hero's half a man, neither here nor there, dead from the gizzard up. Stick him with a pin and see, psst! No feelings! When I came home from Germany . . . I saw most of the war dead were here, not in Africa and Italy. And Roosevelt was dead . . . and we plunged ourselves, all of us, into the noble work of making the buck reproduce itself!
>
> (111)

But even more telling is a statement in the very last minute of the play. Charlie, speaking to Marion, says, "You see, everyone needs a cause to touch greatness" (137). This statement reveals a great deal about Charlie, but even more about Odets.

The Big Knife was received in New York with great interest and mixed feelings. John Gassner indicated that since Odets' rise to prominence, only two young writers, Tennessee Williams and Arthur Miller, had written with such animation. Certainly the force of this animation is felt in such a scene as that in which Charlie is feeling remorseful because of the problems which he has caused Nat, his agent. He says, "Why did I add this burden to that grotesque, devoted soul? Did you ever notice? He moves his lips when he reads" (136). This sort of acute and revealing observation reminds one of the careful artistry of a Rembrandt who so fully caught the nuances of his characters' expressions that he made them seem alive. In another scene, Marion says that ". . . to be faithful . . . gives you that loony, old-fashioned moral grandeur of an equestrian statue in the park" (25). This sort of keen observation and expression has helped to establish Odets as a foremost American playwright.

Writing in *School and Society,* William H. Beyer, after calling *The Big Knife* ". . . bitter, angry, diffused, and garrulous diatribe, a sprawling melodrama of the sinister ways of Hollywood," admits that "in the lesser characters . . . Mr. Odets has given us some sharp, compelling characterizations." However, Beyer did not feel that *The Big Knife* represented a step forward for Odets, and he called the play contrived. Miss Wyatt of the *Catholic World* called the play a "Hollywood nightmare," and looked upon it as a purge for the author, who, she hoped, would go on to write a really excellent play. Wolcott Gibbs, writing in *The New Yorker,* labeled the play ". . . an enormous commotion"; he was disappointed at not finding in it a suggestion of more universal moral implications.

Possibly the most just and balanced evaluation of *The Big Knife* was that written by Kappo Phelan in *Commonweal.* While she was not entirely pleased with the play, she admitted that ". . . the astonishing rhetoric Clifford Odets has welded to his astonishing plot in this particular performance is almost indescribable." She gives a perspicacious estimate of Odets when she writes, "It would seem, adding his promotion to his history, that he [Odets] is angry about his position in our society: a position of a man who thinks to the left and at the same time is holding jobs as far to the right as possible." She makes what seems a legitimate criticism in objecting to the fact that the catastrophe of the play is presented in talk rather than in action.

Most of the criticism of the play dealt with specifics and with the immediate story of the play. As a result, some of the significant, far-reaching implications were lost. Brooks Atkinson pointed out that ". . . one of Mr. Odets' virtues [is] that he always tries to write on the high plane of dramatic art, and he has the talent to do so." Some critics lost sight of this fact, even though Odets himself had said that ". . . essentially it [*The Big Knife*] dealt with the tragedy of lost integrity everywhere."

II. *The Country Girl*

It has been suggested that *The Country Girl* may have been merely a slick potboiler, written by Odets for commercial reasons. Indeed, the author himself stated that the play was without a very serious message and aimed merely to present ". . . certain small aspects of life—and I hope reality." In a recent review, the author accounted for the adroit glibness of the play by saying, ". . . I picked up half my technique here [in Hollywood]. I did . . . [a number of] movies before I wrote *Country Girl*. The movies are a brilliant training school for a dramatic writer." This statement surely seems to be a reasonable explanation of his change in style, and it also represents a rather dramatic reversal of his earlier opinions regarding the effect of Hollywood upon a dramatic talent.

The Country Girl underwent a great deal of revision after the author had set down his initial version. He claims to have written two or three versions of the play before showing it to anyone. His revisions consisted mainly in the ". . . rewriting of certain scenes pertaining to the dramatic structure. I didn't know until the second draft, for example, that Georgie wasn't a destructive, bitchy woman." The play seems, on the surface, to be a psychological study of the actor, Frank Elgin, an alcoholic who is attempting to make a comeback on the stage, and of his effect upon his wife Georgie, and upon his director Bernie Dodd.

Frank, who suffers from a deep and well-established sense of insecurity, has strong paranoid tendencies. He struggles to give the appearance of being easygoing and happy; however, in doing so, he is merely playing a role. His wife realizes this and she explains him to Bernie very acutely when she says, "He doesn't like to make the slightest remark that might lose him people's regard or affection." (*The Country Girl,* Acting Edition, p. 41. All subsequent references will be to this edition.)

However, despite this surface indication that *The Country Girl* is primarily a psychological play, it is not consistently so. Odets claimed to be trying to combine ". . . a certain linear drive of story with psychological drive." In doing so, he often tended to become more concerned with the social than with the psychological elements of the play. Throughout the drama, Odets, as Harold Clurman has noted, ". . . constantly asks, 'What helps a man to live?' 'What today injures man's spirit?' 'What enhances or diminishes the creatively human in him?'" When Odets comes to grips with these questions, he answers them in terms of social rather than purely psychological forces. Obviously, these terms are not mutually exclusive; Frank's drinking stems from his insecurity which is, in this case, a psychological problem. However, it was brought about by social forces, by the uncertainty of an actor's existence, by the poverty which kept Frank at a bare subsistence level for the ten years during which he was unable to find any employment aside from small parts or an occasional role as an understudy. When Frank finally regains his confidence and shows signs of conquering his problems, he does so because he has gained social approval, because he is once more being applauded as the great actor who had previously gained widespread recognition and acclaim.

Had *The Country Girl* been more exclusively a psychological play, it is doubtful that Odets could have changed the role of Georgie so drastically in the various versions of the script. Had Georgie been presented as the nagging wife, as she had been conceived by Odets earlier, Frank's weakness would have been pitiful and psychologically understandable and explicable. But in the final version of the play, Frank's weakness is understandable only on social grounds and, in essence, Odets'

implications are not markedly different from those in his earlier proletarian plays. Frank's psychological composition is relatively transparent; the social forces which have engendered the actor's psychological problems are delineated with much more restraint than are the purely psychological forces; but they become a strong underlying theme in the overall structure of the play.

The Country Girl cannot really be said to have more than two significant characters in it. Georgie and Frank are well developed; but the six remaining characters, with the possible exception of Bernie, never really come to life, nor does Odets show evidence of any real interest in them. Cook, the producer, is a stereotype of a businessman who is looking out for his investment. He is edgy, insensitive to the feelings of others, dynamic in his actions. He is capable of giving encouragement only to someone whose worth has been proved and publicly acclaimed. When Frank most needs encouragement, it is consistent with Cook's personality that he should pounce on him as he does, saying, "Well, this does it! . . . That wife of yours can help you start packing!" (60). It is only when Frank has evoked unrestrained and unprecedented applause from the New York audience that Cook can say, "Frank, a lot of things . . . are said in the heat and toil of the day. I hope you'll accept my apologies" (73). And then he admits that he is attempting to make peace with Frank only because he has in mind some new contractual arrangements. Cook is not significantly different in personality from Tom Moody in *Golden Boy* or from Marcus Hoff in *The Big Knife.* However, his character is so barely sketched in, that one finds it difficult to feel any strong emotions for or against him.

Paul Unger, the author of the play in which Frank is to make his return to the theatre, is quietly intelligent, sensitive, sympathetic. Though he is generally very complacent, he can rise to action when goaded into doing so. When Cook abuses Frank, it is Unger who, white-faced and angry, tells him, "You're the boss, Mr. Cook, but you can't talk that way to an actor in any show I'm on. I won't permit it" (60). Paul represents the voice of social conscience heard in so much of Odets' work; but this voice is somewhat hushed in *The Country Girl.* The author does not give it the opportunity to expostulate at length as in the earlier plays. He is free to admit that ". . . in *The Country Girl* my point of view was held in abeyance." *Time's* review of the play pointed out that "the real story . . . is a compact little tragedy of misunderstanding." There is social protest in the play, but it is intimated rather than frankly stated. Although there is probably no single reason for this, one cannot ignore the fact that in the years following World War II congressional committees were very active in their investigations of literary works of social protest. Such writers as Albert Maltz and Ring Lardner, Jr., were taken into custody and questioned about their political philosophies. The year 1950 was not one in which an author could safely criticize existing social institutions in any but an indirect manner.

Nancy Stoddard, the eighteen-year-old actress who is to play opposite Frank in Unger's play, is presented very sketchily and never is seen as a total personality. However, she is very useful in the play because Frank's reactions to her illustrate significant facets of his own personality. Early in the play, when Frank and the company of Unger's play are in the theatre rehearsing, Frank forgets his lines. Nancy, who has already memorized all the parts in the play, prompts him; and Frank, looking grumpily at her, cautions, "Never usurp the stage manager's position, dear. Older actors don't like it" (22). As the play continues, Frank, because of his basic insecurity, tends to use Nancy as a scapegoat. When he mixes up his lines, he hastens to say to Bernie, ". . . that line mixup—it was the kid's fault all the time!" (42). Frank is jealous of Nancy's youth and of her acting ability; she constantly serves to remind him of what he might have been had he had more stability. She makes him painfully aware of his own inadequacies, inadequacies of which he needs no reminder. When he tells Georgie that ". . . the whole company—none of them like me. . . . They all want me to fail!" (57-58), his defenses are down; his paranoia is evident. However, when his defenses are not down, his paranoia becomes evident in other ways, and his abuse of Nancy is obviously a manifestation of his psychological condition.

Nancy finally becomes instrumental in helping Frank to gain the inner security which he requires in order to make his comeback. As he is playing opposite her, he forgets that he is playing a role and begins to live his part. He strikes out and slaps Nancy repeatedly until she makes a hysterical exit. The curtain falls and the audience, for the first time since the play has opened, gives its tumultuous acclaim to Frank's performance. It is at this moment that Frank begins to regain his self-confidence; his past is behind him and he is now going to be able to rise above it. When Georgie had said, "People don't go back" (49), Frank was filled with doubt about his future. But now he knows that his direction will be as he willed it. At the same time, his human relationships will change because, with success, he will be less inclined to feel that the world is against him. His relentless striking of Nancy marked a turning point in his life. Into this act went all of his pent-up bitterness.

In *The Country Girl,* man's ego is studied carefully and the effect of the wounded ego upon man's total situation is explored. Elements of this problem have been studied and presented forcefully in other Odets plays; however, in none of his earlier plays has Odets been so fully concerned with the problem, nor has he so sharply focused his interest upon a single character. Ja-

cob, in *Awake and Sing!,* suffered a great wound to his ego during his later years, and his suicide was an outgrowth of this wound. The wounded ego was again dealt with in *Night Music,* but, for Steve Takis, suicide was not a solution; instead Steve grew in strength and, as the play closed, was much more in control of his own destiny than he had been when the play opened. It is on a similar hopeful note that *The Country Girl* concludes.

The tension in the play is largely the result of the interaction of the personalities of Frank and Georgie. Each tends to blame the other for the disappointment which characterizes his life. Frank, unable to admit that it is his own weakness which has made him an alcoholic, fabricates a story which places the blame on Georgie. He tells of her violent acts when he has had to leave her alone to act in plays; but, in so doing, he is simply imputing to her his own tendencies. He excuses his drinking by calling attention to the fact that Georgie, too, was a drinker, but that when he starts drinking, she stops. He lies about Georgie's past when he tells Bernie that she was "Miss America" in the late 1930's. The motivation for this lie is obviously Frank's desire to enhance his own prestige by showing that a "Miss America" could fall in love with him. He introduces a note of tragedy into their lives when he tells of the child which they lost in the 1940's; his implication is that this unhappy event caused their social and spiritual decline. Only by losing himself in fantasy can Frank bear to think of what his life has been. The lies about his past become so real for him that they cease to be lies at all.

Odets, in depicting Frank as he does, is dealing with mendacity in individual terms rather than on a more broadly social level such as one might note in such earlier works as *Paradise Lost* and *Awake and Sing!* In all of the earlier plays, as well as in *The Big Knife,* the author was concerned with the false standards which society imposes upon man. Men were depicted as being the victims of the socio-economic milieu in which they found themselves. *Rocket to the Moon* and *Clash by Night* present mendacity on a more individual level than is found in the earlier plays, but the characters of these two plays lie to each other more than to themselves. In each of these plays there is a romantic triangle; in each there is the deception generally made necessary by such a situation. But in the play at hand, the leading character is involved in a self-deception of such proportions that truth and fantasy have merged in his own thinking. It is for this reason, perhaps, that he is such an effective actor; he can live most convincingly the life of the fictitious character whom he is portraying; when he begins slapping Nancy during a performance, he turns in a brilliant performance, but, at the same time, relieves his personal animosity towards the girl.

Despite outward appearances, Frank is introverted. His drinking has tended to shut the world out of his life. Even though he realizes what the consequences of his weakness might be for him and his wife, he cannot exist without the stimulation of alcohol. He buys cough medicine with a high alcoholic content and uses it in place of liquor until Georgie takes it from him. Especially tense is the scene in which she confiscates the cough medicine and nags him to reveal the location of the other bottle which she is sure he has hidden nearby. Frank lies to her very convincingly, but the moment she leaves the room, he pulls from the bottom of his trunk the bottle which he has placed there. Living with the shame and full realization of his own failure and weakness, Frank has had no choice but to withdraw into himself. He has not the strength to do otherwise. Only as the play closes has anyone cause to suppose that Frank might find the strength to mend his broken life.

However, Odets does not attempt to give an explicit answer to the question of whether a person who has lived so selfishly and who has such extreme weakness of character to contend with can be redeemed simply by having his one great talent recognized. Viewing Frank as objectively as possible, one would be forced to admit that the chances of his personality's undergoing any real transformation would be very slight indeed. Frank is actually unable to grow up. He represents, as much as any Arthur Miller or Tennessee Williams protagonist, the prototype of the failure of modern American man. He is insensitive to his wife's need for inner security, and her total effort is directed towards humoring him and looking after him. The major question is whether Frank is worth this sacrifice.

Georgie's marriage to Frank is not fully explained by Odets. Presumably she was overwhelmed by his charm and by the glamor which attended his early theatrical successes. Georgie is completely aware of the amount of responsibility which she is shouldering in her marriage and she often tends to look upon herself as a martyr. Apparently she had hoped, in marrying Frank who was so much older than she, to find a father-husband. Indeed, she tells of her loneliness as a child during the long periods when her father was on the road in vaudeville, and says to Frank, "[I] might not have married you if I'd had a father" (33). She goes on to tell Frank that he does not believe in himself, but her attempt to dominate him so completely results in his being deprived of any opportunity to be independent. She is not entirely culpable in this, however; Frank has not the self-control and will power which enable a man to stand alone. Her motivation in being overly protective of Frank is, in all fairness, basically selfless. Her marriage has been disappointing because Frank is unable to assume the role of leadership which Georgie has convinced herself she wants her husband to assume. She cannot even get Frank to make relatively simple deci-

sions, because he is always afraid of hurting her. She says to him, at one point, ". . . come on, Frank, tell me what you want me to do. I won't love you less. . . . If I go on the road with you . . . tell me straight out anything that's on your mind. Don't shuffle" (33).

This is Georgie's self-created illusion of what she would have her husband be. However, were Frank to take command of the situation, Georgie would be thoroughly miserable. She has assumed a protective role and, in a sense, her relationship to Frank is more that of mother than that of wife. It is for this reason that Georgie, contrary to the behavior of the average woman, frequently makes allusions to the fact that she is old. When Nancy calls a mirror a pier-glass, Georgie says that ". . . only old ladies like me" (49) still use that terminology. Actually, Georgie is in her thirties and is represented as being quite attractive.

Georgie's protectiveness, the result of misplaced maternal feelings, has virtually emasculated Frank. Any hope which might exist for him is contingent upon his getting away from her overpowering influence upon him. As the play closes, there is not any indication that Frank is to gain this liberation. Indeed, Odets, in an interview, indicated that ". . . the action is resolved by Georgie sticking with Frank and Bernie going off alone. But the real interpretation of what will happen to these people is for the reader or audience [to decide upon]." Odets considers this ending the best technical job he has ever done.[1]

The critical reception of **The Country Girl** was notably varied. It ranged from Brooks Atkinson's estimate that ". . . **The Country Girl** is the best play he [Odets] has written for years, perhaps the best play of his career," to George Jean Nathan's comment in *American Mercury* that "he [Odets] is theatrical not in the sense of true theatre, but in the sense of falsified stage." Basic disagreement over specific points characterized much of the criticism of the play. For example, William Beyer wrote in *School and Society* that ". . . the opening scene of the actor's try-out reading is so labored and perfunctory both in its concept and in its execution that we were immediately apprehensive as to the play's development." On the other hand, Miss Wyatt wrote in *Catholic World,* "Act I holds the most interest."

All but a few critics considered the play to be generally a sound technical achievement. Margaret Marshall, reviewing the play for *Nation,* wrote, "The play is well made. Mr. Odets knows the language and ways of the theatre. He also knows how to build a scene and how to induce a rising tension. . . . The situation, if small, is interesting." *Time* considered Odets' characters in the play to be "bitingly real" and noted that the play had ". . . passages of fierce feeling that only Odets could write." The reviewer for *Commonweal,* Walter Kerr, called the play ". . . well balanced [with] passages of quiet, careful motivation . . . followed by inevitable and satisfying flareups; nothing is tacked on; everything moves with easy confidence." It is this architectonic quality which makes *The Country Girl* a technically sound achievement.

Few critics have written of the play with the perspicacity of John Mason Brown. In his review in the *Saturday Review,* he recognized *The Country Girl* as a competent play, and he realized that "Odets' career got off to a poor start in starting too well. It began with a climax." Only the critic for *Newsweek* could see in *The Country Girl* ". . . a strictly theatrical piece with the same vigor and dramatic skill that he [Odets] once dedicated to causes and social significance."

The most widely acclaimed strength of the play was Odets' presentation of Frank and Georgie. *Life* called them ". . . almost too excruciatingly real to watch, but too absorbing to ignore." Harold Clurman, whose criticism of the play Odets felt to be most significant, praised the author's ". . . talent for living dramatic speech, for characterization, for intensity of feeling."[2] He went on to call Odets a poet of the theatre and noted his ability to write with immediacy and intimacy. But, most important of all, Clurman said that Odets previous successes had been bold revolutionary plays, but that their success had been ". . . partly due to the mood of the thirties and our foolish appetite for novelty." In this statement, Clurman seems to have come to the heart of the matter; those who had criticized Odets for abandoning his soapbox were the very critics who would have condemned him for lacking versatility had he continued to write the sort of plays that the 1930's demanded. Odets, in the 1940's and 1950's, moved from dead themes which had ceased to have meaning to those he considered more vital and timely.

In *The Country Girl,* Odets had set as his task ". . . to take simple elements and make something sharp and theatrical out of them. I stated a fact, the story of these people, rather than speculated a fact."[3] The play accomplished the author's basic aim and the public received it well. As a motion picture it also enjoyed a modicum of success. But more important than anything else, *The Country Girl* gives evidence not only that Odets' social commentary can be expressed in a more restrained manner than had hitherto been evident in his works, but also that this restraint did not result from a weakening social concern. It came from a broadening of his interest in the matters which vitally affect man in his social relationships.

III. *The Flowering Peach*

The Flowering Peach, produced in New York in December, 1954, marks a departure from Clifford Odets' previous plays both in scope and in style of presentation. Deeply allegorical, *The Flowering Peach* is a retelling of the story of Noah and the Ark, freely adapted from the Book of Genesis. The play might be called a modern retelling of the story; the dialogue is modern, many of the situations are presented in a modern context, and the men dress in modern clothing. However, the women are clothed in traditional Oriental costumes, and the author's desire seems to be to create a feeling of timelessness which would tend to give the play a greater universality.

The Flowering Peach is Odets' most poetic and most highly imaginative play. The characters are lovable and convincing; the allegory is constantly present, but not intrusive; the humor is light, natural, and pervasive. Long before Odets had thought of writing *The Flowering Peach,* Harold Clurman had observed that ". . . he is never literal and his power with words [represents] a blood tie with the sources."[4] It is Odets' blood tie with his sources that makes *The Flowering Peach* a genuine artistic triumph. To the traditional story of Noah and the Ark, Odets brings a deep understanding of Jewish family life. He captures the warmth of the family much as he had in *Awake and Sing!* and in *Paradise Lost.* His approach has shifted from the almost clinically objective point of view of *The Country Girl*; in *The Flowering Peach,* it becomes warmly subjective.

Odets' blood tie with his sources in *The Country Girl* was found in his prolonged association with the theatre; his blood tie in *The Flowering Peach* is represented by his continued concern with the family as the fundamental unit of society—a concern equally prominent in his earlier, more angry writings. But in *The Flowering Peach* Odets has become mellow. If, in *Awake and Sing!* he could have a perturbed Jacob say, "This is a house? Marx said it—abolish such families," then the matriarchal Esther in *The Flowering Peach,* upon discovering that her son Shem has almost sunk the Ark by hoarding manure in his quarters, can have the compassion to say, as Bessie Berger might have, "But if it's for the family, why throw it overboard?" *The Flowering Peach* as reproduced in *The Best Plays of 1954-55,* ed. Louis Kronenberger, p. 197. All subsequent references will be to this edition of the play. Esther is able to bear the confinement of the Ark, the uncertainty of the future, the constant bickering among the members of her family, because the family is together and this, to her, is the most significant satisfaction she can envision.

The family becomes the symbol of regeneration, of stolid continuance in the face of the most frightening and widespread adversity, represented by the flood. This symbol is reinforced as the play concludes; the women who have been aboard the Ark—Rachel, Leah, and Goldie—are great with children when the waters recede. The repopulation of the earth is to begin. Noah sees a tree blossoming and asks his son, Japheth, "What kinda tree is so beautiful?" Japheth replies, "It's a flow-ering peach, Poppa" (203). When Noah comments that it is April, the implication is obviously one of rebirth and fertility; for Noah comments further that the tree is ". . . from the new earth" (203).

The Odets version of the Noah story was not concerned with reproducing the details of the biblical version. Odets used his source merely as a point from which to work. Noah, when he first appears, is rather addled. He has just wakened from a dead sleep in which he has dreamed of the destruction of the world. His wife, on hearing this, blames such a fanciful musing on Noah's tendency to tipple. She tells him, "You had enough to drink," when he puts the jug to his lips. He responds, "You should be satisfied that I drink, otherwise I'd leave you" (180). This uncomplimentary banter is basically good-natured, and no real offense is intended by it. Noah and Esther, having been married for sixty years, understand each other very well.

Noah is deeply concerned that he should have had a dream tantamount to a visit from the Almighty. He is a common man and very old. He is not sure of his ability to persuade his three sons, Ham, Shem, and Japheth, to help him build an Ark. He knows that his own strength is not great and, examining his hands, he says, "See them bones? That ain' hands no more, it's bones! . . . Why did You pick me . . . ? Honorable Sir . . . ? For what?" (189). Noah is profoundly and unquestioningly reverent, but he feels that the task which God has set for him is too great for his strength and for his abilities.

When Noah sends his unmarried son, Japheth, to bring Shem to him, he does not dare to have Japheth tell Shem that he must leave his harvest because Noah has had a prophecy; Shem is too practical to inconvenience himself during harvest time in order to gratify his fa-ther's whim. So Noah instructs Japheth to tell Shem that ". . . a big building proposition came up! The Customer is very impatient, can't wait. . . . Needs an estimate right away" (181). He knows that with this lure he can bring Shem to him. He still, of course, has doubts regarding his ability to convince Shem that he should leave his harvest to help in the construction of the Ark. Shem is hard-headed. When he hears Noah's story, he is respectful for a time, though doubtful. Fi-nally, Japheth indicates that he believes the story of the dream but that despite this, as a protest against God, he will refuse to go on the Ark if it is built. Shem can re-strain himself no longer and snaps at Japheth, "Poppa's in his second childhood an' you're not outta your first!" (184).

Ham is even more doubtful than Shem. He asks Noah how he can possibly gather together all of the animals which God has said to go on the Ark. Noah, who has no answer for his sons, is himself concerned about the problem of gathering the necessary pairs of animals. The family bickers, and tempers become short until the tension is finally broken by the appearance of what looks like a mouse. It frightens the women and is the occasion for a great deal of screaming. However, the mouse turns out to be a gitka and it runs directly into Noah's hands. The family is deeply impressed as Noah announces, "God has sent us a gitka" (184). Then Japheth cries out to the family to look out the window: pairs of animals are advancing down the road and a whirring of wings in the air heralds the arrival of pairs of birds which will accompany Noah and his family on the Ark.

Thus does God come to Noah's aid to convince the oth-ers that the dream was authentic and not merely a fig-ment of Noah's imagination. This is the first publicly revealed miracle through which God helps Noah. It rep-resents the first major turning point in the narrative; Noah will have the aid of his sons in the building of the Ark. Noah gives thanks to God, saying, "Oh Lord, our God, the soul is rejoiced in Thee and Thy wonders. Here the family . . . is united to serve You as You asked" (185). Fundamentally, Odets is emphasizing here that the family, which, with the marriage of two sons, has drifted apart, is now being reunited through adver-sity. The unity of the family tends, more and more, to become a central social issue in the play. The family is presented as the fundamental unit of the human race; one family, according to the Noah legend, lived through an incredible experience so that the human race might continue on the face of the earth.

In reviewing *The Flowering Peach,* Harold Clurman, writing in *Nation,* spoke of Odets' identification of him-self with both Noah and Japheth. "Noah," wrote Mr. Clurman, "is the essential, instinctive Odets; Japheth the rational, thinking Odets." Odets, at this point, seemed to be at a spiritual crossroads. Noah was the simple, ever-faithful servant of God; but Japheth, por-trayed by Odets as a character suggestive of Job, was at once believing and protesting. Japheth, who believed in the validity of his father's dream long before Ham and Shem did, based his belief upon human reason and ob-servation. He told his brothers, "It hasn't rained since early spring . . . floods are possible, I mean. If Poppa says he had the dream, he had it" (183). Japheth tells Shem that if he decides not to help build the Ark, it will not be because he doesn't think the flood is imminent, but rather because he ". . . might decide to die with the others. . . . Someone, it seems to me, would have to protest such an avenging, destructive God!" (184). Shem, who at this point is unwilling to believe in the truth of his father's dream, shows himself to be much more conventional and much less rational in his accep-tance of the prevailing religious faith than is Japheth;

he is profoundly shocked, not because Japheth believes in the dream, but because his thinking brother has baldly implied that God might be avenging and destructive.

Japheth is unmarried, and this is a source of great concern to his parents. In an exchange with Noah, during which Noah again prods Japheth to take a wife, Japheth responds, "How can I take a wife in times like these?" Noah tells him that God wants him to take a wife because ". . . the new world will need babies, bushels an' bushels of babies." Japheth, with a characteristically skeptical question, brings the scene to a climax by asking, "And what about the bushels of babies who will die in the flood? . . . is this vengeful God the very God I was taught to love?" And thus saying Japheth announces that he cannot continue to work on the building of the Ark: "I cannot work for this brutal God!" (187). So saying Japheth takes his leave of the family, thereby causing the work on the Ark to come to a standstill. Noah still has his unquestioning faith and can say with genuine conviction that ". . . The Lord is good for anybody an' everybody, at all times!" (188). But he is now in a crucial situation because the time of the flood is fast approaching. An old man who has not the physical strength and vitality to do the sort of work of which Japheth is capable, he bemoans his lack of vigor and goes to his rest that evening with dejection. His sleep is so troubled that Esther becomes alarmed and calls her sons to waken him. Upon doing so, they find that Noah is no longer an old man; he has been miraculously transformed into a strong ". . . young man of fifty, with eagle-bright eyes and reddish hair" (189). God has performed this miracle so that the course of events which He has predetermined shall not be impeded.

So strong are the family ties in the play that Japheth cannot really leave the family, and he returns to help complete the Ark. Life is difficult for the entire family; when Noah goes into town, people cast stones at him; and other members of the family are rebuked by those about them. As the time of the flood approaches, there are signs from heaven to indicate that an unusual event is nigh; these signs are observed only by the members of Noah's family. Shem, once the most dubious of the sons, is struck dumb when he observes these signs, and becomes the son who most firmly believes in the coming of the flood. He says in dismay, "The sun is rising in the west and setting in the east! Why don't people see it? Where are their brains?" (190).

Throughout the action of the play, Shem, the businessman of the family, is portrayed as an opportunist. He accepts his faith largely on opportunistic grounds. He tends to play both ends against the middle in a rather amusing way. For example, because he believes in the inevitability of the flood, he sells all of his land. Obviously, the flood, if it eradicates the lives of all earthly

creatures save those in the Ark, will bring about a situation in which the conventional economic system will be meaningless. Nevertheless, Shem hoards the proceeds from the sale of his goods and attempts to evade the payment of taxes on his gain. Similarly, it is Shem and his wife Leah who nearly sink the Ark after it is adrift for many days by hoarding manure. From this manure Shem intends to make ". . . dried manure briquettes," which will be sold after the waters have receded. Noah is appalled by Shem's hoarding and, in a humorous scene, says, "On the Holy Ark he's makin' business! Manure! With manure you want to begin a new world!" (197).

Ham is the playboy among Noah's sons. He is impetuous and, for the most part, forthright. He no longer loves his wife Rachel who feels towards Japheth a deep love which Japheth reciprocates. Ham is in love with Goldie, the young woman who saved Japheth from being beaten by an aroused throng of people and who is the only human outside Noah's immediate family to be taken on the Ark. It is, of course, hoped by Noah that Japheth and Goldie will marry.

Once the family is aboard the Ark, Ham seduces Goldie and then demands further attentions from her, securing her assent by threatening to tell those on board what they already have reason to suspect: that the two are having an affair. Despite this, Ham is portrayed with sympathy and one does not receive the impression that he is despicable. Indeed, the Ark begins to become a place of rather casual moral conduct. Noah tries to resist and suppress this tendency; however, Esther accepts it and deals tactfully with the four who are involved in illicit romances. It is Esther who tries to persuade Noah to permit these four to be married; even as she is on the brink of death, she says to Noah, "Marry the children . . . for the sake of happiness in the world" (201). But Noah is adamant; and, though he finds it very painful to deny his wife's dying wish, he must say to her, "Old friend, it hurts me to refuse you, but it stands in the books for a thousand years." Esther protests that all the books are in the water now and that perhaps Noah does not really know the wishes of God. But Noah assures her that God has concern for them and that He will provide for them a promised land. To this Esther, now much more the rationalist than she has ever been previously, retorts, "The children, their happiness . . . is my last promised land" (202).

In essence, the understanding Esther is denying the intractable God of the Hebrews, the God to whom Noah pays unquestioning homage, and is putting her family first, again emphasizing the extreme social importance of the family. This is Odets writing of any typical Jewish mother. Noah and Esther have, through this scene, become universalized symbols of Man and of Woman. The male upholds the greater laws of the universe; the female upholds the family, the seat of human love and of biological continuance.

Noah serves as a reassuring testament to the endurance of the laws of the Hebrews. He is not a learned man, but he knows and understands the law of his faith. When, in Scene V, three ancient patriarchs appear to ask Noah to take them on the Ark in order that the Old Law be preserved, Noah has to refuse them because God has appointed who is to go. The men point out that they ". . . know the Old Law *behind* the Old Law," but still Noah must carry out God's command. The implication clearly is that the obedient servant gains favor in the eyes of God. It is not necessary that this servant know the Old Laws behind the Old Laws; it is necessary only that he know the will of God and carry it out faithfully and unquestioningly.

Japheth's role in *The Flowering Peach* is a most interesting one. He, among the sons, is the mainstay of the family. His problem is one which involves the principles upon which his life has been based. Japheth, from a rise in the land, looks down upon the landscape below him and says, "Those roads down there! . . . They're not cobwebs, those roads, the work of a foolish spider, to be brushed away by a peevish boy! Those roads were made by man, crazy not to be alone or apart! Men crazy to reach each other! Well, they won't now" (192). But Rachel reminds Japheth that the Ark is the only hope now, and that the only idealism depends upon man's survival. Esther reinforces this point when she tells Japheth that it is hollow to die in protest, that the only real protest is to ". . . have your own sons an' teach them!" (193).

Ultimately, Noah knocks Japheth out and has him carried onto the Ark. Once he regains consciousness, Japheth is insistent that the Ark should have a rudder and should be steered. Noah protests that this was not God's intention; again, reason and faith are sharply in conflict.

The Flowering Peach has been grossly misunderstood. Few people, apparently, were able to see that the story was actually very timely and that Odets' message was pointedly directed at man in the midst of the twentieth century. The play was written during a time of grave international tensions which might easily have erupted into a nuclear war that could have resulted in the sort of mass annihilation brought about by the flood in the Noah story. But Eric Bentley, who wrote enthusiastically about the play in *New Republic*, considered ". . . the drama of ideas . . . a subplot" and viewed the family romance as the main plot. While he called *The Flowering Peach* ". . . the best American play I have ever reviewed in these columns," he felt that the subplot was troublesome.

The play, which ran for one hundred and thirty-five performances on Broadway, received much adverse criticism for its presentation of frequent family squabbles on the Ark. It must be remembered, however, that the members of the family were under immense and constant emotional strain during the entire action of the play and that the confinement on the Ark, which lasted for nearly a year in the Odets version of the story, was condensed by the author to a bare minimum. The bickering was necessary to depict the tensions which existed, and it would hardly have been convincing to present a more harmonious and complacent family.

The Flowering Peach was also criticized by some for lacking the social indignation of the author's early works. This criticism was best countered by John Mason Brown, who pointed out that the play, had it been written by Odets twenty years earlier, ". . . would have quavered with energy, been fired with indignation, and probably ended with all the passengers on the Ark organizing a union." Brown goes on to commend Odets for the compassion, humor, and gentle affirmation of *The Flowering Peach,* and to note the play's significance ". . . in a world once again imperiled."[5]

The play is called ". . . literal and human in conception" by Miss Wyatt, the reviewer for *Catholic World*, who also notes that the freedom with which Odets has handled the biblical version of the Noah story adds charm and warmth to the play. *Time* also spoke favorably of the play's ". . . child-like scrambling of time and place." Robert Whitehead commented in *Theatre Arts* that, ". . . [Odets'] work reflects . . . strikingly certain American national characteristics: rebelliousness [Japheth], virility [Noah], and violence coupled with tenderness, sentiment and humor [also Noah]." *Newsweek* applauded Odets for having mellowed while having ". . . lost none of his feel for words and none of his real sense of theatre."

Among those who felt that *The Flowering Peach* did not represent a step forward for Odets was Maurice Zolotow, who, writing in *Theatre Arts*, stated that Odets seemed to be looking for something in ". . . the mythology of orthodox Judaism," but he did not quite know what it is. As a result, according to Zolotow, ". . . the play is dissolved in murky confusion."

Also among those who felt that the play did not meet expectations was Gerald Weales, who, in *Commentary,* objected to the dullness of the play and to the fact that Odets' Noah did not have ". . . a more valid relation to his surroundings." He felt that the play lacked the vigorous language of *Awake and Sing!* and that Odets, writing as an American Jew, lost much of the humor of the European Jew. Wolcott Gibbs, in *The New Yorker,* objected that ". . . the humor not only is generally out of key with lofty pathos but often . . . has the embarrassing effect of presenting the Almighty as an accessory clown." Weales also stated that "any new tradition would have to lie where Odets, in his early plays, vaguely sees it, in the communities with a Jewish population dense enough to allow its members to retain a group personality even while they absorb everything that is more widely American." Weales did not think that Odets sufficiently established the background of the folk play to have **The Flowering Peach** present a convincing degree of dramatic validity.

A reading of **The Flowering Peach** is vital to anyone who would view Odets as a mature and well-developed artist rather than as a radical playwright who wishes to use the stage as a soapbox. Unfortunately this most significant Odets play has not been published in its entirety, so is not easily available to the public. It is to be hoped that this most unfortunate omission will one day be remedied.

IV. THE THIRD MAJOR PERIOD

The third major period in Odets' creative life, represented by the three dramas written between 1949 and 1954, has been fruitful indeed, for it has marked the most varied period in his writing. He has, during this time, turned his attention to social problems with which, in the 1930's, he would not have been conversant. However, Odets has not grown in popularity. He has suffered from the sort of criticism which bemoaned the passing of the angry Odets of the depression years.

It is exceedingly difficult for anyone familiar with the Odets of **Waiting for Lefty** and **Golden Boy** to judge his later works strictly on their own merits. It must be remembered that the fiery Odets who, in 1935, had seen three of his plays received by New York audiences with unrestrained enthusiasm, had come of age at a time when the social and economic issues brought about by the Great Depression were in the forefront of most minds. He wrote with force and with deep personal feeling of these issues and his writing met an immediate social need. His writing during this period was irresistibly forceful although it was not always artistically exemplary. Odets was so completely caught up in the social issues of the 1930's that he was not concerned with the artistry of his productions.

It was only as the pressing issues of the 1930's had become less pressing and had drawn nearer to solution that Odets was able to enter a phase of artistic experimentation which, in the lives of many artists, occurs much earlier. **Waiting for Lefty** was written in three days of impassioned and feverish activity; **The Country Girl** passed through three distinct versions before anyone was permitted to read it. **Till the Day I Die** was written as a *tour de force* in a matter of days and was presented almost immediately; **Clash by Night** was rewritten nine times before its final presentation. Obviously, the Odets of the 1940's and 1950's was grappling with new techniques and with new social problems. His underlying concerns are often the same in the later plays as they were in the early ones, but the timeliness of the later plays is not always immediately apparent.

With the beginning of World War II, the issues of the Depression era became history. Many people apparently expected Odets to continue writing about them as though they were still vital; but the author turned to more generalized social issues. The later plays mark a redirection of the author's interests, but not a retrogression in his ability as a playwright. They stand as evidence of his versatility, of his artistic concern, and of his ability to write with restraint of the same issues which he once mounted a soapbox to proclaim abroad.

Notes

1. A. Aulicino, "How the *Country Girl* Came about, in the Words of the People Involved," *Theatre Arts,* XXXVI (May, 1952), 57.

2. *New Republic,* CXXIII (December 11, 1950), 29-30.

3. Aulicino, *op. cit.,* p. 55.

4. "The First 15 Years," *New Republic,* CXXIII (December 11, 1950), 29.

5. "On the Crest of the Waves," *Saturday Review,* XXXVIII (January 15, 1955), 30.

Selected Bibliography

PRIMARY SOURCES

Awake and Sing! New York: Covici-Friede, 1935.

The Big Knife. New York: Random House, 1949.

Clash by Night. New York: Random House, 1942.

The Country Girl. New York: Dramatists' Play Service, Inc., 1949. Acting Edition.

The Flowering Peach. New York: Dramatists' Play Service, Inc., 1954. This play is available presently only in typescript. An abridged version appears in *The Best Plays of 1954-55,* edited by Burns Mantle and Louis Kronenberger, New York: Dodd, Mead and Company, 1955.

Golden Boy. New York: Random House, 1937.

"I Can't Sleep: A Monologue." *New Theatre and Film,* III (February, 1936), 8-9.

Night Music. New York: Random House, 1940.

Paradise Lost. New York: Random House, 1936.

Rocket to the Moon. New York: Random House, 1939.

Six Plays of Clifford Odets. New York: Random House, 1939. This volume was also issued in the same year in the Modern Library Edition, in which the pagination was identical and the contents are as follows: Preface by Odets; *Waiting for Lefty; Awake and Sing!; Till the Day I Die; Paradise Lost; Golden Boy; Rocket to the Moon*; Introductions by Harold Clurman to *Awake and Sing!, Paradise Lost,* and *Golden Boy.*

Three Plays by Clifford Odets. New York: Covici-Friede, 1935. Contents: *Waiting for Lefty; Awake and Sing!* and *Till the Day I Die.*

Waiting for Lefty and *Till the Day I Die.* New York: Covici-Friede, 1935.

SECONDARY SOURCES

PUBLISHED WORKS

Bentley, Eric. *The Playwright as Thinker.* New York: Harcourt, Brace and Company, 1955. A consideration of the conceptual patterns and trends in Odets' plays; excellent presentation of Odets as a realist.

Clurman, Harold. *The Fervent Years: The Story of the Group Theatre and the Thirties.* New York: Alfred A. Knopf, 1945. Presents Odets in relation to the training he received in the Group Theatre; also presents intimate insights by one of his closest friends and most understanding critics.

ARTICLES ABOUT ODETS

Brown, John Mason. "The Man Who Came Back." *Saturday Review of Literature,* XXXIII (December 9, 1950), 26-27. Interesting insights on "the new Odets" as exemplified in *The Country Girl* and *The Big Knife.*

Clurman, Harold. "The First 15 Years." *New Republic,* CXXIII (December 11, 1950), 29-30. Basically a review of *The Country Girl,* though the author views Odets in perspective and comments on his basic poetic ability.

Edward Murray (essay date 1968)

SOURCE: Murray, Edward. "*Rocket to the Moon*." In *Clifford Odets: The Thirties and After,* pp. 72-93. New York: Frederick Ungar Publishing Co., 1968.

[*In the following essay, Murray takes issue with the prevailing critical view that Odets's* Rocket to the Moon *is a structurally flawed play, arguing instead that the work is dramatically unified and demonstrates rich characterization, "unforgettable dialogue," and a deft use of symbolism in its treatment of the theme of love.*]

> A man falls asleep in marriage. And after a time he wants to keep on sleeping, undisturbed. I'm surprised how little I've thought about it. Gee!—What I don't know would fill a book.
>
> —Ben Stark, *Rocket to the Moon,* p. 351

Rocket to the Moon: A Romance in Three Acts, which was first presented by the Group Theater at the Belasco Theater on November 24, 1938, is one of Clifford Odets' finest plays. As the dramatist himself once remarked: "*Rocket to the Moon* [reveals] a depth of perception, a web of sensory impressions and a level of both personal and social experience not allotted to the other [early] plays" ("Preface" to *Six Plays,* p. ix). When the Theater Group at UCLA staged *Rocket to the Moon* a few years ago, Odets told the journalist Cecil Smith that the play was "about love and marriage in this country. They're playing it as of 1939 but I should think its theme would be as relevant and poignant today as it was then." *Rocket to the Moon,* as Odets rightly pointed out, "is widely performed in Europe and by the more advanced little theater organizations" (*Los Angeles Times Calendar,* August 26, 1962, pp. 9-10). For some reason, however, *Rocket to the Moon* has never been popular in America. Perhaps the explanation lies in the curious but persistent critical myth that the structure of the play is faulty. Another reason may be that in Act Three Odets is determined to treat his subject in an uncompromising fashion and refuses to give the audience—save for one unconvincing moment—a happy but spurious climax and conclusion.

The charge that *Rocket to the Moon* has a defective structure was made at the time the play was first produced; and, as is so often the case in criticism, that complaint has been perpetuated by one unthinking critic after the other down to the present moment. In the *Time* review of the 1939 production, for example, the writer claims that *Rocket to the Moon* "does not move in a straight line," and that Act Three "wobbles all over the place." Although the word "wobbles" suggests movement of some kind, Rosamond Gilder's review of the play in *Theater Arts* asserts that the last two acts are "static." Even the ordinarily perceptive Harold Clurman argues in *The Fervent Years* that Odets' play is badly constructed and thematically confused. I shall return to Clurman's specific criticism later. The subject again came up for discussion in 1962 when Cecil Smith interviewed Odets on the occasion of the UCLA production of *Rocket to the Moon.* Odets maintained that most people over the years simply "failed to understand the structure" of the play. A close analysis of the dramatic action in *Rocket to the Moon* should make clear that Odets' play is much more successfully integrated than critical opinion over the years has allowed.

Rocket to the Moon is a return to the tight, narrowly focused form of *Awake and Sing!.* Whereas *Golden Boy* extends over eighteen months, has twelve scenes, five sets and nineteen characters, *Rocket to the Moon* covers about two months, has four scenes, one set and eight characters. Which compares more closely with the twelve-month time-sequence, four scenes, one set and nine characters of *Awake and Sing!* than with the more expansive and fluid *Golden Boy.* Needless to add, of course, the *basic* form in all three plays is identical. The setting of *Rocket to the Moon* is a dentist's waiting room in a New York City office building; the time is summer and, as I hope to show in due course, the intense heat is made to function both structurally and thematically in the play.

About two-thirds of Act One is introductory in nature. The audience learns that Ben Stark, the dentist, and his wife, Belle, are unhappily married; that the couple are childless and struggling economically; that Ben is sorely frustrated in a number of ways—for example, he is a sensitive man who reads Shakespeare and often suspects that he is in the wrong profession; and, that Cleo Singer, the dentist's young and attractive secretary—who is likewise frustrated sexually and vocationally—represents a possible threat to the uncertain Stark marriage. The point of attack arrives when Belle's father, Mr. Prince, who has had everything in life except love, hurls a challenge to the similarly suffering Ben—which challenge constitutes the dramatic problem of the play:

PRINCE:

> Iceberg, listen . . . why don't you come up to see the world, the sea gulls and the ships to Europe? . . . When did you look at another woman last? The year they put the buffalo nickel on the market? Why don't you suddenly ride away, an airplane, a boat! Take a rocket to the moon! Explode! What holds you back? You don't want to hurt Belle's feelings? You'll die soon enough—

STARK:

> I'll just have to laugh at that!

PRINCE:

> Laugh. . . . But make a motto for yourself: "Out of the coffin by Labor Day!" Have an affair with—with—with this girl . . . this Miss Cleo. She'll make you a living man again.

> (p. 350)

The major questions of the play, then, are clear: Will Ben have an affair with Cleo? If so, will he thereby solve the problems of his life and make a more satisfying existence for himself? Is love the answer to Ben's problems?

The protagonist's first response to Prince's challenge is frightened and peevish resistance. Throughout the play Ben Stark views his father-in-law as some kind of "devil." The name "Prince" is, of course, significant in this connection, as is the older man's "aristocratic air" (p. 339). After Prince's exit, Frenchy, a chiropodist from an office down the hall, enters:

STARK:

> I don't understand human nature, not the off-color things. Suddenly [Prince] tells me he wants to be an actor! I like normal people, like you.

FRENCHY:

> Hell, who's normal nowadays! Take that kid of yours, that Cleo—

STARK:

> Sometimes people embarrass me. The most ordinary people suddenly become sinister—

FRENCHY:

> Sinister? They're just sleepy.

STARK:

> What about Miss Singer? You were saying—

> (p. 352)

Odets' writing here reveals a sensitive grasp of psychological processes, and in presentation it is skillfully indirect. For it is apparent that Ben Stark is unconsciously alarmed by the image of himself which he dimly perceives in Prince. Even the reference to his father-in-law's desire to be an actor reflects Ben's own submerged Shakespearean longings. Not only promiscuous love, but even artistic aspirations appear disconcertingly abnormal to this frustrated middle class dentist. (The thematic link between *Golden Boy* and *Rocket to the Moon* should be obvious here.) Frenchy's line—"Hell, who's normal nowadays!"—is picked up later in the play and expanded upon in terms of the theme. Similarly, Frenchy's remark that Ben is not "sinister" but merely "sleepy" looks back to the point of attack—"Out of the coffin by Labor Day!"—and forward to Act Three, when the chiropodist urges his friend to, "Leave the morals out" and to "be practical" (p. 405). The final line of the exchange between Ben and Frenchy focuses the attention of the audience on the all important Cleo Singer. And when the girl makes her next appearance, Odets says: "Because of [Ben's] previous scene with Prince [Cleo] now presents a challenge to him which he might never have come to alone" (p. 355). One should note here that in the previous scene between Ben and Prince reference was made to the Hotel Algiers, a place across from Ben's office which caters to lovers (p. 345), and the hotel becomes an important symbol in the play—as can be seen, for example, from the excellent conclusion to Act One:

STARK:

> (*impatiently*) Mrs. Stark is not the terrible person many people think she is!

CLEO:

> (*dismayed*) Oh, I didn't mean anything. . . .

STARK:

> (*almost savagely*) She's one of the most loyal, sincere and helpful persons I've ever met!

CLEO:

(*in a small voice*) I'm sure she is, I'm sure of that. . . .

(CLEO *now disappears into the operating room. For a moment* STARK *stands there, wagging his head. His eye falls on the dental magazine. He picks it up, looks at the ad and then throws the magazine across the room. As he begins to fill his pipe his glance turns to the window, right. He moves over to the window and looks out at the Hotel Algiers.* CLEO's *voice from the operating room threshold turns him around with a guilty start. In a small contrite voice.*) Pardon me . . . did I tell you before? Your wife expects you home at seven.

STARK:

(*annoyed*) Yes, thanks—you told me—thanks!

CLEO:

(*meekly*) You're welcome, Dr. Stark.

(CLEO *disappears into the operating room again.* STARK *looks after her annoyed. For a moment he stands reflectively. Finally he strikes a match and begins to light his pipe.*)

(pp. 356-357)

In Act Two, Scene One, Ben and Cleo are drawn increasingly together and their obvious attraction for each other becomes a painful, and at times even a somewhat ludicrous, state of frustration. The point, I believe, needs to be emphasized. Throughout **Rocket to the Moon,** Odets—and this is one measure of his achievement—successfully walks a tightrope between the serious and the comic. Not many dramatists are capable of engaging the emotions of a sympathetic audience in the fate of a seemingly banal romance—what on the face of it could seem more unpromising than the affair of a middle-aged dentist and his young secretary?—and still have the tact to control the mood and tempo of the action with a light touch of irony and humor. Consider the conclusion of Scene One:

CLEO:

Don't want to be lonely, never left alone! Why should I cry? I have a throat to sing with, a heart to love with! Why don't you love me, Dr. Stark? I was ten, then fifteen—I'm almost twenty now. Everything is in a hurry and you ought to love me.

STARK:

Cleo please. . . .

CLEO:

You're good, you're kind, you're like a father. Do you love your wife? I'm intuitive—I know you don't!

STARK:

(*making a last effort to stop her*) Cleo!

CLEO:

We're *both* alone, so alone. . . . But I won't have it that way. I'll change life.

STARK:

You're wonderful. . . .

CLEO:

You don't deserve me. Not you or any other man I ever met.

STARK:

(*in an agony of indecision*) Cleo, dear. . . .

CLEO:

(*shyly*) I'll call you Benny in a minute! (*After a throb of hesitation.*) Ben! Benny! . . . (*They are standing off from each other, poised on needles.*) Don't be afraid. . . .

STARK:

. . . No? . . .

CLEO:

Love me . . . Love me, Ben.

STARK:

. . . Can't do that. . . .

CLEO:

(*moving forward a step*) Put your arms up and around me.

STARK:

Cleo. . . . (*Now they move in on each other. Everything else gone, they are together in a full, fierce embrace, together in a swelter of heat, misunderstanding, loneliness and simple sex.*)

(pp. 379-380)

There is a lyrical breathlessness here, a balance of romantic urgency and wry humor, and a strong dramatic line, that is far from common in the modern theater.

In Act Two, Scene Two, Ben and Belle have a serious confrontation, and the wife exits in a cold fury:

[BEN]:

wags his head angrily, strides around the room several times. Finally he looks out of the window, examining the Hotel Algiers. A sense of resolution grows into his appearance. Suddenly he puts his hand to his heart, not having noticed before how strongly it is beating.

(p. 395)

The turning point, as is usual in this type of structure, occurs at the conclusion to Act Two:

STARK:

   . . . Tonight we'll be together, Cleo. . . . Alone, alone together. . . .

CLEO:

   I don't trust you.

STARK:

   You're more important to me than anything I know. Cleo, dear. . . .

CLEO:

   What happened?

STARK:

   Nothing. I only know I love you, Cleo.

CLEO:

   (*after a pause, suddenly*) Then hold me tight, Ben. Kiss me, love me—kiss me till I can't be kissed no more. Hold me. Don't let me be alone in the world, Ben. . . . Don't let me be alone. . . . (STARK *moves to her and they embrace passionately.*)

                                   (pp. 397-398)

Thus, Odets focuses the dramatic question first projected at the point of attack and developed throughout the action; moreover, the playwright foreshadows the crisis and climax, both of which become obligatory, since Ben *must* answer the question: Will he "let [Cleo] be alone in the world?" Will he stay on that rocket to the moon? Or will he return to Belle—and all that that return implies?

Conflict is maintained throughout the final act of the play. The entire resolution—crisis, climax and conclusion—explodes within the restricted space of the last four pages of the published text. Cleo asks: "What do you say, Ben? Don't stand there like a dead man . . ." (p. 414). Which line looks back to the point of attack, when Prince tells Ben: "Make a motto for yourself: 'Out of the coffin by Labor Day!'" (p. 350). Cleo's question also prepares the audience for the following crisis:

CLEO:

   (*almost crying*) Don't discuss [Prince], Ben. Tell me what *our* plans are. What'll you do with me?

STARK:

   Cleo, I can't talk now. . . . This man standing here . . .

CLEO:

   No, you have to tell me now. Where do I stand? . . .

STARK:

   (*evasively*) Stand? . . .

PRINCE:

   (*harshly*) In short, will you leave your wife? (STARK *is silent, unable to make an answer.* CLEO *looks at him appealingly.* PRINCE *stands in the background, unwilling to provoke* CLEO'S *wrath.*)

This is, of course, the point toward which the tension of the play has been mounting—that moment in which the fate of Ben, Belle and Cleo must be decided and the theme realized in full. The climax flows immediately out of the crisis:

STARK:

   (*lost*) Nothing. . . . I can't say. . . . Nothing. . . .

CLEO:

   You'll let me go away? (*She gets no reply from him. Half stunned, she seats herself. Finally.*)

CLEO:

   I'd like to hold my breath and die.

PRINCE:

   (*softly*) He'd let you do that, too.

STARK:

   (*to Prince*) You're a dog, the lowest dog I ever met!

—:

   (*To Cleo*) Do you know what this man is trying to do?

CLEO:

   (*crushed*) I don't care.

STARK:

   (*gently*) Listen, Cleo . . . think. What can I give you? All I can offer you is a second-hand life, dedicated to trifles and troubles . . . and they go on forever. This isn't self-justification . . . but facts are stubborn things, Cleo; I've wrestled with myself for weeks. This is how it must end. (*His voice trembling.*) Try to understand . . . I can't say more. . . .

                                   (p. 415)

Cleo then decides that none of the men in the play are worth her love. Nevertheless, she will go on searching for the right man. Prince advises her: "You'll never get what you're looking for! You want a life like Heifetz's music—up from the roots, perfect, clean, every note in place. But that, my girl, is music!" (p. 416). In the three plays discussed in this section—*Awake and Sing!, Golden Boy* and *Rocket to the Moon*—music is used as a symbol of the good life, perhaps of the "perfect" and hence the ultimately unattainable life. An increasing tension is discernible in Odets' work between what the dramatist wants to believe and the limits that reality establishes on romantic dreams. The tension, as I have suggested, was there from the beginning; for example, in *Awake and Sing!* Jacob's broken phonograph records are juxtaposed to Ralph's revolutionary gestures and the romantic flight of Hennie and Moe. In *Rocket to the Moon,* however, the urgency of young Cleo's search for love seems a bit wistful in the somber context of the play. Listening to Cleo's parting words one is reminded of the futile longings of Lorna Moon at the crisis in *Golden Boy.* Here, once again, is Lorna:

> Somewhere there must be happy boys and girls who can teach us the way of life! We'll find some city where poverty's no shame—where music is no crime!—where there's no war in the streets—where a man is glad to be himself, to live and make his woman herself!
>
> (p. 316)

This is Cleo:

> Don't you think there's a world of joyful men and women? Must all men live afraid to laugh and sing? Can't we sing at work and love our work? It's getting late to play at life; I want to *live* it. . . . You see? I don't ask for much. . . .
>
> (p. 416)

It may be, however, *too much.* In *Golden Boy* the lovers end badly, but Frank Bonaparte is present to suggest better days in the future. Similarly, Ralph's conversion in the last act of *Awake and Sing!* foreshadows a world in which love can grow and mature in dignity. At the conclusion of *Rocket to the Moon* Odets does not wholly resist the temptation to add a positive note before the curtain descends on an otherwise realistic play:

PRINCE:

(*at the door*) Go home, to my daughter. . . .

STARK:

(*slowly rises from his seat; calls Prince back*) Poppa, wait a minute. . . . For years I sat here, taking things for granted, my wife, everything. Then just for an hour my life was in a spotlight. . . . I saw myself clearly, realized who and what I was. Isn't that a beginning? Isn't it? . . .

PRINCE:

Yes. . . .

STARK:

And this is strange! . . . For the first time in years I don't feel guilty. . . . But I'll never take things for granted again. You see? Do you see, Poppa?

PRINCE:

Go home, Benny. . . . (*He turns out the lamp.*)

STARK:

(*turning out the other lamp*) Yes, I, who sat here in this prison-office, closed off from the world . . . for the first time in years I looked out on the world and saw things as they really are. . . .

PRINCE:

(*wearily*) It's getting late. . . .

STARK:

(*almost laughing*) Sonofagun! . . . What I don't know would fill a book! (PRINCE *exits heavily.* STARK *turns out the last light, then exits, closing the door behind him. The room is dark, except for red neon lights of the Hotel Algiers and a spill of light from the hall.*)

Slow curtain

(p. 418)

Although Odets avoids having Ben run away with Cleo in the manner of Moe and Hennie in the earlier play, he spoils his ending with this unconvincing final dialogue. I would not, though, call this a serious defect in a structure otherwise noted for its clear, plausible, rising line of action. As Otis Ferguson says: "[*Rocket to the Moon*] is as tight a piece of dramatic joining as you will find, marvelous in the ingenuity with which the play moves forward by the use of three men, two women, two commentators, one dentist's office. It is not only that this ease in the the form means release from formalities as such. In this story of likely people trying to find their way out of the likeliest of difficulties (likely but not humdrum, it must be emphasized) the freedom from strain gives it the complete scope of honesty in dealing with the problems of people who have somehow to live and who dream of living happily." Consequently, it is difficult to understand the persistent claim that the structure of the play is faulty. *Rocket to the Moon* moves in a straight line of development; it is neither "static" nor "wobbly." Odets felt, as I have said, that most people "failed to understand the structure." Close analysis of the action seems to support the playwright's contention.

A word is in order on Odets' use of the hot summer weather in the action of the play. The torrid heat allows the playwright, as Rosamond Gilder has pointed out, to bring various characters on stage, for Ben Stark's office appears to be the only room with a water-cooler. More important, however, is that the oppressive summer intensifies the frustrations and passions of the characters. As might be expected, the stifling atmosphere mainly underscores the romantic and sexual emotions of Ben and Cleo. At one point, for example, Prince mops his brow and stares out thirstily at the Hotel Algiers, which place, as I have shown, becomes a symbol of Ben's desire for Cleo. Belle jealously objects to Cleo going about the office without stockings and wearing her hair in an upsweep (p. 336). In Act Two, while Ben is occupied on the telephone, Cleo hastily adjusts her under-garments. When Ben returns, Cleo says: "I never adjust my shoulder straps or girdle in public, as some women do. God knows, it's so warm I'm practically naked underneath"; to which—"with surprising asperity"—Ben replies: "You musn't say things like that!" (p. 366). Hence Odets, through repeated references to the heat and to Cleo's body, contrives to keep the urgency of love and sex constantly in the foreground of the action. But the blistering summer weather also creates a slight aura of fantasy about the events on stage, and at times lends a touch of "other worldliness" to the characters' drab lives. Thus Cleo remarks: "People in the city have a sweet kind of dizziness in the summer" (p. 375). "They're frying eggs on the sidewalk," Cooper, another dentist, says. "The public is staggering around" (p. 375). Clearly, then, a good deal of that "web of sensory impressions" in *Rocket to the Moon* which Odets spoke of in his "Preface" to the *Six Plays* derives from the dramatist's careful manipulation of atmosphere.

The characters in *Rocket to the Moon* are among the most realistic and complex that Odets has created. For example, Prince tells Cleo that Ben "lost his enterprise, years ago. He's no more resourceful. . . . My good daughter made him like that—afraid to take a chance" (p. 368). Later Cleo repeats this charge to Ben: "You don't go *out* to things any more. It's your wife's fault" (p. 374). It would be an easy task for a dramatist to push the entire responsibility onto the woman—the destructive bitch is a favorite character of American writers—and to whitewash the hero. But Odets refuses the easy way. "I'm what I am," says Ben, "it's not Belle's fault!" (p. 349). Perhaps Ben's troubles, one might argue, extend back to his early days in an orphan home (p. 348), for a child deprived of a mother's love may grow up feeling strangely inadequate. This lack of certainty about himself may account for Ben's need to have the approval and love of others. "My husband lets people walk all over him—" Belle informs Cooper. "Don't you think you're taking advantage of his good nature?" (p. 338). Indeed, Ben's sensitive, brooding nature probably impelled him away from the world long before he had met Belle. Odets makes the point that Ben was interested in botany as a young man (p. 330), and I have already commented on Ben's fondness for Shakespeare. Probably Ben became a dentist because that line of work seemed more "practical," and because he felt that Belle would not marry a man who wanted to be a florist. (The thematic link between *Golden Boy* and *Rocket to the Moon* should, once more, be manifest.) Hence, both socio-economic and psychological forces help to account for Ben's plight. Reference to antecedent causal factors, of course, does not mean that Belle Stark has made no contribution to her husband's unhappiness. A different woman may have helped Ben to overcome the past, may have encouraged him to realize himself more fully. Unfortunately, however, Belle

could not be that woman because she too has been twisted psychologically by circumstances in the past.

For Belle Stark is the product of an unhappy marriage. She informs Ben that her parents were "always quarreling" (pp. 330-331). Belle has an intense grudge against her father—"If you'd seen the life of hell he gave my mother," she tells Ben, "you'd understand" (p. 331)—and the suggestion is present that Belle has developed an unconscious enmity, or at least a resentment, toward men as a result of her early experience as a child. It is also suggested that Belle may be unsatisfactory as a sexual partner due to the Puritanical influence of her mother: "In the bargain," Prince complains to Ben, "[Belle's mother] had more respectability under the blankets than you have on Fifth Avenue!" (p. 347). An unfavorable background then has damaged Belle, too. "Ben, you have to love me all the time," she says. "I have to know my husband's there, loving me and needing me" (p. 335). Instead of making Belle timid and pliable, though, circumstances have molded Belle into a cold, harsh, aggressive person. In a way, Ben and Belle have exchanged "masculine" and "feminine" roles, inasmuch as Ben is rather passive and Belle is more active. One is reminded here of the same reversal of roles in *Awake and Sing!* and of the outrage against nature which accounted for the warped characters in *Golden Boy. Rocket to the Moon,* however, suggests a more complicated approach to character and environment than Odets demonstrated in his earlier plays.

Part of Belle's difficulty derives from the fact that she is unable to have children—there may be a combination of biological and psychological factors here—and hence she remains deeply frustrated in her "natural" role as a woman. Belle does not want her father to move in with the Starks because she believes that a husband and wife should live alone (p. 331). Yet—ironically—it is partly due to the fact that the couple *are* alone that they remain unhappy. Frustrated motherhood would seem to account for Belle's overprotective attitude toward Ben: "Any day now," she remarks to her husband, "I'm expecting to powder and diaper you" (p. 330). To complicate matters further, it is precisely the lack of children that renders Belle more insecure and jealous about Ben's possible waywardness. "You don't have children to hold you together," Prince tells Ben. "You're almost forty . . . a time for special adventures" (p. 349). Belle's general insecurity, the foundation of which was established in childhood but which has been perpetuated through the conditions of her marriage, manifests itself in other ways beside mere sexual jealousy. As Frenchy informs Ben: "every generous impulse on your part brings [Belle] closer to insecurity" (p. 353). Consequently, Belle has felt compelled to dislike Ben's Shakespeare teacher, Dr. Gladstone, evidently simply because Ben loved the man (p. 359). Such factors as these make Ben's announcement at the end of the play—"I insist this is a beginning"—seem rather hollow. "It's Labor Day on Monday," Prince reminds Ben; and one cannot help but feel that Ben, rather than making a "beginning," is returning to his "coffin" (p. 418).

Mr. Prince is another complex character. As is true of so many modern writers, Odets gives the audience options on how to interpret the man. Was Prince the cause of the unhappy marriage that produced Belle? Or was he the victim of a frigid and destructive woman? Perhaps the truth lies in a combination of factors? At any rate, Prince blames his wife and daughter for his misfortunes: "The two of them, my wife included—with their bills they ate holes in me like Swiss cheese . . ." (p. 341). In his directions Odets says that Prince is an "extremely self-confident man" (p. 339); but in the action of the play Prince manifests an intense desire to live with Ben and Belle. Why? To be sure, Prince is fond of his son-in-law; however, he dislikes Belle very much, and he is clearly aware of his daughter's rejection of him. Why then should he wish to move in with the couple? Apparently Prince is not as "self-confident" as Odets suggests; beneath the man's bluster there exists a loneliness, a dread of old age, and a hunger for love. "There are seven fundamental words in life," Prince tells Ben, "and one of these is love, and I didn't have it! And another one is love, and I didn't have it! *And the third of these is love, and I shall have it!*" (p. 409, italics in original). When Ben suggests that Prince was unfaithful to his wife, the older man stoutly defends himself: "Never! *But never!* Not once did I make a sexual deviation!" (p. 347, italics in original). No doubt, it was Belle who told Ben that her father was unfaithful to her mother. Should the audience believe Belle? Or is Prince correct in his claim of innocence? True, Prince has a yearning for Cleo; but his wife is dead now and his sexual longings in the present offer no proof of the man's past behavior. Similar ambiguity surrounds the question of Prince's artistic talent. "Without marriage," Prince asserts, "I would have been one of the greatest actors in the world!" (p. 347). Now it appears extremely unlikely that Prince might have been a *great* actor—but is there *any* truth to his claim? Ben seems dubious (p. 348). Odets, however, says: "There is about [Prince] the dignity and elegant portliness of a Jewish actor, a sort of aristocratic air" (p. 339). Prince declares that his wife "insulted [his] soul" (p. 347). Which remark echoes Jacob's belief expressed in *Awake and Sing!*: "Remember, a woman insults a man's soul like no other thing in the whole world!" (p. 48). In both instances, however, one feels that the man speaking has, in one way or another, contributed to his difficulties with woman. One is forced to conclude, then, that Prince, like the other characters in the play, is far from a simple creation.

The foregoing discussion of structure and character should make plain that love is the main subject matter of **Rocket to the Moon**. In *The Fervent Years*, Harold Clurman maintains that Odets' theme is confused. "As originally planned," says Clurman, "the play was about a meek little dentist ravaged through the love of a silly girl. . . . In the actual writing of the play the theme was transformed to that of the difficult quest for love in the modern world." But aren't there some suspiciously neat and oversubtle distinctions here? As my analysis of the play's action shows, there is nothing seriously defective about Odets' thematic structure. Why can't Ben *and* Cleo—and Prince, *and* Belle, *and* the others—all reveal the "difficult quest for love in the modern world"? In fact, that "quest" constitutes the "spine" of the play. Clurman also argues that Cleo steals the last act. This is not correct. Ben remains the protagonist from the point of attack, through the development and turning point, to the resolution. After the climax, it is true, Cleo tends to move toward the foreground—as did Hennie in *Awake and Sing!*—but this temporary advance is not evidence of gross structural defect. Furthermore, the conclusion of the play belongs to Ben. True, Odets injects a false note of optimism at the end when Ben says: "I insist this is a beginning," but Prince's statement that Monday is Labor Day—with its connotation of a "coffin"—and his weary attitude, tends to qualify the positive assertion. Further proof that there is no confusion between Ben's search for love and "the difficult quest for love in the modern world" lies in a consideration of Cleo, Cooper and Frenchy as agents in the "spine" of the play.

Some critics disparage Cleo Singer. Clurman, for example, calls her "rattle-brained," "silly" and "trivial"; John Gassner brands her "unimportant" and "commonplace"; Edmond M. Gagey regards her as "cheap" and "silly." Others feel that her awakening at the end of the play is unconvincing. In my opinion, Cleo Singer is Odets' most appealing female character, and one of the most attractive and forceful characters ever created by an American dramatist. Only some of Tennessee Williams's heroines have as much vitality on the stage as Cleo; but with the exception of Maggie in *Cat on a Hot Tin Roof*, all of Williams's memorable women are pathological cases. It must be a dour critic indeed who is not charmed and captivated by young Cleo, and compelled by her urgent desire to "live." Nor is her behavior at the end of the play so alarming; in fact, there is no real transformation. For Cleo has merely glimpsed the truth about Ben; her original desire to find love has not altered—indeed it has been intensified. Moreover, is it correct to say that Cleo's sentiments are too lofty for such a young girl? Aside from the fact that the average person expects a character in a play to be more articulate than such a one would be in life—what is so intellectually involved in Cleo's decision to go on searching for love? Every young person has felt the same desire. Nor would an acquaintance with, say, Plato's "Symposium" be a prerequisite for understanding such feelings.

Throughout the play Cleo expresses a desire for love and a sense of personal dignity. "Mrs. Stark," Cleo complains to Prince, "she thinks I'm a dummy. Do this, do that!—I'm a person!" (p. 342). This is in Act One. In Act Three, Cleo informs another unacceptable male: "No man can take a bite out of me, like an apple and throw it away" (p. 411). Similarly, Cleo yearns for fulfillment in love throughout the play. "Nobody loves me!" she wails. "Millions of people moving around the city and nobody cares if you live or die" (p. 372). "Don't you think life is to live all you can and experience everything?" she asks Ben. "Isn't that the only way you can develop to be a real human being?" (p. 374). "I'm a girl, and I want to be a woman," she declares at the end, "and the man I love must help me be a woman!" (pp. 416-417). Cleo, I believe, remains in character throughout the action of the play. Of course she has altered somewhat—"I have more confidence than when I came here," she announces (p. 417)—but that change has been made credible. Luise Rainer, then Odets' wife, thought that Cleo should have married Prince. R. Baird Shuman says: "Such an ending would have been in character with Cleo . . . and would have been a more conclusive ending than the one which Odets insisted upon." Given such a faulty interpretation of a central character, one is not surprised when Shuman concludes that, although **Rocket to the Moon** "does represent a broadening in Odets' interests and social concerns, it does not mark an artistic advance for him."

Phil Cooper is another Odetsian character in search of love. In his case, however, economic problems are even more insistent than they are in the lives of, say, Ben or Cleo: "Who's got time to think about women! I'm trying to make a living! . . . Is there a man in our generation with time to think about women? Show me that man and I'll show you a loafer!" (p. 352). In Act Two Cooper returns to this theme:

> If only they invented hydrants in the streets which give out milk and honey! . . . we'd be happier people. . . . Don't I try? Can anyone accuse me of indifference to my work? Why can't I make a living? I'm falling apart by inches. (*Suddenly sobbing.*) Where can I sail away? To where? I'm ashamed to live! An ostrich can hide his head. Diphtheria gets more respect than me! They coddle germs in laboratories—they feed the white mice twice a day. . . . Why don't somebody coddle *me*? (*Controlling himself now.*) What did I do to my fellow man? Why am I punished like this? (*Trembling again on the brink of sobs, but holding them back.*) Where is the God they told me about? Why should an innocent boy and an old lady suffer? I ask you to tell me, what is the Congress doing? Where are they in the hour of the needs of the people? . . . Where will it end if they can't use millions of Coopers?
>
> (p. 376)

"O'Neill's and Steinbeck's proletarian heroes are often characterized by their lack of verbal coherence," says Robert Brustein, "but Odets' heroes are singular for their extreme verbosity. Rather than being speechless in the face of their dilemma, they never stop talking about it." Alan S. Downer points out that Odets has "an absolute ear for human speech," and that in this respect "he has been unequalled in the modern theater." It is important to add, however, that, as Gerald Weales says, "with Odets, colloquial speech is not simply reproduced; it takes an artistic form . . . [it is] a kind of literary prose." Phil Cooper is a "natural" lover frustrated by the circumstances of his life. "In my younger days I was inclined to poetry," he remarks. "In my older days I'm inclined to poverty" (p. 337). God might be, as the Church says, Love, but Mrs. Cooper is dead and "life is a war" (p. 376).

Perhaps Frenchy, the bachelor, is the chief raisonneur in the play. When Ben says: "A man would be a mad idealist to want a honeymoon all his life," Frenchy corrects him: "No, he'd be a woman. . . . The man who worries for the bucks is not the one to kiss his wife behind the ear" (p. 352). The conflict between the "love ethic" and the "business ethic," a prominent theme in modern literature, is on view here. Later in the play Frenchy is more articulate on the subject of love in our time:

FRENCHY:

(*with extreme seriousness*) . . . Love, for most people, is a curious sensation below the equator. Love—as they call it—is easy—even the rabbits do it! The girl I want . . . she'd have to be made in heaven. That's why I wait—

STARK:

You're that good, you think?

FRENCHY:

(*correcting him*) That *bad*, Doc! *She'll* have to be the good one. This is why: Love is a beginning, a jumping-off place. It's like what heat is at the forge—makes the metal easy to handle and shape. *But love and the grace to use it!*—To develop, expand it, variate it!—Oh, dearie me, that's the problem, as the poet said!

STARK:

Yes, I see your point. . . .

FRENCHY:

Who can do that today? Who's got time and place for "love and the grace to use it?" Is it something apart, love? A good book you go to in a spare hour? An entertainment? Christ, no! It's a synthesis of good and bad, economics, work, play, all contacts . . . it's not a Sunday suit for special occasions. That's why Broadway songs are phony, Doc!—Love is no solution of life! Au contraire, as the Frenchman says—the opposite. You have to bring a whole balanced normal life to love if you want it to go!

STARK:

Yes, I see your point.

FRENCHY:

In this day of stresses I don't see much normal life, myself included. The woman's not a wife. She's the dependent of a salesman who can't make sales and is ashamed to tell her so, of a federal project worker . . . or a Cooper, a dentist . . . the free exercise of love, I figure, gets harder every day.

(p. 404, italics in original)

This is the same viewpoint, the reader will recall, that Odets expressed in *Awake and Sing!* and *Golden Boy,* namely, that there can be no real love until the social environment is "healthy," until lovers can "bring a whole balanced normal life to love." Need one be a Marxist in order to concur with this evaluation of a serious contemporary situation?

The theme of love, as Odets remarked in 1962, remains relevant. Unless human nature changes, and the conditions of modern life are drastically altered, the theme should continue to be relevant. Surely it is silly to go on speaking of Odets in terms of "proletarian drama." In making Odets a stereotype figure of the thirties, the commonplace caricature of his career neglects the fact that his plays written during the Great Depression transcend that specific era and, by projecting continuing spiritual and emotional conflicts arising from our general social situation in this broken century, assume universality. Although Odets appeared to be waving a red flag in *Waiting for Lefty,* one would have to be a member of a certain Congressional committee to locate signs of ideological unAmericanism in, say, *Rocket to the Moon.* Odets persisted in mouthing tough slogans as late as 1939 when, in the "Preface" to *Six Plays,* he said: "We are living in a time when new art works should shoot bullets" (p. ix). Odets' practice, however, was another matter. Gerald Rabkin and other critics overemphasize the importance of the Marxist metaphor in Odets' work in the thirties. There are, as I have attempted to show, many things other than economic going on in the early plays. By focusing too narrowly on the Marxist dimension of *Awake and Sing!, Golden Boy* and *Rocket to the Moon,* Rabkin—and, I repeat, he is certainly not alone here—undervalues not only the other elements in said plays but also all the pieces written after the thirties. This simply will not do. The approach is much too narrow. Even the writer in *Time* magazine was perceptive enough to note this fact in 1938:

The reason Odets has gained and held a public that, by and large, does not share his Leftist ideas is obviously not the ideas themselves but his rich, compassionate, angry feeling for people, his tremendous dramatic punch, his dialogue, bracing as ozone. In every Odets play, regardless of its theme or its worth, at least once or twice during the evening every spectator feels that a fire hose has been turned on his body, that a fist has connected with his chin.

Yet even this concedes too much to Odets' "Leftist ideas" in respect to his better plays of the period. During the thirties Joseph Wood Krutch never tired of reminding his readers that Odets' plays did not depend for their appeal on Marx. Radicalism is apparent in *Awake and Sing!*—which survives in spite of its agit-prop ending—but Marxism disappears almost from view in *Golden Boy* and *Rocket to the Moon. Golden Boy,* as Krutch points out, "may be very readily though not inevitably interpreted in the Marxian terms which Mr. Odets would no doubt insist upon," but the play owes its "excellence to a warmth of imagination rather than to an intellectual creed." Elsewhere Krutch says of *Golden Boy*—but his remarks could as well be applied to *Rocket to the Moon*—that "Odets keeps his political theories in the background where they belong and writes a play which does not depend for its appeal upon a concern with his economic opinions. The agonies of his characters are real and affecting, whatever one may think of the reasons for their existence." These are wise words, and many a contemporary critic would profit from a consideration of them prior to taking another look at Odets' early work. Finally, almost every approach to Odets in the past has been prone to overemphsize theme in his plays, and to neglect the means through which the dramatist expresses his view of life. In the first part of this study I have sought to illuminate Odets' dramaturgy—his complex construction, his rich characterizations, his unforgettable dialogue—and in the analytical chapters that follow I shall continue to stress both the "what" and the "how" of the plays. For Odets is a dramatist—not a philosopher—and as such he is one of the finest writers we have produced in the American theater. And this judgment rests, I believe, not only on three plays of the thirties, but also on three pieces written *after* the thirties.

References

Brustein, Robert. "America's New Culture Hero," *Commentary,* XXV (February 1958), 123-129.

Clurman, Harold. *The Fervent Years.* New York, 1945.

Downer, Alan S. *Fifty Years of American Drama* 1900-1950. Chicago, 1951.

Gagey, Edmond M. *Revolution in American Drama.* New York, 1947.

Gassner, John. "The Long Journey of a Talent," *Theater Arts,* XXXIII (July 1949), 25-30.

———. "Anton Chekhov," *A Treasury of the Theater* (New York, 1960), 205-206.

————. "Introduction," *Play-Making* by William Archer (New York, 1960), v-xxxi.

Shuman, R. Baird. *Clifford Odets.* New York, 1962.

Weales, Gerald. *American Drama Since World War II.* New York, 1962.

————. *A Play and Its Parts.* New York, 1964.

EDITIONS CITED

Six Plays of Clifford Odets. New York: Random House, 1939 (includes *Waiting for Lefty, Awake and Sing! Till the Day I Die, Paradise Lost, Golden Boy* and *Rocket to the Moon*).

Michael J. Mendelsohn (essay date 1969)

SOURCE: Mendelsohn, Michael J. "The Early Plays: Written in Anger." In *Clifford Odets: Humane Dramatist*, pp. 21-42. Deland, Fla.: Everett/Edwards, Inc., 1969.

[*In the following essay, Mendelsohn examines Odets's early plays, highlighting his development as a young playwright and noting, especially, his achievement of "a characteristic style and a personal set of artistic standards" that elevated his work beyond propaganda and social realism.*]

I. WAITING FOR LEFTY

Clifford Odets was at the peak of his political involvement when he wrote *Waiting for Lefty,* his first produced play. This play of labor union strife is so often pointed to as the typical leftist drama of the Thirties that the comment is as trite as it is oversimplified. The drama is militant, propagandistic, and strident, but, unlike so many of the angry plays of the period, it is also frequently human and touching. Part of the importance of the work certainly lies in the acclaim it received; since subtlety is not one of the play's strong points, the fact that audiences were able to lose themselves in such a direct assault is in itself a good indication of the mood in that turbulent depression year, 1935. Harold Clurman referred to the play as "the birth cry of the thirties" and it is quite natural that the drama has assumed for him a large, almost mystic halo. Those less emotionally involved with the play may find that in retrospect it is hard to become so excited as this. Great drama is indestructible; *Waiting for Lefty,* for all its merits, too often seems as dead as last year's newspaper.

There are many fine qualities about *Waiting for Lefty,* not the least of them being that the author approached his work with imagination and technique that far surpass what might be expected from a first play. As a result, *Waiting for Lefty* displays an artistry generally ab-

sent from other labor plays of the period. In a series of vignettes, sharply telescoped in time, the drama takes up the story of several characters associated in different ways with the proposed taxi drivers' strike. As Odets envisioned the structure, it was related to that of a minstrel show, with various characters emerging from the darkened stage into the spotlight to tell their stories. Although seemingly episodic in structure, *Waiting for Lefty* has a basic unity imposed upon it, first by the theatrical framework of the strike meeting and second by the gradually developed thesis that everyone involved is a part of Lefty.

Since *Waiting for Lefty* is a short play dominated almost completely by theme, the incidents of the theatrical frame are few. The drivers meet to consider a strike vote; various drivers come forward to relate recent incidents in their own lives and various stooges of management try to keep them under control; finally, word is received that Lefty, the awaited leader, will never arrive because he has been assassinated; this climactic event prompts one of the men to take the initiative and call for a strike vote.

But there is a double framework involved in *Waiting for Lefty,* and Odets never lets his audience forget the significance of his dramatic point. Time and again as the play builds its intensity, he wrenches the audience away from a scene with a violent reminder that there is a strike to be considered, action to be taken. The interplay between personal lives and collective action is masterfully handled: Joe and Edna need food for their children; a strike will provide it. The "young hack" can't afford to marry at all; a strike will enable him to do so. Dr. Benjamin is fired by an anti-Semitic hospital board; the clenched fist offers the solution. Each character is a fragment of Lefty, and the wait that is taking place is actually a wait for the submerging of the individual in the group.

Each scene adds to the intensity that is necessary for the play's success. By the end the pace is unrelenting, and all that remains is the achievement of a new leader's birth in Lefty's death. A crucial part of the message of labor solidarity is that many spring up where one dies. And so Lefty, very much alive in spirit, arrives in the body and voice of Agate Keller. Odets is doctrinaire, not existential. As a result, unlike the wait for Godot, the wait for Lefty is not in vain.

To present these events, Odets employs what may seem at first a peculiar assortment of characters. He is obviously striving to universalize his situation; undeniably there *were* members of the disrupted middle class and even some professional men trying to earn a few dollars as cab drivers in 1934. Still, the play seems rather oddly unbalanced. Of the five flashback scenes, three concern non-proletarians: a laboratory scientist, an interne, and an actor. The incongruity of the situation is heightened, as John Howard Lawson later observed, by Odets' insistence on having the strike group addressed at the end as "stormbirds of the working class." But Odets could hardly do otherwise. The writers of the Left had little acquaintance with true workers. Odets was dealing with people he knew. Middle-class himself, he was directing his polemics at an audience that was also largely middle-class. Industrial workers who attended his performances did not need the prodding of such a theme; it was the middle class and the intellectuals who needed the lesson. Like so many other American authors of the period, Odets found himself attracted to proletarianism as a state of mind. It was a theoretical or spiritual involvement whose advocates accepted the task of committing their own group to the cause of worker solidarity.

It is revealing that the scene with the unemployed actor is omitted in the Random House published version, *Six Plays of Clifford Odets.* Odets later stated that the reason for the omission was his decision that the problem was not sufficiently universal, that it had special meaning only for actors. Since the scene is the most militant and radical one in the play, a more likely reason for its omission was the calming of the playwright's extremism by 1939.

Waiting for Lefty is notable as the only one of Odets' plays to employ the theatricalist devices of direct address to the audience and actors planted in the auditorium. Both are well adapted to this play. While these techniques appear at first to belong to the anti-illusory theatre of Brecht or Wilder, Odets uses them for a totally different purpose. The basic assumption of the anti-illusionist writer is that the audience, aware that it is in a theatre, may constantly be reminded that it is viewing a play; the basic assumption of the illusionist is that effective drama can best be achieved if the audience forgets it is in a theatre and believes it is viewing not a play, but life. Odets, far from suggesting to the viewer that this is a play, works doubly hard to create the illusion of a strike meeting in a union hall. Almost in the manner of Pirandello, Odets blends the theatre and life, the imitation and the actual, so that the audience is never quite certain which is which. These techniques as well as the bare stage and the entire simplicity of the production made it admirably suited for use by small theatre groups or even for union meetings, and much of the play's success resulted from its use by such groups all over the country.

The dialogue of *Waiting for Lefty* first revealed Odets' tremendous power. In the true and touching words of Edna, wife of one of the taxi drivers, the dramatist

demonstrates his exceptional ability for expressing the abstract of the class struggle by means of the concrete of family life:

> You got two blondie kids sleeping in the next room. They need food and clothes. I'm not mentioning anything else—But we're stalled like a flivver in the snow. For five years I laid awake at night listening to my heart pound. For God's sake, do something, Joe, get wise. . . . I'm turning into a sour old nag.
>
> (i)

And a little later she exclaims, with even more power,

> I know this—your boss is making suckers outa you boys every minute. Yes, and suckers out of all the wives and the poor innocent kids who'll grow up with crooked spines and sick bones. Sure, I see it in the papers, how good orange juice is for kids. But damnit our kids get colds one on top of the other. They look like little ghosts. Betty never saw a grapefruit. I took her to the store last week and she pointed to a stack of grapefruits. "What's that!" she said. My God, Joe—the world is supposed to be for all of us.
>
> (i)

On the other hand, Odets also displays his early tendency to end with an overwrought curtain speech, a passage excessively charged with emotion:

> Hear it, boys, hear it? Hell, listen to me! Coast to coast! HELLO AMERICA! HELLO. WE'RE STORMBIRDS OF THE WORKING-CLASS. WORKERS OF THE WORLD. . . . OUR BONES AND BLOOD! And when we die they'll know what we did to make a new world! Christ, cut us up to little pieces. We'll die for what is right! Put fruit trees where our ashes are!

Such a speech may be exactly what an audience wanted to hear from a militant playwright; yet somehow on the printed page the ring is hollow. Most people go to a national political convention to cheer the speakers, no matter what they say or fail to say. In the same way, most of the audiences for *Waiting for Lefty* had to arrive at the theatre with a preconceived set of opinions, and when they heard the old familiar tune, "Workers of the world, unite," they were entranced mainly by the vigor with which it was shouted. Thus in his first play Odets showed his audiences tantalizing glimpses of effective playwriting embedded in large doses of prepackaged Marxist stimulation.

II. *TILL THE DAY I DIE*

In the play written to serve as a curtain raiser for *Waiting for Lefty,* when the latter drama was brought to Broadway, Odets abandoned the New York setting and characters he knew so well. *Till the Day I Die* represents the playwright's only excursion outside the United States for a setting until his non-localized *The Flowering Peach* many years later. (One minor exception is

Odets' unproduced play about a Cuban rebellion written in 1938, which Odets called "the only really poor play I ever wrote." And it is interesting that he blamed its shortcomings on the fact that he was not really familiar with the people and the area he was writing about, a statement equally applicable to his earlier play about Germany.) Of Odets' eleven produced plays, *Till the Day I Die* is the slightest. As one of the first anti-Nazi plays written in the United States, its importance is historical rather than dramatic.

In this play as in *Waiting for Lefty,* Odets uses a series of brief scenes. However, the method employed is a straight narrative-sequential one rather than the series of vignettes used in the labor play. In seven scenes Odets depicts the degradation and death of Ernst Tausig, a Communist Party underground worker in the Germany of the new Fuehrer. Like so many political plays, this one makes certain assertions that are only slightly related to fact: one, that there was widespread organized opposition to Hitler within Germany; the other, that the Communist Party in Germany was the focal point and guiding light in that opposition. Unfortunately for the playwright, the march of events in Europe proved both of these ideas false. The latter belief dissolved especially suddenly with the signing of the Berlin-Moscow pact in the summer of 1939.

Apart from such political considerations, *Till the Day I Die* fails to be very convincing in its picture of an anti-Nazi underground. The playwright's constant emphasis on physical torture serves more to numb the reader than to make him angry or sympathetic. The mood of this play, in contrast to the steady heightening of mood in *Waiting for Lefty,* rapidly presents a suicide, a murder, and a handsmashing scene. After all of this violence, the second suicide, that of the central figure, is almost an anti-climax. More important, the doctrinaire message which precedes the pistol shot, strikingly similar to the equivalent scene at the end of *Waiting for Lefty,* is again too emotional for the occasion.

The other aspect of the play which is most obviously contrived is the scene depicting one of the Nazis as a homosexual. It is weak because it is so completely irrelevant, adding nothing to either the plot or the characterization. If Odets is interested in demonstrating that all Nazis are perverts and all Communists noble, he fails badly.

At the same time, the play has its merits. Again Odets manages to put the anti-Nazi underground abstraction into human terms. One of the workers exclaims, apropos of nothing that has gone before, "I used to be crazy on tulip bulbs. For years I spent my weekly salary on them" (i). Ernst, the play's hero, is a violinist; thus the

destruction of his hands is doubly immoral. (The same concept recurs in *Golden Boy.*) And again Tilly, Ernst's common-law wife, recalls small details of her early life:

> I had a nice coat once. I had a mother. I had a father. I was a little girl with pigtails and her face scrubbed every morning. I was a good child. I believed in God. In summer I ate mulberries from our own tree. In late summer the ground was rotten where they fell.
>
> (vii)

These and other poignant, humanizing touches show the playwright to advantage, but the net effect of *Till the Day I Die* is hampered by Odets' failure to invest his characters and his situation with a sufficient degree of verisimilitude. For a play which is framed in terms of historical realism, such a failure is disastrous.

III. Awake and Sing

Early in 1935, with the exciting success of *Waiting for Lefty* assured, Odets dusted off *Awake and Sing,* actually completed in draft form two years earlier. Now audiences had an opportunity to see what Odets could do in three full acts. The results were remarkably pleasing. If Odets disappointed those who were expecting another diatribe, *Awake and Sing* must have been a happy surprise to those who suspected that he was incapable of anything more than direct propaganda.

The story centers in the struggle of the two youngest members of the Berger household to escape their environment. In spite of what often appear to be overwhelming odds, the girl, Hennie, leaves at the end; she uses the escape hatch thoughtfully provided by the playwright. But her brother, Ralph, will remain, presumably to fight for a better life for himself and his generation. Some of the plot material employed by Odets left him vulnerable to valid comparisons to soap opera. Nonetheless, even this reliance on fairly obvious plot devices (an inheritance, an illegitimate child, a timely suicide) fails to destroy what is essentially a warm and vibrant picture of the struggles of a Bronx family.

Each character is important in this well-knit play, but apparently old Jacob—ineffectual as he must often seem—is Odets' spokesman. No one in the play pays the slightest bit of attention to Jacob's prophecies, even though each of the characters is to some degree a part of the general depravity of which he speaks. Even Ralph doesn't understand his grandfather; yet, at the end, Ralph comes alive in the death of the old man, thus fulfilling one of Jacob's key prophecies: "For years, I watched you grow up. Wait! You'll graduate from my university" (I). Further underscoring the character's importance, the statement of the playwright's theme is given to Jacob who demands of his grandson, "Go out and fight so life shouldn't be printed on dollar bills" (I).

Underlying *Awake and Sing,* as in so many twentieth century plays, is a noticeable attitude of economic determinism: the evil is in the system, not in the people. The Berger household contains neither hero nor villain. Moe Axelrod is the character who best demonstrates Odets' attitude on this matter. A bitter disabled veteran, Moe sees clearly the need for escape. His cynicism and his hard shell cover, in true sentimental tradition, a sensitive heart. He is the detached, calm observer of life, able to see the foibles of others, yet unable to keep his own emotions in check when touched. In another perspective, Moe is a traditional character between the old (Jacob) and the young (Ralph). The generation that is really warped, Odets indicates, is Bessie's and Myron's; chained to their own bourgeois attitudes and slogans, they are leading a hopelessly false life. (They can squander fifty cents on Irish sweepstakes because someone a block away once won; Myron, the father, says, and perhaps even believes, "Merit never goes unrewarded" I). Because this group is so hopelessly set in its ways, Odets skips over the middle generation and confers Jacob's mantle of hope on Ralph and Hennie. That inheritance of hope motivates Ralph's optimistic utterance at the final curtain. Oddly, the character who leads the way for this rebirth is the embittered but romantic realist, Moe.

Much of the unfavorable criticism of the play centered in the concluding scene, in which Hennie decides to desert her baby and run off with Moe. Krutch, for example, insisted that it was an afterthought, crudely tacked on. There is no doubt that the ending combines Odets' instinct for dramatic effect with his bent for intellectual propagandizing. The combination of Hennie's departure and Ralph's emotional affirmation of faith in the future, provides a characteristic conclusion for an Odets play. Some years ago, asked whether or not he would alter the ending if he were re-writing the play, Odets stated in a letter to me:

> I think *Awake and Sing* should stand as it is. It is true that on the part of the children in the family a "manifesto" is stated (and that the manifesto perhaps does not have the psychological density of certain earlier despairs) at the end of the play; but much in the first two acts of the play points towards the burgeoning insights on the parts of the young folks. What critics seem to carp at is the cultural (or ethical) meanings of the insights arrived at.

More recently, the playwright again reaffirmed a belief in the honesty of the ending. But he added a qualification which suggests that Odets grew to recognize that there are more factors involved in such a decision than there were a quarter of a century ago: "I believed it then, and I believe it now. I think I believed it more *simply* then." (Interview)

The situation at the end of *Awake and Sing,* considered objectively, would not seem to offer much chance for Moe and Hennie to live happily ever after; Odets did

not write fairy tales. Yet optimism is present in the very act of their escape. With Hennie beside him there is a hope that Moe will lose his shell of bitterness and make something of himself in the new society. Moe's conflict has been strictly internal. The one Moe says, "A guy in France has the right idea—dropped his wife in a bathtub fulla acid" (I), while his alter ego can say, "A certain place where it's moonlight and roses. We'll lay down, count stars. Hear the big ocean making noise" (III). Moe has had much in life to make him bitter, but he is still capable of compassion. He points the way for Ralph and thus for all the new generation.

Much of what is best about Odets is on display in *Awake and Sing.* Even relatively minor characters such as Uncle Morty and Sam Feinschreiber are clearly and lovingly etched. Yet the most important quality revealed by Odets in this early play is to be found in the language. The playwright's ability to hear and transcribe the cadences of immigrant Jewish speech is firmly established in *Awake and Sing.* "You gave the dog eat?" (I). "You wanted to make for yourself a certain kind of world" (II). "But you should act. Not like me. A man who had golden opportunities but drank instead a glass of tea" (II). Equally well he hears Morty, now a big man in the garment district, as he employs his heavy-handed sarcasm:

MORTY:

> He had Caruso. Who's got more from life?

BESSIE:

> Who's got more?

MYRON:

> And Marx he had.

MORTY:

> Marx! Some say Marx is the new God today. Maybe I'm wrong. Ha ha ha. . . . Personally I counted my ten million last night. . . . I'm sixteen cents short. So tomorrow I'll go to Union Square and yell no equality in the country! Ah, it's a new generation.

> (III)

Morty refers here to a new generation, one of many such references in the play. This emphasis on a continuing lack of communication between generations adds a contemporary slant to *Awake and Sing.* At the latest revival of this play (at the Charles Theatre in Boston in the fall of 1967) it was this dimension of the play that saved it from appearing dated, that helped make it relevant to a contemporary audience.

As in *Waiting for Lefty* Odets ably employs the poet's technique of suggesting much with something small. In such economy there is an inherent effectiveness clearly recognized by every fine dramatist. For Odets the whole concept of frustration in a Bronx tenement is expressed with a meaningful concrete object. "What the hell kind of house is this it ain't got an orange!!" says Moe (I). Ralph is often the self-pitying yet touching mouthpiece for such statements: "It's crazy—all my life I want a pair of black and white shoes and can't get them. It's crazy!" (I). Again, he berates his mother because he has never had skates, and Bessie, her pride severely wounded, responds in kind: "He didn't have skates! But when he got sick, a twelve year old boy, who called a big specialist for the last $25 in the house? Skates!" (II). In such a discussion neither party is right or both parties are right. The overtones of simple desire for escape from drudgery are present in all these lines.

Another aspect of Odets' dramatic craftsmanship is evident in the manner in which he uses anticipation. Jacob's suicide, for instance, is thoroughly prepared though not, fortunately, with Ibsen's heavy handedness. First, he is allotted the task of walking the dog on the roof; later Moe looks at a newspaper and comments on all the financiers who are jumping to their deaths. Having thus planted the literal plausibility of the suicide, Odets provides the emotional motivation in the senseless act of plain meanness committed by Bessie when she smashes Jacob's beloved records. Hennie's pregnancy is similarly hinted at when she returns sick from a trip to the movies. The plan to marry her off to the unsuspecting Sam is foreshadowed at the outset in Sam's pathetic gift of chocolate peanuts, unfeelingly received by Hennie: "Loft's week-end special, two for thirty-nine" (I).

Awake and Sing appears in retrospect to contain much of the ebullience of O'Casey's *Juno and the Paycock,* and the Odets play suggests O'Casey's in other ways as well. There is, for example, the remarkably astute use of idiomatic language, qualities for which both playwrights have been justly admired. But beyond that is the mood, the "state of chassis" that exists in both worlds: O'Casey's Ireland and Odets' New York are equally out of joint.

Only the ending, in spite of the playwright's insistence on its merit, seems forced and unreal. Ralph's sudden transformation, his rebirth, his passionate utterance of the call to arms are even less credible than Hennie's decision to topple normal conventions. Hennie's walkout is acceptable, if only in John Gassner's terms of "the libido acting up in an intense girl"; Ralph's rapid maturity, triggered by nothing more compelling than watching his sister leave her husband and child, is not as convincing.

IV. *PARADISE LOST*

While it showed overtones of O'Casey, *Awake and Sing* also provided for audiences the first indication that Odets was evolving an American-Chekhovian style. As in Chekhov, not much that is overt really happens; the conflicts are toned down, the crises muted. The most startling physical action of the play is Bessie's destruction of her father's phonograph records. But if Odets' attraction to Chekhov was hinted at in *Awake and Sing,* it appeared in even larger measure in *Paradise Lost,* the fourth Odets play presented in 1935. His knowledge of the Russian master manifests itself in the plotting, the characterization, the dialogue, the theme, and even in the mood, all of which reflect not a slavish imitativeness, but an astute adaptation of Chekhovian mannerisms to an American milieu.

Odets' immediate reaction to the comparisons drawn by several unappreciative reviewers was purely defensive. Following the opening of *Paradise Lost,* he asserted angrily that he had never read *The Cherry Orchard.* But the playwright had brought the trouble on himself by writing a preliminary publicity release on the play which called direct attention to Chekhov:

> By the time I came to write . . . *Awake and Sing* I understood clearly that my interest was not in the presentation of an individual's problems, but in those of a whole class. In other words, the task was to find a theatrical form with which to express the mass as hero. . . . Our confused middle class today—which dares little—is dangerously similar to Chekhov's people. Which is why the people in *Awake and Sing* and *Paradise Lost* (particularly the latter) have what is called a "Chekhovian quality." Which is why it is sinful to violate their lives and aspirations with plot lines.
>
> (["**Some Problems of the Modern Dramatist**"] New York *Times,* Dec. 15, 1935)

In spite of a number of such protestations by Odets and Clurman, however, *Paradise Lost* clearly demonstrates Odets' close kinship with Chekhov.

The mood of wistful melancholy which pervades the play until just before the end and the frequent use of very adroit humor suggest Odets' conscious cultivation of Chekhovian atmosphere. Though Odets breaks the pattern in the final acts of some plays, both playwrights normally avoid emphatic curtains. Shunning climax, the first two act endings in *Paradise Lost* suggest only increasing futility. There are, as well, other obvious points of comparison. Violence is avoided. Both dramatists make extensive use of allegory. Furthermore, the repetition of certain lines by Odets' characters is reminiscent of Gaev's "Cannon off the red." (Clara says, "Have a piece of fruit," and Ben repeats "four stars" as a term of approbation.) Most of all, the characters speak in a vacuum, listen without hearing, respond unresponsively. Like their counterparts in Chekhov's plays, they wander in and out rather aimlessly. There is even an example of mysterious off-stage sound, so deftly employed in *The Cherry Orchard*: at the final curtain, as Leo crosses the stage, "a short fanfare is heard without." If lingering on such comparisons is academic, disregarding them completely is dishonest. To ignore Odets' relationship to Chekhov would be to ignore an important facet of Odets' technique.

In Leo Gordon's household are Leo and his wife, three grown children, and an old family friend, Gus Michaels. Each has his problems, but these individual problems, like the characters themselves, tend to blur and agglomerate. Furthermore, each character seems unaware that his own problem is but another manifestation of the general decay of society, middle-class sterility, or outmoded values tenaciously clung to. Gus Michaels dreams of a return to the old days, the beautiful summer nights "before the Big War. . . . Oh, it was so beautiful in those days!" (II). Like Chekhov's Firs, he lives in the past, in reminiscences of Schoemacher's Ice Cream Parlor. And he holds his Masonic pin in almost the same reverence that the others show for Ben Gordon's little track trophy. Leo's values center in his books and in Emersonian slogans. He wonders what mysterious force is affecting his neatly-ordered universe: ". . . what is happening here? Once we were all together and life was good" (II). Sam Katz is concerned about his childless marriage. Julie Gordon lives in his own special dream world of stock market analysis, his aimlessness underscored by Odets in a stage direction: "He starts out one exit, but changes his mind and goes the other way. It doesn't quite matter where he goes is the intention here" (II). But most alarming of all the parts of the middle-class picture is the breakdown in Clara Gordon's morality; rather than face bankruptcy and disgrace, she is willing to agree to the arson proposition suggested by Leo's partner.

Thus the characters in *Paradise Lost* are intended to merge into a composite picture of a futile middle class. But two characters who stand out from the rest distinctively are Kewpie and Pike. Both are onlookers and commentators on the Gordons' society. Kewpie, the arrogant and ruthless taxi driver, like Yasha in *The Cherry Orchard,* believes in direct action. He knows exactly what he wants and how to get it. Pike, the furnace man, addresses everyone as "Citizen" in the quaint manner of the French Revolution. The playwright's radical spokesman in *Paradise Lost,* he also becomes Leo's guide and mentor.

What actually happens in *Paradise Lost* is relatively simple and relatively unimportant except as it combines with and underscores the theme. The picture that finally emerges is one of an entire household—in fact a miniature society—struggling to overcome the erosion of that society. Profoundly disturbed by what he considered the inability of the middle class to turn from the fetishes that surrounded it, Odets here attempted to portray an entire class floundering aimlessly, heedless of the fact that it is trapped by forces beyond its control. *Paradise*

Lost might almost be subtitled "the education of Leo Gordon," although what Leo learns is not exactly clear. In the course of three years, Leo observes one son dying of encephalitis, another son killed in a holdup, a daughter frustrated in love because of economic conditions, a business partner of twenty-two years become an embezzler, and even his wife tempted by dishonesty under the pressure of the depression. Leo's learning process is painful, and perhaps the rather unsatisfactory ending—another of Odets' early, overwrought curtain speeches—is a direct result of the playwright's unwillingness to be more specific about what Leo intends to do with his newly-gained insight. Odets' brave attempt to raise Leo to tragic stature in the final speech fails badly. The acquisition of wisdom through suffering brings a fitting end to the reign of Oedipus; it is not sufficiently plausible for Leo Gordon.

The subplots add to the picture Odets is sketching. In one, Pearl Gordon, the daughter of the family, finds she cannot marry Felix because in the depression a musician cannot get a job. The situation is a direct extension of the episode of "The Young Hack and His Girl" in *Waiting for Lefty.* In a more interesting subplot, Leo's partner, (who constantly and bitterly complains about his wife's supposed inability to conceive a child—"a woman with a mix-up inside"—) proves to be impotent. And still more interesting is the story of the elder son. Ben has been fed on a diet of ego-inflating lies all his life. His career as a track star and the entire flimsy structure of the Dale Carnegie cult of self-love make Leo and Ben Gordon the direct ancestors of Willy and Biff Loman. Some of Ben's dialogue leaves no room to doubt that Arthur Miller was well acquainted with this play when he wrote *Death of a Salesman*:

BEN:

> But I saw Alfred Bond yesterday—the big A.A.U. official—he says not to worry, a swell berth waiting for me in Wall Street. Will we make money! All the books you can read, Leo. A concert career for Pearlie . . . And Gus can have a better stamp collection than the King of England! Just be patient.

LEO:

> Who said anything to you, Ben?

BEN:

> I'll make good!

GUS:

> You certainly got that magnetism, Ben.

LIBBY:

> My Ben can be anything he wants.

(I)

Most of the characters worship Ben, and a small trophy from one of his track successes is the tangible idol. Yet Pearl sees her brother clearly enough to refer to him as a person "who thinks he owns the world because he won some medals. The great genius who never earned a nickel in his whole life" (I). Eighteen months after his bravado speech and marriage in Act I, Ben is dead, victim of a policeman's bullets in an armed robbery, victim even more of a peculiarly warped version of life.

The ending of the play is perhaps the most preposterous thing that Odets ever wrote. Leo Gordon's final speech must be included here only to point out how much Odets was on occasion capable of misjudging what an audience might tolerate. Leo, about to be dispossessed from his house, his business ruined by an unscrupulous partner, his son slowly dying, his other son already dead, gazes into the future and sees the glory of the promised land:

> Clara, my darling, *listen to me.* Everywhere now men are rising from their sleep. Men, men are understanding the bitter black total of their lives. Their whispers are growing to shouts! They become an ocean of understanding! *No man fights alone.* Oh, if you could only see with me the greatness of men. I tremble like a bride to see the time when they'll use it. My darling, we must have only one regret—that life is so short! That we must die so soon. Yes, I want to see that new world. I want to kiss all those future men and women. What is this talk of bankrupts, failures, hatred . . . they won't know what that means. Oh, yes, I tell you the whole world is for men to possess. Heartbreak and terror are not the heritage of mankind! The world is beautiful. No fruit tree wears a lock and key. Men will sing at their work, men will love. Ohhh, darling, the world is in its morning . . . *and no man fights alone!* (Clara slowly comes down to her husband and kisses him. With real feeling. Every one in the room, Leo included, is deeply moved by this vision of the future. Leo says): Let us have air. . . . Open the windows.

It is hard to realize that these lines are from the same pen that produced the action-packed and intensely dramatic *Waiting for Lefty* only a year earlier. If it requires a large amount of suspension of disbelief for a reader to accept Ralph Berger's idealistic curtain speech in *Awake and Sing,* it requires an impossible amount to accept it from Leo Gordon.

Paradise Lost was one of the most controversial of Odets' efforts. The actors enjoyed it, and Clurman, who directed it, praised the play highly in his introduction to the Random House edition. In his own 1939 preface, the playwright admitted a preference for *Paradise Lost* over his other early plays: "*Paradise Lost,* poorly received as a practical theatre work, remains my favorite in this group." But the audiences as well as the critics were unhappy with the play. Odets tended to bleed easily when attacked and to boil quickly when aroused. Of course, Odets was not the only playwright to engage in

an occasional feud with the drama critics, but his was especially energetic. Odets fought back by hitting at his detractors in a newspaper article quoted by Clurman in *The Fervent Years*:

> The young writer comes out of obscurity with a play or two. Suppose he won't accept the generous movie offers. Why, that means he's holding out for more. Suppose he accepts—an ingrate, rat, renegade. . . . If he's written two plays about the same kind of people, everyone knows that that's all he can write about. But when he writes about a different class, he is told to go back where he came from and stick to his cast (or caste). . . . Suppose he rapidly follows one play with another, why he's writing "quickies"! But if they come further apart, it is a sure sign he's already written out. If the reviewers praise him on Tuesday, it's only because they're gentle, quixotic fellows. But watch them tear him apart on Wednesday! . . . The young writer is now ready for a world cruise!
>
> (pp. 157-158)

But this strained sarcasm made little impression on the group attacked; the New York critics are a notoriously thick-skinned lot. Both Odets and Clurman probably expressed in their statements the normal protectiveness of a parent for a homely offspring.

V. *The Silent Partner*

Odets' next play was never produced, a fact which always bothered the playwright. In his 1939 preface to the *Six Plays,* Odets mentioned "The Silent Partner" fondly, stating: "Rightfully that play belongs in this collection in the place of *Rocket to the Moon,* for of the two it was conceived and written first. Revisions have changed it, but in terms of inner and outer progression, it belongs among the first six, part and parcel of a 'first-period' group." In an interview with John McCarten of *The New Yorker* he once referred to it as "the best labor play ever produced in this country or in any other country," and later he reaffirmed this opinion (adding the even more specific comment that it surpassed Hauptman's *The Weavers*).

The one scene published from "The Silent Partner" indicates that it is a more violent version of *Waiting for Lefty.* When one of the characters suggests an end to the strike, she is attacked by another of the wives:

> You might take a lesson from the lowly banana, Mrs. Finch—stick to your bunch or you'll get skinned! All of you listen . . . you've none of you died yet. A little hardship? Yes! But you've had that before. You been raised up to it and it comes easy and natural by now. Well grit your teeth and hang on a little longer. Stop naggin' your husbands. They're voting on the question right this minute up at the Labor Temple and they want you to be right with them and see this fight to a finish, no matter what they decide. Those of us really interested in our children will be with the men in that fate-

ful hour when the showdown comes with the Company. First they said to us, "Accept or perish" and now they say, "Accept or be shot," Well, we won't bend the knee.

—(*New Theatre and Film,* March 1937)

The dialogue of this single scene reveals that the play is a continuation of Odets' angry phase, a carry-over from *Waiting for Lefty* and *Till the Day I Die.* "The Silent Partner" was considered, discussed, revised, and re-revised several times between late 1936 and mid-1939, but it remained unproduced in spite of the playwright's confidence in it. Clurman has suggested why:

> No play of Odets had a wider scope, a greater variety of characters, or more exciting scenes. But the play, intuitively sound in its basic perception, was very weak in all its central characters and situations. The maturity that the Italian baker was supposed to possess was exactly the quality that Odets himself lacked. His play revealed more instinct than accomplishment, more rough substance than created form. I spoke to Odets at great length about this. If he could imbue these central characters with the life he meant them to have, this would be his most important play and he would indeed be the writer everybody hoped he would become. He needed to work hard rather than to push the play into production. Odets listened to me as if bemused. He was having his problems with Luise Rainer. He was somehow unsure of everything, more bewildered in a way than he had ever been as the obscure young actor of our crazy company. Odets was now his own greatest problem.

(*The Fervent Years,* p. 174)

If arbitrary divisions are helpful, "The Silent Partner" may be placed at the end of Odets' earliest writing period. These years, from 1931, when he made his first efforts, to 1936, when he wrote "The Silent Partner" and completed his first film script, saw Odets emerging as a dynamic young writer with recognized ability. He was developing a characteristic style and a personal set of artistic standards. But he was still known and admired more for his anger than for his ability. A small item in the New York *Times* July 24, 1935 perhaps best illustrates the kind of reputation that surrounded him. With John Howard Lawson and three other writers, Odets called on Luigi Pirandello, who was visiting New York in mid-1935. Pirandello apparently wanted to talk about literature, but his visitors were more interested in politics. Pirandello claimed that "politics and social questions 'are of the moment' but that 'an artistic moment lives forever.' He insisted that Mr. Odets' plays were good plays 'not because they are social, but because they are artistic.'" The *Times* reporter, apparently somewhat overwhelmed by the whole exchange, added, "The conference broke up with some rancor."[1]

Note

1. Lawson later reflected on the episode: "Our visit to Pirandello was a wonderful comedy of errors. He thought we were young admirers coming to render homage. As he gradually realized that we were in his Hotel Room to ask him why he accepted Mussolini, (and he himself had urged that the press be present to witness our homage), his fury was wonderful to behold. What struck me about Pirandello at the time was his lack of any respect for serious problems. After all, he could have had the courtesy, and the decency toward American writers, to answer us with dignity and to defend his own point of view. But he was far too frightened, too eager to serve his masters, to handle the situation with even a minimum of self-control." John Howard Lawson to the author, April 30, 1962.

Bibliography

I. BY ODETS

PLAYS:

The Flowering Peach. In *The Best Plays of 1954-1955,* ed. Louis Kronenberger. New York: Dodd, Mead, 1955. (condensed)

[A Scene from] *The Silent Partner, New Theatre and Film,* IV (March 1937) 5-9.

Six Plays of Clifford Odets. New York: Random House, 1939. (Contains *Waiting for Lefty, Till the Day I Die, Awake and Sing, Paradise Lost, Golden Boy,* and *Rocket to the Moon* as well as a Preface by Odets and Three Introductions by Harold Clurman.)

Waiting for Lefty (original version), *New Theatre,* II (February 1935), 13-20.

ARTICLES:

"Some Problems of the Modern Dramatist," New York *Times,* Dec. 15, 1935, Sec. XI, p. 3.

II. SECONDARY SOURCES

BOOKS:

Clurman, Harold. *The Fervent Years.* New York: Hill and Wang, 1957.

———. Three Introductions. *In Six Plays of Clifford Odets.* New York: Random House, 1939.

Lawson, John Howard. *Theory and Technique of Playwriting and Screenwriting.* New York: G. P. Putnam's Sons, 1949.

PERIODICALS:

McCarten, John. "Revolution's Number One Boy," *New Yorker,* XIII (Jan. 22, 1938), 21-27.

* * *

I gratefully acknowledge permission to use excerpts from the following works: Random House, Inc., which holds the copyrights for Odets' *Paradise Lost* (in *Six Plays of Clifford Odets*) and *The Big Knife* (1949), as well as the excerpt from the Preface to *Six Plays of Clifford Odets,* 1939; Viking Press, Inc., for the excerpt from Odets' *The Country Girl,* copyright 1951; and Alfred A. Knopf, Inc., for the passages from Harold Clurman's *The Fervent Years,* copyright 1945. (Pagination in this book is from the later paperback edition, Hill and Wang, Inc., 1957, by arrangement with Alfred A. Knopf, Inc.)

Gerald Weales (essay date 1971)

SOURCE: Weales, Gerald. "'With brutal sentimentality.'" In *Clifford Odets: Playwright,* pp. 83-90. New York: Pegasus, 1971.

[*In the following essay, Weales critiques* Till the Day I Die, *claiming that while its purpose was "to convince an audience of outsiders of the evils of Nazism and of the need of a united front to fight Germany," the work fails because its "artificiality" and "theatricality" make "one doubt not only the immediate dramatic experience but the objective situation that it is trying to uncover."*]

When, after the opening of **Awake and Sing!,** the Group Theatre decided to move **Waiting for Lefty** to Broadway, it apparently occurred to no one to honor those other playwriting Group actors, Elia Kazan and Art Smith, by bringing *Dimitroff* along. A conscious decision to ignore the earlier agitprop would have been sound on aesthetic and practical grounds, but Harold Clurman—who did an influence reversal bit in *The Fervent Years* when he said that Art Smith's post-*Lefty* labor play, *The Tide Rises,* "showed the Odets influence already at work"—gave no indication that he knew *Dimitroff* existed. When Odets sat down to turn out a companion piece for **Lefty** [**Waiting for Lefty**], he may have acknowledged the work of his two friends by choosing to write an anti-Nazi play. Of course, it was a logical subject to choose. During 1934, as a glance through the pages of *New Masses* and *New Theatre* would indicate, the Left had shown a growing preoccupation with Nazi Germany. Not the Left alone. The first anti-Nazi plays, disasters all, reached Broadway in the season of 1933-34—Adolph Phillipp's adaptation of Theodore Weachter's *Kultur,* Richard Maibaum's *Birthright* and Leslie Reade's *The Shatter'd Lamp.* In the fall of 1934, more serious, more highly respected playwrights turned to the subject—Elmer Rice with *Judgment Day* and S. N. Behrman with *Rain From Heaven.* Since Rice had disguised his Nazis as mythical Balkans and Behrman had chosen to work in his usual drawing-room setting, the time was ripe for a direct propaganda assault. Who better to make it than the most celebrated young radical playwright in America and what better occasion.

Till the Day I Die was "a hasty job—done in four nights," Odets told Percival Wilde in a letter quoted in Wilde's introduction to the play in *Contemporary One-*

Act Plays from Nine Countries (1936). This hurry is still obvious in the printed and reprinted (**Six Plays**) script, not simply in the play's artistic deficiencies, but in the kind of sloppiness that lets the stage directions for Scene IV read "The same as 3," when the set of II is called for, and that fails to sort out the confusions that arise when one compares the cast list to the actual characters. (The discrepancy in the second case and an apparent reference in Scene V to the Soviet-French pact of May 2 suggest that the printed text may not be the one first performed.) *Day* [**Till the Day I Die**], directed by Cheryl Crawford, and *Lefty* opened at the Longacre on March 26, 1935. With a few exceptions—Richard Watts, Jr. in the New York *Herald Tribune* and Edith J. R. Isaacs, who called it "so far ahead of anything else that Odets has done . . . that it escapes comparison with them"—the reviewers dismissed **Day** by attacking it, ignoring it or offering yes-but praise to the playwright for tackling the subject. The play ran for 136 performances, well into July, but it was presumably the **Lefty** half of the bill that sustained the run.

Although **Day** never had the vigorous post-Broadway life that **Lefty** did, it became a usable anti-Nazi play for workers' theaters, and it had its small share of trouble from censors, official and unofficial. In Philadelphia, for instance, the New Theatre was kept from staging it in April 1935 by the threat of having its license revoked. The most dramatic incident occurred in Los Angeles where William Ghere (now Will Geer), who was directing the **Lefty-Day** double bill in a small theater, was kidnapped by four "Friends of New Germany" and severely beaten; according to *Variety,* his "Attackers told Ghere they objected to a scene where Hitler's picture is torn from the wall." Merit aside, one possible reason why **Day** was never as popular as **Lefty** is the confusion that must have affected potential producers in the face of the Leftist attempt to be at once pacifist and anti-Nazi. The conflict—so obvious in retrospect in names like League Against War and Fascism and "Anti-Fascist and Peace" (a category in the New Theater League's 1938 catalogue of plays)—must have worked, however unconsciously, on the theater group which had to choose between disowning war with Albert Maltz (*Private Hicks*) and Irwin Shaw (*Bury the Dead*) and joining Clifford Odets in an implicit call to arms.

In the making of **Till the Day I Die,** as in the writing of **Waiting for Lefty,** Odets used whatever material came to hand. He admitted, in his letter to Percival Wilde, that "the genesis of many of the ideas used is hazy in my mind." That explains the complications about the "letter" in *New Masses* on which the play was admittedly based ("To be blunt, it sounds like it," snarled Richard Lockridge). After acknowledging the "letter" in the program and in a note accompanying the published play, Odets discovered—when he was approached for royalties—that what he remembered as a letter had been a short story in letter form. During 1934, *New Masses* occasionally ran a column "Voices from Germany," in which anecdotes, often fictional, were printed. On more than one occasion excerpts from F. C. Weiskopf's *Those Who are Stronger* appeared (the book, *Die Stärkeren* was published in Prague that year), and it was one of these that gave Odets the starting point for *Day*. What he got from Weiskopf were the details of the way the Nazis worked to break down the captured underground worker (the pattern of torture and release) and to make him appear a traitor to his friends (forcing him to accompany the Radical Squad on raids, stationing him at the door so that prisoners on the way to cross-examination would see him, providing him with new clothes to make him look like a paid stool-pigeon, issuing a bogus underground leaflet accusing him of selling out). The protagonist of the Weiskopf story breaks and informs and, presumably with his own blessing, is killed by his brother. In *Day,* Ernst Tausig commits suicide to keep from breaking; thus Odets converts Weiskopf's theme of revolutionary discipline to one of self-discipline.

Odets's debt to Weiskopf is a great deal less than that to Karl Billinger (Paul W. Massing). Billinger's name turned up first in Richard Watts's column, which found the recently published *Fatherland* similar in tone to Odets's play. Early the next year, in his attack on *Paradise Lost,* James T. Farrell said bluntly that *Day* "was based on notes from Billinger's *Fatherland*." To Percival Wilde, who listed many of the borrowings in his introduction, Odets admitted that he may have seen a chapter of the Billinger book in *New Masses*. Indeed, he had. Since the book came out in March 1935, it would have been possible for Odets to have seen an advance copy of it, but all the evidence points to "In the Nazis' Torture House" (*New Masses,* January 1, 1935) as the source for most of Scene III of *Day*. This is an abridged and heavily edited version of Chapter II ("Columbia") of *Fatherland,* but everything that Odets used is in the *New Masses* version. Some of the borrowing is very direct. The stage directions for the scene (the card-playing, beer-drinking guards, the prisoners lined along the wall, the guns and blackjacks on the table) come from Billinger, as do two of the sequences—the young trooper's knocking down the old man, the tormenting of the boy caught delivering pamphlets. Even the lines—particularly in the second case—come directly from Billinger. The contest between the first and second troopers, to see which can knock his man down first, is a dramatization of a practice that is only described in *Fatherland,* and other incidents (the abusing of the World War I veteran, the typing mix-up from Scene II) appear to be based on comments elsewhere in the chapter. Wilde suggested that the "nucleus of the first scene" came from Billinger's few lines on mimeographing, but such an assumption—which depends on Odets's having read more than the *New Masses*

excerpt—is unnecessary since Weiskopf's Martin also ran an underground press.

Despite the extensive pilfering from Billinger, *Till the Day I Die* is plainly Odets's play—not so much because there are occasional exchanges that are unmistakenly his (Tilly: "He's your brother." Carl: "That won't sell a postage stamp!"), as because the propaganda impulse of the play is tempered by a theatricality that sentimentalizes heroes and villains alike.

Essentially, *Day* is the story of Ernst Tausig, although it is told less in terms of what he does (until he pulls the final trigger) than in what is done to him. Scene I establishes, in a few lines, his love for Tilly, his affection for his brother Carl, his easy friendship with the other workers. That done, the arrest takes place and we are ready for his testing. Although his violin-playing hand is smashed in Scene II and he is beaten in Scene III, he really has no existence as a character in Scenes II through IV, for these are exhibition scenes (see the Nazi horrors!) in which Ernst is either ingredient or observer. Although Scene V has some of the excitement of a thriller in its last few minutes, as Tilly and Carl outsmart the police, and a presumably touching meeting between Ernst and Tilly, it is largely expositional, continuing the account, begun by Major Duhring in Scene IV, of how Ernst will be used. Ernst is of course not in Scene VI, the meeting at which, on Carl's plea and with Tilly's reluctant vote, he is blacklisted. He returns in the final scene, a broken man—despised by Carl, who thinks he has informed, and pitied by Tilly—with just strength enough to clear his name (for the sake of the baby Tilly is carrying) and to protect the cause by committing suicide. "Let him die," Carl says at the end and, after the shot, "Let him live."

At one level, Ernst's story is a Communist cautionary tale like Bertolt Brecht's *Die Massnahme* (1930), an exercise in revolutionary theory in which the individual must be willing to sacrifice himself for the group: "*You did not pronounce the verdict: / Reality did.*" This is presumably the point of Carl's speech in VI, his insistence that "There is no brother, no family, no deeper mother than the working class." Yet *Till the Day I Die* is not a *Lehrstück,* as *Die Massnahme* is, not a didactic play designed more for the performers than the audience. For all its Communist orientation, *Day* is a propaganda play that wants to use Ernst's story to convince an audience of outsiders of the evils of Nazism and of the need of a united front to fight Germany. As such, it embodies two contradictions—one structural, one ideational. The play about party loyalty implicit in Ernst's suicide is not the best vehicle for a direct anti-Nazi statement; after all, one of the forces driving him to death is the "spy-psychosis," as Billinger called it, the climate of suspicion that marks the underground organization. Within the propaganda play, it is difficult to decide whether we are to be moved toward Ernst's dreams of a future when "Brothers will live in the soviets of the world," or toward the action implicit in Major Duhring's "'Red Front' I can't say to you. . . . But 'United Front'—I say that." Are the *for* (the Communist future) and the *against* (the Nazis) of the play inseparable? It is as though the play were teetering between the old Communist line of exclusiveness ("If you want to register an emotional protest against Nazi polity, Mr. Odets requires that you join the Communist brethren," wrote Brooks Atkinson) and the Popular Front, which would not become official until it was blessed the next August by the Seventh World Congress of the Communist International. Perhaps Odets had not gone beyond lip service to cooperation, as Bill Shulman insisted in *Socialist Call*: "It remained for Odets to present to the American audience the only united front an American Communist can conceive, a united front of members of only the Communist Party." In any case, the neat line—politically and dramatically—of *Waiting for Lefty* is missing in *Day* which may be why Odets had to end it with Carl's sentimental rhetoric rather than an equivalent of the STRIKE! cry.

For the most part, *Day* was taken simply as an *against* play, an anti-Nazi statement. There are problems with that reading in both the positive characters and the Nazis themselves. Since Ernst and his friends oppose the Hitler regime from the beginning, there is no conversion with which the audience can identify, by which it can be drawn into the fight. In fact, the plot, insofar as it works at all, leads the audience into defeat and destruction. Ernst's suicide is supposed to be a positive act (like the one in *The Big Knife*), but, robbed of its Brechtian message, it is simply a romantic gesture and understood as such only because audiences have a latent attachment to what might be called the Sydney Carton syndrome. Certainly, Ernst has little existence as a character. He cannot survive on idiosyncrasies (like the man with one shoe off at the meeting, or the tulip-loving Baum) and he is never realized in depth. One reason is that Ernst's scenes are not self-contained (like those in *Lefty,* like the Nazi scenes here) but depend on an emotional freight that he needs to bring into them but that he never has. Another is that he and Tilly and Carl sound like posters when they speak about the future or the cause. Compare the last line of *Fatherland,* the wry "Come on, back to the trenches!" (which might have come out of *Awake and Sing!*) with Carl's benediction over Ernst. At most, Ernst comes through as a demonstration piece. We see him in three stages: whole, breaking, broken. If he is to serve the propaganda play at all, it is as victim not exemplar.

What of the Nazis who destroy him? Although they do terrible things in the play, they come across as not very formidable. The casual violence of the troopers in Scene III is the most frightening since it reflects the too famil-

iar behavior of minor power figures in an environment which condones official violence. It is framed, however, by two comic exchanges between Peltz and Weiner, Odets's addition to his Billinger borrowing, which rob the central section of force by insisting—look, stage comics, stage violence. Funny Nazis abound. Popper, the detective, is a comic turn, a frustrated authoritarian figure whom no one accepts as such. If the leaflet-reading at the beginning of Scene IV were not evidence enough that Edsel and Martin are a misplaced vaudeville team, the assumption would be confirmed by the fact that Robert Lewis (as Martin) made himself up to look like one of the Three Little Pigs. Perhaps the other Nazi characters (Duhring aside) were also to be played for laughs. Frau Duhring is obviously a broad caricature and her first slapping Ernst and then fastidiously discarding her glove is ludicrous ("the author wishes to make her contemptible," Wilde said, "yet he succeeds only in making her impossible"). Leon Alexander in his *Daily Worker* review said that the humor, which he found "tedious and nasty," was "directed mainly at homosexuality," which would make even Captain Schlegel comic. There would be a precedent; the first scene of *Dimitroff*—in which Goebbels fondles van der Lubbe while he, Goering and Hitler instruct the boy about burning the Reichstag—is presumably a joke.

Yet the play was obviously not funny, nor intended to be. It is simply that the ineffectuality implicit in the comic figures lessens the Nazis as opponents; and the caricaturing technique, used in conjunction with those comic figures, infects all the others, turning them into grotesques as well. Schlegel's homosexuality (which would have been an expected touch any time after the Ernst Roehm purge) allows for a kind of mock delicacy which heightens the falseness of his sadistic bit in Scene II (crushing Ernst's hand while talking about Beethoven's Opus 61). His verbal duel with Duhring casts doubt on that character—if the idea of a Communist, Jewish Nazi, lured into the service of Hitler because of his marriage, is not already a bit thick. Perhaps I am looking back on the play from the vantage point of all those wartime movies when variations on Schlegel (the cultured sadist) and Duhring (the anti-Nazi Nazi) crowded the screen, but I think not. Even at the time reviewers recognized that Odets was exposing the Nazis, as Percy Hammond put it, "with brutal sentimentality." The play does not fail because the characters are unrealistic, but because the artificiality does not work in a total artistic context, as it does in *Awake and Sing!*; instead, as the play moves from comedy to brutality to sentiment, the theatricality imposes the kind of overstatement that makes one doubt not only the immediate dramatic experience but the objective situation that it is trying to uncover. As a practical propaganda play, *Day* is deficient because it gives a valid artistic reason for any ostrich in the audience to hide his head. On the other hand, those willing to recognize the dangers of

Nazism are falsely comforted by the play's excessive reliance on sentimental melodrama. Major Duhring's suicide scene, like the killing of the Hitler figure at the end of Rice's *Judgment Day,* is a theatrical solution to a non-theatrical problem. "This is all wish-fulfillment," wrote Rudolf Wittenberg in one of the most perceptive commentaries written on the play.

Unlike **Waiting for Lefty,** in which the specific situation can be generalized, *Till the Day I Die* is inescapably fixed in 1935. Probably the weakest of Odets's plays, it is interesting largely because—a few sketches aside—it is his last piece of pure propaganda and—since "The Silent Partner" and "The Cuban Play" were not produced—his last public attempt to deal directly with an important social situation. It exposed not only the Nazis, but his own limitations.

Notes

The items in the biblioclots that follow are not formal footnote references. They simply list the sources of quotations and unusual bits of information not identified in the text. They will be of interest only to those readers who want to check my assumptions or pursue a particular subject further. The entries are as short as possible. The New York City newspapers are identified by title only (*Sun* rather than New York *Sun*); other newspapers carry the city name unless it is already in the text. Except for a rare item, publication information on the books cited seemed unnecessary in this context.

. . . .

Watts, *Herald Tribune,* March 31, 1935; Isaacs, *Theatre Arts,* May 1935; *Variety,* May 29, 1935; Lockridge, *Sun,* March 27, 1935; Odets on letter, *Harper's,* September 1966; Weiskopf story, *New Masses,* November 6, 1934; Farrell, *Partisan Review and Anvil,* February 1936; Atkinson, *Times,* March 27, 1935; Shulman, *Call,* April 6, 1935; Lewis's make-up, Helen Deutsch, *Herald Tribune,* April 28, 1935; Alexander, *Worker,* April 1, 1935; Hammond, *Herald Tribune,* April 7, 1935; Wittenberg, *New Theatre,* April 1935.

Bibliographical Note

PRIMARY SOURCES

Six Plays (New York, Random House, 1939, now in Modern Library), contains *Waiting for Lefty* (short version), *Awake and Sing!, Till the Day I Die, Paradise Lost, Golden Boy* and *Rocket to the Moon.* The complete version of *Waiting for Lefty,* originally published with *Till the Day I Die* (New York, Covici-Friede, 1935), is available in *Representative Modern Plays: American,* ed. Robert Warnock, Chicago, Scott Foresman, 1952, pp. 551-579. *The Big Knife* (New York, Random House, 1949) and *The Country Girl* (New

York, Viking, 1951) are available in acting editions from Dramatists Play Service. Random House published *Night Music* (1940) and *Clash by Night* (1942).

SECONDARY SOURCES

Much more valuable for my purposes were Harold Clurman, *The Fervent Years* (New York, Hill and Wang, 1957; originally published in 1945 by Knopf);

Gabriel Miller (essay date 1989)

SOURCE: Miller, Gabriel. "The Tragic Vision: *Golden Boy* (1937) *The Big Knife* (1949)." In *Clifford Odets,* pp. 62-93. New York: Continuum, 1989.

[*In the following essay, Miller traces Odets's development of a new dramatic style, one based on symbol and allegory, in his tragedies* Golden Boy *and* The Big Knife, *noting that the central theme of both works is "the soul's yearning for a secure haven in this world."*]

> Essentially it [*The Big Knife*] dealt with the tragedy of lost integrity everywhere.
>
> —Clifford Odets

> It was his duty to keep the Kingdom of the Movies free from the ancient enemy of the people—Art.
>
> —Ben Hecht on Louis B. Mayer

"So many artists today stand in relation to Hollywood as our hero in relation to his double career." So wrote Harold Clurman in his introduction to **Golden Boy,** which he called Odets's "most subjective play." Odets, indeed, made his first trip to Hollywood before writing **Golden Boy**: in 1936 he signed a four-week contract to write **The General Died at Dawn** for producer/director Lewis Milestone, and he was paid $27,500 for his work on that film. Odets had been courted by Hollywood before; he was offered a number of deals after **Waiting for Lefty** opened, and Harold Clurman noted that MGM, which financed part of **Paradise Lost,** went as high as three thousand dollars per week.

Odets's attitude toward Hollywood was, however, always ambivalent. He was attracted by the money, the technical expertise of films, the audience they attracted, and the potential for saying something important to that audience. At the same time, he disliked the Hollywood product and the negative influence it had on people, and he made his reservations clear as early as Jacob's speeches in **Awake and Sing!** In 1936 he told the *New York Times* "I won't be party to the fraud the screen has been perpetuating on the public for years. Boy gets girl. Life is swell."

The General Died at Dawn, the one film that bears Odets's name from this period, is a dull adventure-romance concerning an American named O'Hara (Gary

Cooper), who helps the Chinese peasant revolt against the wicked General Yang (Akim Tamiroff), and in the process wins the heart of Judy (Madeleine Carroll). The dialogue makes some allusion to the plight of the worker—"You ask me why I'm for oppresed people? Because I got a background of oppression myself, and O'Haras and elephants don't forget. What's better work for an American than helping fight for democracy?"—but this motif was eclipsed by the film's most famous lines: "Judy darling, we could have made wonderful music together—a circle of light and warmth," and "Someday, maybe there'll be a law to abolish the blues. Maybe a constitutional amendment, for all of us." The release of the film prompted Frank S. Nugent to ask, "Odets, Where Is Thy Sting?"

While working on the film Odets was taken to a boxing match by Lewis Milestone:

> I had two tickets to the Canzoneri-Ambers championship fight, and knowing Clifford had never seen a prizefight, I invited him to come along. During the prelims he paled and pulled out his notebook. When it seemed to me he was too busy writing to see the main event, I complained that I had bought two very expensive seats and that he could write at home. His reply was "You have just given me a very fine play, and what's more it will make money for the Group." He appeared to be very happy.[1]

Odets later told Elia Kazan that he would soon have a hit show for the Group that he was then calling "The Manly Art" or "Golden Gloves." The play *Golden Boy* did turn out to be the Group Theatre's greatest hit despite mixed reviews. And it came at a critical time, for the Group had dispersed, most of them to Hollywood, after the failure of their previous play *Johnny Johnson* by Paul Green, so *Golden Boy* served as the vehicle that brought the Group back together and allowed them to function for another three years. The play ran on Broadway for 250 performances; there was a West Coast production, and even engagements in London and Paris.

It was also the first Odets play sold to the movies. Directed by Rouben Mamoulian, with a script credited to four screenwriters, Columbia Pictures' *Golden Boy* opened in 1939, and it even featured one member of the Group in the cast, Lee J. Cobb, playing Mr. Bonaparte. The play was then revived in 1952, with Odets directing and John Garfield starring. (Odets had wanted Garfield to star in the original production, but was overruled by Clurman, who chose Luther Adler.) At the time of his death Odets was even working on a musical version about a black boxer who falls in love with a white woman; the play was completed by William Gibson and it opened in 1964 with Sammy Davis, Jr., starring as Joe.

John Garfield starred in the Broadway opening of *The Big Knife* as well. When Odets wrote the play, he had been living in Hollywood on and off for almost thirteen years (the same length of time Charlie Castle has been in Hollywood in the play), though he did move back to New York in 1948 where he wrote the play. The reviews were generally unkind, most critics unaccountably coming to the defense of Hollywood at Odets's expense; *Variety* called Odets "the champ sorehead of show business." The play did manage to run for 108 performances, primarily because of the box-office appeal of John Garfield.

In *The Fervent Years* Harold Clurman wrote that "for Odets . . . Hollywood was a sin." To a large extent this was true, for until the end of his life, Odets had difficulty reconciling his attraction to Hollywood with his need to produce significant art for the theater. It is certainly easy to read *Golden Boy* as a metaphor for that division in Odets and *The Big Knife* as a highly subjective apologia as well. But this is merely to skim the surface, for in both these plays Odets managed to transform his personal conflicts into explorations of broader issues related to his constant themes: the soul's difficult journey on earth, and its need to find a haven, a home. As Charlie Castle says in *The Big Knife,* "We're homesick all our lives," and this human dilemma is ultimately more important than the discovery of personal reference in the writer's work. In both plays Odets was able to project aspects of contemporary American experience into the realm of tragedy, exploring the dividedness of the spirit in two distinctive protagonists living in different times and in very different worlds.

Golden Boy is a different kind of play than *Awake and Sing!* and *Paradise Lost,* for in writing it Odets was experimenting with new techniques, baffling the critics, who apparently expected him to continue in the same vein as his earlier work. His desire to break away from the realistic/naturalistic mode of *Awake and Sing!* was evident in *Paradise Lost,* where he imposed a symbolic framework within the play, involving the characters of the Gordon children and, to a certain extent, Sam Katz. This device, unfortunately, weakened the play's thematic unity, and while *Paradise Lost* is among Odets's richest works, its awkard structural duality ultimately defeats the characters' emotional interplay.

Golden Boy, on the other hand, works best as a symbolic play. Odets clearly intended it as an allegory; indeed, he subtitled an early draft *An American Allegory.* Yet it is Odets's particular accomplishment in *Golden Boy* that his characters are so vividly presented as to transcend their allegorical functions and propel their personal conflict into the realm of tragedy. In order to stimulate a tragic apprehension, dramatic characters must engage an audience's sympathy and passion more fully than can be done either in simple allegory or in the realistic, slice-of-life antidramas of Odets's early career. *Golden Boy* thus represents a departure from his previous practice, for, instead of attempting to minimize theatrical involvement and impact, here Odets exploits the conventions of theater to heighten the formal eloquence of his story.

This play's most obvious conventional feature is the introduction of broad theatrical types; suddenly Odets peoples his stage with readily identifiable heroes and villains. At the center of the play stands Joe Bonaparte, a larger-than-life, emotionally engaging protagonist whose aspiration to be *somebody* in America at length leads to his death. Joe's is a story of thwarted potential, unfolding within an overriding mood of doom. It follows the classic tragic formula of an individual's rise to power and subsequent fall, precipitated by the recognition of irreparable error committed in the use of that power; for this he suffers and dies, having exhausted all the possibilities of his life. Odets moves his hero toward an action that causes great suffering, and then by exposing the consequences of the deed reveals to him the true nature of his ambition. The actions of other characters are related closely to various stages of this hero's passage. Joe's story, however, is more than a tragic study of the danger of courting success in America, for Odets is again exploring herein his favorite theme, the soul's yearning for a secure haven in this world. At this level **Golden Boy** reaches beyond the quintessential American dilemma that supplies its plot, attaining a dimension of universal significance in its symbolic progress.

This play also departs from Odets's past practice in its utilization of space. In the first two plays the characters are confined to the living area of the home, as Odets demonstrates their spiritual and emotional entrapment by contriving a sense of physical constraint. This closed setting also conveys Odets's suspicion of the family itself as a kind of trap that the individual must escape if he is to achieve personal fulfillment. The impulse to escape, however, remains an ambivalent one, since the family home represents also the striver's ultimate goal, as the source of emotional support and place of belonging that is the soul's prime object.

In **Golden Boy** Odets opens up the stage to encompass various settings: Moody's office, the Bonaparte home, the park, and the dressing room. Joe, who is Odets's first major protagonist, cannot be confined to the living room; he needs to go out into the world and see what is there. Accordingly, the audience's sense of possibility expands as Joe moves about the stage, extending its space until it becomes its own world, rich in imaginative potential. The proscenium, emphasized in the earlier plays, seems to disappear here, along with any suggestion of permanent walls, thereby transporting character and action beyond real space into metaphysical space, and this liberation of setting heightens the audience's sense of exhilaration in Joe's journey of discovery.

Joe himself is initially introduced in a deliberately theatrical manner: rather than entering prosaically, he seems to materialize on stage at a significant moment, as if summoned by dramatic necessity. The play has opened upon Moody, a fight manager, arguing with his girlfriend Lorna about her decision to leave him. Tired of waiting for Moody's wife to divorce him and evidently determined to force the issue of their relationship, Lorna feels trapped but is afraid to leave Moody. Like **Awake and Sing!**, **Golden Boy** thus begins on a characteristic Odetsian note of movement and stasis, involving a character's need to break out and frustrating inability to do so. Moody, too, is trapped, not only by his wife's demand for five thousand dollars as the price of a divorce, but also by his failure to find a boxer who can revive his managerial career. As for any hope that his current mediocre fighter, Kaplan, might win him some money, Lorna remarks, "It's the twentieth century . . . no more miracles." Regretting this lack of miraculous potential in the present, Moody, like many Odets characters, reverts to the past, the twenties, when he was successful and there was plenty of money. Lorna undercuts his reverie by mentioning that her mother died in 1928, and this exchange provides the first of many instances of the linkage of success and death, a dominant thematic concept in this play. Then, when Moody kisses Lorna, promising to give her anything she wants, Joe appears. Odets's stage direction is significant: "Suddenly a youth is standing at the office door. Lorna sees him and breaks away." Moody's reaction is, "Don't you knock when you come in an office?"

Joe's entrance is reminiscent of Hilda Wangel's in Ibsen's *The Master Builder*. The protagonist of that play, Halvard Solness, is introduced as a man preoccupied with youth, lamenting his own waning creative powers and a marriage that has trapped him. His longing for youth and love is answered just as he is thinking of it, when, in a marvelous theatrical coincidence, Hilda (youth) comes knocking at his door and changes his life. Moody's line, thus, is Odets's acknowledgment of a debt to Ibsen. On a literal level, Joe functions in the same way as Hilda. Moody longs for a miracle, a winning boxer who will reverse his professional decline and personal fortunes, while Lorna wants love and the sense of family lost at her mother's death, and Joe will answer both their longings. Lorna instantly recognizes this, for when she sees him, she moves away from Moody.

Joe's mode of theatrical entrance becomes a motif in the play, a stylistic device that confirms his story's symbolic thrust. In act 1, scene 2, which takes place in the Bonaparte home, Joe's brother Frank and his father are discussing him, and again he appears unnoticed, this time "in the shadows." Odets's use of lighting here underscores visually Joe's estrangement from the home image, for he has committed himself to Moody's world in scene 1. In act 2 scene 3, he once more appears as Moody and Lorna are kissing, after Lorna has again threatened to leave, this time because of Joe. When Joe enters he is followed by Eddie Fuseli, a gangster who serves as the embodiment of the shadow from the earlier scene; Eddie is the epitome of Joe's worst self. Joe's final "appearance" is in act 3, scene 2, when Fuseli is threatening Lorna with a gun, and once again his sudden entrance is timed to break up another man's confrontation with Lorna. The repetition is significant, for it is Joe's movement toward Lorna that comprises the symbolic progress of the play.

Odets's treatment of the hero typifies his adherence to the Nietzschean tragic system, whereby the playwright designates action and character to function as metaphysical complements to the physical world. Nietzsche's theory, in *The Birth of Tragedy* appropriately, draws upon Schopenhauer's definition of music as a universal language, the "immediate language of the will." Nietzsche explains that music, which he associates with the Dionysian strain, stimulates the imagination to embody the immaterial world:

> Image and concept . . . gain a heightened significance under the influence of truly appropriate music . . . music incites us to a symbolic intuition of the Dionysiac universality; [and] it endows that symbolic image with supreme significance.

Music, then, is Odets's metaphor for the soul, the immaterial, that mode of exaltation that Joe strives after but cannot attain. The energy of this creative inspiration, represented in his violin playing and his love for Lorna, supplies the play's Dionysian dimension.

The Apollonian element, in Nietzsche's words "the transcendent genius of the *principium individuationis,*" inheres in Joe's desire for more material success, his will toward individuation, which is metaphorically embodied in his determination to become a boxer. The need to break free of the spiritual anonymity and poverty arising from his immigrant status and to revenge himself on those who have excluded him—his family name and his cockeye are emblematic of past pain—makes Joe a readily sympathetic figure. However, if the Nietzschean tragic pattern is to be realized, the hero must "deliver us from our avid thirst for earthly satisfaction and remind us of another existence and higher delight." Ultimately Joe, too, must comprehend the error of his pursuit of success and revenge and then willingly embrace his own death; thus, in Nietzsche's words, he realizes himself "not through his victories but through his undoing."

Odets, moreover, seeks to superimpose this tragic model of a contemporary story in order to articulate the distinctive American experience. In an essay entitled **"Democratic Vistas in Drama,"** published in the *New York Times* after **Golden Boy** opened, Odets quoted Whitman's complaint about the lack of an authentic American drama:

> In his essay "Democratic Vistas" written in 1871, Walt Whitman wrote: "Of what is called the drama or dramatic presentation, in the United States, as now put forth at the theatres, I should say it deserves to be treated with the same gravity, and on a par with the questions of ornamental confectionery at public dinners, or the arrangement of curtains and hangings in a ballroom. . . .
>
> "I feel with dejection and amazement that among writers and talented speakers, few or none have yet really spoken to this people, created a single image-making work for them, or absorbed the central spirit and the idiosyncrasies which are theirs—and which, thus, in the highest ranges, so far remain entirely uncelebrated and unexpressed."[2]

Agreeing with Whitman that the modern theater had failed to express the American spirit, Odets then advanced a rather bold claim for the time, that the movies had, at least partially, supplied the lack:

> Let us, for once, give the movies some credit. They have spoken to this people. The movies have explored the common man in all of his manifestations—out of the Kentucky mountains, out of the Montana ranch house, out of the machine shop, from the docks and alleys of the great cities, from the farm, out of the hospitals, airplanes, and taxicabs.
>
> The movies are now the folk theatre of America. But they are still not what Whitman asked for in 1871. . . . Hollywood producers will tell you gladly that they are not interested in presenting their themes "significantly." They are not interested in interpretation or criticism of their material. Their chief problem, they contend, is the one of keeping the level of human experience in their pictures as low as possible. They keep to primary colors with the expected result: The good will be rewarded, the wicked punished; success lurks around every corner; love is only a matter of the right man looking the right girl in the eyes; and so on and so on and so on.[3]

The movies' treatment of theme therefore remaining "puerile in every respect," Odets concluded with the suggestion that the theater adopt the movies' themes but "tell the truth where the film told a lie." The playwright committed to this high cultural calling could thus become in Whitman's term a "celebrator and expressor" of the American experience.

In pursuit of this calling, Odets utilizes in **Golden Boy** a cinematic scenic format that, as mentioned earlier, diverges sharply from the tightly knit structure of the earlier plays. The later play's succession of brief scenes and multiple settings was undoubtedly influenced by Odets's recent Hollywood screenwriting experience. This important technical innovation also represents a probably deliberate imitation of the basic form of the gangster film, which became, in the early thirties, a significant expression of the popular culture, uniquely suited to dealing with the traumatic societal upheaval of the Depression years.

Like *Golden Boy* the gangster film typically features an aggressive, violent protagonist of immigrant descent, whose obsessive rise to prominence in the mob is played against scenes of (usually idealized) family life. Odets echoes this pattern, only substituting a devoted father for the widowed mother more common to the family model of the movies, and the change more likely reflects Odets's own troubled relationship with his father than any conscious variation on the film genre. In the play as well as in the movie versions, the nurturing family functions as a counterpoint to the characteristically violent success story. Consequently, the destruction of the family, and often, the substitution of a false family for the real one become recurrent themes in these films; likewise, in *Golden Boy* Joe rejects his family/father for successive surrogate fathers in the fight game, and this betrayal of the values of home eventually leads to his undoing.

The most meaningful affinity between the gangster film and Odets's play is to be found in their makers' corresponding rejection of the demands and essential rewards of modern life: Robert Warshaw claims that the gangster film rejects "Americanism itself."[4] In making this rejection the film genre offers no alternative, either political, social, or economic, to the bleak picture of corruption and degradation conveyed in its narrative. Neither does Odets, and this is consistent with his attitude in the previous plays, where criticism of the system is implied, but no blueprint for the future is offered. Here, however, Odets provides a central character who, unlike Ralph, Jacob, or Leo, recognizes the moral emptiness of his society, and this rejection moves *Golden Boy* into the realm of authentic tragedy.

Like tragedy, the gangster film insists that man is a being capable of success or failure. The gangster fiercely pursues his finite goal and succeeds, in Warshaw's words, in "emerging from the crowd," defying the anonymity of the city. Nevertheless, like any "tragic" hero, he must be defeated at last, often dying alone in the street. The gangster figure has asserted himself as an individual, but he must die because of it. The genre thus echoes the conventions of tragedy but finally falls short of it: whereas tragedy chronicles a protagonist's doomed struggle with necessity and forces him (and the audience that views his story) to acknowledge the inevitability of his fate, it also celebrates man's need to give meaning to his fate. The gangster film, on the other hand, ultimately offers no real meaning, no sense of nobility to account for the ambition and the downfall of its protagonist. If the Apollonian sense of individuation

is celebrated, the Dionysian, musically symbolic connection with the infinite, that which "breaks the spell of individuation and opens a path to the maternal womb of being" is missing. In the character of Joe Bonaparte, however, Odets not only gives expression to the human condition in the American city of the 1930s, but also celebrates a broader human experience as well. For if this fighter and Apollonian individualist pursues the finite goal of success and fails, his complementary aspiration toward the infinite imparts nobility and meaning to his struggle and his fate.

The first act reveals the three major settings of the play: Moody's office, the Bonaparte home, and the park—each locale representing an alternative in Joe's struggle to come to grips with himself and the conflicting possibilities offered to him. The Bonaparte home is a kind of haven, a nourishing paradise where—unlike the Berger house of *Awake and Sing!*—it is possible to grow and produce "fruit." In the second draft of *Golden Boy,* Odets gave Mr. Bonaparte this speech, which was eliminated from the final version:

> I think sometimes in terms of a citrus grove. I like to think to raise such trees and distribute to a world of children the fresh, natural juices of the fruit.[5]

In this impulse Mr. Bonaparte is related to Jacob in *Awake and Sing!* and Leo Gordon in *Paradise Lost,* all kindly, moral men who "love to slice philosophical salami," though unlike them, he seems unconcerned with the economic situation or even his own poverty. He is in love with life and his children and external troubles seem unimportant in comparison. Joe's ambition for material success does not impress him, for he feels "a good life 'sa possible," achievable in an attitude of self-acceptance and contentment with the simple pleasures of living:

> You say life'sa bad . . . well, is pleasure for you to say so. No? The streets, winter a' summer—trees, cats—I love a them all. The gooda boys and girls, they who sing and whistle—very good! The eating and sleeping, drinking wine—very good! I gone around on my wagon and talk to many people—nice![6]

Even Mr. Carp, his best friend, cannot convince this amiable man that his philosophy has no place in modern-day America.

Carp is the serpent in the Edenic garden of the Bonaparte home, countering Mr. Bonaparte's native optimism and his hopes for Joe's career in music with gloomy cynicism:

> In the end, as Schopenhauer says, what's the use to try something? For every wish we get, ten remains unsatisfied. Death is playing with us as a cat and her mouse!

(p. 249)

The reference to Schopenhauer is important, for Carp proves to be prophetic in his assessment of Joe's pursuit of the American dream. Briefly, Schopenhauer posited that conflict between individual wills is the cause of continuous pain and frustration, and the world is thus a place of unsatisfied wants and unhappiness. Man's intellect and consciousness are mere instruments of the will, while music, the ultimate expression of the soul, provides a means of momentarily transcending the conflict, investing human life with higher significance. Odets's reference to Schopenhauer through Carp confirms the Nietzschean tragic model in the play, for Carp's discussions with Mr. Bonaparte provide in themselves harmless instances of the clash of opposites that causes conflict.[7]

The fateful significance underlying the two friends' contrasting outlooks is emphasized most powerfully in scene 2, when Mr. Bonaparte shows Carp the violin that he has bought for Joe's twenty-first birthday; Carp comments that "it looks like a coffin for a baby." (The coffin image recurs in scene 3, when Moody, disgusted with his ex-wife's constant demands for money, declares, "If I had fifty bucks I'd buy myself a big juicy coffin.") Carp's remark, then, not only prefigures Joe's death but also taints the redemptive music motif with a suggestion of abortive effort. Again, the transcendent impulse seems linked, in Odets's world, with a movement toward renunciation and death.

Joe, unlike Ralph Berger or any of the Gordon children, is a strong, decisive character capable of achieving success; in so doing he rejects his father's home, where he learned music and was encouraged to develop his talent. For Joe, a boy growing up in America, the old-world values of Europe, represented by his father, are not enough—one of many thematic motifs in *Golden Boy* is the generational conflict between the European immigrant and his son. In this context music represents an extension of the European sensibility that cannot survive on the streets of America. Joe, like many first-generation Americans, must reject the ways of the father completely, although in embracing the values of the new land and its ethic of "making it," he risks losing his soul. Joe's rejection of his home suggests that Odets felt the temptations and pressures of the American economic condition were undermining the nurturing influence of the family; certainly his immigrant families, torn between the conflicting demands of two cultures, find little peace or sustenance in the new world.

Joe replaces his father with two successive surrogate fathers who seek to advance his career as a fighter: Tom Moody, his manager and chief rival for Lorna, and Eddie Fuseli, the gangster who eventually comes to dominate Joe's career. Moody serves as a kind of transitional figure here, his values falling somewhere between those of Mr. Bonaparte and his antithesis, Fuseli. Odets even demonstrates a certain affection for Moody, a man down on his luck and in need of a good fighter to revitalize his career as a manager. Joe appears, as discussed earlier, as if in answer to this need, and his declared allegiance works to rejuvenate the older man's spirits. Moody is also in need of a divorce from his wife so that he can marry Lorna, a much younger woman, and so he sees Joe not only as his economic salvation, but a "spiritual one as well." In act 1 Moody longs for the twenties, when the economy was booming and he was successful; he is like the country itself, decimated by the Depression, nostalgic for a former glory and hoping for some miraculous, youthful talisman to revive him. But Moody does not know what to do with the two young people who seem ready to perform this miracle for him: he wants only to exploit Joe's talent, regardless of his best interests or of the spiritual dilemma that troubles Joe, and, when the need arises, he exploits Lorna as well. When Joe seems doubtful as to whether to continue fighting, Moody uses Lorna, along with the promises of fame and fortune, to seduce him back to the ring. In consequence, he eventually loses both Joe and Lorna.

Jealous of Moody's hold on Lorna and increasingly impatient for greater success, Joe gravitates toward Eddie Fuseli, Odets's first truly loathsome character. Basically an outgrowth of the gangsterlike Moe Axelrod and Kewpie, but without any redeeming characteristics, Fuseli is clearly the villain of the play, and when Joe adopts him as his manager, his fall is complete.

A strong link between the two is established in the manner of his first entrance: he comes onstage unnoticed, interrupting a conversation between Moody, Tokio, and Lorna. Shortly after saying hello, he "drifts out of the scene on his cat's feet." A few minutes later, when Joe joins the conversation, he appears "unseen by others" and listens. Thus Odets is emphasizing that Fuseli, like Joe, is a figure of the theatrical world, a poetic double who will figure prominently in the drama of the soul that will unfold.

A significant element in Fuseli's resemblance to Kewpie involves the homosexual overtones with which Odets characterizes the two gangsters' relationship to the young men they befriend. There is in *Paradise Lost* some suggestion of such an attachment between Kewpie and Ben, and in *Golden Boy* Odets provides similar hints about Fuseli's attraction to Joe. When they first meet, the stage directions read, "curiously Eddie is almost embarrassed before Joe"; later Moody calls him a "queen." In addition, Odets associates Fuseli with a cluster of phallic images. After his initial appearance, Lorna comments, "What exhaust pipe did he crawl out of?" Later in the play he threatens her with a gun until Joe appears to stop him. The exhaust pipe image, further, links Fuseli to the Dusenberg that Joe buys and that eventually becomes his "coffin," as he rides it to his death. The gun and the car are two of the central iconographic images of the gangster film, and their prominent use here indicates that Joe's embracing of Fuseli constitutes another Odetsian indictment of the success ethic of America.

Other image patterns are equally suggestive. Just before Fuseli's entrance Moody is complaining to Lorna about getting Joe away from the influence of his home; he employs a vivid simile to express his concern: "We can't afford no more possible bad showings at this stage of the game. No more apparitions, like suddenly a fiddle flies across the room on wings!" (p. 274). After Fuseli appears, Moody once again waxes poetic: "Every once in a while he shoots across my quiet existence like a roman candle!" The images are similar but with widely differing connotations: Joe is described in transcendent terms, Eddie in phallic, violent ones. Once more, in the reiterated flight image, the linkage of music with death is reinforced.

These two image patterns become fused in the final scene of act 2 that takes place in a dressing room before a fight. Here the disparate elements of Joe's world converge, as Mr. Bonaparte, Lorna, Moody, and Fuseli all appear in the scene. Mr. Bonaparte's dissociation from this setting is emphasized in Lorna's greeting to him "What brings you to this part of the world?" and when Joe confronts his father he irrevocably breaks with his true father:

> I have to fight, no matter what you say or think: This is my profession! I'm out for fame and fortune, not to be different or artistic! I don't intend to be ashamed of my life!

> (p. 298)

Shortly before this, he has remarked to Moody, "Eddie's the only one who understands me." Having thus rejected both his father and Moody, he tells Tokio, his trainer, "Now I'm alone. . . . When a bullet sings through the air it has no past—only a future—like me." The image pattern thus echoes Moody's twin similes and confirms Joe's new spiritual allegiance to Fuseli. The act ends when Joe has knocked out his opponent. Returning to the dressing room, his "eyes glitter" and his hands are broken; this changed Joe exults, "Hallelujah! It is the beginning of the world!" Odets's stage directions are significant: "Joe begins to laugh loudly, victoriously, exultantly." He seems almost demonic, and Fuseli, Odets writes, "watches with inner excitement and pleasure."

However, Joe's most important relationship in the play is with Lorna Moon. Her name has overt symbolic overtones, but she functions effectively as a realistic character as well. On one level she feels that she is a "tramp from Newark," survivor of a rough childhood, and she looks to Moody, a man old enough to be her father, to make her respectable. She is impatient for Moody to get a divorce from his wife and marry her because, like Kewpie and Moe, she is anxious for a home. In Moody she is looking for a combination father and husband; Lorna wants what Joe seeks to escape.

When she meets Joe, however, her values are overturned, as she responds to the young man's tenderness and artistic aspiration. She is that familiar movie type, the cynical city girl who was really waiting for true love to rescue her from herself. In her two scenes in the park with Joe, her symbolic function is established, and they are the most expressionistic scenes in the play. Odets emphasizes carousel music and the changing colors of the traffic lights, seemingly projecting his characters into a world apart, where their true inner selves can be revealed. In act 1, scene 4 Lorna compares herself to a butterfly, a traditional symbol of the soul, and Joe literalizes the image when he asks her, "What does your soul do in its perfumed vanity case?" In the next scene, which takes place in the Bonaparte home, she reveals that she was once an airplane hostess, and Odets repeats the airplane image from *Awake and Sing!* again conjuring up the dream of leaving the earth behind in aspiration for a better life. Here Lorna seems to become a personified spirit of the music with which Joe needs to identify himself; he even explains this spiritual need to her in personal terms:

> With music I'm never alone when I'm alone—Playing music . . . that's like saying, I am a man. I belong here. How do you do world—good evening!" When I play music nothing is closed to me. I'm not afraid of people and what they say. There's no war in music.

> (p. 263)

In this scene, however, Lorna is trying to persuade Joe to pursue his boxing career, though she will intuit the error of her ways by the end of the scene. Joe, too, despite his obvious attraction to Lorna, leans toward the other world, and he moves from this discussion of music and the soul to his desire to buy a car, which is "poison" in his blood.

Lorna's name supplies the most obvious symbolic undercurrent in Joe's attraction to her. The moon was a popular symbol among the Romantic poets, particularly Wordsworth and Coleridge, as the ultimate inspiration of poetic reverie and heightened imaginative consciousness. An effective example is found in Wordsworth's short poem, "A Night-Piece," where a glimpse of the moon affords the poet, "whose eyes are bent to earth," a glimpse of the infinite:

> He looks up—the clouds are split
> Asunder—and above his head he sees
> The clear Moon, and the glory of the heavens.

There in a black-blue vault she sails along,
Followed by multitudes of stars.

The moon again appears in a climactic scene in *The Prelude,* where viewing it, Wordsworth has a glimpse of "the soul, the imagination of the whole." Clearly, then, Joe must move toward this moon figure in the play, toward a reconciliation with the Dionysian spirit of the eternal. Lorna's name is not, as Margaret Brenman-Gibson writes, a symbol of the "cool, inhospitable, unattainable woman" for Joe has the ability to attain her if only he could resist the Apollonian ambition and understand his true nature.

Lorna, too, will be worthy of Joe when she recognizes her salvation in him and not in Moody, and she does so in act 2, scene 2, the second and last park scene. She is no longer trying to keep Joe away from music; Joe even compares her to his music: "You're real for me the way music was real." He wants her to teach him love and to be his family, his new life. The music in this scene is provided not by a carousel, but by a whistling duet that Joe and Lorna perform. After trying to resist him, even struggling with herself, Lorna admits to Joe that she wants him: "I've been under sea a long time! . . . Take me home with you."

Joe finally unites himself with Lorna after killing the Chocolate Drop in the fight ring. Now he understands how he has violated his own nature:

> What will my father say when he hears I murdered a man? Lorna, I see what I did. I murdered myself, too! I've been running around in circles. Now I'm smashed! That's the truth. . . . But now I'm hung up by my finger tips—I'm no good—my feet are off the earth!
>
> (p. 315)

Lorna then declares her love for Joe and consoles him:

> We have each other! Somewhere there must be happy boys and girls who can teach us the way of life! We'll find some city where poverty's no shame—where music is no crime—where there's no war in the streets—where a man is glad to be himself, to live and make his woman herself!
>
> (p. 316)

Obviously she is referring to death, for no such place can exist in the real world. Joe understands this, realizing that in order to salvage his soul he must separate it from his body, and the language of his declaration strangely echoes Wordsworth's "A Night-Piece":

> We'll drive through the night. . . . You're on top of the world then. . . . That's it—speed! We're off the earth—unconnected!
>
> (p. 316)

After the poet has been inspired by the moon, as noted before, Wordsworth likewise emphasizes speed:

There in a black-blue vault she sails along,
Followed by multitudes of stars, that, small,
And sharp, and bright, along the dark abyss
Drive as she drives: how fast they wheel away.

The play concludes in the Bonaparte home where Frank announces the deaths of Joe and Lorna to Mr. Bonaparte, Moody, and Fuseli. The play's final words, "Joe . . . come, we bring-a him home . . . where he belong," are spoken by Mr. Bonaparte, and they recall Joe's description of music to Lorna in act 1, scene 4 as well as the ending of O'Neill's *The Hairy Ape.* Odets labored over the ending, changing the final speech a number of times before settling on this rather elegant coda. In one draft Mr. Bonaparte flatly says, "Let us go there . . . and bring the bodies home." In another draft the conclusion is even less satisfying, as Frank cries, "What waste, what waste . . . what ugly [foul] waste." The final version, in contrast, conveys an acknowledgment that the true closure of the soul's longing comes only in death—perhaps it is the only true paradise. Or possibly, as Odets demonstrates here in his compelling tragic vision, paradise must rather be sought in the transcendent power of art to unify and pacify the conflict of wills that undermines the human condition.

Odets began writing *The Big Knife* in 1948, copyrighting it as "A Winter Journey." He changed the title, it seems, late in 1948, having extensively revised the play a number of times. In explanation, Odets said that the earlier title implied "a difficult passage in one's life," whereas the new one alluded to "a force that moves against people." This comment, in fact, illuminates an unresolved problem in the play, for one title emphasizes character, the other exterior forces operating on character. Much of the criticism of the finished play would focus on the protagonist, Charlie Castle, as an insufficiently developed character who was seemingly swallowed up in Odets's vitriol against Hollywood. The early drafts confirm that Odets was struggling to balance the exploration of character with the representation of forces operating from outside it.

When *The Big Knife* opened on Broadway in 1949, it was Odets's first play there in eight years. The critics were not kind, as was generally the case for the plays after *Golden Boy;* even Harold Clurman and Joseph Wood Krutch, always supporters, dismissed *The Big Knife.* The play has fared no better with more recent critics of Odets, and it has rarely been revived.

Much of the disparagement centers on the play's biographical parallel, the critics complaining that Odets, who worked in Hollywood for many years after the collapse of the Group Theatre, was protesting too much. Having made a great deal of money there, now, it seemed, he was suddenly offering an extended bombastic apology for having abandoned his art and the "serious" work of the theater. Clurman criticized the play as defeatist and suggested that Odets was attempting to project his own sense of guilt onto society. More recently, Gerald Rabkin, in his study *The Drama of Commitment,* questioned the protagonist's climactic "act of faith," and unfavorably comparing the play to *Golden Boy,* wrote that *The Big Knife* presents no social alternative as does the earlier play.[8] Some of this criticism, particularly the biographical issue, is beside the point. Readings such as Rabkin's are more disturbing and need to be answered, for *The Big Knife* remains one of Odets's most widely misinterpreted and yet most compelling plays. (Only Edward Murray has attempted to deal with it in detail.)

Both Clurman and Rabkin imply that in this play Odets tried to write a serious tragedy, in a sense, to duplicate the strengths of *Golden Boy,* and simply failed. However, despite its many similarities to that earlier success, *The Big Knife* is sufficiently different in structure and technique to indicate that Odets was attempting here to convey his tragic vision in a very different mode. *The Big Knife* is, in fact, closer in form to *Awake and Sing!* and *Paradise Lost* than to *Golden Boy,* its action confined to a single set, "the playroom" of Charlie Castle's house in Beverly Hills. The sense of entrapment is made even stronger, for if the stage space of the two early plays was shared by family and friends, now it is a lone protagonist's space. Charlie remains at the center of the play, onstage continually until he goes upstairs to kill himself at the end. Other characters enter and leave this space, but no one stays for very long; it is as if everyone has access to the world outside the stage except Charlie, who is confined to the Hollywood castle that his own name betokens.

This intensive, and thematically significant, use of setting provides a strong resemblance to Ibsen's *A Doll's House,* a play that shares various motifs with *The Big Knife,* among them the exposure of a fatal secret from the past. Like Charlie Castle, Ibsen's Nora is confined to the drawing room of her home, and during the course of the play various characters, including her husband and children, become part of her world and then leave. She is the devoted wife and mother, nothing more, and while the others have access to the world outside the drawing room, Nora does not. Ibsen's point is that Nora, as a woman, is trapped in her society, just as she is trapped in her room, without scope for realizing any wider potential. Until she takes her life into her own hands and decides to transform herself, she remains a doll in a doll's house, neither a woman nor a human being. Her walking out at the play's end provides not only a spiritual release but a physical one as well, for by that time the audience has begun to feel as confined as Nora.

While the structures of the two plays are thus alike, the circumstances of their protagonists' captivity are quite different. Plainly, Nora is victimized by her society, locked into a box by the social dictates of her world; her conflict, then, is between herself and her husband and the larger world that her husband represents. Nora is a person who is acted upon, and until the end of the play she does not react to oppose or escape the restraining conventions of her situation. Charlie Castle, on the other hand, is trapped in a predicament primarily of his own making. Formerly a man of deep political conviction, a talented actor, and a loving husband, he is now a wealthy studio star playing endless variations of the same superficial role, estranged from his wife and son, and extremely dissatisfied with himself. The central issue of this play, as in *Golden Boy,* involves the protagonist's conflict of identity, here polarized in Charlie Castle's sense of his true self, represented by his real name Charlie Cass, and the corrupt self represented by his stage name Charlie Castle. Again, life has posed contrasting opportunities, entailing self-defining choices, and again the terms of choice require a dedication either to idealism or to materialism. The Hollywood environment exerts pressure on Charlie to surrender to his worst impulses, but Odets makes clear that this society, however flawed, is not the primary culprit, and that his protagonist, unlike Ibsen's, is and always was free to make his own choices. Charlie Castle's sense of detainment in the playroom that is Hollywood results from his belated recognition of the falsity of the values he has chosen to act upon in life.

Nevertheless, the Hollywood setting is important to the play's thematic design. In an interview before the Boston opening of the play, Odets declared:

> The big knife is that force in modern life which is against people and their aspirations, which seeks to cut people off in their best flower. The play may be about the struggle of a gifted actor to retain his integrity against the combination of inner and outer corruptions which assail him, but this struggle can be found in the lives of countless people who are not on the wealthy level of a movie star. I have nothing against Hollywood per se. I do have something against a large set-up which destroys people and eats them up. I chose Hollywood for the setting for *The Big Knife* because I know it. I don't know any other company town. But this is an objective play about thousands of people, I don't care what industry they're in.[9]

This, of course, is rather disingenuous, for Hollywood is, as Odets was aware, more than a conveniently familiar "company town"; the very name of the place serves as perhaps the primary symbol of those cultural forces that endanger the "integrity" of the idealist in America. Edmund Wilson wrote, "Everything that is wrong with the U.S. is to be found there in rare purity." Certainly that is the basic premise of most literary representations of the Southern California scene; and the aspect of Hollywood most pervasively emphasized in the literature is its artificiality, as in Nathanael West's memorable image of a rubber horse at the bottom of a swimming pool in *The Day of the Locust*. For writers this falsity of environment underscores the betrayal of the promise of America: those who succeed in Hollywood learn that such material success is empty, while those who fail only see the chasm between dreams and reality all the more clearly.

Two prominent thematic motifs in **The Big Knife** are the abuse of sexuality and the meaninglessness of work, both problems commonly attributed to the hedonistic life-style of the moviemakers' society.[10] Sexual freedom was a prime component of the Hollywood image, at least until the lurid sex scandals of the twenties; by the midthirties Hollywood literature had replaced the orgiastic tone with one of either sexual revulsion or indifference, suggesting that the revelry of the past had given way to disillusionment and exhaustion. Similarly, the wild energy that had fueled the growth of the film industry had given way, in its heyday, to a complementary attitude toward the work itself. The work ethic, always a basic component of the American experience, was somehow betrayed in Hollywood, where the rewards were excessive, and the stories of people, especially writers, paid enormous sums for not working became legendary. The work, moreover, has always been seen as trivial, nonfulfilling, and debilitating.

Odets's characters and dialogue build upon these connotations of the Hollywood setting. The atmosphere of unreality is pervasive: Charlie's "playroom," where all of the action takes place, is itself a false front for the man he is not, for the piano and the paintings by Maurice Utrillo, Georges Rouault, and Amedeo Modigliani embody an artistic pretension that is belied by the movie industry and Charlie's films themselves. Even Charlie's professional name, Castle, is a glibly regal substitute for the more mundane Cass. In one of the play's most vivid exchanges, Charlie sums up Hollywood's affectation for his neighbor, Dr. Frary, explaining that "we all wear these beautiful expensive ties in Hollywood. . . . It's a military tactic—we hope you won't notice our faces."[11]

Another such façade of success and respectability is discredited in the portrayal of the various marriages in the play. The destructiveness of sexuality in its divorce from love and commitment has concerned Odets in earlier plays; here it becomes obsessive. Charlie Castle and his wife are separated when the play begins. As Charlie says, "The place is hell on married life!" Charlie hopes for a reconciliation with her, but the depth of their estrangement is revealed when, in act 2, Marion tells him what Hollywood has done to him and their relationship:

> You've taken the cheap way out—your passion of the heart has become a passion of the appetites! Despite your best intentions, you're a horror . . . and every day you make me less a woman and more the rug under your feet!

> (pp. 62-63)

Meanwhile Charlie is indulging in an affair with the wife of a close friend, Buddy Bliss, who is likewise struggling to save his marriage. Charlie also has had an affair with Dixie Evans, who was with him in the car on the night of the accident in which a child was killed, and the concealment of this incident has fused the implications of sexual infidelity with the betrayal of friendship (Buddy Bliss was blamed for the accident) and the reckless, hit-and-run destruction of life. Near the end of the play when the studio fears that Dixie will talk about the incident, it is suggested that Charlie marry her to prevent her testifying against him in court. The dispassionate calculation of this proposal only reinforces the emptiness of the marriage bond in this Hollywood society.

The prime exemplar of Hollywood values in the play is the studio head, Marcus Hoff. In a lengthy speech in which he tries to persuade Charlie not to listen to Marion's plea that Charlie leave Hollywood and not sign a fourteen-year contract with the studio, Hoff delivers the industry's basic business pitch, based on the priority of moviemaking over the personal commitments of love and family. Feigning emotion for effect, he complains of his own wife's suicidal neurosis as an unpardonable interference in his business life:

> One day, in my office—Smiley was there—Frank Lubner, a pioneer in the industry—I drank a light scotch and soda and I began to cry. I don't think I wept like that since I was a boy. Because I saw, by a revelation of pain, that my wife had determined, in her innermost mind, to destroy me and my career out of wilful malicious jealousy! You ask me why? I ask you why! But from that day on I realized an essential fact of life: the woman must stay out of her husband's work when he's making her bread and butter! The wife of a man in your position should have the regard and respect to advance his career! . . . Because sometimes it becomes necessary to separate ourselves . . . from a wife who puts her petty interests before the multiplicity of a great career!

> (p. 41)

Charlie's own dissipated life-style is in part a byproduct of his disgust with his work, which he considers trivial and beneath contempt. In his films he plays a variation of the same role again and again from a series of properties that the studio buys for him. Charlie has, in effect, become a studio property himself, and by the time the play opens, this mechanization of his life and his art has become intolerable, although he continues to enjoy the money and the luxury of star status. Unlike Joe Bonaparte, or any other Odets protagonist, Charlie Castle is not aspiring toward material success when introduced; he has already achieved it and accepted it, and now he must deal with the implications of that acceptance. Charlie has seemingly realized the American dream, but the painfully divided consciousness resulting from his recognition of the various betrayals involved in the achievement make Charlie a tragic protagonist comparable to Joe Bonaparte in the exploration of the corruptibility of the American ideal.

Odets makes occasional oblique references to *Golden Boy,* both to emphasize the connection and to separate this new play from it. While talking to his best friend, a writer, Hank Teagle, Charlie observes:

CHARLIE:

When I came home from Germany . . . I saw most of the war dead were here, not in Africa and Italy. And Roosevelt was dead . . . and the war was only last week's snowball fight . . . and we plunged ourselves, all of us, into the noble work of making the buck reproduce itself! Oh, those luscious salmon eggs of life!

HANK:

If you feel that deeply . . .

CHARLIE:

Get out of here? Does the man in your book get out of here? Where does he go? What, pray tell, does he do? Become a union organizer? Well, what does he do?

HANK:

Charlie . . . I can't invent last-act curtains for a world that doesn't have one. You're still an artist, Charlie.

(p. 111)

The Big Knife, then, represents a world that differs from Joe Bonaparte's more deeply than in its wealthy setting. *Golden Boy* was set in a period when the seeds of World War II were being planted; now the war is over, leaving behind it the postmodern world, wherein people's hopes for the future have been drastically reduced. Charlie's reference to becoming a union organizer is a direct reference to Joe's brother Frank in *Golden Boy,* where Frank represented an alternative to the success world of boxing. But the implication here is that Frank's idealism and activism are now out of place and only another pipe dream.

The loss of a kind of innocence is this fallen world is indirectly evoked in the beginning of the play as well, when the gossip columnist Patty Benedict speaks of Charlie's killing "that child in your car." In the context of the *Golden Boy* parallel, Odets is referring symbolically to Joe's essential youth and idealism—he, too, was killed in a car—and possibly to Ralph and the Gordon children as well, inhabitants of another time and another place. Charlie seems to be related to these characters and yet somewhat beyond them. There is an aura

of hopelessness about him that did not figure in the earlier plays, although Odets, again, does not allow the implication that this man's life holds no possibilities. Hank's protest, "You're still an artist," implies that the artist still possesses some power in society and may still act on his principles.

Charlie Castle is thus carefully differentiated from Joe, and he is also a more complex character. *Golden Boy* ends with Joe's realization that materialism will not make him happy and that the pursuit of it has tainted his soul. But Charlie is partly in love with his success, and he has been capable of sacrificing most of his integrity to it. Joe kills himself after he murders the Chocolate Drop, but Charlie manages not only to live with a killing, but even to let his friend go to jail in his place and then to sleep with that friend's wife. He does, however, stop short of deliberate murder: when the studio boss hints that Dixie Evans may be killed in order to ensure her silence about the accident, Charlie at last rebels against the cold-blooded evil of the business and his own implication in it.

Like other Odets drafts, the early version of **The Big Knife** is overly long and very preachy; in final form, its action is more compact and suggestive, and the forward movement more direct. The basic story outline remains the same, but Odets eliminates certain characters and cuts the parts of others in order to focus more narrowly on his central figure. Charlie's business manager, Harold Waterman, has an extended scene in the first draft but is only an offscreen presence contacted by telephone in the final version, while the character of a publicity agent named Jerry White is simply incorporated into Buddy Bliss. In the early drafts Buddy is an actor who knew Charlie when they were young men struggling to find work in New York. Still struggling, he has become Charlie's stand-in. In the final version the youthful association is retained, but Buddy's function changes.[12]

Odets's most revealing cuts and changes, however, relate to the character of Charlie Castle himself. In the early drafts Charlie is an incessant whiner and complainer, constantly moaning about what a terrible place Hollywood is while at the same time enjoying all of its rewards. Most unfortunately, he seems to blame the place and not himself for the moral surrender he has committed there. By the end of act 2, as a result, his suicide comes as rather a relief, which is clearly not what Odets had in mind. This early Charlie is also endowed with a more detailed past than the final version, but the detail only serves to simplify him, turning him into a typical agitprop character from the thirties, an effect Odets wanted to move away from by 1948. The overt politicization of his character is apparent early in the play when Charlie speaks to the gossip columnist Patty Benedict about the death of his parents:

They were both killed in the Ludlow Massacre in 1912. That's one of the great scandals of what they call "the

History of the American Working Class." Federal troops wiped out a whole tent colony of miners and their families who were striking for a better wage.

Meanwhile, Charlie's abandonment of his past is emphasized by his wife's identification of the symbol of what he has become:

> You're debased. . . . Like the currency. In fact you're currency itself—every gesture and word modulated. Every real human impulse made negotiable.

Odets also introduces the subject of anti-Semitism in the early versions, which is interesting in itself, for although he was Jewish, this subject is rarely addressed elsewhere in his work. Charlie mentions that he was raised by his aunt and uncle after his parents' death. His aunt was not Jewish and, although married to his uncle, she was not, according to Charlie, fond of Jews. Later, when Charlie quotes his uncle, Patty remarks, "That's a very Jewified remark." Charlie replies, "I have nothing against Jewified remarks." Odets apparently seeks not only to allude to anti-Semitism in Hollywood, but also to associate Jewishness with the more moral aspects of Charlie's nature, from which he has distanced himself. This association extends also to the studio head, Marcus Hoff, a man of no moral fiber, whom Charlie calls an "apocalyptic beast" (a remark that was removed in the final draft), and Nat Danziger, Charlie's agent, who, despite a sweet nature, tends to look the other way for the sake of business. At one point utterly repelled by Hoff, Nat cries, "That a man like you is now a Jew to shame and harm my race!" This and all other references to Jewishness were also cut, as distractions from Odets's focus.

The Charlie of the early versions is obviously too completely an idealist, his change too simplistic. The final version exhibits little of this background, retaining only the information that Charlie was raised by an aunt and uncle and was once a stage actor in the East. This pared-down portrait is more suggestive than the original, not reducing Charlie or society to convenient stereotypes, but implying that the main flaw resides in Charlie, as Charlie himself is to some extent aware. He is an exceptionally imaginative man, and his qualities as an artist are attested by those around him. Odets emphasizes both that Charlie is (or at least was) an artist and not just another pretty face, and that Hollywood is fatal to Charlie because there is something within him that responds too readily to its lure. At the same time Hollywood represents the larger world, and when he surrenders to it, he becomes entangled in a web of fate. The play, indeed, unfolds as a series of circumstances that work to enmesh this protagonist in a horrific nightmare of his own making. Perceptive about his own ambition and the stimulation he receives from power and success, Charlie is also disgusted by his capitulation and remorseful about ignoring the dictates of his better self.

At last his conscience overwhelms him as his imagination confronts him with the image of a damnable man. In an early draft he remarks, "To myself I am not an institution—I'm a weak, self-disgusted, very human man, very ordinary, guilty, . . . lonely . . . trapped."

Near the end of the finished play Charlie remarks to Nat Danziger, "It's too late, from *my* point of view. I can't go on, covering one crime with another. That's Macbeth. . . . Macbeth is an allegory, too: one by one, he kills his better selves" (p. 135). Clearly, Odets had *Macbeth* in his mind when he wrote ***The Big Knife***; in an interview he referred to Dixie Evans as "Banquo's ghost." Like Macbeth, Charlie Castle is an extremely tormented character, perhaps the most suffering character in Odets's canon. In Edward Murray's words he is a character, "sickened by compromise and driven to self-destruction in an effort to expiate his sins." ***The Big Knife,*** therefore, is more than a simple attack on Hollywood, because Charlie's dilemma results as much from the divided nature of his own soul, torn between conflicting values and unable to reconcile them, as from the moral emptiness of his environment.

The early versions, in fact, display a number of references to *Macbeth* that were cut from the final. Near the play's end, for example, Charlie says to Marion, "Macbeth doth murder sleep." He then alludes to a web of deceit and hints at his suicide: "Burnham wood is moving up. I hope you know Shakespeare." There are also a number of references to blood, images of which permeate Shakespeare's play. In a scene later cut from the early portion of the play, Patty says to Charlie, "Blood's more saleable than water, sweetie. A thimbleful of blood is relished now and then by the best of readers." After Charlie's suicide, his butler comments, "All that blood, all that blood and water. . . . Ain't no blood left in him." Most important is Charlie's description of Hollywood:

> I'm afraid of Hollywood because it's a tough, desperate world. They play for keeps here. It's as deadly as anything you read in Shakespeare, plots, intrigues, revenge, and cynicism—it's here, including corruption, intimidation, suicide and murder for succession.

In the tragic career of Odets's Macbeth figure, Hollywood, epitomized in the character of the producer Marcus Hoff, plays the role of Shakespeare's witches, tempting Charlie with wealth and fame undreamed of when he was a poor boy growing up in Philadelphia. There he read the authors in his uncle's library—Jack London, Upton Sinclair, Henrik Ibsen, and Victor Hugo:

> Hugo's the one who helped me nibble my way through billions of polly seeds. Sounds grandiose, but Hugo said to me: "Be a good boy, Charlie. Love people, do good, help the lost and fallen, make the world happy, if you can!"

(p. 9)

Having elected, instead, to pursue the promise of riches and power conveyed in Hoff's visions of moviemaking glory, Charlie now feels imprisoned by compromise and a life that violates his better nature. The burden of guilt generated by the fatal accident and its tangled consequences only objectifies the deeper sense of self-ruination that plagues him in the recognition that his success is hollow, that he has subverted his idealism and wasted his art for an ignoble goal. Marion voices this sense of spiritual loss in her complaint about the man Charlie has become:

> Charlie, you're half asleep right now! I haven't seen you sparkle since the day Billy was born! You used to take sides. Golly, the zest with which you fought. You used to grab your theatre parts and eat 'em like a tiger. Now you act with droopy eyes—they have to call you away from a card game. Charlie, I don't want you to sign that contract—you've given the studio their pound of flesh—you don't owe them anything. We arrived here in a pumpkin coach and we can damn well leave the same way!
>
> (p. 22)

Charlie, however, knows that in his case no such fairy-tale exit is possible, for he has become too far embroiled in the ugly business of faked glamour and casual destruction. Throughout act 1 he agonizes over whether or not to sign the new fourteen-year contract with Hoff's studio; his compliance is at last extorted when Hoff threatens to expose Charlie's part in the hit-and-run accident. Critics have argued that this early capitulation robs the play of its dramatic tension, when its effect, rather, is to deflate the melodrama of Charlie's predicament, focusing the remaining action instead upon the emotional disintegration caused by his entanglement. Charlie's own sense of fatal incrimination is reflected in Smiley Coy's remark, "Just keep in mind that the day you first scheme . . . you marry the scheme and the scheme's children," which supplies a clear analogy to Macbeth's lament, "I am in blood stepp'd in so far that, should I wade no more, returning were as tedious as go o'er" (act 3, scene 4).

Odets's central thrust in the play is to bring Charlie to a final awareness of what he has become. Already in act 1 he seems to be aware of the falseness of his position, but he is not yet ready to accept fully his personal implication in the corruption he sees around him. Macbeth, too, knows his crimes, but only at the banquet scene does he reach his breaking point, when the true horror of his own nature is exposed to him. Charlie, likewise, proceeds toward his breaking point, remarking his progress of enlightenment in act 3, scene 1: "Murder is indivisible, Smiley. I'm finding that out. Like chastity, there's no such thing as a small amount of it.

I'm finding that out" (p. 62). Finally, in act 3, scene 2, when he says to Marcus Hoff, "Now . . . I realize what I am," his understanding echoes Lady Macbeth's in a prior scene:

> Nought's had, all's spent,
> Where our desire is got without content:
> 'Tis safer to be that which we destroy
> Than by destruction dwell in doubtful joy.
>
> (act 3, scene 2)

At last he recognizes that in subverting his better self he has destroyed his family as well, that the comfort and joy he enjoys is very "doubtful" indeed.

Charlie's internal conflict is revealed primarily through his conversations with Hank Teagle, a close friend and a writer who has decided to renounce the Hollywood life-style and return East to work on a novel. Teagle is Marcus Hoff's opposite number, a kind of Banquo figure, reminding Charlie of what he once was and what he could do if only he could regain his youthful idealism. Teagle has even proposed to Marion, vowing to take her back to New York, to a more normal and fulfilling life; like Banquo, he will have the "heirs," whereas the wasted potential of Charlie/Macbeth will ultimately yield him nothing.

During a central conversation between the two friends Teagle tells Charlie about the book he is writing, "I still try to write out of Pascal's remark: 'I admire most those writers who tell, with tears in their eyes, what men do to other men.' This book is about a man like you" (p. 109). Explaining why he wants to take Marion away from the Hollywood environment, Hank expands the Hollywood metaphor to encompass an entire contemporary state of mind:

> Marion's future interests me deeply. No. I don't think she'll be happy here with you! I don't want Marion joining the lonely junked people of our world—millions of them, wasted by the dreams of the life they were promised and the swill they received! They are why the whole world, including us, sits bang in the middle of a revolution! Here, of course, that platitude carries with it the breath of treason. I think lots of us are in for a big shot of Vitamin D: defeat, decay, depression, and despair.
>
> (p. 109-10)

Finally, he charges that Charlie is destroying himself trying to choose between moral values and success, sarcastically recommending that he simply yield to the Hollywood ethic: "Your wild, native idealism is a fatal flaw in the context of your life out here. Half-idealism is the peritonitis of the soul—America is full of it! Give up and really march to Hoff's bugle call!" (p. 110). When Hank leaves, Charlie is still torn, unable to act.

Only when the studio pushes him to acquiesce in the murder of Dixie Evans does Charlie decide to take his fate into his own hands.

The conclusion of *The Big Knife* is in certain respects similar to *Golden Boy,* as Charlie breaks with Marcus Hoff and so makes himself a Hollywood outcast. When he tells his agent Nat and then Marion that he now recognizes his own culpability and the degradation of his life, Odets employs an Ibsenian stage device to reinforce the suggestion of clearing sight, of startling enlightenment. As in *A Doll's House,* Charlie twice turns on a lamp in act 3, scene 2, once as he says, "Now I realize what I am" (p. 134). The second time, when he says good-bye to Marion, he observes, "Keep meaning to put larger bulbs in these lamps" (p. 139). In his farewell Charlie also remarks, "Aren't the times beyond us, cold and lonely? Far away as the stars." The image echoes Odets's use of the moon in *Golden Boy,* at once a death image and a romantic symbol of aspiration that moves the lovers beyond the bounds of the physical world. Embracing Marion, he pledges to her a better future, then goes up to the bath to slash his wrists. For Charlie, as for Joe Bonaparte, death represents the only way out of a spiritual dilemma.

Charlie's suicide is discovered by Smiley Coy and Marion when they notice a water spot behind the stairs, ominously recalling Lady Macbeth's inability to remove the blood spots from her hands during her mad scene. Charlie's suicide here precipitates Marion's madness, for after viewing the body, she begins screaming "help," the word that concludes the play. Odets's final stage directions read: "Hank has his arms around her, but the word does not stop and will never stop in this life" (p. 147). It is Odets's most devastating ending, indicating a tragic loss so profound that Marion, unlike Lorna, is unable to comprehend it.

The loss of Charlie Castle attains the dimension of tragedy because the man has come to recognize the futility of his worldly success as well as his own implication in the sordid business of maintaining it. Like Macbeth, he is guilty of a series of crimes committed in the pursuit of an ephemeral glory and in defiance of his own higher nature. Yet, like Shakespeare's overreacher, he is consistently portrayed as a man of stature, clearly superior to the Hollywood types who surround him, and commanding the love and loyalty of Marion and Hank Teagle, the two most sympathetic characters in the play. Just as Macbeth's preeminence as a soldier is established by the wounded soldier at the play's beginning, and his personal virtues attested by his wife and by Duncan, Charlie Castle's integrity and potential are indicated by the deference and affection of his friends and confirmed in the extraordinary perceptiveness he displays in judging his own actions. The weighty catalog of his sins is thus matched by the nobility of his spirit.

Ensnared at the last in a mounting calamity of his own making, he destroys himself as "a final act of faith," a victim, like Macbeth, of the dagger of his own ambition.

Notes

1. Quoted in Margaret Brenman-Gibson, *Clifford Odets, American Playwright: The Years from 1906-1940* (New York: Atheneum, 1981), p. 426.

2. Clifford Odets, "Democratic Vistas in Drama," *New York Times,* 21 November, 1937, sec. 11, p. 1.

3. Ibid.

4. Robert Warshaw, "The Gangster as Tragic Hero," in *The Immediate Experience* (1962. Reprint. New York: Atheneum, 1974), p. 130.

5. This early draft of *Golden Boy,* dated 1937, is in the Billy Rose Theatre Collection of the New York Public Library at Lincoln Center.

6. Clifford Odets, *Golden Boy* in *Six Plays of Clifford Odets* (New York: Grove Press, 1979), p. 247. All further references to the play are from this edition and are cited in the text.

7. Carp's quotes from Schopenhauer are more extensive in the earlier versions of the play.

8. Gerald Rabkin, *Drama and Commitment* (Bloomington: Indiana University Press, 1964), pp. 197-98.

9. Quoted in Edward Murray, *Clifford Odets: The Thirties and After* (New York: Frederick Ungar Publishing Company, 1968), pp. 160-61.

10. For a full discussion of the characteristics of Hollywood fiction, refer to Carolyn See, "The Hollywood Novel: The American Dream Cheat," in David Madden, ed., *Tough Guy Writers of the Thirties* (Carbondale: Southern Illinois University Press, 1968), pp. 197-217.

11. Clifford Odets, *The Big Knife* (New York: Random House, 1949), p. 106. All further references are to this edition and are cited in the text.

12. All quoted material not in the published version of *The Big Knife* is from "A Winter Journey, First Draft" dated 1948, in the Billy Rose Theatre Collection of the New York Public Library at Lincoln Center.

Bibliography

PRIMARY SOURCES

PLAYS

Three Plays by Clifford Odets. New York: Covici-Friede, 1935. (Includes *Waiting for Lefty, Till the Day I Die,* and *Awake and Sing!)*

Waiting for Lefty and Till the Day I Die. New York: Random House, 1935.

Paradise Lost. New York: Random House, 1936.

Golden Boy. New York: Random House, 1937.

Six Plays of Clifford Odets. New York: Random House, 1939. (Includes *Waiting for Lefty, Till the Day I Die, Awake and Sing!, Paradise Lost, Golden Boy,* and *Rocket to the Moon.*) Reprinted by Grove Press, 1979.

The Big Knife. New York: Random House, 1949.

PLAYS PUBLISHED IN PERIODICALS

Waiting for Lefty (Original version). *New Theatre* 2 (February 1935): 13-20.

SCREENPLAYS (ALL ADAPTED FROM PREVIOUSLY PUBLISHED.)

The General Died at Dawn. (Paramount). 1936. Excerpts in Sidney Kaufman, "Odets's First Film," *New Masses* 20 (July 28, 1936): 12-13.

MUSICALS BASED ON ODETS'S PLAYS

Odets, Clifford, and Gibson, William. *Golden Boy.* New York: Atheneum, 1965. (Reprint. New York: Bantam Books, 1966). Although Odets's name appears as a co-author, the work is primarily Gibson's.

ARTICLES AND ESSAYS

"Democratic Vistas in Drama." *New York Times,* sec. 11 (November 21, 1937): 1-2.

SELECTED SECONDARY BIBLIOGRAPHY

Brenman-Gibson, Margaret. *Clifford Odets, American Playwright: The Years from 1906-1940.* New York: Atheneum, 1981.

Clurman, Harold. *The Fervent Years (1945).* Reprint. New York: DaCapo Press, 1975.

Murray, Edward. *Clifford Odets: The Thirties and After.* New York: Frederick Ungar, 1968.

Rabkin, Gerald. *Drama and Commitment: Politics in the American Theatre of the Thirties.* Bloomington: Indiana University Press, 1964.

Warshaw, Robert, *The Immediate Experience* (1962). Reprint. New York: Atheneum, 1974.

Michael Woolf (essay date 1995)

SOURCE: Woolf, Michael. "Clifford Odets." In *American Drama,* edited by Clive Bloom, pp. 46-69. Basingstoke, England: Macmillan, 1995.

[*In the following essay, Woolf surveys Odets's career as a playwright, arguing that his critical reputation is more complex than the common view of him as a prole-* tarian writer, and asserting that the two "myths" about Odets—namely, that he was mainly a Marxist dramatist and that his creativity suffered after his association with Hollywood in the 1940s—are both inaccurate and fail to recognize his larger contributions to American literature.]

> One day Cheryl Crawford, one of the Group's directors, asked me to read half a dozen scripts which were being considered for production. I went through them with little interest, until I came to the last, whose vivid characterization, pungent dialogue and effective dramaturgy revealed a brilliant new talent . . . The play was *Awake and Sing!,* by Clifford Odets.[1]

Elmer Rice's judgement was fairly representative in the mid 1930s. In contrast, Margaret Gibson recorded the tone of the obituaries that followed Odets's death in 1963:

> The newspapers and magazines with few exceptions printed obituaries which were strangely personal, some faintly accusatory, others supercilious; almost all were offhand.[2]

By the 1960s Odets's writing had been largely forgotten and his intellectual and liberal reputation had been bruised by his willingness to testify to the House Committee on Un-American Activities in 1952. For a few years in the 1930s Clifford Odets had enjoyed popular and critical success. In one year, 1935, in a surge of creative energy, Odets completed four plays that were produced by the Group theatre company. The plays were *Waiting for Lefty, Awake and Sing!, Paradise Lost, Till the Day I Die.*[3] Much of his critical reputation came out of those plays and depends to a degree on the perceived value of that year's work. Such a view is a distortion and simplification of what is, in reality, a complex career.

Odets's career has been made murky by a number of myths through which he has tended to be seen. In the first of these, he is placed firmly in the context of the proletarian literature movement of the 1930s. In fact, only a one-act play, *Waiting for Lefty,* can be wholly placed in the context of agit-prop theatre. Indeed, few of Odets's characters are of a strictly proletarian background. More commonly they are drawn from the lower-middle and middle classes. Odets never had a coherent ideological basis in his plays beyond a generalised concern for the impoverished, what Leslie Fielder calls 'sentimental radicalism', and a desire to represent 'ordinary' people in a serious manner.[4] Harold Clurman knew Odets's work as a director and as a founder of the Group theatre:

> There was in it a fervour that derived from the hope and expectation of change and the desire for it. But there was rarely any expression of political consciousness in it, no deep commitment to a coherent philoso-

phy of life, no pleading for a panacea. 'A tendril of revolt' runs through all of Odets' work, but that is not the same thing as a consistent revolutionary conviction.[5]

In part, the reading of Odets as a kind of ideologue of the 1930s Left is, as Arthur Miller indicates, a symptom of the radical imperatives of the times,

> As always, we were trapped into estimating writers by what they apparently stood for rather than by what they were actually doing, by the critical propaganda surrounding them rather than by their literary deeds.[6]

From a current perspective, Odets's political radicalism appears to be rhetorical addition to the plays, a flourish that often has little or no organic place in the dramatic developments portrayed on the stage. More often than not they arise in moments of forced epiphany. The meanings of the work appear beyond and beneath the virtually obligatory rhetoric of the 1930s Left.

The other myth that serves to distort his significance is that of Hollywood. The notion that Hollywood is destructive of the creative writer and that Odets is (another) victim of that process is used to explain what is perceived as creative failure post-1940. There is a common association often made between Hollywood and wealth and the death of creativity that is used, by Arthur Miller for example, as a means of neatly categorising Odets's experience. 'What had he been doing in Hollywood but wasting his talent making money?'[7] This view contains two potential distortions. The first is that Odets's creativity dried up after 1940. While Odets certainly produced less for the theatre, he wrote extensively for the cinema and, in 1948, produced *The Big Knife* which, in Edward Murray's view, is one of Odets's most important works: '*The Big Knife* is a powerful drama—disturbing, wild and unforgettable—something which comes when an artist has driven his vision to an extreme.'[8]

The other notion that Hollywood somehow weakened Odets's creative power ignores the fact that, ostensibly at least, Odets was enthusiastic about the positive impact of working in the film industry. 'What the critics don't realize is that I picked up half my techniques here . . . The movies are a brilliant training school for a dramatic writer.'[9]

There may also be some tendency to see *The Big Knife* as autobiographical in some sense or other. Whatever the source, a common view is that Hollywood had, in combination with other factors, somehow sapped his energies as an author. Joseph Wood Krutch's view is representative of a number of similar perspectives:

> Odets's *The Big Knife* and *The Country Girl*[10] reflected the author's new life as a Hollywood scenarist and though they attracted renewed attention to a writer with great theatrical talent neither had the strong individuality which first distinguished him.[11]

However, a number of other factors combined at the end of the 1930s to undermine those conditions that had encouraged Odets's creativity. On a personal level, a failed marriage enforced a thread of bitterness which became manifest in *Clash by Night* (1941). On a more political level, the outbreak of war signalled the failure of 1930s radicalism to alter the world in ways imagined in the rhetoric of the times. Above all, perhaps, the Group theatre disbanded.

Odets's early career was shaped by the Group theatre and the years of its existence, from 1930 to 1940, coincided with the years of his greatest productivity:

> To some degree . . . the fate of the company and of this writer were entwined. It was the success of his plays in 1935 which cemented the success of the company and it was the gradual disengagement of the company from his 1941 play, *Clash by Night,* which marked its dissolution.[12]

Odets's talent was nurtured and nourished by the Group and his plays were profoundly influenced by his experiences there. He recognised this fact in an interview in 1961: 'Without the Group Theatre I doubt that I would have become a playwright.'[13]

The founders, Lee Strasberg, Harold Clurman and Cheryl Crawford, together created what was close to a commune or community of actors and writers:

> Their primary aims were to establish new and more vital relations between actor and author, between actor and actor, and above all, between the authors and the society in which they lived. They were not committed to social and political radicalism, especially at the start, but were in search of serious, non escapist scripts, preferably with social implications. Only by living, rehearsing, discussing, working and thinking together—they felt—could they realize the full possibilities of a permanent acting company and as a result achieve in their productions greater unity and more significant social connotations.[14]

The formal objectives of the group coincided with Odets's view of what constituted the purpose and meaning of theatre while the community gave him personal support and affirmation in contrast to what had been an unhappy, even suicidal, childhood and youth. He has been described as 'happier and more secure in the collective life of the Group than he had ever been in the booming twenties'.[15] Harold Clurman gives some indication of the life-style of the Group theatre:

> We were all living in remarkable fashion. At least half the Group had moved into a ten-room flat on West Fifty-Seventh Street near the railroad tracks. The rent was fifty dollars a month, for besides its unfavourable location, the house was a neglected old brownstone with insufficient heat and a generally damp atmosphere.
>
> Meals were provided for through a common fund, marketing was done by the two girls, and the cooking was

attended to in turn by four or five of the men who had a knack for it. Clifford Odets's virtuosity in this field was confined to potato pancakes and hot chocolate . . .[16]

The collapse of the Group in 1940 can, with the other political and personal matters, offer a coherent explanation for the relative decline in Odets's productivity that is at least as convincing as the Hollywood myth.

In any case, it is clear that there are alternative contexts through which his writing can be viewed. In this chapter, a number of perspectives will be offered on the significance and meanings of Odets's work which will balance both the excessive critical enthusiasm of the 1930s and the subsequent neglect from the 1950s onwards. The discussions will indicate how, in one view, Odets can be read within the context of Jewish-American literature of the period. *Awake and Sing!*, for example, represents a recurrent theme in Jewish-American writing of the transformed family structure. The secularisation of family life leads inexorably to the diminution of patriarchal authority, traditionally associated with the function of a religious head of the family. One impact of this process of transformation is to create an emergent mother, a Bessie Berger figure, as the central force of the family. In other ways, Odets reflects Jewish-American experience: in the use of Yiddish-English as a dramatic language; in the emphasis on father-son relationships and the conflict between generations; in the expression of a secularised version of a Messianic myth as a form of socialist Utopianism.

Odets can also be read in the context of Romantic literature in so far as he creates a sequence of characters longing for some idealised version of experience. That these idealised images are frequently distorted into crassly commercial shapes reveal Odets as a social critic of a commercialised, acquisitive, consumer society. He was not, however, a simple realist. Many of the plays work through contrasting metaphorical structures, use epiphany as a catalyst, and they construct sequences of action followed by consequences that bring the whole closer to didactic fabulation than realism. The symbolic conflict between the violin and boxing in *Golden Boy* and Joe's death belong more to moral fable than the randomness of reality. The conflicting models of suicide and birth, employed and re-employed in many of the plays, is similarly a structure owing much to fable.

The Depression is the filter through which much experience is recorded. Fears and insecurities bred in the 1930s persist throughout Odets's plays and become a part of his perception of human experience: a permanent state of unease. In another respect, Odets reflects the legacy of the 1930s in, for example, *The Big Knife*, where Hollywood success is seen as a kind of double betrayal of both the values of the theatre and an earlier

radicalism. In another sense, *Golden Boy* draws upon boxing in two respects: as a popular theme in the movies of the time and as a pathway to self-improvement for young men in immigrant communities with little access to the more conventional channels of advancement.

Odets needs to be seen, as the following discussion of the plays themselves indicates, both as a representational figure whose concerns and methods of expression are symptomatic of the times and as a playwright whose work sought to address broad issues of human behaviour, passion and aspiration. This chapter considers Odets within the context of Jewish-American writing, with regard to his treatment of love and aspiration, as a form of American Romantic, and in relation to the economic, cultural and political experiences of the 1930s.

The tendency to categorise Odets as a writer contained and bounded by the 1930s distorts the real value of the work which encompasses the emotional signs of those nightmarish times but goes beyond them. The significance of this work is, primarily, in the combination of a quasi-Romantic perception with a social concern for immigrant experience perceived through a Jewish-American consciousness formed in a time of turmoil.

Waiting for Lefty (first produced 1935) was unashamedly an agitprop production. It is also the only play by Odets that is unarguably a political drama with a clear radical intention. Interest in it now is primarily historical. It was presented in a double bill with *Till the Day I Die*, which similarly has historical rather than dramatic interest. It is an early example of anti-Nazi theatre. Together, these two plays offer an insight into the domestic and international preoccupations of American radicals in the mid-1930s and contain a few signals of the issues and techniques that Odets was to develop in further plays. The use of contrasting motifs of suicide and birth as dichotomies reflecting despair and hope is characteristic of Odets's dramatic strategy and is first expressed in *Till the Day I Die*. Scene iv concludes with the Major's suicide while scene v opens with the announcement by the young woman, Tilly, of her pregnancy. It is presented explicitly as a sign of optimism and hope in the future:

TILLY:

Till the day we die there is steady work to do. Let us hope we will both live to see strange and wonderful things. Perhaps we will die before then. Our children will see it then. Ours!

ERNST:

(*bitterly*) Our children!

TILLY:

I'm going to have a baby, Ernst . . .[17]

Waiting for Lefty demonstrates the talent Odets was to refine later with regard to the use of shifting registers. An easy transition from everyday speech to a rhetoric that builds on everyday speech patterns but elevates them towards a language of poetry signals Odets's political objectives: to elevate the language of the poor and, thereby, to suggest the potential for nobility in the dispossessed. Odets's dramatic language affirms the importance of the experiences of the poor and the exploited. Art is made out of everyday experience and this also, clearly, relates to Odets's general political sympathies. The play was also interesting in that it was constructed precisely to be presented in any hall. It required no scenery or special theatrical device. In short, it was an attempt at a play about, for and by an economic and social group rarely served by the theatre of the times.

Far more interesting than these two plays, however, was *Awake and Sing!* (1935). It was, in fact, the first play written by Odets though it was produced later in the year. It was a skilful play that raised issues of greater complexity and interest than those presented in the politically driven plays *Waiting for Lefty* and *Till the Day I Die.*

Awake and Sing! is Odets's first exploration of tension and disintegration within the family. The Berger family is dominated by the mother, Bessie, who prefigures the satirical monster-mothers of the 1960s who found vivid expression in comic form, particularly in novels such as Philip Roth's *Portnoy's Complaint,* Wallace Markfield's *Teitelbaum's Window,* Bruce Jay Friedman's *A Mother's Kisses* and, in a comic essay, Dan Greenburg's *How to be a Jewish Mother.*

The figure of Bessie reflects the secularisation of Jewish-American family life and a subsequent shift of authority from the father to the mother, the male to the female. Authority traditionally resided in the male because of the father's predominant role as religious head of the household. This invested in the male figure a moral authority and power that shaped roles within the family. The Berger family, like many Jewish-Americans, was secularised and, as a consequence, the patriarchal figures become impotent or comic or defeated. The grandfather Jacob is, as the name signifies, a quasi-patriarchal figure whose power exists only in rhetoric. His rages, remnants of power, are ineffective and treated as inconsequential.

All the fathers in the play are ineffectual figures without clear function. Within the opening seconds Myron, Bessie's husband, is undermined by his daughter:

RALPH:

> Where's advancement down the place? Work like crazy! Think they see it? You'd drop dead first.

MYRON:

> Never mind, son, merit never goes unrewarded. Teddy Roosevelt used to say—

HENNIE:

> It rewarded you—thirty years a haberdashery clerk![18]

The opening exchange reveals both the diminution of the father as a moral authority and the coruscating irony which is typical of the female figures in the Berger family.

Exactly the same inversion of traditional structures is enacted in the relationship between Jacob and Bessie: Jacob is reduced from father to child in a role reversal and distortion that has fatal consequences. This process of family reversal has, certainly, comic potential but it also has, as Odets makes clear, a dimension measured in anguish not only in laughter:

BESSIE:

> Go in your room, Papa. Every job he ever had he lost because he's got a big mouth. He opens his mouth and the whole Bronx could fall in. Everybody said it—

MYRON:

> Momma, they'll hear you down the dumbwaiter.

BESSIE:

> A good barber not to hold a job a week. Maybe you never heard charity starts at home. You never heard it, Pop?

JACOB:

> All you know, I heard, and more yet. But Ralph you don't make like you. Before you do it, I'll die first. He'll find a girl. He'll go in a fresh world with her. This is a house? Marx said it—abolish such families.

BESSIE:

> Go in your room, Papa.

JACOB:

> Ralph you don't make like you!

BESSIE:

> Go lay in your room with Caruso and the books together.

JACOB:

> All right!

BESSIE:

> Go in the room!

JACOB:

> Some day I'll come out I'll—[19]

Jacob is sent to his room by his daughter, signalling an inversion that is symptomatic of the kinds of pain suffered by the fathers in relation to daughters and wives.

This has, of course, some comic potential and is expressed in the relationship of Hennie with her husband Sam. Sam is a victim of Bessie's plot to make him marry Hennie and accept her child as his own. In the frequent family battles that ensue, Sam, weak, gullible and ineffectual, leaves his home and goes to Bessie's house. Odets puts into Jacob's mouth a commentary on this inversion that is both precise and comic: 'In my day the daughter came home. Now comes the son-in-law.'[20]

Many of the play's themes are reflected in Jacob's exchange with Myron in Act II:

MYRON:

> People can't believe in God in Russia. The papers tell the truth, they do.

JACOB:

> So you believe in God . . . you got something for it? You worked for all the capitalists. You harvested the fruits from your labor? You got God! But the past comforts you? The present smiles on you, yes? It promises you the future something? Did you found a piece of earth where you could live like a human being and die with the sun on your face? Tell me, yes, tell me. I would like to know myself. But on these questions, on this theme—the struggle for existence—you can't make an answer. The answer I see in your face . . . the answer is your mouth can't talk. In this dark corner you sit and you die. But abolish private property!

BESSIE:

> (*settling the issue*) Noo, go fight City Hall!

MORTY:

> He's drunk.[21]

The speech, in the first case, signals the process of secularisation through which the option of God is seen to have become irrelevant and to offer no comfort in the past, present or future. The ironic consequence is to render Jacob powerless except in a rhetorical sense. The absence of God renders the patriarchal voice feeble, without a basis for authority, permitting the dismissive responses of the daughter, Bessie, and the son, Morty.

Furthermore, the speech contains a view of human experience that permeates Odets's work. In short, the Depression is the filter through which Odets perceives human experience throughout most of his writing career. Such a perspective sees existence as a 'struggle' and characterises life as defined through fear, insecurity, marginality. Characters in *Paradise Lost* (1935), *Golden Boy* (1937), *Rocket to the Moon* (1938) and *Clash by Night* (1941) cling to security at the edge of a precipice and are forced to construct fragile, illusory defences against despair and defeat. The lower-middle-class Bergers or the middle-class Gordons in *Paradise Lost* share a sense that what they have, security and status such as it is, is menaced by forces outside themselves. Ironically, the stronger characters are the conservative voices like Bessie whose objectives are to maintain what there is through an essentially stoical rather than activist stance.

Jacob also gives voice to that most American of all dreams for a 'piece of earth' and a place in the sun. This Edenic vision of a oneness with nature sits uncomfortably with the actuality of the experience represented, which is remorselessly urban, where the only space is upward, on the roof, from where, ultimately, Jacob jumps to his death. This reveals the extreme fragility of dreams of alternative experience constructed in the shape of the unattainable.

Throughout Odets's writing characters construct dreams to confront reality. These dreams are in essence of two kinds: they are either Edenic notions of return to some lost paradise and/or Utopian constructs of some ideal socialist society; or they are 'false gods', consumer goods and objects into which the characters invest and accumulate meanings the objects themselves cannot carry.[22] Within *Awake and Sing!* both kinds of dreams coincide. Sam's wife Hennie 'looks for a star in the sky' while her brother Ralph gathers images of what he has been deprived of and invests in them accumulated meanings that reveal the extreme fragility of the dreams.[23] From a socially critical point of view, they express Odets's implicit criticism of a society which has translated aspiration into commerce and possessions. Ralph's discontents are expressed in these forms: 'It's crazy—all my life I want a pair of black and white shoes and can't get them. It's crazy.'[24] 'I never in my life even had a birthday party.'[25] 'You never in your life bought me a pair of skates even—things I died for when I was a kid.'[26]

An exchange between Myron and Bessie precisely captures the manner in which material objects are elevated into false poetic alternatives to a harsh actuality. A saxophone and a picture in a calendar are transformed into magic objects in what is a rare direct exchange between husband and wife:

MYRON:

> Yesterday a man wanted to sell me a saxophone with pearl buttons. But I—

BESSIE:

> It's a beautiful picture. In this land, nobody works . . . Nobody worries.[27]

It is a moment when the characters come closest to some kind of nobility, in that real vulnerability is exposed and the humanity expressed in aspirations that can find neither concrete form nor complete expression. The visions are impoverished but momentarily achieve the status, poetry and intensity of vision that is, nevertheless, unshared and misplaced. In the construction of such symbols, Odets approaches a Romantic perception of the world.

There are, then, throughout this play, paradises lost and malformed. Bessie destroys Jacob's record of Caruso singing 'O Paradiso'. Moe seeks his paradise with Hennie at the end of the play: 'A certain place where it's moonlight and roses. We'll lay down, count stars.'[28] He offers Hennie (his nickname for her is Paradise) an escape route. The play ends inevitably ambiguously. Hennie seeks this paradise with Moe by abandoning her child. Ralph is symbolically reborn to establish a polarity with Jacob's suicide which re-enacts the dichotomies established in *Till the Day I Die*:

> Did Jake die for us to fight about nickels? No! 'Awake and Sing', he said. Right there he stood and said it. The night he died, I saw he was dead and I was born. I swear to God, I'm one week old![29]

The ambiguities of the play's conclusion contain and modify what might be read as radical optimism. Hennie leaves in pursuit of paradise and Ralph goes nowhere. Images of hope are potential rather than realised and they are formed in shapes that correspond to forms of illusion. It is appropriate that Odets's fourth play of 1935 should have been called *Paradise Lost.*

Paradise Lost, as the preceding discussion suggests, takes many of the themes and issues from *Awake and Sing!* and relocates them in a middle-class context. Fear and insecurity are shown to encompass not just the poorest groups in society. Surprisingly enough, it is Odets's favourite play among those written between 1935 and 1938:

> *Paradise Lost,* poorly received as a practical theatre work, remains my favourite play in this group. While not unmindful of its harsh and ungracious form, I must be permitted to say that our modern audiences, critics included, still must have their plays, like salt-water taffy, cut to fit the mouth. *Paradise Lost* shares with *Rocket to the Moon* a depth of perception, a web of sensory impressions and a level of both personal and social experience not allotted to the other plays here.[30]

This is an odd judgement in that the play thematically adds little to the issues raised in *Awake and Sing!* but is far more impoverished in its language as it loses the verbal energy invested in the speech of the Bergers by the Yiddish-English constructions.

In *Paradise Lost*, 'Odets crams his stage with evidence of collapse and decay'[31] and creates fragile versions of a past seen to contain positive images of promise and hope frustrated in the harsh present. Each of the characters appears to have lost some personal vision of paradise:

LEO:

> Clara, my beautiful Clara, what is happening here? Once we were all together and life was good.[32]

For Gus, the paradise was in pre-war America:

> 'I can't explain it to you, Mr. G., how I'm forever hungerin' for the past. It's like a disease in me, eatin' away . . . some nights I have cried myself to sleep . . .'[33]

For all the hopeful rhetoric with which the play concludes, Malcolm Goldstein's summary seems most apt: 'The immigrant's dream of finding an earthly paradise in the new world is seen to have become a nightmare of economic and moral bankruptcy.'[34] In this play, Odets most markedly fails to integrate a political stance with the logic of the play. Leo is bankrupt and without business and home. One of the homeless, Paul, describes Leo's predicament at the conclusion of the play in terms that point to the harshest of realities:

PAUL:

> I look at you and see myself seven years back. I been there. This kind of dream paralyzes the will—confuses the mind. Courage goes. Daring goes . . . and in the nights there is sighing. I had my house in the United States. Like you. Did you have a business?

LEO:

> Yes.

PAUL:

> Like me. you had a sorta little paradise here. Now you lost the paradise. That should teach you something. But no! You ain't awake yet.[35]

Leo's epiphanous vision that 'Heartbreak and terror are not the heritage of mankind!'[36] appears to confirm rather than contradict Paul's assessment. The play does not resolve its contradictions and is, in a sense, redundant in that it replays, in a weaker form, the preoccupations of *Awake and Sing!*

In contrast Odets used new experience for *Golden Boy* (1937). Thematically, the play drew upon the popularity of boxing movies in Hollywood and, indeed, Odets saw the play as something of a money-raiser for the Group. It has much of the structure of a popular fable with the central character choosing between alternatives symbolised as the opposite ends of some kind of spectrum. Joe Bonaparte chooses boxing over the violin and so abandons one set of values, implicitly more cultured and cultivated, for others that are only materialistic. In an increasingly Faustian resonance in Odets's later work, this choice brings him financial reward but also ends in despair, moral defeat and, ultimately, death.

In one sense, the play marked a transition from the earlier to the later plays. The atmosphere of economic unease and material striving is sustained, as are the Romantic projections of a world elsewhere. There is, for example, little or no distinction between Moe's dreamed world at the end of *Awake and Sing!* or Jacob's 'place in the sun' and Lorna's response to Joe's despair in *Golden Boy*:

JOE:

> But my hands are ruined. I'll never play again! What's left, Lorna? Half a man, useless . . .

LORNA:

> No, *we're* left! Two together! We have each other! Somewhere there must be happy boys and girls who can teach us the way of life! We'll find some city where poverty's no shame—where music is no crime!—where there's no war in the streets . . .[37]

The characteristics of Odets's later work are also apparent here, particularly in the use of symbol and allegory. For Gabriel Miller, '*Golden Boy* . . . works best as a symbolic play. Odets clearly intended it as an allegory; indeed, he subtitled an earlier draft *An American Allegory*.'[38]

The nature of the allegory is recurrent in the later work. A set of ethics are presented, and figures abandon or betray these in return for financial reward. In *Golden Boy* the ethics betrayed are symbolised in the violin whereas boxing is the symbol for the 'sell-out' to materialism. The contrast is given a more familiar form in *The Big Knife*: theatre versus Hollywood. Harold Cantor summarises this pattern in Odets's work as 'the individual's barter of moral principle for money, power and status'.[39] In these plays, the Faustian element becomes the means through which Odets points the didactic nature of the fable.[40] The protagonists are separated from a version of an elemental self to which, for one reason or another, they are unable to return.

In *Rocket to the Moon* (1938) Odets gave a shape and form to this notion of an elemental self in the figure of Cleo. The influence of Whitman and Emerson has been noted in this aspect of Odets's work and it signals an important shift. The 'salvation' offered in Odets's earliest work was, at least superficially, collective and political from the exhortation to STRIKE at the end of *Waiting for Lefty* to Leo's vision at the end of *Paradise Lost*:

> Everywhere now men are rising from their sleep. Men, men are understanding the bitter black total of their lives. Their whispers are growing to shouts! They become an ocean of understanding! *No man fights alone.*[41]

By *Rocket to the Moon*, the path towards some form of salvation is personal and driven by a notion of discovery of the hidden self that has to be freed. The symbol of singing not only echoes Whitman's, 'I celebrate myself, and sing myself', but is, from *Awake and Sing!* onwards, used to signal this form of personal path towards salvation through perceptions that transcend realities. Escape becomes an act of the imagination as much as physical movement. In the earlier plays the personal co-exists with the political and collective. By *Rocket to the Moon* the individual has become the focus for what is almost a form of transcendental imagination.

In the climax of *Rocket to the Moon*, Cleo is forced to choose between her lovers but the choice she makes is archetypally American and Romantic: for freedom, space, love and the pursuit of joy. All this is symbolised by the idea of singing:

> if there's roads, I'll take them. I'll go up all those roads till I find what I want. I want a love that uses me, that needs me. Don't you think that there's a world of joyful men and women? Must all men live afraid to laugh and sing? Can't we sing at work and love our work? It's getting late to play at life; I want to live it.[42]

In gaining her liberation, she drives Prince and his son-in-law, Stark, to reconciliation and Stark towards a transformed consciousness:

> Yes, I, who sat here in this prison-office, closed off from the world . . . for the first time in years I looked out on the world and saw things as they really are . . .[43]

For Arthur Miller, *Rocket to the Moon* is Odets's 'one real success as a writer'.[44] It is apparent that the play looks back towards Whitman and forwards towards the kinds of transformations that were to be characteristic of the work of Jack Kerouac, John Clellon Holmes and the writers who became known a few years later as the Beats.

In *Night Music: A Comedy in Twelve Scenes* (1940), the two aspects of Cleo's voice are divided. Rosenberger is 'a partisan of life, liberty and happiness', the embodiment of an archetypal American view of the world.[45] Fay Tucker achieves the insight to become another version of Cleo, a Romantic who articulates the potential to transform and transcend reality: 'Night Music . . . If they can sing, I can sing. I'm more than them. *We're* more than them. . . . We can sing through any night.'[46] What is in *Awake and Sing!* a political and personal response becomes, in this context, an individual vision of transformation.

In this play Odets also returned to another recurrent theme in his work. In his introduction to the published edition, Harold Clurman succinctly summarises Odets's treatment of the theme of homelessness:

The play stems from the basic sentiment that people nowadays are affected by a sense of insecurity; they are haunted by the fear of impermanence in all their relationships; they are fundamentally *homeless,* and, whether or not they know it, they are in search of a home, of something real, secure, dependable in a slippery, shadowy, noisy and nervous world. This search for a home—for security of a truly human sort—takes many forms, including the comic.[47]

In *Paradise Lost* and *Awake and Sing!,* for example, homelessness was expressed as a threat in the Depression, where eviction was a real and present danger. That version exists in *Night Music* but it is more explicitly broadened into a metaphorical context where what is missing is both a physical home and a sense of belonging.

Like many of Odets's characters, Steve Takis is from immigrant stock and this enforces his sense of marginality in relation to America. The play traces this notion of finding and defining a notion of home and he appeals to the detective Rosenberger to create for him and others like him an America that can offer a sense of location:

> Make this America for me. Make this America for her and her family—they're shivering in their boots. Where is Wilbur Harris? He fell off the freight an' lost a leg. Where's Joe Abrams? Teddy Bannister? In jail. Dan Lowe is pushin' up the daisies—TB. The sweetest little girl on our block—she's peddling it on the streets! An' where are those other pals of my cradle days? Hangin' up by the ears from coast to coast . . . those harmony boys who mighta been! *Make this America for us!*[48]

Rosenberger's role signifies how close Odets gets at time to creating fables. Rosenberger is ostensibly a detective who is about to retire but who is also dying of cancer. In effect, he is a forerunner of J. B. Priestley's inspector in *An Inspector Calls* in that he acts as a *deus ex machina* and as a sage. He protects Steve and Fay, his girlfriend, but guides them towards a version of enlightenment and alternative optimism. Thus he is, even with his Jewish name, a spokesperson for American values as 'a partisan of the pursuit of life, liberty and happiness'. The key significance of Rosenberger is that he embodies a kind of magical synthesis or reconciliation between America and its immigrants. The figure is at once both Jewish moral activist and American sage. He embodies the dual dimensions of Odets's vision in the combination of American vision and Jewish moral consciousness.

At various points, Rosenberger expresses the moral direction of the play and offers commentary on the evolution of events: 'I'll tell you a secret, Miss Tucker. All the dead and living are cheering for you when you are a good person.'[49] In relation to the generational divide treated in the play, he signals a clear commitment to the future and to youth rather than age: 'The function of the parent is to make himself unnecessary. Unfortunately, only animals and birds know it.'[50]

Night Music confronts a number of themes and issues that are recurrent in Odets's work but through a lighter perspective and, at times, in some bizarre contexts; the cause of Steve's problems is the unpredictable behaviour of two performing monkeys he is charged with looking after. This was a departure in tone for Odets and, certainly, the least realist of all the plays except *The Flowering Peach* (1954). A reading of that version of the Noah story in conjunction with *Night Music* focuses attention on the degree to which other, more ostensibly realist, plays—*Golden Boy* is a clear example—deviate from realism and move in the direction of fabulation. There is also in *Night Music* a sustained approach to the issues raised and a consistency of tone that is not always apparent elsewhere. Harold Clurman's view is that 'among his longer plays it is the most integrated in its feeling and the most completely conceived'.[51]

Night Music presents homelessness and isolation in that most urban, and isolating, of American cities: New York. In this, Winifred Dusenberry argues that Odets offers a perspective on an archetypal American condition:

> In one sense Americans are so used to moving that they are never homeless and may speak of a casual hotel room as home, but in another they are forever homeless, because 'home' is not the place where they live, but the place where they lived as a child.[52]

Odets's tone darkened in 1941 in *Clash by Night,* a play clearly reflecting his matrimonial problems. The play is permeated by discontent. Two couples are contrasted; the married couple, Jerry and Mae, have a marriage torn by conflict and which ends, finally, in the murder of Mae's lover.

There are three forms of discontent expressed in the play. In the first place, the character Peggy expresses a common predicament: 'Great expectations, great disappointments'.[53] Dreams manifestly exceed the capacity of reality to realise them. Mae's lover Earl exactly expresses the distance between actuality and aspiration and tells us that, 'I don't enjoy my life . . . I enjoy only the dream of it.'[54]

Another more concrete discontent derives from the failure of relationships. Odets's view of married life is almost always marked by infidelity, tension and emotional isolation. As in *Rocket to the Moon,* the relationship between husband and wife is desperately poor but, in this bleak version, no possible reconciliation is projected. There is a dark vision of isolation in Jerry's view of human experience:

> You could wake up some day an' find you're an old man with a tool kit under your arm an' they don't want

you—not even your wife. Like my father—my mother didn't speak to him for three years before she died.[55]

Mae's view of her marriage enforces the sense of a chasm between aspiration and fulfilment. Her romantic, quasi-heroic dream meets the realities of the human condition:

> I guess I'm a hold-over from another century! Didn't there used to be big, comfortable men? Or was it a dream? Today they're little and nervous, sparrows! But I dream of eagles . . .[56]

Mae's comment contains the other form of discontent that runs through the play. In short, to be discontented is seen almost as part of the general human condition, a malaise generated by a form of nostalgia for some version of a mythic, more heroic, past. The play is particularly bleak, and some of Odets's personal unhappiness is manifest in the despair, but **Clash by Night** also endorses Joseph Wood Krutch's assessment:

> No one that I know can more powerfully suggest the essential loneliness of men and women, their inability to explain the varied forms assumed by the symbols of their desire, and the powerlessness of any one of them to help the other.[57]

It was seven years before Odets's work next appeared and, in 1948 and 1950 in **The Big Knife** and **The Country Girl,** he drew upon his own experience in Hollywood and in the theatre for subject matter.[58] **The Big Knife** echoes both *Faust* and *Macbeth* ('Is this a dagger which I see before me?') and revisits many of the concerns previously discussed. It is a moral fable which contains the notion that success betrays past values. To achieve worldly fame and fortune is, in this context, to be damned like Faust and driven, like Macbeth, from one act of betrayal to another:

> Like Macbeth, he is guilty of a series of crimes committed in the pursuit of an ephemeral glory and in defiance of his own higher nature.[59]

The central character is a successful film actor, ironically, in the light of his rootlessness, named Charlie Castle. His wife Marion is the voice of his conscience and the embodiment of the values of the theatre. Exactly like Joe Bonaparte in **Golden Boy,** Charlie is caught between two ends of ethical possibility: theatre versus Hollywood (violin versus boxing). The dichotomy between the two locations is perceived in terms that contrast both ethics and artistic integrity. In that respect, Odets's play belongs within the context of a quasi-genre of anti-Hollywood literature (frequently produced in Hollywood) which includes such disparate works as Nathanael West's novel *The Day of the Locust,* F. Scott Fitzgerald's novel *The Last Tycoon* and includes relatively recent works such as the play *Tales from Hollywood* by Christopher Hampton and the popular musical *City of Angels.*

That aspect of the play is, perhaps, less interesting than the manner in which Odets melds that concern with matters that are expressed elsewhere in his work. The idea of separation from some notion of paradise creates a state of perpetual yearning which approaches Edenic and Zionistic intensity in both Charlie and Marion. Charlie's insight that 'We're homesick all our lives, but adults don't talk about it' signals the kinds of discontent that Odets's characters frequently suffer and that is, as in **Clash by Night,** a symptom of human pain.[60]

The key confrontations in the play are between Charlie and Hank, Marion's lover, who is also, significantly, a writer but who has, in contrast to Charlie, retained his integrity. He is able, therefore, to offer explicit and implicit commentary upon the events of the play and these are invested with moral authority: 'I know that Marion stands in your life for your idealism . . . and that you've wounded her and it.'[61] The novel that Hank is writing is a mirror of the play itself: 'It's a fable about moral values and success', he says.[62]

The Big Knife is simple in its structure and clear in its moral intention. The exchange between Charlie and Marion early in the play expresses the essence of the play's meanings:

CHARLIE:

> . . . I'm Hoff Federated's biggest star. I'm worth millions to them in ice-cold profits! Hoff's got me by the tail and he won't let go and you know why!

MARION:

> Tell him you're leaving Hollywood for good. Promise him never to make pictures for anyone else.

CHARLIE:

> Just what do you expect me to do? Pick up without a backward glance—and what? Go back and act in shows?

MARION:

> What's wrong with shows? You started in the theatre. We'd go back to New York, yes—the theatre can still give you a reasonable living. And away from this atmosphere of flattery and deceit we might make our marriage work.[63]

The Hoff contract is a precise translation of a Faustian pact into the Hollywood environment. Success is a kind of spiritual and moral failure as Hank indicates: 'You still know that a failure is the best of American life.'[64]

The play is simple in moral structure and ends in Charlie's suicide, which is the only path left back to the abandoned self:

HANK:

> He . . . killed himself . . . because that was the only way he could live. You don't recognize a final . . . a final act of faith . . . when you see one . . .[65]

While it is tempting to see this play as essentially auto-biographical, such a view minimises the degree to which Odets invents Hollywood as a social construct and is over-simplistic in the context of his creative vision. Of the play Odets said, 'I wanted to write a play about the moral value of success.'[66] The play is a record of the betrayal of radical heritages and artistic integrity.

Hollywood offers Odets, in short, an effective context in which to develop further his vision of mankind as isolated from the source of creative integrity, betraying essential values and corrupted, above all, by money. Commercial success correlates with moral and artistic failure. Odets creates a form of revolt in the rejection of American materialism—the pursuit of the dollar—in favour of faithfulness to a version of an essential and creative self that can transcend, as it does for the actor in *The Country Girl,* the material deprivations and emotional turmoils of life.

There is a better case for seeing *The Country Girl* as at least containing reference to Odets's experience with the Group. The interest in the play derives largely in the character of Frank Elgin, an actor who in effect overcomes domestic and drink problems because, in some underlying sense, he remains true to his art. There is, in addition, a ring of authenticity in the interaction of author, producer, director which suggests that Odets could effectively use personal experience to create the material for what is, in this context, a minor piece of work.

Odets's last produced play, *The Flowering Peach,* is of interest largely because of the manner in which it serves to redirect attention back to the earlier plays, particularly *Awake and Sing!* and *Paradise Lost,* in two ways. It recreates the biblical Noah in the shape of a Jewish family that recalls, at least in part, the Bergers in their speech patterns and in the family tensions they represent. The play also offers the most explicit version of fable in Odets's work. Its interest, though, is largely historical and it exists in published form only in a truncated version. Edward Murray's judgement that the play is 'remarkable . . . "mature" in both form and content' is difficult to share.[67] The text available reflects Odets's skill with varying registers: the movement from biblical to Yiddish-English language structures is used for comic effect and Noah's rage at his frequently rebellious sons is, in context, an effective comic device:

Noah:

> On The Holy Ark he's makin' business! Manure! With manure you want to begin a new world? Everybody's life he put in danger!

Esther:

> Poppa's a hundred per cent right.[68]

What the play demonstrates is that Odets's gift had not, at least in theatre, survived the conditions in which it was formed. The early 1950s were in many respects uncongenial times for Odets. His testimony to the Committee on Un-American Activities created a considerable degree of uneasiness in the years that followed and, perhaps above all, he found no topic out of which his theatre could be built. In essence, the 1930s had given him the Depression and all its consequences, which sustained his work well beyond the 1930s, while Hollywood had, in the 1940s, given him another major context in which to create drama. *The Flowering Peach* is a retrospective piece going back to the kinds of family structure and idioms that had been used to make the much more powerful play *Awake and Sing!* some 20 years earlier.

The best of Odets's work can be found predominantly in the 1930s and to a degree in the 1940s, when he appeared, perhaps more than any other American playwright, to be the figure most representative of his times which, in retrospect, are more complex and ambiguous than they appeared to be. His considerable talent was to encompass these complexities and express them in forms that were passionate, articulate and, at times, profound. There are many contexts and perspectives in which Odets's work may be placed but Arthur Miller offers in summation, perhaps the most appropriate of views:

> He was an American Romantic, as much a Broadway guy as a proletarian leader, probably more so. To call him contradictory is to say he was very much alive and a sufferer.[69]

Notes

1. Elmer Rice, *Minority Report: An Autobiography* (London: Heinemann, 1963) p. 343.

2. Margaret Brenman Gibson in *New York Times,* 13 June 1965, cited in Edward Murray, *Clifford Odets: The Thirties and After* (New York: Frederick Ungar, 1968) p. 113.

3. All dates cited in relation to Odets's plays are to the date of first production.

4. Leslie Fiedler, *To the Gentiles* (New York: Stein & Day, 1972) p. 128.

5. Harold Clurman, *The Fervent Years: The Story of the Group Theatre and the Thirties* (London: Dennis Dobson, 1964) pp. 150-1.

6. Arthur Miller, *Timebends: A Life* (London: Methuen, 1988) p. 228.

7. Ibid., p. 240.

8. Edward Murray, *Clifford Odets: The Thirties and After* (New York: Frederick Ungar, 1968) p. 181.

9. In an interview with Joe Hyams for the *New York Herald Tribune,* 1959, cited by R. Baird Shuman, *Clifford Odets* (New York: Twayne, 1962) p. 30.

10. *The Country Girl* (1952) was published in the UK as *Winter Journey* (London: Samuel French, 1955).

11. Joseph Wood Krutch, *The American Drama since 1918: An Informal History* (New York: George Braziller, 1957) p. 320.

12. C. W. E. Bigsby, *A Critical Introduction to Twentieth Century American Drama* (Cambridge: Cambridge University Press, 1982) vol. 1, p. 163.

13. Clifford Odets, 'How a Playwright Triumphs', in Gabriel Miller (ed.), *Critical Essays on Clifford Odets* (Boston, Mass.: G. K. Hall, 1991) p. 75.

14. Edmund Gagey, *Revolution in American Drama* (New York: Columbia University Press, 1947) p. 168.

15. Malcolm Goldstein, *The Political Stage: American Drama and Theater of the Great Depression* (New York: Oxford University Press) p. 93.

16. Harold Clurman, op. cit., pp. 103-4.

17. Clifford Odets, *Till the Day I Die,* in *Six Plays* (London: Methuen, 1987) p. 139.

18. Clifford Odets, *Awake and Sing!,* in ibid., p. 41.

19. Ibid., pp. 55-6.

20. Ibid., p. 78.

21. Ibid., p. 73.

22. Harold Clurman used the phrase in his obituary of Odets in the *New York Times.* He sees the notion as having a centrality in both Odets's work and his life:

> His central theme was the difficulty of attaining maturity in a world where money as a token of success and status plays so dominant a role. This has very little to do with being a 'reformer'. His very flesh experienced the lure of those false gods. He struggled against their temptations all his life.

> (Cited by Murray, *Clifford Odets*)

23. *Awake and Sing!,* p. 79.

24. Ibid., p. 42.

25. Ibid., p. 46.

26. Ibid., p. 66.

27. Ibid., p. 94.

28. Ibid., p. 98.

29. Ibid., pp. 100-1.

30. Clifford Odets, Preface to the 1939 edition of *Six Plays,* reprinted in *Six Plays* (London: Methuen, 1987), p. vii.

31. Bigsby, op. cit., p. 174.

32. *Paradise Lost,* p. 193.

33. Ibid., p. 207.

34. Goldstein, op. cit.

35. *Paradise Lost,* pp. 228-9.

36. Ibid., p. 230.

37. *Golden Boy,* in *Six Plays,* p. 316.

38. Gabriel Miller, 'Odets and Tragedy: *Golden Boy* and *The Big Knife*', in Gabriel Miller (ed.), *Critical Essays on Clifford Odets* (Boston, Mass.: G. K. Hall, 1991) p. 173.

39. Harold Cantor, *Clifford Odets: Playwright—Poet* (Metuchen, N.J., and London: Scarecrow Press, 1978) p. 48.

40. The same kinds of resonances can be found in what is probably Odets's best film work in *The Sweet Smell of Success* (1957). The pursuit of wealth at the expense of morality along 'the golden ladder' in 'a dog eat dog' world leads inexorably towards disaster for the central figure. The alternative values are located in the figure of a musician. The film, co-written with Ernest Lehman and directed by Alexander Mackendrick for United Artists, has many of the characteristic concerns and structures of Odets's later work.

41. *Paradise Lost,* p. 230.

42. Clifford Odets, *Rocket to the Moon,* in *Six Plays,* p. 416.

43. Ibid., p. 418.

44. Miller, *Timebends,* p. 233.

45. Clifford Odets, *Night Music: A Comedy in Twelve Scenes* (New York: Random House, 1940) p. 154.

46. Ibid., p. 160.

47. Harold Clurman, Introduction to *Night Music,* p. viii.

48. *Night Music,* p. 180.

49. Ibid., p. 169.

50. Ibid., p. 155.

51. Clurman, Introduction to *Night Music,* p. viii.

52. Winifred L. Dusenburry, '*Night Music* and Homelessness', in Miller, *Critical Essays,* p. 220.

53. Clifford Odets, *Clash by Night* (New York: Random House, 1942) p. 49.

54. Ibid., p. 99.

55. Ibid., pp. 126-7.

56. Ibid., p. 78.

57. Krutch, op. cit., p. 272.

58. There are several confusions about the title of this play and they derive from the fact that the first UK production of *The Country Girl* (1952) was retitled *Winter Journey* and published under that title by Samuel French in 1955. The reason for this UK change of title was that a popular musical also called *The Country Girl* was in production on the London stage in 1952. The confusion really derives, however, from the fact that Odets had used *A Winter Journey* as the working title of *The Big Knife*. For a full description of these troublesome matters, see Robert Cooperman, *Clifford Odets: An Annotated Bibliography, 1935-1989* (Westport, Conn., and London: Meckler, 1990) pp. 11-12.

59. Miller, 'Odets and Tragedy', p. 194.

60. Clifford Odets, *The Big Knife,* in *Golden Boy, Awake and Sing!, The Big Knife* (Harmondsworth, Middx: Penguin Books, 1963) p. 193.

61. *The Big Knife,* p. 248.

62. Ibid., p. 249.

63. Ibid., p. 200.

64. Ibid., p. 251.

65. Ibid., p. 272.

66. Cited in Murray, *Clifford Odets,* p. 161.

67. Ibid., p. 116.

68. Clifford Odets, *The Flowering Peach,* in Louis Kronenberger (ed.), *The Best Plays of 1954-1955* (New York and Toronto: Dodd, Maed, 1955) p. 197.

69. Miller, *Timebends,* p. 229.

Christopher J. Herr (essay date 2003)

SOURCE: Herr, Christopher J. "'A Real Artist of the People': Odets' Post-Group Plays." In *Clifford Odets and American Political Theatre*, pp. 125-43. Westport, Conn.: Praeger, 2003.

[*In the following essay, Herr argues that Odets's late plays*—Clash by Night, The Country Girl, *and* The Big Knife—*offer "a skeptical examination of popular culture" in America, in which the dramatist generally "condemns popular culture for its simplistic forms and false promises."*]

"SUAVE AND SWANK JUNK": THE POETICS OF KITSCH

Odets' early Group plays articulated the promises and failures of the American marketplace largely through a language of abundance; his later plays, however, shift to a focus on images of popular culture as the expression—however distorted—of the people's voice. Ralph Willett has commented that "however corny the images of beauty and contentment circulated by popular culture, they at least provide a language through which the inarticulate can express their desires. Odets' respectful use of the clichés of popular song and film is a measure of his authentic sympathy for the classes he writes about and of his identification with their yearning hopes."[1] Odets, always fascinated with popular forms, insisted they could be turned toward progressive ends. For example, he argued in "Democratic Vistas in Drama" that film was the art of the people, with cultural and political power rooting far deeper than its superficial form. Widespread acceptance made film and other mass media ideal vehicles—as advertisers well knew—for reaching audiences with their messages. For example, following World War II, television boomed even more rapidly than radio had in the 1920s. In 1948, there were only twenty-eight stations in the country and 172,000 television sets; by 1955, 32 million sets were in use, and by 1960, almost 90 percent of households had one.[2] With his longing for connection to a large group of like-minded people, Odets naturally gravitated toward the reach and scope of popular forms. His best work was built upon an expression of American's common experience.

However sweet this dream, Odets was conscious throughout the 1930s and 1940s that a folk culture uniting people in common artistic and social endeavor was far from reality. As early as *Golden Boy* and *Night Music,* he had depicted popular culture as a flawed vehicle for the promises of democracy. Such sharp criticism continues in Odets' post-Group plays. For example, the bloody climax of *Clash by Night* takes place in a movie projection booth; Jerry Wilinski strangles his adulterous friend Earl while "a typical Hollywood 'product'"—described by one character as "Suave and swank junk" (226-227)—plays onscreen. Indeed, Odets weaves into his late plays—*Clash by Night, The Country Girl,* and *The Big Knife*—a skeptical examination of popular culture that continues his career-long examination of the American marketplace. More often than not, he condemns popular culture for its simplistic forms and false promises. Just as consumer capitalism preached plenty while denying basic desires to many of its participants, Odets suggests, popular culture promised uplift and artistic pleasure but delivered only clichéd blandishments to an increasingly narcotized public.

Odets' tightrope-walking ambivalence toward popular culture also reflects an ongoing discussion that pervaded American intellectual life from the 1930s onward. Since the rise of radio and the popularization of sound film in the late 1920s, culture had been increasingly enmeshed in a process of artistic reproduction and commodification that made it difficult to separate uplifting forms of art from culturally debilitating ones, and even more difficult to avoid the changes new technologies would bring. As Gus Michaels warns the Gordons in **Paradise Lost,** "Television's coming in, sure as death" (*SP* [*Six Plays*], 161). Odets dramatizes his society's anxieties about the place of these new cultural forms in American democracy.

The cultural object—play, film, popular song, World's Fair, radio program, television program—is inextricable from the economic system that produced it. Recognizing that "[m]odern advertising is born with one foot in the world of goods and the other in mass culture,"[3] Odets shows this connection, depicting how the marketplace increasingly shaped both form and content, both the production and reception of cultural objects. Furthermore, as a number of critics of the 1930s, 1940s, and 1950s argued, popular forms elided gaps between high and folk culture, blending everything into a "midcult" manufactured for and by popular consent and cemented in place by prevailing economic structures.[4] In 1938, about the same time Odets wrote **"Democratic Vistas in Drama,"** an art critic for the *Partisan Review,* Clement Greenberg, argued that mass production techniques, universal literacy, and a demographic shift to urban centers had resulted in the development of an (popular) ersatz culture he derided as kitsch.[5] For Greenberg, true art was necessarily elitist because it challenged accepted notions; any attempt to popularize art invariably adulterated it, resulting in a weak, commercialized imitation: "Kitsch, using for raw material the debased and academicized simulacra of genuine culture, welcomes and cultivates this insensibility [to the values of genuine culture]. It is the source of its profits. Kitsch is mechanical and operates by formulas. Kitsch is vicarious experience and faked sensations."[6]

For Greenberg, kitsch parasitized the forms of avant-garde art without a concomitant progressivism in content, imperiling the avant-garde through cheap repetition. Furthermore, while concerned about the effects on audiences, he worried even more about the development of artists. Because kitsch contained within its form a predetermined emotional response, it was immediately accessible to the popular audience and therefore profitable. This potential, Greenberg suggests, placed enormous pressures on writers to "modify their work under the pressure of kitsch, if they do not succumb to it entirely."[7] The result was a kind of contamination in which the impurities of kitsch poisoned whatever remained of true art. For example, the methods of advertising, which depend on quick recognition and emotional identification, tend toward kitsch. In this view,

technology makes popular art something to be bought and sold, cultural commodities stained a priori by their intimate connection with mass production, until they become what Leo Lowenthal called in 1950 "manipulated consumer goods."[8]

If, as their detractors argued, mass media elided the difference between high art and kitsch, they also elided the personal differences among consumers of popular culture. As the products became standardized, the responses did as well; the individual melted into the mass. This process was seen as self-perpetuating, a demonic machine whose continual operation was more important than the product it generated. Dwight MacDonald, more open early in his career toward the regenerative possibilities of popular culture, by 1950 had declared that "the Lords of kitsch sell culture to the masses. It is a debased, trivial culture that voids both the deep realities (sex, death, failure, tragedy) and also the simple spontaneous pleasures. . . . The masses, debauched by several generations of this sort of thing, in turn come to demand trivial and comfortable cultural products."[9] The individual mark of the aesthetic had been superseded by the mechanisms of production and consumption.

Not all writers about popular culture decried its effects. Gilbert Seldes, for example, located the origins of popular art in the American democratic tradition, arguing that much of American high art was an elitist project, virulently critical of the average person. Drawing a direct line from the Age of Jackson through Whitman and Emerson, Seldes argued that while the mass media often failed to achieve their goals, and while they were shot through with commercialism, there was nevertheless hope for the "popular arts," as he called them: "[P]ersistence of change reflects the one emotion all Americans hold in common . . . the future is theirs to create. It is a confession that the present is not perfect and an assertion that nothing in the present can prevent us from changing for the better."[10] Nevertheless, Seldes' optimistic assertion is undercut throughout the rest of his essay by a partial dismissal of the achievements mass media had made. Thus, even the defenders of popular forms of culture were forced again and again to admit to the paucity of "real" culture in mass media, arguing instead—as Odets did in **"Democratic Vistas in Drama"**—for their seemingly unlimited potential.

Theodor Adorno, a sharp critic of mass culture, nevertheless suggested in 1954 that the commercialism of mass media was perhaps more a matter of degree than of kind:

> It would be romanticizing to assume that formerly art was entirely pure, that the creative artist thought only in terms of the inner consistency of the artifact and not also of its effect on the spectators. Theatrical art in particular cannot be separated from audience reactions.

Conversely, vestiges of the aesthetic claim to be something autonomous, a world unto itself, remain even within the most trivial product of mass culture.[11]

Odets and the Group had struggled with this quandary; theatre was a social art dependent on a real and powerful connection between the stage and the audience. The difficulty—onstage and in the studios—was how far the writer had to budge to meet that audience.

Odets' fervent romanticism gave him deep sympathies with Seldes' democratic view. Still, as his work on Broadway and in Hollywood attests, the opportunity to reach a large audience placed pressures on the mode of production itself, creating an interchange of anticipation and expectation between artist and audience, playwright and company, screenwriter and producer. Indeed, Walter Benjamin had argued in 1935 that systems of mass production had radically changed the way in which art was created, or rather *produced*: "To an ever greater degree the work of art reproduced becomes the work of art designed for reproducibility."[12] Benjamin seemingly applauds this emancipation of art from ritual, arguing that a more political orientation offers hope for social change. But the politicization of art brings a deeper danger of mass control, since along with modes of production, it changes the audience as well; individuals see themselves as part of a mass, or, worse, are part of a mass without realizing it. In Benjamin's view, this sort of social control is the aesthetic counterpart to Fascism; rather than fostering democratic change by expressing the will of the people, it defuses political action through artistic expression: "Fascism sees its salvation in giving those masses not their rights but instead a chance to express themselves."[13]

Benjamin's analysis articulates the mixed feelings Odets exhibited toward his plays and screenplays. Of course, the mass media and the theatre operate in different ways, the former by highly efficient reproduction and the latter by the far more inefficient repeated singular event; it is perhaps disingenuous to compare them. As Odets recognized, theatre was the least effective—and on Broadway, probably the least democratic—way to create a truly popular art. But his bouncing back and forth between Hollywood and Broadway makes such comparisons inevitable; furthermore, his own writings invited them. For example, by characterizing film audiences as imitative and credulous in **"Democratic Vistas in Drama,"** he participates in the blanket critique of mass culture of the late 1930s and early 1940s "whereby the fat cat, capitalist 'lords of kitsch' set about ventriloquizing an inert and prefabricated mass of consumers."[14] At best, in the essay, Odets claims that the "people" need to be challenged with an accurate look at their world; at worst, he refuses them autonomy to resist the narcotic power of popular culture.

Odets does not interest himself in the differences between work as a playwright and work as a screenwriter in **"Democratic Vistas."** The contrast between the debased movie world and the theatre is one of intention rather than method. However, his analysis is not disingenuous. In fact, Odets' plea for a new, socially committed, and popular drama ends with an affirmation of the nobility of the masses: "A writer of talent could begin a great career that way—as 'celebrator and expresser.' Great audiences are waiting now to have their own experiences explained and interpreted for them." For Odets, the politically democratic must be reconciled with the culturally and economically democratic; popular art must speak to and for the people. It is this responsibility of the artist to the people—an attitude that characterized all of Odets' work from the Group onward—that gives his plea a ring of authenticity.

"Democratic Vistas" is one example of how in the late 1930s inclusion of anti-Fascist fellow travelers in the Communist Popular Front had encouraged left-leaning intellectuals to embrace (however tenuously) the political potential of popular culture, while remaining distant from the masses for whom it was intended:

> Even in the broadened cultural base of the Popular Front period, intellectuals could still see themselves as missionaries, offering the masses an alternative folk culture (or through the social agency of Hollywood Popular Fronters, a "progressive" film culture) that was more germane to their interests than what was seen as the debilitating political effects of commercial popular culture.[15]

Beginning with the Soviet-German nonaggression pact, however, arguments against popular culture increasingly identified such culture with the dangers of Communism, suggesting that only Communists, who had weak intellects and bad taste, could find popular culture useful.

Rooted in the social upheaval of the 1930s, the political arguments against popular culture reached their apex in the Cold War. Disenchantment with Stalinism fueled the belief that popular culture could only be a dangerous form of social control. Accordingly, following the war, there was a virtual rewriting of American intellectual history (led by MacDonald and Bernard Rosenberg) that argued that the true tradition of American arts was elitist and noncommercial. They valorized those artists who tried to operate outside the cultural marketplace, who refused the pressures of the "people" to produce a certain kind of art, and who were seemingly immune to economic pressures. But Andrew Ross notes that "this is a claim . . . that depends on forgetting the enormous efforts of the thirties, when intellectuals *en force* devoted themselves, in however imaginary a fashion, to the task of politically creating a culture that would be both national and popular."[16] Odets' dream of a democratic, collective art—his "Charlie Theatre"—was increasingly out of step with the times.

During HUAC investigations into Communist influence in the film industry, fears of popular culture as social control surfaced again. Odets, the Hollywood Ten, and others were accused of hijacking scripts for their Communist propaganda, though ironically, "the one area in which Hollywood's Communists had very little impact was in the films they made. . . . the producers controlled the final product."[17] The committee's motives were complex (and often questionable), but its stated goal was to protect audiences from "subversive" content. Fearful of what secret messages might do to unsuspecting mass audiences, the investigations—first of the Dies committee in the late 1930s, then the blacklist of the 1940s and 1950s—in effect defined art as what was morally inoffensive and politically mainstream: the popular by negation.

The film industry had attempted for years to ward off investigations and outside censorship by self-policing. The Motion Picture Code (MPC), adopted in 1930, was a direct outgrowth of the long-standing belief that art had direct, measurable effects on audiences. It aimed, in essence, to control behavior by controlling aesthetic content:

> It has often been argued that art in itself is unmoral, neither good nor bad. This is perhaps true of the *thing* which is music, painting, poetry, etc. But the thing is the *product* of some person's mind, and that mind was either good or bad when it produced the thing. And the thing has its *effect* on those who come into contact with it. In both these ways, as a product and the cause of definite effects, it has a deep moral significance and an unmistakable moral quality. . . . In the case of the motion pictures, this effect may be particularly emphasized because no art has so quick and so widespread an appeal to the masses. It has become in an incredibly short period, *the art of the multitudes.*[18]

As HUAC would, the MPC places responsibility upon the "good or bad" mind of the individual who creates, rather than the viewer of the movie, institutionalizing the critique of mass culture as an irresistible force. The MPC, designed to keep the government out of the film industry, unwittingly gave HUAC investigators moral and political ammunition for their attacks.

Once the fear of subversive effects was established, the debate centered on what constituted "bad" content. HUAC's conservatism demonstrated that in the hostile political mood of the times, any liberal content was liable to charges of Communism. Though some of those investigated were in fact Communists, others were accused of fostering subversion with politics that ten years earlier had been mainstream New Deal liberalism. It is not surprising, then, that Odets, the clarion voice of the leftist 1930s, was among those against whom the backlash was directed. The price these workers were paid for their leftist attachments was, in part, the threat of

economic and political destruction; most of those named by the committee lost their jobs. The blacklist was more than just an economic sanction, however. Symbolically, the threat to remove connections between artist and audience, preventing the "infection" of a large number of people with subversive ideas, confirms the committee's fear of the popular arts and suggests that, even among conservatives, a belief in—or fear of—real social change through popular art had never disappeared.[19]

Odets' conflicting testimony in front of HUAC underscores the difficulty of separating the political effects of popular culture from the economic conditions of its production. In his personal files, there is a copy of a speech that was apparently prepared—but never delivered—by Odets to the committee:

> Not poor myself, I am convinced by every feeling, the experience & thoughts of my not-especially-endowed life, that capitalism must in the name of everything human & sacred be replaced by socialism. . . . the great struggle in the world today, so painful & tormenting, so confusing, is about this one subject: shall human values make the economics or shall economics make the values? I am proud, even defiant to stand where I do. This is my statement.
>
> (LCA, undated)

The fact that Odets never delivered this statement highlights his personal insecurities, as well as larger economic and political pressures placed on writers. Blacklisted, Odets would never have been able to reach the people he wanted to reach; still, he remained unwilling to cooperate fully with the committee. Certainly, Odets' ambivalent HUAC testimony gives evidence of the popular artist's place in the midcentury political climate. Nevertheless, it is the plays that best evince Odets' growing distrust of popular culture, as well as his ongoing romantic yearning for a full democracy, life with all the trimmings.

"THE ANTI-PICNIC FACTS": *CLASH BY NIGHT*

Odets' critique of the effects of popular culture was greatly tempered in *Night Music* by his romantic optimism. But in *Clash by Night* (1941), the mood becomes ominous, the critique of popular culture almost completely damning. Opening a few weeks after Pearl Harbor, *Clash by Night*'s tension mirrors the political climate into which it was born. Newspaper reviewers were quick to sense the shift that Odets' attitudes had taken, and few were more pleased by the new grimness than they had been with the optimism of *Night Music*. Even with generally high praise for Tallulah Bankhead as Mae and Lee J. Cobb as Jerry, the reviews were far more negative than Odets or his producer Billy Rose (who promised the play would win the Pulitzer Prize) could have anticipated. John Anderson of the *Journal-American* called *Clash by Night* "one of Mr. Odets' worst plays, a rambling, episodic, lurid, and rather pretentious drama," while Burns Mantle deplored its "unsympathetic, uninteresting subjects" and noted that it is "completely unrelieved in mood and tone." The reviews caught the increasing frustration with the unfulfilled promises of American life that had driven the play.

An article Odets wrote for the *New York Times* in 1942, **"Genesis of a Play,"** excerpts journal entries tracing the development of *Clash by Night.* One early entry, for example, suggests that "[p]art of the theme of this play is about how men irresponsibly wait for the voice and strong arm of Authority to bring them to life" (NYT, February 4, 1942). Thus, in the title and themes of the play there is evidence of Odets' continued concern with the dilemmas of American culture: individual freedom without social responsibility, abundance without participation, morality without humanity, appetite without understanding. There is in Odets' conception of the play, in fact, a connection between these appetites and the tendency he speaks of to submit to authority unquestioningly, for unthinking complicity in the economic and cultural marketplace parallels an unthinking complicity in the political marketplace. As critical of the prevailing order as *Awake and Sing!, Clash by Night* demonstrates how the foundations of democracy are undercut when the responsibilities of the individual are subverted into the quest for material goods. The critique of popular culture that Odets began in *Golden Boy* and *Night Music* finds its most vitriolic expression in *Clash by Night.*

The play opens with Mae and Jerry Wilinski, seven years married, sitting on their porch with friends Joe and Peggy. While the others are absorbed in watching the moon rise, Mae is occupied with visions of escape: "An old song was running through my mind (*singing softly*) 'I'm the Sheik of Araby, this land belongs to me. At night when you're asleep, into your tent I'll creep. . . .' Anyone remember that song?" (*CBN* [*Clash by Night*], 4). Memories of this and other popular songs return to Mae throughout the play, assuming increasing emotional importance. More importantly, they provide her with a language to express her desires and fears. When Joe and Peggy leave, Mae tells Jerry why Joe ought to marry Peggy: "She happens to be very much in love with that self-centered gent. She wants him to creep into her tent and he won't" (15). Born from a popular song, Mae's idea of love offers escape and excitement to contrast with the boredom of her life with Jerry. Her use of the song also contrasts Jerry's wide-eyed wonderment at the beauty and distance of the moon and stars with Mae's familiarity with popular culture. Mae's song expresses unfulfilled desires, a sense of longing, and half-articulated hopes. In that sense, it is like the folk tune that Jerry's father plays on his concertina: "It's a Polish song. . . . about the little old house, where you wanna go back, but you

can't find out where it is no more, the house" (10-11). Music in this play has subtly shifted, from Poppa Bonaparte's "great cheer-up" in *Golden Boy* toward the language of the dispossessed and disaffected.

Mae's preoccupation with the mythologies expressed in popular culture is also reflected by her reaction to Jerry's friend Earl, a film projectionist who embodies for Mae the desires excited in her by the movies. Even if his job is, as he says, "good pay but dull work" and he suggests that "they're not happy, those movie people, none of them," Mae nevertheless expresses her longing for the "money, cars, and chauffeurs" that to her signify the exotic life of the films (27). The sixty dollars a week that Earl earns in the booth is a small fortune compared with the scratching and saving she must do with Jerry. It is also significant, then, that the night in which Jerry confronts them, they have been to the "amusements"—amusement is precisely what Mae desires. Her cynical irritation with Jerry, a carpenter on the WPA projects, emphasizes desperation with "life on the installment plan" (94): "You talk too much Jerry. You jump on everything like it's a plank and you're gonna saw it in half" (6). The first act, therefore, sets up a contrast between the bright, almost utopian promises of a vague land where the Sheik of Araby creeps into your tent and the hot, small Staten Island home where Jerry and Mae live with their crying baby, barely making ends meet.

Perhaps the clearest delineation of the contrast between real and ideal comes in act 1, scene 2, at an ocean pavilion. Amid a score of contemporary references to news events, sporting events, popular music, and politics, Earl begins his crude seduction of Mae. The background of this scene, including the seemingly irrelevant tangents, is more important than the actual seduction, for it indicates the scope of the problem as Odets saw it, the connection between popular culture and social responsibility. Indeed, the plot of *Clash by Night* is nothing original. It concerns the development of a love triangle over the course of a long hot summer and culminates in the violent death of one of the participants. But the way in which Odets frames the seduction within the context of 1941 America, against the background of a popular culture that fills lives on the verge of war with false images of bliss, deepens Odets' "triangle play" into an analysis of American idealism.

In the pavilion scene, contemporary references abound: Father Coughlin, the Giants, the songs "Mexicali Rose," "The Beer Barrel Polka" and "Avalon," and the rhumba, in addition to references to Steinbeck's *Of Mice and Men.*[20] Such references don't merely ground the play in the familiar; they offer a departure point for the play's dark mood. Certainly, the audience was expected not only to recognize the references to popular culture but also to react to the juxtaposition of the play's dark foreboding with "happy" popular songs. To an extent, they did. For example, Charles Gentry of the *Detroit Evening Times* remarked when the play opened its pre-Broadway run that **Clash by Night** had "poetry, social significance and a timeliness which is amazing" (October 28, 1941). Odets worked outward from a core of specific references to a general indictment of the culture's false promises. Mae's bewilderment at the power of popular songs, expressed most clearly in her comment to Earl about the song "Avalon," recalls the utopian visions that filled Odets' earlier plays: "It gives me the jim-jams . . . always gets me. I used to sell sheet music in the dime store. A place called Avalon. . . . no worries there, sort of flowers in the winter, I don't know how all that stuff gets in a song, but it does. . . . Well, keep smiling! I don't blame Jerry for what he is" (75-76).

Mae's adoption of "Avalon" to express her bewilderment, like her use of "The Sheik of Araby" as a short-hand expression of discontent, demonstrates the visceral power of popular culture. Language is co-opted by the popular song and the advertising slogan; it slides into romantic cliché. Likewise, Mae's "keep smiling" refusal to consider the consequences of searching for the chimerical "Avalon" dooms her escape attempt to failure. In fact, all the characters wander through the play without a sense of direction; thus, Mae characterizes Earl as "one of those who needs a new suit or a love affair, but he don't know which" (80). To add this sense of purposelessness, Odets uses the action of constant drinking throughout the play. From the first scene on the porch to the final scene where a drunken Jerry kills Earl, alcohol figures prominently in **Clash by Night.** It is another narcotic, another attempt at escape. As Earl puts it, "That's why I drink this varnish, lady—to get unborn" (103-104). Odets had made a similar connection in "The Silent Partner," where the baker Corelli says of popular culture: "Many workers is such dope fiend—baseball and boxing dope fiend, movie dope fiend" (LCA, dated 1936).

The success of **Clash by Night** depends on the success of the popular culture critique. Gabriel Miller, for example, finds the play flawed because the use of popular culture is fundamentally undeveloped:

> [T]he gimmick only suggests that Odets' play is not much more meaningful than the average film, or the cited popular songs, "The Sheik of Araby" and "Avalon." The attempted criticism of popular culture is ambitious, but the terms of the charge are not fully explored in this play. . . . Because Odets has established no adequate connection in the play between the personal and the social, his sudden attack on the popular culture is as vague as his treatment of economics, fascism, and war.[21]

Miller's analysis, while in part true, nevertheless undervalues Odets' participation in the larger debate about popular culture as not only a symptom of the American malaise but also a contributing cause. The popular reflected a powerful belief system of a great number of people. For Odets (and HUAC), the popularity made it meaningful, but also dangerous.

Unlike intellectual critics of popular culture, Odets does not condemn it as inherently flawed, stained by easy accessibility; rather, he warns those who buy its promises unthinkingly. In the key passage of the play, Joe, who has stood aloof from the adulterous trio, tells Peggy:

> We're *all* afraid! Earl, Jerry, Mae, millions like them, clinging to a goofy dream—expecting life to be a picnic. Who taught them that? Radio, songs, the movies—you're the greatest people going. Paradise is just around the corner. Shake that hip, swing that foot—we're on the Millionaire Express. Don't cultivate your plot of ground—tomorrow you might win a thousand acre farm! What farm? The dream farm! Am I blue? Did you ask me if I'm blue. Sure, sometimes. Tricky Otto comes along, with a forelock and a mustache. Then he tells them why they're blue. "You been wronged," he says. "They done you dirt. Now come along with me, Take orders park your brains, don't think, don't worry; poppa tucks you in at night!" . . . And where does that end? In violence, destruction, cripples by the carload! But is that the end for us? No, sweetheart, not while a brain burns in my head. And not because we're better than them. But because we know the facts—the anti-picnic facts. Because we know that Paradise begins in responsibility.
>
> (217)

Like Leo Gordon, Ralph Berger, or Agate Keller, Joe's statement is a call to arms, but unlike the earlier plays, Joe's call is born from fear rather than hope.

Miller is partly correct in arguing that Odets has not prepared the audience for Joe's strong and specific attack on popular culture toward the end of the play with other explicit criticisms. But there are implicit criticisms throughout the play. No audience could be unaware of the utopian promises of the American Dream that are the targets of Joe's criticism, just as they would recognize the popular songs used earlier in the play (or the ones parodied in his speech) and the ongoing debate about the uses of popular culture. Odets' play is shaped so much from the common stuff of the world that it seems mundane and petty—the dreary Staten Island setting irritated a number of critics—but the underlying premise is utopian. Odets' call, through Joe, is not to annihilate popular culture but to recognize its power and understand the social ramifications of that power. He calls for individual responsibility toward the social, rather than individual surrender to the mass implied by Kress' Fascism. Thus, a well-grounded person such as Abe, Earl's fellow projectionist, can dismiss the films he screens as "propaganda for the bug house" (227) and focus instead on his work and family, "Make a plan. Have respect—do your work with respect" (230). Only then can the paradise promised by the American myth and shaped by the forms of popular culture be achieved.

"This Whole Movie Thing is a Murder of the People"

If **Clash by Night** concerned itself with the utopian dreams of individuals within a social order, Odets' next two plays, **The Big Knife** (1949) and **The Country Girl** (1950), are at once both more removed from, and more entwined with, such concerns. Many have suggested that by the time **The Big Knife** was written, Odets was trapped in Hollywood "in a system to which he finally could envisage no alternative. And the images of popular culture, which had expressed the youthful dreams of the depression era, were no longer drawn upon when the theme became decay and exhaustion in middle age."[22] To be sure, specific references to popular culture decline in the later plays—popular music, for example, virtually disappears—and while Odets' work is never free of contemporary references, they don't serve the same central purpose in these two plays as they had in the earlier ones.

Nevertheless, the characterization of Odets as a Hollywood "lackey" ignores the complexities of his dual career as well as his expressed ambivalence about both the theatre and film industries. **The Big Knife** and **The Country Girl,** in fact, marked the beginning of a six-year return to Broadway. Furthermore, analysis of either play is incomplete without an understanding of the relationship between them. Even more important is an understanding of the relationship among the plays, popular culture, and Odets' Hollywood career. These two plays are, in one sense, Odets' attempt to allegorize his own life against the backdrop of the American Dream, to do what he once wrote in his journal, "I will reveal America to itself by revealing myself to myself" (B-G, xiv).

First produced in 1950 and directed by Odets, **The Country Girl** was received by the newspaper reviewers as some of his best work. John Chapman of the *News* called it "tight, taut, and trim" (November 11, 1950); Kenneth Tynan noted that the London production was "quite an important evening in the English theatre."[23] Though Harold Clurman dismissed it as "lightweight Odets" (*New Republic,* December 11, 1950), Brooks Atkinson called it "the best play Odets has written for years. Only **Awake and Sing!** stands above it in the lexicon of his career" (NYT, November 19, 1950). Overall, it was hailed as a triumphant return to the theatre for a writer who had been lured from the stage for Hollywood and whose previous play, **The Big Knife,** had been dismissed as a bitter self-reproach at selling out to the film studios. It is ironic, then, that such praise (except from Clurman, who knew Odets better than the others and who had given advice during the development of **The Country Girl** came for a play that Odets held in low regard.

Odets was not pleased with **The Country Girl** mainly because he had written it specifically with the box of-fice in mind: "I set down deliberately to write a success."[24] Writing a play to make money was not new for Odets; the pressures placed upon him by the Group forced him to consider financial questions as well as artistic ones. **Golden Boy,** for example, was written specifically for money. Odets recognized the differences between the two, however; in **Golden Boy** he had found a popular form for his examination of the American Dream that he hadn't in **The Country Girl.** Nevertheless, he was unable to dismiss his "theatre piece" entirely:

> It does have about it a certain kind of psychological urgency, because if you are creative, things do creep in despite the conscious impulse. For instance, there crept into that play a central problem of my own life. And this did give a certain urgency and heat to much that went on in the script. I didn't *mean* for that problem to come out; I cannily and unconsciously disguised it. But that is unconsciously what came out in the writing of that play.[25]

Still, Odets found it ironic that the least ambitious, the least socially oriented of his plays was among the most popular. He had once more gained access to the audience he always wanted but this time with a play he felt said nothing really important.

The Country Girl is tightly structured, a compelling psychological study of the interdependence between the aging alcoholic actor Frank Elgin, his younger wife Georgie, and the theatre director Bernie Dodd. It is deep in characterization, integrated in feeling and form, and moves toward a convincing ending with a sense of purpose. Elgin's breakdown and rehabilitation and the shifting relationship between Bernie and Georgie are compelling, and there is a never a sense of unreality or falsity about the theatre scenes. Nevertheless, there is a slick feeling to the play that supports Odets' claim that it was manufactured from the outside in, and only as the play was being written did any depth of feeling enter. As if in confirmation, shortly after **The Country Girl** was produced on Broadway, Odets wrote an essay in the *New York Times* (April 22, 1951) titled **"Two Approaches to the Writing of a Play"**—about the same time Odets was working with his young playwrights from the Actor's Studio. He had once again been thinking about the crucial relationship of form to content, and in the essay, he delineates the method he used in **The Country Girl** and the method by which he normally wrote:

> In the first case, the writer sits down to "fabricate," without personal affiliation or personal relatedness to the material; he is reporting an objective event, performing a technical operation or what you will, but fabricating he is. The second writer, with equal technical grasp of his medium, begins always with the premise of expressing a personal state of being.

Odets felt that "fabrication" like **The Country Girl,** however skillful, could never quite reach the highest level of creative work. For him, form always followed the expression of personal states of being.

Apart from the tacit criticism of his own play and its reception, there is also in *The Country Girl* and the essay an implicit criticism of the theatre industry itself. Furthermore, his indictment of the theatre parallels the criticism of the film industry he had given in *The Big Knife*. In that play, Charlie Castle, the compromised film star, asks, "Don't they slowly, inch by inch, murder everyone they use? Don't they murder the highest dreams and hopes of a whole great people with the movies they make? This whole movie thing is a murder of the people" (70). While "false" theatre is obviously not as dangerous as the "murderous" consequences of a dishonest movie industry, Odets suggests that, just as Hollywood appropriates the dreams of America to make money, theatre is easily trapped within a mind-set that makes a play a commercial rather than an artistic entity. Like kitsch, commercial theatre appropriates the forms of true art to mask its inferior content; it is inherently dishonest. As an industry, then, theatre is capable on a large scale of the kind of falseness inherent in a "manu-factured" play.

Still, in spite of the fact that "the creative and deeply felt play is the exception rather than the rule with us, and our theatre the poorer for it," Odets remained unwilling to abandon Broadway. The indictment of theatre in *The Country Girl* is less vehement than his criticism of Hollywood in *The Big Knife*. For example, Bernie tells Georgie at the end of *The Country Girl,* "I'm interested in theater, not show business. I could make a fortune in films, but that's show 'biz' to me." When Georgie responds, "What do you call this play, Literature?" Bernie is forced to acknowledge the parallels between the two industries: "That's true: it's show business trying hard to be theater" (*TCG* [*The Country Girl*], 103). Still, Bernie's admission of the true nature of the show he is directing does not deny the fact that there is something useful in it, for the young playwright Unger and for Frank, especially. Bernie believes that "[a] man like Elgin, giving his best performance—he has the magic to transform a mere show to theater with a capital T!" (103).

There is a chance at redemption in *The Country Girl* that never surfaces in *The Big Knife,* as is readily seen in a comparison of their final lines. In *The Country Girl,* Georgie says, "Wrestle, Bernie. You may win a blessing. But stay unregenerate. Life knocks the sauciness out of us soon enough" (124). On the other hand, the final words in *The Big Knife* are Marion's "Help! . . . Help!! . . . Help!!!," a screaming that the stage direction indicates *does not stop and will never stop in this life*" (*TBK* [*The Big Knife*], 77). The final line of *The Country Girl* also had personal meaning for Odets: "It is one of my favorite lines, 'wrestle and you

may win a blessing. In my life I don't 'wrestle' enough. Perhaps an ease of expression of a fluid emotion or simply a fear of losing others' affection if I persisted and pushed" (LCA, dated July 21, 1953). Giving this line to Georgie at the end of the play makes even stronger the connections implied by Odets' setting his play in the theatre. For him, art was a struggle with strong forces, of which the desire for acceptance or affection is one of the most powerful.

Odets' assertion of hope at the end of *The Country Girl* is paralleled in the hopeful ending of his *Times* article. Writing about his playwriting class, Odets asserts, "No theatre need worry for its future while such young people are working and waiting in the vestibules of our common life." The idea of a common life, the collective experience that recalls his work with the Group, is contrasted to the mechanistic, isolated, profit-oriented film industry he pillories so mercilessly in *The Big Knife*. In fact, theatre is held out to Charlie in *The Big Knife* as the only possible source of hope; his wife, Marion, tells him (in virtually the same words Clurman would later use to Odets), "The theatre can still give you a reasonable living." Charlie responds caustically, "The theatre's a stunted bleeding stump. Even stars have to wait years for one decent play" (15), but *The Big Knife* nevertheless offers a lingering belief in theatre as liberating social art. Though there is the dangerous possibility that theatre will grow false in seeking money, the creative individual working for the common good always possesses the possibility of redemption. Odets' criticism of the theatre is thus made not from despair, but from a hopeful belief of the possibilities inherent in the medium.

On the other hand, the film industry is depicted throughout *The Big Knife* as a parasitic form of popular culture that uses the social myths for private ends and thereby devalues them. The voice of conscience in the play, Hank Teagle, tells Charlie:

> I don't want Marion joining the lonely junked people of our world—millions of them, wasted by the dreams of life they were promised and the swill they received! *They* are why the whole world, including us, sits in the middle of a revolution! Here, of course, that platitude carries with it the breath of treason. I think lots of us are in for a big shot of vitamin D: defeat, decay, depression, and despair.
>
> (57)

The film industry is unredeemable; it denies the very connections it claims to create. Charlie's marriage is failing, he has an affair with his best friend's wife, and he is involved in the cover-up of a fatal accident in which he was involved. He becomes isolated and despairing, crying out to Marion: "Look at me! Can you face it? Look at this dripping fat of the land? Could you ever know that all my life I yearned for a world and people to call out the best in me? How can life be so empty? But it can't be. It can't! It's proven—statistics and graphs prove it—we are the world's happiest" (72). Charlie's disbelief expresses for Odets the entire American ethos: the mindless waste of talent and social impulse in the pursuit of money. The kitschdom of Hollywood wears the form of utopia, but the shell is hollow. Like Joe Bonaparte, Charlie chooses suicide over disconnection.

Marion's plea for help underscores the isolation Odets felt was inherent in the industry, the difficulty the individual faced in creating something useful in a culture where only conformity was rewarded. As Odets was aware, the moral pressure to conform obviates any chance at individual expression; as Charlie says in *The Big Knife,* "Free speech is the highest priced luxury in the country today" (11).[26] Nevertheless, it is not necessary to accuse Odets of bad faith or greed in his early encounters with Hollywood to understand the vitriol of *The Big Knife* in his later career. As he delineated in **"Democratic Vistas in Drama,"** he was excited about the potential audience that film could reach and about the possibilities of disseminating a positive social message to millions of people. But as Michael Denning has pointed out, "[T]he great paradox of film and broadcasting" is the fact that only huge sums of capital can create a truly widespread culture.[27]

Odets—like Charlie, the Steinbeckian "fat of the land"—felt trapped in an industry that could not be swayed by other than economic interests; even the most "radical" films of the radical 1930s were not particularly so. For example, Colin Schindler notes that the film version of Steinbeck's *The Grapes of Wrath* (dir. John Ford, 1940) was anticipated with inordinate worry that it would cause unrest around the country. But Schindler suggests that the film was transformed into something more religious rather than political in tone, far more optimistic than Steinbeck's novel, especially its final appeal to the people: "We're the people that live. Can't nobody wipe us out. Can't nobody lick us. We'll go on forever, Pa. We're the people." The democratic appeal to the people is here wedded to the economic machinery of the popular culture industry: "[Producer Daryl] Zanuck was interested in the triumph of the common man because it was his patronage upon which Twentieth Century's prosperity was founded."[28]

In two articles written for the *New York Times* about his work in Hollywood—the first titled **"Writer Tells Why He Left Hollywood"** (July 25, 1948) and the second titled **"In Praise of a Maturing Industry"** (November 6, 1955)—we get perhaps the clearest encapsulation of Odets' vacillation about popular film. The first article explains his leaving for Hollywood in 1943 as a reaction to the poor reception of *Night Music* and *Clash by Night.* He speaks of his pleasure and education during

his work writing and directing *None but the Lonely Heart,* but suggests that further attempts to make another "human motion picture" were rebuffed because "none of it fitted into recognizable Hollywood schemata." Odets sharply criticizes the Hollywood mentality that "desire[s] to make every movie as accessible as chewing gum, for which no more human maturity of audience is needed than a primitive pair of jaws and a bovine philosophy"; nevertheless, he is ultimately unwilling to forgo entirely the "dream of a Renaissance to come."

Still concerned with the idea of "how our American cultural world is to move on with human health," Odets places his hope once more in the theatre, where, despite those who seek profits, "the search for the reality of the age (whatever that is!) may still be spread upon our stage." There is in the 1948 article, then, the criticism of popular culture that reappears in *Clash by Night* and *The Big Knife.* Hollywood is damned, not because of its dependence upon technology but because technology has been co-opted by commodity capitalism. What could have been democratic has become Fascistic; as Charlie says in *The Big Knife*: "Don't you see them pushing man off the earth and putting the customer in his place?" (18).

However, the production of three more Broadway plays (plus revivals of *Night Music* and *Golden Boy,* the latter of which Odets directed) in the years between 1947 and 1955 and the trauma of testifying in front of HUAC in 1952 make it a different Odets who writes about the film industry in 1955. Coming after years of theatrical work, his 1955 article (written after Odets had seen the film version of *The Big Knife,* which he liked very much) can't be quickly dismissed as self-justification for being in Hollywood. In the article, he argues that "American filmmakers are turning more and more to screen subjects of realism and importance. . . . Moviemakers are aware of the problems of the world and its people." Odets suggested in a later interview that this was because the large studios had broken up after the war, allowing independent producers to work on more interesting projects.[29] By the end of his career, then, Odets had formed an uneasy truce with the film industry, though he never surrendered (either on Broadway or in Hollywood) the goal of creating a people's art. In these plays, Odets attempted to elucidate a connection between popular culture and American life. He tried to show how popular forms both embodied the American Dream and betrayed it, how the democratic ideal of a people's art was problematized by a commodity capitalism that measured everything in terms of financial success.

"I'll Tell You a Mystery . . .": *The Flowering Peach*

Odets' last play, **The Flowering Peach,** seems out of place in his dramatic chronology. It is set outside contemporary times and in distant lands; it lacks the political fervor of his early plays or the bitterness of his post-Group plays. Nevertheless, in important ways, the play serves as a fitting bookend to his work. Covering the story of Noah and his family before, during, and after the flood, the play harks back to *Awake and Sing!* in its depictions of a loud, boisterous Jewish family bound together by struggle and love. It has a maturity beyond most of the Group plays and a humor virtually absent from *The Big Knife* and *The Country Girl.* Indeed, many contemporary commentators found it to be among his best plays. Brooks Atkinson called it "beautiful. His finest [play] in fact" and noted that Odets is not setting himself up "as an oracle. He does not pretend to have the magic formula" (NYT, December 29, 1954). John Gassner remarked that *The Flowering Peach* appeared to be the personal testament of a rueful man content to accept contradiction and shortcomings in man and the world.[30]

Certainly, *The Flowering Peach* is less strident than Odets' earlier plays. Odets remarked, "I couldn't have written *The Flowering Peach* twenty years ago. As you grow older, you mature. The danger is that in broadening, you may dilute your art. A growing writer always walks that tightrope" (NYT, December 26, 1954). But for all the dissimilarities from his earlier work, Odets offers enough similarities in *The Flowering Peach* to mark it clearly as his own. For example, he again examines the theme of responsibility, which had concerned him in *Clash by Night* and afterward. Noah, called to build the ark, fears ridicule: "I don't want it! I'm too old everybody should laugh in my face. . . . Pass me by—Pass me by. Please" (*TFP* [*The Flowering Peach*], 11). The family, too, was drawn from the same middle-class Jewish life that inspired the Bergers. Odets, in fact, used his Uncle Israel, in whose kitchen he had spend many of his best childhood days, as the model for Noah. The defiant son, Japheth, borrows idealism and strident longing from Ralph Berger and Steve Takis.

But perhaps the most striking characteristic of *The Flowering Peach* is that it marks a return to allegorical visions of plenty that dominated the earlier plays. The main tension in *The Flowering Peach* exists between Noah and his youngest son, Japheth. They disagree about how the world is to be used, how imperfect people are supposed to fit into God's perfect plan. Before he is knocked unconscious by Noah and dragged onto the ark, Japheth refuses to board. He chooses rather to die in the coming flood, declaring, "Someone . . . would have to protest such an avenging, destructive God!" (19). Japheth's reasons for resistance are made clear in a speech to Rachel; looking down at the roads crisscrossing in the valley, Japheth exclaims, "Those roads down there! The patterns they make! They're not cobwebs, those roads, to be brushed away by a peevish boy! Those roads were made by men, men crazy not to

be alone or apart! Men, crazy to reach each other! Well, they won't now" (49-50).

The sense of community that Japheth sees in the roads is in direct conflict with Noah's divine mission to take the family out of the world and begin again. In one sense, the conflict depicted in the play mirrors the increasing tensions of the Cold War. The possibility of world annihilation increasing with the invention and testing of ever more dangerous weapons of mass destruction—the play premiered the year after America's first successful test of the hydrogen bomb, and after the Soviets revealed that they had the atomic bomb—allows a reading of *The Flowering Peach* that is both literal and allegorical. Japheth's outrage is the outrage of the leftist romantic against the blind power represented by Noah. Noah wins the first part of the conflict by getting Japheth on the ark, but the troubles resume when Japheth tries to get Noah to see that putting a rudder on the ark is not disrespectful to God: "God didn't tell you to invent the hoe and the rake and yet you did! . . . God doesn't want the respect of a slave upon its knees!" (68-69). When the ark threatens to sink, the old man finally capitulates, and everyone aboard undergoes a transformation. As Japheth says, "I have a strange feeling that God changed today" (74). Complete surrender to God's will embodied by Noah's autocratic manner eventually becomes a joint responsibility between human action and divine guidance. Odets is thus able at the end of the play to suggest that human life requires human action and commitment to others: "It's in man's hands to make or destroy the world" (85).

At the end of the play, the ark has safely landed, the conflict is seemingly resolved, and though the world has been destroyed, it has also been re-created. Even Japheth remarks that "the world looks washed" (82). Nevertheless, the question remains about what kind of world has been created. Early on, for example, Noah told Japheth that he should take a wife because "the new world will need babies, bushels and bushels of babies." Though Japheth counters with "And what about the bushels of babies who will die in the flood?" (29)—a question the play never satisfactorily answers—the use of the word "bushel" to indicate human beings equates human beings with a product of the natural world but also a product produced for consumption. Still, there is a shift by the end of the play. When the ark lands, the human beings aboard it have become both the producers and the consumers of the natural bounty; there is a balance, an easiness of production that works outside of the destructive marketplace characterizing most of Odets' previous plays.

The Flowering Peach looks back to the earliest plays in its hopeful ending, as Noah, his sons, and their wives set forth to begin the world anew after the flood. The image of the flowering fruit tree once more reappears as a symbol of bounty, seemingly freely offered. But there is, as Noah reminds us, a price to pay for this rebirth. The outside world is destroyed, and even on the ark, Esther dies on the journey. Her loss is an indication of how difficult it is to "be fruitful and multiply" (83), that plenty implies sacrifice and loss. Indeed, throughout the play, Esther has been the dominant symbol of bounty and abundance, the glue that holds the family together and provides it with material and spiritual sustenance. Like Bessie in **Awake and Sing!,** she is almost always involved in the preparation of meals and often uses food as a way to control situations; at one point, when Noah's visions become too much for her, she declares that "we'll eat supper—that's real" (19). Later, when they pack for the ark, she takes to wearing a hat with fruit on it (Noah jokes that "with such a hat, you couldn't go hungry" [45]), thus identifying her visually throughout the rest of the play with images of abundance. Indeed, they know she is dead finally because her hat has fallen off.

The Flowering Peach, in one sense, reads like an escape fantasy, the escape from a world where people are commodified. The world is washed clean; it is freed from all connections to a corrupt life, from the world where Noah is harassed in the town's market, where the businessman Shem bribes the tax collector. But Odets' hope is tempered by a realization that great effort is necessary to begin change and a recognition that change may in fact be minimal. There is an indication that everything will proceed within the family much as it did before the flood. Noah decides to live with his son Shem because "it's more comfortable" (83), and Shem, through hard work and careful planning, has acquired more cows and more material goods than all the others on the ark. It is in this tempered vision of a new paradise, one that recognizes the power of the marketplace and hopes rather to turn its benefit for good, that we see the greatest difference between early plays like **Waiting for Lefty** and **The Flowering Peach.** The radical message of Keller's "put fruit trees where our ashes are!," which seemed possible in the radical atmosphere of the 1930s, had become by the era of Eisenhower and HUAC a sentiment expressed quite differently: "I hope everyone gets everything their hearts desire" (83). Odets, the fiery political playwright of the 1930s who wanted audiences to "tear down the slaughter house of our old lives" (SP, 30) had become, with his last play, content to "tell you a mystery" (**TFP,** 85).

Notes

1. Ralph Willett, "Odets and Popular Culture" *South Atlantic Quarterly* 27 (1970) 74.

2. James T. Patterson, *Grand Expectations: The United States, 1945-1974* (New York: Oxford UP, 1996) 348.

3. Pasi Falk. *The Consuming Body* (London: Sage, 1994) 178.

4. "Midcult" is a term coined by Dwight Macdonald to define the popularization of high culture for the benefit of the masses. Andrew Ross notes, "Midcult's institutions included the Book-of-The-Month Club, NBC radio's 'music appreciation' hours, the Great Books series and many other self-educational programs that Macdonald satirized as Howtoism" (*No Respect: Intellectuals and Popular Culture* [New York: Routledge, 1989] 57).

5. Clement Greenberg, "Avant Garde and Kitsch," in *Mass Culture. The Popular Arts in America,* Bernard Rosenberg and David Manning White, eds. (London: The Free Press of Glencoe, 1957) 98-110.

6. Greenberg, 102.

7. Greenberg, 103.

8. Leo Lowenthal, in *Mass Culture. The Popular Arts in America,* Bernard Rosenberg and David Manning White, eds. (London: The Free Press of Glencoe, 1957) 55. There was debate surrounding the use of the term "mass culture" as opposed to "popular culture" from the beginning. Critics such as Adorno and Greenberg, who saw the development of popular forms of culture as a system of control that fostered a largely unthinking audience, often referred to these forms as "mass" culture. Others tended to refer to popular forms as merely "popular" culture, emphasizing the democratic aspect of art, which was not produced for or by an elite ruling class. David Manning White, for example, argued that popular culture is a form that allows large audiences access to high culture. For White, it is not the technology, but how it is used, that is important. In Odets' case, his ambivalence toward popular culture and his frequently expressed hopes that it could, as White argues, reach large audiences with worthwhile art, undercuts the narcotizing effect of popular culture he describes in some of his plays.

9. Dwight Macdonald, "A Theory of Mass Culture," in *Mass Culture. The Popular Arts in America,* Bernard Rosenberg and David Manning White, eds. (London: The Free Press of Glencoe, 1957) 72.

10. Gilbert Seldes, "The People and the Arts" in *Mass Culture The Popular Arts in America,* Bernard Rosenberg and David Manning White, eds. (London: The Free Press of Glencoe, 1957) 87.

11. T. W. Adorno, "Television and the Patterns of Mass Culture," in *Mass Culture: The Popular Arts in America,* Bernard Rosenberg and David Manning White, eds. (London: The Free Press of Glencoe, 1957) 474.

12. Walter Benjamin, "The Work of Art in the Age of Mechanical Reproduction," in *Illuminations,* Harry Zohn, trans. (New York: Schocken, 1969) 224.

13. Benjamin, 241. Frederic Jameson has argued, in fact, that advanced capitalism is a necessary historical condition for the development of popular culture. As mass production shifted the West toward a standardized and frenetic consumer capitalism, for the first time, it was possible for culture to become truly popular. As a result, the practices, if not the aims, of the advertiser and the artist were becoming more alike: "With the coming of the market, [the] institutional status of artistic consumption and production vanishes: art becomes one more branch of commodity production" ("Reification and Utopia in Mass Culture," *Social Text* 1 [1979]: 136-137).

14. Ross, 35.

15. Ross, 49.

16. Ross, 62.

17. Ellen Schrecker, *Many Are the Crimes: McCarthyism in America.* (Boston: Little, Brown, 1998) 317.

18. Quoted in Gerald Mast, ed. The Movies in Our Midst: Documents in the Cultural History of Film America (Chicago: U of Chicago P, 1982) 322.

19. The effects of the "blacklist" and the "graylist" against those in Hollywood who refused to cooperate with the committee are documented by Larry Ceplair and Steven Englund in their excellent book *Inquisition in Hollywood: Politics in the Film Community, 1930-1960* (Garden City, NY: Anchor/Doubleday, 1980). They note that the power of the committee to both find and punish suspected Communists was enormous and suggest that while "virtually no Communists or former Communists escaped exposure, the lives and careers of the frequently named artists were even more lastingly blighted" (372). George Groman suggests, however, that even those witnesses who did cooperate suffered "loss of reputation and ability to make a living" ("Waiting for Odets: A Playwright Takes the Stand," in *Politics and the Muse: Studies in the Politics of Recent American Literature,* Adam J. Sorkin, ed. [Bowling Green, OH: Bowling Green State U Popular P, 1989] 65).

20. Harold Cantor emphasizes the influence of Steinbeck's *Of Mice and Men* in this scene in the character of a drunken man who has been paid to ignore his wife's affair and who wanders through the scene from time to time muttering "fat o' the land," Lennie and George's catchphrase in the Steinbeck novella. (*Clifford Odets: Playwright-*

Poet. [Metuchen, NJ: Scarecrow, 1978] 118), and Gabriel Miller takes the analogy further, identifying Jerry as a sort of Lennie, "[a] strong, sweet, childlike man" (*Clifford Odets.* [New York: Continuum, 1989] 140). This seems in keeping with Odets' assertion, "Personally I am of the opinion that Steinbeck and myself are the two young American writers who see clearly what must be done and are doing it, each in our way" (TIR, 15).

21. Miller, *Clifford Odets,* 138.

22. Willett, 78.

23. Kenneth Tynan, *Curtains* (New York: Atheneum, 1961) 21.

24. Michael J. Mendelsohn, "Odets at Center Stage," interview with Odets. *Theatre Arts* (May 1963) 16-19, 74-76; (June 1963) 28-30, 78-80

25. Mendelsohn, "Center Stage," 19.

26. The idea of conformity and repression troubled Odets through the second half of his career. Even as late as 1961, in a speech before the National Women's Committee for Brandeis University, Odets argued that "our writers today seem conformists. They are afraid to offend. They have dropped their swords and . . . have gone to bed with the dragon they should have killed. They are in TV where the pay is fast and certain and where they are dominated completely by the advertising agency mentality that pays them their wages; they are there to sell merchandise and not much more" (LCA, January 30, 1961) Of course, by the next year, Odets himself would be writing for television. Still, his concern about conformity taps into an ongoing concern in American culture following the war. HUAC and McCarthy reflected a deepening distrust of difference, a repressive attitude that would eventually help to breed the discontents of the Beat Generation and, later, the social upheaval of the 1960s.

27. Michael Denning, "The End of Mass Culture," *International Labor and Working Class History* 37 (Spring 1990) 15.

28. Colin Schindler, *Hollywood in Crisis: Cinema and American Society, 1929-1939* (London and New York: Routledge, 1996) 77-78.

29. Mendelsohn, "Center Stage," 28.

30. John Gassner, *Theatre at the Crossroads* (New York: Holt, Rinehart, Winston, 1960) 155.

Selected Bibliography

Adorno, T. W. "Television and the Patterns of Mass Culture." *Mass Culture: The Popular Arts in America.* Bernard Rosenberg and David Manning White, eds. London: The Free Press of Glencoe, 1957: 474-488.

Benjamin, Walter. "The Work of Art in the Age of Mechanical Reproduction." *Illuminations*. Harry Zohn, trans. New York: Schocken, 1969: 219-253.

Cantor, Harold. *Clifford Odets: Playwright-Poet*. Metuchen, NJ: Scarecrow, 1978.

Ceplair, Larry and Steven Englund. *Inquisition in Hollywood: Politics in the Film Community, 1930-1960*. Garden City, NY: Anchor/Doubleday, 1980.

Denning, Michael. "The End of Mass Culture." *International Labor and Working Class History* 37 (Spring 1990): 4-18.

Falk, Pasi. *The Consuming Body*. London: Sage, 1994.

Gassner, John. *Theatre at the Crossroads*. New York: Holt, Rinehart, Winston, 1960.

Greenberg, Clement. "Avant Garde and Kitsch." *Mass Culture: The Popular Arts in America*. Bernard Rosenberg and David Manning White, eds. London: The Free Press of Glencoe, 1957: 98-110.

Groman, George L. "Waiting for Odets: A Playwright Takes the Stand." *Politics and the Muse: Studies in the Politics of Recent American Literature*. Adam J. Sorkin, ed. Bowling Green, OH: Bowling Green State U Popular P, 1989. 64-78.

Jameson, Frederic. "Reification and Utopia in Mass Culture." *Social Text* 1 (1979): 130-148.

Macdonald, Dwight. "A Theory of Mass Culture." *Mass Culture. The Popular Arts in America*. Bernard Rosenberg and David Manning White, eds. London: The Free Press of Glencoe, 1957: 59-73.

Mast, Gerald, ed. *The Movies in Our Midst: Documents in the Cultural History of Film America*. Chicago: U of Chicago P, 1982.

Mendelsohn, Michael J. "Odets at Center Stage." Interview with Odets. *Theatre Arts* May 1963. 16-19, 74-76; June 1963. 28-30, 78-80.

Miller, Gabriel. *Clifford Odets*. New York: Continuum, 1989.

Odets, Clifford. *The Big Knife*. New York: Dramatists Play Service, 1949.

———. *Clash By Night*. New York: Random House, 1942.

———. *The Flowering Peach*. Dramatists Play Service, 1954.

———. *Six Plays*. New York: Methuen, 1982.

———. *Three Plays*. London: Victor Gollancz, 1936.

———. *The Time Is Ripe: The 1940 Journal of Clifford Odets*. New York: Grove, 1988.

———. Billy Rose Theatre Collection, The New York Public Library for the Performing Arts. T-Mss 1981-008.

Patterson, James T. *Grand Expectations: The United States, 1945-1974*. New York: Oxford UP, 1996.

Ross, Andrew. *No Respect: Intellectuals and Popular Culture*. New York: Routledge, 1989.

Schrecker, Ellen. *Many are the Crimes: McCarthyism in America*. Boston: Little, Brown, 1998.

Seldes, Gilbert. "The People and the Arts." *Mass Culture: The Popular Arts in America*. Bernard Rosenberg and David Manning White, eds. London: The Free Press of Glencoe, 1957: 74-97.

Shindler, Colin. *Hollywood in Crisis: Cinema and American Society, 1929-1939*. London: Routledge, 1996.

Tynan, Kenneth. *Curtains*. New York: Atheneum, 1961.

White, David Manning. "Mass Culture in America: Another Point of View." *Mass Culture: The Popular Arts in America*. Bernard Rosenberg and David Manning White, eds. London: The Free Press of Glencoe, 1957: 13-21.

Willett, Ralph. "Odets and Popular Culture." *South Atlantic Quarterly* 27 (1970): 68-78.

ABBREVIATIONS

B-G: Margaret Brenman-Gibson, *Clifford Odets, American Playwright: The Years From 1906-1940*. New York: Atheneum, 1981.

CBN: Clifford Odets, *Clash by Night*. New York: Random House, 1942.

LCA: Clifford Odets, Billy Rose Theatre Collection, The New York Public Library for the Performing Arts.

NYT: *New York Times*.

SP: Clifford Odets, *Six Plays*. New York: Methuen, 1982

TBK: Clifford Odets, *The Big Knife*. New York: Dramatists Play Service, 1949.

TCG: Clifford Odets, *The Country Girl*. New York: Viking Press, 1951.

TFP: Clifford Odets, *The Flowering Peach*. New York: Dramatists Play Service, 1954.

TIR: Clifford Odets, *The Time Is Ripe: The 1940 Journal of Clifford Odets*. New York: Grove, 1988.

FURTHER READING

Bibliography

Demastes, William W. *Clifford Odets: A Research and Production Sourcebook*. New York: Greenwood Press, 1991, 209 p.

Extensive bibliography of works by and about Odets, as well as "an overview of the author's life, play synopses and critical overviews, production histories and credits," and holdings of unpublished archival material on Odets.

Criticism

Brenman-Gibson, Margaret. *Clifford Odets, American Playwright: The Years from 1906 to 1940.* New York: Atheneum, 1981, 748 p.

Book-length bio-critical study of Odets that purports to evaluate his plays in the context of both his life and "the prevailing historical forces" that shaped his childhood and his early years as a playwright.

Cantor, Harold. *Clifford Odets: Playwright-Poet.* Metuchen, N.J.: The Scarecrow Press, Inc., 1978, 235 p.

Attempts to correct the current assessment of Odets as a "failed" writer, claiming that his plays, "despite their flaws," demonstrate "a depth and complexity" that "lift them out of the category of social realism into the realm of evocative parables and allegories in dramatic form."

Goldstein, Malcolm. "Clifford Odets and the Found Generation." In *American Drama and Its Critics: A Collection of Critical Essays,* edited by Alan S. Downer, pp. 133-46. Chicago: University of Chicago Press, 1965.

Briefly surveys Odets's career as a playwright, asserting that in his post Depression-era works, the author failed to break new ground but continued to repeat the same stories of "class-consciousness" and was unable "to free himself completely . . . from the materialist theme with which he began his career."

Griffin, Robert J. "On the Love Songs of Clifford Odets." In *The Thirties: Fiction, Poetry, Drama,* edited by Warren French, pp. 193-200. Deland, Fla.: Everett/Edwards, Inc., 1967.

Describes Odets as a poet and "imaginative spokesman" of the 1930s in America, saying that despite the sentimentality and didactic tone of his Depression-era works, they demonstrate a "vitality of characterization" and a "core of humanitarianism" that elevates them above pure propaganda.

Miller, Gabriel, ed. *Critical Essays on Clifford Odets.* Boston: G. K. Hall & Co., 1991, 282 p.

Compendium of previously published reviews and essays on Odets, as well as interviews with the author and a few essays published for the first time in this edition.

Mishra, Kshamanidhi. "Clifford Odets' *Awake and Sing!*: A Leftist Play." *Research Bulletin (Arts)* 18, no. 1 (April 1987): 69-81.

Discusses Odets's blending of religious and Marxist ideology in *Awake and Sing,* which the critic interprets as a leftist drama.

Shuman, R. Baird. "Clifford Odets: From Influence to Affluence." In *Modern American Drama: Essays in Criticism,* edited by William E. Taylor, pp. 39-46. Deland, Fla.: Everett/Edwards, Inc., 1968.

Briefly surveys Odets's career as a playwright, emphasizing especially the two major factors that propelled his work for the theater: first, the social forces of the Great Depression in America, and second, the founding of the Group Theatre in 1931.

Additional coverage of Odets's life and career is contained in the following sources published by Gale: *American Writers Supplement,* **Vol. 2;** *Contemporary American Dramatists*; *Contemporary Authors,* **Vols. 85-88;** *Contemporary Authors New Revision Series,* **Vol. 62;** *Contemporary Literary Criticism,* **Vols. 2, 28, 98;** *Dictionary of Literary Biography,* **Vols. 7, 26, 341;** *DISCovering Authors Modules: Dramatists*; *Drama Criticism,* **Vol. 6;** *Drama for Students,* **Vols. 3, 17, 20;** *Encyclopedia of World Literature in the 20th Century,* **Ed. 3;** *Gale Contextual Encyclopedia of American Literature*; *Literature Resource Center*; *Major 20th-Century Writers,* **Eds. 1, 2;** *Major 21st-Century Writers*; *Modern American Literature,* **Ed. 5;** *Reference Guide to American Literature,* **Ed. 4; and** *Twayne's United States Authors.*

Christina Stead
1902-1983

(Full name Christina Ellen Stead) Australian novelist and short story writer.

The following entry provides an overview of Stead's life and works. For additional information on her career, see *CLC,* Volumes 2, 5, 8, 32, and 80.

INTRODUCTION

Australian-born author Christina Stead is considered an important novelist of the twentieth century, as well as one of Australia's leading literary figures. An expatriate for much of her life, Stead possessed a keen awareness of the underlying social and cultural forces of her native country, Europe, and the United States—a broad and far-reaching perspective that is reflected throughout her multifaceted body of work. She is best known for her semiautobiographical novels, *The Man Who Loved Children* (1940) and *For Love Alone* (1944), which explore such topics as family relations, oppression, and the individual's quest for personal identity and freedom. In addition to her insightful social observations and complex exploration of political, social, and psychological themes, Stead is often noted for her deft portrayal of diverse settings and memorable characters, as well as her luxurious and original writing style. After years of suffering critical neglect, Stead's work has been reappraised in recent decades. As a result, the author is now generally regarded as a major literary figure of the twentieth century, appreciated for her political and social commentary and her innovative prose style.

BIOGRAPHICAL INFORMATION

Stead was born in Rockdale, Sydney, Australia, on July 17, 1902, to Ellen Butters and David George Stead, a middle-ranking public servant with the New South Wales Department of Fisheries. Her mother died when she was only two years old, after which she was raised by her father, a socialist and free-thinking atheist who nurtured his daughter's love for storytelling and instilled in her a respect and passion for the natural world. After completing her secondary education at Sydney Girls' High School, Stead attended Sydney Teachers' College, where she co-edited and contributed to the college literary magazine, the *Kookaburra.*

In 1923 she began a five-year bonded teaching period, but as a result of ongoing health concerns, she was released from her teaching commitment in 1925. She worked briefly as a secretary in an architectural firm and then in a Sydney hat factory before saving enough money to move to London, in 1928. There, Stead found employment at Strauss and Company, a grain firm, where she met her lifelong companion and future husband, Wilhelm Blech, an investments manager and intellectual, who later changed his name to William Blake. Blake introduced Stead to leftist intellectuals and writers in Europe and the United States and promoted her work, facilitating the publication of her first books, *The Salzburg Tales* (1934) and *Seven Poor Men of Sydney* (1934).

Over the next few years Stead became increasingly involved in European literary circles and published two more novels, *The Beauties and Furies* (1936) and *House of All Nations* (1938). In July of 1937 Stead and Blake moved to the United States, where they remained until December 1946, mainly residing in areas in and around New York City. During this time Stead began revisiting memories of her early childhood and young adulthood in Australia, drawing on these events for her next novels, *The Man Who Loved Children* and *For Love Alone,* which many critics consider her greatest works of fiction.

While living in the United States, Stead closely studied American society and manners, a preoccupation reflected in her next three novels, *Letty Fox: Her Luck* (1946), *A Little Tea, A Little Chat* (1948), and *The People with the Dogs* (1952). After returning to Europe Stead and Blake experienced a period of transition, marked by poverty and dislocation, resulting in part from the shifting cultural and political climate of that time. Blake's health began deteriorating during this period, and Stead's literary career suffered as a result of disagreements with publishing companies and the couple's leftist political leanings, which prompted low-level harassment from the FBI. Despite these obstacles Stead continued to write, producing several novels that were not published until years later, including *Cotter's England* (1966), *The Little Hotel* (1975), and *Miss Herbert (The Suburban Wife)* (1976).

In 1968 Blake died, leaving Stead with little will to continue writing fiction. The author grew increasingly nostalgic for Australia and permanently returned to her native country in 1974, where she remained until her death, on March 31, 1983. *I'm Dying Laughing* (1986), a novel partially composed during the 1940s and 1950s, was published posthumously by her literary executor, Ron Geering, who edited and restructured the work.

MAJOR WORKS

While Stead is best known for novels written later in her career, her early works have also drawn considerable critical attention. Her first published work, *The Salzburg Tales,* features self-revelatory stories told by a diverse group of individuals, who convene in the Capuchin Wood at night, during the Mozart Festival in Salzburg, to exchange tales. Similar in structure to fourteenth-century literary works, such as Geoffrey Chaucer's *Canterbury Tales* and Giovanni Boccaccio's *The Decameron,* Stead's stories are noted for their gothic attributes and anecdotal quality. The stories in *The Salzburg Tales* achieve cohesion through the figure of the Centenarist, who weaves disparate themes together in his narratives.

Stead's first novel, *Seven Poor Men of Sydney,* set entirely in Australia, combines realist themes and experimental formal techniques and is considered a forerunner of the modernist novel in Australia. The work is comprised of a myriad of perspectives and voices, the most prominent of which are three members of the Baguenault family, Michael, Catherine, and Joseph, who emerge as the narrative's central characters. Michael, a passionate, sensitive, and somewhat fragile individual, struggles against moral and social conventions and questions conformist ways of thinking, a perspective which culminates in his suicide at the end of the work. Michael's unconventional ideals are also reflected in his sister and kindred spirit, Catherine, who is politically active and longs to escape the confines of prescriptive gender roles, while their cousin, Joseph, is a humble individual, who moves through life without questioning his role in the world.

In her next two works, *The Beauties and Furies* and *House of All Nations,* both of which are set in Paris, Stead explores the radical artistic and political movements of the European intelligentsia during the early decades of the twentieth century. Characterized by its sensual and surrealistic treatment of love and politics, *The Beauties and Furies* revolves around the relationship between Elvira Western, a refugee from a provincial domestic life, and Oliver Fenton, a student who is drawn to revolutionary politics. While on the surface the two lovers appear to be fully engaged in their bohemian lifestyle, in reality their participation in both love and politics is shallow and self-serving. Eventually the couple falls prey to Marpurgo, an enigmatic and narcissistic predator.

In *House of All Nations,* a documentary novel, Stead focuses on the financial world of Paris, particularly concentrating on the corrupt inner workings of the male-dominated merchant banking system. Stead parallels the activities of the banking fraternity with the movements of the communist brotherhood, which is composed of political idealists and poseurs. Capitalism, consumerism, and popular-front politics of the 1930s provide the primary themes in the work, although the author also challenges middle-class values and exposes the greed and guile that motivates many of her characters.

In her most successful novels Stead employed autobiographical elements to depict the claustrophobia and callousness associated with a family in turmoil and explore themes related to oppression, personal identity, and the individual's quest for creative freedom. Set in the United States, *The Man Who Loved Children* centers on the Pollit family, which includes the narcissistic patriarch, Samuel, his bitterly disappointed and self-destructive wife, Henny, and his awkward and creative stepdaughter, Louisa, also known as Louie. As the marriage between Samuel and Henny begins to dissolve, Louisa leads her step-siblings in a subtle rebellion, which is ultimately expressed through the staging of a play, written in her own invented language. Although the novel ends tragically, Louisa discovers that through language she is able to counter her father's verbal tyranny and find freedom outside her family life. *The Man Who Loved Children* has inspired a number of critical interpretations. While some scholars emphasize the feminist themes of the work, others have noted its critique of liberal humanism and treatment of Nietzschean concepts.

Stead's next major novel, *For Love Alone,* set in Australia and England, treats themes related to marriage, gender roles, sexuality, oppression, and the confines of provincial life. The protagonist of the work, the rebellious Teresa Hawkins, escapes the narrow confines of the small Australian town where she was born, as well as her oppressive father, and encounters several domineering male figures in her travels. Finally, she experiences sensual awakening and achieves self-knowledge through relationships with an American named James Quick, and her kindred spirit, Harry Girton.

Issues related to consumption and sexual desire provide the major themes for another of Stead's major works, *A Little Tea, A Little Chat,* which is set in New York City during World War II. The protagonist of the work, Robbie Grant, is a womanizer and predatory capitalist, whose sexual and financial exploits are chronicled in detail throughout the work. While he relentlessly and frenetically pursues gratification, Grant also has apocalyptic fears of death and revolution, which manifest in the form of his nemesis, Hilbertson. After seducing numerous women, Grant is finally confounded by the equally duplicitous and materialistic Barbara Downs at the end of the novel. Initially considered one of Stead's lesser achievements, *A Little Tea, A Little Chat* has increasingly drawn critical praise in recent years.

CRITICAL RECEPTION

Critical reaction to Stead's work fluctuated throughout much of her career. While her earliest publications, *The Salzburg Tales* and *Seven Poor Men of Sydney*, were widely praised for their rich and luxurious style, fantastic themes, and imaginative story lines, reactions to her subsequent works were less enthusiastic. *The Beauties and Furies* was generally criticized for its extreme mixture of styles and unconvincing characterizations. And while *House of All Nations* received warm reviews, especially in the United States, *The Man Who Loved Children, For Love Alone,* and Stead's remaining post-World War II works were deemed both critical and popular failures. *Letty Fox: Her Luck* particularly scandalized some critics, who described the novel as immoral and vulgar, while others reacted with confusion to its political nuances. Indeed, in 1947, a ban was placed on the novel by the Australian Literature Censorship Board, which was not lifted until ten years later.

Stead's literary career suffered throughout the 1950s, in part a result of her political affiliations, but also due to her itinerant lifestyle, which some critics believe exacerbated her difficulties with publishers. In 1965, however, with the reissue of *The Man Who Loved Children* by Holt, Rinehart, and Winston, her career experienced a significant boost. This "rediscovery" was facilitated, in large part, by the influential introduction to the novel written by the American poet and critic Randall Jarrell, in which he praised the work's "singularity" and stated that, though it has its "plainly negligible" faults, "it is a better book . . . than most of the novels people call great." In the years that immediately followed, interest in Stead's writings gradually increased, particularly among second-wave feminists, as well as several loyal supporters in her native Australia, especially Ron Geering, whose efforts helped to secure a place for the author in the Australian literary canon.

In recent years scholars have continued to revisit Stead's oeuvre, addressing a number of thematic and formal issues in her work. Foremost among these topics has been her stylistic and narrative techniques. While some critics have focused on the "excesses" in Stead's linguistic style, others have emphasized the methods by which she uses rhetoric and discourse to challenge oppressive forces, and to expose manipulation and abuses of power. Wendy Woodward has noted that "gender struggles, particularly, are located within the language of her characters," adding that this "explicitly foregrounds the production of the subject in language and the essential power play inherent in all linguistic exchange." Other commentators, such as Brian Kiernan, Ann Blake, and Louise Yelin, have explored the significance of setting in Stead's fiction. While Yelin has probed questions related to national identity in the author's work, Blake has noted the influence of "place" on her characterizations. Blake also has observed that whether Stead's novels are set in "Australia, the United States or England seems not to matter," they are always praised "for what is felt to be the authenticity of the settings, in all their aspects—physical, cultural, historical."

A number of critics have also discussed, in one form or another, the nexus of capitalism, patriarchy, and femininity in Stead's writings, especially her novels that deal specifically with consumption and power in human relations, *House of All Nations* and *A Little Tea, A Little Chat*. Some, such as Susan Sheridan and Jennifer Gribble, have questioned the appropriateness of strictly feminist readings of Stead's fiction. Gribble, who has asserted that "feminist critics and women's studies courses have 'appropriated' Stead, despite her firm rejection of feminist ideology and against the grain of her writing," suggests that feminist readings reduce the "stature" and simplified the artistic accomplishments of such works as *For Love Alone*.

As the variety of these readings suggest, Stead's complex body of work resists easy classification and actually invites opposing critical interpretations—characteristics which, according to some scholars, underscore both her originality and universality and reinforce her growing reputation as one of the twentieth-century's most significant, if at times neglected, novelists. Commenting on a number of Stead's literary attributes, Rosemary Lancaster has averred that "the Stead novel is never reductive" but is "subtle, investigative," adding that "within the broad social tableaux she constructs, Stead offers no safe or cut-and-dried picture of how human beings behave." Lancaster concludes that "today she is recognized as one of Australia's most verbally clever (if intellectually daunting) writers; concomitantly appreciation of her social acuity and stylistic diversity has justifiably soared."

PRINCIPAL WORKS

The Salzburg Tales (short stories) 1934
Seven Poor Men of Sydney (novel) 1934
The Beauties and Furies (novel) 1936
House of All Nations (novel) 1938
The Man Who Loved Children (novel) 1940

CRITICISM

Elizabeth Hardwick (essay date 1955)

SOURCE: Hardwick, Elizabeth. "The Neglected Novels of Christina Stead." In *A View of My Own: Essays in Literature and Society,* pp. 41-8. New York: Farrar, Straus and Cudahy, 1962.

[*In the following essay, originally published in 1955 in the* New Republic, *Hardwick lauds Stead's "prodigious talent for fiction," focusing mainly on the novel* The Man Who Loved Children, *which she states is written "in such a magical, abundant, inventive manner that the reading is a pleasure from beginning to end."*]

It is annoying to be asked to discover a book that is neither old nor new. When it must be admitted that the work lacks, on the one hand, the assurance of age and, on the other, a current and pressing fame, our resistance grows and our boredom swells. We feel certain we don't want to read a book no one else is reading or has read. The work being offered to us appears cold and flat, like a dish passed around for a tardy second helping. It is gratifying to our dignity to be able to turn down the offer.

There are many roads to neglect—simple neglect itself, early and late, is far from being the only way. Very often we find that a writer has produced a number of books that were, on publication, well and even enthusiastically received and yet somehow the years passed and the reputation, the fame, the consideration did not quite take hold. The public mind, friendly enough at first, turned out to have been but briefly attracted; the literary mind was, at the moment, fixed upon other points with the helplessness and passion we have all experienced, the realization that our delight is kept in its course by some radar of history or fashion. That there is a good deal of luck, accident, "timing" and sheer chaos in these matters hardly anyone would deny.

People used to say they wanted to be either rich or poor, anything but shabby-genteel, and in the same way a state of extremity is perhaps to be sought in the arts. Attacks upon great work have very nearly the same weight as praise—*bon chat, bon rat.* It is a painful but honorable destiny to be laughed at, scorned as a madman, slandered as immoral or irresponsible or dangerous. Even refusal, being entirely ignored, has in its own way a certain cold and bony beauty.

The notion of a large or small masterpiece lying about unnoticed—a Vermeer in the hayloft—has always stirred men's hearts. To be attacked or to be ignored offer at the least certain surprising possibilities for the future; the work may be dramatically discovered or excitingly defended, reclaimed. The common and lowly fate of most books is shabby gentility. They are more or less accepted, amiably received—nearly everyone is kind about effort and genial in the face of a completed task—and then they are set aside, misplaced, quietly and firmly left out, *utterly forgotten,* as the bleak phrase has it. This is the dust.

The dust seems to have settled rather quickly upon the works of Christina Stead. Her name means nothing to most people. The title of one of her novels, **The House of All Nations,** occasionally causes an eye to shine with cordiality and it may be noted that good things have been heard about this book even if it is not possible to remember precisely what they are. Is it perhaps a three-decker affair by a Northern European once mentioned for the Nobel Prize? The title of her great novel, **The Man Who Loved Children,** doesn't sound reassuring either; the title is in fact, one could remark, not good enough for the book, suggesting as it does a satisfaction with commonplace ironies. (But no title could give a preview of this unusual novel.)

At the present time none of Christina Stead's work is in print. Her name never appears on a critic's or journalist's list of novelists, she is not a "well-known woman writer"; she has written about finance, about Salzburg, Washington, Australia and yet neither place nor subject seem to call her image to the critical eye. Upon inquiring about her from her last American publisher, the information came forth with a *tomba oscura* note: all they had was a *poste restante,* Lausanne, Switzerland, 1947. The facts of her biography seem to be that she is Australian, has lived all over Europe, and lived in America for some time and may still do so. She is, as they say, not in the picture, not right now at least, and therefore one cannot learn much about her past or her future. Yet when **The Man Who Loved Children** appeared in 1940, Rebecca West said on the front page of *The New York Times Book Review* that Christina Stead was "one of the few people really original we have produced since the First World War." Statements of that kind are not a rarity in the public press: the novelty of this one is that it is true. The dust, grimly, meanly collecting, has fallen upon a work of sheer astonishment and success.

The Man Who Loved Children has not been completely buried—it has a small and loyal band of friends. Yet that quaint locution is misleading, because it makes the book sound like a fine but frail old lady living in retirement and occasionally appearing for tea with the selected few. **The Man Who Loved Children** is not a small, perfect, witty book, but a large, sprawling, vigorous work marked by a novelistic, story-telling abundance, the wonderful richness of character and texture the critics are always irritably demanding. It is all this, all story and character and truth and directness, and yet it has been composed in a style of remarkable uniqueness and strength, of truly radical power and authenticity. This book is a genuine novel in the traditional meaning of the term; it is a story of life, faithfully plotted, clearly told, largely peopled with real souls, genuine problems; it is realistically set, its intention and drive are openly and fully revealed; it is also a work of absolute originality.

There has never been anyone in American literature like the great, talkative, tearful, pompous, womanish father, Samuel Clemens Pollitt. Sam is a bureaucrat of the office and the home; he has one of those greedy and restless minds that takes in and chews up everything in sight, like a disposal unit attached to the sink. He expresses himself vividly and tirelessly; his conversation is a rich mash of slogans, baby talk, snatches of old songs, remembered bits of information and nonsense. His very glands secrete his own special cant, his own mixture of self-loving exuberance, sensuality, windy idealism, nature lore, and public service. Pollitt works as a naturalist in Washington, D.C., in the employment of the government. Perhaps one could not seriously describe **The Man Who Loved Children** as a political novel, but in its vastly suggestive way it has something to do with Washington and with politics. It is not easy to imagine Sam Pollitt in any other situation except the one he has here. His free-wheeling, fantastic talents, his active but moderately proportioned ambitions, his dignity and his moralizing fit like a glove his government-post life; a bureaucracy can use his blandly conniving and optimistic nature and assure him a well-settled if not remarkable career. Although he has some specialized knowledge, he is roundly and exhaustively general, like an encyclopedia. His wife sees him as a sort of force who has come into his career, his marriage, his self-satisfaction by the back door. He is "a mere jog-trot, subaltern bureaucrat, dragged into the service in the lowest grades without a degree, from mere practical experience in the Maryland Conservation Commission, and who owed his jealousy-creating career to her father's influence in the lobbies of the capital."

Sam Pollitt's overwhelming cantish vitality is probably not a political thing in itself, but it comes from the lush underside, the slushy, rich bottom soil of the political terrain. His every sentence is a speech to his public, his family is a sort of political party to be used, fulsomely praised, and grotesquely subjected to uplifting sermons. He is literally swollen with idealistic feelings and self-love, with democratic statement and profound self-seeking. He is as fertile of lofty sentiments as he is of children. His little ones clamor about him, blushing and laughing, like an office force, working away, pretending to be playing all the while. Here is an example of Pollitt's fatherly method of expressing himself to his brood:

> "This Sunday-Funday has come a long way . . . it's been coming to us, all day yesterday, all night from the mid-Pacific, from Peking, the Himalayas, from the fishing grounds of the old Leni Lenapes and the deeps of the drowned Susquehanna, over the pond pine ragged in the peat and the lily swamps of Anacostia, by scaffolded marbles and time-bloodied weatherboard, northeast, northwest, Washington Circle, Truxton Circle, Sheridan Circle to Rock Creek and the blunt shoulders of our Georgetown. And what does he find there this morning as every morning, in the midst of the slope, but Tohoga House, the little shanty of Gulliver Sam's Lilliputian Pollitry—Gulliver Sam, Mrs. Gulliver Henny, Lagubrious Louisa, whose head is bloody but unbowed, Ernest the calculator, Little Womey . . . Saul and Sam the boy-twins and Thomas-snowshoeeye, all sun-tropes that he came galloping to see."

Henny Pollitt, the sour mother of Sam's children, is a disappointed daughter of a good and prosperous Maryland family. She is always in debt, always lazy, untidy, hysterical. Although created upon the familiar lines of the disappointed and disagreeable wife, Henny seems completely without antecedents of the literary sort. She is grand and terrifying and inexplicably likeable as she mutters to herself, plays patience, swills tea all day, and screams at the children. As a mother, Henny seems to experience only the most rudimentary maternal feelings; she is as verbose as her detested husband; she is sloppy, mysterious, shabby, a convincing character made up of fantastic odds and ends, leathery grins, stained fingers, squalid lies and brutal hopes. Where Sam presents his family the fruits of his endless moralizing, his flow of nonsense, proverb and hypocrisy, Henny gives them day in and day out the hatred and insult of her heart, the chagrin, anger, poverty, ugliness and rudeness of the world as she knows it. When she goes downtown she returns with tales of an adventure in a street car and "a dirty shrimp of a man with a fishy expression who purposely leaned over me and pressed my bust . . ." or outrageous descriptions of people:

> to whom she would give the go-by, or the cold shoulder, or a distant bow . . . or a polite good-day, or a black look, or a look black as thunder, and there were silly old roosters . . . filthy old pawers, and YMCA sick chickens . . . and all these wonderful creatures, who swarmed in the streets, stores, and restaurants of Washington, ogling, leering, pulling, pushing, stinking,

overscented, screaming and boasting, turning pale at the black look from Henny, ducking and diving, dodging and returning, were the only creatures that Henny ever saw.

Henny's fights with her husband are epics of insult, suffering and sordid vitality. But there is no way of scoring a point on Sam because he is made of words and will not bleed. After a nightmare family collision he goes right on with his imitations of various accents, his horrible but somehow admirable begetting of children, his exploitation and yet honest enjoyment of these children, his reminiscences. No matter what has happened he sleeps comfortably, his bedside table littered with "pamphlets from the Carnegie Peace Foundation, scientific journals, and folders from humanitarian leagues."

The Man Who Loved Children is sordid and bitter. In it Henny commits suicide, one of the little boys shows his feeling about life by hanging himself in effigy, the stepdaughter, Louie, is worked like a horse by the entire household, Aunt Bonnie is exploited and maltreated in the same fashion. The father's oily vanity and ghastly pawings, the mother's lies and shabby dreams: such is actual material of this novel. The grim unfolding of the drama is, nevertheless, done in such a magical, abundant, inventive manner that the reading is a pleasure from beginning to end. The dialogue is realistic and plausible and at the same time humorous, original and exciting in a way that is hardly inferior to Joyce. Sometimes the language is more nearly that of England than of America: people "post parcels," drink tea morning, noon and night, have "elevenses," etc. Still the reader does not find these English turns objectionable—they seem merely another example of the author's incredible gift for amusing and vivid and interesting language. The real triumph of the book is Pollitt. He is modern, sentimental, cruel and as sturdy as a weed. There is no possibility of destroying him. After every disaster, he shoots back up, ready with his weedy, choking sentiments. In the end he is preparing to go on the radio with his "Uncle Sam Hour" and it is inconceivable that the adventure should fail. On the other hand, it will be the tough flowering of all Pollitt's coarse reality.

The Man Who Loved Children is Christina Stead's masterpiece, but all of her work is of an unusual power. *The House of All Nations* is an excellent, interesting novel, large in scale, intelligent, and splendidly detailed. In a novel like *The Salzburg Tales* one can literally say there is talent to burn, and the talent *is* burned in it. These beautifully composed tales are told by people of all sorts and nationalities who are in Salzburg to see the annual presentation of Hofmanstael's *Everyman*. It cannot be called a complete success and yet it would have taken anyone else a lifetime to produce such a strangely gifted failure. *The Salzburg Tales* is long, stately, impressive and unreadable. Her last nov-

els, *For Love Alone* and *Letty Fox,* are also unusual and considerable works. It would be nearly impossible to start out with this author's prodigious talent for fiction and end up without writing something of its own peculiar force and distinction.

In the vast commerce of fame and reputation certain authors are pushed to the front of the counter like so much impatient, seasonal merchandise. It is idle to complain about this and in trying to put Christina Stead's work back on the market one need not insist that she replace anyone, even though there are some highly qualified candidates for retirement. A reminder of her existence should be advertisement enough, especially in the case of such a "genuine article."

R. G. Geering (essay date 1969)

SOURCE: Geering, R. G. "Paris: Love and Money." In *Christina Stead,* pp. 56-85. New York: Twayne Publishers, Inc., 1969.

[*In the following essay, Geering analyzes Stead's* The Beauties and Furies *and* House of All Nations, *focusing on each novel's themes, characterizations, and structural techniques, and calling the latter work a turning point in the author's career and "Stead's greatest intellectual achievement."*]

Only two years separate the publication of *The Beauties and Furies* from that of *House of All Nations,* but so great is the difference between these two novels of life in Paris that we are justified in taking the latter as a turning point in Christina Stead's literary career. *The Beauties and Furies* is her poorest book, but significant in a number of ways. It shows a young writer struggling to expand; not content to fall back on her previous successes, she is on the lookout for fresh subjects. In some respects it harks back to *Seven Poor Men of Sydney* and *The Salzburg Tales*; in others it further anticipates themes, already foreshadowed in the first book, which will receive fuller and better treatment in *House of All Nations, For Love Alone,* and as far ahead as *Letty Fox.* Standing between the early and the later works *The Beauties and Furies* is a strange mixture which, though it has its moments, never succeeds in fusing its elements into one consistent whole. For the present the memories of Australia, it seems, are written out and Christina Stead now turns from the tales told at Salzburg to write about Eruope again but this time in a full-length novel of student life and love in Paris.

In an interview in 1935 already referred to, Christina Stead after discussing *Seven Poor Men of Sydney* is quoted as saying: "My next work of fiction is to be *Student Lovers*—a book containing two or three short novels, of which one, at least, begins in Sydney. This one is *The Travelling Scholar.* These three short novels are, in a sense, love stories."[1] This original plan did not work out—*The Beauties and Furies is* a book about a student lover, the naïve and self-centered young socialist Oliver Fenton and his mistress Elvira Western, but it has grown beyond the scope of a nouvelle. The other projected short novel, *The Travelling Scholar,* obviously grew into the longer (and different) story *For Love Alone,* which was not published till 1944.

I. *The Beauties and Furies*: The Story

The story of *The Beauties and Furies* (whatever may be said of the style in certain places) is ordinary enough. Oliver, handsome, vain and irresponsible, believes he is freeing Elvira from the chains of a bourgeois marriage. Elvira abandons her devoted but dull husband Dr. Paul Western in England, and joins Oliver, who is on a scholarship in Paris. Elvira, though an honors graduate in Arts, has no interest in the politics which Oliver is studying or in the socialism which he (supposedly) is practicing. Despite the excitement of having burnt all her boats and elected for romance, she is not attracted to Paris itself either, and as the story develops she comes to realize the hollowness of her relationship with Oliver. One simple reason for its failure (the main one is Oliver's selfishness) is that she is five years older than he and has eight years of married life with Paul behind her.

In the very first chapter there enters into their lives the strange lace-buyer Annibale Marpurgo, fantast and dandy. The middle-aged Marpurgo, who has an invalid wife he rarely sees, interests himself in the affairs of the young couple and makes the appealing suggestion that Oliver should go into the lace business and make money. Elvira's troubles really begin when she becomes pregnant; after much self-torment she finally decides to accept the advice of Blanche, a French actress Oliver has introduced her to, and have an abortion. Elvira's doubts are increased by the arrival in Paris of a trio of would-be-helpers—the ever sympathetic Paul, his cousin Sara, and Elvira's brother Adam. Marpurgo wants Paul to take Elvira back to England and now does all he can to discredit Oliver in the eyes of the world. The main reason for this is jealousy; Marpurgo has grown fond of the beautiful Coromandel, a young lace-designer with whom Oliver (an incorrigible philanderer) is conducting an affair. But, Elvira having settled for Oliver, abortion, and poverty, Paul returns home defeated. Marpurgo and Oliver both woo Coromandel and the scheming Marpurgo arranges for Coromandel to discover Oliver's attachment to Elvira. As matters worsen for him Oliver turns to Blanche for amorous consolation. Elvira finally learns about Oliver's hypocritical betrayal of her and, completely disillusioned, returns to London. Oliver now takes up with Blanche but she leaves him once his money runs out. Marpurgo (by means of money extracted from Paul) arranges for Oliver to go back to England. The final, ironic scene shows Oliver, who has been drifting helplessly for months, as his old self again, cutting an impressive figure for a beautiful young girl composer he meets on the train. As the book ends he is offering her some of his poems to be set to music.

II. Types of Character

Looking back over these first three books we can now see certain key characters and ideas emerging and the continuous shaping of a few basic themes. One of the dominant character types, who is to undergo further development later on but who, in his early form, is taken about as far as possible in *The Beauties and Furies,* is the Munchausen-figure, the liar and fantasist, the erudite and obscene spellbinder.[2] At his most realistic he appears as Withers in *Seven Poor Men of Sydney,* where, despite his strange qualities, he is set firmly in the prosaic environment of Chamberlain's printing works; on a restricted scale (because here there is no suggestion of evil) he comes into *The Salzburg Tales* as the Centenarist, the man of recondite learning and innumerable stories; and finally he appears in *The Beauties and Furies* as the grotesque and sometimes repulsive Marpurgo, who like Withers is a schemer but a less comprehensible one.

The second important type is the tyrannical father. Once again *Seven Poor Men of Sydney* is the original source—this time not in the shape of a character but in a general description by Kol Blount.

> "Your ideal man is not the balanced, fire-hearted liberal, dripping with humanity and sweetness, who loves his enemies because they are men, weeps and fights for pacifism, employs the poor, encourages talent, educates children, and rules his family life like a patriarch; who never vails his crest, blunts his word; who crushes egotism, but pursues his own will through thick and thin; who believes in morality, but runs with a bunch of nettles to clear the haunts of superstition; who reveals hypocrisy even if it rises in his dearest friend?"
>
> (p. 60)

This type occurs in **"Overcote"** (*The Salzburg Tales*) as the self-advertising free-thinker, the boastful, egoistic schoolmaster who denies his children independence, spoils their chances of marriage and a career, and in his old age gives way to self-pity because they have turned from him; in *For Love Alone* as Andrew, head of the Hawkins family, from whose bonds Teresa must free herself; and in *The Man Who Loved Children* as Sam Pollit, the soupy, domineering, egocentric idealist to whom *The Beauties and Furies* carries no clear analogue.

The third important type to emerge is that of the young woman, trying to break free of the bonds of custom and tradition in order to achieve self-realization. First in this group is Catherine in *Seven Poor Men of Sydney* who is to all appearances emancipated, since she has cast off family ties and all the claims of respectability and given herself (but spasmodically) to the socialist cause. Yet Catherine, unlike Teresa, never achieves fulfilment as a woman—she understands herself well enough but cannot resolve her problems; as she says at the end, she is a woman trying to be a man. In this respect she differs from Elvira, though they have in common a discontent and a desire for a richer life. Elvira is half a rebel— enough to take the first steps to freedom, only to find that she is basically unadventurous and ideologically a thorough bourgeois. In a moment of insight she tries to make Oliver see the truth, but he cannot or will not admit it. "'That's what we are, you see: suburban, however wild we run. You know quite well, in yourself, don't you, two people like us can't go wild? Still it's nice to pretend to, for a while.'"³ Allowing for certain individual differences, Baruch's drawing "La Femme s'échappe de la Forêt" in *Seven Poor Men of Sydney* symbolizes Elvira's as well as Catherine's plight; as he spells it out to Joseph: "'Woman escapes from the forest. It means, the middle-class woman trying to free herself, and still impeded by romantic notions and ferocious, because ambushed, sensuality'" (p. 155).

III. THEME. RELATIONSHIP TO OTHER NOVELS

This passage points to the center of *The Beauties and Furies,* toward a theme which is in danger of being obscured by the antics and the rhetorical extravagances of Marpurgo. The most interesting aspect of this theme is the idea of freedom in and through love and the difficulty of realizing it in modern society. "'The real thought of the middle-class woman,' complained Elvira, 'is the problem of economic freedom and sexual freedom: they can't be attained at the same time'" (p. 127). And Elvira, more honest in self-analysis than Oliver ever could be, terrifies him by admitting as a reason for coming to him: "'. . . I just wanted to see, if in continuing in my own line, you know, just peering, being curious, analysing, being objective, even in love, and I am, I could get any new experiences'" (p. 77). Again in a passage that clearly anticipates the dilemma that Teresa, a more courageous woman, faces and at least partially resolves, she says, "'I find there is no such thing as a spiritual renaissance, at least not for a woman. We are too much nailed to a coffin of flesh, our souls are only plants, they are rooted in an earth of flesh. We need a home, security, comfort for our flesh before the mind can grow'" (p. 170). And (once more reminding us of Teresa) she can still say, wistfully, at the end of her bitter experience: "'I suppose a woman, to be completely rounded, should taste a lot of men's individualities: in a way I believe in free love'" (p. 339).

There are numerous other points of resemblance to *Seven Poor Men of Sydney* and anticipations of *For Love Alone*—indeed *The Beauties and Furies* may

well have been useful in an unintentional way as a sorting ground for some of the later work. The counterpart of Catherine, "a woman of revolution without a barricade," is Oliver, "an arm-chair revolutionary." Oliver is, too, a sham socialist not unlike the Folliots, though they of course have more money. More importantly, Oliver is clearly an early version of Jonathan Crow, Teresa's idealized man in *For Love Alone,* who plays with her affection and loyalty in his cold, selfish way. Crow, like Oliver, fancies himself as an intellectual, but both are second-rate eclectics, shallow poseurs, who toy with people as with the ideas they manage to pick up from their reading. Another (minor) parallel occurs between Adam, Elvira's brother, and Quick, the American, who helps to rescue Teresa from Crow; both these men like to woo in erotic images drawn from Carew's poetry— indeed, Adam once had a mistress named Teresa. The search for love and freedom is far more moving in *For Love Alone,* partly because Teresa is a more interesting and attractive character than Elvira. This personal theme, nonetheless, accounts for the best parts of *The Beauties and Furies.*

IV. SOME CRITICAL OPINIONS

The *Sydney Morning Herald* reviewer received *The Beauties and Furies* fairly favorably.⁴ The "artificial style" which marked *Seven Poor Men of Sydney* and "a leaning towards redundancy" mar "a definite flair for delineation of character and a good sense of dialogue and situation." He says, rightly, that Elvira is well-drawn, an exasperating person but justly handled. He believes (taking refuge in vagueness here) that Oliver, Adam, Coromandel, and Marpurgo all run true to form and that the balance between them is well-preserved. Finally, he says that the book is too long, that the last third flags and that the author needs a firmer grasp of the principles of construction. Parts of this are surprising—notably the failure to observe any essential differences between Marpurgo and Coromandel on the one hand and the other leading characters, and the implication that *The Beauties and Furies* is as good a book as *Seven Poor Men of Sydney.*

Even more favorable are the comments by Roderick, in a brief survey of Christina Stead's work up to 1946, which begin: "The story is told to an obbligato of stinging satire and sharp irony. Its humour is marked by asperity and cynicism. Its dialogue, while at times marred by cloying richness of imagery or by metaphysical concettism resulting in needless obscurity, amply reveals the cultural background of the characters. Exuberance of expression in both dialogue and narrative runs parallel with a striking power of conveying emotional and psychic states in vivid prose."⁵

At the other extreme to Roderick's is the view put forward by Barnard Eldershaw, in an essay which deals with only the first three of Christina Stead's books, that

The Beauties and Furies is the one clear failure. Barnard Eldershaw is, I believe, closer to the truth though, characteristically, she overstates the case against the book. As indicated above, her argument is that Christina Stead's real talent lies in fantasy and therefore she cannot create living characters; *The Salzburg Tales* is the most successful because her limitations do not matter in his kind of work; *Seven Poor Men of Sydney* suffers from the application of "a fantastic, half-grotesque technique to a rational theme" but is saved from the full consequence of this because its weight is thrown on the social rather than the individual element in it. "But," Barnard Eldershaw continues, "in *The Beauties and Furies,* which is an intimate and individual study of a small group of people, the very life of the book depends upon its characterization. No amount of meretricious glitter can animate these sawdust puppets, so that for all its undiminished surface brilliance the book fails, and fails helplessly."[6]

V. The Problem of the Grotesques

The Beauties and Furies is by no means such an utter failure. For one thing Elvira is not a puppet; nor for that matter (though less well presented) is Oliver; even Blanche, a rather stagey creature, has her moments of individuality (as, indeed, Barnard Eldershaw later admits). The real trouble lies, rather, with characters like Marpurgo and (to a lesser extent) Coromandel, who do not function on the same level as the realistically presented characters. Elvira, Oliver, and Paul live fairly commonplace lives and the reader accepts them as they come—in realistic terms; what jolts him is the way Marpurgo, who seems to have come from an altogether different world, is brought into this area of ordinary human relationships and made to operate there. Marpurgo is such a grotesque that any attempts to explain his initial interference in the lives of ordinary people like Elvira and Oliver (even if we are prepared to accept jealousy of Oliver as a motive later on) are bound to fail. Perplexed by his continual obtrusiveness Elvira on one occasion asks him why he torments them, and gets this for an answer:

> "I'm a virtuoso in decadence, disintegration, mental necrosis: if I sit at home, I corrode myself: I can't work in a vacuum. Out, I gather little eschatological flowers to meditate in the hectic nights of the bacillus of Koch. Each of your sorrows is for me an hour of nepenthe: in that hour I build up an endoped dome of misery and failure, doubt and dissolution, ridicule and insufficiency beyond inferno, Eblis, opium, Xanadu. . . ."
>
> (pp. 295-96)

Marpurgo is a grotesque in the Romantic, fin-de-siècle, not the Dickensian, manner and once launched into speech he is apt to rave. Christina Stead refers in one place to "the learned farrago" he goes on with, but the reader can never be sure whether to take him seriously

or not; certainly, he is not presented in a consistently satirical way. In his relationship to Elvira and Oliver he emerges as a rather repulsive grub who feeds on the intimacies of other people's lives, leaving his slime upon them but never satisfying his appetite. Furthermore, and this is what makes him all the more difficult to accept, he is used as observer and commentator, a role for which his personality makes him unsuitable; the reader needs a more normal, reliable person as a guide.

Toward the end of the book Marpurgo bitterly denounces Oliver to his face as a weak, egoistic, cowardly, vain man, "an inkpotvaliant," and then goes on to describe himself as a somnambulist on the brink of insanity. This chapter is to end with the wildly fantastic scene at the Somnambulist Club, but not before Marpurgo has been required to pass judgment (on the novelist's behalf) upon Oliver.

> "You are a dead soul Oliver. You are fooling yourself with all these ideas of revolutions and these friendships with revolutionaries. It doesn't fool anyone but you. . . . You are corrupt like me. You can't be the workers' friend: you'd deceive them as you deceived your other friend—Dr. Western. You've got to be like me. You've got to be a mealymouth."
>
> (p. 323)

And as the book ends Marpurgo again sums up, this time on the relationship between Elvira and Oliver: "'She was just a spell of blessed self-forgetfulness for an academic drudge'" (p. 365).

If we detach Marpurgo from the surroundings of an everyday story and examine him as a kind of gargoyle, he represents quite an achievement of the imagination. He seems to have stepped straight from one of the frankly fantastic sequences in *The Salzburg Tales,* where he could have been in harmony with his surroundings, into a book which must depend finally on its analysis of a more or less commonplace personal relationship between a phoney scholar and a frustrated housewife. Marpurgo tells Paul in his characteristically high falutin way that he was attracted to Elvira because he saw in her an unusual woman in an unusual situation; but all the other evidence suggests that she is a rather ordinary woman caught in an awkward situation. She is certainly not the rare beauty Marpurgo or Oliver would have us believe; for this kind of exotic we have to turn to Coromandel.

A bizarre atmosphere surrounds the early Coromandel sequences and the attempt to link them with the Elvira—Oliver story creates a sense of incongruity. In themselves the scenes at Paindebled's have a grotesque brilliance which is startling, even fascinating, but they are acceptable only as isolated set-pieces. There is a similarly haunting, fantastic quality in the white grotesqueries of the Arnhem chapters in *Letty Fox* but there the poetic force of the scenes is functionally justified because it creates the disturbing and somewhat repellent atmosphere that accompanies the abnormal sensations felt by the heroine in this stage of her search for love. It is no coincidence that the romantic connotations of Coromandel's name should be conjured up by Marpurgo in a conversation where she is entranced by his extravagant talk even though she cannot understand it all. This part (Chapter VII) ends on a note of romantic riot with Coromandel in love not with but through Marpurgo—a love, consequently, that lies not in this world but in the strange and exciting world of dreams. Again it is surely no coincidence that the worst of the stylistic excesses are most likely to occur when Marpurgo is on the stage either in person or in imagination. "Marpurgo edged closer and leaned towards the other table, the lucent epidermis of his face pallid with excitement and self-intoxication; he had reached the rare corybantic hour that he struggled for, his low voice was splintered by the stridor of sorcery, he trembled with the internal dithyrambs of megalomania" (p. 239).

The criticism Nettie Palmer made of **Seven Poor Men of Sydney** applies with greater force to **The Beauties and Furies**—the characters (at least, certain of them) are in danger of being swamped, if not by "the author's personal utterance" then by a headlong rhetoric that makes its way into various segments of the book running over and obliterating their distinctive personal shapes. So it is that Oliver in the later stages begins to think and talk more like Marpurgo, as in his speech to Elvira about the mathematics of love and (even more so) in his speeches to Marpurgo in the final chapter. Here the luxuriance of style that Barnard Eldershaw complains of cloaks rather than expresses the feelings the character is supposed to have. The overindulgence in fantasy reaches one of its peaks in Chapter X in that curious episode where Marpurgo takes Oliver to the Somnambulist Club to listen to the debates of the God-intoxicated eccentrics, crackpots, and astrologers. The Somnambulist Club awakens memories of Swift's crazy Projectors in the Academy of Lagado, with this vital difference—that the Club has little relevance to the book as a whole, whereas the Academy bears directly on the satire of human folly and pride, which is central to *Gulliver's Travels*.[7]

Nevertheless the style of **The Beauties and Furies,** like the characterization, has its redeeming features. As in the previous books it is rich in imagery—vivid and arresting, if sometimes strained.

> Sara, looking at the people standing at the bus stop and on the boulevard seats, and at those visible through the glass screen on the café, thought she saw the scatterings of a population of Saint-Sebastians, of twisting torsos, slightly agonized, with briars twining round them. In the dark of the griping thorax, each carried a little aromatic pot of heart, from whose glossy thick leaves blood dripped. They were lonely, as she was.
>
> (p. 199)

Elsewhere it is incisive in the aphoristic manner favored in **House of All Nations**: "'All middle-class novels are about the trials of three, all upper-class novels about mass fornication, all revolutionary novels about a bad man turned good by a tractor'" (p. 130). And Marpurgo at times expresses himself with a brevity and a sarcasm that make his rhetorical extravaganzas sound all the more histrionic.

> Adam, who took a liqueur whenever it was offered to him, began to recite his own poetic drivel in vers libre, imitations of T. S. Elliot and D. H. Lawrence with a dash of Walt Whitman, a squeamish cocktail. He favoured them with a sonnet he had written to a girl at Leeds University "doing chemistry and bacteriology—I can only go to bed with an intelligence, I like to woo in the images of Donne and Carew."
>
> "Your parents spent a lot of money so that you could get hot in words of more than one syllable," remarked Marpurgo roughly.
>
> (p. 149)

The title derives from a remark by Marpurgo to Oliver. "'It's hard to leave Paris, eh? She has many beauties—and furies'" (p. 220). In his first meeting with Elvira Marpurgo tells her that lace was created for beauties and that she is a beauty who has never reigned, and towards the end of the book he refers to the three furies in Oliver's life as "Elvira, Coromandel, the occasional whore." The final echo of the title is a sardonic comment by the author herself in a passage describing Oliver's deterioration after Elvira's departure. "He noted with shame that his personal habits grew less fastidious: he attributed it to lack of morale, thus doing the work of the furies with the pleasure of supererogation, but it was due to lack of food" (p. 360).

VI. PARIS: THE FINANCIAL WORLD

Moving from **The Beauties and Furies** to **House of All Nations,** from love without money to love of money, is like going from Baudelaire to Balzac and for a novelist this is a step in the right direction. It is Paris again but no longer the enchanting city, home of artists and intellectuals, of lovers and prostitutes who (to Oliver's delight) quote Baudelaire while on the beat; it is the Paris of big business and finance, the city of the capitalist barons and the stock exchange speculators. It is Baudelaire's "Fourmillante cité, cité pleine de rêves"—with a difference, for now the dreams are those of the money-makers. Yet **House of All Nations** depicts a life in its own way almost as fantastic as that of Marpurgo's wildest imaginings despite its thoroughly realistic documentation of modern society. It is a kind of twentieth-century *Arabian Nights,* and the genie it conjures up is money.[8] The description of the Banker in *The Salzburg Tales* is an early sketch of Jules Bertillon in *House of All Nations.* To all appearances a man of the world, Jules lives out his fantasies in his own charming, irresponsible way, responding to calls on his humanity only when he feels in the mood—a prince in a modern fairy tale, who wants to surround himself with gold because it is such a lovely color. The final irony of this epic of money and money-making is that when Jules at last absconds, after having made and lost his millions several times over, the magistrates are unable to discover anything definite about the Banque Mercure, its assets and its operations. It is not as if a great solid structure has collapsed, but rather that the structure is now shown to be what it always was—a shell floating on air. Living in exile (and luxury) with his whole family in Estonia Jules is asked by reporters if he can account for the bank's closing, and his reply is: "'Oh, I should just say it closed from absence of liquidity: a not uncommon weakness with banks nowadays.'" And what happened to the rest of the money? "'You know how those things are! The money just went!'" (p. 772). Mercurial is certainly the word for Jules and his organization.

House of All Nations is a long, densely packed novel of 787 pages, which through its account of the day-to-day life at the bank, Bertillon Frères, seeks to describe the whole business of money-making and its attendant robbery and jobbery in the Paris of the early 1930's. Many books have been written about the search for wealth and power, about misers and millionaires, but few can compare with *House of All Nations* for its authentic and detailed knowledge of what actually goes on behind the scenes, where plans are laid, hunches seized upon, and transactions pushed through. Jules's way of running a bank is, to say the least, unconventional—in fact, he has operated illegally for years on a contre-partie basis, which means, simply, playing the market with his clients' stock in the hope of making big profits. Some of his wealthy clients know or suspect this but are prepared to trust his cool nerve and his genius for gambling. His personality and reputation attract all sorts of people (with all sorts of financial projects) to the bank to do business or just to talk money. Jules is the most important character, but *House of All Nations* is not a novel built round a central figure and treating a certain occupation or social group. Money is a great leveller and in *House of All Nations* there is room for all sorts and classes of men: merchants, economists, lawyers, accountants, bankers, clerks, managers, clients, tellers, customers' men, typists, magistrates, cashiers, industrial magnates, deputies, jurists, brokers and rentiers—and a more miscellaneous bunch of secret go-betweens, shysters, imaginary employees, swindlers, stalking-horses, prostitutes, playboys, servants, family cadgers, society figures, writers, artists, Communists,

cronies, philanderers, and mistresses galore. It is Balzacian in its precise observation, in its accumulation of detail, and in its insistence upon the driving force of human obsession. A novel conceived on such a scale will obviously pose formal problems.

VII. *HOUSE OF ALL NATIONS*: STRUCTURE AND PLOT

The following passage from a review Christina Stead once wrote of Louis Aragon's *The Century Was Young* touches on the characteristics and, by implication, the difficulties of the long novel in our day. The analysis of *House of All Nations* that follows it will show how she has tried to avoid the dangers, as she sees them, of this kind of book.

> Very interesting are two characteristics of long modern novels, exhibited also in this one. All modern artists seem strangely to feel that they are near Judgment Day. They are making summaries of their times and some sink their craft under a load of detail, like the great Joyce and the little Romains; and many, many give us novels of Begat, where we are obliged to run the course from great-grandfather to great-grandson, with the idea of explaining why we are where we are to-day; as though it were necessary to start with Pliny's maps to sail to Japan today. As a result, the hero-with-the-notebook has also come to the fore, dignified brother of the star-reporter-gangbuster.[9]

How is the novelist to organize great masses of material? Thackeray solves the problem in his panoramic *Vanity Fair* by placing two heroines in society and playing off one's fluctuating fortunes against the other's, so that when Becky is on the crest of a wave, Amelia is down in a trough and vice versa. As in *Seven Poor Men of Sydney* Christina Stead has tried in *House of All Nations* to devise the kind of form the book needs. Instead of chopping the material into longish chapter blocks of about the same length she casts it into a number of separate scenes (104 in all) which vary in length according to their importance between two and forty-two pages. Since there is no attempt to construct a series of complicated interlocking stories in the Dickens manner in order to bring numerous characters into relationship with one another, the material can come through in the form of scenes without the jerkiness that would become apparent in a more closely plotted novel. The only connection the minor characters need to have is the cash nexus which links them to the Banque Mercure. This, of course, would not suffice for the main characters; a small group, roughly equal in importance, is to the fore throughout—the Bertillon brothers, Jules and William, the bank economist Michel Alphendéry, the wealthy Dr. Jacques Carrière, the grain merchant Henri Léon, the customers' man Aristide Raccamond and his ruthless, scheming wife Marianne. It is with these that the narrative is concerned and the story itself is simple enough.

The first scene introduces Raccamond, middle-aged, ambitious, and well meaning, in his old-maidish manner. Raccamond was once customers' man at Claude Brothers private bank, recently liquidated, and is now trying to worm his way into Bertillon Frères. Despite Jules's initial distrust of him Raccamond gets the position he wants, partly because he succeeds in persuading Henri Léon to become one of Jules's clients. Jules's instincts about Raccamond were right, as the concluding stages of the novel prove.

In the meanwhile the wealthy Carrière, whose favors Raccamond has been cultivating for some time, comes upon the scene. Carrière is Jules's most bitter enemy. He is a dissolute homosexual, whose jealousy of Jules stems from their schooldays together. Carrière is bent on destroying Jules. In the course of a business talk Jules rashly bets Carrière that the pound sterling will not fall below 122 francs. An agreement is signed whereby if it does Jules will pay Carrière at that rate on all drafts submitted. It so happens that a careless phrase in the document gives Carrière the whip hand, for when sterling does fall (as Jules's most reliable friends predicted to him that it would) Jules finds himself obliged to pay out large regular sums in connection with a brewery in England that has come into Carrière's possession. And these payments will have to continue unless Jules can disprove Carrière's assertion that the brewery has been sold.[10] Carrière bleeds Jules mercilessly, the European slump sets in and Jules, faced with a copy of the agreement with Carrière and letters concerning payments which William at last gets hold of, is forced to admit the truth he has been denying to his brother and Alphendéry for months past.

Matters are now brought to a head by Carrière's toady Raccamond who, genuinely worried about the security of his customers' investments, discovers private ledgers at the bank's Brussels office which reveal the extent of Jules's contrepartie operations over the years. Having bribed his way into possession of these ledgers Raccamond goes almost berserk in rage and self-righteous indignation and tries to blackmail Jules into restoring the share positions of his clients and giving him a partnership with special privileges, which would make him virtual controller of the bank. Raccamond, spurred on by Carrière and Marianne, manages by the violence of his behavior to antagonize almost everybody involved, though (ironically) his cause is basically just. For the first time in his life Jules is thoroughly rattled; he makes half-hearted plans to strike back but he is losing his grip. He has by now turned from his best friends, William and Alphendéry, and has sunk large sums in a crazy aviation combine started by a group of young aristocrats who fail to bring in the money they are supposed to provide, and finally takes the step he has been talking about for months by closing the bank and clearing out with all the money he can lay his hands on.

The consequent public enquiry gets nowhere; people refuse to talk, records are destroyed, broils develop between clients; most people prefer a Jules to a Raccamond anyhow. All the remaining assets are disappearing and, by the end, the Banque Mercure S. A. creditors are paying 208 lawyers. Alphendéry, now working for Léon, receives a telegram from William to say Jules has disappeared, and asking Alphendéry to try to trace him. But no one knows where Jules has gone, and the book ends:

> His old friends, and even the most pertinacious of the creditors, hoped that he went and made immediately a shining new fortune with which he would come home presently to flash in their eyes. For he had by now benefited by the immorality as well as by the mythomania of the financial world and had begun to be relacquered in the minds of the rich. For others, though, it is true, he still remained a rankle and a hurt, the charmer who deceived.

> (p. 787)

House of All Nations is Christina Stead's greatest intellectual achievement—its knowledge of the workings of international finance and its revelation of the fraud, the ruthlessness, the energy, the sheer luck, and the genius that go into money-making, are by any standards remarkable. So detailed is this knowledge in the account of Léon's great scheme for making a fortune out of wheat deals that the reader almost needs to be a professional economist himself to follow the incredibly complex maneuvers, even with the aid of Alphendéry's patient explanations to Jules. This is to say that *House of All Nations* will never be as widely read and enjoyed as some of the other books. But for all its intellectual qualities it is a deeply felt novel too. It is less idiosyncratic in style and tone than its predecessors. One instance of the change is the overwhelming preponderance of dialogue—dialogue, furthermore, of the naturalistic rather than expressionistic kind, in keeping with the method of scenic presentation. Here Christina Stead shows she can write dialogue that establishes character by differentiation. Léon is a superbly realized figure, so too are Raccamond and Jules. If Alphendéry does not measure up to them it is, possibly, because of the double role of actor-raisonneur allotted to him. On the question of dialogue one of the early reviewers, Edwin Berry Burgum makes the point that the volume of talk is in itself a protective device. "When every contradictory impulse is laid bare, no onlooker can tell for certain which will get translated into action." But, Burgum says, speech and action become one and he goes on to quote a remark made by the Comtesse de Voigrand to Jules: "'There are poor men in this country who cannot be bought; the day I found that out, I sent my gold abroad.'" And he comments: "This avowal of her social idealism is not an abstract witticism from Rochefoucauld, but the recollection of an order to her banker."[11]

VIII. Links with the Early Books

House of All Nations is precisely the sort of book that Barnard Eldershaw, judging by her essay, would believe Christina Stead incapable of writing. Today the critic, with the wisdom of hindsight if all else is lacking, ought to be able to observe that its difference from the two previous novels, striking though it may be, is one more of manner and degree than of basic themes and attitudes. A critical view of individuals and of society at large is present in both *Seven Poor Men of Sydney* and *The Beauties and Furies,* and irony colors many of the stories in *The Salzburg Tales.* These elements combine to create the dominant tone of *House of All Nations.* The most characteristic feature of Christina Stead's fiction as a whole is not the fantasy stressed by her early critics but its emotional intensity, the concentrated gaze that sees through appearances and illusions. It is this uncompromising honesty which will help the best of her work to endure—it makes possible the unforgettable Jonathan Crow and Sam Pollit and it gives conviction to the sufferings of the women, Teresa and Henrietta, who are bound to them. This intensity is first fully experienced in *House of All Nations.* Where in modern fiction could we find anything to surpass the controlled ferocity of "A Stuffed Carp," one of the most memorable scenes in a book that is Jonsonian in its exposure of greed, graft, and exploitation?

In addition to an early sketch of Jules in the figure of the Banker, *The Salzburg Tales* also provides us with an embryonic Henri Léon in the person of Henry Van Laer in **"The Amenities."** Van Laer, like Léon, has a rapid, unnatural way of speaking and uses frequent, impetuous gestures. Again like Léon he has an insatiable appetite for women. The Léon character, the dynamic, untutored money-making genius seems to have fascinated our author; he turns up again, with certain modifications, in the protagonist of *A Little Tea, a Little Chat,* Robbie Grant. Furthermore, the main woman in Léon's floating harem, the shrewd, calculating blonde Mrs. Weyman, foreshadows the larger-scale portrait of Barbara, Robbie's blondine. A final link occurs in Alphendéry—economist, leftist, a student (unlike Oliver) with compassion instead of ink in his veins, supremely articulate, who might almost be the Baruch Mendelssohn of *Seven Poor Men of Sydney* moved from the United States to Paris and given a European upbringing.

IX. The Title

All nationalities come to the Banque Mercure and so it is in an obvious way a house of all nations; the critics who have discussed the book seem to assume that the title refers merely to the Bertillon bank. But the title phrase occurs only twice in the text and each time the allusion is to the high-class Parisian brothel also referred to in Nathanael West's *A Cool Million.* The phrase is first used in *Scene Two* where William says to Alphendéry that (despite Jules's opposition) they would be foolish to reject Raccamond because of his bad reputation of crawling to the rich and serving their vices. "'We've got a man to buy tickets for the bouts for clients: I don't see why we can't have a man who knows the prices at the House of All Nations!'" (p. 29).

It occurs again about half-way through the book when Léon tells Alphendéry at the bank that he has lost a batch of important letters in the House of All Nations or, maybe, at his hotel (p. 388). The bank and the brothel are equated—in both, man's concupiscence is given free rein.

X. Jules

Jules has no doubts as to what the motive force behind a bank is. "'It's easy to make money. You put up the sign BANK and someone walks in and hands you his money. The façade is everything.'" This is a characteristic remark; Jules is a thorough skeptic (if not a cynic). Despite his affection for Alphendéry (which, be it noted, does not survive the collapse of the bank) Jules is unable to understand Alphendéry's attachment to humanitarian and political ideals. Jules, in the Balzac manner, is a character built around one dominating idea—the notion that informs his whole philosophy and way of life is that money is the measure of all things. Yet there are other facets to his personality; he is by nature charming and gay, generous and irresponsible, knowing that he can afford to throw his money about because he can always make another fortune.

Like Arthur Miller's Willie Loman he wants not only to be liked but also to be well-liked, and being self-centered is prone to find in his friends indifference and insults where none exist. He is quick-witted and shrewd, but without an ounce of intellect in his make-up—that is why he cannot understand Alphendéry. Like all gamblers he is superstitious and given to hunches and therefore apt to be taken in by flatterers, especially those like the foolish and incompetent Bomba who have the actor's panache.

Jules is an incorrigible liar and a self-deceiver—in time of crisis he is the despair of William and Alphendéry, who do all the hard work and try to save the bank from the consequences of his folly and whose only reward is ingratitude. Furthermore, like all true egoists he can be nasty and petty. In pique he ruins Léon's great wheat scheme, which has the promise of fortunes, because he has not thought of it himself or, more accurately, because he does not really understand it and could never have invented such a brilliant plan himself. Life for Jules is a masquerade but he revels in it and in his best moods his enjoyment is infectious. This is his strength—he dominates by his charm.

Jules is a successful creation because the attractive and the repellent qualities lie side by side with perfect congruity in the one character. Alphendéry's affection for him is thoroughly credible even though he is disturbed by Jules's lack of moral responsibility. Alphendéry sees in Jules a creative talent corrupted and more than once pleads with him to abandon his fantasies and come back to the earth. "Fantasies" is the right word, for Alphendéry with true insight senses that Jules does not really want all the money he is continually dreaming of; as the author says, ". . . he cared not so much for money as for moneymaking, and, when he had got the hang of moneymaking, not so much the making of money as the endless field for speculation and fantasy it yielded him" (p. 597).

A life given over to the pursuit of riches seems to Alphendéry like chasing phantoms, because riches as such have no social value; a true socialist, Alphendéry looks for wealth, which is productive. Jules likes to consider himself a magician; he believes (or says) that big money is won, never earned, but Alphendéry pricks this sort of bubble-blowing easily: "What a race of liars you all are! . . . You work day and night at your schemes and then you love to pretend it's all pure luck; you just lie on your back with your mouth open and luck throws in *pâté de foie gras*'" (p. 311). The idea is significant, nonetheless, of the fantasy Jules indulges in.

XI. THE DIALOGUE

The verbal energy and inventiveness, which takes some strange forms in the previous books, is now being poured into highly articulate dialogue and it is the dialogue which gives vitality and interest to the principal characters. Rich and copious, their speech never lets them down. Since Jules has been under discussion, passages relating to him will serve doubly as illustrations. Here is Jules, in the scene already quoted from:

> "I'm not an old maid playing patience. I want big money and what have I got round me? Savers, hoarders, go-gentlies, abacus gentry back in the carpetbags of the Middle Ages, squirrels, ants, census takers, pennybank campaigners—installment-plan robbers, shilling-a-week shortchangers, Saturday tillshakers, busfare embezzlers, dime defalcators—you're as bad as Etienne. You're honest. It's no good hiding it. All your philosophy hasn't got you farther than scraping and pinching, like the knifegrinder's wife. If you start little, you remain little. If you start with bells on, you end with bells on. I know what I want. I only want to hear from you how it's to be done. You're my technical expert, Michel. I employ you for that. Go to Maître Lemaître or Beaubien and find out how to do it. That's all I'm asking you."
>
> (p. 201)

Here is Jules again, talking to Raccamond, who is worried about the bank's reputation:

> "Raccamond, every woman is a whore, but the whores are the ones who never learned the game: every banker is a poker shark but the Eddie McCaheys are the poor fellows who don't get away with it. What is a whore? A poor girl who never had a chance to go into business with a man and set up a little home of her own. The same with the little swindlers. I'm sorry for them. Haven't you got a heart, Raccamond? Are you all for profit, dignity, reputation? Have you forgotten what sort of business you're in? You'll turn into a crank if you're not careful. And I don't have cranks round me, Raccamond. Listen, there's only one rule in business. Anyone's money is good. That's my rule. When money walks in the door, takes off its hat and says, 'Here I am: I want to live with you,' the least of the polite things you can do, is to say, 'Good day; take a seat.' How else are we to get business? You're crazy if you're waiting for clean money. Did you ever hear of clean money?"
>
> (p. 309)

And, finally, William on Jules, who in the bank's crisis has broken his promise not to gamble on the Paris market:

> "Of course, Jules doesn't know how to tell the truth; he doesn't know what it is. I don't think he knows his own name. He lies about it to himself at night. My name's Evarist Zugger, or let's say, Peter Mugger or better Timothy Hugger: I have twenty million francs, or 150,000,000 francs; I've sold short eighty-five thousand shares yesterday and two million today, that makes a handful of fireworks! What a splendid firebug I am! I'm a genius and my name is Aristide Scarface, I'm a *nervi* from Marseille, I'm Popoff the anarchist, I'm getting the White Russians on Tardieu's payroll, what a smart fellow I am! That's Jules's conversation with himself at night. An eagle of finance who only lays duck eggs, and who doesn't know whether he's a mocking bird or a vulture."
>
> (p. 581)

It is this kind of rhetoric which has taken over from the more formalized poetic monologue discussed in Chapter 2. Occasionally it runs into set speeches of great length where matters of central concern are being elaborated, as in the tremendous denunciation of the money grubbers by Adam Constant, teller, poet, and Communist in *Scene Eight*, "J'Accuse." This might be taken to include a statement of Christina Stead's purpose (or part of it) in writing **House of All Nations.**

> "There are no men in this bank," remarked Constant, "only money galls of one color and another shape: only an infection of monsters with purses at their waists that we wait upon and serve. . . . My dream is, that one day I will get them all down, I will leave them on record."
>
> (p. 80)

Constant's attack has the cumulative force of a Shavian tirade.

XII. ALPHENDÉRY'S ROLE

We should not identify the author with Constant. Adam's is one view, a perfectly intelligible one, of an actor involved in the drama. Alphendery, on the other hand, though also an actor in the same drama, is clearly more detached emotionally than Constant and, as befits his role, a more reliable critic and commentator. It is to Alphendéry that we must look (perhaps because he himself is caught in an ambiguous moral position) for the book's ethical center.

As a socialist Alphendéry is, of course, opposed to the sordid and soulless business of private profiteering and sympathetic toward Constant and Jean Frère, the Communist writer and idealist. It never ceases to amaze Jules that Alphendéry should be so much more concerned with making money for the bank than for himself. Alphendéry could do with more money, for he has a divorced wife and an aging mother to think of. Accordingly, when Jules does bring off a big coup he makes Alphendéry a handsome gift. But the opportunities that lie to hand do not even tempt Michel. As he says to Jules: "'You see, I'm not preaching humanity to you. You have to be born to love of humanity, and trained to it, the way you have to be born to money love'" (p. 198).

When times get bad Alphendéry urges Jules to cut free, pay his creditors (to Jules a monstrous suggestion) and set up with him and William in some more reputable enterprise where they could still make money with their knowledge and wits. Alphendéry's principles, based on personal and social responsibility, are clear and honorable, yet he does to some extent compromise them simply by working for a private bank which must help to perpetuate the system of capitalism. Furthermore, though he has scruples and Jules none, Alphendéry (for reasons of loyalty, affection and even pure fun) is prepared to tag along with many of the bank's doubtful practices.[12] Still, though he enjoys the work and some of the trickery that goes on, he is well aware of his dilemma. He would sooner be elsewhere and when matters get worse he keeps on pleading with Jules to release him. When Jules asks him why he is in this game Alphendéry says it is because he cannot abandon his dependents to poverty for the sake of his principles and because, in the tradition of his family, he has been in finance since he was a boy. When his father died he became the secretary of an Alsatian millionaire, a pro-Dreyfusite and Marxist. So Michel became a fervent Marxist too. "'You see, I have always been a revolutionary at ease, the shadow of a rich man. It would take a violent effort of will to wrench myself out of that setting, and I suppose I will some day. If I go round much longer with Jean Frère I certainly will'" (p. 353). As it happens Alphendéry ends up with Léon—another compromise.

Alphendéry is not only a lucid expounder of technical problems but also a skilful campaigner, as his brilliant performance in court against the pompous fools Rosenkrantz and Guildenstern demonstrates (*Scene Seventy-five*). He tells Stewart, a London broker, all for Christianity and the Empire, that he favors "socialist organization" and, spurred on by Stewart's obtuseness, adds "'I mean a revolution to wipe us all out, all of us who scrounge on others and ravage the wealth of the world—you and Jules Bertillon and me. We must all go'" (p. 328). But in his calmer moments he knows the millennium is not just around the corner.

Alphendéry has a sense of history and this makes his the most comprehensive vision in the book. As early as *Scene Two* he expresses the notion, which the rest of the action is by implication to confirm, that life goes on whatever the corruption that surrounds it, that money-making organizations constitute one of the realities underlying social change, and, indeed, that revolution itself produces new markets. It is this sort of observation that makes *House of All Nations* more than an indictment of capitalism. Alphendéry is, in fact, an exception to the remark about economists made by Oliver Fenton in one of his rare moments of insight.

> "Most of our economists, even our best theoretical Marxians . . . even those who write most intelligently about politics and human nature, write irritating polemic platitudes when it comes to business, because they have never been in it. Business-men are not mannequins of the class war, and individual businesses are not patterns of the decline of capitalism."[13]

XIII. LÉON AND RACCAMOND

Though possessed by the same mania as Jules, both Léon and Raccamond are entirely different personalities from him and from each other. The crude, swaggering Léon domineering and impetuous, exudes vitality. Alphendéry comes to admire him for his quick wits, and the knowledge and skill with which he conducts his business, qualities largely obscured by Léon's meanness in small things, his bewildering, disjointed speech and the almost incredible naïvety of his courting of women. Léon is, in fact, a good judge of character; he appreciates Alphendéry's worth, and quickly sums up the weaknesses of both Jules and Raccamond. He is one of those fictional characters who seem to embody some natural force that guarantees the appropriateness of what they do and say.[14] Not the least of Christina Stead's achievements here is the way Léon becomes, irresistibly, one of the most attractive characters in the whole book. He does not improve morally (that is not the point), but he grows on the reader, for all his roguery, crudity, and boisterousness, as a figure rendered with an artistic sympathy and understanding. He comes through more successfully than his counterpart Robbie Grant of *A Little Tea, a Little Chat,* partly because the characterization conveys this sense of creative delight and partly because, unlike Grant, he is not on stage all the time and so his antics do not become tiresome.

Aristide Raccamond is the fourth of this notable group of large-scale portraits and further proof of Christina Stead's advance in powers of characterization by the time she came to write *House of All Nations.* Once again the character is seen in the round with that artistic objectivity which blends detachment and sympathy. A most unattractive fellow in many ways, a spy and a flatterer, a craven always ready to throw blame on others, an ambitious man who lacks the unashamed drive and the ruthless calculation of his wife Marianne, and who needs her to urge him on, petty and vindictive when he gets the upper hand, Raccamond is still no monster. He is a neurotic who wants rewards for his more or less honest labors, who feels an acute responsibility for the clients who have entrusted their money to him, and who is aghast to learn the extent to which Jules's banking practice affronts conventional morality. The paradox about Raccamond is that, though his behavior is to the contrary, he sincerely believes that there is more to life than money. In a moment of genuine bewilderment he confesses as much to Marianne, but her task is always to win him to the opposite point of view. She is the clear-headed and single-minded one. Raccamond's better feelings contribute to his downfall. He becomes ludicrous and repellent at the end but this is caused by his becoming practically insane with worry, fear, and frustration as he sees his life's work crumbling and all the chances of getting control of the Banque Mercure slipping away. A tougher, self-disciplined man could have won others to stand by his just causes. It is typical of Raccamond that he should believe Alphendéry, the Jew, is the evil genius behind the bank, whereas Alphendéry is more honest than most and has always taken Raccamond's part in arguments with Jules. It is typical of Alphendéry that, on learning Raccamond has stolen the Brussels books, he should say: "'I don't think he's a real blackmailer. . . . I think he's terribly startled at what he's found out'" (p. 645).[15] It is the mixture of Raccamond's motives that gives force and conviction to his frantic behavior in the final stages of the story.

Raccamond is most appropriately named; he brings ruin to the bank. Jules looks upon him as an evil omen from the start. Raccamond even boasts of his destructive power when he is putting the pressure on Jules: "'Raccamond. . . . think of the name: it's going to be synonymous with ruin'" (p. 715). Indeed, names often signify character in *House of All Nations.* Jules is associated with the Banque Mercure, and as an actor says: "'Bertillon is altogether the personage of the old-world Mercury!'" (p. 598). Jules's toady Bomba is full of bombast, and the names Rosencrantz and Guildenstern, Constant and Frère, speak for themselves. Since

Michel's surname is taken, presumably, from the millionaire whose secretary he becomes, it is perhaps not too fanciful to say that it suggests he is living an assumed role—certainly he regards his job as a form of slavery and feels his basic allegiance is to Frère rather than to Jules.

XIV. STYLE

An American reviewer praised *House of All Nations* as a masterpiece which in its savage satire of "the principle of money" brings up to date the theme of Balzac's *La Comédie Humaine.*[16] Not all the reviewers approved: one Australian critic parroted Barnard Eldershaw's "rich and strange" to describe its style—a manifest absurdity because there is nothing in the writing here that is at all comparable to the exotic and luxuriant qualities that Barnard Eldershaw found in the earlier books.[17] The style of *House of All Nations* is far more disciplined and matter-of-fact; it is scored by a sharp and often savage wit and irony, as befits the tough-mindedness that lies behind it. Its characteristic bite is suggested by this description of Stewart:

> An English broker visiting Jules Bertillon both for personal and bank business, cool as a cucumber, in appearance like a gray, superfine badger bristle in a Piccadilly shaving brush, seeming to despise faintly but wholesomely the excitable Gaul, bared his small red lips over his rat teeth and passed upstairs.
>
> (p. 235)

Or this of the employee in one of the tellers' cubicles:

> In the first of these, seated on a high chair, her rosy beauty always framed in that green air, strange behind gilt bars, like a madonna materialized in prison, sat the customers' mail girl, Mlle. Armelle Paëz. She watched and meditated, smiled and got invitations to dinner from all the high-stepping male clients.
>
> (p. 108)

William's speech accords with the general tone of the book. His brand of ironical poetry is often evoked by the exasperating behavior of Jules:

> "I hope he'll come to his senses after this: instead of spending his life with idiotic playboys. So there they are: Prince Jules in a private suite, Claire-Josèphe engaging nurses and bringing surgeons from Paris, Bomba blowing his own kazoo on a platform of gold, Raccamond that great jelly and his Diana-wife hunting in open season on our preserves."
>
> (p. 461)

Finally here is William, irritably, to Raccamond:

> "What do you want now? You've gouged our eyes out, slit our ears, bit our noses, sold our tripes for cat's meat: what else? We've only got our underwear."
>
> (p. 711)

XV. LENGTH AND SCOPE

The Australian critic referred to above also complains that Christina Stead "allows herself to be preoccupied and side-tracked by an infinite variety of queer characters and incidents intensely interesting in themselves, no doubt, but distracting to the reader who seeks, in vain, a stable thread which might lead him out of the maze."[18] It is not true that *House of All Nations* is a confusing book—it has a firm theme and a clear narrative line, and the collapse of the bank (toward which the whole book moves from the start with Raccamond operating in the very first scene) is obviously the "comprehensible climax" that this critic was unable to find. This remark does, however, raise the question of the book's length and scope. Here personal responses will vary, but some comparisons may help to put the matter into perspective.

House of All Nations is a long and densely packed novel, built on the same scale as, say *Pendennis* and *Bleak House,* which did not seem too long to Victorian readers. It is shorter than some of the best-sellers of the twentieth century, for example, *Anthony Adverse* and *Gone with the Wind.* It is certainly an easier book to read and absorb than *The Ambassadors,* or *Ulysses,* or the much shorter *The Sound and the Fury,* all of which have attained the status of modern classics. It has an intensity that some readers would, no doubt, find disturbing; the novelist has seen so much to support the view of life that she presents and she wants to include all the evidence. *House of All Nations* is one of those novels which hammer away obsessively at their themes. It is money, money, money on every page, just as in Richardson's *Clarissa* (a far longer book) it is sex, sex, sex; perhaps novelists really possessed by their subjects are bound to write long books. Christina Stead happens to be this kind of writer—the deeply committed, concentrating, obsessive. And it is this that accounts for the most powerful of her effects in books like *House of All Nations, For Love Alone,* and *The Man Who Loved Children.*

If *House of All Nations* is too long it is because of the hosts of minor figures who swarm over its pages. It is such a rich book, so full of observation and invention that superfluity is a price that has to be paid. Sometimes the characters develop away from the initial sketch given of them. A minor instance of this occurs with Carrière—of some significance, perhaps, as he is the least convincing of the main characters. When he first appears Carrière is described as a "dumpy, red-haired young man." A few scenes later he still has the same arrogant look that is specified in the first description but is now tall and blond. More important, because it seems to show a character taking over from the author, is the case of Davigdor Schicklgrüber, the ugly blond lout, stalking-horse for Lord Zinovraud, the multimillionaire.

The main point about Schicklgrüber is that his apparent stupidity and brutality is probably a cloak for his shrewdness and an aid in collecting women and valuable business information for his master. So we are told, when he first appears, "Davigdor had a vocabulary of two or three hundred words at the most and a lot of those were primitive Anglo-Saxon, also common in low German" (p. 372). And his early speech endorses this description. But within two or three pages Schicklgrüber is talking almost as eloquently as the Bertillons or Alphendéry:

> "Jules, go the right way about it. For instance, you're going to have trouble with this louse Carrière. This self-decorated Christmas tree Carrière has got the first infirmity of feeble minds. He's telling it round that he's going to buy a newspaper. Now, you keep away from all that and you'll win hands down. Never own a newspaper; own journalists: never buy the news-services. Just pay a whisper: never involve a politician—he'll let you down or be let out. And compromise: don't fight."
>
> (pp. 375-76)

It might be argued that Jules himself gets out of hand occasionally. When in a good mood he has an infectious sense of humor which is always running off into fantasy. In a discussion as to the advisability of closing down the bank (a favorite topic) Jules prattles on:

> "We'll scatter and then we'll meet again at a fixed place on a fixed date. We can fly. William still has a pilot's license. Alphendéry gets air-sick but he's necessary because he can hand out the flapdoodle to passport officials and he looks like a Bulgarian or a Spaniard or something. By the way, Michel. Your friends down in the Communist Party must know a lot about faking passports. Why don't you go down and get us a wad of false passports, for Claire and the boys and the twins and William, you, and me."
>
> (p. 211)

Here he is simply enjoying himself and the passage is in character. So too are the hilariously fantastic plans for making money that he talks about in *Scene Forty-seven*; smuggling tobacco into France through naval submarine officers, flooding the market with a new peach brandy, and reviving Monte Carlo by means of a bargain between Jews and the Pope-financial returns in exchange for a Papal bull making divorce easy in the municipality. There seems no limit to his gaiety and inventiveness. But what are we to make of the vicious schemes he puts forward in *Scene Forty-six* for buying up land in some poor country and going to live among the peasants in order to exploit them in truly medieval fashion? Here Jules is said to be in earnest but, even allowing that he is supposed to be an admirer of all kinds of money-makers, the tone (at least) of these speeches seems to jar. It is as if he is being forced into a more villainous role than he deserves.[19]

Despite such inconsistencies, *House of All Nations* is an impressive book. Perhaps the finest of its scenes is

"The Stuffed Carp," which for devastating irony and mordant comedy is unsurpassed by anything else Christina Stead has ever written.

XVI. AN IRONIC MASTERPIECE: "THE STUFFED CARP"

This magnificent scene describes one of the regular dinner visits paid by the Raccamonds to the Hallers, rich clients of Aristide's with an obsession about property of all kinds and about food. Although Haller has not yet brought him much business, Raccamond cannot afford to neglect such a customer and so he regularly comes along to endure the monstrous feasts Madame Haller loves to prepare. The entertaining of the Raccamonds does not spring from friendship or liberality; it is an occasion Haller uses to air his opinions on public affairs and to drain Aristide of useful financial information, and Madame Haller to extract envy and flattery from her less fortunate guests. In her hands, especially, the dinner party becomes an act of tyranny masked by sweetness, a form of display and an occasion for domination. She has piles of priceless possessions, which she can never bear to use, hoarded away—exquisite linen and slips, embroidery and hand-made lace purchased from humble women who have given years and their eyesight to its creation, carpets, curtains, shawls and robes. These and their valuable furniture, which is stored away in case war or revolution should suddenly break out in Europe, are investments more solid than gold.

Madame Haller forces massive quantities of food upon the sycophantic Raccamonds, who are expected to praise everything extravagantly. The feast begins with servings of chicken liver washed down by glass after glass of Cointreau. Then comes the pièce de résistance, the huge stuffed carp; this, with the aid of chartreuse to stimulate the gastric juices, they manage to consume. Now comes the wine, kept for years (and so another cause for self-congratulation) and its flavor gone; this is followed by a miscellany of port, peaches and cream, nuts, sugar, butter, chocolates and honey. Haller at this point starts cheerfully on sausage and Burgundy, and Aristide, protesting, has to follow suit. Tortured by indigestion, green and gasping for breath, Raccamond struggles to the window and stages a partial recovery, only to return to the fray and find tea being served with the chocolates. Madame Haller manages finally to force a splendid Doyenne de Comice pear upon Aristide, specially bought because he needs fresh fruit for his digestion.

Two strands of conversation weave their way through this promiscuous guzzling and gorging. There is Madame Haller's continual fuss about the purity of the food they eat—only one special brand of tinned peaches, a specially prepared butter sent by a country

producer, and so on. The other strand concerns Europe and financial matters, talk that provides a counterpointed comment to the feast. Apparently unaware of the implications, Haller can say:

> "Nothing arouses hate for the ruling classes like excessive taxes and an excessive burden of internal debt. Lenin saw this. He acted as a cathartic; the ruling classes in Russia had stuffed themselves to bursting on interest. You see, the financial papers enable the people to see the Fat People eating."

Raccamond asks, "'You mean the financiers?'" and Haller goes on:

> "Yes I call them the Fat People. Now, human nature teaches us, we know by instinct, that there is something wrong when five per cent of the people stuff and ninety-five per cent have almost nothing to eat and no money to put into interest-bearing bonds at all."

(p. 289)

The Hallers are aghast to learn that their guests love a *pâté de foie gras* which they get in tins from the Dordogne—tinned food is bad enough (when others buy it), but don't they know that *pâté* is made from the diseased livers of overfed geese? The Hallers could not possibly eat it.

Food is the metaphor of this scene. This account of a dinner party is a far more effective denunciation of acquisitiveness and greed, of self-indulgence and hypocrisy, of servility and self-righteousness, than a whole volume of sermons. Fielding often uses similar imagery for satiric as well as purely humorous purposes, but the substance and tone of "A Stuffed Carp" is closer to Swift's "A Modest Proposal."[20] The title is especially appropriate—the carp is omnivorous and so are the people who stuff themselves with food like this. And the reader is free to follow the secondary implications if he cares to.[21]

The experience of the evening leads Marianne to reflect upon money as she and Aristide are on their way home.

> "There's no subject so rich in ideas as Money." Aristide grunted. "I'm thinking," went on Marianne tenderly, with a richer tone than she usually used, "that money is a very pure thing in its way; that's why the Hallers have such curious habits. They have nothing more to do, they do not even need more money—they have enough for avarice. Now they are looking for the absolute. They caught that from their gold bars. It is an absolute. People have such a delicate love for money that if you speak jealously of it or of those who own it, all the dirt falls back on you: people take you for a miserable, poor-spirited person."

(p. 300)

This is a key passage in the book and it confirms the view of *House of All Nations* as a twentieth-century version of the search for the absolute—a theme made memorable by Balzac in his story of Balthazar Claes (*La Recherche de l'Absolu*), who in his zeal to discover the philosopher's stone destroys himself and brings ruin upon his family. In *Scene Seventeen*, one of the few occasions where the author directly addresses the reader, the same idea is explored and this conclusion is reached: "In the old days those that sought the absolute tried to make gold: our own conception is not very different" (p. 136).

Notes

1. *Australian Women's Weekly,* March 9, 1935.

2. The epithet "Munchausen" first occurs in *Seven Poor Men of Sydney,* p. 161, where it is applied by Joseph to Withers.

3. *The Beauties and Furies* (New York, 1936), p. 95.

4. May 22, 1936.

5. *Southerly,* VII, 2 (1946), 88.

6. Barnard Eldershaw, p. 159.

7. The most favorable opinion I have been able to find of *The Beauties and Furies* is a review by J. G. Conant entitled "The Revolutionary Fringe," *New Masses,* August 4, 1936, pp. 25-26. As his title suggests, Conant sees the book as a study of types "who play around the edges of revolutionary realities." But despite the high praise he gives it, Conant also feels that its true significance is liable to be lost through overelaboration of language.

8. Marpurgo introduces himself to Oliver thus: "'. . . I'm a sort of fabulist, the Arabian Nights is my natural background.'" *The Beauties and Furies,* p. 10. In "The Amenities" occurs a description of the elaborate suite of the wealthy business man Henry Van Laer, followed by this passage: "Let no-one think that this is a ridiculous account of the suite of the once-famous Van Laer, for much more fantastic legends are regularly current about the financial wizards and mystery-men of the Stock Exchange who spring up frequently in the nightmarish financial world." *The Salzburg Tales,* p. 277.

9. *New Masses,* January 20, 1942.

10. For a full account of the complexities of the situation see Alphendéry's explanation to Adam Constant, about to go to England as Jules's emissary in this affair. Pp. 500-2.

11. "The House that Jack Built," *New Masses,* June 21, 1938.

12. For example, *Scene Fifteen* (exploiting inflation); and the whole of the contre-partie business.

13. *The Beauties and Furies,* p. 98.

14. To Alphendéry, Jules is the quicksands and Léon the volcano. See p. 370.

15. See, too, p. 539, where Alphendéry, unlike the others, believes the best of Raccamond, and turns out to be right.

16. *Time* Magazine, June 13, 1938.

17. *Sydney Morning Herald,* July 22, 1938.

18. *Ibid.*

19. The two principal passages analyzing Jules are *Scene Nine* and *Scene Seventy-four.* Is there some contradiction in the author's comments? Cf. "vapid cynicism" (p. 88) with p. 597, where we are informed that Jules believes nothing that is told him, "not out of cynicism, but out of the clarity of his nature."

20. See for example *Tom Jones,* Book IX, Chapter V; the eating scene at the inn preceding the seduction of Tom by Mrs. Waters. Tony Richardson, the producer of the recent film, *Tom Jones,* gave a rather different emphasis to Fielding's metaphor and developed a brilliant scene in which the pleasures of eating anticipate the erotic delights to follow.

21. See pp. 283-85 for Madame Haller's ambivalent attitude toward Raccamond.

Selected Bibliography

PRIMARY SOURCES

WORKS BY CHRISTINA STEAD

Fiction: First Publications

The Salzburg Tales. London: Peter Davies, 1934. New York: D. Appleton-Century, 1934.

Seven Poor Men of Sydney. London: Peter Davies, 1934. New York: D. Appleton-Century, 1935.

The Beauties and Furies. London: Peter Davies, 1936. New York: D. Appleton-Century, 1936.

House of All Nations. New York: Simon and Schuster, 1938. London: Peter Davies, 1938.

The Man Who Loved Children. New York: Simon and Schuster, 1940. London: Peter Davies, 1941.

For Love Alone. New York: Harcourt, Brace, 1944. London: Peter Davies, 1945.

Letty Fox: Her Luck. New York: Harcourt, Brace, 1946. London: Peter Davies, 1947.

A Little Tea, a Little Chat. New York: Harcourt, Brace, 1948.

Fiction: Reissues

The Man Who Loved Children. New York: Holt, Rinehart, and Winston, 1965. London: Secker and Warburg, 1966.

Seven Poor Men of Sydney. Sydney: Angus and Robertson, 1965.

For Love Alone. Sydney: Angus and Robertson, 1966.

The Salzburg Tales. Melbourne: Sun Books, 1966.

Miscellaneous

Review of *The Century Was Young* by Louis Aragon, *New Masses,* January 20, 1942.

SECONDARY SOURCES

CRITICAL AND BIOGRAPHICAL

Eldershaw, M. Barnard. "Christina Stead" in *Essays in Australian Fiction.* Melbourne: Melbourne University Press, 1938, pp. 158-81. A good essay but deals with the first three books only.

Roderick, Colin. "Christina Stead," in *Southerly,* VII, 2 (1946), 87-92.

REVIEWS

The Beauties and Furies.

Sydney Morning Herald, May 22, 1936.

New Masses, August 4, 1936. "The Revolutionary Fringe" by J. G. Conant. Controversial and stimulating—in defense.

House of All Nations.

Time, June 13, 1938. Most enthusiastic.

New Masses, June 21, 1938. By Edwin Berry Burgum. Emphasizes political implications; well-written and stimulating.

Sydney Morning Herald, July 22, 1938.

Brian Kiernan (essay date 1971)

SOURCE: Kiernan, Brian. "Christina Stead: *Seven Poor Men of Sydney* and *For Love Alone.*" In *Images of Society and Nature: Seven Essays on Australian Novels,* pp. 59-81. Melbourne, Australia: Oxford University Press, 1971.

[*In the following essay, Kiernan studies the romantic themes and imagery in* Seven Poor Men of Sydney *and* For Love Alone, *noting, especially, Stead's depiction of the city and the sea as "a total cosmic setting" in which her characters enact their "Romantic longings" for escape and self-realization. Kiernan concludes that Stead "is the first major Australian novelist to take the city as a setting and to create from it an image of the metropolis, an image of the great city as the focus of the forces of contemporary life."*]

Both of Christina Stead's first published works, **Seven Poor Men of Sydney** and **The Salzburg Tales,** appeared in 1934, midway through the decade that separates *Ultima Thule* from the last of Henry Handel Richardson's novels, *The Young Cosima.* The contrast between the prosaic psychological realism of Richardson and Christina Stead's much freer, more individual and more experimental mode is striking. Poetic in form, and lyrical (and frequently 'literary') in style, **Seven Poor Men of Sydney** moves beyond the naturalistic tradition which influenced Richardson to explore contemporary life in ways that, as well as being highly individual, acknowledge developments that had occurred in the European novel and which had made *The Fortunes of Richard Mahony* appear so dated when completed. Yet although Richardson and Stead are poles apart, stylistically and formally, their common grounding in a developing European tradition and their common concern with Romantic themes relate them in more than a superficial sense. Christina Stead has specified some of the early influences on her writing:

> At thirteen I began to learn French and soon became an impassioned adept of Guy de Maupassant, whom I regarded as a master of style; later I followed Chateaubriand, Huysmans, Balzac (for expression), Hugo and Zola (for viewpoint), and am influenced by modern French authors, for example, Louis Gilloux in his brilliant *Le Sang Noir* (*Black Blood*). In English and American letters my favorites were Thoreau, Melville, Ambrose Bierce, Poe, along with Bacon (for pithiness alone), Shelley, Shakespeare, and many others, of course.[1]

Many of these influences can be discerned in **The Salzburg Tales,** which draw broadly and parodically on the European tradition from Boccaccio and Chaucer onwards in a sophisticated way that contrasts not only with most of the fiction being produced in Australia before the Second World War, but also with the immature and self-consciously 'literary' indulgences of Christina Stead's own first novel. Yet, although it is not a mature, fully achieved novel, **Seven Poor Men of Sydney** is a remarkable work to have been written out of Australian experience at that time, and is in itself a remarkable first novel that holds a significant place in the by now extensive *œuvre* of a novelist whose reputation at present exceeds that of Henry Handel Richardson.

The non-realistic structuring of **Seven Poor Men of Sydney** on the theme of poverty—in both its economic and metaphorical senses—rather than on the plot and character conventions which Richardson employed, and which were also the usual conventions of the Australian novel, has been explored by most commentators on the novel—most usefully by Barnard Eldershaw,[2] R. G. Geering[3] and Michael Wilding.[4] Kinship, occupation, belief and temperament relate the characters to each other and to wider social groups. But more fundamental than this social network of relationships is the polarization of the basic emotional impulses of the novel embodied in the Baguenaults—the illegitimate Michael, his half-sister Catherine, and their cousin Joseph. Romantic dissatisfaction with life and society, and a humble acceptance of these, are dramatized through Michael and Catherine on the one hand, and Joseph on the other. Michael's incestuous love for Catherine, his search for an ideal unity with her such as was experienced in their youth, and Catherine's insistence to Mendelssohn that Michael is her *alter ego,* point up the adolescent Romantic quality of these characters' drifting search for fulfilment, their *Sehnsucht.* Joseph in his humility, his devotion to his parents, his allegiance to Catholicism and his resigned acceptance of the fulfilment possible in this society contrasts markedly with his cousins. At the end, after Michael's suicide and Catherine's retreat into an asylum for the insane, Joseph marries and years later begins to tell his wife the story of the seven poor men.

Catherine is more important to the novel than the rest of the seven poor men of the title—Tom Withers and Baruch Mendelssohn, printers, Gregory Chamberlain, a comically inept capitalist, owner of the printery, Tom Winter, a Communist librarian, and Kol Blount, a paralysed friend of Michael. These, and other more minor figures, such as the middle-class Romantic socialists Fulke and Marion Folliot, embody aspects of that search for a realization of the possibilities of life that the central characters are seeking—a search which, in this society, is seen to have become fragmented into obsessions with single aspects of existence, such as Winter demonstrates, rather crudely, by his Marxist diatribes. Baruch Mendelssohn's radical political dissertation provides a more intelligent and articulate expression of the dehumanizing effects of the poverty which provides the organizing theme of the novel and contrasts the dreams of past generations of radicals with the reality of capitalist society in the Depression era. The novel as a whole, however, is not concerned simply with economic poverty—indeed the panaceas of social theorists expounded by Winter and Mendelssohn are seen as crude abstractions that only touch on the human possibilities that are being denied—but with the consequences of this economic poverty on the inner lives of the characters and, more, with a metaphorical expression of their distance from the Eden-like state in which their human potential would be realized.

The characters' desires to achieve their Romantic dreams of escape, through love, death, revolution, religion, and the social reality that restricts them are brilliantly imaged through the depiction of Sydney itself. The opening of the novel, 'The hideous low scarred yellow horny and barren headland lies curled like a scorpion in a blinding sea and sky', presents the meeting of the fundamental symbolic forces: the sea, with its ambiguous promise of freedom and death, casting up a rich jetsam and also corpses, and the land ('It was, and remains, a military and maritime settlement'), fenced off, restrictive, supporting the signalling mast by which man's attempts to impose order reach out also across the domain of the sea. This reference to the military establishment anticipates Winter's later remark that 'the shadder of the N.S.W. Corps still blights the wheat fields', and Kol Blount at the asylum similarly expresses the frustrated hopes that this land could have been another Eden had it not been betrayed by civilization:

> 'Why are we here? Nothing floats down here, this far in the south, but is worn out with wind, tempest and weather; all is flotsam and jetsam. They leave their rags and tatters here; why do we have to be dressed? The sun is hot enough; why can't we run naked in our own country, on our own land, and work out our own destiny? Eating these regurgitated ideas from the old country makes us sick and die of sickness. Are we vultures to eat the corpses come down here to bleach their bones in the antipodes?' [*Seven Poor Men of Sydney* (Angus & Robertson, Sydney, 1965), p. 309. Subsequent page references, included in the text in parentheses, are to this edition.]

'Floats', 'worn out', 'tempest', 'flotsam and jetsam', 'rags and tatters', 'destiny', 'sickness' and 'corpses' are part of the whole imaginative texture of language throughout the novel and express the failure of a dream not only of the speaker, for Blount hardly exists as a dramatically individuated voice, but of all the characters and, beyond them, of the society they represent and its historic dream of Australia Felix.

The *fourmillante cité,* with its derelicts, prostitutes and unemployed, its jewellers' shops, Hispano-Suizas and Bentleys, is a nightmare product of dehumanizing economic forces that contrast with the flow of natural forces, of unrestricted life that the ubiquitous imagery of the sea suggests. Michael in particular is aware of and drawn towards surrendering to this flow:

> One day when the school was out on a picnic, the headmaster walked a little way aside with him. 'Your character is like that ship,' said he, looking down from the heights of a bay; 'it can be guided by you, your will the pilot, or cast away, for the immediate gain in a cheap profession, or the pleasures a young man likes, or cast adrift and someone, man or woman, may earn the salvage of it.'
>
> 'I will never be the captain of my soul,' said Michael, interested in the subject. 'I began, and will end, a beachcomber—spiritually, I mean,' he added at the schoolmaster's start; 'guide as you will, Nature is stronger.'
>
> (p. 16)

The headmaster sighs about a lack of 'Doctrine, constitution, order, duty, religion' in this country and opposes the order of civilization to the chaos of Nature, but the city is seen not as an ordering environment but as itself chaotic and as a force that denatures the creatures trapped within it. Michael rejects two views of Nature: his father's view of a tame Mother Nature and the priest's view, presented in the sermon, of Nature as a God-ordained universal order. His father's words anticipate his fate—'You can be absorbed in Nature, as—as in the sea, as if you melted into the sea and were diffused through the oceans of the earth'—as also does the drawing labelled 'Fished up' that he finds when he seeks out Catherine in the city. In casting himself upon the flood of experience, Michael reveals a Romantic longing for love or death, but love first—for Catherine, for Mae Graham, for Marion Folliot. Later, Catherine's verbal slip ('Come sweet sea' instead of 'Come sweet death) when walking along the shore with Fulke Folliot reveals a similarly Romantic equation of the sea with death, death with love.

Melodramatic as these elements are, especially Michael's incestuous love for Catherine, there are indications of the author's awareness of the conventions she is employing. Baruch Mendelssohn provides the author with one means of making a detached judgement of the characters, as when he explains his drawing, 'La Femme s'échappe de la Forêt', to Joseph:

> 'Woman escapes from the forest. It means, the middle-class woman trying to free herself, and still impeded by romantic notions and ferocious, because ambushed, sensuality. . . . Your cousin Catherine, for example.'
>
> (p. 155)

But in Catherine's narrative to Mendelssohn and in the stories told in the asylum, the novel itself surrenders to the characters' Romantic lyrical impulses. Michael, the dreamer, is seen unconvincingly as the artist, the poet. In her narrative, Catherine refers to his reading some of his poems, and Kol Blount in his 'In Memoriam' sings the 'song of Michael' which implies his creativity. There is a lyrical inflation in the prose of these sections that cannot be attributed simply to the characters but is apparent also in the authorial voice—'They heard as a harp twanging in the air for some time after Blount finished'. In Catherine's narrative to Mendelssohn, Michael's three attempts to escape from the city into an ideal Nature turn into the surrealist nightmare of the violin planted in the sand and the sirocco. This, like the stories told in the asylum, seems a delighted indulgence of the author's powers to entertain fantasies and whimsical verbal fantasies, a tendency observable from the opening pages where the ships are seen from far out 'lighted like a Christmas Tree' or the wind that 'with hands in his pockets whistles a tune'. Catherine's narrative and the stories told in the asylum are thematically related to the dramatic situation, but they are developed

in excess of it and fall into an incantatory exuberance of over-writing and the adoption of literary stances that have little to do with what has been established dramatically.

The surest evidence of dramatic control is Joseph, who reveals Christina Stead's ability to explore sympathetically a range of responses apart from the purely Romantic. Joseph himself is not without his Romantic impulses. Like Michael, he is attracted by the promise of the sea:

> He thought of sailing outside the heads and going to the old countries, where the morning sun gilded domes, palaces, royal parks and hives of cities, bigger ports, and where men had a history that looked through millenniums.
>
> (pp. 82-3)

Like Michael, who in his youth has a mystic vision of Nature

> The veils of the flesh were torn; he saw the sun pouring in torrents through translucent creatures with millions of cells. Dehiscent seeds burst, pods split, sheaths flew back, grass sprouted, ants scurried, the sun leapt. . . .
>
> (p. 11)

Joseph has a vision of universal order at the lecture on light and feels sorry for Baruch Mendelssohn, whom he regards as 'the symbol of free thought without regulation, of dispute, confusion, sophistry, of man's untold aberration, anarchy, waste, disappointment'. The cathedral he imagines then, with the five ogival windows through which he perceives all is not chaos, is actualized bleakly in his later visit with Baruch and Winter to St Mary's Cathedral when he perceives that 'People sense some sort of inevitability, and try to run with destiny'. Unlike Michael and Catherine, Joseph does not reject family, religion or the social circumscription of his life:

> He walked slowly along the back road and went along by the Gap; the cool breezes blew in from the ocean. Presently he reached a new stucco semi-detached cottage on the Heights, near the signal station. The little blonde girl lived there. She was sitting on the veranda knitting, but when she saw Joseph sauntering carelessly past, she waved her hand, put down her knitting, and jumped off the veranda.
>
> They walked up and down the paths and Joseph realised for the first time how attractive the small front gardens were with their cement paths and standard roses.
>
> (p. 297)

The reference to the Gap, the breezes from the ocean, the signal station all have their accumulated suggestiveness, particularly with reference to Michael; here, by contrast, is the promise of something redeemed from the tempestuous flow of experience and the impersonal destructiveness of city life—a suburban idyll, neat, contained, a garden protected from the conflicting forces of society and Nature that finally engulf Michael.

Despite the often sharply observed placing of the characters in their social setting and their relationship to each other, the lyrical impulse to relate the characters to a total cosmic setting through the imagery of Nature—the sea, animal and vegetable forms of life, light—conflicts with the dramatic presentation and the characters tend to become antiphonal voices rather than actors. The dramatic structure strains under the energy and conviction with which different viewpoints are put by the characters: the stories told at the asylum represent one tendency—that towards a diffuse Romantic lyricism; another is represented by the political diatribes which reveal not so much a rejection of documentary realism (hardly that) but a similar failure in dramatic control in the novel's concern with the socio-economic plight of the poor. It is readily apparent that the author is seeking to relate the lyrical manifestations of the characters' deepest impulses to their dramatic presentation through their social lives, so as to reveal their frustrations in this society. What is at fault is that, although the tendencies that fragment the novel and dissipate its energies are obviously the product of a single act of the imagination, there is, as Michael Wilding says, 'a disjunction ultimately between the overall theme and organization of the book (poverty), and the individual successful imaginative passages, between the Romantic and the low-life caricature'.[5] In the closest examination the prose of Christina Stead's novels has received, Wilding shows how fundamental the Romantic notes of the grotesque, the macabre and the bizarre are to the successful imaginative realization of society as a nightmare world; at its worst the depiction of society 'drops too easily to mere listing (of place names or objects) or to an imaginative thinness' such as is found in Winter's analysis of capitalist society in terms so crudely stereotyped as to be a burlesque of Marxism. This 'realistic' caricature is one extreme; its opposite is the tendency to surrender to the characters' fantasies in an inflated, rhapsodic prose.

In her maturity as an artist, Christina Stead returned to the Sydney setting in *For Love Alone* (1945), one of her most impressive achievements. Here the characters' Romantic (and romantic) impulses and the socio-economic reality that denies them—for which again the sea and the city provide the images—are brought into a much surer dramatic conflict. Within a structure as conventional as that of *Maurice Guest*—and it is the only Australian novel that would stand comparison with *Maurice Guest* as an exploration of love—*For Love Alone* proceeds in a radically original way to explore the idealistic quest for the transcendent state of love.

From the opening with the narcissistic Andrew Hawkins boasting of his attractiveness to women and his overriding of conventional sexual mores, it is as apparent that a major theme is being announced as it is from the opening of *Women in Love,* and there is a similar sense of a somewhat stilted stylization. This theme of the emotional relationships between men and women is the organizing principle of the novel and is handled in a very Lawrentian way. The postures struck not only by Andrew Hawkins but also by Teresa, who threatens to kill anyone who offends her honour, seem curiously unplaced and couched in a melodramatic 'novelese' until we realize later that the apparent involvement of the author with each character is combined with a dramatic playing off of one against the other.

The much-admired scene of Malfi's wedding shows the almost cinematic technique adopted of scene progression, each scene creating its own mood, adding to and contrasting with the previous scenes to imply the total context of Teresa's life. The scene on the boat on the way to the wedding when the sisters observe the boatman caressing Gladys, the hoyden, suggests their innocence. The mood of the wedding is established from the beginning:

> . . . it was a constant hello'ing and calling out of names, rapid introductions lost in a confusion of smiles and crackling new suits and dresses, a *phew*ing and *ouf*ing over the heat, jokes about the champagne, words and phrases. . . . [*For Love Alone* (Angus & Robertson, Pacific Books, Sydney, 1969) p. 25. Subsequent page references, included in the text in parentheses, are to this edition.]

creating a crowd-scene that conveys the sense of heat, excitement, the 'concupiscent fever' that contrasts with Teresa's proud and, to others, ridiculous reaction to the incident with the bouquet (recalling her earlier speech at the family table about honour) and her virginal aloofness from the good-natured lasciviousness around her. In the scene which follows, Aunt Bea, excited by the wedding and her hopes for her daughter Anne, ventures on the risqué and then embarks on an obsessed, entranced itemization of Malfi's trousseau that conveys her maternal envy and the unreality of her view of marriage. The contrast between Aunt Bea's vicarious dreams of her daughter's marriage as an escape into some fairytale world and her insensitivity to Anne's feelings is implied by Teresa's finding Anne weeping on the bathroom floor. The flimsy gossamer dreams of Aunt Bea's monologue are one extreme; the letter Teresa later receives from Mrs Percy (the madwoman obsessed by sexual guilt whose husband is in an asylum because, Aunt Bea surmises, Mrs Percy 'did not believe in you-know between married people') is another, and one that runs throughout the novel suggesting a relationship between sexual frustration and madness. This free, flowing development of the theme of love and marriage through the contrast of one situation with the next implies the complex of social attitudes Teresa is trapped within and her response to it—now mystification, now aloof awareness that she is destined for something more.

There is no straining to depict society naturalistically; instead the sense of Teresa's involvement in personal relationships is extended outwards to reveal the value in which the institution of marriage is held in this society—the romantic expectations, the fear of being left on the shelf, and the frustrations experienced by Anne, and later by Kitty and Teresa herself. Thus society, rendered in an often strikingly free and colloquial prose style that mirrors the freedom of dramatic development, is presented primarily through Teresa's perception of it and becomes an expression of her personal preoccupations. This expressionism is more obvious in the descriptive passages, as when Teresa makes her way home along the shore from Aunt Bea's after Malfi's wedding:

> From every moon-red shadow came the voices of men and women; and in every bush and in the clumps of pine, upon unseen wooden seats and behind rocks, in the grass and even on open ledges, men and women groaned and gave shuddering cries as if they were being beaten. She passed slowly, timidly, but fascinated by the strange battlefield, the bodies stretched out, contorted, with sounds of the dying under the fierce high moon. She did not know what the sounds were, but she knew children would be conceived this night, and some time later women would marry hurriedly, if they could, like one of her cousins, who had slept the night with a man in one of these very grottoes; and perhaps one or two would jump into the sea. There were often bodies fished up round here, that had leapt when the heart still beat, from these high ledges into waters washed round these rocks by the moon.

(p. 61)

As a rendering of Teresa's inflamed consciousness of sex this is very fine. We are aware of her awkwardness, 'trailing her long skirt, holding her hat by a ribbon', as she makes her way home after the libidinous excitement of the wedding, incongruously alone in this haunt of lovers. Her hearing 'the sounds of the dying' and seeing it as a battlefield suggest her innocence: she knows only family scandal and old wives' tales. To her, love, like death, to which it is here allied in her mind, is one of the ultimate mysteries. As in *Seven Poor Men of Sydney,* the sea ambiguously promises freedom; it is to its edge that the lovers come to escape the restrictions of society, and come also, in a sense, to the edge of life itself. Sensing these mysteries, Teresa envies the life of the fishermen's women who live on the shore 'among the gardens of the sea, and knew their fruits; fish, storms, corpses, moontides, miracles'.

Martha and Elsie, Teresa's normal companions on the boat to work, contrast Teresa's ideals of love with the social expectation of marriage:

> It was not considered respectable among these girls to work after marriage; a girl was supposed to find a man who would keep her, and if she worked after marriage, it was a reflection on man and wife alike. This was Martha's entire theory of marriage. Since she had first got her job at the age of fifteen she had been making her trousseau, which now filled a tea-chest and a trunk. This alone marked her out as a woman with strength of mind; for the law of the boat was that while every girl might start on her trousseau, that is publicly, two or three mornings after her engagement, even her secret engagement, provided her secret engagement was properly given to rumour, a girl was vapid, a dreamer, silly, even pretentious, who worked on her trousseau (in these circumstances called glory-box, bottom drawer, or hope chest) before her engagement. This was observed so strictly that any girl doing sewing on the boat was believed to have a secret engagement to marry.

(p. 108)

This dry, but in its detailing, delighted observation of the prim and calculating social expectations of the other girls developed in this chapter contrasts their 'realistic' appraisal of marriage with Teresa's idealization of love, which would allow her to live in a tent and work her fingers to the bone to keep her lover. But these social expectations are themselves implicitly contrasted with the human misery actualized in the next scene. The school where Teresa works with poor and mentally defective children contrasts ironically with her or the other girls' hopes for the future: George Wadling the Mad Boy, Joe Calton the newsboy, and the retarded Sylvia represent those who have no future at all. There is a comic liveliness established through the antics of poor George that enables this section to avoid, on the one hand, sentimentality, and, on the other, that extraordinary loathing that comes through so powerfully in Lawrence's description of Ursula's similar experiences as a schoolteacher in *The Rainbow*. Our sympathies in the tussle between the headmaster and the unfortunate children are all on the children's side, but they are controlled by a fine dramatic precision that recalls Dickens at his best, as when the headmaster catches George outside the classroom and kicks and pummels him:

> He [the headmaster] shone with clerkly success from head to foot. Georgie, stained, weeping, in an old Norfolk suit of no colour at all, so queered was it by rain and dirt, had given in.

(p. 115)

The colloquial quality of the description of George (a quality of the prose elsewhere also, as in the scene of Malfi's wedding) evokes sympathy and understanding for the unfortunate boy in comparison with the virtues proclaimed by the headmaster—virtues which recall, in a different way, the attitudes of the girls on the morning boat.

The effect of the progression of scenes is not that of a consciously plotted narrative line but a more poetic, associative, elliptical and cinematic development of separate incidents, each of which sets up reverberations which add to, or conflict with, other incidents in Teresa's development. Her responses to experience are implied with immediacy and related to each other rhythmically to produce what Michael Wilding has called a 'psychological drama'. Her sympathy for the school-children and recognition of the hopelessness of their situation is transferred to the self-pitying Jonathan Crow, a transference dramatically implied:

> His tone was brusque and cold, she thought she bored him; but as they passed under the lamp-posts, she looked and saw his starved skin, the sparse stiff hair, the rain-bitten hat, the stuff of his summer shirt, the plain spectacles set in silver over his liquidly sad brown eyes. There was something pathetic in the way he walked, dragging one foot a little, hunching one shoulder slightly, and in his tilted hat and the long twist to his long dark mouth. He had been stamped by poverty. Strange, more curious than insulting, were his sudden grunts, mutterings, his rude sayings. In the midst of her thoughts, he blurted out: 'See that little nipper there? I was a newsboy too, when I was his age—I say, he seems to know you.'
>
> She saw Joey Calton running through the traffic to her.
>
> (p. 125)

Teresa's sympathy for Crow as one who, by his own account, has escaped from the social milieu of Joey Calton is mingled with her idealization of him as someone also embarked on a quest to escape this society and fulfil his self-ideal—'a knight' as she is later to see him. In *For Love Alone* the contrast between Teresa's Romantic impulses and the restricting reality of society, which is again presented primarily in terms of Nature (especially the sea) and the city, is dramatically realized in a way it is not in *Seven Poor Men of Sydney*. In the earlier novel the socio-economic theme conflicts with the other predominant theme of Romantic dissatisfaction; in *For Love Alone* the critique of society is poetically and dramatically related to Teresa's quest for self-fulfilment through love and to her relationship with Crow, who, warped by his poverty, is a distorted version of Teresa's own impulses to flee from the socio-economic restrictions of this society and the marriage relationship that she includes (ambivalently) amongst them.

Teresa's first flight is from the school into the Narara valley, from where she plans to escape into the primitive hinterland:

> . . . if there was an obscure reason for choosing this spot of all spots, it was perhaps that she imagined it as a lonely, dark, dread, endlessly solitary, inhuman place and had heard that a murder had been committed near there.
>
> (p. 139)

The valley promises an escape into idyll: there is the natural plenitude of the 'big-globed fruits fattened on the first rays and the fat midday sun' and here her Aunt Terry and Uncle Ned have maintained a loving life-time relationship. Yet Teresa finds that the forces she is trying to escape extend here also: the rich fruit is left to rot on the ground or is dumped into the harbour to keep the price up (some is scavenged by Joey the newsboy in Sydney); Teresa's cousin Ellen has been jilted and has fallen in love with the son of a ne'er-do-well neighbouring family. The psychological drama is Teresa's encountering again, in her cousin's situation, the problem she is attempting to resolve herself. On an earlier visit Teresa had flirted with one of the Carlin brothers, now married, and she can see her cousin set on a course that she has instinctively rejected herself—to marry the neighbour's son would be to accept this society and one's place in it and to forgo one's ideal. She can see Ellen's situation clearly for 'Teresa was sure that Jerome Carlin was not thinking of Ellen at all'; but she cannot perceive, or admit, the similarity of this relationship to her own with Jonathan Crow, a similarity that even the initials of the two beloved males suggest.

Teresa expresses her preoccupations unconsciously. She wonders if like her cousin Liz, a figure of ridicule to the local men, she might be an epileptic. This irrational fear renews the thematic connection between madness and sexual deprivation suggested earlier by the figure of Mrs Percy. As Ellen and she return from the petting party that has disgusted Teresa, they hear shrieking that recalls the story of the ghost of the convict who had been flogged to death. On their arrival home, her Aunt tells her that the cries they have heard were those of a madman who lives with his mother and is kept in chains. Before going mad he had been about to marry a girl who still hopes for his recovery. Teresa bursts out:

> 'Oh, why didn't they let them get married? . . . Oh, the poor things! But how can they expect mad people to get better if they have no husbands and wives? Why, I should go mad if they shut me up that way. Why, we would all go mad, if we were shut up and not allowed to get married.'
>
> (p. 161)

The sequence of events in the valley, with its recurrent theme of madness, sexual frustration and bondage, is a dramatic externalization of the inner turmoil Teresa is trying to resolve by her flight from the city. A similar psychological organization is apparent in her jumble of personal obsessions during her abortive trek from Narara to Harper's Ferry:

> What was she doing here? What was it for? Why Harper's Ferry? Perhaps it was sixty miles away. Did you pay at Harper's Ferry? She set her teeth, because she knew that if she gave up, *they* would get her, she would be dragged in, she would never get away, she would go back, become their slave, until she was sixty or sixty-five, never know how things were in the world, be what they wanted, an old maid. That never. She felt

rigid as the iron in her will. They would never get her; it would stand there till the end of her day. Also, she would never marry the neighbour's son as a last expedient.

(p. 163)

The unconscious association of distance and life-span conveys her confusion over the dilemma she feels society has confronted her with and which she is attempting both to flee and resolve. But her attempt to escape beyond society into the valley—'Great, fruitful, silent as paradise'—is prevented by the obscene old man. Man is the snake in this Eden.

Crow, the libertarian theorist, recognizes Teresa as 'a free spirit' but throughout he is incapable of making the first move to possess her. When, early in their relationship, they walk along the last cliffs where the continent plunges into the Pacific and know themselves to be surrounded in the dark by other lovers, he cannot approach her, despite their escape from the restrictions of the city and their seeming to be on the edge of limitless possibilities. Crow retreats into self-pity, as when they go, at Teresa's suggestion, to see the sun rise over the harbour from the public gardens; a self-pity that he momentarily forgets:

> Before them was a coppery sky and rolling harbour . . . For a moment, both of them wanted to be out of this misery, and gone to some far island of the Pacific where broken men and women lived, unseen and unlawed, to have their lives in peace and wantonness. Out of a cave underneath their feet a hobo crawled with his bundle of sleeping-paper in his hand. He did not look up at the murmur of voices, but went on down to the water and around out of sight.

(p. 220)

The oceanic promise of the new day awakening before them leads Teresa to repeat the Ulysses theme stated in the prologue—'Where did you come from, O stranger, from what ship in the harbour, for I am sure you did not get here on foot?'—but their Romantic dreams of escape from this society into 'peace and wantonness' are exactly placed by the hobo who rises phantasmagorically beneath their feet, establishing both the unreality of such dreams and the existence of the poverty which is seen by, and through, Jonathan as a perversion of the possibilities of man, a frustration of his deepest impulses.

It is in this dramatically achieved way that the themes of poverty and love (to put them at their simplest) meet in *For Love Alone,* in a way that they do not in *Seven Poor Men of Sydney.* Teresa, while saving to join Jonathan in Europe, thinks that

> In a few months, she would leave them for ever, this herd trampling shoulder to shoulder in its home march. They married, settled down in the Bay or in the sub-

urbs along bus routes to the city, in order to reach their work in the shortest time, and that was the end, then came the marriage-sleep that lasted to the grave. She would sail the seas, leave her invisible track on countries . . . starve in cities, tramp, perhaps shoeless, along side roads, perhaps suffer every misery, but she would know life.

(p. 265)

The 'marriage-sleep' (like Blake's 'marriage hearse') represents to the romantic Teresa the 'mind-forg'd manacles' that have their physical correlatives in the enslaving fetters of poverty which turn men into tramps, women into prostitutes, twist Crow mentally and physically and force Teresa to consider sleeping on the vacant allotment to save the long walk home each night. Her search for a room takes her into this nightmare world of poverty in a scene that recalls a longer comic-grotesque passage in *Seven Poor Men of Sydney,* when Michael wanders through Woolloomooloo before his suicide. Teresa seems to wander down the same street:

> The doors opened on the street. Brawling and drunkenness went on in them; aged, debauched women, filthy, full of liquor, staggered in and out and roomers there would occasionally be thrown out in the street, first their goods, with small vases and basins crashing and cheap silverware clinking and clattering in a delightful smash, then bits of tawdry, or a spare pair of pants, some cracked satin slippers, a hat, and last the personage itself, shouting, quarrelling, but finally bundled out. And there on the pavement the poor thing would stand, swearing and crying, almost sexless, merely degraded. . . .

(p. 266)

A critique of society that proceeds from the basis of sexual relationships is going to seem idiosyncratic unless, as here, the sexual can establish itself within the total context as a measure of the human. That we can accept the phrase 'almost sexless' as being an appropriate measure of how, in this society, the poor are dehumanized victims of economic forces reveals Christina Stead's success in relating Teresa's quest for love to the impediments this society places in the way of personal liberation and fulfilment. The social critique proceeds from the novel's obsessive preoccupation with love as the measure of the possibilities of human life. This obsessive preoccupation is Teresa's chiefly, in that society is presented mainly through her perception of it; but while her idealizing is shown to be ingenuous, the sense of her recoil from such 'reality' as the Woolloomooloo incident presents (it is more nightmare) implies the criticism of a society in which such innocence and concern for human dignity is powerless to do any more than observe. This social criticism is radically related to the dramatic and poetic working of the novel—to Teresa's quest for self-fulfilment through love. It constitutes a radical, because original and fundamental, criticism of society that *Seven Poor Men of Sydney* only announces its intention of providing. In *For Love Alone* the Marxian perception of the relationship between economic and sexual exploitation is absorbed imaginatively into a unified vision of how Teresa's struggle to achieve love involves her rejection of a total society: its class values, morals, education, economic, sexual and family roles. The Marxian element is not obtrusive, as it is in *Seven Poor Men of Sydney,* but pervades and heightens the dramatic presentation of individual human needs subordinated to the demands of capitalist society. It is combined with elements of Nietzschean and Freudian social analyses which relate the individual's instinctual frustrations to a wider criticism of society—that prostitution *and* idealized, romanticized love (such as Teresa's for Crow) are both perversions of human sexuality in a repressive, sexually neurotic society. Such Romantic radical interpretations of the suppression and exploitation of the individual by society are all but explicit in passages such as Crow's diatribes, especially in the chapter entitled 'Property is Everything', and in Teresa's soliloquy:

> Where we have passions that are uncontrollable as in sex, a difficult social web is consciously spun out of them, with the help of oppressor and oppressed, so that practically no joy may be obtained from them, and I believe that it is intended in society that we should have little joy. Religion, morality, consist of the word No! Intended, because the happy man is not willing to become unhappy, nor to slave for a crust of bread, and go dirty, aching. Let a man come along full of the joy of life, bounding, hilarious, hurrahing, and after carefully inspecting him who will not get slapped, they fawn upon him, and take him in, kick him upstairs, give him a few slaves to look after. Then he thinks: 'Why don't they laugh like me?' The laughter of Triumph runs through all the stages of life. He begins to despise, he is irritated, he has become infected with unhappiness; then he is got down. For the poor, those who learn to cry young, they are careful to teach impure, unhappy, harsh laughter, amusements that bring only sorrow—like the lovers in the bay. By 'they', I don't know who I mean. But I am trying to get by them—whoever they are.

(pp. 254-5)

London, the end of Teresa's youthful quest, is the reality against which her dreams of escape and her idealizing of Crow are tested. Socially, London proves as poverty-stricken and debauched as the Sydney she has escaped. She begins to see the reality of Jonathan Crow also: his fascination with sexual exploitation and prostitution, what she sees as his 'naïve confession' about Gloria and his 'schoolboy's scurrility', the difference between the emotionally dependent 'Johnny' and the defensive 'Jonathan' of his letters. Although she has seen Crow as a kindred spirit, an *alter ego,* he is really her opposite, her negative, as their contrasting physical colouring suggests. She wants to embrace life through love; Jonathan is incapable of the surrender of his own personality that would be involved in achieving the

amorous conflicts he dreams of. Repressed, a prey to lascivious fantasies (we are left to wonder whether Bodkin and Burton and Burt exist or whether they are the creations of a lonely man), he dreams of becoming the artist, of writing the *Letters of an Obscure Man* and of becoming the 'casual, delicate, effete, worldly-wise, literary man'. Yet it is Teresa who emerges as the potential artist after she realizes her relationship with Crow is finished, and at the end of the novel she feels she would like to write the story of a confirmed bachelor like Crow. Crow likes to pose as the Nietzschean, 'beyond good and evil' as he says at one stage, as the sadist. Yet the painful and ironically ambiguous scenes of Jonathan alone with Teresa in London, which culminate in the scene in the water-mill, imply, as Teresa then realizes, that it is she who must make the first advance rather than the intellectually ruthless libertarian Jonathan. Crow, apparently the predator where women's affections are concerned, is in fact rendered impotent by his class consciousness; even his sexual relationship with the servant at his landlady's shows him as a submissive victim rather than, as in his (fantasy?) story of his friend Burton's rape, the ruthless exploiter of defenceless working-class women.

The presentation of Crow through Teresa's rapt, adolescent fascination and dawning maturity is a dramatic *tour de force* that is constantly threatening to topple into the melodramatic Romanticism of Crow's own posturing and self-deception. But it is controlled dramatically to reveal his essentially adolescent torments in a psychologically acute way that constitutes a sympathetic realization—that he is Teresa's *alter ego,* perverted by the poverty and self-pity that she overcomes. Where the novel does become melodramatic is with the introduction of the idealized figure of Quick, the wealthy American business man and intellectual. Quick need provide no more than a conventional viewpoint and a device to rescue Teresa: what is worrying in terms of the dialectical dramatic procedure of the novel up to this stage—a procedure which allows the author's apparent complete involvement with the characters at the moment of their experience but weighs each scene against the next implicitly and critically—can be suggested by the scene in which Quick meets Crow:

> He had not been watching long before he noticed a shrewd and unscrupulous-looking man in his thirties, who strolled round the stands and looked sharply at him, perhaps a private dick, he thought. The man was swarthy, oak-complexioned, with a hammered-out distorted and evil face and a syncopated rolling walk which looked like the business stroll of the second-rate spottable spy. Quick felt miserable—was Bow Street or his wife or Axelrode, for any conceivable reason, watching him? Had Axelrode, his old trusted friend, got him into some mess, or had he witlessly signed something? He tried to think. The thin and sly man, who had a tallish hat, rather high heels, a new moustache and horn-rimmed glasses, after staring at him un-

certainly moved off again on his patrol. Not very secretive, thought Quick uneasily, but what dick is? They always wear an expression which says: 'Watch me, I watch you.' He received a shock two minutes later when he raised his head and saw the sly man in front of him, looking at him. This fellow raised his hat, came forward, and said: 'Are you Mr. James Quick? I am Jonathan Crow.'

(p. 429)

Quick's viewpoint is no more than that of the hero of a conventional American crime story, but there seems also to be something of an authorial pressure behind the insistence on Crow's slyness, his unscrupulous looks and evil face, even down to the somewhat ridiculous touch of his new, and therefore deceptive, moustache. In this scene of Quick putting Crow in his place there seems to be a vindictive pleasure in deflating Crow, whom we know already to be an intellectual impostor, even if Teresa may not.

With Quick a debilitating relaxation of dramatic control enters the novel and this is reflected in 'novelese':

> She panted, unable to speak, yielded, released herself in a flurry of darkness, and went towards the stairs. In the hall, on the stairs, and in the upstairs hall just outside the red-headed girl's room, and as they stepped inside her room, in the open door-way, he stopped and held her again in his suffocating embrace. 'My dear girl, my love, my own love.' Each embrace was for her a momentary fainting. During the whole passage, she felt both completely united to the man and yet aware of the awful empire she was giving him over her, and it was always at this moment that she pushed him aside brusquely. It flashed upon her, '*But this is the night of the senses!*' When he grasped her inside her own door, she pushed him away, however, and breathed hard.

(pp. 446-7)

Quick is a *deus ex machina* appearing in the nick of time to provide love *and* money, almost the millionaire seeking the sweet unspoilt heroine of women's magazine fiction. But the novel manages to contain this note of women's magazine fantasy, and by remaining open-ended it avoids the conventional ending these fantasies lead the reader to expect.

In the earlier, climactic scene in the water-mill towards which the whole novel to that stage seems to have been leading, Teresa realizes that having come so far she must still continue to approach the passive, expectant, egoistical Jonathan, now sleeping:

> Jonathan snored. So—always with him, if she had her way? Sleeping there, with cold, dully. She shivered. She thought: 'This is the last of the Houses of Love. Marriage?' She went and leaned over the black pool the wheel spurned. 'What if I should fall in, that he would find me choking the exit in the morning? "Teresa with drowned hair and cheeks of sod—" no, no.'

(p. 408)

This summation of the poetic themes of 'the marriage-sleep' and of water as the flow of experience is Teresa's realization that marriage to Crow would be a denial of life, an end rather than a beginning to her dreams of fulfilling herself through love. The seven houses of love which she has imagined in her first creation as a literary artist are referred to here questioningly, and the question still remains open at the end of the novel.[6] The seven houses seem to correspond to her past experience, though in no clearly allegorical way: there is her adolescent awakening (Pastorale), the excitement engendered beside the harbour at night and her fantasies coloured by the Lindsay *Vision* type of magazine she subscribes to and lends Jonathan (Bacchanale), her love for Jonathan and her privations in Australia while saving to visit him (Creation and *La Folle du Logis*), her experience with Jonathan in London (Heaven and Hell) and the achievement of her 'marriage' (The Last Star). But the night almost spent with Jonathan, who decides instead to catch the eleven o'clock train, is not the last house, the ultimate experience. Neither is her 'marriage' to Quick, as the affair with Girton shows, though again she imagines it is at the time.

Girton also is an *alter ego,* another traveller, and in loving him Teresa makes her choice between sea and city, the flow of experience and the chosen way of life, and in experiencing this choice she finds her true freedom. Before leaving Oxford to return to Quick in London, after spending the night with Girton, she stands at the window and sees the river, and time, flowing away and bearing with it an immense white flower that suggests the passing of the love she has just experienced. Thus she accepts the joyousness of their love without concern about its transience. As she realizes when she returns to the city and Quick, she has passed beyond the 'Seventh House', the limitation she herself has put on experience and which has been conditioned by social mores, and she has become a free spirit:

> . . . and when she understood this, that there was something on the citied plain for all of them, the thousands like thin famished fire that wavered and throve around her, pressing on, she knew why she continued restless and why the men, having so much in the hollow of their hands, kept on striving.

(p. 494)

But although Teresa has broken through to a vision of the future that holds hope for the fulfilment of man's potentialities, the novel recognizes both her fortune and the unlikelihood of society achieving her liberation:

> Outside, near the door of the printing establishment stood the old beggarman to whom the printers threw scraps in paper bags and to whom they gave small change on pay-day. As Teresa glanced, she saw the old man's parasite, a vicious slum youth who had turned up during the last ten days, and taken his receipts, with

a wicked glance at everyone and sly pinches and blows to the old man when no one was looking. The old man a month ago had had a countryman's straight thin form and apple cheeks; in one month he had become pale and bowed, frightened and huddled there, where once he had stood with a simple air. When the old man moved out, which he did at a word from the young rascal, the youth followed him, one bent back following another, and when they went it was a sign for night to come and for all the lights in the court to come on. Teresa, when she passed to and fro, gave the old man what she had, before the youth arrived. This evening she had forgotten.

(p. 498)

The almost allegorical touches of 'one bent back following another' through the generations and the old countryman's quick succumbing to the dehumanizing forces of the city need to be held in balance with Teresa's vision of the future and her personal triumph over all the forces that would constrain her spirit; she herself has forgotten these restraints, as on this evening she forgot to give the old man what she had. The final nightmare meeting with Jonathan outside the pawn shop brings to her the realization that what has happened between them is something that, although over for her, will go on repeating itself between other men and women, as the young beggar suggests poverty also will continue.

Although the characteristic presentation of society in Christina Stead's 'Australian' novels is far removed from the social realism of more conventional Australian novels, the critique of Australian society implied in both of them is amongst the most radical in our literature. They express the deepest personal frustrations experienced by the characters in seeking to attain human dignity and personal fulfilment in Australian society in the Depression era and, explicitly in *Seven Poor Men of Sydney*, the failure of the Australian Dream. In both novels the tensions between the characters' Romantic longings for escape from the social struggle and for self-realization, and the restrictions of capitalist society are brilliantly imaged through the use of the geographical setting of Sydney. City and sea are the extreme poles of Christina Stead's imagery in these novels, and represent the tensions between a dehumanized socioeconomic system and the ambiguous liberation, promised by the expansive sea, which the characters seek to resolve. But the imagery is much subtler than this schematic account might suggest: the characters seek to resolve the contradictions between society and Nature by finding some compromise, a pastoral middle ground where the individual's inner, natural drives can find expression in harmony with the whole external world. Joseph Baguenault finds this compromise in the suburbs: Catherine finds a temporary pastoral refuge in the asylum. To venture farther from society into the hinterland, which seems to offer possibilities of a refuge in Nature

which the sea does not, leads to madness and degeneration, as Michael Baguenault's attempted escapes inland and Teresa's flight towards Harper's Ferry suggest. Between these extremes is a subtle gradation of localized, personal possibilities.

This metaphoric use of the geographical setting of Sydney for correlatives of the characters' emotions and their critical responses to society is all the more strikingly original in the context of the Australian novel, in which the city, when employed as a setting, has most often been depicted with simple realism. Christina Stead is the first major Australian novelist to take the city as a setting and to create from it an image of the metropolis, an image of the great city as the focus of the forces of contemporary life. In her 'Australian' novels, Sydney provides this focus of representative social and ideological developments. In her other works, she is similarly aware of contemporary social and political forces and uses the modern city as their focus. In her vast, satiric exposé of international capitalism, *House of All Nations* (1938), the setting is Paris, in *Cotters' England* (1967) it is London and Tyneside, and in *The Man Who Loved Children* (1940) it is Washington—or, more accurately, Sam Pollit's retreats from the bureaucratic centre of American civilization. These settings, which reflect the author's own long sojourns in various countries since she left Australia in 1928, make her the most cosmopolitan of Australian novelists.

The Man Who Loved Children is generally regarded as Christina Stead's masterpiece and has had critics, especially in America, reaching for superlatives and using it together with novels like *Anna Karenina* and *The Great Gatsby* as a touchstone of modern 'authentic literature'.[7] The question of whether this, or any other of Christina Stead's novels set outside Australia, can be regarded as 'Australian' novels does not really arise. The originality and compendiousness with which the world of the Pollit family is created gives the novel a 'universal' quality and relevance that transcends the specific social and temporal setting. But at the same time *The Man Who Loved Children* is a very American novel and attains its 'universality' through precise evocation of American life and cultural traditions, especially through the comic and pathetic portrait of Sam Pollit, who in his New Deal optimism, individualism and egalitarianism is the heir of the New England Transcendentalists, and symbolic, in a satiric way, of what is self-deceiving, egocentric and escapist in this idealistic cultural inheritance. *For Love Alone,* which draws on similar sources of personal experience in the depiction of the father figure and the use of Harper's Ferry as an Arcadian image, certainly bears comparison with the novel which has been regarded overseas as Christina Stead's masterpiece, and one would want to make the same claims for its 'universality'. Although its imaginative presentation of Australian life will give it a special interest for Australian readers, one that perhaps only they will be able to savour fully, its achievement lies finally in the 'universality' of Teresa's quest for liberation and fulfilment in a civilization that is seen as denying the individual the opportunity to realize his own potential by preventing the great mass of individuals from attaining full human stature and dignity.

Notes

1. S. J. Kunitz & H. Haycraft, *Twentieth Century Authors* (H. W. Wilson, New York, 1942), p. 1330.

2. Barnard Eldershaw, 'Christina Stead' in *Essays in Australian Fiction* (Melbourne University Press, Melbourne, 1938), pp. 158-81.

3. R. G. Geering, *Christina Stead* (*Australian Writers and their Work* series, Oxford University Press, Melbourne, 1969). R. G. Geering, *Christina Stead* (*Twayne's World Author Series,* Twayne Publishers, New York, 1969). This, a fuller study, was written before the above.

4. Michael Wilding, 'Christina Stead's Australian Novels', *Southerly* XXVII, 1 (1967), 20-33.

5. *ibid.,* 24.

6. *For Love Alone* in its correspondence to the author's own experience may be something of a Portrait of the Artist, but it is more like Joyce's *Portrait* in its focus on the individual consciousness rather than on such objective, 'realistic' externals as the family relationship, and in its imagery of sea, moon and *symboliste* city, than in its account of the education of an artistic sensibility. As in Lawrence's *Sons and Lovers,* the theme of artistic development is subsidiary to the love relationships; in *For Love Alone* it is perhaps too subsidiary to these to emerge fully convincingly towards the end.

7. Susan Sontag, *Styles of Radical Will* (Secker & Warburg, London, 1969), p. 36.

Joan Lidoff (essay date summer 1979)

SOURCE: Lidoff, Joan. "Domestic Gothic: The Imagery of Anger, Christina Stead's *Man Who Loved Children.*" *Studies in the Novel* 11, no. 2 (summer 1979): 201-15.

[*In the following essay, Lidoff describes Stead's style, imagery, and technique in* The Man Who Loved Children *as "domestic Gothic," stating that the novel is "pervasively colored by the emotional and metaphorical excesses of a Gothic novel, dominated by the violent emotional forces that seethe beneath ordinary events."*]

Contemporary fiction is urgently seeking techniques for the aesthetic transformation of feminine anger. The rage that is now welling up is an emotion women have traditionally been taught to suppress. In her acute study of British women novelists, *A Literature of Their Own,* Elaine Showalter traces writers' persistent problems with the consequences of repressed anger. She insists on a woman's need for "confrontation with her own violence, rage, grief and sexuality" in order to free her productive energies.[1] On this premise, Freud and the feminists, in spite of their many disagreements, agree. In keeping with the central insights of psychoanalytic thought, women writers today insist on waging the ongoing artistic struggle with form and feeling on their own grounds. All art strives to fashion a voice for experience; women are now determined that the voice and experience of their fiction and poetry be their own, and are rejecting the secondary cultural images that are not grounded in self-definition. Asserting that nurturance and empathy are not separated from aggressive qualities in an individual, they are discovering their own rage. The feeling now searching for expressive form, however, is not just the anger that was formerly denied to women as part of the normal spectrum or emotion but an anger frequently intensified into hostility by its long repression.

This search generates the formal questions: What use can be made of this anger in fiction? What forms will serve to express it? How can its energies enrich and not delimit a work of art? We can look to the past as well as the present for an answer. In spite of prohibitions against it, there has been a mode of expression for anger and other hidden feelings in the work of women writers. The style Christina Stead developed, and perfected in her 1940 masterpiece, **The Man Who Loved Children,** does find an aesthetically productive way to use rage. I call this style the domestic Gothic, and suggest that its imagery may be particularly feminine in both content and technique.

The crucible in which feminine (like masculine) sensibility is forged is the family, and **The Man Who Loved Children** is the quintessential family novel. Its protagonist is not one hero, but a whole family, whose integrated dynamics it portrays as those of a single organism. Stead's characters emerge from the matrix of their family relationships. **The Man Who Loved Children,** says Randall Jarrell, "makes you a part of one family's immediate existence as no other book quite does."[2] We come to know each of the Pollits as we see them in their collisions with each other. Each parent and child has a distinctive personality and mode of manipulation, yet each is wholly engaged in their complexly interdependent collective world.

In the two years of family life the novel explores, the struggles of Sam and Henny Pollit and their relations with their seven children are counterpointed by the progress of the oldest child's adolescence. Louisa, Sam's daughter by a first marriage and Stead's autobiographical counterpart, nearly twelve at the start, begins to find her womanhood and independence, and as the family declines, she grows.

By setting her family history at the beginning of Louie's adolescence, Stead highlights crises of feminine identity important for both Louisa and her stepmother. Louie's puberty evokes Henny's reactions to femininity and sexuality, revealing the self-denigrating feminine world that shapes Louie's character both by her own experience of it and by the way it has shaped Henny. Louie's maturing begins to change the family configuration; always her father's confidante, Louie now begins to shift into an alliance with her stepmother (entering the coalition of the oppressed that binds the women of this novel). The family's collective self-image had been largely determined by Sam; now, the effects of Louie's developing awareness reverberate throughout the Pollit family, bringing to light the repressions and denials by which Sam Pollit has negotiated with all that the feminine world represents. As Louie's pragmatic brother Ernie perceives, "Now, Louie had her own right and wrong, she was already entering their world of power" (p. 106). Her rejection of childlike powerlessness precipitates the beginnings of rebellion against Sam, the figurehead of authority. The disruption in the psychic equilibrium of the Pollit family caused by Louie's changing vision is the real motivating conflict of the plot.

The power of vision, and the power of language to shape vision, is one of Stead's central subjects. This is the power Louie grows to assume. "I never told anyone what it [was] like at home . . . because no one would believe me" (p. 333), Louie cries at the start, wishing she could invent a new language to express what she feels convincingly. The vision she develops in the course of the novel is that of Stead's narrator. Stead creates the language to make her family story credible—a style I call the domestic Gothic, which she perfects in *The Man Who Loved Children.*

Like the Gothic novel, Stead's domestic Gothic allows the revelation of fantasy material, but unlike the Gothic, it operates in the context of nineteenth-century realism. Its settings and situations, characters and events, are realistic, or nearly so. The superficial subjects of *The Man Who Loved Children* are domestic commonplaces constructed from the details of daily life—housework, eating, playing, shopping. Set in an ordinary house in Washington, D.C., not a Gothic castle in an exotic land, the narrative is nevertheless pervasively colored by the emotional and metaphorical excesses of a Gothic novel, dominated by the violent emotional forces that seethe beneath ordinary events. It penetrates the surfaces of personal sentiment and social pretense to expose secret cruelties of family life. Family relationships become psychological struggles of domination, resistance, and humiliation in which female and male, young and old, the powerless and the powerful are locked in relentless opposition.

Through ordinary domestic vehicles, Stead's imagery releases fantasies of the subterranean psychic world. While she uses the technique of the grotesque, Stead never entirely cedes her fiction to the forms of inner consciousness. There are no logical or even psychological impossibilities in it. People may be described in cockroach imagery, but they do not become cockroaches. Rooted in a real time and place, Stead's characters are neither stylized villains nor innocent victims, but complex figures with humanly mixed motivations. The texture of her prose is dense with naturalistic renderings of the material world, but everything in her world is intensified, stained with the violent colors of fantasy life.

Stead's distortions, paradoxically, make her story real. Her fiction is mimetic not so much of ordinary behavior as of the workings of the inner life. Not quite like any we know, the family Stead re-creates for us is closer to what R. D. Laing calls the inner family, that internalized version of family experience that an individual reshapes to accord with his or her fears and desires, resentments, angers and wishes.[3] Stead and her characters create a world of language that penetrates by its very excesses to this psychological core of intensified experience. She turns what Christopher Ricks describes as the "false, overblown, indiscriminately theatrical" rhetoric we use when "we speak to ourselves in the privacy of our skulls"[4] into external speech that exceeds the cadences of normal conversation in order to expose fantasies ordinarily kept hidden and reveal the characters' personal ways of seeing. Similarly, some of the actions of the plot are more psychologically true than literally credible. When Louie poisons her stepmother at the novel's end, she acts out an Oedipal fantasy of murder and liberation. With a realism more psychological than behavioral, Stead turns fantasies into fictional events and uses metaphor and dialogue to expose the emotional distortions of her characters' private realities.[5]

Each of Stead's characters is determined by a different rhetoric, and each is extreme. The Pollits are all acting on the same stage, but reading scripts from different plays: the world of the novel is an ironic suspension of their constantly colliding visions. In Sam and Henny Pollit, Stead distinguishes a masculine and a feminine vision, at such irreconcilable poles that communication is almost impossible. Sam is defined by his rhetoric as Henny is by hers, but their imaginations are profoundly different. Where Henny's is harsh and concrete, Sam's is optimistic and abstract. Their children are amazed at

> this world of tragic faery in which all their adult friends lived. Sam, their father, had endless tales of friends,

enemies, but most often they were good citizens, married to good wives, with good children (though untaught), but never did Sam meet anyone out of Henny's world, grotesque, foul, loud-voiced, rude, uneducated, and insinuating, full of scandal, slander, and filth, financially deplorable and physically revolting, dubiously born, and going awry to a desquamating end.

(p. 14)

Stead exposes the power dynamic that mediates these polarized visions within the family. Sam, "the man who loved children," has the most power, and he uses it to manipulate others to serve his own needs. Like Meredith's egoist, he is innocent of self-knowledge. The masculine vision, in him, derives from a process of generalization that works by denial and repression. Preferring ideas about things to things in themselves, he ignores immediate and individual realities. All weakness and aggression he projects on others. While Sam loves, in all-encompassing abstraction, Henny hates, with vile particularity. Her female vision is chaotic and fantastic, angry and self-denigrating, but particular, energetic, and honest. Fully aware of all her own destructive passions she does not draw a clear line between the turbulent feelings she recognizes within herself and the world outside of her. Louie inherits this feminine vision of self-denigration, which is expressed in grotesque images of monstrousness, dirt, and chaos, but she also wrests from her father the power of definition. When Louie, the young artist, discovers the power of language, she is able to reshape the family perception of reality. Stead's narrative vision is an extension of the feminine vision she has portrayed. It gains its energy from its detailed particularity of observation, unremitting honesty, and willingness to yield to the truths of the inner life.

Like Dickens (who was her earliest literary influence) Stead releases vivid distortions of feeling by grotesque imagery. The grotesque evokes its disturbing effect by blurring boundaries and confounding animate and inanimate, animal and human. One of the roots of the fear it arouses is the recognition it forces on us of those animal elements of our nature which oppose the civilized behavior reason demands. Further, the very process of erasing boundaries[6] threatens us with a recognition of the imminence of chaos. (On this general theme the numerous literary studies of the grotesque agree.)[7] Incongruous combinations and distortions, the sudden transformations wreaked on what had seemed stable shake our basic certainties about the constancy of human form, both physical and psychological. The grotesque awakens our fear that all tends to chaos, and that we are somehow not persevering autonomous entities with enduring shape and purpose. Threatening us with the violation of our physical and emotional integrity, it touches, at the physical extreme, on fears of death, at the psychological, on fears of dissolution of identity. Henny's metaphoric failure to distinguish her own feelings from the world outside of her derives from a way of perceiving that colors all of a character's environment with the suffocating reflections of her own fantasies. This Gothic device reveals internal conflict about the boundaries of one's self.[8]

The cosmic disharmony of the grotesque suggests an extension of personal feelings of fragmentation, pain, and internalized denigration. While there are many sources for such feelings, one is social subordination. Traditionally bound by images of nurturing maternal benevolence, women have been denied outlets of aggression, and have been made the bearers of a competitive culture's discarded values of feeling, introspection, and self-effacement. Stead's domestic Gothic draws on the virtues as well as the damages of that position. It utilizes the permissible access to fantasy and feeling of a constricted subculture to express the angers and frustrations of being so confined.

The power of Stead's style derives from the distinctive features of what she defines as a woman's vision. She has an unusual ability to tolerate chaos and to accommodate fantasy and the everyday world simultaneously. While persistently shunning Sam's style of abstract generalization and denial, Stead is able to establish transcendent meaning from the vast chaos of individual particularity. Her characters are idiosyncratic and at the same time representative.

An extreme character by any standards, Henny Pollit nevertheless emerges from a familiar context shared by her mother and sister and the other women in the novel. Her angry vision is seen as growing out of the enforced dependency and passive submission to outside forces that characterize women's domestic life. Her constant tirades express her lack of coherence as a person (though not as an aesthetic creation). Feeling trapped by her unhappy marriage, Henny projects frustrations on the world around her which her stories populate with astonishing creatures. When she goes downtown to shop she invariably sees characters like

> a dirty shrimp of a man with a fishy expression who purposely leaned over me and pressed my bust, and a common vulgar woman beside him, an ogress, big as a hippopotamus, with her bottom sticking out, who grinned like a shark and tried to give him the eye . . . and waitresses smelling like a tannery (or a fish market), who gave her lip, . . . there were . . . creatures like a dying duck in a thunderstorm, filthy old pawers, and YMCA sick chickens, . . . and women with blouses so puffed out that she wanted to stick pins in, and men like coalheavers, and women like boiled owls and women who had fallen into a flour barrel; and all these wonderful creatures, who swarmed in the streets, stores, and restaurants of Washington.

(pp. 12-13)

Wandering in the alien atmosphere of a freakish, Bosch-like hell, Henny constantly encounters animated objects and animalized people—weird aggressive creatures who act as angry as she feels. She sees herself as a victim who, though constantly scrapping, has no hope of escaping to clearer air. Though subject to the social and personal pressures that encourage women to hate themselves, Henny turns her anger not only on herself but outwards toward the rest of the world as well, visiting on the whole universe her internal tensions and conflicts. While her vision is angry and self-hating, it is not self-deluding like Sam's. For Stead, conventional women are tied to the material world in a way that is both creative and destructive (as she perceives nature itself to be). Henny's apprehension of the natural world feeds her wildly creative imagination; her language is full of animal, aggressive energy.

Stead's descriptions reveal Henny's defective self-esteem. "Haggard, threadbare, over-rouged" (p. 85), Henny is a slatternly witch, distinguished by her dark eyes, "the huge eyeball . . . deep-sunk in the wrinkled skullhole, the dark circle round it" (p. 10). Stead's metaphors for Henny evoke the decay of aging, but more than that, they tend to fragment and objectify her—to portray her in pieces, rather than as a whole, as an inert object rather than as a living being. Henny's appearance reflects her feelings; her skin is wrinkled and her clothes threadbare; to her "life is nothing but rags and tags and filthy rags at that" (p. 171).

In the formative opening metaphors of the novel, Stead introduces the Pollit children as a collective vital force, dashing, tumbling, steaming, and popping like a bubbling volcano, as they flood into Henny's room. When they leave, they

> all rush off like water down the sink, leaving her sitting there, with blackened eyes, a yellow skin, and straining wrinkles: and she would think of the sink, and mutter. . . .
>
> "A dirty cracked plate: that's just what I am! . . . I'm a greasy old soup plate."
>
> (pp. 16-17)

Caricaturing herself in Dickensian fashion as a ludicrous, passive, defective object, Henny collaborates in her own metaphorical denigration. This wry deflation, which evinces her imaginative energy and force, nevertheless diminishes her full humanity. Stead's grotesque metaphors are much like Dickens's, but, more than Dickens's external characterizations, hers are clearly continuous with the creatively realized consciousness of her characters.

Stead's imagery frequently confounds Henny with the house in which she lives:

> She belonged to this house and it to her. Though she was a prisoner in it, she possessed it. She and it were her marriage. She was in-dwelling in every board and stone of it: every fold in the curtains had a meaning . . . every room was a phial of revelation to be poured out some feverish night in the secret laboratories of her decisions, full of living cancers of insult, leprosies of disillusion, abscesses of grudge, gangrene of nevermore, quintan fevers of divorce, and all the proliferating miseries, the running sores and thick scabs, [of] the flesh of marriage . . .
>
> (p. 11)

Marriage takes on a human body as Henny's house becomes her tormented feelings. Pressurized by Henny's confinement in and identity with her surroundings, the dominant imagery of disease in this passage echoes her angry and turbulent emotions. The physical is so intermingled with the psychological that external realities which intrude on her become projections of her internal conflicts and are themselves seen as human. "Toothaches and headaches, the insane anxieties about cancer and t.b." that preoccupy Henny get confused with "the winds, the rattlings and creaking of the old house," as well as with the diseased body of her marriage (p. 16). This loss of boundaries intensifies Henny's misery and imprisonment. All of her life is of a piece, but it is all in pieces.

Stead shows the roots of this fragmentation and angry feminine self-hatred in women's confinement to the sphere of domestic drudgery. Henny shares with the other women in the novel the experience of life as dirty and threateningly chaotic. When she and her daughters visit her mother, Old Ellen Collyer drolly passes on her feminine wisdom to her granddaughter: "Life's dirty, isn't it, Louie. . . . Don't you worry what they say to you, we're all dirty. . . . Only it's all over now; I'm clean now. The worst was when they were all . . . tramping through the house, dirtying it all up. . . . She laughed uproariously. . . . Now, it's different. I'm a decent body, fit to talk to my washerwoman. No more milk on my bodices, mud on my skirts, only snuff on my mustache" (p. 172). During their reproductive years, the shape of these women's lives is determined by immersion in dirt.

Old Ellen is beyond the messiness of birth and childrearing now, by virtue of her age, and laughs, as only the very old and the very young in this novel can. For Henny, the omnipresent dirt mirrors despair. The sheer messiness of caring for children overwhelms her. Returning home, toward the disastrous climax of the book, she retreats to the babies' room filled with disorder, smelling of babies' dirt. The children's cry, "The baby's eating dirt. . . . He's eating dirt," calls her from this messy refuge. "The baby's eating his own crap—shh! excrement, Mother." "And yesterday he ate a caterpillar." . . . "Ooh," cried Evie [the youngest girl] "it's so dirty, it squidged out. . . ." [Stead's ellipsis] "They shrieked with laughter" (pp. 427-28). What is funny to the children and their grandmother is tragic to Henny, for this mess shapes her whole life.

Anthropologist Mary Douglas explains how the definition of dirt a culture formulates in its attempt to impose order on experience reveals patterns of social dominance and subordination.[9] Dirt is symbolically equivalent to disorder. Women who are assigned by a culture to the daily tasks of chasing dirt, are perpetually immersed in chaos. They repeatedly reconfront disorder, without ever gaining the satisfaction of establishing more than the most ephemeral harmony. Moreover, the traditional association of feminine reproductive biology with dirtiness reflects a cultural denigration of femininity.[10]

Daily experience with culturally devalued tasks bound to the disorganized material realm is internalized in these women's self-image. Images of disorder are extended to feelings of uncertain identity and lack of control. The Collyer women's preoccupation with disease (which seems an invasion of the body by unclean, alien elements) is a manifestation of this feminine distress. The conversation, when Henny visits home, which is filled with talk of accidents, disease, and death, dramatizes the enclosed world of inevitable suffering in which all these women seem to live. Their "gossip" begins with an extensive discussion of various ways of committing suicide and concludes with a helpless lament about the plight of all women: "she was going to take permanganate. . . . They found that woman last year . . . who had taken about two hundred aspirins. . . . I'd drown myself. Why not put your head in a gas oven? . . . rat poison is too nasty . . ." (pp. 156-57). And, "Poor Connie died at last. . . . cancer, intestinal cancer—" (p. 159). Joining them, Louie overhears "the end of a discussion about varicose veins, girls in factories with unwanted babies, and clots in the brain and the heart . . ." (p. 162). "When I see what happens to girls [declares Henny] I'd like to throttle my two, or send them out on the streets and get it over with" (p. 160).

These women live with a helpless lack of self-determination. Their own want of self-esteem or feelings of effectiveness and their internalization of the denigrated feminine image the culture promulgates are expressed particularly acutely in the derogation of female sexuality. By setting her novel at the beginning of Louie's adolescence, Stead uses the younger woman's puberty to evoke her stepmother's denigrated and denigrating feelings about sex. In one of her frequent fights with her husband, Henny shouts that

> she wanted to know whether Sam knew that his beautiful genius' clothes were smeared with filth and that most of the time the great big overgrown wretch with

> her great lolloping breasts looked as if she'd rolled in a pigsty or a slaughterhouse, and that she couldn't stand the streams of blood that poured from her fat belly and that he must get someone to look after such an unnatural big beast.
>
> (p. 411)

Henny's natural antagonism to her stepdaughter is eventually modulated into a sense of beleaguered sympathy that comes to unite the two of them in a feminine bond of anger and despair. Henny says she feels sick when she contemplates telling Louie about womanhood and thus dragging her into "all the darn muck of existence . . ." (p. 120). Her revulsion at Louie's new sexuality expresses her attitudes toward her own body as much as it does her conflicts with Louie. The imagery she uses for herself is also degrading, especially when it refers to her sexual functions. When she is pregnant, her bloated figure is as grotesque as her normal haggardness. "I feel full as a tick" (p. 263), she says, or, turning the oceanic imagery often associated with motherhood inside out, "I'm so empty, I feel like a big barrel floating out to sea" (p. 243). When she is angry, her dehumanization is more violent: "My back's bent in two with the fruit of my womb. . . . I go about with a body like a football, fit to be kicked about by a bohunk halfback. . . . such a rotten, helpless, stupid thing . . . I am. . . . going through the bloody mess again . . ." (pp. 253-54).

Sex to Henny is hostile aggression. Passive and misshapen, she portrays herself as the despicable, helpless object of someone else's will. And Henny is, in fact, in some ways helpless. Since she is not trained to support herself or her children financially, social and economic as well as psychological pressures keep her tied to her hated husband, in an endlessly reinforcing cycle of childbearing and dependency. This real passivity intensifies both her anger and her helplessness, regenerating the negative feelings about herself that her grotesque imagery expresses.

Henny's reactions to other women reinforce the feeling that, to her, sex and physicality are dirty and repulsive. Voluptuous women offend her; she insults them as she does Louie, mocking the features that emphasize their sexuality. One woman "had a breath like a salt mine and a great belly like a foaling mare, floating and bloating" (p. 160). Another was "beefier than ever in the hips . . . and great big shoulders lolloping. . . . a ton of beef [with] that great body of hers . . ." (pp. 170-71). Henny's young daughter Evie reflects her mother's feelings in her reaction to her Aunt:

> [S]he shrank from the long, plump, inhuman thigh, the glossy, sufficient skirt, from everything powerful, coarse, and proud about this great unmated mare. . . . "Oh," thought Evie to herself, "when I am a lady with a baby, I won't have all those bumps, I won't be so big

and fat, I won't croak and shout, I will be a little woman, thin like I am now and not fat in front or in the skirt."

(pp. 114-15)

The animality of these big women offends Henny and her daughter, but Henny's disgust reflects her own internal contradictions: she is repelled by sex, but she is actively sexual; she has a lover who is just such an elephantine character as she finds revolting; she reviles childbearing but has six children. Her sensuous metaphors make physical realities repugnant, but it is sensuous things that she notices.

In her memoirs, Simone de Beauvoir observes in her mother the same tension that Stead senses in Henny:

> She had tastes, aversions and desires that were too masterful for her not to loathe whatever went against them . . . [but] her desires did not carry their own justification with them. . . . Thinking against oneself often bears fruit; but . . . my mother . . . *lived* against herself. She had appetites in plenty: she spent all her strength in repressing them and she underwent this denial in anger. . . . A full-blooded, spirited woman lived on inside her, but a stranger to herself, deformed and mutilated.[11]

Henny exposes this deformed and mutilated inner self to public view by her vividly distorted imagery.

Louie inherits Henny's denigrated female self-image and the grotesque metaphoric mode that expresses it. From her parents, both experts at insults, Louie accrues a special collection of epithets exaggerating her size. (She is a "silly fathead," a "great fat lump," a "sack of potatoes.") Henny rants that she will kill "that great stinking monster, that white-faced elephant with her green rotting teeth and green rotting clothes" (p. 410). In the bewilderment of adolescence, Louie sees herself as a gross and clumsy, awkward beast. She becomes the physical embodiment of Henny's vision of the painful mess that is women's lot.

> [M]essiness was only like all Louie's contacts with physical objects. She dropped, smashed, or bent them. . . . She was always shamefaced and clumsy in the face of that nature which Sam admired so much, an outcast of nature. She slopped liquids all over the place, . . . could never stand straight to fold the sheets and tablecloths from the wash without . . . dropping them in the dirt, fell over invisible creases in rugs, was unable to do her hair neatly, and was always leopard-spotted yellow and blue with old and new bruises.

(p. 59)

Louie suffers the "trivial miseries, self-doubts, indecisions, and all those disgusts of preadolescence, when the body is dirty, the world a misfit, the moral sense qualmish, and the mind a sump of doubt . . ." (p. 155).

The only people outside her family she identifies with are "the oddities" who are also "eccentric, ugly, and awkward. . . . She felt at home with them" (p. 71).

Like Carson McCullers's preadolescents, Louie secretly fears that she may be a freak. She makes jokes at school about being Caliban. In the class of her favorite teacher, Miss Aiden, on whom she has a schoolgirl crush, she is overcome by excitement and the "comicality in her heart." Expressing her sexualized enthusiasms, she bursts out with a little essay of puns and jokes which begins, "There was a wedding at the circus! The hermaphrodite married the bearded lady, the giant the dwarf, the fat lady the hungry wonder" reminding one of the circus freaks with whom Frankie is identified in *The Member of the Wedding* (p. 316).

In these images of freaks and outcasts Stead and McCullers express the stresses of female adolescent self-doubt and sexual ambiguity. Louie struggles both with a denigrated image of femininity and with the violence of the disturbing animal feelings she is beginning to recognize within herself. When she argues with her little sister, seeing the "look of terror on her sister's face she felt she was a human beast of some sort. . . . And the worst thing, more terrifying, was the way she villainously held back the animal in her, while it waited to pounce."

Louie is tormented by her anger and lust for destruction. Like Henny, and unlike Sam, she acknowledges the primitive violence within herself. While Henny is the strongest spokesman of the emotional grotesque in the novel, Louie is its agent, and commits the acts of violence that the adults cannot bring themselves to do. Although she shares Henny's vision, Louie struggles to resist the "frightful sloughs of despondency and doubt and uncleanness which seemed to be sucking her down" and counters her self-denigration with a feeling of power (p. 312). Infinite in her expectations of either success or disaster, Louie casts the world in dramatic extremes, but she is more attracted to the role of hero than that of victim. More active than her stepmother, she can turn her internal stresses into a positive source of energy.[12]

One critic accuses Louie of "thinking gothic" and having "a tendency to see great patches of life as Gothic melodrama."[13] But Louie's Gothic sensibility is also Stead's narrative voice. Stead shares with Henny and Louie the legacy of feminine self-hatred that turns anger inward and projects violent fantasies onto the world. For example, when Stead describes the alliance of despised and self-despising female creatures that overcomes antagonisms to unite the women into a coalition of the oppressed, she confounds categories of being in the grotesque animal imagery she has given to her women characters:

> Although Louisa was on the way to twelve and almost a woman, Sam had not suspected this veering. He went on confiding in her and laying the head of his trouble on her small breasts. But Henny, creature of wonderful instinct and old campaigner, had divined almost instantly. . . . This irresistible call of sex seemed now to hang in the air of the house. It was like an invisible animal, which could be nosed, though, lying in wait in one of the corners of this house that was steeped in hidden as well as spoken drama. Sam adored Darwin but was no good at invisible animals. Against him, the intuitions of stepmother and stepdaughter came together and procreated, began to put on carnality, feel blood and form bone, and a heart and brain were coming to the offspring. This creature that was forming against the gay-hearted, generous, eloquent, goodfellow was bristly, foul, a hyena, hate of women the house-jailed and child-chained against the keycarrier, child-namer and riot-haver.

(pp. 37-38)

Stead's narrator shares with her female characters the staunch ability to confront that animal human nature which Sam so persistently denies. Her imagery makes explicit the tensions of the power dynamics that animate family life. Stead employs the techniques of the grotesque to do what Louie wished to do: invent a language that can express every shade of her meaning and convince others of the truth of what she sees. This style, which allows fantasy into the everyday world, permits her to develop the complex, ironic vision that both conveys and places her heroine's struggle for self-mastery and personal power.

One of the particular fantasies that animates Stead's fiction is a distinctly feminine one. In Stead's first published work, *The Salzburg Tales* (1934), a more overt Gothic technique, which permits the expression of fantasies directly as plot, reveals a pervasive conflict about self-assertion. Whenever characters in the tales act directly and achieve love or success, they endure dire punishments, grotesquely imagined. The bloody violence of the tales embodies the fear that realizing sexual or aggressive desires is potentially disastrous.[14] Stead's later work incorporates these fantasies into imagery instead of acting them out as events, but the theme so blatantly exposed in the *Tales* [*The Salzburg Tales*] is a crucial one for women writers. Ambivalence about self-assertion is a central issue of feminine psychology. When women are afraid to act, the blocking of the impulse for self-expression causes frustration, which induces anger. But that anger, particularly, may not be expressed, so it turns inward, along with initial aggressive urges, against the self, and further denigrates women's self-image. In many women, this cycle leads to depression. Melancholy has been more typical of the feminine

voice than rage. As Adrienne Rich has written, we have a long line of women poets "marked by the depressive mood, their sense that to act was to court destruction."[15] For Stead, however, domestic Gothic techniques create a narrative voice, which, though self-denigrating, is aggressive in its expression of anger.

Other women writers have also mined this mode of expression. Critic Ellen Moers starts tracing a feminine Gothic style with Mary Shelley, Emily Brontë, and Christina Rossetti.[16] Carson McCullers and Flannery O'Connor[17] practice variants of the domestic Gothic; contemporary poets (one thinks especially of Sylvia Plath and Anne Sexton) share it too. I do not mean to imply that the grotesque or domestic Gothic are exclusively feminine modes. Other writers, like Dickens and Kafka, share this angry way of perceiving helplessness and pain. Humankind, in the existential twentieth century, is often imagined at a loss in a valueless world, distressed by human nature that is animal as well as cultivated, irrational as well as humane. Assertion is not always distinguished from aggression and is at best ambivalently regarded. One does not have to explain a grotesque style by saying that it expresses the vision of an oppressed subculture; it derives too from individual experience of psychic stress and physical pain and from modes of perception determined by personal family histories. But the family is a social institution as well as a private experience, and some of the perceptions formed by it follow social patterns which many people share. In *The Man Who Loved Children,* Stead represents this domestic Gothic vision as one created from the constraints and strengths of women's life in the family.

The feminine vision Stead depicts and displays in her fiction neither denies nor romanticizes the darker side of experience. Stead draws her imagery from the domestic field of women's daily lives and the self-hatred and distress of their inner lives. Some of the unique strengths of her style—her ability to portray a collective inner life, her awareness of the particularity of the physical world and her respect for individuals, her openness to inner and outer experience can be seen as having their sources in what she defines in *The Man Who Loved Children* as a feminine habit of perception. Her capacity not only to tolerate but to utilize the boundarilessness and chaos that can be so threatening enables her to order the very unyieldingness of human experience to order; she finds a shape for shapelessness. The shakiness of self-definition that results in what psychologists call "weak ego boundaries" Stead uses in a grotesque style where the confusions between self and world are aesthetically effective. While expressing the anger and frustration generated by prohibitions against self-assertion, the domestic Gothic mines the fantasies of the confined inner world, overcomes the ban on aggression and thus releases energies for creative use; it is a style humorous as well as aggressive, and profusely creative.

Notes

1. (Princeton: Princeton Univ. Press, 1977), p. 262.

2. Afterword, *The Man Who Loved Children* (New York: Holt, Rinehart & Winston, 1940; rpt. N.Y.: Bard-Avon, 1965). Originally published in *The Atlantic,* March, 1965, p. 493. All subsequent references to *The Man Who Loved Children* are to this edition, and are indicated in parentheses in the text.

3. R. D. Laing, "Family and Individual Structure," in *The Predicament of the Family,* Peter Lomas, ed. (London: Hogarth Press and The Institute of Psychoanalysis, 1967).

4. "Domestic Manners," *The New York Review of Books,* 17 June 1965, p. 14.

5. In this psychological realism, Stead is evocative of D. H. Lawrence. Her next novel, *For Love Alone* especially, shows significant similarities to *Women in Love.*

6. Freud's interpretation of the disturbing nature of this process is that it takes us back to an earlier state in the development of thought, in which the distinction between imagination and reality is effaced. The uncanny, he says, recalls our primitive inability to distinguish between wish and act, between the inner world of our fears and desires and the outer world of pragmatic action and reaction. Cf. "The Uncanny," *The Standard Edition of the Complete Psychological Works of Sigmund Freud,* trans. and ed. James Strachey (London: Hogarth Press, 1955), vol. 17 (1917-19).

7. Cf. Wolfgang Kayser, *The Grotesque in Art and Literature,* trans. Weisstein and Ulrich (New York: McGraw-Hill, 1963); Lee Byron Jennings, *The Ludicrous Demon: Aspects of the Grotesque in German Post-Romantic Prose,* Univ. of California Publications in Modern Philology, v. 71 (Berkeley: Univ. of California Press, 1963); Arthur Clayborough, *The Grotesque in English Literature* (Oxford: Clarendon Press, 1965).

8. Psychologists clinically define this condition as a problem with "weak ego boundaries," and have found it to be a frequent feminine condition. Psychiatrist Jean Baker Miller suggests that the normal process of female ego development may produce a less autonomously and more relationally defined ego: that part of the problem is defining it as a problem. Cf. Miller, *Toward a New Psychology of Women* (Boston: Beacon Press, 1976).

9. Mary Douglas, *Purity and Danger: An Analysis of Concepts of Pollution and Taboo* (New York: Praeger, 1966).

10. The literary stereotype that defines woman as having a special "close identification with organic life and its perpetuation" (Robert Jay Lifton, "Women as Knower: Some Psychohistorical Perspectives" in *The Woman in America,* ed. R. J. Lifton [1964; rpt. Boston: Beacon Press, 1967], p. 31) draws on and supports women's confinement, in conventional roles, to the self-perpetuating daily care of material needs. Sam Pollit puts this stereotype to its typical derogatory use when he explains to another man why Henny would not share his humanitarian dream of adopting one baby of every race: "The women have to wash the diapers: they are not quite so generous as ourselves." While, as Sam inadvertently demonstrates, women's submersion in immediate physical realities can save them from his style of empty idealism, it can also impose on them destructive limitations. The confinement to "inner space" which Erik Erikson associates with nurturance can also create a feeling of psychological impotence.

11. Simone de Beauvoir, *A Very Easy Death,* trans. Patrick O'Brien (London: Deutsch, 1965; rpt. N.Y.: Warner, 1973), pp. 43, 47, 51.

12. Learning to balance access to their fantasies with pragmatic action in the world is the rhythm of development for all of Stead's independent heroines, Cf. Lidoff, "The Female Ego: Christina Stead's Heroines," *New Boston Review,* Jan. 1977.

13. James Walt, "An Australian Novelist Looks at America," *UNISA,* 4 (Nov. 1969), 38.

14. This pattern takes its purest form in "The Prodigy," a tale of an ambitious and talented young girl who is an exceptional violinist. She is demeaned by progressive humiliations, and finally raped and murdered.

15. *The Washington Post Book World,* 31 Dec. 1972, p. 3. Quoted in *Adrienne Rich's Poetry,* ed. Barbara and Albert Gelpi (New York: Norton, 1975), p. xii.

16. Ellen Moers, *Literary Women: The Great Writers* (New York: Doubleday, 1976).

17. O'Connor's grotesque has, of course, been considered an instrumental technique for expressing a logically ineffable religious vision. I would like to suggest that it can equally well be considered as an expression of personal anger. The arguments of Claire Katz and Josephine Hendin support this view. Cf. Claire Katz, "Flannery O'Connor's Rage of Vision," *American Literature,* 46 (March 1974),

54-67; and Josephine Hendin, *The World of Flannery O'Connor* (Bloomington: Indiana Univ. Press, 1970).

Wendy Woodward (lecture date June 1988)

SOURCE: Woodward, Wendy. "Calling a Spade a Muck Dig: Discourse and Gender in Some Novels by Christina Stead." In *Crisis and Creativity in the New Literatures in English,* edited by Geoffrey V. Davis and Hena Maes-Jelinek, pp. 249-64. Amsterdam: Rodopi, 1990.

[*In the following essay, originally delivered as a lecture in June, 1988, Woodward explores Stead's use of "the masculine genderlect," which she describes as "masculine-gendered discourse [that] narcissistically celebrates itself" and that serves to reinforce male dominance and female subjugation. Woodward focuses specifically on* A Little Tea, A Little Chat, For Love Alone, *and* The Man Who Loved Children.]

Christina Stead's novels repeatedly depict oppression, whether it be of gender, class or age. That the gender struggles, particularly, are located within the language of her characters explicitly foregrounds the production of the subject in language and the essential power play inherent in all linguistic exchange. Stead has her fictional characters speak in their own dialects, which I will refer to subsequently as "genderlects," revealing how each character is inserted within the social formation. Yet those who attempt power over others (Robert Grant in *A Little Tea, A Little Chat,* Jonathan Crow in *For Love Alone,* and Sam Pollit in *The Man Who Loved Children,* among others) are also subjected themselves by rigidly conforming to the identities they have been socialized into. They too, like those they have power over, experience immobilization within a "prison-house of language." Michel Foucault's essay "The Subject and Power" is useful here in the discussion of the individual doubly turned into a subject:

> The form of power applies itself to immediate everyday life which categorizes the individual, marks him by his own individuality, attaches him to his own identity, imposes a law of truth on him which he must recognize and which others have to recognize in him. It is a form of power which makes individuals subjects. There are two meanings of the word "subject": subject to someone else by control and dependence; and tied to his own identity by a conscience or self-knowledge. Both meanings suggest a form of power which subjugates and makes subject to.[1]

Foucault, however, neglects to take cognizance of the gender identity of subjects. Women's experience of being doubly subjected tends to be more extreme in a phallocentric social formation that endorses competition and domination over others. Historically, women have functioned as male property or as signs of interchange between males, as well as having their identities moulded by a consciousness learnt within patriarchal culture. As Simone de Beauvoir maintains of woman in *The Second Sex,* "[S]he is defined and differentiated with reference to man, and not he with reference to her; she is the incidental, the inessential as opposed to the essential. He is the subject, he is The Absolute—she is the Other."[2] And as Luce Irigaray argues in "This Sex Which is Not One," woman is "this mirror entrusted by the (masculine) subject with the task of reflecting and redoubling himself."[3]

This difference between subject and Other is legislated by language. Generally, men's experience of the socio-symbolic contract is more positive than that of women. Thus, though Stead's male characters may be tied to their own identities and entrapped by what Ibsen would term their "life-lies,"[4] their sufferings are ameliorated by the congruency of the dominant ideology with their own. As Cheris Kramarae argues in "Proprietors of Language":

> By and large men have controlled the norms of use; and this control, in turn, has shaped the language system available for use by both sexes and has influenced the judgements made about the speech of women and men. Men have largely determined what is labeled, have defined the ordering and classifying system, and have in most instances created the words which are catalogued in our dictionaries and which are the medium of everyday speech.[5]

Nelly Furman, too, points out in her essay, "The Study of Women and Language," the predominant role that men have played in language:

> It is through the medium of language that we define and categorize areas of difference and similarity, which in turn allows us to comprehend the world around us. Male-centred categorizations predominate in American English and subtly shape our understanding and perception of reality; this is why attention is increasingly directed to the inherently oppressive aspects for women of a male-constructed language system.[6]

To equate all men with collusion in the socio-symbolic contract and all women with oppression by or antagonism towards it is to oversimplify: distinctions should be made between women who might either be "male-identified" or "woman-identified." In "On Female Identity and Writing by Women,"[7] Judith Kegan Gardiner defines the former as those who accept their identity from what has been handed down to them by the Law of the Fathers and whose allegiances are to men, and the latter as those who question the patriarchal social contract, locating their loyalty with other women. Nellie Cotter in *Cotters' England* and Letty Fox in *Letty Fox: Her Luck* are prototypes of the male-identified women, who aim to placate the phallocentric order, while the putative women artists, Catherine Baguenault in *Seven Poor Men of Sydney,* Louisa Pollit in *The Man Who Loved Children,* and Teresa Hawkins in *For Love Alone* embody the characteristics of the woman-identified woman. Elsewhere I have discussed how, in their embedded narratives, they challenge the male symbolic by metaphor derived from the female body.[8] Thus, in a feminine genderlect, women who are "woman-identified" tend to subvert or challenge the masculine genderlect which I would define (according to criteria in Stead's narratives) as an idiolect which seeks to dominate, often in intellectual theorizing, which may be highly self-conscious or self-reflexive, and which is often entered into for its own sake, rather than for any desire to communicate.

This masculine genderlect does not conform to Jürgen Habermas's concept of an "ideal speech situation." Here, all participants have the opportunity, and are equally able, to enter into dialogue in an atmosphere in which no domination over others occurs. Only then is any consensus realisation of truth possible. Habermas, in his theory of communicative competence, stresses the importance of discourse in communicative interaction and considers how the implications of this ideal speech situation ramify into the participants' way of life, into their ideologies and neuroses.[9]

This theory has relevance for reading Stead's novels. Rarely are any interactions free of an atmosphere of dominance so that "communicative interaction" is infrequent in her canon. In addition, a character's discourse becomes the measure of his or her humanity. Those who are linguistically self-reflexive remain trapped within patterns of language which never suggest any possibility of communication with others. Such masculine-gendered discourse narcissistically celebrates itself; any theorizing on the part of the speaker excludes the working class it purports to include, and politically it leads to autocratic rather than democratic behaviour. Thus, Stead illustrates how cultural laws are embodied in language.

THE MASCULINE GENDERLECT AND NARCISSISM

The masculine genderlects are often narcissistic narratives that are self-reflexive and self-preoccupied. Discourse may become a substitute for experience, as it does for Robert Grant in *A Little Tea, A Little Chat.* Grant, an obsessive entrepreneur, is socially inept and caricatured by his alienation from interactive speech situations. His life is a lie, filtered through cliché and euphemism and when Edda says that the blondine (his "mistress") is real, "her body, her hair is real" as opposed to the abstractions of money, Grant frowns, "embarrassed by the word body" (p. 66). Though he does admit that with women he has a "forr-r-mula," he is largely unconscious of the items within it: "a little tea,

a little chat" signifies seduction, the "honey," the sexual act. He reiterates to each woman his need for "an oasis in [his] desert, a rose on a blasted heath" and "a woman, a mother, a sister, a sweetheart, a friend,"[10] thus objectifying women to fit his needs.

His use of language is politically significant: when he takes Miss Grimm to his hotel, "both said they were leftist" (p. 17); he pays lip-service to socialism as he decides that this will help him make more money and that he will not have to pay for the sexual favours of radical-minded women. He is fixated by the narrative possibilities of certain actions and he lives by his stories. After Barbara Kent marries Churchill Downs the Third, he comforts himself:

> He had a surge of energy. He had a true story to tell, something to live for. As he now passed his life in a wilderness of lies, he enjoyed having something authentic to tell and to weep over.
>
> (pp. 173-174)

What he seems to want is not emotion or interaction, but material to discuss: "The talk of love had become a daily hunger with him, he was starving, never satisfied" (p. 195). He is obsessed with the idea that a novel entitled *All I Want is a Woman* should be written about his life and he wants to make the novel a story of "true romance, true love." In blurring the plot of this novel with his life, his literary pretentions are indicative of his desire to command and to have power in planning his own fate. One of his seduction lines to Barbara Kent Downs to cajole her into a relationship with him is "Must be a love story." In foregrounding the literary aspect of all that he does, he transforms his life into an artifact.

Stead has Grant's genderlect conform to the dominant ideology that effaces those not involved in the means of production. In his corrupt world, women are either cattle to be felt all over and judged like beef on the hoof or merchandise: "most had been bargains and most had made delivery at once. He never paid in advance: 'I got no time for futures in women'" (p. 56). He compares Barbara Kent Downs to the commodities of grain and bread, and regards property as a woman to be exploited. Everything that is marketable he equates with the female, feminizing property in "She's there to be stolen" in his Polonius-like advice to his son, Gilbert.

THE MASCULINE GENDER AND THEORIZING

Both Sheila Rowbotham in *Woman's Consciousness, Man's World* and Dale Spender in *Man Made Language,* note the extensiveness of social and linguistic theorizing that silences or marginalizes women by ignoring them. Jane Gallop in *Feminism and Psychoanalysis* speaks derogatorily about the "coherent and thus phallocentric representations of theory."[11] In *For Love Alone,*

Jonathan Crow's relationship with language is as exploitative as Grant's. Theorizing, instead of constituting a sharing of ideas, often becomes a locus for ego battles in the masculine genderlect and Crow's is no exception. In spite of his working class background, as a male and an intellectual, Crow is inserted unproblematically into theoretical practice, which confirms and reinforces the dominant ideology.

Stead has Crow embody the phallocentric, self-conscious "savant" who styles discourse as metalanguage, and who denigrates women by belittling or disregarding them. He never goes beyond his initial relationship with language which is sexually acquisitive and self-concerned. He confesses to Teresa "'What dirty words meant to us as children! It wasn't mumbo-jumbo, it was a new thrill per word.'"[12] Now, as an adult, he collects *bon mots* and phrases in order to impress academically. He congratulates himself: "'Sublimation is the secret spring of style! That's a bull's eye, I'll put that in my next lecture'" (p. 201). His genderlect, like Robert Grant's, is also a means of power over others, and his idiolect is reminiscent of Sam Pollit's in its racism, its male chauvinism, and its fascism with its emphasis on selective breeding (see p. 183). Like Sam in **The Man Who loved Children,** Jonathan categorizes women in his symbolic, telling Clara that "slavery is a kind of instinct with women"[13] and judging them either as Madonnas or as whores. James Quick, who is endorsed by the narrator, comments astutely to Jonathan: "'Why is it every careerist tries to turn his mother into a Madonna—to prove his intellect is a virgin birth, papa had nothing to do with it?'" (p. 434); for Quick it is "the sign of the misogynist" to regard a woman as lacking an identity, functioning merely as a stereotype defined by the male.

Jonathan Crow's interaction with the "maid" at the boarding house in London exemplifies his attitude to woman as whore. That he has a sexual relationship merely out of self-absorption "excited by his own misery" reveals Crow as a Lovelace/loveless type. He also takes vicarious pleasure in narrating to Teresa the story of a "servant" girl's rape:

> "The girl was crying downstairs and telling what was the matter, and Burton yelling upstairs. What a din! Some of the fellows were making a row too. Would you believe it? The landlady didn't believe the girl and sent her up, to satisfy him, and he raped her, and a couple of other fellows did, but we just sat and grinned. What a scene!" he finished reminiscently, but with a sidelong glance at her. Seeing she took it ill, Jonathan swung away to the window with a bitter contemptuous look and looked out.
>
> (p. 339)

To Jonathan, the girl had deserved this treatment for appearing as a sexual being. Earlier he had described how her legs were bare above the knee and that she wore rolled cotton stockings. "He said these words in a lascivious voice, as if there was an erotic meaning in rolled stockings" (p. 338). His ideas illustrate the mistaken popular assumption referred to by Ethel Spector Person that a "female sexuality is inhibited (hyposexual), while male sexuality represents the norm."[14]

In Crow's code, women, especially of the working classes, are to be oppressed; as the drunk in Sydney had called them "sewers," so to Jonathan they are "dustbins." He undermines Teresa just as he had silenced and erased the female listeners to his lecture in Sydney, doubly excluding them saying: "'We, every man jack of us, prefer the beautiful woman to the drudge in books'" (p. 183). His theory of the sexes as "Two races with different needs" defines men as those who impose their needs onto women who "must be selected for motherhood and impregnated by the state" (p. 183).

Throughout her canon Stead satirizes intellectuals who purport to be radical but show little concern for the working class they theorize about, even though they themselves might originate from the working class. Alvin G. Gouldner considers:

> To participate in the culture of critical discourse [. . .] is to be emancipated at *once* from lowness in the conventional social hierarchy. To participate in the culture of critical discourse, then, is a political act.[15]

Stead portrays her intellectual characters as being very conscious of such a rise in social status. The insertions of Crow in **For Love Alone,** Fulke in **Seven Poor Men of Sydney,** Oliver and Marpurgo in **The Beauties and Furies** into this "culture of critical discourse" do not signify political acts in solidarity with the workers themselves, but acts of egotism. Crow, as I have discussed, is always depicted as self-concerned, Fulke's speech at The Workers' Education Association confuses Joseph and the listening seamen; the former, too, had been unable to decipher the "learned dialect" spoken earlier. Oliver neglects to join a protest march because he has an essay to complete and Marpurgo sneers at him: "'After, when you are well-established, you will go footloose among the intellectuals, dazzling them and the masses but well removed by a pretty line of footlights'" (p. 26). Marpurgo tells Coromandel that the "liberation of men is the death of the intellectual as such" (p. 246), yet he himself babbles on in his "learned farrago" or proffers "the usual claptrap" about cabbalistic lore.

Stead portrays implicitly the intellectual's alienation which is inherent in what Gouldner terms CCD, the culture of critical discourse. As Gouldner himself points out, though CCD may be radicalizing, it also "treats the relationship between those who speak it, and others *about whom* they speak, as a relationship between judges and judged."[16] Only in Baruch Mendelssohn in

Seven Poor Men of Sydney does Stead represent an intellectual who does not speak this genderlect and who uses his theory to analyse oppression in a manner that is liberatory for the workers. He even subverts radical discourse, cautioning Joseph:

> "These glib, rhetorical speakers sometimes fire the men but more often betray them. Follow the interest of your class. Become your own tactician, your own Caesar. Don't be afraid to criticise the speaker. Don't become refined, Joseph, your clerical training was a bad start, you always incapacitated yourself by believing in refinement. You could be a fine antique that way, but the workers would stick you in a museum. You can't follow Fulke or me. You must think for yourself. For preference, listen to those of your class who speak simply, with the flowers of rhetoric, with jokes, without cleverness; none of these glancing, glintering, slithering fellers."[17]

Obviously we are meant to endorse the character of Baruch Mendelssohn in his criticism of CCD and in his analysis of class and gender oppression. He considers all capitalist oppression analogous to sexual exploitation, describing the workers's relationship with their boss, Chamberlain, in terms that recognise their subjection to "someone else's power."

> "But it isn't an economic relation at all, ours here, it's a connubial one. We're married to Chamberlain, or we're his concubines. He pets us, snarls, he sees to the general supplies and we get no pin-money at all. [. . .] But I object to living in a harem, first, for natural jealousy, second, because I carefully surveyed myself in the glass this morning and I can certify I'm not an odalisque."

> (pp. 90-91)

Baruch may criticise culture, but, in maintaining the traditional Marxist views, his analysis of the position of women fails to address the relationship between women and the exploited classes:

> "There are no women," interposed Baruch flatly. "There are only dependent and exploited classes, of which women make one. The peculiarities are imposed on them to keep them in order. They are told from the cradle to the grave, You are female and not altogether there, socially and politically: your brain is good but not too good, none of your race was ever a star, except in the theatre. And they believe it. We all believe these great social dogmas."

> (p. 205)

Stead illustrates that the tragedy for women in this social formation is that they *have* to believe these "social dogmas" in order to survive economically. In order to attract the men who are going to reward them with economic security, they have to become "odalisques" or else prostitutes. Here Baruch Mendelssohn's theorizing fails; still, in his criticism of the falsity of the culture of critical discourse, Baruch, as an intellectual, is anoma-

lous in Stead's canon. He is not Jonathan Crow or Sam Pollit who seeks to dominate through his discourse, and on the whole, the narrator seems to sanction Catherine's praise of Baruch's "golden sanity."

POLITICS AND THE MASCULINE GENDERLECT

One of Stead's concerns in presenting the character of Baruch Mendelssohn is obviously to explore the link between class and gender. In later novels the interconnection of these two issues suggest that Stead comes to regard gender as a political issue in itself. In the capitalist ideology of the financiers in *House of All Nations* language as a means of communication breaks down completely. Women are totally excluded from the male conversations, and the male socio-symbolic cannot make sense of them. Female characters, whose discourse differs from that of the male characters, are set up as some sort of an ideal to counteract the excessively competitive, ruthless world of the bankers and financiers. The feminine genderlect here denotes powerlessness and exclusion from the means of production, the masculine genderlect, power and an ability to engage in dialogue.

In *The Man Who Loved Children* Sam Pollit reveals his desire for autocracy. The family becomes a site of struggle as the battles are waged between husband and wife, father and daughter along the lines of language.[18] His essential role is that of a father, as long as the children are young, pre-pubescent, and easily cowed, but Louisa is neither and can beat him linguistically. When he boasts that his system of government might be called "Monoman" or "Manunity," Louisa counters "You mean Monomania,"[19] instinctively and cleverly obliterating the male-nomenclature. Sam as totemic father embodies the Law of culture for his family and is fascistic and patriarchal and, as Daphne Patai argues, fascism, which can be linked to androcentrism and anti-feminism, "*is* the ideology of hypertrophied masculinity."[20] He sees himself as a ruler of his children, a Gulliver in their Lilliput kingdom, or a second Christ, and he seeks to dominate them, moulding them to his ideas.

In, "The Subject and Power," Michel Foucault considers the nature of the modern state which he defines as "a very sophisticated structure, in which individuals can be integrated, under one condition: that this individuality would be shaped in a new form and submitted to a set of very specific patterns."[21] Sam, like Uncle Sam, certainly takes on the power at the head of such a state, subjecting the individualities of his children and wife to his specific pattern, which he also dreams of universalizing. His schemes of paternity recall genetic engineering at its most sinister. He wants to produce "'schemes children, a tribe of giants'" and he tells Naden with admiration about "'schemes for fathering many children [. . .] for preserving man's seed in tubes and fertilizing selected mothers'" (p. 238). That he regards his family as symbolic of "'mankind'" with the tacked on "'and the wiminfolks likewise'" is indicative of his wish for a more widespread dominion.

As men have always initiated terminology, so Sam, like the Judaeo-Christian Adam, takes on the God-given privilege of naming objects in his kingdom. The nomenclature reveals his desire for power: women are defined secondarily as "shemales," with male as the norm;[22] he infantilizes eight-year-old Eve calling her "names of engaging little dusky birds or animals" (p. 63) of his "Little-Womey" because her child sexuality is his to monopolize—speaking to her in a voice "fallen to the lowest seductive note of yearning."

Stead locates the difference between Sam and Henny linguistically and materially: husband and wife seem unable to find a common tongue, because they come from different classes. Here Christine Delphy is apposite in her challenge to the sociological premise that women share the same social class as their husbands. In *Close to Home: A Materialist Analysis of Women's Oppression* she argues that, because this relationship is based on the women's dependence, husbands and wives constitute different "sex classes," that women "form part of *another* mode of production"[23] which is domestic. Stead portrays this difference in her depiction of the relationship between Sam and Henny. Sam, because of his gender, seems automatically now a member of the bourgeoisie, whereas Henny, the domestic worker, comes from the working class. In a sympathetic merging of narrative voice and Henny's narrated monologue the text makes the following claim: "[Sam] thought she was a sort of ignorant servant, and so he paid her almost nothing" (p. 166).

Henny, then, in an effort to make herself understood to Sam, talks to him in what he labels as her "woman's hysterics." They do not even share a common vocabulary: "He called a spade the predecessor of modern agriculture, she called it a muck dig: they had no words between them intelligible" (p. 167). Sam talks in high-flown pseudo-academese classifying the spade within a system of culture. For Henny, however, the spade exists in the everyday and is an implement to be utilized in unappealing labour.

No "ideal speech situation" in which two speakers communicate from an equal base obtains in their relationship. Economically disempowered, Henny's only weapon against Sam is verbal as she tries to speak her fury and despair, but even here she is ultimately powerless. In one interchange he shouts "'Shut up [. . .] shut up or I'll shut you up'" (p. 170) and then does so, quite literally, by slapping her across the mouth.

What Sam most objects to in Henny's speech are her oaths "I wish to God" or "that's the devil of it," yet his expletives are euphemistic, idiosyncratic "By Gee" or "By Jimmy"; "strange oaths" the narrator comments "since he could never swear foul ones" (p. 55). Women, of course, should not swear. Not only is it unseemly but swearing is usually regarded as a masculine domain. Sam's veiled language is congruent with his life-lie, the smug Puritan stance that conceals his rigid authoritarianism. Sam's genderlect very obviously denotes his self-held image of the Great White Father, never the benevolent parent. He is instrumental in setting up and endorsing the socio-symbolic contract that his artist-daughter, Louisa, and his domestic worker/wife, Henny, react so violently against, one with attempted murder and escape, the other with suicide.

CONCLUSION

In the masculine genderlect women lack subjectivity; they are Other to the male self, reflecting mirror-like the image of masculine power back to the male speakers. In Foucault's terms they are always "subject to someone else by control and dependence."[24] Stead illustrates how all linguistic interchanges are based on the power struggles of the androcentric social formation. Differences in genderlect can by attributed, as the narratives suggest by their contextualization, to gender socialization rather than to innate biological characteristics. She portrays both men and women as trapped within the prison-house of language, both doubly subjected by an external power that subjugates and an internalized censor within. Yet, I have argued that women are more likely to be doubly subjected because of the nature of the social formation that privileges the male.

It is obvious where Stead's sympathies lie: she satirizes characters who speak in the masculine genderlect. Sam Pollit is fascistic and destructive; Robert Grant narcissistic and exploitative; Jonathan Crow a sterile intellectual theorist. That these men take on the roles of proprietors of language denotes what Furman describes as "the inherently oppressive aspects for women of a male-constructed language system."[25] If some of the women artists in Stead's novels provide a challenge to this, other male characters like Baruch Mendelssohn in *Seven Poor Men of Sydney*, Ed Massine in *The People With the Dogs*, and Jean Frere in *House of All Nations* both socially and linguistically subvert the binary power structures of the androcentric, capitalist social formation: they do not claim domination over others, nor do they speak in genderlects that denigrate women; their language is never narcissistic, theoretically excluding, or fascistic. Notably, they are all artist figures who communalised their art and their desires: Ed is the community raconteur; Jean, the people's poet; and Baruch, the worker's theorist.

Although Stead has the female artist figures write their own language in their embedded artworks, only in these male characters does she suggest a masculine subjectivity and feminine alienation. Yet Ed Massine and his family are surrounded by burgeoning nature at their country home called Oneida, and Jean Frere's garden (his name, of course, is significant) resembles a new Eden.[26] Both places, Stead seems to suggest, are utopias, literally not-places, as though any alternative to the aggression within genderlects is, if desirable, certainly not attainable.

Notes

1. Michel Foucault, "The Subject and Power," *Critical Inquiry,* Vol. 8, No. 4 (1982), 781.

2. Simone de Beauvoir, *The Second Sex,* trans. H.M. Parshley, 1949, Harmondsworth, Penguin, 1983, p. 16.

3. Luce Irigaray, "This Sex Which is Not One," in *New French Feminisms: An Anthology,* eds. Elaine Marks and Isabelle de Courtivron, Brighton, Harvester, 1981, p. 104.

4. Cited in Dorrit Cohn, *Transparent Minds: Narrative Modes for Presenting Consciousness in Fiction,* Princeton University Press, 1978, p. 81.

5. Cheris Kramarae, "Proprietors of Language," in *Women and Language in Literature and Society,* eds. Sally McConnell-Ginet, Ruth Borker and Nelly Furman, New York, Praeger, 1980, p. 58.

6. Nelly Furman, "The Study of Women and Language: Comment on Vol. 3, No. 3," *Signs: Journal of Women in Culture and Society,* Vol. 4, No. 1 (1978), 182.

7. Judith Kegan Gardiner, "On Female Identity and Writing by Women," *Critical Inquiry,* Vol. 8, No. 2 (1981), 347-61, passim.

8. Wendy Woodward, "The Natural Outlawry of Womankind': Four Artists in the Novels of Christina Stead," *Journal of Literary Studies: Special Issue on Feminist Theory,* (forthcoming).

9. Thomas McCarthy explicates this on the basis of Habermas's work generally in the translator's introduction to *Legitimation Crisis,* London, Heinemann, 1976.

10. Christina Stead, *A Little Tea, A Little Chat,* first published 1948, London, Virago, 1981, p. 23. All references are to this edition and given in the text.

11. Jane Gallop, *Feminism and Psychoanalysis: The Daughter's Seduction, Language, Discourse, Society,* first published 1982, London, Macmillan, 1983, p. 63. See also Sheila Rowbotham, *Woman's Consciousness, Man's World,* Baltimore, Penguin, 1973, and Dale Spender, *Man Made Language,* first published 1980. London, Routledge and Kegan Paul, 1982.

12. Christina Stead, *For Love Alone,* first published 1944, London, Virago, 1981, p. 174.

13. Christina Stead, *The Man Who Loved Children,* first published 1940, Harmondsworth, Penguin, 1983, p. 176. All references are to this edition and are given in the text.

14. Ethel Spector Person, "Sexuality as the Mainstay of Identity: Psycholanalytic Perspectives," *Signs: Journal of Women in Culture and Society,* Vol. 5, No. 4 (1980), 605.

15. Alvin G. Gouldner, *The Future of Intellectuals and the Rise of the New Class. A Frame of Reference, Theses, Conjectures, Arguments, and an Historical Perspective on the Role of Intellectuals and Intelligentsia in the International Class Contest of the Modern Era,* New York, Macmillan, 1979, p. 59.

16. Ibid., p. 59.

17. Christina Stead, *Seven Poor Men of Sydney,* first published 1934, Sydney, Sirius, 1981, pp. 177-78. All references are to this edition and are given in the text.

18. Many critics of the novel have referred to or discussed the differing discourse: Susan Sheridan in "*The Man Who Loved Children* and the Patriarchal Family Drama" observes that the readers witness a "battle of discourses in the novel," in *Gender, Politics and Fiction: Twentieth Century Australian Women's Novels,* ed. Carole Ferrier, St. Lucia Queensland, University of Queensland Press, 1985, p. 139. Terry Sturm in "Christina Stead's New Realism: *The Man Who Loved Children* and *Cotters' England*" considers that Sam has two personalities (his egotism and his idealism) which manifest themselves in two quite different languages, and that Henry, too, is "defined consistently throughout the novel by her speech," in *Cunning Exiles: Studies of Modern Prose Writers,* eds. Don Anderson and Stephen Knight, London, Angus and Robertson, 1974, p. 19. Shirley Walker in "Language, Art and Ideas in *The Man Who Loved Children*" analyses the difference between the "idiom" of Henry, Sam, and Louisa, *Meridian,* Vol. 2, No. 1 (1983), 11-19. This paper, however, locates the different discourses in class and gender.

19. Christina Stead, *The Man Who Loved Children,* ibid., p. 85. Further cited in the text.

20. Daphne Patai, "Beyond Defensiveness: Feminist Research Strategies," in *Women and Utopia: Critical Interpretations,* eds. Marleen Marr and Nicholas D. Smith, Lanham, University Press of America, 1983, p. 161.

21. Michel Foucault, op.cit., 783.

22. See Nelly Furman, "Textual Feminism," in *Women and Language in Literature and Society,* eds. Sally McConnell-Ginet, Ruth Borker and Nelly Furman, New York, Praeger, 1980. She states: "The signifieds of the words *female* and *woman* exclude the masculine. The siginifiers, on the other hand, seem to include the masculine: "fe-male" contains "male," and "wo-man" includes "man,"" pp. 47-48.

23. Christine Delphy, *Close to Home: A Materialist Analysis of Women's Oppression,* trans. and ed. Diane Leonard, Explorations in Feminism, London, Hutchinson, 1984, p. 39.

24. Michel Foucault, op.cit., 781.

25. Nelly Furman, "Textual Feminism," 182.

26. See Ann Snitow, Christine Stansell, and Sharon Thompson, eds., *Desire: The Politics of Sexuality,* London, Virago, 1984. They refer to mid-nineteenth-century, North American Oneida, a Utopian community which, though not feminist in orientation, "did advance the thought and practice of sex radicalism" (p. 7).

Susan Sheridan (essay date 1988)

SOURCE: Sheridan, Susan. "*For Love Alone*: A Quest and a Love Story." In *Christina Stead,* pp. 55-81. New York: Harvester Wheatsheaf, 1988.

[*In the following essay, Sheridan interprets* For Love Alone *as both an "epic" novel and one based on the archetype of the "quest" or journey, saying that it is "romantic," not in the Joycean sense of the "necessary self-exile of the artist" or in the idea of "the necessary independence from men of the feminine heroine," but "in the rather archaic sense of the heroic and idealistic quest for love."*]

A literal 'journey around the world' is the subject of Christina Stead's next published novel, *For Love Alone* (1944). Teresa Hawkins, the protagonist, travels from Australia, the 'Island Continent' of Part 1 to the setting of Part 2, 'Port of Registry: London'. As these names already suggest, the novel is shaped around the structure of a journey, and it is marked by kinaesthetic imagery and allusions to many kinds of literary travels. This emphasis on space, place and movement distinguishes the imaginary world of this novel from its predecessor. Where *The Man Who Loved Children* works by repetition, with the horrors of that domestic repetition echoed in the natural imagery that evokes yet other cycles, *For Love Alone* is a work of endless restlessness, of journeying—physical, geographical, intellectual, erotic—and extends to social relations beyond the domestic circle.

It begins again where *The Man Who Loved Children* left off, in a dramatic scene of the daughter's rebellion against the family patriarch: goaded by his sermonizing and his sexual taunts, Teresa turns on the widowed Andrew Hawkins, threatening, 'I will kill you, father,' while her sister and two brothers look on in mixed horror and amusement.[1] She is an older Louie, a passionate and ambitious young woman, now at the point of entry into adult social and sexual relations: thus the thematic issues around the family are recast. Her heroic stance is also given a different cast, in that she is the narrative's single focus and other characters appear on the scene only to the extent and at the point that they impinge upon her needs and priorities. Around her position at centre stage is grouped a large cast of new characters, most of whom appear only briefly, like the family members, and then move into the background, yielding place to Teresa's lovers.

They all, but especially the lovers, serve to define the kind of world she must come to terms with: as in all of Stead's fiction, they are presented largely through their talk, their monologues, and each of them represents a different kind of discourse on the topics that vitally concern her—sexuality, love, destiny. The father introduces this pattern in the first scene with his hymn to the heavenly harmony of the sexes, mixed with a narcissistic catalogue of his own charms and admirers. But all the other characters' definitions of reality (which are at the same time their self-assertive claims on her attention) are more than matched by Teresa's secret life of fantasy—her reading, art work, daydreams and speculations.

What especially distinguishes this from *The Man Who Loved Children* is the single narrative focus in contrast to the triangular structure of father, mother and daughter/other children in that earlier novel. That shape, and the sense of inevitability about Henny's fate, lends to the novel much of the quality of tragic drama. In contrast the journey shape of *For Love Alone* and its isolated protagonist seeking to be the architect of her own destiny evoke an *epic* form. It certainly fulfils the heroic expectations that are engendered by Louie's final gesture of leaving her father's house to go for a walk around the world, yet it rarely recalls the utopian dimensions of that finale. Teresa's epic journey includes a version of the proposed walk to Harper's Ferry, but that, along with her other ventures, is an ordeal marked by struggle, disappointment, and an outcome quite other than what she had aimed for. Yet it remains heroic in that her aspirations, though modified in detail, are vindicated in their scope. If *The Man Who Loved Children* can be read as the dramatic aspect of Christina Stead's enabling autobiographical myth, *For Love Alone* can be read as its epic phase. Indeed, it evokes, as well as the Homeric epic, many other literary journey structures as well: religious quest, sentimental education, psychological and social *Bildung,* colonial expatriatism, a Joycean flight of the artist and, in the heroine's own words, 'a kind of Darwin's voyage of discovery, as the voyage to Cytherea', to 'our secret desires' (pp. 192-3). But it also 'weaves its epic ambitions', as Lorna Sage puts it, 'into a mock-naive "first novel" format (a young woman's entrance into the world)'.[2]

To the extent that it does evoke this first-novel format, *For Love Alone* deliberately draws attention to its autobiographical basis. Stead is again casting her narrative line into the waters of her own youthful experience. But now, with *The Man Who Loved Children* behind her, she is able finally to make use of materials she had drafted as long ago as the early 1930s in Paris. These included several schemes for a series of stories following the stages of a woman's life, and pages of erotic sketches and lists. She had also worked on pieces entitled **'The Young Man will Go Far'** and **'The Wraith and the Wanderer',** some of which went into *The Beauties and Furies* (1936). Such evidence of earlier attempts to deal with the Jonathan Crow figure might suggest that it was only when she had worked out a way of using this kind of autobiographical material in her fiction, that she was ready, well on in her publishing career, to complete the story. It was perhaps the emotional account-settling with the figure of her father in the previous novel which enabled Stead now to put the young woman at centre stage as the single protagonist.[3]

The material of *For Love Alone* is more directly autobiographical than that of its predecessor. Like Teresa Hawkins, Christina Stead spent her early twenties in Sydney working in an ill-paid office job instead of the teaching for which she had been trained, starving herself of sustenance of all kinds so as to save the fare for her passage to Europe. She too, having finally reached London and the man she had decided years before was the one for her, instead fell in love and went to live with an American who was to be her life partner from then on. These events provide the plot line of the novel. The Sydney setting—the family home at Watson's Bay (Fisherman's Bay in the novel), the city and the university—is left unchanged, though the autobiographical material is transposed in time, as it is in *The Man Who Loved Children,* to take place in the 1930s.

As with the previous novel, the autobiographical reading which is 'authorized' by Stead in interviews sets strict limits to interpretation. She insisted that Teresa's struggle is not for independence but 'to achieve union with a man, that's what it is':[4] and she rejected all such terms as 'liberation', 'escape' and 'expatriate artist', claiming that it was not so much dissatisfaction with

her lot that motivates Teresa as 'the impulse of the young to wander'. It seems clear that she was, in these comments, rejecting two cultural myths that have frequently been invoked in readings of *For Love Alone*: that of the necessary self-exile of the artist from 'his' provincial home (a particularly potent myth in Australian literary culture),[5] and that of the necessary independence from men of the feminist heroine (a myth popular in the 1970s with male and female critics alike).[6]

While these objections on the writer's part can be seen as merely a rather cranky resistance to labels of any kind, they do in fact point to two emphases in the novel that belie both its autobiographical origin and the implications of its title. She is pointing to the fact that it is not a romantic Joycean myth of the artist, despite Teresa's 'being' herself and beginning to write. However it is romantic in the rather archaic sense of the heroic and idealistic quest for love: Teresa like any feminist heroine is determined to break out of the social mould set for her life, to seek out her own grandly conceived 'destiny', but central to that impulse, and to the concerns of the story, is her sexuality and her desire actively to know love. What's more, the novel does not disabuse her of the expectation that she can get for herself 'love, learning, bread', the three things she wants, although in order to get them she has to run the gauntlet of misogynist ideologies and practices in her relationship with Jonathan Crow (who is not only a 'one-horse pedant', as James Quick calls him (p. 416), but a one-horse misogynist). How the novel comes to arrive at such a romantic, even utopian, outcome is an important and intriguing question for any feminist reader to confront. Yet such a reading must also take account of the deeply ironic possibilities of the title, of a heroine named after St Teresa of Avila, and of the epigraph from *Don Quixote,* an exchange between two horses about the nature of love, which concludes: 'you grow metaphysical' (response) 'From lack of food'.[7]

The doubly heroic associations of an *epic* journey into life and a *quest* for love as its meaning are evoked in the novel's prologue, **'Sea People'.** It is a prose poem which gives a positive twist to the colonial-expatriate myth by characterizing Australia, the 'island continent in the water hemisphere', as a locus of legend as rich as the Old World (which is later celebrated in a matching virtuoso piece as 'the land of ice-Cockaigne'; p. 189). Here the European inhabitants appear as born wanderers over the seas of the world ('each Australian is a Ulysses', declares Teresa later, p. 222):

> It is a fruitful island of the sea-world, a great Ithaca, there parched and stony and here trodden by flocks and curly-headed bulls and heavy with thick-set grain. To this race can be put the famous question: 'Oh, Austra-

lian, have you just come from the harbour? Is your ship in the roadstead? Men of what nation put you down—for I am sure you did not get here on foot?'

(p. 2)

The distinction between legend and social reality which is one of the major axes of the narrative is not located in opposing places, the Old and the New Worlds, but rather in two dimensions of the heroine's experience, her mental life of fantasy and speculation and her relations with other people and their constructions of reality. The gap between the two dimensions, a space traditionally for the play of irony, is where will and knowledge operate—the arena of the *Bildung*.

Despite the intense isolation and self-centredness of Teresa, and the steady narrative focus on her, Stead manages to evoke the social presence of cities and people around her. By choosing to set the events of the novel almost a decade later than her own departure from Sydney in 1928, she makes Teresa's harsh regimen of saving and starving coincide with the worst years of the Depression in Sydney. Details of the period confirm her sense of entrapment in senseless and punitive social forms, for instance an official requirement that women teachers who marry must resign from the state education service. Other such details include a lock-out at the factory where her brother, Leo, works, and the dumping of unsold produce in the harbour near their home while her relatives go bankrupt on their orchard block. Teresa's cousins' 'marriage-fever', her retarded pupils' disabilities, her fellow students' dissatisfactions, all function to express this material and spiritual impoverishment and hunger. Even the ideas about sexual and economic oppression introduced by Jonathan Crow articulate a pessimistic determinism, rather than celebrating the Bohemian alternatives that might have been encountered in the 1920s by Stead herself.[8]

Also lacking from the Sydney scene is any representation of the kinds of political engagement that might have captured the imagination of students, at least, in the early 1920s. Such radical political and sexual possibilities only enter the space of the novel with the advent of James Quick and his cosmopolitan friends in London—for it is a major part of his function to make the world come alive for Teresa, as she tells him (p. 390). For the most part, however, Crow's theories of social determinism serve to underline the sharp separation between Teresa's fantasies of freedom and love, and possible social realities. In this novel, the realist details of the Depression years are subordinated to, and expressive of, the urgency of the protagonist's desires. The focus is on the individual, not the collectivity (as it was in the earlier *Seven Poor Men of Sydney*), and on the personal quest rather than the social realities of the early 1930s.[9]

In this protagonist-centred narrative, much of the action goes on in her imagination, or in the talk she listens to, or it is presented as the projection of her imagination into the natural and social world (for instance, the feverish excitement of **'Malfi's Wedding'**, or the sexual 'battlefield' that she senses around her as she walks home in the dark afterwards). Such constant activity of thought and imagination prompted one critic, refuting claims that the novel was shapeless, to characterize it as a 'meditation on love'.[10] A meditation is, of course, the formal structure suggested by Teresa's composition, after the manner of her saintly namesake, entitled 'The Seven Houses of Love'. It is not hard to find parallels in her story with these 'houses' or stations: Pastorale, Bacchanale, Klingsor's Garden ('yearning lust'), the alternating houses of Creation and Imagination, the identical houses of Heaven and Hell ('relation with a single human being') and the last house, Extinction ('to die terribly by will') (pp. 419-21).

Yet the novel creates a multitude of meanings around love/sex/destiny, not only through Teresa's differing experiences of fantasy and relationship, but also through the variety of discourses on those subjects that make up its heterogeneous texture. It is, like all of Stead's, a polyphonic novel of the kind Bakhtin attributes to Dostoyevsky (one of Stead's most admired novelists). In the polyphonic novel there is no single discourse and no hierarchy of discourses established by a unified narrative consciousness. There is always a mixture of discourses, but its constitution changes throughout.[11] In most of Stead's writing, each character's way of speaking is identifiable with a known social discourse rather than appearing to be the effusions of a unique personality.

The novel's early sections are dominated by Teresa's erotic daydreams, furnished by her searches through the literature and art of the past, in tension with all the popular wisdom about marriage picked up from cousins and friends, mixed with strains of her father's lofty Victorian sentiments on sexual beauty, harmony and freedom. Into this mêlée Jonathan Crow introduces a heavy dose of hard-headed Darwinian theorizing on sex and survival (biological and social), and builds on it as the narrative proceeds with a wealth of popularized psychology of the racist and sexist kind predominant in the inter-war years. This discourse almost wins out, as we see in Teresa's despairing decision to 'die by will' because Jonathan has rejected her: accepting his verdict that she has failed in her biological destiny as a woman, she tells herself, 'So much the worse for you, says nature. So much the worse for the woman who can't get a man. I don't care, says nature, die, then' (p. 346). But at this point in the narrative she is 'rescued', and the literary discourses that have always sustained her are supplemented by James Quick's crash course in erotic poetry and obscene limericks, and given a new context of revolutionary political ideas. The evocation of traditional romance, where the woman is not the questor but its object, is prominent in the novel's complex resolution—and something of an embarrassment for feminist readings.

Symphonic Structure

A way of describing the powerful and complex orchestration of journey structure, narrational stance and textual heterogeneity is suggested by a chance remark made by Christina Stead in an interview, that she thought of the structure of her novels as 'symphonic'.[12] The classic symphony is a sonata for full orchestra, developing two major themes with contrasting rhythms through four movements, in which pace and textual density vary. A reading of the novel as analogous to this musical form can enable us to specify the political and textual complexities offered by this narrative of a woman's quest for love.

The first of the novel's four movements carries it as far as the failure of Teresa's journey to Harper's Ferry (Chapter 14). Following the opening scene with the father (which I have discussed earlier), the chapters divide into two groups dealing with the outer life of social reality (family, the wedding, school and friends, the 'iron circle of home and work', p. 85) around an intervening section on Teresa's inner life, which is distinguished by exalted, allusive language, excited rhythms and obscure incidents. In the three chapters concerning her flight to Narara, the two dimensions of inner and outer life are brought into close conjunction as her fantasy of escape attains the status of an expedition. The expedition fails in its practical object, but that is barely noticeable as the scene takes on Biblical resonances. Teresa wanders all day in circles around the valley ('great, fruitful, silent as paradise', p. 163) with Biblical phrases echoing in her head. Pursued along the track by a leering old man waving his penis at her, she thinks of Noah's daughters: 'they were punished who uncovered their father's nakedness. Why would an old man publish his own shame?' (p. 166). None of this is resolved in her conscious mind—indeed, all she comes home with (ignominiously fetched by brother Lance) is the conviction that she will give up teaching and will never marry the boy next door, like her cousin. Yet some unconscious resolution is signalled in the moment she decides to turn back: 'a deep melancholy came over her at the sight and smell of the great valley with all its slopes far and untrodden by her. She loved it. What a hidden life it had' (p. 166). Despite suggestions of the snake in the Garden of Eden it is not so much a knowledge of good and evil that she gains, as an acceptance of the female body evoked by this image of the valley. Her earlier vision of Harper's Ferry was, in contrast to this, 'a lonely, dark, dread, endlessly solitary, inhuman place . . . a drear wild crossing' (p. 139).

In the second movement, which concludes with her departure for London in pursuit of Jonathan, the twin themes of imprisonment and flight that were established in the first movement are taken up again in something like a minor key. It is now her isolation that becomes imprisoning, for her anguish at the 'extreme deed' she has committed in declaring herself to Jonathan has left her with no confidantes. The narrator comments: 'The deeds of the moral inventor are always criminal and their most evil effect is that when done secretly they cut the doer off from society; put around, they attract adherents' (p. 226). Also, with a change of scene to the university milieu, the rest of the social world falls away. Talk dominates, and after Jonathan's departure this narrows down to Teresa's inner monologues as she walks to and from her job. With these compulsive repetitions of talking and walking, the orchestration is less rich and varied, with a more cerebral concentration on the operations of will and determination. The climax of the movement is marked, again, by an expedition, another failed one, when Teresa, having starved herself for three years and in a state of nervous collapse, attempts to sleep out overnight in the vacant lot behind the factory, in order to save more money. As before, this practical goal, and her conviction afterwards that she will not submit to the seductive attentions of her workmate, Erskine, seem beside the point. Again, her confusion is resolved not by rational understanding but by a simple, inexplicable turning away (literally) from her plan. Hidden in the vacant lot, she sees a man come in and relieve himself by the fence:

> In her ignorance of men's ways, she supposed this man was like the man on the road long ago at Narara, and she became very much afraid. She rose, trembling— what excuse could she give if she was seen coming out of the lot at this time of night? She came out boldly; so much the worse, she would explain that she had to fix her stockings. . . . She began to walk down her old route, heel and toe, heel and toe, in the old strong rhythm, carrying her valise.
>
> (p. 287)

The hallucinatory quality of the scene, like the paradisical valley scene, recalls the wandering tales section of the *Odyssey,* a heroic journey which Teresa is to evoke yet again, in the next movement, when her self-imprisonment appears to have become complete and she chides herself for her 'buffoon odyssey'.

Beginning with Part 2 of the novel, and Teresa's arrival in London, the third movement picks up speed, but with a sickening see-saw rhythm as it measures her exchanges with Jonathan. The atmosphere of entrapment and emotional enclosure is intensified as the writing swings back and forth between Jonathan's theories and tales of his sufferings and his friends' sexual exploits, and Teresa's secret searching for the clue to their 'eternal maddening conversation' and her periodic attempts to break away. It is relieved only by the occasional presence of James Quick, Teresa's employer, who is represented not only through his talk but also through his wanderings in the streets of London, where he is a stranger as well. In this movement there are several shifts of narrative perspective away from Teresa and onto Crow or Quick. Its finale takes place in an appropriately dark setting, a deserted sawmill in which Teresa and Jonathan have taken shelter during one of their country walks. The sudden rainstorm sets the mill-wheel in violent motion: 'Grinding and groaning, shrieking, it turned downwards into the boiling pool while the timbers tried to rear part' (p. 407). Across the gaping hole in the mill floor,

> They looked at each other by the light of the flare with unveiled dislike. Teresa, looking at him, released him from her will; it happened suddenly. The harness of years dropped off, eaten through; she dropped her eyes, thought: 'How stupid he is! How dull!'
>
> (p. 408)

It is the decisive moment of release but, again, not a rational decision; nor is she concerned to follow through with her perception of his stupidity and dullness, despite Quick's eagerness to demonstrate this to her. The simple statement, 'She released him from her will', signals the final playing out of the Nietzschean belief that 'Willing emancipateth', which they have both held, but so differently.[13]

The beginning of the fourth and final movement promises resolution as it clarifies much of what has gone before through Quick's response to two bizarre documents, Jonathan's essay on the inferiority of women, and Teresa's 'Seven Houses of Love', subtitled **'A system by which the Chaste can Know Love'**. But with the flowering of the Teresa-Quick relationship, a new double movement begins. A rapid succession of discoveries, sexual and intellectual, is punctuated by moments in which Teresa has to take account of her lover's difference from herself, and of the fact that he loves her in return. She fears that the 'night of the senses' that she has dreamed of will trap her in the 'marriage sleep' that is the usual end of the woman's love story (p. 463). Now that her desires are accepted and loved, she wants to go further, to try out her power with men (p. 464). This conflict is played out in her affair with Harry Girton, and it is their semi-clandestine meeting in Oxford that provides the occasion for this movement's visionary climax. The chapter title from Donne's 'Epithalamium', 'Today put on perfection (and a woman's name)', names *this* incident as her wedding—though not to the man to whom she will return, Quick. Again, the restlessness of desire is imaged in walking, and kinaesthetic imagery is continued in the moment when, alone, she feels 'something of the first feeling of all':

> Down below flowed a great slaty river, smooth but covered with twisted threads of water, swollen with its great flow, and directly under the window was an immense dusk-white flower with drooping petals, surrounded by green and living leaves. . . . 'Time is already floating away', she thought, smiling peculiarly. She was astonished at her feeling of wanting nothing.
>
> (pp. 489-90)

This mythical moment is followed by two further finales, as in many symphonies: one for full orchestra, whom she will return, Quick. Again, the restlessness of the 'citied plain' of human history, and a coda, in which she catches sight of Crow in the street and concludes with the question that revives the whole paradox of desire is imaged in walking, and kinaesthetic imagery is repeated forever, he—and me! What's there to stop it?' (p. 502).

'A YOUNG WOMAN'S ENTRANCE INTO THE WORLD': FEMINIST GENRE CRITICISM

To read this novel as belonging to the genre of personal quest is inevitably to link it with many others by twentieth-century women writers—for instance, Doris Lessing's Martha Quest novels and *The Golden Notebook*. It is also to enter into a well-developed discussion among feminist critics on women's interventions into this genre, the novel of development or of existential quest. I want to look at some examples of this criticism, both for its specific relevance to **For Love Alone** and as an example of what genre criticism has to offer. Broadly defined, considerations of genre raise questions about the kinds of plot, the types of protagonist, the narrative stances and discursive registers that were available to women writers at a given time, and about the uses they made of these devices. Genre has always been gendered, fiction being considered suitable for women to attempt, but not poetry and drama. Within the house of fiction, plots are strictly gendered, as indicated by the gradual elision between 'romance' and 'love story' in the late nineteenth century, and the consignment of the masculine romance under the general name of 'adventure story'.[14] Feminist genre criticism attends to women writers' adaptations (sometimes subversions) of gendered literary genres. As well, the area of genre and gender accommodates questions about the material determinants of these generic codes, their changes over time, and the social conditions of their accessibility to women.

Within feminist criticism there has been much interest in the novel of development, the *Bildungsroman*, as a genre popular with women writers since the early nineteenth century. Feminist critics re-examining definitions of the genre from a gendered perspective in *The Voyage In: Fictions of Female Development* identify 'distinctively female versions of the *Bildungsroman*'. These are described in terms of recurrent narrative structures (the apprenticeship and the awakening) and recurrent thematic tensions 'between autonomy and relationship, separation and community, loyalty to women and attraction to men'.[15] The editors claim that these are specifically female tensions, and while conceding that social constraints produce other conflicts that are not unique to women, they claim that these conflicts are more relentless in women's stories:

> Repeatedly, the female protagonist or *Bildungsheld* must chart a treacherous course between the penalties of expressing sexuality and suppressing it, between the costs of inner concentration and of direct confrontation with society, between the price of succumbing to madness and of grasping a repressive 'normality'.[16]

This would suggest that **For Love Alone** is unusual among women's novels in that Teresa always is quite clear about choosing the anti-social side of each one of these dilemmas. Believing in principle in the expression of sexuality, she scorns conventional female prudery and timidity; but she is susceptible to Jonathan Crow precisely because he talks sex and practises a perverse chastity. Her few direct confrontations with social convention are confusing to others and humiliating to her, such as her refusal to dive for the bridal bouquet at Malfi's wedding and her running away from teaching—but in each case the vivid reality of her fantasy life sustains her conviction that she is doing the right thing. Despite her earlier fear of the madness that she believed to be attendant on sexual repression, she welcomes the willed madness of her isolated dedication to following Jonathan: 'it seemed proof that she was very strange indeed—and to strange persons, strange visions, strange destinies' (p. 265). But finally, having followed the logic of that 'inner concentration' almost to the brink of suicide, Teresa re-emerges, still demanding 'love, knowledge, bread—all these I will have', and seizes what she wants—a committed partnership with a man (but not marriage and suburbia), knowledge of the world, and her own creative work. Triumphant but not free of conflict, she can be read as a twentieth-century sexual rebel who succeeds.

This is, of course, why it is tempting to read **For Love Alone** as a manifesto of sexual liberation, if not of feminism. But the story it tells of 'a young girl's entrance into the world' does not match the pattern of the female *Bildungsroman* traced by the editors of *The Voyage In.* To point this out is not to cast doubt on the value of genre definitions *per se,* but rather to test the outer limits of this currently influential feminist account of the novel of development. My reading of Stead's novel questions this structural model by pointing to its dependence on a psychological theory of individual development and sexual difference, one which deflects attention from the heterogeneity of writing and which is not well equipped to discern the concepts of social structure and change that are deployed in particular fictions.

While the editors of *The Voyage In* readily concede that the balance of tensions within the genre shifts with history, and note in twentieth-century fictions of female development 'a movement from the world within to the world without, from introspection to activity',[17] it seems inadequate simply to gesture towards 'history' itself as the determinant of changing structures. It is as if the differences between **For Love Alone** and Woolf's *The Voyage Out* (a paradigm case for the book's thesis, echoed in its title) could be explained by women's greater access to freedom of movement during the period between the two world wars. Teresa's voyage is equally mental and physical, and what enables her to grasp both independence and love is not so much a changed social world as a different vision of its dynamics and possibilities. Social and personal freedom such as she finds are one possibility, but so too is further entanglement in the 'difficult social web' (p. 254) that is spun to contain human passions.

In all of Stead's fiction, conflict is imaged in hand-to-hand combat between lovers or family members. Compared with the pattern in Woolf's *The Voyage Out* of the individual young woman ranged against overwhelming social and metaphysical forces, Stead constructs a fictional world in which those forces are internalized by the characters and become forces in their own mental life, enacted in the clash of wills in a violent struggle for psychic survival. It is psychology in this sense, as internalized social forces at war within and between persons, that is implied by Stead's self-description as a writer of 'the psychological drama of the person'. This vision of personal conflict and social-historical dynamics enables her to portray 'the young woman's entrance into the world' as ultimately the triumph of the social rebel.

Such a vision is incompatible with the concepts of psychology and social dynamics that are implicit in the feminist criticism represented by the essays in *The Voyage In.* By and large they share the mother-centred psychological theory of sexual difference which we encountered in the previous chapter. The editors quote Nancy Chodorow on sexual difference: 'The basic feminine sense of self is connected to the world, the basic masculine sense of self is separate';[18] the implication is that fictions tracing this development of self will be *essentially* different for women and for men. And so it is proposed, following Carole Gilligan's theory of the different moral development of women and men, that 'A distinctive female "I" implies a distinctive value system and unorthodox developmental goals, defined in terms of community and empathy rather than achievement and autonomy.'[19] The problem with this claim, as with the psychological essentialism proposed by Chodorow, is that it confirms rather than deconstructs the male/autonomy, female/community opposition—a deconstruction that is crucially necessary in order to reveal the dependence of the one (the male side of the opposition) on the suppression of the other. What is cause for concern here is the dominance in U S feminism of a theory of sexual difference that does not directly contest the way phallocentrism constitutes itself upon that culturally constructed difference.

In this structuralist phase in feminist criticism, such a theory of psychological structure is held to underlie and be reflected in common or recurrent literary structures. Thus the 'deep structure' of the women's novel of development or quest is often held to be the loss and redemption of the mother-daughter bond as the psychic economy upon which a woman must develop her autonomous sense of self. Several interesting essays on the twentieth-century female *Kunstlerroman,* the novel of the artist's development, demonstrate the working of this structuralist assumption in relation to that subgroup of *Bildungsromane* to which both **The Man Who Loved Children** and **For Love Alone** could be said to belong. Susan Gubar, finding in the work of Woolf, Mansfield and other modernists an exploration of 'the mother-daughter bond as a release from the solipsism of individual consciousness', lists three shifts in perspective that allowed them to reshape the structure:

> [F]irst, domestic disease or sickness *of* home is imaginatively reconstructed as sickness *for* home in what amounts to a revisionary domestic mythology; second, silent female resistance to or retaliation against the male word transforms itself into fantasies of a woman's language; finally, matrophobia, fear of becoming the mother, turns into matrisexuality, the erotics of mother and child.[20]

But, she says, this modernist-feminist assertion of a 'natural and distinct sphere' fell victim to its conservative consequences, and by the time **The Man Who Loved Children** appears, the utopian project of women's *Kunstlerromane* is all but extinguished 'when the daughter-artist can only respond to her mother's painful cry, "My womb is tearing" with the act of matricide'.[21]

Rachel Blau DuPlessis identifies the two elements in tension in the female novel of development as the love plot and the *Bildungs* plot, and points out the way this tension is exacerbated in the figure of the female artist. In most nineteenth-century female artist novels, the tension is resolved by the triumph of the love plot: formation or development ends, and social integration happens through marriage or not at all—the heroine dies or goes mad. The pattern she finds in some twentieth-century female artist fictions, however, overcomes this split by redefining both love and art: 'The romance plot, which often turns into a stalemate, is displaced . . . and replaced by a triangular plot of nurturance offered to an emergent daughter by a parental couple.'[22] Most often, the mother becomes the muse, and the daughter's task is to complete the mother's work:

This intellectual, aesthetic and ethical defense of the mother becomes involved with the evocation of the preoedipal dyad, matrisexuality, or a bisexual oscillation deep in the gendering process. In these works, the female artist is given a way of looping back and re-enacting childhood ties, to achieve not the culturally-approved ending in heterosexual romance, but rather the reparenting necessary to her second birth as an artist.[23]

Following Judith Kegan Gardiner, she cites **The Man Who Loved Children** as an example of maternal death as a 'necessary enabling act, which distinguishes the useful from the damaging in the maternal heritage'.[24] Now, while that novel could be read in terms of this proposed triangular plot (which, perversely, nurtures Louie's talent by setting it huge obstacles to overcome), it is certainly not the case that **For Love Alone** could be read as displacing the heterosexual romance plot. Stead redefines love and marriage, instead of refusing them or even 'working through' them, as Lessing does in *The Golden Notebook*. **For Love Alone** begins with the symbolic death of the father and establishes the emotional logic of what is to follow: in Teresa's libidinal economy, the sadistic man, in the mould of her father, is the more powerful attraction, despite her fantasy of love as freedom. If she could succeed in loving Jonathan she would redeem the 'murder' of Andrew Hawkins. He, like the father, invites women to 'do the work of passion' for him, a self-confessed 'gadfly of desire' who likes to observe 'scientifically' women's arousal. By denying his own desire and witholding consummation, he embodies that cultural presence of the Father which was discussed in the previous chapter— the denial, the illegitimation, of female desire. Thus he represents the stalemate of heterosexual romance, which Teresa herself breaks with the help of a nurturing male lover. Furthermore, Stead destabilizes this second love-plot by Teresa's insistence on trying out her power over men while remaining loyal to Quick as 'the only love, but not the first and not the last' (p. 496).

DuPlessis claims, too, that the art work represented in these female *Kunstlerromane* 'has a poetics of domestic values—nurturance, community building, inclusiveness, empathetic care' and because these poetics begin with its ethics, not its aesthetics, 'it is very like "life"'.[25] Yet this is manifestly not the case with either Louie's play or with Teresa's 'The Seven Houses of Love'. On the contrary, what strikes one is their profound literariness, and their bringing into play the unresolved conflicts of mental life through the working of fantasy. Teresa's writing, like her namesake saint's visionary work, *The Interior Castle,* articulates the desire for an impossible union. In each, too, desire is struggle as well as ecstasy and the beloved turns out to be also an adversary (Jonathan Crow's initials suggest this aspect of his role in Teresa's quest). Her description of the work, the completion of which will be her death, is *perversely* nurturing, empathetic: 'these pale leaves of poor sterile women, floated off the tree of flesh, would not have been without someone to carry their words, . . . would, dead, dying and to come, have an advocate in the courts of the world' (pp. 419-20).

The point is not that *For Love Alone* is unique, nor that it is deviant from this preferred model in feminist criticism, but that the model is too limited. It tends to set up a literary and psychological norm of femininity; and if, instead of a male model of the *Bildungsroman* that endorses patriarchal values, we now have an established feminist model of psychic and artistic development based on a notion of essential femininity, then we have no more than an inversion of the original patriarchal structure. Secondly, the specific problem posed for feminist readings of *For Love Alone* by this kind of structuralist criticism is how to accommodate both the romance genre (the 'for love alone' element) and the quest or *Bildungsroman* or *Kunstlerroman* (for autonomy, identity, creativity).

A QUEST FOR LOVE

As we have seen, it is far from inevitable that the love-story plot disappears, although some feminist critics tend to wish it away, to insist that although Teresa thinks she is seeking a man's love, she is 'really looking for herself'.[26] It is as if a serious novel about a woman can no longer be a love-story. Yet it is crucial to recognize that the terms of Teresa's quest are about the *world* rather than the self—about the finding or making of a place, a person or persons, from which to know the world, to create its meanings. If anything, it is a *Bildungsroman* of the kind that Bakhtin wrote about as one where not only the protagonist but the world itself was in process of change, and where the protagonist 'is forced to become a new, unprecedented type of human being' because the *foundations* of the world are changing. In such a novel of emergence, 'problems of reality and man's (sic) potential, problems of freedom and necessity, and the problem of creative initiative' are crucial, and the human image 'enters into a completely new, *spatial* sphere of historical existence'.[27] It is this aspect of the novel that achieves completion in the image of Teresa's emergence from the 'womb of time' into the 'citied plain' of history. Her joining with the liberated masses may be read as a utopian resolution to the story of women, men and love, but one which incorporates struggle and change.

Where Stead is most radical in this female *Bildungsroman* is her transformation of the oppositional thematics of love and independence by vindicating Teresa's idealistic quest for both. Her dedication to 'love alone' is portrayed as dedication to a principle, not a person—to a dynamic principle of Eros, of creative struggle. It is love conceived of as a passion, a kind of knowledge

and a kind of power. It links the saint with the sensualist, the individual with the collective history, the human and the natural worlds.

A measure of the transformation performed in Stead's novel can be gained by comparing it with George Eliot's *Middlemarch,* where St Theresa is also invoked as the prototype of the woman questor. Where Eliot's 'Prelude' refers to those 'later-born Theresas' of her time whose ardour 'alternated between a vague ideal and the common yearning of womanhood', Stead's Teresa fuses together in her passion the ideal and the yearning. It is passion which, with her, 'performs the function of knowledge for the ardently willing soul', in Eliot's words. It was Eliot's view that this function could only be performed by a 'coherent social faith and order' such as that which had enabled the original Theresa to realize her ideal of 'an epic life wherein there was a constant unfolding of far-resonant action', but this seemed no longer possible.[28] Eliot's Dorothea turns to secular love as the means of realizing her aspirations, and to a particular man as her guide to knowledge, like many nineteenth-century heroines.[29] The *Middlemarch* pattern, where the unloving scholar is superseded by the loving man of the world, is repeated in *For Love Alone,* but here the heroine need not resign herself to a conventional marriage, to living vicariously through her husband an obscure life of 'incalculably diffusive' beneficial effects. There is no 'coherent social faith and order', nor even the promise of a new one, like that held out by Will Ladislaw in *Middlemarch.* Yet there is the principle of love as creative struggle which Teresa defends and demonstrates: having taken on the position of social rebel, she continues the experiment of living her life against the grain of the dominant culture.[30]

A solution to the problem of what status to afford the love story has been offered by feminist and other critics' accounts of the operation of irony in Stead's narrative. Stead certainly entertains the possibility of Teresa's quest for love being read ironically: she has Quick declare that her devotion to Jonathan was 'just the illusion of a love-hungry girl' and Teresa agrees that she 'can't believe I ever loved that man' (p. 502). In this light, the pattern is banal: first she picks Mr Wrong because she is only an idealistic and inexperienced girl, and then she is rewarded by the appearance of Mr Right. But Mr Right has no monopoly on wisdom, and the relationship with him is deliberately destabilized by the encounter with Girton (Teresa's college education, perhaps?). An ironic reading may point to the truism that 'self-deception awaits the idealist',[31] that is, the expression of desire in fantasy and speculation is bound to go wrong and, indeed, that being 'undeceived' and wise to the ways of the world is unquestionably first priority. Yet the very presence of Jonathan Crow's constant lectures on self-interest and the survival of the psychologically fittest is enough to cast a shadow on this reading of the novel; and then there is Teresa's declaration, '*Love is blind* is the dictum, whereas, with me at least, Love sees everything. Like insanity, it sees everything; like insanity, it must not reveal its thoughts' (p. 460).

I would argue, rather, that criticism based on a moral reading of classic nineteenth-century realism *expects* a fictional protagonist to move from innocence to experience, and expects to be assigned by the narrative a superior position of knowledge from which to perceive this progress. Such expectations become banal in the case of the female novel of development because we 'know' that a girl's high expectations of love and autonomy are bound to be disappointed (whether this knowledge is accompanied by 'realistic' patriarchal regret or 'romantic' feminist anger). The move from innocence to experience is not the same thing for a young woman as for a young man. The outcome is likely to be tragic (like Hardy's heroines) or a noble accommodation to a limited sphere (like James's young women) rather than a 'realistic' finding of one's place in the world, a proper and constructive tempering of 'great expectations'.

As a feminist critic sensitive to this difference, Lidoff develops an ironic reading which relegates the 'romance' element of the heroine's quest to the realm of the inner life and classifies the narrator's stance as that of a 'realism' which allows both sympathetic identification and ironic distance.[32] However, I would argue that it is time to drop the dichotomy between realism and romance defined as moral attitudes, and the notion of irony that is its corollary. It is a limiting one for feminist criticism to be stuck with, and particularly so in relation to Stead's tales of women's lives, for they inscribe ideologies of femininity that cannot be definitively assigned to either side of the dichotomy. On this question of the status of love and ideas about love in the novel, Jennifer Strauss suggests that Stead seems to be demonstrating that 'the confusions concerning love, lust and marriage are real confusions, cases not of mere mistaken identity, but of identities overlapping and intertwining'.[33] And Teresa's ideas are inevitably like a wardrobe of hand-me-downs where nothing fits exactly but everything has some usefulness or some attraction. The patriarchal cultural inheritance of a young woman, even if she is trying to 'make over' conventional expectations that she find her place and value in marriage by the creative addition of erotic literature, Nietzschean metaphysics, nineteenth-century social theory, and so on, is bound to fall short of her needs and expectations:

> Teresa knew all the disorderly loves of Ovid, the cruel luxury of Petronius, the exorbitance of Aretino, the meaning of the witches' Sabbaths, the experiments of Sade, the unimaginable horrors of the Inquisition, the bestiality of the Bible, the bitter jokes of Aristophanes and what the sex-psychologists had written. . . . [T]he

> poets and playwrights spoke the language she knew, and the satirists and moralists wrote down with stern and marvellous precision all that she knew in herself but kept hidden from family and friends.

> (p. 76)

Teresa apprentices herself to this philosophy of passion rather as the classic nineteenth-century male *Bildungsheld* was indentured to a philosophy of life. Classically, this hero develops from innocence to knowledge through an exposure to experience that tempers his idealism. The major difference here is that the young woman forges the philosophy herself, out of her fantasies and the scraps of knowledge that she manages to glean from reading and talking.

It is, of course, tested by experience, but not in the banal sense of disillusionment or correction. In her meditations on passion and social mores, she concludes that women must always have desired as she does, but never uttered their desire, not acted upon it (p. 101). Timidity seems to her women's great weakness, and she resolves to act as (she believes) no woman has ever done, in defiance of man-made laws to control passion (p. 93). That her action takes the form of a declaration of love to a frigid misogynist, Jonathan Crow, is an irony with as much comic as tragic potential. Yet however romantically conceived, this 'extreme deed' proves to be the action which makes everything else possible, thus vindicating the seriousness with which this idealist takes her ideas.

Such a reading of the *productive* force of frustrated desires could be applied to all of Stead's fiction, from the heroic *For Love Alone* to the satirical portraits and the deeply ironic later novels. Ideas and fantasies have a material force in the lives of all her characters, whether dangerous or beneficent, and are not conducive to correction and control, as they are in liberal humanism. Characters change direction because of their instincts for psychic survival or destruction, not because of reconsidering their ideas. Stead's construction of 'character' in this way involves a certain deployment of irony, but one that differs from the humanist ideas of classic realism, and which can coexist with a utopian degree of idealism—as *For Love Alone* demonstrates.

Notes

1. Christina Stead, *For Love Alone* (Sydney: Angus & Robertson, 1969), p. 14. Further references to this edition in text.

2. Lorna Sage, 'Inheriting the Future: *For Love Alone*', *Stand,* vol. 23, no. 4 (1982), pp. 34-9, p. 35.

3. Christina Stead, Papers. Box 1, folder 2; see also her 'Another View of the Homestead', in *Ocean of Story,* pp. 513-20, p. 517.

4. Wetherell interview, p. 439.

5. For an early example, see Jean Saxelby and Gwen Walker-Smith, 'Christina Stead', *Biblionews* vol. 2, no. 9 (1949), pp. 37-43.

6. See, for example Brian Kiernan, 'Christina Stead: *Seven Poor Men of Sydney* and *For Love Alone*', in *Images of Society and Nature* (Melbourne: Oxford University Press, 1971), pp. 59-81; Ian Reid, '"The Woman Problem" in Some Australian and New Zealand Novels', *Southern Review* (Adelaide), vol. 7, no. 3 (1974), pp. 187-204.

7. Putnam's translation of *Don Quixote,* quoted by R. G. Geering, *Christina Stead* (Sydney: Angus & Robertson, 1979), p. 119.

8. See Drusilla Modjeska, *Exiles at Home: Australian Women Writers, 1925-1945* (Sydney: Angus & Robertson, 1981), pp. 20-5.

9. These are more fully documented in Ian Reid, '"The Woman Problem" . . .'.

10. Michael Wilding, 'Christina Stead's Australian Novels', *Southerly,* vol. 27, no. 1 (1967), pp. 20-23, p. 28.

11. I refer to the account of Bakhtin by Julia Kristeva, *Desire in Language,* trans. Leon S. Roudiez *et al.* (Oxford: Basil Blackwell, 1980), pp. 64-72.

12. R. J. Schofield, 'The Man Who Loved Christina Stead', *Bulletin,* May 22 (1965), pp. 29-31, p. 31.

13. Ian Reid, '"The Woman Problem" . . .', pp. 108-10.

14. Tony Davies, 'Transports of Delight: Fiction and its Audiences in the Later Nineteenth Century', in *Formations of Pleasure,* ed. Formations Collective (London: Routledge & Kegan Paul, 1983), pp. 46-58, p. 56.

15. Elizabeth Abel, Marianne Hirsch and Elizabeth Langland (eds), *The Voyage In: Fictions of Female Development* (Hanover and London: New England University Press, 1983), Introduction, pp. 11-12.

16. Ibid., pp. 12-13.

17. Ibid., p. 13.

18. Ibid., p. 10, quoting from *The Reproduction of Mothering* (Berkeley: University of California Press, 1978), p. 169.

19. Ibid., p. 10, referring to Gilligan's *In a Different Voice: Psychological Theory and Women's Development* (Cambridge, Mass.: Harvard University Press, 1982).

20. Susan Gubar, 'The Birth of the Artist as Heroine', in *The Representation of Women in Fiction,* ed. Carolyn Heilbrun and Margaret Higonnet (Baltimore and London: Johns Hopkins University Press, 1983), pp. 19-59, p. 39.

21. Ibid., p. 50.

22. Rachel Blau DuPlessis, *Writing Beyond the Ending* (Bloomington: Indiana University Press, 1985), p. 91.

23. Ibid., p. 94.

24. Ibid., p. 99.

25. Ibid., p. 103.

26. Diana Brydon, *Christina Stead,* ([London: Macmillan, 1987]) p. 82; Joan Lidoff, *Christina Stead,* p. 58.

27. M. M. Bakhtin, *Speech Genres and Other Late Essays,* trans. Vern McGee (Austin: University of Texas Press, 1986), pp. 23-4.

28. George Eliot, *Middlemarch* (London: Oxford University Press, 1947), pp. xv-xvi.

29. Nancy Miller, discussing this theme in *Villette,* comments on 'the way in which female desire as quest aligns itself uneasily with the question of mastery . . . , mastery and knowledge within an academy': 'Changing the Subject', p. 112.

30. This comparison with *Middlemarch* was developed in my earlier essay: Susan Higgins, '*For Love Alone*: A Female Odyssey?', pp. 441-3.

31. R. G. Geering, *Christina Stead,* p. 112.

32. Joan Lidoff, *Christina Stead,* ([New York: Ungar, 1982]) pp. 59-60.

33. Jennifer Strauss, 'An Unsentimental Romance', *Kunapipi,* vol. 4, no. 2 (1982), pp. 82-94, p. 92.

Select Bibliography

MAJOR WORKS BY CHRISTINA STEAD

BOOKS

(The details refer to first publications; editions used in this study are given in the endnotes.)

Seven Poor Men of Sydney (London: Peter Davies, 1934; New York: D. Appleton-Century, 1935).

The Beauties and Furies (London: Peter Davies, 1936; New York: D. Appleton-Century, 1936).

The Man Who Loved Children (New York: Simon & Schuster, 1940; London: Peter Davies, 1941).

For Love Alone (New York: Harcourt Brace, 1944; Peter Davies, 1945).

POSTHUMOUS PUBLICATIONS

Ocean of Story, The uncollected stories of Christina Stead, edited with an afterword by R. G. Geering (Ringwood, Victoria: Viking/Penguin, 1985).

INTERVIEWS (A SELECTION)

Wetherell, Rodney, 'Interview with Christina Stead', *Australian Literary Studies,* vol. 9, no. 4 (1980), pp. 431-48.

CRITICAL WORKS ON CHRISTINA STEAD

ARTICLES, ESSAYS AND REVIEWS

Higgins [Sheridan], Susan, '*For Love Alone*: A Female Odyssey?', *Southerly,* vol. 38, no. 4 (1978), pp. 428-45.

Kiernan, Brian, 'Christina Stead: *Seven Poor Men of Sydney* and *For Love Alone*', in *Images of Society and Nature* (Melbourne: Oxford University Press, 1971), pp. 59-81.

Reid, Ian, '"The Woman Problem" in Some Australian and New Zealand Novels', *Southern Review* (Adelaide), vol. 7, no. 3 (1974), pp. 187-204.

Sage, Lorna, 'Inheriting the Future: *For Love Alone*', *Stand,* vol. 23, no. 4 (1982), pp. 34-9.

Saxelby, Jean and Gwen Walker-Smith, 'Christina Stead', *Biblionews,* vol. 2, no. 9 (1949), pp. 37-43.

Schofield, R. J., 'The Man Who Loved Christina Stead', *Bulletin,* May 22 (1965), pp. 29-31.

Strauss, Jennifer, 'An Unsentimental Romance', *Kunapipi,* vol. 4, no. 2 (1982), pp. 82-94.

Wilding, Michael, 'Christina Stead's Australian Novels', *Southerly,* vol. 27, no. 1 (1967), pp. 20-33.

CRITICAL THEORY AND BACKGROUND

Abel, Elizabeth, Marianne Hirsch and Elizabeth Langland (eds), *The Voyage In: Fictions of Female Development* (Hanover and London: New England University Press, 1983).

Bakhtin, M. M., *Speech Genres and Other Late Essays,* trans. Vern McGee (Austin: University of Texas Press, 1986).

DuPlessis, Rachel Blau, *Writing Beyond the Ending* (Bloomington: Indiana University Press, 1985).

Gubar, Susan, 'The Birth of the Artist as Heroine', in *The Representation of Women in Fiction,* ed. Carolyn Heilbrun and Margaret Higonnet (Baltimore and London: Johns Hopkins University Press, 1983), pp. 19-59.

Kristeva, Julia, *Desire in Language,* trans. Leon S. Roudiez *et al.* (Oxford: Basil Blackwell, 1980).

Miller, Nancy K., 'Changing the Subject: Authorship, Writing and Gender', in *Feminist Studies/Critical Studies,* ed. Teresa de Lauretis (Bloomington: Indiana University Press, 1986), pp. 102-20.

Modjeska, Drusilla, *Exiles at Home: Australian Women Writers, 1925-1945* (Sydney: Angus & Robertson, 1981).

Louise Yelin (essay date 1988)

SOURCE: Yelin, Louise. "Sexual Politics and Female Heroism in the Novels of Christina Stead." In *Faith of a (Woman) Writer,* edited by Alice Kessler-Harris and William McBrien, pp. 191-98. New York: Greenwood Press, 1988.

[*In the following essay, Yelin traces Stead's changing views of "the relationship of sexual politics and female heroism" in her novels of the 1940s, saying that these works "echo, in small, the evolution in Stead's vision from the exuberant if equivocal optimism of the early books to the growing pessimism of the later ones."*]

Christina Stead's career as a novelist spans three continents—Australia, Europe, and North America—and the middle half of the twentieth century. Her novels wander over territories as broad and varied as those she actually traversed, encompassing working-class life in Sydney in the 1920s (**Seven Poor Men of Sydney, For Love Alone**), international finance and politics in Paris in the 1930s (**House of All Nations**), the life of a middle-class family in New Deal Washington (**The Man Who Loved Children**), and the marginal existences of declassé rentiers in post-war Europe (**The Little Hotel**) and of working-class, women's, and bohemian subcultures in England in the 1950s and 1960s (**Cotters' England, Miss Herbert**). Yet underlying this evident diversity of character and setting is an imaginative terrain whose contours remain more or less constant.

Perhaps the most pervasive features of Stead's novelistic world are the political vision which shapes it and the delight she takes in language. Stead is surely a political writer, with a leftish disposition, as numerous critics have remarked and Stead herself has suggested.[1] Political in her case means a preoccupation with the ways that the familiar features of our world—love, say, or families, or finance, for that matter—are not given in nature but are rather products of struggle, arenas in which power is contested.[2] Conversely, *politics* for Stead also involves the tracing of what one of her characters somewhat cryptically identifies as "the influence of Marx on character,"[3] which I take to mean that view of the world that regards persons more or less as products of their circumstances. Stead's preoccupation with language links her with other contemporary writers. Her novels investigate, among other things, the processes of signification and the conditions and determinants of meaning. But their main energy lies in a linguistic excess that takes a number of different forms across an unusually wide stylistic register: intense lyricism coupled with closely observed descriptions, aphoristic brilliance, heightened reproduction of the ordinary speech of quite distinct groups of people.

While politics and language structure Stead's imaginative world and define it in relation to the world that she and her novels inhabit, they do so quite differently at different times. Indeed, the meanings of both *politics* and *language* as well as the relationship between them change in significant ways over the course of her long and distinguished career. Stead's early novels are concerned with explicitly social and political themes; the novels written during the 1940s transpose her political vision from public life to the more "private" world of the family and shift their focus from questions of class, loosely, to questions of gender; her late novels describe the commodification of both public and private life and represent the fragmentation of a world composed entirely of words. These changes, and especially the narrowing of Stead's novelistic world, mark the trajectory of a left-wing female intellectual through a literary culture initially somewhat receptive, later indifferent, and finally hostile to the left.

The novels Stead published in the early and mid-1940s occupy a central place in her *oeuvre,* both chronologically and thematically. In the early novels, the heroes, generally, are men whose heroism tends to involve public gestures of one kind or another. The late novels are lacking in both heroes and heroism, unless we consider as heroic the author's act of recording the disintegration of the novels' world. In the novels of the 1940s, however, the heroes are young women whose heroism is largely defined by their rebellion against the limitations of gender. Taken together, then, these novels examine the relationship of sexual politics and female heroism. But the changes in their notions of female heroism—from the heroic imagination of Louisa Pollit in *The Man Who Loved Children* to the romantic longings of Teresa Hawkins in *For Love Alone* (1944) to the satirical pragmatism of Letty Fox in *Letty Fox: Her Luck* (1946)—echo, in small, the evolution in Stead's vision from the exuberant if equivocal optimism of the early books to the growing pessimism of the later ones.

The Man Who Loved Children, the autobiographical novel rightly regarded as Stead's masterpiece, vividly portrays the life of a middle-class family in Washington, D.C., in the late 1930s. In dramatizing the struggles of its heroine, Louisa Pollit (age eleven when the novel begins) to grow up in a household whose members are constantly at war with each other, and to free herself from the sadistic tyranny of her father and the self-loathing of her mother, *The Man Who Loved Children* offers us a myth of feminine survival.

The portrayal of the Pollit family articulates a vision of radical sexual difference, manifesting the opposition—in all senses—between the mother, Henny, and the father, Sam.[4] First, Stead at once evokes and parodies in Henny and Sam the conventional identification of woman and nature, man and culture: thus, Henny refers to her family as a brood, while Sam calls it a tribe but treats it as an extension of himself. In addition, Stead delineates feminine and masculine world-views, opposing Henny's particularity, imagination, and pessimism to Sam's moralizing abstraction and scientific optimism:

> What a moral, high-minded world their father saw! But for Henny there was a wonderful, particular world, and when they went with her they saw it: they saw the fish eyes, the crocodile grins, the hair like a birch broom, the mean men crawling with maggots, and the children restless as an eel, that she saw. . . . Sam, their father, had endless tales of friends, enemies, but most often they were good citizens, married to good wives, with good children (though untaught), but never did Sam meet anyone out of Henny's world, grotesque, foul, loud-voiced, rude, uneducated, and insinuating, full of scandal, slander, and filth, financially deplorable and physically revolting, dubiously born and going awry to a desquamating end.[5]

These divergent visions, in turn, engender the Pollits' quite distinct verbal forms or discourses (as well as endow the novel with much of its linguistic richness): for Henny, the tirade and catalogue; for Sam, the secular sermon and a private, comic language composed out of the "verbal tatters of Artemus Ward" (p. 301).[6]

The novel's vision of the Pollits as polis is not only a fable of difference but also and equally one of domination. (One could profitably read **The Man Who Loved Children** as an illustration of Michel Foucault's notion that "the family" is an arena in which relations of knowledge and power are organized.)[7] Sam attempts to control his family by constant intrusions into Henny's and the children's lives, by repeated assertions of a will-to-knowledge that is also a will-to-power. Often, Sam's will is exercised through manipulation of language, as if by naming and renaming the inhabitants of his world he might denude them of their power to disturb his order and render them harmless. Although delight in language offers Sam a structure of illusions which mediates his attempts to alter his world and to create an alternative to it, Sam's word-play is defensive, ultimately a sign of his weakness and puerility. Indeed, Sam's children resist, revelling in the chaotic particularity of their mother's world, and an unspoken bond develops, in the course of the novel, between Henny and Louisa, Sam's daughter by his first wife. This bond, which Henny identifies as "the natural outlawry of womankind" (p. 244; the rhetoric of nature is singularly inappropriate), represents an alliance between the principal victims of Sam's tyranny. This tyranny, especially as it takes the form of apparently gratuitous sadism, suggests Sam's own weakness and, more generally, the obsolescence of the rule of the patriarch. (Stead comically evokes the latter in a slip of the pen made by Sam's daughter Evie, who begins a letter to him with the salutation "Dead Dad.")

While Stead is primarily concerned in *The Man Who Loved Children* with what might be called politics *in* the family, the novel is shaped by her characteristic social vision and depicts the Pollit family not in isolation but as it is inscribed within a wider network of social relations in a particular time and place. The novel's setting—Washington, Baltimore, Annapolis, and Harper's Ferry—is a politicized landscape marked by the Depression, the New Deal, and the intersection of the cultures of North and South.[8] Here we encounter Henny as a decayed Southern aristocrat from a fading Baltimore family and Sam as a New Deal liberal, a government bureaucrat (a naturalist, like Stead's father) who believes that science and reason will enable him to raise his family above his own working-class origins.[9] From this vantage point, Sam's domination within the family is revealed as a function of his relative powerlessness in the world "outside." Thus, while Henny borrows money from anyone who will lend it, Sam blindly insists that the Pollits survive without credit, which he echoes his Puritan ancestors in equating with usury. His refusal to acknowledge that Henny's "sordid secrets" have been feeding the family (p. 477) is an act of bad faith which sustains him for a time, until bankruptcy finally forces him to confront the family's debts. While Stead uses the collapse of credit in *House of All Nations* to suggest the demise of the liberal political order, here, in the puncturing of Sam's illusions it delineates a crisis in liberal and patriarchal ideologies.

This crisis is vividly realized in Louisa's rebellion against her father's authority. Louisa's struggle is remarkable not only for its confidence and intensity, but also because it is carried out in writing—for example, in a play she writes in a language she invents for the occasion, a tragedy entitled *Herpes Rom* in which a father (Herpes Rom, or the snake man) murders his daughter. (When Sam angrily asks her why she does not write in English, she replies, in what might be the novel's greatest moment, "Did Euripides write in English?" (pp. 374-77).) If writing enables Louisa to articulate her anger, it is also a means of paying homage and a source of solace and delight—equipment for living, to borrow Kenneth Burke's phrase.[10] Louisa's writings—a cycle of poems she writes for a beloved teacher, the diary she keeps in code, so Sam cannot read it, the stories she tells her brothers and sisters—are among the novel's chief pleasures. Writing, moreover, Louisa surpasses both Henny and Sam, whose considerable verbal resources are dissipated in their vocal squabbling: by writing, that is, she transcends their *spoken* reality and, as her author does, successfully marries Henny's particularity to Sam's comedy.[11]

But writing alone cannot ensure Louisa's passage into adulthood; she must also overcome the crippling limitations of sexual difference, if not difference itself. In the novel's vision of how she does so lies its myth of feminine survival. On the one hand, Louisa appropriates the prerogatives of men, announcing, "I am triumphant, I am king." (p. 320) On the other hand, she invokes the solidarity of women, repudiating Sam's authority to speak for her mother by asking, "What do you know about my mother? She was a woman." (p. 488) To thrive, then, Louisa must be *both* woman and king. This resolution, which ignores the logical impossibility of the dyad woman/king, can be seen either as a symptom of the novel's central problem, a restatement of its question, "Can women have power?" or as a way of magically endowing women with the power of men.

The novel's climax is similarly ambiguous. Louisa, made wretched by the constant war between her parents, resolves to poison them, but changes her mind after placing cyanide in one teacup. Henny, though, notices what Louisa has done, seizes the poisoned cup, drinks the tea, and dies. For a girl to grow up, Stead seems to be saying, she must kill her mother. Or, alternatively, she must escape from her family and refuse the passivity and self-hatred that deform the feminine character, her own as well as her mother's. Thus, in the last pages of the novel, Louisa looks at her family as if from a great distance, and the book ends with her running away to take a "walk round the world" (p. 491). Unlike the heroines of nineteenth-century fiction, Louisa gets away with murder. By rewriting the nineteenth-century plot that punishes characters for their transgressions, Stead has invented a new mythology, a cultural script appropriate to a modern age.[12] But the myth belongs to the world of fantasy, as is evident in the way that the novel projects its resolution—Louisa's escape—into a future that it does not describe.

In fact, the meaning of Louisa's escape and therefore of the novel's denouement is rather more ambivalent than we have suggested and bears closer examination. The novel ends—quite conveniently—before Louisa actually reaches womanhood (she is still in her mid-teens), so that she can be said to evade the constraints of sexual difference by not having fully to experience them. Moreover, her escape is largely made possible—enacted in as well as enabled—by her writing. Literature, or vision, or the word is to be her mode of transcendence and also her way of solving the conundrum of women and power. As with so many characters in novels, her power is preeminently the power of narrative: that is, the power to tell her story or to make fictions. But Stead is not giving us a simple apotheosis of woman as author, for if *The Man Who Loved Children* manifests the power of the word, it just as surely indicates, for Louisa as for Henny and Sam, that the power of the word is poor compensation for powerlessness in the world. While Louisa's writing offers equipment for living, it does not substitute for the power to transform the world. In this respect, it suggests Stead's view, in 1940, of her own literary production.

Like *The Man Who Loved Children,* Stead's next two novels, the autobiographical *For Love Alone* and *Letty Fox: Her Luck* are preoccupied with relations between the sexes and with the question of women and power. The two novels present different versions of the future that is projected at the end of *The Man Who Loved Children*: the protagonists of both novels are young women facing conflicts involving their sexuality, their ambitions, and their circumstances. Although both Letty Fox and Teresa Hawkins, the heroine of *For Love Alone,* are survivors, neither is heroic in quite the manner of Louisa. Taken together, then, these two novels revise the myth of female heroism that underlies *The Man Who Loved Children.*

For Love Alone asks under what conditions it is possible to be both "woman and freeman"[13] and argues that love, in all its complexity, is one of the conditions in question. (Thus, the novel attempts, among other things, a provisional definition of *love.*) That Teresa sees herself as a *freeman* while Louisa insists that she is king can be read not only as a figure for the identification of power with masculinity, but also as a sign of the ever-contracting space in which Stead's characters enact their destinies. For Teresa, in any case, love represents the only possibility of escape from the stifling poverty of Sydney, from the tyranny of her father and the claustrophobic life of her family, and from the sterile existence of the old maid. But *love* in this novel is equivocal in somewhat the same way as writing is in the earlier book. For one thing, love often takes the form of domination and can hardly be imagined except as property relations or even fantasized except as it is represented in the canonical texts of the Western erotic tradition from Ovid to Sade: that is, love is inscribed within the discourse of European bourgeois and patriarchal hegemony.[14] (In this respect, love can be distinguished from writing in *The Man Who Loved Children* for in *For Love Alone* there is no movement beyond a gendered language such as we encountered in the earlier book.) In addition, although the novel seems to call for a transformation of bourgeois and patriarchal social relations,[15] it offers little hope of its being brought about. Accordingly, Teresa's heroism is limited more or less to the sphere accorded women within bourgeois and patriarchal social orders, the terrain of "private life," and takes the form of attempts to define for herself the meaning of love and a commitment to create, in love, an alternative to the exploitation and oppression that prevail in the world at large.

There is no such alternative or enclave in *Letty Fox: Her Luck.* Like its two predecessors, this novel asks whether (or how) its protagonist's ambitions can be realized. But Letty's desires are neither heroic, like Louisa's, nor romantic, like Teresa's, but pragmatic, in keeping with the cynicism that is the novel's dominant mood: Letty seeks "to get married and join organized society" and wants "to be a metropolitan."[16] In its scrutiny of these aspirations—Letty's scrutiny, for the most part, since the novel is told in the first person—the novel measures them not against ideal values like love or heroism but rather against the decadence and exploitation that pervade the world it describes.

Letty Fox, in short, is a satire which relentlessly exposes the commodification of culture, politics, and "personal life," especially in the world of the left-wing intelligentsia in New York in the 1930s and 1940s. Among the targets of Stead's satire is "radical chic," as one critic points out.[17] But *Letty Fox* also laments the degeneration, in the 1940s, of the idealism and activism that made the thirties a "younger, healthier world" (p. 476). Similarly, the novel's satire of the world of letters is an indictment of a literary culture that cannot accommodate Stead's apparently idiosyncratic talents. (Stead wrote *Letty Fox* soon after a stint as a screenwriter at MGM.) Although Letty herself is verbally inventive, words in *Letty Fox* lack the power they have for Louisa or even Sam Pollit. More important, most of what passes for culture in this novel is debased by the mass-production and marketing of words and images—as in Letty's work writing copy for advertisements—or is the sterile product of a quest for aesthetic purity. Finally, the law of the marketplace—illustrated in numerous kinds of traffic in flesh—and the universal exploitation of everyone by everyone else underlie the depiction of "private life" in *Letty Fox.* Here, parents neglect their children (abdication by both mothers and fathers replaces the paternal tyranny of the two previous books), and children desert their parents; men exploit women, and women victimize men. Marriage is the principal site of this parody of mutuality, but only briefly, for it is mainly important as an occasion for alimony—a form of legal extortion and therefore a paradigm for social relations generally in *Letty Fox*—and for divorce, which ensures that "the family" is little more than an aggregation of women who compete for attention from men.

While Letty does not share the values of the culture she inhabits, she does not, like Louisa or Teresa, actively confront it. But even though she appears to give in to the prevailing cynicism and despair, she wins our sympathy because she never yields completely. If Letty's complicity in a culture whose values she cannot endorse separates her from her author, the critical stance she adopts toward her world nevertheless defines the only possibility Stead sees for female heroism in a decidedly unheroic age. This critical stance, of course, resembles that of Stead herself, whose novels reveal the shabbiness of the dismal world we live in and at the same time insist that this is not the only imaginable world.

Notes

1. See, for example, Terry Sturm, "Christina Stead's New Realism: *The Man Who Loved Children* and *Cotters' England,*" in Don Anderson and Stephen Knight, eds., *Cunning Exiles: Studies of Modern Prose Writers* (Sydney: Angus and Robertson, 1974): 9-35; Grant McGregor, "*Seven Poor Men of Sydney*: The Historical Dimension," *Southerly* 38 (1978): 380-403; Jose Yglesias, review of *Dark Places of the Heart* (The American title of *Cotters' England*), *The Nation,* 24 October 1966, pp. 420-21; Yglesias, "Marx as Muse" (Review of the reissue of *The Man Who Loved Children*), *The Nation,* 5 April 1965, pp. 368-70; Michael Wilding, "Christina Stead's Australian Novels," *Southerly* 27 (1967): 20-33; Bell Gale Chevigny, "With Rake-offs for the Pope" (review of the reissue of *House of All Nations*), *Village Voice,* 4 October 1973, p. 21.

2. Here Stead can profitably be read in conjunction with feminist theory, particularly theories of feminism as politics. For recent examples, see Maria Ramos's reinterpretation of Freud in "Freud's Dora, Dora's Hysteria: The Negation of a Woman's Rebellion," *Feminist Studies* 6, no. 3 (Fall, 1980): 472-511, and Michele Barrett, *Women's Oppression Today: Problems in Marxist Feminist Analysis* (London: Verso editions, 1980).

3. *Seven Poor Men of Sydney* (1934; reprint ed., Sydney: Angus and Robertson, 1965), p. 120.

4. Stead took the name Pollit from Harry Pollit, a leader of the British Communist Party. Samuel Clemens was one of her father's favorite humorists (the other was Artemus Ward, whose linguistic style forms Sam's): thus, Samuel Clemens Pollit. Cf. John B. Beston, "An Interview with Christina Stead," *World Literature Written in English* 15 (1976): 93-94.

5. *The Man Who Loved Children* (reprint ed., New York: Avon, 1966), pp. 13-14. All subsequent references to this novel appear parenthetically in the text.

6. Henny's tirades are like the torrent of invective which Northrop Frye identifies as a feature of satire, in *Anatomy of Criticism* (1957; reprint ed., New York: Atheneum, 1965), pp. 223, 236. Joan Lidoff finds in the novel a "satiric realism of observation", cf. ("Home is Where the Heart Is," *Southerly* 38 (1978), p. 371).

7. See, for example, *History of Sexuality, Volume I: An Introduction,* trans. Robert Hurley (New York:

Pantheon, 1978), pp. 108-14; and Jacques Donzelot, *The Policing of Families,* trans. Robert Hurley (New York: Pantheon, 1980), pp. 217-34.

8. Jose Yglesias observes that the setting gives the novel political relevance ("Marx as Muse," p. 369).

9. Although Stead disavows any abstract intention in creating Sam Pollit, she does see some merit in Jonah Raskin's remark that Sam is the American liberal who is also totalitarian. ("Christina Stead in Washington Square," *London Magazine,* NS, 9, 11 [1970]: 74-75, 77; cf. Mary Kathleen Benet, who sees Sam as "the 'liberal' exemplar of the imperialist period of capitalist expansion.") (Introduction to the Virago edition of *Letty Fox: Her Luck.*)

10. Graham Burns sees Louisa's project as a challenge to Sam's monopoly of language, a moral struggle involving the "authority of the written word" ("The Moral Design of *The Man Who Loved Children,*" *Critical Review,* no. 14 [1971]: 50-51, 55). Stead describes her own delight in writing—clearly the model for Louisa's—in "A Writer's Friends," *Southerly* 28 (1968): 163-68.

11. Joan Lidoff points out that the novel is written with Henny's particularity ("Home is Where the Heart Is," p. 375).

12. This may be one reason for the interest in Stead on the part of feminist critics. Stead herself says of Louisa, "It's the child's viewpoint that I'm faithfully reproducing. We live through agonies and grow up perfectly straight. What happens to Louie doesn't upset her so much. She has some concept that what she's done is bad, but children are capable of very cool thinking. . . . People who do serious things are not necessarily scarred." (Beston, "Interview," p. 92).

13. *For Love Alone* (reprint ed., Virago Modern Classics, London: Virago, n.d.), p. 224. All subsequent references to this novel appear parenthetically in the text.

14. In the novel's most intensely lyrical passage, Teresa muses, in metaphors drawn from the language of land-tenure, on the "short season" woman has for love. She reads Ovid, Virgil, de Sade, etc., delighted to find her fantasies reflected there, "for she found nothing in the few words of women that was what they must have felt." (pp. 72-76).

15. Susan Higgins notes Stead's "radically critical insight into bourgeois social relations." See "Christina Stead's *For Love Alone*: A Female Odyssey?" *Southerly* 38 (1978), 429.

16. *Letty Fox: Her Luck* (reprint ed., Virago Modern Classics, London: Virago, n.d.), pp. 4, 235. All

subsequent references to this novel appear parenthetically in the text.

17. Mary Kathleen Benet, Introduction to the Virago edition of the novel.

Jennifer Gribble (essay date 1991)

SOURCE: Gribble, Jennifer. "Christina Stead's *For Love Alone*." *Critical Review*, no. 31 (1991): 17-27.

[*In the following essay, Gribble contends that feminist readings of* For Love Alone *reduce its stature and simplify its artistic accomplishments, especially with regard to Stead's complex treatment of love in the novel.*]

Twenty years ago, in what is still in my view the best article on Christina Stead's *The Man Who Loved Children,* Graham Burns described it as a great and innovatory work that had received scant analytical attention (*The Critical Review*, xvi, 1971). In the intervening decades, attention has burgeoned, all too little of it closely analytical. Most notably, feminist critics and womens' studies courses have "appropriated" Stead, despite her firm rejection of feminist ideology and against the grain of her writing. Stead's writing is in fact these days quite widely read as a significant contribution to feminist theory and a challenge to "pre-feminist criticism", which means, variously, "liberal-humanist", "conventional", "moral", and even "Leavisite". No Stead novel has been more thoroughly de-natured and reduced in stature by this process than the work on which, together with *The Man Who Loved Children,* Stead's critical reputation must surely rest.

For Love Alone might seem to lend itself admirably to the cause: young girl cuts off her ties with the patriarchy, defies the constraints on women in 1930s Australian society, painfully finances her passage to England where she shakes off the misogynist grip of her lover, and establishes herself as an independent woman (though she falls in love with a man and seems more or less satisfied with the outcome). Dressed up as many of these accounts are in the language of recent theory, they come down to strangely old-fashioned simple conceptions of novels as summarizable plots complicated by characterization and diverse intersecting discourse. I know of only one recent account of *For Love Alone* that fixes its attention on the extraordinary quality of Stead's prose, and the critical questions it raises, and that is Nicholas Jose's suggestive few pages in *Meridian,* October 1987. Jose describes the novel as "a peculiar case of the teller seeking her defining tale. If it is only intermittently successful, that is because the undifferentiated multiplicity Stead would convey is ultimately inimical to art. Hence the clumsy, tendentious framework that encumbers the passages of vibrancy,

immediacy and insight" (p. 110). His argument is that the novel gropes its way backwards to the essential and the elemental "to understand self-realization by going back to its opposite, the chaotic energies of an unformed yet forming self".

I would argue that the passages of "vibrancy, immediacy and insight" take their bearings from a controlling vision that represents art of a high order. In the novels that precede *For Love Alone,* Stead progressively works through her autobiographical sources until, in *The Man Who Loved Children,* she is able to look unflinchingly at the idea of "love", and the range of meanings it has within the context of Pollit family life. The astonishing capacity of Sam and Henny's sexual relationship to regenerate itself out of the clash of their mismatched personalities hints at a mysteriousness in sexual love that clearly requires the sustained focus of *For Love Alone.* And it is shaped by Louie Pollit's discovery of the Nietzschean "will-to-power" as, veritably, the "life-force." In *For Love Alone,* Teresa's search for love is so immediate and so deceptively picaresque in its rendering of what Henny Pollit thinks of as "life's put-together and rough-and-tumble" that the novel's disciplined and probing thinking about the larger questions of what love actually is and how it feels and what it does to and for people, has gone largely unnoticed. This "thinking", as one might expect of a considerable novelist, goes on not simply at the level where ideas are exchanged and emotional transactions effected, but in those areas of experience most closely in touch with "the essential and the elemental". So that in my reading, "the chaotic energies" are part of the territory this novel opens up, in pursuit of a self that by its very nature never finally is, nor can be, "formed."

Stead professed herself always "a believer in love" as the source of all human creativity, and she often drew an analogy between the work of art and the love relationship: "every work of art should give utterance [to], or indicate, the awful blind strength and the cruelty of the creative impulse, that is why they must all have what are called errors, both of taste and style: in this it is like a love affair . . . the passion, energy and struggle, the night of which no one speaks, the creative act" (To Thistle Harris, April 6, 1942, reprinted in *Meridian,* October 1989, p. 146). "Awful", "blind", "strength", "cruelty", "creative", "impulse", "errors": the words point precisely to the distinctive power and the complex tone of this novel in particular.

When Teresa Hawkins declares "everything in the world is produced by the act of love", "I have been in love all my life", it is in the name of love as a fundamental creative force that she speaks. This is the sense of love that sustains her search for a love that is particular and personal, giving its quite unironic appropriateness to the novel's title. That title, not of Stead's choosing, nevertheless picks up Andrew Hawkins' dictum in the first chapter, that "love alone unites humans", and its echo in the conclusive wisdom of James Quick: "we are united by love alone". The ironies that play over that sense of love as motivation and attainment have received some attention. A further, and unnoticed, irony attaches to "alone", a word that reverberates throughout the novel. Teresa, who believes that she can, if necessary, live for herself "alone", but yearns for union, discovers that although we may be united by love alone, we are also rendered solitary by it. Her journey is in part a discovery of the inherent isolation, the loneliness, of loving.

Such an emphasis is characteristic of Stead, whose views of the way things are is far from comforting. Her somewhat tendentious insistence that she was a "naturalist", like her father, simply recording what she saw, raises questions about form, and other moral shapings and judgments, that need to be considered. It also points up the importance, in all her novels, of the natural world, as source of those energies and impulses that link human and non-human nature, and as source of the images that engage her. imagination and structure her work. This is signalled in **"Sea People"**, the brief prelude with which *For Love Alone* opens: a vision of lives set down on the sea-board of an island continent, but made restless voyagers, responsive as they are to the swell of the tides and the passage of ships, the sun and the moon and the "heavenly constellations". The relationship between what seems fixed, determined, geographically and culturally, and what seems to be the free and liberating play of impulse, is the larger theme of Teresa's journey and of the many journeys that compose it.

Stead's habit in all her novels is to explore her characters' talking, and what the characters in *For Love Alone* have to say to one another about love is an important aspect of this novel's enquiry, though I can only touch on it here in so far as it relates to the different kind of writing I want to hold in focus. These are moments that might loosely be called symbolic, or, to borrow from another novelist who thought that "the via media to being, for man and woman, is love, and love alone" (D. H. Lawrence, *Study of Thomas Hardy*), they are "organic units of consciousness with a life of their own, and you can never explain them away, because their value is dynamic, emotional, belonging to the sense consciousness of the body and the soul" ("The Dragon of the Apocalypse"). These epiphanies form the very basis of the novel's thinking about love, though they take their place in the ordinary flow of incident, confirming Teresa's sense, and the novel's, of "how extraordinary real life is".

That thinking about what love is, or might be thought to be, begins with the opening sentences of Chapter 1:

Naked, except for a white towel rolled into a loincloth, he stood in the doorway, laughing and shouting, a tall man with powerful chest and thick hair of pale burning gold and a skin still pale under many summers' tan. He seemed to thrust back the walls with his muscular arms; thick tufts of red hair stood out from his armpits. The air was full of the stench of brown seaweed and old fish nets. Through the window you could see the water of the bay and the sand specked with flotsam and scalloped with yellow foam, left by the last wave.

(London and Sydney [1978], 1986, p. 5)

This chapter, which climaxes in Teresa's furious "I will kill you, father", has been seen as "the symbolic death of the father", and a certain similarity between Andrew Hawkins and Sam Pollit has helped to license the view that there is some "emotional account settling" going on here.

Hawkins' flaunting himself before his captive women in a homely scene where they sew their outfits for their cousin's wedding is shrewdly observed, but with some amusement and affection, and certainly not with anything so simple as rejection. His bragging of conquest ("I have been much loved"), his laying down the law, is inseparable from his physical and intellectual vitality, his being at ease with his own body and at home in the world of water and sand with which the writing identifies him. This chapter represents one kind of writing that is characteristic of Stead at her best, in which self-engrossed rhetoric becomes the vehicle for serious enquiry. Hawkins is not only the decisive voice in shaping Teresa's conception of love as "the via media to being" and source of many of the energies that empower her; his views on the question of love are to be explored and echoed by the novel's many voices. One after another they unroll: the sense of love as primitive idyll—his recollection of a bare-breasted, but modestly clad, black woman; from there to love as idealism; love as a meal-ticket ("I could have married a rich girl"); love as the marriage of true minds ("one poor girl, Paula Brown, wrote to me for years, discussing things"); love as sacred ("your mother and I were united by a great love, by a passion higher than earthly thoughts"); love as servitude ("in the peace and sanctity of a man's home he feels the love that is close to devotion"); and love as sexual gratification ("yes, sex . . . on the other side of the barrier of sex is all the splendour of internal life, a garden full of roses . . . sweet-scented, fountains playing"); love as above all, the fulfilment of emotional needs ("what do we look for in a woman—understanding!").

Teresa's and the novel's focus on "love" has often been described as "obsessive", and Jose, for one, sees the re-iteration of the word as draining it of significance. On the contrary, I think that, both here and in the enquiry flowing from this opening, attention is directed to the gap between what is said about love, a word that is made to do duty for many meanings ("language is simply not large enough", Teresa reflects), and the experience itself ("all the ecstacies are things within for which there is no name"). Informing the present discussion is the battle of wills and wits that links Hawkins and Teresa, the humiliations inflicted in the name of love: "I don't know where you got your face of a little tramp, Trees, a ragamuffin . . . I personally cannot stand ugliness, Trees. I worship beauty." Love is in the air, in the very atmosphere of family life, with cousins and friends marrying and the Hawkins children alert to each others' silent burden of sexual maturing. "Trees is always moaning about love", as her father puts it, and there are many questions to which she would like an answer. Disingenuousness and genuine speculation make her ask Hawkins what he would do if he loved more than one person. (It so happens, he confesses, that the unique and sacred love he had had for their mother has been followed by another more recent love.) And love is in the physical atmosphere too. The "Concupiscent fever" of Malfi's wedding, "a hundred degrees in the shade and getting hotter", the hot rooms of Teresa's love orgies, entertain Hawkins' view that "love is warmth, heat. The sun is love", in the context of uncomfortable actualities.

Two sequences are now juxtaposed: Malfi's wedding, a distinctively Australian epithalamium, and Teresa's walk home through the moonlit gardens of the bay. It's the second of these I want to discuss, while indicating how it draws on the first for some of its power. The wedding is kept up by the congregated voices of family and friends, caught in their variety of tones and timbres, but dominated by Aunt Bea, whose excruciating, genial commentary establishes the tone. Her jokes about chamber-pots and hot first nights and little strangers unforgettably convey the embarrassment and unease that attend social celebrations of sexual union. Though Stead's view of her, and of the wedding ritual, is demonstrably more tolerant than Teresa's, seeing the role it plays not only in glossing over and cheapening what should be powerful mysteries, but in providing hope and consolation in hard times. Teresa's rebellious, critical presence dramatizes her sense that this is a conspiracy and a lie. Malfi is marrying a man whom she knows, and knows Teresa knows she knows, Malfi does not love. ("Don't think too badly of me", she whispers.) And the ritual so faithfully detailed, from hope-chest to feasting to throwing the bouquet, seals the couple into their life-long commitment. Yet Teresa's vehement phrases reveal identification with, rather than the dissociation she intends from, the scrum of girls who jostle for the bouquet: "a miserable mass writhing with desire and shame, grovelling before men, silent about the stew in which they boiled and bubbled". To avoid being left on the shelf, and to be initiated into this love business, all the girls say, it is necessary to have a young man, or, as Teresa would say, a "lover", so that you can then

read "How She Became a Happy Bride". But Theresa is reading Ovid and other erotic classics, and enamoured of Watteau's painting, feels herself on a journey to a Cythera of "secret desires", travelling towards something that is merely travestied in the social and sexual coercions she sees around her.

The concupiscent fever of the wedding and her own vague romantic yearnings dissolve into a moonlit scene. The tide is high and full, the ocean flooding the reefs. The headland is covered by black shapes that individuate as man and woman, white gloves laid to one side, or as lovers looking into eyes that reflect the moon:

> From every moon-red shadow came the voices of men and women; and in every bush and in the clumps of pine, upon unseen wooden seats and behind rocks, in the grass and even on open ledges, men and women groaned and gave shuddering cries as if they were being beaten. She passed slowly, timidly, but fascinated by the strange battlefield, the bodies stretched out, contorted, with sounds of the dying under the fierce high moon. She did not know what the sounds were, but she knew children would be conceived this night, and some time later women would marry hurriedly, if they could, like one of her cousins, who had slept the night with a man in one of these very grottoes; and perhaps one or two would jump into the sea. There were often bodies fished up round here, that had leapt when the heart still beat, from these high ledges into waters washed round these rocks by the moon.
>
> (p. 61)

What Teresa hears bewilders and fascinates her. The scene seems to stretch out, limitless in its vision of human lives driven by forces she recognizes without consciously understanding. There is a gap between her knowledge of consequences—desire, impregnation, desertion, death—and the reality of these stretched out and contorted bodies uttering their orgasmic cries. In this force-field of desire, the gravity as well as the naturalness of the passage from birth to copulation and death is registered in suggestive phrases that point forward and back through the narrative, underlying all its characters' talk about love. The physical extremity that grips the body in particular echoes that shocking glimpse she has just had of her cousin Anne on the bathroom floor, writhing in what is possibly anguish, possibly desperate self-gratification. ("It's because she's not married", Teresa says, simply and intuitively.) That physical extremity also anticipates her own solitary erotic fantasies, "the voluptuous swimming and rolling by herself in the deep grass of the garden", instinctively discovering the rhythms of desire. And the orgasmic cries, so indeterminate in tone to the timid and fascinated consciousness of the girl, locate in sexual union something that is driven, unfree, yet exultant, a leap with the heart still beating, launching the self into the unknown of what makes for life and death. On the one hand, it is the urgency that holds her brother Leo and his girl together in the moonlight; on the other, it is something that specifies itself in her image of "moon-struck fish". In a startlingly immediate way, this passage raises questions for Teresa and for the novel about what love is like as a physical experience, what its social consequences might be, about the relationship between its pleasure and its pain, and about how an individual meaning can be discovered in this battlefield of driven need by imagination, courage, honesty.

Journeys towards Cythera become the means of exploring and unfolding those qualities in Teresa's nature: first the journey of erotic fantasy, and then the journey to a version of pastoral at Harper's ferry. The account of her "carnal intoxications", her orgies, catches their quality of carnival indulgence, but it tries for something more difficult too, the physical sensations of a maturing body in search of pleasure:

> Her room, the door ajar, invited her, blazing to her with the gem-like colours of past saturnalia, the heavy air thickened with fables of lust, beckoning without beckoning, self-content, streaming with sylphs of ancient style and Priapic hosts, shaken from floor to ceiling with the presence of monsters, no heavier than smoke. The door and window open, inviting them, made her stand still on the landing for a few moments as she looked into her room, trembling with expectancy, as certain of joy as if it were a grotto of the satyr-woods, breeding the miracles of incarnated desire, waiting for a rustle, a voice, unheard by them downstairs but heard by her. She deceived herself with joy, hoping for a powerful hallucination; if she could hear or see them only once! It was the hot, intolerable hour, the hour when in hot countries the sun begins to embrace the earth and crush it with his weight; when he changes everything in it. At this time, there is no more love, conscience, remorse, or sin. In that room, in the furnace, she understood herself and knew what was wrong with the world of men. She felt like a giantess, immense, somehow growing like an incommensurable flower from a root in the earth, pouring upwards into the brazen sky, "the woman clothed with the sun". At this hour each day, the sun, reckless, mad with ardour, created her newly. This was the hour when she lived as a heart lives inside a beast, she was the blood and the convulsion; outside was a living envelope, the world.

> (p. 100)

Critics of the excesses of Stead's prose are apt to have this kind of passage in mind, pulled out of context and made to represent her writing in general. The experience with which this passage deals is in its very nature intense, and indeed one rarely treated in fiction: the somewhat uneasy comedy of *Portnoy's Complaint* might come to mind here. Stead's most immediate emphasis is on the feelings generated in this atmosphere heated from within by "the fables of lust" and from without by "the intolerable hour", and on the powerful auto-erotic rhythms of Teresa's body's moving towards the climax of its convulsive act. Unlike the riot of images that furnish Teresa's private movies, however, the images that shape the writing here draw on that larger imaginative life to which I have been referring: to the naked vulnerability of love, the stretched-out body gripped by the lover's beating heart, to the sun as the source of warmth and desire, creator of the growing that establishes being in the world. At the same time, the prose registers a certain frenetic bravado in Teresa's solitary love-making. In her urgency of physical desire she must take the sun as her lover; the phrase "reckless, mad with ardour" is made to pivot, making either or both the sun and the girl its subject. The sense of power and self-sufficiency her ecstasy brings is one which shuts out the world of men, and seeks to transcend and annihilate not only its more oppressive moral categories, "conscience, remorse and sin", but also what is conventionally understood by the word "love" itself. What kind of freedom is this, that brings her to articulate her anguished cry "send me a lover soon, I must, I must, I beg, I beg"?

The journey to Harper's Ferry is, in its way, an extension of this solipsism. Some form of pastoral has haunted Teresa's imagination, fed by Hawkins' Pacific atoll stories and by the El Dorados of primitive sensuality, of nymph and satyr and fleshly women, she sees in the pages of the bohemian coterie magazine, *The Quarterly* (succinctly dismissed by Jonathan Crow as "the green colony"). The ironic deflations that await her among the orchards of Narara, with their "big globed fruits fattened on the first rays and the mid-day light of the sun", may seem to come a little too easily until they are looked at more closely. The simple kindness of her aunt and uncle reassure and repel this motherless girl in search of her origins. They hold her embittered and over-educated cousin Ellen in a domestic prison not unlike the one Teresa has just renounced in her grand romantic gesture. (Ellen, now twenty-nine, is so desperate for marriage that she is submitting to the crude courtship of "the boy next door", Jerry Carlin, son of the local rouseabout. And there is also the inset story of another cousin, Lily, who takes fits and parades through the town without her corsets: "all the men looked".) As Teresa and Ellen return from the Carlins', an evening visit heavy with sexual innuendo and behind the scenes sexual play, Teresa hears what she recognizes as "the cry of the chase I am on":

> a human yell pealed out through the wood, marvellously loud, ringing through the air as if carried by the high airs and after two or three shouts, dying slowly, groaning away into the empty grass paddock beside them, as if tingling in the grass roots as they were treading on the neighbouring ruts. The young girl, in a paroxysm too great for fear, looked at her cousin, expecting some violent sign in her. Ellen lowered her head and trudged on against the hill. It was inconceivable! When she was opening her mouth to speak to Ellen, as if out of her own mouth, the cry pealed again,

a little farther behind, but ringing tremendous, from the things on the land, from some martyred and bleeding field, or a giant old tree being murdered in the wood there. What a cry! And there again!

(p. 158)

Terrified by the sound, and by her cousin's passive response to it, Teresa has the instinct that it is a cry inside her own head. And in a sense, so it is: at least it's the articulation of her own despairing, exultant cry and of the frustrated crying she hears on every side. Like the cry of the lovers in the bay, its tone makes its blood-chilling, primitive announcement: exultation or agony, seeming to link the solitary self with the very groaning of creation, coming out of the night, under cover of darkness, from the heart of the country-side. Buried in the cottage lurks a story as Gothic as anything in *The Salzburg Tales*: a young man has gone mad on the eve of his wedding, is separated for ever from his fiancée down in the valley, and is kept, by his mother, in chains. It's the kind of bold stroke Stead quite often somehow manages to get away with. Teresa, too, searches erotic fable for the knowledge it brings to her body and imagination. Stead's frame of reference here is, I think, Nietzschean—the Nietzsche of *The Birth of Tragedy,* describing the dionysian experience in which the inmost self sounds from "the abyss of being" to become one with the "Primordial Being", enabling a subjective knowledge that cannot be grasped by the objective intelligence. But it is through this moment of apprehension that Teresa is able to articulate her growing sense that "we would all go mad if we were locked up and prevented from marrying". And the question of what pleasure or need is appeased by the lover in chains foreshadows the next phase of Teresa's journey. One of the most telling things we hear about Jonathan Crow is that he has more than once intervened to prevent his brother's wedding.

And as she walks on towards Harper's Ferry, through the "great fruitful silent paradise of abandoned orchards", through a valley from which there seems no exit, a place nostalgic in its evocations of fruitfulness, "the wild grass, crooked apple-trees turning back to nature . . . festoons and knots of sour apples", the lyricism of the writing celebrates all that has led her here, without map or compass, in search of what she associates with the first stirrings of love in early adolescence. Those thoughts renew themselves now, more fully charged with romantic and sexual yearning. She is thinking of making love generously, to "a beautiful man" (a phrase associated, early on, with Andrew Hawkins) when hungry, lonely, sexual desire begins to pursue her, first as a fear and then materializing in the shape of an old man following her and exposing himself on the isolated road. The indignation of this girl who has yearned for nakedness: "we can't see naked men, we're robbed of our pleasure", sends her groping

for the law and takes us back to the novel's opening: "in the Bible they were punished who uncovered their father's nakedness". This grotesque parody of sexual pursuit points forwards, as well as backwards, however: again, it is not fanciful to see the impotent sexual display as a foreshadowing of all that Jonathan Crow represents. It is worth noting that Stead has Crow anticipate some of the cruder commentary we are beginning to hear about these aspects of the book in terms of sexual politics and psychopathology of the sado-masochistic variety. What there is to admire in the Harper's Ferry sequences is an unusual play of intelligent imagination between what we might call Teresa's self (her ideas, her imagination, her responsive senses) and the world that meets and challenges and is forming that self: between that which is barely articulate and even ultimately inarticulable, and the world in which it may come to consciousness.

The chase Teresa is on develops into that protracted drama of mutual approach and recoil explored in depth and in detail by Stead. It is the destiny of Crow, self-appointed guru of love, preaching free love in the suburbs, to bring Teresa to a sense of how *un*freeing love can be and what it can do to the love-needy body. (The account of the starving girl saving for her passage to England, bitterly aware that her scarecrow frame is losing all attractiveness, has a particular poignancy.) Crow is embarked, both formally and informally, on the attempt to define "the sexual question" (another warning to Stead's critics here), to nail it down by the experiments he conducts with his women students and disciples, and by pithy, clever, iconoclastic statements culled from his reading in Freud and Krafft-Ebing and Havelock Ellis. He is also, as he keeps telling Teresa, in a phrase that at once invites her and puts her out of the running, "looking for a woman" and terrified of being caught by one. Woman, in his view, is biologically and socially programmed to hunt. Teresa acknowledges in herself and in all women the role of huntress, claiming not only the *right* of women to declare themselves in love, but seeing generous self-offering as a way in which love may be experienced and understood. Crow's appeal to the iconoclast and plain-talker in Andrew Hawkins' daughter is seen as part of his attractiveness. Stead shows Crow's systematic humiliation of Teresa, each miserly gesture in her direction weighed and measured and withdrawn, met again and again by her devotion to the task of teaching this self-pitying, cynical, moody boy from the slums the joy of living. "Can I love this man", she asks herself, and behind the rapture lies a range of questions about romantic love and sexual frustration that are explored by Stead with a remarkable poise. I'm thinking here particularly of the passage where Teresa struggles for detachment after she arrives in London and must take the measure of Crow's strange personality, and the endless, deadlocked dance of humiliation and submission that goes on recharging itself.

More remarkable still I find the moment of insight that cuts through years of discussion and duplicity and self-deception. A long-deferred excursion to the Berkshire border recalls, in an ironic way, Teresa's excursion to sunny Harper's Ferry. The countryside is wet and muddy, and at nightfall they are forced to spend the night together in the shelter of a deserted, unfinished sawmill. It is Teresa's idea to get the rusty mill-wheel going by removing its wedges and opening the sluices, so that the water begins to fall faster and faster into a deep pool, "black and now agitated with a horrible swirling, as it began to lead its true life". Beleaguered by roaring winds and stamping rain, they settle into uneasy, separate sleep, until the floor begins to tremble and they realize that the mill wheel is turning dangerously. There is nothing laboured about the images here: the black vortex below the rotting floor boards, the turning wheel, the temporary shelter. Unobtrusively, they play their part in what happens, suddenly, when Crow and Teresa, woken from sleep, find themselves poised on either side of the beckoning hole:

> They looked at each other by the light of the flare with unveiled dislike. Teresa, looking at him, released him from her will; it happened suddenly. The harness of years dropped off, eaten through; she dropped her eyes, thought: "How stupid he is! How dull!" He looked sullenly at her, with hatred, crueller and more vicious than teased lust. He half shut his eyes and turned his head away. When his eyes returned to her, they had a natural look, but he was a stranger.

> It's cold," she said in a whistling voice. "I'm hopping it," said Jonathan.

(p. 408)

And he does, removing the light, leaving Teresa alone in the dark while he just catches the last train to London. It is again an intimation from "the abyss of being". Exposure to the night, to the natural forcefulness of wind and water, to the treacherous depths with their threat or promise of death, throws up a truth about this death-bound relationship that Teresa has until now been unable to acknowledge.

Her restless journeying seems to come to an ending in her love for James Quick, her employer. Quick is in every way Crow's opposite: an eloquent and ardent wooer, imaginative, gregarious, candid. The edgy jealousy with which he sounds out Crow as a way of understanding the girl he has come to love suggests Stead's even-handed dealing with a figure as recognizably based on her husband, Bill Blake, as Andrew Hawkins is on David Stead. Journey now becomes courtship: "every part of the country became a part of their desire and consummation", leading at last to the miraculous journey that "she could not foresee and that no-one could build up out of lonely flesh":

> in the night, waking, she found for him a terrible human passion of pity and love, such as she had never felt for any man or woman on earth. She said to herself: 'This is my husband, I know it for sure.'

(p. 457)

What she has come to recognize, she thinks, is the truth about love: "This is love with a man". But a continuing restlessness in her is a sign that the journey is not done. She wants more fully to take the measure of "love and man, from whom she had been wrongly, feloniously, separated for so long". And finding herself "half-mad" for love of Harry Girton, Quick's friend, she must acknowledge that love "comes again, it does not die with marriage, it is not once for all". Her journey to Oxford with Girton allows her to test the boundaries of her love for Quick and the large moral questions about "truth", "fidelity" and "freedom" that have been kept living throughout the novel.

Quick has said repeatedly, early on, "you are free, I will share you with another man who is worthy of you". In the grip of her brief affair with Girton, she feels that love has nothing to do with moral or social constraints; that love is by its very nature, "free":

> She had reached the gates of the world of Girton and Quick and . . . it was towards them she was only now journeying, and in a direction unguessed by them; and it was towards them and in this undreamed direction that she had been travelling all her life and would travel, further, without them."

(p. 494)

The heady rapture of this qualifies its sense of having arrived. When she discovers that the affair with Girton is no more than "a foray from which she brought back milk and honey for her own affair with James", it is then that she says "I am thinking I am free". That sense, too, is to be qualified by some of the new truths she has discovered about love: the need to play a part with Quick "because she loved him, and in order to give him happiness", a loving mendacity that includes not burdening him with her real feelings and not telling him the truth about Girton. And yet in an important sense love has been "the via media to being", and the freedom she glimpses now is the freedom to travel further "without them", a freedom that makes her essentially solitary and committed to the labyrinth of concealment.

Neither in Quick nor in Girton does the novel arrive at a sense of love that equates it with a happy ending. In fact, the ending sounds a distinctly bitter note as she sees, as through a nightmare vision, in the streets of London, "a peculiar, sliding, fumbling figure go by, the typical self-pickled bachelor. . . . The vile-faced man, the bent-backed man, walking crowded with all the apparatus of melodrama was Jonathan Crow! They looked at each other, and he saw her eyes, ghastly to him, pale vapours in brilliant eye-balls, fastened upon him". And the novel ends on Teresa's reflection: "it's dreadful to think that it will go on being repeated for ever, he—and me! What's there to stop it?"

This final encounter makes what may seem an enigmatic and even despairing counter-assertion to Teresa's love for Quick. But it is consistent with the way in which the novel allows that welling up, out of the surface of talk and subjective impression, of a deeper experience that checks and challenges and illumines. Crow floats into Teresa's vision here not as a recognizable person, but as an image—an almost anonymous representation of frustration and self-enclosure—and then comes into focus in a shape that challenges her to self-recognition. What she recognizes, in so far as it can be summarized, is what the novel's powerful and tough-minded vision of love has been unfolding. That love is neither rational nor readily articulable, having to do with energies and drives that lie below the level of consciousness, amoral no matter how essential it is to relate love to the moral considerations that shape lives and commitments. That love is a hazarding of the self, drawing vulnerable bodies to the edge of annihilation. And that love is finding solitariness and accepting constraint, even at journey's end in what looks like freedom and knowledge.

Nick Mansfield (essay date March 1992)

SOURCE: Mansfield, Nick. "'This Is Not Understanding': Christina Stead's *For Love Alone*." *Southerly* 52, no. 1 (March 1992): 77-89.

[*In the following essay, Mansfield discusses the significance of "the structuring principle of journey" to the formation of the protagonist's "selfhood" in* For Love Alone.]

In *For Love Alone,* Christina Stead presents a protagonist defined by her continual contest with masculine power. Teresa Hawkins seeks some provisional freedom from this power in a selfhood that is contentious and experimental. The structural principle of this selfhood is a quest that knows no fixed goal, and that is undertaken in the various discourses of love she encounters. In the same way that Teresa's quest has no destination, Stead refuses to endorse any particular type of love as ideal. Teresa's selfhood is constructed from a series of struggles with powerful others, rather than oriented towards the revelation of some particular truth or ideal.

For Love Alone never distinguishes Teresa from the structuring principle of journey, whether it be trekking to Harper's Ferry, walking the streets of Sydney to and from work or voyaging across the world. This journeying is not some ultimate image of Australian national

experience; neither is it some attempt to appropriate or parody Joyce's use of *The Odyssey,* nor is it the frame of a female Bildungsroman, constructing some archetype of feminist freedom. Journeying in Stead, as *The Man Who Loved Children* intimates, is a form of selfhood in which an all-smothering power is circumvented by a voluntarist project of experimenting with change, understood as open-ended and ineluctable.

Teresa engages in a series of specific struggles with threatening or seductive antagonists—her father, the marriage law of Sydney society, Jonathan Crow and James Quick. Each of these antagonists is associated with a particular type of love—autoeroticism, oppressive marital conformity, a loudly proclaimed ideology of "free" love, a warm urbanity, a Romantic passion and so on. These loves are manifested in discourses that are wielded upon Teresa, sometimes violently, sometimes with a deceptive consideration. Teresa must recognize the strategy hidden in each of these discourses, and design for herself a way of living through and beyond them. The reader is not asked to choose between these various loves so much as understand them as the crucial and inevitable staging-posts in Teresa's open-ended journey towards an imagined freedom, a journey that knows no ideal destination, and seeks no resolution in either consummation or revelation.

Thus Teresa is not on a journey that ends with arrival. In many minor but important ways, the text makes this reading impossible. The second half of the novel defines London as a "port of registry" rather than a point of arrival. The Harry Girton episode displaces any simple *stasis* Teresa's relationship with Quick might imply. Teresa is described as "too formed by adversity and too firm and ambitious by nature to take pleasure in her marital union alone"[1]; she is "idea hungry, ambitious and energetic" (p. 461); "her hunger had made her insatiable, and she was not content, as he thought she would be, with what he told her, she was not at all satisfied with the end of physical craving; she wanted to try men" (p. 464). Even the conclusion of her relationship with Girton implies irresolution. "I am thinking I am free", she says. It is impossible for her to be settled into a final or resolved situation. R. G. Geering is confused by Teresa's failure to conform to the satisfied wife of romance stereotype; he writes:

> Teresa's restlessness, her sense of awakened powers, emotional and intellectual, and her desire for freedom are much more in keeping with the rebellious, idealized young woman of the early chapters than a passive and contented wife would be.[2]

Stead does not merely reject this stereotype "a passive and contented wife" because it is too pale. Such a resolution would be inconsistent with the type of heroism that has been constructed for Teresa. Her journey knows no destination because any neat resolution would belie the narrative's understanding of selfhood in terms of change and experiment rather than meaning and truth.

In Louie Pollitt's case, this experimentation is notionally linked with the aesthetic. Louie invents a new language in which to represent her relationship with her father. Her creativity is the most optimistic alternative to Sam's power. Teresa's journey finds a similar coherence and impetus in Teresa's prose-writing. "The Seven Houses of Love" is both an enigmatic summary and a useful instrument of her journey. Critics have been too willing to see Teresa's art as the fruit of her arrival in a stable relationship, succumbing to the sentimental formula that identifies art with love. Yet, "The Seven Houses of Love" is unfinished. Rather than transcending the chaos and contingency of her daily life in order to signal Teresa's achievement of meaningful heroism, it becomes involved in that life, sharing its shape and encouraging its movement.

The novel's opening scene dramatizes Teresa's struggle with her father. Although, on the naturalistic level, Andrew Hawkins seems to successfully repress any resistance Teresa might offer to his prestige and authority, we find on close reading evidence of a different process that can only succeed in designing her eventual triumph, reducing him from the naked tyrant of this scene to the effete nay-sayer of the rest of the book's first part. The two enter into conflict, not as patriarchal father repressing a daughter he will never understand, but as two powerful figures attempting to dominate the language of Eros. Hawkins is defined as "naked" and "powerful": "Naked, except for a white towel rolled into a loin-cloth, he stood in the doorway, laughing and shouting, a tall man with powerful chest and thick hair of pale burning gold and a skin still pale under many summers' tan." (p. 5)

Hawkins' speech is identified as an act of physical power. The intention to communicate meaning becomes secondary. His aim is not to define the nature and meaning of love, his ostensible topic. The fact that he is "laughing and shouting" takes precedence over whatever he is saying. He aims to use his naked body, which he sees as a source of prestige and the guarantee of his sexual charisma, in order to exhibit a primitivist, solar love that will intimidate Teresa, who he knows is fascinated with the erotic classics, and exclude her from the discourse of love he believes he controls. He says:

> "Yes, Trees is always moaning about love, but you don't know, Trees, that love is warmth, heat. The sun is love and love also is fleshly, in this best sense that a beautiful woman gladdens the heart of man and a handsome man brightens the eyes of the ladies. One blessed circle, perpetual motion."
>
> (pp. 7-8)

This description of love in heroic, Apollonian imagery is not an attempt to define or discuss love as much as an assertion of personal power grounded in confident control of a certain type of language. The attempt to arrogate the discourse of love to himself at Teresa's expense is the main purpose of Hawkins' speech. He constantly returns to the theme of the inadequacy of her response to his heightened sensibility; imagining an ideal garden of sexuality, he says:

> "There are temptations there, but the man sure of himself and who knows himself can resist them and direct his steps into the perfumed, sunny, lovely paths of sex. Oh!" he cried, his fine voice breaking, "who can tell these things to another, especially to you, Trees? You are too cold, you have never responded to me, and my soul, yes, I will use that word, had such great need of understanding!"
>
> (p. 12)

The imagery here keeps alive the association between Hawkins' sexuality and the sun, as well as advancing his claim that his sexuality is somehow archetypal. Not only is the "man sure of himself" possessed of an unusual ability and destiny, but he is also capable of a speech so refined it can only take place at the limits of language, where the voice breaks and the difficulties of communication can only be overcome by a rhetorical question. Yet, the political aim of this discourse is never forgotten. Hawkins' autoeroticism attacks Teresa by excluding her from the eternal cycle of sexual compatibility and satisfaction, because of her refusal to respond to him. He has constructed this elaborate monologue in order to assert his dominance over the language of love which he fears she may use to evade his power.

Teresa's first counter-attack against this power parodies his speech by reversing his self-indulgent description of how his body has been caressed by loving female hands (pp. 6-7):

> "I told you I would kill you if you insult me. I will do it with my bare hands. I am not so cowardly as to strike with anything. I know where to press though—I will kill you, father."
>
> (p. 14)

Andrew Hawkins answers Teresa with a "terrifying roar" (p. 15). His speech again subordinates intended meaning to political force. Yet by a deft reversal of her father's language, Teresa alerts us to the fragility of his power and her ability to circumvent it. Henceforth, he will become only a marginal presence in the book.

Teresa attacks the whole basis on which Hawkins' prestige depends—his fanciful language of his own sexuality—by appropriating it from him and turning it to her own uses. She indulges, like he does, in an exultant nudism, leaning out naked from her bedroom window (pp. 72-3). She relates to her body in an equally auto-erotic way: "her voluptuous swimming and rolling by herself in the deep grass of the garden and her long waking nights were part of the life of profound pleasure she had made for herself, unknown to them." (p. 73)

This last phrase shows that although she does not assert the social meaning of her autoeroticism in the same way as her father, its purpose is to define a new life for her in contradistinction to that of her family. In the same way that love was not the topic of Hawkins' speech as much as the source of a language that had a fundamentally political function, love in Teresa's world is a way of exempting herself from the oppressive life of her family. "Love" is what is missing in the Hawkins' household. By orienting her life according to the strictures of this love, Teresa is constructing for herself another life, beyond the one that entraps her.

In the same way that Teresa confronted her father by threatening his body, the guarantee of his language, she confronts his authoritarian love, defined in terms of the sun, with a dark liquid love she associates with the moon:

> The full moon shone fiercely on the full-bellied sea. A woman who had known everything, men's love and been deserted, who had the vision of a life of endless work and who felt seedy, despairing, felt a bud growing on its stalk in her body, was thirsty; in her great thirst she drank up the ocean and was drowned.
>
> (p. 74)

In contrast to the idyllic, eternal cycle of man's perfect compatibility with woman, we have here a vision of powerful, almost Gothic solitude. This dark consuming figure directly threatens the Arcadian fantasy of Teresa's father not only by the opposition of moon to sun, and of female to male, but of an abject, amoral power to his phallic absolutism. Teresa enters into the language of love offered to her by her father in order to find within his domain some principle of love she can oppose to his. Her aim is to contradict and threaten his power base and engineer some escape from the futile household over which he presides. Her success in discovering this love explains why the novel almost ignores Hawkins after the first chapter. Although he can exercise some bullying domestic power, he is unable to maintain control over the discourse of love in which the greater contest takes place. The contest between Hawkins and Teresa is not simply between the exhausted, in-authentic egotism of the old and the authentic passion of the young. Nor is it simply the struggle between the oppressive masculine and the liberating feminine principles. These contests are mere positions in the discourse of love that produces Teresa and Hawkins as characters, and measures the distance between them. In the end, it is not "love" that is important here, as much as the way the languages of love produce the relationship between the characters.

Thus, when Teresa expatiates on the theme of "love", we are not simply being asked to endorse her position, and see it somehow as an exemplary theory of human sexual relationships. We cannot and should not accept her version of love as that which is preferred by the text. Her confidence in her own superior powers (p. 76), her sense of being inspired and her overly Romantic luxuriance in her own sexuality do not combine into an ethic. The truth of her discourse of love is not the issue. What is important is Teresa's will to see beyond the social life around her by contradicting the behaviour of others. The love for which she sees herself fitted is not part of a coherent or even intelligible discourse of love as much as an abstraction of her rejection of the social conditions around her. Her nakedness is not the escapism of the autoerotic but the assertion of a mode of being alternative to social constriction. Thus, the overly Romantic content of her thought becomes part of a whole moment of articulation independent of its surface content and value. It becomes the process of opposition by which Teresa constitutes herself. The significance of Teresa's discourse of love is not its "meaning" as a discussion of love—the book soon abandons its issues as immature—but the selfhood it makes possible.

Teresa attempts to free herself from the dominant discourses of love around her by threatening them with their own terms. In the same way that she parodied her father's image of hands caressing his naked body, she opposes the word "love" to the orthodox marriage law of Sydney society, formulated by her friends Martha and Elsie into "the law of the boat":

> A girl, before the diamond ring, belonged to Martha's category of the Great Unwanted. Martha was the wit of the party, a village gossip of the forbidding, dangerous, upright, churchly kind, with a rapid, penetrating eye, who could strip a congregation down to its underlinen and who, completely integrated, feared neither man nor God; . . . Teresa's other friend, this Elsie, was also an Engaged Girl.
>
> (pp. 108-9)

The social law is defined here as co-ordinated gossip. What Stead labels ironically a "theory of marriage" (p. 108) is merely a regimen of power enacted in language. Its landmarks are "rumour" and the capitalized categories of the Great Unwanted and the Engaged Girl.

Teresa explodes this theory by introducing into it its missing term, "love". She opposes the word "love" to the sacred lore of marriage:

> Teresa said: "Everything in the world was produced by the act of love, it would be queer not to think about it," but so wrapped up were they in husbands-to-be, they seemed never to have heard of love. They knew all the scandals in the newspapers, of course, and much about whether Mrs X was found on the lap of Mr Y or not. For all the men they had names: boy friends, fiancés,

husbands, and co-respondents, and there were flirts, engaged couples, married couples, and misconduct, but they recoiled at the improper words, *love* and *lover*.

(p. 110)

Teresa aims to intimidate the social rituals of romance and marriage by threatening them with the possibility of their own authenticity. "Love" and "lover" are omitted from the gossips' lexicon of marriage because these words speak of sexual conduct without a precise moral or social location, or reference to the logic that defines the success and failure of marriage. The word "love" allows Teresa to transgress the law of the boat. By plucking a dormant term from the discourses of love around her, she frees herself from their entrapment. Thus Teresa creates a place for herself by contriving an opposition in language. She takes a word and uses it superficially, with a trivial or even platitudinous meaning, turning it against the languages that have been wielded upon her.

This understanding of language as a locus of struggle for a liberating selfhood is borne out in several ways in Teresa's relationship with Jonathan Crow. At first, Crow's language seems to Teresa to vitalize her image of love, empowering her by uncovering a life for her in contradistinction to "the law of the boat". Yet we are quickly aware that his facility in language has made him insincere. When he writes a love-letter to Teresa, we are told: "So easily did he write now after all those essays and letters, in engaging, acceptable confidences, with a soft, modest indiscretion; it flowed like peaceful maundering, he scarcely knew what he had written." (pp. 200-1)

Yet this does not seem to matter to Teresa. In one scene, she allows herself to be "stirred" by his appeals (p. 220), while showing only superficial interest in them— "she paid no attention, she thought it was a mania of all young graduates" (p. 218). She recognizes the hollowness of his rhetoric while remaining free to pursue its energy. His discourse of free love does not make a convert of Teresa. Instead, it allows her to improvise in her own style, derived from her reading and secret life: she compares Australians to Egyptians (p. 222). Teresa's aim is not to invite a serious discussion of the truth and meaning of love. She finds in Jonathan's speech an antagonism to contest and pass beyond, something that, intentionally or not, inspires her own metaphorical journey. By recognizing the hollowness of Jonathan's speech while at the same time allowing it to move her, Teresa invests in a superficial reading of his language in order to promote her movement towards freedom. In the same way that she had proposed an undefined honour as some resistance to her father, and a polemical love as an alternative to "the law of the boat", Teresa reads Jonathan's speech incompletely and naively for the freedom it allows her, rather than for any authentic

meaning. In this way, she succeeds in resisting the power he attempts to impose upon her, as well as freeing her own language and its creative play. Out of the "free" love Crow pretends is his mission, Teresa appropriates her freedom.

Thus, Jonathan is constructed as an instrument of her will, rather than a serious object of her affection:

> She cast about for a man to love; the nearest man was Jonathan, but she ran over the others. Dr Smith, a man resembling Crow in the office, the medical student on the boat. She went to and fro to work for two days, thinking over what she must do. She must put herself to the test, could she write to poor Jonathan telling him she loved him? Am I afraid, she asked herself. Yes? Then I must. This is the proof. If I haven't the courage for this, I'll fail everywhere. I'll never get anything done.

(p. 225)

Here, Jonathan is merely "the nearest man". His rhetoric and Teresa's Romanticism are subordinate to her determination to test her will. This is what love means here. Love, however defined, fades in the face of the issue of the orientation of the self on its imagined journey towards freedom. *For Love Alone* is not a book about love. It is naive of a critic like Laurie Clancy to argue: "there is no other novel of Christina Stead's that deals with its theme—of love and the proper relation of the sexes—in such a single-minded and almost obsessive way."[3]

The word "love" is not a stable object of the novel's purpose. There is no attempt to clarify love or purge it of its confusions in order to reveal it in its heroic authenticity. In Teresa's relationship with Jonathan, love is never a single thing. It switches quickly and sometimes imperceptibly between the topic that inspires Teresa's confident experimenting with words and the ideal with which she identifies Jonathan in order to test her strength of character.

The construction of Jonathan as the test or proof of Teresa's will becomes particularly important while they are separated. The night his boat sails, Teresa walks up onto the headland and looks out to sea:

> Her dark heart moved over the sea with the throbbing of a ship. The ship had already passed beyond all this coast and was in new waters. "What would a man do?" thought the girl. "Would he let this accident stand between himself and his love? Would he if he loved me? No. And I am worthy of him . . . I will make him love me.

(pp. 244-5)

The journey of Teresa's heart and Jonathan's journey are synchronised with one another. In this passage, Jonathan performs two distinct functions. Firstly, he is the measure against which she assesses her behaviour. She understands her obligations purely in terms of what he would do. Jonathan loses his individuality to become archetypal man. In the sentence "Would he if he loved me?" this confusion is important. Jonathan comes to function now as a type, an abstraction of himself, deprived of any naturalistic individuality.

This abstraction of Jonathan is furthered in the second important function he performs here. He becomes an object of love defined not in terms of sexuality, but *worthiness,* an essential quality of self, not of relationship. Relieved of his burden of sociological and psychological meaning, Jonathan is fictionalized, as the quasi-literary stereotype "the knight of poverty" (p. 248). Jonathan is transformed into a literary type in order to become the centrepiece of Teresa's discipline. By becoming fictionalized, Jonathan allows Teresa to enact a complicated repudiation of her old social self, her life among the "boobies" (p. 243). Her anorexic refusal of her own body becomes a rejection of her family life: she is disgusted by a surprise party planned for her (p. 255); she rejects the conventional role of a woman, becoming indifferent to the catcalls of men (p. 258); and eventually she rejects her home, planning to live somewhere else, even in a vacant lot. This disciplined repudiation of the self is notionally connected to delirium, reinforcing its connection with a higher irrational exigency she identifies with Jonathan's name. Yet, this madness is not a real psychological condition as much as a way of "getting out of certain situations" (p. 288). Her orientation towards Jonathan is thus merely the name and symbol she affixes to a process of much wider meaning, what she calls vaguely "her great destiny" (p. 285).

Because it is a process that is ongoing and can have no simple end, all the goals of Teresa's quest for worthiness prove illusory. When she arrives in England she finds she is unable to share Jonathan's intellectual life, because she has studied the wrong subjects and texts (p. 296). She condemns herself for not having cultivated "her physical passion for him" (p. 328). Teresa tries to keep alive the Jonathan who, by his absence, has inspired her journey. Yet she has already been confronted with the possibility that this Jonathan is a fraud, bearing no relation to the "real" Jonathan. She finds that "she had never loved Jonathan" (p. 328).

Again the struggle between them is to take place in language. They both construct discourses from which the other is to be excluded. Jonathan offers an account of the gang rape of a maid by a group of his friends, a story he uses to bludgeon Teresa with the violence of a sexual demi-monde from which he loudly proclaims her exclusion. The sexual violence of this episode, and the aggressiveness of Jonathan's choosing to narrate it, are reminiscent of some of his cynical and exclusive

speeches in Sydney before his departure. Then, his discourse of sex inspired Teresa's own language which has grown to demand of Jonathan a specific function he can no longer fulfil. Out of the languages, firstly of pagan pleasure and secondly of quest for worthiness, Teresa constructed a journey of love that no longer needs him. Now she fictionalizes this journey in the form of her prose piece "The Seven Houses of Love". In the mill episode, she tries to decide whether Jonathan can be accommodated by this new language of progress and quest:

> So—always with him, if she had her way? Sleeping there, with cold, dully. She shivered. She thought: "This is the last of the Houses of Love. Marriage?" She went and leaned over the black pool the wheel spurned. "What if I should fall in, that he would find me choking the exit in the morning? 'Teresa with drowned hair and cheeks of sod—' no, no."
>
> (p. 408)

Here, contemplation of an image derived from her own writing produces for Teresa a revelation of her own power. Her attainment of power is her rejection of Jonathan as a possible character in Marriage, the last of her Seven Houses of Love. Her decision to live on is synchronised with her rejection of Jonathan both as an object of love and a source of fiction. He next appears soliciting her charity in making connection with Quick. The intellectual sparring between Jonathan and Quick has been predetermined by Quick's rejection of Jonathan's "crackpot egotism" (p. 416), and his enthusiasm for Teresa's writing. "The Seven Houses of Love" thus rejects Jonathan as a possible character and surpasses him by engaging Quick. There is no equivocation here: Quick stands for the moment when Jonathan's redundancy is made manifest in the rejection of his writing for Teresa's.

By becoming the resting-point of Teresa's quest, Crow frees her from the restrictions of her father's narcissistic authority and her peers' normative pressure. As an object of this quest, however, he is proved absurd. Quick renders him "extinct" (p. 462) by simultaneously embracing Teresa and praising her writing. These three episodes are tactfully synchronized. Yet it would be over-simplifying things to see this complex development as an ideal destination of Teresa's real quest. Diana Brydon reduces the book's ending to such an idealized point of arrival, both sexual and artistic, when she writes: "[Stead] saw sexual and creative fulfillment as inseparable and she believed they could only result from relationships of absolute equality."[4]

Here, the identification between sexuality and art is reduced to a simple liberal feminist formula, the idea that Teresa's relationship with Quick is to be seen as exemplary of an open marriage built on sexual satisfaction and encouraging the vocational self-fulfillment of both partners. This seems somewhat anachronistic, but more importantly, it seems to belie the imagery and language used to describe the moment of Quick's and Teresa's consummation in terms of delirium and ongoing struggle rather than resolution and equilibrium:

> All through the night, he moaned in his sleep and cried, for what he foresaw, the struggle to come and that it must be fought through, because this was the woman to hold him and there was no solution but a bitter one . . . it seemed to her, in this sad long night of the man weeping and foreseeing that he would be tormented by his women, that this was the consummation of life.
>
> (pp. 456-7)

This consummation defines love as unstable and necessarily antagonistic, rather than a simple and stable resolution. Although tempered by Quick's humanistic urbanity, and experienced by Teresa as a near triumph, this "love" is still subject to the process of confrontation and overcoming that has determined and measured Teresa's quest throughout the novel, and that does not end here. Quick himself "naturally supposed that the life he offered her would not eventually satisfy her" (p. 461). He accepts the role Teresa demands of him—he becomes another figure to be redefined and surpassed. This wrestling frees her into what the novel calls living "from day to day" (p. 462) and a provisional self-formulating freedom. Teresa's journey is still conceived as a journey of self in which Quick is merely one more stage:

> Teresa did not worry about her sisters, and she was so ungrateful as not to worry even about James Quick. Her hunger had made her insatiable, and she was not content, as he thought she would be, with what he told her, she was not at all satisfied with the end of physical craving; she wanted to try men.
>
> (p. 464)

Over and above sexual desire is an undefined longing that Quick cannot neutralize. It is most fully defined here as the ambiguous longing to "try men". This need for experiment is dramatized and celebrated in her relationship with Harry Girton. Girton provides her with a model of deracinated social life, of *kinesis* in *stasis,* that summarizes her emotional reality throughout the novel. Girton's desire to be "unknown to all that know me" soothes Teresa (p. 487), providing her with an image of a life in "some unknown region" free from "relatives, home, living, and holy dying". The Romantic imagery and rhetoric associated with Girton are summarized in the notion of repudiating one's established social self. This radical simplification of the self is a consequence of the life of provisionality and experiment she has constructed with Quick, realized both in his tolerance of her amour with Girton and his earlier approval of a draft of her autobiographical writing. She thinks of her

love with Quick as "the only love, but not the first and not the last" (p. 496). Out of this paradoxical love she will be able to design for herself "a life apart". Teresa's relationship with Girton is an experiment that furthers the long process of self-creation we have seen in *For Love Alone.* Under the sign of Quick's sacrifice of himself to her, Teresa contrives a provisional freedom—"I am thinking I am free", she says (p. 496). This emphasis on a provisional rather than an absolute freedom is important. Freedom, like ideal love, is never imagined in the novel as an ultimate destination of Teresa's quest. It is merely the term used and needed to orient that quest and the fictional end of the relationships of struggle and overcoming that have marked it out.

This provisionality, defined so clearly in the paradox of an only love that is in a sequence that it neither begins nor ends, defines Teresa's quest as one made up of positions, neither superior nor inferior to one another. She comes to occupy these positions in turn, without needing them to be collapsed into meaning or telos. We are reminded early in her relationship with Quick that "her chief anxiety was to live from day to day" (p. 462). Each of Teresa's struggles outlined above—with her father, the "law of the boat", Jonathan Crow and finally Quick—is all-absorbing. She struggles to outline some provisional freedom by experimenting with the languages of love. Her "great destiny" is merely the sequence made up of these absorbing conflicts. The struggle unfolds in significant stages juxtaposed with one another, rather than by a process of gradual evolution. Dramatically, the stages are linked by chance rather than by meaningful design. They are not held together by unity of purpose as much as by the consistency of the book's discourse, its marshalling of a variety of the languages of love as the way of outlining the trajectory of a selfhood constantly seeking change and development.

Given such a development—significant stages in a coordinated discourse of love—it is appropriate that when the book seeks a coherent image for Teresa's experience, it finds it in her draft prose-piece "The Seven Houses of Love". Teresa's notes for this work define a progress by way of the paradoxical operation of the will producing affirmation out of opposition:

> To die terribly by will, to make death a terrible demand of life, a revolt, an understanding, such as rives life, blasts it, twists it. To die by the last effort of the will and body. To will, the consuming and consummation. To force the end. It must be dark; then an extraordinary clutching of reality. This is not understanding, not intellectual, but physical, bitter, disgusting, but an affirmation of a unique kind.
>
> (pp. 421-2)

The "death" outlined in this passage is not resolution but affirmation. Out of opposition, the will uncovers an intensity of life that both extinguishes and affirms, consumes and consummates. This intensity repudiates "meaning" (or understanding) in order to embrace a sort of Dionysian affirmation. This is an articulate summary of the paradoxical nature of Teresa's selfhood. Out of conflict, the old self is displaced by a new self— not as part of a meaningful journey towards enlightenment and fulfillment as much as an affirmation of vitality. This selfhood is provisional, at times directly fictional, and constructed in the various languages of love the book marks out in stages. "The Seven Houses of Love" encourages this journey, summarizes its structure and abstracts its logic—especially its refusal to betray the vital process of affirmation by forcing "understanding".

Notes

1. Christina Stead, *For Love Alone,* London: Arkon, 1982, p. 458. All page references in the text are to this edition.

2. R. G. Geering, *Christina Stead,* New York: Twayne Publishers Inc., 1969, p. 118.

3. Laurie Clancy, *Christina Stead's* The Man Who Loved Children *and* For Love Alone, Melbourne: Shillington House, 1981, p. 28.

4. Diana Brydon, *Christina Stead,* Houndmills: Macmillan Education, 1987, p. 15.

Elizabeth Perkins (essay date spring 1992)

SOURCE: Perkins, Elizabeth. "Learning to Recognize Wicked People: Christina Stead's *A Little Tea, A Little Chat.*" *World Literature Written in English* 32, no. 1 (spring 1992): 13-25.

[*In the following essay, Perkins disagrees with the view that Stead's* A Little Tea, A Little Chat *lacks "a conventional moral centre," asserting that "the narrative point of view insists on some moral perspective without prescribing what it should be, and that the novel has a positive, if not a simplistically uplifting, tendency."*]

A Little Tea, A Little Chat is the second book of Stead's New York trilogy, which includes *Letty Fox: Her Luck* (1946) and *The People with the Dogs* (1952). Each novel, Stead said, contains characters based on people she knew and whose stories "happened that way" (Beston 89). *A Little Tea, A Little Chat,* published in 1948, ten years and four novels after *House of All Nations,* continues Stead's critique of capitalism and commerce, begun in *House of All Nations,* and her study of the kinds of people in whom capitalism brings out the worst. *A Little Tea, A Little Chat* has not been highly regarded by most critics, who, to some extent, share the opinion that "exposing pettiness and vice seems hardly worth the effort when none of the characters is attractive enough to elicit our concern" (Lidoff 149). Because almost all of its characters are corrupt or self-serving or foolish dupes, the story seems to lack a conventional moral centre. Moreover, authorial criticism, minimal in any of Stead's writing, seems even slighter in this novel. This intellectual maturity, which leaves the placement of a moral perspective to its readers, is one of the strengths of Stead's work. This essay discusses a possible perspective for reading *A Little Tea, A Little Chat,* suggesting that the narrative point of view insists on some moral perspective without prescribing what it should be, and that the novel has a positive, if not a simplistically uplifting, tendency.

Stead often said that New York was one of her favourite cities and that she particularly liked its people, something that might surprise readers on first encountering the New York trilogy. *A Little Tea, A Little Chat* is perhaps the least popular of Stead's novels because its depiction of capitalism and wartime profiteering in New York, apparently by people Stead knew, seems unrelieved by satire or by the presence of any admirable and effective character to provide a gleam of moral enlightenment. On Stead's evidence, absence of authorial condemnation cannot be attributed to a belief in the existence of absolute evil, which requires no explanation (Beston 90). It cannot be said, however, that *A Little Tea, A Little Chat* adopts an amoral position in which greed, treachery, and viciousness are merely depicted without comment. A sound argument has been made to suggest that this novel should be read sequentially with *Letty Fox: Her Luck,* which shows the effect of capitalism on middle-class women (Mercer). The portrait of Robert Owen Grant in *A Little Tea, A Little Chat* is undoubtedly that of a man of ability who is thoroughly corrupted by the self-interest encouraged by the worst aspects of capitalism. Yet, Grant's relationship to capitalism is different from that of characters in the earlier novels.

In one of the finest studies of wickedness in English literature, Milton's epic poem *Paradise Lost,* there is a memorable recognition of wickedness in the confrontation between Satan and the Cherub Zephron in the fourth Book. Satan arrogantly claims that, "Not to know me argues yourselves unknown" (1.830). When the Cherub replies that Satan has lost the shape of undiminished brightness by which he was known in Heaven, and that his Glory has departed from him

> abasht the Devil stood,
> And felt how awful goodness is, and saw
> Vertue in her shape how lovely, saw, and pin'd
> His loss;
>
> (11.846-49)

Stead's stories seldom show awe-inspiring goodness and the lovely shape of virtue, for even their fantasy is based in reality. However, they do point out to those who believe in capitalism, socialism, marriage, family love, romantic love, passion, and the hundred varieties of friendship and attachment depicted in their pages what may become of these ideals and virtues in the post-lapsarian world.

In *A Little Tea, A Little Chat* the worst characters do not stand abashed, although Grant finally begins to dream that he is sinking in the filthy mud of a battle-field (375). Like much of Stead's work, this novel seems to adopt the epigraph from Denis Diderot's dialogue, *Le Neveau de Rameau,* which she used for *House of All Nations*:

> On est dédommagé de la perte de son innocence par-celle de ses préjugés. Dans la société des méchants, où le vice se montre à masque levé, on apprend à les con-naître. [*One is compensated for loss of innocence by loss of prejudices. In the company of wicked people, where vice shows itself unmasked, one learns to recognize them.*]

A central didactic device in Stead's writing, and notably in *A Little Tea, A Little Chat,* consists of allowing characters to show themselves unmasked.[1]

In *A Little Tea, A Little Chat,* the mask of vice is raised, showing readers the face of twentieth-century bourgeois capitalism as Swift or Goya might have shown it.[2] In *Rameau's Nephew,* the Nephew, Lui, a sycophant and consummate mime, living, as he admits, like a parasite on the corrupt wealthy families of eighteenth-century Paris, shamelessly exposes himself and his patrons to Moi, the interlocutor whom he accosts in the gardens of the Palais-Royal. In *A Little Tea, A Little Chat* Grant believes his mask is firmly in place as he mesmerizes others with his self-absorbed monologues and conversation, justifying to himself his treachery and shabbiness. His mask is lifted, nevertheless, by the mimetic style and by the many subtleties of Stead's narrative, which provides little authorial comment, but considerable narrative irony.

The concept of mimesis is appropriate in considering Stead's mode of narration and suggests a key to the kind of realism that most critics have identified in her writing. Stead was adamant that her fictional characters be based on real people, because, as she told Joan Lidoff, "you can't invent people, or they're puppets" (Lidoff 217). Like the fictional characters created by most writers, any one of Stead's characters is a composite of people she knew or of whom she had heard. Just as Rameau's nephew has an astonishing capacity to mime, so Stead's narrative shows a remarkable mimetic skill, which can be appreciated for what it is without wishing on it the pruning and shaping that critics tend to recommend. In *A Little Tea, A Little Chat* the characters create themselves in dialogue, concealing themselves from themselves, but not from the reader.

From Stead's own comments, Robert Grant is based on Alfred Hurst, a close friend and business partner of her husband, William Blake. Hurst, who, like Grant, had a son, dictated Stead's own movements for some years while Blake accompanied him on various money-making ventures to different countries, including Spain and Canada (Whitehead 237-38). Blake supplied much of the inspiration for a number of Stead's characters and, as Annette Segerberg suggested, it is likely that David Flack, Grant's loyal and sincerely socialist friend, is based on Blake (Segerberg 20). Blake's warmth and loyalty seem to have suggested the best qualities of Grant's only honest male friend, a clever but unambitious economist, and perhaps Flack's daughter, Edda, an aspiring cartoonist, writer, and linguist, is a partial self-portrait of Stead. A more detailed portrait of Blake's brilliance as an economist and sincerity as a socialist is seen in the character of Michel Alphendéry in *House of All Nations.* Both Alphendéry and Flack are essential to the critique of European capitalism between the wars in *House of All Nations* and of American of capitalism during the Second World War in *A Little Tea, A Little Chat.* Alphendéry and Flack see wickedness unmasked around them, but because they are warm, loyal, and humane, these clever, competent men often comply with the wickedness of their friends. The failure of good men to make any effective stand against the corruption of which they are aware helps to explain how human wickedness flourishes.

House of All Nations depicts capitalism practised by the élite and aristocracy of the "Old World." *A Little Tea, A Little Chat* depicts the kind of capitalism practised by the bourgeoisie of the "New World," and this partly accounts for the sober tone of the latter novel. "New World" capitalism is shown as sordid and unimaginative because it attempts, as Grant and his associates do, to reconcile capitalism with puritanical moral values distorted almost beyond recognition. Money, not gold, is the centre of their worship. This colours the tone of the novel, distinguishing it from *House of All Nations,* where, it has been said, the authorial tone suggests "a wistful inclination towards what might be called an idealized condition of which gold is an emblem" (Holmes 266).

These bourgeois New York businessmen, however, pursue their self-interests without imagination and they have no comprehension that self-interest might be served by altruism. It would be beyond the ability of Grant and his associates to understand the wisdom of Alphendéry's remark in *House of All Nations* that "altruism is selfishness out with a pair of field glasses and imagination" (100). Wisdom, to March, for example, is knowing that "corruption, vice and crime were the essence of human nature, [and] that the fools, the lambs, did not know it" (97). Grant is seduced by the sophisticated refugees from Europe, an "international scum" of the worst types depicted in *House of All Nations*: "Vice was understood; it was, to them, maturity. It was their life-blood; it gave them food" (166). Grant needs no instruction in vicious business practices, but he adds hypocrisy to delusion, for his prudery colours what he thinks is his wisdom in seeing the world as "a hardworking, well-behaved, respectable place in which a few devil-may-care men and women, pricked on by their own temperament, found vice irresistible, discovered, but kept to themselves, the great secret that there is gaiety in vice" (97). There is irony in seeing the timid, hypocritical, self-pitying Grant as one of the devil-may-cares.[3]

Grant is distanced from the fictional Henri Léon, and from the real Alf Hurst, who was a Romanian Jew. Grant's mother was "a tough, coarse old woman" who, as a girl, worked in the Lancashire cotton mills (14). Grant knows he was named after the social reformer and educational pioneer Robert Owen, who, between 1800 and 1825, converted the cotton mills of New Lanark into a progressive co-operative, offering workers and their families education and social justice and proving that altruism was enlightened self-interest that would bring all the rewards a capitalist might desire. Robert Owen Grant, however, apart from knowing the cotton trade, has nothing in common with his namesake. Robert Owen built his fortune steadily from the age of nine, through hard work, intelligence, and vision, and in the 1830s his name became synonymous with the new word, "socialism," used to describe the social aspirations of the workers (Cole 31). Grant, too, "knew cotton from boyhood" (14), but when the novel opens in 1941 he is making his spending money in a few hours daily on the Cotton Exchange, has married a wealthy woman, and in his numerous other ventures always takes on partners to sign the documents: "He always had the impression that these adventurers would make a mistake and that whoever lost . . . he would be able to wrangle a profit out of it for himself" (14).

In certain company, Grant declares himself a socialist, partly because he believes in socialism as an idea, but also because he believes that women committed to socialism will give freely of themselves and their time without expecting monetary reward. After entertaining two women with drinks "and various extravagances," he says he is a radical and advises them to read Bellamy's *Looking Backward* (15). Irony is paramount here. *Looking Backward 2000-1887*, published by a New England journalist in 1888, is among the best-known of the hundreds of Utopian novels written in English in the last decades of the nineteenth century, and for several generations was used as a primer in socialist lecture courses. Its thesis is a moral indictment of capitalism and an advocation of what Bellamy calls Nationalism; that is, a scientifically state-organized economy of supply and demand based on highly developed statis-

tical information. The Utopia is made possible through the moral enlightenment of citizens no longer obsessed with personal possessions and consumerism and converted to a domestic austerity that is compensated for by a wealth of beautiful and imaginative public parks, landscaping, architecture, sculpture, and other arts. Although Bellamy's Utopia shares the conservative social values that appear in a distorted form in Grant's lifestyle, nothing could be further from Bellamy's vision than Grant's business exploitation of national needs and shortages, and his secretive, sordid, domestic arrangements.

Grant is also a perversion of all that Robert Owen represents. His name is another example of Stead's grim wit, often at its best when she chronicles the state of contemporary socialism. Grant's avowed socialism represents the impulse he has towards altruism, but he practises a gross form of capitalism that he is too craven to affirm. The basis of Robert Owen's philosophy was that people are entirely the result of their environment. As the socialist historian G. D. H. Cole says, Owen's "[c]o-operative communities were attempts to change men's hearts and minds by placing them in a new environment better adjusted to the needs of the new social conditions" (Cole 7-8). Narrative irony, therefore, appears whenever Grant makes one of his frequent declarations that he would have been a better man if he had been brought up in a different country, where there was "a law to stop me putting my hands in other people's pockets," (19) or "[i]n another country, different civilization, set of values, more education" (158). These attempts to shift the responsibility for his acknowledged corruption on to something beyond his control, and his anxiety to see himself as "wholesome, a constructive type" (36), distance Grant further from the brilliant, boldly unashamed characters in *A House of All Nations*.

Grant's social context is established in the first pages. It is enlarged during the narrative of his shoddy, lucrative business deals and his pitiably contemptible search for a domestic oasis, for "three women in one, the sweetheart, the wife and the mother" (110). As in the opening of some other novels by Stead, the main action is not clearly separated from the material that forms background detail and staffage. The novel's mimetic realism forces readers to postpone their identification of the major figures until the narrative narrows its focus.

The first chapter begins in 1941, with a description of Peter Hoag, a Manhattan bachelor and businessman with many partners but no special business, whose life is devoted to helping the financial deals and private affairs of a group of friends, including Grant. These men "loved the United States intensely, ferociously, with terror and greed" (4). When it appears that Grant Associates sold rare alloys essential to the Nazi war effort, exporting them in cotton bales sent from South America, it seems that theirs is the love of maggots feeding on a gangrenous sore in a living body. The narrative describes a "prank" in which Hoag and his friends, through financial chicanery, manipulate the suicide of a corporation president and prepare to mulct another president by marrying him to the lover of one of the pranksters, who would himself marry her after she divorced the unsuspecting president. It then focuses on another woman whom Hoag picks up in the street. This is Mrs Barbara Kent, English-born and part Russian, who has been living off of men all her life and who now meets Grant in a fur warehouse in which he has a financial interest. As has been said often about other Stead novels, exposing the sex and cash nexus is part of Stead's critique of western society. In Grant's relationship with the blonde Mrs Kent, however, the sex and cash nexus has a ghastly kind of pathos, for if Grant had been capable of more than "a schoolboy's and seducer's tin pan alley view of love" (374), he would have loved the blondine. Four years later, the grimly comic story of Grant's business deals and sexual engagements that comprises the novel comes to an end. Grant and the blondine live like *petit bourgeois* landlords in a basement apartment, sharing creature comfort and malice, until Grant dies of a heart attack brought on by the appearance of Hilbertson, his mysterious Nemesis.

Grant works in the neighbourhood of Wall Street, described by Stead in her synopsis of the novel as a place that, lacking any principle, had "no patriotism, had only the passion for profit" (Geering, "From the Personal Papers" 424). The day after Pearl Harbour, Grant and Flack sell all of Grant's government bonds, "many others being ashamed to sell at that moment," and buy steel shares. When Grant proposes forming a shipping company in Valparaiso to send contraband to Japan, "Flack was found sufficiently pusillanimous to shake his head at this idea, while laughing" (52). Examples of Grant's wartime profiteering and exploitation of national and international emergencies are often ludicrously accompanied by Grant's visions of himself as a benevolent reconstructionist of postwar European economies.

The difference between Grant and Diderot's Lui, who also preys on his society, is that Lui never attempts to conceal from himself or his interlocutor the cynicism and viciousness of his conduct, which he believes is appropriate to the Paris he inhabits. Grant deliberately conceals from himself the truth of his conduct through an amazing series of evasions that should not deceive anyone, but do finally deceive even the sharp and critical Edda. The process of watching Grant deceive good people as well as bad makes *A Little Tea, A Little Chat* an instructive experience, if reading pleasure is not dependent on the need to empathize with fictional charac-

ters. Grant succeeds because few people wish to learn what Stead (and Diderot) plainly depict.[4]

Much of the narrative deals with Grant's relationships with women, which, apart from his involvement with the blondine, always end in his material advantage, although he gains little sensual pleasure from his encounters. When Stead said that the "basic myth" of *A Little Tea, A Little Chat* was that of Don Juan (Geering, "From the Personal Papers" 424) she was referring to Grant's promiscuity, not to his prowess, for there is nothing to suggest that Grant and his women share sexual excitement or release. The aridity of Grant's sexual adventures is emphasized by the passages depicting the delighted day-dream that surrounds Grant's son Gilbert when he falls in love with Celia Grimm, a white fighter for black rights who has earlier rejected Grant. Grant's sexual chauvinism provides fine feminist comedy when he expresses horror because some of his women leave him for an elderly Greek, who succeeds with women because he "thinks of them, too!" when he makes love. Grant mentions a few of his own exploits and exclaims, "I don't need that for my pleasure. I'm not a pervert" (280).

Stead often remarked that love and sexuality were greatly important to her, repeating in an interview a few months before her death, "I'm a believer in love. That's really my religion. Why, I don't know. I think it has something to do with creativity" (Geering, "Talking" 9). The inability to love and a lack of creative imagination are basic traits in Grant's character. The timidity that underlies his meanness and treachery and his appalling treatment of women make him not so much a monster, as several critics have called him, as a ludicrous caricature of masculinity. The banality and prudery that accompany Grant's every vicious act are Stead's indictment of the class he represents.

The title of the novel derives from the euphemism Grant uses for a short sexual meeting, usually in his rooms, to which he has taken a woman on the pretext of making a long-distance telephone call. Sometimes he refers to such encounters as "a party," and he would be shocked if anyone were to give them a more accurate name, as he is shocked when Edda, attempting to see the blondine as something more than a commodity, says, "Yes, even the blondine is real, her body, her hair is real" (66). In this conversation with the Flacks, Grant comes close to appreciating the difference between the reality of the commodity, whether it is a woman or a shipment of wheat, and the factitious nature of the speculations by which it changes hands. But he is so upset by Edda's reference to the living body of the woman that in the end Edda apologizes: "'Look, I didn't say body in a wrong way. The word body is a good word, too,' said Edda, ashamed" (67). Grant, however, "could not think about his sexual life. This was repugnant to him" (31).

This hypocritical prudery is part of the evasiveness, timidity, and lies by which he lives. The effect of these traits in action may be illustrated by two events: the death of Myra Coppelius, which shows Grant in his most evil act, and the play he attempts to write, an incident that shows him in his most ludicrous role.

Grant represents human egotism in an acute form when he confuses the idea of "love" with the measurement of what a woman is prepared to give him or to do for him. Grant often begs women to "show" their love for him in scenes recalling a similar scene in *King Lear,* which Shakespeare almost makes great drama, but which Stead's novel reveals more accurately as consummate, unheroic egotism. The narrative repeats again and again Grant's "sweet" song to women: "I'm looking for a woman; my life is empty. It's up to you . . . A fair field and no favor, you prove to me you're the woman I'm looking for. That's all I ask" (41). One of the women who is seduced by this appeal is Myra Coppelius, the wife of a philandering mid-western doctor, who comes to New York and works as a salesgirl when her husband's affairs become too upsetting, because "she loved him deeply" (29). She once undressed for Grant, to show him she was not ugly, but would only kiss him, saying, "I would fall in love with you, but to you I am only a woman you take upstairs" (30). Although her sincerity is beyond Grant's understanding, he compares her favourably with Barbara Kent when his accounts show that he has spent $23,000 in six months on the blondine: "Too much, little Coppelius works honestly for a living, she's Sea Island-staple, the other's rotten" (30). Nevertheless, Grant brings about Myra Coppelius's death. He cajoles her into buying him a second-hand car, promising that he will pay for it later and that after the war they will go to Europe together "and try to build a new life, do something for someone who needs it" (175). He tells all of his friends that a rich woman is buying him a car "as a gift, for love" (176) and harasses Mrs Coppelius to make the purchase as a pledge of her love, begging her to pay for it in her name, as "he had momentary difficulty in releasing his funds" (182). Later, however, Grant decides to cut back on "the expenses of love":

> [H]e now told Mrs Coppelius that he could not help her with the car, he thought she had acted rashly in taking an odd word of his, a sort of boyish enthusiasm, for gospel, and after all she had no written word from him. She must grow up, not believe in fairy princes, said he: she would be happier.
>
> (195)

As it is Christmas, he is "hurt" when Mrs Coppelius does not send him a card, as he had hinted that she might make the car over to him as a gift and that he might then make her a gift of some satisfactory sum, "to avoid income-tax" (196). Three days before New Year's Eve he is lonely, thinking "I must be loved this afternoon; I must make up for all my headaches," but on arriving at Mrs Coppelius's hotel he learns that she has just fallen from the seventh floor (197). Terrified at his close encounter with "Azrael"—he only dares to think about death in this metaphor—he joins his friends at a bar and "thanked his luck that he had not mentioned Mrs Coppelius to any of them recently" (197). Grant's mind cannot suppress the event, however, and the death of Mrs Coppelius reappears in distorted forms in the stories he tells later in the narrative. There are a number of similar suicides in Stead's fiction, but the intention here is not to reflect on their social, psychological, or metaphorical significance. In the context of literary realism, to narrate the cause of such a death is to do no less than lift the mask of human evil.

Evidence that Edda Flack is partly a self-portrait of Stead appears early in the narrative when Grant pesters the girl to write his life story. Edda is seventeen, a "slender, sharp-tongued young brunette" (31) who instinctively dislikes Grant and once drew a caricature of him, describing him as "avaricious, long-nosed, thin-haired, with a sniffing belly" (103). The caricature gives him a huge "woman-hunting nose," a representation from which Grant never recovers: "Grant locked the caricature away in a drawer but took it with him wherever he went—he could not throw it away" (32). He seldom alludes to it openly, but offers to give Edda his life story and a formula that will make it a bestseller, the central figure being a thinly disguised version of what Grant imagines himself to be:

> This American says, "I like to construct," says he's a moral engineer, "I like to construct lives, too." Now, Edda, make it simple, don't be clever, don't be sardonic—I beg pardon, I don't mean anything wrong, but no words like mur-murmur—like you said about me, unnecessary, uncalled-for: people don't buy spoiled goods.
>
> (37)

It is not necessary to identify Edda with the author to appreciate the irony that writing to formula is quite foreign to Stead's work. A mercenary motive that prompts a writer to depict only wholesome characters could not be further from the composition of *A Little Tea, A Little Chat.*

Grant pesters Edda with ideas for the work, which finally becomes a play, and engages Karol Karolyi, a Polish refugee writer, to write the script for him, but he does not pay the writer or his typist. Grant pursues the play, finding several absurd titles relating to his need for an ideal woman: "Dream Girl," "The Rainbow Girl," "My Narrow Paradise," "All I Want is a Woman." Karolyi, with a somewhat more original concept of box-office success, calls it "The Subway Princess." A grotesquely ironic scene occurs when, after one extraordinary reading of the play, Grant is alarmed at Karolyi's sparse dialogue, expands the script himself, and holds another reading in the presence of an actress as egotistical as he, whom he hopes to interest in the play:

> She was a powerful, corpulent, vain animal, a sort of Grant in skirts. They sniffed at each other, and liked each other at the first glance. The gross man went up to the gross woman, put his arm partly round her waist, and kissed her on the shoulder, "A Polish woman taught me to do that; I was going with her to reconstruct Poland after the war, arrange to supervise spinning and clothes, but she died. You remind me of her.
>
> (356)

Flack reads for them, while Grant bursts with pride at the dialogue that he has titivated with many of his catch-phrases; Karolyi's words are represented in italics:

BERTIE:

> [*to the maid*] *Let any woman in who is less than five feet four.* I advertised for a dream girl. With an innocent air, sweet ways, loyalty. And a waist that can go through a wedding ring!
>
> (356)

The actress is unimpressed, reminding Grant that she does not have that kind of waist. Undeterred, Grant points out the box-office appeal of lines like these:

LULA:

> *It's a town on the Fall Line.* I'm looking for the right man and when I find him, I'll settle down and forget my ambitions and make breakfast for him.
>
> (357)

The actress, whose vocabulary is as coarse as Grant's is prissy, announces that she has heard enough after the following lines:

BERTIE:

> *I've never been to New Jersey, but I'd love to travel—with you.* I'm looking for the right woman and if you are the right woman, then we'll go when the war is over and reconstruct . . .
>
> (357)

The scene ends in chaos as Alf Goodwin, one of the most disreputable of Grant's friends, launches into a mad tirade because Grant purchased for him a packet of underpants of the wrong size. This is the end of Grant's attempts to make capital from writing, a venture directed entirely by egotism and a need to reconstruct his life story closer to his heart's desire. It also allows Stead to satirize would-be writers and the dream of the bestseller.

Myra Coppelius is the most tragic of Grant's victims, but he betrays everyone with whom he has contact, including fine characters such as his old housekeeper, Mrs MacDonald, and Miss Robbins, his loyal confidential secretary. Miss Robbins has no illusions about him: "Her low pay, common sense, and firmness of character had prevented her from ever loving him, ever admiring him; but she spoke about him to no one" (200).

The novel's realism makes it unnecessary to explain why good women, and Flack, remain loyal to Grant: in real life unworthy people do attract love and loyalty. Only occasionally is the reader given the satisfaction of hearing Grant criticized: by Edda or Celia Grimm, or by his son Gilbert. Although Gilbert's interest in psychological self-analysis is caricatured, there is power in his deduction that "Dad has never quite emerged from that cloud of infantile personality. He is obsessed by his own impulses. He sees the world as driven by the same, and he attributes these impulses to others" (125).

Grant, however, has his revenge. He betrays Celia and his son to the police when Celia goes south to organize the black workers; and while Flack goes down to bail them from jail with his own money, Grant writes an anonymous letter to the Department to which Edda was applying as a foreign-language secretary, accusing her of immorality and Communist views, and she loses the job. Nevertheless, at the end, with some belief in a plan that Edda and Flack, who is now quite ill and unsalaried, although still working on Grant's affairs, would accompany Grant to Rome, the girl partly trusts her father's friend: "They had no attraction for each other as man and woman, but each was tired of the long contest of wills" (379).

Barbara Kent (later Downs) wins in her contest with Grant, partly because she is as ruthless as he, which attracts him, and partly because he is truly susceptible to her physical appeal. Stealing documents showing that Grant has already made over most of his property to his two sons, she has him in her power by the end of the story and decides to live with him, although she dislikes him and is tired of him (244). The narrative allows her some integrity in that she has a natural love of men (240) while seeing them as her best and most legitimate means of livelihood. In her synopsis, Stead describes the blondine as "a worthless woman, a leech on men, whose corruption seems to be at one with the corruption of that society" (Geering, "From the Personal" 424). Yet, the blondine appears less despicable than Grant. Similarly, Grant's rich wife, who has elected to sleep her life away as the best means of coping with it, and March's silly, coquettish wife Angela seem not so much contemptible as culpable of taking one of the poorer of the options available to them.

Betty Goodwin, who conducts a long-standing affair with Grant, loyally nurses her husband as he succumbs to mental illness, while Grant, although not abashed by her goodness, is "astonished and flattered" and "often felt a bit queer" about the selflessness of her devotion to himself (381). Livy Wright, a business-like woman, teases Grant about his sweet talk, in a scene reminiscent of an incident, apparently involving Hurst, that Stead described in a letter to Thistle Harris in 1943 (Williams 161). Livy, despite her astuteness, is also cheated by Grant when she buys two New York properties, believing, like Mrs Coppelius, that "the houses were a sort of gauge from her to Grant" (376). Grant refuses to assist with the payments and, when she is forced to sell, buys the houses cheaply through an agent.

Female characters are chiefly responsible for the novel's positive moments. Celia Grimm encourages Gilbert's passage from naive moral enthusiasm to mature commitment and integrity, and the woman involved in the hoax at the beginning of the story has a change of heart, dismaying Hoag and his friends by remaining loyal to the company president.

A writer less committed to realism might have rescued the Flacks, as their intelligence, courage, and loyalty to each other, and David's loyalty to Grant, deserve a better fate. An adequate examination of the character of Flack has not yet been published but would make a useful comparison with that of Alphendéry in *House of All Nations*. There is also scope for a comparison of Flack's and Grant's attitudes to money-making that would be interesting to the student of capitalist mores. Midway through the story, Flack becomes seriously ill: "Supposing himself in excellent health, because gay and garrulous, he had not been near a doctor for years, and had been overcome by an incurable though not painful disease" (256). Flack's illness may be read as an image for the *laissez-faire* of cultured, benevolent socialists, who, not sufficiently aggressive and committed, trust their idealism to survive in a corrupt environment without itself becoming corrupt.

Two mysteries hover in the background of Grant's life: one is the story of Laura in Italy, with ironic Petrarchan overtones; the other is the figure of Hilbertson in New Orleans. Laura, wealthy and a secret anti-fascist, might indeed have become Grant's ideal love, and even in New York he retains traces of the refinement he learnt from her. Yet, with the possibility of their reunion as the war and the novel come to an end, he remains true to himself, cheats her of her property, and tells her that he has contracted "a very unpleasant, even disgraceful, disease . . . He believed Laura could easily die of a broken heart now, and then his title would be clear in Rome" (378).

It is some consolation to watch the emergence of Hilbertson, who first appears in a faked record compiled by March to show that Barbara Kent is connected with enemy espionage. Hilbertson is apparently a former business partner, but Grant seems afraid to mention his name and does not want to visit New Orleans again. A woman informant writes from New Orleans: "Hilbertson stays at home like a bear with a sore head: but everyone says he still speaks of getting you. What did you do to that guy anyway?" (196). Hilbertson, however, remains obscure; he is possibly a friend of Laura's, possibly a victim of Grant's promises, but certainly a man who believes he has "some unfinished business" with Grant (379). As Grant settles into mundane domesticity with the blondine, Hilbertson comes closer, inquiring about Grant, first through March, then through the black housekeeper, Marsha. The reader and the blondine meet him only on the penultimate page of the book: "a very tall, strong, but bent, old man, with blue eyes and big hands . . . well dressed and [with] that imposing air of a man who had once had great charm and had not wasted it with prostitutes, a man who still carried in him his passion" (392-93). This "splendid old man," who appears to be all that Grant is not, invites the blondine out for tea, but does not keep the appointment. Instead, he calls on Grant, who, seeing Hilbertson at the door with his hand in his pocket, stammers a few sentences and collapses. When the blondine returns, Grant is dead. Classic Nemesis or Hollywood cliché, Hilbertson is a fitting climax to the story of a man who thrives in a factitious society and is guilty of the classical sin of betrayal of self and of fellow men and women.

In *A Little Tea, A Little Chat* enterprise and daring are reduced to pure cheating, even among friends, and the adventures in buying and selling that in *A House of All Nations* fascinate even the non-materialist reader, become mean and tedious tricks. The moral distance between the novels recalls the decline of Lucifer, from a proud rebel Angel to a squat malicious toad, in *Paradise Lost*. The blondine believes she is "in the centre of a kind of exchange of values" and that "everything was for sale" (194). In Grant, however, a perverted impulse towards altruism corrupts this simple commercialism. He makes treacherous promises because he needs to see himself as a good, generous man, just as he believes he is a superior socialist because he could, if he wished, donate one million dollars to socialist causes (362). Before he dies he is puzzled by a dimly perceived "moral question" (385). The novel leaves readers to identify this moral question as they wish: perhaps it is simply that capitalism cannot satisfy the best instincts of humankind. As Diana Brydon suggests, "[c]apitalism makes sexism and fascism seem inevitable" (Brydon 107). Capitalism, Stead's narrative implies, should not attempt to take on the virtues of human love, cooperation, and mutual support.

The narrative's steady unmasking of Grant is the more effective because the characters, unlike the reader, do not learn the depths of Grant's depravity. Most critics are intolerant and unimpressed when the narrative mimes Grant's monologues and sweet talk, yet in real life these lies can be effective, and it is not incredible that many people are deceived by Grant. Grant's success, paradoxically, is one reason why **A Little Tea, A Little Chat** is not wholly a depressing or pessimistic view of society. It shows that society for the most part is comprised of people who do not habitually cheat each other and do not expect to be cheated, lied to, and deceived.

Notes

1. The concept of unmasking is raised briefly in an interesting article by Denise Brown, "Christina Stead's 'Drama of the Person'".

2. See the reveiwer in the *San Francisco Chronicle* who wrote of this novel, "Swift and Goya could not have done it any better" (Williams 177).

3. Diana Brydon, in a brief but thoughtful commentary on the novel, suggests that Grant is "not a hypocrite so much as morally bankrupt" (106).

4. Bruce Holmes makes this point in greater depth when quoting Aphendéry's respect for Diderot, suggesting that Alphendéry "is motivated by the Marxist's wish to benefit man by a proper application of materialism, but this paradoxically entails the expression of spiritual values . . ." He quotes Alphendéry's remark that one must be born and trained to a love of humanity, as one must be born to money and love (268). My point is that in emphasizing the discrepancy between socialism and capitalism, Stead's writing implies spiritual or non-material values, just as it demonstrates the importance of honesty by creating corrupt and self-deceptive characters.

Works Cited

Bellamy, Edward. *Looking Backward 2000-1887*. 1888. Cambridge, Mass.: Harvard University Press, 1967.

Beston, John. "An Interview with Christina Stead." *World Literature Written in English* 1 (1976): 87-95.

Brown, Denise. "Christina Stead's 'Drama of the Person.'" *Australian Literary Studies* 2 (1987): 139-45.

Brydon, Diana. *Christina Stead*. Women Writers. London: Macmillan Education, 1987.

Cole, G. D. H. *The Life of Robert Owen*. 1925. New introduction by Margaret Cole. London: Frank Cass, 1965.

Geering, R. G. "Talking into the Typewriter: The Letters of Christina Stead." *Southerly* 1 (1990): 3-19.

———. "From the Personal Papers of Christina Stead: Extracts and Commentaries." *Southerly* 4 (1990): 399-425.

Holmes, Bruce. "Character and Ideology in Christina Stead's *House of All Nations*." *Southerly* 3 (1985): 266-79.

Lidoff, Joan. *Christina Stead*. New York: Frederick Ungar, 1982.

Mercer, Gina. "Christina Stead—A Radical Author: Patterns of Thesis and Antithesis." *The Given Condition: Essays in Post-Colonial Literatures. Span* 21 (1985): 137-51.

Milton, John. *The Complete Poems*. London: Dent, 1980.

Saxelby, Jean and Gwen Walker-Smith. "Christina Stead." *Biblionews* 14 (1949): 37-43.

Segerberg, Annette. "A Fiction of Sisters: Christina Stead's *Letty Fox* and *For Love Alone*." *Australian Literary Studies* 2 (1989): 15-25.

Stead, Christina. *A Little Tea, A Little Chat*. 1948. London: Virago, 1981.

———. *House of All Nations*. 1938. London: Angus and Robertson, 1974.

———. "Christina Stead: An Interview." By Ann Whitehead. Australian Broadcasting Commission 13 Aug. 1973. *Australian Literary Studies* 3 (1974): 230-48.

Williams, Chris. *Christina Stead: A Life of Letters*. Melbourne: McPhee Gribble, 1989.

Susan Sheridan (essay date December 1993)

SOURCE: Sheridan, Susan. "Re-reading Christina Stead." *Southerly* 53, no. 4 (December 1993): 42-6.

[*In the following essay, Sheridan attempts to answer the question of whether it is possible to read Stead's satirical novels of masculinity and money, namely* House of All Nations *and* A Little Tea, A Little Chat, *through the lens of a feminist political agenda as works "articulating relations between capitalism and patriarchy."*]

I measure my re-reading of Stead's fiction from the publication of my book, which was the study of her novels about women, starting with **The Man Who Loved Children** and ending with **I'm Dying Laughing**.[1] Since that time, I've been re-reading the novels I had to leave out of that book, in particular the ones which could be described as "the novels about men". **House of all Nations** and **A Little Tea, A Little Chat** share a concern with the masculine world of money and sex, the two great commodities that circulate among men and bond them together.

It wasn't, I must say, a purely voluntary return and re-reading. In fact I'd rather thought that I might have a break from the inevitably close, uncomfortably familial relationship I'd developed with Stead's ghost as I wrote the book. But then I realized, as I guess most academics do, that having published a book I was now considered something of an expert on Stead, and people would invite me to offer yet FURTHER thoughts on her work. I realized that my relationship to Christina Stead would be an ongoing one, more like a family relationship which, for better or worse, becomes part of oneself, than like the voluntary relationship one forms with a new acquaintance or lover—the strictly "ELECTIVE affinity" which was Stead's preference over the "iron bonds" of family life.

In the book I had courted the risk of identifying the qualities of her writing with the qualities of her women characters, especially the "monstrous passions" embodied in Nelly of *Cotters' England* and Emily in *I'm Dying Laughing,* and seeing the monstrosity as a manifestation of their entrapment, as women, within patriarchal constraints. How, I had to ask myself, could the feminist approach I had developed to reading her novels about women be adapted to read her novels about men? Did "their" texts have to be read differently? What monstrous passions drove them? Was the object of satire the same, or different? Most people read the "men and money" novels as satires on capitalism, and classify them as "political". But I had argued that *Cotters' England* and *I'm Dying Laughing* were also political novels, in the sense that they challenged the boundaries between public and private. Was there a way to re-read *House of All Nations* and *A Little Tea, A Little Chat* as "political" in this sense also, as articulating relations between capitalism and patriarchy?

To test these concepts of the satirical and the political in my feminist reading-position, I turned to *House of All Nations.* Stupendous, amazing, what an appallingly energetic vision of the world as a giant brothel—but there was too much going on, I couldn't get the text in focus, I felt battered by it. And so, perversely, as masochists will, I plunged further into discomfort and disorientation and re-read *A Little Tea, A Little Chat,* the novel I want to talk about here.[2]

It's a most unloved book—few people I know have read it. But it is focussed, excessively so, on a central figure. It is a portrait of Robbie Grant, a Manhattan businessman who deals in commodities and women. He and his cronies are war-profiteers on two fronts, the sexual and the economic. The title echoes his favourite euphemism for the sexual connections which he pursues constantly, the pursuit and clinching of the deal being his true passion, rather than pleasure or even possession. The major action of this novel, which spans the years 1941-1945, concerns his pursuit of "the Blond-ine", a woman in whom he is convinced he has met his match. This pursuit passes through various stages (all of them duly measured in financial terms by Grant) from the initial wooing through Grant's investigation of reports that the Blondine is a spy (set up by his business cronies and rivals), several brief marriages on her part, and a farcical attempt on his part to flee the country to escape paying for her subsequent divorces. All this takes place in a crowd of minor characters, his cronies, employees and "girls", whom he involves in these and other schemes by using Volpone-like promises of gain.

Robbie Grant, perhaps the most monstrous of all Stead's egotistical exploiters (male and female), is a superbly vile man. He is the ultimate trader in women and money, which become, in the novel, the two sides of the coin that is exchanged between men in the capitalist commodity market. Through his portrait, Stead scrutinises masculine desire. Appropriating Freud's question, the woman writer asks What, after all, does a man want? The question is explored through his relations to women and to property—and, as well, to other men. Women/money are the means of exchange between men, sites on which they confirm their masculinity and mediate their homosocial desire. As Eve Kosofsky Sedgwick defines that desire, it is "the affective or social force, the glue, even when its manifestation is hostility . . . that shapes an important relationship", one which may be deeply homophobic at the same time as it connects and confirms men as power-brokers in patriarchy.[3]

What is distinctive about Stead's satirical texts is the way they construct "character" as the vehicle of the critique, where it operates not as moral character but as caricature,[4] a figure whose major features are highly exaggerated, who performs himself repeatedly, in constant movement but always remaining the same. The caricature always has a huge balloon of speech issuing from its mouth: Stead has Robbie Grant, like all her monomaniacal protagonists, speak himself into fictional existence, obsessively and repetitively. But speech does not serve its usual novelistic function of "revealing character" either by dramatizing or by ironic indirection. Discourse-as-power has a peculiarly literal significance in the case of Stead's monomaniacs who, distinguished by their capacity for monologue, speak in order to impose their will on others. Grant, for instance, speaks in order to get a deal, a screw, or a favour, imposing his will by means of his self-characterization.

Speech also imposes limits on the interpretive positions available to readers of the novel. For example, Grant claims to be a Marxist, and to abide by his "strait-laced" working class origins (his mother, a Lancashire mill-girl, named him Robert Owen!). For the reader, this appropriation of Marxism works so as to rob it of its potential as a privileged critical discourse, as offering an "objective" position, in the name of Reason or Science, from which to judge him.

Indeed, there is no position of superior knowledge made available in the text, neither political nor psychological. Grant's son, Gilbert, exhibits an obsession with analysing motives and outcomes that could have been set up as a counterpoint to his father's ruthlessness. But the reader is denied much confidence in such a position of knowledge. Gilbert's striking analysis of his father as an infantile personality, surrounded by a "cloud of flesh" (p. 120) is ironically placed as the view of a complacent armchair social critic, a sentimentalist innocent of the ways of the world. Psychology, it is suggested, is too limited in its scope to "master" such a phenomenon as Robbie Grant.

Alternatively there is an angle on Grant provided by Edda Flack, a young woman who is unique in not succumbing to his charm. It is not a discursive position of knowledge so much as performative stance: her name, after the Scandinavian story-collections, suggesting that she occupies the story-teller position. She plays an emblematic minor role, signifying a possible but unarticulated narrative perspective as the critical observer who does not claim to explain the character who is the object of the satire, although she is in no doubt about the ethical issues at stake.

It is Edda who draws a cartoon caricature of Grant which hurts his pride. He is motivated to replace Edda's cartoon with his own, self-authored portrait, which he makes several attempts to have written, either as a best-selling novel called "All I Want is a Woman" or as a Broadway smash hit called "Dream Girl". Grant wants to describe his life as a sentimental, romantic story of his relations with women—as the "real truth" behind his ruthless businessman persona. This motif in the novel constitutes in itself a powerful critique of the ideological split between public and private. It also performs a further function of providing the novel with a reflection on its own textuality, a rehearsal of other forms which this text could have taken. (This often happens in Stead's novels.) Is it, then, Edda's cartoon caricature that Stead has actually written?

Edda's and the narrator's position is one of fascinated but critical observation of a homosocial world and the monstrous passions that animate it. But, as with Stead's satirical portraits of women, the critical distance is not fixed. Indeed, it fluctuates under the strain of attraction to and admiration for the very objects which the narrative critically constructs. Stead works in close-up, her ethnographic thick description effecting a kind of saturation in its object of observation.

This causes the narrative to tread a dangerous line in irony, remaining close to its objects, rather than consistently maintaining the critical distance necessary to perform the classical function of satire, that is, of "castigating the vices of its time and place". But if the

purpose of such castigation is, literally, to purify, then Stead makes no such claim. She does not deny her involvement with her objects in order to claim a pure position of opposition, and this is the case with her male as much as with her female monsters. I do not mean by this a personal involvement with their real-life prototypes, of the kind that Hazel Rowley traces in her biography of Stead, but rather that she risks immersing herself in the element in which her creatures swim, an immersion which enables her to understand how they operate at the same time as she exercises her power over them. Here is, perhaps, the satirist who loves her objects, not in the Christian way of loving the sinner while hating the sin, but in something like the naturalist-observer's desire to possess her objects through knowledge. Christina Stead as satirist is one I want to re-read.[5]

Notes

1. *Christina Stead* (Harvester Wheatsheaf Key "Women Writers" Series, 1988).

2. *A Little Tea, A Little Chat* (Virago, 1981): further references in the text are to this edition.

3. *Between Men: English Literature and Male Homosocial Desire* (Columbia University Press, 1985), p. 2

4. Thanks to Judith Barbour and Lesley Stern for a stimulating discussion about the uses of caricature in response to an earlier version of this paper.

5. Stead often characterized her stance as a novelist as that of the naturalist observing the human species, but in the context of Foucault's work on the relations between knowledge and power, such a stance could not be regarded as innocent. I have elaborated on this theme in "The Woman Who Loved Men: Christina Stead as Satirist in *A Little Tea, A Little Chat* and *The People with the Dogs*", *World Literature Written in English*, 32:1, 1993.

Jennifer Gribble (essay date 1994)

SOURCE: Gribble, Jennifer. "England with the Lid Off." In *Christina Stead,* pp. 94-111. Melbourne, Australia: Oxford University Press, 1994.

[*In the following essay, Gribble examines Stead's three English novels—*Cotters' England, The Little Hotel, *and* Miss Herbert (The Suburban Wife)—*noting, especially, her delineation of the protagonists in these works to expose "a society that clings to its fictions, unable to tell, or to face, the truth about itself."*]

> I'd like to take ye with me, show you a bit of
> England with the lid off . . . Aye, it's a bit different
> from your green and pleasant fields.
>
> *CE [Cotters' England]* 46

Nellie Cotter's phrase recalls a famous passage from Dickens,[1] and Stead's critique of the working-class, expatriate and middle-class life of postwar England has something of the later Dickens' sardonic comedy and critical incisiveness. This bleakest phase of her writing exposes a society that clings to its fictions, unable to tell, or to face, the truth about itself. The apparent candour with which her protagonists offer to lift the lid masks suppression and self-deception. They impose their narratives with increasing wilfulness. The seeds of this development lie of course in Letty Fox and Robbie Grant: by now the quest for love has become utterly voracious, a parody of all that is creative. Stead and Blake, exiled from America by the McCarthyist purges, living in a succession of temporary dwellings in or near London, experience at firsthand the debilitation, hopelessness, and 'semi-starvation' of postwar British life.

At the same time, Stead's own approach to narrative continues to be speculative and innovatory. The interplay between the story that is told and the story that can't be told is most strikingly exploited in the fate of Robbie Grant. Stories can kill, as well as console. Now, however, we are more often left to construct the untold stories for ourselves. Narrative sequences are glimpsed, but not assimilated or developed. Expressing and repressing anxieties and desires, they dramatise the different levels of consciousness, and the power relations, to which the formal analysis of Foucault's poststructuralism would direct attention.[2] In this way, the form of these late novels, developing out of the narrative indeterminacies of **The Salzburg Tales,** is fashioned into an appropriate expression of false consciousness.

As always, however, it is Stead's 'drama of the person' that makes these fractured lives compelling. Nellie Cotter is one of Stead's most terrible creations. We are made to inhabit her consciousness, and to see the fictions it sustains for what they are: survival strategies that permeate the effort to build a better life in the aftermath of war.

COTTERS' ENGLAND

Just as Stead finds in local idiom and speech rhythms a key to the restless and rapid behaviours exposed in the New York trilogy, so she hears in the seductive croon of Tyneside all the paradoxes of the familial and communal intimacies to which it appeals. Lulling cadences and ritual endearments carry with them the insidious and the brutally destructive. Living with a 'decaying family' in the 'dark, dank, weary town of Newcastle',[3] Stead found her image of working-class life. Her social analysis proceeds always by lifting the lid on households of various kinds. The novel moves between 'the grind and grudge of working class life' (*CE* 231) in the industrial north, with its back-to-back houses, and post-

war London in which people and terraces prop each other up. The British 'cot' evoked in Nellie's early diatribe against modern urban tower blocks is a nostalgic tribute to the Cotters' tenement in Bridgehead. It is also a model for the ad hoc commune set up in her London terrace to perpetuate the traditional yeoman values of the cottage. Around these firesides, however, and on the 'cot' on which so many transient sleepers find uneasy rest, domestic comfort is travestied. Stead defended her title (it was published in America as **Dark Places of the Heart**) on the grounds that 'it's what the Cotter family thought about England'.[4] The view from the cot reflects the perspective of the viewer: the attic window, seen from the outset by Nellie as a place of threat ('It was a big drop' *CE* 9) and transformed near the end with one of her characteristic flights of metaphor ('we have an attic window only, open on the swamp of stars' *CE* 344), becomes the vantage point from which Uncle Simon recalls his youthful cloud-scapes, and Nellie enforces her sinister, destructive visions on the vulnerable Caroline.

Vision, point of view, reflection and reflective patterns are foregrounded. The novel's most striking scenes explore the externalising and confrontation of inner experience, and are associated with window and mirror, with individual solipsism and the formative constraints of family and class. 'Cotters' England' is identified by Nellie's husband George Cook as 'the England of the oppressed that starved you all to wraiths' (*CE* 216). In answer to her accusation that his pursuit of an ILO job in Europe is 'class betrayal' he accuses her of sentimentalising the class struggle: 'a worker's a figment to you, Nellie . . . someone for you to mother and maunder over. You're just a plain Fleet Street sobsister.' (*CE* 214) And if he, like Nellie, is shaping the socialist struggle in the light of his own ego, this is because, as Stead sees it, the 'rescue mission' of postwar England is in the hands of the victims themselves, entrapped and self-consuming. Nellie is inclined to identify herself with 'the strange old witch' London, 'all trial and error like my own life' (*CE* 37). With her witch-like enticements and her emaciated, deformed body, she is Stead's most powerful embodiment of the corruption of domestic nurture, 'mothering and maundering' over those she purports to save, selling out on the class struggle and her youthful political ideas in the name of 'truth' as she herself sees it.

Stead's claim to write what she sees (demonstrated as convincingly here as in any of her novels) is parodied in Nellie the journalist: 'Write what you see, Caroline sweetheart.' (*CE* 38) She resigns from her leftwing journal when not allowed to see things her way. The truth claims of narrative are increasingly under scrutiny as Stead's belief in its shaping power is more and more tempered by her sense of the human needs that put it to consolatory and often duplicitous use. A network of anecdotes form a psychological jigsaw puzzle in which the pieces gradually compose themselves into what appear to be significant, though never conclusive, relationship. Through the discursive surface there erupt epiphanic moments that subvert all talk. The constant interplay of the Cotters' points of view hints at a 'story' that is never told, of incest, seduction, unexplained deaths and disappearances.

The Cotters' communal guilt is glimpsed in a series of Pinteresque[5] scenes in which first Nellie, then her brother Tom, revisit the family home. Here lived Thomas Cotter, the gregarious father on whom Nellie models herself, accused by her of a long history of infidelity; here lives his demented widow, Ma Cotter, said by Nellie to have 'worshipped' him and to have exacted the cost of sexual betrayal by neglecting her children. (Tom's recollections of being starved sit oddly with the counter claim that he was indulged by a mother who delighted to cook for her men.) And Peggy, the youngest, institutionalised for eight years for an unspecified mental illness. The clandestine sexual activities by which she relieves her present role as household prisoner and drudge invite speculation about the nature of the 'illness'. And Uncle Simon, pathetic and cantankerous, whose solitary self-gratification is mercilessly exposed by his sisters, a 'parasite' who nevertheless pays the rent. Violent and incestuous feelings explode in harrowing incidents. Peggy's savage whipping of the old man 'from me knees to me forehead' (*CE* 119) as he attempts to relieve himself in a bucket under the sink; Nellie's wordless exposure of her naked breasts, taunting and mocking him; the feast of chicken, undercooked and inedible, which also loses its accompanying potatoes when the old mad mother throws them into the fire so that she can wash and polish the vegetable dish.

Nellie's precocious 'mothering' of her siblings (which has clearly involved sexual initiation and extreme possessiveness) is further played out in the blitz-weakened tenement she inhabits in London. Nellie's pattern of communal living, while it seems to embody the plucky cheerfulness and cooperation of postwar England, seasoned by socialist principles that replace the old bourgeois family, enables Nellie to tyrannise over the homeless and deserted waifs she shelters. Gasping and puffing as she chain-smokes her way through the night, Nellie is merciless in her 'glorious long chats'. Camilla, deserted wife and struggling writer, is the first of many audiences for the tale of Nellie's own perfect union: 'what George and I have is the flower of perfection. Physically, George is a wonderful man, it's joy, it's heaven; there's nothing like it when it's natural and sweet; a blessed union.' (*CE* 17) George's infidelities gradually emerge, however, and Nellie is under the 'strange tyranny' of the lesbian prostitute Johnny Sterker and her friends. As Nellie travels the country to conferences and George pursues his career abroad the couple

are seldom together. But she clings to her story of blessed union, and her desperate, characteristically melodramatic plea to be allowed to join him in Geneva succeeds in the end. Nellie's erotic appeal to a younger George, and her continuing ability to 'tease and stir' make plausible the tenuous survival of the marriage. Their night scenes are loudly available. Preparing for bed in her faded men's pyjamas, with a boot lace round her 'bunch of scallions', consuming raw onions, brandy, a last cigarette, spitting blood and smoking in George's face, she is an unlikely seductress as she cries 'want a real good fight, pet?' (*CE* 305)

'Nellie's a thrilling woman. She can make you see things her way, though you knew it wasn't so' (*CE* 145) says Eliza, George's first wife, who lives in the household as his 'sister'. Like Robbie Grant, Nellie is convincingly endowed with the power to attract the assent of her victims. What prevents her repeating spiel ('the dead end of the lonely road'; 'love is a terminal disease'; 'it's the bloody men') from becoming tiresome to the reader is the way in which it unfolds Stead's analysis of her contradictions, inner torments, haunted dreams and desires. The gloating journalese in which she dwells on the miseries of her friends shows a vicarious feeding off their suffering. The pathetic Caroline, refugee from a broken marriage, caught up in the incestuous dynamics of Nellie's relationship with Tom, is selected to act out the role of Nellie's own weakened and despairing self.[6] Caroline is compelled to 'see' Nellie's great vision of sacrificial death: 'have you a great passion for me, Caroline? Will you do what I say? Then I would be the thing I am meant to be, the great leader—some saw in me.' (*CE* 266)

If Stead risks melodrama here, it is to underline the element of mania in Nellie, drawing its strength from the illness and delirium of her victim. The 'dishonour' to which Caroline refers in her suicide note links Nellie's seduction of her to the suicide of a young girl who has reputedly died for love of Johnny Sterker. The scene in which Nellie forces Caroline to see the inner meaning of their relationship also illumines the meaning of the suicide. Grotesquely clad in Tom's old airman's clothes, an expression of her possessive love and longing for him, and an ironic impersonation of him, Nellie drives Caroline to the attic window to look down on the climax of the two-day orgy with the women friends she keeps hidden from George and Tom:

> A number of naked women were rounding, breaking, wrestling, weaving together in the back yard between the brick walls, the high fence and the tree. The moonlight showed that some were rosy in the daytime, others wore the colours of night-lighted fish and they were like queer fish, a seahorse, an old man snapper, a gar, a toadfish, a puffball and one rather awkward and hesitant was as yet, only a woman: and what was more ludicrous, partly dressed.
>
> *CE* 292

The moonlight imparts a surreal colouring to these interweaving forms, and a narrative vantage point beyond that of the watcher invites consideration of Stead's own views of the 'disorder' of lesbian relationships. Transforming themselves from half-recognisable daily and female selves into 'queer fish', they project a mocking view of female self-sufficiency and cooperation. The animal imagery, as always in Stead's writing, defuses moral judgement. These queer fish are no more queer than Robbie Grant or Henny Pollit; the orgy, 'rounding, breaking, wrestling, weaving together' in its various stages of coupling, copulation, satiety, courtship and ritual dance, is no more or less a travesty of the creative mysteries of love than the sex parties of Grant and his cronies. The shocking effect of the scene comes rather from Nellie's rape of Caroline's sensibility and her trust. Wordlessly identifying, in her look of animal intelligence, with these lunar cavortings, she pinions Caroline with an arm and a 'beak'. Caroline's subsequent leap to her death causes Nellie only a passing nightmare and a letter to Tom that rewrites the death as a martyrdom: 'she was a born saint and a born victim . . . I'll be glad of a word of comfort. I wish I had you here to pour out my thoughts. I need a good bout of introspection to relieve my feelings. Will you come down?' (*CE* 306)

Tom is Nellie's tacit ally and competitor in the seduction of women. And he is perhaps the chief cause and symptom of her insatiable sexual and emotional hungers. She brags of the bond with Tom in terms that recall her 'perfect union' with George: 'a communion that comes only once in a life, if it comes at all. He could never have with anyone else what he had with me.' (*CE* 153) It is through Nellie's prying and scheming that the long history of their relationship is uncovered: her seduction of him in latency (associated with her own initiation into the fringe-anarchist circle of the mysterious 'Jago'), her destruction of his first marriage, her successive interventions in his relationship with the dying Marion, with Camilla, Caroline, and Eliza. Her story that he has 'an incurable disease' (a literal translation of one of her favourite metaphors for life) and her accusation that he is a 'shadow man', a mirror reflection, are refashioned, with her journalist's flair, to suit the personality and circumstances of each new woman. It is a story that serves her possessive and jealous feelings. It is fuelled by a deep-founded hostility to men and their power over women. And it expresses sexual rivalry in its perverse identification with, or parody of, the stereotypical male role and with Tom's particular destructive impotence and coquettishness. Shared and intimate knowledge enables each to deflate the other's rhetoric, and 'the wonderful story of love and misery' Tom delights to tell in his seductive croon echoes Nellie's sobsister singing. Like her, he is attracted by victims, the

dying Marion, the ailing Caroline. His sensitivity to the ongoing misery of life at Bridgehead is registered. And yet, as Nellie affirms, he is a shadowy figure.

Tom speaks of himself as a man detached from his own history, and this detachment is most clearly seen in his relationships with women. In the scene in which he performs his 'shadow' self, posturing impotently naked in front of Frieda's mirror, he recognises a divided self: 'a gold man, skin and hair youthful, red lips and hopeful smile', and an old, 'wasted, hungered man' (*CE* 243). The scene has behind it the force of an earlier moment, in which Nellie and Tom find themselves at one of the country fairs of their childhood, in the 'Palace of Mirrors', 'a playing card king' and a 'spindling hatchet witch', hand in hand, offering to each other, and identifying, their reflected selves, repeating the childhood dance, so that 'there was a string of them in the dusty narrow corridor, a ballroom of the strangest people, but always the same two' (*CE* 182). It is another of Stead's fine epiphanies; like birds in long grass they stretch and strut, enigmatic creatures only half-way human, the 'distortions of human beings' locked into the repetitive self-performings of their fractured, mirroring selves.

In the stories he tells, however, Tom projects an identity detached from its history. Strange things happen to Tom, and his anecdotes carry an air of unreality. The line between the things that happen to him and the things he makes happen is blurred. People glimpsed on a train vanish suddenly—a little emblem of his habit of making people disappear. There's another 'Tom Cotter' for whom he is mistaken, and a man who seems to mistake him for somebody else. Tom tells the story of a man in a pub who says '"you're the man who came down from Scotland with a child of nine years, aren't you? I said no. He said to me, I recognise you because I happened to be over in Wisbech and you were there and the child was never heard of again."' (*CE* 252) Only later does it emerge, in an aside, that Tom has been in Scotland. We also learn, by the way, that he has had a child. That child, however, seems to have disappeared from his life without trace. This suppression, and the paranoia with which he denies the story, take on a sinister edge, underlined by Nellie's hints of the 'evil' in Tom's past: 'You ought to do what I ask without questioning. I know. You know I know.' (*CE* 255) If there's a story of seduction, incest, death, almost surfacing again and again out of the Cotters' history, Nellie clearly plays a central role in it, and in its suppression. 'We're all guilty', she says. But we're never sure exactly of what. Was the child the product of Nellie and Tom's earlier incestuous relationship? It's an interpretation that can't be ruled out, and the possibility makes a telling link with other young people who are suddenly removed: the young boy from the Jago circle who dies in mysterious circumstances, the suicides of Johnny Sterker's and Nellie's protégées. Tom tells his story of maternal neglect, and he tells a story recalling the Harper's Ferry story in *For Love Alone,* of a young man who has been literally imprisoned by his mother.

Most significantly, however, the suppression of the child's story is linked with the suppressed story of Uncle Sime.[7] Following the death of Ma Cotter, Peggy transforms the Bridgehead house into a boarding house for men (after callously evicting Uncle Sime and appropriating his life savings). Tom, who has proclaimed his intention to marry a girl he has met at a dance, is called back up north by 'a horrifying thing'. An unnamed 'old man' (but answering to the description and whereabouts of Uncle Sime) has tried to drown himself in the swamp, taunted by a youth who destroys his illusion that he is a house-owner. This possible, shadowy sequel to the story of Uncle Sime is allowed its bitter, ambiguous resonance as another of Tom's disaster stories, or as the perfect emblem of Cotters' England.

The Cotters are Stead's bleakest study of love corrupted at its sources by familial proximities, where weaknesses are known and exploited, where all are guilty. This time it is not the bourgeois, but the proletarian family she has in her sights. As in *The Man Who Loved Children,* the roles of victim and aggressor are blurred and shifting. Nellie's sexual taunting of Uncle Sime wordlessly raises the narrative issues of exploitation and guilt early on, implicating him in a history of incestuous relationship. Stead, like Foucault, sees narrative as a process of simultaneous inscription and erasure. By the end of *Cotters' England* Uncle Sime has become a non-person, denied his name and history, in a process that begins with his rejection by the family and ends in his attempt to destroy himself and in Tom's suppression of their relationship to each other. At the same time, Stead's narrative has traced that history—of the rent payer, the needy and wily brother and uncle, the careful hoarder, the moraliser and patron. But Nellie and Tom survive. Hand in hand, smiling, they are photographed at the funeral of George, although the photograph is suppressed as unsuitable for such a sad occasion. They are riven with contradictions. Committed to reaching back and lifting up their suffering brothers and sisters, they take on the role of exploiters of those they purport to champion and protect. In this way, the novel suggests, they express the ideological contradictions of postwar Britain in the capitalist doldrums, attempting to embrace the welfare state. The people most deserving of its welfare, its children, its old people, become its victims. Notions of 'progress', improvement, and cooperation are undermined by the destructive and habitual patterns created by solipsistic needs and hungers.

THE LITTLE HOTEL

'Everyone knows the English are a fallen nation', jeers Mme Blaise at her friend Mrs Trollope, 'and you know it, too, Trollope and Wilkins, cousins who sleep together, or you would not be hiding like cowards, misers, insects that you are, lower than the hotel rats of whom you make friends, rich people and grudging every penny, going shabby. I am tired of your company.' (*LH* [*The Little Hotel*] 177) But next day it is 'forgive me, darling. You are my best friend.' (*LH* 179) The moral shabbiness of postwar Britain is set, in Stead's next novel, within a Europe recovering from one war and speculating on the next. At the Hotel Swiss-Touring everyone has something to hide. English expatriates in retreat from the Labour Government jostle for space and status with other exiles. Stead finds here a new model of communal living for her social microcosm, suggesting how the most trivial of daily transactions illumine larger territorial and national rivalries, and how postwar readjustment is undermined by hidden guilts and collaborations.

'If you knew what happens in a hotel everyday', begins the as yet unidentified narrator, confidingly addressing her conjectural audience. The apparent candour recalls Nellie Cotter. Mme Bonnard, too, is an avid collector of other people's stories. Again, the offer to reveal plays against the impulse to conceal, in this hotel-keeper as in her guests. The tantalising incompleteness of her narrative account-keeping is signalled when a woman telephones from Geneva, a former guest, needing to talk, hinting at death, murder, suicide, terrors. This is the suppressed repeating story glimpsed in the collage of life stories Mme Bonnard has to unfold, an indeterminate narrative in which the details and linkages are subtly suggested, never finally stated. In this short novel, which brings together several stories Stead wrote between 1952 and 1968,[8] the hopeful questers of her earliest novels are replaced by becalmed travellers whose stories were better not told.

Once again, however, narrative buoyancy is sustained by Stead's delighted observation of human behaviour. The comedy of the mad Mayor of B. (who may also, or instead, be the Mayor of A.) sheds its light on the secret fears and xenophobias of the other guests. Arriving 'incognito' from Belgium in his chauffeured limousine to partake of injections and shock treatment, he is the source of some amusement for the servants, over whom he tyrannises with deranged memos and 'documents'. The connection between Mme Bonnard's aside 'they were still shooting collaborators in Belgium' (*LH* 26) and the Mayor's fanatical anti-German obsession and fear of being recognised is never pressed. But untold fears and guilts clearly link his story with that of the virulently anti-communist and racist American Mrs Power ('I cannot approve of the extermination of peoples and yet you might say [Hitler] was like a surgeon cutting out the disease. Yes, people have seen it, Darwin saw it, he was of a fine old family' *LH* 38). Later still, it is revealed that Mme Blaise's wealth derives from the Nazis.

The prejudices and the decencies of the British Empire and American democracy are nicely exposed in the manners of their representatives. At the same time, the pathetic Miss Abbey-Chillard, dying, despite her British hauteur, perhaps of love, at the age of thirty-five, and the overbearing British matron, nick-named 'the Admiral', exemplify the pathos of the death-throes of Empire. So, too, does the dying relationship of Lilia Trollope with Yorkshire-born Mr Wilkins, retired rubber planter. And the unfolding stories of all three exploited women are connected with that of the unlikeable Mme Blaise, victim of a miserable marriage. In one of Stead's unforgettable dinner parties,⁹ food becomes the metaphor for other greeds and hungers, and celebration licenses uneasy or chilling revelations. The occasion commemorates the date, twenty-seven years before, on which 'the cousins' fell in love. Lilia opens up her vein of public musing on Wilkins's settled indifference, his refusal, long after her divorce, to marry her, and his gradual appropriation of her fortune (the chart he keeps of world-wide money flow is seen by Lilia as the chart of her life). Miss Chillard makes the relevant point succinctly: 'the woman is an Eurasian, that is why the man won't marry her' (***LH*** 90). The designs of the Swiss doctor, Blaise, who keeps his estranged wife at the hotel, visiting her, it emerges, mainly to feed her drug dependency, are more sinister: 'I don't think she will ever leave here alive. I am glad for her to stay here for life. Marriage is a curse and the more I am free of her the better I feel.' (***LH*** 130) The weakness of the pound, the probable cheapness of Swiss francs during the next war, and the financial shelter offered by South American dictatorships, provide the staple conversation, while negotiations between Wilkins and the Pallintosts, an English couple from whom he hopes Lilia will buy him a car, make part of the evening's sociability. With varying degrees of brutality, the men flaunt their predatory natures in the faces of their women. Wilkins treats Lilia with the contempt of the long-married while maintaining his British fiction of respectability, Dr Blaise encourages his wife's morbid fascination with disease (she circulates some of his photographs of diseased bodies as they digest the hors d'oeuvres) and openly threatens her. The colourful Princess Bilis is being two-timed by the gigolo she plans to marry and set up in business after her next face-lift. The party trick of her dog, Angel, who will sing 'D'ye ken John Peel' on request, complements the droll exposure of the human performers.

And yet, across the abysses, allegiances habitually re-establish themselves. Lilia and Wilkins go off to dance 'in a pretty coupling, their faces lit up' (***LH*** 133). The Blaises next day unite conspiratorially to snub their hosts of the night before. In a complex gesture, Lilia uses the money that was to have bought a cigarette-case for Wilkins to send Miss Chillard to her doctor in Zermatt to meet an ambiguous love or death: a recognition of fellow-suffering, perhaps, or an act of social ap-

peasement to one who has patronised her relentlessly. Similarly inscrutable is her visit to Mme Blaise, who has rejoined the doctor—a home visit that ends in her death. It is through Lilia's account of Mme Blaise's will that we are left to construct the end of this story: her fortune goes to the maid she suspects of being Blaise's mistress (she is demonstrably the mistress of his establishment). But the condition is made that she will marry Blaise. Death, murder, or suicide: we end in the indeterminate narrative with which we began.

Or not quite. There is also the unresolved story of Lilia Trollope: 'I do not know if they ever saw each other again' (***LH*** 191), Mme Bonnard concludes, of 'the cousins'. Lilia's thoughts and feelings have made a deeper register for the narrative throughout. A woman of limited understanding (as her pronouncements on politics suggest) but of good instincts, she has been weighing up her chances of survival as a divorcée of fifty in London. She leaves Wilkins for that unknown future, having been little more than a 'witness' to the demise of Mme Blaise. In this way, she plays out the narrative role of Mme Bonnard and of Stead. Mme Bonnard's omniscience is progressively undermined and, as the stories she initiates themselves take over, at times completely abandoned. The vigilant espionage by which she and her husband possess themselves of the secrets of their guests and servants is ironically accompanied by the piecemeal revelation that her own marriage is unloving and her husband philandering. But she sustains her tone of amused observer to the end, recognising, like her creator, that sharp observation of behaviour, and the discovery of hidden secrets and illuminating connections, finally yield only the sense of how impenetrably mysterious life stories really are. In its understated play of narrative possibilities, ***The Little Hotel*** nevertheless provides comic and pathetic insights into those stories, and into the cultural history that has helped to shape them.

MISS HERBERT (THE SUBURBAN WIFE)

The last of Stead's English novels, the last novel she was to publish, is a sharp little fable about London literary life. A drama in five succinct acts, it charts the process that transforms its 'beautiful, well-educated, classy heroine'¹⁰ into a fifty-year-old divorcée, like Lilia Trollope, alone in London. This middle-class right-wing literary life forms part of Stead's sequence of antithesis-and-comparison: Eleanor's name echoes Nellie's, and there are connections between their journalistic literary parasitism. A further connection is suggested in parallels between the narcissism of a working class locked into its self-enclosed version of struggle and the narcissism of middle-class self-admiration. As unerring as Stead's rendering of Nellie's Northern croon is her rendering of Eleanor's braying jollity: the tones and attitudes of a social élite rallying round and making do, ever ready with cliché. Eleanor meets the challenge of wartime rationing with a cheerful frugality, always busy and adaptable, and continues to put up 'a good fight' (**Letters 1** [**A Web of Friendship: Selected Letters (1928-1973)**], 339) in the lean postwar years. But the particular quality of stoic British spirit that saw England through the wars is deeply inhibiting, in Stead's view, to any fundamental social change or renewing creativity. And Eleanor is incapable of the kind of passion that wracks Nellie. If Stead's habitual play of narrative suppressions and possibilities feels more formulaic in this novel, it is because the passionate self that surfaces on rare occasions in Eleanor has no credible connection with the resolute shallowness of her given personality. 'You must not write about someone you at heart despise', Stead reflected (**Letters 1,** 339). She completed the novel in 1958, attempted to destroy it in 1969, and did not publish it until 1976. During these years, of course, she continued to wrestle with a very different writer-protagonist, the heroic Emily Wilkes. Stead's detachment from Eleanor is betrayed in uncharacteristic narratorial explanations and justifications. The attempt to understand why Eleanor prostitutes herself to Grub Street values conveys scant sympathy. Conceived so completely as its representative, Eleanor is too deeply immersed in the values of her 'particular phase of capitalism'[11] to challenge them with any conviction. For once, Stead's satire suffers from divided impulses. Her own experiences of literary agencies and hack work is represented, as echo and parody, in Eleanor's. Impotence, and more than a hint of self-contempt, are registered in the corrupting effect of such enforced labour. And this blunts the political thrust of Stead's concern about its wretchedness, exploitation, and lack of bargaining power.

Playing against the story Eleanor has been telling herself about herself are the literary versions of that story, together with representative women's stories from the cultural store.[12] It is Quaideson, the elderly publisher, who articulates the novel's real 'story' in the form of a speculation: 'you yourself must have a story worth anything ever written; how does it happen that a woman like yourself—a fine-looking and, I can tell, sensually aware woman, aware of the sensual values—is living alone?' (**MH** [**Miss Herbert**] 284)

And Stead is astute about what goes into the making of the story. The opening 'Playtime, Maytime' sets Eleanor among a group of lively, educated women friends whose 'open' discussion of their futures and their sexual relationships reveals ignorance and inner constraints. Eleanor's naked self-contemplation becomes an image of all that is being discussed but scarcely fathomed. Her sexual coyness, and the strange blend of calculation and unselfconsciousness (recalling both Elvira Western and

Tom Cotter) with which she sees herself as a highly-prized social commodity that attracts a well-defined social role, reflect 'Mumsie's' upbringing.

Eleanor's pre-war career of meaningless sexual indulgence is a parody of Teresa Hawkins' search for 'freedom' and 'knowledge'. Like Letty Fox, Eleanor is intent on marriage, 'my own home', 'my own children', 'and then I want to be a person in my own right' (**MH** 12). But her extended fling is 'off the record', not, like Letty's, a means to the end. The dirty linen she handles in her below stairs life as a chambermaid becomes, to her writerly imagination, a metaphor for her immersion in the sordidness of fugitive sex and the picaresque bohemian life: 'one grand riot of beastliness, so that I will know the whiff of it all my life' (**MH** 16). In the repeated transactions of her later life, sexual and literary activities become interchangeable aspects of society's debasement of creativity. Bourgeois sexual hypocrisy continues to be Stead's target. The sequence in which Eleanor discovers the 'Hostel for Young Ladies' run by her mother's 'New Religious Society' to be home to the 'harem' of Count James von Ulse, respected missionary and dedicated ladies' man, helps direct her towards a more settled life. It is at his wedding in Paris that she meets Edward Thieme, who seems to touch on 'some great instability in her, a cold inky well in which the self she enjoyed would be lost' (**MH** 67).

She deflects this threat in the name of the suburban dream: 'I'm a romantic woman, and I feel society, I mean nature, owes me a happy life. I like things in their place, I like beauty in things and tranquillity, decency' (**MH** 60). The pivot between 'society' and 'nature' reflects her divided self. Her marriage to Heinrich Charles, the young Swiss-German organiser with the Religious Society, fulfils social expectations while 'nature', in the shape of a lyrical blackbird, insists that she recognise 'I am to marry a man I don't love' (**MH** 85). Stead's fable is stark in its view that conventional middle-class marriage has little to do with love, and that 'Venus unknown to Venus', as Thieme has called her, is peculiarly susceptible to the considerations that shape such marriages: the sense of time running out, consideration of class status ('Henry' is seriously 'thinking of becoming British' **MH** 77), the sense of herself as marketable commodity. She settles with ease into her new role ('perfect hostess', loyal wife, respectable married woman), and proceeds to rewrite her story. The episode where she sheds her friend Diana because of her unconventional liaison—'Henry is rather old-fashioned' (**MH** 89)—incisively demonstrates the power of middle-class manners to deal brutally with other people's feelings.

Matching social ambitions mask concealed personal agendas. Henry sees Eleanor as his passport to social success: 'I'll have an English wife and children' (**MH** 81). His social climbing, racism, anti-Semitism (he is half-Jewish), and inflexibility, are ironically interwoven with the reassuring fiction of marital happiness they offer one another. Not only does Eleanor come to believe in this orderly married 'love' as the suburban happiness to which she is entitled, but, as she copes with housekeeping on a small budget, and with child-bearing and rearing as she frugally manages the 'boarding home' which is their source of secondary income, she identifies this 'down-to-earthiness' as what she has been looking for in her bohemian days. Meanwhile Henry's flirtatiousness with the au pair, the 'notes' on polygamy and divorce he may or may not have planted for Eleanor to read, his barely concealed disaffection and frequent absence, are met by her acquiescent silence: 'they seemed happy'; 'I suppose this is just a marriage growing up' (*MH* 117).

Stead drives to the point of absurdity Eleanor's clinging to this fiction as Henry makes his emancipation increasingly clear. He sends Eleanor and the two children 'back' to her father and brother. After a while he sends a photograph of his new 'wife' and child. Months and years pass as Eleanor still declares, at intervals, 'he has come to his senses'. Henry, too, has an astonishing power to rewrite history, accusing Eleanor of deserting him to join her brother's 'social experiment farm' (a reference to the affair George's wife is enjoying with a village man), and, as his files reveal, telling a different version of his unhappy marriage to a succession of mistresses. She is still contemplating a down-to-earth talk with him when the final indignity of her position shocks her into seeking a divorce. Eleanor's complicity in the marital farce makes her less a victim than a co-conspirator, eliciting none of the pity in writer or reader of Lilia Trollope's briefer story.

Eleanor's desultory attempts to write in these years underline her marketing of herself as a commodity. The story of 'Deb and Russ at Sunnytop Farm' aligns her family with the official version of family life derived from her staple reading in children's stories and the women's magazines for which she writes articles on child care and domestic matters. A radically different version of her own life is provided by 'Brief Candle', the story she touches up for her father, in which Sabrina, the village flirt, casts a spell over all the men. Eleanor's suppressed, passionless career as a seductress is ironically invoked, as is the story of Marge, George's errant wife, whose affair engages Eleanor's fascinated attention, envy, and official disapproval. The middle-class father's myth of the woman as love-object complements the mother's image of mystic maidenhood to create a daughter whose destiny is a puzzled oscillation between the two roles.

It now becomes clear that her earlier sexual adventuring, the marriage, and the writing career she takes up to support herself and her children, are successive stages of her self-prostitution. In Cope Pigsney (one of several names that point up the satire's acid note), Eleanor meets 'the kind of man who attracted her violently' (*MH* 223). A red-faced blond with greasy hair and a gentleman's accent, a forty-minute telephoner like herself, he is a knowing literary hack feeding off gossip. Cope, 'the guinea pig', will try anything, and his wife Bronwyn confides her distaste for him: 'there is something he does which I hate' (*MH* 233), an unspeakableness that may be literary or sexual or both. The files he encourages Eleanor to keep in preparation for their collaborative 'diary' of the London literary scene suggest Stead's ambivalent view of the writer's compulsion to record: 'set down with spite or devilment, greedily listened to with a rascally ear, she later found them precious, titillating . . . sometimes she would flush suddenly. This is prying! It's sneaking! But then writers must have material, mustn't they?' (*MH* 249) The collaboration is wryly characterised as a displacement and perversion of sexual attraction. Eleanor and Cope get high on sexual scandal. She finds herself pondering the Pigsneys' married life with 'a pure sexual fever' (*MH* 242). When Bronwyn turns cold towards Eleanor and threatens to leave Cope, Eleanor wonders, with the disingenuousness that always shields her from unpleasant reality, 'Could it have been over me? Surely not!' (*MH* 252)

Part 5 sees Eleanor as the woman of fifty, marking her independence by adopting her mother's impeccably-connected maiden name, Miss Herbert. Footslogging around employment agencies attempting to sell marketable versions of herself, she glimpses the self others now see—'I look old-fashioned, fussy, a suburban wife and mother' (*MH* 265). The image of herself restored to her by the publisher Quaideson is consistent with the work she finds in his agency, 'piracy-with-permission, the shameless authors agreeing to be cut up in order to sell' (*MH* 274). The elderly pornographer's manuscript 'The Old Curiosity Shop' and an apartment furnished with 'ironmongery' and miscellaneous paraphernalia of death indicate preferences that Eleanor is happy to accept as 'mature sex'. She divines that she is required to act out his fantasies of bondage and necrophilia in 'classic poses' and 'love portraits', as he calls them:

> She liked to stand exposing her smooth, powerful body in the quiet old rooms in some noble or perverse pose; she felt perfectly feminine. Mr Quaideson had explained to her in the beginning that love and pleasure were best in the imagination: nothing can disguise the crudity of ordinary sexual love.
>
> *MH* 289

Like all Stead's excursions into the Gothic, this sequence seems as appropriate as it is bizarre. This final turn of the fable returns to the opening, drawing attention once again to the Miss Herbert who has invited this consummation. The image of the naked Eleanor, held for our contemplation, embodies the fable's meaning with arresting directness. Her naked self-exposure remains a mockery of self-offering and self-fulfilment. Desire is transmuted into pose. The object of love, the female body, a commodity like any other, adapts to the needs of the marketplace. The desires of the man and the woman are self-mirroring. Quaideson's impotence and Eleanor's narcissism meet. The unawakened Venus, still sensuous, is the perfect partner for the 'obscure senses' of the predatory male viewer. After Quaideson's death, she continues to turn aside from the possibility of a compatible relationship (with the landscape writer Huie) and from the passion she feels, momentarily, for Paul Waters, her daughter's friend, and looks towards her role as middle-aged mother-in-law. A career of selling and sacrificing herself has purchased her modest success as a literary agent. If, as Stead suggests, Eleanor typifies her phase of capitalism, she is intended to command sympathy as its victim: 'one whose emotional life is turned into petty living and yet personally brave'.[13] Clearly, however, her literary production, notably the life story she now plans, will simply write large her consoling fictions. Meanwhile, the unauthorised version, the vehicle of Stead's unrelenting irony, has simultaneously not only undermined the credibility of those fictions, but exposed the limits of Stead's engagement with this particular 'drama of the person'.

Notes

1. *Dombey and Son* (Penguin, Harmondsworth, Middlesex, 1982), ch. 47, p. 738: 'Oh for a good spirit who would take the housetops off . . . and show a Christian people what dark shapes issue from amidst their homes.'

2. 'What is an Author?' in *Modern Criticism and Theory: A Reader,* David Lodge (Longman, Essex, 1988), 197-210.

3. [Chris] Williams [*Christina Stead: A Life of Letters* (McPhee Gribble, Melbourne, 1989)] 186-8.

4. [Jonah] Raskin ['Christina Stead in Washington Square', *London Magazine,* 9, 2 (1970)] 71.

5. See *Letters 1* 296, on Stead's reading of Pinter.

6. This, I think, is what redeems an episode which, as Margaret Walters points out in her introduction to the 1980 Virago edition, 'trembles on the edge of absurdity'.

7. As Brydon notes [Diana Brydon, *Christina Stead*], 137, Stead's working title for the novel was 'Uncle Syme'.

8. 'The Hotel Keeper's Story', 'The Woman in the Bed'.

9. Don Anderson discusses these in 'Christina Stead's Unforgettable Dinner Parties', *Southerly,* 39, 1 (1979), 28-45.

10. Stead, quoted in Williams, op. cit., 290.

11. Quoted in Williams, op. cit., 206.

12. [Susan Sheridan, *Christina Stead*], 102-3, discusses Verdi's Leonora and Milton's Sabrina.

13. Williams, op. cit., 206.

Bibliography

PRINCIPAL WORKS BY CHRISTINA STEAD

FICTION

(The details refer to first publications; editions used in this study are given in the Note on Texts and Abbreviations)

The Salzburg Tales (Peter Davies, London, 1934; D. Appleton-Century, New York, 1934).

The Man Who Loved Children (Simon & Schuster, New York, 1940; Peter Davies, London, 1941).

For Love Alone (Harcourt Brace, New York, 1944; Peter Davies, London, 1945).

Dark Places of the Heart (Holt, Rhinehart & Winston, New York, 1966). Published in London as *Cotters' England* (Secker & Warburg, London, 1967).

The Little Hotel (Angus & Robertson, Sydney, 1973; Holt, Rhinehart & Winston, New York, 1975).

Miss Herbert (The Suburban Wife) (Random House, New York, 1976).

LETTERS

A Web of Friendship: Selected Letters (1928-1973), ed. R. G. Geering (Angus & Robertson, Sydney, 1992).

INTERVIEWS

Raskin, Jonah, 'Christina Stead in Washington Square', *London Magazine,* 9, 11 (1970), 70-7.

BIOGRAPHY

Williams, Chris, *Christina Stead: A Life of Letters* (McPhee Gribble, Melbourne, 1989).

CRITICAL REFERENCES

BOOKS

Brydon, Diana, *Christina Stead* (Macmillan, London, 1987).

Sheridan, Susan, *Christina Stead* (Harvester Wheatsheaf, Hemel Hempstead, Herts, 1988).

ARTICLES, ESSAYS AND REVIEWS

Anderson, Don, 'Christina Stead's Unforgettable Dinner Parties', *Southerly,* 39, 1 (1979), 28-45.

Brydon, Diana, "'Other Tongues than Ours": Christina Stead's *I'm Dying Laughing*', *Australian and New Zealand Studies in Canada,* 2 (1989), 17-26.

A Note on Texts and Abbreviations

Page references for quotations from Stead's work are taken from the editions listed below, and the following abbreviations used:

CE: Cotters' England (Virago, London, 1980)

LH: The Little Hotel (Angus & Robertson, London, Sydney, 1973)

MH: Miss Herbert (The Suburban Wife) (Random House, New York, 1976)

IDL: I'm Dying Laughing (Virago, London, 1986)

Letters 1: A Web of Friendship: Selected Letters (1928-1973) (Angus & Robertson, Sydney, 1992)

Louise Yelin (essay date 1998)

SOURCE: Yelin, Louise. "Unsettling Australia: *The Man Who Loved Children* as National Family Romance." In *From the Margins of Empire: Christina Stead, Doris Lessing, Nadine Gordimer,* pp. 17-37. Ithaca, N.Y.: Cornell University Press, 1998.

[*In the following essay, Yelin places Stead's* The Man Who Loved Children *in a genre she calls "the national family romance," asserting that "as a novel about an American family written by an Australian woman with affiliations in the American and European Left,* The Man Who Loved Children *is a discursive site in which national identity is contested."*]

In 1928, Christina Stead, chafing at the restrictions of a provincial existence lived in the house of her repressive, overbearing father, left Sydney and went to London.[1] Not long after arriving there, she found a job as secretary to a man named William Blech (later changed to Blake), a cosmopolitan American economist, Marxist polymath, and writer who was working as associate manager in a grain importing and exporting firm. Early the next year, Stead agreed to accompany Blech to Paris, where he was to work in a private investment bank. By February 1929, the two had become lovers, beginning what was to be a lifelong relationship. (They were married in 1952, after his first wife finally agreed to divorce him.)

Throughout the 1920s and early 1930s, Stead and Blake lived in Europe, primarily in London and Paris. Stead, encouraged by Blake, became a writer, publishing three books in the early 1930s and sometimes also working in the bank where he was employed.[2] In 1935-36 they lived in New York, where they were involved in the left-wing culture associated with *New Masses.* They returned to Europe to write in 1936, living first in Spain and then, when Franco threatened the Spanish Republic, in France and later in Belgium. In 1937 they returned to New York, where they remained through the war years. (They left the United States in 1946, fleeing anticommunist persecution.) Throughout this period, Stead was affiliated with left-wing cultural institutions in both Europe and the United States. She was the secretary to the English delegation to the First International Congress of Writers, held in Paris in June 1935, and she read manuscripts and wrote reviews for *New Masses.* Stead's European wanderings and her experiences working in the bank are reflected in **House of All Nations,** a Rabelaisian satire of capitalism published (in New York) in 1938.

In **The Man Who Loved Children** (1940), Stead shifts her setting from Europe to the United States and turns her focus from the public world of finance to the putatively private world of the family. The family is situated in a politicized landscape—the area around Washington, D.C.—that superimposes the United States in which the novel was written on the Australia of the author's childhood. As a novel about an American family written by an Australian woman with affiliations in the American and European Left, **The Man Who Loved Children** is a discursive site in which national identity is contested.

The Man Who Loved Children belongs to the genre of the family romance, which Marianne Hirsch defines, elegantly glossing Freud, as an "interrogation of origins . . . which embeds the engenderment of narrative within the experience of family."[3] The novel sets the trajectory of its protagonist, Louisa Pollit, age eleven when the novel begins, against the marriage of her father, Sam, and stepmother, Henny, antagonists in a battle between the sexes. Louisa's adolescence is punctuated by the increasingly violent quarrels of her parents, by Sam's intrusive attempts to assert control over his children, and by the poverty that follows when Sam loses his position as a naturalist in the Conservation Bureau. For much of the novel, Louisa is suspended between Sam and Henny, shifting her allegiances and antagonism from one to the other. Her zigzagging between maternal and paternal poles is abruptly brought to a close when she decides to free herself and her siblings by killing her parents. She changes her mind, but Henny, noticing that she has already put cyanide in a teacup, takes the poisoned drink and dies. The novel ends soon afterward when Louisa runs away to take "a walk round the world" (491).

This summary conveys the extravagant turn that resolves the plot of **The Man Who Loved Children,** but it does not do justice to the novel's portrait of a family at once ordinary and astonishing or the richness of the novel's language. More important, in its focus on the family story, the summary suppresses the significance of the novel's represented world, the United States, and does not account for the way it grafts American onto Australian subject matter. In this chapter, I examine the novel's depiction of the Pollit family, its representation of an American scene, and its deployment of Australian discourses of race, class, and gender. The traces of Australian material that mark the novel's portrayal of an American family play out the hybrid, unstable national identifications of the author and inscribe *The Man Who Loved Children* in a genre I call the national family romance.

PATRIARCHAL PATHOLOGIES: THE POLLITS AS POLIS

The Pollit family is represented in *The Man Who Loved Children* as a polis: a locus of conflicts between husband and wife, parents and children; a set of hierarchies of difference and domination.[4] At the head of this order is Sam Pollit, the novel's version of a paternal tyrant. Samuel Clemens Pollit, named for "Mark Twain" and Harry Pollitt, chairman of the British Communist Party during the years of the Popular Front, suggests white men's power over women, children, and colonized racial others.[5] Sam is challenged in the novel, chiefly by Henny and Louisa. But, like patriarchy itself, Sam is hardy, resilient, and capable of withstanding the threats he encounters.

Sam's position in the family is illuminated by Michel Foucault's notion of the family as a "microcenter" or "transfer point" in which relations of pleasure, power, and knowledge are organized.[6] Yet *The Man Who Loved Children* exposes slippages between sexuality and gender that Foucault frequently ignores. Sam treats all the members of his family as sources of pleasure and objects of power and knowledge. He appears to his sons and daughters alike as the personification of authority: "Their father was the tables of the law, but their mother was natural law; Sam was household czar by divine right, but Henny was the czar's everlasting adversary, household anarchist by divine right" (36). But he singles out his daughters as targets of his invidious notions of sexual difference. He infantilizes the compliant Evie, but his treatment of the resistant Louisa is ambiguous. On the one hand, he identifies her as an extension of himself.[7] On the other hand, he insists that she recognize sexual difference—sexuality itself—as a disability that renders women vulnerable to men's power and especially their erotic aggression.

Sam is a classifier: "child namer," cataloguer, record keeper, world maker, and system builder. He is based on Stead's father, the naturalist David Stead.[8] To Sam, Tohoga House, the family home, is a museum, an archive, a repository of things and persons to be described

and categorized. As a naturalist, he resembles the early-20th-century primatologists that Donna Haraway describes. His obsession with taxonomy recalls the order of primatology that, as Haraway explains, "works by the negotiation of boundaries achieved through ordering differences."[9]

The continuities between patriarchal domination of women and colonial domination of feminized racial others are illustrated in an episode that describes Sam's trip to Malaya as a member of an anthropological mission. Sam's particular combination of racism and liberalism and his desire "to know my fellow man to the utmost . . . to penetrate into the hearts of dark, yellow, red, tawny, and tattooed man" (50) make him a latter-day comic echo of Joseph Conrad's Kurtz who belongs, initially at least, to the party of enlightenment. And, like Conrad's Marlow, Sam encounters in the colonial scene a test of his mettle and his manhood. Sam regards Malaya as a reflection of his own beliefs, values, and preconceptions and as an arena in which to realize his ambitions:

> In a short time he had fallen madly in love with Malaya and saw her as a great country, unplundered, untouched, undreamed of, brimming with natural wealth, which would make all of its soft-skinned people rich and happy. All that was needed was understanding and the eviction of the People of Greed. He himself was helping mightily the people, he believed, by getting to know them and finding out their different types and entirely addled strains. He could tell the indigenous Malays from the new imports from India, Hailam from Canton, Hohkien from Teochiew, and he tried to have a friend in each of these and many other strains. He felt like a kind of Livingstone going into the heart of the darkest unknown, as he put it, the heart of man.
>
> (213)

Sam's version of "Malaya" resembles a figure in Orientalist discourse as Edward W. Said describes it. (It also recalls Australian versions of eugenics.) Sam conflates the biological and the cultural ("strains," "types") and confuses description and judgment ("addled"). He identifies Malaya—or Malayans—with "other peoples variously designated as backward, degenerate, uncivilized, and retarded, . . . [with] elements in Western society (delinquents, the insane, women, the poor) having in common an identity best described as lamentably alien."[10] And he "Orientalizes" Malaya, producing it both as an object of knowledge and as a passive, inert, feminized object of desire. Soon afterward, he imagines himself as the husband of Chinese, Indian, Malay, and Cingalese women and the father of a multiracial "phalanstery" (219).

Sam's adventures in Malaya suggest the self-importance, muddle-headedness, and irrelevance of ostensibly liberal, "scientific" versions of the colonial project. He is defeated by the tropical heat and humidity. He despises those he calls the "People of Greed," but he benefits from their exploits. He compiles notes for a comprehensive report on the mission, but he cannot complete the report without the assistance of his Chinese secretary. By extension, Stead suggests, the liberal colonialism for which Sam speaks depends on the exploitation of native subjects without whom he cannot realize his project of enlightenment. Indeed, the letters he writes his family belong to the genre of imperial travel writing, a genre in which, as Mary Louise Pratt explains, Europeans writing "about non-European parts of the world went (and go) about creating the 'domestic subject' of Euroimperialism."[11] But Sam's predicament also points to Stead's own situation, that of a white colonial intellectual at once critical of and complicit in the colonial order that makes her career possible.[12]

Henny is Sam's principal antagonist. She challenges Sam's authority, mocks the rationality he professes, and attacks his commitment to science and morality. As Julia Duffy points out, Henny incarnates what M. M. Bakhtin identifies as "the essential principle of grotesque realism, degradation, that is, the lowering of all that is high, spiritual, ideal, abstract." Her characteristic mode of utterance is the tirade, a torrent of abuse that dramatizes "carnival liberties and carnival truths."[13]

> "Look at me! My back's bent in two with the fruit of my womb; aren't you sorry to see what happened to me because of his lust? I go about with a body like a football, fit to be kicked about by a bohunk halfback, an All-America football, because of his lust, the fine, pure man that won't look at women. . . . To you he's something wonderful; if you know what he is to me, something dirty, a splotch of blood or washing-up water on my skirts."
>
> (253-54)

But Henny's linguistic fecundity does not enable her either to escape or to transform the "proliferating miseries" that make her marriage a "life sentence" (11).

In the impasses that she incarnates, Henny appears as the voice of abjection, as Julia Kristeva explains it. Henny's grotesque intensity dramatizes the "violence of mourning for an 'object' that has always already been lost"; here she suggests the mother who died when Christina Stead was an infant and was always already lost in (to) the conscious life of the author. Henny also evokes the archaic mother feared, Kristeva explains, for the "generative power" that "patrilineal filiation has the burden of subduing."[14]

Henny plays a part as well in the family seen as an economic unit. She lives on credit, subsisting and sustaining her family on her debts. In the very first episode of the novel, she discovers that her wealthy brother has refused the loan she has requested. The climax of the novel is set in motion by the loss of Tohoga House, the home that Henny and Sam have rented from Henny's father, David Collyer, believing that he will leave it to them when he dies. When Collyer dies broke, Tohoga House is sold to pay his debts, and the Pollits are forced to move from their beloved Washington to a seedy quarter of Annapolis. After Sam loses his government job, Henny tries unsuccessfully to patch up the holes in the family finances by pawning her few valuables, pilfering the meager savings of her son Ernie, and borrowing from a notorious usurer. But Sam cannot or will not admit that she is feeding the family.

As an unacknowledged foundation of the family's existence, Henny's debts signify her exploitation: that is, they link her and, by extension, the women she stands for to the proletariat whose exploitation supports the structure of capitalism. Here *The Man Who Loved Children* revises American, left-wing, 1930s configurations of class and gender whereby the proletariat is gendered masculine and the bourgeoisie seen as feminine or effeminate.[15] In addition, Henny's debts and the plot that flows from them inscribe *The Man Who Loved Children* in the tradition of Dickens and Balzac, novelists whom Stead consistently identified as influences.[16] In this respect, *The Man Who Loved Children* might be seen as Stead's homage—an acknowledgment of here debt—to her literary forefathers.

Unlike Henny, who wallows in abject femininity and dramatizes the power of passivity, Louisa exemplifies two distinct strategies of gender. On the one hand, she refuses the disabilities of women and claims the privileges of men. In response to Sam's meddling and prying, she thinks to herself, "I am triumphant, I am king" (320). On the other hand, she insists on the prerogatives of difference. When Sam praises her mother (his first wife, who died when she was an infant), she retorts, "What do you know about my mother? She was a woman" (488).

Louisa's self-identification as a woman coincides with the development of a tenuous bond between herself and Henny, a bond that expresses the "natural outlawry of womankind" (243-44). But this connection is fleeting, and their fragile solidarity entails Louisa's tacit acceptance of the common lot of "every woman" (13), vulnerability to sexual innuendo, harassment, and assault.

Another locus of Louisa's maternal identification is Harpers Ferry, West Virginia, home of her mother's family, the Bakens. In Louisa's personal mythology, the Bakens and Harpers Ferry summon up a maternal domain uncontaminated by the father's law. At the end of the novel, when Louisa runs away from home, her intended destination is Harpers Ferry. She is attempting to recover or recapture a place untouched by Sam. But the Baken family belongs to the same patriarchal regime as the Pollits. The head of the family is the stern and puritanical grandfather Israel Baken, and all but one of Louisa's uncles tyrannically dominate their submissive wives.

In addition to taking refuge in a female solidarity more imagined than real, Louisa attempts to ignore the constraints of gender by appropriating the prerogatives of men. According to Diana Brydon, Stead, too, refused to acknowledge her gender as a handicap: perhaps this gesture of refusal reinscribed her affiliation with a Left in which gender was subordinated to class as an analytic category.[17] Louisa wants to assert her claim to a heroism exempt from the disabilities of sex. If this desire propels her to run away, the sequel, *For Love Alone,* suggests that even women's wanderings make them vulnerable to the sexual power of men.[18] In *The Man Who Loved Children,* however, the adolescent Louisa evades some of the constraints of gender by being young enough not to have to experience them.

Louisa's refusal of gender constraints is also conveyed in her relation to a bourgeois, patriarchal, predominantly European literary tradition like the genealogy that Stead fashioned for herself. Throughout the novel, Louisa lays claim to the enabling narratives of "her" culture, finding in them models she can emulate or fantasies that console her. Louisa identifies mainly with male heroes. One important prototype is Hans Christian Andersen's ugly duckling (59-60), a male creature whose gender is not mentioned in *The Man Who Loved Children.*[19] Another is Friedrich Nietzsche, an important influence on Stead herself.[20] Louisa also reads *The Pilgrim's Progress* and a biography of John Brown. And she attacks Sam by quoting at him Byron's "Ode to Napoleon Buonaparte": "The Desolator desolate, / The tyrant overthrown; / The Arbiter of other's fate, / A Suppliant for his own!" (267). (Louisa substitutes "tyrant" for Byron's "Victor.")

Like Teresa Hawkins, the protagonist of *For Love Alone* who sees herself as an Australian Ulysses, Louisa puts herself in the place of men. She rewrites the scripts that construct women as objects of men's desire or symbols of men's heroism and identifies herself with (male) heroes who are agents, not victims, of patriarchal cultural hegemony.[21] But if identifying with male heroes is a fantasy that compensates for women's powerlessness, it does not enable Louisa, as an aspiring writer—or Stead, as an established one?—to transform the gendered cultural text she lays hold of.

Louisa's literary efforts dramatize the narrow compass in which she can assert herself. To celebrate her father's birthday, she attempts to rewrite Shelley's *The Cenci,* the story of Beatrice Cenci, executed in 1599 for the killing of her father, a brutal, corrupt count. Louisa's play, titled *Tragos: Herpes Rom* ("Tragedy: The Snake

Man"), is written in an invented language; it is about a father who kills his daughter.[22] When Sam asks why her play is not written in English, she replies, in what might be the novel's finest moment, "Did Euripides write in English?" (377). But her protest against paternal despotism is ineffective because no one understands the invented language in which it is expressed. Whatever Louisa's intent, *Herpes Rom* reproduces the patriarchal script in which the mother cannot prevent the father's victimization of the daughter. Like Lucretia Cenci, who cannot save Beatrice from the collective power of father, state, and church, and like Henny Pollit, who cannot save Louisa from the onslaughts of Sam, the mother in *Herpes Rom* cannot help her daughter, who dies at the end of the play. Like Sam's letters home, Louisa's writings pose questions about Stead's own project, that of a colonial woman writer: Can Stead establish her own authority, or is her writing a mimicry of metropolitan and patriarchal originals?

The end of the novel replays Louisa's oscillation between her parents. In her rebellion against Sam, she identifies with Henny. She runs away, then, to escape Henny's destiny: confinement and unpaid labor in the patriarchal family.[23] But Louisa is a survivor, and her survival links her with the surviving parent, Sam. She is, after all, at least partly responsible for Henny's death. Is the daughter's freedom dependent on the destruction of the mother? Of what the mother represents? Or does Louisa's role in Henny's death signal her complicity in the male dominance—and especially the antifeminism—that pervades the Pollit polis, the patriarchal, misogynist Australian culture in which Stead was reared, and the international and American Left in which she later found a home in exile? Unresolved, these questions linger in Louisa's resemblance to Sam and to the snake man, fathers who strangle, suffocate, or otherwise do away with the femininity incarnated in daughter and mother alike. They are prompted, too, by Stead's own affiliation with a masculine (European) novelistic tradition and with a Left in which feminist commitment and feminine identifications are devalued.

CIVIL WARS

Stead wrote *The Man Who Loved Children* in the late 1930s in the United States, where it was published before it was published elsewhere. The novel is set in an American scene contemporary with the moment in which it was written. Stead represents her novel as American literature and herself as an American writer by inserting her text into American cultural debates.[24] In other words, *The Man Who Loved Children* is an attempt to perform an American identity for itself and its author alike. But this performative project, enabled in part by the value that the Popular Front placed on Americanness, is disrupted by the pedagogical imperatives of Stead's Australian (colonial) history.

The American identity of *The Man Who Loved Children* is announced, at least implicitly, in the very first scene, in Henny Pollit's notion of her marriage as a "civil war" (11). Throughout, Stead presents the violent quarrels that divide the Pollit family as a retelling of the American national story. The Pollits' conflicts unfold in an area bounded by Washington, Baltimore, Annapolis, and Harpers Ferry. These places are not only sites of such important events in American history as John Brown's raid but also a crossroads, a microcosm of the entire national landscape, in which North and South intersect. Stead's version of the American national legend is based on an analogy between the husband and the victorious North and the wife and the defeated South, but these oppositions are undermined by her ambivalence toward North and South, husband and wife, and by ambiguities in her treatment of class as a conceptual category.

Throughout the novel, Sam is identified not only with the North but also with the artisan class from which he springs and with bourgeois liberal ideology. The Pollits' Baltimore, a domain of puritanical attitudes toward alcohol and culture, belongs to the North. Sam also exemplifies an androcentric, racist liberalism at once universal and quintessentially American.[25] He sees himself as the great white father and as a representative of the "United States of mankind" (71, 202-3). And, at the end of the novel, he proposes to pull his family up out of poverty by spreading his message of cultural enlightenment on a radio show called the *Uncle Sam Hour.*[26]

In addition to the historical or legendary characters such as Franklin Delano Roosevelt and the Horatio Alger heroes that Sam himself explicitly takes as models, he evokes figures who represent diverse aspects of American culture. These include Artemus Ward, Herman Melville's Ahab (and Melville himself), and Mark Twain. Ward, a nineteenth-century journalist and humorist, wrote sketches in an idiosyncratic, pseudo-folksy dialect that sounds like baby talk. In Sam's incessant chatter, a pastiche composed of the "verbal tatters of Artemus Ward" (301), Stead simultaneously emphasizes his misogyny and trivializes it: "If I had my way no crazy shemales would so much as git the vote! Becaze why? Becaze they is crazy! . . . if they ain't got childer, they need childer to keep 'em from going crazy; en if they have childer the childer drive em crazy" (108).

Stead's allusions to Melville work in several different ways.[27] Toward the end of the novel, when the Pollit family is virtually starving because Sam has lost his job, he catches a marlin and decides to boil it for its oil, which he plans to use for cooking and heating the house (436-44). The minutely detailed description of Sam's elaborate preparations and the anticlimactic yield of just one gallon of oil make the marlin-boiling scene a trav-

esty of Melville's "Try-Works" chapter.[28] In *Moby Dick,* the boiling of the oil in the Pequod's try-works occasions in Ishmael a vision of the "redness, the madness, the ghastliness of others" (354) and a meditation on sorrow and mortality (chapter 96). The boiling of the fish oil in *The Man Who Loved Children* produces a stench that permeates the house and occasions Henny's remark that "my life has been one blessed fish chowder!" (437). Substituting chowder for mortality, Henny punctures Sam's self-deluding optimism and undercuts Ishmael's metaphysical concerns.

Melville is not simply an object of parody but also a figure for Louisa's aspirations and, by implication, for those of the author herself. Soon after the fish-boiling episode, Louisa recites from *Moby Dick,* "'Bear me out in this, thou great democratic God! who didst not refuse to the swart convict Bunyan the pale poetic pearl: Thou who didst clothe with doubly hammered leaves of finest gold, the stumped and paupered arm of old Cervantes'" (444). Here, Melville—along with the writers that he invokes, Bunyan and Cervantes—signifies the literary heritage to which Louisa lays claim. In identifying with Melville and his canon of male geniuses maimed, imprisoned, impoverished, or unappreciated in their own day, Louisa asserts her ambition and inserts herself into a tradition of "kingly commons" (*Moby Dick,* 105) at once democratic and patriarchal, European and American. Like her unspoken rejoinder to Sam, "I am triumphant, I am king" (320), Louisa's appropriation of Melville is an attempt to refuse her own subjection to hierarchies of difference.

In the novel's national allegory and its condensed American geography, the Pollits are identified with the North, and Henny's family, the Collyers, with the South. In Sam's ascendancy over Henny, the subordination of women is transcoded as the defeat of the South by the North. But ambiguities undermine the implied analogies and expose the Old South—a "residual" formation in Raymond Williams's terms—as a nostalgic myth.[29]

Henny's childhood home in Frederick, Maryland, is an estate with a name redolent of the Old South, Monocacy. (The Monocacy River runs through Frederick and Harpers Ferry.) Under the aegis of Henny's sharp-tongued mother and alcoholic, Faulknerian, ne'er-do-well brother, the now dilapidated estate emblematizes Henny's history: a belle who could not catch the kind of husband she was brought up to marry, she had to settle for Sam.

As Stead's identification of Sam with the North is amplified through echoes of *Moby Dick,* her identification of Henny with the South is elaborated through allusions to *Gone with the Wind.* Stead disliked Margaret Mitchell's novel. Her antipathy may have been reinforced by pressure from her agent and publisher to satisfy the tastes of the literary marketplace by writing popular romances.[30] Indeed, the one clear reference to *Gone with the Wind* in **The Man Who Loved Children** suggests that popularity—sales—requires a serious distortion of reality:

> [Henny] made herself some tea, and then got into bed, to try and read the saga of upland Georgian gentility, which she had three times abandoned because she, Henny, had "no fancy big buck niggers to wait on her and lick her boots": but once more she threw it away. Where, indeed, was she to find heroes to succor her and how could she succeed in business with her spendthrift ways. "I'm a failure all right," said Henny; "and why don't they write about deadbeats like me—only it wouldn't sell!"
>
> (414)

Here, Henny voices Stead's critique of Mitchell, a critique that associates **The Man Who Loved Children** with a tradition of novelistic realism that, from Cervantes onward, exposes the sentimental excesses and implausibility of romance. These excesses are conventionally coded as "feminine."[31]

The Man Who Loved Children has no equivalent of an Old South that dies, as does Scarlett's mother, Ellen O'Hara, or survives, as do Ashley and Melanie Wilkes, by accommodating itself to the rapacious commercial tendencies associated with the New South of Scarlett O'Hara and Rhett Butler. Scarlett thrives by working hard, by outright stealing, by exploiting the labor of convicts and former slaves, and by marrying three men whose money she puts to good use; Henny is destroyed by debts. Scarlett is virtually unaffected by motherhood; Henny, whose nicknames Moth, Mothering, Motherbunch, and Pet identify her with maternity, is dragged down by Sam's sexual demands and her children's insatiable needs. **The Man Who Loved Children,** set in the 1930s, exposes the era depicted in *Gone with the Wind,* the 1860s and 1870s, as a depression-era fantasy.[32]

But Stead reinscribes as well as revises the assumptions that underlie Mitchell's text.[33] She demystifies Mitchell's racist romanticization of the South, while she is, like Mitchell, skeptical about the virtues of the dominant (northern, liberal) culture. Both Stead's version of American history and Mitchell's dramatize the exploitation and victimization of women by men: for both writers, that is, gender is also a marker of class. The two writers—the white, Southern woman and the left-wing, Australian-born woman—conflate gender oppression and geographical marginality or subordination. In *Gone with the Wind* the defeat of the South is enacted in the marriages of white northern men (both, ironically, former overseers of slaves) who take possession of white southern women ("white trash" and an impoverished plantation aristocrat) and symbolically of the South itself. Scarlett escapes the common fate of these two women, but Henny's situation resembles theirs. Unable to turn her marriage to account, she is proletarianized by her subjection to Sam, whose racism belies his liberalism, and to the imperatives of maternity.

Henny insists that Sam is not the self-made man that he claims to be. She declares that Sam's rise in the world is not the result of his own efforts but rather of his dependence on her father and thus of his exploitation of her:

> "You took me and maltreated me and starved me half to death because you couldn't make a living and sponged off my father and used his influence, hoisting yourself up on all my aches and miseries . . . boasting and blowing about your success when all the time it was me, my poor body that was what you took your success out of. . . . A brute, a savage, a wild Indian wouldn't do what you did."
>
> (136)

Henny elaborates Stead's class-conscious analysis of gender, but her parroting of racist platitudes undermines the critique of *Gone with the Wind*. Here, she describes herself as the victim of a man worse than a "wild Indian," but she also identifies with the "wretched beggars, Chinks and niggers" she was brought up to hold in contempt, regarding Sam as "the family carpetbagger" who imposes his hypocritical morality on all those he tyrannizes at will (253).

If Henny represents one model of opposition to Sam and the American cultural values that he exemplifies, Louisa's maternal kin, the Bakens of Harpers Ferry, represent another. Louisa's grandfather Israel is reminiscent of John Brown himself. The tiny library of Israel's gentle son Reuben is the source of Louisa's literary and political inheritance, *The Pilgrim's Progress, Paradise Lost,* and James Redpath's *The Public Life of Captain John Brown* (148). At the end of the novel, after Henny's death, when Sam tries to regain control over Louisa, she invokes the Bakens and the heritage they represent: "'You remember when you used to take me to see the Lincoln Memorial, walking along the Reflecting Pool from your office on Saturdays. I learned from him, not from you. . . . When I was at Harpers Ferry, I only thought about John Brown. I always thought Israel Baken was just like him—my grandfather. Not a Pollit, thank goodness, not one of you'" (488).

Despite the palpable tyranny of Israel Baken, Harpers Ferry represents—to Louisa, at least—an imagined alternative to her father's authority. In giving Louisa Harpers Ferry as a maternal or matrilineal heritage, Stead presents the "walk round the world" on which Louisa embarks at the end of the novel as a daughterly declaration of independence that announces a third

American revolution, following on John Brown's second and Thomas Jefferson's first. At the same time, Stead articulates a cultural politics that opposes both racism and the masculinist bias of an—"the"?—American cultural tradition that canonizes texts such as *Moby Dick* and, as Jane Tompkins rightly argues, refuses cultural authority to the devalued femininity inscribed in works such as *Gone with the Wind*.[34] **The Man Who Loved Children** negotiates an alternative to an antiracist tradition that is implacably patriarchal if not misogynist and a woman's tradition that is irretrievably racist.

In situating **The Man Who Loved Children** in debates about American culture, canonical and popular, high and low, Stead produces it as an American text. But the novel bears the marks of its origins, as if Louisa's declaration of independence—or Stead's—were inaugurating yet another revolution that remains to be fulfilled. In identifying with John Brown, Louisa imaginatively aligns herself with but also displaces the black slaves on whose behalf he raided the arsenal in Harpers Ferry. Suppressed, in this retelling of an American tale, are the stories of particular African Americans, the race plot that underwrites the colonization of America and Australia alike, and hence the Australian beginnings of this American novel.

UNSETTLING AUSTRALIA

"Oh yes, I am an Australian. Of course I'm an Australian."

—Christina Stead quoted in Joan Lidoff, *Christina Stead*

The terrain on which the battle of the sexes unfolds is not only the family construed as microcosm, or polis, not only an American political landscape, but also an Australian milieu like the one in which Christina Stead herself grew up.[35] In some respects, Stead is always writing "about" Australia even when she sets her novels elsewhere, as she herself implies when she says that she set her novel in the United States to shield family members living in Australia.[36] "Australia" is a source of pressure on the manifest content of **The Man Who Loved Children**. This pressure remains for the most part beneath the narrative surface, but it erupts periodically, marking the novel or leaving traces in details that appear incongruous in the American scene that Stead portrays.

One of these eruptions occurs in a climactic scene in the novel, the family party held to celebrate Sam's return from Malaya. This gathering is described as a "family corroboree" (236), a word that, according to the *Oxford English Dictionary*, originates in the Port Jackson dialect of Australia and denotes a warlike or festive dance of Australian natives. In this episode, Sam chas-

tises Henny, Louisa transfers her allegiance from father to mother, and a telegram arrives announcing the death of Henny's father. Immediately afterward, the last Pollit child is born, rumors circulate that Sam is not the child's father, and Sam loses his job. During the party, Sam's father, Charles Pollit, dramatizes scenes from *Great Expectations*, following the lead of his namesake, Charles Dickens.

Throughout **The Man Who Loved Children,** allusions to *Great Expectations* comment on the history of the Pollit family. *Great Expectations* also operates as a metonym for the story of Australian colonization in general and for Stead's history in particular.[37] In Dickens's novel, Pip has to confront the "criminal" source of his expectations in the wealth of the convict Magwitch, whose punishment for theft is "transportation" to Australia. In foregrounding Pip's connections to British crime and law, *Great Expectations* elides the Australian consequences of Magwitch's fortunate fall, the appropriation of aboriginal lands that makes possible the "sheep farming" that underwrites Pip's transformation into a "gentleman."[38] (Dickens also distorts the later history of those brought to Australia as convicts, very few of whom became rich.) The colonial racial script suppressed in *Great Expectations* also plays a part in Stead's own family history: her paternal grandfather—the model for Sam Pollit's father—was influenced to emigrate to Australia by Dickens's novel.[39]

The Pollits' family life is another instance of the eruption of "Australian" matter in the American environment of **The Man Who Loved Children**. Henny apparently personifies an American cultural type, the déclassé Southern belle, and Sam's association with his namesakes, Uncle Sam and Samuel Clemens, makes him an exemplary American. But their marriage is not connected to the 1930s American scene. The depression is virtually unmentioned in the novel and, strangely, plays no part in Sam's losing his job. If we recover the Australian genealogy of Henny and Sam, however, we can account for apparently incongruous or idiosyncratic narrative details. The marriage of Henny and Sam belongs to the Australia of Stead's childhood and adolescence, and Sam and Henny themselves recall early-twentieth-century Australian articulations of race, class, gender, and family.[40] The novel's relentlessly binary vision of gender—"their father was the tables of the law, but their mother was natural law"—represents the rigid sexual division of labor and "gender apartheid" that Australian historians and sociologists have traced in this period.[41]

Henny's grotesque femininity and exaggerated, even parodic fecundity transcribes material and ideological changes in early-twentieth-century Australia. The sociologist Desley Deacon explains that during this period there was a decline in the situation and status of middle-class and elite women relative to those of men in the same classes.[42] Changes in the Australian economy led to policies and institutions that defined productive labor as the province of men, relegated women (identified as wives and mothers) to the home, and reconceptualized women's domestic labor as nonwork.[43] Married women in this era lacked legal protection. They had limited property rights but no guaranteed rights either in the guardianship of the children or to the family's accumulated wealth.[44]

In addition, this period saw what the sociologist Kerreen Reiger identifies as the "rationalization" of domestic life. As Reiger explains, "experts" attempted to extend "the principles of science and reason to the operation of the household and the management of personal relationships," while the infant welfare movement focused on maternal adequacy—or, more often, inadequacy.[45] Henny's helter-skelter notion of motherhood—"they grow up whether you look after them or not," she says (427)—makes her both target and victim of the ideological strategies that these Australian scholars describe. Similarly, Henny's conflation of marriage and maternity, her fatalistic sense of marriage as a life sentence, recalls the discursive construction of compulsory marriage and motherhood as the "cornerstone of femininity."[46] Judged in terms of the demand that the mother supervise all aspects of a child's existence or the idea of the home as a haven for men,[47] Henny will inevitably be found wanting. Yet these are precisely the criteria that guide Sam's "scientific" and managerial view of Henny's laissez-faire housekeeping.

Like Henny's abject domesticity, Sam's public spiritedness has an Australian provenance in the values of the new middle class. This class, consisting of workers "who depended on the sale of education, technical and social skills, or 'cultural capital,'" was consolidated in the late nineteenth and early twentieth centuries through the exclusion of women, Asians, and "other races."[48] Early in the novel, Sam lectures his children about his vision of an "ideal state," a "system" that he calls "Monoman or Manunity": "Monoman would only be the condition of the world after we had weeded out the misfits and degenerates. . . . People would be taught, and would be anxious to produce the new man and with him the new state of man's social perfection" (51).[49] (The children are not impressed.) The eugenic fantasia that Sam spins out reaccentuates early-twentieth-century Australian population ideology that articulates "the 'White Australia' immigration policy; . . . state intervention in matters of education [and] welfare, . . . religious debate over purity and decadence, scientific debate over evolution and degeneracy, [and] political debate over socialism and liberalism."[50] In addressing his children as potential citizens of his ideal state, Sam also echoes the exponents of the Australian infant welfare movement.[51]

Between 1913 and 1920—roughly the years of Stead's adolescence—the government was professionalized. Professional government workers attempted to reform the family by intensifying the sexual division of labor and the asymmetrical organization of gender. Sam Pollit's angle of vision and the rhetoric in which he expresses his beliefs in progress reproduce the idiolect of the new middle class, a "language of science, technology and expertise."[52]

The Australian beginnings of Stead's text can also be traced in what appears—to a late-twentieth-century American reader, at least—as a jarring depiction of families and children. The Pollit family is characterized by extreme violence, both physical and emotional, but the violence is presented almost dispassionately. This incongruity situates the novel at the juncture of two distinct historical moments. Between 1880 and 1940 there was a shift in Australia from criminal to family law in juridical attempts to resolve family violence. One consequence of this shift was the emergence of the "family" as an entity in need of treatment.[53] The conceptualization of childhood changed in similar ways. The old idea that a child is responsible for her or his behavior gave way to ideas of children as victims of either the environment or their families.[54] Louisa's emergence, apparently unscathed, from the clamor and violence she witnesses daily and the matter-of-fact attitude she takes when she decides to poison her parents are residues of earlier constructions.

In numerous interviews and in her own autobiographical writings, Stead acknowledges the Australian takes origins of her American story. Indeed, in her account, Australia takes priority over America, the novel's represented world. Susan Sheridan observes that Stead retrospectively legitimates her novels by asserting that they tell authentic, autobiographical truths.[55] The statements Stead makes about the Australian provenance of *The Man Who Loved Children* are instances of these assertions. Stead's claims of authenticity, Sheridan argues, sanction some ways of reading the novels and preclude others, notably those that interpret them as works of imaginative fiction (15-18). These claims attempt to foreclose the narrative or discursive construction of a hybrid—in this case, Australian American—national identity. At the same time, they prohibit reading practices that explore such constructions. The performative construction of American identity in *The Man Who Loved Children* is not subverted by exclusionary conceptions of "Australianness" or "Americanness"; rather, it is retrospectively prohibited by Stead's insistence on the literal truth of what she writes.

The authority that Stead assigns to the cluster Australia-autobiography-authenticity apparently forbids a reading that regards the Australian material I have been describing as subject to repression in *The Man Who Loved*

Children. By extension, the claims of authenticity preclude readings that emphasize the "affinity," to borrow Balibar's term, between family and nation or between the family romance as Freud and psychoanalytic critics and historians such as Hirsch and Lynn Hunt conceive it and the genre that I want to call the national family romance. Yet the word Stead uses to describe the Australian material in her novel invites just such a reading.

Stead presents the relationship between "Australia" and "America" as one of translation; she says she took experiences from her childhood in Sydney and dropped them, whole and entire, into the area around Washington, D.C. The word she uses for this operation, however, invites scrutiny: she says she "transported" Watson's Bay to the Chesapeake.[56] *Transportation,* presumably, is a metaphor. But unlike its synonyms *transposition* and *translation,* "transportation" is also a metonym, one that evokes an Australian colonial history and specifically the convict past that, as Robert Hughes argues, was subject to amnesia, repression, or distortion in the collective national consciousness of Australia in later years.[57] This distortion is reproduced in Stead's account of her grandfather's emigration: Samuel Stead is inspired by the story of Magwitch, but he omits—or his granddaughter sometimes does when she retells his story—the sentence of transportation and penal servitude that sent Magwitch to Australia.

The narrative of Australian colonization, a story of "transportation" in both the literal and the figurative senses, is absent from *The Man Who Loved Children,* yet it underwrites all the stories told in the novel. Like repressed material, like identities that are lost in cases of amnesia, and like the constellation of abjection that Kristeva delineates, "Australia," ostensibly privileged in Stead's account of her own literary production, also signifies what is forgotten or misremembered: the mother (the maternal origin) that is always already lost. "America," ostensibly devalued but narratively prominent, evokes the paternal or symbolic order to which other orders are subject.

In *The Man Who Loved Children,* then, "Australia" and "America" contend for dominance. This contention is grafted onto the family story that occupies the narrative surface of the novel. Louisa's oscillation between mother and father is played out in her identification with the "natural outlawry of womankind" and her assumption of kingly (masculine) prerogatives. This oscillation not only rewrites the family constellation of Stead's childhood but also inscribes the hybrid, contested national identity of the novel itself.

At the end of the novel, Louisa leaves her family. Her declaration of independence is an attempt to escape from mother and father alike. Louisa's escape recalls Stead's exile from Australia, an exile that leaves behind what cannot be acknowledged and must therefore be forgotten. Reproducing the repression of the abject mother, Louisa's escape reinscribes Stead's allegiance to the father—the United States in the guise of the liberal/tyrannical Uncle Sam—and her identification, however equivocal, with the America in which she wrote *The Man Who Loved Children.* It also suggests Stead's continuing affiliation with a Left in which women's concerns were subordinate or secondary. But if, in allying itself with the liberal cultural politics of the Popular Front, *The Man Who Loved Children* reproduces the swerve toward the father that is the characteristic gesture of Stead's life and career, its sequel, *For Love Alone,* exposes the perils of male identification and exile alike.

Notes

1. The details of Stead's life are drawn from Rowley, *Christina Stead: A Biography.* Rowley says that Stead later denied that she had left Australia because of its cultural inferiority (64). Stead fictionalizes her exile from Australia in *For Love Alone* (1944); see Chapter 2, below.

2. On Stead's early career, see "A Writer's Friends."

3. Hirsch, *Mother/Daughter Plot,* 9; cf. Lynn Hunt's definition of the family romance as the "collective, unconscious images of the familial order that underlie revolutionary politics . . . a kind of collective political unconscious . . . structured by narratives of family relations" (*Family Romance of the French Revolution,* xiii). See also Freud, "Family Romances."

4. The family has been the main focus of critical attention since 1965, when *The Man Who Loved Children* was reissued. See my "Fifty Years of Reading"; Boone, "Of Fathers, Daughters, and Theorists," and the expanded version of this essay in his *Libidinal Currents,* which appeared after I wrote this chapter; Brydon, *Christina Stead*; Gardiner, *Rhys, Stead, Lessing,* and "Male Narcissism"; Lidoff, *Christina Stead*; and Sheridan, *Christina Stead.*

5. Stead, "Interview" (with Beston), 93-94. Gardiner, *Rhys, Stead, Lessing,* 134. Sam's beliefs and values resemble what Donna Haraway designates as the "Teddy Bear Patriarchy" of the American Museum of Natural History and Carl Akeley, doyen of its Africa Hall (*Primate Visions,* chap. 2).

6. Foucault, *History of Sexuality,* 1:82-83, 92-93, 103.

7. Boone, ("Of Fathers, Daughters, and Theorists," 516 and passim, and *Libidinal Currents,* 328 and passim), and Gardiner (*Rhys, Stead, Lessing,* 137, and "Male Narcissism," passim) comment on Sam's narcissism.

8. Stead reflects on her father's influence in "A Writer's Friends" and "A Waker and a Dreamer." See also Rowley, "How Real Is Sam Pollit?" 505.

9. Haraway, *Primate Visions,* 10.

10. Said, *Orientalism,* 207.

11. Pratt, *Imperial Eyes,* 4.

12. Sam's letters are taken verbatim from a letter that David Stead wrote his family while on a mission for the Australian government (Rowley, *Christina Stead,* 263, and "How Real Is Sam Pollit?").

13. Duffy, "Grain of the Voice," 50-51; Bakhtin, *Rabelais,* 19, 27-28. Henny is based on Stead's stepmother, Ada, David Stead's second wife, but Stead invented her language (Rowley, *Christina Stead,* 260). Lidoff links the grotesque imagery that describes Henny and the "domestic gothic" that defines Stead's own style (21, 38).

14. Kristeva, *Powers of Horror,* 15, 77. Boone links Henny's "subversive if ambivalent power . . . to a repressed female history distorted by the lens of patriarchal vision" ("Of Fathers, Daughters, and Theorists," 528). Lidoff sees Henny as the powerful figure of the pre-oedipal mother (33).

15. On the gendering of class in (male) Marxist writers in the 1930s, see Rabinowitz, *Labor and Desire,* 8, 22, 47.

16. See Stead, "Uses of the Many-Charactered Novel" and "A Waker and a Dreamer."

17. Brydon 4. See Rabinowitz 6 and passim, and Stead, "Writers Take Sides."

18. See Chapter 2.

19. Randall Jarrell describes *The Man Who Loved Children* itself as a "neglected masterpiece," that is, an ugly duckling only later recognized as a swan (Afterword, 492, 500).

20. On the influence of Nietzsche in *The Man Who Loved Children,* see Rowley, "Christina Stead: The Voyage to Cythera," 1; Walker, "Language, Art, and Ideas"; R. Baker, "Christina Stead: The Nietzsche Connection"; and Stewart, "Heaven and Hell."

21. Cf. Brydon: "The female artist learns to proceed through subterfuge, identifying her models in male heroes conceived by men and seeing no irony in that identification" (70).

22. On the revisionary force of the play, see Gardiner, *Rhys, Stead, Lessing,* 135, and Arac 188. Sheridan argues that the play dramatizes a "nullification of female subjectivity" (48).

23. Boone reads this ending as a revision of the "psychosexual dynamics . . . of oedipal narrative"; unlike Oedipus, whose patricide leads to union with the mother, Louisa's matricide leads to separation from the father ("Of Fathers, Daughters, and Theorists," 537).

24. See my "Fifty Years of Reading" for a discussion of the national identities attributed to the novel by reviewers. In a 1941 application for a Guggenheim Fellowship, Stead described her project as an "addition to *American* literature" (quoted in Harris, "Interrogating Ideologies," 5; emphasis added). In the 1942 edition of *Twentieth-Century Authors,* she identified herself as Australian American.

25. On Sam as a liberal, see Arac; Yglesias, "Marx as Muse"; and Stead, "Christina Stead in Washington Square."

26. Late in her life, Stead expressly denied that Sam was intended to represent Uncle Sam ("Christina Stead in Washington Square," 73-74, and "Interview" [with Wetherell], 443).

27. M. H., reviewing the novel in 1940, and Day Thorpe, reviewing the 1965 reissue, noticed the Melville connection.

28. Stead said that this episode was based on an incident from her childhood and denied that she meant to parody Melville. ("A Waker and a Dreamer," 490; letter to Robie Macauley, 20 September 1965, Harry Ransom Humanities Center, University of Texas, Austin). The echoes of Melville illustrate Bakhtin's notion that an utterance encounters "alien words that have already been spoken about it" ("Discourse in the Novel," 276).

29. Williams, *Marxism and Literature,* 122.

30. Stead complained that her agent represented John Steinbeck and *Gone with the Wind* and was pushing her to write books that sell. Letter to Stanley Burnshaw, 31 August 1942, Burnshaw Collection, Harry Ransom Humanities Center, University of Texas, Austin.

31. On romance and the feminine, see Langbauer, *Women and Romance.*

32. Jane Tompkins historicizes the romance element of *Gone with the Wind* as "true to what so many were thinking and feeling at the time" ("All Alone," 195).

33. I thank Margaret R. Higonnet for pointing this out.

34. Tompkins 191.

35. On the influence in *The Man Who Loved Children* of early-twentieth-century Australian intellectual life, see Walker; R. Baker; Stewart; Green, "*The Man Who Loved Children*"; and Reid, *Fiction and the Great Depression.* For Stead's reading of Australian authors, see "Interview" (with Wetherell), 446.

36. Stead, "Christina Stead: An Interview," 242; Rowley says that Stead changed the locale to make the book marketable in the United States (*Christina Stead*, 261).

37. See Chapter 2 for a discussion of *Great Expectations* as an intertext in *For Love Alone*. Said discusses *Great Expectations* as part of a "history of speculation about and experience of Australia" (*Culture and Imperialism*, xiv-xvi.) Peter Carey, in *Jack Maggs*, published after I wrote this chapter, takes *Great Expectations* as his point of departure.

38. Prior ownership by indigenous people of the land that became Australia was not recognized until June 1992 (Curthoys, "Citizenship and National Identity," 25).

39. Stead, "A Waker and a Dreamer," 481-82; Lidoff 203.

40. Rowley says that Stead set the novel in the 1930s because the America she knew was contemporary (*Christina Stead*, 261).

41. Matthews, *Good and Mad Women*, 148.

42. Deacon, *Managing Gender*, 153-54.

43. Matthews 58.

44. Rowley, *Christina Stead*, 27-28; Allen, "Breaking into the Public Sphere."

45. Reiger, *Disenchantment of the Home*, 3; on the infant welfare movement, see Deacon, *Managing Gender*, 212; Matthews 78.

46. Matthews 112.

47. Reiger 172, 38.

48. Deacon, *Managing Gender*, 4 and chap. 4.

49. Arac identifies Sam's vision of Monoman with United States imperialism (179).

50. Matthews 74-75. On the "White Australia" policy, see also Ward, *Nation for a Continent*, 30-32.

51. Deacon, *Managing Gender*, 212.

52. Ibid., 210, quotation from 206.

53. Allen, "Invention," 20.

54. Reiger 168.

55. Sheridan 15. See notes 22 and 24, this chapter.

56. Stead, "Another View," 515.

57. Hughes, *Fatal Shore*, xiv-xv.

Works Cited

Allen, Judith. "Breaking into the Public Sphere: The Struggle for Women's Citizenship in New South Wales, 1890-1920." *In Pursuit of Justice: Australian Women and the Law*, ed. Judy MacKinotty and Heather Rodi. Sydney: Hale and Iremonger, 1979. 107-17.

———. "The Invention of the Pathological Family." *Family Violence in Australia*, ed. Carol O'Donnell and Jan Craney. Melbourne: Longman and Cheshire, 1982. 1-27.

Arac, Jonathan. "The Struggle for the Cultural Heritage: Christina Stead Refunctions Charles Dickens and Mark Twain." *Cultural Critique* 2 (Winter 1985/86): 171-89.

Baker, Rebecca. "Christina Stead: The Nietzsche Connection." *Meridian* 2, no. 2 (1983): 116-20.

Bakhtin, M. M. "Discourse in the Novel." In *The Dialogic Imagination* 259-422.

———. *Rabelais and His World*. Trans. Helene Iswolsky. Bloomington: Indiana University Press, 1984.

Boone, Joseph Allen. *Libidinal Currents: Sexuality and the Shaping of Modernism*. Chicago: University of Chicago Press, 1998.

———. "Of Fathers, Daughters, and Theorists of Narrative Desire: At the Crossroads of Myth and Psychoanalysis in *The Man Who Loved Children*." *Contemporary Literature* 31 (1990): 512-41.

Brydon, Diana. *Christina Stead*. Totowa, N.J.: Barnes and Noble, 1987.

Burnshaw Collection. Harry Ransom Humanities Center, University of Texas, Austin.

Carey, Peter. *Jack Maggs*. New York: Knopf, 1998.

Curthoys, Ann. "Citizenship and National Identity." *Feminist Review* 44 (Summer 1993): 19-38.

Deacon, Desley. *Managing Gender: The State, the New Middle Class, and Women Workers, 1880-1930*. Melbourne: Oxford University Press, 1989.

Duffy, Julia. "The Grain of the Voice in Christina Stead's *The Man Who Loved Children*." *Antipodes* 4, no. 2 (1990): 48-51.

Foucault, Michel. *The History of Sexuality*. Vol. 1, *An Introduction*. New York: Pantheon, 1978.

Freud, Sigmund. "Family Romances." 1908. *The Standard Edition of the Complete Psychological Works of Sigmund Freud*. London: Hogarth, 1959. 9:237-41.

Gardiner, Judith Kegan. "Male Narcissism, Capitalism, and the Daughter of *The Man Who Loved Children*. *Daughters and Fathers*, ed. Lynda Boose and Betty S. Flowers. Baltimore: Johns Hopkins University Press, 1989. 384-99.

———. *Rhys, Stead, Lessing, and the Politics of Empathy*. Bloomington: Indiana University Press, 1989.

Green, Dorothy. "*The Man Who Loved Children*: Storm in a Teacup." *The Australian Experience: Critical Essays on Australian Novels*, ed. W. S. Ramson. Canberra: Australian National University Press, 1974.

Haraway, Donna. *Primate Visions: Gender, Race, and Nature in the World of Modern Science.* New York: Routledge, 1989.

Harris, Margaret. "Interrogating Ideologies: Christina Stead's American Sequence." Paper delivered at a special session on Stead at the annual meeting of the MLA, San Francisco, December 1991.

Higonnet, Margaret R., ed. *Borderwork: Feminist Engagements with Comparative Literature.* Ithaca: Cornell University Press, 1994.

Hirsch, Marianne. *The Mother/Daughter Plot: Narrative, Psychoanalysis, Feminism.* Bloomington: Indiana University Press, 1989.

Hughes, Robert. *The Fatal Shore.* 1986. New York: Vintage, 1988.

Hunt, Lynn. *The Family Romance of the French Revolution.* Berkeley: University of California Press, 1992.

Jarrell, Randall. Afterword. *The Man Who Loved Children.* By Stead. 492-503.

Kristeva, Julia. *Powers of Horror: An Essay on Abjection.* Trans. Leon Roudiez. New York: Columbia University Press, 1982.

Langbauer, Laurie. *Women and Romance: The Consolations of Gender in the English Novel.* Ithaca: Cornell University Press, 1990.

Lidoff, Joan. *Christina Stead.* New York: Ungar, 1982.

Matthews, Jill Julius. *Good and Mad Women: The Historical Construction of Femininity in Twentieth-Century Australia.* Sydney: George Allen and Unwin, 1984.

M. H. "Christina Stead's Fantastic Gallery." Rev. of *The Man Who Loved Children. New York Times Book Review* 20 October 1940: 7.

Pratt, Mary Louise. *Imperial Eyes: Travel Writing and Transculturation.* New York: Routledge, 1992.

Rabinowitz, Paula. *Labor and Desire: Women's Revolutionary Fiction in Depression America.* Chapel Hill: University of North Carolina Press, 1991.

Reid, Ian. *Fiction and the Great Depression: Australia and New Zealand, 1930-1950.* Melbourne: Arnold, 1979.

Reiger, Kerreen M. *The Disenchantment of the Home: Modernizing the Australian Family, 1880-1940.* Melbourne: Oxford University Press, 1985.

Rowley, Hazel. *Christina Stead: A Biography.* New York: Holt, 1994.

———. "Christina Stead: The Voyage to Cythera." *SPAN.* Newsletter of the South Pacific Association of Commonwealth Literature and Language Studies. April 1988. 33-45.

———. "How Real Is Sam Pollit? 'Dramatic Truth' and 'Procès-Verbal' in *The Man Who Loved Children.*" *Contemporary Literature* 31 (1990): 499-511.

Said, Edward W. *Culture and Imperialism.* New York: Knopf, 1993.

———. *Orientalism.* New York: Pantheon, 1978.

Sheridan, Susan. *Christina Stead.* Bloomington: Indiana University Press, 1988.

Stead, Christina. "Another View of the Homestead." In *Ocean of Story* 513-20.

———. "Christina Stead: An Interview." With Ann Whitehead. *Australian Literary Studies* 6 (1974): 230-48.

———. "Christina Stead in Washington Square." Interview with Jonah Raskin. *London Magazine* ns 9, no. 11 (1970): 70-77.

———. *For Love Alone.* 1944. Rpt. London: Virago, n.d. [1978].

———. "An Interview with Christina Stead." With John B. Beston. *World Literature Written in English* 15 (1976): 87-95.

———. "Interview with Christina Stead." With Rodney Wetherell. *Australian Literary Studies* 9 (1980): 431-48.

———. *The Man Who Loved Children.* 1940. Rpt. New York: Avon, 1966.

———. "Uses of the Many-Charactered Novel." Draft ms. in the papers of the League of American Writers. Bancroft Library, University of California, Berkeley.

———. "A Waker and a Dreamer." In *Ocean of Story* 481-93.

———. "A Writer's Friends." In *Ocean of Story* 494-502.

———. "The Writers Take Sides." *Left Review* 1, no. 11 (August 1935): 453-62.

Stewart, Ken. "Heaven and Hell in *The Man Who Loved Children.*" *Meridian* 2, no. 2 (1983): 121-27.

Thorpe, Day. Rev. of *The Man Who Loved Children,* by Christina Stead. *Washington Sunday Star* 7 March 1965.

Tompkins, Jane. "All Alone, Little Lady?" *The Uses of Adversity: Failure and Accommodation in Reader Response,* ed. Ellen Spolsky. London: Associated University Presses, 1990. 190-96.

Walker, Shirley. "Language, Art, and Ideas in *The Man Who Loved Children.*" *Meridian* 2, no. 1 (1983): 11-20.

Ward, Russel. *A Nation for a Continent: The History of Australia, 1901-1975.* Richmond, Victoria: Heinemann Education, 1977.

Williams, Raymond. *Marxism and Literature.* Oxford: Oxford University Press, 1977.

Yelin, Louise. "Fifty Years of Reading: A Reception Study of *The Man Who Loved Children.*" *Contemporary Literature* 31 (1990): 472-98.

Yglesias, Jose. "Marx as Muse." Rev. of *The Man Who Loved Children,* by Christina Stead. *Nation* 5 April 1965: 368-70.

Ann Blake (essay date 1999)

SOURCE: Blake, Ann. "A Political Sense of Place." In *Christina Stead's Politics of Place,* pp. 35-50. Nedlands, Australia: University of Western Australia Press, 1999.

[*In the following essay, Blake emphasizes the controlling influence of "place" in Stead's fiction, especially in terms of the way in which geographic and social location, in a materialistic sense, informs all of her characterizations, stating, "If the centre of [Stead's] fiction is 'the drama of the person,' it follows in her case that the material circumstances of the person's life are decisive."*]

Stead's practice was always to write closely from life and so her novels are set in the many places in which she lived or, more precisely, in the locations where she got to know the people on whom she modelled her characters. The path of her travels, from Australia to Europe, to the United States, and then back to Europe and England, is easily traced through her writing. A more settled life would have meant producing a series of novels with the same setting, or so it seemed to her:

> But we were always in a different country, and typing in the hotel bedroom. I got used to it . . . On the other hand, if I'd always lived in one setting and my books turned out the same . . . Well, who knows?[1]

Stead's oeuvre thus falls chronologically into four national sections: Australian, French, American and finally English. This neat sequence, however, is broken by the two autobiographical novels of her childhood and young life in Sydney: *The Man Who Loved Children* and *For Love Alone.* Both these novels, based on Australian material, were composed in the United States and, in the case of *The Man Who Loved Children,* then 'transferred', as she put it, to an American setting. Such discrepancies between place of setting and place of composition, as occurred with these autobiographical novels, happened frequently with Stead, who was not a fast writer. Often she was writing of a place where she had lived after she had moved on somewhere else. For instance, she completed the last American novel she finished, *The People with the Dogs,* after her departure

from the United States for Europe. Stead did, as she claimed, work from what she had seen, but often this meant from the places she had immersed herself in and then carried around in her head. In a bizarre way, this transnational pattern continued briefly even after her death. The massive novel *I'm Dying Laughing: The Humourist,* set in the United States and France, was finally made ready for publication by her literary trustee, Ron Geering, in Australia. He worked from boxes of manuscripts that Stead had brought from the United States, carried around Europe, taken to England and brought from there to Sydney. But if much worked over outside the United States, that novel too derives from first-hand knowledge—indeed, from a long acquaintance with the central figures and their setting.

This characteristic closeness to her material was there from the start. Among the earliest surviving manuscripts of Stead's work is a short story, as yet unpublished, called 'The Student of Naples', written in 1928-29 when she was first in London. Stead here is drawing on a few hours' visit, when her ship to England called in at Naples. In her discussion of these early writings, Anita Segerberg remarks that they show a strong political bias in defence of the oppressed, and then singles out for praise this story's depiction of place: 'The atmosphere of Naples, its streets and people are recreated so vividly'.[2] This is a judgment repeated again and again by critics and reviewers of Stead. Whether the novels are set in Australia, the United States or England seems not to matter. The response is the same: they are praised for what is felt to be the authenticity of the settings, in all their aspects—physical, cultural, historical. Australian readers and others who know Sydney admire *Seven Poor Men of Sydney* and *For Love Alone* for their evocation of the city and its harbour in the 1920s. In one of the earliest extended critical discussions of Stead's fiction, H. M. Green, writing cautiously of *Seven Poor Men,* a book he found impressive but flawed, gave warm praise for its depiction of Sydney:

> Yet *Seven Poor Men,* incomplete and one-sided, uncharacteristic of any country as is the life that it presents, was yet somehow the first novel to convey an impression of Sydney as a world city, one of the foci of world life: it is full of glimpses of crowds and scenes and places; shabby, bedraggled, gaudy, or simply illustrative of episodes in ordinary everyday life, all of which are characteristic and alive.[3]

Quoting this passage in his own discussion of *Seven Poor Men,* Michael Wilding points out that in this novel, which has no single hero, the 'city itself becomes a character' and acts as one of the novel's unifying forces, the 'literal and detailed' writing making a 'vivid, authentic recording of Sydney's geographical and social particularity'.[4] Moving on chronologically from Australia to Paris and *The Beauties and Furies,* Hilary Bailey begins her introduction to that novel by speaking of place in Stead's fiction. She comments that many of Stead's best novels are based in 'foreign cities' and registers the strong impression made by these locations when she says: '[t]he cities themselves produce the kind of action the characters are involved in'. She then adds a general comment praising Stead's commanding handling of place:

> All [the novels] demonstrate her almost uncanny ability to absorb, and use, not just the physical location of the countries and cities she writes about but also the atmosphere and ethos they produce.[5]

These phrases constitute the ultimate tribute to the novelist as writer of place: such an authentic representation of a specific place is produced that it seems to exist prior to and outside the fiction. Randall Jarrell's tribute to Stead is more sophisticated in its understanding of literary illusion and reality, but no less favourable. His introductory essay to **The Man Who Loved Children,** 'An Unread Book', probably the best piece of criticism on Stead's work, emphasizes above all the lifelike quality of the novel—a tribute, he admits, paid annually by thousands of reviewers to hundreds of novelists, but here deservedly: 'reality is rare in novels'.[6] The different locations in the novel—Washington, Ann Arbor, Harpers Ferry, Singapore—are 'entirely different and entirely alive'.[7] This is indeed a writer who can create the illusion of recognition, of making us see something that seems familiar, though, as Jarrell knows, it is Stead's creation, an effect of reality, and not the thing itself.

An instance of the power of Stead's English novels to impress readers with equally convincing representations of place is the testimony of Rodney Pybus, a Tynesider. For Stead to choose as one of the two main settings of **Cotters' England** the north-east industrial area of Tyneside strikes him as a characteristically 'bold gesture', and one matched by her success in capturing the 'atmosphere', the physical qualities and the local accent. Through a remarkably accurate re-creation of 'Tyneside accents and rhythms', Pybus claims, Stead taps into 'the energies of English society still largely neglected in the novel'.[8] Not many novels have been set in Newcastle, but Pybus is also pointing out that, as in **Seven Poor Men of Sydney,** Stead is writing about the working class. As Segerberg gives tribute to the early short story of Naples as a recording of a place in authentic detail, and a story with a strong political commitment, Pybus registers both these qualities in **Cotters' England.**

Stead liked to 'get things right', and saw herself as a writer who tried to be 'accurate'. In a long letter written in New York in reply to questions from her friend Nadine Mendelson, then a child, about 'how, what, when, where' she wrote, she described how she worked and what books she studied:

> if one of my characters is supposed to be tubercular, I read medical treatises on tuberculosis, if he has to write an essay on, say, Tariffs and Free Trade, then I have to study tariffs and free trade. More than that, if possible, I like to find a writer on tariffs and free trade who has the peculiar mental quirks that my character is meant to have.

When it came to 'character-analysis and presentation', the method was essentially similar:

> I study books of diagnosis, such as doctors use. There is a prescribed system of diagnosis: you begin at the top of the head and end at the feet, taking in posture and all the rest. Medical students are told to practice this instantaneous general diagnosis on everyone that they see in the subway or street, and it is excellent training for a writer. There are many other ways of acquiring proficiency in an art for which there are no art schools and no teaching masters.[9]

While this may be a neat, tidy and incomplete account of her practice, its essential points reappeared when Stead later ran a course on novel writing at New York University, and again put down her thoughts on writing. She advised her students to build up characters by paying attention to detail, observing the signs like careful physicians, and to work from the outside in. Place in her novels is built up in the same way as character. Closely observed, vividly rendered details combine to form precise images that give an effect of authenticity. A fund of recent direct observation was essential to her. She wrote to Florence James from Paris about plans for a book: 'I want to start one altogether in a Paris setting, in case we leave Paris for good, as Bill so often promises'.[10] Her attachment to this same practice lies behind the explanation she sent her brother from New York for not writing an Australian story:

> my bits of local colour have been incorporated or indefinitely held over, and I couldn't get up a 'synthetic' Australian novel . . . One of these days I dearly hope to come to see Australia and once more get some local colour.[11]

Underpinning Stead's method was, of course, a commitment to a materialist view. Place shapes people; we are the product of our environment. In her notes for the novel course, she wrote: 'In general we are formed by our society and our own nature makes a slight variation'.[12] And this principle permeates her fiction; occasionally it is even explicitly stated. In **For Love Alone,** James Quick, one of the fictional versions of Blake, offers a materialist interpretation of Jonathan Crow: '"You're a poor man and women frighten you because they're an expense"'; and a little later he adds: '"I regard you as a function of your setting, and so I am able to separate you from your detestable opinions"' (440-1). Stead's thinking about real people ran on the same lines. Her remarks, already mentioned in chapter 1, about why she herself left Australia are one instance: 'We felt

we belonged to the sea. It wasn't a question of leaving Australia, nothing to do with that at all.'[13] Similarly, it was the spaciousness and easy climate of Australia that explained what she and Blake both recognized as a distinctive Australian walk.[14] Her description of the people she met in Newcastle-upon-Tyne is a more extended comment informed by this way of thinking:

> They are all obsessed with their physical (geographical, topog; geolog; stratig; etc) situation, and I suppose that it is the fact that they are living right on their living (coal measures) and that the country behind is open bare desolate country, picturesque and wild . . . I see too, now, partly where Peter [Peter Kelly, Anne Dooley's brother] gets his wonderful vision of the country. (But they don't all have it: e.g. the population in the Back Room which is also typical of N/C).[15]

From her fiction, the gloomy Jonathan Crow offers a memorable instance of a complex figure built up through details of his gait, physique, clothes, doleful tones—all seen as bearing witness to his poverty and the slum house in which he has grown up. He walks with Teresa down to the waterside, after dark, when 'the streets, especially near the parks, were filled with loungers who solicited the women walking by' (124). Teresa is harangued by a drunk and Jonathan growls to her that it is her fault: 'You see if women didn't try to make themselves so different . . . you wouldn't get this'. The narrative runs on, following her thoughts:

> His tone was brusque, and cold, she thought she bored him; but as they passed under the lamp posts, she looked and saw his starved skin, the sparse stiff hair, the rain-bitten hat, the stuff of his summer shirt, the plain spectacles set in silver over his liquidly sad brown eyes. There was something pathetic in the way he walked dragging one foot over a little, hunching one shoulder slightly and in his tilted hat, and in the firm twist to his long dark mouth. He had been stamped by poverty. Strange, more curious than insulting, were his sudden grunts, mutterings, his rude sayings. In the midst of her thoughts, he blurted out; 'See that little nipper over there? I was a newsboy too, when I was his age—'.
>
> [125]

At this early stage, he admires Teresa's 'grit', while she is impressed by his association with the university and by how he has suffered for learning, his 'noble ideal'. But the lines that mark the cruelty, self-pity and distorted emotionality that Quick discovers in him later are already clear. Crow is, of course, not the only figure presented in his setting; his life interacts with others, and contributes to the overall significance of this novel of struggle for emotional and sexual liberation. But to consider just this one figure in his environment and in the fabric of her novel is to identify something of the attraction of the novel form to Stead: it offers the greatest scope to express the complex interactions of human life. This is the thought that surfaces in her review of

Malraux's *Man's Hope* (*L'Espoir*): 'Malraux has achieved that perfect synthesis and simulacrum of life of which the novel alone is capable, an international, local and personal history'.[16]

A consideration of place in her work is a means of perceiving the nexus between Stead's style and her underlying political orientation. She emerges as the exponent of her own distinctive version of socialist realism; one who writes in harmony with that enlightened understanding of the Marxist conception of the material basis of existence that still leaves room for the power of the individual will. Marx's pronouncement that 'being determines consciousness' was not to be equated with a 'narrow economic determinism', as Stead's fellow Australian the communist novelist Judah Waten observed.[17] To separate an interest in character and in place is in the end simply impossible in Stead's work. If the centre of her fiction is 'the drama of the person', it follows in her case that the material circumstances of the person's life are decisive.

It is tempting to link the materialist strain in Stead's writing not only to her own circumstances and to the intellectual influence of her study of psychology and of Marxism but also back to her father's work as a biologist and botanist. Stead publicly claimed that in her practice as a novelist she followed his method, his point of view. 'I was brought up by a naturalist and I *am* a naturalist', she said.[18] On several occasions she spoke of observing the living creatures in her father's collection at close quarters, and then of human beings as one more species of living organism. The analogy between the novelist and the naturalist came in handy for her when she was asked to respond to questions about the lack of explicit judgment in her novels: like her father, she insisted, she was an observer of life. One did not pass judgments:

> I'm not at all critical. When you're a little girl and you look in an aquarium and you see fish doing this and that, and snails and so on, you don't criticize and say that they should be doing something else.[19]

Whether Stead's writing can be seen as influenced more by a scientific outlook or more by Marxism, her fiction is always sensitive to the particular place where an individual's experience is located. The naturalist's approach to human existence might seem to define place in broader terms such as environment or habitat, with all their connotations of formative interaction between place and life form. But Stead's fiction, however materially based, does not make a simplifying approximation of human existence to the animal or vegetable. For people, places exist in all their specificity, and with all their distinctive cultural and historical implications. The figures in her fiction are subject to and shaped by the history and culture specific to a place, and not just by 'habitat'.

It is clear, then, that 'place' must be understood in the broadest sense. Bailey's comment, previously quoted, that Stead is able to 'absorb, and use, not just the physical location of the countries and cities she writes about but also the atmosphere and ethos they produce' is a step towards that wider definition. Place can include much that goes under the umbrellas of geography and history—both the natural features of a location and all that men and women have done to them—as well as, in turn, the effects of the location and its climate on the people. But though it embraces local practices, attitudes and beliefs, this wider sense of place, as Leonard Lutwack helpfully points out, is not synonymous with a social system.[20] For 'place' to be present, the writing about it must retain always the distinctive physical properties of the surroundings of a particular way of life. The New Zealand critic Terry Sturm captures very well this deep and wide-ranging, yet specific, sense of place in Stead when he comments on *Cotters' England,* and notices how place and the 'impinging past' are brought into the novel. The past is present in the novel not as an objective history, he says, but in the changing perspectives of varied dramatic situations. And in the same way, the awareness of place in Stead is also built up from shifting, personal views:

> History and environment, then, suffuse the novel as part of its 'drama of the person', and not as an abstraction from it. The title itself conveys the author's aim: England, in the novel, is England as it is experienced by the Cotters, and the process is carried into the novel in very detailed ways.[21]

Ralph Fox, the Marxist critic and novelist whom Stead loved and admired, wrote that a novelist must be concerned with the creation of 'human character', rather than with his or her own moods, or political arguments. In his critical study *The Novel and the People,* he declares that what is wrong with contemporary writers—he is writing in the mid-1930s—is that, though they lack Zola's passion and genius, they still insist on writing about ordinary people:

> The modern novelist, abandoning the task of creating personality, or a hero, for the minor task of rendering ordinary people in ordinary circumstances, has thereby abandoned both realism and life itself.

This preoccupation with the ordinary

> isolates life from reality, and eventually, through the destruction of time and the inner logic of events, the mutual interaction of the characters and the outer world is lost; it is an approach which in the end kills creation by denying the historical character of man.[22]

Though Stead's fiction consistently fails to produce the positive revolutionary hero Fox looked for—'man changed by the world and man changing the world'[23]—she shares his underlying political orientation towards a material historical view. She makes her readers think constantly of the interaction between the characters and the outer world and of their place in time.

That she relocated *The Man Who Loved Children* from Australia to the United States might seem to undermine this conception of Stead's approach to her work. A novelist who transposes an autobiographical novel of family life from one continent to another can hardly be defined as writer for whom particular places are greatly significant. But this case is worth examining because rather than demolishing the argument about the significance of place, it in fact confirms it.

From the first, American readers spotted traces of the process of revision in *The Man Who Loved Children.* Elizabeth Hardwick noted: 'Sometimes the language is more nearly that of England than of America: people "post parcels", drink tea morning, noon and night, have "elevenses," etc.'. Hardwick, an early admirer of Stead, found these 'English turns' (of phrase) not objectionable but amusing.[24] Jarrell, too, noticed an 'occasional awkwardness or disparity' and excused it as the result of Stead creating 'from an Australian memory an American reality' (35). Ian Reid, however, has argued that slips like these undermine any coherent sense of place in Stead's fiction: the setting cannot be 'identified'. He makes this criticism briefly in the opening paragraphs of an essay that in fact goes on to suggest a telling relationship between place and structure in the *Puzzleheaded Girl* novellas. In his opinion, the settings of the novels are blurred, and do not permit clear grouping of Stead's fiction under national headings, as has been a common critical practice. This is a point of view that, at least in relation to *The Man Who Loved Children,* has some substance.

What concerns Reid is Stead's practice of hanging on to an identifiable piece of material—a character, location or situation—and reusing it, transplanting it from one text to another. There is no denying that Stead does this: the unhappy wife running a boarding house for a snobbish, ambitious husband in the short story 'Accents' reappears as a stage in Eleanor's life in *Miss Herbert (The Suburban Wife).* In this instance, though, Stead reworks material within the same fictional national setting—England. Reid's argument depends on Stead's practice of transplanting material across fictional countries, the outstanding example of this being *The Man Who Loved Children,* with its relocation of her childhood from its Sydney setting to Washington. Further, he points to Australian idioms in *The Salzburg Tales,* and to *For Love Alone* (chapter 12), where the name Harpers Ferry is borrowed from West Virginia and given to Teresa's remote destination in northern New South Wales.[25]

Certainly, some relocated details in *The Man Who Loved Children* are not as convincing in their new

American settings as they might have been originally: Grandpa Pollit's Dickensian performances, for example, or Henny's Piccadilly recitation: 'Offal baw the R.A. Show and yet a chappie has to go: the only thing in Picadilleh I wegard as being silleh' (119). Just plausible in Washington, both would be more at home in a British colonial setting. Sam Pollit's mission to Singapore, which derives from David Stead's, seems to be less likely when the father 'becomes' an American and the British Empire link between the two countries disappears.

But any argument that Stead's fiction cannot be grouped nationally, grounded largely on *The Man Who Loved Children,* is at once weakened when it is recognized how much that novel is a unique case, the only book of hers transposed from 'where it happened' to another location. To those curious as to why she did this, something so at odds with her usual fictional practice, Stead consistently declared that her purpose was to spare her family: her father was still alive when the book appeared. Perhaps her efforts to get the details right helped her to ignore any qualms she might have had in exposing her family by her use of private, intimate material. But Rowley's biography reveals that it was in fact the publishers who insisted that the story be transplanted.[26] That there is no trace of Stead admitting this publicly is to be expected. One of her most cherished ideas of herself as a writer was her independence. She liked to think that she was totally apart from the commercial world of publishing; that she 'wrote'—she was not 'a writer'; and that she wrote for herself and no one else. No editor or publisher ever told her what to do.[27] But of course they did: on this occasion and also later, asking for revisions of *I'm Dying Laughing* and excisions of anti-Semitic references from *Miss Herbert.* From this information, not available to Reid when he wrote his essay, it is clear that the transposition of this autobiographical novel across continents does not, as he argued, undermine the notion of Stead as a 'national novelist'. Nor does it weaken her commitment to the material significance of place: on the contrary. Once committed to the recasting, almost certainly not her idea in the first place, she made enormous efforts to embed every aspect of her novel deeply in American life. She attacked this task by reading American history, literature and folktales, as well as by travelling about, exploring and investigating every aspect of the physical location she chose, Washington and the Chesapeake Bay, as closest to the original Sydney Harbour setting. Sam Pollit's enthusiasm for Darwinism and scientific meliorism have been convincingly replanted in the brave New World of the United States, his work in the fisheries to the Atlantic Ocean, and his language games follow Uncle Remus and the American humorous writer Artemus Ward. Henny becomes a convincing Baltimore belle, 'expecting to have a good time at White House receptions' (119). Even if some Australian fossils re-

main, Stead's efforts to reintegrate her story into its new setting testify to her persistent belief in the shaping power of place.

The distinctive aspects of Stead's creation of place emerge sharply when her work is set in the context of traditional literary criticism—that is, where descriptions of place are related to the conventionally identified components of the novel: to plot, character, symbol and atmosphere. There is no obvious point of contact between Stead's fiction and more recent theories of narrative that turn away altogether from a mimetic understanding of fiction as offering to relate to the actual world. Fiction is often now seen as working within a system of narrative, following its laws and conventions, its value not to be found in its relation to the world outside but within its own narrative domain. To shed light on writers' responses to specific actual places, or their re-creation in fiction, is no concern of the structuralist critic. And even in critical studies that relate evocation of place to other traditionally defined aspects of the novel, it is much easier to see how Stead's novels do not quite fit the critics' categories than how they do. Gillian Tindall's study *Countries of the Mind,* a book subtitled 'The Meaning of Place to Writers', is a case in point. For the writers Tindall considers, as for Stead, location is more than a 'setting'; but where Tindall goes on consider how it may be 'germane to the very theme and plot of the story', in Stead its role is enmeshed in her people's lives. Place is there in all its particularity, but not in its own right; she is not a writer whose original inspiration is a setting. Tindall is concerned with the literary re-creation of place and her focus is on writers in whose work

> these physical settings, these real places, from railway-wracked London to a remote tropical trading post, are essentially put to use as metaphors, emblems or examples for ideas that transcend a particular time and place. In them, a local habitation and a name are given to perennial human preoccupations.[28]

Tindall's phrase 'perennial human preoccupations' belongs to a humanist tradition. Stead may go far towards satisfying the expectations of a humanist reader, while writing a different kind of fiction. When in *For Love Alone* she describes the high cliff near Sydney Heads known as The Gap, a frequent place for suicides, she associates the horror of the place with the despair of young, poor, pregnant women, and with Teresa's frustrated virginal state. The place lives in the reader's memory, but not as a timeless metaphor for youthful despair. In general, Tindall's emphasis on literary re-creation of place is, in an enlightening way, at odds with the effect of Stead's writing, where place does not assume 'a quality of universality which transcends the particular'.[29] In Stead, a particular place may assume a symbolic significance, but at the same time it exists within its specific historical, material context. This dual quality of the writing of place is described well by Wilding in the context of **Seven Poor Men** and the description of the military camp on South Head: it is 'present in the novel to establish themes, symbolic within the fictional structure. But it is also indisputably real.'[30] The Gap is a physical location where desperate young women respond to the conditions of their lives, and hurl themselves to death; and it is a symbol of the consequences of the clash of sexual desire with conventions of female premarital chastity, the shame of remaining single and all 'the complex conditioning processes to which women were subjected in the 1930s'.[31]

Put against accounts of changes in the presentation of place in fiction from the nineteenth century to the twentieth, Stead ends up being out of step historically as well. In *The Role of Place in Literature,* Lutwack describes the novel moving throughout the nineteenth century closer to historic and scientific documentation, and ultimately to Zolaesque naturalism.[32] In this century, writers for the most part have turned away from detailed definition of place and from the deterministic construction earlier writers had put on it. Perhaps today place does exert less influence on people than in earlier times. People are more mobile. Place itself is less distinctive: cities, regrettably, have become less varied. But Lutwack's point is that fiction is now less concerned with tracing links between people and places. Earlier in this century, modern writers stressed the separation of place and people in the alienation of people from their world. No longer creatures of place, these fictional figures were to be understood in relation to the individual unconscious. Alienation is for Stead little more than a bourgeois affectation. As a writer, her practice is precisely to expose the roots of those so-called alienated, deracinated figures who may not feel at home, but who are nevertheless shaped by their setting.

A male figure who recurs in Stead's fiction embodies her respect for that outside world as a shaping force and something, therefore, that the novelist must study. One instance of this figure is James Quick in **For Love Alone.** Quick has the engaging habit, on arriving in a new city, of walking around it (as Bill Blake did), carefully learning it, absorbing it, getting to know the names of the streets, the uses of the buildings past and present, the styles of decoration, the minute details of its life. Other figures who share this habit with Bill Blake appear in the novels and short stories. For Blake, there was more at stake here than the tourist's pleasure in seeing and knowing. These were eager investigations into the material and economic conditions under which people lived, and Stead's re-creation of them in her fiction suggests a respectful understanding of their purpose.

This practice of concrete inquiry, lovingly re-created here in an imagined figure, also provides the foundations of Stead's own fiction, and contributes to its idio-syncratic realist mode. So much can be documented from the preparations Stead made to write **Cotters' England.** Letters and a notebook from this time give authentic and detailed illustration of her materialist practice as a writer of place. In 1949 Stead went to stay with Anne Dooley's family, the Kellys, in Newcastle-upon-Tyne to gather material for the novel. As well as observing the family at close hand, Stead went about the town, worked in the local Communist Party office and read voluminously in the local library. This was 'background reading'—the phrase she used—with a vengeance. Evidence of the comprehensiveness of her attention to placing her people in their setting is preserved in twenty packed pages of single-spaced typed notes. Nevertheless, after all these detailed researches into place, Stead still does not fit into the categories of writer of place as defined by Tindall in *Countries of the Mind.*

The title of Tindall's book is a phrase now familiar from contemporary discussions of place in relation to identity and regional and national difference. In this context, ideas of a nation are not seen as materially based but rather as myths that have their own history. Notions of England and Englishness evolve and are refined and then, mediated through literary and other cultural sources, impose themselves as 'countries of the mind'. In an essay entitled 'England: A Country of the Mind', G. J. B. Watson writes of how this process worked in his own case. In his Northern Ireland childhood, 'England' was the country portrayed in radio programs and the books he read, and it remains, in spite of frequent visits and of having lived there for a time, indelibly that 'country of the mind'. The oppositional construction of place, as 'home' as against 'other', foreign or 'abroad', may, as explicitly political accounts argue, produce more sinister, oppressive effects, when myths of national identity and authentic Englishness are manipulated to define those in power, and to label others, in disaffected 'troublesome' groups, as non-English. Stead, the internationalist, was well aware of the process by which myths of England, or any other country, evolve and are absorbed, and hold sway over the mind: 'pure chauvinism clothed in romance' was her phrase for it.[33] Not all novelists are as wary as Stead of the influence of such myths.

And characters in their novels may be enveloped in them. Indeed, within a single text, different figures may each have constructed their own cherished country of the mind, and, as a result, as Alexander Gelley puts it, 'complex and even contradictory valorisations' of a place may be 'brought into play'.[34] Certainly, this is the case with Stead's novels: she is a writer who feeds greedily on an ironic awareness of the constructed nature of individual reality. Personal myths of physical places or national identities, overlapping or conflicting, build up a mosaic of impressions of the one fictional setting, and the reader must find a way to make sense of the picture offered by the narrative as a whole, with virtually no judgmental comment from the narrator. But if this constructed place is seen through the draperies of the characters' myths, as Angela Carter says, Stead's 'passion for the material truths of human reality' simultaneously puts the reader in touch with the 'essence' of the place.[35]

Notes

1. Joan Lidoff, 'Interview with Christina Stead', in *Christina Stead,* New York: Ungar, 1982, 193.

2. Anita Segerberg, 'Getting started: The emergence of Christina Stead's early fiction', *ALS,* 13, 2, 1987, 126.

3. H. M. Green, *A History of Australian Literature,* rev. D. Green, vol. I, Sydney: Angus & Robertson, 1961, 1158.

4. Michael Wilding, *Studies in Classic Australian Fiction,* Sydney: Association for Studies in Society and Culture, 1997, 161, 164.

5. Hilary Bailey, 'Introduction', in Christina Stead, *The Beauties and Furies,* London: Virago, 1982, v.

6. Randall Jarrell, 'An unread book', in Christina Stead, *The Man Who Loved Children,* Harmondsworth: Penguin, 1970, reprinted 1983, 21.

7. ibid., 22.

8. Rodney Pybus, '*Cotters' England*: In appreciation', *Stand,* 23, 4, 1982, 42.

9. To Nadine Mendelson, n.d., late 1937 or early 1938, *Selected Letters 1,* 81.

10. To Florence James, 12 November 1933, Florence James papers, Manuscript Section, State Library of New South Wales.

11. To Gilbert Stead, 21 December 1937, *Selected letters 1,* 75.

12. Notebook for 'Workshop on the Novel', Fall 1943, Christina Stead papers, MS 4967, NLA.

13. Rodney Wetherell, 'Christina Stead: Interviewed by Rodney Wetherell', *ALS,* 9, 4, 1980, 432.

14. Stead mentions this 'Australian walk' in her story 'Street Idyll'; see ch. 7, p. 156.

15. Stead to Bill Blake, 29 October 1949, Christina Stead papers, MS 4967, NLA.

16. *New Masses,* 15 November 1938, 1-2.

17. *Realist Writer,* a publication launched in the 1950s in Sydney to which Stead subscribed.

18. Wetherell, interview, 441.

19. ibid. Stead seems to have felt that her practice at one stage had not followed this non-judgmental principle and spoke of making a conscious shift: 'With *The People with the Dogs* I decided, "I can't go on criticizing"'. John Beston, 'An interview with Christina Stead', *World Literature Written in English,* 15, 1, 1976, 91.

20. Leonard Lutwack, *The Role of Place in Literature,* Syracuse, NY: Syracuse University Press, 1984, 57.

21. Terry Sturm, 'Christina Stead's new realism: *The Man Who Loved Children* and *Cotters' England*', in Don Anderson & Stephen Knight, eds, *Cunning Exiles: Studies of Modern Prose Writers,* Sydney: Angus & Robertson, 1974, 22-3.

22. Ralph Fox, *The Novel and the People,* London: Cobbett Press, 1944, 90.

23. ibid., 91.

24. Elizabeth Hardwick, 'The neglected novels of Christina Stead', *New Republic,* 1955, reprinted in *A View of My Own,* New York: Farrer, Strauss & Cudahy, 1964, 47.

25. Ian Reid, 'Form and expectations in Christina Stead's novellas', *Literary Criterion,* 15, 3-4, 1980, 48.

26. Rowley, 261.

27. Equally, she claimed that she paid no attention to readers' expectations. An interviewer noted that the novellas collected in *The Puzzleheaded Girl* had appeared first in magazines. Asked if this place of publication had had any effect on her style, she replied: 'No, there was no effect whatsoever. I never write for anyone.' See Jonah Raskin, 'Christina Stead in Washington Square', *London Magazine,* 9, 2, 1970, 71.

28. Gillian Tindall, *Countries of the Mind: The Meaning of Place to Writers,* London: Hogarth Press, 1991, 10.

29. ibid., 3.

30. Wilding, *Studies in Classic Australian Fiction,* 164.

31. Diana Brydon, *Christina Stead,* Women Writers series, Basingstoke: Macmillan Education, 1987, 85.

32. Lutwack, *The Role of Place in Literature,* 19-20.

33. 'The writers take sides', *Left Review,* 1, 11, August 1935, 462.

34. Alexander Gelley, *Narrative Crossings: Theory and Pragmatics of Prose Fiction,* Baltimore: Johns Hopkins University Press, 1987, 7.

35. Angela Carter, 'In love with the tempest', *Sunday Times,* 10 April 1983, 44.

Select Bibliography

WORKS BY CHRISTINA STEAD

FICTION

The Salzburg Tales, London: Peter Davies, 1934.

Seven Poor Men of Sydney, London: Peter Davies, 1934.

The Beauties and Furies, London: Peter Davies, 1936.

The Man Who Loved Children, New York: Simon & Schuster, 1940.

For Love Alone, New York: Harcourt Brace, 1944.

The People with the Dogs, Boston: Little, Brown, 1952.

Dark Places of the Heart, New York: Holt, Rinehart & Winston, 1966; *Cotters' England,* London: Secker & Warburg, 1967.

The Puzzleheaded Girl, New York: Holt, Rinehart & Winston, 1967.

Miss Herbert (The Suburban Wife), New York: Random House, 1976.

I'm Dying Laughing: The Humourist, edited and with a preface by R. G. Geering, London: Virago, 1986.

NON-FICTION AND LETTERS

A Web of Friendship: Selected Letters (1928-1973), edited with a preface and annotations by R. G. Geering, Pymble: Angus & Robertson, 1992.

INTERVIEWS

Beston, John, 'An interview with Christina Stead', *World Literature Written in English,* 15, 1, 1976, 87-103.

Lidoff, Joan, 'Interview with Christina Stead' [1973], *Aphra,* 1976, reprinted in her *Christina Stead,* New York: Ungar, 1982, 180-220.

Wetherell, Rodney, 'Christina Stead: Interviewed by Rodney Wetherell', *ALS,* 9, 4, 1980, 431-48.

MANUSCRIPT SOURCES

Christina Stead papers (drafts, MSS, notebooks and miscellaneous correspondence), MS 4967, NLA.

Florence James papers, Manuscript Section, State Library of New South Wales.

CRITICAL, HISTORICAL AND THEORETICAL WORKS

Bailey, Hilary, 'Introduction', in Christina Stead, *The Beauties and Furies,* London: Virago, 1982.

Brydon, Diana, *Christina Stead,* Women Writers series, Basingstoke: Macmillan Education, 1987.

Carter, Angela, 'In love with the tempest', *Sunday Times,* 10 April 1983, 44.

Fox, Ralph, *The Novel and the People,* 1937, London: Cobbett Press, 1944.

Gelley, Alexander, *Narrative Crossings: Theory and Pragmatics of Prose Fiction,* Baltimore: Johns Hopkins University Press, 1987.

Green, H. M., *A History of Australian Literature,* rev. D. Green, 2 vols, Sydney: Angus & Robertson, 1961.

Hardwick, Elizabeth, 'The neglected novels of Christina Stead', *New Republic,* 1955, reprinted in *A View of My Own,* New York: Farrer, Strauss & Cudahy, 1964.

Jarrell, Randall, 'An unread book', in Christina Stead, *The Man Who Loved Children,* 1965, Harmondsworth: Penguin, 1970.

Lidoff, Joan, *Christina Stead,* New York: Ungar, 1982.

Lutwack, Leonard, *The Role of Place in Literature,* Syracuse, NY: Syracuse University Press, 1984.

Pybus, Rodney, '*Cotters' England*: In appreciation', *Stand,* 23, 4, 1982, 40-7.

Reid, Ian, 'Form and expectations in Christina Stead's novellas', *Literary Criterion,* 15, 3-4, 1980, 48-58.

Rowley, Hazel, *Christina Stead: A Biography,* Port Melbourne: William Heinemann Australia, 1993.

Segerberg, Anita, 'Getting started: The emergence of Christina Stead's early fiction', *ALS,* 13, 2, 1987, 121-38.

Sturm, Terry, 'Christina Stead's new realism: *The Man Who Loved Children* and *Cotters' England*', in Don Anderson & Stephen Knight, eds, *Cunning Exiles: Studies of Modern Prose Writers,* Sydney: Angus & Robertson, 1974, 9-35.

Tindall, Gillian, *Countries of the Mind: The Meaning of Place to Writers,* London: Hogarth Press, 1991.

Watson, G. J. B., 'England: A country of the mind', in R. P. Draper, ed., *The Literature of Region and Nation,* Basingstoke: Macmillan, 1989, 147-59.

Wilding, Michael, *Studies in Classic Australian Fiction,* Sydney: Association for Studies in Society and Culture; and Nottingham: Shoestring Press, 1997.

TEXTS AND ABBREVIATIONS

Quotations from Christina Stead's fiction follow the recent editions listed below. Details of first publication may be found in the Bibliography.

The Salzburg Tales, with a new introduction by Lorna Sage, London: Virago, 1986.

Seven Poor Men of Sydney, Sydney: Angus & Robertson, 1974.

The Beauties and Furies, with a new introduction by Hilary Bailey, London: Virago, 1982.

The Man Who Loved Children, Harmondsworth: Penguin, 1970, reprinted 1983.

For Love Alone, Sydney: Angus & Robertson, 1974.

The People with the Dogs, London: Virago, 1981.

Cotters' England, Sydney: Angus & Robertson, 1974.

Miss Herbert (The Suburban Wife), New York: Random House, 1976.

I'm Dying Laughing: The Humourist, edited and with a preface by R. G. Geering, London: Virago, 1986.

The following abbreviations are used for frequently cited sources:

ALS: *Australian Literary Studies*

NLA: National Library of Australia

Rowley: Hazel Rowley, *Christina Stead: A Biography,* Port Melbourne: William Heinemann Australia, 1993

Selected Letters 1: *A Web of Friendship: Selected Letters (1928-1973),* edited with a preface and annotations by R. G. Geering, Pymble: Angus & Robertson, 1992

Fiona Morrison (essay date 2000)

SOURCE: Morrison, Fiona. "A 'Cruel Book': Menippean Satire and the Female Satirist in *I'm Dying Laughing.*" In *The Magic Phrase: Critical Essays on Christina Stead,* edited by Margaret Harris, pp. 224-40. Brisbane, Australia: University of Queensland Press, 2000.

[*In the following essay, Morrison interprets Stead's posthumously published novel* I'm Dying Laughing *as a menippean satire, but she argues that the satirical form is complicated by the fact that this is a text written by a female author about "a left-wing woman writer," which results in a complex narrative that contains "a multiplicity of identifications based on contested proprieties of genre, femininity, politics and authorship."*]

The prevailing critical view of *I'm Dying Laughing* is that it is at best an unwieldy but crucial example of Stead's later work, and at worst, illegible. Begun in the 1940s, worked on throughout the 1950s and a little in the 1960s, abandoned as an unfinished magnum opus in the 1970s and published posthumously in 1986, the textual history of *I'm Dying Laughing* displays the complexities of the multiple locations of production and reception consistent with Stead's expatriate career and

political affiliations.[1] In this essay, I extend a number of recent critical positions that have sought to address both legibility and complexity in *I'm Dying Laughing.* Increasingly, considerations of nation and nationality in Stead's work, and of *I'm Dying Laughing* in particular, have been matched by readings of gender, genre and class. Specifically, such critics as Susan Sheridan and Louise Yelin have called for an elaboration of Stead's role as a political satirist: thus Sheridan offers a challenge to feminist literary critics to investigate how satire operates in Stead's "woman-centred" novels, suggesting that feminist criticism, hitherto interested in "affirmative representations of women", has baulked at *Letty Fox, Cotters' England, Miss Herbert* and *I'm Dying Laughing.*[2] I maintain that a comprehensive feminist reading position for Stead must consider her later satires as examples both of her fearless use of genre, and of the complex and diverse operations of gender, sexuality and national identity in these texts. Stead's satires on women exhibit rich and complex relationships among the rhetorical, discursive and gendered structures of satire, recognising the nuances of ideological frameworks and political consequences.

Of all Stead's texts, *I'm Dying Laughing* most emphatically foregrounds politics, political conscience and their relation to textual practice. Her account of a left-wing woman writer struggling to survive in an increasingly right-wing literary and political milieu is structured through the generic forms of menippean satire, and it is as a menippean satire that *I'm Dying Laughing* participates in a genealogy of radical political satire. Using the mixed forms and rhetorical structures of menippea, Stead's project is to record the life of a political woman writer from the American mid-west, Emily Wilkes, whose ultimately tragic experience articulates the complexities of political identity and radical American politics in the 1930s and 1940s. The strange and uneasy alliance between female authorship and menippean satire in *I'm Dying Laughing* allegorises the extensive contradictions in the political and personal life of this central character. The further ambivalence of Stead's satire resides not only in the two-way mechanisms of censure and delight familiar in satire, but also in the ironically prolific elaborations of a satire by a political woman writer on the left, about a political woman writer on the left and her satires about herself and others. In *I'm Dying Laughing,* therefore, the formulations of female authorship and "woman-centred" menippean satire present a complex narrative economy of same-sex discipline and desire that works with a multiplicity of identifications based on contested proprieties of genre, femininity, politics and authorship—proprieties contested by dislocation, mixed category and excess.

Stead was a leftist, but not of the joining variety; she claimed to hate conflict and meetings. She existed "alongside but not in" the Communist Party, a sympathetic outsider to American left-wing politics.[3] "Alongside" is an elaboration of a marginal position that eschews rigid affiliation in order to retain imaginative mobility. To sustain the degree of observation required for authorship, Stead declared that the writer must be able to "see both sides": her own option for association over membership allowed her to move from the inside to the outside of certain categories. Like "renegade", the political tag that the Howards so fear in *I'm Dying Laughing,* "alongside" indicates a strategic knowledge of classificatory boundary or limit. As an Australian expatriate, Stead's location on both political and national margins enabled her to scrutinise the hypocrites, the renegades and the "radical chic" of American radical politics, as well as to pursue her enduring interest in exploitation, tyranny and monomania. In addition, Stead's self-positioning "alongside" (notoriously misogynist) party lines meant that she was well situated to examine the cross-over between the personal and the political, and hence the contradictory dynamics of authorial and financial ambition, political allegiance and artistic autonomy for the political woman writer (Christina Stead, Ruth McKenney and Emily Wilkes) that form the key drama of *I'm Dying Laughing.*

Despite her strategic distance from party membership, *I'm Dying Laughing* demonstrates Stead's passionate engagement with concepts of political betrayal and political exile as forms of radical individualism and extreme alienation. Hazel Rowley reports this of Stead's reaction to *Jericho,* a film about the Resistance that Stead and Blake saw in 1950:

> [Stead] who by then had begun to write *I'm Dying Laughing* in earnest—"wept like a fool. I'd never known until then how far this 'traitor' theme I am treating had got under my skin . . . I felt how dreadful dreadful dreadful it is for R McK (the only friend I have in that category) to betray. I never thought her anything but *Gargantua, a crazy out-of-size drawing*".[4]

Although political betrayal and exile were everyday realities in the McCarthyist environment of the late 1940s and early 1950s in which the first drafts of *I'm Dying Laughing* were written, the tragic category of political traitor overturns Stead's initial satiric identification of Ruth McKenney, on whom she modelled Emily Wilkes, with Rabelais's Gargantua. For Stead, the Rabelaisian transgression of limit and decorum was an attractive operation of inventive, because maverick, outsideness. However, since Stead's expatriate status and the politics of her marriage meant that stable ideological coordinates were crucial, political betrayal was a kind of transgression that was unforgivable, and demanded an energetic and relentless portrait of the degeneration of corrupt American socialists.

I'm Dying Laughing is therefore a satire about the left, from the left, which examines the slow "turn" from the

principles of Communism to the practices of capitalism during the McCarthyist period in America. In 1973, Stead offered these historical coordinates for her political satire:

> It was all about the passion—I use passion in almost the religious sense—of two people, two Americans, New Yorkers, in the thirties. . . . They were politically minded. They went to Hollywood. They came to Europe to avoid the McCarthy trouble. Of course, they were deeply involved. And then, they lived around Europe, oh, in a wild and exciting extravagant style. But there was nothing to support it. At the same time they wanted to be on the side of the angels, good Communists, good people, and also to be very rich. Well, of course . . . [sic] they came to a bad end.[5]

Although *I'm Dying Laughing* satirises the contradictory desire to be "on the side of angels . . . and also very rich", Stead's use of passion "in almost the religious sense" indicates a tragic kind of suffering. The lack of ideological strength or system to support the pressures of the desire to be left-wing and also wealthy determines a combination of satiric and tragic treatment indicated in the tone "of course . . . they came to a bad end". Desire for success and money, accompanied by fear of failure and obscure poverty, are thematised as the "American dilemma"—the often paradoxical and often productive relationship between collective action and individual survival at the heart of American national identity. Stead uses the weak and renegade Howards as a serio-comic portrait of the consequence of the corruptions of capitalism for left political thinkers and writers. In her portrait of this marriage between two radical Americans of different classes, Stead activates themes of American national identity, political activism and ideological commitment within a shifting economy of earning power, popular fame and authorial integrity.

Emily Wilkes, the central character of *I'm Dying Laughing,* declares of one of her many political writing projects:

> I've got an idea. I'm going to write a horror book, about the most dreaded figure in American society, a failure . . . And the terrible aching poignancy of knowing, in a way, for they know, it's all a mistake, and these hectic, drab lives are living for nothing, because the country's mindless, and life here is without a system; and it could be better . . . We're all so pressed down on every side, like a fish at the bottom of the ocean, as Mike Gold says, with dollars, dollars.
>
> (pp. 148-9)

Emily's book of horror will satirise American commitment to the cult of the wealthy and successful individual to the detriment of any equitable social system, and in this sense Emily's book is an outline of the menippean satire that satirises her; a satire that launches a critique of the contradictions at the heart of American political, national and gender identity, and the way in which the left-wing American, "pressed down on every side" by the demands of capital, is vulnerable to corruption. While the object of satire is clear on one level, the proliferation of genres and of satiric texts by author and subject obscures the precise direction of attack. Part of this obscurity relates to the way in which the "horror book" uses a mixture of satire and tragedy. Introducing Derrida's work on genre, Derek Attridge suggests that "the question of genre—literary genre but also gender, genus and taxonomy—brings with it the question of the law, since it implies an institutionalised classification, an enforceable principle of non-contamination and non-contradiction".[6] In this sense, genre is an odd categorical imperative that legislates against "mixture" and by doing so points up the lapses of genre's putative purity, because when a limit is suggested, so are contamination, proliferation and decomposition. Stead's title and her character's signature phrase, "I'm dying laughing", indicate a self-conscious combination of the tragic and the comic. It is this contradictory, and therefore impure, satiric mixture that provides the basis for Stead's representation of ambivalence, transgression and monstrosity. The serio-comic text by the woman satirist about a woman satirist is a grotesquely mixed text that demonstrates the limit case of "pure" genre through its gleeful transgressions of taxonomy.

For Marxist critics such as Fredric Jameson (for instance in *The Political Unconscious,* 1989), it has been vital to re-position theories of genre as part of a critical and dialectical juncture between history and aesthetic production. It is in this materialist sense that the specifics of period and of literary genealogy form an indispensable historical horizon for Stead's use of menippean satire in *I'm Dying Laughing.* For example, *I'm Dying Laughing* is avowedly based on Ruth McKenney and Richard Bransten, an American couple of Stead's political acquaintance from the late 1930s. Both Stead's closeness to her "real people" sources and the text's self-conscious identification of literary patrilineage display the reciprocal relationship of satire to the world of history, ideology, text and structure for which Jameson argues, and upon which this reading of female-authored satire rests.

Stead's texts consistently "re-mark" on a preference for hybrid forms such as romance-epic and serio-comic satire.[7] So the first book of *I'm Dying Laughing* opens with an epigraph from Rabelais's *Gargantua and Pantagrue!* (1564): "I'm thirsty" is a translation of Gargantua's birth cry as Gargamelle gives birth to him at a feast of tripe, making an explicit connection between Gargantua and the character of Emily Wilkes. Stead, writing to Edith Anderson about her visits to Ruth McKenney in London in the late 1940s and early 1950s, explained that she would head for Chelsea "to see Mme. Gargantua perform".[8] Stead had obviously read Rabelais, and her debt to him was as potent for her later novels as her earlier debt to the European realists of the nineteenth century. Louise Yelin makes the point that Ralph Fox, a figure of great importance to Stead, "praises the philosophical novel of Rabelais and Cervantes, among others. Fox's figure . . . of the satirical novel as a powerful 'instrument' in political struggle, like Stead's figure of the pen as a scalpel, authorises the Rabelaisian project of *House of All Nations*".[9] Having written the female Quixote in *For Love Alone,* and the female rake in *Letty Fox,* Stead tackles the female Gargantua in *I'm Dying Laughing,* unknowingly following Mikhail Bakhtin's view that Rabelais was the most significant existing link to the antique menippean tradition.

Satire is the literary art of diminishing or derogating a subject by making it ridiculous and evoking towards it attitudes of amusement, scorn or indignation. Satire, which typically uses weapons of parody and caricature, mobilises laughter to attack vice or folly existing outside the work itself, in Stead's case, left hypocrisy in the form of Ruth McKenney-Emily Wilkes. Contemporary definitions of satire such as "wit or humour founded on fantasy or a sense of the grotesque or absurd", and "an object of attack for the other; or fantasy and a moral standard; or indirection and judgement", account for the kinds of satire used by Stead, Ruth McKenney and Emily Wilkes.[10] This combination of the delights and variety of grotesque fantasy and the attack on an implicit moral standard feature strongly in indirect satire rather than the more direct forms of classical political satire. Combination is a keynote of menippean satire as a famously indirect form of satire. Satire derives from the Latin, *satur,* meaning "full", a denotation that subsequently underwent a transition from "fullness" to "miscellany" by its application to *lanx.* The *lanx satura,* or the full plate of various kinds of fruit, comes to describe a medley, a method that derives from the Greek Menippeus who used a mixed form to ridicule philosophical opponents. Thematically, therefore, menippean satire was most concerned with "right learning or right belief, a theme that often called for ridicule or caricature of some intellectual or theoretical fraud".[11]

In *Anatomy of Criticism* Northrop Frye designates this form the "anatomy" after a major English instance of the type, Burton's *Anatomy of Melancholy* (1621). Such satires are usually written in prose and feature a series of extended dialogues and debates (often conducted at a banquet or a party) in which a group of loquacious pedants, literary people and representatives of various professions or philosophical points of view make ludicrous the attitudes and viewpoints they typify by the arguments they urge in their support. In the modern period, menippean satire markedly shifted into other modes and genres such as tragedy and the novel, although a principal emphasis on the forms of variety has been retained. Dialogues, conversations, picaresque narratives, traveller's narratives, anatomies and mock lectures form the menippean variety in *I'm Dying Laughing*. Examples of this variety include: the travel between Hollywood, New York and Paris; house hunting in Hollywood and Paris; and detailed accounts of material possessions, grandeur and dining out. Emily's monologic tirades about Cicero or Versailles (pp. 419 ff.) operate as learned anatomies or mock lectures. Vittorio's lecture about the war (pp. 240 ff.), and Suzanne's account of the Occupation demonstrate the way in which menippean characters, obsessed by particular ideas, dramatically expose the shortcomings both of themselves and of others.

In *I'm Dying Laughing* the prerequisite rhetorical variety of prose satire is exemplified in five main textual modes: labyrinthine exchanges between Emily and Stephen (Emily does most of the talking); the Howards' interaction with larger groups of people, including their children and tutors; Emily's monologic tirades, including lists of food; "learned anatomies" from select characters; and lengthy descriptions of Emily's indiscriminate textual production and proliferating plans for new texts, both commercial and "serious". Eugene Kirk's catalogue of menippean textuality reads like a check list for the heteroglossic aspects of *I'm Dying Laughing*:

> Neologisms, portmanteau words, macaronics, preciosity, coarse vulgarity, catalogues, bombast, mixed languages and protracted sentences were typical of the genre, sometimes appearing all together in the same work . . . a jumble of flagrantly digressive narrative, or again a potpourri of tales, songs, dialogues, orations, letters, lists, and other brief forms, mixed together. Menippean topical elements included outlandish fictions and extreme distortions of argument (often paradoxes).[12]

The following excerpt from Emily's voyage to Europe illuminates Stead's wonderful use of unconventional diction, usefully testifying to Stead's "ear" for idiom in her rendition of the pungency and idiosyncrasy of direct speech:

> I'm just one hundred and one per cent hayseed and ignoramus, the big, brainless American wonder from Hix-in-the-Stix. They've got so much culture over there they throw it away like, Uncle said, we threw away beefsteaks and turkeys in the garbage cans at Christmas around Camp Upton. I'm hoping to eat out of their garbage cans. Unless there's a sentry.

> (p. 11)

Emily's Rabelaisian coarseness, her puffed up invective, ostentatious flights of fancy and her wonderful rambunctiousness are exemplified in the vitality and strangeness of her language.

I'm Dying Laughing is a menippean satire about the greed and corruption of a couple who subscribe to Communist ideals, but who find themselves unable to live without the comforts of capitalism. Food, central to satire's traditions of the mixed plate and the materiality of the body, is variously troped throughout Stead's work as a form of consumption indispensable to production, and thus invariably present at representations of the decadent greed of capitalism. Feasting is also a favourite subject of grotesque realism, involving both loquacity and the lower bodily stratum, and in *I'm Dying Laughing* the generativity and excesses surrounding food are part of an ambivalent economy of censure and delight; food represents a degenerative downward spiral of insatiable desire and partial gratification, as well as an energetic and impressive production of speech and text. Several lists of food provide useful epideictic examples of the equivocal relationship between the inside and the outside in the form of Emily's eating, talking and earning. Emily says to her "astringent" husband that she has the "figure and avoirdupois of the Child of Moby Dick", but makes detailed and tantalising lists of her favourite foods, consumed on "the theory that I work better" (p. 58, see also p. 165). Emily's wonderful lists of food reflect her logic that, as the means of production, copious consumption will result in her copious and profitable production of text.

Let us take the banquet or party as an example of the menippean aspects of Stead's text. A number of critics have noted Stead's penchant for the dinner party or family dinner as the scene of melodramatic crisis or exchange of positions.[13] Frye's identification of menippean characters as "pedants, bigots, cranks, parvenus, virtuosi, enthusiasts, rapacious and incompetent professional men of all kinds" and his claim about the scene of satire are also apposite to *I'm Dying Laughing*: "disorderly, crowded, packed to the very point of bursting. The deformed faces of depravity, stupidity, greed, venality, ignorance and maliciousness group closely together".[14] The "Holinshed Party," the "Straightening Out" and Olivia's eleventh birthday in Part One, are good examples of these menippean dynamics. In both France and the United States, the contradictions of the Howards' politics are rehearsed at the feast-banquet, although the crowded scenes of pedantry, invective and venality do change tone with geographical location. In France, feasting is less the Hollywood-Land of Cockaigne site of carnival (pp. 60, 71), and more a desperate black-market decadence, which marks the Howards' decline into amorality and a move towards tragedy. The behaviour of the Howards in obtaining and dining out on blackmarket food in France is contradictory to their communist principles, and a gesture of desperation against the poverty and political complexity of post-war Europe.

Stead's satiric targets are the same as those of Roman satirists such as Horace and Juvenal: the corrupting effects of fame and the lofty and hubristic delusions inspired by superficial success. However, a number of satiric commonplaces (other than the feast) are used to lampoon capitalist venality and hypocrisy in particular, only some of which I will mention here: Stephen's "gift" to Emily of an amethyst necklace (p. 63), Stephen's gold smuggling (p. 348), debt/lotteries (pp. 260-1, 406), the use of children as capital—the so-called "rape of Olivia" (p. 95) and "The Struggle for Christy" (pp. 380ff). These episodes thematise the indiscriminate and corrupt pursuit of capital to support an insupportable lifestyle as Emily and Stephen Howard frantically prostitute themselves and their children in order to sustain an increasingly corrupt world. Another important mode of Emily's exploitation of her children relates to her improper maternity, which is another of the stable of satiric tropes on grotesque femininity and female excess.

The working-class Emily Wilkes aspires to write a satiric-tragic text of radical revolutionary proportions in the style of Dreiser's *An American Tragedy* (pp. 350ff). However, it is her "humourist" material, involving the stories of her family and small town American life—"family hokum, a belly-laugh or two and a shovelful of sentiment" (p. 137)—that earns her "serious" money. Her addiction to luxury—a combination of disposition and an aristocratic marriage—forces her to continue with her humourist pieces, linking gender, genre and pecuniary motive in her commodification of her own regional origins and class position. Instead of writing "Toonerville tales", Emily Wilkes wants to produce a critique of the revolutionary movement, "the way I see it and what's wrong with it", a political ambition outside the traditional orbit of female authorship. She calls this writing project the "cruel book": "I'd try to put a finger on essential human weaknesses; the ignorance and self-indulgence that has led us into Bohemia . . . I ought to say how everything becomes its opposite not only outside the besieged fortress but in" (pp. 71-2). Stephen's response to the proposed "cruel book" that would articulate the contradictions and oppositions within and outside the left is that: "It might be an epitaph of American socialism"; but Emily declares that: "It would be for the real rebels, the real labour movement, against all vampires who take all that's best in the world, even the name of the most sacred causes and use them for promotion; shepherds killing and eating the lambs" (p. 72). This is the Howards' story, and so the cruel book Emily desires to write in fact writes her, including her genius and her "bohemian" self-indulgence.

The complexity of *I'm Dying Laughing* develops because Emily is both the object of Stead's satiric discipline, and increasingly the narcissistic object of her own satiric writing. Stead's "cruel book" about Emily Wilkes and her various texts anatomises the unstable situation ("how everything becomes its opposite") within the "besieged fortress" occupied by American radicals in the late 1940s, as well as thematising the complex relation of the boundaries between the inside and the outside. Stead's and Emily's texts represent radical satires in the tradition of the eighteenth century, which themselves deployed the mixed tradition of menippean satire, and which necessarily incorporated into their textual bodies the caricatures and stereotypes to which they would retort. This structure of irony and parody suggests an infinite regress that works through figures of repetition, doubling and difference in the female-authored satire of the female satirist.

The consistent doubling of the Stead and Wilkes texts (the "horror book", the "cruel book" and "The Monster") requires an account of the ways in which gender and satiric form are entangled in *I'm Dying Laughing.* Women, whilst tremendously represented as *objects* of satire, have not historically been *authors* of satire. Satire has been a masculine province because satire takes up the authority to judge and name, and because social prohibition against satiric authorship did not extend to men. The main complication for the female author lies in the attitudes of satire towards women, who are frequently its targets. If satire often takes femininity and female authorship as objects of satiric attack, what are the consequences for female narrative authority? What happens when satire, a mode invested in dominance, is taken up by minorities it traditionally satirises? Can the minority Other establish the necessary subject position to launch a satiric attack, and what difference does gender make in the construction of a satiric persona as well as in the very writing of satire?

In other words, if there has been no real tradition of female satire, how and why might Stead take up the authorship of satire in the twentieth century? How does the woman writer assume the authority and the knowledge of the public sphere built into the authorship of satire if the woman satirist, or scold, has been the object of satire, and rarely its subjective "I"?[15] If, as Sheridan asserts, there can be no simple revision of the traditional paradigm of male satirist as subject and his feminine/effeminate object, the nature of the woman writer's use of satire to satirise women must inevitably lie somewhere along the spectrum of a complex rewriting, or a complicitous critique, or a strategic complicity. The antifeminist female satirist must certainly find a legitimate place from which to speak within hostile conventions designed to silence women's critical and shrewish voices, at the same time as disciplining that voice. Stead's worldly legitimation to write satire was at least partially founded in a radical literary and political affiliation with menippean satirists such as Rabelais, Cervantes and Burton, and political theorists such as Ralph Fox. For the rest, she simply ignored the hierarchical restrictions of gender and genre, and by dramatising the category of female satirist as volcanic virago, proceeded to engage fully with the violence, intrusiveness and immediacy of menippean satire.

As *House of All Nations, Letty Fox* and *A Little Tea, A Little Chat* indicate, Stead's investment in sexual difference was as a limitation to be overcome by aspiration to the public sphere of homosocial exchange and masculine discursive practice and privilege. Politics and science authorised her writing, and class rather than gender was considered to be the important category in the radical politics of the time. Susan Sheridan suggests that "The tendency to read her as a naturalist writer has been reinforced by Stead herself, who always responded to questions about narrative moral and political judgements by declaring that she was a 'naturalist', like her father before her, and would no more condemn certain kinds of behaviour than she would criticise a dingo for being a dingo."[16] Stead's claim to truthfulness of observation within the naturalist model was a claim to "objectivity". However, Stead's claim to naturalistic mimetic interest as a guarantee of gender indifference is not borne out by her satires on women. Emily Wilkes and Nellie Cotter are not like Robbie Grant or Jules Bertillon. We can see from *I'm Dying Laughing, Letty Fox, Cotters' England* and *Miss Herbert* that the central women are depicted through an armoury of sexually specific grotesque tropes in the line of writers like Rabelais and Cervantes. Without the triumvirate of masculinity, money and sex of the male-centred satires, Stead's woman-centred satires are clearly more aggressively menippean in their portrait of feminine excess and impropriety.

In fact, Stead was deeply invested in an antifeminist and homophobic ethics of sexual difference, and hence her mimicry of a "masculine" genre should present little ambiguity in the effect or destination of satiric tropes about femininity. Yet, the view Stead attributes to Letty Fox, that "mere observation is not enough. The examiner must take part . . . sympathy and antipathy are two instruments of observation" (*LF* [*Letty Fox*], p. 458), indicates her ambivalent engagement with femininity. Sheridan argues that in Stead's satires on men "the critical distance" between author and object "is not fixed; indeed, it fluctuates under the strain of attraction to the very objects the narrative critically constructs . . . Stead as satirist does not deny her involvement with her objects in order to claim a pure position of opposition." Sheridan speculates that this fluctuating closeness to a masculine satiric object is "something like the naturalist-observer's desire to possess her objects through knowledge."[17] The "fascinated critical distance" to which Sheridan refers is also a feature of the satires that take femininity rather than masculinity as their target. When the masculine Other of sexual difference is the feminine "same", I suggest that the quality of intensive engagement is equally close but increasingly am-

bivalent, and that the object of satire (femininity, female ambition, monstrosity) becomes increasingly ambiguous.[18]

For the "woman who loved men" satire was taken up as a "major textual mode of opposition" but not as a "powerful means of critique and protest against patriarchal domination."[19] Stead is optimistic about the "stern and marvellous precision" of the "satirists and moralists" (*FLA* [*For Love Alone*], p. 76), but not for specifically feminist purposes, because she saw politics as a matter of class and environment rather than gender. Stead, "having learned the lessons of the masters," is "adept at satirising women" using misogynist tropes which have traditionally been the mainstay of classical satire.[20] The orientation and the energies of misogynous satire are not strategically redirected; they work with and through Stead's ambivalence about Emily's vitality and genius. Stead's deployment of misogynist and homophobic satiric tropes are unapologetically modelled on a number of male-authored satires of decadence and corruption. Nevertheless, the gender and textual politics of Stead's satire of women cannot be made to answer to a naively affirmative nor to a wholly misogynist view of women since satiric irony is unable to work in only one political or moral direction, and therefore Stead's misogyny unravels, rebounds and redirects. The portrait of Emily, while invested in gynophobia and misogyny, does not simply produce a vilifying caricature. Stead's text reiterates Emily's impressive ability to retain the power of the tongue as well as the authority of authorship. The tremendous generativity of the unusual, vital woman in terms of her raw satiric energy is palpable in the exaggerations, accretion and rhythm of her language. The text treats Emily as a genuine serio-comic writer of genius, with aspirations to revealing something of tragic experience and therefore something lasting. The double direction of satire resides in the fact that although Emily is thoroughly satirised by the kind of book she herself desires to write, Stead treats her "female Gargantua" as a suitably serious object of intense and intimate observation.

In *I'm Dying Laughing* satiric direction is distinctly unstable; like many satires it is ambivalent in its effects, oscillating between censure and delight, and the cautionary "showing forth" of the monstrous satiric object means that monstrosity also attaches itself to the author of satire. Destructive self-reference is finally the price satire pays to articulate any point of view at all. That Emily takes her own monstrosity (of text, body size, region and gender) as a subject for a humorous allegory of American dilemmas provides a case in point: "A typical American Middle-Western Mamma, with a beer-barrel waist, overstuffed dewlaps, panting about looking for an ice-cream soda" (p. 310). The female satirist satirising a female satirist who satirises herself as well as others, introduces a number of occasions for a reflexive account by the text of its own genre, and in this sense, women's satire becomes the object of its own interrogation. The doubled relationship between the self-conscious mobilisation of satire as a mode by Stead, and also by Emily Wilkes (the "humourist" Stead's text satirises) makes for a knot of problematics in the arena of female satire and gender identification, doubling and difference.

When Emily arrives in Paris, one of her many ideas for a new book concerns an autobiographical sketch of herself "Emily Wilkes, in *Double or Nothing*; by Emily Wilkes". She drafts a version of herself as her subject. She is encouraged to make this choice because of her "fame, however decayed, shot through and mistaken" (p. 191), and sees increasing satiric and textual capital in her own grotesque notoriety. During her time in France she elaborates this idea a number of times (e.g. p. 230), reaching a crescendo in chapter 16, "Subjects for Emily", which concentrates on material for Emily's writings of all kinds. Emily suggests to Stephen that this idea is something in her "best style" that would *sell*. In her lengthy synopsis of *The Sorrows of a Really Fat Person like Me*" (pp. 301ff.), Emily's relentless commodification of her political and personal life slides schizophrenically and incoherently between "she" and "me", between subject and object, and between public and private.

The allegory is a blackly humorous commodification of her own past. Emily's tall tale includes a regional story of her fascination with grotesque (because very fat) people from rural Arkansas. Intriguingly, she comments that they "don't earn." She surmises that "I suppose you have to be fatter still to earn a living in a circus" (p. 301). This collocation of fatness, earning power and grotesque spectacle is telling for its insight into the fat lady's self-exploitative (self-commodifying) view about writing and money.[21] It is also a bitter self-dramatisation, with "Some gruesome, funny details. All sorts of superstitions" (p. 302), and strongly features Emily's ambivalent signature claim, "I nearly died laughing." It illustrates Emily's monstrous willingness to sell her own monstrosity—to prostitute her own suffering as a supposedly "humourous" account of her life that will please the punters and hold off the debtors. At the Holinshed Party in Hollywood, Godfrey Bowles' claims about Emily's "exploitation of her own personality" and "pronounced cult of her own individuality" (p. 100) have, it seems, come true. Emily's real corruption in *I'm Dying Laughing* is signalled by this kind of narcissistic and masochistic textual self-framing as a desperate bid (or gamble) to keep earning.

The dizzying menippean feat of the female satirist satirising a female satirist who satirises herself poses the question: who exactly has become the object of satire? Jayne Lewis' assertion that "satire by women interna-

lised suspicions about itself and was fraught with a deep and debilitating ambivalence about the satiric enterprise" is one that pinpoints the complexity of double and triple identifications within a generic paradigm of the censure of, and delight in, excess and transgression.[22] The threat of absorption or consumption, and the temptations of projection, increase through the operations of Same, indicating an unstable formulation of female intimacy and the ways in which women write about women, either satirically or panegyrically. Simultaneous identification with, and discipline of, the unruly body and powerful tongue of the female satirist mark out the territory of doubling and difference within sexual and textual identity that is held together in *I'm Dying Laughing* by the breadth and muscular re-combinations afforded by menippean satire.

Stead's thematisation of the grotesque and exhilarating possibilities of renegade law-breaking is matched by a satiric and tragic portrait of the loss of categorical coordinates and structuring principles, such as political faith. Stead's thematisation operates through a demonstration of the delights and dangers of contradiction and excess in body, text and speech, and in *I'm Dying Laughing,* textual bodies and bodily texts transgress established limits to the extent that they threaten political systems of location and classification. The stable homology of woman-local-private is threatened with an expatriate violation of boundary and rule and therefore the grotesque potential of mixed category. The carnival inversions of Emily's decline into a basement and perpetual dressing gown (pp. 330, 416) suggest that the feminine grotesque is an indispensable component of Stead's grotesque realism, but also indicates that the disruptive excess and overabundance of the mixed menippean form is harnessed to a portrait of political and personal degeneration. In this reading of the trajectory of political satire in its relation to gender and sexuality, Stead's satirical anatomisation of Emily's Wilkes as the marvellously and horrifyingly generative grotesque feminine is too profoundly ambivalent to be part of a *strategic* feminist project. Yet, while it is caught fast in misogynist satirical tropes of the fat lady-female comic, it is also desirous of Emily's carnivalesque vitality, individuality and excess. Ambivalence rather than dialectics, figured as the contradictory combination of death and laughter suspended together in a continuous present, is the carnivalesque mode *par excellence.*

Menippean satire has always posed problems for the closure of texts: both Emily's and Stead's texts are unfinished. The closing moments of Stephen's suicide and Emily's final and extreme marginality rehearse the satirist's position as alienated and self-immolating, and if Emily's penultimate identification with Marie Antoinette as the corrupt, tragic victim of revolution leaves little comic potential, it is the dissolution of her unfinished serious work ("The Monster") that suggests the devastating negations of tragedy. The ultimate ambivalence of Emily's inconclusive end on the steps of the Forum Romanum presents a cautionary tale about the transgression of limit as the breaking of filiation (outlawry), but also about that moment of laughter that indicates pure invention, imperfection, freedom and ambition; a cathexis that does not sublate contradictions, but holds them momentarily in suspension. As with Emily's "Pagliaccio" laughter (pp. 399-400), which verges on hysteria, her laughter at the end of *I'm Dying Laughing* powerfully ruptures discursivity and systematicity with anarchic excess, foregrounding the body and indicating the dialectical desire on the part of the satirist and the reader to enclose and incorporate the ungovernable subject within a system, and the impossibility of such a closure: "She began to laugh and could not stop. She lay on and rolled about the steps, endless laughter" (p. 447).

Notes

First published in this volume. This essay is a version of part of Fiona Morrison's doctoral thesis, "Out of Bounds: Three Expatriate Australian Women Writers, 1890-1990 (Henry Handel Richardson, Christina Stead, Janette Turner Hospital)" (University of Sydney, 1999).

1. In my thesis, "Out of Bounds: Three Expatriate Australian Women Writers, 1890-1990", work on Stead's expatriation involved the recuperation of the salient political, historical and generic specifics that might underwrite the "readability" of *I'm Dying Laughing*. See also Margaret Harris, "Christina Stead's Human Comedy: The American Sequence", *World Literature Written in English* 32, no. 1 (1992), pp. 42-51.

2. Susan Sheridan, "'The Woman Who Loved Men': Christina Stead as Satirist in *A Little Tea, A Little Chat* and *The People with the Dogs*", *World Literature Written in English* 32, no. 1 (1992), p. 3; and see Louise Yelin, "Christina Stead in 1991", *World Literature Written in English* 32, no. 1 (1992), pp. 52-4.

3. Letter to Stanley Burnshaw (29 September 1938), Burnshaw Collection, Harry Ransom Humanities Center, University of Texas, Austin, Folder 1.

4. Christina Stead, letter to Edith Anderson, 13 July 1950, cited in Hazel Rowley, *Christina Stead: A Biography* (Melbourne: William Heinemann, Australia, 1993), pp. 361-2 (my emphasis). This biography is an invaluable source of primary documentation and commentary on Stead's politics.

5. Joan Lidoff, "Interview with Christina Stead", *Christina Stead* (New York, Ungar, 1982), p. 181.

6. Jacques Derrida, *Acts of Literature,* ed. Derek Attridge (London and New York: Routledge, 1992), p. 181.

7. For a commentary on "mixed mode" see also Diana Brydon, "'Other Tongues Than Ours': Christina Stead's *I'm Dying Laughing*", *Australian and New Zealand Studies in Canada* 2 (1989), pp. 17-26.

8. Christina Stead, letter to Edith Anderson, 20 January 1950: in a later letter to Anderson, 11 October 1950, Stead again refers to Gargantua in connection with Ruth McKenney/Emily Wilkes (Rowley, *Christina Stead,* pp. 361-2). Rabelais had been a literary outlaw for Renaissance and Augustan critics, his excessive texts defying the decorum of the well-made textual body. In the 1930s, Bakhtin was to reclaim Rabelais as a genuinely populist author, and Popular Front ideologies also reclaimed him for a counter-hegemonic folk tradition. Bakhtin's work on menippean satire is inseparable from his work on the novel, since the types of novel he privileges are centrally formed by serio-comic energies. Bakhtin argues that the emerging novel absorbed the carnivalesque energies of menippean satire, and his discussion of this absorption provides apposite analytic categories for my reading of *I'm Dying Laughing*.

9. Yelin cites Ralph Fox, *The Novel and The People* (1937). She argues for an historically specific matrix of left textual politics in "Representing the 1930's: Capitalism, Phallocracy and the Popular Front in *House of all Nations*" (in this volume).

10. Ronald Paulson, *The Fictions of Satire* (Baltimore: Johns Hopkins University Press, 1967), p. 6.

11. Eugene P. Kirk, *Menippean Satire: An Annotated Catalogue of Texts and Criticism,* Garland Reference Library of the Humanities, vol. 191 (New York: Garland, 1980), p.xi. David Musgrave's work on menippea has also been invaluable: "Figurations of the Grotesque in Menippean Satire", Diss. University of Sydney, 1998.

12. Kirk, *Menippean Satire,* p.xi.

13. E.g. Don Anderson, "Christina Stead's Unforgettable Dinner Parties," *Southerly* 39 (1979), pp. 28-45, and Tina Muncaster, "The Pleasures of Text and Table: Appetite and Consumption in *I'm Dying Laughing*," *Southerly* 53, no. 4 (1993), pp. 106-15.

14. Northrop Frye, *Anatomy of Criticism: Four Essays* (Princeton: Princeton University Press, 1957), pp. 311-2; Alvin P. Kernan, "A Theory of Satire", *Satire: Modern Essays in Criticism,* ed. Ronald Paulson (Englewood Cliffs, N.J.: Prentice Hall, 1971), pp. 253-4.

15. For a comprehensive overview of satires by women in the seventeenth and eighteenth centuries, see Jayne Lewis, "'Compositions of Ill

Nature': Women's Place in the Satiric Tradition", *Critical Matrix* 2, no. 2 (1986), p. 45. In addition, Felicity Nussbaum's discussion of Mary Wollstonecraft's feminist use of satire is useful: "Gulliver's Malice: Gender and Satiric Stance", *Gulliver's Travels: Case Studies in Contemporary Criticism,* ed. Christopher Fox (Boston and New York: Bedford Books, 1995), pp. 321-3.

16. Sheridan refers to Rodney Wetherell, "Interview with Christina Stead", *Australian Literary Studies* 9 (1980), p. 441: *Christina Stead* (Hemel Hempstead: Harvester, 1988), pp. 14-15. Virginia Blain's discussion of the intersection between scientific naturalism and fictional naturalism is illuminating, in "*A Little Tea, A Little Chat*: Decadent Pleasures and the Pleasure of Decadence", *Southerly* 53, no. 4 (1993), pp. 20-35, an essay pertinent to many of my concerns here. [Included in this volume.]

17. Sheridan, "'The Woman Who Loved Men'", pp. 11, 8.

18. Sheridan, "'The Woman Who Loved Men'", pp. 8, 11.

19. Sheridan, "'The Woman Who Loved Men'", p. 2.

20. Sheridan, "'The Woman Who Loved Men'", p. 3.

21. See Patricia Parker, *Literary Fat Ladies: Rhetoric, Gender, Property* (Methuen: New York, 1987). Parker's work reads romance, rather than satire, but her work on female garrulity and the copious female body as signs of rhetorical dilation is suggestive in relation to female excess.

22. Lewis, "'Compositions of Ill Nature'", p. 45.

Bibliography

1: Works by Christina Stead

Manuscripts

Christina Stead's unpublished papers are held in the National Library of Australia Manuscript Collection: Christina Stead Papers, MS 4967. Other Stead and Blake material is held elsewhere within the collection. Significant Stead correspondence is held in the Harry Ransom Humanities Research Center, University of Texas, Austin, and there are smaller holdings in other libraries in the United States, including the Berg Collection, New York Public Library and at Yale University, New Haven.

Major works

House of All Nations. New York: Simon & Schuster, 1938; London: Peter Davies, 1938, offset from the Simon & Schuster edition; New York: Holt, Rinehart & Winston, 1972, offset from the Simon & Schuster edi-

tion, with the omission of 7pp. with lists of characters and businesses in the novel; New York: Avon, 1974; Sydney: Angus & Robertson, 1974, 1981, offset from the Simon & Schuster edition, with omission of lists of characters etc.

For Love Alone. New York: Harcourt Brace, 1944; London: Peter Davies, 1945; Sydney: Angus & Robertson, 1966, with introduction by Terry Sturm, subsequently in various hardback and paperback impressions, as Pacific, Sirius, and Angus & Robertson Classics: as Imprint, 1990, with an introduction by Peter Craven, repr. Sydney: ETT, 1999; Virago, 1978, offset from 1966 Angus & Robertson edition, with introduction by Mary Kathleen Benet; New York: Harcourt Brace Jovanovich paperback, 1979, reprints 1944 Harcourt Brace edition. Translated into Italian, 1947; French, 1948. Film, dir. and screenplay Stephen Wallace, UAA Films, 1986.

Letty Fox: Her Luck. New York: Harcourt Brace, 1946; London: Peter Davies, 1947; Sydney: Angus & Robertson, 1974, with introduction by Meaghan Morris, offset from 1946 Harcourt Brace edition, subsequently as a Sirius paperback, and Imprint, 1991, with introduction by Susan Sheridan; London: Virago, 1978, offset from 1946 Harcourt Brace edition, with introduction by Mary Kathleen Benet; New York: Harcourt Brace Jovanovich paperback, 1979, reprints 1946 Harcourt Brace edition. Translated into Italian, 1953.

A Little Tea, A Little Chat. New York: Harcourt Brace, 1948; London: Virago Modern Classics, 1981, with introduction by Hilary Bailey. Translated into French, 1990; Italian, c. 1994.

[*Dark Places of the Heart*]. New York: Holt, Rinehart & Winston, 1966; *Cotters' England.* London: Secker & Warburg, 1967, offset from 1966 Holt, Rinehart & Winston edition; Sydney: Angus & Robertson, 1974, offset from 1966 Holt, Rinehart & Winston edition, with afterword by Terry Sturm, subsequent impressions as Angus & Robertson Classics and Sirius (without afterword); London: Virago, 1980, offset from 1966 Holt, Rinehart & Winston edition, with introduction by Margaret Walters.

Miss Herbert (The Suburban Wife). New York: Random House, 1976; London: Virago Modern Classics, 1979, offset from 1976 Random House edition; New York: Harcourt Brace Jovanovich paperback, 1981, offset from 1976 Random House edition.

I'm Dying Laughing: The Humourist. Ed. R. G. Geering. London: Virago Press, 1986; New York: Henry Holt, 1987, offset from Virago, including Geering introduction (in paperback, 1990); Harmondsworth: Penguin, 1989, offset from Virago, including Geering introduction.

2. Works about Christina Stead

Biographies

Rowley, Hazel. *Christina Stead: A Biography*. Melbourne: William Heinemann Australia, 1993.

Selected Interviews

Lidoff, Joan. "Christina Stead: An Interview". *Aphra* 3, nos. 3 & 4, pp. 39-64. Repr. in *Christina Stead*. New York: Ungar, 1982, pp. 180-220.

Wetherell, Rodney. "Interview with Christina Stead". *Australian Literary Studies* 9, no. 4 (October 1980), pp. 431-48. Repr. as "Christina Stead Talks To Rodney Wetherell". *Overland,* August 1983, pp. 17-29.

Criticism

(i) Monographs

Lidoff, Joan. *Christina Stead*. New York: Ungar, 1982.

Sheridan, Susan. *Christina Stead*. Hemel Hempstead, Herts.: Harvester Wheatsheaf, 1988.

(ii) Articles

Anderson, Don. "Christina Stead's Unforgettable Dinner-Parties". *Southerly* 39 (1979), pp. 28-45.

Blain, Virginia. "*A Little Tea, A Little Chat*: Decadent Pleasures and the Pleasure of Decadence". *Southerly* 53, no. 4 (1993), pp. 20-35.

Brydon, Diana. "'Other Tongues Than Ours': Christina Stead's *I'm Dying Laughing*". *Australian and New Zealand Studies in Canada* 2 (1989), pp. 17-26.

Harris, Margaret. "Christina Stead". "Christina Stead's Human Comedy: The American Sequence". *World Literature Written in English* 32, no. 1 (1992), pp. 42-51.

Muncaster, Tina. "The Pleasures of Text and Table: Appetite and Consumption in *I'm Dying Laughing*". *Southerly* 53, no. 4 (December 1993), pp. 106-15.

Sheridan, Susan. "The Woman Who Loved Men: Christina Stead as Satirist in *A Little Tea, A Little Chat* and *The People with the Dogs*". *World Literature Written in English* 32, no. 1 (1992), pp. 2-12.

Woodward, Wendy. "Christina Stead in 1991". *World Literature Written in English* 32, no. 1 (1992), pp. 52-4.

Texts and Abbreviations

Throughout this volume, quotations from Christina Stead's works refer to the following editions, using the abbreviations listed. In many cases, the editions cited are new impressions of earlier printings (not always by the same publisher): consult the Bibliography for details.

For the reader's convenience, I have supplied page references to Christina Stead's works in those reprinted essays which did not originally include them. Quotations from Stead's works have been checked and silently amended where necessary.

FLA: *For Love Alone*. 1944. Sydney: ETT, 1999.

LF: *Letty Fox: Her Luck*. 1946. Sydney: Angus and Robertson (Imprint Classics), 1991.

Nicole Moore (essay date 2001)

SOURCE: Moore, Nicole. "'A Monster of Indecision': Abortion, Choice and Commodity Culture in Christina Stead's *The Beauties and Furies*." *Southerly* 61, no. 2 (2001): 142-57.

[*In the following essay, Moore regards the the indecision of Elvira, the protagonist of* The Beauties and Furies, *over whether to have an abortion, as reflective of modern woman's inability to achieve individuation within "commodity culture," stating that the heroine's inability to decide derives from her recognition that all choices are false, and that there is "no situation in which she is expressible as 'free.'"*]

Judith Kegan Gardiner suggests that a conviction in the power of individual choice could be Christina Stead's legacy as a writer:

> [. . .] concerns about female identity recur in her work from its beginning to its end without resolution, held to a subordinate place by firm moral and political convictions: "the choice is coming; the choice has come." Perhaps her conviction that individual choice can triumph over debilitating circumstances of gender, culture and generation [. . .] is her strongest legacy.
>
> (*Rhys, Stead, Lessing and the Politics of Empathy* 82)

"The choice is coming", the lapsed Marxist Emily declares in Stead's *I'm Dying Laughing* (74), between joining the revolution and reactionary lassitude, between acting and assuming responsibility, or remaining an impediment to the socialist future. In *The Beauties and Furies,* Stead's third novel, Elvira is a bourgeois English housewife, run away to Paris to her young and handsome lover, unintentionally pregnant and chronically unable to decide what to do about it. Choice for her is an agony. Her lover, Oliver, characterises her life, her character as "involuntary", thus determined for her, and her indecision is a temporising that delays choice between her lover and husband, Paris and London, and between identities, "lover-women and mother-women", as she outlines (*The Beauties and Furies* 217). About her, Oliver exclaims to himself: "What a woman she was! She was a monster of indecision: there was something grand and frightening about a life so involuntary"

(173). Elvira delays her decision about the pregnancy to such an extent that her temporising and vacillation make up almost half of the plot. Her aboulia is pathological—she *is* (and struggles with) the "monster of indecision". Her disease or her pathology derives directly, Stead elaborately shows us, from the ideological primacy of choice in modern capitalism.

The logic of either/or, the rhetorical dualism structured by and under the primacy of choice, is its connection, complexly embodied in the commodity form, to capitalism. 'Choice' is not merely ideological and is also more than a structure of feeling, following Raymond Williams. It can perhaps be thought of as a mode of action and denial, transferred from basic economic relations into the intersubjective realm, transforming relations between subject and object, self and other, person, labour, commodity, even past and present. It is present in the process of abstraction that transforms use value into exchange value and the primacy of choice also supposes, and perhaps thus produces, the individual who chooses. Indecision is agony or disease in capitalism: an agony of too much to choose from or effectively nothing to choose between. I want to explore Stead's writing of abortion and indecision as an assay of the conventional dualisms of abortion plots—the conflict between necessity and danger, desire and horror, the ordinary and the abject, the conventional and the criminal—and as such, an assay of their structuring dichotomies, especially a materialist/psychological divide. *The Beauties and Furies* has abulia at its heart because it baulks at authorising the individuation of modern women in capitalism, it seems to me. This is even as it pursues and explores that very possibility, as a central project for a gendered cosmopolitan modernism. Stead's narrative consistently mocks any of Elvira's decisions or self-affirmations as convenient and cynical, especially her resolution of the indecision, the final procuring of the abortion. Blanche, marginalised, dependent actress and seducer, sex worker, is Elvira's adviser and Oliver's lover. With her, one day, *shopping,* Elvira is *bored* and passively succumbs, under the impossibility of her decision, to attend her appointment with the *sage femme.*

The episode, with its surrounding events, exposes the ideological masquerade of 'free choice'. All at the same moment, Elvira is shopping, Oliver is paying for sex at the same brothel as Elvira's brother, Blanche is looking after Elvira as a cynical means to gain financial support from Oliver. 'Choice' as a defence of abortion can position women in relations of consumption to their bodies and their reproductivity. Somehow, their maternity or refusal of maternity is chosen, as goods and services are in the market economy. In the process, choice reifies the relation between body and subjectivity. Reproductive choice as a model resists the positioning of maternity as production, as a labour and not a commodity,

and as a different positioning of women in *interested* relation to market mechanisms of exchange. Steven Connor, in his work on theories of value, critiques Luce Irigaray's analysis of gender and commodity relations in her essay in *This Sex Which is Not One,* arguing that her analysis of the "double alienation" of women (into a commodity and into abstracted exchangability) confuses the commodity form and money itself (172). He suggests that, in the process, Irigaray's analysis takes the capitalist abstraction of 'woman' too far from masculine labour power. Gayatri Spivak, in a new return to the question of the abstraction of exchange value, points to a confusion arising from Engels' translation of Marx from the German. Exchange value and use value are both abstractions, she insists, by virtue of being values, attending to the importance of this abstraction to global industrial forms and mechanisms of exchange (4). Connor notes, as others have, that one of the central problems of Irigaray's analysis is that it seems to make it impossible to speak of the alienation of female labour, even as labour itself becomes increasingly feminised (172). Spivak's emphasis on the process—on abstraction or alienation—can give me, I hope, some pause from which to view the either/ors at stake in this debate: labour/commodity, use/exchange, self/body, choice/no choice. I want to try and place them in some form of stasis, viewing sexuality, modern sexuality, from within commodity culture, as historians of the late modern are increasingly insisting that critics must (cf. Matthews "Normalising"). Stead's narrative explores an interwar commodification of erotic relations, in which sexuality and reproductivity become positioned as opposite choices and married motherhood and a single desiring sexuality are alternative consumable identity categories: "lover-women or mother-women". Elvira's aboulia exposes these as false predicates, these mind/body, lover/mother, sex/reproduction either/ors as unreal choices and her anxiety is the agony of nothing to choose; the agony of no situation in which she is expressible as 'free', to freely choose.

Oliver and Elvira argue and quibble about the abortion, unable to decide for pages and pages of *The Beauties and Furies.* Their discussions are self-conscious about the history and representation of unwanted pregnancy as a public issue. Occasionally they evolve into a debate between the material and the 'instinctual' natural, Stead using the opportunity to satirise Oliver's schoolboy socialism:

> She went on: 'All day I was thinking of the girls who are abandoned and who commit suicide.'
>
> He said, trying to catch her thoughts:
>
> 'Isn't it strange, when they say the maternal instinct for life is so strong?'
>
> She looked straight at him. 'It's not that; it's the money. Where would I be now if I didn't have Paul or you to

look after me?' She had a slightly contemptuous satisfaction at seeing the thoughts in his face.

(124-25)

Elvira's situation here accords with Wilding's reading of Stead's radical socialist vision in *The Puzzleheaded Girl* (1968), valuing a preoccupation with the "deforming" effects of poverty on the individual and the isolated alienation of the human condition under capitalism (151, 154). Kegan Gardiner argues that this "Marxist humanism ignores gender and so misses the story's moving ambivalences about the connections among individual psychology, gender and politics" (Gardiner "Caught" 27). Kegan Gardiner is concerned to nominate psychology and gender as particular concerns of Stead's that are exterior to a Marxist framework and, in doing this, tellingly nominates their *ambivalences* as opposed to the invoked static dogma of a social or material theory of determination. In identifying the situation of the individual in history for Stead, as the "problem of defining female identity under capitalist patriarchy" (*Rhys, Stead* 54), Kegan Gardiner outlines this problem as one balanced between the psychic and social realms of individuation. Notably, she positions sexuality (as does Wilding to some degree) as an asocial, ahistorical dilemma of identity constitution, invoked by Stead as a problematic indeterminate force, unaffected by morality or politics. "Female identity in Stead's work is constantly struggling for definition against overwhelming forces—in her earliest and some of her latest work, the disruptions of female sexuality and the engulfing power of parents" (Kegan Gardiner, *Rhys, Stead* 55). The "disruptions of female sexuality" are unwanted pregnancy in *The Beauties and Furies* and *Letty Fox,* as well as in the novellas of *The Puzzleheaded Girl* and, similarly to sensuality and feminine desire in *For Love Alone,* they are read as overwhelming forces outside the control of the subject, Freudian drives isolated from social practices and economic conditioning.

I want to explore the notion that this construction of the 'overwhelming' power of sexuality and pregnancy is parallel to, or even a feature of, a pattern of personal alienation enacted as a condition of capitalism. Rather than removed from or opposite to each other, the sexual and the material can be seen to be much more complexly interwoven in Stead's explorations of commodified erotics than Kegan Gardiner's reading can perhaps acknowledge. As a reworking of the Marxist and feminist conjoining of patriarchy and capitalism, Stead's construction of sexuality as a plot for the expression of capitalist alienation nevertheless rejects, even parodies any association between sexuality and a natural moral authority. Unlike other modernists' more liberal reliance on instrumental psychology, also, a woman's alienation from her body in pregnancy is figured not as a template for organic madness but as a paradigm of her alienation from her body as object in commodity culture. Women and workers are alienated by their exclusion from the ownership of production and exchange, and women are alienated from their bodies in their role as commodities of exchange between men, by the fetishising logic of exchange and surplus value in capitalism. Stead's Marxism would write patriarchy as a feature of capitalism. Outside the sustaining economy of the nuclear family, the middle class single woman has no ideological authority for her maternity and her decision is marriage or abortion (not madness and not suicide, interestingly); a choice between Engels' slavery of the wife, "the cabbage wife" (174), as Elvira describes herself, or the tenuous economic conditions of the sexworker, dependent, as Blanche is, on an earning man's favours.

Reproductive control is a commodity choice, in this context, to be reached for or deliberated over as another good or service. This is Blanche telling Oliver the process of Elvira's eventual and still hesitant decision to go through with the abortion:

> "She only decided this afternoon. She got tired shopping; she felt sick and she suddenly said, "Oh, I can't go through with it," so I popped her into a taxi and off to the nurse's before she could regret. She hesitated at least ten minutes in the street below the surgery, as it was, until I said, "Well, here you are, you may as well go through with it: be a sport," and she said, "What's the odds, I'll do it." And there you are, *mon ami.* Do I get a vote of thanks or not?"

(216)

She "can't go through with" the pregnancy, not the abortion. Elvira's abortion is an explicit rejection of the conditions of pregnancy and maternity, rather than the desperate act of a woman forced into a situation that requires abortion of her. Her decision is nevertheless immensely protracted and difficult. She hesitates another ten minutes in the street and she does it, finally, under pressure to 'be a sport' and do Oliver a favour, as Blanche is doing Oliver a favour, unknown to Elvira. Elvira has given five hundred francs to Blanche to arrange the "little operation", of which at least one hundred Blanche regards as her cut. She discusses the affair with her café circle and one of her friends/clients declares: "Can you believe the Western woman gave Blanche five hundred francs to arrange a little business for her? Satan finds some suckers still for idle Blanche to do" (211). Blanche and Elvira compete in the economy of sexual dependence and Blanche responds to the above: "I work for my living: it's more than this Western woman does, the dear little thing" (212). Blanche supports her daughter on these earnings: "she will live bourgeois. Bourgeois!" she declares (218). Elvira's surname makes her representative here, both the cabbage wife and the *declassé* mistress.

Elvira declares, under the nurse's window, "there are lover-women and mother-women—I am the first sort"

(217). This distinction figures her abortion as the explicit *rejection* of maternity, not an experience or factor of maternity as most readers seem to presuppose when employing psychoanalysis to discuss abortion in women's writing (Judith Wilt, Debrah Kelly Kloepfer, Kegan Gardiner, Hollenberg). Her abortion is not a plot of "maternal choice", as Judith Wilt would suggest, but an explicit rejection of the dominant construction of all women as always potentially maternal. It is a positioning of the woman outside the space of the offered maternal, in a rejection of it in favour of the desiring lover position, desiring and engaged in the masculine world of exchange and comparison (choice?) and yet woman, yet the feminine. Indeed, in the modernist canon, the lover-woman is the new feminine subject, in contest with the excluded organic wife and mother. Her 'newness' posits the modernist separation of reproduction and sexuality as a movement of emancipation, a freeing up of the exploitative bonds of the patriarchal sexual contract. This positing is rhetorical for Elvira, however, as most of her speeches are in *The Beauties and Furies*. Abortion's possibility as the agent of this separation is restricted in her case in that her abortion is in Oliver's interests, represented by Blanche, more than her own. The spectre of this possibility is nevertheless present; the lover-woman can experience her passion, her sexuality prior to and without maternity, even if this is only in the role of the sex worker, the woman valued for her sexed corporeality in economic terms, explicitly as commodified labour.

Elvira got tired shopping, felt sick. She makes her decision to alleviate the condition of modernity—boredom—and projects the agency granted to her as shopper, by consumer culture, towards her own body and the dilemma of her alienated pregnancy. *The Beauties and Furies* makes clear that the two positions available to women become *déclassé* mistresses are as *flâneuse* or sex worker. The contrasting and self-conscious figure of Blanche is crucial in this critique of gender relations as economic relations. Her figure is also a distilling of modernity or the *style* of modernity in the cynical, urbane, marginalised modern woman, whose 'career' is show girl and *amateur* prostitute and whose 'family' is abandonment, single motherhood, abortions; in modernism an exclusively metropolitan destiny. The text never holds up traditional family values as a feasible alternative, however. Elvira's own contradictory imaginings of the maternal/suburban are inadequate, as either the "back-yard" in which women are grown as cultivated vegetables, the cabbage (174) or the "pumpkin wife" (84), and as mothers, the rooted, fleshy source of life, accepting the role of plants, passive, ornamental, natural:

> Women are too much nailed to our coffin of flesh, our souls are only plants, they are rooted in an earth of flesh. We need a home, security, comfort for our flesh

before the mind can grow. That is because we are the carriers of life . . .

(175)

Abortion is an animating rejection of the vegetable natural—a revealing choice of trope distinct from the convention that writes the sexuality of working class women as animal.[1] In both conventions abortion remains an unnatural return to the rational realm of culture and agency. Stead undercuts Elvira's maternal pathos with satire: "Oliver listened to her simple pomp with smiling, Paul with disillusioned eyes." The desiring position is coveted and imitated by women but no role is available to them outside the economic prescriptions of the feminine as practice. Even their self-description is without authority.

Commodity culture's logic is the temporality of the *new*.[2] Women themselves are the 'new' subjects, Dymphna Cusack's "women as they are" (as she declared about her novel *Jungfrau,* published also in 1936 (ix)), constituted as interesting to and interpellated by the new modernist discourses. Unwanted pregnancy and abortion are represented as temporal crises, threatening to the orientation of the woman subject in time, between past and future, the old and new. Abortion is both psychic and social, relational, context-bound and the progress of narrative time places the experiencing subject in history. The late modern feminine subject is positioned as shopper/*flâneuse,* in relation to her managed and regulated body, defined as object elsewhere by medicine and the biological sciences, delimited by the posited plasticity of the body, the 'making' of physical beauty (Matthews "Building the Body"). Stead's writing of the feminine modern doesn't allow a space outside commodity culture for the experience of the everyday and her everyday explicitly includes the sexual and reproductive experiences of women. Abortion becomes commodity in the expansion of economic logic into the private sphere; no longer natural crime nor witches' magic. The two positions, of cabbage-wife and lover-whore, are differently placed in relation to commodity culture, and in *The Beauties and Furies* this is a writing of the inter-constitution of patriarchy and capitalism. The inorganic of commodity culture, roaring technologism, the fetishising of the material, the 'man-made', draws a line which excludes the organic 'cabbage wife', the fleshy mother-woman, who occupies the space of the private, the home, the interior (Walter Benjamin *Charles Baudelaire* 168), apparently excluded from the domains of worker and consumer, as the modes of being-in-capitalism. The lover-woman finds her place as sex worker, producing desire, in exchange for dinners and hotel rooms, constructed as the woman of artifice, of fashion, made and producing, a machine for desire, as she is in the fictions of Jean Rhys and Colette. Walter Benjamin places her in the modern city, in Paris cafes and theatres, walking the boulevards and arcades, herself as whore, representing *ambiguity*. Ambiguity is close to ambivalence but significantly is not an emotion, nothing present or felt in herself. She's an image, instead, or an abstraction and, for Benjamin, this abstraction is stasis or a point of standstill.

> Ambiguity is the figurative appearance of the dialectic, the law of the dialectic at a standstill. This standstill is Utopia, and the dialectical image therefore a dream image: a fetish. The arcades, which are both house and stars, provide such an image. And such an image is provided by the whore, who is seller and commodity in one.
>
> (Benjamin 171)

The lover-woman is seller and commodity in one: her mode is self-distantiation, the shop-keeper of her body. The "rationalisation of reproduction" writes pregnancy as product and the female body as instrument. In that context, the modern feminine subject, aborting her fleshy, vegetable pregnancy, struggles to achieve a middle class individuality, rational, controlling, consuming or 'choosing' the technology that has regulated her.

Elvira and Blanche are in the company of the characters of other Western European and English women novelists: Olivia, in Lehmann's *Weather in the Streets,* Anna from Jean Rhys' *Voyage in the Dark* (1934), Colette's characters, especially in the short story "Gribiche" (1937) and Anaïs Nin's first person moderns, all of them 'marginal' women in the masculine world of commerce and bars in the capitalist metropolis. Insofar as a feminine literary modernism is evident in Australian writing before 1950, no characters seem to accord so distinctly with Elvira or Blanche, or even Letty Fox, Stead's Parisian and New Yorker women, as do these French and English representations. The 'flowering' innocence and virginal abstraction of Thea in *Jungfrau,* for example, are qualities already disallowed in the modern sophisticate of the European metropolis, whose sexed identity is identified much more clearly as an economic resource. *The Beauties and Furies* is directly concerned with the possibility of a feminine modern and in ways similar to but also critical of the abortion plots of Lehmann, Rhys and Colette. *The Weather in the Street* and *Voyage in the Dark,* similarly to *The Beauties and Furies,* pursue the effect of socially unsanctioned sex and love on single (in)dependent women—their social isolation and economic insecurity—and plot in pregnancy as the unfortunate but inevitable effect of their condition in capitalism. Stead's text is comic and darkly cynical, however, offering an ironised rendering of what for Lehmann manifests as melancholy and for Rhys is desperation.

In writing the abortion dilemma as the dilemma of the 'marginal' woman in capitalism, distanced from her body and herself in increasingly hegemonic systems of objectification, unable to 'decide' her own abortion plot, Stead also allows the marginal woman to confront her own construction as surface and reflection in the aesthetic of the modern. Elvira's attempts at self-definition abound in *The Beauties and Furies,* filtered and mediated by the cynicism of Blanche and the idealisation of Oliver, and yet they are never authoritative, remaining in contest with the web of references from which they emerge. The marginal woman is financially insecure and thus emotionally so, and necessarily predatory in a way pre-constructed for her in the writings of sexuality in modernity. Blanche invokes Baudelaire's writing of the modern Parisian woman when, soon after Elvira's abortion, she drunkenly admits to the infatuated Oliver that she (and everyone else) has syphilis. She quotes Baudelaire on the fatal poison of passion embraced—the languid death of internal decay (221)—and they discuss this while Elvira waits at home for Oliver in pain after the abortion. When Oliver finally returns to Elvira, he reads to her, first "the scene in the lying-in hospital in James Joyce's *Ulysses,* then some of his poems" (231). This intertextuality and the self-conscious invocation of a modernist canon seems to me a reconsideration of women's sexuality and reproductivity as mythic cultural clichés. Elvira's pregnancy figures in the context of other tropes of femininity that are self-conscious references to the over-coding of femininity in literature and modern culture.

This is the writing of femininity's literariness, its fabulous mythical history of roles, in the context of an explosion of references to the feminine as cliché: Coromandel the hamadryad and her mad, opera singing mother; Paul's virginal, middle-class cousin, waiting-to-be-wife; Elvira's lover-women and cabbage wives; the Baudelaire-quoting prostitute who seduces Oliver when he emerges from a week of tending to Elvira after her abortion: "Je suis belle, ô mortels!" she recites (233). Drunken Blanche is "playing a part" with her excessive stage accent (221); she is a lovely "bird of prey" (220), a "Circe" declares Oliver (222). Finally she pulls on "her airs of '*grande dame*'" (224) and to put him off asks "You know the Frog Princess? In the daytime, when you have seen me, I am only an ugly frog, ugh!" (225). The baroque style of *The Beauties and Furies* means this list of referencing is almost endless; it is the tissue of which Stead makes the life of the Paris cafe set as style, as reference. To a large extent, the concern of the novel can be seen to be the fabulous 'nature' of womanhood, showcasing a variety of archetypes, mythological, literary, theatrical; all of them powerful via associated meanings and stories but none of them 'natural' or real. They are all masquerades, witnessed by the male characters, who have the power of a gaze and thus grounded identity. They are the beauties and furies, and *embonpoint* and parturition are just part of one stereotypical feminine role, one which occasions a heightening of women's relation to men and their specificity as women, in the representational history of the feminine. Reading to Elvira, Oliver picks up a French grammar book and reads an example of an *adjectifs dans la liaison*: "Ex.: Divi(n)-*n*enfant" (237). In the meantime, Elvira is in pain and long suffering under his shouts and effusiveness (231).

The 'new' and ironic play of feminine archetypes is a modernist topos in *The Beauties and Furies,* highlighting available modes of subjectivity in order to underline their breakdown, their refashioning, the Nietzschean challenge to system and morality construed as anti-conventional by the avant-garde. It is the monstrous modern feminine, monstrous in its transformation, as masquerade, metaphor and allegory; femininity as performance, as practice, as it has been re-identified by Irigaray and Judith Butler, among others. Susan Sheridan suggests that Stead's fiction proposes "that we *are* what we act, that femininity is lived as it is performed in society and culture. [Her writing] enacts splits between these patriarchal ideologies and women's desires, yet both are presented as equally part of their reality, and not, as in liberal humanism, as the shadow and the substance of experience" (13). Brigid Rooney pursues performativity in Stead further, in a reading of *The Man Who Loved Children.* Stead's Marxism is at work in the performative model perhaps because it is an anti-humanist Marxism, cynical and savagely revealing of patriarchal capitalism's ability to critically disable women, in their interpellation within impossible roles. The ordinary role of abortion as revelation, as a truth effect, is in abeyance in *The Beauties and Furies,* covered over by layers of intertextuality and irony. As more instrumentalist modernists like Eleanor Dark do, Stead employs Freudian plots as diagnostics, analysing the symptoms of femininity. Unlike Dark, however, her speculation about these doesn't invoke the dangerous pathological instability of the feminine 'natural', then grounding the legal and psychological discourse of abortionist trials in the 1920s and 1930s, in discounting the conscious ability of the aborting woman to act and choose, beyond a victim role. Instead, Stead's ironising of femininity as performance can also be gentle and sympathetic, and her monsters and pathologies speak their symptoms as marks of oppression, as instruments of social critique.

Abortion for the feminine modern is often a vertiginous and exposing threat to sanity, as it is in Cusack's *Jungfrau,* a crucial moment of reckoning when identity breaks down into its constitutive parts: memory, pain, language, time/space. Dark's *Prelude to Christopher,* Olive Moore's *Fugue* and the *Weather in the Streets,* Olivia's pain-induced delirium, all invoke the spectre of insanity as a correlate of reproductive misadventure and abortion. The abortion in Jean Rhys' *Voyage in the Dark* has occasioned readings of this collapse of identity as characteristic of feminist modernism, in its lapses in narrative progression and logic, its breakdown in the structures of language, the shifts in time and space, speaking position and points of view.[3] For Deborah Kelly Kloepfer, Anna's abortion scene is the climax of the "hallucination and syntactical rupture" of the text: "the boundaries of language begin to break down, a disorder that is reflected in the structure of the text" (74). She reads this as the irruptions of the maternal into the patriarchal symbolic, from Julia Kristeva's pre-oedipal semiotic, exposing itself in the nonsense of language, as the anti-logic disrupting the either/or.

> At the moments of most intimate confrontation with the maternal form—the mother's death, the daughter's abortion—the text almost abandons the surrounding thetic structure. As the novel progresses in the "present," syntax and chronology are increasingly ruptured by the maternal subtext, mother as both memory and rhythm break through the surface of English life and language.
>
> (Kloepfer 74)

The writing of Elvira's abortion, its aftermath, her metritis and pain, is similarly a reworking of the conventions of narrative time and space, but its dissonances are not as easily read as the irruption of the Kristevan maternal, I'd suggest. Blanche suggests that "Love is a tête-à-tête: a third person spoils it: a child is a third person. It is the woman's fault. She loves the child more than the father." But Elvira explicitly rejects the oedipal model to declare her identity as lover woman, under the abortionist's window (217), and the cachet of oedipality in writing maternity as a site of nostalgia and excessive meaning is explicitly resisted. I could suggest that this is part of the resistance of Stead's texts to the reading method by which poststructuralist psychoanalysis privileges modernist challenges to narrative convention as the only access to a political or feminist alternative meaning, outside language. History, memory, consumption, production and labour relations are all contexts in which sexuality is deeply imbricated in *The Beauties and Furies,* and Stead's attention to deconstructing or undercutting the aspirations of Elvira expose her as a mere petulant product of those contexts, including language.

In keeping with Elvira's distinction between mother-women and lover-women, her abortion aftermath writes her as daughter, the marginal modern, refusing the linking of absorption with the role of mother and her context of the bourgeois family and oedipality; that is, allowing abortion to be a refusal of this. She waits at home, fevered and jealous of Oliver's time, lonely and self-pitying: "New pains, a spasm coming every ten minutes, had begun early in the evening and were now intense: the back of her head throbbed, her heart beat heavily and she was fevered. . . . She only was alone . . . She was alone and disgraced here" (237). Oliver has left her to wander Paris and Elvira is in pain and acutely conscious of her position or role, abandoned and 'fallen'. Her uterus is inflamed and her pain is measured as fever and impatience by Stead: "Her escapade brought her pain, fever and impatience. She had the metritis that Blanche had warned her of" (238). This fever escalates as spiralling self-concern and jealousy.

> She blushed and cried in her fever. She could see the sullen sky with its lacklustre powdered stars. Never had she seen so high, so ominous and still a night. Now she was sure Oliver was with another woman.
>
> (237)

> She looked up at the still, breeding night, the soundless, close-wrapped night, and imagined it full of a thousand bedded loves, millions of murmurs in the dark of rooms, square miles of tumbled pillows, and somewhere amongst them Oliver's seraphic white smile, which could be seen in the dark, smiling into someone else's knotted hair and little ear. Pure tears of suffering fell down her face.
>
> (237)

The motif of the changing night sky is pervasive in *The Beauties and Furies*. It works as a changing reflection of a character's emotional state, cynically and obviously contradictory, as "so high, so ominous" is different to "close wrapped", the "breeding night". Elvira's cell-like solitude is opened into this mirror; her onanistic emotional journeys, her atomisation and alienation from the sky watch it become the city, Paris, which is in love, which is sex. The sky is her reflection, part of her solipsistic subjectivist preoccupations. This *is* her interior, a preoccupation with the external, with Oliver, and a raving elaborate imaging of the city of lovers, from which she, the half maternal, the image of the older, discarded, invalid wife (for she is none of these) is excluded or anxiously avoiding this exclusion. Her fears manifest and crowd her, become the city of lovers and she declares that she will return to Paul, her husband, who would have looked after her in this moment, "in this pass" as she calls it. For her, the abortion aftermath is helplessness and isolation and, even as Elvira rails against her fears and moans in pain, Stead's biting satire leaves her pleas as cliché, shallow and flimsy, assumed for show. Even as Oliver lies to her, having spent the evening with a young prostitute who recites Baudelaire, Elvira's complaints are hollow and petulant. "'I am in such pain,' she moaned. 'You were away when I was in introuble.'"

Her changing night-scapes, her oscillating fears, her solipsistic emotional fluctuations are all features of her alienation, her position as chattel and object, whose very fears and physical pain require witness, whose logic is a semiotic of surface. As this scene allows, Elvira's characteristic aboulia is constituted in abortion. Even as abortion is an act and its procurement a deci-

sion, an end to something and a return to something, so it is also a suspension of her life as process, an interruption to relation and continuity and in that interruptiveness abortive, a suspension of action, making her invalid. This is temporisation, invalided, indecisive, in a space of *playing for time*; (Molly Bloom's lying-in bed, the bed scene in Olive Moore's *Fugue*, Thea's body distantiation in *Jungfrau*). Time is suspended in a space outside history. Notions of progress and future are hostage to immediacy and then to the call of the past, the play of memory, of a distanced space brought closer through time (consider Anna's maternal extra-colonial in Rhys's *Voyage in the Dark*). Elvira's temporised space is not maternal, however. The vacillating movement of equivalences that is her equivocation is not in a space of fulfilment or unity, but rather its fluidity is in the pendulous movement of anxiety; of trauma and denial; the hysteric's refusal/suspension of the demand of the father's either/or; that is, the time/space of the daughter. Abortion is her return from interruption, her access to the old space of the lover-woman, a nostalgia not for the maternal but for the child's oedipal moment, time starting again. The foetus gone, she herself becomes child: "With a young man, she was young. She would give up the child. They would start again, children, hand in hand: they would give each other pure glances untouched by blame or regret" (162).

This confrontation with her own construction as surface is the consequence of Elvira's impossibility, the material condition of the bourgeois woman outside the middle-class family. Her abortion exposes her as chattel and object to herself; exposes her self-distantiation and her alienation from the roles and narratives of the family. Not maternal, she attempts a return to the role of the daughter and thus reinvokes the authority of the father, returning from the interruption of her temporisation to once again the logic of the either/or. These impossibilities challenge and collapse the ideologies that place sex and reproduction in a causal relation, and highlight their roles within hegemonic mechanisms of fetishising consumption and objectification. The modernism of the metropolis includes the character of the marginal woman as trope, a symptom of the modern as *style,* as Raymond Williams invokes it: as self-generating reference, cynical and disenchanted and at odds with convention, so far as convention designates the traditional bourgeoisie content with itself. *The Beauties and Furies* asks this marginal woman to choose to act for herself and, in her inability to do this, Elvira exposes the impossibility of this modernist trope as anything but trope, exposes it as a trope of its self concern, enacting an atomisation that makes its embodiment unbearable, impossible. She is the monster of indecision and it is this same monster, consumer capitalism, the condition of boredom, that entraps her.

Notes

1. Olivia in Rosamund Lehmann's *The Weather in the Streets* describes herself, when pregnant, as a vegetable, a "marrow", passive and unconscious.

2. Rita Felksi's work on the gender of modernity relies on Gianni Vattimo's definition of modernity as "that era in which being modern becomes a value, or rather, it becomes the fundamental value to which all other values refer" (99). She makes an argument for shifts in temporal measures as the condition of the modern, rather than more material factors, and these shifts are towards the "necessary value of the new" (170).

3. See Judith Kegan Gardiner (*Rhys, Stead*) for further comparison between Stead and Rhys.

Works Cited

Benjamin, Walter. *Charles Baudelaire: A Lyric Poet in the Era of High Capitalism.* Trans. Harry Zohn. London: Verso, 1983.

Collette. *The Collected Stories of Collette.* Ed. and Intro. Robert Phelps. New York: Farrar Strauss Giroux, 1983.

Connor, Steven. *Theory and Cultural Value.* Oxford, UK and Cambridge, US: Blackwell, 1992.

Correspondence of Literature Censorship Board, Canberra, Regarding Christina Stead's *Letty Fox* and *A Little Tea, A Little Chat.* Australian Archives, Canberra, Series A425/1 Item 1949/1976.

Cusack, Dymphna. *Jungfrau.* [1936] Intro. Florence James. Ringwood, Vic: Penguin, 1989.

Dark, Eleanor. *Prelude to Christopher.* [1934] Sydney: Halstead Press, 1999.

Devanny, Jean. *The Butcher Shop.* [1926] Intro. Heather Roberts. Auckland: Auckland University Press, 1981.

Ellis, Havelock. *Sex in Relation to Society.* London: Heinemann, 1937.

Felski, Rita. *The Gender of Modernity.* Harvard University Press, 1995.

Ferrier, Carole. *Jean Devanny, Romantic Revolutionary.* Melbourne: Melbourne University Press, 1999.

Hollenburg, Donna. "Abortion, Identity Formation and the Expatriate Woman Writer: H.D. and Kay Boyle in the Twenties." *Twentieth Century Literature* 40.4 (1994): 499-517.

Irigaray, Luce. *This Sex Which is Not One.* Trans. Catherine Porter and Carolyn Burke. Ithaca, N.Y.: Cornell University Press, 1985.

Kegan Gardiner, Judith. *Rhys, Stead, Lessing and the Politics of Empathy.* Bloomington and Indianapolis: Indiana University Press, 1989.

———. "'Caught but not Caught': Psychology and Politics in Christina Stead's 'The Puzzle-headed Girl'." *World Literature Written in English* 32.1 (1992): 26-41.

Kloepfer, Debra Kelly. *The Unspeakable Mother: Forbidden Discourse in Jean Rhys and H.D.* Ithaca and London: Cornell UP, 1989.

Lehmann, Rosamund. *The Weather in the Streets.* [1936] London: Virago, 1981.

Matthews, Jill Julius. "Normalising Modernity". *UTS Review,* Special Issue "Localising Modernity", 6.1 (2000): 4-10.

———. "Building the Body Beautiful." *Australian Feminist Studies* 5 (1987): 17-34.

Moore, Olive, (Constance Vaughan). *Fugue.* [1932] London and New York: Serpent's Tail, 1993.

Nin, Anaïs. *Under a Glass Bell.* [1948] London: Penguin, 1978.

Rigg, Julie and Julie Copeland, eds. *Coming Out! Women's Voices, Women's Lives.* Melbourne: Nelson and Australian Broadcasting Corporation, 1985.

Rhys, Jean. *Voyage in the Dark.* [1934] Harmondsworth, Middlesex: Penguin, 1982.

Rooney, Brigid. "She Casts Herself as Revolutionary: Performance and Performativity in Christina Stead's *The Man who Loved Children.*" *Current Tensions: Proceedings of the 18th Annual Conference, ASAL.* Eds. Sharyn Pierce and Philip Neilson. Association for the Study of Australian Literature, 1997. 129-136.

Rowley, Hazel. *Christina Stead: A Biography.* Port Melbourne, Vic.: William Heinemann, 1993.

Sheridan, Susan. *Christina Stead.* London: Harvester, Wheatsheaf, 1988.

Spivak, Gayatri Chakravorty. "From Haverstock Hill Flat to U.S. Classroom, What's Left of Theory?" *What's Left of Theory? New Work on the Politics of Literary Theory,* Eds. Judith Butler, John Guillory and Kendall Thomas. London and New York: Routledge, 2000. 1-39.

Stead, Christina. *The Beauties and Furies.* [1936] London: Virago, 1982.

———. *Lettie Fox: Her Luck.* [1946] Sydney: Angus and Robertson, 1983.

———. *I'm Dying Laughing.* Ed. R. G. Geering. London: Virago, 1986.

Vattimo, Gianni. *The End of Modernity: Nihilism and Hermeneutics in Postmodern Culture.* Baltimore: The Johns Hopkins UP, 1988.

Wilding, Michael. "Christina Stead's *The Puzzle Headed Girl*: The Political Context." *Words and Word-smiths: A Volume for H.L. Rogers*. Ed. G. Barnes, J. Gunn, S. Jenson, L. Jobling. Sydney: Department of English, University of Sydney, 1989. 147-173.

Williams, Raymond. *Marxism and Literature*. Oxford: Oxford University Press, 1977.

———. *The Politics of Modernism: Against the New Conformists*. London: Verso, 1989.

Wilt, Judith. *Abortion, Choice and Contemporary Fiction: The Armageddon of the Maternal Instinct*. Chicago: University of Chicago Press, 1990.

Rosemary Lancaster (essay date 2008)

SOURCE: Lancaster, Rosemary. "'All that Glitters': Illusory Worlds in Christina Stead's *The Beauties and Furies* (1936) and *House of All Nations* (1938)." In *Je Suis Australienne: Remarkable Women in France, 1880-1945*, pp. 124-50. Crawley, Australia: University of Western Australian Press, 2008.

[*In the following essay, Lancaster studies Stead's "mix of documentation, satire and fantasy" in her depiction of 1920s and 1930s Paris in her novels* The Beauties and Furies *and* House of All Nations. *She calls the former "a counterfoil for exposing western capitalist oppression" and the latter "a stinging Balzacian 'comédie humaine' of her times."*]

The end of World War I, marked by the signing of the Armistice on 11 November 1918, was only officially over when the Peace Treaty of Versailles was enacted on 18 January 1919.[12] But the treaty, over whose terms the Allies hotly argued, left Germany embittered, France vengeful, and Britain and the United States occupying different middle ground, the whole enterprise being termed 'an unhappy compromise' by the British diplomat, historian and politician Harold Nicolson, and a 'Carthaginian [or no] peace' by the economist John Maynard Keynes.[3] Clearly, the punitive territorial, military and economic measures the treaty imposed on Germany fanned national resentments on which Hitler and his Fascist followers capitalised. The 1920s, then, in France, as elsewhere, were uneasy years. At the same time international alarm gathered momentum during the stock market frenzy that grew out of postwar inflation in America and peaked in the world-shattering Wall Street Crash of 1929.[4] The 'roaring twenties', what the French called the 'années folles', were heady but precarious times. When the Australian Christina Stead stepped onto French soil in 1929 she entered a land of political uncertainties that had been festering for eleven years. That world became the setting for her two 'Paris'

novels: **The Beauties and Furies** (1936) and **House of All Nations** (1938)—one a counterfoil for exposing western capitalist oppression, the other, the fictional model of a Europe in the throes of economic collapse and political turmoil. In the latter, she made France the example of nations facing financial crises even as Hitler was unnervingly rising to power.

Christina Ellen Stead was born in Sydney on 17 July 1902. Her childhood was not a happy one, or so her writings betray. Her mother died when she was two and her strict though clever naturalist father expected her to nurture her younger siblings more than girls in most families did. A distrust of family relationships is everywhere apparent in her oeuvre. On the other hand the young Christina was intelligent, inquiring and articulate, and a wide and discerning reader, largely thanks to her father's influence and fecund mind. As a teenager she yearned to travel, deepen her understanding of literature, acquire cultivation and see the world. In fact she was to remain a restless spirit, even when she returned to Australia in 1974. By then she was a widow and seventy-two.

Stead left Australia for England in 1928. On arrival in London she found work with a company of grain merchants, where she met her future life partner and husband, the brilliant economist and writer, William Blake.[5] Their relationship, an emotionally and intellectually enduring one, was to see them live an itinerant working life as they moved between Europe and America, initially on business affairs, later as authors involved in publication and translation in addition to their respective writing careers. Her work, which includes novels, novellas and short stories, draws imaginatively on her and Blake's singularly nomadic existence and notoriously on the wide range of people she met as she moved between countries and abodes. On those grounds she was somewhat spurned as a 'cosmopolitan' writer by her Australian contemporaries,[6] although she never denied her roots and wrote creatively about her homeland from abroad.[7] Nonetheless, her first novel, **Seven Poor Men of Sydney**, in progress when she and Blake arrived in Paris in 1929, was received to acclaim when it was published in 1934. It covered a career that spanned forty-nine years until her death in 1983. Today she is recognised as one of Australia's most verbally clever (if intellectually daunting) writers; concomitantly appreciation of her social acuity and stylistic diversity has justifiably soared.[8]

When Blake and Stead moved to Paris he took up a senior post and she a position as a secretary in their merchant company's American Travelers' Bank. They would remain in Paris until 1935, when political uncertainty and Blake's not entirely unwitting role in the bank's dubious affairs obliged them to leave.[9] The events and her job, which inspired **House of All Na-**

tions, gave Stead a firm insight into the running of international banking organisations and the complexity of deals made behind closed office doors. But she and Blake also enjoyed an interesting social life, amicably spent in the cafés and bars close to the office and their rented rooms. Where Stead was quiet and shy, Blake was gregarious and talkative, but both were insatiably curious, well read and politically aware; together they befriended numerous Anglo-Saxons in transit, as were they. Itinerancy is, indeed, one of Stead's major literary themes. It is pathetically the case in *The Beauties* [*The Beauties and Furies*], whose English protagonists, more talk than action, waste the chance offered by their travels to emotionally learn and grow.

Judging by her letters, Stead blossomed in Paris under the spell of her ebullient and attentive companion. With his appetite for life, history, food, languages, places and fun, Blake feted her around the city, introducing her to its wonders and charms with the purpose of a teacher and the devotion of one in love.[10] At the time she facetiously wrote to her Sydney friend, Nellie Molyneux:

> To be fed, sunned, dressed in grand chic, petted, educated, loved, indulged, taken (intelligently) all over Paris, musiced, champagned, cabareted, zooed, parked, taxied, walked and otherwise ambulated, that I regard as misery of the last order.[11]

Such words reveal much, of course, about the lifestyle Stead led, the activities she enjoyed and the extent of Blake's zeal—infectious, one gathers, judging from a further hyperbolically-phrased comment to her friend:

> I am very unhappy. There are only 5,000 bookstores, artstores, flowershops, little dogs and cafés in Paris: only 40,000 little girls with a grand air and futurist dresses, poets with capes, 3-foot sombreros and sharp faces, waiters, taxi-drivers and petit-rentier bourgeois reading the Bourse quotation, students, Montmartrois and incroyables: only 10,000 beautiful facades, iron balconies, kaleidoscope windows, giant pillars, gold, silver, green and red decors, chaste or abandoned— there is only, in Paris, the most charming, civilised and decorative of cities whose native gaiety is intelligent, sustained and elegant: therefore, I am very miserable here. I am contemplating returning to Darlinghurst, or Murrurundi.[12]

Stead's time in Paris, when governments in Europe were tottering and the stock exchange was volatile, aroused her moral consciousness to levels of intensity she was never to forgo. The Great Depression, capitalist profiteering, the rise of Fascism and the spread of Communism were political realities that deeply concerned her. Blake's Marxist persuasions she quickly and fervently espoused.[13] In June 1935, in Paris, while Hitler was having literature he deemed threatening burned, she attended the Popular Front's First International Congress of Writers for the Defence of Culture, an anti-

Fascist writers' lobby, where she encountered such literary notables as Gide, Aragon and Malraux. There, commonly ideologically bound, the 220 attendees, all leftist in persuasion, most Communist in creed, thrashed out how they might best address the new dictatorships plaguing Europe and the perceived weaknesses of the capitalist paradigm. For her part, she was the British delegation's unofficial secretary and her report on the event, **'The Writers Take Sides',** while representing the commitment of the group, positioned her as one who would repeatedly argue against the 'disorders', 'anomalies' and 'decadence' of the 'bourgeois world'.[14] Alternatively, she never saw herself as a propagandist or proletarian writer, but rather as one who offered a picture of what she observed. If Leftist in leaning, she was able to see faults within all political systems and from all points of view. What she could not tolerate was hypocrisy, injustice and dishonesty.[15] She believed what mattered in the getting and practice of wisdom was open-mindedness, debate and healthy incertitude. Equally, she conditionally considered the impact and theoretical contributions of Darwin, Nietzsche and Freud. It is that rich ferment of 1930s events and ideologies that gives *The Beauties* and *House of All Nations* their contemporary edge. Few of their characters come through their adventures unscathed by the worlds that bred them or the societies that challenge their beliefs and ideals.

* * *

In the opening chapter of *The Beauties* Christina Stead proffers a striking image of a showy 1930s Paris, conjured up in the words of one of her most decadent (and articulate) characters, the malevolent Marpurgo. The significance of his words sharpens, ironically enough, as the novel unfolds. The Paris its naïve but hedonistically motivated English protagonists romantically seek turns out to be a corrupt and tawdry world, though they are content, in the seeking, to indulge in its titillations as their relationship rapidly fails. The 'land of enchantment'[16] Marpurgo hails in his thinly disguised jaded wisdom is a place of ready seductions and glamorous veneer. Paris, he remarks, is the place where

> . . . there are more false diamonds and false eyelashes than anywhere else, where the gowns are more elegant, the complexions more enamelled, laces finer, shoes smaller, heels higher, the gait more billowy, the fans better painted and the breasts set more to advantage, than in all the world; where that violent liquor love concealed in the heart's smoky hard jewel, is finer strained and thicker distilled, more adulterated and oftener aspersed, the blood flows wilder in passion and revolt, the beds are oftener stained with blood and love and the river oftener thickened with blood and tears: the garden of lovers, joy of youth, nest of revolution, city of thrice-fired blood![17]

There is a warning to be had in Marpurgo's appraisal, if not at the point of its pronouncement to his young love-blinded English listeners, come to Paris to embark on an adulterous affair, then within the larger spectrum of what both 'Paris' novels thematically portray. *House of All Nations,* too, points to a city of low ideals. There the characters are predominantly involved in the type of frenzied banking operations that characterised Paris in the anxious lead-up to World War II. They too, even more than the protagonists of *The Beauties,* look to the transient delights the capital offers, not with any measure or discernment, but with the lust and profligacy that befits the greedy rich and self-serving ambitious and bold.

The Beauties and *House of All Nations* are early examples of that sparkling Stead mix of documentation, satire and fantasy. The Paris she evokes is one she observed and knew well, though the larger-than-life characters that move within in it—visitors, locals, opportunists—are overwhelmingly of the ne'er-do-well, egotistical kind: at once the products and the exploiters of the societies from which they spring. The authorial view, then, is no kindly one. Stead looks upon a 'grab and graft'[18] world, epitomised in the flawed characters of her invention who seek gratification or advancement by taking from others what they can. In *The Beauties* that world is a recognisably not-so-gay post-1920s one, stringently portrayed it all its expatriate (and local) decline: the idle English lovers, drifting habitués of the city's cafés and bars, find little in the course of their adventures to satisfy their dreams. In *House of All Nations,* the focus is, rather, on the city's financial milieux and the kind of risky capitalist enterprises that spectacularly rose and fell in the unstable economic climate that followed the Crash and prevailed in the jittery Europe of pre-World War II. But Stead looks, too, to the literary legacy of Balzac and Maupassant, each a merciless critic of the capital's coveters of money, sex and power.[19] In *House of All Nations,* especially, she constructs a stinging Balzacian 'comédie humaine' of her times.

The Beauties opens with the heroine, Mrs Elvira Western, travelling across the French countryside by train, on her way to Paris to meet her student lover, Oliver Fenton, who has pledged his love and munificent desire to pluck her from her staid marriage and bourgeois home.[20] On her lap lies his letter, calling her to Paris, which she reads while making acquaintance with a fellow traveller, the Italian Marpurgo who later callously intrudes on their lives. But the letter, despite its effusiveness, reveals an elopement that is both escape and escapade: Oliver imagines Elvira 'at home', 'grumping over a meal' with her bourgeois doctor husband, Paul, or seated by the fireside 'contented in habitual melancholy'[21] and reminds her that he has risen from his English working-class origins to become a scholar and participant in Paris's revolutionary affairs. 'Wake up,' he urges, 'come to life before it is too late: before the thorns interlock and crib you forever . . . enjoy the youth and young love you never had . . . I'll breathe my whole life into you.'[22] In the event, Oliver's Prince Charming promises prove short-lived. What follows in the book is but the relation of the affair's inexorable disintegration as the lovers deliberate the pros and cons of a commitment of which they quickly tire.

Stead's characters typically speak in the idiom that betrays their ingrained traits. At times they are given to self-reflexive perspicacity; more often they are oblivious to their flaws. Oliver's letter, pompously composed with its mixture of florid phrasings and banal amorous overtures ('I love you, you love me, we both love each other: you be good to me and I will be good to you'), smacks of infatuation, despite his claim that he is 'not a boy'.[23] Paris he describes with clichéd sentimentality as the land of poetical sighs, whose beauty he conflates with Elvira's even before she sets foot on its soil:

> On moonlight nights, when everyone walks with his shade, I pretend we are here together. You are the moon of beauty and I a moonstruck poet. My little glass of water on the bedroom table, when the moon sails high above the narrow street, shines with one eye, a little moon, and I go out. The skies are starling-dark—your hair; the town and its towers discoloured—your breast; the river, curdled, bubbling—your voice; the glistening brown-buds of the first-sprouters—your eyes.[24]

As for himself, he beguiles, 'How can any woman resist my entreaties . . . How can any young woman resist Paris in the spring? How can you resist me in the spring?'[25] If Elvira is beautiful, Paris, he believes, will raise her to new heights of continental charm. Part of his mission is to smarten her up, though, for all he pretends to be her liberator, it is not her character he hopes to alter, but, quite simply her looks. He enjoins:

> A French woman built like you would build up her bosom. I'll take you to a dressmaker who will study your style, and bring out your femininity. You must go, the very first thing, to the Printemps, or to Antoine, and have your hair done too. Oh, you'll spend fortunes on yourself before you've been in Paris long. You'll be quite a different woman . . . You'll be splendid when you're dressed like a French woman. Everyone will say, How adaptable she is.[26]

In fact, despite what Paris offers—a fresh start, a different appearance, sexual freedom, geographical distance—neither Elvira nor Oliver finds the spirit or will to change. Oliver, a compulsive philanderer, retains the ideal of possessing a 'woman playing in a house', her 'hand wandering over the ivories . . . a woman, a soft, reluctant voice, music, flowers';[27] the soon pregnant Elvira, after much prevaricating upon whether or not to keep Oliver's child, opts for an abortion, and returns to her husband, her linen and bourgeois ease. The wakers are after all sleepers. The fairy-tale has no substance at all. What Marpurgo cynically calls a 'perfectly modern love-affair'[28] is no more than a shabby holiday fling.

The Beauties is not a novel of events; its characters, despite much puffing and blowing, do not practise what they preach: leopards who do not change their spots, chained to attitudes they barely forsake, touting fuzzy ideals they are too lazy to uphold. As such they are typical Stead representatives of the faint-hearted and aimless, the very opposite of the energetic and purpose-ful (though no less morally thin) characters of *House of All Nations,* still less of those others of her novels who have the courage to act and reform.[29] In that respect *The Beauties* is a scathing indictment of human self-delusion and lethargy.

Much of *The Beauties* is concerned with failed ambi-tions and unrealistic ideals, no more than in the arena of professional endeavour and political affairs. For the bushy-tailed Oliver, a doctoral student of history, ostensibly in Paris to hone his thesis on the Workers' Move-ment in France, 1871-1904, the time seems ripe for him to give expression to his professed Leftist ideals. Throughout the novel he engrosses himself in the odd protest meeting, the odd café debate, enough to con-vince himself he is an activist and the friend of the poor. Of his part in the workers' United Front protest of 27 May 1934, an allusion to France's real response to the wrath unleashed by the Left on the Right in the wake of the Stavisky affair, he grandly recalls:[30]

> He had been called 'camarade' so often during the day, had seen so many red flags and so many sinewy arms lifted into the air, had heard the 'Internationale' and 'The Young Guard' so often, that he was no longer himself, a piecemeal student grubbing on collegiate benches, but a glorious foot-soldier in an army millions strong, sure of battery, but sure of victory.[31]

In fact the hollowness of Oliver's professions is every-where apparent, whether in the form of his 'arm-chair' politicking,[32] or his talent for intellectual expediency. His thesis, conveniently cast in the past is, he reckons, distant enough to make archival research easier, and re-mote enough from British affairs not to offend English examiners of a conservative or xenophobic mind. In other words, he hopes 'to look like a socialist who knows the amenities'[33] and how to get on in the world. Others, his observers, are hardly fooled. Marpurgo, not one to mince words, pronounces him 'a coward . . . the summit of well-bred nonentity . . . an inkpot-valiant', for whom 'Marxism is just the newer label for a smart young man who must be up to date', and atten-dance at workmen's meetings a means 'to be in the swim'.[34] For Elvira's husband, Paul, who comes to Paris to fetch Elvira home, he is a fence-sitter, 'not a Lenin-ist, or a Stalinist, or a Marxist, and not a Trotskyist ei-ther, but some shade of opinion of his own he has worked out . . . in between cafés and scribbling in . . . Archives'.[35] Thus is the presumed hallowedness of aca-demia exposed as no less open to abuse than the busi-ness of business or any other selfishly spurred human enterprise.

Political and professional insincerity are key issues in Stead's work. She and Blake were committed to their writing and their Marxist beliefs; materialism she de-tested; creativity she valued in others and practised with zeal. Oliver emerges as a failure in *The Beauties* not because he is a Marxist but because he cheats the sys-tem he pretends to embrace and the proletariat he claims to serve. Over that kind of duplicity Stead casts an un-forgiving eye. Whatever the different motivations of pseudo-socialist Oliver, bourgeois Elvira and lip-serving Marxist-cum-capitalist Marpurgo, they exhibit equal measures of hypocrisy. When Marpurgo urges the intel-ligent Oliver to get into business it is because he recog-nises in him double standards he shares. He may exude good taste: in food, in books, in liqueurs, in the gentle-manly pursuit of chess, but his little extravagances are paid for because of the success of his employers' dirty work ethic and his own complicity. There is something perversely anomalous in his private obsession with hand-made lacework, collected with the passion of the connoisseur, and his dealings as a lace-buyer for sellers of shoddy garments and marked-up job lots. The myth of Paris, seat of art and learning, is challenged by Stead's gallery of careerist rogues: not only Oliver, master of the intellectual short cut, but also by Mar-purgo and the opportunistic 'depression' and 'post-war' bosses he serves.[36] In *The Beauties,* the 'grab and graft' mentality of the consumer society is seen for the mod-ern canker it is. Stead looks to the nature of lace pro-duction as a real and metaphoric measure of how the economic power base lies in the hands of the exploit-ative few. 'We're not in the candlestick age', argues one of Marpurgo's managers . . .

> . . . we don't wear knee-breeches and ruffles . . . lace is proletarian now . . . What you want is pretentious, embossed, cheap, washable flowing stuff to put on cheap voile nighties . . . To-day you've got to be a cheap-jack, a thug, a bastard. You've got to forget art and steal your competitor's best selling design . . . This is an age of decay—you can plunder . . . You've got to be a man of your time.[37]

In *The Beauties* Stead develops the 'drama of the person' with attention to psychological detail.[38] While some 126 characters traverse the pages of *House of All Nations,* in the former the three characters of Elvira, Oliver and Marpurgo take centre stage. But individuals in Stead's work are but products of broad class systems that govern their gender and determine their lives. If the system is fallible they may rise above it; more often the strong exploit it and the weak buckle or comply. Not Marxist to the fanatical letter, but Marxist in orientation and sentiment, Stead looks to the never straightforward issue of human effort in the context of the tenets the West has imposed. Capitalism is a prime target; rising Fascism she disquietingly portrays. In *The Beauties* Marpurgo's Marxism barely conceals his capitalist cun-ning and Oliver, despite his assertions, is but a smug capitalist bourgeois. As for Elvira, Paris in the spring differs little from London in winter, the domestic hearth from the drab Paris hotel rooms in which she and Oliver thrash out the tedious binds of their affair. She is, and will remain, locked into the patriarchal values on which she was raised. If *The Beauties* is a domestic drama (where *House of All Nations* looks to the world of commerce), it is the sexual politics of her era Stead explores. Not a feminist in the strict sense (all human oppression concerned her and women, she thought, could be as conforming or conniving as men), her female characters are nonetheless trapped in established gender roles. For Stead's unbecoming fictitious trio the prevailing system rules.

Stead makes much of Elvira's beauty. *The Beauties'* title refers, at least in one of its uses, to the physicality of the bodies women have learnt to flaunt (or sell). Elvira knows her attractiveness gets her what she wants, even though it inhibits her from cultivating a deeper than skin-deep self. According to the cynical Marpurgo she is the classic 'enchantress',[39] 'putting out her flowers', 'spread[ing] her charms around', giving men 'the benefit of her eyes', the 'thought of her body'.[40] But for Elvira male approval is enough; the admiration (or love) of others is not returned; rather it feeds her vanity and confirms her belief that her body is the source of her power. One senses it on the occasion when Oliver spies on her as she emerges from her bath. Parading naked before the mirror, she passes her hands over her body, carries her breasts in her hands, kisses her arms, a shoulder, then, clothed in a gown, executes a kind of self-anointment (albeit with the most standard of feminine aids):

> She wandered about the room, giving her body hundreds of small attentions, using ear and nose syringes, sponges, files, scissors, chamois leather, swan's-down puffs, sticks of orange-wood, creams, powders, and the rouge that Oliver had brought her home.[41]

Elvira may resent having been a 'slave of the kitchen and bedroom'[42] and a 'hearthside wife',[43] but what she demands of her lovers effectively keeps her where she is. Love is possession. Life is making, not working towards, love. Men chase women. Women play 'the eternal game of hide-and-seek'.[44] Oliver forges a career. Despite being a Master of Arts, Elvira fritters her days away. Oliver is a 'playmate';[45] sleeping with him is 'an experiment'.[46] Uncommitted and idle, she perpetuates a feminine condition against which she bucks just long enough to persuade her that her old lifestyle is easier to maintain. But, like most Stead characters, Elvira pays a price for her selfish ways. Apathy brings boredom; changing partners, not convictions, brings satiety; travel is wandering; wandering breeds irresponsibility. Like an Emma Bovary, out for the grand passion, but not the investment of a loving self, Elvira opts for the instant gratifications of the flesh: sex without attachment, marriage (and adultery) without the trouble of motherhood. 'There are lover-women and mother-women', she confesses. 'I am the first sort.'[47] Paris, then, can offer nothing new to one who seeks no newness of self. A hotel room sought as another bed is not a Sleeping Beauty's boudoir. Oliver's choice of 'an old-fashioned hotel, with high, grand, elegant rooms, long brocade curtains'[48] is not received by the jaded Elvira with the same naïve joy. Looking upon 'the yellow-plated bedstead; the wallpaper covered with red palm-leaves', she remarks: 'It's so trite . . . Think of all the couples who have slept here before us! They make it stale.'[49] Then: 'Life's a pattern, and we're just shuttles rushing in and out.' For Elvira, life is mechanical. In it, one can have no creative role.

No single character is to blame in *The Beauties.* Rather, together its players construct an untenable world of unworkable ties. The arrival of Elvira's husband in Paris brings about an unsuitable *ménage à trois.* In his wake comes his cousin Sara, hoping to pick up the luckless man on the rebound and get the lover she never had. Hovering in the background is Elvira's cynical brother, accompanying the English cohort, with ready but bad advice. But Paris is also untenable because it is only ever considered a short-term solution to long-term ills. Paul, weak, dull, and indulgent, in Oliver's opinion, a 'big, tender, kind mug',[50] gives up the chase and retreats to England, his surgery and his home. Finally, he generously but foolishly separately finances Elvira and Oliver home. Oliver, fatigued by Elvira's unpredictable changes of heart, finds solace in a French woman, the exotic and buxom Coromandel, potentially a better companion, but, he tells Marpurgo, taken up casually as 'one of those romances of your city of light and love'.[51] For him, conceited and imprudent, infidelity begets infidelity as he sets out to prove his questionable manhood, lurching first into the arms of the unreliable Blanche, Elvira's prostitute café friend, then, while Elvira is recovering from her abortion, into those of a one-night stand. If, as he boasts to Marpurgo, 'the French women bring it out in you',[52] he looks neither far nor deeply to prove his point, and it is unsurprising that the scheming Blanche cheats him out of the money he lends her and that their affair is short lived.

Elvira's solution, while different from her juvenile paramour's, is comparably selfish and weak. Both 'sell out' to the 'amenities' in the strongest sense of those recurrent Stead terms. For Elvira, the call of possessions is too easy and too great. The values of Stead's bourgeois characters are generally too entrenched to be budged, and while she rarely intervenes to moralise, the choices they make and the opinions they offer speak for themselves. Marpurgo, vicious but not blind, is right in observing that Elvira, who 'loves her habits', is a 'pampered girl'.[53] 'Property', her husband recognises, is what she 'loves'.[54] Tired of her grubby hotel room, Elvira soon longs for her cluttered house, packed with the belongings of eight years of married life: 'curtains, silver dressing-table ware, vases [and] doyleys', 'soaps and cleansing materials always in stock',[55] hardly enough to fill the emotional desert she inhabits and the spiritual emptiness she rues. Elvira is at fault in having expected a miraculous make-over in Paris, but so too, Stead implies, is the feminine condition on to which she clings. She is an unwary spokeswoman for the oppressed of her sex when she bemoans:

> I came away with Oliver . . . but it is not just charm I was looking for, it was—a new life, a bath of the soul. I thought his charm and love would act like cold cream, and his inexperience like an astringent and give me a new skin, take away my mental wrinkles. Well, I find there is no such thing as a spiritual renaissance, at least not for a woman. We are too much nailed to a coffin of flesh, our souls are only plants, they are rooted in an earth of flesh. We need a home, security, comfort for our flesh before the mind can grow.[56]

When Oliver tells her he will look back to 'this great spring all my life' when they 'first joined hands and began to walk along the crazy pavement with flowers and moss coming through all the cracks', she rejoins: 'How suburban . . . That's what we are, you see: suburban, however wild we run . . . We are not fire and dew.'[57] It is that lack of vitality, that defeatism, that settling for banality that locks Elvira into her lot. 'Fire and dew', energy and spirit, attributes Stead admired, are not in her command. The melancholy of which Elvira complains is the cost born of willed subservience and pathological inertia.

The Beauties' title assumes its full meaning as the book grinds to its inevitable end. There the characters wind up their continental affairs as egotistically and destructively as each sees fit. Effectively, the 'beauties' (pretty, youthful Oliver and Elvira, clever Marpurgo and Coromandel) become 'furies' just long enough to vent their discontent on others before they slip back into old lives or oblivion. When Marpurgo slyly tells Oliver: 'It's hard to leave Paris, eh? She has many beauties—and furies',[58] he means that Paris provides the seductions one hopes to find. Later, he extrapolates, Oliver's 'three furies' are 'Elvira, Coromandel, the occasional whore'.[59] But each of the book's characters exhibits a 'fury' of his or her vengeful kind. Marpurgo, jealous of Oliver's relationship with Coromandel, maliciously contrives a meeting between her and Elvira to expose Oliver's infidelity. Subsequently he writes to Paul telling him of Oliver's treachery, enough to encourage the cuckolded man to call his wife home. After a final argument with Elvira, Oliver runs off with Coromandel, who inveigles him into the country, giving her time to ruin his chances of reconciliation with his lover and for Elvira to pack up and leave.

The romantic Paris Oliver envisaged as he set out on his amorous quest seems emptied of his presence, when, returning to the city with Coromandel, he looks upon the spectacle of its throng. While he reckons he will always 'mourn' it as 'the country of the heart',[60] it hovers before and above him as a place to which he no longer belongs. The last glimpses of the city before the book's close are ironically his. It is not the Paris he promised Elvira, the Paris of pen and paper, of cliché and dream, but rather the Paris that will continue to hum and thrive well after he has gone:

> The Place de l'Opéra was like quicksands and undertows with regiments of all ages and kinds drifting back and forth across the roads as the circular traffic stayed and went. There stood the solid cavernous sepia Opera-house, and down the Boulevard de la Madeleine the thick old rich Chinese pavilioned and lanterned scene, with the stuff of boughs above. There was Lancel's corner-shop, with a large inverted lily in its glass bed, the first sun on the windows of the Grande Maison de Blanc. The people tapped to work . . . High above the mansards were the thin filaments of night-signs—Fumez-les-Gitanes, Marivaux, Pathé-Polydor, Eversharp, Le-Touquet-Paris-Plage.[61]

Early in *The Beauties* Marpurgo tells his newly-made English friends that of those who embark on spiritual adventures 'some never reach them, lying becalmed off Cytherea':[62] the quest is of no avail. The significance of the remark resounds in the book as the protagonists' ill-conceived plans come undone. Cytherea, the mythical island of love and destination of lovers, famously depicted in Watteau's painting of 1717, is a recurrent Stead metaphor of journeys that fail.[63] In *The Beauties* it melds with the image of sleep: the 'sleep' of romantic fancy, moral capitulation and human unconcern. Towards the end of the book, in one of its more curious episodes, Marpurgo takes Oliver to his Somnambulists' Club, the meeting place of crackpot philosophers and, it appears, an opium den. In it Marpurgo speaks to the drugged Oliver as one who is 'a dead soul':[64] 'You're somnambulists walking in a world of phantoms: you're shadows', he says of Oliver's kind.[65] The warning is compounded when, just before Oliver leaves for home, he dreams of an entombed woman who rallies—terrible, irresistible—then, as he goes to kiss her, sinks back into the earth: 'In an instant she was cold and I was grasping a stone'.[66] The last pages of *The Beauties* see the lovers return to their former lives. Whatever they rued in Paris in small moments of lucidity is over. No sentimental education occurred. Elvira at home, we learn, has another 'young pup';[67] Oliver, journeying back to England by train is seducing another girl with the same old ploys. It will take more heroic characters than those of *The Beauties* to see Stead give expression to her belief that only through struggle, endeavour, enquiry and a willingness to adapt can human beings rise above those social forces that stifle human creativity and independence of action and mind.

House of All Nations, Stead's most historically-driven novel, refers outrageously, even fantastically, to the

1930s world in which she moved. A mammoth work of around 800 pages and 104 scenes, it rampages through the lives of its smart but rapacious protagonists, each scrambling for wealth in a toppling world. The time is 1931-32, the political mood one Stead understood well. Her characters, caught up in the thick of their daily deals, must nonetheless reckon with the web of historical phenomena that impinges on their business lives: the precarious peace that followed World War I; the Depression; the growing threat of German Fascism; the memory of the Russian Revolution; unrest in China and Japan; discontent in Spain; impending war. The book's cavalcade of careerists are ever mindful of the might (or machinations) of the real political leaders of the time: Mussolini, Hitler, Hoover, Roosevelt, Ramsay MacDonald, Churchill. But influencing all their chancy ventures is the stock market crash and the fear that France, hanging on to the gold standard when England had devalued the pound, might itself be forced to devalue the franc and face the economic Depression that was rampant elsewhere. The volatility of the novel's aptly-named Banque Mercure mimics that of a string of real banks and financial empires—Dawes, Kreuger, Insull, Credit-Anstalt—to which, moreover, its characters nervously allude. In this, her testament to 1930s economic instability, Stead lets fact and fiction calamitously interweave. More discerningly, she posits her characters' wheelings and dealings as evocative of a Europe entering a new and risky political phase. Just as they engage in underhand gambles and swindles, each coveting personal wealth and power, so she envisages a world whose countries, vying for political supremacy, were already set upon paths of clandestine operation and unsure accords. Of that world the Banque Mercure, seat of competing ambitions and dicey pacts, is both an illustrative fictional instance and a complex metaphor.

Stead knew when she arrived in Paris she had come to the 'capital of the modern world'.[68] It was then the international centre of high finance as much for the big-time investor as for those who controlled economic flow. So it is for the Banque Mercure, run as 'a sort of cosmopolite club for the idle rich and speculators of Paris, Madrid, Rio, Buenos Aires, New York, London, and points farther east and west'.[69] To its doors are welcomed the moneyed of all nations, behind them grand deals are made. Much of the novel's action takes place within its walls: on the lower floors the clients gather to do business with brokers, tellers, secretaries, cashiers; along its corridors rumours are spread and decisions forged; in the upper storeys, inhabited by senior management, the best customers—those most likely to fill the bank's vaults—are received, feted, flattered and deceived. But it is in the office of the charismatic bank manager, Jules Bertillon, that, unbeknown to the many, the rashest schemes are hatched and realised. There, over the course of the narrative, the major characters assemble to thrash out the bank's future and secure their careers: William Bertillon, Jules's stable and practical brother and partner; Richard Plowman, faithful but gullible family retainer; Michel Alphendéry, loyal investments manager and uncomfortable socialist in a capitalist world; Henri Léon, one-time grain merchant, valuable client and ideas man; Count Jean de Guipatin, affable investor; Aristide Raccamond, the wily customers' man who eventually betrays Jules and the firm. When Alphendéry introduces Léon to the kind of 'mercurial money crowd'[70] the bank sets out to lure, he proffers a damning picture of the fast cash contacts postwar men like Jules cynically made:

> South Americans who make money every two or three years in some new mining grab . . . a few old Spanish land hogs, a few Hollywood skyrockets, a few Eton playboys . . . consolidated squirearchies . . . conserved Napoleonic dough, society figures who remember where they came from and how far: not too rusty, not too incautious . . . People who eat their cake and have it . . . A few Chicago street walkers with packing-house fortunes, married to phony counts, a few French hereditary bankbooks, a few postwar youngsters, motordrome and flying aces, born in a bedeviled world, crazy to make a fortune, amoral and playing for big stakes.[71]

If Jules's bank is a place of dubious morals (ironically, the real 'House of All Nations' was an exclusive 1930s Paris brothel), it suits its more knowing investors, in for the quick return. Far from being daunted by economic uncertainty, the shrewdest amongst them relish the chance to profit from others' naïvety and ruin. Stead is clearly fascinated by the frenzied buoyancy and restless energy of the age. One feels it in the rhythm of the book, in the cinematic succession of scenes, the breakneck progress of narrative event, the cut-throat conversations that unfold. In *House of All Nations* 'mercurial money' begets mercurial activity; risk-taking is all; a *carpe diem* incaution prevails. Jules, 'full of ideas as a hive of bees',[72] plunges from hunch to caprice to act, hoping to 'make real money in a dissolving world';[73] 'every crisis', he reckons, 'is a storm of gold'.[74] As Alphendéry maintains in terms that would make Marx, his touted god, turn in his grave:

> This is a new Napoleonic age, a new Commune age. Revolution! Why, it always produces new markets! All new money is made through the shifting of social classes and the dispossession of old classes. Today we have it. Property is changing hands, losing its old owners all the time. This is the time to move in.[75]

Of the mixed reception of her novel in America, Stead claimed, 'it was badly received in Wall Street, because it was so true.'[76] 'Those boys told me everything', she admitted of her Travelers' colleagues.[77] That 'everything', epically transformed, was evidently manna from heaven for one of her social acuity. Early on in their jobs she and Blake realised their American manager, Peter Neidecker, was running a crooked business by fiddling the books, though Blake, in particular, felt caught between moral principle and fidelity to his nonetheless warm and generous superior. Amongst other shady practices, Neidecker was 'bearing' the market. The bank was no more than a 'bucket house', financing speculative stock market deals with the clients' money in order to resell when the market rose—or so they planned. Blake resigned, but the bank limped on until it crashed in July 1935. Neidecker and his two partners (his brothers) absconded with some of the bank's funds, but were subsequently caught in America and later tried—not the fate of Stead's elusive Jules, although the parallels between fictional and real conmen she hardly disguised.[78]

Stead put her experience to immediate literary advantage, recontextualising it to proffer a picture of capitalist mayhem at a time when her own Leftist persuasions were firming and the capitalist nations were apprehensively observing changing political and economic trends. The book, which she later agreed was 'a staggering satire on the capitalist system', is a kind of negative portrayal of her own world view.[79] Indeed, at the time she was involved in Blake's Marxist circles, borne out in their combined journalistic affiliations with the London-based pro-communist *Left Review,* and the American *New Masses* which Blake had supported in earlier days.[80]

House of All Nations is neither a 'proletarian' novel nor a 'revolutionary' novel in the strict sense of those genres. It does not focus upon strikes, workers, and unions, nor, other than incidentally, upon revolts and wars. 'Everyone is still waiting with baited [sic] breath for *the* left novel', she wrote to her friend Stanley Burnshaw, before the book appeared. 'It can't be mine, as there is no member of the lower classes in my bank novel and even—I think this shows the highest moral courage—one of my chief moral heroes is a blueblooded *Count.*'[81] Of course this does not detract from the strength of what it does say. Inspired by the Marxist novelist, literary critic and scholar Ralph Fox—to boot, a loved friend and mentor—she believed a work should be 'artistic' rather than 'propagandist' and 'functional', and that characters who speak for themselves don't need authors to judge or explain the way they behave.[82] But Stead, like Fox, *did* present character from a Marxist materialist perspective. Unlike the social realist, she believed the private and public self are not separable, that we are not born in ivory towers; that we are defined by the social and economic contexts in which we are immersed. In the deep Lukácsian sense, her characters are 'world historical beings', forged from the social forces at work in their lives.[83] As Diana Brydon remarks, '[in Stead] character is politics', 'inner and outer realities' are 'seamlessly one'. With her, the 'novel of character', ideologically and historically driven, is inextricably the 'novel of ideas'.[84]

In *House of All Nations* Stead focuses upon the West's 'sell outs', those who abuse or exploit the prevailing system, for which, she shows, the capitalist society is ideologically prone. Her characters, or at least those of them who hold public sway, are the rich who rob the poor: Marx's privileged; the class that has the money to make more money, and the mental acumen (read cunning) to keep it so. Duping the people was always Marx's great lament; the capitalist strategy, he reckoned, was to keep the worker in the dark, happy, presumably, to have a job rather than none at all. Jules and his entourage give no thought to those under them. 'I don't care a hoot for them',[85] Jules spins off, when asked of their use to mankind. In his universe labour is cleanly divided into those who manage and those who toil. 'We make it: the smart people', he tells Alphendéry.[86] And later: 'I come from a breed of men who have harvested, for generations, what others have sown, or dug, or made'.[87] Fleecing the people is literally how he phrases it in his trademark cynical way. 'I'm a sheep shearer', he explains. 'The lambs eat grass and grow wool and I clip it.'[88] He is, he knows, at the profitable end of the production line. It is not lost on his close colleagues, no better than he, that Jules is 'a robber by instinct, [a] sharpshooter of commerce by career . . . [a] child of his age'.[89] If he shamelessly calls himself a 'gilded pickpocket' and a 'postwar man'[90] to his rich hangers-on, he is, to their benefit, 'Hermes',[91] the Greek god of luck and patron of merchants and thieves.

Jennifer Gribble's study of money mythomania in *House of All Nations* rightly points out the role of 'gold' in its protagonists' lives.[92] It is their fantasy, their obsession, their poison, their ruin; it is their professional business and the bank's keepings; ultimately, it is the fortune that was never there. In a key scene, entitled 'In Praise of Gold', the narrator conjures up all that the word 'gold' has long universally inspired: not merely because of its materiality, its lustre, its 'brightness, softness, purity, rarity', but its 'lifelong association' with 'the idea of ultimate wealth, perennial ease, absolute security'.[93] Gold, real and imagined, governs Stead's main characters' private and public lives. In the novel's opening chapter Léon, tired of a night on the town, thrusts money into the hands of the prostitutes he has been entertaining to get rid of them by paying their next taxi fare. They are but commodities—spoiled goods, to be sure. Alphendéry sends money to his poor mother and unfaithful wife to keep them out of his way. Near the novel's end Jules shows Raccamond a vault of gold, partly borrowed and planted, to trick the man into thinking the bank coffers are full. In between, the Banque Mercure lurches between liquidity and insolvency, sudden loss and shaky gain, until, as Léon puts it, the 'golden opportunity' had demonstrably gone.[94] But beyond the legendary power gold has to purchase what one will, it is, in Marxist terms, that great marker of bourgeois greed. Having it, amassing it, rather than needing it, is what beguiles. 'I've got always to be thinking about money', Jules concedes,[95] 'I like glitter, brilliance . . . [if I left the bank] I'd be unable to resist the splendor of the façade'.[96] Repeatedly Stead's characters look to money not for its 'use' value, but for the measure of power its quantity confers. 'I want highflying cash, beautiful cash, in platoons . . . I want it big, rich, and plentiful, and all mine', Jules dreams.[97] Hence his disdain for the 'little man':

> . . . and what have I got round me? Savers, hoarders, go-gentlies, abacus gentry back in the carpetbags of the Middle Ages, squirrels, ants, census takers, penny-bank campaigners, installment-plan robbers, shilling-a-week shortchangers, Saturday tillshakers, busfare embezzlers, dime defalcators.[98]

Jules's view that 'if you start little, you remain little' is precisely the capitalist attitude that the rich have the will for betterment and the poor can't help themselves.[99] In fact, the gold in which the Banque Mercure deals is hardly gold at all, but, rather, paper money, stocks and shares that are never realised. For Jules, 'gold isn't wealth: positions in markets is wealth'.[100] 'Brokerage,' affirms William, 'is the true gold mine.'[101] 'Gold is a commodity, and we're not into commodities', Jules explains. 'We're in grapples, clinches, blackmails, plunges, lucky breaks, long odds, lowdowns, big gambles.'[102] In essence, gold—on their terms—is the means to advantage, status and power, earned not by manual labour—the lot of the worker—but by professional know-how. In the words of one of Jules's unreliable advisers: 'The greater the "superstructure of graft", the greater the "surplus-value".' A Marxist opinion indeed, if unwarily mouthed.[103]

The vulnerability of the corporate authority to corruption is a key issue in *House of All Nations* that binds together its multitudinous thematic threads. Concealment of questionable practice in the private organisation, is, in Stead's exposé, too easily had. The modus operandi of the Banque Mercure is neither well known within, nor properly publicly declared, though its more astute and wealthy clients are happy to turn a blind eye to what they understand in the hope that their investments (and complicity) will duly be bounteously returned. As the novel progresses and managerial discussions proliferate, making up much of its volume, so the reader is made privy to the rorts the bank enfolds: antedated contracts, ghost companies, inactive branches abroad, 'paper' directors who don't meet, tax avoidance schemes, unpublished balance sheets, tips for the averted, hush money for the alarmed . . . 'A bank is a confidence trick', Jules brags to his acolytes. 'If you put up the right signs, the wizards of finance themselves will come in and ask you to take their money.'[104] And, again, more cynically, of the Banque Mercure: 'This isn't a bank: there's a sign outside saying BANK and when they [the ordinary people] see it they come inside

and drop their cash on the counter. If I put up the sign BARBER they'd come in just as automatically looking for a shave.'[105] What is meant, of course, is that the capitalist system thrives on human ignorance and gullibility.

Jules's hubris is eventually his downfall, even if, in a rebuff to the comfortable closure of the 'goodies and baddies' narrative, he doesn't get what the reader might think he deserves. A series of bad decisions makes him the victim of others' sly plans. When he signs a complex bet with his arch enemy and former schoolboy rival that the pound sterling will not fall below 122 francs, the gamble turns sour. The pound drops and the terms of the agreement are such that he is obliged to pay up large and regular sums unless he can prove the hidden underhand facets of the deal. In addition, the envious Raccamond, keen to assist Jules's rival in the hope of assuming control of the firm, sets out to uncover Jules's frauds. Bribing his way, he accesses two anonymous ledgers held in the bank's Brussels office that reveal the extent of its *contrepartie* deals: Jules had long been illegally short-selling his clients; in reality they didn't own the investments they thought they had; transactions were but book entries that concealed bets made on the stock market against their accounts. Rightly indignant over the swindling of his personal clients, but nonetheless bent on serving his own ambitions to rise, Raccamond blackmails Jules into a confession that sets in motion the latter's demise. The clients demand their money. The bank fails. Had Jules swallowed his pride and endorsed an ingenious wheat scheme thought up by the brilliant Léon, he may have earned resources that could have saved the bank and his career.

Speaking at a League of American Writers congress in 1939, Stead defended her penchant for the 'many-charactered novel' as a 'seductive form'. The novel, she reckoned, had to be multi-layered, complexly socially inclusive, chaotically diverse, capturing both the disordering energy of political and economic forces and the intensity of human experience. It had to be what she termed the 'novel of strife': social panorama recording social flux; social flux complicated by characters who bring to the prevailing order the stamp of their own passions, contradictions, tensions and drives.[106] Hers are frenetic characters caught up in the tangle of their private, social and professional lives. In that, the Stead novel is never reductive in the way much politically committed literature is, but, rather, subtle, investigative; the relationship between individual and society is everywhere evident, but individual ego is rarely lost from view. 'I write characters, because, really I'm a character writer,' she said. 'I'm interested, not in plot but what they do with their lives and what their lives do with them.'[107] In *House of All Nations* the characters are not all straightforwardly bad; rather, they are complex, unpredictable creatures, capable of warmth and cruelty, loyalty and betrayal, creativeness and destructiveness, imaginativeness and calculation. Within the broad social tableaux she constructs, Stead offers no safe or cut-and-dried picture of how human beings behave.

Jules, despite his intrigues, comes across as strangely likeable: devious but charming, elegant but insouciant, 'mercurial and often lethargic',[108] a 'harlequin' creature[109] who gives credence to the paradox that 'everyone adores a successful thief',[110] that ingenuity, dash, spontaneity and exuberance are preferable to predictability and dullness. Repeatedly Jules is referred to by the narrator, his entourage, his enemies and his clients as Mercury, 'a flier, a dancer—a messenger of the gods',[111] flighty, insubstantial, but 'full of a fantastic, ingenuous, and disarming charlatanry',[112] 'frail', but 'brave, full of go and gaiety',[113] reckless (where William is grounded), irrational (where Alphendéry is logical), fitfully generous, unprincipled, dreamy, engaging, playful, perverse.

Riotous characters abound in Stead's novels but so, too, do the ideologically thwarted and the morally fraught, none more so than the uneasy Alphendéry, the bank's so-called 'mystery man'[114] and *éminence grise*.[115] Tagged a 'scholar', 'idealist' and 'Utopian' by the bemused Bertillons because of his Marxist beliefs,[116] he nonetheless clings to his job as Jules's faithful servant, chief advisor, and, until Jules unfairly dismisses him, as the steady hand of his sinking ship.[117] But Alphendéry's motives are not entirely unselfish. His altruism is theoretical rather than lived. The bank offers him security, and, although he lives a Spartan life, it enables him to provide for his absent wife and mother without being tied down. He may speak at revolutionary meetings, visit his comrades, spout Marxist rhetoric, but, once relieved of his bank position, he takes up work with the go-ahead capitalist Léon. Just occasionally he yields to pangs of guilt, casting him as a somewhat compromising spokesman for the inequitableness of the distribution of capitalist wealth. In a scene entitled 'Façade':

> The more Michel looked at façades, fine furnishings, crystal panes, brass rods, chased mirrors, carved frames, and soft carpets, the more depressed he became, the more was he convinced that he had to leave the bank and find another job. This came not only from his natural penchant for simplicity but also from a constant guilty picture in his mind's eye: a ganger sweating on the permanent way and the subtitle 'these stones, grilles, mahoganies came that way.' It was too much: it was too good.[118]

In fact, *House of All Nations* accords little narrative space to the opponents of the mad world of high finance it portrays. Only a few isolated characters speak up in the wilderness of their whirligig age: the aptly named Jean Frère and Adam Constant, their small band of country-loving followers (Frère works a rural property) and their not wholly liberated wives—voices for the Marxist faithful, brothers in shared ideals. Where all around them the 'grab and graft' mentality is rife, they are those who have opted for frugality, friendship, social reform and simple lives. In a key scene entitled 'J'Accuse' (a patent allusion to France's most divisive anti-Semitic court case),[119] Constant, junior teller with the Bertillons, bent on going to China to serve Chiang Kai-shek, lays down with missionary purpose what is one of the novel's most sobering arraignments of the capitalist scourge. 'There are no men in [the Banque Mercure],' he regrets . . .

> . . . only money galls of one color and another shape: only an infection of monsters with purses at their waists that we wait upon and serve . . . My dream is, that one day I will get them all down, I will leave them on record. I want to show the waste, the insane freaks of these money men, the cynicism and egotism of their life, the way they gambol amidst plates of gold loaded with fruits and crystal jars of liqueurs, meats pouring out juices, sauces, rare vegetables, fine fancy breads, and know very well what they are doing, brag, in fact, of being more cunning than the others, the poor . . . 'Knowledge, money, real love, power', they say, 'are too good for the people . . . we must keep them all to ourselves.'[120]

Constant's food thematic, conjuring up capitalist superfluity, recurs in a formidable narrative guise in one of the book's satirical highpoints: 'A Stuffed Carp' (Scene 42). For Stead's 1938 editor it was 'one of the great comic scenes in English literature';[121] for her first biographer, 'an ironic masterpiece';[122] for Don Anderson, one of those 'unforgettable [Stead] dinner parties' in which man metaphorically eats man.[123] The character of Raccamond—as blackmailer but also victim—gathers up in his bulky and gluttonous person the worst traits of the capitalist 'fat' people his equally reprehensible host reproves.

Nowhere in *House of All Nations* does Stead bring private and professional ambition into such awful synchrony as in this, her most relentless tableau of bourgeois consumption and display. Extending over forty-two pages, the scene plots the progress of a gargantuan meal, ostensively offered to the Raccamonds by their business acquaintances the Hallers in generous friendship but seized upon by both couples as an opportunity to get out of it what they can: Mme Raccamond, the guiding hand behind her husband's professional ruses, looks to her husband to win Haller to his custom; Haller, a retired investor, hopes to wheedle business information from the crafty Raccamond; Mme Haller, eager for congratulation, thrills at the chance to exhibit her household possessions and culinary skills. Shot through with parodic interpolations that complement the diners' table talk—itself as richly reflective as is the food of the ghastly values they espouse—Stead has constructed a social send-up worthy of a Balzac, but with the gutsy edge and gastronomic innuendo of a Rabelais. As the diners gorge their way through countless dishes, so ingestion becomes satiety and lasting the course (or courses) becomes power play.

Stead delights in group settings, people depicted playing off people, taking advantage of one another, contesting values, exercising authority, exerting control. Mme Haller's dinner occasion is a chance to show the amazed (but secretly contemptuous) Raccamonds how much she owns and how much she knows. Having given Mme Raccamond a woman-to-woman glimpse of her vast stores of linen, lace, crystal vases (all hoarded as saleable goods should a revolution occur)—'feel it', she tells the poor woman, as each item is slipped from its chest, fingered and returned—the meal gets under way.[124] Hoping to impress her guests beyond endurance by plying them with food they can barely stomach but are obliged to consume, Mme Haller's game of domination unfolds. Inexorably, dish after dish arrives; wines and liqueurs are copiously poured; inescapably, the Raccamonds are presented with their large, unwanted serves: chicken livers washed down with liqueurs; sausages and red wine; the *pièce de résistance* and pinnacle of the 'ordeal'—a 'huge, stuffed jellied and nobly decorated carp', accompanied with 'roe, jelly, and stuffing, and a small dish of macaroons';[125] breads, cakes, nuts, honey and red-wine tea; finally, 'a splendid Doyenne de Comice pear',[126] slyly presented to Raccamond to help him recover from the indigestion that, part way through the event, had caused him to reel. After 'a hailstorm of protestations and inquiries, refusals and moral suasions', as the guests plead sufficiency, Sophy Haller 'won'.[127] Her ritual battle—perversely meant to punish and seduce the flagging customers' man—leaves her remorseful but triumphant: her handiwork (the carp) is sadly demolished, but her effusive hospitality prevails. Raccamond, changing hue over the evening from pasty white to green to mauve, is shown up for what he is: a 'great blubber of voracious male'.[128]

As the diners ply their knives, so the conversation—another challenge—moves to and fro. While Mme Haller prises compliments from her overfed feasters, assuring them of the purity of her gastronomic medley, they ponder the world's problems, tossing off their opinions, refuting each other's ideas. Haller, an ex-capitalist and converted Leninist, embraces the Russian revolution for the 'Fat People' it overthrew: 'Lenin saw [the injustice]', he contends, '. . . the ruling classes in Russia had stuffed themselves to bursting on interest'; financers, he concludes, are the same: 'There is something wrong when five per cent of the people stuff and ninety-five per cent have almost nothing to eat and no money to put into interest-bearing bonds at all'.[129] Raccamond's feeble defence of the 'sound', 'hard-working', 'saving', 'modest' bourgeoisie,[130] of which he is smugly one, is deplored as Haller speaks up for social 'moderation' as 'a wise use of liberty, a wise limitation

of plenitude'.[131] The chocolates arrive and are consumed. As the exhausted guests head home, Mme Raccamond resolves that one day she will achieve her highest aspiration and 'wash [her] hands in gold coins'.[132]

The 'Stuffed Carp' scene is quintessential Stead at her wordsmith best. As the guests pontificate on politics and food, and descriptions of the sumptuousness of the meal accrue, the book's major themes collide—power, money, social advancement, political expedience, human hypocrisy. After all, the discourses of gastronomical indulgence and of financial amassment share similar vocabularies. In Jules's office, around the Hallers' table, it is 'quantity', 'gross intake' that counts. The 'richness' of Mme Haller's menu, the 'surfeit' of food that makes up the spread, the 'stocks' she flaunts, the 'large amounts' she serves are transferable Marxist concepts and terms, relevant to Jules's banking ethos and relevant to 1930s greed. Consumption and expansion are fundamental principles of the capitalist credo. Stead's novel, then, is 'multi-voiced', 'hybrid', in the true Bakhtinian sense: discourses intrude on one another; words are never semantically neutral or naïvely used.[133] Her characters say what they say, but invariably mean (or hide) more. So too does Stead, inflecting her narrative with parodic overtones, pushing her obsessive characters to the verge of the caricatural, watching them fall into the traps they set, inviting the reader to savour not only their rankled humour, but also that of authorial interjection, sardonic comment, witty aside, social *aperçu*. Stead's is a refracted writing. The metaphoric intention, the satirical edge is always there. Her characters are given autonomy in the way they speak and live, but they are not spared from being exposed. Despite (and because) of themselves, they are revealed for what they are.

The imbrication of plot and metaphor and of character and social exposé save ***House of All Nations*** from being 'just' a story or 'just' a political treatise: Stead's is indeed the 'drama of the person', but the drama evolves from the seething world events in which she, like her characters, was embroiled. Their lives—her invention—point repeatedly to the broad canvas of 1930s crises. The emptiness of the Banque Mercure's vaults at the book's close is both the inevitable outcome of Jules's rashness and a metaphor for France's actual economic insubstantiality. Jules's wealth is illusory, but so, Stead infers, is that of a France dependent on a dangerously fluctuating stock market and precarious monetary schemes. So she gathers up telltale images, even as she lets the narrative unfold. The bank, variously 'a hollow jewel',[134] a 'phantom bank',[135] a 'citadel of invisible gold',[136] is eventually exposed for the shell it is. When Jules vanishes as if in a puff of smoke to another country in his brother's plane—Mercury winging to another land—he leaves behind him destroyed accounts, partial records, falsified documents and insolvent clients. As the law courts settle down to do business on the dust of what remains, the memory of Jules lingers on, some believing in his return with fresh fortunes, others nursing the losses he bequeathed. Their financial baron has become the stuff of myth and his empire an unfulfilled dream.

The collapse of the Banque Mercure foreshadows what Stead, writing after the novel's time frame of 1931-32, knew had occurred in France by 1933. By then the Wall Street Crash legacy had spread. By choosing to stay on the gold standard in 1931, France (unlike England and the United States), had merely stalled what occurred in time: inflation, the Depression, the doubt that the Left, after a sweeping victory in 1932, could restore economic confidence and growth. France, the 'house of all nations', seemingly impervious to ruin, proved in fact to be no less vulnerable than any other country to rampant economic disarray. But Stead's world view, filtered through the forebodings on which her characters expound, intimates there was worse to come. The Banque Mercure's disintegration fictionally mimics the 'crumbling' of Europe,[137] and the mounting events that Churchill, fearing the worst, had the insight to call 'the gathering storm'.[138] By 1938, when *House of All Nations* appeared on the shelves, its shadowy predictions were becoming realities. In 1938 Hitler invaded Czechoslovakia, the first country to fall victim to his expansionist program; in 1939 the Nazi-Soviet Pact was signed; in September, following Hitler's invasion of Poland, Britain declared war on Germany. The Second World War had begun. There is something darkly premonitory in Stead's evocation of the Banque Mercure's frightened clients from across borders lobbying for allies as they tot up the implications of the catastrophe Jules had left behind: 'All the clients banded themselves together in national protective associations, and thus the next European war began in little.'[139] Even as the novel closes, Stead seemingly looks ahead to the nervous unity that would propel 'all nations', Europe's especially, beyond the false utopias to which, in the early 1930s, so many had unguardedly clung.

Notes

1. In this chapter page numbers refer to Christina Stead, *The Beauties and Furies* (BF), Virago Press, London, 1982, and *House of All Nations* (HN), Angus and Robertson, London and Sydney, 1974.

2. Famously negotiated in the 'Hall of Mirrors' at Versailles, it was attended by seventy delegates and twenty-six nations from which Germany, Austria, Hungary and Russia were excluded. In a subsequent paring down of the peace participants, the final conditions were negotiated by the 'Big Three': the United States, France and Great Britain, and ratified by the League of Nations on 10 January 1920.

3. Harold Nicolson, *Peacemaking 1919,* Constable, London, 1933; new edition, Methuen, London, 1964, p. 84; John Maynard Keynes, *The Economic Consequences of the Peace,* Macmillan, London, 1919, and Harcourt Brace Jovanovich, New York, 1920, vol. 2.

4. After preliminary bank losses across America, the market spectacularly collapsed on 29 October ('Black Tuesday'). Although much debated, it is widely believed to have started the Great Depression.

5. Blake was born Wilhelm Blech of German Jewish parents in 1894 in New York. He anglicised his name in 1937.

6. Anne Summers, 'The Self-Denied: Australian Women Writers—Their Image of Women', *Refractory Girl,* vol. 2, nos 9-10, Autumn 1973, p. 10; Elizabeth Hardwick, 'The Neglected Novels of Christina Stead', *A View of My Own: Essays in Literature and Society,* Farrar, Strauss and Cudahy, New York, 1951, pp. 41-48.

7. Asked if she had wished to escape from Australia, she replied, 'I was not escaping, I liked Sydney. Sydney was fine. And as for the suggestion that I found the culture narrow—that's ridiculous. I was full of Australian culture. I wanted to go abroad', Rodney Wetherell, 'Interview with Christina Stead', *Australian Literary Studies,* vol. 9, no. 4, October 1980, p. 435.

8. For a review of the evolving critical evaluations of Stead's work see Diana Brydon, *Christina Stead,* Macmillan Education, London, 1987, ch. 8 ('Stead and Her Critics'), pp. 159-73.

9. Hazel Rowley, *Christina Stead: a biography,* Minerva, Port Melbourne, Victoria, 1994, p. 165.

10. Of Blake she writes: 'I have seen some parts of Paris inside-out, but always under the wing of Mr Blech, who is a marvellous raconteur, rapporteur—a great memory and ingenuity and enthusiasm—and who will not leave my side for even two hours', letter to Nellie Molyneux, 2 April 1929, in RG Geering (ed.), *A Web of Friendship: selected letters, Christina Stead (1928-1973),* Angus and Robertson, Sydney, 1992, p. 15.

11. ibid., p. 16.

12. ibid. A *petit rentier* is a small-time investor; *incroyables* are 'amazing ones'.

13. Set down by Blake in *Elements of Marxian Economic Theory and Its Criticism: an American looks at Karl Marx,* Cordon, New York, 1939.

14. *Left Review,* vol. 1, no. 2, July 1935, pp. 453-62. The article is Stead's only official statement about the political responsibility of writers.

15. 'I am not puritan nor party, like to know every sort of person; nor political, but on the side of those who have suffered oppression, injustice, coercion, prejudice, and have been harried from birth', SJ Kunitz and H Haycroft, *Twentieth Century Authors,* H. W. Wilson, New York, 1942, p. 1330.

16. One of Stead's early titles for *The Beauties and Furies,* letter to Gwen Walker-Smith, Geering, *Selected Letters,* p. 33.

17. BF, p. 18.

18. HN, p. 199.

19. Stead read French literature avidly in Australia, exploring the holdings of the Sydney Municipal Library in her teenage years (Kunitz and Haycroft, *Twentieth Century Authors,* p. 1330). In 1980 she confessed to Rodney Wetherell: 'I fell overboard for Balzac . . . [he] was one of my main discoveries', 'Interview', p. 243.

20. An early title for the book was *The Lovers in Paris,* letter to Gwen Walker-Smith, 23 September 1930, Geering, *Selected Letters,* p. 33.

21. BF, p. 2.

22. BF, p. 3.

23. ibid.

24. BF, p. 2.

25. BF, pp. 1-2.

26. BF, p. 13. Printemps is a large department store in Paris. Stead, a plain woman, reputedly took great care to look good (Hazel Rowley, *Christina Stead,* p. 136). On meeting her in Paris, Nettie Palmer records Stead's intense interest in smart fashion and her 'lightly elegant' appearance', *Nettie Palmer: her private journal 'Fourteen Years', poems, reviews, and literary essays,* ed. Vivian Smith, University of Queensland Press, 1988, p. 154.

27. BF, p. 22.

28. BF, p. 142.

29. Notably Teresa in *For Love Alone* (Harcourt Brace, New York, 1944; Peter Davies, London, 1945; Virago, London, 1978).

30. Stavisky, a Jewish stockbroker and confidence trickster, was involved in the early 1930s in a series of scandalous financial frauds. After his suspicious death it was revealed that certain members of the incumbent Radical Socialist Party had been associated with his deals. When the government dismissed the right-wing Prefect of police for supporting anti-government demonstrations, the right wing revolted and a series of riots, culminating in a mass demonstration on 6 February, ensued. Seventeen people were killed and, although the Third Republic survived, the government duly resigned. But the left supporters of the time had genuinely feared a right-wing pro-Fascist coup, and the events led to the formation of anti-Fascist leagues and the Popular Front in 1936, detailed in Paul Jankowski, *Stavisky: a confidence man in the republic of virtue,* Cornell University Press, Ithaca, New York, 2002.

31. BF, p. 138.

32. BF, p. 102.

33. BF, p. 26.

34. BF, pp. 324-25.

35. BF, p. 159.

36. BF, p. 47.

37. BF, pp. 41-2.

38. 'Sometimes I start with a situation, sometimes with a personality. I never question or argue. I'm a psychological writer, and my drama is the drama of the person', Jonah Raskin, 'Christina Stead in Washington Square', *London Magazine,* vol. 9, no. 2, February 1970, p. 75.

39. BF, p. 28.

40. BF, pp. 28-9.

41. BF, p. 70.

42. BF, p. 131.

43. BF, p. 175.

44. BF, p. 157.

45. BF, p. 80.

46. BF, p. 79.

47. BF, p. 217.

48. BF, p. 12.

49. BF, p. 29.

50. BF, p. 139.

51. BF, p. 229.

52. ibid.

53. BF, p. 323.

54. BF, p. 206.

55. BF, p. 133.

56. BF, p. 175.

57. BF, pp. 98-9.

58. BF, p. 226.

59. BF, p. 321.

60. BF, p. 364.

61. ibid.

62. BF, p. 21.

63. *The Embarkation for Cytherea.* Some commentators believe the work depicts a departure *from* Cytherea, Venus's birthplace, and, as such, symbolises the brevity of love.

64. BF, p. 331.

65. BF, p. 325.

66. BF, p. 376.

67. BF, p. 374.

68. Letter to Nellie Molyneux, 1 March 1929, Geering, *Selected Letters,* p. 12.

69. HN, p. 19.

70. HN, p. 23.

71. HN, p. 38.

72. HN, p. 24.

73. HN, p. 130.

74. HN, p. 18.

75. ibid.

76. Wetherell, 'Interview', p. 441.

77. Ann Whitehead, 'Christina Stead: An Interview', *Australian Literary Studies,* vol. 6, no. 3, May 1974, p. 238.

78. Initially Blake and Stead worked in the American & Foreign Discount Corporation, associated with the Travelers' Bank, but moved to the Travelers' office, 18 Rue de la Paix, some time in 1931, Rowley, *Christina Stead,* pp. 109 and 141. On the bank's collapse, see ibid., pp. 178-80. According to a letter Stead wrote to her friend Florence James dated 17 October 1935, Neidecker gave her his 'full permission' to write a book based on the bank, though, as Rowley remarks, he clearly never imagined she knew what she did, ibid., p. 191.

79. Whitehead, 'Interview', p. 238.

80. The *Masses,* founded in 1911, was renamed the *New Masses* in 1926, and ran as a pro-Communist, anti- Fascist journal until 1948.

81. Letter to Stanley Burnshaw, 2 October 1936, cited in Hazel Rowley, 'Christina Stead: Politics and Literature in the Radical Years, 1935-1942', *Meridian,* vol. 8, no. 2, 1989, p. 151.

82. Stead met Fox, a Marxist historian and literary critic, in London in 1934. Though not proved, it is thought they may have briefly been lovers before Fox's untimely death in 1937 in the Spanish Civil War. Stead remained indebted to Fox's Marxist reflections on novel writing, set down in the posthumously published *The Novel and the People* (London, Lawrence and Wishart, 1937; Cobbet Press, London, 1944).

83. Georg Lukács, *The Historical Novel* (1938), tr. Hannah and Stanley Mitchell, Penguin, Harmondsworth, 1981.

84. Brydon, *Christina Stead,* p. 169.

85. HN, p. 199.

86. ibid.

87. HN, p. 201.

88. HN, p. 200.

89. HN, p. 86.

90. HN, p. 181.

91. HN, p. 164.

92. Jennifer Gribble, *Christina Stead,* Oxford Australian Writers, Oxford University Press, Oxford, 1994, pp. 37-45.

93. HN, p. 135.

94. HN, p. 566.

95. HN, p. 197.

96. HN, p. 592.

97. HN, p. 333.

98. HN, p. 201.

99. ibid.

100. HN, p. 157.

101. HN, p. 236.

102. HN, p. 158.

103. HN, p. 442. The capitalist principles of superstructure and surplus-value were elaborated by Marx in Volume I of *Das Kapital* (1867), notably in Parts 4 and 5. Those principles were further defined in Volume IV (*Theories of Surplus-Value*), published posthumously by Karl Kautsky between 1905 and 1910. Stead's understanding of Marx's theories is borne out in *House of All Nations* both in the ambitions of her characters and the overtly Marxist terminologies they use.

104. HN, p. 115.

105. HN, p. 251.

106. League of American Writers papers, Bancroft Library, University of California, Berkeley, California.

107. Wetherell, 'Interview', p. 444.

108. HN, p. 89.

109. HN, p. 171.

110. HN, p. 144.

111. HN, p. 503.

112. HN, p. 87.

113. HN, p. 88.

114. HN, p. 595.

115. HN, p. 179.

116. HN, p. 253.

117. When asked if Alphendéry was based on Blake, Stead replied, 'He was Alphendéry', Whitehead, 'Interview', p. 238.

118. HN, p. 530.

119. See Chapter 2, endnote 45.

120. HN, pp. 80-81.

121. Boxed records, cited in Rowley, *Christina Stead*, p. 233.

122. RG Geering, *Christina Stead*, Twayne Publishers, New York, 1969, p. 83.

123. 'Christina Stead's Unforgettable Dinner Parties', *Southerly*, vol. 39, no. 1, 1979, pp. 42-5.

124. Hoarding as a capitalist 'fetish' for possessing—for having the potential to buy without selling, or purchasing or selling later—is discussed by Marx in *Das Kapital*, vol. I, Part 1, ch. 3.

125. HN, p. 283.

126. HN, p. 298.

127. ibid.

128. HN, p. 284.

129. HN, p. 289.

130. ibid.

131. HN, p. 296.

132. HN, p. 300.

133. Mikhail Bakhtin theorised that languages are incapable of neutrality, that words are 'heteroglossic' or multi-layered, and cannot be separated from the social, historic and cultural contexts from which they spring, Michael Holquist (ed.), *The Dialogic*

Imagination: four essays (1975), tr. Caryl Emerson and Michael Holquist, University of Texas Press, Austin and London, 1981.

134. HN, p. 23.

135. HN, p. 130.

136. HN, p. 240.

137. HN, p. 634.

138. *The Second World War,* vol. 1, Cassell and the Book Society, Sydney, 1948.

139. HN, p. 767.

Bibliography

PUBLISHED SOURCES

Anderson, Don, 'Christina Stead's Unforgettable Dinner Parties', *Southerly*, vol. 39, no. 1, 1979, pp. 28-45.

Brydon, Diana, *Christina Stead,* Macmillan Education, London, 1987.

Geering, RG, *Christina Stead,* Twayne Publishers, New York, 1969.

Geering, RG (ed.), *A Web of Friendship: Selected Letters, Christina Stead (1928-1973),* Angus and Robertson, Sydney, 1992.

Gribble, Jennifer, *Christina Stead,* Oxford University Press, 1994.

Hardwick, Elizabeth, 'The Neglected Novels of Christina Stead', in *A View of My Own: Essays in Literature and Society,* Farrar, Strauss and Cudahy, New York, 1951, pp. 41-8.

Lukács, Georg, *The Historical Novel* (1938) (trans. Hannah Mitchell and Stanley Mitchell), Penguin, Harmondsworth, 1981 (first published 1962).

Marx, Karl, *Capital* (trans. Eden Paul and Cedar Paul, Dent, London), Dutton, New York, 1957. Online, Marx/Engels Internet Archive, <htpp:www.marxists.org>, viewed 22 May 2007.

Marx, Karl, *Theories of Surplus-Value,* Foreign Languages Publishing House, Moscow, 1963. Online, Marx/Engels Internet Archive, <htpp.www.marxists.org>, viewed 22 May 2007.

Raskin, Jonah, 'Christina Stead in Washington Square', *London Magazine,* vol. 9, no. 2, February 1970, pp. 70-7.

Rowley, Hazel, 'Christina Stead: Politics and Literature in the Radical Years, 1935-1942', *Meridian,* vol. 8, no. 2, 1989, pp. 149-59.

Rowley, Hazel, *Christina Stead: A Biography,* Minerva, Port Melbourne, 1994 (first published 1993).

Smith, Vivian (ed.), *Nettie Palmer: Her Private Journal 'Fourteen Years', Poems, Reviews, and Literary Essays,* University of Queensland Press, 1988.

Stead, Christina, 'The Writers Take Sides', *Left Review,* vol. 1, no. 2, July 1935, pp. 453-62.

Stead, Christina, *House of All Nations,* Angus and Robertson, London and Sydney, 1974 (first published 1938).

Stead, Christina, *The Beauties and Furies,* Virago Press, London, 1982 (first published 1936).

Summers, Anne, 'The Self-Denied: Australian Women Writers-Their Image of Women', *Refractory Girl,* vol. 2, nos. 9-10, Autumn 1973, pp. 4-11.

Wetherell, Rodney, 'Interview with Christina Stead', *Australian Literary Studies,* vol. 9, no. 4, October 1980, pp. 431-48.

Whitehead, Ann, 'Christina Stead: An Interview', *Australian Literary Studies,* vol. 6, no. 3, May 1974, pp. 230-48.

FURTHER READING

Bibliographies

Beston, Rose Marie. "A Christina Stead Bibliography." *World Literature Written in English* 15, no. 1 (April 1976): 96-103.

> Bibliography of works by and about Stead, including reviews of her books as well as longer essays.

Ehrhardt, Marianne. "Christina Stead: A Checklist." *Australian Literary Studies* 9, no. 4 (October 1980): 508-35.

> Bibliography of Stead's publications, including works she translated, contributions to periodicals and collections, and interviews. Ehrhardt's bibliography also includes a listing of critical and biographical materials about Stead, including theses and dissertations.

Biography

Williams, Chris. *Christina Stead: A Life of Letters.* London: Virago, 1989, 341 p.

> Book-length biography of Stead based on her letters and archive materials from her estate, and including numerous photos, a select bibliography, and a listing of first publications by the author.

Criticism

Adie, Mathilda. *Female Quest in Christina Stead's* For Love Alone. Lund, Sweden: Lund University, 2004, 221 p.

> Book-length study that "undertakes an intertextual exploration of female quest in Stead's novels," focusing primarily on *For Love Alone.*

Arac, Jonathan. "The Struggle for the Cultural Heritage: Christina Stead Refunctions Charles Dickens and Mark Twain." *Cultural Critique* 2 (winter 1985): 171-89.

> Argues that *The Man Who Loved Children* offers a "conscious revisionary polemic" or "refunctioning" of the cultural heritage of Charles Dickens and Mark Twain, saying that in the composite figure of Samuel Clemens Pollit, specifically, the author provides "an exploration, at once critical and imaginative, into the cultural meanings that Dickens and Twain have taken on in their historical afterlife."

Blake, Ann. "Christina Stead's *Miss Herbert (The Suburban Wife)* and the English Middle Class." *Journal of Commonwealth Literature* 26, no. 1 (1991): 49-64.

> Probes the reasons why there is such a large gap in years between when Stead finished *Miss Herbert (The Suburban Wife)* and when the book was published.

———. "Christina Stead's English Short Stories." *Southerly* 53, no. 4 (December 1993): 146-60.

> Highlights Stead's negative treatment of England in four short stories she wrote while living in London during the 1950s.

———. "Christina Stead's Tyneside Novel: *Cotters' England.*" *Durham University Journal* 86 (July 1994): 271-79.

> Emphasizes the importance of "place" in Stead's novel *Cotters' England,* stating that the setting of Tyneside, England, is not simply a specific location in the story but "is rather a detailed, sensuous evocation of a whole social and cultural milieu in all its varied specificity."

———. "A Reconsideration of Christina Stead at Work: Fact into Fiction." *Australian Literary Studies* 18, no. 1 (May 1997): 12-20.

> Traces the artistic method by which Stead created the character of Elinor Herbert, in the novel *Miss Herbert (The Suburban Wife),* from the real-life figure of Florence James, a fellow-author and friend of Stead's, drawing on evidence found in manuscript notes in the author's papers.

Brown, Denise. "Christina Stead's 'Drama of the Person.'" *Australian Literary Studies* 13, no. 2 (October 1987): 139-45.

> Emphasizes "the dialectical principle of unity" as a crucial feature of Stead's novels, stating that the author's interest in duality reflects "the main tenets of her work."

Brydon, Diana. "Resisting 'the tyranny of what is written': Christina Stead's Fiction." *Ariel* 17, no. 4 (October 1986): 3-15.

Maintains that Stead's "notion of novelistic form," reflected in the "interdependent," "democratic," circular, and open-ended style of her novels, is a key organizing principle in her work.

———. *Christina Stead.* Basingstoke, England: Macmillan Education, 1987, 188 p.

Study of Stead and her work that is, according to the critic, the first to consider how her "status as a woman affected her fiction and the first to focus on those elements of her writing that are most immediately relevant to women."

Clancy, Laurie. *Christina Stead's* The Man Who Loved Children *and* For Love Alone. Melbourne, Australia: Shillington House, 1981, 46 p.

Comparative study of Stead's two novels *The Man Who Loved Children* and *For Love Alone,* exploring the relationship of the two texts and concluding that both works are central to the author's success as a novelist.

Davenport-Hines, Richard. "Christina Stead (1902-1983)." In *World Writers in English, Volume II: R. K. Narayan to Patrick White,* edited by Jay Parini, pp. 701-19. New York: Charles Scribner's Sons, 2004.

Includes a biography of Stead, a critical summary of her publications, and a selected bibliography of works by and about the author.

Eldershaw, M. Barnard. "Christina Stead." In *Essays in Australian Fiction,* pp. 158-81. Melbourne, Australia: Melbourne University Press, 1938.

Examines the "qualities of richness and strangeness" in Stead's first three books of fiction, *The Salzburg Tales, Seven Poor Men of Sydney,* and *The Beauties and Furies,* arguing that whereas the author's fantastic style succeeds in works that rely less on characterization and a realistic theme, such as *The Salzburg Tales,* it fails in those that depend on these elements, such as the latter two novels.

Fagan, Robert. "Christina Stead." *Partisan Review* 46, no. 2 (1979): 262-70.

Traces Stead's publishing career and development as a writer, examining in the process a number of her novels, including *A House of All Nations, The Man Who Loved Children,* and *For Love Alone.*

Gardiner, Judith Kegan. "Emphasizing Politics: Christina Stead's Fiction." In *Rhys, Stead, Lessing, and the Politics of Empathy,* pp. 50-82. Bloomington: Indiana University Press, 1989.

Highlights the central importance of politics and female identity and sexuality in Stead's fiction, stating that "with Stead, though she resists such labels, the problem of defining a relationship between the individual and history becomes the problem of defining female identity under capitalist patriarchy."

———. "'Caught but not caught': Psychology and Politics in Christina Stead's 'The Puzzleheaded Girl.'" *World Literature Written in English* 32, no. 1 (spring 1992): 26-41.

Studies Stead's characterization of her protagonist Honor Lawrence in her novella *The Puzzleheaded Girl* in order to shed light on the author's "understanding of the psychology and politics of women's alienation under capitalism."

Geering, R. G. "The Achievement of Christina Stead." *Southerly* 22, no. 4 (1962): 193-212.

Surveys Stead's work as a novelist and short story writer, asserting that "she has strong claims to be regarded as one of our few important novelists, whose best work will endure when many of our more widely known writers will be read for historical and sociological interest rather than for literary merit."

———. *Christina Stead.* Melbourne, Australia: Oxford University Press, 1969, 48 p.

Monograph that surveys Stead's career as a writer and that examines, specifically, the concerns and themes that unify her literature, such as "the tensions of family life, the pressures and constrictions of society, the search for personal freedom, the burdens of money and poverty, fake idealism, and the corrosion of political beliefs."

Green, Dorothy. "Chaos, or a Dancing Star? Christina Stead's 'Seven Poor Men of Sydney.'" *Meanjin Quarterly* 27, no. 2 (June 1968): 150-61.

Describes *Seven Poor Men of Sydney* as a "meditative lyric," and attempts to correct previous misreadings of the novel by stating that its central focus is not Michael but Catherine, and that the fates of the seven men and women in the narrative are not the fates of separate characters but "the possible fates of one character, Catherine, the directions that are open to her."

Hammett, Kristin. "Remembering the Thirties: Christina Stead's *For Love Alone* and *I'm Dying Laughing.*" In *And in Our Time: Vision, Revision, and British Writing of the 1930s,* edited by Antony Shuttleworth, pp. 221-42. Lewisburg, Pa.: Bucknell University Press, 2003.

Focuses on Stead's depiction of the 1930s in her novels *For Love Alone* and *I'm Dying Laughing.*

Harris, Margaret. "Christina Stead's Human Comedy: The American Sequence." *World Literature Written in English* 32, no. 1 (spring 1992): 42-51.

Demonstrates the ways in which Stead's so-called American sequence of novels, including *Letty Fox: Her Luck, A Little Tea, A Little Chat, The People with the Dogs,* and the posthumously published *I'm Dying Laughing,* are thematically integrated and written by the author to be read as "episodes in her Human Comedy."

Jarrell, Randall. "An Unread Book." In *The Man Who Loved Children,* by Christina Stead, pp. v-xli. New York: Holt, Rinehart and Winston, 1965.

Influential introduction to the 1965 reissue of *The Man Who Loved Children,* in which the critic explores the author's original treatment of the Pollit family in her novel, praising its "singularity" and claiming that the work "makes you a part of one family's immediate existence as no other book quite does."

Lidoff, Joan. *Christina Stead.* New York: Frederick Ungar Publishing Co., 1982, 255 p.

Book-length study that considers Stead's two autobiographical novels, *The Man Who Loved Children* and *For Love Alone,* to be her greatest achievements as a writer. Lidoff's book also includes an interview she conducted with Stead in June, 1973.

Mackenzie, Manfred. "*Seven Poor Men of Sydney*: Christina Stead and the Natural/National Uncanny." *Southerly* 56, no. 4 (summer 1996-97): 201-18.

Contends that Stead's first novel, *Seven Poor Men of Sydney,* "concerns itself with the possibility of a distinctively Australian 'nationness,'" a concern the critic sees inscribed in the life and death of the character Michael Baguenault.

Reid, Ian. "Form and Expectation in Christina Stead's Novellas." *Literary Criterion* 15, nos. 3-4 (1980): 48-58.

Highlights Stead's use of "place" in her collection of novellas, *The Puzzleheaded Girl,* as a method of providing structural unity in her work.

Roderick, Colin. "Christina Stead: *Seven Poor Men of Sydney.*" In *20 Australian Novelists,* pp. 190-215. Sydney: Angus and Robertson, 1947.

Summarizes and critiques Stead's first seven books of fiction, culminating with *For Love Alone,* which the critic calls "the best novel she has yet written." Roderick's essay includes an excerpt from Stead's first novel, *Seven Poor Men of Sydney.*

Rooney, Brigid. "Christina Stead." In *A Companion to Australian Literature since 1900,* edited by Nicholas Birns and Rebecca McNeer, pp. 235-46. Rochester, N.Y.: Camden House, 2007.

Surveys Stead's career as a writer, emphasizing her "classifying gaze of author-as-naturalist" in her work and concluding that "few writers have crossed so many boundaries to immerse themselves so comprehensively in, or to document so accurately and fearlessly, such a range of peoples, places, and societies."

Rowley, Hazel. "Christina Stead: Un-Australian?" *Southerly* 53, no. 4 (December 1993): 47-57.

Discusses Stead's neglect by critics in her native Australia because of the "un-Australianness" of her work, then goes on to show the many references to her homeland in her novels, though nearly all of these are set in locales other than Australia.

Segerberg, Anita. "Getting Started: The Emergence of Christina Stead's Early Fiction." *Australian Literary Studies* 13, no. 2 (October 1987): 121-38.

Studies both the published and unpublished work from Stead's first literary phase, from 1921 to 1937, asserting that "it is sometimes in her early work that some of Stead's preoccupations as a writer manifest themselves most clearly, preoccupations that later became submerged in her fiction."

———. "A Fiction of Sisters: Christina Stead's *Letty Fox* and *For Love Alone.*" *Australian Literary Studies* 14, no. 1 (May 1989): 15-25.

Demonstrates through unpublished letters and other material written by Stead that the author originally intended the figure of Letitia, from *Letty Fox: Her Luck,* to be Teresa's sister in her previous novel, *For Love Alone,* and that, as such, *Letty Fox* should be grouped with Stead's earlier two autobiographical novels, *For Love Alone* and *The Man Who Loved Children.*

Sheridan, Sue. "The Woman Who Loved Men: Christina Stead as Satirist in *A Little Tea, A Little Chat* and *The People with the Dogs.*" *World Literature Written in English* 32, no. 1 (spring 1992): 2-12.

Examines Stead's satiric and ironic treatment of "masculine desire" in her novels *A Little Tea, A Little Chat* and *The People with the Dogs.*

Stewart, Douglas. "Glory and Catastrophe." In *The Flesh and the Spirit: An Outlook on Literature,* pp. 235-38. Sydney: Angus and Robertson, 1948.

Praises the characterization and tragic power of Stead's *For Love Alone,* saying that the novel demonstrates "a profoundly original talent . . . , something wild and fierce and fearless that tempts one to use the word 'genius.'"

Williams, Christine. "Christina Stead's Australia—'Easily the Largest Island.'" *Southerly* 53, no. 1 (March 1993): 80-95.

Studies Stead's letters to determine her views of Australian culture during the 1920s, "and to consider to what extent they remained consistent throughout her life."

Woodward, Wendy. "Writing Differences and the Ideology of Form: Narrative Structure in the Novels of Christina Stead." *Theoria* 68 (December 1986): 49-57.

Examines how "the ideology of gender determines the forms of women's writing," citing examples from Stead's novels to illustrate her points.

———. "Concealed Invitations: The Use of Metaphor in Some of Christina Stead's Narratives." *Southerly* 53, no. 4 (December 1993): 80-95.

Maintains that "the metaphorical mode" of Stead's fiction "interrogates the masculinist nature of 'the long literary tradition' of Western culture and its use of metaphor."

Yelin, Louise. "'Buffoon Odyssey'? Christina Stead's *For Love Alone* and the Writing of Exile." *Yale French Studies* 1, no. 82 (1993): 183-203.

Contends that the ambiguous nature of Teresa's "heroic adventure" in Stead's novel *For Love Alone* "raises questions about the status of the (self-)exile of white women from European colonies or former colonies and, by extension, about the status of their writing."

Additional coverage of Stead's life and career is contained in the following sources published by Gale: *British Writers Supplement,* **Vol. 4;** *Contemporary Authors,* **Vols. 13-16R, 109;** *Contemporary Authors New Revision Series,* **Vols. 33, 40;** *Contemporary Literary Criticism,* **Vols. 2, 5, 8, 32, 80;** *Contemporary Novelists,* **Eds. 1, 2, 3;** *Dictionary of Literary Biography,* **Vol. 260;** *Encyclopedia of World Literature in the 20th Century,* **Ed. 3;** *Feminist Writers; Literature Resource Center; Major 20th-Century Writers,* **Eds. 1, 2;** *Major 21st-Century Writers; Novels for Students,* **Vol. 27;** *Reference Guide to English Literature,* **Ed. 2;** *Reference Guide to Short Fiction,* **Ed. 2; and** *World Writers in English,* **Ed. 1.**

Italo Svevo
1861-1928

(Born Aron Hector Schmitz; also wrote under pseudonym E. Samigli) Italian novelist, short story writer, essayist, and playwright.

The following entry provides an overview of Svevo's life and works. For additional information on his career, see *TCLC*, Volumes 2 and 35.

INTRODUCTION

Italo Svevo is considered one of the most original and innovative authors of twentieth-century Italian literature. Although he wrote plays, essays, and short stories, he is best known for his longer works of fiction, including the novels *Una vita* (1892; *A Life*), *Senilità* (1898; *As a Man Grows Older*), and *La coscienza di Zeno* (1923; *Confessions of Zeno*), which examine the psychological development of ordinary protagonists and anticipate the formal and narrative concerns of early twentieth-century modernism. Throughout his career Svevo was particularly concerned with the everyday issues of the average man or woman in European society, and he openly explored such themes as personal identity, ineptitude, loss of vitality, and death, as well as the frustrations of the struggling artist and the decadence of the middle class. Svevo was greatly influenced by the theories of Sigmund Freud, and with the publication of *Confessions of Zeno* is credited with introducing the modern psychoanalytic novel. Known for both his thematic and formal experimentations, the author employed stream-of-consciousness and pioneered the use of the interior monologue as a narrative technique. Although Svevo received little critical notice for most of his literary career, he is currently regarded as one of the most important Italian novelists since Giovanni Verga and a seminal figure of European literature. C. P. Snow has claimed that Svevo's gift is "something like an absolute candour. In a certain range of emotional experience, no one could be more unselfsparingly honest. It is that special kind of truth-telling that makes him so funny and so sad." Snow concludes that "in the wider field of the novel," Svevo occupies "his own singular place."

BIOGRAPHICAL INFORMATION

Svevo was born Aron Hector Schmitz on December 19, 1861, to a patriarchal Jewish family that had migrated from Hungary to Trieste, then a port city of the Austro-Hungarian Empire. His parents, Francesco and Allegra Moravia Schmitz, embraced Italian culture and history, and while they observed some Jewish customs, they were not particularly religious. At the age of twelve Svevo was sent to Germany to complete his secondary education at a commercial school in Segnitz, in Bavaria, where he studied philosophy and the German language. While in Segnitz he was exposed to progressive social ideals and began to read widely, immersing himself in the works of William Shakespeare, Ivan Turgenev, and Johann Wolfgang von Goethe. It was during this time that Svevo first became inspired to pursue a literary career. At the age of seventeen he returned to Trieste and began studying business at the Istituto Superiore Commerciale Revoltella. While Svevo's father was unaware of his son's literary leanings, his younger brother, Elio, understood and encouraged his aspirations.

As a result of financial difficulties with his family, Svevo left school in 1880 and found work as a clerk at the Unionbank, a job he endured for nineteen years. He began contributing to the Triestine newspaper, *Indipendente,* during this time and published his first article, "Shylock," in 1880, under the pseudonym E. Samigli. With his brother's support, the author continued to study literature in his spare time, familiarizing himself with Italian authors as well as the works of French naturalists, such as Gustave Flaubert and Emile Zola. In 1886 Svevo suffered a great personal loss, when Elio died after a long illness; bitter and discouraged, he found solace and comfort only in writing. At his own expense, he published his first novel, *A Life,* in 1892 and introduced his official pseudonym, Italo Svevo, which highlighted his dual cultural heritage as an Italian and Swabian.

In 1893 Svevo began teaching French and German correspondence part-time at the Istituto Commerciale Superiore Revoltella, later known as the University of Trieste. Three years later he married his cousin Livia Veneziani. Svevo continued to write, and he self-published his second novel, *As a Man Grows Older,* in 1898. The following year he left his position at Unionbank and began working for his wife's family business, a job that was financially rewarding but increasingly demanding of his time, leaving him little opportunity to pursue his true interest in writing. Although the author attempted to give up literature, his efforts to renounce his "secret vice" were ultimately unsuccessful.

In 1904 he became acquainted with the Irish writer James Joyce, who had come to Trieste to teach English. Svevo, who had longed to improve his knowledge of English, became Joyce's pupil. These lessons provided the two authors an opportunity to discuss literature, as well as their own writings, and resulted in a long-lasting friendship, from which both figures drew encouragement and support. After twenty-five years of literary silence Svevo began writing his third novel, *Confessions of Zeno,* in 1919, which he published in 1923, once again at his own expense. After years of critical neglect the author's work finally began to find an audience in the mid-1920s, initially in France and eventually in the rest of Europe. Over the next two years Svevo was treated as a celebrity, giving lectures and interviews, and he began preparing new editions of his long-neglected novels. In 1928, however, the author suffered a broken femur in a car accident. Svevo died, unexpectedly, several days later, on September 13, 1928, in Treviso, Italy.

MAJOR WORKS

With his first work of fiction, *A Life,* Svevo began to explore themes to which he would return throughout his career, including ineptitude; the struggles of the frustrated artist; the banality and decadence of middle-class life; the crises of the modern individual; and issues related to old age, disease, and death. The protagonist of the novel, Alfonso Nitti, is a young man who finds work at a bank in Trieste but has trouble adjusting to city life and the tedium of his low-paying job. He is deemed incompetent and suffers harsh reprimands from his superiors. While Alfonso is timid and introspective by nature, he eventually befriends Annetta, his boss's beautiful and arrogant daughter. Annetta, characterized as vain and spoiled, treats Alfonso as an inferior, but Alfonso is intrigued with her nonetheless and enjoys the new-found respect he receives at the bank as a result of this relationship. Their flirtation ultimately results in a seduction, but instead of marrying Annetta, thereby improving his personal and professional situation, Alfonso retreats, using his mother's illness as an excuse to leave her. When he returns to Trieste, Alfonso has lost everything. He is demoted at work and shunned by Annetta, and the novel ends with his suicide. According to some critics, *A Life* serves as Svevo's "spiritual autobiography" and reflects, through the anti-hero, Alfonso, his own efforts to establish an identity and overcome frustration and anxiety. Scholars have also observed that while Svevo borrows aspects of the objective and naturalistic nineteenth-century novel in his depiction of the social and cultural problems of the Triestine bourgeoisie, his presentation of the shifting trends occurring within the European middle class and his portrait of the modern individual as anti-hero reflect his prescient understanding of twentieth-century concerns.

For his second novel, *As a Man Grows Older,* Svevo also drew from the anxieties and events of his own life, in his depiction of the protagonist, Emilio Brentani, an inexperienced thirty-five-year-old bachelor. In the novel Emilio lives with his spinster sister, Amalia, and leads an uneventful and unfulfilling life, marked only by the fading glory of having authored a novel in his youth. He is also friends with Balli, a sculptor who pursues his hedonistic aestheticism without restraint. Emilio's life changes when he falls in love with Angiolina, a younger and more experienced woman of the working class, whose respectability is questionable. Caught up in his newly awakened passion, Emilio ignores Angiolina's vulgarity and infidelity. After Amalia dies of an illness, however, Emilio follows Balli's advice and ends the affair, thereby returning to his dull existence. At the end of the novel the characters of Angiolina and Amalia blend together in Emilio's mind into a single feminine image. As the title suggests, *As a Man Grows Older* is concerned with themes related to old age and youth, stagnation and vitality. Emilio, still many years from suffering the debilitating effects of aging, is nevertheless spiritually old and easily overcome by the inertia, introspection, and resignation that mark his personality and stifle his vitality. As with Svevo's first novel, this work shares characteristics of the nineteenth-century social novel, although its inquiry into the psychological make-up of the protagonist and other characters signals an affinity with the preoccupations of modernist literature.

Generally considered Svevo's masterpiece, *Confessions of Zeno* is also acknowledged as the first Italian psychoanalytic novel and a seminal work in the development of contemporary fiction. Experimental in both form and content, the novel is comprised of dual narrative lines—an external story, which features episodes in the life of the protagonist, Zeno Cosini, that are recorded in a loosely structured diary form, and an internal narrative line, which reveals the depths of the human mind, as the protagonist explores his own subconscious in search of the motivations that have influenced his life. Zeno is a fifty-six-year-old, successful businessman in Trieste, who is plagued by his obsessive preoccupation with real and perceived pains and physical failings. More than anything else he is concerned with his nicotine addiction and decides to seek treatment through the newly discovered therapy of psychoanalysis. At the suggestion of his analyst, Zeno begins to keep a diary, using free association to recover dreams, repressed memories, latent emotions, and impressions. The act of smoking is an important part of this exploration for Zeno, as each cigarette recalls a series of forgotten associated experiences, which, in turn, reveal and offer insight into the protagonist's anxieties. In addition to themes related to the psychological development of the individual, the novel explores issues of memory and the paradoxical coexistence of the past and present, as they simultaneously materialize within human consciousness. Some scholars have also noted the prominent role of humor in *Confessions of Zeno,* a feature that distinguishes the novel from Svevo's previous works. Comic elements primarily manifest in the character of Zeno, who, as he recalls events from his past, uses humor to interpret the absurdities and eccentricities that have marked his life.

CRITICAL RECEPTION

Although it received a handful of favorable reviews, Svevo's first major work, *A Life,* was generally met with critical silence. This silence marked the beginning of the so-called "Svevo case," a term used to describe the author's inability to gain notice from Italian critics, which beleaguered his reputation in his native country until the post-Fascist era. Scholars have identified several factors that may have contributed to the critical neglect Svevo suffered for most of his literary career, including his Jewish heritage and dual cultural identity, as well as his decision to inhabit and write about Trieste, an international city, as opposed to a mostly or completely Italian setting. Some commentators have also observed that Svevo's unusual literary style, choice of subject matter, and tendency to use anti-heroic characters set him apart from other writers of his generation, prompting many reviewers to ignore his work entirely. After his next novel, *As a Man Grows Older,* was treated with similar neglect in 1898, Svevo ceased writing for publication, later remarking that he had resigned himself to "a unanimous judgment (there is no more perfect unanimity than silence) and for twenty-five years I abstained from writing. If it was a mistake, it was mine."

In the early 1900s Svevo met James Joyce, who encouraged the author to continue writing and dispelled his uncertainties about his previous work. As a result of this support Svevo completed his third novel, *Confessions of Zeno,* and published the work in 1923, after twenty-five years of literary silence. Once again, Italian critics paid little attention to the novel. Joyce circulated the work among French critics, who were intrigued by Svevo's style and promised to introduce the author to the French public. At about the same time, the Italian poet Eugenio Montale published a significant study of Svevo's works in his periodical, *Esame,* which finally brought him to the attention of Italian readers. Meanwhile in France, Parisian critics Benjamin Crèmieux and Valèry Larbaud devoted an entire issue of *Le navire d'argent* to Svevo's writings, which garnered the author recognition in France and, eventually, the rest of the world. Svevo's experimental fiction, which had once alienated him from critics, found a receptive audience in readers more familiar with modernist narrative and literary techniques. Numerous articles followed this success, and Svevo was hailed as the "Italian Proust."

In the years following Svevo's death, scholars increasingly began to appreciate his literary achievements, focusing on both his formal and thematic innovations and assessing his significance within European literature. Some critics, such as Renato Poggioli and C. Roland Wagner, characterized the author as a "bourgeois writer," emphasizing the honesty of his writings and his deep understanding of the "ordinary" aspects of human life. C. P. Snow traced Svevo's influence on subsequent generations of writers, such as Kingsley Amis and William Cooper, while François Bondy described him as one of the fathers of existential literature, who perceived in the human event "a mode of existence rather than a sequence of actions." Bondy also claimed that Svevo was one of the first authors to explore the "darksome country" of old age.

A number of commentators, such as Renata Minerbi Treitel and, more recently, James Wood, have discussed the incorporation of comic and tragic elements in Svevo's writings, particularly *Confessions of Zeno.* Woods has described the work as "the great modern novel of the comic-pathetic illusion of freedom." Questions related to identity and selfhood, as well as Svevo's treatment of the relationship between the genders, have also prompted critical studies in recent decades, such as those by Elizabeth Fifer, Roland A. Champagne, and Giuliana Minghelli. As a result of these and many other assessments, in both English and Italian, Svevo's stature in world literature has increased significantly. Whereas he suffered years of critical neglect during his lifetime, today he is generally regarded as one of Italy's most significant twentieth-century authors, commended for both his original approach to narrative and his preoccupation with existential questions related to identity and the human condition. Renato Poggioli has declared that Svevo's primary concern in all his work is "the value of man," adding that the author was "endowed with such bourgeois honesty and common sense as to refuse to transform his indulgent egoism into any set of theories, any 'egotism.' A kind of innocent wisdom was the real source of his greatness and originality. He was with everybody, including himself, a man of the world." Poggioli concludes that "in the annals of literature very few books will remain so youthfully fresh as the pages of a writer like Svevo, who spent all his life in drawing a 'portrait of the artist as an old man.'"

PRINCIPAL WORKS

Una vita [*A Life*] (novel) 1892
Senilità [*As a Man Grows Older*] (novel) 1898
La coscienza di Zeno [*Confessions of Zeno*] (novel) 1923

Terzetto spezzato (play) 1927

Una burla riuscita [*The Hoax*] (short story) 1928

La novella del buon vecchio e della bella fanciulla e altri scritti [*The Nice Old Man and the Pretty Girl, and Other Stories*] (short stories) 1929

Corto viaggio sentimentale e altri racconti inediti [*Short Sentimental Journey, and Other Stories*] (short stories) 1949

James Joyce (lecture) 1950

*Commedie (plays) 1960

Diario per la fidanzata, 1896 (diary) 1962

Further Confessions of Zeno (play and short stories) 1969

*This work includes the plays *Ariosto governatore, La rigenerazione, Le ire di Giuliano, Le teorie del conte Alberto, Il ladro in casa, Una commedia inedita, Prima del ballo, La verità, Terzetto spezzato, Atto unico, Un marito, L'avventura di Maria, Inferiorità,* and *Con la penna d'oro.*

CRITICISM

C. P. Snow (essay date 1961)

SOURCE: Snow, C. P. "Italo Svevo: Forerunner of Cooper and Amis." In *Essays and Studies, 1961: Being a Volume of Fourteen of the New Series of Essays and Studies Collected for the English Association,* edited by Derek Hudson, pp. 7-16. London: John Murray, 1961.

[*In the following essay, Snow describes Svevo as an "attractive and idiosyncratic" writer, who has "his own singular place" in the novel genre, and traces his influence on such writers as Kingsley Amis and William Cooper.*]

Towards the end of the twenties, smart young men used to demonstrate that they were in the swim by introducing the name of Svevo into literary articles. Svevo was being talked about in Paris; no one seemed quite clear why he was so important, but somehow the name had a gnomic ring, rather as, say, the name of Musil had in the early fifties. A cluster of legends began to drift foggily across the Channel—that Svevo (who was recently dead—that was the one hard indisputable fact) had been an immensely rich Jewish financier who tossed off two or three masterpieces in the midst of conducting gigantic industrial negotiations.

What kind of masterpiece? On that opinion was vaguer. For safety's sake, his name was usually tagged on to those of Proust and Joyce. Then in 1930 and 1931 appeared translations of his two best known novels, excellent and racy translations by Beryl de Zoete. At last some of us actually got down to reading him. Quite a few literary people were touched by those books, so sad, funny, quirky, and unforced; to one or two of us, thinking of the novels we hoped to write, totally dissatisfied with the aesthetic (represented by Joyce and Virginia Woolf) round us, and trying to work out a new one, he meant rather more. But then his name began to slip out again, as mysteriously as it had slipped in; the kind of writing of which he was a part went underground; when it reappeared, its younger practitioners had not so much as heard of him, although at one or two removes they owed him a certain debt.

In fact, his books wear well, and he was an interesting man, although the legends about him are pleasing examples of biographical transmogrification. He was born in 1861, in Trieste, then the chief port of the Hapsburg Empire. His real name was Ettore Schmitz. His family was Jewish: that is about the one point where the legends approximate to the truth, and even that is misleading. The Schmitzes had been assimilated for a couple of hundred years. They thought of themselves as indistinguishable from the Italian-speaking commercial middle-classes of Trieste, among whom they lived. Like nearly all the characters in Svevo's books, they were strongly Italian in sentiment, and the only passionate political feeling Svevo ever had was the desire to see Trieste part of Italy.

He was an unbeliever, but just once in his life, after his mother's death, he tried to get comfort from the faith. The faith then, and always in his books, meant the Catholic faith. In that, as in so much else, except his gift, he belongs to the Triestine *bourgeoisie*—in middle age a fattish, bald, comfortable, timid man, arriving regularly at his favourite café, fond of his food, devoted to his wife and child, talking of himself as old when, in northern countries, a contemporary might admit to a brisk middle age.

His great riches? His Napoleonic business moves? They did not exist. He was nothing like so successful a business man as, say, Mr. Wallace Stevens: he did not even get as far in business as Stendhal, the Consul of Civitavecchia, got in his public life, and was nothing like so ambitious about it. As Svevo himself wrote, when he thought his writing had come to nothing:

> I can't help smiling when my critics, out of benevolence, not being able to do me the pleasure of acclaiming me as a great writer call me a great financier and a great industrialist. I am neither the one nor the other.

He always did, conscientiously and with resignation, what he was asked to. That was all. Until he married, he was working as a high-class bank clerk, at a salary corresponding in present-day terms to about £600 per annum. When he married, his wife's family pulled him out of the bank and made him manager of their family firm, which manufactured nothing more glamorous than varnish for the keels of boats. In this job, which gave little scope for dazzling coups, he was modestly prosperous, and in his later life was perhaps earning what would now be equivalent to £3,000 to £4,000 per annum. The remarkable thing, when one reads his attempts to describe business transactions in *The Confessions of Zeno,* is that he did so well. He was conscientious and steady, but he had about as much feel for the commercial life as Charlotte Brontë had for the higher education of young women.

The truth is not dramatic, but fairly natural. He was really a born writer; but he was also a timid, hypersensitive and unusually realistic man. He just did not see how he could ever make a living out of writing. His family, which in his childhood had been well enough off to educate him in Germany, had lost its money; so at eighteen he found himself in the Trieste branch of the Union Bank of Vienna. As usual, he accepted his fate. In the bank he did his best. At nights he behaved like other aspiring young writers, sketched out plays, wrote short stories, went round the artistic cafés of Trieste, in his diary solemnly discussed his own work. Occasionally he saw himself in print. Trieste had its *salons* and its cultivated circles, which, although they now seem to an outsider to have shown a good many Austrian traits, were vehemently Italophile and Irredentist. They had their own newspaper, the *Independente,* for which Svevo was sometimes allowed to write.

It was out of this world, of clerks, petty officials, small businessmen, of offices and cafés, of the girls of good family the young men hoped to marry and the impoverished girls they fell in love with, that Svevo built his first novel, *Una Vita.* It was published at his own expense (it would not have cost him much) by the local firm of Vram in 1892. (It has never been translated into English.) Few first novels have ever had less success; it was reviewed in three papers, including the *Independente*; he sent a copy to the German novelist Paul Heyse and got back a letter of guarded praise asking why he wrote about such insignificant people. It always remained to Svevo the favourite among his books: but after its publication he felt unavailing as usual, resigned as usual, slightly more hypochondriacal and troubled about his cigarette-smoking, just as conscientious at the office, a bit of a muff.

At this stage he fell in love, not with a person so much as a family, the Veneziani. The father was all he was not, a tough and effective business man, there were four unmarried daughters. Svevo duly drifted into love with the haughty and beautiful one, not being clear in his muffish way that she loved his best friend. Meanwhile, the ferocious Veneziani mother had decided that he was compromising the plainest of the daughters, who had fallen for him. As usual kind, absent-minded, unable to

say no, Svevo could not see a way to evade marrying her, and marry her he dutifully did. This situation is described with exquisite naturalism and self-mockery in *The Confessions of Zeno,* which is drawn very closely from the life. He did make the minor alteration of giving Zeno's wife a squint, which Svevo's wife in real life did not in fact possess—but, as she says sweetly and candidly in her memoir of her husband—'Augusta (Zeno's wife)—so different from me physically but in whom Svevo drew my moral portrait.'

Incidentally, Signora Svevo's book (*Vita Di Mio Marito,* Edizione dello Zibaldone, Trieste, 1951) is one of the most amiable and unpretentious of its kind. It does not set out to be a work of art or penetration, it just sets down some facts with simplicity, candour and love. Relatives of good writers ought to take it as a model—and study the egregious memoir of Dostoievski's daughter as the best example of how not to do it.

The marriage was a very happy one, to Svevo's muffish surprise. 'Didn't you know marriage was like this?' said his young wife, not long out of school, to Svevo, who had had his love affairs. To his astonishment, she did, and he didn't. His standard of domestic content went up: also his standard of living, since he was soon lugged out of the bank. Meanwhile, in 1898, he published his second novel, *Senilità* (also from Vram, also at his own expense. English edition, 1931; *As A Man Grows Older,* translated by Beryl de Zoete).

It is the story of a minor Triestine functionary, still not forty despite the title, falling in love with a working-class girl whom he cannot marry. A good many critics, especially Italians, have come to consider it his best work. At the time it did even worse than his first novel. Once again he had three reviews, two of them from Trieste papers. Once again he had a letter from Paul Heyse, even more guarded in its praise, even stronger in its regret that the characters were so insignificant. No writer was ever more discouraged by criticism, or the lack of it, than Svevo. That reception went pretty near to drying him up for over twenty years. As his wife says, with her usual sweet-natured realism: 'If *Senilità* had had any success, I am certain that he would have continued to write, although the needs of his family would have prevented him from abandoning his work (at the varnish firm) to dedicate himself completely to art.'

As it was, Svevo soldiered on, through his forties, through his fifties. He wrote scraps and notes, but his literary hopes he had driven out of sight. He became even more conscientious at his job, and travelled often to England, where the Veneziani had just started a subsidiary varnish factory at Charlton: Svevo's impressions of London were largely gained through the somewhat desolate journey between Charlton and his hotel in Russell Square. He had occasional autumnal love-affairs:

the *novelle* describe several of these, in which the poor old gentleman really wants to go home to his wife and put his feet up.

During this whole period, from 1898 until 1922, he had one single piece of luck, the only real piece of luck in his literary life. In 1907 he wanted to improve his spoken English, and he arranged to have lessons from a young teacher in Trieste, who happened to be James Joyce. Joyce, who was twenty years the younger man, promptly assured Svevo that he, Joyce, who had published almost nothing, was the greatest writer alive. The lessons continued. At the end of one of them, Svevo, in trepidation, without a word, feeling ineffectual and out-faced, slipped an uncut, yellowed copy of **Una Vita** into Joyce's pocket.

Now Joyce had some of the unpleasing characteristics of megalomania, but he had the pleasing ones too; he decided Svevo was a very good writer, and from that moment the entire efforts of the C.P.S.U. (B) would not have budged him. To the incredulous Trieste intelligentsia, he declared that Svevo was the only interesting Italian writer. If Italians complained that Svevo could not write Italian, well, so much the worse for them. On this point, modern Italian critics would most of them agree that Joyce was right. Svevo was faced with a problem which does not beset English writers to the same degree: what language to write in? Not so much by conscious choice as because it was necessary for the content of his books, he wanted to write in an easy, un-rhetorical, flat, general-purpose prose, a good deal nearer the colloquial language than most Italian of his period. But what colloquial language? At home, the Svevos and their friends talked Triestine, which is a dialect or language something like Venetian, and more unlike Tuscan than, say, the spoken speech of Mr. Faulkner's characters is unlike the spoken speech of North Oxford. Svevo made a compromise; he did not write in Triestine, but it is Triestine which lies at the root of that relaxed, intimate, buttonholing style.

At the time, apart from cheering Svevo up, Joyce's praise did not have any practical results. Svevo spent a little more time with his notebooks; he may have drafted one or two *novelle*. His gentle, dutiful sadness grew with age. The war separated his family. He was alone in Trieste, which in his view was fighting on the wrong side. Everything he had hoped for had come to nothing, and he was a kind, despondent, ageing man. The glummer his life became, though, the more his hypochondria grew. No one could see less point in living—but he was convinced that his obsessive cigarette-smoking was shortening his life, and that was a most serious matter. He was frequently vowing that this one really must be the last cigarette. He got interested in psychoanalysis, partly because he was a literary psychologist himself, partly because it might be able to stop him smoking.

After 1918, with Trieste Italian at last, with his daughter marrying, with his first grandson, he had a wave of high spirits. He wrote articles for the new Italian nationalist paper in Trieste, for a public which now knew him only as a comfortable business man. In 1922, he took a summer holiday in Poggioreale, which looks out over the Istrian gulf. Then, suddenly, it all pelted out: his comic, sad, muffish life, his hero-worship for his father-in-law, his marriage, his hypochondria about smoking, his depressed love-affairs. He wrote the first draft of a very long novel in a fortnight. No critical success of this century has been written so fast. The book in its final form is about 200,000 words long. He must have written 14,000 words a day. There is nothing mysterious about this outpouring. It was the result of being bottled up, discouraged, experiencing, for twenty years. The nearest equivalent I can think of is Stendhal, in very similar circumstances, after a literary career of unqualified failure, suddenly setting to and writing *La Chartreuse de Parme,* which is half as long again as Svevo's book, in a month.

La Coscienza di Zeno was published in the summer of 1923, by Cappelli, a Bolognese firm, again at the author's expense (English edition, 1930, **The Confessions of Zeno,** translated by Beryl de Zoete). It fell absolutely flat. It got a shade more notice than its predecessors; in Trieste, where Svevo was by now something of a figure, he had five reviews, in Bologna three (inspired, one cannot help suspecting, by his publishers), four more in the rest of Italy. It was disaster. Svevo had no hope left. He was not merely sad, he was becoming melancholic. His heart symptoms got worse. To write another book was unthinkable; this was the end.

On a morning in 1925, he was sitting at breakfast with his three grandsons. He was sixty-three. A letter was brought in. He opened it absent-mindedly and began to read. His wife says that she never in their life together saw his face so radiant. The letter was from Valery Larbaud, and began:

> Dear Sir and Master, Since I received and read **La Coscenza di Zeno,** I have done all I can to make this admirable book known in France. My propaganda has so far been only word of mouth, but nevertheless effective as you will see. . . .

The letter said, in effect, that a circle of French writers had taken up Svevo. They were just about to write articles on him in the new intellectual magazine *Commerce,* in the *Nouvelle Revue Française,* and in the *Revue Européenne.*

It was the first public appreciation Svevo had ever had. He was suffused with joy. Just as he had been totally downcast by neglect, so he was totally elated by this bit of notice.

He owed it, at least partially, to Joyce, who had made him send copies of **Zeno** [**The Confessions of Zeno**] to two Frenchmen, Larbaud and Crémieux, and two Englishmen, Ford and T. S. Eliot. There is also a strong presumption that Joyce had done some talking behind the scenes. Anyway, it was the French, Larbaud and Crémieux, who made Svevo's reputation. They did it with skill and devotion, and within a couple of years literary people all over the world had heard of him. It is unusual, of course, for a writer to make his name in a foreign country before his own: it is even more unusual for that foreign country to be France.

From then on, Svevo basked in a state of modest inflation. The young Italian writers, led by Eugenio Montale, followed the French lead; there was a Svevo Club in Florence; even in Trieste, people heard of his fame. He was not a suspicious man; he took praise simply and with delight. His literary life had come right. Diffident as he used to be, he felt this praise was just. 'I always knew I should do something,' he said, happily, quite untruthfully.

He was afraid he would die before the translations came out. He still did his duty at the office. He was still worried about his physical symptoms: he had never managed to stop smoking; and in his sixties, he remained by no means reassured about the effect of smoking on the lungs. In fact, he died in a motor accident, when his chauffeur, during a holiday trip near Treviso, rammed the car into a tree. It was a kind of sad, Svevo-ish joke, and on his death-bed he lived up to it. Timid as he had always been, he nevertheless managed to be stoical. He told his daughter: 'It isn't much to die'. He asked for a cigarette and was refused. He muttered: 'This really would be the last cigarette'.

How good a writer was he? Except for **Una Burla Riuscita** (**The Hoax,** translated by Beryl de Zoete) the shorter works are not significant. He stands by the three novels. Superficially, the first two of these, **Una Vita** and **As a Man Grows Older,** are so different from **Zeno** that they might be by a different writer; he is always a bit wordy and repetitive, but the first two are as formally composed as Flaubert's or Turgeniev's novels, whereas, on the outside. **Zeno** is self-consciously of the early twenties, beginning with a note from a psychoanalyst, split up into chapters without any but the most tenuous narrative line. Nevertheless the differences do not mean much. It is possible to argue that, in structure, **Una Vita** is the most original of the three, **As a Man Grows Older** the most perfect, **Zeno** the least integrated, but it is only at a secondary level that, reading Svevo, one makes such comparisons. One does not think of reading him for novel architecture, any more than one really reads him for the evocation of the background of Trieste, effective in a subdued fashion though that is. Everything that Svevo wrote is set there, and the beau-

tiful city, beautiful as Quebec is beautiful, not so much because of the buildings in detail but because of the shape of the streets, the colour, the light and water, looks down on Svevo's sad old men, his young optimistic bumblers, the affectionate girls. But that is by the way. And so is his depiction of character, which is subtle, but not, particularly in the first two novels, very strongly projected. His characters are not embossed as the great projective writers' are, but as one reads one thinks 'How true, how life-like'.

His special gift is something different again. It is something like an absolute candour. In a certain range of emotional experience, no one could be more unselfsparingly honest. It is that special kind of truth-telling which makes him so funny and so sad. An unavailing young man finding that he is expected to marry the wrong girl—a respectable elderly man taking a mistress who is too much for him—in all the situations where self-respect is at its most precarious, Svevo tells the truth in a manner fluid, straightforward, naked to life.

It is that quality which has given him an influence on an interesting stream of modern novels. The best part of Mr. Kingsley Amis's work—as, for example, in the Margaret-Dixon scenes in *Lucky Jim*—shows a truthfulness which bears a family resemblance to Svevo's. This is not so surprising as it sounds, for Mr. Amis is the latest member of a literary chain. Part of *Lucky Jim* is owed (in an entirely proper sense) to an intelligent study of Mr. William Cooper's *Scenes from Provincial Life*. Part of *Scenes from Provincial Life* is owed to an intelligent study of **Zeno** and William Gerhardi's *The Polyglots*. Part of *The Polyglots* is owed to an intelligent study of Chekhov and (this is the one link of the chain that cannot be documented, although it is certain that Svevo studied Chekhov's master, Turgeniev) I am prepared to bet that that was also true of **Zeno**.

This is one of the clearest cases on record of direct literary transmission. Many of the things one can say of Svevo apply, with greater or lesser force, to the other writers. For instance, all of them, despite the knowingness of Cooper and Amis, are unworldly: they are lost in a mysterious, inconsequential, and often hilarious universe: everything that happens is about as probable or improbable as anything else. It is that unworldliness which gives them their innocence: without it their art would be too cheeky by half.

Of these writers, Svevo is certainly the least professional. He is not always easy to read. On the other hand, he is in some ways the most original and the deepest-natured. I do not want to claim too much for him. He is not a great writer. He is, however, an attractive and idiosyncratic one. He may very well be, as Italian critics have asserted, the best Italian novelist since Verga. In the wider field of the world novel he has his own singular place.

François Bondy (essay date winter 1967-68)

SOURCE: Bondy, François. "Italo Svevo and Ripe Old Age." *Hudson Review* 20, no. 4 (winter 1967-68): 575-98.

[*In the following essay, Bondy remarks that Svevo "looms as one of the first explorers of that darksome country that is old age," and describes the author as "one of the fathers of that 'existential' literature that sees in the event a mode of existence rather than a sequence of actions."*]

> Strange! I feel so young and am at the same time so different from what I was in my youth! Could this be ripe old age?
>
> —Italo Svevo, **"Umbertino"**

In Italo Svevo, fables play a part close to that allotted to them in the work of Franz Kafka—the last author for whom Svevo showed enthusiasm and one to whom he intended to devote a study. One of Svevo's last fables is entitled **"The Mother."** A chick born in an incubator will not resign himself to being motherless. In a neighboring garden he spots some chicks thronging around a hen—whom, in his ignorance, he calls a giant chick—who protects her brood with her ample, warm body. "Cucco," the chick, feels that this being is surely his mother, and when the hen, by scratching on the ground, produces worms for her chicks, Cucco rushes in, delighted to have understood his mother's intentions better than the others, and gobbles up the worm. The hen hurls herself at the intruder and beats him with mighty strokes of her beak. Cucco thinks at first that these are vehement caresses, but, wounded, he takes to his heels. The mother hen, stopped by a hedge, stares at Cucco with red, furious eyes and says, "Who are you, you who steal the food I procure with so much effort?"—"I am Cucco," the chick says humbly, "but you, who are you, and why have you inflicted these wounds on me?" To this double inquiry the hen responds majestically, "I am the mother"—and turns her back on him.

This fable may have been written somewhere around 1926, at the time when Svevo's third and last novel, **The Confessions of Zeno,** met with sudden literary fame in France, where it had been discovered thanks to James Joyce, Valery Larbaud, Adrienne Monnier and several other writers. At that time, Italian criticism—with the one exception of the poet Eugenio Montale—was totally unaware of his work; the influential *Corriere della Sera,* though it had accorded a review to Svevo's first novel, *A Life,* did not deem it necessary to speak of *Zeno.* The publisher Treves refused to reissue the novels that were out of print, even though the author was offering to share the cost. And now, suddenly, Italy had to come to terms with a reputation "made in Paris" by numerous writers: those just named as well as

Benjamin Crémieux, André Thérive, Nino Franck, and still others. It was the hour Svevo had been waiting for for a quarter of a century, the hour of belated recognition. Yet here is what he could read then in the Italian periodicals:

> Italo Svevo, a Triestine merchant, author of mediocre novels, viewed among us with the indifference he deserves, finds himself suddenly proclaimed a great writer by a decadent Irish novelist living in Trieste, Joyce; by a decadent poet from Paris, Valery Larbaud; and by a critic, Benjamin Crémieux, who, because he is competent in matters of French literature, passes in France for a connoisseur of Italian literature, of which he has some notions among people who have none. What are the merits of Svevo? The fact that more than any other Italian he has espoused a passive and analytical literature which reached its peak with Proust, and which will be considered a decadent art as long as it is held that art must be the work of living and active men, and that a painter is more deserving than a mirror.

This verdict, from the year 1927, stems from the young Guido Piovene—who, nevertheless, was to become an enlightened critic and a thoroughly "analytical" novelist. But this Svevo did not live to see, any more than he was able to note his profound influence on one part of the new Italian literature—one thinks of Vittorini, of Leo Ferrero, of Alberto Moravia—which was to claim kinship with his sobriety and place him above every other Italian writer of his generation.

In the *Corriere della Sera,* the important critic Giulio Caprin was writing: "If this unrecognized Italian is destined to be recognized some day by Europe, it will have to be accomplished through some other language, and, in any case, through *some* language. Svevo is an antiliterary curiosity in Italian literature."

The mother hen of the fable who wounds poor Cucco with her beak is without any doubt Italian culture—that culture of which Ettore Schmitz, the "Italian Swabian" Italo Svevo, Triestine irredentist, wanted to be the legitimate son, without her ever consenting to recognize him as such. In all the vast *oeuvre* of the illustrious Benedetto Croce I fully believe that the name of Svevo is not mentioned a single time; otherwise Bruno Maier, the Svevo scholar, could not have failed to make note of it in his works.

In the period when Svevo considered the theatre his true mode of expression—"form of forms," he writes, "the only one that can render life in its immediacy"—he sent a play to Pirandello, who had been his guest in Trieste, asking him for his judgment and advice, but he never received an answer.

Only one writer read with care the two first novels of Svevo: Paul Heyse, a once famous German novelist, who wrote the author to express his regret at seeing him go astray by placing at the centers of his tales weak and flabby creatures instead of vigorous characters. Indeed, *A Life* was originally to have been entitled *An Inept One,* and Svevo, who knew *Hamlet* by heart and was full of Turgenev and of Chekhov, as of Jean-Paul Richter and Flaubert, never created anything but "non-characters," prey to the difficulty of being. He thus could not benefit from Heyse's well-intentioned counsel. Nevertheless, until his sixty-fifth year, Svevo was not accorded by any Italian writer even the attention, full of reservations as it was, granted him by the German author, to whom so many young writers were submitting their manuscripts.

Svevo was by no means indifferent to the fate of his writings: "The greatest unanimity is that of silence," he sighed after the failure of his second novel, *As a Man Grows Older.* He renounced publication for twenty-five years. But for the happy accident of the meeting and friendship with James Joyce, he would undoubtedly not have ventured to publish another work. But Svevo's relations with society are marked by humor and a radical irony. And his own disillusionment with the dream of literary fame appeared to him as a comic element of which he made use, exactly as of other great experiences: sickness, old age, death. A story that must date from the period of **"A Mother"** bears witness to this; it is entitled *A Hoax.* Its hero, Mario Samigli, is a "sexagenarian littérateur." His antagonist, Enrico Gaia, a traveling salesman known for his practical jokes, represents cunning and vitality incarnate. (A figure of this sort appears in all of Svevo's narratives, as Doctor Miracle does all through *The Tales of Hoffmann.*) Samigli, like Svevo himself, and like Emilio, the hero of *As a Man Grows Older,* has written in his youth a novel that went unnoticed. We are in Trieste, just after the war. Relations with Vienna, the former capital, are broken off; Gaia avails himself of this to make Samigli believe that a great Viennese publisher is offering him two hundred thousand crowns for the translation rights of that novel. Samigli is persuaded to sign a contract with our traveling salesman who purports to be the publisher's representative, and a bank draft is solemnly handed over to him. Why does Mario let himself be snared when the joke is obvious, all the more so since the two pranksters cannot control their guffaws through the whole affair? "It can be said," writes Svevo, "that Mario was a poor observer, a literary observer, hence one of those who can be effortlessly deceived, for if they should happen to make an exact observation, they must forthwith transform it by applying concepts to it. Whoever has had a few experiences is never lacking for concepts, because the same lines and colors can be adapted, as the case may be, to the most diverse things, and a littérateur insists on considering all of them."

So, for Svevo, it is the man of letters who is most easily duped, because he projects his desires and his ideas onto the tiniest scrap of reality, especially when his vanity is at stake.

Svevo was first appreciated in Paris and not, as he probably expected, in Vienna. By 1918 he had translated into Italian a book by Sigmund Freud. He followed closely Austrian intellectual life and, at the same time, thought of his glory in Italy. But Gaia thinks of it, too, in behalf of Samigli, and tells him, "You will retain ownership of the Italian language rights. I thought of that, for who knows what value this novel will acquire for Italy once it is known that it was translated into all languages?" And he reiterates, "Italy remains yours." As for Mario, he would have been content with a more modest sum, if only the novel could come out soon. "I am no longer young," he excuses himself, "and I should like to see my novel translated before I die."

The sentiment that here contributes to the success of a hoax had just been, for Svevo, a painful experience. In July he had written the head of the House of Treves, asking him to reissue *As a Man Grows Older*: "I am sixty-five years old, and I have no time to lose." The publisher replied that he was obliged, much to his regret, to return the manuscript that Svevo had considerably revised. "We are swamped for three more years, but your novel, in its day, would have deserved a kinder fate." In the short story, all this feeds the comedy. Not even the most flagrant contradictions can shake Samigli's faith. Svevo insists, "The littérateur's habit to cross out a phrase that dissatisfies him leads him into readily accepting that others should modify their statements. While elaborating on reality, he eliminates whatever jars. So here he eliminated."

One notes in this tale to what degree the Italian patriot felt himself belonging to the German culture of Central Europe. Although he had been a member of the "Patriotic League" of Trieste, national conflicts play not the slightest part in his work. He had chosen Italianness, just like his father, Schmitz, who had married an Italian woman, but he did not include literature in this commitment. Despite the all-important formative years he spent in a Bavarian school, Svevo wrote in Italian, not by a deliberate choice, but quite naturally. Neither Joyce nor contemporary French critics could associate Svevo with Austro-Hungarian literature. It was necessary, first, that the writers who were spiritually most akin to him—Kafka, Musil—be revealed. Until then the name of Svevo had to remain linked to those of Joyce and Proust, with the interior monologue, the stream of consciousness, the analyzing and distorting memory. Today Svevo takes his place quite naturally in that literature of "Cacania," along with the Croat Krleža, the Hungarian Karinthy, the Pole Bruno Schulz, and other writers of the bygone multilingual monarchy. His German translator, Piero Rismondo, and Edouard Roditi,[1] among others, have sufficiently demonstrated it. For the rest, there is no reason to sever Svevo from a more occidental tradition. The Proust-Marcel, Joyce-Dedalus, Svevo-Zeno relationships are the same: they attest to the identity of, and the distancing between, existence and work in a manner previously unknown. Illness, conceived of as a backing away from time to set it and its relation to active life into perspective, brings Svevo close to Proust, as does a sense of literature not as reflecting but as completing life.[2]

In Svevo's consciousness all is distance, like Trieste, far from Vienna, at the periphery of the Hapsburg Empire, but far, too, from Italian culture. It is literature which is in the margin of existence for this writer who was long employed in a bank and became a very active industrialist. There is a distance also between Svevo and the language he writes. We shall come back to this later. Every erotic relationship in the narratives of Svevo is a vain attempt to overcome the coldness of being, to abolish the distance between the self and the other, between self and self—and makes it only more manifest. Illnesses and aches likewise mark a distance from immediate life. But these ills pale before old age, the phase of life when involvement in active existence decreases, when humorous observation of passions and follies is sharpened. Humor mediatizes what has been lived, which it combines with other realities in unexpected relationships. Irony refracts all happenings and turns upon itself. This irony is not only an acid wit, it is above all an instrument of analysis, the apprenticeship of disillusion. Like La Rochefoucauld, Schopenhauer, Nietzsche and Freud, Svevo is a writer who "unmasks."

Svevo's spoken language is the Triestine dialect, mixed into which are fragments and syntactic forms of German and Slovene—remote indeed from classical Italian. Svevo himself has sternly judged his relationship to "good Italian," as sternly as Kafka judged his relation to the German tongue. But Svevo's self-criticism is more justified and does not have the character of gratuitous self-castigation. And yet, that impoverished language, often "incorrect" in its syntax and vocabulary, is it only the product of a deficiency? Svevo did not know well the Italian literature of his day. Among contemporaries, only Pirandello suited him. He had read diligently Machiavelli and Guicciardini, and only his father's bankruptcy prevented him from going to live in Florence to familiarize himself with "Tuscan." The first character created by Svevo, Alfonso Nitti, hero or "antihero" of *A Life,* scrutinizes his reading matter for expressions that Petrarch would not have used. Svevo's sincere doubts about his own style are apparent in his letters to friends whom he asks to go over his writings.[3]

Yet, from the outset of his literary career, Svevo was the enemy of fine writing. For him, literature is an investigation of the real, a quest for truth, and he rejected all formal beauty. In a letter of 1908 to his daughter La-

etitia, then aged ten, he writes "Abasso i poeti!" and he illustrates this exclamation with a little tale. Of two carpenters, one makes cupboards and the other describes them; both in the wood used and in the manner of fabrication, these cupboards become stranger and stranger, until he pretends to be making living cupboards that feed on clothes. "You see," Svevo concludes, "that's how things are. You describe a bit this way, a bit that way, and in the end nothing is real."

His own literature could be "true" only if it remained "anti-literary"—which it was, if one is to accept the opinion of Giulio Caprin cited above. It is a literature in which a word never suggests the *other*: every word is weighed in its nexus with things, and, beyond that, in its quality of micro-action or action-substitute. "Language offers satisfactions to a small part of the organism. It simulates a battle, when the battle is already over and lost. It wants to wound and caress. It moves among immense transferences, and if the words are incandescent, they burn the one who pronounced them."

Zeno makes fun of the psychiatrist who took his confessions at face value:

> The doctor believes a bit overmuch in these blessed confessions. He won't return them to me for corrections. But, good God! having studied only medicine, he has no idea what an effort it is to write Italian for those of us who speak (but do not know how to write) in dialect. A written confession is always mendacious, and we, it's with each Tuscan word that we lie! One will choose to relate what is easily expressed, and will set aside a fact because it's too much trouble to consult a dictionary. . . . There you have exactly what governs our choice when we insist on one episode from our life rather than another. It will be understood that in dialect our story would no longer have the same aspect.

And he provides an example:

> It seems that the doctor made an inquiry also into the subject of Guido. He maintains that, chosen by Adelina, he could not have been such as I describe him. He has discovered close by the spot where our psychoanalytical sessions took place a vast stockpile of wood that had belonged to the firm Guido Speier & Co. Why had I never mentioned it?

> Why? So as not to aggravate the difficulties of an already extremely difficult exposé. This omission proves merely that a confession written by me, in Italian, could be neither complete nor sincere. In a stockpile like that there exists an innumerable variety of woods, which we designate in Trieste by barbarisms borrowed from our dialect, from Croatian, from German, from French even (for example, *zapin,* taken from the word *sapin,* but which no longer has the same meaning). Where would I have found the proper vocabulary? I would have had to go to Tuscany, and there, old as I am, look for work with a wood merchant. By the way, the woodpile of the firm Guido Speier & Co. never yielded anything but losses.

Now, this example—and this is truly Svevian—fails to convince, for the relationship of Svevo and Zeno is not one of identity but of ironic distancing. If Zeno has concealed the existence of this great reserve of wood, it must surely have been for reasons other than linguistic insufficiency. By 1926, an Italian critic, Umberto Morra, had correctly perceived Svevo's relation to his language. "The defects are so evident that the first judgment passed on these books will always be a condemnation: they are badly written . . . But we note a peculiar obsession with not learning, the fear that a surer writing routine would be only a mask." Svevo's language has been termed "Triestine merchants' esperanto," but it always had to be admitted that Svevo achieves a very special precision and power of suggestion, that he finds expressions that are striking, transparent, appropriate to the capturing of the most complex psychological phenomena.

He was by no means indifferent to language. "The word does not merely express. It has a weight, and it has been possible to maintain that our character is formed more by what we say than by what we think." Svevo avoids all play with assonance. "Perhaps," he writes in a study devoted to Joyce, "it is an effect of our destiny that we cannot sufficiently play with words, that they should be our masters rather than our servants." But one could equally assert that punning carried to the point of linguistic mystique makes the word master, whereas Svevo, if he does not exactly dominate language, is not dominated by it either. Today, the "incorrect" Italian of Svevo passes for a model of writing. It has loosened the tongue of a whole new Italian literature—I am thinking of Pavese, of Vittorini, and even of Silone—which unmasks rhetoric and has only an ironic relationship to the great sonorous flights. Besides, it is less the vocabulary of the Triestine dialect than the German syntax that makes Svevo's language so personal to Italian ears.

It is the marginal Italian of the cosmopolitan Austro-Hungarian port—that language so different from "good Italian"—that furnished Svevo with his instrument for particular psychological analysis, and also for irony toward that analysis. A language without artifice, sober, was most apt to convey comic situations, not only those born of the contrast between rhetoric and reality, but also those which, beyond language, are comic by virtue of their situation—what could be called "clown's" comedy, if we recall that Zeno has often been judged "Chaplinesque." It is in comedy that Svevo best realized himself. And it is there, too, that one can best sense an evolution. In each of his three novels there is a personage whom we see from within, facing a world seen from without. This difference of perspective is most strongly marked in the first book, *A Life.* Only Alfonso Nitti seems to practice introspection, step back from things, while all others appear as emanations of a blind

and elemental will to live; they are unable to put themselves to the question. Alfonso Nitti is "inept" at living and commits suicide. The others succeed or fail in their careers, plot, perish, but they derive their criteria from life itself and not, like Nitti, from a view of life, from a critical stance. *A Life* unfurls as yet along the mainstream of naturalism, where different milieus—banking, the petty bourgeoisie, the peasantry—are scrutinized fairly systematically. It was needful for Svevo to kill Nitti in order for him, afterward, to make Emilio and Zeno live.

In *As a Man Grows Older,* the contrast between Emilio and his sculptor friend Stefano is no longer so pronounced. Stefano, whom no success has crowned, but who is sure nevertheless of his art, proclaims aesthetic principles that are those of Svevo himself. Emilio's sick sister is also seen from the inside, and not only through Emilio's eyes. *A Life* is rich in proto-comic situations, but they are lived out without humor, as they must be lived by a young man like Alfonso. If Emilio, at thirty-five, is presented as an aging man—Svevo finally entitled his novel *Senilità* [in English, *As a Man Grows Older*], although he first wanted to call it "Emilio's Carnival"—the precocious decrepitude manifests itself in the deliberate gap between action and observation, in the progressive movement of disillusionment, in Emilio's becoming aware that he wants to conquer the "flirt" Angiolina (we shall find a girl of this type in Moravia's *The Empty Canvas* and in Dino Buzzati's *A Love Affair*) only to provide himself with a source of warmth, invaded as he is by his own internal cold, and to acquire that elemental vitality of which he feels himself deprived, but with which, ultimately, he will be able to do nothing, because nothing in him really demands it. Love as an experiment and as cure by rejuvenation, what can it be if not an old man's love? Thus Emilio already heralds Zeno, the "vecchione," the "vegliardo," who will secure for themselves the possession of girls by means of money and gifts, and will try to convince themselves that they are performing for the girls a paternally educational mission. "Starting with a certain age, all passion passes through paternity."

The greater the inner coldness, the nearer the natural end, and the more sexuality, in Svevo, becomes the subject of tragicomedy: the eternal return is experienced as an unending search for novelty. In love, the "old man" endeavors not to see himself as the conquered or bought girls see him, but the effort remains unsuccessful. Zeno is greatly surprised that Felicita, the proprietress of a tobacco shop, should repeat to him, "I assure you you don't disgust me." He hadn't given it a thought, and he replies spontaneously, "You don't disgust me either"—and Felicita bursts out laughing. The fairly horrible comedy that Svevo extracts from the relation between sexuality and senility arises from the difference in response between the partners, each of whom, because of what he expects from the relationship, applies himself to playing the role that would best meet the other's expectations.

Like all great humor, Svevo's emerges from where tragedy is born: from love, old age, death. Distance is established when existence is flat against the immediate, close enough to be gasping for breath.

Georg Lukács, in his recently published *Aesthetics,* stresses the kinship between Kafka and Chaplin. In the very sense in which Lukács means it, this kinship applies also to Svevo. Zeno is a bourgeois clown. For him, clumsiness becomes destiny. In the most celebated episode of *Zeno,* the marriage proposal, Zeno sets himself successively, in a single evening, to conquering three sisters: first the most beautiful, whom he loves; then the youngest; and, finally, by accident, Augusta, the squint-eyed, whom he is then obliged to marry. In this scene it is apparent, too, that, except for the "inept" Nitti, Svevo's heroes do not undergo true "defeats," but that, on the contrary, they stumble onto happiness over failed actions and accidents—for Augusta will be for him the ideal spouse.

Another example of this felicitous stumbling: in the last chapter of the novel, Zeno is caught unawares by the war as he is picking roses; he cannot go home, he is dragged off on journeys, he throws himself into speculations and makes a fortune. And Mario Samigli, the failed novelist, victim of the "hoax," also profits by the war, for he banks the phoney draft from the imaginary publisher, and buys it back with Austrian crowns since devaluated, thus realizing a tidy profit to console him for his misfortune.

Whereas Augusta, conquered by Zeno (without his wanting it) will be for him a marvelous helpmeet; the beauteous Ada, who rejected his advances, is disfigured by Basedow's disease; and Zeno's rival whom she marries, Guido Speier, the capable fellow, makes bad business deals and ends up the victim of a ridiculous suicide meant to have been only simulated—an episode which, in turn, will be a scene of high comedy. It is in *Zeno,* too, that we encounter numerous scenes of macabre humor, such as the burial of Guido Speier. Zeno and his colleague Nilini are immersed in so passionate a conversation about the stock market that they get involved in another funeral procession headed for another cemetery:

> When we got to the point where, habitually, the carriages stopped, Nilini stuck his head through the door and emitted a cry of astonishment. The carriage was still following the cortège wending its way to the Greek cemetery.
>
> "—Was Mr. Speier Greek, then?" he inquired.

Indeed, we had left behind the Catholic cemetery and were off to some other burial ground—Jewish, Greek, Protestant or Serbian.

"—Perhaps he was a Protestant," I murmured at first.

But no! He had definitely been married in the Church. Then I exclaimed, "They must be making a mistake!" thinking that they were going to bury him in someone else's grave.

Suddenly Nilini burst into laughter, uncontrollable laughter that hurled him exhausted to the depths of the carriage, his hideous mouth wide open. "—We were wrong!" he shouted.

As soon as he could restrain his hilarity, he covered me with reproaches. I should have known where we were going, been cognizant of the time . . . Here we were participating in the funeral of an unknown.

I was no more in a mood for laughter than I was disposed to accept his reproaches. Why hadn't he, for his part, opened his eyes? I hid my displeasure, for the stock market mattered more to me than the obsequies. We got out of the carriage to orient ourselves, and took the path to the Catholic cemetery. The cab was following us. The members of the other dead man's cortège looked at us with surprise. Doubtless they could not explain to themselves why, after having honored the deceased with our presence up to the entrance of his final resting place, we were dropping him at the finest moment.

Nilini, impatient, was walking ahead. He asked the gatekeeper:

"—Has Mr. Speier's funeral procession arrived yet?"

The gatekeeper remained unastonished by this rather comic question. He answered that he knew nothing about it.

One is reminded of the demise of the friend, Copler, who, being sick, is visited by Zeno and discovered dead. Thence Zeno goes off to dinner at his father-in-law's, and in order not to spoil the evening, pretends that Copler is "doing much better." But he gets drunk and describes Copler's death. Very embarrassed by this blunder, he then declares that it was only a joke. At last, Zeno remarks pensively:

> I was never "his" again: I wasn't even present at his funeral. We had so much to do at home and in town that there was not an hour to be spared for him. Sometimes he was spoken of at table, but only as a joke, in memory of that dinner at which, half drunk, I had several times killed and resurrected him. It even became an adage in the family. If it happened that a newspaper announced and then denied someone's death, we would say, "It's like poor Copler."

Other comic situations take off from sickness, from suffering. Zeno begins to limp the moment a friend explains to him how many muscles are needed to set the foot in motion (we grasp then why Svevo chose the name Zeno). And this limp becomes an ailment that will never leave him. Likewise, the triple marriage proposal is made more comic by Zeno's passing the evening in hobbling from one girl to the other.

The comic in Svevo, then, is the relation of a social reality to a corporeal reality, whether it is a case of love, disease, or death. And discourse is only one of the means—not always the most significant—with which this false relation is realized.

Alongside of situational comedy, there is the one that flows from verbiage, from description, and which affects only the reader. In contradistinction to situational comedy, perceptible to the very persons in the story, one could here speak of humor. Thus Zeno, intoxicated, finds himself next to his sister-in-law Alberta, who wants to know his views on love, and he tells her:

> "A woman is an object whose price varies a good deal more than that of any commodity on the market."
>
> Alberta did not get my meaning very well. She thought that I was expressing the banal truism that a woman's worth varies with her age. I made myself clearer: a woman's worth may be great in the morning, zero at noon, very great a little later, and distinctly negative in the evening. I explained the concept of negative value: a woman takes on negative value when a man reckons within himself what sum he would pay gladly to know her far away from him.

Alberta being incapable of understanding this reflection, he illustrates it in a very direct manner, and comedy of expression becomes situational comedy.

A more indirect humor characterizes the fragment entitled **"Short Sentimental Journey,"** and the evocation of Laurence Sterne by this title is all the more significant. The insurance company inspector who, on the train, engages Aghios in conversation, speaks of the low prices of commodities during his youth. "He caresses his low prices," thinks Mr. Aghios, "as if they were his dear deceased parents."

The psychoanalyst for whom Zeno writes his confession is a source of continuous humor, for **Zeno** is a psychoanalytical novel, but also one that makes fun of psychoanalysis. When the doctor imparts to Zeno, in the wake of his confessions, certain solemn verities, Zeno thinks:

> I prefer laughing about these asininities to discussing them. Which did not prevent the doctor, while proffering them, from assuming his air of Christopher Columbus disembarking in the New World. What a man! Realizing that I had had the desire to go to bed with two very beautiful women, he gravely asked himself for what reasons. Who but he could have invented questions like that?

Svevo considered psychoanalysis a marvelous discovery because of its double relationship—conscious and unconscious—to humor, all the more so as sexuality was at the center of its thought. Psychoanalysis is at once a manifestation of and occasion for mistrust—occasion because it relies too much on words. For Svevo, basically, psychoanalysis is literature, and, for that reason, suspect like all literature. But in the same way that his antiliterary novels belong to literature. his anti-Freudian commentaries stay in the domain of psychoanalysis.[4]

For Svevo, psychology and irony merge. He has the feeling that "the *I* is the most important being in this whole vast world," but also that the world knows nothing about it. The immense and uprooting events lived by the *I* can be "distanced" by psychology, as can the banal and mundane events happening to "just anybody." The *I,* that unique face, is itself only a mask. Nothing is so impersonal, so rigorously subject to laws, as is perfect egocentricity. The truly personal factor is the ability to bypass egocentricity slightly, to observe oneself with irony. It is not a method of changing this *I*; but since another Being is not possible, at least another Way of Looking. . . .

From his first writings on, Svevo inserts into his tales reflections on the enjoyment of pain or of the recollection of pain. "The sensation of having to be much happier now than he was a few minutes before was not pleasing to him. For pain, especially when it is past, has a fascinating force of attraction, and, for weak natures, it is a satisfaction to become submerged in it." (*A Life.*) In **"Short Sentimental Journey,"** Aghios meditates: "Pain remembered is not always pain. At present, he felt in it the intensity of life. Ah! why couldn't he feel again that impatience and that pain! What a new lease on life!"

To be set free from pain, then, is not happiness. Similarly, the analysis of the cause of a malady does not set one free from it. "Strange that the analyzing of the causes of a too painful sentiment should not suffice to destroy or even to shade it! It could be the matter of a misunderstanding, a reparable error, a moment's blindness, a word. But after the analysis, all is as before: a pain, a setback, a passionate desire."

Svevo has spoken of psychoanalysis in these terms:

> What writer could renounce thinking of psychoanalysis? I got to know it in 1910. My neurotic friend rushed to Vienna to undergo treatment. The knowledge I thus acquired was the only happy consequence of his therapy. He let himself be analyzed for two years and came back utterly undone, abouliac as before, but his aboulia henceforth aggravated by his conviction that he was so constituted and could not be otherwise.
>
> (*Saggi e pagine sparse,* p. 175; published posthumously.)

To unmask a hidden social relationship is not yet a revolution: to unmask the artifices of a psychology is not yet a metamorphosis. To clarify, to transform: for

Svevo, these realms remain perfectly distinct. He removed from his work the dimension of the future; what concerns him is clarification directed toward the past, and not transformation brought to bear on the coming. If the dimension of futurity does exist for him, it is solely in order to apprehend the past from the standpoint of the present in its possibilities and its indeterminacy, at the point where it is open and not yet fatality. The present is a hypothesis; the past remains charged with the unknowable.

If the future as such is missing from Svevo's work, it is because the old man plays a bigger part in his work than he has in all previous literature. (Beckett, and Faulkner, in some aspects of his work, are also writers of old age.) One can legitimately compare Svevo to Joyce and Proust on the one hand, and to Kafka, Schnitzler, and Musil, on the other, but this particular remains Svevo's own. For Stephen Daedalus, Marcel, Josef K., Anatol, Ulrich are young or just barely ripening men.

Alfonso Nitti, the only young man in Svevo's *oeuvre,* experiences a difficulty of being: life and he himself collaborate on his destruction, less so by the pressure of threatening forces in society than because these forces find in him the complicity of a lack of will to live, of a corrosive doubt that urges him toward renunciation. By suicide, Nitti amputates his future. Emilio, in **As a Man Grows Older,** is already an old man in the making, even though he is only thirty-five. In the letters that Svevo, then aged forty, was writing to his wife, he speaks of himself as a man already on the threshold of ripe old age; he lavishes on his wife paternal advice—notably that she should remarry upon his death. Since Lao-Tse, whom his mother, according to legend, carried for eighty years, and who was born white-haired, there has probably not been such a "born old man," for it is in the works of his old age that Svevo found fulfillment. The "Zeno after Zeno" of his last narratives, and the nameless "old man" complete Svevo's world, along with those few figures that recur as regularly as the masks of the commedia dell'arte: the hussy, the worthy wife, the friend bursting with obscene vitality.

In his final tales, Svevo abandons any attempt to individualize: there are now only silhouettes, ciphers, that remind one of the *nouveau roman.* Why the masks? In his ripe old age, man lives repetitions rather than the unique, but Svevo's old men are by virtue of this all the more avid for new and unique experiences. The older Svevo gets, the more his personages resemble one another, and the more he takes his distance by means of abstraction, by ironic generalizations with which the tale is shot through. His old men seek exclusively one more renewal of the "warmth" of life, albeit well aware that this quest ends in the grotesque. Today when gerontology has become a science, and when the world contains more old people (and more young ones) than

ever—one recalls the apocalyptic vision of the overpopulated world at the close of **Zeno!**—Svevo looms as one of the first explorers of that darksome country that is old age.

Svevo had not the pitiless judgment of Knut Hamsun, who, in his nineties, wrote in his last book, "Advanced age brings no wisdom, old age has only itself to bring,"—but down to his last stories, his last letters, Svevo does not for an instant fudge this reality, he nurtures no illusion. There is humor, breeziness and—let us say it, although Svevo did not care for modish terms—an existential awareness of aging, which, for him, is an experience of incomparable potency, even if it is a matter of impotence, and a repertoire of new possibilities (or lacks). Above all, aging permits one to see different ages in a new perspective.

In his last (unfinished) novel, **The Old Man,** begun in the summer of 1928 (Svevo died on September 13 from the consequences of an auto accident), we can read the following:

> I continue to struggle between past and present, but at least hope does not intrude any more, the anguished hope for the future. In consequence, I always live in a mixed time, for that is man's destiny; yet grammar knows of pure times, which seem to be made for the animals, which, when they are not frightened, live in a crystalline present. But for the old man (well, yes! I am an old man, it is the first time I am saying it, and it is the first benefit from my new aptitude for concentration) the amputation by which life loses what it never possessed, the future, simplifies his existence, even if it makes it so denuded of meaning as to tempt one to tear out his last remaining hairs. . . . I have meditated so long about this problem that even my inactive life has provided me with the chance for an experiment that could be clarified if it were repeated with finer instruments, which is to say by putting in my place someone more skilled in precise observations.

And here are the concluding lines of this fragment:

> To be old, the livelong day, without a moment's respite! And with each instant to grow older yet! I accustom myself painfully to being what I am today, and tomorrow I must resume the effort to reënsconce myself in my seat grown still more uncomfortable. Who can deny me the right to speak, to shout, to protest? All the more so as protest is the shortest path to resignation.

In **"The Nice Old Man and the Pretty Girl,"** a friend wants to convince the old man that advanced age is in itself an illness, but earns this answer: "The old man is merely weak. He is nothing other than a young man grown weak." And, in another tale, this reflection: "Strange! I feel so young and am at the same time so different from the young man I was! Could this be old age?"

Old age, then, is that experience that could not be deduced from anything if one did not feel it: "If there were no old men in this world, it would be impossible

to imagine that from the rosy face of the child expressing all of life still inchoate there would emerge this
hard pasteboard face whose lines life traces one after
the other without any care for harmony, these lines of
which some may signify a perhaps painful thought, others the suffering of the flesh itself that twists and becomes misshapen because it is over- or underfed. All
these scars that efface the original traits, unless they
make of them, in the same material, a caricature!"

To grow old is to diminish; but illness, the difficulty of
living of the "inept" also constitute a diminution. Man
then turns away from life, and everything goes on as if
the vital process could be conveyed only thanks to this
slowing down. In life, it is the representation of this ap-
titude for being, and not defeat, that interests Svevo.
His sickly or hypochondriacal old men are, in truth, of
a surprising vitality, thus the "veglione" who, twice a
week, pays a visit to the proprietress of the tobacco
shop. Zeno succeeds in his speculations: the bungler
comes off better than the clever ones.

Is there a connection between this and Svevo's life?
During long years he led a dreary existence as a minor
bank employee, teacher in a trade school, analyst of the
foreign press for a newspaper. Thereafter, through his
marriage to the daughter of a wealthy industrialist, Veneziani, he was led into concerning himself with business, and ended up in the skin of a competent entrepreneur.

The parallel between this career and the lives of the
characters in his books is obvious. But Svevo never
made of failure a criterion of intellectuality. The man
with artistic aspirations who is obliged to submit to the
prosaic demands of a job appeared to him comic rather
than touching. In the conflict between the bourgeois and
the artist—on which Thomas Mann was to feed his
work—Svevo is not on the artist's side; what interests
him is the conflict, the opportunity for him to exercise
his irony at the expense of the bourgeois and the artist
alike. Failure is not the seal of a superior vocation, but
success, in turn, is not the confirmation of a gift, nor
necessarily the fruit of an activity. Svevo's personages
meet with success in time of war, by virtue of troubled
circumstances, through inflation, accidents, strokes of
luck; these are gains stemming from a game at the edge
of catastrophe. Thus the successes, in their dispropor-
tion to the effort, assume a character as comic as that of
the failed actions and the chains of misfortune.

The old man maintains a distance proper to the observer, but can he cross this distance that relegates him,
in other people's eyes, to his specificity of an old man?
In **"The Confessions of an Old Man,"** Zeno attempts
to establish with his son Alfio better relations than those
he had with his father. One remembers the "death of the
father" in **Zeno,** which recalls Kafka's short story, "The

Verdict"; in it, the dying man with a last—perhaps involuntary—gesture strikes his son: "I had prepared myself so much better than my father to understand the
new, and yet I did not know how to put up with Alfio.
He always said that between us there was even more
than the difference in age, and that the war separated
us. Yet it seemed to me that I was in a position to
fathom this new world; and when I was treated as an
imbecile, it made me furious."

To prove to his son how well he understands him, Zeno
buys from him one of his pintings. For Alfio is a modernist painter. And Zeno contemplates this canvas until
it gets to mean something to him. But immediately
thereafter he ruins everything he has just achieved. An
old friend comes to see him, and with him Zeno cannot
refrain from speaking humorously about this picture.
"After all," he says to justify himself, "laughter is the
last exercise permitted to an old man." When this friend
asks him whether the canvas in question represents an
earthquake, he answers that "before this catastrophe,
the houses were exactly in the same state," and he explains how he had tried to straighten out these houses
and people them by means of an intense contemplation.
When Alfio defends his work, Zeno gets angry, calls
him a cretin, and the long effort to communicate over
the gap of generations is wiped out at a stroke:

> Strange, this rapport between fathers and sons! No
> amount of effort one may expend can save it. I who
> had always said that I knew nothing about painting was
> flying into a rage because my son was yelling that he
> was quite of the same opinion. . . . All the theories I
> had deduced from my relations with my father were of
> no avail, for toward him I had behaved quite differ-
> ently. And yet I continued to be gentle and courteous.
> When, at table, a disagreement erupted, I always took
> Alfio's side. I gave him money when he asked me for
> it. I said nothing but sweet things to him. To be sure, I
> must have looked strange and not at all affectionate.
> While I caressed him, there was in me something like a
> howl: how good I am, how good I am! The feeling of
> being so good threatens to lead us into being less good.

Thus ripe old age is not wise renunciation, but distanced observation of what still unblemished vitality accomplishes. For Svevo, advanced age becomes what
youth is to other writers: the laboratory of the vital process. Old age is not only a slowing down, but also, in
relation to the future which tends toward zero, an extraordinary speeding up. "I am a rocket," says the "vecchione." In **The Confessions of Zeno,** illness was still
conceived in the perspective of therapy, as a transitional
stage that can be shortened or ignored, and not as the
fundamental condition of life. With advanced age, it's
something else again. Zeno, to be sure, does not become a sage. So little does he renounce that, in one of
the tales, **"Idleness,"** he evokes the Voronoff cure. And
he asks himself whether, seeing a beautiful woman, one
would not then feel compelled to climb the nearest tree.

The experience of advanced age is that one grows old for others, and through the gaze of others, for oneself. "All the other old men seemed to me much older than I was." To enunciate this reflection is already to deny it. Thus Zeno's objectivity can be traced back to the awareness of subjectivity. All phases of life (reflection, formulation, and, in this sense, "literature") become so many compensations and corrections brought to bear on the "life lie," a notion that reminds us how much Svevo, like Joyce, owes to the influence of Ibsen.

It can be said that all of Svevo's work deals with the relations between life and literature.[5] It is indeed the only relationship that does not exist solely through an ironic refraction and which, for this very reason, is the premise of irony.

Svevo is one of the fathers of that "existentialist" literature that sees in the event a mode of existence rather than a sequence of actions. He is at the antipodes from a literature of violence that seeks in paroxysm the proof of authentic existence rendered in the raw. The literature of expunged distance is the tendency that encompasses Hemingway, the cinema, action painting. But distance so lucidly experienced becomes a problem and prepares forthwith the future abolition of distance. In Beckett, this continuous examination, this self-observation, will become a *sotto voce* soliloquy.

Where mediation is so important, it is a question less of Being than of Perceiving, of passion than of humor, of the immediate than of stepping aside. In the game of past and present the absence of a future creates a limited space comparable to the Sartrean "wall," *"in camera,"* and "sequestration."[6] This narrow space partakes of the laboratory. It is understandable that it should have been precisely Sartre who said that Svevo represents Italy's most important contribution to modern literature. And also that Alain Robbe-Grillet claims him as precursor of the *nouveau roman,* because Zeno's time is "a sick time" and incarnates a consciousness for which nothing is natural any more:

> What Italo Svevo tells us is that in our modern society nothing is *natural* any more. And there is no reason even for being sad about it. We can perfectly well be happy, talk, make love, make deals, make war, write novels; but none of this will any longer be done without thinking, as one breathes. Every one of our actions reflects about itself and becomes loaded with questioning. Under our gaze, the simple gesture we make of stretching out our hand becomes bizarre, awkward; the words that we listen to ourselves pronouncing sound suddenly false; the time of our spirit is no longer that of the clocks; and novel writing, in its turn, can no longer be innocent.

One could trace another kinship: that between Svevo of the "micro-events" and Nathalie Sarraute. But the lost innocence of literature places Svevo more particularly among the descendants of Flaubert—with literature considered as a false consciousness reacting to literary creation. Svevo is as removed from Zeno the contemplator as the latter is from Zeno the doer, and there lies the source of his radical irony. It behooves us to admire that this double refraction does not stop the tale in its tracks. In this connection, one reads with interest the famous drunkard's vow in the **Diary,** [*Diario per la fidanzata*] in which Svevo renounces literature "once and for all"—as, hundreds of times, he renounces smoking, until, on his deathbed, he asks for his "last cigarette."

The complexity of reflection does not impair the naïveté of an action rich in comic situations which makes one think of Goldoni, a name it is right to invoke because Goldoni, who wrote in Venetian and French, likewise had an ambiguous relation with "Tuscan."

With his way of linking reality and the mask, reflection and force, Svevo could have been a playwright, and at least one of his plays, **The Misunderstanding**—which Camus intended to adapt—proves his gifts in this area where all encouragement was denied him. The theme of this play is yet another successful "hoax," but one which miscarries, because the servant who is supposed to frighten his master for laughs, actually kills him.

Despite his "Cacanian" cultural foundation, Svevo is certainly an Italian writer, by the fulgurating transition between reflection and situation. The distancing is created by "ineptitude," sickness, old age. Formally, it is a creation of style. But spatially, it is Svevo's destiny and is called Trieste. Trieste, province and cosmopolitan city, with Central Europe for hinterland, did not enjoy a cultural climate comparable to that of Prague, even though it produced poets and essayists of merit: Saba, Stuparich, Slataper, the "Anonymous of Trieste," and others I don't mention. Trieste was a port and a commercial center, and not a cultural focal point. Svevo will not frequent literary cafés like those of the Prague writers, but the Stock Exchange Café at the Tergesteo palace. Trieste is far from the cultural centers of the Empire, and from those of Italy as well, and Svevo, with a German father and Jewish-Italian mother, is a very Triestine mixture.

Did the Jewish origin play the same role in Svevo's life as it did in Kafka's? An important Italian critic, Giacomo Debenedetti, has insisted on interpreting Svevo altogether from this factor: his humor, his taste for fables and parables, his "shlemihls," his far-away gaze which makes him a stranger to the world he belongs to. Yet it seems to me difficult to attribute such importance to this factor. In his letters to his fiancée and (subsequently) wife—published in two volumes by Zibaldone—Svevo mentions occasionally that he belongs to the Jewish community, but rather as a pitcturesque element. One may, if one so desires, take into consideration the fact that both Svevo and Proust had Jewish mothers, and, above all, that Svevo was the inspiration for Joyce's Leopold Bloom. But what characterizes Svevo is not one of his numerous roots, it is their very diversity, the variety of factors, the mixture—the premise of critical objectivity, of distanced and humorous awareness of traditions and opinions. Every given is mediatized by its relation to some other given. An intelligence nourished by all high cultures—Russian, German, French and, thanks to Joyce, English and American—on an impoverished terrain, here is a fact that had to stress the distance between "life" and "spirit."

Svevo was seeking Italian roots. But the mother hen refused to recognize a "Cucco" born from an incubator. And Italo Svevo, the "Italian Swabian," did not mix in his irredentist Italian patriotism with his literature. Nothing would have seemed more unsuitable to him than to write a "patriotic novel"—which Italian criticism would definitely have noticed. To the extent that, later on, Central European nationalisms were to turn out more enfeebled and fragile than the declining culture of the Hapsburg Empire, the writer of the periphery could assume a central position in modern culture.

To make of distance the motif of an *oeuvre* was attempted later, and by all manner of means and procedures, but ripe old age retains over all of them the advantage of the natural, precisely because more than all catastrophes—and **Zeno** ends with the evocation of a cosmic catastrophe—aging is the image of inexorable fate.

The (belated) influence of Svevo on Italian literature is considerable. By 1930 Guido Piovene records it, not without uneasiness: "One might ask oneself for the reasons of Svevo's success with so many young writers," he wrote in the *Neue Zürcher Zeitung*. Because for him—or "for us," as he then put it—Svevo remained "the prisoner of that ambiance of positivism which it is our most vital task, our most ardent hope to vanquish." The tranquil prose of Svevo survived this "task" and this "ardor." And Piovene himself—who was actually just the man to understand Svevo, once his political involvements were shaken off—has recently invoked, at the Leningrad colloquy, the Triestine writer as "the most remarkable case in Italy" of a novel "that has a traditional external appearance without really being that" (*Esprit,* July 1964: "Novel and Reality," p. 29).

But precisely because Svevo, the outsider, became father to an entire new literature and because his posthumous influence has been so powerful, it is remarkable that he should have remained alone—at least until Beckett—to explore the realm of old age, from the "aging" Emilio to the "vecchione," the "vegliardo," the "buon vecchio," the "Zeno after Zeno," and that he should have met the challenge: the transmuting into pure hu-

mor of the terror of existence, the cold and the dread of life without future.

Notes

1. Cf. "Zeno ressuscité des morts," *Preuves,* Nr. 148, February 1955.

2. P. N. Furbank's *Italo Svevo, The Man and the Writer* (University of California Press, $6.00) is oddly divided into 250 pages on "the man" and 70 pages on "the writer." It is useful as a biography, especially on the subject of the family origins and the cultural milieu of Trieste; but does not contribute as much to an understanding of the work. Piero Rismondo, Svevo's translator into German and author of some of the best essays on his writing, in the postface to the German translation of *A Short Sentimental Journey and Other Stories* (Rowohlt, 1967) praises Furbank's book, but adds tersely, "The real monograph on Svevo has yet to be written."

Even so I am surprised that George Steiner, assessing the importance of Svevo on the occasion of Furbank's book (*The New Yorker,* June 3, 1967), should find Svevo an engaging yet minor and provincial writer, as compared to Robert Musil. I would rather agree with Michel David who calls Svevo *"Un provincial plus universel que la plupart de ses illustres contemporains,"* or with a recent opinion of Guido Piovene who wrote about the *Epistolario* ("La Stampa," 3.12.66): "Svevo ignored D'Annunzio and started with the *verismo* of the late 19th century, getting rid of its heaviness and using it for quite different effects. From realism he distills new acid vapors. There is in him a new tragic feeling and at the same time a music, a vital mirth, a poetry *in sordina* which our literature had not yet known. No other Italian novelist resembles him. If he belongs to any family, it would be the family of Chekhov and Gogol."

Svevo himself was quite aware of his "provincialism" and cultural limitations. Discussing in a letter to Valerio Jahier an obviously unfavorable comparison of his own books with Proust's, he writes: "Ours were utterly different destinies! His so much more fine than mine; a coarse man like myself could not possibly resemble the most perfect product of such a refined civilization."

But does Svevo really believe that a writer is only what his civilization and background permit him to be and that he stands to Proust as Trieste does to Paris? To Svevo a contemplative mind (and a writer for him is just a special case of a contemplative mind) would always be something else than a "product" of any given circumstances. I see in the quoted passage a genuine modesty and the recognition of a true superiority, but also a diffident hint of something else. Of his own evident "inferiority" Svevo is nearly convinced, but perhaps not quite.

3. On his relation to the Italian language and the beginning of his fame in a foreign country, Svevo writes to Giuseppe Prezzolini (November 21, 1925): "I am hopeful that I shall become known in Italy. At first I had given up and by my own silence approved everyone else's. I then had the luck to find these generous Frenchmen whose strong praise staggered me. I do not deny that I thought (without, however, saying so, in order not to harm myself) that they appreciated me all the more because they did not have a subtle enough understanding of our language. After all, I have grown up in a region where till seven years ago our dialect was our true language. My prose could only be what it is and, alas, it is too late now to get my legs straightened."

When speaking of other writers, Svevo is always self-disparaging and often clowning. Thus in a letter written in English to Cyril Drucker in March, 1927, on his preparation of a lecture on James Joyce, he writes: "Of *Ulysses* I knew only very few pages, of which I talked a great deal, in order to make them appear more. I was now obliged to read it; and set to work immediately. I got home. It was simply awful. Whole phrases remained for a long time a mystery to me, and the vocabulary did not help me very much. . . . The worst of it was that the reading of the book lasted so long that when I reached the end I had quite forgotten the beginning."

Svevo's perceptive remarks on Joyce prove that in this letter he does not do justice to his critical understanding. He comments, however, often with self-confidence, and even pride, on his own novels: "I wrote *Una Vità* at a time when several novelists wrote differently but not better than I did, and sometimes wrote too well" (Letter to Enrico Rocca, April 1927).

4. For Svevo's attitude toward Freud one should read his letters of 1928 to Valerio Jahier. An exhaustive study on the subject of psychoanalysis in its relation to the work of Svevo and other writers in Trieste can be found in Michel David, *La psicoanalisi nella cultura italiana,* (Boringhieri, 1966), 373-440. Svevo knew very well two persons who had undergone psychoanalytical treatment with disastrous effects, and he thought that Freud's discoveries meant more to literature than to the cure of mental disease. Nevertheless, he, the translator of Freud's essay on dreams, believed or pretended to believe that Freud would appreciate *Zeno* as a writer's contribution to psychoanaly-sis. Could he have been unaware that the psychoanalyst in this novel is a figure of fun, and that Zeno Cosini's self-analysis ignores his childhood, his mother, and has much less relation to Freud than the pessimism of *A Life* had to Schopenhauer?

Michel David is primarily concerned with psychoanalysis as it penetrated Italian culture, and does not fully explore its implications for Svevo. There are at least three different aspects to be considered: a) the new way of exploring "anti-literary" truth; b) the new danger of superimposing pat formulas on individual situations; and c) the further danger of creating a two-edged instrument, since psychoanalysis may destroy a "disease" which intellectually is worth more than any cure. Would not mental health, as restored by the analyst, mean the loss of the "sick" and oblique attitude to "real life" so essential to the one who contemplates? The greatest virtue of the writer remains linked to failure rather than to the kind of success which a cured mental patient could expect. "You may be right," Svevo wrote to Valerio Jahier, "to think that the benefits one might get from psychoanalysis could be counterbalanced by the harm it does."

5. The *Epistolario* (Dall'Oglio, 1966) has been issued as the first of four volumes of *Collected Works*. A book of 900 pages, it inexplicably lacks an index: this makes it impossible to find what Svevo wrote about Freud or Joyce, for instance, without perusing hundreds of pages. The *Epistolario*—like the diaries—has all the quality of "Svevian comedy" that one finds in the novels and stories. In one letter, for example, he analyses "these strange twin diseases of mine. The first, which I believe innate, is the incapacity to reach the immediate representation of any reality in the form in which others feel it. The second is a terror of my own idea which makes me unable to stay close to it for any length of time."

One of the many letters to his wife (July, 1897) shows particularly well—as the editor Bruno Meier points out—how the letters lead to the narrative prose. Here Svevo describes humorously the failure of his attempt to link literature and reality in the "experiment of marriage," and goes on: "I was created for rebellion, indifference, corruption, always excited by what could be and never obedient to what is." Svevo's interest in the "possible" as opposed to the "real" comes very close, indeed, to Musil's "conjecturalism" (a word which, I believe, Baudelaire was the first to use in this sense).

6. The reference here is to the French titles of works known in America as "The Wall," *No Exit,* and *The Condemned of Altona.* (Tr.'s note.)

C. Roland Wagner (essay date 1970)

SOURCE: Wagner, C. Roland. "Italo Svevo: The Vocation of Old Age." *Hartford Studies in Literature* 2, no. 3 (1970): 214-28.

[*In the following essay, Wagner calls Svevo a bourgeois writer, whose art resulted from "his gradual reconciliation to his role as an ordinary man in an ordinary world."*]

> The sounds drift in. The buildings are remembered.
> The life of the city never lets go, nor do you
> Ever want it to. It is part of the life in your room.
> Its domes are the architecture of your bed.
> . . . .
>
> It is a kind of total grandeur at the end,
> With every visible thing enlarged and yet
> No more than a bed, a chair and moving nuns,
> The immensest theatre, the pillared porch,
> The book and candle in your ambered room . . .
>
> —Wallace Stevens, "To an Old Philosopher in Rome"

The writings of Italo Svevo record the spiritual autobiography of a man who moved from the youthful sadness, even the bitterness, of living in a godless and absurd world, to the gaiety, the merry wisdom, of living easily with absurdity. Like Proust, Svevo finally sublimated some of the energy originally devoted to the infantile quest for the Romantic Mother and turned it to spiritual and even comic uses. But more worldly and earthly than Proust, more completely the philosophical materialist, Svevo found his way not so much into the Heavenly City of art and essence as up and down the commercial streets of everyday Trieste.

Limited though his artistic achievement certainly is, Svevo's dual commitment to the world and the spirit is a magnificent refutation of the Romantic dictum, enunciated by Tonio Kröger, that a "properly constituted, healthy, decent man never writes, acts, or composes . . . ," that a "banker who isn't a criminal, who is irreproachably respectable, and yet writes—he doesn't exist." Svevo was both a bourgeois businessman and a bourgeois writer. His basic values stemmed from his middle class inheritance: his spirituality grew more from his worldly than from his artistic vocation. His greatest successes as an artist stemmed from his success as a man. His art was the culmination of his gradual reconciliation to his role as an ordinary man in an ordinary world.

In many ways, of course, and even to the end of his life (he died in 1928 at the age of sixty-seven as a result of an automobile accident), Svevo was not a "properly constituted, healthy, decent man." Like the heroes of his stories there was a good deal of the *schlemiel* about him. (The original title, "The Inept One," of Svevo's first novel—subsequently published as *A Life* in 1893—is revealing; even more so is the response it evoked in one publishing house that declared it could never publish a novel with such a title.[1]) His handling of the details of business and family life, although devoted, was never quite up to the mark. Yet, like Tonio's, his moral standards were bourgeois, and he condemned himself primarily because he could not achieve the kind of success that was expected of him. Romantic as well as bourgeois, he yearned to escape from his responsibilities to the world that nurtured him and judged himself severely for his subversive wishes.

Unlike Tonio Kröger, however, who, startled by the accusation that he is a "bourgeois manqué," finally takes his stand among the artists while making the bourgeois and the normal his precious subjects, Svevo thought of himself primarily as a "bourgeois manqué." Whatever his youthful dreams of artistic success, he took his basic stand among the bourgeois, not only condemning himself for failing to be bourgeois enough, but rooting whatever limited success he was capable of—and it increased as he grew older—in bourgeois soil. Most of the artists of recent times who glimpse the spiritual vocation define it in fundamental, or extreme dialectical, opposition to the bourgeois values around them. They tend to overlook the distinction between central and peripheral bourgeois values, between consequential values celebrated but only partly realized, and petty values actually lived. They reject the inner core of the bourgeois world. Svevo, however, when he began to see some of the weaknesses of what Emerson called the "good models"—his father became prematurely senile as a result of a financial catastrophe that overtook the family when Svevo was nineteen[2]—never questioned the central values they embodied, and gradually himself became capable of living by those values. His spirituality, like his idiosyncratic style of life, developed within the framework of his respect for the bourgeois. He was Blake's fool, certainly, and persisting in his folly he became wise, but the wisdom he achieved was not alien to the wisdom of the world: it was the fuller realization of worldly wisdom.[3]

Svevo's heroes feel old, old in their youth. They are frightened by the fires of feeling, of their own uncompromising demand for absolute gratification. They want to be young again; they want to satisfy their mysterious yearning for an inaccessible object, but at the first chance of any success they retreat into "senility," into a boredom that protects them from a terrifying reality. Schopenhauer's influence is evident: need and boredom are the two poles of human life; but for Svevo, wiser than the Romantic Schopenhauer, there is no escape in denial of the Will, no solution to the antinomies of desire in quietistic self-surrender. Yet "senility" for Svevo is not the final word either. As his heroes grow older, they become capable of a different sort of escape: not total or even partial denial of the Will but mature sublimation of some of its energy. Instead of remaining attached to romantic wish-fulfillments or yielding to postromantic despair at finding that infantile wishes cannot be completely satisfied, Svevo's heroes begin to modify their demands in the face of reality. Old age ceases to be merely a protection against feeling and becomes rather a positive vocation in itself. Instead of renouncing existence altogether in the style of Schopenhauer, Svevo affirms it in the style of Freud: the neurotic pattern itself becomes the frame of a truer liberation; need and boredom, youth and old age, are metamorphosed into a passionate order that retains the values of the original elements without their illusions. The writing begins to reveal new comic and spiritual dimensions, the minor writer becomes a major wonder worker, the infant becomes a man.

But this does not occur until Svevo's heroes (and Svevo himself, apparently) approach the age of sixty. (Genitality at sixty! What a comment on the world we live in!) Not until *Confessions of Zeno* (1923), published thirty years after *A Life,* is the vision adequately expressed; and not until just before his death, in his very last writings, does Svevo's style really embody the victorious spiritual tone. The superficial Flaubertian detachment of *A Life* should not mislead us into presuming an equivalent detachment in the author. The style is not really of a free man, but of one who, like the hero himself, has artificially placed himself in the position of senile observer to avoid the emotional whirlwinds of mortal men. The voice of the author seems to be telling the reader: no comment is necessary, this is the horror that life really is. Unfortunately Svevo has no clear standard of his own by which to measure his hero's failures. He sees Alfonso Nitti's failure, his illusions, his despair, but he does not see them in the light of any higher good. The naturalistic technique is a screen for lack of commitment. The result is that, in spite of his obvious intentions, Svevo implicitly suggests to us that his own self-hatred and self-pity are as unironic and unredeemed as the self-hatred and self-pity of his hero. He does not stand firmly on his *own* ground and look out towards Alfonso's problems. He does not really believe in his own detachment. It is reasonable to presume, I think, that Svevo wrote this novel primarily to reject a part of himself that he did not want (although he knew that it was there) and did not have enough confidence in the better part left within to offer it as at least a dream of health.

By the time he came to write *As a Man Grows Older* (1898), Svevo began—but only just barely—to see the feasibility of old age as a positive vocation. His thirtyfive-year-old hero, Emilio Brentani, is not much different from the twenty-two-year-old Alfonso Nitti; he is an old-young man who has lost whatever youthful vitality he once possessed, in whom passion flares up one last time before he moves into the "monotonous, colorless" existence of "an after dinner sleep dreaming" of his youth. Romantic need is pursued to its joyless end, not, this time, in suicide, as in *A Life,* but in the "quiet" and "security" of a banal existence devoid of all hope.

Yet there are hints of something new now, not in the actual life of the hero but in the somewhat altered perspective of the author. Svevo's insights into human nature are so much profounder here than in his first novel that one is tempted to agree completely with P. N. Furbank that the "center" of *As a Man Grows Older* is its scrutiny of unconscious human motivation. Svevo's great contribution to the development of the modern novel, according to Mr. Furbank, is his extension of the concept of the unconscious from the special and unusual case, already familiar in the work of Stendhal and Dostoevsky, to the everyday and ordinary one. The "ineffectual" Brentani is chosen, not to illustrate "fantastic or catastrophic irruptions of the unconscious," not as an "exception to the general law of human existence but rather as a striking example of it."[4]

What appears to me as even more important than this new "knowledge," however, is the greater compassion that accompanies it, a compassion that not only suggests Svevo's increased involvement but his more authentic detachment. The *tone* of the novel as much as its central subject—the subject that elicited that tone and the tone that found that subject—is what makes this a novel on the verge of greatness. Its accent of tender, yet firm analysis, its disciplined control of its apparently formless elements, suggests increased mastery of the primitive sources of experience. The old selfhatred, the old desire for unlimited gratification, have been substantially modified by a saner love of self and other, a maturer comprehension of reality.

But the novel is only on the verge of greatness, I think, not truly great. There is too much in it that has not been liberated. Its great virtue—its amazing power of compression—is at the same time its great fault: it is *too* tight, *too* suggestive, ever fearful of plain statement and free laughter. Rich potential for comedy lies just beneath the calm, melancholy surface of its language, now appearing, now disappearing, in the cloudy atmosphere that pervades the novel. At one point Svevo describes Emilio's response to the news of his mistress' interest in another man:

> Nor did it need any particular effort for him to simulate indifference; his expression had become, as it were, crystalized by his initial effort and he felt as if he could almost have fallen asleep with that stereotyped, calm smile on his face. His simulation was so intense it penetrated far beneath the skin.[5]

Again, Svevo describes Emilio's response to the sight of a strange woman who he thinks is his mistress. He has been frantically chasing the woman in the street and finally overtakes her:

He looked her full in the face with the calm, ironic expression which he had taken so much trouble to prepare. He was startled to see the unknown face of an old woman, all dried up and wrinkled.

But this potential could only be actualized in the language of ambiguity; the vision, although certainly an earned vision, could only be a vision of sadness. Its half-hidden comedy could not completely free itself from its source in the infantile sense of an unjust universe; bitterness is not yet disinfected by comic self-awareness. The spiritual and the comic have still to be joined to create a new world, not just a new accent.

The spiritual and the comic finally fuse in Svevo's later works: the comic note is somewhat stronger in *Confessions of Zeno,* the spiritual dominates the last pieces. Although the bitterness and self-hatred never completely disappear, they are transfigured by the power of a mature imagination. Because of the effect of World War I on his private life and because of his own latent powers of maturation, Svevo's confidence in himself as man and writer increased enormously.[6] The same neuroses, the same problems, even, to some extent, the same solutions, are evident in the works of old age, but the tone has altered fundamentally. The neurotic quest for the Absolute, whether for complete safety or for romantic ecstasy, has become a comic pursuit of health and bourgeois happiness. The "appetite for the absolute," the "nostalgia for unity" which Camus speaks of, is not merely confronted, as it is by the existentialists, but is mastered and altered by sanity and insight. *Zeno* is a shout of freedom. Its openly expressed despair and its comic wildness tell us that Svevo is at last capable of coming to terms with experience. The painful insights, the half smiles of the earlier works have become an unqualified joyousness issuing from a profound spiritual calm. Svevo is one of the very few writers of modern times who finally transcends the sadness of being a modern man. And yet, how modern he is!

Zeno Cosini has the same basic weaknesses as Svevo's earlier protagonists, only more so. He too is the man "born old," in quest of the youth he never seems to have experienced; he too is the pursuer of an impossible security, who yet demands fulfillment of an absolute ecstasy. But he exhibits his infinite desires in a new and bewildering variety. He is, in fact, a genius of neurosis, containing within himself most of the faults we have learned to associate with the modern soul. He is Nietzsche's slave, unconsciously inflicting punishment on himself out of resentment against the strong man, Dostoevsky's Underground Man, hyperconsciously attempting to make sense of the world at the same time that he is aware of its senselessness, Kafka's burrow-building creature of the earth, creeping back into his "lair" (as Zeno puts it) to protect himself from the external enemy and finding that an unknown internal enemy has created a mysterious whistling in his walls—he is, in short, the modern castrated, consumer-oriented, alienated man, incapable of finding meaning in any of the normal tasks of life.

And Svevo himself cannot be separated from his hero. Inside Zeno's confused mind, flesh of his psychosomatic flesh, Svevo can now expose himself utterly. He draws us into the very center of Zeno's fantasies. We experience them as real because Svevo still needs to believe in them: the comedy of neurosis is rooted in the unsatisfiable wishes of his heart. But although irresistibly inside Zeno, Svevo is outside too. The comic structure of illusions provides its own gentle criticism. Svevo does not *altogether* believe in them. Without repudiating the neurotic self that was once the victim of its illusions, he discounts the illusions. They are thus seen for what they are—seen through—and, as authentic expressions of human need, celebrated: they are made transparent both morally and aesthetically.

> . . . for after life is done and the world is gone up in smoke, what realities may the spirit of a man boast to have embraced without illusion, save the very forms of those illusions by which he has been deceived?[7]

Hence it is that Mr. Furbank properly takes issue with the suggestion of the Italian critic Debenedetti that "self hatred" is the clue to Svevo's attitude towards Zeno.[8] This simplistic interpretation overlooks the ironies embodied in Svevo's tone, the sanity of his perspective. The ironic love for his hero and for himself which began to emerge in *As a Man Grows Older* comes fully into the open here. Zeno's neurotic defeats are seen as strategies for survival, strategies devised not so much by the hero as by Nature herself—that "insane experimentalist"—who smiles benevolently upon ineffectual sub-men in touch with her hidden processes and frowns at "healthy" types whose superficial successes generate deeper and more destructive illusions. Svevo's lenient judgment of Zeno is in marked contrast to his more rigorous, though still comic, judgment of the conventional hero. Thus, in the person of Zeno, Svevo not only caricatures the insane bourgeois quest for mechanical control of all the conditions of life and the insane bohemian deification of sickness and failure—both typical of late nineteenth-century European decadence—but offers his hero as a "healthy" contrast to these absolutes. Svevo is indeed our contemporary.

But is even Mr. Furbank's analysis adequate to the complex moral ironies of the novel? Does Zeno merely stand as a judgment on the excesses of others; is his basic virtue merely "survival," or is it possible to say that he stands also as a touchstone of real health—at least a modest degree of real health? Is it possible that Zeno himself, as well as Svevo, becomes somehow aware of the fantasies he lives by, that the aging Zeno, looking back on his "foolish" life, has in a sense overcome the limits of his neurosis? The question of tone is all-important, of course, and I think that the tone of the novel does imply, through the interpenetration of author and hero, that Svevo has communicated his own success as a man to the perspective of the neurotic Zeno.

Take the short introduction to the novel, in which Zeno informs the reader of his difficulties in remembering the details of his past life. (The whole novel is composed of a series of free associations written down for Zeno's psychoanalyst, Dr. S., as part of treatment.) Believing that the "good" patient is required to remember everything from his past, he finds himself frustrated in his attempt to do a perfect job of reporting:

> Remember my own infancy, indeed! Why it is not even in my power to warn you, while you are still an infant, how important it is for your health and your intelligence that you should forget nothing. When, I wonder, will you learn that one ought to be able to call to mind every event of one's life, even those one would rather forget? Meanwhile, poor innocent, you continue to explore your tiny body in search of pleasure; and the exquisite discoveries you make will bring you in the end disease and suffering, to which those who least wish it will contribute. What can one do? It is impossible to watch over your cradle. Mysterious forces are at work within you, child, strange elements combine. Each passing moment contributes its reagent.[9]

The passage, like so many in Svevo, is remarkable for its ability both to characterize Zeno's neurosis and to suggest how he has learned to resolve it. Zeno reveals his compulsive need to be a perfect patient, his insane quest for absolute health, his will to preserve his defenses and avoid true analysis. At the same time, the comic flavor of the passage suggests that the tragic conflict between the pleasure principle and the reality principle has been freed of infantile bitterness. Although his explicit statement contradicts the idea of reconciliation, Zeno's comic inflection carries him towards a lyrical acceptance of an uncertain fate. Finally, even the illusions he lives by, bathed in the transparent light of comedy and truth, can be seen to have lost some of their insistence: perhaps Zeno himself, not merely Svevo, sees them for what they are.

The passage suggests in miniature how we can most fruitfully read the novel as a whole. There is moral progress hidden beneath the cycles of need and boredom, of neurotic yearning and neurotic disappointment. But it is expressed not in the gradual or even sudden shedding of illusions by the hero, but in the gaiety with which he recounts his early experiences, the genuine poise he eventually achieves within the limits of his eccentricities. At no point does Zeno ever explicitly recognize the nature of his basic illusions: the sound of his voice and the new found powers of his mind are almost our only clues.

Occasionally, there are slight but significant modifications even in Zeno's overt behavior that supplement the basic inward metamorphosis; but it is easy for the modern reader, bemused by existentialist assumptions of the inevitability of human weakness, to ignore these elusive indicators of moral improvement. An example is Zeno's smoking problem. From beginning to end, Zeno's days are "filled with cigarettes and resolutions to give up smoking" (p. 9). He refuses to accept the analyst's interpretation that he feels guilty about smoking because he is unconsciously competing with his father and needs to punish himself by attributing a poisoning effect to the tobacco. He prefers to continue smoking like a Turk and to continue resolving to give up smoking. Hence we may not take with sufficient seriousness the remark that as he grows older his "resolutions are less drastic" (p. 9). We may assume that Zeno's masochism is irrepressible; and the resolutions, after all, do continue: "Now that I am old and no one expects anything of me, I continue to pass from cigarette to resolution and back again" (p. 10). We would be mistaken, however, if we did not take the hint of slight improvement seriously as well as comically. For it is precisely because of the *mildness* of the claim that we can assume that it has a high probability of truth. (Zeno's more typically perfectionist claims about his health and strength are expressed in such extreme terms that we immediately estimate their probability as close to zero.) Although the ratio of seriousness to comedy is impossible to determine exactly, there is some indication that Zeno has progressed.

Zeno's fantastic marriage also proves his ability to change for the better. He chooses Augusta, the ugly squinting daughter of Signor Malfenti—the powerful Father from whom Zeno wishes to derive masculine strength and abundant health by marrying one of his four daughters—only because he is refused by the two attractive daughters, Ada and Alberta, and the fourth, Anna, is still a child. When it turns out that Augusta makes the best possible wife for Zeno, the reader is inclined to laugh at the comment that real life makes on Zeno's hyperconscious rationalism and compulsiveness, and laugh still more at Zeno's remark that he "discovered that far from being a blind beast driven by another's will, I was a very clever man" (p. 140). The fact remains that Zeno *is* a clever fellow, but not in the sense that he wishes to think himself clever. He does not have the kind of control of his person and his destiny that he thinks is possible—a conscious and completely rational control of irrational forces. But he is clever, or, rather, wise in deeper ways: in the irrepressible hope that first led him to Augusta even after being rejected by the other sisters, and in his real capacity to appreciate her qualities as a wife. Zeno's "damned good luck" (as Malfenti terms it) in both marriage and business stems in part from a certain humility he possesses together with a profound piety towards the unpredictable elements of existence. His grandiose dream of reason and health certainly contradicts his piety and prevents him from pursuing a direct path to true harmony, but it never interferes with his appreciation of whatever chance good arrives along his crooked way. Unlike Dostoevsky's Underground Man, he can take pleasure in what he receives even if it comes to him in apparent denial of the principles of his existence.

It is easy to see that Zeno, like his creator, remains from beginning to end basically bourgeois in his moral orientation. It is perhaps not so easy to see that Zeno learns to modify his behavior in the light of the best of bourgeois principles, that he does not merely continue to live a comically dual life of attempted gratification and accompanying guilt. Zeno's ambivalent devotion to his brother-in-law Guido (Ada's husband) is an example of ethical advancement in the midst of psychological sickness. Certainly it is true, as both Ada and the psychoanalyst insist, that Zeno disliked Guido more deeply than he wishes to realize, and that his honorable attempt to recoup Guido's financial losses was in part compensatory activity grounded in guilt. But Zeno does not claim that he loved Guido—he even recognizes that he disliked him to some extent—merely that he "stood by him as if he had been my brother, and helped him in every way I could" (p. 364). Again, Zeno's modest and complex claim is a strong counterweight to Ada's simplistic attempt to blame Zeno and Dr. S's reductive analysis. Zeno learns to function with ambivalence, with the impossibility of moral perfection, and yet without abandoning bourgeois ideals of self-mastery and moral obligation. His insight, still somewhat touched by comic exaggeration, is part of the central wisdom of the novel as a whole:

> Goodness is the light that in brief flashes illuminates the darkness of the human soul. A burning torch is needed to light the way . . . and the human intelligence must choose by its light the way it will have to take afterwards in the dark. So that one could continue to do good always, and that was the important thing. When the light returned to guide one it would neither surprise nor dazzle. Perhaps I should even blow it out straight away, as I should have no need for it; for I should have learnt how to keep my resolution, how not to lose my way.
>
> (pp. 302-303)

Zeno has learned that bourgeois metaphysics may be superficial, but that central bourgeois values are basically sound and worthy of committing oneself to in the darkness.

It is sometimes argued by those who reject the notion of Zeno's maturation that the comical "psychoanalysis" he undergoes, although perhaps true as science, is essentially worthless as therapy. It cannot be denied that Svevo is dubious about the value of orthodox therapy:

it does not follow that he rejects a psychoanalytic standard for judging mental health; it does not follow that his hero Zeno fails to achieve a substantial degree of maturity in response to his psychoanalytic experience. It is true that, after the doctor begins to make his interpretations and points the way to the possibility of real, i.e., moderate health, and further suggests that his patient is not as sick as he would like to believe, Zeno promptly quits psychoanalysis and hopefully pursues urine analysis, preferring the "sweet" sickness of diabetes to those curable psychosomatic ills with which the doctor insists on burdening him (pp. 378-379). Yet in spite of his resistance, the free voice of Zeno's spirit grows more secure. He does not gain intellectual insight into his problems, but he undergoes an authentic experience which brings him some of the fruits of insight.

Zeno enters psychoanalysis out of attachment to his romantic and bourgeois needs: he unconsciously thinks that he will be able both to satisfy and to protect himself from his infantile wishes. He expects to find in his free associations the paradisiac maternal world that has been lost. A crucial point in his analysis is reached when he evokes a number of powerful images that appear to be literal reproductions of the past. Each takes him further into the haunted past of sibling rivalry, incest, and patricide, but each is curiously mixed with images of spiritual joy. ("The room was quite white, indeed I had never seen such a white room, nor one so entirely flooded with sunlight. Could it be that the sun was really shining through the walls?" [p. 370].) The abreaction is overwhelming: "I was bathed in perspiration while creating the images, and in tears when I recognized them" (p. 368). But Zeno is unable consciously and intellectually to "educate" himself in accordance with the analyst's objective interpretation of the images. (Svevo complicates this by suggesting that the analyst's need to play God contributes to the partial failure of treatment.) He does not see the enormous significance of the fact that when the images are gone, his "memory of them was free from any excitement or agitation. I remembered them as one remembers an event one has been told by somebody who was not present at it" (p. 369). He does not see that images of anxiety have been transformed into transparent images of freedom; that, to some extent, analysis has helped liberate him from neurotic attachment to the past, but that he is unconsciously avoiding the enlargement and support of his moment of freedom.

The full meaning of the title, **La Coscienza di Zeno,** now becomes clear. *Coscienza,* meaning both "conscience" and "consciousness," comprehends the dual perspective of the novel. We have seen how the comic strategies of self-examination and self-justification, the less-than-tragic battles of superego, ego and id, make up the bulk of the novel; but we have also seen that the *consummation* of consciousness is part of the novel, implicit throughout in the comedy, explicit in the spirituality (and the comedy) of the final wonderful chapter "Psychoanalysis." The novel invisibly progresses both within each moment and through its various moments—both vertically and horizontally, as it were—from conscience to consciousness, from consciousness in the sense of self-judgment to consciousness in the sense of spiritual victory.

After freeing himself from those guilt-haunted images, Zeno finally begins to find in the present sufficient food for spiritual satisfaction. At first he hopes to re-evoke similar images, similar visions from the past, but this time without the pain and the tears. He wants to "see once more in December the roses of May" (p. 374). What he finds, without full understanding but with a fullness of experience, takes the place of his nostalgic visions: he calls it his "physiological theory of color" (p. 374), but it is no more, and no less, than a poetry of the present, a phenomenology of the mind. He discovers the vocation of old age, that joy in a December that surpasses all seasons. Gazing out the window one evening at a "pale red sky," he notices a white cloud taking on the "marvelous shade of pure tender green":

> it was clear to me that all my attention and love had been given to that shade of green, for its complementary color was produced on my retina, a brilliant red that had nothing to do with the luminous, but pale red of the sky. I gazed in enchantment at the color that I had myself brought into being. My great surprise came when I opened my eyes again, for then I saw that flaming red spread over the whole sky and cover up my emerald green, so that for some time I was unable to see it. So I had actually found a way of painting nature! I naturally repeated the experiment several times. The strange part was that I had actually endowed the colors with movement. When I opened my eyes again, the sky would not at once take on the color from my retina. There was a moment's hesitation during which I could just detect the emerald green from which the red had sprung, and which seemed to have been destroyed by it. It emerged now from within and spread in all directions like a giant conflagration.
>
> (p. 375)

Zeno here innocently experiences, without understanding, what Svevo discovered, with the disillusioned understanding of old age—the free imagination, the imagination as spirit, no longer constrained by the quest for Truth, no longer only in the service of infantile superego and id, but free, in the words of Santayana, to "spread its silent light over all nature and all essence."[10] In company with other modernists, but without the usual existential anxiety that follows upon the discovery of nothingness, Svevo brings subject and object into new relation. He permits the self to experiment with the "brilliant red" of its own nature without losing contact with the "pure tender green" of its polar opposite. Fan-

tasy and reality are thus joined to produce the emancipated off-spring of an enraptured spirit.

Svevo has transformed the senility of his old-young men into a vocation of old age, a self-overcoming that has reduced their need to find the roses of May in December and the imagined securities of December in May. But only reduced it. It is the distinctive mark of Svevo's writing, even after his great discovery, that tone and statement never cease to remind us of the bonds that bind the spirit to its earthly habitation. When Zeno reports his visionary "theory of color" to his analyst, the latter insists that Zeno's retina has merely "become ultra-sensitive from so much nicotine" (p. 375). Svevo's irony is directed as much at the new freedom of Zeno's imagination as at the philistinism of the doctor. Even where his explicit statement appears to be wholly committed to the ideal of spirit, as in the following fragment—which states the theme of a sequel to **Zeno** that Svevo began to write in 1928—the accent, edging towards parody, implies the limits to spiritual freedom. The voice is that of the old Zeno, looking back in wonder at his earlier "confessions":

> So now, who am I? Not the one who lived but the one who described. Oh! The only real part of life is meditation. When everyone understands this as I do, they will become writers too, life will become literature. One half of humanity will spend its time reading and studying what the other half has written, and contemplation, freed from the sordid business of living, will be the great business of existence.[11]

The lyricism of Svevo's last writings goes far beyond **Zeno** in its devotion to the life of the spirit, but never abandons the comic context of everyday reality. The aging writer becomes the poet of the banal, the transfigurer of our crazy world and our crazy conflicts. One is reminded of Nabokov, who, according to Denis Donoghue, "places his fiction, deliberately, half-way between the banal and its corrective parody."[12] But Svevo lacks the high style, the ear for rhythms, of Nabokov: he is not the "master of surfaces and structures," only their shy lover. And Nabokov, I think, lacks the worldly wisdom of Svevo, his ripe sense of the human condition. Eugenio Montale writes of the enormous "love of life that pulsates through [Svevo's late works], the power of renouncing everything that they display."[13] Not a creator of new visions, Svevo is yet a visionary—a clear-eyed visionary of the commonplace. The light of his mind shines upon the merely neurotic condition of his aging heroes and produces an otherworldly glow that might seem alien to their ordinary predicaments. Yet so masterful is Svevo's control of his material—the vision seems thoroughly earned—that we are convinced that the light comes, in part at least, from the workaday world itself.

The secret of Svevo's late lyrical power lies in his fearless submission to the contradictoriness of experience, to the creative tension between the ideal and the real, between maturity and immaturity. The tension is grounded in a profound calm, the ambiguity in clarity, the complexity in a wonderful simplicity. Until his last day, Svevo wished to recapture his youth, dreamed impossible dreams, was frightened of death. Yet his late writings show an extraordinary ability to distance his fears and wishes, to translate them into themes for poetic discourse. Their combination of the intensest love with the extremest disillusion is unusual at any time: it has almost disappeared in our day. The synthesis of style and subject matter in *Zeno* brought Svevo to the point where technique became thoroughly subordinate to subject, form totally subserving a liberated content. There is no longer any concern with "art" in these late works. They are documentaries of the spirit, meditations on a single subject in many guises, reflections on the relation of mind to its object. In spite of their lack of ostentation, they remind one of the music of the baroque, its central pulse. The problem they all concern themselves with is this: how to live with the apparent fact that Nature's principal concern is to delude men and then to kill them. The solution: to live the life of an "old, old man." Mario Samigli in *The Hoax* (1928), the old man in **"The Story of the Nice Old Man and the Pretty Girl"** (written in 1926, published posthumously), and Signor Aghios in **"Short Sentimental Journey"**[14] (written in 1925, published posthumously) are all facets of the "old, old man," dim reflections of the single central Self—serene commentator on their weaknesses and delusions—that lodges within them all. Like Zeno, these ordinary men are hardly aware of their latent potentialities. They have settled down, as they think, to a world without imagination or hope, but somewhere within themselves they are still in quest of an unacknowledged Absolute, they are still composing "notes toward a supreme fiction" which they take to be literal truth. They cry out in their dreams for some unknown food which cannot be found in their ordinary lives. Each of these old men is vulnerable, unconsciously ready to submit once more to illusions provoked by hidden passions. Each is aroused one last time by the hope stimulated by the possibility of literary success, sexual gratification, or brotherly love, and each is finally forced to return to the routine, the saving grace of small satisfactions and their accompanying frustrations, and to the reality of death.

But, as in the case of Zeno, these old men experience, without understanding, new resources of the mind as they bring to light their unconscious desires. They begin to lose and to love the world around them, to extract the eternal essence from its temporal embodiments, to focus their new-found energies on transparent objects instead of cloudy images of themselves. Yet only Svevo thoroughly comprehends what is happening to them, only Svevo completes for us what nature in them (in Schopenhauer's words) merely "stammered forth." He teaches us how the passions offer their own antidote to the absolute illusions they generate, how their deification can become food for the disintoxicated spirit. The old man in **"The Story of the Nice Old Man and the Pretty Girl,"** after having experienced his renewal of sexual passion, his subsequent heart attack and his terror, is seated by "the stove into which he liked to throw bits of coal and watch them burn."

> Then he shut his dazzled eyes and opened them to go on with the same game. This is how he passed the evenings of days which had been quite as empty.

> But his life was not to end in this way. Some organisms are fated to leave nothing behind them for death, which merely succeeds in seizing an empty shell. All that he could burn, he burnt, and his last flame was the finest.[15]

The same fuel the old man has burned in the service of his romantic illusions, he now begins to burn for the spirit's sake. There is no other fuel for the spirit. Indeed, for Svevo, always the naturalist and the comedian, the spirit itself is totally dependent on the material conditions of its existence. Salvation, therefore, can be no more than a temporary harmony in a sea of uncertainty. The passions will continue to generate fresh illusions and new absolutes which will again prevent the spirit from attending to its true vocation; but eventually these too can for a time become themes for its disenchanted vision, these too can become objects of unanxious love.

Notes

1. See P. N. Furbank, *Italo Svevo: The Man and the Writer* (London, 1966), p. 30.

2. See Furbank, p. 22.

3. Cf. Renato Poggioli, "A Note on Italo Svevo," in *The Spirit of the Letter* (Cambridge, 1965), pp. 171-179.

4. Furbank, pp. 163, 165-166.

5. *As a Man Grows Older,* tr. by Beryl De Zoete (New York, 1949), pp. 86-87 and p. 90.

6. Furbank, ch. 6, *passim.*

7. George Santayana, *Platonism and the Spiritual Life* (London, 1927), p. 89.

8. See Furbank, p. 184 ff.

9. *Confessions of Zeno,* tr. Beryl De Zoete (New York, 1958), p. 4. All subsequent citations are from this edition and will appear in the text.

10. *The Realms of Being* (New York, 1942), p. 824.

11. Quoted (and tr.) by Furbank, p. 147. For another version, see Italo Svevo, "An Old Man's Confessions," tr. Ben Johnson, in *Further Confessions of Zeno* (London, 1969), p. 27.

12. See Donoghue's review of Andrew Field, *Nabokov: His Life in Art,* in *The New York Review of Books,* August 3, 1967, p. 5.

13. See his Introductory Note, *The Nice Old Man and the Pretty Girl and Other Stories,* tr. L. Collison-Morley (London, 1930), p. 11.

14. These three novellas, the last of which is unfinished, can be found in *Short Sentimental Journey and Other Stories,* various translators (Berkeley and Los Angeles, 1967).

15. *Short Sentimental Journey,* etc., tr. L. Collison-Morley, p. 94.

Renata Minerbi Treitel (essay date spring 1972)

SOURCE: Treitel, Renata Minerbi. "Schopenhauer's Philosophy in Italo Svevo's *La coscienza di Zeno.*" *Modern Fiction Studies* 18, no. 1 (spring 1972): 53-64.

[*In the following essay, Treitel treats the paradoxical relationship between the comic tone and tragic vision of* Confessions of Zeno, *linking this dichotomy to the pessimistic philosophy of Schopenhauer and concluding that Svevo's "pessimistic vision" foreshadows "an atomic holocaust."*]

Taken at face value, Italo Svevo's **La Coscienza di Zeno** displays two opposite and irreconcilable moods which confront the reader with a seemingly paradoxical experience. The paradox lies in the fact that even though for the greater part of the novel there is a prevalence of the comic vein, the unexpected and masterful shift at the end of the book bespeaks despair, tragedy, pessimism.

How can a reader make sense out of this apparently unfounded change? Is he faced with an author's arbitrariness, or are there perhaps in the novel itself hidden seeds that might help explain this disregard for cohesion and reveal a unity of purpose and of vision? The understanding of this abrupt shift is crucial to judging the novel as one whole organic unity as well as conferring on Zeno some of the human dignity of which he seems entirely deprived in the course of the novel.

At one point in the story, Zeno confesses his familiarity with Schopenhauer.[1] Significantly enough, the name of the philosopher comes up in connection with some colored optical games which a lonely and bored Zeno indulges in towards the end of the novel. The game itself, played to while away time, is less important than the fact that Zeno, for one instant, betrays his knowledge of the master himself: Schopenhauer.

It is the opinion of the present writer that an explanation of **La Coscienza di Zeno** in the light of Schopenhauer's ideas may be a way to dispel the paradox created by the two moods of the novel. In fact, and to quote from Schopenhauer, "the source of the ludicrous is always the paradoxical."[2] But, because any paradox brings together two contrasting views of one same object, it is only natural to infer that the other side of the ludicrous must be the tragic or the pessimistic. No doubt, under the unfaltering streak of humor that pervades the novel, the perceptive reader can easily detect touches of pessimism. A real study of the book will confirm this assumption and reveal the main mood of **La Coscienza di Zeno** as one of deep, bitter pessimism.

Furthermore, Svevo's characterization of Zeno seems to substantiate Schopenhauer's assertion that "the life of every individual, if we survey it as a whole, . . . and only lay stress on its most significant features, is really always a tragedy; but gone through in detail it has the character of a comedy" (S, I, 415).

The comic and the tragic, and their resolution into a pessimistic body of ideas or, in other words, the discrepancy between the appearance of **La Coscienza di Zeno** and its reality is evident at three distinct levels: first, in Zeno's philosophical sickness; second, in his strange state of alienation as a result of such sickness; and, last, in the partial-to-nonexistent hope of salvation at the personal as well as at the universal levels. Each one of these levels reflects in one way or another the enormous impact of Schopenhauer's ideas on Svevo.

Zeno's philosophical sickness—as explored in great detail by Treitel[3]—has deep Schopenhauerian overtones. In the light of Treitel's study, it can be boldly stated here that in **La Coscienza di Zeno** the central concern of the main character pivots around the vanity and suffering of life. And such, as it is well known, is one of Schopenhauer's main concerns and the topic of Chapter XLVI of *The World as Will and Idea* (S, III, 382).

Zeno's concern about the vanity and suffering of life manifests itself in his metaphysical sickness which, according to the study made by Treitel, hides Svevo's use of paradox in handling Zeno. The paradox is evident not only between Zeno's sickly-comic appearance and his pessimistic *Weltanschauung,* but it is underscored by Svevo's choice of names for the main character of his novel. Treitel advances the possibility that Zeno's metaphysical sickness is a lifelong process which, starting from a rather light-hearted concern for man and life, ends up in a full-fledged body of ideas which reveals Zeno's conversion from frivolous optimism to deep-set pessimism. To quote from Treitel: ". . . at the end of **La Coscienza di Zeno,** Zeno finds personal, meaningful, but otherwise extremely painful answers to the metaphysical questions that lie at the basis of his dilemma. His answers consistently show the pessimistic drift of the book: man is evil, life is painful, death is the organizer of life, . . ."[4]

Since Zeno's metaphysical ideas echo many of the thoughts expressed almost a century earlier by the German philosopher Arthur Schopenhauer, it might be pertinent at this point to explore the close kinship between Zeno and Schopenhauer.

Schopenhauer's pessimism unwinds itself in a never-ending sequence of visions of evil. For him, life is basically evil because all it offers to man is suffering; it is evil because pain and boredom are its basic stimuli; and finally it is evil because, when considering life and death, he sees the triumph of the latter at the expense of life, which, to Schopenhauer, is but a chain of miseries or evils ending up in nothingness.

Also for Zeno life is suffering. He reaches this conclusion in middle age when, away from his family and away from his occupations, he discovers the true essence of life as made up of pain and love, pain and love being *"la vita insomma"* (*Z* [*La Coscienza di Zeno*], p. 477) and the origin of man's suffering.

Zeno proclaims that unhappiness or, rather, *"la miseria e il dolore"* (*Z*, p. 407) are the only realities of life; but it is Schopenhauer who exclaims: ". . . how essential to all life is suffering" (*S*, I, 401). He even adds: "If we should bring clearly to a man's sight the terrible sufferings and miseries to which his life is constantly exposed, he would be seized with horror; . . ." (*S*, I, 419). Like Schopenhauer, Zeno believes that no happiness is possible for man and that suffering is man's lot in life:

> *La legge naturale non dá diritto alla felicitá, ma anzi prescrive la miseria e il dolore. Quando viene esposto il commestibile, vi accorrono da tutte le parti i parassiti e, se mancano, s'affrettano di nascere. Presto la preda basta appena, e subito dopo non basta piú perché la natura non fa calcoli, ma esperienze. Quando non basta piú, ecco che i consumatori devono diminuire a forza di morte preceduta dal dolore e cosi l'equilibrio, per un istante, viene ristabilito.*
>
> (*Z*, pp. 407-8)

And he sees unhappiness and pain even at birth as when, over a cradle holding a sleeping infant, he muses that even an innocent creature is bound toward "[*il*] *dolore e* [*la*] *malattia*" (*Z*, p. 25).

Through personal experience, Zeno evolves a concept of life which embraces the polarity: boredom-pain. He reaches this awareness in early adulthood when he realizes that boredom is the essence of his life: *"La mia vita non sapeva fornire che una nota sola senz'alcuna variazione, abbastanza alta e che taluni m'invidiavano, ma orribilmente tediosa. . . . Puó essere che l'idea di sposarmi mi sia venuta per la stanchezza di emettere e sentire quell'unica nota"* (*Z*, p. 82). Just as boredom spurs him to marriage, so does boredom of married life spur him to adultery. Zeno's life alternates between pain and boredom, and boredom and pain he sees in other people's lives as, for instance, when he sums up Carla's recollection of life as *"tutte le sue ore di noia e di dolore"* (*Z*, p. 215).

The above ideas are to be associated with Schopenhauer's belief that man's ". . . life swings like a pendulum backwards and forwards between pain and *ennui*. . . . After man ha[s] transferred all pain and torments to hell, there then remain[s] nothing over for heaven but ennui" (*S*, I, 402).

If boredom spurs man to action, action ends up for man in suffering, misery, and, finally, disease and death. Zeno discovers that life resembles disease because it proceeds by *"crisi e lisi"* (*Z*, p. 479) but, and here again Zeno echoes Schopenhauer, *"a differenza delle altre malattie la vita é sempre mortale. Non sopporta cure"* (*Z*, p. 479).

Zeno is obsessed with the idea of death, and he sees life as a struggle ending in death; but here as elsewhere Zeno merely echoes the philosopher who says: "The life of the great majority is only a constant struggle for this existence itself, with the certainty of losing it at last" (*S*, I, 403). Treitel points out that "Zeno lives confronting one certainty only: death"[5] and that he sees death as *"la vera organizzatrice della vita"* (*Z*, p. 100). However, Zeno's ideas on death, like those on life, seem to stem from Schopenhauer: "It is clear that as our walking is admittedly nothing but a constantly-prevented falling, so the life of our bodies is nothing but a constantly-prevented dying, an ever-postponed death" (*S*, I, 401).

As Zeno matures, he realizes that he is moving closer and closer to death. His feelings about death are expressed very clearly by Schopenhauer: "Everything lingers for but a moment, and hastens on to death" (*S*, III, 269). Zeno's preoccupation with death grows with age, and yet, like Schopenhauer, he condemns suicide as an action *"indegna per un uomo"* (*Z*, p. 378) because he sees it as an expression of immaturity only. That suicide is not alien to Zeno's own thinking is proven by the following comment he makes on Guido: *"Se non gli riusciva di ammazzarsi prima,* anche lui [underscoring is mine] *prima o poi sarebbe arrivato alla maturitá"* (*Z*, p. 379). Zeno puts the problem in terms of personal maturity rather than in moral terms, and, in some way, he reflects Schopenhauer's opinion that suicide is also part of the vanity of life: ". . . suicide, the wilful destruction of the single phenomenal existence, is a vain and foolish act" (*S*, I, 515) because the will to live ensures the survival of the species.

Thus, Zeno and Schopenhauer share the belief in life's basic evil and in death's inevitability as the only realities for man. But their agreement can be carried one step further.

Schopenhauer's pessimism makes its inroads also into the nature of man whom he thought deprived of the will to change his nature. Schopenhauer believed that man is driven by the will to live—a powerful, blind force independent of knowledge (S, I, 421), working unceasingly toward its goal: the reproduction of the species. In no man better than Zeno is it possible to see man's impotence in the face of this blind, strong, life force. At the beginning of the novel, Zeno believes that he can change himself: "*Sono un po' bizzarro, ma mi sarà facile di correggermi*" (**Z**, p. 155). Every stage of the novel shows Zeno's desperate attempts at being what he is not. However, Zeno discovers by sheer experience of life that he cannot change his nature. Not only is he what he is, but he seems to move as if impelled by a force outside his rational volition. In the course of the novel he slowly comes to the realization that changing one's nature is only a delusion.

There is in Zeno an opposition between his mind that wills change and an unknown force which keeps him on his course of lies and deceptions. No matter how hard his mind analyzes the facts and decides what is right and what is wrong, an unknown force grips Zeno at every turn and makes change for him an impossibility. Zeno is truly driven. He is driven to marriage through his admiration for a healthy man—his opposite—in the hope to recover his own health: "*é evidente che non fu una risoluzione quella che mi fece procedere verso la meta ch'io ignoravo*" (**Z**, p. 83). He marries "*quella delle sue figliole che non volevo*" (**Z**, p. 93), and, in all, he lets things happen to him. He cannot change because "*c'é una lieve paralisi nel mio organismo*" (**Z**, p. 138), and just as he keeps playing the violin because he cannot bring himself to stop, so does he keep on with his psychoanalytic treatment "*solo perché m'é sempre stato tanto difficile di fermarmi quando mi muovo o di mettermi in movimento quando son fermo*" (**Z**, p. 451).

The change that Zeno to all appearances desires, but which he cannot bring about, never takes place because the basic contention of **La Coscienza di Zeno** is that man cannot change his nature. But it takes Zeno a lifetime of optimistic attempts to learn the sad truth, for the accumulation of all his failures at changing himself results in a slow erosion of the optimism which has set Zeno in pursuit of change. By the time Zeno comes to this realization, mainly that change is not possible, he has matured enough to be able to accept its implications. But, again, Zeno's ideas on this problem are a mere reflection of Schopenhauer's ideas as presented in *The World as Will and Idea*.

According to Schopenhauer, "most existences . . . act according to the laws of their nature,—i.e. of their will" (S, II, 337), and man has no hold over it:

> Everyone believes himself *a priori* to be perfectly free, even in his individual actions, and thinks that at every moment he can commence another manner of life, which just means that he can become another person. But *a posteriori,* through experience he finds to his astonishment that he is not free, but subjected to necessity; that in spite of all his resolutions and reflections he does not change his conduct, and that from the beginning of his life to the end of it, he must carry out the very character which he himself condemns, and as it were, play the part which he has undertaken, to the very end.

> (*S*, I, 147)

The above explains why psychoanalysis cannot change Zeno although it helps him reach *knowledge* of his personal will:

> Will is first and original; knowledge is merely added to it as an instrument belonging to the phenomenon of will. Therefore every man is what he is through his will; and his character is original, for willing is the basis of his nature. Through the knowledge which is added to it he comes to know in the course of experience *what he is,* i.e., he learns his character. Thus he *knows* himself in consequence of and in accordance with the nature of his will. . . .

> Therefore [man] cannot resolve to be this or that, nor can he become other than he is; but he is once for all, and he knows in the course of experience what he is.

> (*S*, I, 378)

The above also explains why all of Zeno's attempts at changing himself fail miserably, because a true follower of Schopenhauer cannot will anything that is contrary to the nature of his will.

In the course of the novel, Zeno complains of an unfair will which deprives him of the power to act. Things happen to Zeno: he does not will rationally; he cannot will. He is prey to the incessant flow of life and, paradoxically, he succeeds best by not acting. But this too is in agreement with Schopenhauer who says: ". . . the nature of life throughout presents itself to us as intended and calculated to awaken the conviction that nothing at all is worth our striving, our efforts and struggles; that all good things are vanity, the world in all ends bankrupt, and life a business which does not cover expenses" (S, III, 383).

Throughout the novel, Zeno seems to leave action in favor of chance, rationalizing that for him times come back so that nothing ever changes. And with this reflection he explains his illimited, false optimism. In this too **La Coscienza di Zeno** reflects Schopenhauer's dictum: "throughout and everywhere the true symbol of nature is the circle, because it is the schema or type of recurrence" (S, III, 267).

Thus, optimism only skims the surface of the novel. The true contention of the book, mainly that life is evil and that man cannot change his nature, is reminiscent of Schopenhauer who felt that ". . . *optimism* . . . appears not merely as an absurd, but also as a really *wicked* way of thinking, as a bitter mockery of the unspeakable suffering of humanity" (S, I, 420).

Therefore, in the light of the above explanations, the paradox raised by the comic and the tragic in *La Coscienza di Zeno* finds an adequate solution when Zeno's philosophical ideas are likened to Schopenhauer's. Zeno's central concern pivots, like Schopenhauer's, around the vanity and suffering of life, and Zeno, like the philosopher, evolves truly pessimistic insights into life and into man.

Another aspect of the paradox attached to the main character of *La Coscienza di Zeno* is the subtle interplay between Zeno's apparent madness and Zeno's profound wisdom. This paradox again presents the reader with the two contrasting moods running side by side throughout the novel. However, even while laughing at the touches of insanity in Zeno, the reader will find a satisfactory resolution of the two moods only in the surprising realization that his apparent madness—cause and reason of so much laughter in *La Coscienza di Zeno*—is only a cover for Svevo's, not Zeno's, pessimistic insights into the special position of the genius or the thinking man in the midst of a bourgeois society. This pessimism is attributable to Schopenhauer's influence on the novelist.

In dealing with Zeno, Svevo often uses words like *pazzo* (**Z**, p. 99), *casa di salute* (meaning asylum) (**Z**, p. 39), *certificato di pazzia* (**Z**, p. 55), and he makes other characters in the novel see Zeno as a man who has been slightly touched by some sort of madness. However, a close reading of the novel will not fail to impress the reader with the obvious fact that Zeno is a thinker and that his capacity for abstract intellectual processes brings about his alienation from his environment and his unhappiness.[6]

Zeno's predicament—mainly his state of alienation as a result of his philosophical sickness—reflects Schopenhauer's ideas on genius, madness, and the alienation of genius.

Without by any means implying that Zeno be considered a real genius, he undoubtedly stands out from the society around him by way of his philosophical disposition. In this sense, he shares in the fate of the thinking man as viewed by Schopenhauer. In the light of Schopenhauer, Zeno is a budding genius because he is able to see "all that is essential and significant . . . and what is accidental and foreign" (S, I, 321) he leaves out of his vision. To quote from Schopenhauer: "Genius . . . knows not individual things but Ideas" (S, I, 251).

The above point, however, proves further Schopenhauer's pessimistic contention concerning the basic evil of life, because for Zeno—the Schopenhauerian genius of

sorts—the capacity to think is one more source of suffering. In fact, Schopenhauer suggests that "the higher the organism the greater the suffering."[7] In his own words: "Thus, in proportion as knowledge attains to distinctness, as consciousness ascends, pain also increases, and reaches its highest degree in man. And then, again, the more distinctly a man knows—the more intelligent he is—the more pain he has; the man who is gifted with genius suffers most of all" (S, I, 400).

Furthermore, a reconciliation between Zeno's apparent madness and Zeno's growing wisdom can be achieved by reference again to Schopenhauer who points out the close and "direct" connection of genius and madness, ". . . I have known some persons of decided, though not remarkable, mental superiority, who also showed a slight trace of insanity. It might seem from this that every advance of intellect beyond the ordinary measure, as an abnormal development, disposes to madness" (S, I, 248). He goes on to show his view of the relation between genius and madness. For Schopenhauer, both the madman and the genius are capable of transcending the particular in things "in order to see in things only their Ideas" (S, I, 251), or, in other words, to go beyond the particular which "is raised through [their] way of contemplating it, to the Idea of the thing, to completeness" (S, I, 251). Schopenhauer even adds: ". . . we must therefore assume that there exists in all men this power of knowing the Idea in things, and consequentially of transcending their personality for the moment, . . . The man of genius excels ordinary men only by possessing this kind of knowledge in a far higher degree and more continuously" (S, I, 252).

Zeno is neither a genius nor an ordinary man. He is above the ordinary men of *La Coscienza di Zeno* by possessing higher insight into the nature of things, but he never reaches the level of the genius. If he is insane within the world of *La Coscienza di Zeno,* neither is he what Schopenhauer would call a "great genius" (S, I, 246). Zeno lingers in limbo between Bedlam and paradise without quite belonging to the one or to the other.

It is the fate of the genius, according to Schopenhauer, to be queer and isolated from those around him, "for his mind and theirs have no common grounds and never meet."[8] So does Zeno share in the fate of genius, as expounded by Schopenhauer, by way of his alienation, of his isolation, and by the "queerness" which is his hallmark throughout the novel.[9] He shares in the "unsociability of the genius; [for he is] thinking of the fundamental, the universal, the eternal; [whereas] others are thinking of the temporary, the specific, the immediate."[10] And to quote from Schopenhauer again: "As a rule, man is sociable just in the degree in which he is intellectually poor and generally vulgar."[11]

However, the clearness of consciousness which makes Zeno so different from those around him is his only redeeming quality because it lifts him "out of the endless stream of willing" (S, I, 254), conferring on him for one fleeting moment the peace necessary to behold the scheme—or lack of scheme—of the universe. That his peace is transformed into despair by the end of the book adds weight to that speck of dignity that Zeno earns, in the eyes of the reader, only through the exercise of his intellect, because as his knowledge increases so does his despair at the human corruption.

Treitel points out that in *La Coscienza di Zeno* happiness and health are linked to minds void of ideas and that it is Zeno's tragedy to think. In the face of shallow, child-like characters, Zeno is the only one who evolves mentally, and this evolution is shown by his constant lack of health and lack of happiness. Again, this is truly Schopenhauerian philosophy which teaches that "to be happy, one must be as ignorant as youth."[12]

Thus, Svevo subtly uncovers his thoughts concerning his own society and, perhaps, his own position within it; through Zeno he seems to suggest that the price for attaining the true knowledge of life is unhappiness. Once more, another aspect of the paradox underlying *La Coscienza di Zeno* and its resolution into a pessimistic body of ideas can be explained by reference to Schopenhauer.

Paradox adds to paradox in *La Coscienza di Zeno,* for if Zeno's philosophical disposition causes his ridicule, his alienation, and, finally, his disease, it is also that very disposition that provides a glimmer of hope in some sort of minute, personal salvation before Zeno's plunge into the depths of black despair. This imperfect sort of salvation—insufficient as it is to save Zeno—is also attributable to Schopenhauer.

At the beginning of the novel, Zeno finds everyday salvation in his marriage of convenience to Augusta. His marriage not dictated by love, is a spiteful action done to get rid of the uncomfortable feeling of rejected suitor. Augusta is well aware of this when she cries out after the wedding ceremony, *"Non dimenticheró mai che, pur non amandomi, mi sposasti"* (*Z*, p. 180). Yet, Zeno paradoxically achieves a very happy relationship with his wife and finds in her a source of strength and understanding. Zeno's marriage and subsequent happiness in his married state are to be related to Schopenhauer who thought that "marriages of convenience . . . are often happier than marriages of love" (S, III, 371). In fact, in *La Coscienza di Zeno,* passion as represented by Zeno's relationship to Ada and Carla, and Guido's to Ada, is doomed. This is clearly in agreement with the German philosopher who thought that "love is a deception practiced by nature . . ." (S, III, 370).

If marriage of convenience provides Zeno with some salvation at the domestic level, he will yet achieve a greater sense of salvation which is very Schopenhauerian in nature.

Because of his philosophical disposition, Zeno moves toward the partial kind of personal salvation and happiness which Schopenhauer attributes to the man of intellect, for "there can be no victory over the ills of life until the will has been utterly subordinated to knowledge and intelligence."[13] In other words, "what the bridle and bit are to an unmanageable horse, the intellect is for the will in man" (S, II, 426) because "nothing reconciles so thoroughly as a distinct knowledge" (S, I, 396); so, if knowledge is source of suffering, as it was pointed out earlier, knowledge is also one way to partial salvation.

Zeno achieves a certain liberation from the powerfully-driving will and a certain recovery of happiness by an intelligent contemplation of life. In this, he again echoes Schopenhauer who firmly believed that "clearness of consciousness" lifts man "out of the endless stream of willing" (S, I, 254).

Zeno's partial liberation from the will that drives him stems from the clarity with which he looks at things, at people, and at the intellectual honesty with which he objectively registers what he learns to see. In fact, at the end of the book, his knowledge about man and life, pessimistic as it is, is only a result of his life experiences. In this, too, he follows Schopenhauer who displayed a remarkable distrust for all sorts of textbooks and who felt that "philosophy purifies the will. But philosophy is to be understood as experience and thought," because ". . . if anyone spends almost his whole day in reading, . . . he gradually loses the capacity for thinking. . . . Experience of the world may be looked upon as a kind of text, to which reflection and knowledge form the commentary" (S, II, 254).[14] This is true for Zeno who, almost at the end of the book, conquers knowledge through life experience thus achieving what Schopenhauer calls "the intelligent contemplation of life:"[15]

> *Fu un vero raccoglimento il mio, uno di quegl'istanti rari che l'avara vita concede, di vera grande oggettivitá in cui si cessa finalmente di credersi e sentirsi vittima. In mezzo a quel verde rilevato tanto deliziosamente da quegli sprazzi di sole, seppi sorridere alla mia vita ed anche alla mia malattia.*

However, if for Schopenhauer the intelligent contemplation of life is a road to salvation and a road away from life's suffering, man cannot yet totally avoid the evils of life. This is what happens to Zeno who does conquer inner harmony through contemplation of life but for whom the hard-begotten inner harmony lasts for a fleeting moment. Historical developments reveal to Zeno deeper insights into man's true nature pushing him into the abyss of despair with which *La Coscienza di Zeno* ends.

As Zeno is engulfed by World War I, his inner world—center of metaphysical anguish for so many years—suddenly expands into the outer world, and, in the calamity of cosmic disease, Zeno's former disease becomes frivolous and unimportant even in his own eyes. Zeno discovers that the possibility to devote a lifetime to meditate on the disease of life was a game possible because of the peace and lull of pre-war times. In Zeno's own words: *"appresi che ci fu a questo mondo un'epoca di tanta quiete e tanto silenzio da permettere di occuparsi di giocattoli simili"* (*Z,* p. 466). The realization of the present in the light of the past gives way to the final wave of despair with which the book ends. A now mature Zeno holds man responsible for the defacement of nature. He feels that man has prostituted his intelligence to his own detriment—intelligence giving way to "furbizia" (*Z,* p. 479), strength to weakness—and that man's intelligence, now at the service of modern technology, has corrupted nature and, finally, man himself. Zeno's Schopenhauerian discovery of evil as intrinsic to man and to life destroys the last shreds of his optimism.

The beginning of the present paper raised the question of whether a reconciliation between the comic tone of the novel and the tragic vision of its ending is possible. At this point, the answer is affirmative because, as this study has tried to show, the flippant tone is only a way to mask the pessimistic strain that intimately links the two parts of **La Coscienza di Zeno.** The reconciliation is possible on aesthetical grounds, in that the underlying continuity of thought establishes the essential unity of this novel. More important, a reconciliation is possible in philosophical terms by a *rapprochement* to the philosophy of Schopenhauer, who sees life as comic and tragic at the same time. This dichotomy is present in Zeno himself. Zeno is comic, absurd, ridiculous, inadequate every time a single, insignificant, everyday act of his life comes into focus. But, when taking Zeno's fate in relation to the cosmos—as Svevo does at the end of the book—the reader is reminded of Schopenhauer's black pronouncement: ". . . under the firm crust of the planet dwell powerful forces of nature, which, as soon as some accident affords them free play, must necessarily destroy the crust, with everything living upon it . . ." (*S,* III, 395-396).

La Coscienza di Zeno hides under a layer of humor, of clownishness, of ridicule, a tragic vision of man and of destiny. In this novel, Zeno travels from ignorance to knowledge. His last vision is one of black pessimism and makes his regained health and happiness meaningless. His final vision embraces the recovery of cosmic health in a universe deprived of man and of life.

In this novel, Svevo seems to overreach Schopenhauer himself and to carry Schopenhauer's pessimism one step further by denying even the philosopher's idea of salvation and immortality "which rests on the assured survival of the species."[16]

Svevo's pessimistic vision—almost prophetic of our times—foreshadows an atomic holocaust.

Notes

1. Italo Svevo, *La Coscienza di Zeno* (Milano: Dall'Oglio Editore, 1964), p. 453. All citations are from this edition and are indicated in the text by the abbreviation (*Z*) and page number in parenthesis.

2. Arthur Schopenhauer, *The World as Will and Idea,* translation from the German by R. B. Haldane and J. Kemp (London: Routledge & Kegan Paul Ltd., 1964), 3 Vols., II, 271. All citations are from this edition and are indicated in the text by abbreviation (*S*), volume and page number in parenthesis.

3. Renata Treitel, "Zeno Cosini: The Meaning behind the Name," *Italica,* 48 (1971), 234-245.

4. Treitel, p. 244.

5. Treitel, p. 238.

6. Treitel, pp. 239, 244.

7. Will Durant, *The Story of Philosophy* (New York: The Pocket Library, 1957), p. 324.

8. Durant, p. 335.

9. Treitel, p. 235.

10. Durant, p. 335.

11. Schopenhauer, "Wisdom of Life," *Essays,* p. 24, cited by Will Durant, *The Story of Philosophy,* p. 335.

12. Durant, p. 327.

13. Durant, p. 329.

14. "Books and Readings; Counsels and Maxims," *Essays,* cited by Durant, p. 332.

15. Durant, p. 333.

16. Erich Heller, *Thomas Mann: The Ironic German* (New York: The World Publishing Company, 1965), p. 59.

Elizabeth Fifer (essay date summer 1973)

SOURCE: Fifer, Elizabeth. "The Confessions of Italo Svevo." *Contemporary Literature* 14, no. 3 (summer 1973): 320-31.

[*In the following essay, Fifer observes that in Svevo's fiction "women are not independent of men's fantasy lives" and argues that because "they are dreamed up in the minds of men," these women are "simultaneously forbidden and sacred," but "still have the greater power."*]

Italo Svevo's narrators form their first impressions of women so unclearly that reality must forcibly intervene: myopia as neurosis. Bruised but finally unrepentant, they fortify their former images with the addition of some saving rationalization. These narrators, as many have noted,[1] are constantly being shocked by "sudden" observations. From Alfonso Nitti of *A Life,* through his "son," Emilio of *As a Man Grows Older,* all the way to Zeno of *The Confessions* [*The Confessions of Zeno*], each has his rude awakening:

> But I am ashamed not to have realised earlier that I was heading for a disaster. I had to deal with a most single-minded nature, but by continually dreaming about her I had transformed her into a consummate flirt. My fierce resentment when she at last made me understand she did not want me was quite unjust. But I had so closely interwoven dreams with reality that it was hard for me to believe she had actually never even kissed me.[2]

According to Svevo, women are not independent of men's fantasy lives. Each narrator goes through a meticulous mental preparation for his woman and with great difficulty distorts her reality until it conforms to his ideals. Kissing a prostitute, Emilio imagines his Angiolina to be "the pure virginal moonlight."[3] When he realizes his dream has not been made flesh, he only raises it one level, to include all women. She has never been an individual to him so Emilio can, without difficulty, elevate her behavior into a principle (again of his own making) and withdraw to admire a new creation, his excuse for her. "It was useless to punish her," he began to think, "she was only the victim of a universal law" (*A* [*As a Man Grows Older*], p. 91). Angiolina has not changed during this process—indeed, she has never appeared at all, except insofar as she understands Emilio's need for her, and, in order to use him, anticipates what is required to fulfill his fantasy.

François Bondy calls this circle of hypocrisy "the fairly horrible comedy" Svevo finds in the relations between old men and young girls, which arises "from the difference in response between the partners, each of whom, because of what he expects from the relationship, applies himself to playing the role that would best meet the other's expectations."[4] The Pantalone-Isabella relationship of paternal eroticism is archetypal. For Svevo's fantasizing narrator, the acceptance of an old man's rejuvenation by benevolence is *quid pro quo* for a young girl entering a liaison with him. The girl is paid to fit into the man's image. She is never fooled, for she does not need his dream, only his money. Indeed, throughout Svevo's fiction one has a sense of attractive women sequestered in small rooms with their quiet, hopeful mothers, pretty girls like the one in **"The Nice Old Man and the Pretty Girl,"** flying about in trams, waiting for a situation:

> For her the adventure was so clear-cut that she could not lie about it, as he did. She must not break off the

relationship for the moment. . . . The young girl fell in with the old man's ways. When he wanted her, she came; she went off when he had done with her.[5]

A fantasy may work for the paternal "protector and educator" of young girls, but how can it accommodate itself to a man who wants to step outside these roles?

Zeno, like the rest of these males, does not see a woman apart from certain fixed social roles, most frequently that of mistress. The woman's family often helps to enforce the Svevian fantasy: Angiolina's grasping mother excites Emilio's suspicions more than her daughter's blatantly sordid activities; Zeno's sympathy is roused as much by her mother's timidity as by Carla's own need. Perhaps an older Zeno can be excused for thinking of his mistress in a stereotyped fashion, but how can the young Zeno propose to a woman and marry her without at least recognizing her basic personality outside of what he desires from her for himself? Svevo handles the marriage with great irony, sending Zeno into the Malfenti's home by way of the father, Giovanni, crafty financier, of whom Zeno admits: "I clung to him in the hope of enriching myself" (*C* [*The Confessions of Zeno*], p. 75). Narrowly escaping marriage with another girl whose name, years later, he has trouble remembering, he turns to a firm figure he can believe in, admire, and imitate—a mature man who will guide the youth to financial (and personal) riches.

Judging from the position of Svevo's typical narrator toward women, it does not seem at all "odd," as Zeno imagines, to approach marriage by way of the father, attaching himself wholly to this man as if some "fate" had decreed it. The subconscious nature of his decision to marry into the Malfenti family is further underscored by the inseparability of the daughters, whose names all begin with "A," and his rejection at first glance of his future bride, Augusta: "Well, that was the end of one of the four girls with the same initial, as far as I was concerned" (*C,* p. 81). By a further irony, Augusta the squint-eyed becomes the best wife, even though she is his third choice on the night of their engagement.

Through bitter experience Zeno learns that merely because a woman's beauty stimulates him, he cannot impose any fantasy he wants upon her. However, his realization that Ada is not flirting with him, even though she is attractive enough to succeed, only drives him to a further subjectivity in regard to feminine beauty. Just as Emilio raises his deception with Angiolina to disillusionment with the whole sex, Zeno raises his deception about the character of his mistress Carla to the level of a philosophy of women. He can accept his feelings about her, in this way, without having to accept her. Just as the others appropriate their women's families into their feelings about the girls, Zeno begins to think of feminine beauty as separable from the female, to be judged by the way he responds to it, having nothing to do with her personality. Such beauty is an element apart, another stimulus surrounding the woman which enhances his desire for her. That he desires her and what he desires in her are products of his own vision and should not be confused with the bearer of the beauty. It is his own feelings and not her that he worships:

> When, several hours later, I began dreaming about Carla, it seemed to me that joy and sorrow conflicted in her face. But when I knew her better I found nothing of all this, and was forced to recognize once again that feminine beauty can simulate feelings which are wholly foreign to it, just as the canvas on which is painted a battle scene has nothing heroic about it.
>
> (*C* [*The Confessions of Zeno*], p. 168)

It is a small step from declaring women chameleons to saying that only men have souls, and that men, by their adoration of women, lend them the illusion of profundity.

Entering a wife's or mistress' family, the Svevian protagonist, far from adjusting his character to theirs, carnivorously attempts to bring the family into himself. Zeno is in an undifferentiated state with Augusta, where he believes she shares his ego. She becomes his conscience, and he placates her in his dreams by offering her a bite of his mistress Carla's neck as he is devouring her: "To calm her I said: I won't eat her all up: I will leave a little for you" (*C,* p. 180). The unprecedented honesty of this dream gives the waking Zeno a brief moment of satisfaction.

The narrator's shortsightedness lies in the nature of the personal neurosis Svevo creates for him. Zeno is intensely self-hating, searching for his justification in the world without, and, once finding it in a woman, internalizing her identity. He must then destroy her, within him, as he would destroy an image of himself, were he to fall in love with it. His initial impression of her must be so overwhelming that he surrenders himself. He believes that Carmen, his brother-in-law Guido's secretary and mistress, is the most beautiful woman he has ever seen. She serves the traditional romantic purpose of making the narrator more interesting to us, the more infatuated he becomes with her. When she applies for a job in Zeno's office, he thinks slyly, "What sort of post? In the bedchamber?" (*C,* p. 252). Ada, Guido's wife, is also forced to see her husband's mistress, as Augusta saw Carla in Zeno's dream. She visits the office unexpectedly to find the beauteous Carmen there. The mistress, admittedly a "caricature" of the good woman, outshines the wife with the brillance of her beauty. Both women's appearances are a direct result of Zeno's feelings. He does not love Carmen, so her beauty dazzles him. He loves Ada, so her "wifely" beauty is at this moment "unobtrusive" to him. He lifts his percep-

tion to another universal law. Feminine beauty can only become real to him through possession. Without the fact of possession, beauty becomes hazy and finally fades. If the object of desire is unattainable, it hardly matters that one has desired.

This antiromanticism is his best defense against his obsession with women; his extreme ambivalence from love to hatred to indifference arises because his cynicism is only a mask:

> On the other hand I really loved Ada at that moment; and it is a strange feeling to love a woman whom one has desired passionately but never possessed, and who now means nothing to one. On the whole the situation is the same as it would have been if the women had yielded, and it is interesting as proving once more how little importance we ought to attach to certain things that for the time being fill our whole horizon.
>
> (*C,* p. 255)

By making the woman's attraction trivial, Zeno saves his feelings from seeming so. He further emphasizes the ersatz nature of love when he observes that although his brother-in-law Guido was never so energetic as when he was in love, "very little of the business invented by him when he was in love bore any fruit" (*C,* p. 255).

Svevo's heroes, disbelieving in the power of women and refusing to see them with any sense of their separate reality, are yet domineered by their visions of mother, daughter, and sister in the women around them. The protagonists are minimal, waiting for others to make the first move. Alfonso Nitti waits for his mother to die before he commits a romantic suicide. Aghios' **"Short Sentimental Journey"** is, significantly, away from his wife. "Running away was already more than justified,"[6] the narrator says of middle-aged Aghios. He contrasts this legal spouse with Aghios' dream, so like the dream of the other protagonists, of "ideal woman, at least, without legs or lips" (*S,* p. 205). Because their lives seem worthless to them, the men feel that any woman they meet must be tainted also. These very women whom they despise are part of them, both boundary and barrier, beyond which lies Aghios' "scheme of joy and hope," the promise of escape, giving the lie to the mundane drabness of their own souls.

Stricken with the curse of a modern Midas, these inoffensive men become whatever they see, whatever can give them a shape, an identity. When they find themselves displeased with the new identities, be they fantasy or nightmare, this only furthers their desperation to find something which will take them beyond all they know. Their trip outside is an attempt to penetrate more deeply within themselves. Zeno allows his friend's illness to stimulate his own hypochondria:

> I discovered something terrifically complicated which seemed to get out of order directly I began thinking about it.
>
> Even today, if anyone watches me walking, the fifty-four movements get tied up in a knot, and I feel as if I shall fall down.
>
> (*C*, pp. 108, 109)

Using Tullio as an excuse, Zeno experiences his own neurosis, recognizing with mingled horror and fascination that his illness is psychosomatic.

The functions of Signor Aghios' phantom lover depend upon the imagination of her seducer. A journeying middle-aged man has but a limited selection of roles for a woman: "she serves primarily for love, but sometimes also as a thing to be protected and saved" ("**S**" ["**Short Sentimental Journey**"], p. 205). His narrow imagination circumscribes the whole of his life. He is forced to protect a young man instead of the lovely creature of his dreams. The rake steals Aghios' money to repay a debt and marry. Old men who have the dream, Svevo seems to be saying, would do better to give youth a chance. He has Aghios deliver the damning prophecy, as is usual with the protagonists, in a distanced, academic manner, as if citing a natural law by rote which he himself neither comprehends nor would obey: "She [Mother Nature] is always busy. There are so many of us! She eliminates only those who are no longer of service" ("**S**," p. 283). After the young man robs the middle-aged one, the manuscript is left unfinished, indicating that this lesson was expressed too cruelly even for the author. His protagonists let themselves in for disaster by preparing an experience in their minds before it happens, to avoid any shock. The outrage life perpetrates upon them is to allow their fantasies to become real.

Women are not guiltless in this round of pretension. Emilio sees not only his desire for Angiolina but her expectations for the course of their affair. He plays in part a role she has designed for him, speaks of his love as magical "possession," and echoes Zeno's submission to Augusta's masochistic fantasy. When Zeno finally turns to Augusta after Ada and Alberta, she accepts him with a humble "You need a woman, Zeno, to live with you and look after you. I will be that woman" (*C*, p. 134). Zeno reflects later that it was at this moment that he gained certainty.

The nice old man in Svevo's short story is an exaggerated miniature of Emilio, also a philanthropist who seems to completely accept his mistress' sexual fantasy about him, even to her taking other lovers, from the first moment he sees her on the tram. In the proper tradition of the "coup de foudre," her eyes meet his and he begins to think—about his wife's death, about incest, about youth. He decides that because she is pretty, he will buy her. Insidiously, the girl eats of his substance—the reverse of Zeno's dream, where he eats his mistress—both literally and figuratively, diminishing his finances and causing him the physical over-exertion which finally kills him. Instead of his buying youth from her, she has sold him old age.

Through third-person distancing Svevo keeps his male figures ineffectual. We see Emilio's obsession with Angiolina both as a middle-aged bachelor would see her—from without, and also from within, as she really is. When the story is entirely first-person narrative, he uses someone unreliable, like Zeno, who is always changing his mind. He filters a seemingly stable woman in this way until her image is rendered ludicrous by the aberrations of her observer. A contradiction and subsequent frustration is created in the heroes by use of these unreliable narrative voices; they say one thing and do another, feeling ridiculous in front of a woman who is given no such depth or ambiguity of characterization. They do not reflect on themselves but see only what is revealed of them by the women. Their women-mirrors are therefore to blame when misfortune arises. Emilio and Zeno feel that everyone, but most of all women, is laughing at them.

This dual reaction of dependency and withdrawal arises because women are used for mutually exclusive purposes. Not only do the men go to them for support, nurturing, and focus, but they also use women for invidious comparisons. Going to women for help, they force themselves to reject any offering—to accept would be too painful. Caught between a worldly renunciation of feminine wisdom, suffering for mistakes they make because they will not take advice and cannot figure things out on their own, they suffer loss of self-respect when they find it necessary to conform to the ideas of wife or mistress.

Zeno begins to think of acts of self-destruction, like chain-smoking, as being beneficial because they are self-assertive. He admits with glee to wanting to kill his brother-in-law on the Via Belvedere, delighted with this untenable urge rising from his subconscious to compel him to acts of unreasoning violence. What keeps him from killing Guido is, he thinks, not his love for Augusta, nor is it that her sister is to be married to the would-be victim. He must see his excuse as his own: "I had got engaged to Augusta just in order to have a good night. How should I be able to sleep if I killed Guido?" (*C*, p. 141). Zeno uses Augusta's contrasting nature as moral norm, the better to savor his crimes, as Emilio uses Angiolina's immorality to put the edge on his love:

> In my contemplative mood . . . I was able to smile at life and at my malady. Women played a great part in both. Even the details of a woman's body . . . her feet, her waist, her mouth—were enough to fill my

days. . . . Even when I was not thinking of my mistress, I still thought of her in the sense that I craved forgiveness for thinking of other women as well. . . . I have never known life without desire, and illusions sprang up afresh for me after every shipwreck of my hopes, for I was always dreaming of limbs, of gestures, of a voice more perfect still.

(*C,* pp. 363-64)

Whatever virtue the women have is perverted by Zeno into a foil for his sinfulness. Augusta's unsuspecting tenderness, after Zeno has just betrayed her with Carla, pushes him over the edge into the delicious sickness of guilt: "When I saw her so gentle and so completely without ill-feeling my shivering fit grew worse and my teeth began to chatter" (*C,* p. 191). The nicer she is to him, the worse he becomes in fantasy. By perfecting her behavior toward him, in a strange way Augusta plays into Zeno's desire to suffer. He admires in himself what she would abhor and defeats her symbolically in his mind.

The only strength Svevo will give to his "heroine" Augusta is her actual ability to laugh at her foolish husband. Her smile and her laugh startle Zeno with their gaiety and seeming oblivion to his suffering. In the sanitarium where she has left him interred to give up his smoking habit, he "suddenly felt that her smile, which I loved so much, was mocking me" (*C,* p. 41). He goes from this fantasy to one in which Augusta wants to get rid of him to make love to his doctor, completing this neurotic circle of making her assets into liabilities. When a girl does treat Zeno with evident disrespect, as in the scenes with little Anna Malfenti, the reader is so used to this being fantasy that it seems surreal. Svevo increases this unreality by having only the two hear the insult and by having the little girl quite "normal" when the other people are about:

> When I was going away she would join me at the door and ask me prettily to bend down to her; then rising on the tips of her toes, she would put her mouth right up to my ear and say in a whisper, so that nobody could hear: "But you're mad, quite mad!" The comic part is that when the others were there the little hypocrite treated me very politely.

(*C,* p. 93)

Only a woman can help Zeno in this plot he has concocted against himself because he believes, as he tells his analyst Dr. Copler, that they are the cause of his disease. They actually cure him only by deflecting guilt from its true origin in his own psyche, effectively shielding him from this recognition.

In the case of justified anger, denigration of the woman-as-object is much more easily accomplished. With Emilio's fantasy it is certain that its object is both despicable and despising. Zeno's route is inevitably more circuitous. From Alfonso Nitti's suicide on, the urge to self-destruction in Svevo's men searches only for an excuse to be realized. In *As a Man Grows Older* a woman can be found who is at last both seductive and rejecting. None of the threats Zeno imagines have the power to really frighten him—in Emilio's case, the woman is harmful enough to make his love for her itself a neurosis.

The more Angiolina increases his love, the more she enforces his self-hatred. Until he begins to feel like a fool, he does not even know he is involved with her. Her unfaithfulness begins to pique him more and more. Although Emilio would like to think of himself and Angiolina as virgins, from the first kiss he is longing to know of her infidelity: "Was it he then who had initiated her into an art of which he himself was but a novice?" (*A,* p. 19). He longs to avenge himself on her, as punishing father, masochistically drawn to her the more she flaunts his love. He watches her day and night, imagining what he cannot see, relishing the waiting more than the meeting. All is in the anticipation; the absurdity of his own life seeks any manner of interrupting boredom.

"Do you really desire all the pretty women you see?" (*C,* p. 163), Dr. Copler asks his patient anxiously. Emilio's evil demon is also this creature, the pretty woman, whose parts exist only to give him stimulation, "the kind of adventure which begins by admiring a shoe or a glove or a skirt" (*C,* p. 164). Women are fragmented into a mysterious conglomeration of body images, which are disturbing if one possesses them but even more so if one does not. The fantasy of sex is more compelling than its fulfillment, although Zeno has remarked previously that a woman's beauty seems to fade without the fact of possession. It is not possession but dreams of possession which in the end are the strongest: "I thought of all the women who were walking along the streets, and whose secondary sexual organs, just because they were hidden, became so important, whereas they disappeared altogether in the woman you possessed, as if the very fact of possession had atrophied them" (*C,* p. 164). Emilio's guilty "son" Zeno carries on the earlier man's hatred of women without any justification. Zeno would like to torture even the patient Griselda he married.

Women are troublesome: Signora Nitti expecting her son to comfort her like a husband when she is dying; a pretty bus driver wanting an old man to be young. Angiolina is the vessel into which Emilio pours the bitterness of age. As with the nice old man, women are Emilio's death instrument, impressing on him the need for withdrawal from life. His sister dies during the course of the affair, but he scarcely notices her gradual withering away and thinks of her as a child when she is dead. Only his paternal passion for Angiolina has meaning for him: "waiting was inexpressibly painful to him . . . he knew that if he were to go home without having seen his mistress he should know no peace" (*A*, p. 154). The development of the protagonist's disgust with himself is the development of the narrative; he goes from stage to stage in it, propelled by the self-hatred that he projects onto the woman he loves. Similarly, when Ada will not marry Zeno he feels "anger and contempt" instead of sorrow.

These Svevian men are existentialists to the extent that they believe there are no more adventures to be had; yet despite the authenticity of their disillusionment, they continue to search for some justification in women. They always get exactly the opposite from what they think they want in their fantasies, be it success or, more perversely, the lack of it. Zeno longs to be disappointed, so Svevo gives him a stable life, a good mistress, and has his bosom enemy die by his own hand. Emilio's Gethsemane comes when he realizes his mistress does not have enough interest in him to torture him even after he has waited all evening for her. When she arrives he has a difficult time making her do to him even half as much as he has done to himself: "She did not take much notice, thinking she could pacify him with a few caresses" (*A*, p. 155).

As if escaping from their own consciences, these men go to women to become children again, in the spirit of irresponsibility. Instead of losing all sense of moral responsibility, however, the heroes begin to feel somehow that they should be consciences not only for themselves but for their women as well. Emilio feels he must justify Angiolina's behavior in some way, and Zeno imagines the secret lives of his mistress and his brother-in-law's escapades with Olympian forgiveness. This ambivalence is nowhere more clearly expressed as in **"The Nice Old Man,"** [**"The Nice Old Man and the Pretty Girl"**] where paternal love kills the seducer with its recriminations. His anger at the pretty girl's misdeeds is really anger at his own impotence. Her evil deed is not running to the young rake with the smart umbrella but visiting and exciting him, the old man, in his illness:

> A bliss and pain indescribable. At a given moment he became obsessed with the idea that the girl certainly had other lovers, all as young as he was old.

> Perhaps the old man ate and drank too much. He was anxious to show off his strength. I do not wish to imply that that is why the old man fell ill.

> (**"N"** [**"The Nice Old Man and the Pretty Girl"**], pp. 86, 87)

The authoritarian father who abruptly summons and dismisses his daughter wishes to possess the object of his fantasy and yet have her be as guilty of promiscuous love as he appears to be to himself. Misplaced in

his old age, desire is not an emotion he nurtures easily. A passive aggressor who lets the old man kill himself over her, the pretty young girl must acquiesce to him because she needs him. No sooner do old men dream up a story than they expect to live in it. At this point the girl herself is released, and the old man's body proclaims the grotesqueness of the association.[7]

Yet the old man is willing to accept that his young girl has other lovers, so long as she will continue to serve as a symbol to him. Like Pantalone, he feels "he must forbid her all irregular relations and above all relations with old men" (**"N,"** p. 115); only he is allowed to love. With his guilty fears about his age, his narcissism increases. Her visits are not the cause of his illness; he will not let doctors prohibit them. He passes alternately from the role of Romeo to that of Polonius, fancying himself a philosopher who will teach the girl about life through "moral lectures" prepared beforehand. Of course this is just another way of thinking about the young girl. When the flimsy pretense of education is over, the old man faces only the girl. He relives his experiences with her as prohibition. Dying, he remains unregenerate and continues to think "if youth had been all it should be, old age could never have learned to sin" (**"N,"** p. 126).

Because they are dreamed up in the minds of the men, all the women in Svevo's fiction are simultaneously forbidden and sacred. Woman alive, outside man's fantasy of her, would be too forbidding. She must live a world apart, without influence, her life unknown, her talents and personality virtually ignored. Although locked as objects inside their men's fantasies, women still have the greater power. Zeno's squint-eyed wife is the best choice he could have made, frustrating him with her patience and goodwill. Emilio's fickle and voluptuous mistress has the sexual strength to make him forget his intellectual emptiness and has him believing at the end that such is his need for her that she "only exists in order that I may live" (*A*, p. 229). When she runs away with a bank thief, his anger against her for removing herself from his fantasy is transformed into anger against her for her immorality, and he defends himself before her mother with the assertion that he tried to "correct Angiolina and to point out the straight road to her" (*A*, p. 230). The fantasy of women reaches its final degradation when it kills the old man. He dies of a kind of moral turpitude, in a vain effort to escape the consequences of his act by writing treatises on youth and age. Although his dream has already died before him, the girl still gets his money because he is too lethargic by that time to change his will.

Notes

1. Jean Murray, "The Progress of the Hero in Italo Svevo's Novels," *Italian Studies,* 21 (1966): "In seducing Annetta, he [Alfonso Nitti] was trying to

prove himself superior to her and the revelation of how inferior she really was broke him completely. For he was idealistic, and unable to reconcile his dream with reality. . . . The uncomplicated view of life held by Angiolina is part of her attraction for Emilio. She is so different from him, and in trying to make the conquest he is probably trying to prove to himself that he is really as young and gay as she is. She was the projection of his self image . . . although aware that her attraction was merely sensual and that the affair probably would not last, the discovery that her point of view was equally selfish and that the decisions were not all his as he had imagined, shocked him into action" (pp. 92, 94).

2. Italo Svevo, *Confessions of Zeno,* trans. Beryl de Zoete (1930; rpt. London: Secker and Warburg, 1962), p. 91; hereafter referred to parenthetically as *C.*

3. Italo Svevo, *As a Man Grows Older,* trans. Beryl de Zoete (1949; rpt. New York: New Directions, 1968), p. 19; hereafter referred to parenthetically as *A.*

4. François Bondy, "Italo Svevo and Ripe Old Age," trans. John Simon, *The Hudson Review,* 20, No. 4 (Winter 1967-68), 585.

5. Italo Svevo, "The Nice Old Man and the Pretty Girl," in *Short Sentimental Journey and Other Stories,* trans. L. Collison-Morley (London: Secker and Warburg, 1967), p. 87; hereafter referred to parenthetically as *N.*

6. Italo Svevo, "Short Sentimental Journey," in *Short Sentimental Journey and Other Stories,* trans. Ben Jonson, p. 204; hereafter referred to parenthetically as *S.*

7. "Every erotic relationship in the narrative of Svevo is a vain attempt to overcome the coldness of being, to abolish the distance between the self and others, between self and self—and makes it only more manifest" (Bondy, p. 580).

Stephen Kolsky (essay date January 1987)

SOURCE: Kolsky, Stephen. "Italo Svevo and Mario Equicola: A Strange Encounter." *MLN* 102, no. 1 (January 1987): 128-40.

[*In the following essay, Kolsky focuses on Svevo's unfinished drama,* Ariosto governatore, *arguing that the author's "most pressing preoccupations are to be found in this fragment," in which he openly discusses politics and allows "himself to be 'uncovered' more completely than in any other of his fictional works."*]

The first efforts of a major writer have always been of interest to literary critics partly because of the light they throw on the writer's subsequent development, partly as first literary statements. Svevo's first attempt at literature is no exception. Scholars have studied *Ariosto governatore,* of which only the first scene was actually written, with some enthusiasm because a number of Svevo's principal themes are prefigured in this fragment.[1]

The play's historical setting allows a partial disguise for the head-on clash of ideologies between its two protagonists. One can see why, at this stage, Svevo was inclined to use the dramatic form rather than a more dispersive one like the novel: it seems that, for once, Svevo wished to express his conflicts as clearly as possible without needing to have recourse to the complexities that the novelistic form could offer him. Critics have used the *Ariosto governatore* to confirm their view that in this first attempt at writing the most important themes in Svevo's work are already present *but* only in embryo, that is, they were to be developed and amplified in his later writings.

In this article I will argue that Svevo's most pressing preoccupations are to be found in this fragment. However, it will be my contention that it is in this play that Svevo allows himself to be "uncovered" more completely than in any other of his fictional works. This will be the first and last time he will do so, preferring in later works to become more and more "hidden". The play can be regarded as having been written in an "open" or "sincere" mode in contrast to his three major novels which, in varying degrees, were all written in the ironic mode. Critics have so far preferred to stress other aspects of Svevo's play. One of his most astute critics, Eduardo Saccone, revising an earlier opinion, sees this youthful work as grappling with one of Svevo's most essential themes:

> Oggi, però, sarei forse disposto a leggere anche di più in questo brano [the second part of Ariosto's principal speech]: a scorgere nell'individuazione di un mondo diviso in servi e padroni, come l'emblema del nodo problematico che lo scrittore era destinato ad analizzare.[2]

I would add that Svevo rarely discusses politics in such an open fashion as he does in this play and one can only be struck by the *honesty* of this attempt to tackle the problems that beset the bourgeois writer. It is likely that the play remained unfinished due to Svevo's realization of just how much of himself he had revealed.

Saccone's reading shows other characteristics of Svevo's writing, the most important feature of which is, however, the head-on collision between two characters, a form of representation that will be taken up in ever more complex and subtle ways in his three major novels.[3] Yet the contradiction remains: if the young Svevo accepted at this stage that literature should deal with problems relating to the writer's experience of reality, in this case the problem of commitment, then why should he have set the play in the Renaissance?

Svevo himself in the *Profilo autobiografico* states that amongst the authors he read were two Renaissance writers, Machiavelli and Guicciardini, both Renaissance intellectuals, notorious for their interest in power, politics, and the State.[4] It was perhaps these concepts that attracted Svevo, rather than a pure interest in the Renaissance (it is noteworthy that Machiavelli and Guicciardini represent opposing trends in the political thought of Renaissance Florence, an early example of Svevo's preoccupation with oppositions.) Moreover, Svevo does not mention any Renaissance poets. The decision to write a play with Ariosto as its chief protagonist may have had a more precise reason: Ariosto was and is still considered one of the greatest poets of the Italian Renaissance and, as such, a glory of Italian literature. For someone wishing to prove his *Italianità* there could be no better way than choosing an Italian figure acceptable to Risorgimento ideology. According to this hypothesis, Svevo intended to demonstrate his loyalty to the Italian cause by dropping, if only on the surface, his attachment to things German and by taking up the cause of Italian culture. He was helped in this task by Francesco De Sanctis who, by Svevo's own admission, was "il coordinatore dei suoi studi letterari."[5] It is almost unthinkable that Svevo did not read at some time De Sanctis' *Storia della letteratura italiana* in which there is a chapter on Ariosto's most famous poem, the *Orlando Furioso*. The nineteenth-century critics's analysis of the poem aims to demonstrate how unconcerned Ariosto was with the realities of his time. Thus De Sanctis' praise of the poem as a fine work of art is intended at the same time to be a harsh condemnation. He characterizes the poet in the following terms: "Ludovico è innanzi tutto un artista." The *Orlando furioso* has claimed a unique place in Italian literature "come opera di pura arte, il lavoro più finito dell'immaginazione italiana."[6] It is noteworthy that De Sanctis' concern ends where Svevo's begins, in that the Triestine writer is preoccupied with the effect that creating a famous literary work has on one's lifestyle. *His* Ariosto has already written the *Orlando furioso* and is chiefly concerned with the effects that this epic poem has had on his existence. In a way, the *Ariosto governatore* is a "riposte" to De Sanctis' position. From another point of view the *Ariosto governatore* anticipates Svevo's own autobiography by many years; the anxiety that late fame brought to a mature Svevo by the tardy recognition of *La coscienza di Zeno* is well known. Svevo seems to have been obsessed right from the very beginning of his career with the problems arising from literary fame and although it is ironic that he did not achieve such fame until almost the end of his life, the recognition of this problem forms

part of his concern about the isolated position of the intellectual in bourgeois society. For this reason the play is set in the Garfagnana, which represents the peak of Ariosto's formal court career because he had been appointed Governor of that small province by the Duke of Ferrara. Yet, at the same time, this office emphasized the poet's isolation and distance from the capital of the Ferrarese state and from courtly life, as represented by the courtier Mario Equicola. Ariosto's position in society is emphasized by the annotation made by Svevo in the list of characters, in which he is the only one to have his status specified "governatore." His power is materialized on stage by the actual setting, which is the Governor's house, and in particular "una stanza riccamente ammobigliata" (*Diario*, [*Diario per la fidanzata*] p. 222). However, this power is illusory in many ways, since the position of the Governor depends on the real power of the Duke in distant Ferrara; Ariosto is subject to the policies and whims of someone he cannot hope to influence. Thus, the stage-setting is at once indicative of the extent of his power and its limitations.

In order to write the *Ariosto governatore* Svevo needed biographical information on the poet. As is evident from the list of the characters at the beginning of the play, Svevo mixed historical fact with fiction. The existence of Alessandra Benucci is well documented, but this is not the case for another character who would have appeared if Svevo had finished the play, Matteo Benucci, who seems to be an invention on Svevo's part. The inclusion of Mario Equicola in the play must have necessitated further historical research by Svevo, for, as we shall see later, this figure was not at all well studied at the time when Svevo began writing his play. The question of Svevo's sources for *Ariosto governatore* has so far been neglected by scholars even if it is clear that the writer would have needed to consult historical works: "Ettore si pose a comporre una comedia sopra l'Ariosto" (*Diario,* p. 219). In order to inform himself about Ariosto's life, Svevo would have had at his disposal a source which was reliable and easily obtainable, the standard early nineteenth-century biography of Ariosto by Baruffaldi.[7] Here are recorded the basic facts of Ariosto's existence which would have enabled Svevo to form some kind of picture of the poet's struggles in his everyday life. If it is a relatively easy matter to identify the probable source of Ariosto's life used by Svevo, it is a different matter with Mario Equicola. Interest in Mario Equicola only gained momentum in the second half of the 1880's. Thus, the work of contemporary scholarship would not have been available to Svevo. At the time when Svevo was composing his play, Equicola was even more obscure than he is today.[8] The question that needs to be answered is where did Svevo first come across the name of Equicola, let alone any hints concerning his personality. Even if Svevo used his intuition as to what constituted the core of Equicola's character, nevertheless he had to know, even in general terms, the career Equicola had and other such basic information. There is one mention of Equicola in Baruffaldi's biography of Ariosto. It occurs by way of a quotation from Ariosto's *Orlando furioso,* not the 1532 edition but the earlier one:

> Mario Equicolo è quel, che gli è d'appresso,
> Che stringe i labbri, e manda in su le ciglia,
> E fa con man di tutti i detti d'esso
> Di stupor segno e d'alta maraviglia.[9]

Equicola is presented in these lines of poetry as a servile and timeserving personality who lives off the greatness of others. In these few lines Equicola is shown as having no characteristics of his own. Entirely devoted to an appreciation of other writers, everything about him is exaggerated and comical. In contrast to Svevo's original treatment of Ariosto as someone suffering from the success that the *Orlando furioso* brought him, Equicola seems to follow very much the path of historical tradition which represents Equicola as a typical sycophantic courtier. An interpretation along these lines, though not presented in negative terms, is offered by the then standard authority on Italian literature, Tiraboschi. This literary historian had not neglected Equicola in his survey of Italian literature. He places him within the restrictions that are imposed on a writer in a court society:

> Il favore di cui i Gonzaghi furon liberali alle scienze meritava che molti scrittori essi trovassero encomiatori delle loro gloriose imprese.[10]

Tiraboschi further fosters this impression of Equicola as a servile courtier by a well chosen quotation from Bandello which portrays Equicola as the almost perfect courtier, a type of man that any court would be pleased to have because of all the qualities with which he was endowed.[11] It would not have been too difficult to analyze the information that Tiraboschi gives on Equicola and use it in a way not intended by the author, that is, presenting Equicola as the archetype of courtly servility. It is my opinion that this is precisely what Svevo did.

Once Svevo had this barest outline it is true that he could have directly set about writing his play. However, I think it possible that he may have turned to a primary source, using the information found in Tiraboschi. It is not impossible that Svevo consulted Equicola's most important work firsthand, the *Libro de natura de amore.*[12] If Svevo consulted the *Libro* he would have found much of interest to him, particularly in the section of the fifth book entitled "Virtù, diligentia, modi, et arte di conciliarci benivolentia."[13] The title sums up Equicola's attitude to court society viewing the individual courtier in terms of his ability to win for himself, by adhering to the rules of court behaviour, the highest honours open to him. According to Equicola, the court-

ier must do nothing to attract unwelcome attention and must be ready to drop any personal opinions he may have:

> Quello amabile reputamo, che a loco et tempo secundo suo et d'altri conditione, quanto et quando si conviene sa giocosamente ragionare senza offendere altri, senza latrare, et senza mordere.[14]

Any matter that is liable to give rise to controversy is abandoned in favour of social conservatism and jovial conversations. By using "la virtù de la urbanità" the courtier will be able to obtain nearly everything that will be necessary for a comfortable existence (*Libro,* f. 168r).

From what has been said, it is clear that Svevo had the opportunity of obtaining enough historical information to produce the portrait of Equicola as it is found in **Ariosto governatore.** It is also true that no evidence has been discovered which will allow a more precise determination of which books Svevo actually consulted. But because of Svevo's choice of someone as obscure as Equicola, one can be fairly certain that he needed to have recourse to the kind of sources I have indicated. It might be argued that Equicola is only a name attached to a preconceived idea and as a consequence, historical research would not have been necessary. In my opinion such a response begs the question. In the first place, **Ariosto governatore** is an historical drama. While it is true that Matteo Benucci was a character invented by Svevo, the other three were taken from historical reality (Ariosto, Equicola, and Alessandra Benucci). Svevo needed at least a basic knowledge of Ariosto's biography in order to be able to set his play in the Garfagnana. From there he might choose to invent certain events, such as the meeting between Ariosto and Equicola, which certainly did not take place there.[15]

It is now the moment to discuss the fictional encounter between Ariosto and Equicola in the first scene (and only scene) of the play. It is obvious that Ariosto and Equicola produce a vivid sense of opposition as far as their characterization is concerned. However, a curious point has so far gone unnoticed by the critics, that is, the significance of the first stage direction which reads: "Lodovico Ariosto e Mario Equicolo entrano a braccetto." (**Diario,** p. 222) I think a symbolic meaning can be ascribed to this stage direction. Even though clear and precise oppositions are incarnated in the characters of Ariosto and Equicola, nevertheless, the stage direction seems to suggest that a vital interaction takes place between the two. Ariosto may have been attracted at one stage by the position propounded by Equicola but which he now forcefully rejects in the play. Equicola, then, can be said to represent the easy way out: the chase after material benefits at the cost of a social conscience.

The entire fragment of the play is articulated around the notion of appearances. Implicitly there is a choice of whether to rebel against the existing social order or to accept it in its entirety. Equicola holds the second view:

Se poi col mio venire non vi causai piacere
Abbiate compassione . . . Non fatelo vedere.

(*Diario*, p. 222)

Equicola can only see surfaces whereas Ariosto can feel essences. It is the bonds between fellow human beings that come in for scrutiny in the opening section of the play. This is seen in the use of the term "amico" joined to the concept of "giusto amico." Verbs of interrelating are equally revealing, particularly Equicola's distinction between "amare" and "stimare." Human relations are seen to be computed by considerations of fame and the acquisition of wealth. Finding an acceptable rapport with other human beings is something that torments Ariosto. For Equicola the concept of "stimare" replaces that of "amare" (*Diario*, p. 222). Equicola can see things only in terms of success or lack of it. He completely avoids the question of Ariosto's "senilità" ("Ciò non mi cale," (*Diario*, p. 222). Equicola's discourse brings together images of life and vitality. With reference to Ariosto, terms such as "vostro carattere focoso" and "vivida forza di gioventù" are frequently used in Equicola's misreading or *méconnaissance* of Ariosto's behaviour. Equicola's traditional definition of the poet is in direct conflict with the pessimistic view presented by Ariosto. In the play Ariosto has already reached the peak of his poetic career and has found that success was not all that it was meant to be. The realization of fame has not made life any easier for the poet. Ariosto's attitude may be seen as a projection of the young Svevo's hopes and fears. It is well known how, in his later years, when fame had come to the mature Svevo, the writer found his new position almost untenable. Thus, writing, implying fame and success, was a problem for Svevo from the very start of his "career". Equicola perceives Ariosto's poetry and success in terms of a precocious *Dannunzianism,* associating with the poet certain key elements such as inspiration, youthfulness and worldly success. The poet then is seen as the embodiment of a social myth, that is, someone who, unlike ordinary mortals, is freed from the travails of the struggle for life. Ariosto, on the other hand, conceives of the poet in quite another vein: he is the victim of the social system, the impotent bystander of the struggle for life ("ma esso patisce e langue/sotto una larga piaga e continua a sparger sangue" (*Diario*, p. 222)). One might think that the first scene of Svevo's play contrasts the tormented Romantic poet with a poet cast in the mould of a Carducci or a D'Annunzio. However, what distinguishes Svevo's poet is his sense of social injustice: as an outcast he feels the weight of the social system. The poet is oppressed, in this interpretation, by social injustices, but can do nothing about them, "langue/sotto."

Equicola's response to Ariosto's position brings out the contradictions of the socially aware bourgeois poet:

la vostra piaga è ben nascosta et io non la discerno
fra tutti questi beni che la vostra vita adornan.

(*Diario*, p. 223)

It is the word "nascosta" that I wish to emphasize here. Equicola's accusation seems to be very accurate and hard-hitting if applied in a wider autobiographical sense to Svevo's own lack of commitment. Ariosto does not tackle this problem in depth. His principal speech (p. 223) does indeed describe the *piaga,* first of all in existential terms. There abound abstractions and an abstract sense of alienation from bourgeois values and expectations. The generalizations of the first part of Ariosto's major speech sound hollow because they do not attempt to locate the social or historical source of the poet's malaise, this "male/che è la vita" (*Diario*, p. 223). The insistence of this theme is relayed to the reader by the constant repetition of key words, in particular, the past participle *vissuto* which conveys this sense of alienation and disappointment with what life has to offer. This procedure of highlighting important concepts extends to other words. Probably the most blatant use of this device is the following line:

fredda la gloria, fredda la vita e freddo il cor.

(*Diario*, p. 223)

This distancing from Equicola's definitions of the poet as a vital and forceful creature is further emphasized by the simile of the colour of Ariosto's hair, in other words, the senility of the writer. Youthful illusions have gone forever and will never return because the poet has been through a learning process which has revealed life to him in all its brutality.[16]

The second half of Ariosto's speech is concerned with analyzing the roots of the poet's predicament. The poet is neither a revolutionary nor an unthinking upholder of the system. But the nature of the poet's position prevents him from being more than a sympathizer of the oppressed masses. His intellect can perceive the divisions in society ("io vidi," *Diario,* p. 223). Yet, the poet himself recognizes that he is no more than a passive receiver of disturbing truths about society:

. . . I gridi
degli oppressi *toccarono* il mio cuor, lor compagno
mi fecero . . . e ne piansi. (my italics)

(*Diario*, p. 223)

The poet does not act; the two verbs "toccarono" and "fecero" seem to lead the verses to a crescendo, perhaps to an important action. However, the reader is disappointed—all the poet can manage is tears. Only the poet's sensibilities are touched by the fact of social oppression. Anger and the will to change seem to be absent even though Ariosto claims to be the *compagno* of the oppressed. This occurs solely on the emotive and intellectual levels. Thus any socialist connotations of the word *compagno* are severely limited because of the poet's inability or refusal to change his or others' state. The *io* of the poet is oppressed from two directions: the first from the socially oppressed, "lor compagno mi fecero," and the second, from those of his own class, ". . . meditai sul mio stato/e mi trovai coi grandi" (***Diario***, p. 223).

Interestingly, Ariosto's discourse focuses on the poet's genius as the feature which distinguishes him from the others. Instead of putting forward an economic analysis, difference is seen in terms of intelligence or genius, something that is not the fault of the poet (a gift of nature) nor anything he can do much about. By claiming that he himself is a victim, Ariosto, in this way, manages to free himself from any social responsibilities.[17] Although Ariosto makes it quite clear that he has abandoned those concepts that differentiate him from the others, such as *genio* and *gloria,* it cannot be said that his material position has greatly changed, as can be judged by Equicola's comments. Two interpretations of Ariosto's political stance are possible at this point. The first is much kinder than the second in that it takes into account the impotence of the individual trapped in bourgeois society and who, nonetheless, feels his position as a predicament. The second interpretation sees Ariosto's position as an act of bad faith which allows a sense of pity for the oppressed to become an act of solidarity. Thus he avoids a sense of guilt which could arise from total inaction on the poet's part. It is perhaps this aspect which will achieve predominance in Svevo's later works. The protagonists of his three major novels all seem to bear the stamp of this conflict to a greater or lesser extent.

Equicola's reply to Ariosto is sharp, with a touch of cynicism to combat the poet's views. It is as if, towards the end of the fragment, Ariosto's bad conscience is embodied in Equicola who plays on Ariosto's inability to change his situation. The courtier points out the poet's reluctance to exchange his existence for another, particularly of the kind represented by Equicola.[18] Apart from this cogent attack on Ariosto's philosophical stand, the rest of Equicola's discourse is built on weak premises. He refuses to acknowledge the divisions within society, preferring to talk about *ognun,* thus moving the discourse onto the individual level away from grand issues. Equicola's home-spun philosophy smacks of stoicism:

> . . . E ripartita
> la buona e la cattiva sorte in parti eguali,
> ha nella vita ognun e piaceri e grandi mali.
>
> (***Diario,*** p. 224)

According to this interpretation, which will be refuted by Ariosto, there is nothing that can be done to alter the conditions of existence. Moreover, Equicola raises inaction to the dignity of action, in other words, sympathy for the oppressed is an end in itself and does not require any further deed on the part of the poet:

> Quell'ingiustizia adunque che voi piangete tanto
> diggià fu cancellata da questo vostro pianto.
>
> (***Diario,*** p. 224)

In his turn, Ariosto accuses Equicola of being unfeeling, of refusing to face the situation. Ariosto's challenge is couched in interesting terms, using the metaphor of numbers ("sol le cifre aman"). Ten years later Svevo would take up the theme of numbers in his first novel *Una vita* where the banking world is seen as a closed circle bounded by financial calculation, a world to which it is almost impossible to gain access if you happen to be an outsider. The banking world attempts to remove reality from within its boundaries and transform it into a set of figures or calculations. Contact with external social reality is purposely avoided. Figures themselves become the substitute for reality. Thus it can be seen that there is a logical progression in Svevo's work from the first fragment to the first novel which complicates the original idea to the point of ambiguity and uncertainty.

It might seem strange to claim that *Ariosto governatore* represents the clearest indication of a political consciousness in Svevo's work when the writer himself states that he did not finish the first scene because he recognized "l'astrusità dell'idea." On the other hand, it could be argued that Svevo broke off just at the moment when his character, Ariosto, would have had to make a firm commitment to political change. Hence Svevo's reluctance to go on with the play. If the ideas are "abstruse," there are attempts within the play to define such ideas which would perhaps make the author vulnerable in the future. *Ariosto governatore* is one of Svevo's clearest political statements. It deals comprehensively with the writer/intellectual and his relationship with the rest of society. The play presents the reader with a first attempt at working out the social implications of writing: Ariosto, tormented by self-doubt, yet unable to break out of the vicious circle in which he is trapped, and Equicola, firmly attached to bourgeois values which make his position more certain and more secure than that of the poet.

It has been argued in this article that the *Ariosto governatore* occupies a crucial position in Svevo's works and this is underlined by a comment that Elio Schmitz makes in his diary concerning the genesis of the play:

> Questa volta, però, gli feci firmare una obligazione
> nella quale promette che fino al 14 Marzo finirà tutto

l'*Ariosto governatore,* altrimenti mi pagherà, per il corso di 3 mesi, per ogni sigaretta che fuma 10 soldi.

(Diario, p. 221)

Svevo's failure to finish the play, that is, his refusal or impotence to state the basic features associated with his experience of writing, is mirrored in his inability to stop smoking. According to Elio's comment, Svevo will be punished for the act of smoking. Thus, right from the beginning, smoking and writing are closely connected, as they will be in Svevo's greatest novel *La coscienza di Zeno.* Writing for Svevo will always fall under the sign of impotence; in this respect the *Ariosto governatore* is at once typical of Svevo's literary production and at the same time exceptional in that he will never again have the courage to be so honest.

Notes

1. I wish to thank John Gatt-Rutter for his stimulating comments in the early stages of the preparation of this article. *Ariosto governatore* was first published by G. Spagnoletti in "La giovinezza e la formazione letteraria di Italo Svevo," *Studi Urbinati di storia, filosofia e letteratura,* NS (1953), 179-221. This work was republished with various corrections by B. Maier in his edition of *Lettere a Svevo. Diario di Elio Schmitz* (Milano: Dall'Oglio, 1973).

   The play is often mentioned in passing: the more interesting contributions include R. Barilli, *La linea Svevo-Pirandello* (Milano: Mursia, 1972), where, in the critic's opinion, we find "uno Svevo già interamente se stesso" (p. 19), but his characteristic themes, although present, are found "in misura contratta e implicita" (p. 19). Another important contribution is E. Saccone, *Il poeta travestito* (Pisa: Pacini, 1977), in which the historical significance of the play in Svevo's *opus* is recognized; however, at the same time, the critic detracts from its importance: "L'argomento è trito" (p. 31).

2. E. Saccone, pp. 31-37.

3. G. Spagnoletti, pp. 208-209.

4. *Profilo autobiografico* in Italo Svevo, *Opera Omnia,* III (Milano: Dall'Oglio, 1968), p. 800: "Si trattava finalmente di conquistarsi un po' di cultura italiana".

5. *Profilo,* p. 800: "Poi fu introdotto nei suoi studii un qualche ordine dalla conoscenza delle opere di Francesco De Sanctis."

6. Francesco De Sanctis, *Opere,* ed. N. Gallo (Milano-Napoli: Ricciardi, 1961), p. 457, p. 465.

7. Girolamo Baruffaldi Giuniore, *La vita di M. Lodovico Ariosto* (Ferrara: Stampa del Seminario

1807). See also G. Fatini, *Bibliografia della critica ariostea (1510-1956)* (Firenze: Le Monnier, 1958), item n. 728 (p. 173).

8. For a brief survey of later critical opinion of Equicola's character see S. D. Kolsky, *Mario Equicola. A Biographical Reappraisal,* unpublished Ph.D. thesis, University of London, 1981, pp. 4-10.

9. Baruffaldi, pp. 260-261. The biographer's observation on Ariosto's treatment of Equicola may have provided Svevo with a precise line of investigation or at least reinforced his original idea:

   > Queste smanie e dibattimenti dell'Equicola a approvazione di tutti i detti del *Furioso* furon dipinti forse dall'Ariosto, ricopiandoli scherzevolmente dal vivo.
   >
   > (p. 261)

   First of all it is interesting to note that Baruffaldi's reading represents a misinterpretation of the text because the person in question is not Ariosto but another poet, the Unico Aretino. However, in spite of this error, Baruffaldi puts across an important trait of Equicola, his exaggerated servility, particularly toward those who have won fame and riches.

10. G. Tiraboschi, *Storia della letteratura italiana,* tomo VII, parte III (Firenze: Molini, Landi e Co., 1812), pp. 967-969.

11. G. Tiraboschi, p. 967.

12. S. Pesante, *Le cinquecentine della biblioteca civica di Trieste. Catalogo breve* (Trieste, 1974). I am using the 1525 edition of the *Libro* published by Lorenzo Lorio da Portes in Venice.

13. *Libro,* f. 165r.

14. *Libro,* f. 169r.

15. For Equicola's biography see D. Santoro, *Della vita e delle opere di Mario Equicola* (Chieti, 1906) and S. D. Kolsky, *Mario Equicola.*

16. Disillusionment, which experience brings in its wake, is symbolized here by the whiteness of Ariosto's hair. The sense of disillusionment is further reinforced by the repetition of "tutto" which gives a sense that once everything has been tried and tested there is nothing left except brutal reality.

17. Cognition as an act of the intellect is seen as perhaps the only valid bastion against bourgeois convention and inauthenticity.

    Svevo's own comment on the play is indicative in this context: "più che scritto ci ho pensato." Intellection is perhaps the one activity which is fully in the control of the poet. And this can account for the predominance of verbs of knowing in Ariosto's central speech ("conoscere," "il saperlo" and so on).

18.   . . . di cangiar non accetto
     contuttociò la vostra gran sorte colla mia.

                                        (*Diario,* p. 223)

Beno Weiss (essay date 1987)

SOURCE: Weiss, Beno. "Short Stories." In *Italo Svevo,* pp. 122-33. Boston: Twayne Publishers, 1987.

[*In the following essay, Weiss surveys Svevo's short stories, sketches, and narrative fragments, arguing that while many of these writings are "marred by sketchiness, incompleteness, and incongruities," they nevertheless "illustrate the development of Svevo's literary experimentalism."*]

We have already seen that Svevo's earliest attempts at writing were for the theater. Elio's diary informs us that in 1881 his brother was also dabbling in short stories, which were never completed. It was not until 1888, however, that the fledgling author made his first appearance as a writer of fiction on the pages of *L'Indipendente,* which serialized his short story "**Una lotta**" ("**A contest**").[1] His "minor" narrative writings are a potpourri of mainly undated short stories and tales of different lengths, some fragmentary and others sketches of future works never brought to completion. Only seven were ever finished: "**Una lotta,**" "**L'assassinio di Via Belpoggio,**" "**La tribù,**" "**La madre,**" *Una burla riuscita,* "**La novella del buon vecchio e della bella fanciulla,**" and "**Vino generoso.**" An eighth, "**Lo specifico del dottor Menghi,**" appears to be complete, except for a fragment missing on the first page. This narrative production—in addition to his plays—belies Svevo's claim of having given up literature after the critical failure of *Senilità* and until the beginning of World War I. What is clear is that, though he may not have submitted many of his creative writings for publication, he continued to practice his craft and to experiment with new narrative forms and techniques.

PUBLISHED WRITINGS AND FINISHED WORKS

"**Una lotta**" seems to be a parody of chivalric romance. The hero, Arturo Marchetti, is a frail, neurotic, but witty poet and theorizer, who at the age of thirty-five feels his youth is slipping away; he regards Rosina as his Dulcinea, and tries like Don Quixote to affirm his heroic spirit. His bravura in threatening his physically more powerful rival, Ariodante Chigi—a handsome, vigorous but inarticulate athlete—and the inevitable deflating result, reveal him to be a true prototype of Svevo's antiheroic characters. The story, written contemporaneously with *Una vita,* anticipates certain basic motifs and characters that Svevo will develop more fully in his novels: the dreamer, the theorizer, the individual whose propensity to think and reflect renders him unprepared for life. Indeed, Arturo resembles Emilio Brentani—both suffer from precocious "senility," both are full of unfulfilled desires. Finally, the contest between Arturo and Ariodante presages those between Alfonso and Macario, Emilio and Stefano, Zeno and Guido. The structure, the language, the intermingling of direct and indirect discourse, but above all the ironic contrast between the rivals whose characterizations are deftly achieved, all reveal Svevo's growing mastery.

Svevo's second short story is far more serious and complicated. Written in 1890 and serialized once again in *L'Indipendente,*[2] "**L'assassinio di Via Belpoggio**" ("**Murder on Belpoggio Street**") is clearly reminiscent of Dostoyevski's *Crime and Punishment*: an impoverished street-porter, Giorgio, kills Antonio, a casual drinking companion, and robs him of a substantial sum of money in a dark street of Trieste. Like Raskolnikov, Giorgio feels superior to his fellows and has absolutely no remorse for what he has done. Indeed, he sees himself as the wronged party: it was all the fault of Antonio who ought not have shown him the money. The murderer quickly becomes entangled in an intricate snare of motives, conscience, and fears. His true punishment is psychological; the torment of isolation from others makes him abominable to himself until he is arrested and confesses to the murder.

Giorgio is an *inetto,* at odds with both social classes, the middle class that has rejected him as an outcast, and the subproletariat that refuses to accept him. In the brutal attack on Antonio, Giorgio's monotonous and squalid life suddenly becomes dramatic. Like the servant in *Inferiorità* who kills his master, Giorgio frees himself momentarily from his sense of inferiority. The euphoria, however, is fleeting and he falls back immediately into his inherent inadequacy.

In "**L'assassinio di Via Belpoggio**" Svevo produced something more than a successful thriller. The style is simple, direct, fresh, and vigorous; the somber tone is very persuasive; and the picture of Trieste's low life is vivid and convincing. The story already reveals the mastery of psychological observation and analysis for which Svevo will eventually be esteemed.

In 1897 Svevo wrote "**La tribù**" ("**The Tribe**"), his only political narrative. It appeared in *Critica sociale,* the prominent socialist magazine published by Filippo Turati (1857-1932), one of the founders of the Italian Socialist Party in 1892.

The narrative, signed Italo Svevo, deals with a nomadic tribe that settles in a fertile region of the desert. The tribal tents and neat little houses soon disappear, giving way to rich mansions on the one hand and squalid hovels on the other. The tribal leader, Hussein, asks young Ahmed to help the tribe out of its predicament, but Ahmed, who has studied European economic systems, can only suggest the ways of capitalism: first factories, then exploitation, and finally equality. Hussein finds this process too long and tells the tribe that they should skip the first two phases and start with the last. Ahmed, who insists on building a factory, is expelled from the tribe, and the tribesmen thus reach a state of happiness.

Although Svevo's solution to the capitalistic system seems vague, a fabulous and ephemeral resolution to the problem, and although one may view the tale as a parody of Marxist dialectical materialism, or, as Mario Fusco suggests, "an unexpected and humorous hypothesis of Marxist doctrine,"[3] "La tribù" does reflect Svevo's commonsense view of morality and utopian socialism, and clearly points out the incompatibility between progress and happiness. Hussein and his people succeed in a classless society by avoiding the internecine evolutionary class struggle between capitalists and oppressed proletariat. Svevo propounds a philosophy of sense and moderation, and his veiled message is that the functioning of any society, even a primitive and classless one, requires ideals and moral standards.

"La tribù," more charming that persuasive, is memorable for Svevo's laconic wit and the irony of the political allegory.

Composing fables was one of Svevo's lifelong habits. They are central to many of his stories and particularly to his third novel, and Svevo frequently experimented with the form.[4]

"La madre" ("The Mother") concerns several chicks hatched in an incubator who suffer because they do not have a real and nurturing mother,[5] unlike a nearby brood with a mother hen that watches over them with great care.

First written in 1910 and revised for publication in 1927,[6] "La madre" deals in allegorical form with Svevo's exclusion from the Italian literary establishment. The garden with the hen and its homogeneous population of animals represents Italy; while the one with the incubator, populated by chicks of various colors and shapes, is an obvious reference to the city of Trieste at the crossroads of *Mitteleuropa,* the melting pot of various religions and nationalities. The mother, "who was said to be able to give every delight and therefore satisfy ambition and vanity" (131), stands for the Italian establishment, which, until the very last phase of Svevo's career, refused to acknowledge his artistic merits. Indeed, even after the so-called discovery of Svevo by the French literati and Montale, he ran into all sorts of difficulties in trying to have the second edition of *Senil-*

ità published. Furthermore, his writings were attacked by critics like Guido Piovene, who, in a vitriolic review of *Senilità,* wrote: "What is Svevo's merit? Of having come close, more than any other Italian, to that passively analytic literature, which found its apogee in Proust; but it is inferior art, if art is meant to be a product of living and active men. . . ."[7] And finally, the ostracism of the chick Curra reflects not only Svevo's exclusion from the strongholds of Italian culture and learning, but also his position as a Jew without a "true" sense of belonging and acceptance, particularly during the rise of fascism.

Una burla riuscita (*The Hoax*), completed in 1926, is a long narrative divided into eight segments; it takes place in Trieste during the last days of World War I.[8] Mario Samigli is an unassuming but devoted office clerk who in his youth published an unappreciated novel entitled *Giovinezza* (Youth).[9] Forty-three years later he has still not gotten over his neglect by the critics. Though he no longer writes for publication, he secretly composes fables whose protagonists are sparrows. Gaia, a former poet who has become a successful traveling salesman, is envious of Mario's faithful commitment to literature. He decides to play a hoax on his friend, leading him to believe that an important Viennese publishing house is interested in buying the rights to his novel. Mario naively falls for the ploy and signs an attractive contract with one of Gaia's accomplices. When eventually he finds out the truth, he confronts Gaia and gives him a sound thrashing. Though the author's ego is deeply wounded, financially the hoax turns out to be rather profitable for him. A speculation performed with nonexistent funds, together with the confusion resulting from the entrance of the Italian Army into Trieste and the collapse of the Austrian currency, give the author a handsome profit of seventy thousand lire.

Aside from the obvious similarities with Svevo's own literary experiences—Lavagetto calls it "a parable of his own existence"[10]—*Una burla riuscita* is extremely important in that it offers an insight into Svevo's self-image as an author right after the initially unsuccessful publication of *La coscienza di Zeno.* Like his namesake and creator, the character Samigli derives relief from the psychic pain of his existence by writing fables. Thus, literature takes on a double valence: protection and shield against the world, and escape and potential cure for his frustrations. In essence, fables are symbolic expressions of wish fulfillment akin to dreams, in which the author finds cathartic release from the tensions and anxieties produced by repressed emotions. Indeed, as the narrator says, Gaia's practical joke remains "powerless against his dreams" (64). The story also offers a psychological study of the motives behind practical joking. Svevo echoes Freud when he explains that Gaia's love for practical joking "was a relic of his suppressed artistic tendencies"; and that he resented Mario because he had remained faithful to his art and become a "silent witness against him" for having given up and repressed his own poetry (92).

"La novella del buon vecchio e della bella fanciulla" (**"The Story of the Nice Old Man and the Pretty Girl"**), written in 1926, deals with the last love affair of an old man who is clearly the aged successor of Zeno.

During the war in Trieste, while the guns are rumbling in the distance, a rich elderly gentleman meets a young and beautiful girl who quickly becomes his paid mistress. The affair does not last very long because he suddenly falls ill, stricken with angina—no doubt precipitated by the romance—that limits all his activities. One day, as he looks out of his window, he sees her in the company of an attractive young man. Both jealous and guilty for having taken advantage of his wealth to seduce her, he sets out to reform her and write a thesis on the relations between the aged and the young, between health and disease. The girl's reeducation becomes a mere pretext for a profound and desperate examination of his own existence. The narrative ends with the old man's realization that his physical strength is insufficient to bring his thesis to completion. He wraps the pages of his manuscript in a sheet of paper on which, as a final reply to his quest, he writes several times: *Nothing.* The next day he is found dead amidst his writings, with a pen in his mouth.

The story, written in the third person with nameless protagonists, reminds us of Zeno's affair with Carla, and his attempts to appease his guilt feelings. Though similar, the two adventures differ considerably—in this narrative Svevo is merciless toward both the cynical "good" old man and the compliant, mischievous young girl. Both are willing and ready to corrupt and be corrupted by money. Love, as in *La rigenerazione,* is seen as a cure for old age and as an escape from degrading physical and emotional conditions. Ironically, however, the cure proves to be fatal for "our old man."

Like most of the short stories written during Svevo's Zeno period, **"Vino generoso"** (**"Generous Wine"**), begun in 1914 and revised in 1926, is full of psychological insights and probings on the themes of disease and old age. A sickly old man narrates the story of his niece's wedding. The doctor has given him permission to break his diet and take part in the festivities like everyone less. Taking advantage of this precious and singular opportunity, the old man eats and drinks to excess not because of thirst and hunger, but "from a craving for liberty" from the pills, drops, and powders that have become part of his life. That night he has a nightmare in which all the members of the wedding party call for his death; he, however, offers his daughter's life in ex-

change for his own. Once awake, he blames the wine, and in order to avoid the recurrence of such a dream, decides to follow the doctor's orders and go back to his diet.

The "generous wine" of the title suggests the opening of doors leading to the subconscious. As the old man becomes more absorbed in analyzing his inner self, guilt and remorse come to the surface. He regrets, in particular, having married the wrong woman and having given up his socialist ideals. The dream clearly shows the late Svevo's familiarity with Franz Kafka's (1883-1924) work. The narrator is caught in a nightmarish tangle of guilt feelings and remorse. His lucid mind, notwithstanding the effects of the wine, finds itself confronting an incomprehensible state of existence. The simplest human conviction—that one deserves respect, affection, and good health, that one has a place in the world—has no basis in his world of altered reality.

"Lo specifico del dottor Menghi" (**"The specific of Dr. Menghi"**), one of Svevo's few contributions to science fiction,[11] also concerns itself with the influence of Darwinism. The narrative, written in pseudoscientific and philosophical language, deals with the experiments of Dr. Menghi who, on his deathbed, asks his colleague Dr. Galli to read to the Medical Society a paper dealing with a special serum he has discovered. What follows is the reading in the first person of Dr. Menghi's paper.

The story, written most likely in 1904,[12] contains in a nutshell many of Svevo's favorite themes: the elusiveness of health and the ever-lurking presence of disease, the *senectus* theme and its corresponding debilitating and degenerative effects, the death of a loved one and the ambiguous relationship between son and parent, a skeptical and ironic treatment of doctors and their magical cures. The precarious energy that fascinates Dr. Menghi and constitutes life, and the delicate physiological balance in terms of chemical, physical, and functional processes, maintained by a complex of mechanisms, is what Svevo seems to be searching for both literally and figuratively. Dr. Menghi's specifics, with their potential effect on this vital balance, are very much like the two opposite poles of the Basedowian lifeline that mesmerizes Zeno, namely, the symptomatic characteristics of Graves' disease: hypoactivity and hyperactivity. The story is also significant because it reveals Svevo's attitude toward science, and especially toward those scientists who undertake experimentation without regard for its potentially evil results. "You thought you were helping people," says the doctor's mother, "but instead your invention is nothing but a new scourge" (381). This ominous accusation will be realized, of course, in the momentous ending of *La coscienza di Zeno.* The scientist or individual, although essentially good and well meaning, is tempted by his desire for knowledge to experiment selfishly with life and to end up in a hell of his own making—a very timely theme indeed. Svevo remains faithful to Darwin's law of evolution and "rejects any initiative that might risk modifying the natural equilibrium of the existing forces in nature, however imperfect or unjust the equilibrium might be."[13]

FRAGMENTS AND SKETCHES

The sheer volume of unfinished works in Svevo's canon indicates the great difficulty he experienced in bringing his ideas to fruition. Many of these fragments abound in autobiographical data relevant to Svevo's hesitancy and ambivalence about writing, as well as to his ongoing concern with the shifting functions of reality, memory, and death. The fragment **"Incontro di vecchi amici"** (**"Old friends meet"**; ca. 1912) deals with an unsuccessful writer of unfinished stories. Roberto, like Svevo, compensates for his lack of success by becoming a businessman.[14] The character Roberto reappears as an old man in two other unfinished stories, **"L'avvenire dei ricordi"** (**"Along memory lane"**; 1923) and **"La morte"** (**"Death"**; 1925), in which the narrator's reminiscences act as a repetition and re-creation of the past, thus slowing the approach of death. Svevo's constant focus on memory and death is also apparent in **"Proditoriamente"** (**"Traitorously"**; 1923), a drab meandering narrative that proffers the philosophical message that death is always looming, insidiously awaiting its next victim.

Svevo also explored various theories about the nature of humankind, ranging from the tenets of natural science to the influence of superstition and psychoanalysis. **"La buonissima madre"** (**"The Very Good Mother"**; circa 1919) offers an imaginative reworking of Darwin's theory of natural selection, and echoes Svevo's suspicion—openly stated in his 1907 article **"L'uomo e la teoria darwiniana"** (**"Man and the Darwinian Theory"**)—that man has not, in fact, evolved. In **"Il malocchio"** (**"The Evil Eye"**; circa 1917), Svevo utilizes both superstition and psychoanalytic theory to depict the irrationality and absurdity of human existence, and also to express his well-founded suspicions of modern technology and scientific achievement.

Like his other works, Svevo's fragments reveal his willingness to experiment with more open narrative structures. **"Orazio Cima"** (ca. 1917) and **"Corto viaggio sentimentale"** (**"Short Sentimental Journey"**; 1925-26) are both shaped and given meaning by the consciousness and psychological attitudes of the narrators. The narrator of **"Orazio"** presents us with a tableau of conflicting values and ideologies, while in the second story the mendacious narrator offers an equally distorted picture of reality. By far the more experimental of the two stories, **"Corto viaggio sentimentale"** has no principal character other than the narrator's consciousness, no plot, and no structure. Written under the influence of James Joyce, it became Svevo's longest, albeit unfinished, short story; he referred to it as "a long, long serpent curled up in [his] desk drawer."[15]

SVEVO'S LAST WORKS

In preparation for his projected fourth novel Svevo wrote four alternative segments, in addition to the unfinished **"Il vecchione,"** that seem to be related components for a work intended to crown his literary career.[16] According to Gabriella Contini, although these contain similarities with *La coscienza di Zeno,* and although Zeno reappears as the author/protagonist, Svevo meant to write a novel quite distinct and separate from his previous masterpiece. In her controversial book *Il quarto romanzo di Svevo* Contini argues that the projected novel consists of diverse fragmentary segments, some of which are constituent parts (**"Le confessioni del vegliardo,"** **"Umbertino,"** **"Il mio ozio,"** **"Un contratto"**), while others are preparatory (*Rigenerazione,* **"L'avvenire dei ricordi"**), lateral (**"Orazio Cima"**), or subsidiary (**"Vino generoso,"** **"La novella del buon vecchio,"** **"Viaggio sentimentale,"** **"Incontri di vecchi amici,"** **"Proditoriamente,"** **"La morte"**).[17] Such a novel, according to Contini, is a work in progress, made up of interlocking segments that are readable and comprehensible only if considered in an intertextual relationship.

Regardless of whether Svevo intended these later works to form a fourth novel, it is clear that an idée fixe marks all of Svevo's works written after *La coscienza di Zeno* and serves to bind the disparate parts together. Svevo's overruling concern with old age and declining health is particularly evident in the "constituent parts" of the narrative, in which he picks up where he left off with his third novel, and in which the already-aged Zeno ages still more.

A man of leisure, cut off from all activity, Zeno turns to the past. Rereading his ten-year-old writings, Zeno realizes that what he had already narrated in *La coscienza* was not the most important part of his life. Surprisingly, he seems to have forgotten his past, except for the part recorded in the novel. Faced, however, with his previous confessions, he can suddenly recall other elements of his past. Thus, he begins to inquire philosophically about the meaning of life and to study his past objectively, as if it belonged to someone else. He asks "And now what am I? Not the one who lived, but the one I described."[18] Zeno is surprised to see how the written word can transform life. He envisions a time when, for therapeutic reasons, everyone will be compelled to write, "life will be literalized. . . . And contemplation will be the main business of the day, shielding us from the horridness of actual living. . . ."[19] This realization prompts Zeno to resume writing his diary, which raises the question of whether at the conclusion of *La coscienza di Zeno,* the protagonist was really cured. In any case, as he resumes writing, we may assume that Zeno's former and present writings must have some beneficial effect for him.

In **"Un contratto"** (**"A Contract"**), with the advent of peace and a bad business deal that wipes out practically all the money made during the war, Zeno realizes that he no longer has the enterprise required for the more competitive peacetime economy. Aware of his incompetence, Zeno knowingly allows himself to be maneuvered into signing a contract making young Olivi a partner of the business, and relinquishing to him virtually all control. Although Zeno regards it finally as a defeat of old age and a victory of youth, he can't help but smile at the socialist administrator who behaves like a typical capitalist, exploiting his employees and cutting their wages.

In **"Le confessioni del vegliardo"** (**"An Old Man's Confessions"**)[20] and **"Umbertino,"** Zeno deals with family relations and attempts to fix on paper the present (with all its gradations) and the recent and distant past. Zeno, who still has virtually all of his classic foibles, tries to come to terms with his children, committing the same disastrous mistakes that marred the relationship with his own father. His docile wife Augusta, completely taken with her menagerie, fails to notice the continuous crises he endures on account of his age. Zeno's only consolations are his young grandson, Umbertino, who distracts him with his innocence and curiosity from the dreary routine of his life, and his nephew, Carlo, the son of Ada and Guido Speier.

In **"Il mio ozio"** (**"This Indolence of Mine"**) Zeno closely analyzes his inertia and discovers that even the present—himself "and the things and people round him"—is made up of various tenses. His "major and interminable present" is his retirement from business and the inertia of his daily life. In this forced indolence he becomes even more preoccupied with the degeneration of his aged body. The companionship of Carlo—very much his father's son—who has his medical degree, stimulates Zeno's curiosity, particularly with the notion that it is the sexual organs and not the heart that sustain our whole organism. According to Zeno, "Mother Nature is a maniac," who maintains life within an organism as long as it is able to reproduce itself. In view of this Zeno sets out to hoodwink Mother Nature by taking a mistress, which for him is equivalent to "going to the chemist's" (146). The cure, however, has a sobering effect when his mistress Felicita, a tobacconist,[21] educates him in his present role as an old man. Zeno, with his unmistakable sense of humor and lack of resolve, decides that it will be his last "fling," and then he adds slyly that he occasionally still keeps "cheating" nature.

With **"Il vecchione"** (**"The Old, Old Man"**),[22] written in 1928 and consisting of only a few pages, we have the beginning of the proposed sequel to *La coscienza di Zeno.* A seventy-year-old Zeno, narrating in the first person, relates how on his way home from an outing he felt compelled to greet a pretty young girl as she passed near his car. When Augusta inquires who she is, Zeno explains that she is the daughter of their friend Dondi. Augusta points out that he is mistaken because Dondi's daughter is older than she, and, therefore, like herself, she too must be an old woman. This encounter triggers in Zeno a myriad of involuntary memories in which time becomes confused as he ponders his life's experiences.

Zeno finds himself constantly frustrated in an absurd and hostile world, in which he is unable to find his proper place. The trivial incident with the pretty girl, like the Proustian madeleine, evokes a rush of memories and the past floods back in its entirety, enabling him to re-create his earlier experiences, but at the same time exposing the illusory nature of his early ideals.[23] He discovers that the past can be recovered by memory, preserved, and even improved in his writings. As he had done once before for his failed psychoanalysis, he records his observations in great detail and analyzes his responses to them, finally rediscovering his vocation as an author. He resolves to write the book that will permit him to "pull himself together" and "rehabilitate" himself (136). Writing assumes a hygienic purpose, because in his memoirs time is crystallized and can always be located if one "knows how to open to the right page" (137). By reading his former and present memoirs, he will find the past always at hand and protected from all confusion.

Zeno's constant concern with the processes of remembering and forgetting reveals his psychological sophistication. The past is forever vanishing, not only materially, but in our minds as well. Time that destroys everything is Zeno's real villain. Still, the past remains enclosed in his unconscious, waiting for the trigger that will release it. But even this recovered past is only a fragment of its totality, since each man's truth is relative to his own needs and psychological constitution.

During the last years of Svevo's life old age became the only subject of his writings. Having written so much about it as a metaphysical condition, as a psychological attitude, and mental frame of mind, Svevo now faced it also in a social and literal sense. Now that he was old and experiencing true old age, he described it as being languid, weakening, and dirty; he saw it as an abject state of enfeeblement.[24] He acquired a new concept: no longer spiritual and emotional, but "physical and chronological" senility.[25] The task was no longer establishing a relationship between the past, the present, and the future, but rather functioning solely in the present. "My situation has simplified itself," says the Old, Old Man, "I continue to struggle between the present and the past, but at least hope—anxious hope for the future—does not intrude. So I go on living in a mixed tense. This is man's destiny. . . ."[26] Old age becomes a privileged point of observation from which life is examined and seen with death on one side and youth on the other. Man's condition is seen as a grammatical problem and lived in a "mixed tense," between past and present; for Svevo there is no future, no ultimate grammatical tense: the present serves only to create future memories. The aged Zeno, in all his manifestations, is a misfit because he vacillates between tenses, between youth and old age. He has always lived in the wrong tense and time.

It is difficult to arrive at an organic assessment of Svevo's numerous and fragmentary narrative writings, often marred by sketchiness, incompleteness, and incongruities. Nonetheless, both his early stories and his post-Zeno production, clearly illustrate the development of Svevo's literary experimentalism. After discovering a fully stratified dimension of memory and time in *La coscienza di Zeno*, in his later stories Svevo created a form based entirely on the present. This "presence," together with the elimination of the future, becomes the conditioning factor of Svevo the man and writer. It explains why he describes, dwells, and lingers on details, often deviating carelessly from the theme at hand. The author arrives also at a juncture where he creates not only an open-ended narrative form—innovative for his time—but also a new relationship between himself and his narrator/protagonist. Indeed, in these "further confessions" Svevo and Zeno become an organic whole no longer separate and distinct. Zeno's presence is that of Svevo, who is also beginning to be cut off from his commercial activity because of age and ill health. He too has lost the future and savors, after many years of struggle and defeat, the present fruits of his literary labors. As he tries to come to terms with his long-awaited success, he ponders his personal obsessions and philosophical anguish over the fate of man, an isolated flimsy spirit condemned to wither and die, while the world that encircles him and assails him remains in a time reduced to the present and a reality made up of a series of discontinuous moments. All this is presented by Svevo in a bristling style, in a work whose inexorable introspective analysis, tempered with irony and sagacity, presages a work to be set beside the great *La coscienza di Zeno.*

Notes

1. It was serialized on 6, 7, 8 January 1888. Now available in Luciano Nanni, *Leggere Svevo. Antologia della critica sveviana* (Bologna: Zanichelli, 1974), 380-87. Except for "Una lotta," all the short stories and fables are in Svevo, *Racconti, Saggi, Pagine.* Numbers in parenthesis refer to this edition.

2. It appeared in nine installments between 4 and 13 October 1890.

3. Fusco, *Svevo,* 215-16.

4. Svevo wrote many fables, now collected in *Racconti, Saggi, Pagine,* 751-63.

5. It appears that the Venezianis owned an incubator appropriately called "La Foster-Mother" and that while in England, Svevo inquired as to its proper functioning. Cf. Svevo, *Epistolario,* 426.

6. Svevo wrote three versions of the tale: the 1910 version has been lost to us; the second was published on 7 December 1924 in *Sera della Domenica* (Svevo considered it "mutilated"), and the third appeared on 15 March 1927 in *Il Convegno.* See Svevo, *Epistolario,* 830.

7. Guido Piovene in *La parola e il libro,* no. 9-10 (September-October 1927), 253.

8. The story is based on a real-life incident as well as on a dream. Cf. Furbank, *Svevo,* 136-37.

9. Samigli, of course, is the name Svevo used to sign his first writings in *L'Indipendente.*

10. Lavagetto, *L'impiegato Schmitz,* 112.

11. In the original MS one reads under the title: "Short story of a fantastic nature. Warning: you are requested not to laugh . . . right away. No. 298." In Svevo, *Saggi e pagine sparse,* ed. [Umbro] Apollonio [(Milano: Mondadori, 1954),] 388.

12. In a letter dated 4 May 1904 Svevo signed off in a postscript: "The inventor of Annina [the name of the serum] and all its applications, practical and impractical." See *Epistolario,* 400.

13. Fusco, *Svevo,* 221-22.

14. Most likely, it was written when Svevo, like Roberto Erls, had become a successful businessman and no longer suffered the humiliation of failure, so well described in *Una vita.* The treatment of the inferiority complex suggests also that Svevo was by now familiar with Freud's ideas.

15. Svevo, *Epistolario,* 770. See 768, 796, 799, 809 for other references to his difficulties with the story.

16. It is difficult to establish their order of composition, except for "Le confessioni del vegliardo" which bears the date 4 April 1928. The English edition of the sequel to Zeno, which includes the play *La rigenerazione,* is appropriately entitled *Further Confessions of Zeno.*

17. Gabriella Contini, *Il quarto romanzo di Svevo* (Turin: Einaudi, 1980), 28-30.

18. "Le confessioni del vegliardo," *Racconti, Saggi, Pagine,* 372.

19. Ibid.

20. The manuscript bears no title. The present title was chosen by Umbro Apollonio. Cf. Svevo, *Corto viaggio sentimentale e altri racconti inediti,* ed. Umbro Apollonio (Milan: Mondadori, 1966), 411.

21. Svevo ironically links love and tobacco into one organic pleasure.

22. In a letter to B. Crémieux (16 May 1928) Svevo indicates that the story's title will be "Il vecchione." In a subsequent letter to Marie Anne Comnène [Crémieux] (19 August 1928), he uses the title "Il vegliardo." Cf. *Epistolario,* 876-77, 888.

23. By now Svevo was familiar with Proust's writings and most likely was influenced by them when he wrote "Il vecchione."

24. At this point in his life Svevo was weighed down by many ailments: he suffered from chronic asthma and emphysema (as a result of smoking 60 cigarettes a day), arteriosclerosis, intestinal disturbances, arthritis, nervousness (for which he took tranquillizers), and baldness. Cf. Carlo Baiocco, "Intervista alla signora Letizia Svevo Fonda Savio" in *Analisi del personaggio sveviano in relazione alle immagini di lotta e malattia* (Roma: Centro Informazioni Stampa Universitaria, 1984), 126-29.

25. Maier, *Svevo,* 121.

26. "Il vecchione," *Racconti, Saggi, Pagine,* 138.

Selected Bibliography

PRIMARY SOURCES

The standard edition of Svevo's works in Italian is *Opera Omnia,* ed. Bruno Maier (Milano: dall'Oglio Editore): vol. I, *Epistolario,* 1966; vol. 2, pt. 1, *I romanzi (Una vita & Senilità,* 1927 ed.), 1969; vol. 2, pt. 2, *I romanzi (La coscienza di Zeno & Senilità,* 1898 ed.), 1969; vol. 3, *Racconti, saggi, pagine sparse,* 1968; vol. 4, *Commedie,* 1969.

[The Uniform Edition, published by Secker and Warburg, consists of the following volumes:

I. *Confessions of Zeno,* translated from the Italian by Beryl De Zoete, with a Note on Svevo by Eduardo Roditi (1962)

II. *As A Man Grows Older,* translated from the Italian by Beryl De Zoete (1962)

III. *A Life,* translated from the Italian by Archibald Colquhoun (1963)

IV. *Short Sentimental Journey and other stories,* translated from the Italian by Beryl De Zoete, L. Collison-Morley and Ben Johnson (1967)

V. *Further Confessions of Zeno,* translated from the Italian by Ben Johnson and P. N. Furbank (1969)]

NOVELS

A Life. Translated by Archibald Colquhoun. London: Secker & Warburg, 1963. Vol. 3 in the Uniform Edition of Svevo's Works.

Confessions of Zeno. Translated by Beryl De Zoete. London: Secker & Warburg, 1962. Vol. 1 in the Uniform Edition of Svevo's Works.

SHORT STORIES

"The Tribe." In P. N. Furbank, *Italo Svevo the Man and the Writer.* London: Secker & Warburg, 1966, 217-23.

Short Sentimental Journey and Other Stories. Translated by Beryl De Zoete, L. Collison-Morley, and Ben Johnson. London: Secker & Warburg, 1967. Vol. 4 in the Uniform Edition of Svevo's Works. The volume includes "The Hoax," "The Story of the Nice Old Man and the Pretty Girl," "Generous Wine," "Traitorously," "Argo and his Master," "The Mother," "Short Sentimental Journey," and "Death."

Further Confessions of Zeno. Translated by Ben Johnson and P. N. Furbank. London: Secker & Warburg, 1969. Vol. 5 in the Uniform Edition of Svevo's Works. The volume includes "The Old, Old Man," "An Old Man's Confessions," "Umbertino," "A Contract," "This Indolence of Mine," and *Regeneration* (a play).

PLAYS

Regeneration. A Comedy in Three Acts. Translated by P. N. Furbank. In *Further Confessions of Zeno.* London: Secker & Warburg, 1969.

SECONDARY SOURCES

BOOKS

Baiocco, Carlo. *Analisi del personaggio sveviano in relazione alle immagini di lotta e malattia.* Rome: Centro Informazione Stampa Universitaria, 1984. Analyzes illness in its various manifestations by reconstructing Svevo's own medical knowledge.

Contini, Gabriella. *Il quarto romanzo di Svevo.* Turin: Einaudi, 1980. Although there are similarities between *La coscienza* and the fragmentary writings for his projected fourth novel, Svevo intended to write a distinct and separate novel, viewed by Contini as a work in progress, composed of linking segments that are readable and comprehensible only if considered intertextually.

Furbank, P[hilip] N[icholas]. *Italo Svevo, The Man and the Writer.* London: Secker & Warburg, 1966. First full-length biographical study in English. Extremely well written, it furnishes abundant and valuable data, and includes a critical analysis of Svevo's major writings.

Fusco, Mario. *Italo Svevo. Conscience et réalité.* Paris: Éditions Gallimard, 1973. Lacanian psychoanalytic study of Svevo's writings; Fusco shows that there exists a fundamental narcissistic relationship that ties Svevo to his works.

Lavagetto, Mario. *L'impiegato Schmitz e altri saggi su Svevo.* Turin: Einaudi, 1975. Four essays focusing on the relationship between author and his *écriture*. In this Freudian and Marxist study, the critic maintains that Svevo tried to create a fictitious personality for himself.

Maier, Bruno. *Italo Svevo.* 5th rev. ed. Milan: Mursia, 1978. Historical, eclectic approach; Maier studies disease, senility, death, originality, and life's unpredictability as the fundamental themes of Svevo's work. His introspectiveness, autobiographic nature, and behavioral difficulties are also those of other Triestine writers.

Nanni, Luciano. *Leggere Svevo. Antologia della critica sveviana.* Bologna: Zanichelli, 1974. Extremely useful anthology of critical writings on Svevo. Volume includes synopses of Svevo's novels, short stories, and plays.

Roland A. Champagne (essay date 1999)

SOURCE: Champagne, Roland A. "Calling into Question Psychoanalysis with an Ethics of Reading: An Other Look at Italo Svevo's *La coscienza di Zeno.*" *Italiana* 8 (1999): 41-53.

[*In the following essay, Champagne characterizes* Confessions of Zeno *as a fictional autobiography, which "responds to Freud's 'talking cure' by presenting the otherness of the self as a postponement of finality," or "an inability to find identity."*]

Italo Svevo's **Confessions of Zeno** (**La coscienza di Zeno,** 1923) is remarkable as a fictional autobiography that responds to Freud's "talking cure" by presenting the otherness of the self as a postponement of finality, as an inability to find identity. Svevo is the pseudonym of Ettore Schmitz (1861-1928) who was himself born in a Jewish family of German descent in the Austrio-Hungarian town of Trieste. He wrote in Florentine Italian, thus further using his plural otherness to express the alienation that his narrator Zeno Cosini expresses within himself.

Emmanuel Lévinas (1906-1996), the French ethical philosopher whose writings inspire us to think about reading as an ethical act,[1] provides an opportunity to return with a French perspective to the writer who was himself inspired by the French, that is, the French Naturalists. Lévinas, in fact, allows us to see how Svevo subverts the determinism of the Naturalists and Freud's psychoanalysis. Lévinas's ethical call from the other, what he calls solicitude, becomes in this example the beginning of a dialogue with oneself in which humor is the vehicle for constantly delaying a retrievable unity of the self, thus exemplifying the inherent failure of psychoanalysis to totalize the self. From the recognition of the existence of the other (what Lévinas calls *hypostase*) in himself, Zeno Cosini proceeds with a dismantling of psychoanalysis from the inside. Effectively, **Confessions of Zeno** exemplifies anti-psychoanalytic psychoanalysis.[2] In other words, by using irony and humor to displace the serious identity of the self, Zeno creates an autobiography that never achieves analysis. Instead, Zeno is caught in dialogic frenzy with his other, unable to realize that "analysis presupposes the detachment of the writer from his subject, a perspective impossible to achieve when the subject is the self."[3] Zeno cannot actualize his desires for his self. No closure is possible regarding his dreams of "never again": neither in his desire to quit smoking cigarettes nor in his desire to stop being unfaithful.

The ethical reading of Zeno entails the relationship of the narrator with this self he calls "I." Zeno's guilt, which drives him to write and to search for his self, is a reflection of the plural voices already speaking to him before the story begins. Lévinas's categories of *hypostase* (recognition of the other), the welcoming of the other, and the *illéité* (the impersonal third agent) constitute three stages through which Zeno develops his questioning of the integrity of the self by use of humor. These three stages correspond to the formation of the ego, the id, and the superego in Freudian theory and yet question the Freudian voices as components of the same self and its unified identity. In **Confessions of Zeno,** there can be no "progress" toward the analysis of the self's identity because the self reveals itself to be heterogeneous by its nature. The narrator's very name, Zeno, is a play on the Eleatic philosopher who, as Jorge Borges reminds us, said in his second paradox that "movement is impossible because before a moving body can reach a given point, it must traverse half the distance and before that, half of that half, etc."[4] Hence, the affirmation of the unity that cannot be divided is affirmed through Zeno and his followers. This pre-Socratic Zeno was a follower of Parmenides, whom Lévinas rejects in favor of a pluralism which refuses totalizing unity.[5] For Svevo, there is no unity nor movement with Zeno Cosini's narrative that reflects an uncanny lack of self-knowledge. Cosini desires change and an identity different from his smoking, unfaithful one. But he constantly delays accomplishing his quest. Even the end of his narrative cannot be final. Zeno Cosini's autobiography simply stops "saying," as Lévinas would describe it. At that point, Zeno the chemist responds to his others by engaging in a dialogue that can only implode because, as Lévinas remarks, death is the other's death.[6] When Zeno Cosini comprehends that he is incapable of giving a unifying sense to this self, which becomes other to his speaking voice, the only alternative is the death of that other and consequently his own assumed, univocal self.

The unique quality of Lévinas's ethical call is that it does not conquer. Instead, it provides the invitation for a bilateral contract between the text and its reader, Lévinas's "Said"(*Dit*) and "Saying" (*Dire*). Hence, the reader is not overwhelmed by the text as if it were already "Said" (*Dit*) once and for all. Nor is the text itself ever conquered or exhausted by the reader. For Lévinas, reading does not entail a victory that is often associated with a military, male model of reading. Rather, the feminist reader responds to the call, according to Lévinas, with Abraham, Jacob, or Moses as the model insofar as they responded to the call of the Other with *me voici,* that is, "here I am." This *me voici* is a declaration of relationship to the Other and an insistence of a relative place and perspective of the "I" within the world of the Other. For the reader, this means that an ethical reading entails the recognition of the place of the Other relative to the reader as a consequence of the reading. Regarding **Confessions of Zeno,** when the narrator speaks of Florentine Italian as "our inelegant dialect,"[7] one has to be suspicious of the private language Zeno shares intimately with Ada as a sign of his inferiority because he is relying upon it to explain himself throughout his narrative. Actually, the diffuse self that is being displayed with this "inelegant" language is an elegant subversion, or commentary, on the inability of psychoanalysis to produce a coherent self through the method of the "talking cure." The self keeps unraveling as the text is "said." Lévinas tells us that the "Saying" voice needs to reply.

L'HYPOSTASE AND THE SUBVERSION OF THE EGO

Svevo's narrator Zeno Cosini solicits his reader's response to the speaking "I" with its constant self-deprecating and ironic stances. It is as if Svevo is winking his eye behind the mask of Zeno. The humor of Zeno is often at the expense of the status of the narrator himself both among his colleagues in the story and among his readers who have to wonder constantly about the reliability of the speaking voice with so little confidence in himself. For Svevo's heroes, failure is often endemic, in the sense of a disease which wears away at their psyches.[8] So Zeno is not the prototype. In fact, he is almost part of a tradition of failure and incompletion that could constitute part of Svevo's vision about the nature of the self. This self is calling out with its sense of incompletion to see if others are hearing the cry of a

confession that is the conscience of the "I" speaking to itself with a judgmental voice.

The reader's recognition of Zeno's relative fragmentation of the self into various parts begins the communal, bilateral act of an ethical reading. This is the role of the self in the world for Lévinas, what he calls *hypostase,* "the very event of our relationship with others."[9] This "event" orients an ethical reading toward its first stage, that is, the recognition that others are there in the face of the speaking "I." With Zeno Cosini as narrator, the reading points inward toward the narrator who is hearing the call of his other with the initial question "See my childhood?" (3) which provides the invitation for the reader to revisit with Zeno the fifty years since his childhood to explain his fascination with such present-day phenomena as "the last cigarette," the title for his first chapter. Of course, the "last" is postponed indefinitely throughout his "confession." Instead, Zeno looks backward toward his origins with the psychoanalytic search for first causes in childhood experiences. His initial dialogues are with his doctor, who recommends to Zeno that he write in order "to get a clear picture of yourself" (5). This self to be discovered is distinct from Zeno's speaking voice and theoretically is the ego who can provide cures for such ills as Zeno's smoking, limping, and infidelity. The event of this recognition of himself as other somewhere in the past is not a clear-cut acceptance of the methods of psychoanalysis. As Dr. S. mentions in his preface to Zeno's autobiography, we are reading his "patient's hostility" (vii) to psychoanalysis. This hostility is never patently manifest. Through Zeno's irony and his ability to laugh at himself, he calls into question the value of going back and forth between these others that constitute whoever he is. In effect, Zeno thus demonstrates Lévinas's *hypostase* as being a restless recognition in which the other is seen as exiled in an uncanny marginalized space. Writing is supposed to expose the eccentric angle of vision necessary to the traveler who is willing to reveal the relationship to the other.[10]

The question of Zeno's infidelity is crucial to his search for the integrity of his own internal others. Zeno and the women in his life are often the subject of hilarious anecdotes about Zeno's supposed incompetence at determining how to please them. A pertinent matter is Freud's own inability to have psychoanalysis answer his question about what a woman wants. While the "talking cure" does not ever specifically answer Freud's question about women, Zeno, for his part, is also confused as his "writing cure" cannot unravel his own version of the problem: "One of the great difficulties of life is guessing what a woman wants. Listening to what she says is no help, for a whole speech may be wiped out by a single look, and even that is no guide if one is alone with her, by her own invitation, in a cozy, dark little room" (323). However, he has wrongly stated the problem by placing the responsibility on what woman, as Zeno's other, wants. He is not really interested in knowing what a woman wants. Instead, she becomes an excuse for his own inexplicable lust in that his sexual behavior is a response to her "invitation," that is, her call to him with her "single look." For Lévinas, welcoming the call of the other calls into question the freedom of the subject. And there is the rub for Zeno, as it is for his reader who soon learns about Zeno's purported otherness in the admission that "evidently I am quite different from other people" (17). The affectation of difference soon wears thin as the reader realizes that Zeno is not as different as he claims to be. Where his difference does make a mark is with his self which must become fragmented because it cannot bear the narrator's scrutinizing its cohesion and unity.

Lévinas was much influenced by the reflections of Maurice Blanchot, so much so that he even published a collection of essays on his work. In that monograph, Lévinas comments that Blanchot's concerns about the false openness of dialogue point toward "a purring which closes the openings of communication as soon as they occur."[11] This "purring" is a sound calling from within and appealing for an inward directed acknowledgment of the self's fragmentation which controls the apparent openness of communication. Blanchot's purring is a development of the link between Lévinas's distinctions of the Said and the Saying. The apparent openness of the Saying is already being controlled by the divided self which has inserted its purring otherness into the Said of the language being used for dialogue. Rather than an open-ended sensitivity toward the other, in fact language is always already marked by the speaker's divided self. The previously cited passage from Zeno's writing cure about his quandary regarding what women want is a good case in point. His obsession about his own infidelities has marked his confession before it starts. His own guilt about not being able to control either his lust or his smoking provokes his remarks on a woman's wants in order to mask his lack of responsibility. Literally he is "unable to respond" to his self's call for attention to its plural nature.

Zeno tries to slip away from the reader's attribution of responsibility to the speaking voice. He asks: "did I really love cigarettes so much because I was able to throw all the responsibility for my own incompetence on them?" (10). Zeno's reiterated incompetence, one failure after another, is an example of what Blanchot calls textual purring. The word "incompetence" apparently absolves the speaker of guilt in the acknowledgment of the lack of ability to judge. However, this is too naive for a speaker intent upon "a sense of victory over oneself" (10). Svevo's reader must not be fooled by this narrator whose very name suggests the irony which will be a hallmark of the confession. This is the irony Socrates used so well by pleading ignorance while ma-

nipulating his students' answers with the maieutic. Zeno the philosopher was pre-Socratic, and Zeno Cosini's self likewise exists prior to the questions posed within his confession, which after all is not only a revelation but an admission of guilt. Zeno Cosini's self is about to reveal its plural nature as well as admit its subversion of the speaking voice. Far better is it that the writing cure represent the speaking voice than for it to remain silent. Zeno admits that "I had desired my father's death, but had not dared to say so" (48). Here is his self-destructive silence for which he admits criminal guilt (if only Heidegger and de Man had listened to Zeno![12]): "the fact that I had remained silent about it made it a crime which weighed heavily on my mind" (48).

Zeno's call to a talking performance is also an enticement to show himself to be a fool in front of others. As Naomi Lebowitz points out, "of course, Zeno's babbling is a symbol of modern decadence."[13] He avoids action by talking about it. Now, by using Freud's infamous "talking cure," Zeno seeks to arrive at some future cure through his analysis by Dr. S. The solution is to talk about his past and relate it to his present problems. Zeno's foolishness in the past is a recurring issue. Zeno's role as a competitive suitor for three Malfenti daughters generates considerable laughter at his expense. Freud defines jokes as "the intended criticism of the inner resistance."[14] Svevo's "inner resistance" is between the two meanings of his "confessions" found in the Italian word *coscienza*: consciousness and conscience. Zeno resists the "consciousness" demanded by Dr. S., only to have his conscience criticize him to the benefit of Lévinas's reading subject. Zeno is reading himself, as Dr. S. is reading Zeno, who is glossed by Svevo, who in turn is masked by Ettore Schmitz, and finally who is seen by the glasses of a reader through the ethics of Lévinas. All these interventions reveal the texts of Zeno's jokes about himself as palimpsests about what is actually being said. For example, Zeno thought that his mediocre violin playing could seduce Ada. In fact, the limping Zeno was upstaged by Guido Speier, whose walking stick made Zeno envious and whose violin-playing elicited from the Malfenti father the comment that "you will hear a violinist such as one does not often hear" (106). Zeno admits to being a fool as he limped along without a walking stick and returning home without having serenaded the daughters with his violin. Then, when Zeno decides to avow his love to Ada, he mistakenly approaches her sister Augusta in the darkened room and tells the wrong sister he loves her. His weakened leg, his lack of opportunity, and his general lack of self-knowledge all subverted the intended performances by the ego or speaking voice. Finally, Zeno proposes to all three sisters and succeeds in marrying the one for whom he seems least inclined and to whom he is perpetually unfaithful.

This talking cure, however, was assigned to writing by Dr. S. who would then analyze Zeno's writing, rather than his speaking voice on a couch. The writing cure is bridging the past and the future. As Anthony Wilden remarks about Zeno's confessions, "words imply time and impose order."[15] The framing of these words is within the time and order of psychoanalysis. Zeno's psychiatrist, Dr. S., has published the typescript of Zeno's writing cure in revenge for Zeno's having terminated the analysis and then refusing to pay. The irony is that Zeno's voice admits to all sorts of self-humiliation, such as his desire to kill the above-mentioned Guido, because Zeno assumes that this writing, "the thing no one knows about, and which leaves no trace, does not exist" (138). Of course, Lévinas introduces writing as "the trace" to Jacques Derrida who elaborates its role within a deconstructive writing. For Lévinas, the trace of writing is a memory of a face-to-face relationship, not only of the writer with the writing but also of the writer with the anxiety that generated that writing—in Zeno's case—his worries about his smoking and his infidelities.

This conscious ego of Zeno is not so much in control as Dr. S. would have his writing cure reveal. Instead, as Leslie Rabkin observes, "Zeno has precisely the disease he covets, that of self-reflexive analytic consciousness."[16] This "analytic consciousness" leads Zeno to subvert his conscious self and to provide explanations for what the self is saying. The critical voice[17] reflects a diseased or separated self, unable to retain its integrity. For example, Zeno would have his reader believe that the nicotine from his cigarettes has generated his need for women, and that his two problems, smoking and infidelity, must therefore be linked. However, the links between the two are not so much physiological as metonymical, grounded in the act of writing which suggests to the speaker links which had not been obvious in the past. A future is being written through the writing cure's trace of the speaker's anxieties. Zeno's writing cure is not the same as Freud's talking cure because the writing can curl back upon the self, provide a trace by which the process of the self can be tracked and revealed in all its contradictions. The lying of the writing, that is the mendacious nature of a reflective or self-aware written narrative, leads Zeno's ego to see its division and to recognize the other side which is being revealed by the laughter at the ludicrous nature of the ego facing its own incompetence and inability to control the pain within. At one point, Zeno is so influenced by his limping friend Tullio that he himself begins to limp painfully. Zeno tries to ignore the pain and allow his self to speak: "The pain I was suffering made me talkative, as if I were endeavoring to shout it down" (133). The pain is the other side of the story. This side appears through the laughter generated by the text against the ludicrous situation of an ego facing Zeno's self, that voice which Freud calls the Id, the reservoir of the libido and the source of instinctive energy. However, for Zeno, it is the voice calling from the other side of his self, the voice which he ignored until the lying became known as such.

THE WELCOMING OF THE OTHER IN THE ID

Lévinas remarks that "to welcome the other is to call my freedom into question."[18] This is so because my spontaneity is no longer operative. This response to alterity has a special significance in an ethics of reading Zeno's story about himself. Therein, the reader is struck by the disparity between the story's power as a wedge separating Zeno's narrating self, the I, from the discovered other within, the "me" that is formed by objectifying the self among others on the outside. Zeno realizes that he is a comic presence and recognizes this by portraying that side of his self that appears to be self-deprecating. However, as the reader moves through Zeno's confessions, it becomes apparent that the narrating I sees a split within himself and is able to speak about an inner other who is incompetent and awkward when trying to find his place within society.

Svevo was influenced by the French Naturalists at the end of the nineteenth century, who found the circumstances of society as a formative influence on the individual. Following upon Taine's focus on the determinism of what he called race, milieu, and moment (basically genetic, cultural, and historical determinism), Svevo internalizes the circumstantial realism of the Naturalists with the insights from psychoanalysis. The effect is Zeno who is threatened by the expectations of others. His failures at satisfying those expectations make him a comic spectacle and also an expert at internalizing a self which is protected from the derision of others. This is his id which is distinct from his ego and provides the libido by which he fantasizes about the sexual prospects of seducing all three of the eldest Malfenti sisters, of whom there are four. The fourth sister, Anna, thinks that Zeno is mad. This madness reveals Zeno's other as being misunderstood within the rational, bourgeois world in which he finds himself. Even Zeno's narrating I, his ego, cannot control the energy Zeno manifests for affairs, his smoking, and his physical limp. All these are controlled by the id and present realities beyond the grasp of Zeno's searching ego.

As Lévinas contends that the others limit my freedom, Zeno's otherness certainly calls into question the degree of control his ego has over his activities. Within the *Confessions of Zeno,* Svevo appears to be simply restating Freud's argument that the unconscious often subverts repressed knowledge. However, with Zeno, there is the additional problem that knowledge itself is a disease[19] that leads to the destruction of the cohesion of the subject. In contrast with Guido, Zeno discovers that "all the knowledge I had acquired was used by me for talking and by him for action" (261). Freud's talking cure becomes in Zeno a retrogressive disease. Rather than a unified subject or self assumed by the Freudian proponents of depth psychology, Zeno's id introduces the awareness that the self is a plural entity with various voices contributing to the chorus that appears to be univocal. Zeno's narrating I welcomes this id by identifying its force as "my ludicrous fancy" (254). His appellation "ludicrous" means playful and signifies the judgment of others about the lack of having a place in their world. Hence, Zeno's otherness must find a place for itself and plays at being the ego's other within himself.

Among women, Zeno's ego appears sexist as he tries to seduce them and usually manifest his incompetence in this realm also. However, women are victorious over him because he is not in control of his presence among them. The narrating I judges that "for a woman to remain passive is a form of giving consent" (335) and thinks that thereby he can be victorious. His confessions have been identified as "not confessions at all but attempts to hide the truth."[20] However, once again, he has the uncanny ability to become the victim when he thinks that he should have the upper hand. With women, he feels constantly guilty about his infidelities and displays his ineptitude in his marriage to Augusta. This reminds me of Livia Veneziani Svevo's comment about Italo's abandoning his wedding ring after complaining that it was strangling him.[21] Zeno also felt strangled by his fidelity and ashamed of his infidelities. Although his ego portrays women as inferior to male strategies of seduction, he becomes the foil for their wiles. Zeno is the one who is seduced into playing a passive, subjugated role. Zeno's narrating I insists upon stating that he will never be unfaithful again, that he will now have his last cigarette, and that he must stop imitating the limping Tullio. Yet Zeno's freedom is always undermined by his cowardice in acting. The id plays his other side and cause him to blush and thus to admit his own submissiveness to the orders of alterity, that is, the apparently passive women who reveal his ego as truly passive in relationship to his id's subversive power.

Zeno tries to identify what it is that makes him "manly." As in his love relationships with women, his friendships with men are marked with the narrating I's concerns about fidelity and confidence among friends. While knowledge is disease in the aging Zeno, the commitment to friendship is also allied by Zeno's ego with sickness: "my devotion to him [Guido] seems to me a clear symptom of disease" (259). An anti-intellectual posture thus looms within Zeno's narrative in that the recognition of his ties to others threatens his sense of a healthy individuality. The threat stems from his lack of ability to control the kind of relationship he has with others. When Zeno admits his plot to kill Guido, he rationalizes the act with a comic attitude that reveals

more than it appears: "But to kill someone, even treacherously, is more manly than to wound a friend by betraying his confidence" (142). This "manly" attribute should more accurately be translated as "humanly" because the concern about betraying a confidence is the same one he has about his sexual infidelities.

Zeno's apparent distinctions between men and women reveal his discomfort with his language. As Robbe-Grillet observes, Svevo was just as *unheimlich,* uncanny and not at home, with his own language as were Kafka and Joyce.[22] Zeno's narrating self admits that it is even mendacious for him to try and confess under the influence of alcohol. He is constantly misrepresenting, whether it be to his wife or to his reader. However, it is the reader who provides Zeno with a third voice, that of his superego, to intervene between Zeno's ego and id and thus give him insight into what this mendacious use of language finally produces.

L'ILLÉITÉ: HOW FORGETTING SAVES THE SUPEREGO FROM ITSELF

Lévinas coins the term *illéité* from the Latin demonstrative pronoun to speak about the necessity of the third party to bring reality to a relationship. The third party is a grounding of the relationship between me and you by providing contextual information by which to gauge the relationship. For the reader, this third party exists outside the reading act and provides a gauge by which to judge the effectiveness of what was understood by the reading. As Zeno reads himself into his confessions, he too needs the third party to check whether he has been cured psychoanalytically as Dr. S. had guaranteed. Zeno's writings were supposed to have led him to the cure. However, he begins to doubt the effectiveness of the cure (399) as he continues to gaze just as lustfully at young women as he did before his writing.

Freud's superego often edits the workings of both the ego and the id. Not wholly outside either the conscious or the unconscious, the superego moves from the realms of both the ego and the id. Lévinas's *illéité* originates from the action of the superego's movement between the conscious and unconscious realms to provide a critique of Zeno's confessions. Within the confessions Zeno provides a voice from afar that causes him to blush when he lies (379), to judge his behavior as foolish or comical, and yet continue to use irony throughout his writing because, as the narrating ego claims, "a written confession is always mendacious" (384). However, the written confession was used on the advice of Dr. S., Zeno's psychoanalyst, and reflects the need of psychoanalysis for naming a sickness. In Freud's opinion, to name the cause of the sickness is to help resolve it because, in the psycho-analysis of the relationships between past and present, human foibles are recorded, explained, and theoretically resolved. The lies of Zeno the writer threaten the very core of Zeno the analysand's condition as a recorder of his past. Instead of remembering the past, he is re-creating it in a fashion that justifies the image his superego has already made of himself. This replication is for the sake of the reader, so that the reader may laugh at Zeno the buffoon and at the psychoanalytic which is subverted by Zeno's lies. Zeno even admits to inventing details of his childhood (395) to Dr. S. in order to become more Oedipal in the psychoanalyst's eyes. In effect, to the reader, Zeno becomes more pathetic and even more human as he steps aside from his narrative and speaks about his relationship, and the relationship of his narrative to Dr. S. Zeno thereby attempts to create his own personality rather than to allow it to be created by the psycho-analyst. He realizes that his lying about his past allows him to escape being determined by it. The cure could not come from the analyst, but was really a matter of "self-persuasion" (413). But which of Zeno's voices is going to persuade which voice? It is the voice that listens to the third person, Lévinas's *illéité*, which finally persuades the reader that autobiography merely leads to an explosion of the links between the past and the present in a single self. Zeno looks to the future in an apocalyptic vision where he will no longer be haunted by disease: "there will be a tremendous explosion, but no one will hear it and the earth will return to its nebulous state and go wandering through the sky, free at last from parasites and disease" (416). The irony that "no one will hear it" provides a problematic setting to this otherworldly cure.

Nevertheless, Zeno is, and always has been, very concerned about the future. He does want to be "cured" despite Freud's contention that psychoanalysis does not guarantee a cure. Hence, what Zeno wants may be outside the purview of the method he is using. And indeed Zeno steps outside the psychoanalytic structure of the self by subverting the tripartite constituents of the mind. Zeno's superego is continually asserting resolutions about changing his behavior which suggest that his ego is not in control of the past being described. When Zeno came home to Augusta after being with Carla, "all was soon forgotten in a health-giving bath of good resolutions" (224). Forgetting the past ensues from a projection into the future. Similarly, Zeno's resolutions to have his last cigarette or to become faithful to one woman are postponements of the end, a denial of a teleology between past and present, and an affirmation by Svevo that especially the narrating autobiographical voice must listen and respond to the call of the other.

Notes

1. This is one of my first essays into this topic is more fully developed in my book *The Ethics of Reading According to Emmanuel Lévinas* (Amsterdam: Rodopi Publishers, 1998). I am es-

pecially thankful to Professor Mancini for his inspirational courses on Svevo at the Ohio State University in the early 1970s, which provided me with the opportunities to explore Svevo through Mancini's published essay "Svevo e la recente critica anglo-americana," *Forum Italicum* 4.4 (1970): 590-605.

2. Although P. N. Furbank contends that Svevo "seriously believed at the time of writing Zeno that he was making a contribution to psycho-analytic literature" (*Italo Svevo, The Man and the Writer* [Berkeley: U of California P, 1966] 177), the tone of self-mockery throughout *Confessions of Zeno* leaves little doubt that Svevo was playing with the methods of psychoanalysis through the interactions of Dr. S. and Zeno.

3. Bruno Maier, *Italo Svevo* (Milan: Mursia, 1968) 81.

4. Jorge Luis Borges, *Other Inquisitions, 1937-1952*, trans. Ruth L. C. Simms (Austin: U of Texas P, 1964) 110.

5. Emmanuel Lévinas, *Le Temps et l'autre* (Paris: Presses Universitaires de France, 1994) 20 ff.

6. Emmanuel Lévinas, *Face to Face with Lévinas*, ed. Richard A. Cohen (Albany: State U of New York P, 1986) 26.

7. Italo Svevo, *Confessions of Zeno,* trans. Beryl de Zoete (New York: Vintage, 1989) 101. All subsequent references to this text will be given by page number after the citation.

8. *Una vita* (1893) and *Senilità* (1898) are two other narratives by Svevo in which ineptness and failure are the hallmarks of their heroes. These "qualities" are commentaries about their homelessness and displaced nature in a capitalist society in which self-worth is measured by accumulation and possession, neither of which Svevo's principal characters are capable of mastering. Zeno himself could not master the double-entry accounting which young Olivi tried to teach him in order to be successful in his business partnership with Guido (261).

9. *Le Temps et l'autre* 34.

10. Most of these characteristics have been recently developed by Edward Said (*Representations of the Intellectual* [New York: Pantheon, 1994] 61 ff.) as appropriate for the intellectual. Thus, Zeno could bespeak more profundity than his mask of failure and folly conveys. Said also recalls James Joyce's Stephen Dedalus's admiration for Lucifer's *non serviam* ("I will not serve") in *A Portrait of the*

Artist as a Young Man (1916). Zeno is also so inspired appropriately since Joyce was a good friend of Svevo in Trieste during the early 1920s.

11. Emmanuel Lévinas, *Sur Maurice Blanchot* (Montpellier: Fata Morgana, 1975) 32.

12. See the discussion of Heidegger's and de Man's silences regarding their collaboration as a rejection of the ethical stance adopted by Lévinas in Roland A. Champagne, "Jacques Derrida's Response to the Call for Ethics," *International Journal of Social and Moral Studies* 6 (Spring 1991): 3-18.

13. Naomi Lebowitz, *Italo Svevo* (New Brunswick: Rutgers UP, 1978) 127.

14. Sigmund Freud, "Jokes and their Relation to the Unconscious," *Complete Psychological Works of Sigmund Freud,* vol. 13, trans. and ed. James Strachey and Anna Freud (London: Hogarth, 1960) 111.

15. Anthony Wilden, "Death, Desire and Repetition in Svevo's Zeno," *Modern Language Notes* 85.1 (1969): 104.

16. Leslie Y. Rabkin, "Beyond Health and Disease: Psychoanalysis and Italo Svevo's *The Confessions of Zeno,*" *Literature and Psychology* 37.1-2 (1991): 77.

17. The critical voice echoes the Greek etymon *kritein* meaning "to divide."

18. Emmanuel Lévinas, *Totality and Infinity,* trans. Alphonso Lingis (Pittsburgh: Duquesne UP, 1969) 85.

19. Rabkin 79 ff.

20. Paula Robison, "Svevo: Secrets of the Confessional," *Literature and Psychology* 20.3 (1970): 102.

21. Livia Veneziani Svevo, *Memoir of Italo Svevo,* trans. Isabel Quigly (Marlboro, VT: Marlboro P, 1990) 33.

22. Alain Robbe-Grillet, "Zeno's Sick Conscience," *For a New Novel: Essays on Fiction,* trans. Richard Howard (New York: Grove, 1965) 92.

Works Cited

Borges, Jorge Luis. *Other Inquisitions, 1937-1952.* Trans. Ruth L. C. Simms. Austin: U of Texas P, 1964.

Champagne, Roland A. "Jacques Derrida's Response to the Call for Ethics." *International Journal of Social and Moral Studies* 6 (1991): 3-18.

———. *The Ethics of Reading According to Emmanuel Lévinas.* Amsterdam: Rodopi, 1998.

Felman, Shoshana. *Jacques Lacan and the Adventure of Insight: Psychoanalysis in Contemporary Culture.* Cambridge, MA: Harvard UP, 1987.

Freud, Sigmund. *Complete Psychological Works of Sigmund Freud.* Trans. and ed. James Strachey and Anna Freud. London: Hogarth, 1960.

Furbank, P. N. *Italo Svevo: The Man and the Writer.* Berkeley: U of California P, 1966.

Joyce, James. *A Portrait of the Artist as a Young Man.* New York: Viking, 1963.

Lebowitz, Naomi. *Italo Svevo.* New Brunswick: Rutgers UP, 1978.

Lévinas, Emmanuel. *Totality and Infinity.* Trans. Alphonso Lingis. Pittsburgh: Duquesne UP, 1969.

———. *Sur Maurice Blanchot.* Montpellier: Fata Morgana, 1975.

———. *Face to Face with Lévinas.* Ed. Richard A. Cohen. Albany: State U of New York P, 1986.

———. *Le Temps et l'autre.* Paris: Presses Universitaires de France, 1994.

Maier, Bruno. *Italo Svevo.* Milan: Mursia, 1968.

Mancini, Albert. "Svevo e la recente critica Anglo-Americana." *Forum Italicum* 4.4 (1970): 590-605.

Rabkin, Leslie Y. "Beyond Health and Disease: Psychoanalysis and Italo Svevo's *The Confessions of Zeno.*" *Literature and Psychology* 37.1-2 (1991): 72-87.

Robbe-Grillet, Alain. "Zeno's Sick Conscience." *For A New Novel: Essays in Fiction.* Trans. Richard Howard. New York: Grove, 1965. 89-94.

Robison, Paula. "Svevo: Secrets of the Confessional." *Literature and Psychology* 20.33 (1970): 101-14.

Said, Edward. *Representations of the Intellectual.* New York: Pantheon, 1994.

Svevo, Italo. *Confessions of Svevo.* Trans. Beryl de Zoete. New York: Vintage, 1989.

———. *Una vita* (1893) and *Senilità* (1898). *Opera omnia.* Vol. 2. Ed. Bruno Maier. Milan. Dall'Oglio, 1966-69. Translated in English as *A Life.* Trans. Archibald Colquhoun (London: Secker & Warburg, 1963).

———. *As a Man Grows Older.* Trans. Beryl de Zoete. London: Secker & Warburg, 1962.

Svevo, Livia Veneziani. *Memoir of Italo Svevo.* Trans. Isabel Quigly. Marlboro, VT: Marlboro P, 1990.

Wilden, Anthony. "Death, Desire and Repetition in Svevo's Zeno." *Modern Language Notes* 85.1 (1969): 98-119.

Giuliana Minghelli (essay date 2002)

SOURCE: Minghelli, Giuliana. "The Crying of the Statues: Art and Women in *Senilità*." In *In the Shadow of the Mammoth: Italo Svevo and the Emergence of Modernism,* pp. 102-26. Toronto: University of Toronto Press, 2002.

[*In the following essay, Minghelli examines* As a Man Grows Older, *asserting that in this work Svevo uncovers artists' "desire to transfigure" and "compulsion to represent the self in the other" through the characters of Angiolina and Amalia. Minghelli concludes that in this novel "the male dream and the women's resistance" engender "a hybrid artifact, a screaming statue."*]

'Je m'adore dans ce que j'ai fait.'[1] Pygmalion's words in front of Galathea's statue can be heard as an insistent echo in Svevo's second novel, *Senilità,* a text that, more than any other by Svevo, obsessively uses the metaphor of figural representation. The two artists, sculptor Stefano Balli and writer Emilio Brentani, seek, like Rousseau's Pygmalion, a representation of the other, the living Angiolina and Amalia, that would help them achieve a successful self-production.[2] Even though the dreams of Emilio and Stefano differ radically, both artists are in search of a body to incarnate them. In *Senilità,* however, Galathea lends her body only to walk away from the artist, leaving behind a shattered dream. Both Angiolina, objectified as a body without dreams, and Amalia, a body consumed by dreams, participate as subversive agents in this figurative process.

In his uneventful life, Emilio 'abbisognava di puntelli per sentirsi sicuro' [needed props to feel safe].[3] One of these crutches is Stefano Balli, who 'era men colto, ma aveva sempre avuto su [Emilio] una specie d'autorità paterna' [was not as educated, but always held over Emilio a sort of paternal authority (*S* [*Senilità*], 335)]. This friendship, that was 'piú intima di quanto Emilio per prudenza avrebbe desiderato . . .' [more intimate than Emilio's caution would have desired (*S,* 336)], grew from a common interest in the 'arti rappresentative nelle quali andavano perfettamente d'accordo perché in quelle arti esisteva una sola idea, quella cui s'era votato il Balli' [representational arts about which they were in perfect agreement because in those arts only one idea existed, the one to which Balli subscribed (*S,* 336)]. Later, when the friendship with Stefano becomes rather strained because of Emilio's love for Angiolina, the narrator explicitly notes: 'L'arte del Balli era veramente l'unico punto di contatto fra i due amici' [Balli's art was really the only point of contact between the two friends (*S,* 456)]. Art seems to substitute for a true intimacy, not only between the two friends but also between Emilio and the other crutch in his life, his sister Amalia.

Emilio's literary interest has shaped the solitary and grey relationship with his sister, with whom he used to spend uneventful evenings studying and reading. Life breaks into their monotonous existence with the same glitter and promises to be found in the first enticing pages of a novel. Thus, when Emilio narrates his encounter with Angiolina, Amalia listens intently:

> col medesimo aspetto, [con cui] ella aveva letto quel mezzo migliaio di romanzi che facevano bella mostra di sé, nel vecchio armadio adattato a biblioteca . . .
>
> (*S,* 337)

[with the same attitude she had when reading those five hundred novels, elegantly shown off in the old armoire that had been converted into a library . . .]

But the narrator immediately specifies that Amalia 'non era passiva ascoltatrice, non era il fato altrui che l'appassionasse' [was not a passive listener, it was not somebody else's destiny to move her (*S,* 337)]. Collaborating with Emilio in the 'artificial construction' of Angiolina, Amalia surreptitiously lives her own 'romanzo': 'ella guardava dentro di sé sorpresa ch'essendo fatta cosí, non avesse desiderato di godere e di soffrire' [she looked inside herself and was surprised that although she was made in that way, she had not desired to suffer or enjoy life (*S,* 337)]. The image of Angiolina projected by Emilio's dream dispels Amalia's 'senilità.' The unconscious state of renunciation in which she had lived is replaced by the consciousness of a different self, championed by Angiolina, a woman 'che abbatteva tutti gli ostacoli e somigliava ad Amalia stessa' [who overthrew all obstacles and resembled Amalia herself (*S,* 382)]. Amalia's 'romanzo' is a self-discovery. The resigned 'senilità' that has enclosed and isolated brother and sister in their own thoughts is challenged by the common project of an unattainable representation of life. Emilio and Amalia enter into the same adventure, but with the difference that Amalia's 'senilità' cannot be sublimated, being a 'tristezza senza parole' [sadness without words (*S,* 418)], for 'la parola non guariva Amalia' [the word did not heal Amalia (*S,* 421)]. While Emilio will stubbornly project his plot on to Angiolina, Amalia, unable to represent her life, or, rather, prevented from doing so, will be consumed by the 'corsa vertiginosa dei suoi sogni' [vertiginous race of her dreams (*S,* 495)]. The repressed word will leave behind only an unconscious monologue, the delirious words of a dying woman.

Angiolina is the fourth and pivotal member of the quartet. Her story remains outside the text, the invisible loom on which the threads of the story of Emilio, Amalia, and Balli merge into a figure. The free and seductive 'figlia del popolo' [daughter of the people (*S,* 447)] is the surface upon which the eye of the sculptor, the dream of the poet, and Amalia's desire for 'life' project their images and illusions. But only the two artists, the sculptor Balli and the writer Emilio, have the prerogative of representing their dreams, thanks to the possibility of giving them a body, the body of the woman.

The dionysian Balli and his melancholic friend are separated not only by temperament but by two conflicting artistic credos, two conflicting modes of self-production. While Emilio, revels in a 'sentimentalità da letterato' [sentimentality of the man of letters (*S*, 342)] that continuously embellishes Angiolina's image to create a romantic and unlikely *Ange,* Stefano aims to regain '[la] semplicità o ingenuità che i cosidetti classici ci avevano rubate' [the simplicity or ingenuousness that the so-called classics had robbed from us (*S*, 336)]. As a first programmatic gesture, he clips the wings of Emilio's *Ange,* who then precipitates to earth as a vulgar *Giolona.*

> Chi avrebbe potuto far capire ad Emilio che la fantasia dell'artista s'era fermata su quell'oggetto, proprio perché in tanta purezza di linee ci aveva scoperta un'espressione indefinibile, non creata da quelle linee, qualche cosa di volgare e di goffo, che un Raffaello avrebbe soppresso e ch'egli tanto volentieri avrebbe copiato, rilevato?
>
> (*S*, 452)

> [Who could have explained to Emilio that the fantasy of the artist rested on that object, precisely because in such a purity of lines he had discovered an indefinable expression, something vulgar and awkward not created by such lines, that a Raphael would have suppressed and that he so willingly copied and put into relief?]

Balli's attraction to Angiolina runs counter to Emilio's; while the latter pursues an ideal representation of the woman, Stefano's eye is caught by the reality that persistently reasserts itself to pollute the perfection of the ideal, an allegory which he wants to represent in the work of art. Stefano's aesthetic, in contrast to the confused dreams of Emilio, is articulated as an artistic manifesto at the beginning of the novel:

> aveva continuato a correre la sua via dietro a un certo ideale di spontaneità, a una ruvidezza voluta, a una semplicità o, come egli diceva, perspicuità d'idea da cui credeva dovesse risultare il suo 'io' artistico depurato da tutto ciò ch'era idea o forma altrui.
>
> (*S*, 335)

> [for all his life he had run after a certain ideal of spontaneity, a desired roughness, simplicity or, as he put it himself, perspicacity of idea from which he thought his artistic 'self' should have emerged cleansed of other people's ideas and forms.]

The roughness pursued in Balli's artistic ideal will guarantee the triumph of his subjectivity over any 'otherness,' whether of form or content. In art as in life Balli seeks a strength that is self-contained and uncontaminated by the world.

The whirl of contrasting passions that envelopes the four protagonists of the novel is filtered both by the second-rate writer Emilio and his sculptor friend through narcissistic acts of representation. Through Angiolina and Amalia, Svevo keenly uncovers the artists' desire to transfigure, the compulsion to represent the self in the other and worship that self in the other. Angiolina and Amalia, whose desire is conveniently ignored or frustrated by the male characters, do not passively lend their bodies to the artists' dreams, but rather resist and indirectly critique them. As a result, the male dream and the women's resistance to it engender a hybrid artifact, a screaming statue.

WHAT IS HIDDEN IN A STATUE?

The scene in Balli's studio when Angiolina poses for a sculpture frames, through Emilio's eyes, the representational act that obsessively invests the woman throughout *Senilità*. Despite the opposing strategies followed by Emilio and Stefano in the project of reading and writing the self, and the different media used, the sculpting session articulates an intersubjective relationship between the artist and his object that functions as a leitmotif in at least two other crucial scenes of the novel: namely Amalia's death and Angiolina's final assumption into Emilio's artistic pantheon.

> Su una base informe poggiava inginocchiata una figura quasi umana, le due spalle vestite, evidentemente quelle d'Angiolina nella forma e nell'atteggiamento. Fatta fino a quel punto la figura aveva qualche cosa di tragico. *Pareva fosse sepolta nell'argilla, facesse degli sforzi immani per liberarsene.* Anche *la testa* su cui qualche colpo di pollice aveva incavate le tempie e lisciata la fronte, *appariva come un teschio coperto accuratamente di terra acciocché non gridasse.*—Vedi come *la cosa* sorge—disse lo scultore, gettando un'occhiata, una carezza su tutto il lavoro.—L'idea c'è già tutta; è la forma che manca.
>
> (*S*, 455; emphasis mine)

> [On a shapeless base an almost human figure rested kneeling, both shoulders dressed, obviously Angiolina's in shape and attitude. Modelled to that point the figure conveyed a tragic sensation. *It seemed to be buried in clay, and to be exerting itself desperately to emerge to freedom.* Even the *head,* on which a few thumb strokes had hollowed out the temples and smoothed over the forehead, *appeared like a skull carefully covered with earth to prevent its screaming.*—See how *the thing* rises—the sculptor said, throwing a glance like a caress over the whole work.—The idea is all already there, only the form is missing.]

The living Angiolina, under the weight of the idea, kneels down, encased in dead matter like an obedient *thing.* The head, shaped by the violent touch of the sculptor, has been reduced to a skull silenced as if to prevent a scream. In order to achieve form, the 'I' of the artist, his 'pure and transparent' idea, has killed the living body, has suffocated the other.[4] Pygmalion's anxieties before the living Galatea are unknown to Balli's unproblematic search for self-recognition. The contrasting perceptions of the work-in-progress continue to unfold, moving between Balli's illustration of his idea and the narrator's—and Emilio's—critical view of it:

> Ma l'idea non la vedeva che lui. Qualche cosa di fine, quasi inafferrabile. Doveva sorgere da quell'argilla una prece, la prece di persona che per un istante crede e che forse non avrebbe creduto mai piú. Il Balli spiegò anche la forma che voleva. La base sarebbe rimasta grezza e la figura sarebbe andata affinandosi in su fino ai capelli, che dovevano essere disposti con la civetteria del parrucchiere piú modernamente raffinato. I capelli erano destinati a negare la preghiera che la faccia avrebbe espressa.

> (*S*, 455)

> [But he was the only one to see the idea. It was something subtle, almost intangible. A prayer had to emerge from the clay, the prayer of a person that for a moment has faith and who perhaps will lose it forever. Balli also explained the form that he wanted. The base would remain rough and the figure would become more and more refined up to the hair, which would be made up following the coquetry of the most modern and exquisite hair-dresser. The hair was destined to negate the prayer that the face would express.]

Totally absorbed in his 'idea,' which is invisible to Emilio, Balli does not see the violence involved in his allegory. It is Emilio's gaze that reveals the distorted limbs of the woman disguised under the beautiful surface of the 'finished' figure. The scream of pain rising from the buried figure will reach human ears only sublimated in a 'pure' transcendent voice: from the silenced skull will rise only an unutterable prayer.

Since initially 'ad Emilio non parve che l'argilla riproducesse alcun tratto della faccia d'Angiolina' [for Emilio the clay did not seem to reproduce any trait of Angiolina's face (*S*, 456)], the sculptor teaches him how to 'look.' As a result 'Emilio vide quella somiglianza evidentissima' [Emilio saw that evident resemblance (*S*, 456)], a resemblance that interestingly is perceivable only 'quando si guardava quella testa da un solo punto' [when one watched that head from one single point (*S*, 456)], namely Balli's uncontaminated perspective. Angiolina does not recognize herself in the shapeless clay. From the beginning of her posing for the sculpture, she is far from being contained in Balli's concept. In fact, the sculptor notices with disappointment and 'disgust':

> Quella beghina non sapeva pregare. Piuttosto che rivolgerli piamente, ella lanciava con impertinenza gli occhi in alto. Civettava col signor Iddio.

> (*S*, 455)

> [That hypocrite did not know how to pray. Rather than piously look to the sky, she glanced up with impertinence. She flirted with God.]

Angiolina's face, notwithstanding Balli's directions, holds an expression of challenge rather than supplication, ultimately defying his fantasy. At the end of the session, the artist covers the statue's sleeping face; this Angiolina will never awake from his dream.

The molding of Angiolina's statue constitutes a powerful metaphor of the violence involved in the production of the 'figure' of the woman. The scene of Amalia's agony, because of the anaesthetizing gaze that Stefano and Emilio cast on her body, constitutes an actualization of the violence contained in the sculpting session. The scream suffocated in Angiolina's statue finds a voice in the dying Amalia, even as her death is sublimated into an aesthetic experience.

> Amalia era livida; la sua faccia aveva il colore del guanciale su cui si proiettava. Il Balli la guardò con evidente ammirazione. La luce gialla della candela si rifletteva luminosissima sulla faccia umida d'Amalia, tanto che pareva luminosità sua; *il nudo cosí brillante e sofferente gridava. Pareva la rappresentazione plastica di un grido violento di dolore.* [. . .] Il Balli disse:— Pareva *una buona dolce furia.* Non ho mai visto qualche cosa di simile—. S'era seduto e guardava in aria con quell'occhio da sognatore con cui cercava le idee. Era evidente, ed Emilio ne provò soddisfazione: Amalia moriva amata dell'amore piú nobile che il Balli potesse offrire.

> (*S*, 495; emphasis mine)

> [Amalia was livid: her face had the color of the pillow on which her shadow was projected. Balli looked at her with evident admiration. The candle's yellow light was brightly reflecting on Amalia's wet face, so that it seemed to be her own luminosity; *the naked skin so brilliant and suffering was crying out. It seemed the plastic representation of a violent scream of suffering.* . . . Balli said:—She seemed *a good sweet Fury.* I have never seen anything like it—He seated himself and looked in the air with that dreamy eye in search of ideas. It was obvious: Amalia was dying loved by the purest love that Balli could offer. Emilio felt satisfaction.]

'It seemed the plastic representation of a violent scream of suffering,' directly recalls the previous description of the statue. While Emilio critically discerns an image of death in the 'thing rising' from Balli's hands, he willingly participates, in the case of Amalia's scream, in the transfiguration of the dying woman. The living form approximating death titillates the artist's imagination, but his representation, as in Angiolina's statue, strives to cover up the fundamental reality of death. Thus, Amalia, the ignored messenger from the realm of the dead, is exorcised into a paradoxically unthreatening Fury ('a good sweet Fury'). In both cases, the artistic gaze effaces the woman, art competing with death in its powers of erasure.

Angiolina eventually escapes from both the 'mortuary sheet' imposed upon her by Balli and the suffocating dream of Emilio. On the other hand, Amalia, thrust back into Emilio's stifling 'senilità,' dies literally suffocated in the inconsistent clay of her dreams. A similar control over the two women is exerted within the narrative structure through the manipulation of the narrative point of view. While the inaccessibility of Angiolina's point of view creates a shadow where her subjectivity is hidden *and* protected from any manipulation, Amalia's thoughts, as they emerge in the narration, occasion her imprisonment in the shadow of Emilio's adventure. His story not only hides Amalia's in his 'cono d'ombra' [the cone of his shadow (Benedetti 1991: 206)], but it co-opts it for his own search for meaning.[5] From the moment Amalia's softly spoken dream of happiness is overheard by Emilio and betrayed to Balli, the narration represents the progressive ravaging of Amalia's interiority. As the 'illness' strips her of all her clothes, revealing her fragile nudity, the narration lifts away the layers of her consciousness one after the other, leading her to death 'misconosciuta e vilipesa' [misunderstood and vilified (*S,* 484)]. In the final babbled and broken words of her agony, she, too, is left as a screaming statue, an object for the gaze of the two artists.

For the guilty Emilio, Balli's 'purest love' constitutes a white shroud, the last beautifying and redeeming act that accompanies the woman into the silence of death. The aggressive love of the older woman for Balli, 'una seconda Angiolina che lo veniva a turbare nelle sue abitudini, ma un'Angiolina che gli faceva ribrezzo' [a second Angiolina who came to disturb his habits, but an Angiolina who repelled him (*S,* 415)] is again transfigured by the sculptor to simultaneously capture and suppress the scream. The mold of a *good sweet Fury,* imposed by Balli's 'dreamy eye' onto Amalia, forever hides the menacing sexuality of the other, a disturbing and embarrassing desire which threatens to disrupt the stories of Stefano and Emilio.

The cold ennobling 'love' of the artist, a necrophilic love for the object, taints Emilio's love for Amalia as well. Confronted with her death, Emilio casts *his* 'artistic eye' on his dying sister in the search for a beautifying image.

> Guardò a lungo Amalia sperando di poter nuovamente piangere. L'analizzò, la scrutò, per sentire tutto il suo male e soffrire con lei. Poi guardò altrove vergognandosi; s'era accorto che nella ricerca di commozione era andato *alla ricerca di immagini e di traslati.*
>
> (*S,* 492; emphasis mine)

> [He looked at Amalia for a long time hoping to be able once again to cry. He analysed her, he scrutinized her to feel all her pain and suffer with her. Then he looked away with shame; he realized that in the attempt to be moved, he had gone *in search of images and metaphors.*]

> Sempre guardandola egli pensò:—Ella morrà!—Se la *figurò* morta, quietata, priva d'affanno e di delirio. Ebbe dolore di avere avuta quell'idea poco affettuosa.
>
> (*S,* 493)

> [Still looking at her he thought:—She will die!—He *imagined* her dead, still, without pain and delirium. He was pained to have had such an unloving idea.]

No prayer that would transcend the reality of death and absolve the guilty Emilio rises from Amalia's bed, only a 'humble protest,' immediately translated into 'il lamento della materia che, già abbandonata, disorganizzandosi, emette i suoni appresi nel lungo dolore cosciente' [the moaning of matter which, already abandoned, on the way to decomposing, emits the sounds learned in long conscious suffering (*S,* 500)]. Her scream finds an articulation as the voice of silent and shapeless *matter.*

But in the moment that death carries Amalia's story away into silence, its materiality scornfully defies any act of representation on the part of the two artists. Death, simultaneously evoked and hidden in Stefano's 'transparent' allegory of Angiolina's statue, comes to the surface here with a vengeance. The dream of the artist is cast off; matter refuses all disguises and relapses into its chaos. The spectacle of death stages the unveiling of the naked truth: that the two artists live vicariously through the body of the woman. If Angiolina, as some critics have repeatedly observed, metaphorically stages the elusiveness of life (Saccone 1977: 275), Amalia stages the materiality of death; one, following her own desire, disappears in the blinding light of the city, the other in the shadows of a long ceaseless night.

Seeing Grey: Emilio's Artistic *Senilità*

Balli's representational violence unveils the violence inherent in Emilio's repression of Amalia and her threatening desire, his egotistical preoccupation with perpetuating an image of his sister that is neither problematic nor menacing: 'Non aveva saputo tutelare la vita della sorella; avrebbe ora tentato di conservarne intatta la riputazione' [he had been unable to protect his sister's life; he would try now to keep her reputation intact (*S,* 497)]. Nevertheless it would be a mistake to assimilate Emilio's desire with Balli's dream of mastery and his pursuit of the idea as a faithful mirror of the self (Robinson 1971). Art is for Emilio a delicate collaborative project, an effort to dream symbiotically with the other.[6] It is Emilio's desire to *collaborate* with the woman (a desire also implicit in his preoccupation with the 'tutela' and education of Amalia and Angiolina) that radically separates him from Balli. While Angiolina, as we will analyse later, resists Emilio's symbiotic dream, Amalia, because of her own desire for a 'story,' participates in Emilio's creation, though, in the process, subverting it with a silent but radical critique.

> ad Emilio piacque di aver creata nella sua mente un'Angiolina ben diversa dalla reale. Quando si trovava con la sorella, amava quell'immagine, l'abbelliva, vi aggiungeva tutte le qualità che gli sarebbe piaciuto

trovare in Angiolina, e quando capí che anche Amalia *collaborava* a quella costruzione artificiale, ne gioí vivamente.

(*S*, 381; emphasis mine)

[Emilio was pleased to have created in his mind an Angiolina very different from the real one. When he was with his sister, he loved that image, he embellished it, he added all the qualities that he would have liked to find in Angiolina, and when he understood that even Amalia *was collaborating* in that artificial construction, he deeply enjoyed it.]

Amalia is a precious partner; thanks to her, a much longed for 'sweetness' is insinuated into Emilio's adventure. In the shadow of Amalia, Emilio can endlessly enrich and correct his fantastic idyll like a work of fiction through collaborative dreaming with her sister, and, exactly like the man in the shadow of the compliant mammoth, live his private dream in the world. As in the fable, the story of association and mutual contamination is also a story of betrayal, as the man, in pursuit of his desire, abandons the faithful mammoth.

From the moment Emilio starts an intimate relationship with Angiolina, the 'senilità' that united brother and sister and allowed their symbiotic dream of a more energetic life becomes so burdensome to Emilio that he shies away from Amalia as if from 'una persona inquietante, di cui si doveva evitare la vicinanza' [an unsettling person, whose closeness had to be avoided (*S*, 496)]. Even after Amalia's death, Emilio will unconvincingly reiterate the distance separating him from his sister: 'Amalia stessa era stata insignificante nella sua vita' [Amalia herself had been insignificant in his life (*S*, 501)]. But the poet's symbiotic contamination with his sister survives this last rejection and betrayal, growing instead in significance with the unfolding of the novel. It is 'the ennobling thought of Amalia' that finally will grant a fictional fulfilment to Emilio's love (life) story.

Shockingly for Emilio, the mammoth has desires too, and even though it eventually dies, the presence of its unwritten story opens a powerful critique of the weak and unfaithful man. Even if contained in Emilio's story, Amalia's voice, when heard, reveals the silences on Emilio's part and advances her own interpretation of 'senilità.'[7] During the night at the opera, Amalia's thoughts emerge independently in the narration stirred by the music of Wagner's *Die Walküre*:

Ma, assorbito da quella musica, il suo grande dolore si coloriva, diveniva ancora piú importante, pur facendosi semplice, puro, perché mondato d'ogni avvilimento. [. . .] Mai non s'era sentita tanto mite, liberata da ogni ira, e disposta a piangere lungamente, senza singhiozzi. [. . .] La magnifica onda sonora rappresentava il destino di tutti. La vedeva correre giú per una china, guidata dall'ineguale conformazione del suolo. Ora una sola cascata, ora divisa in mille piú piccole, colorite tutte dalla piú varia luce e dal riflesso delle cose.

(*S*, 428)

[But, absorbed in that music the sorrow gained color, became even more important, although simpler and pure because cleansed of any humiliation. . . . She never felt so peaceful, freed from any anger, and willing to cry for a long time, without sobbing . . . The marvellous wave of sound was representing everybody's destiny. She saw it running down a hill, guided by the uneven formation of the ground. Now a single waterfall, now divided into a thousand smaller ones, all colored by the most varied light and the reflection of things.]

Amalia, now betrayed and abandoned to her solitude, wilfully embraces Wagner's grandiose celebration of the impassivity of destiny and finds there that artistic sublimation of her sorrow she cannot otherwise attain. Emilio, on the other hand, still in the swing of his passion, maintains a detached critical eye on the performance. Unaddressed by the narrator, the story of *Die Walküre*—the doomed incestuous love between the siblings Siegmund and Sieglinde—hovers over the estranged brother and sister. Although incestuous overtones are present in the relationship of Amalia and Emilio, the core of their drama is their different attitudes towards destiny. While Amalia resigns herself to fate, and, unlike Sieglinde, is finally crushed by it, Emilio refuses to submit to an idea of destiny, that is, to confront the limitation of his character, namely, that 'senilità' that binds him in a metaphorical incest with his sister.

It is only later on, on the eve of his loss of both Amalia and Angiolina, and at the sight of a truly Wagnerian sea storm, that Emilio reaches an insight into his weakness similar to Amalia's at the opera:

Al sibilare del vento si univa imponente il clamore del mare, un urlo enorme composto dall'unione di varie voci piú piccole. [. . .] Ad Emilio parve che quel tramestío si confacesse al suo dolore. Vi attingeva ancora maggiore calma. *L'abito letterario* gli fece pensare il paragone fra quello spettacolo e quello della propria vita. Anche là, nel turbine, nelle onde di cui una trasmetteva all'altra il movimento che aveva tratto lei stessa dall'inerzia, un tentativo di sollevarsi che finiva in uno spostamento orizzontale, egli vedeva l'impassibilità del destino. Non v'era colpa, per quanto ci fosse tanto danno. [. . .] Emilio pensò che la sua sventura era formata dall'inerzia del proprio destino.

(*S*, 487-8; emphasis mine)

[The hissing of the wind was joined by the imposing clamor of the sea, a huge cry made of the union of various smaller voices. . . . Emilio had the impression that such noise suited his sorrow. He gained an even greater peace from it. *Literary habit* made him draw a comparison between that spectacle and the one of his own life. Even there, in the eddy, in the waves that transmitted from one to another the movement that subtracted each of them from the initial inertia, an attempt to rise that ended in a horizontal movement, he saw the impassiveness of destiny. Even in the midst of such destruction there was no guilt. . . . Emilio thought that his misfortune was due to the inertia of his own destiny.]

Brother and sister think the same thoughts as if they were contrapuntal and diachronic stages of the same consciousness. Emilio's reflection—'se gli fosse stato imposto di forzare con la propria voce i clamori del vento e del mare, egli sarebbe stato meno debole e meno infelice' [If it had been imposed on him to confront with his own voice the roar of the wind and sea he would have been less weak and unhappy (*S,* 488)]— echoes Amalia's slightly more passive interrogation: 'Piccola e debole, ella era stata abbattuta; chi avrebbe potuto pretendere ch'ella reagisse?' [Little and weak, she had been knocked down; who could have expected a reaction from her? (*S,* 428)]. Amalia is able to reflect on and question her own 'senilità' when her brother does not have the insight to do so, and her consciousness lucidly precedes her brother's in her final realization: 'Nella sua vita non c'erano però catene; ella era del tutto libera, e nessuno le chiedeva né risoluzione, né forza, né amore' [In her life there were no longer any chains; she was totally free, and no one asked of her either resolution, strength, or love (*S,* 382)].

Although Emilio's resignation to destiny before the tempest is similar to Amalia's after the concert, there is at least one important difference. While for Amalia 'the marvellous wave of sound' *purifies* her sorrow of any humiliation, for Emilio the 'impassiveness of destiny' is simply a way to *disguise* individual responsibilty: 'even in the midst of such destruction there was no guilt.' These different moral reactions find an explanation in Amalia and Emilio's different view of their 'senilità.' In coherent pursuit of his self-deception, Emilio eagerly shares his 'guilt' for their sad existence with Amalia: 'Come erano stati colpevoli lui e Amalia di prendere la vita tanto sul serio!' [How guilty he and Amalia had been in taking life so seriously! (*S,* 487)]. Amalia, on the other hand, gave earlier on in the story a very different reading of her own 'senilità':

> Ella aveva parlato altre volte d'amore, ma altrimenti, senz'indulgenza, perché non si doveva. Come aveva preso sul serio quell'imperativo che le era stato gridato nelle orecchie sin dall'infanzia. Aveva odiato, disprezzato coloro che non avevano obbedito e in se stessa aveva soffocato qualunque tentativo di ribellione. Era stata *truffata!*
>
> (*S,* 376; emphasis mine)

> [She spoke other times of love, but differently, without indulgence, because one should not. How seriously she took that imperative that had been shouted in her ears since her childhood. She had hated, despised those that did not obey and she had suffocated in herself any attempt at rebellion. She had been *cheated*!]

The significance of 'senilità' for brother and sister diverges, but not because it splits into the opposing terms of resigned old age and youth (Saccone 1977: 178). If

Emilio recognizes their 'senilità' as a choice and a guilty one, Amalia's reflection reveals surprisingly that 'senilità' for her is an imposed trait, something that she had been tricked into, a repression of her desire. While Emilio embraces 'senilità' as a self-defence, Amalia sees herself as deceived into a false religion.

Beguiled by Emilio's example of 'voluntary resignation to the same sad destiny,' Amalia awakens to dreams induced by the passions of Emilio and Stefano. Nevertheless, she is deprived of the means to project her own story, which, repressed, finally finds a powerful, if resigned, staging as inescapable 'destiny' in Siegmund and Sieglinde's story. Unable to attain an affirmative sublimation independently, Amalia yields to Wagner's representation, and, once more, although this time willingly and consciously, she embraces somebody's else destiny, 'the destiny of everybody.' If it is true that 'ella non esce dal sistema, non mette in discussione il mondo che l'ha prodotta' 'she does not escape the system, she does not put in question the world that produced her (Saccone 1977: 180)], Amalia's 'silent revolution' (Benedetti 1991: 210) still manages to unveil Emilio's disguises and the illusion that art stands above the pain of life as a universal and ideal consolation. 'L'arte [. . .] che canta ed eleva il destino di questi vinti' [The art . . . that sings and ennobles the destiny of these defeated (Saccone 1977: 180)] seals Amalia's destiny as if it were a shroud. 'Era nata grigia' [she was born grey (*S,* 336)] comments the artist Balli, thus essentializing a 'greyness' to which the narrator already from the start condemned Amalia 'piú vecchia per carattere o forse per destino' [older by character or perhaps by destiny (*S,* 329)]. If there is any consolation in the sublimation of art, it is a privilege only to be shared by the artist for whom the spectacle of ruin and destruction entails aesthetic enjoyment *and* the added pleasure of seeing his responsibility dissolved. Thus Emilio reflects after Amelia's death: 'Era passata la morte, il grande misfatto, ed egli sentiva che i propri errori e misfatti erano stati del tutto dimenticati' [Death had passed by, the final misdeed, and he felt that his mistakes and misdeeds had been totally forgotten (*S,* 500)].

Amalia's death simultaneously stages an artistic, moral, and material erasure. But confronted with the spectacle of her death, the artists' sublimation miserably pales. Emilio as well as Balli will not accomplish a representation either of life (Angiolina) or death (Amalia). Significantly, Emilio's final allegory of the crying Angiolina, a last fragmentary artistic disguise, is obtained only by re-enacting the passage of death, and killing Amalia one last time: '[Angiolina] conservò inalterata la sua bellezza, ma acquistò anche tutte le qualità d'Amelia che morí in lei una seconda volta' [Angiolina kept her beauty intact, but she acquired too the qualities of Amalia who died in her a second time (*S*, 505)]. The only sublimation the morally bankrupt artist will fully enjoy will be the one afforded by the other's death.

Sporadic as they are, Amalia's reflections further our understanding of her condition; unlike her brother, she does not usually indulge in the creation of mystifying images. Nonetheless, following the night at the opera, Amalia surprises her brother by putting on a disguise in an attempt to escape her destiny. Emilio finds her slowly strolling in the sunny streets wearing 'dei colori azzurri, chiari, su una stoffa grezza' [clear blue colors on a rough fabric (*S*, 429)]. Her thin figure awkwardly stands out on the Corso, the stage of Angiolina's triumphant walks. She is as incongruous an apparition as the rough linen against the cheerful color of the dress. Amalia's disguise fails to erase the 'destiny' inscribed on her thin body by Emilio, who brings her back home to the 'vestito abituale, grigio come la sua figura e il suo destino' [everyday dress, grey as her figure and her destiny (*S*, 429)]. On the other hand Emilio's body never objectifies him; he can carry his sadness around the city without being essentialized in the greyness of a dress. It is rather a subjective perception of the other, one that 'ved[e] grigio e sent[e] grigio' [sees grey and feels grey (*S*, 400)], the whole world, his sister included.

The inertia and sense of defeat that condemns Amalia finds in Emilio'case a convenient and dignified disguise in his 'abito letterario.' While Amelia, at the *Walküre*, reaches a kind of self-knowledge, Emilio searches in that same music for a suitable moral disguise for his subjectivity.

> Egli credeva che il suo amore e il suo dolore si sarebbero presto *travestiti* nel pensiero del genio. No. Per lui si movevano sulla scena eroi e dei, e lo trascinavano con sé lontano dal mondo ove aveva sofferto. Negl'intervalli egli cercava invano nel ricordo qualche accento che avesse meritato *un travestimento* simile. L'arte forse lo guariva?
>
> (*S*, 428; emphasis mine)

> [He believed that his love and his sorrow soon would have been disguised by the mind of the genius. No. For him heroes and gods were moving on the stage, and taking him away from the world where he had suffered. In the intermissions he searched vainly in his memory for some feeling that deserved such *a disguise*. Was art healing him?]

Seen in this context the novel's first tentative title, *Il Carnevale di Emilio,* acquires its full meaning, shedding light on *Emilio's 'senilità.'* From such a Carnival, the 'sosia,' the uncanny double, must be banned: Amalia is unable to masquerade, because she *is* one of the masks Emilio wears, the stark reminder of an existential complicity that 'the artist,' pursuing his sunny muse, has to suppress.

'PER SOGNARE IN DUE': THE POET'S SYMBIOSIS WITH THE MUSE

The complicity between Emilio and Angiolina is of a totally different nature and lies exactly in that 'artistic' territory from which Amalia is excluded. Although the same desire for a collective dream with the other punctuates the poet's relationship with his muse, Angiolina, unlike Amalia, is baffled by Emilio's desire for collective fantasizing. Before such a desire, she opposes an indifferent resistance:

> La donna ch'egli amava, *Ange,* era sua invenzione, [. . .] essa non aveva *collaborato* a questa creazione, non l'aveva neppure lasciato fare perché aveva resistito.
>
> (*S*, 358; emphasis mine)

> [The woman he loved, *Ange,* was an invention of his, . . . she did not *collaborate* on this creation, she didn't even let him pursue it for she resisted it.]

Ironically, to overcome such a resistance and live his fantasy, 'pur di renderla dolce' [more in the manner of Amalia] 'e indurla a entrare in quelle idee, *per sognare in due*' [in order to make her sweet and induce her to enter those ideas, *to dream together* (*S*, 447; emphasis mine)], Emilio will be the one *collaborating with the other's dream,* making Angiolina's lies his own. Started as an attempt to appropriate the other, Emilio's desire for a symbiotic dreaming will yield an unexpected surprise: Emilio will be the one appropriated. An ironic example of this collaboration at a parodically degraded 'artistic' level is the letter Emilio and Angiolina write to the tailor Volpini, the only collective creation of their relationship and the meeting point of the well-packaged lies of the rhetorician and Angiolina's 'lies': 'Angiolina era potuta sembrare superiore nell'interpretazione della lettera del Volpini; la risposta colò intera dalla penna esperta di Emilio' [Angiolina might have seemed more insightful in the interpretation of Volpini's letter; the reply flowed entirely from Emilio's skilled pen (*S*, 464)]. Beyond the failed attempt to dream together, it is in the ambiguous relationship between the artist and the muse that the complicity between Emilio and Angiolina lies, a complicity that starts from the moment Emilio enters into his artistic adventure.

Emilio's literary ambition, a senile *and* adolescent expectation of an unspecified future, waltzes arm in arm with Angiolina in the narration, and, thus, from the very beginning of the text, the problem of self-representation and the representation of the other are one and the same thing. If Balli molds reality, Emilio seems to be waiting for a mold from the outside, a mold that would give form and direction to his life and his art.

> Viveva sempre in un'aspettativa, non paziente, di qualche cosa che doveva venirgli dal cervello, l'arte, di qualche cosa che doveva venirgli dal di fuori. . . .
>
> (*S*, 330)

[He lived always in an impatient expectation of something that should have come to him from the mind, art, or something that should have come from the outside. . . .]

Angiolina represents that hoped-for mould. The encounter with Angiolina, 'l'evento che segna uno scatto nella *senilità* di Emilio' [the event that marks a change in Emilio's *senilità* (Palumbo 1976: 71)], is immediately interpreted as the possibility of living a long-awaited dream, of 'composing,' of uttering well-rehearsed words.

> Fece piovere sulla bionda testa le *dichiarazioni liriche* che nei lunghi anni il suo desiderio aveva maturate e affinate [. . .]. Ebbe il sentimento che da tanti anni non aveva provato, *di comporre, di trarre dal proprio intimo idee e parole*: un sollievo che dava a quel momento della sua vita non lieta, un aspetto strano, indimenticabile, di pausa, di pace. *La donna vi entrava!*
>
> (*S,* 330-1; emphasis mine)

[He showered the blond head with all the *lyric declarations* that his desire had matured and refined through the years . . . He felt, as he had not felt for many years, *as if he were composing, drawing ideas and words from his interiority*: a relief that gave to that moment of his not too happy life a strange aspect, unforgettable, of pause, of peace. *The woman was entering it!*]

We enter the narration *because* Angiolina, the muse, enters it, opening the floodgates of Emilio's fantasy. But from the first moment, Angiolina plays the paradoxical functions of both a mould (the idealized 'musa' or 'dea') and an artistic and sexual object to be moulded by the artist. The poet is therefore caught in an unresolved tension between two opposite desires: to enclose the woman in an unspecified artistic ideal and to dream symbiotically with the muse. *Senilità* narrates the failed attempt to share an already written romance with an unsuspecting muse, the failed making of a 'romanzo' (both love story and novel). It is exactly in the gap that separates the 'romanzo' already written and interpreted by a unified subjectivity (the idyll rehearsed for years in Emilio's mind) and the living flesh and blood of the experience that Emilio's story unfolds. 'Senilità' is the paradoxical yearning for an already written story. In this sense Emilio's adventure is truly quixotic, Emilio being the last hero of a now impossible romance, and therefore possibly the initiator of a new genre, the modernist novel that represents not Emilio's time past 'ma un tempo che egli sa bene di non aver mai posseduto, ma solo *sognato,* sperato' [but a time that he knows well he never possessed, but only *dreamed* and hoped for (Saccone 1977: 191)].

Nevertheless, both Emilio's striving for a symbiotic dream and the Balli-like attempt to enclose the muse in an image fail before Angiolina's indifference. A kalei-

doscopic number of images are worn and cast off by Angiolina as she *resists* representation with the defiance of an impenetrable mask: 'aveva sulla faccia una *mancanza assoluta di espressione*' [she had on her face an absolute lack of expression (*S,* 396; emphasis mine)]. Emilio deploys all his rhetorical weapons to reduce the threatening indifference of the woman to a reassuring and frozen dream image: 'le vedeva la compostezza e la serietà della buona infermiera dolce e disinteressata' [he saw her with the composure and seriousness of a good nurse, sweet and disinterested, (*S,* 437)] a decorous posture that recalls the dignified corpse of Amalia. In flight from the familial nest where he is attended by the grey vestal, Emilio tries to recreate with Angiolina the same reassuring nest, inhabited though by a golden muse (expressed, for example, in his dream of the mountain).

In this sense, Angiolina is radically different from the woman tiger, protagonist of Emilio's first novel, a hybrid creature that contains the woman within the male fantasy and through which Emilio can vicariously suffer and rejoice. Angiolina is rather the *indifferent* woman whose resistance threatens to annihilate both the man and the artist. As Sarah Kofman notes when reflecting on the figure of woman in Freud's writings: 'What makes woman enigmatic here is no longer some 'inborn deficiency,' some sort of lack, but on the contrary her narcissistic self-sufficiency and her indifference; it is no longer the woman who envies man his penis, it is he who envies her for her unassailable libidinal position, whereas he himself—one may wonder why—has been impoverished, has been emptied of this original narcissism' (1985: 52). Not only Angiolina, the narcissistic beauty, but Amalia as well represents such a threat: 'Amalia non gli apparteneva nel delirio; era ancora meno sua che quando si trovava nel possesso dei suoi sensi' [Amalia did not belong to him in delirium; she was even less his than when she was in full possession of her senses (*S,* 482)]. Pygmalion's narcissistic contemplation and perpetuation of his self in the other is now only possible for Emilio *with* the collaboration of the other. But unlike Galathea, Angiolina pre-exists the dream of the poet. Ungraspable, she walks in the world with all the color and warmth of his fantasy, an irrepressible other without whom there is no representation for the self, but whose presence also disrupts that representation.

Along with Angiolina, the medium has to be held partly responsible for the ambiguous and ungraspable character of Emilio's representations. While clay obediently yields under the ordering gesture of the artist, words seem to arrange themselves around gravitational points beyond the will of the writer. The first paragraph of *Senilità* attracts our attention to this immateriality and ambiguousness of language, by opening with the cautious *prime parole* that an unspecified 'he' addresses to an equally unspecified 'she.'[8]

> Subito, con le prime parole che le rivolse, volle avvisarla che non intendeva compromettersi in una relazione troppo seria. Parlò cioè a un dipresso cosí:—T'amo molto e per il tuo bene desidero che ci si metta d'accordo di andare molto cauti—. La parola era tanto prudente ch'era difficile di crederla detta per amore altrui, e un po' piú franca avrebbe dovuto suonare cosí:—Mi piaci molto, ma nella mia vita non potrai essere giammai piú importante di un giocattolo.
>
> (S, 329)
>
> [Immediately, with the first words he addressed to her, he wanted to warn her that he did not intend to compromise himself with too serious a relationship. Thus, he spoke more or less as follows:—I love you a lot and for your own good I want us to agree to move very cautiously—. The word was so prudent that it was difficult to believe it was said for somebody else's sake, and if it would have been a little more sincere it should have sounded like this:—I like you a lot, but in my life you will never be more important than a toy.]

Given the abstraction of the dialogic situation and its actors, this *incipit* could be read as a classical invocation of the muse, yet one which, when transcribed into the secular world of **Senilità,** becomes an unabashed act of seduction. At the same time it is an invocation of and a careful distancing from the muse's power to make the poet go astray from his comfortable if mediocre path.

But another effect of this opening paragraph is to concentrate all attention on the 'first words,' as if they were the real protagonists of the story. The first action is a word, a word uttered to distance oneself, a step backward from a yet invisible other. As Emilio steps backward from his engagement with Angiolina, from the start torn between desire and caution, the narrator, 'che è tutt'altro che ai margini o dietro la storia che sta narrando' [who is far from being at the margins or hidden behind the story that he is telling (Palumbo 1976: 96)], steps away from his character by laying bare Emilio's complex defence strategy in the pursuit of a safe passion. But the narrator steps down as well, though less noticeably so, from his role as a writer who could univocally narrate the story. The narrator's insistence on approximating the phrasing of Emilio's intentions amounts to a denunciation of the word as an opaque screen, a manoeuver which, even more importantly, acknowledges his own participation in the deceptiveness of discourse.[9] Emilio's desire for truth proceeds with the narration, and, with the narration, is constantly sidetracked into detours and disguises. Where could Emilio find a better fellow traveller than Angiolina in the undertaking of this insidious adventure?

There is an intrinsic contamination between the travesties and deceptions of the artist and the muse's disguises. Here lies the fundamental complicity between Angiolina and Emilio. John Locke puts his finger on the founding trait that ties the artist to the woman: 'Eloquence, like the fair sex, has too prevailing beauties in it to suffer itself ever to be spoken against. And it is vain to find fault with those arts of deceiving wherein men find pleasure to be deceived' (cited in Johnson 1989: 38). No other words could be a more appropriate admonition for Emilio. The poet's rhetoric and the woman's beauty compete in creating parallel worlds, losing themselves in a merry-go-round of deception. So if Emilio states over and over that 'la menzogna doveva essere tanto connaturata in quella donna, ch'ella non se ne sarebbe liberata mai' [lying must have been such a second nature to that woman that she would never have been able to free herself from it (*S, 402*)], the narrator immediately corrects the statement by saying:

> Egli dimenticava quanto in altri momenti aveva percepito tanto chiaramente, cioè il fatto ch'egli aveva stranamente *collaborato* a vedere in Angiolina ciò ch'ella non era, ch'era stato lui a creare la menzogna.
>
> (S, 402; emphasis mine)
>
> [He forgot what in other moments he had perceived so clearly, that is the fact that he had strangely *collaborated* in seeing in Angiolina what she was not, that he had been the one to create the lie.]

Angiolina's own travesties neatly mirror the rhetorical masquerades Emilio uses to disguise his feelings, each corresponding in its turn to new biographies of Angiolina. The impossibility of representing the other, the woman, because of her active resistance, really amounts to the impossibility of representing oneself announced in the very *incipit* of **Senilità.** It should not be any surprise to Emilio then that 'Col Balli che non la possedeva, ella si *smascherava,* con lui no!' [With Balli who did not possess her, she *unmasked* herself; with him, no! (S, 458)] Emilio's complicity with Angiolina is marked by his sense of guilt, but Angiolina, unlike Amalia, is no victim of Emilio's moral self-chastising. To his mystifications she opposes 'il riso forte delle Baccanti' [the strong laugh of the Bacchanti (S, 385)]; 'lieta, ingenuamente perversa' [happy, ingenuously perverse (S, 359)] she dissolves Emilio's ambiguous juggling with truth and lies into a Dionysian celebration of joy beyond innocence and guilt.

Jacques Derrida, in his reading of the inscription of woman in Nietzsche's texts, explores the complicity between woman, life, and seduction, referring to it as a constellation of 'the veiled and veiling effects' enacted by femininity, and the 'veiling' performed by the artist. While for women the veiling is merely 'an affair of decency and modesty,' for the poet, who is involved in the deceptive choreographies of truth and untruth, the veiling becomes the fundamental act of creating meaning (Derrida 1979:51). In **La coscienza di Zeno** these two movements are intricately woven together during Zeno's dream of Carla, when he indulges in the all too familiar pleasure of Svevo's 'artists' of painting on the joyful and indifferent surface of the woman's face the depth of sorrow, 'una lotta fra la letizia e il dolore' [a struggle between happiness and sorrow (CdZ, 665)]. Once confronted with the reality of Carla, Zeno comes to the conclusion that she lives on a smooth surface oblivious to any profundity:

> la *bellezza femminile simula dei sentimenti coi quali nulla ha a vedere.* Cosí la tela su cui è dipinta una battaglia non ha alcun sentimento eroico.
>
> (*CdZ* [*La coscienza di Zeno*], 665; emphasis mine)
>
> [*Feminine beauty simulates feelings with which it has nothing to share.* Similarly the canvas on which a battle scene is depicted has no heroic feeling.]

Nor may we assume does the painter.

The world of appearance and deception in which the woman lives, rather than being inherently her own, is the defining domain of artistic production. Woman is trapped on the surface; if she cannot live on that surface and reflect the deceptions of the eye of the other (the male artist and creator), she is refused any possibility of survival, and, like Amalia, must disappear into the unformed world of matter. In this system only the woman as artist, an artist that competes with the male artist for control and the ability to create her own fiction, could survive. The woman is artistic, or (a much more troubling possibility!) the artist is truly feminine. If Angiolina's language and gestures are traces, signs of other men, this very mimetic character unites her with Emilio: 'Emilio subí l'influenza dell'amico persino nel modo di camminare, parlare, gestire' so that 'il Balli [. . .] quando si trovava accanto il Brentani, poteva avere la sensazione d'essere accompagnato da una delle tante femmine a lui soggette' [Emilio suffered the influence of his friend even in his way of walking, speaking, gesticulating [so that] Balli . . . when he was near to Brentani could have the sensation of being accompanied by one of the many women he had subjugated (*S,* 336)].

In this context it is interesting that the first time Emilio feels he is possessing the Angiolina of his dreams is when he, at the moment of abandoning her, succeeds in getting a cry of anguish out of her, of painting sorrow on her face, leaving his trace—or better, finding the trace of Amalia.

> Gli camminava accanto la donna nobilitata dal suo sogno ininterrotto, da quell'ultimo grido d'angoscia ch'egli le aveva strappato lasciandola, e che per lungo tempo l'aveva personificata tutta; persino dall'arte, perché ormai il desiderio fece sentire ad Emilio d'aver accanto la dea capace di qualunque nobiltà di suono o di parola.
>
> (*S,* 434)

> [They walked along, the woman ennobled by his uninterrupted dream, and by that last cry of anguish that he elicited by leaving her. That last cry completely personified her for a long time. Emilio's desire transformed her into an artistic symbol; he felt next to him a goddess capable of every noble sound or word.]

Once again a cry ennobles the woman, taming her in the image of a 'crying beauty' ('donna amante, sempre però donna triste e pensierosa' [the woman lover, always though a woman sad and thoughtful (*S,* 505)]), an image that recalls the 'sweet Fury' whose cry sublimates an obtrusive and uncontrollable passion. The tension between the self (of the artist) and the other, namely an attempt to contain the threat of the overwhelming sexuality of the Beauty and the Fury, finds in these oxymorons a concise but ambiguous rhetorical formulation. Emilio's muse is a hybrid creature: Angiolina's inspiring beauty *needs* Amalia's sweetness and sorrow to grant the fulfilment of his dream.

In the final symbol of Angiolina standing on the altar, the poet accomplishes the painting of sorrow (the veiling) on the indifferent surface.

> Egli la vide dinanzi a sé come su un altare, la personificazione del pensiero e del dolore [. . .]. Ella rappresentava tutto quello di nobile ch'egli in quel periodo avesse pensato od osservato.
>
> (*S,* 505)

> [He saw her in front of him as if on an altar, the personification of thought and sorrow. . . . She represented everything noble that he thought or observed in that period.]

It is notable that, in order to achieve a final representation of his experience, the 'letterato ozioso' [idle man of letters (*S,* 505)] has to resort to a statuesque image to try and save himself from the snares of words, and this final image of Angiolina brings back, curiously reelaborated, Balli's screaming statue. With a striking inversion, Angiolina, the former kneeling worshipper before the 'priest'—'nel suo lungo mantello di tela [Balli] aveva un aspetto sacerdotale' [in his long cloth cloak [Balli] had a priestly look (*S,* 456)]—becomes the goddess on the altar, while the artist, powerless worshipper, now stands before her. Has Emilio thereby achieved his dream of collaboration? Is he giving up the 'disguises'? Or is this only the ultimate disguise?

In the fragmentary story **'In Serenella,'** the character dreams of a gigantic pietà emerging from the horizon, representing '[la] Donna che consola l'Uomo inginocchiato e riposante nel suo grembo' [the Woman who consoles the Man kneeling and resting on her lap ([*Opera Omnia*] 1968: 356). This dream, which Emilio repeatedly tried to impose on Angiolina, finds its ironic actualization in *Senilità*'s final image.

Si! Angiolina pensa e piange! Pensa come se le fosse
stato spiegato il segreto dell'universo e della propria
esistenza; piange come se nel vasto mondo non avesse
piú trovato neppure un *Deo gratias* qualunque.

(S, 505)

[Yes! Angiolina thinks and cries! She thinks as if the
secret of the universe and of her own existence had
been explained to her; she cries as if she did not find
any *Deo gratias* in the whole wide world.]

If Angiolina is the one in need of consolation, we could
observe that the artist, absent from this final representation, plays the role of the 'Deo gratias qualunque.'
Nevertheless, in spite of Emilio's desire to be needed,
the final transfiguration of Angiolina is but another attempt to hide her indifference. The divinity/muse is no
mater dolorosa and definitely she *does not need* the
worshipper. Thus, unable to accomplish his dream of
symbiosis with Angiolina or Amalia, Emilio is left only
with the consolation of being able to represent it: he finally elevates the ideal symbiosis between *senilità* and
life on to an altar.

The question remains open regarding the relation between woman's 'truth,' living on the indifferent surface,
and the truth of the poet, the veil of sorrow that redeems the woman. Derrida, commenting upon Nietzsche's text, describes the relation in these terms:
'"Truth" can only be a surface. But the blushing movement of that truth which is not suspended in quotation
marks casts a modest veil over such a surface. And only
through such a veil which thus falls over it could 'truth'
become truth, profound, indecent, desirable. But should
that veil be suspended, or even fall a bit differently,
there would no longer be any truth, only 'truth'—
written in quotation marks. *Le voile/tombe*' (1979: 59).

Is Emilio's representation of truth with or without quotation marks? 'Perché circondare quell'avventura di
tanti particolari e pensieri strani? Era un'avventura solita
. . .' [Why surround that adventure with so many details and strange thoughts? It was a common adventure
. . . (*S*, 391)]—so Emilio reflects, and, after so doing,
keeps on laying veils over the surface, thereby introducing profundity, indecency, and desire into the
'avventura solita.' In Emilio's case the suspicion arises
that the poet's intent in dropping the veil, however, is
not to create profundity and indecency but rather to
cover it. For him, the *opacity* of the surface is what is
indecent, putting him closer to Hofmannsthal—'Truth *is
hidden* in the surface'—than Nietzsche. The 'simbolo
alto, magnifico' [noble, splendid symbol (*S*, 505)] therefore constitutes the final veil, but a veil which, by hinting at a hidden profundity, creates the truth of the surface. The indifferent surface of Angiolina's face teaches
the secret of the universe, of existence. Tears roll down
her indifferent cheeks as if no veil could piously cover
her indecent *pudendum*. Thus 'truth,' woman's belief in

the superficiality of existence, exposes the poet's truth
at the conclusion of *Senilità,* and as a result *the veil is
suspended between meaning and its negation.* Svevo,
through the representation of Angiolina, transcends the
logic of the enchantress (truth) turned hag (non-truth),
opting for Derrida's third affirming woman, 'a dissimu-
latress, an artist, a dionysiac. And no longer is it man
who affirms her. She affirms herself, in and of herself in
man' (1979: 97).

* * *

While Balli experiences the artifact only as the frozen
embodiment of his idea (his self), Emilio experiences
the shock of the unpredictable life of the other as it escapes, like Galathea, from the marble of a reified imagination. As in Rousseau's *Pygmalion,* the artistic creation epitomizes for Emilio the repetitive vacillation of
character rather than the Bildungsroman's teleology of
selfhood. While in Rousseau's *Pygmalion* the artist creates the woman out of nothing—it is in coming to life
that Galathea questions the artist's subjectivity—in *Senilità,* and despite Emilio's boast of knowing Angiolina
'come se l'avesse fatta lui,' [as if he made her himself
(*S*, 453)], Angiolina and Amalia refuse to revert to the
stillness of the dream, and by so doing they call it into
question. Although Emilio creates out of his fantasy the
woman-tiger, a hybrid figure similar to Pygmalion's
goddess, a *monstrous* concatenation of self and other—
'Aveva sofferto e goduto con essa sentendo a volte vivere anche in sé quell'ibrido miscuglio di tigre e di
donna' [With her, he suffered and loved, and at times he
felt that hybrid mix of tiger and woman living within
his very self (*S*, 430)], the woman, the radical other in
Senilità, pre-exists any such 'figure.' Even the final hybrid of Angiolina and Amalia is but a reflection of Mar-
gherita, Balli's lover, whose face expresses 'vivacità e
sofferenza' [liveliness and pain] an allegory not of mastery but of recognition and desire, the unavoidable and
sought after *complicity* of the subject with its object, of
artist and woman, in the form of an ambiguous symbiosis. The oxymoron is but the expression of a utopian
contamination between self and other, a contamination
called love.

The creative act, which, once played out, reveals the
unavoidable contiguity and promiscuity of self and
other, is not quite accomplished by either Stefano or
Emilio. Emilio's 'simbolo alto e magnifico,' the 'figure,'
the rhetoric within which he has enveloped his dream
throughout the narration, ends up covering, like the
sheet Stefano drapes over the unfinished statue of Angiolina, the unknowable contours of the woman, and,
conversely, the unknowable contours of the self as a
'lenzuolo mortuario' [death shroud]. *Le voile/tombe.*

285

Notes

1. Rousseau, 'Pygmalion,' 1226. See the discussion of this brief 'scène lyrique' in de Man 1979: 160-87.

2. Bárberi Squarotti, 356-65. Squarotti suggests a parallel between Emilio and Pygmalion when he points out how Emilio's fantasy of a 'donna ideale' is achieved by negating the reality of woman.

3. Italo Svevo, *Senilità,* in *Romanzi,* ed. Mario Lavagetto (1993: 335). Hereinafter cited in the text as S; all translations are mine.

4. Cf. *La Coscienza di Zeno.* In a daydream, Zeno changes the features of the woman to lend her the qualities of fine porcelain: 'Un sogno pericoloso perché può conferire nuovo potere alle donne di cui si sognò e che rivedendo alla luce reale conservano qualche cosa delle frutta, dei fiori e della porcellana da cui furono vestite' [A dangerous dream because it can give a new power to the women whom you dreamed about, so that once you see them in the daylight they keep something of the fruit, flowers and porcelain that decorated them (CdZ, 578-9)]. Balli's representation is founded on this very reification of the woman.

5. For discussions of point of view in the novel see Palumbo 1976, Saccone 1977, and Benedetti 1991. Palumbo puts the narrator, the ironic 'coscienza di Svevo,' at a higher level than the character, from which he oversees the reconstitution of meaning through the shifting perspectives of the story. Benedetti agrees with Saccone that 'il predominio del punto di vista di Emilio è innegabile' [the predominance of Emilio's point of view is undeniable (205)], but then proceeds to analyse crucial instances in which the thoughts of Amalia (and Balli) emerge in the story. See Baldi 1998 for a comprehensive analysis of the narrative perspective in the novel.

6. Miceli-Jeffries observes how the figure of the woman can play a double role: 'da una parte opera come oggetto di desiderio, di possesso e di piacere o felicità, e dall'altra come processo di autoidentificazione e di scoperta da parte dei protagonisti' [on the one hand, she functions as an object of desire, possession and pleasure or happiness, and, on the other, as a process of self-identification and discovery (1990: 353)].

7. See Benedetti 1991 for a detailed analysis of all the instances in which Amalia's thoughts are narrated.

8. For a structural analysis of the *incipit* of the novel, see Guglielminetti 1964: 135-7.

9. Correctly, Biasin reads *Senilità* as 'uno studio in forma romanzesca della comunicazione umana, della problematicità della parola' through which unfolds 'la critica serrata di Svevo alle falsità del linguaggio' [a study in novelistic form of human communication, and the problematicity of the word . . . Svevo's stringent critique of the falsities of language (Biasin 1984: 137)].

Bibliography

Works by Italo Svevo

Unless otherwise indicated, the source for Svevo's short works is Bruno Maier, ed., *Opera Omnia,* vol. 3, *Racconti, saggi, pagine sparse* (Milan: dall'Oglio, 1968).

Novels

Senilità [1898]. In *Romanzi,* ed. Nunzia Palmieri. Turin: Einaudi-Gallimard.

La coscienza di Zeno [1923]. In *Romanzi,* ed. Arrigo Stara. Turin: Einaudi-Gallimard.

Unfinished Short Stories

'In Serenella'

Secondary Sources

Baldi, Guido. 1998. *Le maschere dell'inetto: Lettura di 'Senilità.'* Turin: Paravia.

Bárberi Squarotti, Giorgio. 1989. 'La donna ideale: Svevo, D'Annunzio, non senza Leopardi.' *Lettere Italiane* 41 (3): 356-65.

Benedetti, Laura. 1991. 'Vivere ed essere vissuti: Amalia in Svevo's *Senilità.' Italica* 68 (2): 204-16.

Biasin, Gian Paolo. 1984. 'Un *Deo Gratias* qualunque: Svevo, il linguaggio, il sapere.' *Italica* 61 (2): 134-46.

de Man, Paul. 1979. *Allegories of Reading.* New Haven, CT: Yale University Press.

Derrida, Jacques. 1979. *Spurs: Nietzsche's Styles/ Éperons: Les Styles de Nietzsche.* Chicago: University of Chicago Press.

Guglielminetti, Marziano. 1964. *Struttura e sintassi del romanzo italiano del 900.* Milan: Silva.

Johnson, Barbara. 1989. 'Gender Theory and the Yale School.' In *A World of Difference.* Baltimore: Johns Hopkins University Press, 32-41.

Kofman, Sarah. 1985. *The Enigma of Woman.* Ithaca, NY: Cornell University Press.

Lavagetto, Mario. 1993. 'Introduzione' to Italo Svevo, *Romanzi,* ed. Mario Lavagetto. Turin: Einaudi-Gallimard, ix-lxxix.

Miceli-Jeffries, Giovanna. 1990. 'Per una poetica della senilità: la funzione della donna in *Senilità* e *Un amore.*' *Italica* 67 (3): 353-70.

Palumbo, Matteo. 1976. *La coscienza di Svevo.* Naples: Liguori.

Robinson, Paula. 1971. '*Senilitá*: The Secrets of Svevo's Weeping Madonna.' *Italian Quarterly* 55: 61-84.

Rousseau, Jean-Jacques. 1961. 'Pygmalion.' In *Oeuvres complètes,* ed. Bernard Gagnebin and Marcel Raymond. Vol. 1. Paris: Gallimard.

Saccone, Eduardo. 1977. *Il poeta travestito.* Pisa: Pacini.

ABBREVIATIONS

CdZ: La coscienza di Zeno

S: Senilità

Richard Robinson (essay date September 2006)

SOURCE: Robinson, Richard. "From Border to Front: Italo Svevo's *La coscienza di Zeno* and International Space." *Journal of European Studies* 36, no. 3 (September 2006): 243-68.

[*In the following essay, Robinson emphasizes the "linguistic unease" of Svevo's writings and argues that by employing a "deterritorialized vernacular" in such works as* Confessions of Zeno, *the author was ready to promote himself as "a new type of novelist, free from the tyrannical laws and sacred lists of the national canon."*]

INTRODUCTION

Italo Svevo's native Trieste is a paradigmatic border city. A topographical map reveals the city's curious position: a Mediterranean port adjacent to Central Europe, it is on the upper rim of the Balkan peninsula. A series of twentieth-century political maps confirms this confusion of place. The major port of the Austro-Hungarian Empire, Trieste was incorporated into Italy after the First World War; made a Free Territory, which was divided into Italian and Yugoslav zones, after the Second World War; and then passed back to Italy in 1954.

To many contemporary writers, critics and historians, such as Fulvio Tomizza, Claudio Magris, Elizabeth Schächter, Jan Morris, Katia Pizzi and Glenda Sluga, Trieste has invited metaphorical and theoretical disquisitions on its anomalous character. It is, in the words of some of these authors, a 'small compendium of the universe', a 'microcosm', a 'city of contrasts' which resists monolithic identity, a 'problem', a nationless 'nowhere', always marked on the map by hatching

(Tomizza, 2000: 7; Magris, 1997; Tomizza, 2000: 35; Sluga, 2001; Morris, 2001). Katia Pizzi has, in the pages of this journal and in her book *A City in Search of an Author,* pointed to the neurosis and 'constant provisionality' of Triestine identity (Pizzi, 1998: 220; Pizzi, 2001).

It has been commonplace to locate Svevo in the hybrid cultural milieu in which Ettore Schmitz, with Jewish, German, Hungarian and Italian antecedents, could give himself another bilocated pseudonym: Italo Svevo, 'the Italian from Swabia'.[1] In fact Svevo himself, in his 'Profilo autobiografico', felt the need to explain that his name was formed out of a 'crucible which amalgamated heterogeneous elements' ('crogiolo assimilatore degli elementi eterogenei'), and hinted at the possible intellectual and spiritual advantages of being at such a crossroads of ideas and cultures (Svevo, 1968b: 799).

Fulvio Tomizza, an Istrian novelist, has ranked Svevo as a great Central European writer, like Musil, Kafka, Lukács and Andric (Tomizza, 2000: 68). Tomizza claims that all writers from the Italian north-east (Friuli-Venezia Giulia), from Svevo to Claudio Magris, have one foot outside the Italian frontier, whether they like it or not, and begin to write in order to proclaim or discover how different, or even how slight, their Italian identity is (Tomizza, 2000: 99-100). Giuseppe Antonio Camerino has also written on Svevo as a *Mitteleuropäisch* writer, comparing aspects of his work to that of Kafka, for example (Camerino, 1994).

Critics point to how Trieste, alternatively a 'nowhere' or a microcosm of everywhere, has had an inhibiting or liberating effect on the cultural attitudes of its writers. Elizabeth Schächter has defined the paradox. Trieste's élite 'had access . . . to a far richer cultural diet than their counterparts in Italy'; however, though 'one read Freud, Ibsen *et al.* . . . there was also a sense of Trieste as a literary periphery, a cultural backwater without a specific literary identity' (Schächter, 2000: 12, 16). This has led border writers to feel themselves inadequately attached to a national culture but bursting with cosmopolitanism: as under-represented and over-determined. Naomi Lebowitz has written that in Svevo's case 'geographical alienation was an emblematic climate for the homeless, weightless, bourgeois, superfluous man relentlessly portrayed in modern literature as politically useless, socially decadent, and psychologically anxious'; Trieste is here an 'advantage', at least if this crisis-laden modernist *Weltanschauung* can be considered as such (Lebowitz, 1978: 2).

This border strangeness has led to bold claims about the representation of the city in Svevo's fiction. Eugenio Montale, in a lecture given in 1961 on the centenary of Svevo's birth, spoke passionately of the inescapable *triestinità* of his novels. Trieste is the symbolic, non-naturalistic 'personaggio-città' (city as character) of *Una vita*; it breaks into and gives life to the characters of *Sentilità* (Montale, 1985: 128, 132). In *La coscienza* [*La coscienza di Zeno*] Trieste is not a background to the dominating figure of Zeno but 'the tissue, the very warp' ('il tessuto, l'ordito primo') from which he is made, 'so strong that it could be said to produce the characters themselves' ('così forte che si direbbe produttore delle stesse figure') (Montale, 1985: 138). Trieste, with its 'many-spirited life' ('vita multanime'—a coinage) or 'double spirit' ('doppia anima', in Scipio Slataper's phrase) is an intensely European but distinctly singular place. To Montale, the typical Svevian character—hypochondriacal and neurotic but somehow stable, besieged but nonetheless able to muddle through—is inconceivable as anything other than Triestine (Montale, 1985: 138, 142).

More recently, Elvio Guagnini has regarded Trieste as indispensable to a complete understanding of *Una vita,* which moves from documentary naturalism (showing the inability of its hero to adapt to hostile class conditions) to a more symbolic and existential mode. Guagnini states that it would be difficult to conceive of the genesis and development of *Una vita* without the city and all its contradictions (Guagnini, 1994: 171). Elizabeth Schächter also argues that Svevo's native city is both 'physical topography and psychological space' which 'is the very essence of his novels' (Schächter, 2000: 2-3).

Others, however, have been struck by the inconspicuousness of Trieste in Svevo's writing. According to Sergio Pacifici, the Svevian anti-hero looks out on to one of the 'narrowest [landscapes] in modern Italian fiction'; there is no 'feeling of society' or 'of history unfolding' in the novels (Pacifici, 1967: 156). J. M. Coetzee remarks that 'Svevo's writing career stretches over four turbulent decades in Trieste's history, yet strikingly little of this history is reflected, directly or indirectly, in his books' (Coetzee, 2002: 59). These readers might say that although Svevo had wanted James Joyce to write a *Portrait* of Trieste, he failed to do so himself (Joyce, 1966: 335).[2]

Indeed, in the simplest terms Zeno pays only occasional attention to his home space; and the novel's fame is as a comic psychological novel. The 'confessions' are a pastiche of a psychoanalyst's casebook, a catalogue of *lapsi* and parapraxes, condensations and substitutions, phallic symbols, Oedipal triangles, dream sequences, jokes and lies. The introspective anti-hero, with his evasions, repressions and self-justifications, constructs for himself an *inner* life which largely occludes historical and social detail. The first-person narration is a prolonged recollection which turns a conscience and a consciousness, both meanings of which are implied by *coscienza,* from the inside out. The local realist world has receded; states of mind have taken the place of place.

This is not only explained by those classically modernist reasons: what Lukács called the 'bad infinity' of abstract potentialities in consciousness which modernism fetishistically recorded, or the privileging of time (the Bergsonian-Proustian *durée*) over notions of fixed external spaces (Lukács, 1963: 24). For the Triestine, or more broadly the Central European, the sense of dislocation—being out of place—can lead to a neurotic obsession to write, as an internal exile, about one's deracinated identity. But for Svevo, I would argue, it connected to a certain unwillingness or lack of confidence in creating a setting securely embedded in national space. What is missing is the confident realist particularism of Balzac's Paris or Dickens' London. Montale's claim for the Triestinity of the novels is, in fact, based on this idea that the city appears as an indeterminate image or symbol of place—there is no mimetic reflection of city space: the Triestine writer is 'not connected to a folklore . . . or to a local colour, rather to the image of a city like no other in Italy' ('[non] legato a un folclore . . . o a un color locale, bensì all'immagine di una città che in Italia non somiglia a nessun'altra') (Montale, 1985: 120-1).

This essay elaborates how this fictive image of space, and of what Istrians call the citizenship of the *apolidi* (people without polity or nation), can be understood through the figure of the border (Bettiza, 1999). I concentrate on two manifestations of border space. The first, by considering the dialect of *triestino* (what a Joyce biographer recently called a 'living encyclopaedia of cultures, nations and languages'), conceives of space-in-language (McCourt, 2000: 52). *La coscienza* reveals the asymmetry of Triestine and Italian identity in the gap between local dialect and national language. Like his author, Zeno is problematically caught between speaking his Triestine mother tongue and writing in the distant form of Italian. This supposedly 'regional' *triestinità* is finally seen to be central to the complex and destabilized epistemology of the novel. In the final chapter, Zeno is stranded on the Austro-Italian border on the day war breaks out between these combatant nations. This episode is not an external adjunct to the novel's interiority, an eleventh-hour shift to the realist mode. As he negotiates the military cordon, Zeno—a victim of the Central European atopia where national teleologies disappear into blank space—is increasingly representative of the floating, 'extraterritorial' modernist subject (Steiner, 1972).

WOODEN WORDS: TUSCAN AND TRIESTINE

We are made quietly aware of the Triestine dialect during the course of the novel. Zeno points out, for example, that the nurse in the sanatorium is a 'pure' dialect speaker; and that Carla's broad vowels lend a certain foreignness to the way she talks—she is more adept at local love songs, transcribed with their strange-looking collection of x's and z's ('Fazzo l'amor xe vero, Cossa ghe xe de mal' (Svevo, 1988: 222)), than with the masterpieces of Italian opera.

Though a member of the commercial upper-middle class, Zeno is nevertheless a dialect speaker, though he can gingerly venture into standard Italian. For example, hurrying to the *Tergesteo* in order to meet his prospective father-in-law, Zeno intends to ask for Ada's hand in marriage, but rather than worrying whether he will be accepted or not, he occupies himself solely with the choice of asking the all-important question in *lingua* or in *dialetto*. He can switch between the two, but the co-existence of a stern 'big' language and a more natural 'little' dialect creates inhibiting social dilemmas, even amongst Triestines of the same class.

Zeno's first meeting with Guido Speier—his rival in love, partner in business and inimical friend—is dramatized (in the presence of Ada) as a type of competition in *echt* Italian-ness. Zeno asks Speier (who has just arrived in Trieste) if he is German, to which Speier replies that, although his name might suggest this, documents show that his family had been Italian for centuries ([*Zeno's Conscience*] Svevo, 2001: 109; Svevo, 1988: 101).[3] Speier talks Tuscan fluently; he has been 'rinsed in the Arno'—that is in the national language modelled on the Tuscan dialect, and adopted in the mid to late nineteenth century by the new nation state (Moloney, 1977: 4).[4] In the familiar role of the grumbling provincial, Zeno laments that he is not a 'good' Italian; he is condemned—at least it is with Ada—to the Triestine *dialettaccio* (the pejorative suffix suggesting coarseness and dissonance). It is strikingly illogical, and wholly in keeping with the lapses and impulses of Zeno's conversational outbursts, that he should choose to attack Speier for being German—i.e. an alien trespassing on Italian soil—on the very grounds of which, as a dialect speaker uncomfortable with Italian, he is uncertain himself.

From the point of view of linguistic space, there is a further irony. Zeno repeatedly refers to *toscano* as synonymous with *italiano,* drawing attention to the very regionality of the national standard language. The historical disposition of space had, over the centuries, placed one language at the core, and the other at the periphery: Tuscany now stands for Italy. But as Samuel Beckett pointed out in his essay on *Finnegans Wake,* the *toscano* written by the Florentine Dante—in his attempt to resist Latin and pave the way for a communal language of state—was itself an ideal, synthetic language, which had imported elements from the other dialects of the peninsula (Beckett, 1961: 17-18).[5] Zeno feels inferior because of what he perceives is an easy commerce between a core language and the nation, but in fact no such territorial relationship had existed.

The most central irony, of course, is that Zeno tells us about his *dialettaccio* in written Italian. It is within this unnatural medium that he has to attack the doctor for his failure to understand that the dialect speaker, when forced to translate himself into the national language, will involuntarily distort and mislead. Zeno makes the following complaint:

> The doctor puts too much faith also in these damned confessions of mine, which he won't return to me so I can revise them. Good heavens! He studied only medicine, and therefore doesn't know what it means to write in Italian for those of us who speak in dialect and can't write it. A confession in writing is always a lie. With our every Tuscan word, we lie! If he knew how, by predilection, we recount all the things for which we have the words at hand, and how we avoid those things that would oblige us to turn to the dictionary! This is exactly how we choose, from our life, the episodes to underline. Obviously our life would have an entirely different aspect if it were told in dialect.
>
> (Svevo, 2001: 404)

> (Il dottore presta una fede troppo grande anche a quelle mie benedette confessioni che non vuole restituirmi perché le riveda. Dio mio! Egli non studiò che la medicina e perciò ignora che cosa significhi scrivere in italiano per noi che parliamo e non sappiamo scrivere il dialetto. Con ogni nostra parola toscana noi mentiamo! Se egli sapesse come raccontiamo con predilezione tutte le cose per le quali abbiamo pronta la frase e come evitiamo quelle che ci obbligherebbero di ricorrere al vocabolario! È proprio così che scegliamo dalla nostra vita gli episodi da notarsi. Si capisce come la nostra vita avrebbe tutt'altro aspetto se fosse detta nel nostro dialetto.)
>
> (Svevo, 1988: 381-2)

The narrator here purports to explain why *La coscienza* is not more Triestine. How can Zeno compose a portrait of his Triestine self when he cannot *write* in *triestino*? It is a question which relates to Svevo's narrowness of landscape, the relatively silent local space in his novels. Zeno tells us that he is compelled to write a more generalized account of his life, using or misusing terms which his doctor can then frustratingly match to his preformulated Oedipal mould. Zeno must include material which the foreign-familiar *lingua* expects of him, or omit that which it cannot accommodate. He thus writes not as he speaks—as a subject of the borderland between the Germanic, Latin and Slav worlds—but in the limited palette of usable *italianità*. The entirely different or 'other' appearance (*tutt'altro aspetto*) of the Triestine is unrepresented.

True to his anti-Freudian Freudianism, Zeno turns his anxiety into another suppression, a joke. Zeno repeats that 'a confession made by me in Italian could be neither complete nor sincere' (Svevo, 1988: 414) ('una confessione fatta da me in italiano non poteva essere né completa né sincera' (Svevo, 2001: 391)), and illustrates this with a particular example of an omitted confession—which, significantly, is a kind of paradox. The doctor, who wants to prove that Zeno's hatred of Guido Speier remained profound and undimmed, gleefully pins a great deal of significance on the fact that Zeno had never mentioned Speier's huge timber yard, a seeming proof that he had been commercially successful at some point in his career. The explanation, Zeno would have us believe, is rather less psychological than linguistic:

> In a lumberyard there are enormous varieties of lumber, which we in Trieste call by barbarous names derived from the dialect, from Croat, from German, and sometimes even from French (*zapin,* for example, which is by no means the equivalent of *sapin*). Who could have given me the appropriate vocabulary? Old as I am, should I have found myself a job with a lumber dealer from Tuscany?
>
> (Svevo, 2001: 414)

> (In un deposito di legnami ci sono varietà enormi di qualità che noi a Trieste appelliamo con termini barbari presi dal dialetto, dal croato, dal tedesco e qualche volta persino dal francese (*zapin* p.e. e non equivale mica a *sapin*). Chi m'avrebbe fornito il vero vocabolario? Vecchio come sono avrei dovuto prendere un impiego da un commerciante in legnami toscano?)
>
> (Svevo, 1988: 391)

Zeno does not confess to the existence of Speier's timber yard because he does not have the Italian vocabulary. It is a mimetic crisis, however comic: he cannot match the word to the wood, nor the wood to the word. He is stranded between two places: in declining to work for a Tuscan timber merchant, he also fails to fashion himself as a true 'barbarian' of Trieste.

Is Zeno, always seeking to excuse his own mendacity in the hope of escaping the charges that will be brought against him by his doctor, speaking (that is, writing) in bad faith? Brian Moloney, who emphasizes the complete unreliability of the narrator, believes that Zeno misleadingly adduces linguistic rather than psychological reasons in order to throw the reader off track, and to discredit the manuscript as a psychoanalytical document (Moloney, 1972: 313; Moloney, 1998: 85). Moloney wryly observes that Zeno continues to write in the same language in which he wrote the other chapters: 'Non continua a scrivere nella stessa lingua in cui ha scritto gli altri capitoli?' (Moloney, 1998: 89). How can Zeno's implication, that he is now using a meta-language which circumscribes all that has come before, be sustainable? Naomi Lebowitz points out that the inevitability of the lie in written confessions has a long tradition (she cites Montaigne and Heine); the plea is thus 'conventional and unconvincing', a 'ridiculous ascription of cause' (Lebowitz, 1978: 125). Lebowitz feels that we surely should not be taken in by such a literal rationalization.

I would first argue that though Zeno's is a special pleading, it is demonstrably close to Svevo's own statements about his Triestinity. What is often unambiguously seen as authorial irony at the narrator's most brazen self-justification, is not as detached as it may seem. This passage from the **'Profilo autobiografico',** for example, aligns Svevo with Zeno:

> [Svevo] was well aware that his language could not be embellished with words he did not feel. One can tell a story effectively only in a living language, and his living language could only be Triestine, which did not need to wait until 1918 to be felt as Italian.
>
> (Moloney, 1974: 111)

> (D'altronde [Svevo] ben sapeva che la sua lingua non poteva adornarsi di parole ch'egli non sentiva. Non si può raccontare efficacemente che in una lingua viva e la sua lingua viva non poteva essere altra che la loquela triestina, la quale non ebbe bisogno di attendere il 1918 per essere sentita italiana.
>
> (Svevo, 1968b: 806)

There was both a feeling of inferiority and of scornful pride in Svevo's perception of his own defective prose. He was unable to efface his Triestine self in the practice of writing 'pure' Italian. Domenico Cerneca and Serge Vanvolsem, amongst others, have pointed out some of the marks of Triestine dialect: the German grammatical influence of *zu* on the Italian use of *di*; the use of a Triestine lexicon of non-standard locutions or of archaisms; the mistaken use of the subjunctive (Cerneca, 1972; Vanvolsem, 1994).[6] The end result was, according to P. N. Furbank, 'a kind of "business" Italian, almost an esperanto—a bastard and graceless language totally without poetry or resonance' (Furbank, 1966: 172).

Svevo was famously mistrustful of what he thought of as ornate writing. For example, his resistance to D'Annunzio—contrary to Joyce's reverence for the poet—was not only based on his wish to undermine the Italian's veneration of the Nietzschean Superman, but also on linguistic grounds, as the following biographical episode reminds us:

> [Svevo] challenged Joyce to find any page by D'Annunzio which did not contain at least one meaningless sentence and, opening one of the Pescarese writer's books at random, read the following passage: 'The smile which pullulated inextinguishably, spreading among the pallid meanders of Burano lace . . .'
>
> (Gatt-Rutter, 1988: 231)[7]

The aesthetic glories of Italian language enjoyed by his contemporaries—adepts of the canon, linguistic virtuosi—were unavailable to Svevo, who thus struck an attitude of verbal utilitarianism. Unlike Joyce, he could get on with writing about the complexities of human consciousness without worrying too much about the words.

Zeno's self-justification is built into the novel as a pre-emptive defence, an authorial manoeuvre which anticipates the Italian charges of anti-literariness that surely enough would continue to be levelled against Svevo. The self-exculpatory plea may be in the spirit of his *Witze* (or witticisms—the substantial timber yard that vanishes into thin air) and is certainly not free from irony. But here J. M. Coetzee can venture to say that Zeno is speaking 'from the heart' (Coetzee, 2002: 59). At such moments Svevo-Zeno, unable to transcribe an inner voice, seems to some to be genuinely dislocated by the irreconcilability of written *lingua* and spoken *dialetto*. The author is caught in the same bind as the narrator: how can I write a *good* book about Trieste (and my Triestine self) in Italian, a distant written form with which I am uncomfortable? And, obversely, how can I write a book about Trieste (and my Triestine self) in *good* Italian?

Elizabeth Schächter's analysis of the focalization and diegetic levels of *La coscienza* (the relationship between the older narrating and younger narrated self, how the truth claims of the narrative are affected by the in-built readerly position of Dr S., the psychoanalyst) recognizes how Zeno exploits his sense of linguistic deficiency (Schächter, 2000: 132). However, she concludes: 'The reader's task of unravelling the truth from the falsehoods is made more difficult by Zeno's apparent linguistic inadequacies, but all we have are Zeno's words on which every hypothesis and interpretive act seem to founder and collapse'. Or, in the words of M. Lavagetto which she then quotes, 'the reader is forced to surrender any illusion of truth . . . is a prisoner of (a fictional) pretence which reveals itself as such': 'il lettore è costretto a dimettere ogni illusione di verifica . . . si trova prigionero di una finzione che si denuncia come tale' (Schächter, 2000: 133). Thus, even if we should continue to emphasize the complete unreliability of Zeno's narration, the dialect question remains inseparable from the epistemological status of the novel as a whole.

Whether Zeno's dialect plea is the author's prime motive for the paradoxical mode of telling with truthful mendacity, or an egregious example of untrustworthy narration, is a circular question; it is a Möbius strip, a Cretan Liar paradox, a Catch-22.[8] The excluded dialect-speaking author creates an unreliable narrator; the narrator tells us, unreliably, that his confessions cannot be believed because he is an excluded dialect speaker. If we believe Zeno's claim that he lies with every Tuscan word, then that claim is false: he is speaking true (but still in standard Italian). The aporia in which the novel fails to ratify itself is, in Derridean terms, the classic Western anxiety of logocentrism: Zeno's/Svevo's writing is merely supplementary to his speaking, a distorting shadow of what is felt to be an original spoken meaning.

Zeno affords a new conspicuousness, even if some take it to be spurious, to the Triestine periphery. His border language cannot be dismissed as the latter component of a binary between 'internal' formalist-narratological and an 'external' territorial-linguistic problematic. In this novel the political space between dialect and language proves to be a hermeneutic gap in which the narrative deconstructs itself.

ZENO IN NO MAN'S LAND

The narrative of **La coscienza,** then, is built on paradox. This connects to a point often made: that Zeno's name is designed to recall that of the paralogician, Zeno of Elea (Wilden, 1969: 106; Weiss, 1987: 71; Gatt-Rutter, 1988: 315).[9] The Eleatic space-time continuum is infinitely divisible; the world is stasis rather than universe. Thus the fleet Achilles can never catch the tortoise: he is a moving object condemned to constant pursuit, moving through the eternal intermediate gradations of space but never reaching his final destination (Borges, 1970: 237).[10] Temporally, the point at which the arrow leaves the bow (now!) is always before or after that moment: it may be wound to the bow-string, or it may be in the state of flight, but it is always, at a given time, at rest.

These paradoxes relate to Zeno's compulsive resolution-making—most famously to give up cigarettes, but also to leave his mistress Carla. Zeno nominates a last cigarette, a last time with Carla, and these final moments—which convince him of his worthy and refashioned self—are so sweet that he continually repeats the cycle. Fearful of the unknown thereafter, Zeno is trapped in his desire for the ultimate rather than the terminal. As Beno Weiss has said, this is connected to Zeno's procrastination and inability to finish things (his law or chemistry degree, his course of psychoanalysis), and to his obsession with calendrical dates, which allow him to count and divide the *durée* of time in order to decelerate it (Weiss, 1987: 57-8). This is typical of Zeno's non-linear, pre-Socratic philosophy of the world.

Zeno's relationship with his father was largely inert while the latter was alive; conducted posthumously, it is open-ended, restless, and torturously unfinished. Zeno, of the last initial letter, is the Omega seeking an Alpha-wife—neither Ada nor Alberta but Augusta. His tall stories were designed to conquer the first 'A', but as he says, he was like the marksman who hit the bullseye, but that of the target next door (Svevo, 2001: 83; Svevo, 1988: 78). In a caricature of the Freudian *lapsus,* Zeno famously goes to the wrong funeral, not that of his 'friend' Guido: this is another of Zeno's missed destinations and also an example, in psychotherapeutic jargon, of his failure to achieve closure with his suicide brother-in-law.

In his determination not to reach his destination, Zeno Cosini is thus like his Eleatic namesake. However, what has been missed by critics is that the psychological spaces of the novel eventually incorporate Zeno's movements on the international border as well. The Triestine frontier irrupts into the secure interiority of the novel as space becomes, in Lebowitz's words, an 'obsessive term in the last part of the novel' (Lebowitz, 1978: 26). She is referring to the way the last section famously opens out on to the cosmos. But Zeno's journey outside of Trieste during the onset of war is an important middle term: the space between warlike nations broadens the interpersonal animosities—hitherto confined to the drawing rooms, bedrooms and offices of the city—that have characterized the novel. The outbreak of war between Italy and Austria is not a mere contingency to seal up the period of Zeno's comfortable Habsburg life, but adds to the established Svevian pattern of illogic and absurdity.

Brian Moloney, in his chapter on *La coscienza* as a type of war novel, has challenged this idea that the last part of the novel merely uses the war, otherwise conspicuous by its absence, as a structural device to separate Zeno from his hostile personal relationships. Rather, he argues for its primary importance, proposing that it was the war that inspired Svevo to write the novel, and that the last chapter fully reveals the ontological meaning of the preceding chapters: 'io avanzo l'ipotesi che sia stata la guerra a ispirare a Svevo il romanzo, e che l'ultimo capitolo riveli pienamente il significato ontologico dei capitoli precedenti' (Moloney: 1998: 99). I would also like to concentrate on these final, dated pages of Zeno's writings by relating this ontological readjustment to the way Trieste's peacetime border is shown to be metamorphosing into a wartime front.

Zeno's penultimate diary entry, dated 26 June, tells the story of how, a month before, war had caught up with him. Zeno has just discovered that his family is safe and sound in Turin, and thus feels able to recount the story in his diary. He compares himself to a man living calmly in a building whose ground floor had caught fire; he is now stranded in his home town (Svevo, 1988: 399-400; Svevo, 2001: 423). The war previously seemed to be happening in another time and in another place, but time (the day war broke out) and place (the Austro-Italian border) converged upon him. He stumbled into the midst of war—or it stumbled into him. 'The war has overtaken me', 'the war and I met' (Svevo, 2001: 423-4) ('La guerra m'ha raggiunto!'; 'la guerra ed io ci siamo incontrati' (Svevo, 1988: 399-400)): this peculiar grammatical agency is explained by the strange reversal which, instead of sending Zeno to the front, sends the front to him.[11]

He acknowledges that events unfolded in a way which was both a little violent and a little comical. On 23 May, the day on which unbeknownst to him war between Italy and Austria was officially declared, he is staying with his family in his villa in Lucinico, a village near what is now the border town of Italian Gorizia—Slovenian Nova Gorica. Along with a dose of Carlsbad salts he must also take a two-hour morning walk, an obligation of his cure, the reward for which will be a coffee when he returns home. Zeno is given a reason for his constitutional—namely to find his daughter some roses—which pleases him: he ominously has a destination and a purpose.

Having met a peasant neighbour and reassured him that his potato field will not become a theatre of war (which it did), Zeno then comes across a troop of soldiers. The scene of his encounter with the Austro-Hungarian army, rag-tag and polyglot, gives a brief glimpse of the way a formerly unified political space (the Habsburg Empire) is in the process of dissolving into mutual bafflement and incompatibility. This is the beginning and not the end of war, but the soldiers are in some disarray—aging, shabbily dressed, malodorous (they reek of game), and equipped with weaponry (such as the Durlindana bayonet) more suited to the nineteenth than to the twentieth century.

In an echo of Zeno's own dialectal dilemmas, the German lingua franca is shown to be comically inadequate in such a disparate multinational army. The sentinel who stops him on the corner of the road shouts '*Zurück!*', but this is the only word of German he knows. Zeno repeats the word and retreats. When he comes across the same platoon on the top of the hill, he is at least able to conduct a conversation in German with the commanding officer, who is nevertheless not a native speaker (otherwise it would not be notable that he could speak German properly (Svevo, 1988: 405; Svevo, 2001: 428)). This time Zeno is disadvantaged by his own relative lack of fluent German.

He is watched by the other soldiers, *cinque mammelucchi* or five 'Mamelukes' (Svevo, 1988: 405; Svevo, 2001: 428), interestingly rendered in an earlier translation as 'five Czech soldiers', though this national designation is not made directly in the Italian ([*Confessions of Zeno*] Svevo, 1989: 407). It is clearly a broad pejorative, signifying Zeno's haughty contempt of the soldiers, but also has a historical relevance to the Mamelukes themselves, Circassian slaves who became military rulers in Egypt and Syria from the thirteenth century.[12] The offensive term hints at the way Slav peoples from all corners of the Austro-Hungarian Empire had been drafted into the army and, in a classic imperialist strategy, ended up by defending and expanding the hegemony of those who had originally subjugated them.

Zeno is finally insulted by the officer in German and escorted down the hill by a Slav corporal who does his duty by shouting '*Marsch!*' and acting sternly while still in sight of the other soldiers. But Zeno tells us that the corporal 'spoke rather decent Italian' (Svevo, 2001: 430) ('parlava discretamente l'italiano' (Svevo, 1988: 406)), and that he reverted to this more natural though still foreign tongue when out of sight of his superior. Zeno is thus prevented from drinking his coffee, but still politely inquires whether it would be possible to cross the military frontier for his hat and coat.

This episode is indeed 'un poco buffo'; Svevo used to entertain friends by putting on an act as a conscript of Franz Josef's army (Gatt-Rutter, 1988: 337). Furbank has emphasized how the wildly farcical tone of the last chapter returns to the first comical section with Zeno in the sanatorium, voluntarily imprisoning himself and then escaping from this wretchedly smoke-free zone (Furbank, 1966: 202). The disintegration of the ramshackle Empire's army is probably best captured in Jaroslav Hasek's subversive comic novel *The Good Soldier Svejk,* directly contemporary to Svevo's. The scene is a miniature of the collapse of the motley Austro-Hungarian army and its patchwork empire. Technically, the little group on the hill, including Zeno, are all subjects of the same state—a sovereignty of the absurd whose failure of language signals the imminent failure of state.

But part of the burlesque of this last section is the unexpected threat of violence—Zeno is after all held at gunpoint, and will be cut off from his family. War will have a particular type of tragic outcome for the border citizen. Svevo described elsewhere the meeting on a tram—likewise, on the day that war was declared—between an Italian mother, whose son was to fight for Italy, and the wife of an Austrian officer. Each recognizes the anguish of the other; they almost but do not quite embrace one another: 'neither of them dared—it would have been a protest against the war' ('Nessuna delle due osò. Sarebbe stata una manifestazione contro la guerra'). As Moloney suggests, Svevo opposed 'the mystical and untruthful rhetoric of patriotism' ('la mistica e la falsa retorica del pattriottismo'): the women stop short of uniting themselves in grief at the prospect of heroic (male) sacrifice (Moloney, 1998: 101). But there is a particular sharpness to the *Triestines* not daring to embrace—it would reassert, in wartime, a supranational civic autonomy. Zeno notes of his employees that they 'have all gone off to fight on this side or that' (Svevo, 2001: 423) ('sono andati a battersi di qua o di là' (Svevo, 1988: 400)). The border city is now internally riven along national lines, and war will initiate, in certain cases, a type of localized fratricide typical of Central and Eastern European history.

On the train from Gorizia to Trieste Zeno has a view of the 'Sassonia di Trieste', a mild green area of the Karst particularly picturesque in May. As the train stops to let eight or nine others head towards Italy, he thinks of the border as splitting open:

> The gangrenous wound (as the Italian front was immediately called in Austria) had opened and needed material to nourish its purulence. And the poor men went there, snickering and singing. From all those trains came the same sounds of joy or drunknenness.
>
> (Svevo, 2001: 433)
>
> (La piaga cancrenosa (come in Austria si appellò subito la fronte italiana) s'era aperta e abbisognava di materiale per nutrire la sua purulenza. E i poveri uomini vi andavano sghignazzando e cantando. Da tutti quei treni uscivano i medesimi suoni di gioia e di ebbrezza.)
>
> (Svevo, 1988: 409)

Zeno adds the metaphor of the border to his lexicon of ailments: the front is a physical wound, a purulent infection which—in the expected paradox—does not require disinfection but rather the nourishment of trainloads of soldiers on a one-way journey. The pathos of the high-spirited generation of 1914 (here 1915) derives from a later disillusionment—Svevo's knowledge that the north-east of Italy, quite narrow in comparison with the Western Front, nonetheless sucked in and decimated huge numbers of soldiers on both sides. The battle lines drawn up on the day of Zeno's walk, on either side of the Isonzo, remained fatally stable until the Caporetto retreat of 1917, and the subsequent collapse of the Austro-Hungarian Empire. (This is the same territory in which Hemingway sets *A Farewell to Arms*: the most bravura passage describes Fredric Henry's participation in the retreat—a scar on the collective Italian memory.)

The shock of this wartime section in *La coscienza* depends on a preceding lack of portentousness: the novel finally reveals that it has no need to plant signposts to the bloody losses of the Isonzo, Caporetto and the Piave precisely because it is sited there. This gives a spatial inflection to Moloney's argument that in Svevo's view war was not 'other' or elsewhere, but rather a natural and paradigmatic continuation of the human condition (Moloney, 1998: 103).

By superimposing Zeno's route upon the co-ordinates of the battle lines established on the same day, we note that it is a circle which does not quite close—another missed destination. Zeno walks eastwards from Lucinico, crossing the Isonzo to the Gorizian side. He then walks back towards Lucinico, to a point at which he can see his villa again, but finds himself behind a troop of soldiers. He is stopped there by a sentinel, but still intent on his coffee climbs the neighbouring hill next to the road, only to come across other members of the regiment. He is marched back away from Lucinico and ends up going to Gorizia where he fails to make telephone contact with his family at the villa. He is advised more than once that the quickest way to Lucinico from Gorizia is now via Trieste, a geographical nonsense, but nevertheless he takes a train to the city. The small village of Lucinico 'becomes' Italian, and Gorizia (or in

German, Görz: a couple of miles away but an important defensive position) remains Austrian. For the duration of the war Zeno's wife and children find themselves in Italy, and Zeno, trapped in his own backyard, in Austria.

In the retelling of the story we are aware of exponentiality—how an irritant to Zeno's daily routine becomes a cause for concern, a threat, an emergency, and then a final rupture. Furbank has noticed that in this final chapter the 'pace accelerates and becomes staccato as we return from Zeno's inner life to his antics in the face of present circumstances'; and that '[t]ransition huddles on transition'. This adds 'a further Chinese box effect' to the narrative framing (Furbank, 1966: 202-3).

It also helps to visualize the spatial amplification of the chapter, which is consistent with Zeno Cosini's Eleatic paradoxes: his walk around and across the border is a final geo-political fable to add to the paralogician's list. It is certainly a comic episode, and reminds us that the philosophical paradoxes are themselves playful. Zeno sets off from a starting-point knowing that his point of return was easily accessible. But although within sight of his own house, he is tantalizingly unable to get there, ultimately failing to join Z(eno) to L(ucinico). He himself recognizes the absurdity of being told that the best way to get from Gorizia to Lucinico is via Trieste: motion through Julian space becomes stasis. He is also stuck in time before and after, one moment enjoying a holiday walk in May, the next witnessing the fires of Trieste, unaware of the absolute moment of the outbreak of war (which takes place while he is on a train—i.e. in transitional space).

This emphasis on the anti-empirical, surreal potentiality of the novel's representation of its international space does not imply that the border was necessarily an apolitical figure to Svevo. For example, in his essay on peace and war, **'Sulla teoria della pace',** together with the draft fragments 'Pace e guerra' and 'Sulla guerra', Svevo argues in favour of Italy's participation in the newly formed League of Nations, and proposes that borders should be weakened or opened (Svevo, 1968a). State-enforced borders prohibit free economic exchange and healthy competition. According to Svevo, the disposition of private property—based on unfettered competition between individuals—is better regulated than the brute power which the state applies to territory and which inevitably leads to the collision of borders and to war.

The conservative, free market economic model that Svevo advances in this essay—more as the businessman Schmitz than the writer Svevo—modulates into a more utopian cosmopolitanism. Some territorial possessions should be sacrificed by nations in the interests of humanity. Svevo proposes quixotic experiments with open borders; frontiers should be reduced to the extent that they are simple signs which warn the newcomer that certain laws apply and should be complied with, like the Swiss cantons or the interstate borders of the USA (Svevo, 1968a: 653). Peace treaties, including the contemporary Paris Conference, are criticized for quibbling and getting bogged down by border questions whenever they can: they ratify the idea of the border as a point beyond which one cannot pass, like a brick wall. In the broader, non-economic sense, the border impedes life as well as capital (Svevo, 1968a: 660-1).

Svevo wrote 'Sulla teoria della pace' in 1919, when he began *La coscienza.* Read alongside one another, it can be seen that it is precisely because the border is a problematic political site—pressured by competing *polities*—that it becomes invitingly symbolic and overdetermined in narrative too. It also perhaps strengthens the idea that the border and the war were inevitably associated in Svevo's mind and work: if *La coscienza* is to be regarded as a type of war novel, as Brian Moloney proposes, the fact that it is eventually drawn to the theatre of the front gains in significance.

In his final diary entry, written in March 1916, nine months after the border adventure, Zeno reports his own health but the illness of mankind. For the first time, he feels himself free of hypochondria and is defiantly dismissive of the use of psychoanalytical therapy—the barb is aimed at his first reader, Dr S. The jolting tonal shift in the final pages of *La coscienza* has been compared to the ending of Thomas Mann's *Der Zauberberg* (1924), as both interns of the sanatorium are forced to break away from the seclusion of their illness (Furst, 1968; Moloney, 1998).[13] Both books are conceived on a relative scale of sickness and health, and have ordinary heroes who—unlike other fatally ill characters—manage to escape their confinement when war begins. As a terminal epidemic breaks out across Europe, Hans Castorp and Zeno Cosini find that they are rid of their phantom diseases. The novels are both pessimistically open-ended, and their survivors, strange Darwinian creatures indeed, are hardly to be regarded as 'safe' (Furst, 1968: 499). Castorp marches off to the murderous front, while Zeno's unreliable narration of his present 'recovery' and future health is purely conjectural—as differing interpretations of this final section, and the subsequent fragment 'Le confessioni del vegliardo' (which relates Zeno's post-war resumption of his 'conscience' and neuroses), make clear (Weiss, 1987: 91; Moloney, 1977: 16-17).[14] Perhaps most importantly, as Moloney has convincingly argued, Zeno's health is a dangerous, self-deceptive sickness: 'his conscience was cauterized by the war . . . Zeno surrounds himself with a misty, imaginary harmony' ('la sua coscienza è stata cauterizzata dalla guerra . . . Zeno si circonda di una nebbia di armonia immaginaria' (Moloney, 1998: 108)).

Zeno's final vision is of a dystopia in which machines rule, disease proliferates, and mankind kills itself. This anticipates the atomic and nuclear ages, and acutely understands—prophetically or not—that it will be the psychologically sick or weak who will be dangerously empowered by the new weaponry. However, the contemporary impact of these closing lines should not be understated: the 'ordigni', the high-technology weapons, are already laying hundreds of thousands to waste.

Zeno chokes like a Malthusian at the thought of abundant man filling up the spaces of the earth, occupying every square yard: 'Who will cure us of the lack of air and space?' (Svevo, 2001: 436) ('Chi ci guarirà dalla mancanza di aria e di spazio?' (Svevo, 1988: 412)). There is a desperate social Darwinist plea—Svevo had read Herbert Spencer—that machines, in making obsolete the survival of the fittest, have fatally damaged the law of natural selection (Svevo, 2001: 436): 'Ed è l'ordigno che crea la malattia con l'abbandono della legge che fu su tutta la terra la creatrice. La legge del più forte sparì e perdemmo la selezione salutare' (Svevo, 1988: 413). The envisaging of a silent explosion with which the novel ends, and with it the return to a nebulous world ('terra nebulosa') without mankind and without disease, has a certain ideological ambiguity. Furbank feels—again returning to the problem of whether the narrator ever speaks 'from the heart'—that this is the moment in which Zeno's voice modulates into that of the author (Furbank, 1966: 176). Moloney, on the other hand, emphasizes that the appeal of apocalypse as a *pharmakon* is being heavily ironized ('L'apocalisse di Zeno: altro che *pharmakon*' (Moloney, 1998: 111)). While Svevo's general pacifism would certainly not allow for anything curative in the poison of war, it should be noted that Zeno's hope for a new world purged and purified, the technophobic longing for a more natural world, together with alarm at the growth of the masses, were nonetheless symptomatic of certain extreme but not so uncommon feelings of modernist alienation, as John Carey has illustrated (Carey, 1992).

When, after a long period of discouraged silence, Svevo came to write *La coscienza,* it was not in a contemporary but in a historical, even nostalgic, mode. Trieste had been delivered from Italy to Austria (former members of the Triple Alliance), but at a cost: the First World War. Thus, *La coscienza* counterbalances what had become a suddenly anachronistic Habsburg world with the horrors of Caporetto, the neuroses of the *mal du siècle* with a vision of the abyssal modern. There is a sense, then—not to be confused with Svevo's irredentist happiness at Trieste becoming Italian—that there has been a dangerous shift from a border-less to a bordered world. Svevo may not quite be like Joseph Roth, the great elegist of vanished supranational Habsburg space—a Jewish Austro-Slav outsider, another kind of *apolide,* whose nostalgia was increasingly conditioned

by the Nazi threat. The association might remind us, however, that *La coscienza* can be read not just as a war novel or a post-war novel but as anticipating the later 1930s spirit of the *entre deux guerres.*

The supervention of the border into Zeno's consciousness at a local Triestine level pinpoints the schism between the world's nations that is about to be enacted. The novel does not leap quite as violently as it may seem from an individual's introspective urban life to his cosmic projections. The contested international border is the mediate term of a *spatial* modulation—into a world suffocated by its lack of open spaces (by proliferating mankind, and thus warring nations), and thence to that of a 'terra nebulosa'. Zeno echoes his philosopher-namesake in conceiving of mankind's infinite 'progress' in empty space, and in prophesying a destruction of linear time.

By lifting place out of the text, we are not led outwards to reified naturalist settings but further inwards to metaphor and form. As Franco Moretti has said, 'near the border *figurality rises*: spaces and tropes are entwined; rhetoric is dependent on space' (Moretti, 1998: 43). *La coscienza*'s border is suddenly put centre stage, where it reveals itself not as incidental local colouring but as a territorialized conundrum, a trope of space. The final Eleatic paradox of the novel, a comic meeting of diachronic and synchronic states, occurs when the decelerating subject is stranded between Italy and Austria: bourgeois Western man in no man's land. Svevo intentionally interposes his home border between Zeno and his destination, thereby drawing the suppressed locus of the novel into its map of psychological and philosophical co-ordinates.

BORDER MODERNISM: THE LANGUAGE OF MISTRUST

As the text foresaw, *La coscienza,* by 'lying with its every Tuscan word', did indeed manifest its Triestine identity in its own chill reception: what Svevo himself called 'an utter lack of understanding and a glacial silence' ('un'incomprensione assoluta ed un silenzio glaciale') (Svevo, 1968b: 809). Readers elsewhere in Italy thought the book foreign and unpatriotic; Triestines felt that it treacherously misrepresented the city (perhaps in not representing it at all). Bruno Maier powerfully expressed this contemporary rejection:

> The 'barbarian' Triestine, the Italo-German writer who betrayed his hybrid origins in his very pseudonym, could not, with his unpleasant, clumsy jargon, full of Germanic traces and of dialect remnants, bristling with ungrammatical constructions and with incorrect vocabulary and syntax, be admitted to the noble castle of Italian literary tradition.
>
> (Il barbaro triestino, lo scrittore italo-tedesco che sin nello pseudonimo adattato tradiva la sua ibrida origine, con quel suo gergo ingrato e rozzo, pieno di calchi ger-

mani e di residui dialettali, irto di sgrammaticature e d'improprietà lessicali e sintattiche, non poteva essere accolto nel nobile castello della tradizione letteraria italiana.)

(Furst, 1968: 493)

The 'Svevo case', the 'Svevo question', the 'Svevo campaign'—in other words the battle within Italy for the acceptance of supposedly badly written novels such as those of Svevo—was caught up with the political programme of an increasingly Fascist state. As Maier's summary suggests, one reviewer of *La coscienza* was disturbed by the author's unpatriotic combination of forename and surname: the battle was lost before the front cover had been opened (Gatt-Rutter, 1988: 317-18). And it was a symptom of the nationalist (recently irredentist) culture of 1920s Trieste that the poor reception of *La coscienza* in Italy was led by critics from that country's newly redeemed city in the north-east. Svevo's fellow Triestines felt that the novel had somehow insulted their home town (Gatt-Rutter, 1988: 321-8).

We know that Joyce helped secure Svevo's European reputation, but it was Eugenio Montale who was the first Italian to champion him. Montale's article in Milan's *L'Esame*, 'Omaggio a Italo Svevo' (1925), inspired other young Italian writers of his generation to take up Svevo's cause (Montale, 1985). In 'I limoni', Montale opposes himself to the laureate poets ('i poeti laureati'—the festooned prize winners, the hyper-educated) who use archaic or *recherché* words (Montale, 1948: 13).[15] Montale was the first Italian to understand that Svevo's modernity, his acute psychological understanding of the contemporary mind, had been neglected during and partly because of the 'dittatura dannunziana'—the Byzantine 'stilismo' of D'Annunzio and his school (Montale, 1985: 78). There is a sense in which Montale understood, as Fascism was beginning to take hold, that appreciating 'European' works such as *La coscienza* was a resistance to atavistic cultural conformity.

Zeno's musings about his *dialettaccio* show us that Svevo not only anticipated the initial coolness of his novel's reception, but also that, in maintaining the Swabian part of his *italianità,* he was eventually ready to advance a modern identity for himself as a new type of novelist, free from the tyrannical laws and sacred lists of the national canon. Lebowitz has paired Svevo and Pirandello as regional writers who overcame the problem of dialect and 'discovered new languages that could interpret as well as describe their deracinated visions': Svevo thus made 'of his "defect" a part of his strength' (Lebowitz, 1978: 191-2). In his 'modern anthology', Alain Robbe-Grillet sees Svevo (at least linguistically) as a prototypical *nouveau romancier,* for his lack of appeal to the *belles lettristes,* and his proud conviction to *say things badly* (Robbe-Grillet, 1965: 98).

This inability to master and emulate traditional literary languages, a refusal to play by the rules of the novel, is what makes such writers fit to change the direction of the genre. As Moretti has pointed out, the novel has metamorphosed in what he has termed the 'semi-peripheries' of the world-system: the patrilineal line is broken and a new form—the Russian novel of ideas, Latin American magic realism—evolves (Moretti, 1998: 196). Svevo was a nephew rather than a son to Italy. *La coscienza,* perhaps Italy's first modernist fiction, may be seen as an example of one such generic shift in the psychological novel.[16] By the 1960s Montale noted that Svevo had moved, in reverse, from the ambiguity of *Weltliteratur* to 'the world of our highest national literature' ('[il mondo] della nostra più alta letteratura nazionale')—i.e. to the belated membership of a canonical élite (Montale, 1985: 143).

Robbe-Grillet has identified dialect (along with time, Zeno's libido and even his gait) as another form of sickness in *La coscienza.* The narrative insincerity and ill health of Zeno reflect on the lost innocence of the novel, which must speak false to ring true. Robbe-Grillet, perhaps surprisingly, connects Svevo's sick language to its provenance in the imperial borderlands, reminding us that irredentist Trieste is comparable to 'Kafka's Germano-Czech Prague, and Joyce's Anglo-Irish Dublin—the birthplace of everyone who is not at ease with his own language' (Robbe-Grillet, 1965: 105).

The idea of this linguistic unease, clearly relevant to Svevo's modernist vernacular, has been developed in Gilles Deleuze and Félix Guattari's notion of Kafka's 'minor literature' and the deterritorialization of language. Seen alongside Kafka, Svevo (as a border Triestine in the shadow of great Italian literature) also undertakes 'the minor practice of a major literature'. Rather than attempting a reterritorialization (an 'artificial enrichment', a Joycean 'exhilaration and overdetermination' of language), Svevo chooses the path of deterritorialization: like Kafka and Beckett, though not as radically or self-consciously, he finds 'his own point of underdevelopment, his own *patois*' in the poverty of language (Deleuze and Guattari, 1986: 18-19).

This type of border literature is imprisoned in a partly foreign language, flat and functional, which forces complexity to be made elsewhere, not at the particular verbal level. We thus come to read the stiff prose of *La coscienza*—in some respects like Kafka's German officialese, the prose of mistrust—as the deterritorialized idiom of *Mitteleuropa.* This is not the experimental aesthetic of a rarefied cosmopolitanism, but an atopian modernism whose poetics are, in Robert Musil's phrase, 'without qualities'.

Notes

1. Svevo had in fact been educated in Segnitz, in Bavaria rather than Swabia, but probably intended the name to be taken as a synonym for non-Prussian, non-Austrian Germanity.

2. 'When will you write an Italian work about our town?': letter to Joyce from Ettore Schmitz.

3. Place names are geo-political signs. In *La coscienza,* surnames point to the novel's hybrid locus: not only Guido Speier, but Zeno's dying friend Enrico Copler (who comes from a village in Austrian Styria and is a bilocated Germanic-Italian, like Italus the Swabian), the shady Dr Coprosich (who, though supposedly an irredentist, is nonetheless trusted by the Imperial Courts, and whose name has a Slavic as well as scatological ring), and Tacich, the Dalmatian who is dismissed as a provincial by Guido.

4. This is a paraphrase of Manzoni, who journeyed to Florence to 'rinse his clothes in the Arno'.

5. Beckett wrote: 'Dante did not adopt the vulgar out of any kind of local jingoism nor out of any determination to assert the superiority of Tuscan to all its rivals as a form of spoken Italian . . . He did not write in Florentine any more than in Neapolitan. He wrote a vulgar that could have been spoken by an ideal Italian who had assimilated what was best in all the dialects of his country, but which in fact was certainly not spoken nor ever had been.' For Beckett, this ideal Italian, constructed in defiance of the medieval Latin audience's intolerance of innovation, is analogous to the modernist language of *Finnegans Wake* and its hostile reception; both Dante and Joyce 'saw how worn out and threadbare was the conventional language of cunning literary artificers, both rejected an approximation to a universal language' (Beckett, 1961: 17-18).

6. Cerneca makes a useful distinction between the inner and outer languages: 'The dialect takes first place in that the fundamental texture of the inner discourse, the humus from which Svevian characters emerge, suffer, and live their psychological ordeals, is precisely the Triestine dialect. However, later after conception, the characters shift at the language level and take up the Italian cloak through a sometimes more or less conscious effort . . . Svevo's linguistic expression . . . is represented by a dialect-language in which the dialect tries to melt and burn itself out without leaving any traces (even though it does not always succeed) and in which the beat goes on underneath, more or less openly, to make itself felt' (Cerneca, 1972: 85).

7. No Italian text is quoted.

8. In fact in one episode *La coscienza* resembles Joseph Heller's novel *Catch-22*. In order to convince his father of his sanity, Zeno produces a certificate of proof of mental health, to which his father despairingly replies, 'Ah, you really are crazy' (Svevo, 2001: 35) ('Ah! Tu sei veramente pazzo!' (Svevo, 1988: 33)). Both Zeno and Yossarian, in their imaginary or willed illnesses, are subjects dispossessed of truth, tragicomically condemned to procuring medical certificates, but only to prove themselves false to a hostile authority (the nation, the army, the father).

9. The name of Zeno of Citium, the founder of Stoicism, is also present. Weiss relates Cosini's conclusion that there is no cure to life, and his final, tranquil acceptance of this idea, to Stoic philosophy (Weiss, 1987: 90).

10. A well-known exposition of the paradoxes is in Jorge-Luis Borges' essay 'Avatars of the Tortoise'. The second paradox is expounded as follows: 'Achilles runs ten times faster than the tortoise and gives the animal a headstart of ten metres. Achilles runs those ten metres, the tortoise one; Achilles runs that metre, the tortoise runs a decimetre; Achilles runs that centimetre, the tortoise, a millimetre; fleet-footed Achilles, the millimetre, the tortoise, a tenth of a millimetre, and so on to infinity, without the tortoise ever being overtaken.'

11. We find the same reversed agency in Svevo's explanation of the revival of his urge to write: 'I regarded myself as having been convicted and sentenced and certainly *if Italy had not come to me,* I would not even have thought I could write' (my italics) (Gatt-Rutter, 1988: 291).

12. The Mamelukes were also a ruling caste within the Ottoman Empire until the nineteenth century. The Austro-Hungarian Empire took over former Ottoman lands in Bosnia during that century, which could explain the curious transmigration of this term.

13. Zeno constructs his own prison bars, though he too has a spell in a Triestine institution to cure himself of smoking. Furst stresses the biographical Germanic influence on Svevo, and his alienation from the Italian literary tradition, which has contributed to him being perceived as 'modern' and European. Furst comments on the incomplete closure of both novels but contrasts the essentially comic tone of *La coscienza* with the *ernste Spiel* of *Der Zauberberg,* and discusses their differences in narrative technique and literariness. See also Moloney (1998: 102).

14. Beno Weiss writes: 'At the end of his analysis he [Zeno] emerges as a whole and authentic human

being, fulfilled and even contented, able to work and function in society as well as anyone else—perhaps even better, because of his capacity to laugh at life' (Weiss, 1987: 91). Brian Moloney's view is in opposition: '[Zeno] has not achieved wholeness or integrity. He has merely acquired the precarious superiority of the jackal who suddenly finds himself in a jungle temporarily deserted by its fiercest predators' (Moloney, 1977: 16-17).

15. Montale signed the anti-Fascist manifesto. He probably wrote the poem 'I limoni' soon after reading *La coscienza*. It begins: 'Ascoltami, i poeti laureati / si muovono soltanto fra le piante / dai nomi poco usati: bossi ligustri o acanti'.

16. This is obviously a generalized claim: *La coscienza* is compared in this respect to Luigi Pirandello's earlier novel, *Il fu Mattia Pascal* (1904).

References

Beckett, S. (1961) 'Dante . . . Bruno . . . Vico . . . Joyce', in *Our Exagmination Round his Factification for Incamination of 'Work in Progress'*, pp. 1-22. London: Faber and Faber.

Bettiza, E. (1999) 'Noi senza nazione e senza odi etnici', *La Stampa,* 18 April.

Borges, J. L. (1970) 'Avatars of the Tortoise', in *Labyrinths: Selected Stories and Other Writings,* pp. 237-43. Harmondsworth: Penguin.

Camerino, G. A. (1994) 'Italo Svevo: significato e caratteri di una poetica mitteleuropea', in N. Cacciaglia and L. Fava Guzzetta (eds), *Italo Svevo scrittore europeo: atti del convegno,* pp. 15-29. Florence: Leo S. Olschki Editore.

Carey, J. (1992) *The Intellectuals and the Masses: Pride and Prejudice among the Literary Intelligentsia, 1880-1939.* London: Faber and Faber.

Cerneca, D. (1972) 'Dialectical [sic] Error and Linguistic Complex in Italo Svevo', *Modern Fiction Studies,* 18: 81-9.

Coetzee, J. M. (2002) 'The Genius of Trieste', *New York Review of Books,* 26 September, pp. 58-60.

Deleuze, G. and Guattari, F. (1986) *Kafka: Toward a Minor Literature,* trans. D. Polan. Minneapolis: University of Minnesota Press.

Furbank, P. N. (1966) *Italo Svevo: The Man and the Writer.* London: Secker and Warburg.

Furst, L. R. (1968) 'Italo Svevo's *La coscienza di Zeno* and Thomas Mann's *Der Zauberberg*', *Contemporary Literature,* 9: 492-506.

Gatt-Rutter, J. (1988) *Italo Svevo: A Double Life.* Oxford: Clarendon Press.

Guagnini, E. (1994) 'Esordi di Svevo: città, letterature e società triestina', in N. Cacciaglia and L. Fava Guzzetta (eds), *Italo Svevo scrittore europeo: atti del convegno,* pp. 161-74. Florence: Leo S. Olschki Editore.

Joyce, J. (1966) *Letters of James Joyce,* ed. Richard Ellmann, vol. 2. London: Faber and Faber.

Lebowitz, N. (1978) *Italo Svevo.* New Brunswick, NJ: Rutgers University Press.

Lukács, G. (1963) *The Meaning of Contemporary Realism,* trans. J. and N. Mander. London: Merlin.

McCourt, J. (2000) *The Years of Bloom: James Joyce in Trieste 1904-1920.* Dublin: Lilliput Press.

Magris, C. (1997) *Microcosmi.* Milan: Garzanti.

Moloney, B. (1972) 'Psychoanalysis and Irony in *La Coscienza di Zeno*', *Modern Language Review,* 67(2): 309-18.

Moloney, B. (1974) *Italo Svevo: A Critical Edition.* Edinburgh: Edinburgh University Press.

Moloney, B. (1977) 'Italo Svevo and the European Novel'. Inaugural lecture, University of Hull.

Moloney, B. (1998) *Italo Svevo narratore: lezioni triestine.* Gorizia: Editrice Goriziana.

Montale, E. (1948) 'I limoni', in *Ossi di Seppia.* Verona: Arnoldo Mondadori Editore.

Montale, E. (1985) 'Italo Svevo nel centenario della nascita', in G. Zampa (ed.), *Carteggio Svevo-Montale, con gli scritti di Montale su Svevo.* Milan: Mondadori.

Moretti, F. (1998) *Atlas of the European Novel 1800-1900.* London and New York: Verso.

Morris, J. (2001) *Trieste and the Meaning of Nowhere.* London: Faber and Faber.

Pacifici, S. (1967) *The Modern Italian Novel from Manzoni to Svevo.* Carbondale and Edwardsville: Southern Illinois University Press.

Pizzi, K. (1998) '"Silentes Loquimur": "Foibe" and Border Anxiety in Post-War Literature from Trieste', *Journal of European Studies,* 28: 217-29.

Pizzi, K. (2001) *A City in Search of an Author.* London: Sheffield Academic Press.

Robbe-Grillet, A. (1965) *Snapshots and Towards a New Novel,* trans. Barbara Wright. London: Calder and Boyars.

Schächter, E. (2000) *Origin and Identity: Essays on Svevo and Trieste.* Leeds: Northern Universities Press.

Sluga, G. (2001) *The Problem of Trieste and the Italo-Yugoslav Border: Difference, Identity, and Sovereignty in Twentieth-Century Europe.* Albany: State University of New York Press.

Steiner, G. (1972) 'Extraterritorial', in *Extraterritorial: Papers on Literature and the Language Revolution,* pp. 14-21. Harmondsworth: Penguin.

Svevo, I. (1968a) 'Sulla teoria della pace', 'Pace e guerra' and 'Sulla guerra', in *Opera omnia,* ed. Bruno Maier, vol. 3, pp. 649-62. Milan: Dall'Oglio.

Svevo, I. (1968b) 'Profilo autobiografico', in *Opera omnia,* ed. Bruno Maier, vol. 3, pp. 799-810. Milan: Dall'Oglio.

Svevo, I. (1988) *La coscienza di Zeno.* Milan: Mondadori.

Svevo, I. (1989) *Confessions of Zeno,* trans. Beryl de Zoete. New York: Vintage.

Svevo, I. (2001) *Zeno's Conscience,* trans. William Weaver. London: Everyman.

Tomizza, F. (2000) *Alle spalle di Trieste.* Bologna: Bompiani.

Vanvolsem, S. (1994) 'La lingua e il problema della lingua in Svevo: una polimorfia che non piacque', in N. Cacciaglia and L. Fava Guzzetta (eds), *Italo Svevo scrittore europeo: atti del convegno,* pp. 433-48. Florence: Leo S. Olschki Editore.

Weiss, B. (1987) *Italo Svevo,* Twayne's World Author Series. Boston: G. K. Hall.

Wilden, A. (1969), 'Death, Desire, and Repetition in Svevo's *Zeno*', *Modern Language Notes,* 84: 98-119.

Paolo Puppa (essay date 2006)

SOURCE: Puppa, Paolo. "Italo Svevo, Dramatist." In *A History of Italian Theatre,* edited by Joseph Farrell and Paolo Puppa, pp. 312-22. Cambridge: Cambridge University Press, 2006.

[*In the following essay, Puppa considers Svevo's often-neglected dramatic writings and contends that despite their "many deficiencies," these works "are genuinely reflective of developments in the European theatre of the time," and "in certain respects more so than with any other Italian dramatist of the early twentieth century."*]

Italo Svevo's very considerable dramatic talent was never fulfilled. The thirteen scripts which he composed without any hope of seeing them performed in his lifetime and without the support of theatre companies, circuits, commissions or the attention of public or critics were almost totally ignored in his day.[1] This is not of course the only example of a dramatist being neglected by the theatre establishment of his time, but in the case of Ettore Schmitz, the name on Svevo's birth certificate, the bare stage mirrors his abortive literary career, producing a painful double failure. A novelist can, technically, continue writing even in the absence of publication, but for a dramatist the refusal of a stage constitutes a death-sentence. Svevo's habit of continuously modifying his scripts and effectively treating them as work in progress makes their dating very difficult: some estimates put them at the end of the nineteenth century, others in the years following World War I. *Un marito* (*A Husband*) is a special case since the manuscript is dated 1903, when the author was forty-two (he was born in Trieste on 19 December 1861). The language of these 'armchair plays'[2] sounds odd, never having been actually spoken by actors who could make it natural and speakable. The diction is laboured, not really authentic, a mixture of the German prevalent in commercial circles in Habsburg-dominated Trieste, the English which he studied for business purposes, and the dialect spoken in his home and traces of which remain in the bitter-sweet rhythms of his lively *Atto Unico* (*One-Act*), with its domestic scenes in the style of Giacinto Gallina.

Svevo's cultural horizon when he begins to 'imagine' plays is still naturalistic, that is, aimed at a close reproduction of everyday life, but in spite of, or perhaps because of, this dilettante background and complete absence of any demand from an audience, his 'amateur' works are genuinely reflective of developments in the European theatre of the time, and are in certain respects more so than with any other Italian dramatist of the early twentieth century, including Pirandello. This remains true in spite of the many deficiencies in plot construction and typologies of situation forced on him by current convention: it remains true in spite of the mismatch between the interpersonal, objective structure of drama itself and the tendency towards the subjective in Svevo's narrative work, and even in spite of the chaotic interweaving of overlapping time-frames in his plots. The brief, amusing Schnitzlerian monologue, *Prima del ballo* (*Before the Ball*), in which the young female protagonist waiting at the door for her carriage to take her to the ball muses over the suitors proposed by her family and her own romantic fancies, is a good example of Svevo's 'stream of consciousness', but is far removed from the rhythms of dialogue. Ettore Schmitz may seem quite unsuited to the stage yet he had a genuine vocation for the theatre, even if we ignore the welter of anecdotes about his precocious talent, about his acting ambitions despite a stammer and lisp and his willingness as a young journalist to take on theatre reviews for the local, mildly irredentist, *Indipendente*.

All of Svevo's work is centred on the motif of the failed artist, around whom he created a gallery of portraits of *fin de siècle* characters, each one condemned to anonymity and disappointment, unlike the happy, dissipated and spoiled young men of D'Annunzio's theatre. This theme recurs in Svevo's narrative works where such characters find themselves strangely paralleled by medical practitioners of all kinds (as happens in *La coscienza di Zeno* (*The Confessions of Zeno*), peopled as it is by psychoanalysts, directors of clinics, specialists and/or ordinary doctors, not to mention lowly nurses, and which gives off an odour of ether or iodine which, in its obsessive intensity, is equalled only by Molière's farces). By the very use of a nom de plume (firstly E. Samigli and then Italo Svevo), Ettore Schmitz gives evidence of the disapproval of the economic environment (the Stock Exchange!) in which he moved.

His abandonment of writing parallels his move away from his inherited Judaism, similarly suppressed but surviving not least in the persistently macabre and grotesque tones in his work. Many of the conflicts within the family circles in his plays can be traced back to his own family situation as son-in-law to the Veneziani family, wealthy, assimilated Jews, or more precisely converts to Catholicism who were unswerving in their observance of Catholic rites. We find such a situation in *L'avventura di Maria* (*Maria's Adventure*), possibly written in the period immediately preceding World War I, where the male protagonist talks of 'repatriating' after business trips between Florence and Trieste which are in reality pretexts for erotic escapades. Maria is a variant of a recurring prototype, a nervous violinist who is expelled from the bourgeois household after capriciously falling in love with Alberto, the head of the family, a businessman married to her childhood friend. The triangle is eventually broken and normality restored, thus preventing the bourgeois/artist couple realising their love-dream. This sounds like a rather sad allegory for the formal prohibition imposed on Ettore Schmitz's writing by his full-time job at his underwater-paint factory, as well as a general allusion to the incompatibility between art and middle-class work.

Un marito and *La rigenerazione* (*Regeneration*), both structured on interlocking relationships, are his most ambitious plays. The former follows the ideological swings of the protagonist, the lawyer Federico Arcetri, who in the distant past had stabbed to death his unfaithful wife, Clara, after finding a number of letters indicating her *probable* infidelity. Meantime he has taken a second wife, Bice, and when the curtain rises the mother of the first wife strides on to the stage carrying other letters, this time belonging to the second wife and proving that she too is *perhaps* unfaithful, and demanding that the husband repeat his act of murderous revenge. At the same time, in a parallel situation, one of Federico's clients has also killed his wife, whom he had

caught *in flagrante*. Federico at first undertakes to defend him but later, tired of 'serving as an example of untainted honour', declines the uxoricide's case. At first sight this is no more than a straightforward tale of cuckoldry, but the social status of the characters, upper-middle class, is significant. Even when writing a play in the knowledge that it will not be performed, the author to some extent adjusts to the expectations of the stalls by providing characters of an elevated social status, similar to his own personal position following his marriage.

On first reading, the play seems to fall into the category of nineteenth-century *pièces bien faites*. Svevo, an enthusiastic theatregoer, was certainly familiar with the repertoire of Dumas *fils* and Scribe, who were very popular in Trieste at that time. Scribe regularly makes use of mislaid letters, handkerchiefs and eavesdropping from behind screens. (The central element in another of Svevo's plays, *Una commedia inedita* (*An Unpublished Play*), is the screen from behind which a potentially cuckolded husband checks on the adulterous tendencies of his wife, who is involved with an aspiring lover, who happens to be a playwright). There is no shortage of letters in *Un marito,* both in the traumatic memory of the motive for the killing and the newly discovered correspondence of the second wife. Clearly, this is no longer a well-made play: by 1903 these devices had worn thin. In keeping with the rejection of action in late nineteenth-century drama, nothing actually happens on stage. If reality is uncertain, if identity and guilt gradually disappear, feelings of jealousy, the urge to commit murder, the Othello complex are also bound to decline. Svevo's work anticipates a wider movement, a peaceful protest against the crime of honour, which finds its fullest expression in Pirandello's *Cap and Bells* some fourteen years later.

On the other hand, there is no shortage of vaudeville touches in Svevo's play, which contains dialogue and situations worthy of Feydeau, or reminiscent of some witty central-European operetta sparkling with smart repartee: for example, the brother-in-law, a doctor, tells Federico that he will have to 'take the bull by the horns', before remembering that 'horns' are a synonym for cuckoldry. In the third act, Bice convinces Federico that the letters he has found were just an innocent attempt on her part, after being neglected and humiliated by her husband for so long, to distract him from his infatuation with the dead Clara, leading us to expect a happy ending, such as Svevo often contrived elsewhere. In the already mentioned *Una commedia inedita,* the protagonist forgives his wife whom he has caught with her lover, because he realises he has been a neglectful husband, too wrapped up in his business affairs, and so must share the blame. In *La verità* (*The Truth*), Silvio Arcetri, who has the same surname as the Federico of *Un marito,* uses a blatant lie backed up by zealous witnesses to persuade his wife, who has caught him in bed with the dressmaker, to come back to him. In *Le ire di Giuliano* (*Giuliano's Rages*) the couple overcome the problems caused by tension and incompatibility of character and stay together in order to carry on their business and maintain their property. In *Le teorie del conte Alberto* (*Count Albert's Theories*), the protagonist gradually abandons his adherence to rigid Darwinian convictions in matters of heredity and, in spite of initial doubts about her family origins, marries Anna. In *L'avventura di Maria,* Alberto and Giulia decide to stay together, partly for the sake of their only child but in spite of Alberto's affair with a touring violinist.

However, in a sudden shift of plot in *Un marito,* the wife of the couple's friend Paolo claims to have seen Bice in a carriage letting Paolo caress her hand. Federico, finding himself once more compelled to assume the executioner's part, declines to face the truth and takes on a new role, that of the trusting friend: 'I know, Bice, that you were ready to betray me, and I also know that you didn't, but not out of any virtue of yours. I forgive you.' From a case of actual cuckoldry actually punished in the past, the script moves to one of hypothetical cuckoldry in the present, accepted by the victim with a resignation worthy of Hamlet. This equivocation, a disconcerting departure from the binary logic of realist plots where the truth or falsity of a real act leads to the condemnation or forgiveness of the supposedly guilty party, undermines both the playful and the opposing, complementary (or dramatic) dimension involved in adulterous situations, and steers developments towards an ambiguous outcome. Federico resorts to various legalistic arguments to persuade his wife to fall in with his theatrical display of noble feelings, his 'peace-offering', and drags her along to the sick-bed of his dying mother-in-law, thinking that in her confusion she might mistake Bice for her dead daughter Clara—a sort of ghost of his first wife who has been symbolically present from the opening of the play and whose portrait has been hanging in the lawyer's severe office, like an Ibsenite fetish, or a lugubrious Fury whose presence hangs over the action.

The intrusion of the dead on the stage creates a murky, funereal atmosphere in *Un marito. Terzetto spezzato* (*A Broken Trio*), which seemingly unfolds in the style of farce, is similarly conceived, and is yet another variant of the clash between the economic and artistic sides of the author's life. The script seems to promise nothing more than another spiritualist séance set up to evoke a dead wife. The séance is arranged by the widower, who is worried about the coffee-merchandising business where his partner is his best friend, obviously his wife's former lover, as well as an aspiring man-of-letters now inconsolable because he has lost his inspirational Muse. Both men need the woman for their own professional purposes, but she derides them in a very unmetaphysi-

cal way. The situation in *Un marito* is of a different order. In killing his wife for an obsolete 'question of honour', Federico has transformed her into some sort of superior reality, an icon of unattainable desire, a saint to be worshipped. Married love has vanished with his first wife, the murdered Clara, and he is now totally inhibited sexually.

The plot hinges on the disturbed relationship between husband and wife, as in Ibsen and Pirandello. If he really married Bice in a vain attempt to dispel the ghost, she took him for a great romantic hero, the violence of whose passion could lead him to commit murder, only to find that he is a spent force, interested only in making money. Earlier in his life when he fell in love, he was committed to the study of law and of great juridical ideas based on the humanitarian spirit and tolerant solidarity. Later he moved quite cynically into civil law, taking on not merely administrative but financially remunerative cases. Federico now seems almost a double of Ibsen's master-builder, Solness, who gave up building churches to God in favour of producing simple houses where couples lived out their loveless lives. In Svevo's case, it may be that lawyers and architects are metaphorical allusions to his own thwarted literary ambitions. There is a fundamental ambiguity in the relationship between man and woman, as in any exchange of affection or power, making it a mere tangle of attraction and repulsion. This is also the case in the unfinished *Con la penna d'oro* (*With a Golden Pen*) where the two cousins, the rich Alberta and the unfortunate Alice, each interpret in her own way the reciprocal, constantly changing feelings of love and hatred that bind them together, each taking in turn the roles of persecutor and victim; as again in the almost Hegelian relationship between master and servant in *Inferiorità* where, after a bizarre drawing-room game, the naïve but spiteful waiter kills Alfredo Picchi and then puts on his hat and coat.

While attending the consulting rooms of the analyst, Edoardo Weiss, and considering those of Freud, Svevo seemed to veer in the direction of the Scandinavian dramatists, Ibsen and Strindberg. At the end of *Un marito,* Federico undergoes a regeneration of an ontological nature. The play demonstrates the absurdity of the crime of honour from both a moral and a juridical point of view, but it also underlines the lack of any consistency or coherence in the individual. There is no need to destroy yourself, as Ignazio does literally in Svevo's youthful *Il ladro in casa* (*The Thief in the House*), when he falls from the roof almost as though to compensate for the trouble he has caused his family through his repeated irresponsibility. It is sufficient to fall silent, to leave things unsaid, to let strange symptoms and inconsistent conduct reveal the inner self. The rejection of the myth of male honour coincides with the humiliation of the ego. Federico discovers in practice the ambiguity of the self. At the end, as he and Bice go off to give their performance at the bedside of the aged Arianna, all relationships seem to demonstrate the impossibility of being defined or of assuming a distinct identity. Law has been abolished, lawyers put to flight, fathers deprived of their power. In any case, the couple have no children. The spoken word has now lost all authority, all credibility. All that remains is an area of lawlessness, confirmed by one significant statement made by Paolo, the only father in the play, to clarify his pedagogical methods:

> My Guido is accustomed to the strictest injustice. When he behaves well I always manage to punish him for some trivial reason; when he behaves badly I do the same, but not always. I praise him only when I myself feel well, physically and morally. He has learned from this that he is not in charge of his own destiny but has to submit to capricious and unreasonable chance . . . confronted with this gloomy prospect, with this harshness and injustice, he despairs, and in a few years he will have lost most of his congenital illusions.[3]

Before Federico kills Clara, we learn that he had dreamed about her death. The homicidal impulse resurfaces in *Rigenerazione,* where dreams have a more literal sense. The principal character aspires to return to the past and accepts the possibility of rediscovering his youth. If the earlier play had a tight, compact structure, like a sonata with interlocking motifs, the later work is a prolix and, in many ways, unfinished symphony, a choreographed, multi-figured fresco, focused on the theme of regression. However, the parental roles remain as confused as before. The protagonist is husband, father, grandfather, lover and, now that the function of the dominant father in the earlier play has been suppressed, interacts continually with the others in each of these roles according to external stimuli and his attempts to subdue them. The wealthy, retired textile merchant, Giovanni Chierici, leads an apathetic existence. All passion spent, he lives quietly in the loving care of Anna, his wife-nurse who looks after his sleep and his digestion in the way she does with the numerous pets in the house and garden. Boredom rules over his forgetful universe (he cannot remember people's names), and his only pleasure is taking a walk with his grandson. In this twilight world the protagonist suddenly agrees to undergo an operation to recover his youth, though the author himself appears uncertain of his age.[4] What Zeno attempted with his writing, Giovanni attempts with his body, his skin, making the Faustian journey not metaphorical but literal. He will not be having the surgical operation for sexual reasons, according to his honourable claims. If the other old men, the prying merchants from the Stock Exchange who scurry along to see the physical effects of his operation, reduce the motives of this central-European Frankenstein to an attempt to seduce the maids, Giovanni has his own agenda. He intends nothing less than to 'see one more time' his past

lovers, now long gone, to rediscover the vision now lost but once aroused by those exuberant girls he later abandoned, particularly the lovely Pauletta.

Behind his craving to evoke the ghosts of the past, behind this spiritualist voyeurism, we sense the obsessions that haunt Svevo, the obsession with ageing, or the obsessive need to end the eternal conflict between fathers and sons, that gulf which, in so much proto-Expressionist drama at the turn of the century, is the substitute inside the family for class conflict, but which also humanises it. Giovanni is not a lawyer (unlike Federico in *Un marito*), and not even a writer, but his real difference from Federico is that he surrounds himself with a multiplicity of women, starting with Anna, the wife with whom he has played out the pleasant but exhausting charade of middle-class family solidarity, overlaid with a touch of Epicurean hedonism, or at least absence of tension. But behind the tepidity and torpor of married life there is a brooding resentment (a hint of the uxoricide of *Un marito*) surfacing in the second intermezzo, where the serving maid Rita urges uxoricide but only in the safe dimension of dream. Giovanni returns to his wife in the end, in a sort of twilight farewell, making repeated but enigmatic declarations of love:

GIOVANNI:

> I loved you so much.

ANNA:

> Will you kiss me?

GIOVANNI:

> Kiss? No, certainly not. I love you. I never wanted to kill you. I love you. For your sake I will love all your pets, birds, cats, dogs. And I will work for you. I will gladly work for you. For your sake I will save people and care for them. That is the duty of us youthful old people.[5]

Rita herself, the Goldonian maid, is the bodily representation of the myth of guiltless Eros, the embodiment of the fantasies of Giovanni's youth, the sentimental relic of times past. Giovanni gives life to private associations, mixing time and desire, indulging his own visions, depriving the others of any objective existence, making them clusters of associations inside his own being. Rita miraculously becomes Pauletta, a parody of Goethe's Gretchen, caught up in an episode which causes our hero to sink briefly into the low comedy of the Atellan farce. With Rita, Giovanni constructs a *mise-en-scène* of a stolen but interrupted kiss, complete with legalistic bickering and attempts to outflank her feigned defences: the saddest of seductions. It is melancholia that, as in *Un marito,* connects this scene with others, connects Rita the actress and Pauletta the character, as previously Bice and Clara. The ambiguous rapport between the girl and the old man parallels that between father and daughter so common in Scandinavian and Pirandellian theatre. Rita's mother's name is Giovanna, a name similar to Anna, the name of the protagonist's wife. The girls who ought to flourish in the figure of the maid were never actually possessed in the past, because of their very availability and their overwhelming desirability. Giovanni makes this confession to his wife:

GIOVANNI:

I found the whole world turned upside down. Kissing didn't mean anything any more. I kissed Rita . . .

ANNA:

Yes, like a father kisses his daughter.

GIOVANNI:

(*impatiently*) OK—like a father kisses someone else's daughter.

(p. 561)

There is, however, a third woman on the stage, Emma, Valentino's widow, a daughter in mourning like the stepdaughter in *Six Characters in Search of an Author.* An unloving father and a daughter without a husband—an odd couple! When she finds her father sunk in his biblical (therefore Jewish) sleep, like Lot, in a state of, she believes, post-coital drunkenness, she immediately decides to marry the awkward Enrico, the dead man's friend (and yet another Zeno-surrogate) so that he will protect her against her rejuvenated father. The peaceful, bourgeois drawing-room cannot fail occasionally to evoke another scene, the adjacent cemetery. There is an anxious link between the two, the Futurist automobile that has replaced the horse-drawn carriage but has multiplied its ancient destructive power. Often in the later Svevo, as though prophesying his own demise, there are buses or cars that bring metaphysical or baroque tremors to the *Ville industrielle.* Rather than doctors, it is the car that expresses fear and desire for death, its dark form casting a shadow over Giovanni's senseless operation. The nightmarish fear of losing Umbertino, the spoiled grandson, of seeing him crushed under the wheels of a car, the ritual of dressing him in preparation for going out, the insistence that he hold his grandfather's hand are in reality obscure sacrificial formulae. As in **"Il buon vecchio e la bella fanciulla"** (**'The Old Man and the Pretty Girl'**), the novella written at the same time as *Rigenerazione,* loving the girl implies for the old man the urge to annihilate her, to get her out of the way so that he can then possess her completely in his grief, perhaps even through writing (even if on this occasion he is a boy). At the end of the play, freed of the temptation to repossess his old ghosts, Giovanni advances the dismal proposal of conjugal friendship.

In a contemporary story, **"Vino generoso,"** similar tensions appear, ineffable in the sense that they stem from impulses that are not confessable but are the very essence of dreams. Here an old man who gets drunk at his daughter's wedding dreams he is in a cave and condemned to be put to death in some strange ritual. In this modern version of Euripides' *Alcestis,* no one is prepared to take his place. The old man has no hesitation in calling for his young daughter to save him, and does this so loudly that when he sobers up, his wife (the usual ingenuous wife of all Svevo's œuvre) in a paradoxical flash of insight interprets these screams of death as expressions of love. The ancient myth of Iphigenia or, in the Christian tradition, the myth of Jacob, with allusions to the already mentioned biblical Lot, are all in evidence here, with Bacchus not far off to help overcome the moral resistance of the elderly protagonist. Pointedly, in the *novella,* the old man at the end experiences an acute feeling of guilt for having brought into the world creatures condemned in their turn to die and be devoured, a fate like being possessed by one's father, as in the myth of Chronos, the cruel god who devoured his children.

There are many flashes of Jewish humour in the witty thrusts and sophistry of *Rigenerazione.* In addition to denying the univocal meaning of words, to oscillating between the mendacity of every confession and the authenticity of every deceit, Svevo's witticisms explode in a stunning display of paradoxes and rhetorical figures that turn the Trieste drawing-room into a sophisticated Wildean comedy set. The spectator is embarked on a journey towards a ground zero of logic, with sketches equalling anything produced by such contemporary comics as Achille Campanile, featuring doctors who bury their mistakes and thieves who steal everything other than a second head. The script is sprinkled with popular sayings, as for example the now obsolete 'going to the well' as a metaphor for sexual initiation. Speaking no longer guarantees winning a case, or imposing an outlook. Speaking is a means of resisting drawing-room nihilism, and if it brings the stage to life, it ends up nevertheless by invalidating it, as in the central crisis of the child who is thought to have been killed by a car but is resurrected to make a farcical reappearance moments later. While still in full mourning, people manage to make jokes in an effort to overcome their grief. The driver who was believed to have accidentally killed the child is dismissed with a ridiculous joke to the effect that he is somebody who 'careers through the streets with his tongue out, flattening people' (*Teatro,* p. 479).

However, Giovanni's satanic attempt at sublimating the Oedipal complex and other parental obsessions, at reconciling offspring with their parents and seeing anew lost Sphynxes does not end in total failure: there remains language, a healer of wounds and a means of putting together broken pieces and of regenerating faith in life, and there remains too the humble ability of what is left of the self to face the shame of its own disintegration.

Notes

1. Only one work, *Terzetto spezzato,* was performed, for one week in April 1927.

2. The image is taken from the *Caprices* of De Musset who, in his disgust with nineteenth-century Parisian theatre, refused to allow his stage works to be circulated. Svevo did not make that choice.

3. Italo Svevo, *Un marito* in *Teatro e saggi,* p. 296.

4. In Act 1, scene 5, the wife declares that her husband is seventy-four, but in the following scene, Guido and Enrico state he is seventy-six while in Act 1, scene 20, the protagonist himself insists he is only seventy-four.

5. Italo Svevo, *La rigenerazione,* in *Teatro e saggi,* pp. 763 and 767.

Bibliography

Scripts

Svevo, I. *Teatro,* ed. G. Contini, Milan, 1986.

———. *Teatro e saggi,* ed. F. Bertoni, introduction by M. Lavagetto, Milan, 2004.

Criticism

Camerino, G. A. 'Svevo e il teatro di prosa', in R. Scrivano (ed.) *Contributi sveviani,* Trieste, 1979, pp. 75-85.

Chia Romonte N. 'Svevo e la commedia', in Romonte (ed.), *Silenzio e parola,* Milan, 1978, pp. 167-74.

Gatt-Rutter, J. *Italo Svevo: A Double Life,* Oxford, 1988.

Guidotti, A. *Zeno e i suoi doppi: le commedie di Svevo,* Pisa, 1990.

Moloney, B. *Italo Svevo: A Critical Introduction,* Edinburgh, 1974.

Puppa, P. 'Svevo e le metamorfosi della scena', in *Parola di scena: Teatro italiano tra '800 e '900,* Rome, 1999, pp. 23-5.

Rimini, R. *La morte nel salotto: Guida al teatro di Italo Svevo,* Florence, 1974.

Saccone, E. *Il poeta travestito (otto scritti su Svevo),* Pisa, 1977.

Vigorelli, G. 'In atto la riscoperta del teatro di Svevo', *Il Dramma,* 44. 3 (1968), 37-49.

FURTHER READING

Bibliography

Bloodgood, Francis C. and John W. Van Voorhis. "Criticism of Italo Svevo: A Selected Checklist." *Modern Fiction Studies* 18, no. 1 (spring 1972): 119-29.
Bibliography of Svevo's writings and a selective list of critical studies of the author's works.

Biography

Gatt-Rutter, John. *Italo Svevo: A Double Life.* Oxford: Clarendon Press, 1988, 410 p.
Extensive biography of Svevo that describes the author as a figure who commands attention "by reason of his moral authority, his artistic rigour," and "his irresistible humour."

Joyce, Stanislaus. *The Meeting of Svevo and Joyce.* Udine, Italy: Del Bianco Editore, 1965, 19 p.
Recounts the friendship and literary relationship between James Joyce and Italo Svevo.

Subrizi, Lilia Ghelli. *Svevo: A Fascination with Melancholy.* Florence, Italy: Il Candelaio Edizioni, 1984, 148 p.
Studies Svevo's life and literary career and investigates the negative critical responses he received in Italy, describing him as an artist with "an emotional capacity sharp enough to acknowledge and accept shortcomings" and a writer with "the courage to go against the national mainstream."

Criticism

Acocella, Joan. "True Confessions." In *Twenty-eight Artists and Two Saints: Essays,* pp. 35-48. New York: Pantheon Books, 2007.
Assesses Svevo's literary career, describing the author as "a thorny item, a one-masterpiece master, but a master nevertheless," and referring to *Confessions of Zeno* as one of the earliest modernist novels in Italy.

Anderson, Mark. "The Private Tool of Writing: Autobiographical Fictions in the Work of Italo Svevo." *Stanford Italian Review* 3, no. 2 (fall 1983): 273-89.
Remarks that Svevo's protagonists are autobiographical, in that they "represent ironized, subjective, and distorted images of their author's past" and provide a version of his life story, but they also contain "the condemnation of its failures and inadequacies."

Bossche, Bart van den. "Unreliability in Italian Modernist Fiction: The Cases of Italo Svevo and Luigi Pirandello." In *Narrative Unreliability in the Twentieth-*

Century First-Person Novel, edited by Elke D'hoker and Gunther Martens, pp. 247-58. Berlin: Walter de Gruyter, 2008.

Declares that "unreliability" plays "a prominent, diverse and at times even dubious role" in the fiction of Svevo and Luigi Pirandello, noting, in particular, that the use of the unreliable narrator is a key component in the "manipulation" and "transformation" of the realist novel into modernist fiction.

Cernecca, Domenico. "Dialectical Element and Linguistic Complex in Italo Svevo." *Modern Fiction Studies* 18, no. 1 (spring 1972): 81-9.

Analyzes Svevo's writing style and asserts that "his language is the result of intricate inner labor," which manifests itself in three directions: "the dialectical, the Italian, and the German." The critic adds that Svevo was "tortured by a true and real linguistic complex common to all regions of multilingual frontiers" and did not realize that his dialect was "the safest platform from which to express himself."

Champagne, Roland A. "A Displacement of Plato's *Pharmakon*: A Study of Italo Svevo's Short Fiction." *Modern Fiction Studies* 21, no. 4 (winter 1975-76): 564-72.

Contends that in his short fiction, Svevo's "creative presentation" of the "ambivalence of living in mixed tenses," or vacillating between the categories of "past, present, and future time," is a "commentary on the act of writing as a displacement of the Platonic myth of *pharmakon.*"

Coetzee, J. M. "Italo Svevo." In *Inner Workings: Literary Essays 2000-2005,* pp. 1-14. New York: Viking, 2007.

Appraises Svevo's literary career and describes his masterpiece, *Confessions of Zeno,* as more than an "application" or "interrogation" of psychoanalysis, but "an exploration of the passions," including "greed and envy and jealousy," in the "tradition of the European novel."

Furbank, P. N. *Italo Svevo: The Man and the Writer.* London: Secker & Warburg, 1966, 232 p.

Includes a short biography and a discussion of Svevo's major works, including *A Life, As a Man Grows Older,* and *Confessions of Zeno,* as well as his last writings and plays. Furbank asserts that Svevo's major novels illustrate the development and rise of the modernist novel "rather beautifully."

Furst, Lilian R. "Italo Svevo's *La Coscienza di Zeno* and Thomas Mann's *Der Zauberberg.*" *Contemporary Literature* 9, no. 4 (fall 1968): 492-506.

Compares Svevo's novel *Confessions of Zeno* with *The Magic Mountain,* by Thomas Mann, and contends that Svevo "finds his rightful place" among the leading progressive novelists of Europe.

Gatt-Rutter, John. "Non-commitment in Italo Svevo." *Journal of European Studies* 3, no. 2 (June 1973): 123-46.

Reviews Svevo's body of work and argues that it shows "indecision" and "equivocation" between two views: "moral revulsion against the actual basis of society, and 'dreams' of a socialist utopia," and "despair in the possibility of any radical change for the better."

Hardwick, Elizabeth. Preface to *Zeno's Conscience,* by Italo Svevo, translated by William Weaver, pp. ix-xii. New York: Alfred A. Knopf, 2001.

Describes *Confessions of Zeno* as a "rich and detailed study of Trieste families" before World War I, a "novel of money and an idle, introspective man's way of hanging on to it," and a "brilliant psychological document about procrastination."

Joyce, Stanislaus. Introduction to *As a Man Grows Older,* by Italo Svevo, translated by Beryl De Zoete, pp. v-xii. New York: New Directions, 1949.

Reflects on the friendship between Svevo and James Joyce and remarks that "it may not be too far-fetched to see in the person of Bloom," one of Joyce's main protagonists, "Svevo's maturer, objective, peaceable temper reacting upon the younger writer's more fiery mettle."

LaPalma, Marina deBellagente. "Wings of Desire: Italo Svevo's *Senilità.*" *Romance Languages Annual* (1989): 156-59.

Examines the character of Angiolina in Svevo's *As a Man Grows Older,* applying Judith Fetterley's critical method of "resistance," by which the reader refuses to accept the inherent patriarchal biases of a text, in order to reveal "the prejudices and myopia of a middle-class man in the last decade of the 19th century."

Lebowitz, Naomi. *Italo Svevo.* New Brunswick, N.J.: Rutgers University Press, 1978, 230 p.

Book-length study of Svevo that charts the development of the author's fiction, reviews the cultural atmosphere in which he wrote, and considers his positions within Italian and European literary traditions.

Moloney, Brian. *Italo Svevo: A Critical Introduction.* Edinburgh, Scotland: Edinburgh University Press, 1974, 140 p.

Second book-length study of Svevo in English that offers a complete review of his work, not only his major publications but his other stories, novellas, plays, and essays.

————. "A Sentimental Ulysses: Sterne, James Joyce and Italo Svevo's *Corto viaggio sentimentale.*" In *Literature and Travel,* edited by Michael Hanne, pp. 111-21. Amsterdam: Rodopi, 1993.

Details the thematic and formal similarities between Svevo's collection *Short Sentimental Journey, and Other Stories* and Laurence Sterne's *A Sentimental Journey* and James Joyce's *Ulysses.*

———. "Italo Svevo (Commercial) Traveller." In *Cross-Cultural Travel: Papers from the Royal Irish Academy Symposium on Literature and Travel, National University of Ireland, Galway, November 2002,* edited by Jane Conroy, pp. 305-13. New York: Peter Lang, 2003.

Discusses Svevo's impressions of England, as documented in letters and various essays, concluding that the author had a "deep affection" for the country and a "keen understanding" of its culture, but adding that his "Triestine background" allowed him to "temper his affection with irony" and his admiration "with detached and informed criticism."

Murray, Jean. "The Progress of the Hero in Italo Svevo's Novels." *Italian Studies* 21 (1966): 91-100.

Studies Svevo's novels *A Life, As a Man Grows Older,* and *Confessions of Zeno,* maintaining that they illustrate the "dilemma of modern man" and document the "eclipse of the romantic hero and the rise and fall of the existential hero."

Poggioli, Renato. "A Note on Svevo." In *Confessions Of Zeno,* by Italo Svevo, translated by Beryl De Zoete, pp. 1-8. London: Putnam & Co. Ltd., 1948.

Assesses Svevo's literary career, concluding that the author was endowed with "bourgeois honesty and common sense," and that "a kind of innocent wisdom was the real source of his greatness and originality."

Russell, Charles Coulter. "Italo Svevo's Trieste." *Italica* 52, no. 1 (spring 1975): 3-36.

Observes that Svevo was unsuccessful in Trieste because he was "out of tune with the patriotic and commercial rhythms of the city," asserting that the "economic tyranny" and rejection that the author experienced in the city forced him to "retreat into his own mind" and "develop what was to be peculiarly his."

———. *Italo Svevo, the Writer from Trieste: Reflections on His Background and His Work.* Ravenna, Italy: Longo Editore, 1978, 249 p.

Investigates Svevo's background and literary career, focusing, in particular, on the author's "shifting relationship with Trieste" and "the significant influence" that the city had on his writings.

Saccone, Eduardo. "Struggles, War, Revolution and Literature in Some Stories by Italo Svevo." In *Literature and Revolution,* edited by David Bevan, pp. 63-71. Amsterdam: Rodopi, 1989.

Identifies "struggle" as an important recurring theme in Svevo's work, noting that the struggles in his writings are usually caused by "a situation of malaise, produced in turn by differences" and "a condition of inequality," whether economic, social or moral, which "in feeding resentment, creates a reservoir" of violence.

Selig, Karl Ludwig. "A Note on the Theatre of Italo Svevo." *Italica* 27, no. 4 (December 1950): 327-29.

Considers Svevo's work as a playwright, concluding that the author "did not possess the technical training" nor the temperament to write drama.

———. "Italo Svevo and 'Solaria.'" *Italica* 30, no. 4 (December 1953): 227-30.

Details critical assessments of Svevo's writings that appeared in *Solaria,* one of "the leading and most important of the Italian literary reviews to have appeared since World War I," and suggests that the contribution of this magazine to the author's career was "paramount and decisive."

Staley, Thomas F. "Italo Svevo and the Ambience of Trieste." *Modern Fiction Studies* 18, no. 1 (spring 1972): 7-16.

Traces several aspects of "Triestine life and thought" that were formative in the development of Svevo's art, arguing that his work "defined itself within the Triestine microcosm of turmoil, turbulence, and disillusionment," and "contributed from its own obsessions, themes, and circumstances to the more universal demands of art."

Wagner, C. Roland. "Italo Svevo." *Contemporary Literature* 9, no. 4 (1968): 554-57.

Surveys the development of Svevo's literary career, arguing that "his maturity was created out of the materials of his despair" and describing his late novels as the "fruit of a spiritual strength and wholeness," which move "easily between the lyrical and the comic," without "ignoring the tragic."

Westwater, Lynn Lara. "Franz Kafka and Italo Svevo: 'A Blur of Languages.'" *Romance Languages Annual* 8 (1997): 342-50.

Explores the multilingualism of Kafka and Svevo, stating that "the quandary of language and of languages" plagued both authors, and that no language was "sufficient to negotiate their commercial, intellectual, and personal lives."

Zatta, Jane. "The Sentimental Journeys of Laurence Sterne and Italo Svevo." *Comparative Literature* 44, no. 4 (fall 1992): 361-79.

Addresses similarities between Svevo's collection of stories, *Short Sentimental Journey, and Other Stories,* and Laurence Sterne's novel *A Sentimental*

Journey, noting that both works suggest "that the possibility of communication resides not in reason" but in "sentiment," and both superimpose "a jour- ney in the mind onto a physical journey." The critic adds that Svevo's work "goes a step farther into the disconnected landscape first mapped out by Sterne."

Additional coverage of Svevo's life and career is contained in the following sources published by Gale: *Contemporary Authors,* Vols. 104, 122; *Dictionary of Literary Biography,* Vol. 264; *Encyclopedia of World Literature in the 20th Century,* Ed. 3; *European Writers,* Vol. 8; *Literature Resource Center*; *Major 20th-Century Writers,* Ed. 1; *Reference Guide to World Literature,* Eds. 2, 3; *Short Story Criticism,* Vol. 25; *Twentieth-Century Literary Criticism,* Vols. 2, 35; and *World Literature and Its Times,* Vol. 7.

How to Use This Index

The main references

Calvino, Italo
1923-1985 .... CLC 5, 8, 11, 22, 33, 39,
73; SSC 3, 48

list all author entries in the following Gale Literary Criticism series:

AAL = *Asian American Literature*
BG = *The Beat Generation: A Gale Critical Companion*
BLC = *Black Literature Criticism*
BLCS = *Black Literature Criticism Supplement*
CLC = *Contemporary Literary Criticism*
CLR = *Children's Literature Review*
CMLC = *Classical and Medieval Literature Criticism*
DC = *Drama Criticism*
FL = *Feminism in Literature: A Gale Critical Companion*
GL = *Gothic Literature: A Gale Critical Companion*
HLC = *Hispanic Literature Criticism*
HLCS = *Hispanic Literature Criticism Supplement*
HR = *Harlem Renaissance: A Gale Critical Companion*
LC = *Literature Criticism from 1400 to 1800*
NCLC = *Nineteenth-Century Literature Criticism*
NNAL = *Native North American Literature*
PC = *Poetry Criticism*
SSC = *Short Story Criticism*
TCLC = *Twentieth-Century Literary Criticism*
WLC = *World Literature Criticism, 1500 to the Present*
WLCS = *World Literature Criticism Supplement*

The cross-references

See also CA 85-88, 116; CANR 23, 61;
DAM NOV; DLB 196; EW 13; MTCW 1, 2;
RGSF 2; RGWL 2; SFW 4; SSFS 12

list all author entries in the following Gale biographical and literary sources:

AAYA = *Authors & Artists for Young Adults*
AFAW = *African American Writers*
AFW = *African Writers*
AITN = *Authors in the News*
AMW = *American Writers*
AMWR = *American Writers Retrospective Supplement*
AMWS = *American Writers Supplement*
ANW = *American Nature Writers*
AW = *Ancient Writers*
BEST = *Bestsellers*
BPFB = *Beacham's Encyclopedia of Popular Fiction: Biography and Resources*
BRW = *British Writers*
BRWS = *British Writers Supplement*
BW = *Black Writers*
BYA = *Beacham's Guide to Literature for Young Adults*
CA = *Contemporary Authors*
CAAS = *Contemporary Authors Autobiography Series*
CABS = *Contemporary Authors Bibliographical Series*
CAD = *Contemporary American Dramatists*
CANR = *Contemporary Authors New Revision Series*
CAP = *Contemporary Authors Permanent Series*
CBD = *Contemporary British Dramatists*
CCA = *Contemporary Canadian Authors*
CD = *Contemporary Dramatists*
CDALB = *Concise Dictionary of American Literary Biography*

CDALBS = *Concise Dictionary of American Literary Biography Supplement*
CDBLB = *Concise Dictionary of British Literary Biography*
CMW = *St. James Guide to Crime & Mystery Writers*
CN = *Contemporary Novelists*
CP = *Contemporary Poets*
CPW = *Contemporary Popular Writers*
CSW = *Contemporary Southern Writers*
CWD = *Contemporary Women Dramatists*
CWP = *Contemporary Women Poets*
CWRI = *St. James Guide to Children's Writers*
CWW = *Contemporary World Writers*
DA = *DISCovering Authors*
DA3 = *DISCovering Authors 3.0*
DAB = *DISCovering Authors: British Edition*
DAC = *DISCovering Authors: Canadian Edition*
DAM = *DISCovering Authors: Modules*
   DRAM: *Dramatists Module;* **MST:** *Most-studied Authors Module;*
   MULT: *Multicultural Authors Module;* **NOV:** *Novelists Module;*
   POET: *Poets Module;* **POP:** *Popular Fiction and Genre Authors Module*
DFS = *Drama for Students*
DLB = *Dictionary of Literary Biography*
DLBD = *Dictionary of Literary Biography Documentary Series*
DLBY = *Dictionary of Literary Biography Yearbook*
DNFS = *Literature of Developing Nations for Students*
EFS = *Epics for Students*
EW = *European Writers*
EWL = *Encyclopedia of World Literature in the 20th Century*
EXPN = *Exploring Novels*
EXPP = *Exploring Poetry*
EXPS = *Exploring Short Stories*
FANT = *St. James Guide to Fantasy Writers*
FW = *Feminist Writers*
GFL = *Guide to French Literature,* Beginnings to 1789, 1798 to the Present
GLL = *Gay and Lesbian Literature*
HGG = *St. James Guide to Horror, Ghost & Gothic Writers*
HW = *Hispanic Writers*
IDFW = *International Dictionary of Films and Filmmakers: Writers and Production Artists*
IDTP = *International Dictionary of Theatre: Playwrights*
LAIT = *Literature and Its Times*
LAW = *Latin American Writers*
JRDA = *Junior DISCovering Authors*
MAICYA = *Major Authors and Illustrators for Children and Young Adults*
MAICYAS = *Major Authors and Illustrators for Children and Young Adults Supplement*
MAWW = *Modern American Women Writers*
MJW = *Modern Japanese Writers*
MTCW = *Major 20th-Century Writers*
NCFS = *Nonfiction Classics for Students*
NFS = *Novels for Students*
PAB = *Poets: American and British*
PFS = *Poetry for Students*
RGAL = *Reference Guide to American Literature*
RGEL = *Reference Guide to English Literature*
RGSF = *Reference Guide to Short Fiction*
RGWL = *Reference Guide to World Literature*
RHW = *Twentieth-Century Romance and Historical Writers*
SAAS = *Something about the Author Autobiography Series*
SATA = *Something about the Author*
SFW = *St. James Guide to Science Fiction Writers*
SSFS = *Short Stories for Students*
TCWW = *Twentieth-Century Western Writers*
WLIT = *World Literature and Its Times*
WP = *World Poets*
YABC = *Yesterday's Authors of Books for Children*
YAW = *St. James Guide to Young Adult Writers*

Literary Criticism Series
Cumulative Author Index

Alegria, Claribel 1924- .... **CLC 75; HLCS 1;**
PC 26
See also CA 131; CAAS 15; CANR 66, 94,
134; CWW 2; DAM MULT; DLB 145,
283; EWL 3; HW 1; MTCW 2; MTFW
2005; PFS 21
Alegria, Claribel Joy
See Alegria, Claribel
Alegria, Fernando 1918-2005 .... **CLC 57**
See also CA 9-12R; CANR 5, 32, 72; EWL
3; HW 1, 2
Aleixandre, Vicente 1898-1984 .... **HLCS 1;**
TCLC 113
See also CANR 81; DLB 108, 329; EWL 3;
HW 2; MTCW 1, 2; RGWL 2, 3
Alekseev, Konstantin Sergeivich
See Stanislavsky, Constantin
Alekseyer, Konstantin Sergeyevich
See Stanislavsky, Constantin
Aleman, Mateo 1547-1615(?) .... **LC 81**
Alencar, Jose de 1829-1877 .... **NCLC 157**
See also DLB 307; LAW; WLIT 1
Alencon, Marguerite d'
See de Navarre, Marguerite
Alepoudelis, Odysseus
See Elytis, Odysseus
Aleshkovsky, Joseph 1929- .... **CLC 44**
See also CA 121, 128; DLB 317
Aleshkovsky, Yuz
See Aleshkovsky, Joseph
Alexander, Barbara
See Ehrenreich, Barbara
Alexander, Lloyd 1924-2007 .... **CLC 35**
See also AAYA 1, 27; BPFB 1; BYA 5, 6,
7, 9, 10, 11; CA 1-4R; 260; CLR 1, 5,
38, 55, 113; CLR 1, 5, 48; CWRI 5; DLB
52; FANT; JRDA; MAICYA 1, 2; MAIC-
YAS 1; MTCW 1; SAAS 19; SATA 3, 49,
81, 129, 135; SATA-Obit 182; SUFW;
TUS; WYA; YAW
Alexander, Lloyd Chudley
See Alexander, Lloyd
Alexander, Meena 1951- .... **CLC 121**
See also CA 115; CANR 38, 70, 146; CP 5,
6, 7; CWP; DLB 323; FW
Alexander, Rae Pace
See Alexander, Raymond Pace
Alexander, Raymond Pace
1898-1974 .... **SSC 62**
See also CA 97-100; SATA 22; SSFS 4
Alexander, Samuel 1859-1938 .... **TCLC 77**
Alexeiev, Konstantin
See Stanislavsky, Constantin
Alexeyev, Constantin Sergeivich
See Stanislavsky, Constantin
Alexeyev, Konstantin Sergeyevich
See Stanislavsky, Constantin
Alexie, Sherman 1966- .... **CLC 96, 154;**
NNAL; PC 53; SSC 107
See also AAYA 28; BYA 15; CA 138;
CANR 65, 95, 133, 174; CN 7; DA3;
DAM MULT; DLB 175, 206, 278; LATS
1:2; MTCW 2; MTFW 2005; NFS 17, 31;
SSFS 18
Alexie, Sherman Joseph, Jr.
See Alexie, Sherman
al-Farabi 870(?)-950 .... **CMLC 58**
See also DLB 115
Alfau, Felipe 1902-1999 .... **CLC 66**
See also CA 137
Alfieri, Vittorio 1749-1803 .... **NCLC 101**
See also EW 4; RGWL 2, 3; WLIT 7
Alfonso X 1221-1284 .... **CMLC 78**
Alfred, Jean Gaston
See Ponge, Francis
Alger, Horatio, Jr. 1832-1899 .... **NCLC 8, 83**
See also CLR 87; DLB 42; LAIT 2; RGAL
4; SATA 16; TUS

Al-Ghazali, Muhammad ibn Muhammad
1058-1111 .... **CMLC 50**
See also DLB 115
Algren, Nelson 1909-1981 ..... **CLC 4, 10, 33;**
SSC 33
See also AMWS 9; BPFB 1; CA 13-16R,
103; CANR 20, 61; CDALB 1941-1968;
CN 1, 2; DLB 9; DLBY 1981, 1982,
2000; EWL 3; MAL 5; MTCW 1, 2;
MTFW 2005; RGAL 4; RGSF 2
al-Hamadhani 967-1007 .... **CMLC 93**
See also WLIT 6
al-Hariri, al-Qasim ibn 'Ali Abu
Muhammad al-Basri
1054-1122 .... **CMLC 63**
See also RGWL 3
Ali, Ahmed 1908-1998 .... **CLC 69**
See also CA 25-28R; CANR 15, 34; CN 1,
2, 3, 4, 5; DLB 323; EWL 3
Ali, Tariq 1943- .... **CLC 173**
See also CA 25-28R; CANR 10, 99, 161,
196
Alighieri, Dante
See Dante
al-Kindi, Abu Yusuf Ya'qub ibn Ishaq c.
801-c. 873 .... **CMLC 80**
Allan, John B.
See Westlake, Donald E.
Allan, Sidney
See Hartmann, Sadakichi
Allan, Sydney
See Hartmann, Sadakichi
Allard, Janet **CLC 59**
Allen, Betsy
See Harrison, Elizabeth (Allen) Cavanna
Allen, Edward 1948- .... **CLC 59**
Allen, Fred 1894-1956 .... **TCLC 87**
Allen, Paula Gunn 1939-2008 . **CLC 84, 202,**
280; NNAL
See also AMWS 4; CA 112, 143, 272;
CANR 63, 130; CWP; DA3; DAM
MULT; DLB 175; FW; MTCW 2; MTFW
2005; RGAL 4; TCWW 2
Allen, Roland
See Ayckbourn, Alan
Allen, Sarah A.
See Hopkins, Pauline Elizabeth
Allen, Sidney H.
See Hartmann, Sadakichi
Allen, Woody 1935- ..... **CLC 16, 52, 195, 288**
See also AAYA 10, 51; AMWS 15; CA 33-
36R; CANR 27, 38, 63, 128, 172; DAM
POP; DLB 44; MTCW 1; SSFS 21
Allende, Isabel 1942- ... **CLC 39, 57, 97, 170,**
264; HLC 1; SSC 65; WLCS
See also AAYA 18, 70; CA 125, 130; CANR
51, 74, 129, 165, 208; CDWLB 3; CLR
99; CWW 2; DA3; DAM MULT, NOV;
DLB 145; DNFS 1; EWL 3; FL 1:5; FW;
HW 1, 2; INT CA-130; LAIT 5; LAWS
1; LMFS 2; MTCW 1, 2; MTFW 2005;
NCFS 1; NFS 6, 18, 29; RGSF 2; RGWL
3; SATA 163; SSFS 11, 16; WLIT 1
Alleyn, Ellen
See Rossetti, Christina
Alleyne, Carla D. **CLC 65**
Allingham, Margery (Louise)
1904-1966 .... **CLC 19**
See also CA 5-8R; 25-28R; CANR 4, 58;
CMW 4; DLB 77; MSW; MTCW 1, 2
Allingham, William 1824-1889 ...... **NCLC 25**
See also DLB 35; RGEL 2
Allison, Dorothy E. 1949- . **CLC 78, 153, 290**
See also AAYA 53; CA 140; CANR 66, 107;
CN 7; CSW; DA3; DLB 350; FW; MTCW
2; MTFW 2005; NFS 11; RGAL 4
Alloula, Malek **CLC 65**
Allston, Washington 1779-1843 .... **NCLC 2**
See also DLB 1, 235

Almedingen, E. M.
See Almedingen, Martha Edith von
Almedingen, Martha Edith von
1898-1971 .... **CLC 12**
See also CA 1-4R; CANR 1; SATA 3
Almodovar, Pedro 1949(?)- .... **CLC 114, 229;**
HLCS 1
See also CA 133; CANR 72, 151; HW 2
Almqvist, Carl Jonas Love
1793-1866 .... **NCLC 42**
al-Mutanabbi, Ahmad ibn al-Husayn Abu
al-Tayyib al-Jufi al-Kindi
915-965 .... **CMLC 66**
See also RGWL 3; WLIT 6
Alonso, Damaso 1898-1990 .... **CLC 14**
See also CA 110, 131, 130; CANR 72; DLB
108; EWL 3; HW 1, 2
Alov
See Gogol, Nikolai
al'Sadaawi, Nawal
See El Saadawi, Nawal
al-Shaykh, Hanan 1945- .... **CLC 218**
See also CA 135; CANR 111; CWW 2;
DLB 346; EWL 3; WLIT 6
Al Siddik
See Rolfe, Frederick (William Serafino Aus-
tin Lewis Mary)
Alta 1942- .... **CLC 19**
See also CA 57-60
Alter, Robert B. 1935- .... **CLC 34**
See also CA 49-52; CANR 1, 47, 100, 160,
201
Alter, Robert Bernard
See Alter, Robert B.
Alther, Lisa 1944- .... **CLC 7, 41**
See also BPFB 1; CA 65-68; CAAS 30;
CANR 12, 30, 51, 180; CN 4, 5, 6, 7;
CSW; GLL 2; MTCW 1
Althusser, L.
See Althusser, Louis
Althusser, Louis 1918-1990 .... **CLC 106**
See also CA 131, 132; CANR 102; DLB
242
Altman, Robert 1925-2006 .... **CLC 16, 116,**
242
See also CA 73-76, 254; CANR 43
Alurista
See Urista, Alberto
Alvarez, A. 1929- .... **CLC 5, 13**
See also CA 1-4R; CANR 3, 33, 63, 101,
134; CN 3, 4, 5, 6; CP 1, 2, 3, 4, 5, 6, 7;
DLB 14, 40; MTFW 2005
Alvarez, Alejandro Rodriguez
1903-1965 . **CLC 49; DC 32; TCLC 199**
See also CA 131; 93-96; EWL 3; HW 1
Alvarez, Julia 1950- .. **CLC 93, 274; HLCS 1**
See also AAYA 25; AMWS 7; CA 147;
CANR 69, 101, 133, 166; DA3; DLB 282;
LATS 1:2; LLW; MTCW 2; MTFW 2005;
NFS 5, 9; SATA 129; SSFS 27, 31; WLIT
1
Alvaro, Corrado 1896-1956 .... **TCLC 60**
See also CA 163; DLB 264; EWL 3
Amado, Jorge 1912-2001 ... **CLC 13, 40, 106,**
232; HLC 1
See also CA 77-80, 201; CANR 35, 74, 135;
CWW 2; DAM MULT, NOV; DLB 113,
307; EWL 3; HW 2; LAW; LAWS 1;
MTCW 1, 2; MTFW 2005; RGWL 2, 3;
TWA; WLIT 1
Ambler, Eric 1909-1998 .... **CLC 4, 6, 9**
See also BRWS 4; CA 9-12R, 171; CANR
7, 38, 74; CMW 4; CN 1, 2, 3, 4, 5, 6;
DLB 77; MSW; MTCW 1, 2; TEA
Ambrose c. 339-c. 397 .... **CMLC 103**
Ambrose, Stephen E. 1936-2002 .... **CLC 145**
See also AAYA 44; CA 1-4R, 209; CANR
3, 43, 57, 83, 105; MTFW 2005; NCFS 2;
SATA 40, 138

Amichai, Yehuda 1924-2000 .. **CLC 9, 22, 57, 116; PC 38**
See also CA 85-88, 189; CANR 46, 60, 99, 132; CWW 2; EWL 3; MTCW 1, 2; MTFW 2005; PFS 24; RGHL; WLIT 6

Amichai, Yehudah
See Amichai, Yehuda

Amiel, Henri Frederic 1821-1881 .... **NCLC 4**
See also DLB 217

Amis, Kingsley 1922-1995 . **CLC 1, 2, 3, 5, 8, 13, 40, 44, 129**
See also AAYA 77; AITN 2; BPFB 1; BRWS 2; CA 9-12R, 150; CANR 8, 28, 54; CDBLB 1945-1960; CN 1, 2, 3, 4, 5, 6; CP 1, 2, 3, 4; DA; DA3; DAB; DAC; DAM MST, NOV; DLB 15, 27, 100, 139, 326, 352; DLBY 1996; EWL 3; HGG; INT CANR-8; MTCW 1, 2; MTFW 2005; RGEL 2; RGSF 2; SFW 4

Amis, Martin 1949- ... **CLC 4, 9, 38, 62, 101, 213; SSC 112**
See also BEST 90:3; BRWS 4; CA 65-68; CANR 8, 27, 54, 73, 95, 132, 166, 208; CN 5, 6, 7; DA3; DLB 14, 194; EWL 3; INT CANR-27; MTCW 2; MTFW 2005

Amis, Martin Louis
See Amis, Martin

Ammianus Marcellinus c. 330-c. 395 .... **CMLC 60**
See also AW 2; DLB 211

Ammons, A.R. 1926-2001 .. **CLC 2, 3, 5, 8, 9, 25, 57, 108; PC 16**
See also AITN 1; AMWS 7; CA 9-12R, 193; CANR 6, 36, 51, 73, 107, 156; CP 1, 2, 3, 4, 5, 6, 7; CSW; DAM POET; DLB 5, 165, 342; EWL 3; MAL 5; MTCW 1, 2; PFS 19; RGAL 4; TCLE 1:1

Ammons, Archie Randolph
See Ammons, A.R.

Amo, Tauraatua i
See Adams, Henry

Amory, Thomas 1691(?)-1788 .... **LC 48**
See also DLB 39

Anand, Mulk Raj 1905-2004 ..... **CLC 23, 93, 237**
See also CA 65-68, 231; CANR 32, 64; CN 1, 2, 3, 4, 5, 6, 7; DAM NOV; DLB 323; EWL 3; MTCW 1, 2; MTFW 2005; RGSF 2

Anatol
See Schnitzler, Arthur

Anaximander c. 611B.C.-c. 546B.C. .... **CMLC 22**

Anaya, Rudolfo 1937- ...... **CLC 23, 148, 255; HLC 1**
See also AAYA 20; BYA 13; CA 45-48; CAAS 4; CANR 1, 32, 51, 124, 169; CLR 129; CN 4, 5, 6, 7; DAM MULT, NOV; DLB 82, 206, 278; HW 1; LAIT 4; LLW; MAL 5; MTCW 1, 2; MTFW 2005; NFS 12; RGAL 4; RGSF 2; TCWW 2; WLIT 1

Anaya, Rudolfo A.
See Anaya, Rudolfo

Anaya, Rudolpho Alfonso
See Anaya, Rudolfo

Andersen, Hans Christian 1805-1875 ...... **NCLC 7, 79, 214; SSC 6, 56; WLC 1**
See also AAYA 57; CLR 6, 113; DA; DA3; DAB; DAC; DAM MST, POP; EW 6; MAICYA 1, 2; RGSF 2; RGWL 2, 3; SATA 100; TWA; WCH; YABC 1

Anderson, C. Farley
See Mencken, H. L.; Nathan, George Jean

Anderson, Jessica (Margaret) Queale 1916- .... **CLC 37**
See also CA 9-12R; CANR 4, 62; CN 4, 5, 6, 7; DLB 325

Anderson, Jon (Victor) 1940- .... **CLC 9**
See also CA 25-28R; CANR 20; CP 1, 3, 4, 5; DAM POET

Anderson, Lindsay (Gordon) 1923-1994 .... **CLC 20**
See also CA 125, 128, 146; CANR 77

Anderson, Maxwell 1888-1959 .... **TCLC 2, 144**
See also CA 105, 152; DAM DRAM; DFS 16, 20; DLB 7, 228; MAL 5; MTCW 2; MTFW 2005; RGAL 4

Anderson, Poul 1926-2001 .... **CLC 15**
See also AAYA 5, 34; BPFB 1; BYA 6, 8, 9; CA 1-4R, 181, 199; CAAE 181; CAAS 2; CANR 2, 15, 34, 64, 110; CLR 58; DLB 8; FANT; INT CANR-15; MTCW 1, 2; MTFW 2005; SATA 90; SATA-Brief 39; SATA-Essay 106; SCFW 1, 2; SFW 4; SUFW 1, 2

Anderson, R. W.
See Anderson, Robert

Anderson, Robert 1917-2009 .... **CLC 23**
See also AITN 1; CA 21-24R, 283; CANR 32; CD 6; DAM DRAM; DLB 7; LAIT 5

Anderson, Robert W.
See Anderson, Robert

Anderson, Robert Woodruff
See Anderson, Robert

Anderson, Roberta Joan
See Mitchell, Joni

Anderson, Sherwood 1876-1941 ... **SSC 1, 46, 91, 142; TCLC 1, 10, 24, 123; WLC 1**
See also AAYA 30; AMW; AMWC 2; BPFB 1; CA 104, 121; CANR 61; CDALB 1917-1929; DA; DA3; DAB; DAC; DAM MST, NOV; DLB 4, 9, 86; DLBD 1; EWL 3; EXPS; GLL 2; MAL 5; MTCW 1, 2; MTFW 2005; NFS 4; RGAL 4; RGSF 2; SSFS 4, 10, 11; TUS

Anderson, Wes 1969- .... **CLC 227**
See also CA 214

Andier, Pierre
See Desnos, Robert

Andouard
See Giraudoux, Jean

Andrade, Carlos Drummond de
See Drummond de Andrade, Carlos

Andrade, Mario de
See de Andrade, Mario

Andreae, Johann V(alentin) 1586-1654 .... **LC 32**
See also DLB 164

Andreas Capellanus fl. c. 1185- .... **CMLC 45**
See also DLB 208

Andreas-Salome, Lou 1861-1937 ... **TCLC 56**
See also CA 178; DLB 66

Andreev, Leonid
See Andreyev, Leonid

Andress, Lesley
See Sanders, Lawrence

Andrew, Joseph Maree
See Occomy, Marita (Odette) Bonner

Andrewes, Lancelot 1555-1626 .... **LC 5**
See also DLB 151, 172

Andrews, Cicily Fairfield
See West, Rebecca

Andrews, Elton V.
See Pohl, Frederik

Andrews, Peter
See Soderbergh, Steven

Andrews, Raymond 1934-1991 .... **BLC 2:1**
See also BW 2; CA 81-84, 136; CANR 15, 42

Andreyev, Leonid 1871-1919 ... **TCLC 3, 221**
See also CA 104, 185; DLB 295; EWL 3

Andreyev, Leonid Nikolaevich
See Andreyev, Leonid

Andrezel, Pierre
See Blixen, Karen

Andric, Ivo 1892-1975 .... **CLC 8; SSC 36; TCLC 135**
See also CA 81-84; 57-60; CANR 43, 60; CDWLB 4; DLB 147, 329; EW 11; EWL 3; MTCW 1; RGSF 2; RGWL 2, 3

Androvar
See Prado (Calvo), Pedro

Angela of Foligno 1248(?)-1309 .... **CMLC 76**

Angelique, Pierre
See Bataille, Georges

Angell, Judie
See Angell, Judie

Angell, Judie 1937- .... **CLC 30**
See also AAYA 11, 71; BYA 6; CA 77-80; CANR 49; CLR 33; JRDA; SATA 22, 78; WYA; YAW

Angell, Roger 1920- .... **CLC 26**
See also CA 57-60; CANR 13, 44, 70, 144; DLB 171, 185

Angelou, Maya 1928- ...... **BLC 1:1; CLC 12, 35, 64, 77, 155; PC 32; WLCS**
See also AAYA 7, 20; AMWS 4; BPFB 1; BW 2, 3; BYA 2; CA 65-68; CANR 19, 42, 65, 111, 133, 204; CDALBS; CLR 53; CP 4, 5, 6, 7; CPW; CSW; CWP; DA; DA3; DAB; DAC; DAM MST, MULT, POET, POP; DLB 38; EWL 3; EXPN; EXPP; FL 1:5; LAIT 4; MAICYA 2; MAI-CYAS 1; MAL 5; MBL; MTCW 1, 2; MTFW 2005; NCFS 2; NFS 2; PFS 2, 3, 33; RGAL 4; SATA 49, 136; TCLE 1:1; WYA; YAW

Angouleme, Marguerite d'
See de Navarre, Marguerite

Anna Comnena 1083-1153 .... **CMLC 25**

Annensky, Innokentii Fedorovich
See Annensky, Innokenty (Fyodorovich)

Annensky, Innokenty (Fyodorovich) 1856-1909 .... **TCLC 14**
See also CA 110, 155; DLB 295; EWL 3

Annunzio, Gabriele d'
See D'Annunzio, Gabriele

Anodos
See Coleridge, Mary E(lizabeth)

Anon, Charles Robert
See Pessoa, Fernando

Anouilh, Jean 1910-1987 ..... **CLC 1, 3, 8, 13, 40, 50; DC 8, 21; TCLC 195**
See also AAYA 67; CA 17-20R, 123; CANR 32; DAM DRAM; DFS 9, 10, 19; DLB 321; EW 13; EWL 3; GFL 1789 to the Present; MTCW 1, 2; MTFW 2005; RGWL 2, 3; TWA

Anouilh, Jean Marie Lucien Pierre
See Anouilh, Jean

Ansa, Tina McElroy 1949- .... **BLC 2:1**
See also BW 2; CA 142; CANR 143; CSW

Anselm of Canterbury 1033(?)-1109 .... **CMLC 67**
See also DLB 115

Anthony, Florence
See Ai

Anthony, John
See Ciardi, John (Anthony)

Anthony, Peter
See Shaffer, Anthony; Shaffer, Peter

Anthony, Piers 1934- .... **CLC 35**
See also AAYA 11, 48; BYA 7; CA 200; CAAE 200; CANR 28, 56, 73, 102, 133, 202; CLR 118; CPW; DAM POP; DLB 8; FANT; MAICYA 2; MAICYAS 1; MTCW 1, 2; MTFW 2005; SAAS 22; SATA 84, 129; SATA-Essay 129; SFW 4; SUFW 1, 2; YAW

Anthony, Susan B(rownell) 1820-1906 .... **TCLC 84**
See also CA 211; FW

Antiphon c. 480B.C.-c. 411B.C. .... **CMLC 55**

Antoine, Marc
See Proust, Marcel

Antoninus, Brother
See Everson, William

Antonioni, Michelangelo
1912-2007 .... **CLC 20, 144, 259**
See also CA 73-76, 262; CANR 45, 77

Antschel, Paul
See Celan, Paul

Anwar, Chairil 1922-1949 .... **TCLC 22**
See also CA 121, 219; EWL 3; RGWL 3

Anyidoho, Kofi 1947- .... **BLC 2:1**
See also BW 3; CA 178; CP 5, 6, 7; DLB
157; EWL 3

Anzaldua, Gloria (Evanjelina)
1942-2004 .... **CLC 200; HLCS 1**
See also CA 175, 227; CSW; CWP; DLB
122; FW; LLW; RGAL 4; SATA-Obit 154

Apess, William 1798-1839(?) .... **NCLC 73;
NNAL**
See also DAM MULT; DLB 175, 243

Apollinaire, Guillaume 1880-1918 .... **PC 7;
TCLC 3, 8, 51**
See also CA 104, 152; DAM POET; DLB
258, 321; EW 9; EWL 3; GFL 1789 to
the Present; MTCW 2; PFS 24; RGWL 2,
3; TWA; WP

Apollonius of Rhodes
See Apollonius Rhodius

Apollonius Rhodius c. 300B.C.-c.
220B.C. .... **CMLC 28**
See also AW 1; DLB 176; RGWL 2, 3

Appelfeld, Aharon 1932- ... **CLC 23, 47; SSC
42**
See also CA 112, 133; CANR 86, 160, 207;
CWW 2; DLB 299; EWL 3; RGHL;
RGSF 2; WLIT 6

Appelfeld, Aron
See Appelfeld, Aharon

Apple, Max (Isaac) 1941- .... **CLC 9, 33; SSC
50**
See also AMWS 17; CA 81-84; CANR 19,
54; DLB 130

Appleman, Philip (Dean) 1926- .... **CLC 51**
See also CA 13-16R; CAAS 18; CANR 6,
29, 56

Appleton, Lawrence
See Lovecraft, H. P.

Apteryx
See Eliot, T. S.

Apuleius, (Lucius Madaurensis) c. 125-c.
164 .... **CMLC 1, 84**
See also AW 2; CDWLB 1; DLB 211;
RGWL 2, 3; SUFW; WLIT 8

Aquin, Hubert 1929-1977 .... **CLC 15**
See also CA 105; DLB 53; EWL 3

Aquinas, Thomas 1224(?)-1274 ..... **CMLC 33**
See also DLB 115; EW 1; TWA

Aragon, Louis 1897-1982 .... **CLC 3, 22;
TCLC 123**
See also CA 69-72, 108; CANR 28, 71;
DAM NOV, POET; DLB 72, 258; EW 11;
EWL 3; GFL 1789 to the Present; GLL 2;
LMFS 2; MTCW 1, 2; RGWL 2, 3

Arany, Janos 1817-1882 .... **NCLC 34**

Aranyos, Kakay 1847-1910
See Mikszath, Kalman

Aratus of Soli c. 315B.C.-c.
240B.C. .... **CMLC 64, 114**
See also DLB 176

Arbuthnot, John 1667-1735 .... **LC 1**
See also BRWS 16; DLB 101

Archer, Herbert Winslow
See Mencken, H. L.

Archer, Jeffrey 1940- .... **CLC 28**
See also AAYA 16; BEST 89:3; BPFB 1;
CA 77-80; CANR 22, 52, 95, 136, 209;
CPW; DA3; DAM POP; INT CANR-22;
MTFW 2005

Archer, Jeffrey Howard
See Archer, Jeffrey

Archer, Jules 1915- .... **CLC 12**
See also CA 9-12R; CANR 6, 69; SAAS 5;
SATA 4, 85

Archer, Lee
See Ellison, Harlan

Archilochus c. 7th cent. B.C.- .... **CMLC 44**
See also DLB 176

Ard, William
See Jakes, John

Arden, John 1930- .... **CLC 6, 13, 15**
See also BRWS 2; CA 13-16R; CAAS 4;
CANR 31, 65, 67, 124; CBD; CD 5, 6;
DAM DRAM; DFS 9; DLB 13, 245;
EWL 3; MTCW 1

Arenas, Reinaldo 1943-1990 .. **CLC 41; HLC
1; TCLC 191**
See also CA 124, 128, 133; CANR 73, 106;
DAM MULT; DLB 145; EWL 3; GLL 2;
HW 1; LAW; LAWS 1; MTCW 2; MTFW
2005; RGSF 2; RGWL 3; WLIT 1

Arendt, Hannah 1906-1975 .... **CLC 66, 98;
TCLC 193**
See also CA 17-20R; 61-64; CANR 26, 60,
172; DLB 242; MTCW 1, 2

Aretino, Pietro 1492-1556 .... **LC 12, 165**
See also RGWL 2, 3

Arghezi, Tudor
See Theodorescu, Ion N.

Arguedas, Jose Maria 1911-1969 .... **CLC 10,
18; HLCS 1; TCLC 147**
See also CA 89-92; CANR 73; DLB 113;
EWL 3; HW 1; LAW; RGWL 2, 3; WLIT
1

Argueta, Manlio 1936- .... **CLC 31**
See also CA 131; CANR 73; CWW 2; DLB
145; EWL 3; HW 1; RGWL 3

Arias, Ron 1941- .... **HLC 1**
See also CA 131; CANR 81, 136; DAM
MULT; DLB 82; HW 1, 2; MTCW 2;
MTFW 2005

Ariosto, Lodovico
See Ariosto, Ludovico

Ariosto, Ludovico 1474-1533 ... **LC 6, 87; PC
42**
See also EW 2; RGWL 2, 3; WLIT 7

Aristides
See Epstein, Joseph

Aristides Quintilianus fl. c. 100-fl. c.
400 .... **CMLC 122**

Aristophanes 450B.C.-385B.C. .... **CMLC 4,
51; DC 2; WLCS**
See also AW 1; CDWLB 1; DA; DA3;
DAB; DAC; DAM DRAM, MST; DFS
10; DLB 176; LMFS 1; RGWL 2, 3;
TWA; WLIT 8

Aristotle 384B.C.-322B.C. .... **CMLC 31, 123;
WLCS**
See also AW 1; CDWLB 1; DA; DA3;
DAB; DAC; DAM MST; DLB 176;
RGWL 2, 3; TWA; WLIT 8

Arlt, Roberto 1900-1942 .. **HLC 1; TCLC 29**
See also CA 123, 131; CANR 67; DAM
MULT; DLB 305; EWL 3; HW 1, 2;
IDTP; LAW

Arlt, Roberto Godofredo Christophersen
See Arlt, Roberto

Armah, Ayi Kwei 1939- . **BLC 1:1, 2:1; CLC
5, 33, 136**
See also AFW; BRWS 10; BW 1; CA 61-
64; CANR 21, 64; CDWLB 3; CN 1, 2,
3, 4, 5, 6, 7; DAM MULT, POET; DLB
117; EWL 3; MTCW 1; WLIT 2

Armatrading, Joan 1950- .... **CLC 17**
See also CA 114, 186

Armin, Robert 1568(?)-1615(?) .... **LC 120**

Armitage, Frank
See Carpenter, John

Armstrong, Jeannette (C.) 1948- .... **NNAL**
See also CA 149; CCA 1; CN 6, 7; DAC;
DLB 334; SATA 102

Arnauld, Antoine 1612-1694 .... **LC 169**
See also DLB 268

Arnette, Robert
See Silverberg, Robert

Arnim, Achim von (Ludwig Joachim von
Arnim) 1781-1831 .. **NCLC 5, 159; SSC
29**
See also DLB 90

Arnim, Bettina von 1785-1859 ...... **NCLC 38,
123**
See also DLB 90; RGWL 2, 3

Arnold, Matthew 1822-1888 ..... **NCLC 6, 29,
89, 126, 218; PC 5, 94; WLC 1**
See also BRW 5; CDBLB 1832-1890; DA;
DAB; DAC; DAM MST, POET; DLB 32,
57; EXPP; PAB; PFS 2; TEA; WP

Arnold, Thomas 1795-1842 .... **NCLC 18**
See also DLB 55

Arnow, Harriette (Louisa) Simpson
1908-1986 ...... **CLC 2, 7, 18; TCLC 196**
See also BPFB 1; CA 9-12R, 118; CANR
14; CN 2, 3, 4; DLB 6; FW; MTCW 1, 2;
RHW; SATA 42; SATA-Obit 47

Arouet, Francois-Marie
See Voltaire

Arp, Hans
See Arp, Jean

Arp, Jean 1887-1966 .... **CLC 5; TCLC 115**
See also CA 81-84, 25-28R; CANR 42, 77;
EW 10

Arrabal
See Arrabal, Fernando

Arrabal, Fernando 1932- .. **CLC 2, 9, 18, 58;
DC 35**
See also CA 9-12R; CANR 15; CWW 2;
DLB 321; EWL 3; LMFS 2

Arrabal Teran, Fernando
See Arrabal, Fernando

Arreola, Juan Jose 1918-2001 .... **CLC 147;
HLC 1; SSC 38**
See also CA 113, 131, 200; CANR 81;
CWW 2; DAM MULT; DLB 113; DNFS
2; EWL 3; HW 1, 2; LAW; RGSF 2

Arrian c. 89(?)-c. 155(?) .... **CMLC 43**
See also DLB 176

Arrick, Fran
See Angell, Judie

Arrley, Richmond
See Delany, Samuel R., Jr.

Artaud, Antonin 1896-1948 ... **DC 14; TCLC
3, 36**
See also CA 104, 149; DA3; DAM DRAM;
DFS 22; DLB 258, 321; EW 11; EWL 3;
GFL 1789 to the Present; MTCW 2;
MTFW 2005; RGWL 2, 3

Artaud, Antonin Marie Joseph
See Artaud, Antonin

Arthur, Ruth M(abel) 1905-1979 ..... **CLC 12**
See also CA 9-12R; 85-88; CANR 4; CWRI
5; SATA 7, 26

Artsybashev, Mikhail (Petrovich)
1878-1927 .... **TCLC 31**
See also CA 170; DLB 295

Arundel, Honor (Morfydd)
1919-1973 .... **CLC 17**
See also CA 21-22; 41-44R; CAP 2; CLR
35; CWRI 5; SATA 4; SATA-Obit 24

Arzner, Dorothy 1900-1979 .... **CLC 98**

Asch, Sholem 1880-1957 .... **TCLC 3**
See also CA 105; DLB 333; EWL 3; GLL
2; RGHL

Babbis, Eleanor
  See Friis-Baastad, Babbis Ellinor
Babel, Isaac
  See Babel, Isaak (Emmanuilovich)
Babel, Isaak (Emmanuilovich)
  1894-1941(?) . **SSC 16, 78; TCLC 2, 13, 171**
  See also CA 104, 155; CANR 113; DLB 272; EW 11; EWL 3; MTCW 2; MTFW 2005; RGSF 2; RGWL 2, 3; SSFS 10; TWA
Babits, Mihaly 1883-1941 .... **TCLC 14**
  See also CA 114; CDWLB 4; DLB 215; EWL 3
Babur 1483-1530 .... **LC 18**
Babylas
  See Ghelderode, Michel de
Baca, Jimmy Santiago 1952- . **HLC 1; PC 41**
  See also CA 131; CANR 81, 90, 146; CP 6, 7; DAM MULT; DLB 122; HW 1, 2; LLW; MAL 5
Baca, Jose Santiago
  See Baca, Jimmy Santiago
Bacchelli, Riccardo 1891-1985 .... **CLC 19**
  See also CA 29-32R, 117; DLB 264; EWL 3
Bacchylides c. 520B.C.-c. 452B.C. .... **CMLC 119**
Bach, Richard 1936- .... **CLC 14**
  See also AITN 1; BEST 89:2; BPFB 1; BYA 5; CA 9-12R; CANR 18, 93, 151; CPW; DAM NOV, POP; FANT; MTCW 1; SATA 13
Bach, Richard David
  See Bach, Richard
Bache, Benjamin Franklin
  1769-1798 .... **LC 74**
  See also DLB 43
Bachelard, Gaston 1884-1962 ...... **TCLC 128**
  See also CA 97-100; 89-92; DLB 296; GFL 1789 to the Present
Bachman, Richard
  See King, Stephen
Bachmann, Ingeborg 1926-1973 ..... **CLC 69; TCLC 192**
  See also CA 93-96; 45-48; CANR 69; DLB 85; EWL 3; RGHL; RGWL 2, 3
Bacon, Francis 1561-1626 ..... **LC 18, 32, 131**
  See also BRW 1; CDBLB Before 1660; DLB 151, 236, 252; RGEL 2; TEA
Bacon, Roger 1214(?)-1294 ... **CMLC 14, 108**
  See also DLB 115
Bacovia, G.
  See Bacovia, George
Bacovia, George 1881-1957 .... **TCLC 24**
  See Bacovia, George
  See also CA 123, 189; CDWLB 4; DLB 220; EWL 3
Badanes, Jerome 1937-1995 .... **CLC 59**
  See also CA 234
Bage, Robert 1728-1801 .... **NCLC 182**
  See also DLB 39; RGEL 2
Bagehot, Walter 1826-1877 .... **NCLC 10**
  See also DLB 55
Bagnold, Enid 1889-1981 .... **CLC 25**
  See also AAYA 75; BYA 2; CA 5-8R, 103; CANR 5, 40; CBD; CN 2; CWD; CWRI 5; DAM DRAM; DLB 13, 160, 191, 245; FW; MAICYA 1, 2; RGEL 2; SATA 1, 25
Bagritsky, Eduard
  See Dzyubin, Eduard Georgievich
Bagritsky, Edvard
  See Dzyubin, Eduard Georgievich
Bagrjana, Elisaveta
  See Belcheva, Elisaveta Lyubomirova
Bagryana, Elisaveta
  See Belcheva, Elisaveta Lyubomirova

Bailey, Paul 1937- .... **CLC 45**
  See also CA 21-24R; CANR 16, 62, 124; CN 1, 2, 3, 4, 5, 6, 7; DLB 14, 271; GLL 2
Baillie, Joanna 1762-1851 ...... **NCLC 71, 151**
  See also DLB 93, 344; GL 2; RGEL 2
Bainbridge, Beryl 1934-2010 ..... **CLC 4, 5, 8, 10, 14, 18, 22, 62, 130, 292**
  See also BRWS 6; CA 21-24R; CANR 24, 55, 75, 88, 128; CN 2, 3, 4, 5, 6, 7; DAM NOV; DLB 14, 231; EWL 3; MTCW 1, 2; MTFW 2005
Baker, Carlos (Heard)
  1909-1987 .... **TCLC 119**
  See also CA 5-8R, 122; CANR 3, 63; DLB 103
Baker, Elliott 1922-2007 .... **CLC 8**
  See also CA 45-48, 257; CANR 2, 63; CN 1, 2, 3, 4, 5, 6, 7
Baker, Elliott Joseph
  See Baker, Elliott
Baker, Jean H.
  See Russell, George William
Baker, Nicholson 1957- .... **CLC 61, 165**
  See also AMWS 13; CA 135; CANR 63, 120, 138, 190; CN 6; CPW; DA3; DAM POP; DLB 227; MTFW 2005
Baker, Ray Stannard 1870-1946 .... **TCLC 47**
  See also CA 118; DLB 345
Baker, Russell 1925- .... **CLC 31**
  See also BEST 89:4; CA 57-60; CANR 11, 41, 59, 137; MTCW 1, 2; MTFW 2005
Baker, Russell Wayne
  See Baker, Russell
Bakhtin, M.
  See Bakhtin, Mikhail Mikhailovich
Bakhtin, M. M.
  See Bakhtin, Mikhail Mikhailovich
Bakhtin, Mikhail
  See Bakhtin, Mikhail Mikhailovich
Bakhtin, Mikhail Mikhailovich
  1895-1975 .... **CLC 83; TCLC 160**
  See also CA 128, 113; DLB 242; EWL 3
Bakshi, Ralph 1938(?)- .... **CLC 26**
  See also CA 112, 138; IDFW 3
Bakunin, Mikhail (Alexandrovich)
  1814-1876 .... **NCLC 25, 58**
  See also DLB 277
Bal, Mieke 1946- .... **CLC 252**
  See also CA 156; CANR 99
Bal, Mieke Maria Gertrudis
  See Bal, Mieke
Baldwin, James 1924-1987 ...... **BLC 1:1, 2:1; CLC 1, 2, 3, 4, 5, 8, 13, 15, 17, 42, 50, 67, 90, 127; DC 1; SSC 10, 33, 98, 134; TCLC 229; WLC 1**
  See also AAYA 4, 34; AFAW 1, 2; AMWR 2; AMWS 1; BPFB 1; BW 1; CA 1-4R, 124; CABS 1; CAD; CANR 3, 24; CDALB 1941-1968; CN 1, 2, 3, 4; CPW; DA; DA3; DAB; DAC; DAM MST, MULT, NOV, POP; DFS 11, 15; DLB 2, 7, 33, 249, 278; DLBY 1987; EWL 3; EXPS; LAIT 5; MAL 5; MTCW 1, 2; MTFW 2005; NCFS 4; NFS 4; RGAL 4; RGSF 2; SATA 9; SATA-Obit 54; SSFS 2, 18; TUS
Baldwin, William c. 1515-1563 .... **LC 113**
  See also DLB 132
Bale, John 1495-1563 .... **LC 62**
  See also DLB 132; RGEL 2; TEA
Ball, Hugo 1886-1927 .... **TCLC 104**
Ballard, James G.
  See Ballard, J.G.
Ballard, James Graham
  See Ballard, J.G.

Ballard, J.G. 1930-2009 ..... **CLC 3, 6, 14, 36, 137; SSC 1, 53**
  See also AAYA 3, 52; BRWS 5; CA 5-8R, 285; CANR 15, 39, 65, 107, 133, 198; CN 1, 2, 3, 4, 5, 6, 7; DA3; DAM NOV, POP; DLB 14, 207, 261, 319; EWL 3; HGG; MTCW 1, 2; MTFW 2005; NFS 8; RGEL 2; RGSF 2; SATA 93; SATA-Obit 203; SCFW 1, 2; SFW 4
Ballard, Jim G.
  See Ballard, J.G.
Balmont, Konstantin (Dmitriyevich)
  1867-1943 .... **TCLC 11**
  See also CA 109, 155; DLB 295; EWL 3
Baltausis, Vincas 1847-1910
  See Mikszath, Kalman
Balzac, Guez de (?)-
  See Balzac, Jean-Louis Guez de
Balzac, Honore de 1799-1850 ... **NCLC 5, 35, 53, 153; SSC 5, 59, 102; WLC 1**
  See also DA; DA3; DAB; DAC; DAM MST, NOV; DLB 119; EW 5; GFL 1789 to the Present; LMFS 1; NFS 33; RGSF 2; RGWL 2, 3; SSFS 10; SUFW; TWA
Balzac, Jean-Louis Guez de
  1597-1654 .... **LC 162**
  See also DLB 268; GFL Beginnings to 1789
Bambara, Toni Cade 1939-1995 ..... **BLC 1:1, 2:1; CLC 19, 88; SSC 35, 107; TCLC 116; WLCS**
  See also AAYA 5, 49; AFAW 2; AMWS 11; BW 2, 3; BYA 12, 14; CA 29-32R, 150; CANR 24, 49, 81; CDALBS; DA; DA3; DAC; DAM MST, MULT; DLB 38, 218; EXPS; MAL 5; MTCW 1, 2; MTFW 2005; RGAL 4; RGSF 2; SATA 112; SSFS 4, 7, 12, 21
Bamdad, A.
  See Shamlu, Ahmad
Bamdad, Alef
  See Shamlu, Ahmad
Banat, D. R.
  See Bradbury, Ray
Bancroft, Laura
  See Baum, L. Frank
Banim, John 1798-1842 .... **NCLC 13**
  See also DLB 116, 158, 159; RGEL 2
Banim, Michael 1796-1874 .... **NCLC 13**
  See also DLB 158, 159
Banjo, The
  See Paterson, A(ndrew) B(arton)
Banks, Iain 1954- .... **CLC 34**
  See also BRWS 11; CA 123, 128; CANR 61, 106, 180; DLB 194, 261; EWL 3; HGG; INT CA-128; MTFW 2005; SFW 4
Banks, Iain M.
  See Banks, Iain
Banks, Iain Menzies
  See Banks, Iain
Banks, Lynne Reid
  See Reid Banks, Lynne
Banks, Russell 1940- . **CLC 37, 72, 187; SSC 42**
  See also AAYA 45; AMWS 5; CA 65-68; CAAS 15; CANR 19, 52, 73, 118, 195; CN 4, 5, 6, 7; DLB 130, 278; EWL 3; MAL 5; MTCW 2; MTFW 2005; NFS 13
Banks, Russell Earl
  See Banks, Russell
Banville, John 1945- .... **CLC 46, 118, 224**
  See also CA 117, 128; CANR 104, 150, 176; CN 4, 5, 6, 7; DLB 14, 271, 326; INT CA-128
Banville, Theodore (Faullain) de
  1832-1891 .... **NCLC 9**
  See also DLB 217; GFL 1789 to the Present

Baraka, Amiri 1934- .. **BLC 1:1, 2:1; CLC 1, 2, 3, 5, 10, 14, 33, 115, 213; DC 6; PC 4; WLCS**
See also AAYA 63; AFAW 1, 2; AMWS 2; BW 2, 3; CA 21-24R; CABS 3; CAD; CANR 27, 38, 61, 133, 172; CD 3, 5, 6; CDALB 1941-1968; CN 1, 2; CP 1, 2, 3, 4, 5, 6, 7; CPW; DA; DA3; DAC; DAM MST, MULT, POET, POP; DFS 3, 11, 16; DLB 5, 7, 16, 38; DLBD 8; EWL 3; MAL 5; MTCW 1, 2; MTFW 2005; PFS 9; RGAL 4; TCLE 1:1; TUS; WP

Baratynsky, Evgenii Abramovich
1800-1844 .... **NCLC 103**
See also DLB 205

Barbauld, Anna Laetitia
1743-1825 .... **NCLC 50, 185**
See also DLB 107, 109, 142, 158, 336; RGEL 2

Barbellion, W. N. P.
See Cummings, Bruce F.

Barber, Benjamin R. 1939- .... **CLC 141**
See also CA 29-32R; CANR 12, 32, 64, 119

Barbera, Jack 1945- .... **CLC 44**
See also CA 110; CANR 45

Barbera, Jack Vincent
See Barbera, Jack

Barbey d'Aurevilly, Jules-Amedee
1808-1889 .... **NCLC 1, 213; SSC 17**
See also DLB 119; GFL 1789 to the Present

Barbour, John c. 1316-1395 .... **CMLC 33**
See also DLB 146

Barbusse, Henri 1873-1935 .... **TCLC 5**
See also CA 105, 154; DLB 65; EWL 3; RGWL 2, 3

Barclay, Alexander c. 1475-1552 .... **LC 109**
See also DLB 132

Barclay, Bill
See Moorcock, Michael

Barclay, William Ewert
See Moorcock, Michael

Barclay, William Ewert
See Moorcock, Michael

Barea, Arturo 1897-1957 .... **TCLC 14**
See also CA 111, 201

Barfoot, Joan 1946- .... **CLC 18**
See also CA 105; CANR 141, 179

Barham, Richard Harris
1788-1845 .... **NCLC 77**
See also DLB 159

Baring, Maurice 1874-1945 .... **TCLC 8**
See also CA 105, 168; DLB 34; HGG

Baring-Gould, Sabine 1834-1924 ... **TCLC 88**
See also DLB 156, 190

Barker, Clive 1952- .... **CLC 52, 205; SSC 53**
See also AAYA 10, 54; BEST 90:3; BPFB 1; CA 121, 129; CANR 71, 111, 133, 187; CPW; DA3; DAM POP; DLB 261; HGG; INT CA-129; MTCW 1, 2; MTFW 2005; SUFW 2

Barker, George Granville
1913-1991 .... **CLC 8, 48; PC 77**
See also CA 9-12R, 135; CANR 7, 38; CP 1, 2, 3, 4, 5; DAM POET; DLB 20; EWL 3; MTCW 1

Barker, Harley Granville
See Granville-Barker, Harley

Barker, Howard 1946- .... **CLC 37**
See also CA 102; CBD; CD 5, 6; DLB 13, 233

Barker, Jane 1652-1732 .... **LC 42, 82; PC 91**
See also DLB 39, 131

Barker, Pat 1943- .... **CLC 32, 94, 146**
See also BRWS 4; CA 117, 122; CANR 50, 101, 148, 195; CN 6, 7; DLB 271, 326; INT CA-122

Barker, Patricia
See Barker, Pat

Barlach, Ernst (Heinrich)
1870-1938 .... **TCLC 84**
See also CA 178; DLB 56, 118; EWL 3

Barlow, Joel 1754-1812 .... **NCLC 23, 223**
See also AMWS 2; DLB 37; RGAL 4

Barnard, Mary (Ethel) 1909- .... **CLC 48**
See also CA 21-22; CAP 2; CP 1

Barnes, Djuna 1892-1982 .... **CLC 3, 4, 8, 11, 29, 127; SSC 3; TCLC 212**
See also AMWS 3; CA 9-12R, 107; CAD; CANR 16, 55; CN 1, 2, 3; CWD; DLB 4, 9, 45; EWL 3; GLL 1; MAL 5; MTCW 1, 2; MTFW 2005; RGAL 4; TCLE 1:1; TUS

Barnes, Jim 1933- .... **NNAL**
See also CA 108, 175, 272; CAAE 175, 272; CAAS 28; DLB 175

Barnes, Julian 1946- .... **CLC 42, 141**
See also BRWS 4; CA 102; CANR 19, 54, 115, 137, 195; CN 4, 5, 6, 7; DAB; DLB 194; DLBY 1993; EWL 3; MTCW 2; MTFW 2005; SSFS 24

Barnes, Julian Patrick
See Barnes, Julian

Barnes, Peter 1931-2004 .... **CLC 5, 56**
See also CA 65-68, 230; CAAS 12; CANR 33, 34, 64, 113; CBD; CD 5, 6; DFS 6; DLB 13, 233; MTCW 1

Barnes, William 1801-1886 .... **NCLC 75**
See also DLB 32

Baroja, Pio 1872-1956 .... **HLC 1; SSC 112; TCLC 8, 240**
See also CA 104, 247; EW 9

Baroja y Nessi, Pio
See Baroja, Pio

Baron, David
See Pinter, Harold

Baron Corvo
See Rolfe, Frederick (William Serafino Austin Lewis Mary)

Barondess, Sue K. 1926-1977 .... **CLC 3, 8**
See also CA 1-4R; 69-72; CANR 1

Barondess, Sue Kaufman
See Barondess, Sue K.

Baron de Teive
See Pessoa, Fernando

Baroness Von S.
See Zangwill, Israel

Barres, (Auguste-)Maurice
1862-1923 .... **TCLC 47**
See also CA 164; DLB 123; GFL 1789 to the Present

Barreto, Afonso Henrique de Lima
See Lima Barreto, Afonso Henrique de

Barrett, Andrea 1954- .... **CLC 150**
See also CA 156; CANR 92, 186; CN 7; DLB 335; SSFS 24

Barrett, Michele
See Barrett, Michele

Barrett, Michele 1949- .... **CLC 65**
See also CA 280

Barrett, Roger Syd
See Barrett, Syd

Barrett, Syd 1946-2006 .... **CLC 35**

Barrett, William (Christopher)
1913-1992 .... **CLC 27**
See also CA 13-16R, 139; CANR 11, 67; INT CANR-11

Barrett Browning, Elizabeth
1806-1861 ...... **NCLC 1, 16, 61, 66, 170; PC 6, 62; WLC 1**
See also AAYA 63; BRW 4; CDBLB 1832-1890; DA; DA3; DAB; DAC; DAM MST, POET; DLB 32, 199; EXPP; FL 1:2; PAB; PFS 2, 16, 23; TEA; WLIT 4; WP

Barrie, Baronet
See Barrie, J. M.

Barrie, J. M. 1860-1937 .... **TCLC 2, 164**
See also BRWS 3; BYA 4, 5; CA 104, 136; CANR 77; CDBLB 1890-1914; CLR 16, 124; CWRI 5; DA3; DAB; DAM DRAM; DFS 7; DLB 10, 141, 156, 352; EWL 3; FANT; MAICYA 1, 2; MTCW 2; MTFW 2005; SATA 100; SUFW; WCH; WLIT 4; YABC 1

Barrie, James Matthew
See Barrie, J. M.

Barrington, Michael
See Moorcock, Michael

Barrol, Grady
See Bograd, Larry

Barry, Mike
See Malzberg, Barry N(athaniel)

Barry, Philip 1896-1949 .... **TCLC 11**
See also CA 109, 199; DFS 9; DLB 7, 228; MAL 5; RGAL 4

Barry, Sebastian 1955- .... **CLC 282**
See also CA 117; CANR 122, 193; CD 5, 6; DLB 245

Bart, Andre Schwarz
See Schwarz-Bart, Andre

Barth, John 1930- ... **CLC 1, 2, 3, 5, 7, 9, 10, 14, 27, 51, 89, 214; SSC 10, 89**
See also AITN 1, 2; AMW; BPFB 1; CA 1-4R; CABS 1; CANR 5, 23, 49, 64, 113, 204; CN 1, 2, 3, 4, 5, 6, 7; DAM NOV; DLB 2, 227; EWL 3; FANT; MAL 5; MTCW 1; RGAL 4; RGSF 2; RHW; SSFS 6; TUS

Barth, John Simmons
See Barth, John

Barthelme, Donald 1931-1989 ... **CLC 1, 2, 3, 5, 6, 8, 13, 23, 46, 59, 115; SSC 2, 55, 142**
See also AMWS 4; BPFB 1; CA 21-24R, 129; CANR 20, 58, 188; CN 1, 2, 3, 4; DA3; DAM NOV; DLB 2, 234; DLBY 1980, 1989; EWL 3; FANT; LMFS 2; MAL 5; MTCW 1, 2; MTFW 2005; RGAL 4; RGSF 2; SATA 7; SATA-Obit 62; SSFS 17

Barthelme, Frederick 1943- ...... **CLC 36, 117**
See also AMWS 11; CA 114, 122; CANR 77, 209; CN 4, 5, 6, 7; CSW; DLB 244; DLBY 1985; EWL 3; INT CA-122

Barthes, Roland (Gerard)
1915-1980 .... **CLC 24, 83; TCLC 135**
See also CA 130; 97-100; CANR 66; DLB 296; EW 13; EWL 3; GFL 1789 to the Present; MTCW 1, 2; TWA

Bartram, William 1739-1823 .... **NCLC 145**
See also ANW; DLB 37

Barzun, Jacques (Martin) 1907- ..... **CLC 51, 145**
See also CA 61-64; CANR 22, 95

Bashevis, Isaac
See Singer, Isaac Bashevis

Bashevis, Yitskhok
See Singer, Isaac Bashevis

Bashkirtseff, Marie 1859-1884 .... **NCLC 27**

Basho, Matsuo
See Matsuo Basho

Basil of Caesaria c. 330-379 .... **CMLC 35**

Basket, Raney
See Edgerton, Clyde

Bass, Kingsley B., Jr.
See Bullins, Ed

Bass, Rick 1958- . **CLC 79, 143, 286; SSC 60**
See also AMWS 16; ANW; CA 126; CANR 53, 93, 145, 183; CSW; DLB 212, 275

Bassani, Giorgio 1916-2000 .... **CLC 9**
See also CA 65-68, 190; CANR 33; CWW 2; DLB 128, 177, 299; EWL 3; MTCW 1; RGHL; RGWL 2, 3

Berengar of Tours c. 1000-1088 .. **CMLC 124**
Beresford, J(ohn) D(avys)
   1873-1947 .... **TCLC 81**
   See also CA 112, 155; DLB 162, 178, 197;
   SFW 4; SUFW 1
Bergelson, David (Rafailovich)
   1884-1952 .... **TCLC 81**
   See also CA 220; DLB 333; EWL 3
Bergelson, Dovid
   See Bergelson, David (Rafailovich)
Berger, Colonel
   See Malraux, Andre
Berger, John 1926- .... **CLC 2, 19**
   See also BRWS 4; CA 81-84; CANR 51,
   78, 117, 163, 200; CN 1, 2, 3, 4, 5, 6, 7;
   DLB 14, 207, 319, 326
Berger, John Peter
   See Berger, John
Berger, Melvin H. 1927- .... **CLC 12**
   See also CA 5-8R; CANR 4, 142; CLR 32;
   SAAS 2; SATA 5, 88, 158; SATA-Essay
   124
Berger, Thomas 1924- .... **CLC 3, 5, 8, 11, 18,**
   38, 259
   See also BPFB 1; CA 1-4R; CANR 5, 28,
   51, 128; CN 1, 2, 3, 4, 5, 6, 7; DAM
   NOV; DLB 2; DLBY 1980; EWL 3;
   FANT; INT CANR-28; MAL 5; MTCW
   1, 2; MTFW 2005; RHW; TCLE 1:1;
   TCWW 1, 2
Bergman, Ernst Ingmar
   See Bergman, Ingmar
Bergman, Ingmar 1918-2007 ..... **CLC 16, 72,**
   210
   See also AAYA 61; CA 81-84, 262; CANR
   33, 70; CWW 2; DLB 257; MTCW 2;
   MTFW 2005
Bergson, Henri(-Louis) 1859-1941 . **TCLC 32**
   See also CA 164; DLB 329; EW 8; EWL 3;
   GFL 1789 to the Present
Bergstein, Eleanor 1938- .... **CLC 4**
   See also CA 53-56; CANR 5
Berkeley, George 1685-1753 .... **LC 65**
   See also DLB 31, 101, 252
Berkoff, Steven 1937- .... **CLC 56**
   See also CA 104; CANR 72; CBD; CD 5, 6
Berlin, Isaiah 1909-1997 .... **TCLC 105**
   See also CA 85-88, 162
Bermant, Chaim (Icyk) 1929-1998 ... **CLC 40**
   See also CA 57-60; CANR 6, 31, 57, 105;
   CN 2, 3, 4, 5, 6
Bern, Victoria
   See Fisher, M(ary) F(rances) K(ennedy)
Bernanos, (Paul Louis) Georges
   1888-1948 .... **TCLC 3**
   See also CA 104, 130; CANR 94; DLB 72;
   EWL 3; GFL 1789 to the Present; RGWL
   2, 3
Bernard, April 1956- .... **CLC 59**
   See also CA 131; CANR 144
Bernard, Mary Ann
   See Soderbergh, Steven
Bernard of Clairvaux 1090-1153 .. **CMLC 71**
   See also DLB 208
Bernard Silvestris fl. c. 1130-fl. c.
   1160 .... **CMLC 87**
   See also DLB 208
Bernart de Ventadorn c. 1130-c.
   1190 .... **CMLC 98**
Berne, Victoria
   See Fisher, M(ary) F(rances) K(ennedy)
Bernhard, Thomas 1931-1989 ..... **CLC 3, 32,**
   61; DC 14; TCLC 165
   See also CA 85-88, 127; CANR 32, 57; CD-
   WLB 2; DLB 85, 124; EWL 3; MTCW 1;
   RGHL; RGWL 2, 3
Bernhardt, Sarah (Henriette Rosine)
   1844-1923 .... **TCLC 75**
   See also CA 157

Bernstein, Charles 1950- .... **CLC 142,**
   See also CA 129; CAAS 24; CANR 90; CP
   4, 5, 6, 7; DLB 169
Bernstein, Ingrid
   See Kirsch, Sarah
Beroul fl. c. 12th cent. - .... **CMLC 75**
Berriault, Gina 1926-1999 .... **CLC 54, 109;**
   SSC 30
   See also CA 116, 129, 185; CANR 66; DLB
   130; SSFS 7,11
Berrigan, Daniel 1921- .... **CLC 4**
   See also CA 33-36R, 187; CAAE 187;
   CAAS 1; CANR 11, 43, 78; CP 1, 2, 3, 4,
   5, 6, 7; DLB 5
Berrigan, Edmund Joseph Michael, Jr.
   1934-1983 .... **CLC 37; PC 103**
   See also CA 61-64, 110; CANR 14, 102;
   CP 1, 2, 3; DLB 5, 169; WP
Berrigan, Ted
   See Berrigan, Edmund Joseph Michael, Jr.
Berry, Charles Edward Anderson
   1931- .... **CLC 17**
   See also CA 115
Berry, Chuck
   See Berry, Charles Edward Anderson
Berry, Jonas
   See Ashbery, John
Berry, Wendell 1934- ..... **CLC 4, 6, 8, 27, 46,**
   279; PC 28
   See also AITN 1; AMWS 10; ANW; CA
   73-76; CANR 50, 73, 101, 132, 174; CP
   1, 2, 3, 4, 5, 6, 7; CSW; DAM POET;
   DLB 5, 6, 234, 275, 342; MTCW 2;
   MTFW 2005; PFS 30; TCLE 1:1
Berry, Wendell Erdman
   See Berry, Wendell
Berryman, John 1914-1972 ... **CLC 1, 2, 3, 4,**
   6, 8, 10, 13, 25, 62; PC 64
   See also AMW; CA 13-16, 33-36R; CABS
   2; CANR 35; CAP 1; CDALB 1941-1968;
   CP 1; DAM POET; DLB 48; EWL 3;
   MAL 5; MTCW 1, 2; MTFW 2005; PAB;
   PFS 27; RGAL 4; WP
Bertolucci, Bernardo 1940- ...... **CLC 16, 157**
   See also CA 106; CANR 125
Berton, Pierre (Francis de Marigny)
   1920-2004 .... **CLC 104**
   See also CA 1-4R, 233; CANR 2, 56, 144;
   CPW; DLB 68; SATA 99; SATA-Obit 158
Bertrand, Aloysius 1807-1841 .... **NCLC 31**
   See also DLB 217
Bertrand, Louis oAloysiusc
   See Bertrand, Aloysius
Bertran de Born c. 1140-1215 .... **CMLC 5**
Besant, Annie (Wood) 1847-1933 ..... **TCLC 9**
   See also CA 105, 185
Bessie, Alvah 1904-1985 .... **CLC 23**
   See also CA 5-8R, 116; CANR 2, 80; DLB
   26
Bestuzhev, Aleksandr Aleksandrovich
   1797-1837 .... **NCLC 131**
   See also DLB 198
Bethlen, T.D.
   See Silverberg, Robert
Beti, Mongo 1932- .... **BLC 1:1; CLC 27**
   See also AFW; BW 1, 3; CA 114, 124;
   CANR 81; DA3; DAM MULT; EWL 3;
   MTCW 1, 2
Betjeman, John 1906-1984 ...... **CLC 2, 6, 10,**
   34, 43; PC 75
   See also BRW 7; CA 9-12R, 112; CANR
   33, 56; CDBLB 1945-1960; CP 1, 2, 3;
   DA3; DAB; DAM MST, POET; DLB 20;
   DLBY 1984; EWL 3; MTCW 1, 2
Bettelheim, Bruno 1903-1990 .... **CLC 79;**
   TCLC 143
   See also CA 81-84, 131; CANR 23, 61;
   DA3; MTCW 1, 2; RGHL

Betti, Ugo 1892-1953 .... **TCLC 5**
   See also CA 104, 155; EWL 3; RGWL 2, 3
Betts, Doris (Waugh) 1932- ..... **CLC 3, 6, 28,**
   275; SSC 45
   See also CA 13-16R; CANR 9, 66, 77; CN
   6, 7; CSW; DLB 218; DLBY 1982; INT
   CANR-9; RGAL 4
Bevan, Alistair
   See Roberts, Keith (John Kingston)
Bey, Pilaff
   See Douglas, (George) Norman
Beyala, Calixthe 1961- .... **BLC 2:1**
   See also EWL 3
Beynon, John
   See Harris, John (Wyndham Parkes Lucas)
   Beynon
Bhabha, Homi K. 1949- .... **CLC 285**
Bialik, Chaim Nachman
   1873-1934 .... **TCLC 25, 201**
   See also CA 170; EWL 3; WLIT 6
Bialik, Hayyim Nahman
   See Bialik, Chaim Nachman
Bickerstaff, Isaac
   See Swift, Jonathan
Bidart, Frank 1939- .... **CLC 33**
   See also AMWS 15; CA 140; CANR 106;
   CP 5, 6, 7; PFS 26
Bienek, Horst 1930- .... **CLC 7, 11**
   See also CA 73-76; DLB 75
Bierce, Ambrose 1842-1914(?) ...... **SSC 9, 72,**
   124; TCLC 1, 7, 44; WLC 1
   See also AAYA 55; AMW; BYA 11; CA
   104, 139; CANR 78; CDALB 1865-1917;
   DA; DA3; DAC; DAM MST; DLB 11,
   12, 23, 71, 74, 186; EWL 3; EXPS; HGG;
   LAIT 2; MAL 5; RGAL 4; RGSF 2; SSFS
   9, 27; SUFW 1
Bierce, Ambrose Gwinett
   See Bierce, Ambrose
Biggers, Earl Derr 1884-1933 .... **TCLC 65**
   See also CA 108, 153; DLB 306
Billiken, Bud
   See Motley, Willard (Francis)
Billings, Josh
   See Shaw, Henry Wheeler
Billington, Lady Rachel Mary
   See Billington, Rachel
Billington, Rachel 1942- .... **CLC 43**
   See also AITN 2; CA 33-36R; CANR 44,
   196; CN 4, 5, 6, 7
Binchy, Maeve 1940- .... **CLC 153**
   See also BEST 90:1; BPFB 1; CA 127, 134;
   CANR 50, 96, 134, 208; CN 5, 6, 7;
   CPW; DA3; DAM POP; DLB 319; INT
   CA-134; MTCW 2; MTFW 2005; RHW
Binyon, T(imothy) J(ohn)
   1936-2004 .... **CLC 34**
   See also CA 111, 232; CANR 28, 140
Bion 335B.C.-245B.C. .... **CMLC 39**
Bioy Casares, Adolfo 1914-1999 ... **CLC 4, 8,**
   13, 88; HLC 1; SSC 17, 102
   See also CA 29-32R, 177; CANR 19, 43,
   66; CWW 2; DAM MULT; DLB 113;
   EWL 3; HW 1, 2; LAW; MTCW 1, 2;
   MTFW 2005; RGSF 2
Birch, Allison CLC 65
Bird, Cordwainer
   See Ellison, Harlan
Bird, Robert Montgomery
   1806-1854 .... **NCLC 1, 197**
   See also DLB 202; RGAL 4
Birdwell, Cleo
   See DeLillo, Don
Birkerts, Sven 1951- .... **CLC 116**
   See also CA 128, 133, 176; CAAE 176;
   CAAS 29; CANR 151; INT CA-133

Bodker, Cecil 1927- .... **CLC 21**
　　See also CA 73-76; CANR 13, 44, 111;
　　CLR 23; MAICYA 1, 2; SATA 14, 133
Boell, Heinrich 1917-1985 ..... **CLC 2, 3, 6, 9,**
　　11, 15, 27, 32, 72; SSC 23; TCLC 185;
　　WLC 1
　　See also BPFB 1; CA 21-24R, 116; CANR
　　24; CDWLB 3; DA; DA3; DAB; DAC;
　　DAM MST, NOV; DLB 69, 329; DLBY
　　1985; EW 13; EWL 3; MTCW 1, 2;
　　MTFW 2005; RGHL; RGSF 2; RGWL 2,
　　3; SSFS 20; TWA
Boell, Heinrich Theodor
　　See Boell, Heinrich
Boerne, Alfred
　　See Doeblin, Alfred
Boethius c. 480-c. 524 .... **CMLC 15**
　　See also DLB 115; RGWL 2, 3; WLIT 8
Boff, Leonardo (Genezio Darci)
　　1938- .... **CLC 70; HLC 1**
　　See also CA 150; DAM MULT; HW 2
Bogan, Louise 1897-1970 .... **CLC 4, 39, 46,**
　　93; PC 12
　　See also AMWS 3; CA 73-76, 25-28R;
　　CANR 33, 82; CP 1; DLB POET; DLB
　　45, 169; EWL 3; MAL 5; MBL; MTCW
　　1, 2; PFS 21; RGAL 4
Bogarde, Dirk
　　See Van Den Bogarde, Derek Jules Gaspard
　　Ulric Niven
Bogat, Shatan
　　See Kacew, Romain
Bogomolny, Robert L. 1938- .... **SSC 41;**
　　TCLC 11
　　See also CA 121, 164; DLB 182; EWL 3;
　　MJW; RGSF 2; RGWL 2, 3; TWA
Bogomolny, Robert Lee
　　See Bogomolny, Robert L.
Bogosian, Eric 1953- .... **CLC 45, 141**
　　See also CA 138; CAD; CANR 102, 148;
　　CD 5, 6; DLB 341
Bograd, Larry 1953- .... **CLC 35**
　　See also CA 93-96; CANR 57; SAAS 21;
　　SATA 33, 89; WYA
Bohme, Jakob 1575-1624 .... **LC 178**
　　See also DLB 164
Boiardo, Matteo Maria 1441-1494 .... **LC 6,**
　　168
Boileau-Despreaux, Nicolas
　　1636-1711 .... **LC 3, 164**
　　See also DLB 268; EW 3; GFL Beginnings
　　to 1789; RGWL 2, 3
Boissard, Maurice
　　See Leautaud, Paul
Bojer, Johan 1872-1959 .... **TCLC 64**
　　See also CA 189; EWL 3
Bok, Edward W(illiam)
　　1863-1930 .... **TCLC 101**
　　See also CA 217; DLB 91; DLBD 16
Boker, George Henry 1823-1890 . **NCLC 125**
　　See also RGAL 4
Boland, Eavan 1944- ... **CLC 40, 67, 113; PC**
　　58
　　See also BRWS 5; CA 143, 207; CAAE
　　207; CANR 61, 180; CP 1, 6, 7; CWP;
　　DAM POET; DLB 40; FW; MTCW 2;
　　MTFW 2005; PFS 12, 22, 31
Boland, Eavan Aisling
　　See Boland, Eavan
Bolano, Roberto 1953-2003 .... **CLC 294**
　　See also CA 229; CANR 175
Bolingbroke, Viscount
　　See St. John, Henry
Boll, Heinrich
　　See Boell, Heinrich
Bolt, Lee
　　See Faust, Frederick

Bolt, Robert (Oxton) 1924-1995 ...... **CLC 14;**
　　TCLC 175
　　See also CA 17-20R, 147; CANR 35, 67;
　　CBD; DAM DRAM; DFS 2; DLB 13,
　　233; EWL 3; LAIT 1; MTCW 1
Bombal, Maria Luisa 1910-1980 .... **HLCS 1;**
　　SSC 37
　　See also CA 127; CANR 72; EWL 3; HW
　　1; LAW; RGSF 2
Bombet, Louis-Alexandre-Cesar
　　See Stendhal
Bomkauf
　　See Kaufman, Bob (Garnell)
Bonaventura **NCLC 35**
　　See also DLB 90
Bonaventure 1217(?)-1274 .... **CMLC 79**
　　See also DLB 115; LMFS 1
Bond, Edward 1934- .... **CLC 4, 6, 13, 23**
　　See also AAYA 50; BRWS 1; CA 25-28R;
　　CANR 38, 67, 106; CBD; CD 5, 6; DAM
　　DRAM; DFS 3, 8; DLB 13, 310; EWL 3;
　　MTCW 1
Bonham, Frank 1914-1989 .... **CLC 12**
　　See also AAYA 1, 70; BYA 1, 3; CA 9-12R;
　　CANR 4, 36; JRDA; MAICYA 1, 2;
　　SAAS 3; SATA 1, 49; SATA-Obit 62;
　　TCWW 1, 2; YAW
Bonnefoy, Yves 1923- . **CLC 9, 15, 58; PC 58**
　　See also CA 85-88; CANR 33, 75, 97, 136;
　　CWW 2; DAM MST, POET; DLB 258;
　　EWL 3; GFL 1789 to the Present; MTCW
　　1, 2; MTFW 2005
Bonner, Marita
　　See Occomy, Marita (Odette) Bonner
Bonnin, Gertrude 1876-1938 .... **NNAL**
　　See also CA 150; DAM MULT; DLB 175
Bontemps, Arna 1902-1973 ... **BLC 1:1; CLC**
　　1, 18; HR 1:2
　　See also BW 1; CA 1-4R; 41-44R; CANR
　　4, 35; CLR 6; CP 1; CWRI 5; DA3; DAM
　　MULT, NOV, POET; DLB 48, 51; JRDA;
　　MAICYA 1, 2; MAL 5; MTCW 1, 2; PFS
　　32; SATA 2, 44; SATA-Obit 24; WCH;
　　WP
Bontemps, Arnaud Wendell
　　See Bontemps, Arna
Boot, William
　　See Stoppard, Tom
Booth, Irwin
　　See Hoch, Edward D.
Booth, Martin 1944-2004 .... **CLC 13**
　　See also CA 93-96, 188, 223; CAAE 188;
　　CAAS 2; CANR 92; CP 1, 2, 3, 4
Booth, Philip 1925-2007 .... **CLC 23**
　　See also CA 5-8R, 262; CANR 5, 88; CP 1,
　　2, 3, 4, 5, 6, 7; DLBY 1982
Booth, Philip Edmund
　　See Booth, Philip
Booth, Wayne C. 1921-2005 .... **CLC 24**
　　See also CA 1-4R, 244; CAAS 5; CANR 3,
　　43, 117; DLB 67
Booth, Wayne Clayson
　　See Booth, Wayne C.
Borchert, Wolfgang 1921-1947 .... **TCLC 5**
　　See also CA 104, 188; DLB 69, 124; EWL
　　3
Borel, Petrus 1809-1859 .... **NCLC 41**
　　See also DLB 119; GFL 1789 to the Present
Borges, Jorge Luis 1899-1986 ... **CLC 1, 2, 3,**
　　4, 6, 8, 9, 10, 13, 19, 44, 48, 83; HLC 1;
　　PC 22, 32; SSC 4, 41, 100; TCLC 109;
　　WLC 1
　　See also AAYA 26; BPFB 1; CA 21-24R;
　　CANR 19, 33, 75, 105, 133; CDWLB 3;
　　DA; DA3; DAB; DAC; DAM MST,
　　MULT; DLB 113, 283; DLBY 1986;
　　DNFS 1, 2; EWL 3; HW 1, 2; LAW;

LMFS 2; MSW; MTCW 1, 2; MTFW
2005; PFS 27; RGHL; RGSF 2; RGWL
2, 3; SFW 4; SSFS 17; TWA; WLIT 1
Borne, Ludwig 1786-1837 .... **NCLC 193**
　　See also DLB 90
Borowski, Tadeusz 1922-1951 .... **SSC 48;**
　　TCLC 9
　　See also CA 106, 154; CDWLB 4; DLB
　　215; EWL 3; RGHL; RGSF 2; RGWL 3;
　　SSFS 13
Borrow, George (Henry)
　　1803-1881 .... **NCLC 9**
　　See also BRWS 12; DLB 21, 55, 166
Bosch (Gavino), Juan 1909-2001 ..... **HLCS 1**
　　See also CA 151, 204; DAM MST, MULT;
　　DLB 145; HW 1, 2
Bosman, Herman Charles
　　1905-1951 .... **TCLC 49**
　　See also CA 160; DLB 225; RGSF 2
Bosschere, Jean de 1878(?)-1953 ... **TCLC 19**
　　See also CA 115, 186
Boswell, James 1740-1795 ...... **LC 4, 50, 182;**
　　WLC 1
　　See also BRW 3; CDBLB 1660-1789; DA;
　　DAB; DAC; DAM MST; DLB 104, 142;
　　TEA; WLIT 3
Boto, Eza
　　See Beti, Mongo
Bottomley, Gordon 1874-1948 ..... **TCLC 107**
　　See also CA 120, 192; DLB 10
Bottoms, David 1949- .... **CLC 53**
　　See also CA 105; CANR 22; CSW; DLB
　　120; DLBY 1983
Boucicault, Dion 1820-1890 .... **NCLC 41**
　　See also DLB 344
Boucolon, Maryse
　　See Conde, Maryse
Bourcicault, Dion
　　See Boucicault, Dion
Bourdieu, Pierre 1930-2002 .... **CLC 198, 296**
　　See also CA 130, 204
Bourget, Paul (Charles Joseph)
　　1852-1935 .... **TCLC 12**
　　See also CA 107, 196; DLB 123; GFL 1789
　　to the Present
Bourjaily, Vance (Nye) 1922- .... **CLC 8, 62**
　　See also CA 1-4R; CAAS 1; CANR 2, 72;
　　CN 1, 2, 3, 4, 5, 6, 7; DLB 2, 143; MAL
　　5
Bourne, Randolph S(illiman)
　　1886-1918 .... **TCLC 16**
　　See also AMW; CA 117, 155; DLB 63;
　　MAL 5
Boursiquot, Dionysius
　　See Boucicault, Dion
Bova, Ben 1932- .... **CLC 45**
　　See also AAYA 16; CA 5-8R; CAAS 18;
　　CANR 11, 56, 94, 111, 157; CLR 3, 96;
　　DLBY 1981; INT CANR-11; MAICYA 1,
　　2; MTCW 1; SATA 6, 68, 133; SFW 4
Bova, Benjamin William
　　See Bova, Ben
Bowen, Elizabeth 1899-1973 ..... **CLC 1, 3, 6,**
　　11, 15, 22, 118; SSC 3, 28, 66; TCLC
　　148
　　See also BRWS 2; CA 17-18; 41-44R;
　　CANR 35, 105; CAP 2; CDBLB 1945-
　　1960; CN 1; DA3; DAM NOV; DLB 15,
　　162; EWL 3; EXPS; FW; HGG; MTCW
　　1, 2; MTFW 2005; NFS 13; RGSF 2;
　　SSFS 5, 22; SUFW 1; TEA; WLIT 4
Bowen, Elizabeth Dorothea Cole
　　See Bowen, Elizabeth
Bowering, George 1935- .... **CLC 15, 47**
　　See also CA 21-24R; CAAS 16; CANR 10;
　　CN 7; CP 1, 2, 3, 4, 5, 6, 7; DLB 53
Bowering, Marilyn R(uthe) 1949- .... **CLC 32**
　　See also CA 101; CANR 49; CP 4, 5, 6, 7;
　　CWP; DLB 334

Bowers, Edgar 1924-2000 .... **CLC 9**
See also CA 5-8R, 188; CANR 24; CP 1, 2, 3, 4, 5, 6, 7; CSW; DLB 5
Bowers, Mrs. J. Milton
See Bierce, Ambrose
Bowie, David
See Jones, David Robert
Bowles, Jane (Sydney) 1917-1973 ..... **CLC 3, 68**
See also CA 19-20; 41-44R; CAP 2; CN 1; EWL 3; MAL 5
Bowles, Jane Auer
See Bowles, Jane (Sydney)
Bowles, Paul 1910-1999 ..... **CLC 1, 2, 19, 53; SSC 3, 98; TCLC 209**
See also AMWS 4; CA 1-4R, 186; CAAS 1; CANR 1, 19, 50, 75; CN 1, 2, 3, 4, 5, 6; DA3; DLB 5, 6, 218; EWL 3; MAL 5; MTCW 1, 2; MTFW 2005; RGAL 4; SSFS 17
Bowles, William Lisle 1762-1850 . **NCLC 103**
See also DLB 93
Box, Edgar
See Vidal, Gore
Boyd, James 1888-1944 .... **TCLC 115**
See also CA 186; DLB 9; DLBD 16; RGAL 4; RHW
Boyd, Nancy
See Millay, Edna St. Vincent
Boyd, Thomas (Alexander) 1898-1935 .... **TCLC 111**
See also CA 111, 183; DLB 9; DLBD 16, 316
Boyd, William 1952- .... **CLC 28, 53, 70**
See also BRWS 16; CA 114, 120; CANR 51, 71, 131, 174; CN 4, 5, 6, 7; DLB 231
Boyesen, Hjalmar Hjorth 1848-1895 .... **NCLC 135**
See also DLB 12, 71; DLBD 13; RGAL 4
Boyle, Kay 1902-1992 .... **CLC 1, 5, 19, 58, 121; SSC 5, 102**
See also CA 13-16R, 140; CAAS 1; CANR 29, 61, 110; CN 1, 2, 3, 4, 5; CP 1, 2, 3, 4, 5; DLB 4, 9, 48, 86; DLBY 1993; EWL 3; MAL 5; MTCW 1, 2; MTFW 2005; RGAL 4; RGSF 2; SSFS 10, 13, 14
Boyle, Mark
See Kienzle, William X.
Boyle, Patrick 1905-1982 .... **CLC 19**
See also CA 127
Boyle, T.C. 1948- . **CLC 36, 55, 90, 284; SSC 16, 127**
See also AAYA 47; AMWS 8, 20; BEST 90:4; BPFB 1; CA 120; CANR 44, 76, 89, 132; CN 6, 7; CPW; DA3; DAM POP; DLB 218, 278; DLBY 1986; EWL 3; MAL 5; MTCW 2; MTFW 2005; SSFS 13, 19
Boyle, T.Coraghessan
See Boyle, T.C.
Boyle, Thomas Coraghessan
See Boyle, T.C.
Boz
See Dickens, Charles
Brackenridge, Hugh Henry 1748-1816 .... **NCLC 7, 227**
See also DLB 11, 37; RGAL 4
Bradbury, Edward P.
See Moorcock, Michael
Bradbury, Malcolm (Stanley) 1932-2000 .... **CLC 32, 61**
See also CA 1-4R; CANR 1, 33, 91, 98, 137; CN 1, 2, 3, 4, 5, 6, 7; CP 1; DA3; DAM NOV; DLB 14, 207; EWL 3; MTCW 1, 2; MTFW 2005

Bradbury, Ray 1920- ... **CLC 1, 3, 10, 15, 42, 98, 235; SSC 29, 53; WLC 1**
See also AAYA 15, 84; AITN 1, 2; AMWS 4; BPFB 1; BYA 4, 5, 11; CA 1-4R; CANR 2, 30, 75, 125, 186; CDALB 1968-1988; CN 1, 2, 3, 4, 5, 6, 7; CPW; DA; DA3; DAB; DAC; DAM MST, NOV, POP; DLB 2, 8; EXPN; EXPS; HGG; LAIT 3, 5; LATS 1:2; LMFS 2; MAL 5; MTCW 1, 2; MTFW 2005; NFS 1, 22, 29; RGAL 4; RGSF 2; SATA 11, 64, 123; SCFW 1, 2; SFW 4; SSFS 1, 20, 28; SUFW 1, 2; TUS; YAW
Bradbury, Ray Douglas
See Bradbury, Ray
Braddon, Mary Elizabeth 1837-1915 .... **TCLC 111**
See also BRWS 8; CA 108, 179; CMW 4; DLB 18, 70, 156; HGG
Bradfield, Scott 1955- .... **SSC 65**
See also CA 147; CANR 90; HGG; SUFW 2
Bradfield, Scott Michael
See Bradfield, Scott
Bradford, Gamaliel 1863-1932 .... **TCLC 36**
See also CA 160; DLB 17
Bradford, William 1590-1657 .... **LC 64**
See also DLB 24, 30; RGAL 4
Bradley, David, Jr. 1950- ...... **BLC 1:1; CLC 23, 118**
See also BW 1, 3; CA 104; CANR 26, 81; CN 4, 5, 6, 7; DAM MULT; DLB 33
Bradley, David Henry, Jr.
See Bradley, David, Jr.
Bradley, John Ed 1958- .... **CLC 55**
See also CA 139; CANR 99; CN 6, 7; CSW
Bradley, John Edmund, Jr.
See Bradley, John Ed
Bradley, Marion Zimmer 1930-1999 .... **CLC 30**
See also AAYA 40; BPFB 1; CA 57-60, 185; CAAS 10; CANR 7, 31, 51, 75, 107; CPW; DA3; DAM POP; DLB 8; FANT; FW; GLL 1; MTCW 1, 2; MTFW 2005; SATA 90, 139; SATA-Obit 116; SFW 4; SUFW 2; YAW
Bradshaw, John 1933- .... **CLC 70**
See also CA 138; CANR 61
Bradstreet, Anne 1612(?)-1672 .... **LC 4, 30, 130; PC 10**
See also AMWS 1; CDALB 1640-1865; DA; DA3; DAC; DAM MST, POET; DLB 24; EXPP; FW; PFS 6, 33; RGAL 4; TUS; WP
Brady, Joan 1939- .... **CLC 86**
See also CA 141
Bragg, Melvyn 1939- .... **CLC 10**
See also BEST 89:3; CA 57-60; CANR 10, 48, 89, 158; CN 1, 2, 3, 4, 5, 6, 7; DLB 14, 271; RHW
Bragg, Rick 1959- .... **CLC 296**
See also CA 165; CANR 112, 137, 194; MTFW 2005
Bragg, Ricky Edward
See Bragg, Rick
Brahe, Tycho 1546-1601 .... **LC 45**
See also DLB 300
Braine, John (Gerard) 1922-1986 . **CLC 1, 3, 41**
See also CA 1-4R, 120; CANR 1, 33; CD-BLB 1945-1960; CN 1, 2, 3, 4; DLB 15; DLBY 1986; EWL 3; MTCW 1
Braithwaite, William Stanley (Beaumont) 1878-1962 ...... **BLC 1:1; HR 1:2; PC 52**
See also BW 1; CA 125; DAM MULT; DLB 50, 54; MAL 5
Bramah, Ernest 1868-1942 .... **TCLC 72**
See also CA 156; CMW 4; DLB 70; FANT

Brammer, Billy Lee
See Brammer, William
Brammer, William 1929-1978 .... **CLC 31**
See also CA 235; 77-80
Brancati, Vitaliano 1907-1954 .... **TCLC 12**
See also CA 109; DLB 264; EWL 3
Brancato, Robin F. 1936- .... **CLC 35**
See also AAYA 9, 68; BYA 6; CA 69-72; CANR 11, 45; CLR 32; JRDA; MAICYA 2; MAICYAS 1; SAAS 9; SATA 97; WYA; YAW
Brancato, Robin Fidler
See Brancato, Robin F.
Brand, Dionne 1953- .... **CLC 192**
See also BW 2; CA 143; CANR 143; CWP; DLB 334
Brand, Max
See Faust, Frederick
Brand, Millen 1906-1980 .... **CLC 7**
See also CA 21-24R; 97-100; CANR 72
Branden, Barbara 1929- .... **CLC 44**
See also CA 148
Brandes, Georg (Morris Cohen) 1842-1927 .... **TCLC 10**
See also CA 105, 189; DLB 300
Brandys, Kazimierz 1916-2000 .... **CLC 62**
See also CA 239; EWL 3
Branley, Franklyn M(ansfield) 1915-2002 .... **CLC 21**
See also CA 33-36R, 207; CANR 14, 39; CLR 13; MAICYA 1, 2; SAAS 16; SATA 4, 68, 136
Brant, Beth (E.) 1941- .... **NNAL**
See also CA 144; FW
Brant, Sebastian 1457-1521 .... **LC 112**
See also DLB 179; RGWL 2, 3
Brathwaite, Edward Kamau 1930- ..... **BLC 2:1; BLCS; CLC 11; PC 56**
See also BRWS 12; BW 2, 3; CA 25-28R; CANR 11, 26, 47, 107; CDWLB 3; CP 1, 2, 3, 4, 5, 6, 7; DAM POET; DLB 125; EWL 3
Brathwaite, Kamau
See Brathwaite, Edward Kamau
Brautigan, Richard 1935-1984 .. **CLC 1, 3, 5, 9, 12, 34, 42; PC 94; TCLC 133**
See also BPFB 1; CA 53-56, 113; CANR 34; CN 1, 2, 3; CP 1, 2, 3, 4; DA3; DAM NOV; DLB 2, 5, 206; DLBY 1980, 1984; FANT; MAL 5; MTCW 1; RGAL 4; SATA 56
Brautigan, Richard Gary
See Brautigan, Richard
Brave Bird, Mary
See Crow Dog, Mary
Braverman, Kate 1950- .... **CLC 67**
See also CA 89-92; CANR 141; DLB 335
Brecht, Bertolt 1898-1956 ..... **DC 3; TCLC 1, 6, 13, 35, 169; WLC 1**
See also CA 104, 133; CANR 62; CDWLB 2; DA; DA3; DAB; DAC; DAM DRAM, MST; DFS 4, 5, 9; DLB 56, 124; EW 11; EWL 3; IDTP; MTCW 1, 2; MTFW 2005; RGHL; RGWL 2, 3; TWA
Brecht, Eugen Berthold Friedrich
See Brecht, Bertolt
Brecht, Eugen Bertolt Friedrich
See Brecht, Bertolt
Bremer, Fredrika 1801-1865 .... **NCLC 11**
See also DLB 254
Brennan, Christopher John 1870-1932 .... **TCLC 17**
See also CA 117, 188; DLB 230; EWL 3
Brennan, Maeve 1917-1993 ... **CLC 5; TCLC 124**
See also CA 81-84; CANR 72, 100
Brenner, Jozef 1887-1919 .... **TCLC 13**
See also CA 111, 240

Caputo, Philip 1941- .... **CLC 32**
    See also AAYA 60; CA 73-76; CANR 40,
    135; YAW
Caragiale, Ion Luca 1852-1912 ...... **TCLC 76**
    See also CA 157
Card, Orson Scott 1951- ...... **CLC 44, 47, 50,**
    279
    See also AAYA 11, 42; BPFB 1; BYA 5, 8;
    CA 102; CANR 27, 47, 73, 102, 106, 133,
    184; CLR 116; CPW; DA3; DAM POP;
    FANT; INT CANR-27; MTCW 1, 2;
    MTFW 2005; NFS 5; SATA 83, 127;
    SCFW 2; SFW 4; SUFW 2; YAW
Cardenal, Ernesto 1925- .... **CLC 31, 161;**
    HLC 1; PC 22
    See also CA 49-52; CANR 2, 32, 66, 138;
    CWW 2; DAM MULT, POET; DLB 290;
    EWL 3; HW 1, 2; LAWS 1; MTCW 1, 2;
    MTFW 2005; RGWL 2, 3
Cardinal, Marie 1929-2001 .... **CLC 189**
    See also CA 177; CWW 2; DLB 83; FW
Cardozo, Benjamin N(athan)
    1870-1938 .... **TCLC 65**
    See also CA 117, 164
Carducci, Giosue (Alessandro Giuseppe)
    1835-1907 .... **PC 46; TCLC 32**
    See also CA 163; DLB 329; EW 7; RGWL
    2, 3
Carew, Thomas 1595(?)-1640 ..... **LC 13, 159;**
    PC 29
    See also BRW 2; DLB 126; PAB; RGEL 2
Carey, Ernestine Gilbreth
    1908-2006 .... **CLC 17**
    See also CA 5-8R, 254; CANR 71; SATA
    2; SATA-Obit 177
Carey, Peter 1943- .... **CLC 40, 55, 96, 183,**
    294; SSC 133
    See also BRWS 12; CA 123, 127; CANR
    53, 76, 117, 157, 185; CN 4, 5, 6, 7; DLB
    289, 326; EWL 3; INT CA-127; LNFS 1;
    MTCW 1, 2; MTFW 2005; RGSF 2;
    SATA 94
Carey, Peter Philip
    See Carey, Peter
Carleton, William 1794-1869 ... **NCLC 3, 199**
    See also DLB 159; RGEL 2; RGSF 2
Carlisle, Henry (Coffin) 1926- .... **CLC 33**
    See also CA 13-16R; CANR 15, 85
Carlsen, Chris
    See Holdstock, Robert
Carlson, Ron 1947- .... **CLC 54**
    See also CA 105, 189; CAAE 189; CANR
    27, 155, 197; DLB 244
Carlson, Ronald F.
    See Carlson, Ron
Carlyle, Jane Welsh 1801-1866 ... **NCLC 181**
    See also DLB 55
Carlyle, Thomas 1795-1881 ..... **NCLC 22, 70**
    See also BRW 4; CDBLB 1789-1832; DA;
    DAB; DAC; DAM MST; DLB 55, 144,
    254, 338; RGEL 2; TEA
Carman, (William) Bliss 1861-1929 ... **PC 34;**
    TCLC 7
    See also CA 104, 152; DAC; DLB 92;
    RGEL 2
Carnegie, Dale 1888-1955 .... **TCLC 53**
    See also CA 218
Caro Mallén de Soto, Ana c. 1590-c.
    1650 .... **LC 175**
Carossa, Hans 1878-1956 .... **TCLC 48**
    See also CA 170; DLB 66; EWL 3
Carpenter, Don(ald Richard)
    1931-1995 .... **CLC 41**
    See also CA 45-48, 149; CANR 1, 71
Carpenter, Edward 1844-1929 .... **TCLC 88**
    See also BRWS 13; CA 163; GLL 1
Carpenter, John 1948- .... **CLC 161**
    See also AAYA 2, 73; CA 134; SATA 58

Carpenter, John Howard
    See Carpenter, John
Carpenter, Johnny
    See Carpenter, John
Carpentier, Alejo 1904-1980 .. **CLC 8, 11, 38,**
    110; HLC 1; SSC 35; TCLC 201
    See also CA 65-68; 97-100; CANR 11, 70;
    CDWLB 3; DAM MULT; DLB 113; EWL
    3; HW 1, 2; LAW; LMFS 2; RGSF 2;
    RGWL 2, 3; WLIT 1
Carpentier y Valmont, Alejo
    See Carpentier, Alejo
Carr, Caleb 1955- .... **CLC 86**
    See also CA 147; CANR 73, 134; DA3;
    DLB 350
Carr, Emily 1871-1945 .... **TCLC 32**
    See also CA 159; DLB 68; FW; GLL 2
Carr, H. D.
    See Crowley, Edward Alexander
Carr, John Dickson 1906-1977 .... **CLC 3**
    See also CA 49-52; 69-72; CANR 3, 33,
    60; CMW 4; DLB 306; MSW; MTCW 1,
    2
Carr, Philippa
    See Hibbert, Eleanor Alice Burford
Carr, Virginia Spencer 1929- .... **CLC 34**
    See also CA 61-64; CANR 175; DLB 111
Carrere, Emmanuel 1957- .... **CLC 89**
    See also CA 200
Carrier, Roch 1937- .... **CLC 13, 78**
    See also CA 130; CANR 61, 152; CCA 1;
    DAC; DAM MST; DLB 53; SATA 105,
    166
Carroll, James Dennis
    See Carroll, Jim
Carroll, James P. 1943(?)- .... **CLC 38**
    See also CA 81-84; CANR 73, 139, 209;
    MTCW 2; MTFW 2005
Carroll, Jim 1949-2009 .... **CLC 35, 143**
    See also AAYA 17; CA 45-48, 290; CANR
    42, 115; NCFS 5
Carroll, Lewis 1832-1898 . **NCLC 2, 53, 139;**
    PC 18, 74; WLC 1
    See also AAYA 39; BRW 5; BYA 5, 13; CD-
    BLB 1832-1890; CLR 18, 108; DA; DA3;
    DAB; DAC; DAM MST, NOV, POET;
    DLB 18, 163, 178; DLBY 1998; EXPN;
    EXPP; FANT; JRDA; LAIT 1; MAICYA
    1, 2; NFS 27; PFS 11, 30; RGEL 2; SATA
    100; SUFW 1; TEA; WCH; YABC 2
Carroll, Paul Vincent 1900-1968 ...... **CLC 10**
    See also CA 9-12R, 25-28R; DLB 10; EWL
    3; RGEL 2
Carruth, Hayden 1921-2008 .... **CLC 4, 7, 10,**
    18, 84, 287; PC 10
    See also AMWS 16; CA 9-12R, 277; CANR
    4, 38, 59, 110, 174; CP 1, 2, 3, 4, 5, 6, 7;
    DLB 5, 165; INT CANR-4; MTCW 1, 2;
    MTFW 2005; PFS 26; SATA 47; SATA-
    Obit 197
Carson, Anne 1950- .... **CLC 185; PC 64**
    See also AMWS 12; CA 203; CANR 209;
    CP 7; DLB 193; PFS 18; TCLE 1:1
Carson, Ciaran 1948- .... **CLC 201**
    See also BRWS 13; CA 112, 153; CANR
    113, 189; CP 6, 7; PFS 26
Carson, Rachel 1907-1964 .... **CLC 71**
    See also AAYA 49; AMWS 9; ANW; CA
    77-80; CANR 35; DA3; DAM POP; DLB
    275; FW; LAIT 4; MAL 5; MTCW 1, 2;
    MTFW 2005; NCFS 1; SATA 23
Carson, Rachel Louise
    See Carson, Rachel
Cartagena, Teresa de 1425(?)- .... **LC 155**
    See also DLB 286

Carter, Angela 1940-1992 ...... **CLC 5, 41, 76;**
    SSC 13, 85; TCLC 139
    See also BRWS 3; CA 53-56, 136; CANR
    12, 36, 61, 106; CN 3, 4, 5; DA3; DLB
    14, 207, 261, 319; EXPS; FANT; FW; GL
    2; MTCW 1, 2; MTFW 2005; RGSF 2;
    SATA 66; SATA-Obit 70; SFW 4; SSFS
    4, 12; SUFW 2; WLIT 4
Carter, Angela Olive
    See Carter, Angela
Carter, Martin (Wylde) 1927- .... **BLC 2:1**
    See also BW 2; CA 102; CANR 42; CD-
    WLB 3; CP 1, 2, 3, 4, 5, 6; DLB 117;
    EWL 3
Carter, Nick
    See Smith, Martin Cruz
Carter, Nick
    See Smith, Martin Cruz
Carver, Raymond 1938-1988 ..... **CLC 22, 36,**
    53, 55, 126; PC 54; SSC 8, 51, 104
    See also AAYA 44; AMWS 3; BPFB 1; CA
    33-36R, 126; CANR 17, 34, 61, 103; CN
    4; CPW; DA3; DAM NOV; DLB 130;
    DLBY 1984, 1988; EWL 3; MAL 5;
    MTCW 1, 2; MTFW 2005; PFS 17;
    RGAL 4; RGSF 2; SSFS 3, 6, 12, 13, 23;
    TCLE 1:1; TCWW 2; TUS
Cary, Elizabeth, Lady Falkland
    1585-1639 .... **LC 30, 141**
Cary, (Arthur) Joyce (Lunel)
    1888-1957 .... **TCLC 1, 29, 196**
    See also BRW 7; CA 104, 164; CDBLB
    1914-1945; DLB 15, 100; EWL 3; MTCW
    2; RGEL 2; TEA
Casal, Julian del 1863-1893 .... **NCLC 131**
    See also DLB 283; LAW
Casanova, Giacomo
    See Casanova de Seingalt, Giovanni Jacopo
Casanova, Giovanni Giacomo
    See Casanova de Seingalt, Giovanni Jacopo
Casanova de Seingalt, Giovanni Jacopo
    1725-1798 .... **LC 13, 151**
    See also WLIT 7
Casares, Adolfo Bioy
    See Bioy Casares, Adolfo
Casas, Bartolome de las 1474-1566
    See Las Casas, Bartolome de
Case, John
    See Hougan, Carolyn
Casely-Hayford, J(oseph) E(phraim)
    1866-1903 .... **BLC 1:1; TCLC 24**
    See also BW 2; CA 123, 152; DAM MULT
Casey, John (Dudley) 1939- .... **CLC 59**
    See also BEST 90:2; CA 69-72; CANR 23,
    100
Casey, Michael 1947- .... **CLC 2**
    See also CA 65-68; CANR 109; CP 2, 3;
    DLB 5
Casey, Patrick
    See Thurman, Wallace (Henry)
Casey, Warren 1935-1988 .... **CLC 12**
    See also CA 101, 127; INT CA-101
Casey, Warren Peter
    See Casey, Warren
Casona, Alejandro
    See Alvarez, Alejandro Rodriguez
Cassavetes, John 1929-1989 .... **CLC 20**
    See also CA 85-88, 127; CANR 82
Cassian, Nina 1924- .... **PC 17**
    See also CA 298; CWP; CWW 2
Cassill, R(onald) V(erlin)
    1919-2002 .... **CLC 4, 23**
    See also CA 9-12R, 208; CAAS 1; CANR
    7, 45; CN 1, 2, 3, 4, 5, 6, 7; DLB 6, 218;
    DLBY 2002
Cassiodorus, Flavius Magnus Aurelius c.
    490(?)-c. 583(?) .... **CMLC 43, 122**
Cassirer, Ernst 1874-1945 .... **TCLC 61**
    See also CA 157

Author Index

Chandler, Raymond Thornton
See Chandler, Raymond
Chang, Diana 1934-2009 .... **AAL**
See also CA 228; CWP; DLB 312; EXPP
Chang, Eileen 1920-1995 .... **AAL; SSC 28; TCLC 184**
See also CA 166; CANR 168; CWW 2; DLB 328; EWL 3; RGSF 2
Chang, Jung 1952- .... **CLC 71**
See also CA 142
Chang Ai-Ling
See Chang, Eileen
Channing, William Ellery 1780-1842 .... **NCLC 17**
See also DLB 1, 59, 235; RGAL 4
Chao, Patricia 1955- .... **CLC 119**
See also CA 163; CANR 155
Chaplin, Charles Spencer 1889-1977 .... **CLC 16**
See also AAYA 61; CA 81-84; 73-76; DLB 44
Chaplin, Charlie
See Chaplin, Charles Spencer
Chapman, George 1559(?)-1634 . **DC 19; LC 22, 116; PC 96**
See also BRW 1; DAM DRAM; DLB 62, 121; LMFS 1; RGEL 2
Chapman, Graham 1941-1989 .... **CLC 21**
See also AAYA 7; CA 116, 129; CANR 35, 95
Chapman, John Jay 1862-1933 .... **TCLC 7**
See also AMWS 14; CA 104, 191
Chapman, Lee
See Bradley, Marion Zimmer
Chapman, Walker
See Silverberg, Robert
Chappell, Fred (Davis) 1936- .... **CLC 40, 78, 162, 293; PC 105**
See also CA 5-8R, 198; CAAE 198; CAAS 4; CANR 8, 33, 67, 110; CN 6; CP 6, 7; CSW; DLB 6, 105; HGG
Char, Rene 1907-1988 ..... **CLC 9, 11, 14, 55; PC 56**
See also CA 13-16R, 124; CANR 32; DAM POET; DLB 258; EWL 3; GFL 1789 to the Present; MTCW 1, 2; RGWL 2, 3
Char, Rene-Emile
See Char, Rene
Charby, Jay
See Ellison, Harlan
Chardin, Pierre Teilhard de
See Teilhard de Chardin, (Marie Joseph) Pierre
Chariton fl. 1st cent. (?)- .... **CMLC 49**
Charlemagne 742-814 .... **CMLC 37**
Charles I 1600-1649 .... **LC 13**
Charriere, Isabelle de 1740-1805 .. **NCLC 66**
See also DLB 313
Charron, Pierre 1541-1603 .... **LC 174**
See also GFL Beginnings to 1789
Chartier, Alain c. 1392-1430 .... **LC 94**
See also DLB 208
Chartier, Emile-Auguste
See Alain
Charyn, Jerome 1937- .... **CLC 5, 8, 18**
See also CA 5-8R; CAAS 1; CANR 7, 61, 101, 158, 199; CMW 4; CN 1, 2, 3, 4, 5, 6, 7; DLBY 1983; MTCW 1
Chase, Adam
See Marlowe, Stephen
Chase, Mary (Coyle) 1907-1981 .... **DC 1**
See also CA 77-80, 105; CAD; CWD; DFS 11; DLB 228; SATA 17; SATA-Obit 29
Chase, Mary Ellen 1887-1973 .... **CLC 2; TCLC 124**
See also CA 13-16, 41-44R; CAP 1; SATA 10

Chase, Nicholas
See Hyde, Anthony
Chase-Riboud, Barbara (Dewayne Tosi) 1939- .... **BLC 2:1**
See also BW 2; CA 113; CANR 76; DAM MULT; DLB 33; MTCW 2
Chateaubriand, Francois Rene de 1768-1848 .... **NCLC 3, 134**
See also DLB 119; EW 5; GFL 1789 to the Present; RGWL 2, 3; TWA
Chatelet, Gabrielle-Emilie Du
See du Chatelet, Emilie
Chatterje, Saratchandra -(?)
See Chatterji, Sarat Chandra
Chatterji, Bankim Chandra 1838-1894 .... **NCLC 19**
Chatterji, Sarat Chandra 1876-1936 .... **TCLC 13**
See also CA 109, 186; EWL 3
Chatterton, Thomas 1752-1770 ..... **LC 3, 54; PC 104**
See also DAM POET; DLB 109; RGEL 2
Chatwin, (Charles) Bruce 1940-1989 .... **CLC 28, 57, 59**
See also AAYA 4; BEST 90:1; BRWS 4; CA 85-88, 127; CPW; DAM POP; DLB 194, 204; EWL 3; MTFW 2005
Chaucer, Daniel
See Ford, Ford Madox
Chaucer, Geoffrey 1340(?)-1400 ... **LC 17, 56, 173; PC 19, 58; WLCS**
See also BRW 1; BRWC 1; BRWR 2; CD-BLB Before 1660; DA; DA3; DAB; DAC; DAM MST, POET; DLB 146; LAIT 1; PAB; PFS 14; RGEL 2; TEA; WLIT 3; WP
Chaudhuri, Nirad C(handra) 1897-1999 .... **TCLC 224**
See also CA 128, 183; DLB 323
Chavez, Denise 1948- .... **HLC 1**
See also CA 131; CANR 56, 81, 137; DAM MULT; DLB 122; FW; HW 1, 2; LLW; MAL 5; MTCW 2; MTFW 2005
Chaviaras, Strates 1935- .... **CLC 33**
See also CA 105
Chayefsky, Paddy 1923-1981 .... **CLC 23**
See also CA 9-12R, 104; CAD; CANR 18; DAM DRAM; DFS 26; DLB 23; DLBY 7, 44; RGAL 4
Chayefsky, Sidney
See Chayefsky, Paddy
Chedid, Andree 1920- .... **CLC 47**
See also CA 145; CANR 95; EWL 3
Cheever, John 1912-1982 ..... **CLC 3, 7, 8, 11, 15, 25, 64; SSC 1, 38, 57, 120; WLC 2**
See also AAYA 65; AMWS 1; BPFB 1; CA 5-8R, 106; CABS 1; CANR 5, 27, 76; CDALB 1941-1968; CN 1, 2, 3; CPW; DA; DA3; DAB; DAC; DAM MST, NOV, POP; DLB 2, 102, 227; DLBY 1980, 1982; EWL 3; EXPS; INT CANR-5; MAL 5; MTCW 1, 2; MTFW 2005; RGAL 4; RGSF 2; SSFS 2, 14; TUS
Cheever, Susan 1943- .... **CLC 18, 48**
See also CA 103; CANR 27, 51, 92, 157, 198; DLBY 1982; INT CANR-27
Chekhonte, Antosha
See Chekhov, Anton
Chekhov, Anton 1860-1904 ...... **DC 9; SSC 2, 28, 41, 51, 85, 102; TCLC 3, 10, 31, 55, 96, 163; WLC 2**
See also AAYA 68; BYA 14; CA 104, 124; DA; DA3; DAB; DAC; DAM DRAM, MST; DFS 1, 5, 10, 12, 26; DLB 277; EW 7; EWL 3; EXPS; LAIT 3; LATS 1:1; RGSF 2; RGWL 2, 3; SATA 90; SSFS 5, 13, 14, 26, 29; TWA
Chekhov, Anton Pavlovich
See Chekhov, Anton

Cheney, Lynne V. 1941- .... **CLC 70**
See also CA 89-92; CANR 58, 117, 193; SATA 152
Cheney, Lynne Vincent
See Cheney, Lynne V.
Chenier, Andre-Marie de 1762-1794 . **LC 174**
See also EW 4; GFL Beginnings to 1789; TWA
Chernyshevsky, Nikolai Gavrilovich
See Chernyshevsky, Nikolay Gavrilovich
Chernyshevsky, Nikolay Gavrilovich 1828-1889 .... **NCLC 1**
See also DLB 238
Cherry, Carolyn Janice
See Cherryh, C.J.
Cherryh, C.J. 1942- .... **CLC 35**
See also AAYA 24; BPFB 1; CA 65-68; CANR 10, 147, 179; DLBY 1980; FANT; SATA 93, 172; SCFW 2; YAW
Chesler, Phyllis 1940- .... **CLC 247**
See also CA 49-52; CANR 4, 59, 140, 189; FW
Chesnutt, Charles W(addell) 1858-1932 .... **BLC 1; SSC 7, 54, 139; TCLC 5, 39**
See also AFAW 1, 2; AMWS 14; BW 1, 3; CA 106, 125; CANR 76; DAM MULT; DLB 12, 50, 78; EWL 3; MAL 5; MTCW 1, 2; MTFW 2005; RGAL 4; RGSF 2; SSFS 11, 26
Chester, Alfred 1929(?)-1971 .... **CLC 49**
See also CA 196, 33-36R; DLB 130; MAL 5
Chesterton, G. K. 1874-1936 . **PC 28; SSC 1, 46; TCLC 1, 6, 64**
See also AAYA 57; BRW 6; CA 104, 132; CANR 73, 131; CDBLB 1914-1945; CMW 4; DAM NOV, POET; DLB 10, 19, 34, 70, 98, 149, 178; EWL 3; FANT; MSW; MTCW 1, 2; MTFW 2005; RGEL 2; RGSF 2; SATA 27; SUFW 1
Chesterton, Gilbert Keith
See Chesterton, G. K.
Chettle, Henry 1560-1607(?) .... **LC 112**
See also DLB 136; RGEL 2
Chiang, Pin-chin 1904-1986 .... **CLC 68**
See also CA 118; DLB 328; EWL 3; RGWL 3
Chiang Ping-chih
See Chiang, Pin-chin
Chief Joseph 1840-1904 .... **NNAL**
See also CA 152; DA3; DAM MULT
Chief Seattle 1786(?)-1866 .... **NNAL**
See also DA3; DAM MULT
Ch'ien, Chung-shu 1910-1998 .... **CLC 22**
See also CA 130; CANR 73; CWW 2; DLB 328; MTCW 1, 2
Chikamatsu Monzaemon 1653-1724 ... **LC 66**
See also RGWL 2, 3
Child, Francis James 1825-1896 . **NCLC 173**
See also DLB 1, 64, 235
Child, L. Maria
See Child, Lydia Maria
Child, Lydia Maria 1802-1880 .. **NCLC 6, 73**
See also DLB 1, 74, 243; RGAL 4; SATA 67
Child, Mrs.
See Child, Lydia Maria
Child, Philip 1898-1978 .... **CLC 19, 68**
See also CA 13-14; CAP 1; CP 1; DLB 68; RHW; SATA 47
Childers, (Robert) Erskine 1870-1922 .... **TCLC 65**
See also CA 113, 153; DLB 70
Childress, Alice 1920-1994 .... **BLC 1:1; CLC 12, 15, 86, 96; DC 4; TCLC 116**
See also AAYA 8; BW 2, 3; BYA 2; CA 45-48, 146; CAD; CANR 3, 27, 50, 74; CLR 14; CWD; DA3; DAM DRAM, MULT,

NOV; DFS 2, 8, 14, 26; DLB 7, 38, 249;
JRDA; LAIT 5; MAICYA 1, 2; MAIC-
YAS 1; MAL 5; MTCW 1, 2; MTFW
2005; RGAL 4; SATA 7, 48, 81; TUS;
WYA; YAW

Chin, Frank 1940- ..... **AAL; CLC 135; DC 7**
See also CA 33-36R; CAD; CANR 71; CD
5, 6; DAM MULT; DLB 206, 312; LAIT
5; RGAL 4

Chin, Frank Chew, Jr.
See Chin, Frank

Chin, Marilyn 1955- .... **PC 40**
See also CA 129; CANR 70, 113; CWP;
DLB 312; PFS 28

Chin, Marilyn Mei Ling
See Chin, Marilyn

Chislett, (Margaret) Anne 1943- ...... **CLC 34**
See also CA 151

Chitty, Thomas Willes
See Hinde, Thomas

Chivers, Thomas Holley
1809-1858 .... **NCLC 49**
See also DLB 3, 248; RGAL 4

Chlamyda, Jehudil
See Gorky, Maxim

Ch'o, Chou
See Shu-Jen, Chou

Choi, Susan 1969- .... **CLC 119**
See also CA 223; CANR 188

Chomette, Rene Lucien 1898-1981 .. **CLC 20**
See also CA 103

Chomsky, Avram Noam
See Chomsky, Noam

Chomsky, Noam 1928- .... **CLC 132**
See also CA 17-20R; CANR 28, 62, 110,
132, 179; DA3; DLB 246; MTCW 1, 2;
MTFW 2005

Chona, Maria 1845(?)-1936 .... **NNAL**
See also CA 144

Chopin, Kate 1851-1904 .... **SSC 8, 68, 110;
TCLC 127; WLCS**
See also AAYA 33; AMWR 2; BYA 11, 15;
CA 104, 122; CDALB 1865-1917; DA3;
DAB; DAC; DAM MST, NOV; DLB 12,
78; EXPN; EXPS; FL 1:3; FW; LAIT 3;
MAL 5; MBL; NFS 3; RGAL 4; RGSF 2;
SSFS 2, 13, 17, 26; TUS

Chopin, Katherine
See Chopin, Kate

Chretien de Troyes c. 12th cent. - . **CMLC 10**
See also DLB 208; EW 1; RGWL 2, 3;
TWA

Christie
See Ichikawa, Kon

Christie, Agatha 1890-1976 . **CLC 1, 6, 8, 12,
39, 48, 110; DC 39**
See also AAYA 9; AITN 1, 2; BPFB 1;
BRWS 2; CA 17-20R; 61-64; CANR 10,
37, 108; CBD; CDBLB 1914-1945; CMW
4; CN 1, 2; CPW; CWD; DA3; DAB;
DAC; DAM NOV; DFS 2; DLB 13, 77,
245; MSW; MTCW 1, 2; MTFW 2005;
NFS 8, 30, 33; RGEL 2; RHW; SATA 36;
SSFS 31; TEA; YAW

Christie, Agatha Mary Clarissa
See Christie, Agatha

Christie, Ann Philippa
See Pearce, Philippa

Christie, Philippa
See Pearce, Philippa

Christine de Pisan
See Christine de Pizan

Christine de Pizan 1365(?)-1431(?) ...... **LC 9,
130; PC 68**
See also DLB 208; FL 1:1; FW; RGWL 2,
3

Chuang-Tzu c. 369B.C.-c.
286B.C. .... **CMLC 57**

Chubb, Elmer
See Masters, Edgar Lee

Chulkov, Mikhail Dmitrievich
1743-1792 .... **LC 2**
See also DLB 150

Churchill, Caryl 1938- .... **CLC 31, 55, 157;
DC 5**
See also BRWS 4; CA 102; CANR 22, 46,
108; CBD; CD 5, 6; CWD; DFS 25; DLB
13, 310; EWL 3; FW; MTCW 1; RGEL 2

Churchill, Charles 1731-1764 .... **LC 3**
See also DLB 109; RGEL 2

Churchill, Chick
See Churchill, Caryl

Churchill, Sir Winston
1874-1965 .... **TCLC 113**
See also BRW 6; CA 97-100; CDBLB
1890-1914; DA3; DLB 100, 329; DLBD
16; LAIT 4; MTCW 1, 2

Churchill, Sir Winston Leonard Spencer
See Churchill, Sir Winston

Chute, Carolyn 1947- .... **CLC 39**
See also CA 123; CANR 135; CN 7; DLB
350

Ciardi, John (Anthony) 1916-1986 . **CLC 10,
40, 44, 129; PC 69**
See also CA 5-8R, 118; CAAS 2; CANR 5,
33; CLR 19; CP 1, 2, 3, 4; CWRI 5; DAM
POET; DLB 5; DLBY 1986; INT
CANR-5; MAICYA 1, 2; MAL 5; MTCW
1, 2; MTFW 2005; RGAL 4; SAAS 26;
SATA 1, 65; SATA-Obit 46

Cibber, Colley 1671-1757 .... **LC 66**
See also DLB 84; RGEL 2

Cicero, Marcus Tullius
106B.C.-43B.C. .... **CMLC 121**
See also AW 1; CDWLB 1; DLB 211;
RGWL 2, 3; WLIT 8

Cimino, Michael 1943- .... **CLC 16**
See also CA 105

Cioran, E(mil) M. 1911-1995 .... **CLC 64**
See also CA 25-28R, 149; CANR 91; DLB
220; EWL 3

Circus, Anthony
See Hoch, Edward D.

Cisneros, Sandra 1954- .... **CLC 69, 118, 193;
HLC 1; PC 52; SSC 32, 72**
See also AAYA 9, 53; AMWS 7; CA 131;
CANR 64, 118; CLR 123; CN 7; CWP;
DA3; DAM MULT; DLB 122, 152; EWL
3; EXPN; FL 1:5; FW; HW 1, 2; LAIT 5;
LATS 1:2; LLW; MAICYA 2; MAL 5;
MTCW 2; MTFW 2005; NFS 2; PFS 19;
RGAL 4; RGSF 2; SSFS 3, 13, 27; WLIT
1; YAW

Cixous, Helene 1937- .... **CLC 92, 253**
See also CA 126; CANR 55, 123; CWW 2;
DLB 83, 242; EWL 3; FL 1:5; FW; GLL
2; MTCW 1, 2; MTFW 2005; TWA

Clair, Rene
See Chomette, Rene Lucien

Clampitt, Amy 1920-1994 .... **CLC 32; PC 19**
See also AMWS 9; CA 110, 146; CANR
29, 79; CP 4, 5; DLB 105; MAL 5; PFS
27

Clancy, Thomas L., Jr.
See Clancy, Tom

Clancy, Tom 1947- .... **CLC 45, 112**
See also AAYA 9, 51; BEST 89:1, 90:1;
BPFB 1; BYA 10, 11; CA 125, 131;
CANR 62, 105, 132; CMW 4; CPW;
DA3; DAM NOV, POP; DLB 227; INT
CA-131; MTCW 1, 2; MTFW 2005

Clare, John 1793-1864 .. **NCLC 9, 86; PC 23**
See also BRWS 11; DAB; DAM POET;
DLB 55, 96; RGEL 2

Clarin
See Alas (y Urena), Leopoldo (Enrique
Garcia)

Clark, Al C.
See Goines, Donald

Clark, Brian (Robert)
See Clark, (Robert) Brian

Clark, (Robert) Brian 1932- .... **CLC 29**
See also CA 41-44R; CANR 67; CBD; CD
5, 6

Clark, Curt
See Westlake, Donald E.

Clark, Eleanor 1913-1996 .... **CLC 5, 19**
See also CA 9-12R, 151; CANR 41; CN 1,
2, 3, 4, 5, 6; DLB 6

Clark, J. P.
See Clark-Bekederemo, J. P.

Clark, John Pepper
See Clark-Bekederemo, J. P.

Clark, Kenneth (Mackenzie)
1903-1983 .... **TCLC 147**
See also CA 93-96, 109; CANR 36; MTCW
1, 2; MTFW 2005

Clark, M. R.
See Clark, Mavis Thorpe

Clark, Mavis Thorpe 1909-1999 ...... **CLC 12**
See also CA 57-60; CANR 8, 37, 107; CLR
30; CWRI 5; MAICYA 1, 2; SAAS 5;
SATA 8, 74

Clark, Walter Van Tilburg
1909-1971 .... **CLC 28**
See also CA 9-12R, 33-36R; CANR 63,
113; CN 1; DLB 9, 206; LAIT 2; MAL 5;
RGAL 4; SATA 8; TCWW 1, 2

Clark-Bekederemo, J. P. 1935- ...... **BLC 1:1;
CLC 38; DC 5**
See also AAYA 79; AFW; BW 1; CA 65-
68; CANR 16, 72; CD 5, 6; DAM DRAM,
MULT; DFS 13; DLB 117; EWL 3;
MTCW 2; MTFW 2005; RGEL 2

Clark-Bekederemo, John Pepper
See Clark-Bekederemo, J. P.

Clark Bekederemo, Johnson Pepper
See Clark-Bekederemo, J. P.

Clarke, Arthur
See Clarke, Arthur C.

Clarke, Arthur C. 1917-2008 .. **CLC 1, 4, 13,
18, 35, 136; SSC 3**
See also AAYA 4, 33; BPFB 1; BYA 13;
CA 1-4R, 270; CANR 2, 28, 55, 74, 130,
196; CLR 119; CN 1, 2, 3, 4, 5, 6, 7;
CPW; DA3; DAM POP; DLB 261; JRDA;
LAIT 5; MAICYA 1, 2; MTCW 1, 2;
MTFW 2005; SATA 13, 70, 115; SATA-
Obit 191; SCFW 1, 2; SFW 4; SSFS 4,
18, 29; TCLE 1:1; YAW

Clarke, Arthur Charles
See Clarke, Arthur C.

Clarke, Austin 1896-1974 .... **CLC 6, 9;
PC-112**
See also BRWS 15; CA 29-32, 49-52; CAP
2; CP 1, 2; DAM POET; DLB 10, 20;
EWL 3; RGEL 2

Clarke, Austin C. 1934- .... **BLC 1:1; CLC 8,
53; SSC 45, 116**
See also BW 1; CA 25-28R; CAAS 16;
CANR 14, 32, 68, 140; CN 1, 2, 3, 4, 5,
6, 7; DAC; DAM MULT; DLB 53, 125;
DNFS 2; MTCW 2; MTFW 2005; RGSF
2

Clarke, Gillian 1937- .... **CLC 61**
See also CA 106; CP 3, 4, 5, 6, 7; CWP;
DLB 40

Clarke, Marcus (Andrew Hislop)
1846-1881 .... **NCLC 19; SSC 94**
See also DLB 230; RGEL 2; RGSF 2

Clarke, Shirley 1925-1997 .... **CLC 16**
See also CA 189

Dennis, Nigel (Forbes) 1912-1989 ...... **CLC 8**
See also CA 25-28R, 129; CN 1, 2, 3, 4;
DLB 13, 15, 233; EWL 3; MTCW 1

Dent, Lester 1904-1959 .... **TCLC 72**
See also CA 112, 161; CMW 4; DLB 306;
SFW 4

Dentinger, Stephen
See Hoch, Edward D.

De Palma, Brian 1940- .... **CLC 20, 247**
See also CA 109

De Palma, Brian Russell
See De Palma, Brian

de Pizan, Christine
See Christine de Pizan

De Quincey, Thomas 1785-1859 ..... **NCLC 4, 87, 198**
See also BRW 4; CDBLB 1789-1832; DLB
110, 144; RGEL 2

De Ray, Jill
See Moore, Alan

Deren, Eleanora 1908(?)-1961 .. **CLC 16, 102**
See also CA 192, 111

Deren, Maya
See Deren, Eleanora

Derleth, August (William)
1909-1971 .... **CLC 31**
See also BPFB 1; BYA 9, 10; CA 1-4R, 29-
32R; CANR 4; CMW 4; CN 1; DLB 9;
DLBD 17; HGG; SATA 5; SUFW 1

Der Nister 1884-1950 .... **TCLC 56**
See also DLB 333; EWL 3

de Routisie, Albert
See Aragon, Louis

Derrida, Jacques 1930-2004 ...... **CLC 24, 87, 225**
See also CA 124, 127, 232; CANR 76, 98,
133; DLB 242; EWL 3; LMFS 2; MTCW
2; TWA

Derry Down Derry
See Lear, Edward

Dersonnes, Jacques
See Simenon, Georges

Der Stricker c. 1190-c. 1250 .... **CMLC 75**
See also DLB 138

Derzhavin, Gavriil Romanovich
1743-1816 .... **NCLC 215**
See also DLB 150

Desai, Anita 1937- . **CLC 19, 37, 97, 175, 271**
See also BRWS 5; CA 81-84; CANR 33,
53, 95, 133; CN 1, 2, 3, 4, 5, 6, 7; CWRI
5; DA3; DAB; DAM NOV; DLB 271,
323; DNFS 2; EWL 3; FW; MTCW 1, 2;
MTFW 2005; SATA 63, 126; SSFS 28, 31

Desai, Kiran 1971- .... **CLC 119**
See also BRWS 15; BYA 16; CA 171;
CANR 127; NFS 28

de Saint-Luc, Jean
See Glassco, John

de Saint Roman, Arnaud
See Aragon, Louis

Desbordes-Valmore, Marceline
1786-1859 .... **NCLC 97**
See also DLB 217

Descartes, Rene 1596-1650 .... **LC 20, 35, 150**
See also DLB 268; EW 3; GFL Beginnings
to 1789

Deschamps, Eustache 1340(?)-1404 .. **LC 103**
See also DLB 208

De Sica, Vittorio 1901(?)-1974 .... **CLC 20**
See also CA 117

Desnos, Robert 1900-1945 ...... **TCLC 22, 241**
See also CA 121, 151; CANR 107; DLB
258; EWL 3; LMFS 2

Destouches, Louis-Ferdinand
See Celine, Louis-Ferdinand

de Teran, Lisa St. Aubin
See St. Aubin de Teran, Lisa

de Tolignac, Gaston
See Griffith, D.W.

Deutsch, Babette 1895-1982 .... **CLC 18**
See also BYA 3; CA 1-4R, 108; CANR 4,
79; CP 1, 2, 3; DLB 45; SATA 1; SATA-
Obit 33

Devenant, William 1606-1649 .... **LC 13**

Devi, Mahasweta 1926- .... **CLC 290**

Deville, Rene
See Kacew, Romain

Devkota, Laxmiprasad 1909-1959 . **TCLC 23**
See also CA 123

De Voto, Bernard (Augustine)
1897-1955 .... **TCLC 29**
See also CA 113, 160; DLB 9, 256; MAL
5; TCWW 1, 2

De Vries, Peter 1910-1993 ..... **CLC 1, 2, 3, 7, 10, 28, 46**
See also CA 17-20R, 142; CANR 41; CN
1, 2, 3, 4, 5; DAM NOV; DLB 6; DLBY
1982; MAL 5; MTCW 1, 2; MTFW 2005

Dewey, John 1859-1952 .... **TCLC 95**
See also CA 114, 170; CANR 144; DLB
246, 270; RGAL 4

Dexter, John
See Bradley, Marion Zimmer

Dexter, Martin
See Faust, Frederick

Dexter, Pete 1943- .... **CLC 34, 55**
See also BEST 89:2; CA 127, 131; CANR
129; CPW; DAM POP; INT CA-131;
MAL 5; MTCW 1; MTFW 2005

Diamano, Silmang
See Senghor, Leopold Sedar

Diamant, Anita 1951- .... **CLC 239**
See also CA 145; CANR 126

Diamond, Neil 1941- .... **CLC 30**
See also CA 108

Diaz, Junot 1968- .... **CLC 258**
See also AAYA 83; BYA 12; CA 161;
CANR 119, 183; LLW; SSFS 20

Diaz del Castillo, Bernal c.
1496-1584 .... **HLCS 1; LC 31**
See also DLB 318; LAW

di Bassetto, Corno
See Shaw, George Bernard

Dick, Philip K. 1928-1982 ... **CLC 10, 30, 72; SSC 57**
See also AAYA 24; BPFB 1; BYA 11; CA
49-52, 106; CANR 2, 16, 132; CN 2, 3;
CPW; DA3; DAM NOV, POP; DLB 8;
MTCW 1, 2; MTFW 2005; NFS 5, 26;
SCFW 1, 2; SFW 4

Dick, Philip Kindred
See Dick, Philip K.

Dickens, Charles 1812-1870 . **NCLC 3, 8, 18, 26, 37, 50, 86, 105, 113, 161, 187, 203, 206, 211, 217, 219, 230, 231; SSC 17, 49, 88; WLC 2**
See also AAYA 23; BRW 5; BRWC 1, 2;
BYA 1, 2, 3, 13, 14; CDBLB 1832-1890;
CLR 95; CMW 4; DA; DA3; DAB; DAC;
DAM MST, NOV; DLB 21, 55, 70, 159,
166; EXPN; GL 2; HGG; JRDA; LAIT 1,
2; LATS 1:1; LMFS 1; MAICYA 1, 2;
NFS 4, 5, 10, 14, 20, 25, 30, 33; RGEL 2;
RGSF 2; SATA 15; SUFW 1; TEA; WCH;
WLIT 4; WYA

Dickens, Charles John Huffam
See Dickens, Charles

Dickey, James 1923-1997 .... **CLC 1, 2, 4, 7, 10, 15, 47, 109; PC 40; TCLC 151**
See also AAYA 50; AITN 1, 2; AMWS 4;
BPFB 1; CA 9-12R, 156; CABS 2; CANR
10, 48, 61, 105; CDALB 1968-1988; CP
1, 2, 3, 4, 5, 6; CPW; CSW; DA3; DAM
NOV, POET, POP; DLB 5, 193, 342;
DLBD 7; DLBY 1982, 1993, 1996, 1997,
1998; EWL 3; INT CANR-10; MAL 5;
MTCW 1, 2; NFS 9; PFS 6, 11; RGAL 4;
TUS

Dickey, James Lafayette
See Dickey, James

Dickey, William 1928-1994 .... **CLC 3, 28**
See also CA 9-12R, 145; CANR 24, 79; CP
1, 2, 3, 4; DLB 5

Dickinson, Charles 1951- .... **CLC 49**
See also CA 128; CANR 141

Dickinson, Emily 1830-1886 ... **NCLC 21, 77, 171; PC 1; WLC 2**
See also AAYA 22; AMW; AMWR 1;
CDALB 1865-1917; DA; DA3; DAB;
DAC; DAM MST, POET; DLB 1, 243;
EXPP; FL 1:3; MBL; PAB; PFS 1, 2, 3,
4, 5, 6, 8, 10, 11, 13, 16, 28, 32, 35;
RGAL 4; SATA 29; TUS; WP; WYA

Dickinson, Emily Elizabeth
See Dickinson, Emily

Dickinson, Mrs. Herbert Ward
See Phelps, Elizabeth Stuart

Dickinson, Peter 1927- .... **CLC 12, 35**
See also AAYA 9, 49; BYA 5; CA 41-44R;
CANR 31, 58, 88, 134, 195; CLR 29, 125;
CMW 4; DLB 87, 161, 276; JRDA; MAI-
CYA 1, 2; SATA 5, 62, 95, 150; SFW 4;
WYA; YAW

Dickinson, Peter Malcolm de Brissac
See Dickinson, Peter

Dickson, Carr
See Carr, John Dickson

Dickson, Carter
See Carr, John Dickson

Diderot, Denis 1713-1784 .... **LC 26, 126**
See also DLB 313; EW 4; GFL Beginnings
to 1789; LMFS 1; RGWL 2, 3

Didion, Joan 1934- . **CLC 1, 3, 8, 14, 32, 129**
See also AITN 1; AMWS 4; CA 5-8R;
CANR 14, 52, 76, 125, 174; CDALB
1968-1988; CN 2, 3, 4, 5, 6, 7; DA3;
DAM NOV; DLB 2, 173, 185; DLBY
1981, 1986; EWL 3; MAL 5; MBL;
MTCW 1, 2; MTFW 2005; NFS 3; RGAL
4; TCLE 1:1; TCWW 2; TUS

di Donato, Pietro 1911-1992 .... **TCLC 159**
See also AMWS 20; CA 101, 136; DLB 9

Dietrich, Robert
See Hunt, E. Howard

Difusa, Pati
See Almodovar, Pedro

di Lampedusa, Giuseppe Tomasi
See Lampedusa, Giuseppe di

Dillard, Annie 1945- ...... **CLC 9, 60, 115, 216**
See also AAYA 6, 43; AMWS 6; ANW; CA
49-52; CANR 3, 43, 62, 90, 125; DA3;
DAM NOV; DLB 275, 278; DLBY 1980;
LAIT 4, 5; MAL 5; MTCW 1, 2; MTFW
2005; NCFS 1; RGAL 4; SATA 10, 140;
TCLE 1:1; TUS

Dillard, R(ichard) H(enry) W(ilde)
1937- .... **CLC 5**
See also CA 21-24R; CAAS 7; CANR 10;
CP 2, 3, 4, 5, 6, 7; CSW; DLB 5, 244

Dillon, Eilis 1920-1994 .... **CLC 17**
See also CA 9-12R, 182, 147; CAAE 182;
CAAS 3; CANR 4, 38, 78; CLR 26; MAI-
CYA 1, 2; MAICYAS 1; SATA 2, 74;
SATA-Essay 105; SATA-Obit 83; YAW

Dimont, Penelope
See Mortimer, Penelope (Ruth)

Dinesen, Isak
See Blixen, Karen

Ding Ling
See Chiang, Pin-chin

Diodorus Siculus c. 90B.C.-c.
31B.C. .... **CMLC 88**
Dionysius of Halicarnassus c. 60B.C.-c.
7B.C. .... **CMLC 126**
Diphusa, Patty
See Almodovar, Pedro
Disch, Thomas M. 1940-2008 .... **CLC 7, 36**
See also AAYA 17; BPFB 1; CA 21-24R,
274; CAAS 4; CANR 17, 36, 54, 89; CLR
18; CP 5, 6, 7; DA3; DLB 8, 282; HGG;
MAICYA 1, 2; MTCW 1, 2; MTFW 2005;
SAAS 15; SATA 92; SATA-Obit 195;
SCFW 1, 2; SFW 4; SUFW 2
Disch, Thomas Michael
See Disch, Thomas M.
Disch, Tom
See Disch, Thomas M.
d'Isly, Georges
See Simenon, Georges
Disraeli, Benjamin 1804-1881 ... **NCLC 2, 39,
79**
See also BRW 4; DLB 21, 55; RGEL 2
D'Israeli, Isaac 1766-1848 .... **NCLC 217**
See also DLB 107
Ditcum, Steve
See Crumb, R.
Dixon, Paige
See Corcoran, Barbara (Asenath)
Dixon, Stephen 1936- .... **CLC 52; SSC 16**
See also AMWS 12; CA 89-92; CANR 17,
40, 54, 91, 175; CN 4, 5, 6, 7; DLB 130;
MAL 5
Dixon, Thomas, Jr. 1864-1946 ..... **TCLC 163**
See also RHW
Djebar, Assia 1936- .... **BLC 2:1; CLC 182,
296; SSC 114**
See also CA 188; CANR 169; DLB 346;
EWL 3; RGWL 3; WLIT 2
Doak, Annie
See Dillard, Annie
Dobell, Sydney Thompson
1824-1874 .... **NCLC 43; PC 100**
See also DLB 32; RGEL 2
Doblin, Alfred
See Doeblin, Alfred
Dobroliubov, Nikolai Aleksandrovich
See Dobrolyubov, Nikolai Alexandrovich
Dobrolyubov, Nikolai Alexandrovich
1836-1861 .... **NCLC 5**
See also DLB 277
Dobson, Austin 1840-1921 .... **TCLC 79**
See also DLB 35, 144
Dobyns, Stephen 1941- .... **CLC 37, 233**
See also AMWS 13; CA 45-48; CANR 2,
18, 99; CMW 4; CP 4, 5, 6, 7; PFS 23
Doctorow, Cory 1971- .... **CLC 273**
See also AAYA 84; CA 221; CANR 203
Doctorow, E. L. 1931- .... **CLC 6, 11, 15, 18,
37, 44, 65, 113, 214**
See also AAYA 22; AITN 2; AMWS 4;
BEST 89:3; BPFB 1; CA 45-48; CANR
2, 33, 51, 76, 97, 133, 170; CDALB 1968-
1988; CN 3, 4, 5, 6, 7; CPW; DA3; DAM
NOV, POP; DLB 2, 28, 173; DLBY 1980;
EWL 3; LAIT 3; MAL 5; MTCW 1, 2;
MTFW 2005; NFS 6; RGAL 4; RGHL;
RHW; SSFS 27; TCLE 1:1; TCWW 1, 2;
TUS
Doctorow, Edgar Laurence
See Doctorow, E. L.
Dodgson, Charles Lutwidge
See Carroll, Lewis
Dodsley, Robert 1703-1764 .... **LC 97**
See also DLB 95; RGEL 2
Dodson, Owen (Vincent)
1914-1983 .... **BLC 1:1; CLC 79**
See also BW 1; CA 65-68, 110; CANR 24;
DAM MULT; DLB 76

Doeblin, Alfred 1878-1957 .... **TCLC 13**
See also CA 110, 141; CDWLB 2; DLB 66;
EWL 3; RGWL 2, 3
Doerr, Harriet 1910-2002 .... **CLC 34**
See also CA 117, 122, 213; CANR 47; INT
CA-122; LATS 1:2
Domecq, Honorio Bustos
See Bioy Casares, Adolfo; Borges, Jorge
Luis
Domini, Rey
See Lorde, Audre
Dominic, R. B.
See Hennissart, Martha
Dominique
See Proust, Marcel
Don, A
See Stephen, Sir Leslie
Donaldson, Stephen R. 1947- ... **CLC 46, 138**
See also AAYA 36; BPFB 1; CA 89-92;
CANR 13, 55, 99; CPW; DAM POP;
FANT; INT CANR-13; SATA 121; SFW
4; SUFW 1, 2
Donleavy, J(ames) P(atrick) 1926- .... **CLC 1,
4, 6, 10, 45**
See also AITN 2; BPFB 1; CA 9-12R;
CANR 24, 49, 62, 80, 124; CBD; CD 5,
6; CN 1, 2, 3, 4, 5, 6, 7; DLB 6, 173; INT
CANR-24; MAL 5; MTCW 1, 2; MTFW
2005; RGAL 4
Donnadieu, Marguerite
See Duras, Marguerite
Donne, John 1572-1631 ... **LC 10, 24, 91; PC
1, 43; WLC 2**
See also AAYA 67; BRW 1; BRWC 1;
BRWR 2; CDBLB Before 1660; DA;
DAB; DAC; DAM MST, POET; DLB
121, 151; EXPP; PAB; PFS 2, 11, 35;
RGEL 3; TEA; WLIT 3; WP
Donnell, David 1939(?)- .... **CLC 34**
See also CA 197
Donoghue, Denis 1928- .... **CLC 209**
See also CA 17-20R; CANR 16, 102, 206
Donoghue, Emma 1969- .... **CLC 239**
See also CA 155; CANR 103, 152, 196;
DLB 267; GLL 2; SATA 101
Donoghue, P.S.
See Hunt, E. Howard
Donoso, Jose 1924-1996 ..... **CLC 4, 8, 11, 32,
99; HLC 1; SSC 34; TCLC 133**
See also CA 81-84, 155; CANR 32, 73; CD-
WLB 3; CWW 2; DAM MULT; DLB 113;
EWL 3; HW 1, 2; LAW; LAWS 1; MTCW
1, 2; MTFW 2005; RGSF 2; WLIT 1
Donoso Yanez, Jose
See Donoso, Jose
Donovan, John 1928-1992 .... **CLC 35**
See also AAYA 20; CA 97-100, 137; CLR
3; MAICYA 1, 2; SATA 72; SATA-Brief
29; YAW
Don Roberto
See Cunninghame Graham, Robert Bontine
Doolittle, Hilda 1886-1961 . **CLC 3, 8, 14, 31,
34, 73; PC 5; WLC 3**
See also AAYA 66; AMWS 1; CA 97-100;
CANR 35, 131; DA; DAC; DAM MST,
POET; DLB 4, 45; EWL 3; FL 1:5; FW;
GLL 1; LMFS 2; MAL 5; MBL; MTCW
1, 2; MTFW 2005; PFS 6, 28; RGAL 4
Doppo
See Kunikida Doppo
Doppo, Kunikida
See Kunikida Doppo
Dorfman, Ariel 1942- .... **CLC 48, 77, 189;
HLC 1**
See also CA 124, 130; CANR 67, 70, 135;
CWW 2; DAM MULT; DFS 4; EWL 3;
HW 1, 2; INT CA-130; WLIT 1

Dorn, Edward 1929-1999 .... **CLC 10, 18**
See also CA 93-96, 187; CANR 42, 79; CP
1, 2, 3, 4, 5, 6, 7; DLB 5; INT CA-93-96;
WP
Dorn, Edward Merton
See Dorn, Edward
Dor-Ner, Zvi CLC 70
Dorris, Michael 1945-1997 .... **CLC 109;
NNAL**
See also AAYA 20; BEST 90:1; BYA 12;
CA 102, 157; CANR 19, 46, 75; CLR 58;
DA3; DAM MULT, NOV; DLB 175;
LAIT 5; MTCW 2; MTFW 2005; NFS 3;
RGAL 4; SATA 75; SATA-Obit 94;
TCWW 2; YAW
Dorris, Michael A.
See Dorris, Michael
Dorris, Michael Anthony
See Dorris, Michael
Dorsan, Luc
See Simenon, Georges
Dorsange, Jean
See Simenon, Georges
Dorset
See Sackville, Thomas
Dos Passos, John 1896-1970 ...... **CLC 1, 4, 8,
11, 15, 25, 34, 82; WLC 2**
See also AMW; BPFB 1; CA 1-4R, 29-32R;
CANR 3; CDALB 1929-1941; DA; DA3;
DAB; DAC; DAM MST, NOV; DLB 4,
9, 274, 316; DLBD 1, 15; DLBY 1996;
EWL 3; MAL 5; MTCW 1, 2; MTFW
2005; NFS 14; RGAL 4; TUS
Dos Passos, John Roderigo
See Dos Passos, John
Dossage, Jean
See Simenon, Georges
Dostoevsky, Fedor
See Dostoevsky, Fyodor
Dostoevsky, Fedor Mikhailovich
See Dostoevsky, Fyodor
Dostoevsky, Fyodor 1821-1881 ... **NCLC 2, 7,
21, 33, 43, 119, 167, 202; SSC 2, 33, 44,
134; WLC 2**
See also AAYA 40; DA; DA3; DAB; DAC;
DAM MST, NOV; DLB 238; EW 7;
EXPN; LATS 1:1; LMFS 1, 2; NFS 28;
RGSF 2; RGWL 2, 3; SSFS 8, 30; TWA
Doty, Mark 1953(?)- .... **CLC 176; PC 53**
See also AMWS 11; CA 161, 183; CAAE
183; CANR 110, 173; CP 7; PFS 28
Doty, Mark A.
See Doty, Mark
Doty, Mark Alan
See Doty, Mark
Doty, M.R.
See Doty, Mark
Doughty, Charles M(ontagu)
1843-1926 .... **TCLC 27**
See also CA 115, 178; DLB 19, 57, 174
Douglas, Ellen 1921- .... **CLC 73**
See also CA 115; CANR 41, 83; CN 5, 6,
7; CSW; DLB 292
Douglas, Gavin 1475(?)-1522 .... **LC 20**
See also DLB 132; RGEL 2
Douglas, George
See Brown, George Douglas
Douglas, Keith (Castellain)
1920-1944 .... **PC 106; TCLC 40**
See also BRW 7; CA 160; DLB 27; EWL
3; PAB; RGEL 2
Douglas, Leonard
See Bradbury, Ray
Douglas, Michael
See Crichton, Michael
Douglas, (George) Norman
1868-1952 .... **TCLC 68**
See also BRW 6; CA 119, 157; DLB 34,
195; RGEL 2

Dumas, Claudine
See Malzberg, Barry N(athaniel)
Dumas, Henry L. 1934-1968 . **BLC 2:1; CLC 6, 62; SSC 107**
See also BW 1; CA 85-88; DLB 41; RGAL 4
du Maurier, Daphne 1907-1989 .. **CLC 6, 11, 59; SSC 18, 129; TCLC 209**
See also AAYA 37; BPFB 1; BRWS 3; CA 5-8R, 128; CANR 6, 55; CMW 4; CN 1, 2, 3, 4; CPW; DA3; DAB; DAC; DAM MST, POP; DLB 191; GL 2; HGG; LAIT 3; MSW; MTCW 1, 2; NFS 12; RGEL 2; RGSF 2; RHW; SATA 27; SATA-Obit 60; SSFS 14, 16; TEA
Du Maurier, George 1834-1896 ..... **NCLC 86**
See also DLB 153, 178; RGEL 2
Dunbar, Alice
See Nelson, Alice Ruth Moore Dunbar
Dunbar, Alice Moore
See Nelson, Alice Ruth Moore Dunbar
Dunbar, Paul Laurence
1872-1906 .... **BLC 1:1; PC 5; SSC 8; TCLC 2, 12; WLC 2**
See also AAYA 75; AFAW 1, 2; AMWS 2; BW 1, 3; CA 104, 124; CANR 79; CDALB 1865-1917; DA; DA3; DAC; DAM MST, MULT, POET; DLB 50, 54, 78; EXPP; MAL 5; PFS 33; RGAL 4; SATA 34
Dunbar, William 1460(?)-1520(?) .... **LC 20; PC 67**
See also BRWS 8; DLB 132, 146; RGEL 2
Dunbar-Nelson, Alice
See Nelson, Alice Ruth Moore Dunbar
Dunbar-Nelson, Alice Moore
See Nelson, Alice Ruth Moore Dunbar
Duncan, Dora Angela
See Duncan, Isadora
Duncan, Isadora 1877(?)-1927 .... **TCLC 68**
See also CA 118, 149
Duncan, Lois 1934- .... **CLC 26**
See also AAYA 4, 34; BYA 6, 8; CA 1-4R; CANR 2, 23, 36, 111; CLR 29, 129; JRDA; MAICYA 1, 2; MAICYAS 1; MTFW 2005; SAAS 2; SATA 1, 36, 75, 133, 141; SATA-Essay 141; WYA; YAW
Duncan, Robert 1919-1988 .... **CLC 1, 2, 4, 7, 15, 41, 55; PC 2, 75**
See also BG 1:2; CA 9-12R, 124; CANR 28, 62; CP 1, 2, 3, 4; DAM POET; DLB 5, 16, 193; EWL 3; MAL 5; MTCW 1, 2; MTFW 2005; PFS 13; RGAL 4; WP
Duncan, Sara Jeannette
1861-1922 .... **TCLC 60**
See also CA 157; DLB 92
Dunlap, William 1766-1839 .... **NCLC 2**
See also DLB 30, 37, 59; RGAL 4
Dunn, Douglas (Eaglesham) 1942- .... **CLC 6, 40**
See also BRWS 10; CA 45-48; CANR 2, 33, 126; CP 1, 2, 3, 4, 5, 6, 7; DLB 40; MTCW 1
Dunn, Katherine 1945- .... **CLC 71**
See also CA 33-36R; CANR 72; HGG; MTCW 2; MTFW 2005
Dunn, Stephen 1939- .... **CLC 36, 206**
See also AMWS 11; CA 33-36R; CANR 12, 48, 53, 105; CP 3, 4, 5, 6, 7; DLB 105; PFS 21
Dunn, Stephen Elliott
See Dunn, Stephen
Dunne, Finley Peter 1867-1936 ...... **TCLC 28**
See also CA 108, 178; DLB 11, 23; RGAL 4
Dunne, John Gregory 1932-2003 ..... **CLC 28**
See also CA 25-28R, 222; CANR 14, 50; CN 5, 6, 7; DLBY 1980

Dunsany, Lord
See Dunsany, Edward John Moreton Drax Plunkett
Dunsany, Edward John Moreton Drax Plunkett 1878-1957 .... **TCLC 2, 59**
See also CA 104, 148; DLB 10, 77, 153, 156, 255; FANT; MTCW 2; RGEL 2; SFW 4; SUFW 1
Duns Scotus, John 1266(?)-1308 ... **CMLC 59**
See also DLB 115
Duong, Thu Huong 1947- .... **CLC 273**
See also CA 152; CANR 106, 166; DLB 348; NFS 23
Duong Thu Huong
See Duong, Thu Huong
du Perry, Jean
See Simenon, Georges
Durang, Christopher 1949- .... **CLC 27, 38**
See also CA 105; CAD; CANR 50, 76, 130; CD 5, 6; MTCW 2; MTFW 2005
Durang, Christopher Ferdinand
See Durang, Christopher
Duras, Claire de 1777-1832 .... **NCLC 154**
Duras, Marguerite 1914-1996 . **CLC 3, 6, 11, 20, 34, 40, 68, 100; SSC 40**
See also BPFB 1; CA 25-28R, 151; CANR 50; CWW 2; DFS 21; DLB 83, 321; EWL 3; FL 1:5; GFL 1789 to the Present; IDFW 4; MTCW 1, 2; RGWL 2, 3; TWA
Durban, (Rosa) Pam 1947- .... **CLC 39**
See also CA 123; CANR 98; CSW
Durcan, Paul 1944- .... **CLC 43, 70**
See also CA 134; CANR 123; CP 1, 5, 6, 7; DAM POET; EWL 3
d'Urfe, Honore
See Urfe, Honore d'
Durfey, Thomas 1653-1723 .... **LC 94**
See also DLB 80; RGEL 2
Durkheim, Emile 1858-1917 .... **TCLC 55**
See also CA 249
Durrell, Lawrence 1912-1990 .... **CLC 1, 4, 6, 8, 13, 27, 41**
See also BPFB 1; BRWR 3; BRWS 1; CA 9-12R, 132; CANR 40, 77; CDBLB 1945-1960; CN 1, 2, 3, 4; CP 1, 2, 3, 4, 5; DAM NOV; DLB 15, 27, 204; DLBY 1990; EWL 3; MTCW 1, 2; RGEL 2; SFW 4; TEA
Durrell, Lawrence George
See Durrell, Lawrence
Durrenmatt, Friedrich
See Durrenmatt, Friedrich
Durrenmatt, Friedrich 1921-1990 . **CLC 1, 4, 8, 11, 15, 43, 102**
See also CA 17-20R; CANR 33; CDWLB 2; CMW 4; DAM DRAM; DLB 69, 124; EW 13; EWL 3; MTCW 1, 2; RGHL; RGWL 2, 3
Dutt, Michael Madhusudan
1824-1873 .... **NCLC 118**
Dutt, Toru 1856-1877 .... **NCLC 29**
See also DLB 240
Dwight, Timothy 1752-1817 .... **NCLC 13**
See also DLB 37; RGAL 4
Dworkin, Andrea 1946-2005 ..... **CLC 43, 123**
See also CA 77-80, 238; CAAS 21; CANR 16, 39, 76, 96; FL 1:5; FW; GLL 1; INT CANR-16; MTCW 1, 2; MTFW 2005
Dwyer, Deanna
See Koontz, Dean
Dwyer, K.R.
See Koontz, Dean
Dybek, Stuart 1942- .... **CLC 114; SSC 55**
See also CA 97-100; CANR 39; DLB 130; SSFS 23
Dye, Richard
See De Voto, Bernard (Augustine)
Dyer, Geoff 1958- .... **CLC 149**
See also CA 125; CANR 88, 209

Dyer, George 1755-1841 .... **NCLC 129**
See also DLB 93
Dylan, Bob 1941- .... **CLC 3, 4, 6, 12, 77; PC 37**
See also AMWS 18; CA 41-44R; CANR 108; CP 1, 2, 3, 4, 5, 6, 7; DLB 16
Dyson, John 1943- .... **CLC 70**
See also CA 144
Dzyubin, Eduard Georgievich
1895-1934 .... **TCLC 60**
See also CA 170; EWL 3
E. V. L.
See Lucas, E(dward) V(errall)
Eagleton, Terence
See Eagleton, Terry
Eagleton, Terence Francis
See Eagleton, Terry
Eagleton, Terry 1943- .... **CLC 63, 132**
See also CA 57-60; CANR 7, 23, 68, 115, 198; DLB 242; LMFS 2; MTCW 1, 2; MTFW 2005
Early, Jack
See Scoppettone, Sandra
East, Michael
See West, Morris L(anglo)
Eastaway, Edward
See Thomas, (Philip) Edward
Eastlake, William (Derry)
1917-1997 .... **CLC 8**
See also CA 5-8R, 158; CAAS 1; CANR 5, 63; CN 1, 2, 3, 4, 5, 6; DLB 6, 206; INT CANR-5; MAL 5; TCWW 1, 2
Eastman, Charles A(lexander)
1858-1939 .... **NNAL; TCLC 55**
See also CA 179; CANR 91; DAM MULT; DLB 175; YABC 1
Eaton, Edith Maude
1865-1914 .... **AAL; TCLC 232**
See also CA 154; DLB 221, 312; FW
Eaton, (Lillie) Winnifred 1875-1954 .... **AAL**
See also CA 217; DLB 221, 312; RGAL 4
Eberhart, Richard 1904-2005 ...... **CLC 3, 11, 19, 56; PC 76**
See also AMW; CA 1-4R, 240; CANR 2, 125; CDALB 1941-1968; CP 1, 2, 3, 4, 5, 6, 7; DAM POET; DLB 48; MAL 5; MTCW 1; RGAL 4
Eberhart, Richard Ghormley
See Eberhart, Richard
Eberstadt, Fernanda 1960- .... **CLC 39**
See also CA 136; CANR 69, 128
Ebner, Margaret c. 1291-1351 ...... **CMLC 98**
Echegaray (y Eizaguirre), Jose (Maria Waldo) 1832-1916 .... **HLCS 1; TCLC 4**
See also CA 104; CANR 32; DLB 329; EWL 3; HW 1; MTCW 1
Echeverria, (Jose) Esteban (Antonino)
1805-1851 .... **NCLC 18**
See also LAW
Echo
See Proust, Marcel
Eckert, Allan W. 1931- .... **CLC 17**
See also AAYA 18; BYA 2; CA 13-16R; CANR 14, 45; INT CANR-14; MAICYA 2; MAICYAS 1; SAAS 21; SATA 29, 91; SATA-Brief 27
Eckhart, Meister 1260(?)-1327(?) .. **CMLC 9, 80**
See also DLB 115; LMFS 1
Eckmar, F. R.
See de Hartog, Jan
Eco, Umberto 1932- .... **CLC 28, 60, 142, 248**
See also BEST 90:1; BPFB 1; CA 77-80; CANR 12, 33, 55, 110, 131, 195; CPW; CWW 2; DA3; DAM NOV, POP; DLB 196, 242; EWL 3; MSW; MTCW 1, 2; MTFW 2005; NFS 22; RGWL 3; WLIT 7

Eddison, E(ric) R(ucker)
1882-1945 .... **TCLC 15**
See also CA 109, 156; DLB 255; FANT;
SFW 4; SUFW 1

Eddy, Mary (Ann Morse) Baker
1821-1910 .... **TCLC 71**
See also CA 113, 174

Edel, (Joseph) Leon 1907-1997 .. **CLC 29, 34**
See also CA 1-4R, 161; CANR 1, 22, 112;
DLB 103; INT CANR-22

Eden, Emily 1797-1869 .... **NCLC 10**

Edgar, David 1948- .... **CLC 42**
See also CA 57-60; CANR 12, 61, 112;
CBD; CD 5, 6; DAM DRAM; DFS 15;
DLB 13, 233; MTCW 1

Edgerton, Clyde 1944- .... **CLC 39**
See also AAYA 17; CA 118, 134; CANR
64, 125, 195; CN 7; CSW; DLB 278; INT
CA-134; TCLE 1:1; YAW

Edgerton, Clyde Carlyle
See Edgerton, Clyde

Edgeworth, Maria 1768-1849 ... **NCLC 1, 51,
158; SSC 86**
See also BRWS 3; CLR 153; DLB 116, 159,
163; FL 1:3; FW; RGEL 2; SATA 21;
TEA; WLIT 3

Edmonds, Paul
See Kuttner, Henry

Edmonds, Walter D(umaux)
1903-1998 .... **CLC 35**
See also BYA 2; CA 5-8R; CANR 2; CWRI
5; DLB 9; LAIT 1; MAICYA 1, 2; MAL
5; RHW; SAAS 4; SATA 1, 27; SATA-
Obit 99

Edmondson, Wallace
See Ellison, Harlan

Edson, Margaret 1961- ...... **CLC 199; DC 24**
See also AMWS 18; CA 190; DFS 13; DLB
266

Edson, Russell 1935- .... **CLC 13**
See also CA 33-36R; CANR 115; CP 2, 3,
4, 5, 6, 7; DLB 244; WP

Edwards, Bronwen Elizabeth
See Rose, Wendy

Edwards, Eli
See McKay, Claude

Edwards, G(erald) B(asil)
1899-1976 .... **CLC 25**
See also CA 201, 110

Edwards, Gus 1939- .... **CLC 43**
See also CA 108; INT CA-108

Edwards, Jonathan 1703-1758 .... **LC 7, 54**
See also AMW; DA; DAC; DAM MST;
DLB 24, 270; RGAL 4; TUS

Edwards, Marilyn
See French, Marilyn

Edwards, Sarah Pierpont 1710-1758 .. **LC 87**
See also DLB 200

Efron, Marina Ivanovna Tsvetaeva
See Tsvetaeva, Marina

Egeria fl. 4th cent. - .... **CMLC 70**

Eggers, Dave 1970- .... **CLC 241**
See also AAYA 56; CA 198; CANR 138;
MTFW 2005

Egoyan, Atom 1960- .... **CLC 151, 291**
See also AAYA 63; CA 157; CANR 151

Ehle, John (Marsden, Jr.) 1925- ...... **CLC 27**
See also CA 9-12R; CSW

Ehrenbourg, Ilya (Grigoryevich)
See Ehrenburg, Ilya (Grigoryevich)

Ehrenburg, Ilya (Grigoryevich)
1891-1967 .... **CLC 18, 34, 62**
See Erenburg, Ilya (Grigoryevich)
See also CA 102, 25-28R; EWL 3

Ehrenburg, Ilyo (Grigoryevich)
See Ehrenburg, Ilya (Grigoryevich)

Ehrenreich, Barbara 1941- ..... **CLC 110, 267**
See also BEST 90:4; CA 73-76; CANR 16,
37, 62, 117, 167, 208; DLB 246; FW;
LNFS 1; MTCW 1, 2; MTFW 2005

Ehrlich, Gretel 1946- .... **CLC 249**
See also ANW; CA 140; CANR 74, 146;
DLB 212, 275; TCWW 2

Eich, Gunter
See Eich, Gunter

Eich, Gunter 1907-1972 .... **CLC 15**
See also CA 111; 93-96; DLB 69, 124;
EWL 3; RGWL 2, 3

Eichendorff, Joseph 1788-1857 .... **NCLC 8,
225**
See also DLB 90; RGWL 2, 3

Eigner, Larry
See Eigner, Laurence (Joel)

Eigner, Laurence (Joel) 1927-1996 ..... **CLC 9**
See also CA 9-12R, 151; CAAS 23; CANR
6, 84; CP 1, 2, 3, 4, 5, 6, 7; DLB 5; WP

Eilhart von Oberge c. 1140-c.
1195 .... **CMLC 67**
See also DLB 148

Einhard c. 770-840 .... **CMLC 50**
See also DLB 148

Einstein, Albert 1879-1955 .... **TCLC 65**
See also CA 121, 133; MTCW 1, 2

Eiseley, Loren
See Eiseley, Loren Corey

Eiseley, Loren Corey 1907-1977 .... **CLC 7**
See also AAYA 5; ANW; CA 1-4R; 73-76;
CANR 6; DLB 275; DLBD 17

Eisenstadt, Jill 1963- .... **CLC 50**
See also CA 140

Eisenstein, Sergei (Mikhailovich)
1898-1948 .... **TCLC 57**
See also CA 114, 149

Eisler, Steve
See Holdstock, Robert

Eisner, Simon
See Kornbluth, C(yril) M.

Eisner, Will 1917-2005 .... **CLC 237**
See also AAYA 52; CA 108, 235; CANR
114, 140, 179; MTFW 2005; SATA 31,
165

Eisner, William Erwin
See Eisner, Will

Ekeloef, Bengt Gunnar
See Ekelof, Gunnar

Ekeloef, Gunnar
See Ekelof, Gunnar

Ekelof, Gunnar 1907-1968 ... **CLC 27; PC 23**
See also CA 123, 25-28R; DAM POET;
DLB 259; EW 12; EWL 3

Ekelund, Vilhelm 1880-1949 .... **TCLC 75**
See also CA 189; EWL 3

Ekman, Kerstin (Lillemor) 1933- ... **CLC 279**
See also CA 154; CANR 124; DLB 257;
EWL 3

Ekwensi, C. O. D.
See Ekwensi, Cyprian

Ekwensi, Cyprian 1921-2007 .... **BLC 1:1;
CLC 4**
See also AFW; BW 2, 3; CA 29-32R;
CANR 18, 42, 74, 125; CDWLB 3; CN 1,
2, 3, 4, 5, 6; CWRI 5; DAM MULT; DLB
117; EWL 3; MTCW 1, 2; RGEL 2; SATA
66; WLIT 2

Ekwensi, Cyprian Odiatu Duaka
See Ekwensi, Cyprian

Elaine
See Leverson, Ada Esther

El Conde de Pepe
See Mihura, Miguel

El Crummo
See Crumb, R.

Elder, Lonne III 1931-1996 .. **BLC 1:1; DC 8**
See also BW 1, 3; CA 81-84, 152; CAD;
CANR 25; DAM MULT; DLB 7, 38, 44;
MAL 5

Eleanor of Aquitaine 1122-1204 ... **CMLC 39**

Elia
See Lamb, Charles

Eliade, Mircea 1907-1986 .... **CLC 19; TCLC
243**
See also CA 65-68, 119; CANR 30, 62; CD-
WLB 4; DLB 220; EWL 3; MTCW 1;
RGWL 3; SFW 4

Eliot, A. D.
See Jewett, Sarah Orne

Eliot, Alice
See Jewett, Sarah Orne

Eliot, Dan
See Silverberg, Robert

Eliot, George 1819-1880 ...... **NCLC 4, 13, 23,
41, 49, 89, 118, 183, 199, 209, 233; PC
20; SSC 72, 139; WLC 2**
See also BRW 5; BRWC 1, 2; BRWR 2;
CDBLB 1832-1890; CN 7; CPW; DA;
DA3; DAB; DAC; DAM MST, NOV;
DLB 21, 35, 55; FL 1:3; LATS 1:1; LMFS
1; NFS 17, 20, 34; RGEL 2; RGSF 2;
SSFS 8; TEA; WLIT 3

Eliot, John 1604-1690 .... **LC 5**
See also DLB 24

Eliot, T. S. 1888-1965 .. **CLC 1, 2, 3, 6, 9, 10,
13, 15, 24, 34, 41, 55, 57, 113; DC 28;
PC 5, 31, 90; TCLC 236; WLC 2**
See also AAYA 28; AMW; AMWC 1;
AMWR 1; BRW 7; BRWR 2; CA 5-8R;
25-28R; CANR 41; CBD; CDALB 1929-
1941; DA; DA3; DAB; DAC; DAM
DRAM, MST, POET; DFS 4, 13; DLB 7,
10, 45, 63, 245, 329; DLBY 1988; EWL
3; EXPP; LAIT 3; LATS 1:1; LMFS 2;
MAL 5; MTCW 1, 2; MTFW 2005; NCFS
5; PAB; PFS 1, 7, 20, 33; RGAL 4; RGEL
2; TUS; WLIT 4; WP

Eliot, Thomas Stearns
See Eliot, T. S.

Elisabeth of Schonau c.
1129-1165 .... **CMLC 82**

Elizabeth 1866-1941 .... **TCLC 41**

Elizabeth I, Queen of England
1533-1603 .... **LC 118**
See also BRWS 16; DLB 136

Elkin, Stanley L. 1930-1995 ...... **CLC 4, 6, 9,
14, 27, 51, 91; SSC 12**
See also AMWS 6; BPFB 1; CA 9-12R,
148; CANR 8, 46; CN 1, 2, 3, 4, 5, 6;
CPW; DAM NOV, POP; DLB 2, 28, 218,
278; DLBY 1980; EWL 3; INT CANR-8;
MAL 5; MTCW 1, 2; MTFW 2005;
RGAL 4; TCLE 1:1

Elledge, Scott CLC 34

Eller, Scott
See Shepard, Jim

Elliott, Don
See Silverberg, Robert

Elliott, Ebenezer 1781-1849 .... **PC 96**
See also DLB 96, 190; RGEL 2

Elliott, George P(aul) 1918-1980 .... **CLC 2**
See also CA 1-4R; 97-100; CANR 2; CN 1,
2; CP 3; DLB 244; MAL 5

Elliott, Janice 1931-1995 .... **CLC 47**
See also CA 13-16R; CANR 8, 29, 84; CN
5, 6, 7; DLB 14; SATA 119

Elliott, Sumner Locke 1917-1991 ..... **CLC 38**
See also CA 5-8R, 134; CANR 2, 21; DLB
289

Elliott, William
See Bradbury, Ray

Ellis, A. E. CLC 7

Ellis, Alice Thomas
See Haycraft, Anna

Espada, Martin 1957- .... **PC 74**
See also CA 159; CANR 80; CP 7; EXPP;
LLW; MAL 5; PFS 13, 16
Espriella, Don Manuel Alvarez
See Southey, Robert
Espriu, Salvador 1913-1985 .... **CLC 9**
See also CA 154, 115; DLB 134; EWL 3
Espronceda, Jose de 1808-1842 ..... **NCLC 39**
Esquivel, Laura 1950- ..... **CLC 141; HLCS 1**
See also AAYA 29; CA 143; CANR 68, 113,
161; DA3; DNFS 2; LAIT 3; LMFS 2;
MTCW 2; MTFW 2005; NFS 5; WLIT 1
Esse, James
See Stephens, James
Esterbrook, Tom
See Hubbard, L. Ron
Esterhazy, Peter 1950- .... **CLC 251**
See also CA 140; CANR 137; CDWLB 4;
CWW 2; DLB 232; EWL 3; RGWL 3
Estleman, Loren D. 1952- .... **CLC 48**
See also AAYA 27; CA 85-88; CANR 27,
74, 139, 177; CMW 4; CPW; DA3; DAM
NOV, POP; DLB 226; INT CANR-27;
MTCW 1, 2; MTFW 2005; TCWW 1, 2
Etherege, Sir George 1636-1692 . **DC 23; LC 78**
See also BRW 2; DAM DRAM; DLB 80;
PAB; RGEL 2
Euclid 306B.C.-283B.C. .... **CMLC 25**
Eugenides, Jeffrey 1960- .... **CLC 81, 212**
See also AAYA 51; CA 144; CANR 120;
DLB 350; MTFW 2005; NFS 24
Euripides c. 484B.C.-406B.C. .... **CMLC 23, 51; DC 4; WLCS**
See also AW 1; CDWLB 1; DA; DA3;
DAB; DAC; DAM DRAM, MST; DFS 1,
4, 6, 25, 27; DLB 176; LAIT 1; LMFS 1;
RGWL 2, 3; WLIT 8
Eusebius c. 263-c. 339 .... **CMLC 103**
Evan, Evin
See Faust, Frederick
Evans, Caradoc 1878-1945 ... **SSC 43; TCLC 85**
See also DLB 162
Evans, Evan
See Faust, Frederick
Evans, Marian
See Eliot, George
Evans, Mary Ann
See Eliot, George
Evarts, Esther
See Benson, Sally
Evelyn, John 1620-1706 .... **LC 144**
See also BRW 2; RGEL 2
Everett, Percival 1956- .... **CLC 57**
See Everett, Percival L.
See also AMWS 18; BW 2; CA 129; CANR
94, 134, 179; CN 7; DLB 350; MTFW
2005
Everett, Percival L.
See Everett, Percival
See also CSW
Everson, R(onald) G(ilmour)
1903-1992 .... **CLC 27**
See also CA 17-20R; CP 1, 2, 3, 4; DLB 88
Everson, William 1912-1994 .... **CLC 1, 5, 14**
See also BG 1:2; CA 9-12R, 145; CANR
20; CP 1; DLB 5, 16, 212; MTCW 1
Everson, William Oliver
See Everson, William
Evtushenko, Evgenii Aleksandrovich
See Yevtushenko, Yevgenyn
Ewart, Gavin (Buchanan)
1916-1995 .... **CLC 13, 46**
See also BRWS 7; CA 89-92, 150; CANR
17, 46; CP 1, 2, 3, 4, 5, 6; DLB 40;
MTCW 1
Ewers, Hanns Heinz 1871-1943 ..... **TCLC 12**
See also CA 109, 149

Ewing, Frederick R.
See Sturgeon, Theodore (Hamilton)
Exley, Frederick (Earl) 1929-1992 .... **CLC 6, 11**
See also AITN 2; BPFB 1; CA 81-84, 138;
CANR 117; DLB 143; DLBY 1981
Eynhardt, Guillermo
See Quiroga, Horacio (Sylvestre)
Ezekiel, Nissim (Moses) 1924-2004 .. **CLC 61**
See also CA 61-64, 223; CP 1, 2, 3, 4, 5, 6,
7; DLB 323; EWL 3
Ezekiel, Tish O'Dowd 1943- .... **CLC 34**
See also CA 129
Fadeev, Aleksandr Aleksandrovich
See Bulgya, Alexander Alexandrovich
Fadeev, Alexandr Alexandrovich
See Bulgya, Alexander Alexandrovich
Fadeyev, A.
See Bulgya, Alexander Alexandrovich
Fadeyev, Alexander
See Bulgya, Alexander Alexandrovich
Fagen, Donald 1948- .... **CLC 26**
Fainzil'berg, Il'ia Arnol'dovich
See Fainzilberg, Ilya Arnoldovich
Fainzilberg, Ilya Arnoldovich
1897-1937 .... **TCLC 21**
See also CA 120, 165; DLB 272; EWL 3
Fair, Ronald L. 1932- .... **CLC 18**
See also BW 1; CA 69-72; CANR 25; DLB
33
Fairbairn, Roger
See Carr, John Dickson
Fairbairns, Zoe (Ann) 1948- .... **CLC 32**
See also CA 103; CANR 21, 85; CN 4, 5,
6, 7
Fairfield, Flora
See Alcott, Louisa May
Falco, Gian
See Papini, Giovanni
Falconer, James
See Kirkup, James
Falconer, Kenneth
See Kornbluth, C(yril) M.
Falkland, Samuel
See Heijermans, Herman
Fallaci, Oriana 1930-2006 .... **CLC 11, 110**
See also CA 77-80, 253; CANR 15, 58, 134;
FW; MTCW 1
Faludi, Susan 1959- .... **CLC 140**
See also CA 138; CANR 126, 194; FW;
MTCW 2; MTFW 2005; NCFS 3
Faludy, George 1913- .... **CLC 42**
See also CA 21-24R
Faludy, Gyoergy
See Faludy, George
Fanon, Frantz 1925-1961 ...... **BLC 1:2; CLC 74; TCLC 188**
See also BW 1; CA 116; 89-92; DAM
MULT; DLB 296; LMFS 2; WLIT 2
Fanshawe, Ann 1625-1680 .... **LC 11**
Fante, John (Thomas) 1911-1983 .... **CLC 60; SSC 65**
See also AMWS 11; CA 69-72, 109; CANR
23, 104; DLB 130; DLBY 1983
Far, Sui Sin
See Eaton, Edith Maude
Farah, Nuruddin 1945- .. **BLC 1:2, 2:2; CLC 53, 137**
See also AFW; BW 2, 3; CA 106; CANR
81, 148; CDWLB 3; CN 4, 5, 6, 7; DAM
MULT; DLB 125; EWL 3; WLIT 2
Fardusi
See Ferdowsi, Abu'l Qasem
Fargue, Leon-Paul 1876(?)-1947 .... **TCLC 11**
See also CA 109; CANR 107; DLB 258;
EWL 3
Farigoule, Louis
See Romains, Jules

Farina, Richard 1936(?)-1966 .... **CLC 9**
See also CA 81-84, 25-28R
Farley, Walter (Lorimer)
1915-1989 .... **CLC 17**
See also AAYA 58; BYA 14; CA 17-20R;
CANR 8, 29, 84; DLB 22; JRDA; MAI-
CYA 1, 2; SATA 2, 43, 132; YAW
Farmer, Philip Jose
See Farmer, Philip Jose
Farmer, Philip Jose 1918-2009 ..... **CLC 1, 19**
See also AAYA 28; BPFB 1; CA 1-4R, 283;
CANR 4, 35, 111; DLB 8; MTCW 1;
SATA 93; SATA-Obit 201; SCFW 1, 2;
SFW 4
Farmer, Philipe Jos
See Farmer, Philip Jose
Farquhar, George 1677-1707 . **DC 38; LC 21**
See also BRW 2; DAM DRAM; DLB 84;
RGEL 2
Farrell, James Gordon
See Farrell, J.G.
Farrell, James T(homas) 1904-1979 . **CLC 1, 4, 8, 11, 66; SSC 28; TCLC 228**
See also AMW; BPFB 1; CA 5-8R; 89-92;
CANR 9, 61; CN 1, 2; DLB 4, 9, 86;
DLBD 2; EWL 3; MAL 5; MTCW 1, 2;
MTFW 2005; RGAL 4
Farrell, J.G. 1935-1979 .... **CLC 6**
See also CA 73-76; 89-92; CANR 36; CN
1, 2; DLB 14, 271, 326; MTCW 1; RGEL
2; RHW; WLIT 4
Farrell, M. J.
See Keane, Mary Nesta
Farrell, Warren (Thomas) 1943- ...... **CLC 70**
See also CA 146; CANR 120
Farren, Richard J.
See Betjeman, John
Farren, Richard M.
See Betjeman, John
Farrugia, Mario Benedetti
See Bentley, Eric
**Farrugia, Mario Orlando Hardy Hamlet
Brenno Benedetti**
See Benedetti, Mario
Fassbinder, Rainer Werner
1946-1982 .... **CLC 20**
See also CA 93-96, 106; CANR 31
Fast, Howard 1914-2003 .... **CLC 23, 131**
See also AAYA 16; BPFB 1; CA 1-4R, 181,
214; CAAE 181; CAAS 18; CANR 1, 33,
54, 75, 98, 140; CMW 4; CN 1, 2, 3, 4, 5,
6, 7; CPW; DAM NOV; DLB 9; INT
CANR-33; LATS 1:1; MAL 5; MTCW 2;
MTFW 2005; NFS 35; RHW; SATA 7;
SATA-Essay 107; TCWW 1, 2; YAW
Faulcon, Robert
See Holdstock, Robert
Faulkner, William 1897-1962 .... **CLC 1, 3, 6, 8, 9, 11, 14, 18, 28, 52, 68; SSC 1, 35, 42, 92, 97; TCLC 141; WLC 2**
See also AAYA 7; AMW; AMWR 1; BPFB
1; BYA 5, 15; CA 81-84; CANR 33;
CDALB 1929-1941; DA; DA3; DAB;
DAC; DAM MST, NOV; DLB 9, 11, 44,
102, 316, 330; DLBD 2; DLBY 1986,
1997; EWL 3; EXPN; EXPS; GL 2; LAIT
2; LATS 1:1; LMFS 2; MAL 5; MTCW
1, 2; MTFW 2005; NFS 4, 8, 13, 24, 33;
RGAL 4; RGSF 2; SSFS 2, 5, 6, 12, 27;
TUS
Faulkner, William Cuthbert
See Faulkner, William
Fauset, Jessie Redmon
1882(?)-1961 ...... **BLC 1:2; CLC 19, 54; HR 1:2**
See also AFAW 2; BW 1; CA 109; CANR
83; DAM MULT; DLB 51; FW; LMFS 2;
MAL 5; MBL

Faust, Frederick 1892-1944 .... **TCLC 49**
　　See also BPFB 1; CA 108, 152; CANR 143;
　　　DAM POP; DLB 256; TCWW 1, 2; TUS
Faust, Frederick Schiller
　　See Faust, Frederick
Faust, Irvin 1924- .... **CLC 8**
　　See also CA 33-36R; CANR 28, 67; CN 1,
　　　2, 3, 4, 5, 6, 7; DLB 2, 28, 218, 278;
　　　DLBY 1980
Fawkes, Guy
　　See Benchley, Robert (Charles)
Fearing, Kenneth 1902-1961 .... **CLC 51**
　　See also CA 93-96; CANR 59; CMW 4;
　　　DLB 9; MAL 5; RGAL 4
Fearing, Kenneth Flexner
　　See Fearing, Kenneth
Fecamps, Elise
　　See Creasey, John
Federman, Raymond 1928-2009 .. **CLC 6, 47**
　　See also CA 17-20R, 208, 292; CAAE 208;
　　　CAAS 8; CANR 10, 43, 83, 108; CN 3,
　　　4, 5, 6; DLBY 1980
Federspiel, J.F. 1931-2007 .... **CLC 42**
　　See also CA 146, 257
Federspiel, Juerg F.
　　See Federspiel, J.F.
Federspiel, Jurg F.
　　See Federspiel, J.F.
Feiffer, Jules 1929- .... **CLC 2, 8, 64**
　　See also AAYA 3, 62; CA 17-20R; CAD;
　　　CANR 30, 59, 129, 161, 192; CD 5, 6;
　　　DAM DRAM; DLB 7, 44; INT CANR-
　　　30; MTCW 1; SATA 8, 61, 111, 157, 201
Feiffer, Jules Ralph
　　See Feiffer, Jules
Feige, Hermann Albert Otto Maximilian
　　See Traven, B.
Fei-Kan, Li
　　See Jin, Ba
Feinberg, David B. 1956-1994 .... **CLC 59**
　　See also CA 135, 147
Feinstein, Elaine 1930- .... **CLC 36**
　　See also CA 69-72; CAAS 1; CANR 31,
　　　68, 121, 162; CN 3, 4, 5, 6, 7; CP 2, 3, 4,
　　　5, 6, 7; CWP; DLB 14, 40; MTCW 1
Feke, Gilbert David CLC 65
Feldman, Irving (Mordecai) 1928- ..... **CLC 7**
　　See also CA 1-4R; CANR 1; CP 1, 2, 3, 4,
　　　5, 6, 7; DLB 169; TCLE 1:1
Felix-Tchicaya, Gerald
　　See Tchicaya, Gerald Felix
Fellini, Federico 1920-1993 .... **CLC 16, 85**
　　See also CA 65-68, 143; CANR 33
Felltham, Owen 1602(?)-1668 .... **LC 92**
　　See also DLB 126, 151
Felsen, Henry Gregor 1916-1995 ..... **CLC 17**
　　See also CA 1-4R, 180; CANR 1; SAAS 2;
　　　SATA 1
Felski, Rita CLC 65
Fenelon, Francois de Pons de Salignac de la
　　Mothe- 1651-1715 .... **LC 134**
　　See also DLB 268; EW 3; GFL Beginnings
　　　to 1789
Fenno, Jack
　　See Calisher, Hortense
Fenollosa, Ernest (Francisco)
　　1853-1908 .... **TCLC 91**
Fenton, James 1949- .... **CLC 32, 209**
　　See also CA 102; CANR 108, 160; CP 2, 3,
　　　4, 5, 6, 7; DLB 40; PFS 11
Fenton, James Martin
　　See Fenton, James
Ferber, Edna 1887-1968 .... **CLC 18, 93**
　　See also AITN 1; CA 5-8R, 25-28R; CANR
　　　68, 105; DLB 9, 28, 86, 266; MAL 5;
　　　MTCW 1, 2; MTFW 2005; RGAL 4;
　　　RHW; SATA 7; TCWW 1, 2

Ferdousi
　　See Ferdowsi, Abu'l Qasem
Ferdovsi
　　See Ferdowsi, Abu'l Qasem
Ferdowsi
　　See Ferdowsi, Abu'l Qasem
Ferdowsi, Abolghasem Mansour
　　See Ferdowsi, Abu'l Qasem
Ferdowsi, Abolqasem
　　See Ferdowsi, Abu'l Qasem
Ferdowsi, Abol-Qasem
　　See Ferdowsi, Abu'l Qasem
Ferdowsi, Abu'l Qasem
　　940-1020(?) .... **CMLC 43**
　　See also CA 276; RGWL 2, 3; WLIT 6
Ferdowsi, A.M.
　　See Ferdowsi, Abu'l Qasem
Ferdowsi, Hakim Abolghasem
　　See Ferdowsi, Abu'l Qasem
Ferguson, Helen
　　See Kavan, Anna
Ferguson, Niall 1964- .... **CLC 134, 250**
　　See also CA 190; CANR 154, 200
Ferguson, Niall Campbell
　　See Ferguson, Niall
Ferguson, Samuel 1810-1886 .... **NCLC 33**
　　See also DLB 32; RGEL 2
Fergusson, Robert 1750-1774 .... **LC 29**
　　See also DLB 109; RGEL 2
Ferling, Lawrence
　　See Ferlinghetti, Lawrence
Ferlinghetti, Lawrence 1919(?)- .... **CLC 2, 6,**
　　10, 27, 111; PC 1
　　See also AAYA 74; BG 1:2; CA 5-8R; CAD;
　　　CANR 3, 41, 73, 125, 172; CDALB 1941-
　　　1968; CP 1, 2, 3, 4, 5, 6, 7; DA3; DAM
　　　POET; DLB 5, 16; MAL 5; MTCW 1, 2;
　　　MTFW 2005; PFS 28; RGAL 4; WP
Ferlinghetti, Lawrence Monsanto
　　See Ferlinghetti, Lawrence
Fern, Fanny
　　See Parton, Sara Payson Willis
Fernandez, Vicente Garcia Huidobro
　　See Huidobro Fernandez, Vicente Garcia
Fernandez-Armesto, Felipe 1950- .... **CLC 70**
　　See also CA 142; CANR 93, 153, 189
Fernandez-Armesto, Felipe Fermin Ricardo
　　See Fernandez-Armesto, Felipe
Fernandez de Lizardi, Jose Joaquin
　　See Lizardi, Jose Joaquin Fernandez de
Ferre, Rosario 1938- ...... **CLC 139; HLCS 1;**
　　SSC 36, 106
　　See also CA 131; CANR 55, 81, 134; CWW
　　　2; DLB 145; EWL 3; HW 1, 2; LAWS 1;
　　　MTCW 2; MTFW 2005; WLIT 1
Ferrer, Gabriel (Francisco Victor) Miro
　　See Miro (Ferrer), Gabriel (Francisco
　　　Victor)
Ferrier, Susan (Edmonstone)
　　1782-1854 .... **NCLC 8**
　　See also DLB 116; RGEL 2
Ferrigno, Robert 1947- .... **CLC 65**
　　See also CA 140; CANR 125, 161
Ferris, Joshua 1974- .... **CLC 280**
　　See also CA 262
Ferron, Jacques 1921-1985 .... **CLC 94**
　　See also CA 117, 129; CCA 1; DAC; DLB
　　　60; EWL 3
Feuchtwanger, Lion 1884-1958 .... **TCLC 3**
　　See also CA 104, 187; DLB 66; EWL 3;
　　　RGHL
Feuerbach, Ludwig 1804-1872 ..... **NCLC 139**
　　See also DLB 133
Feuillet, Octave 1821-1890 .... **NCLC 45**
　　See also DLB 192

Feydeau, Georges 1862-1921 .... **TCLC 22**
　　See also CA 113, 152; CANR 84; DAM
　　　DRAM; DLB 192; EWL 3; GFL 1789 to
　　　the Present; RGWL 2, 3
Feydeau, Georges Leon JulesMarie
　　See Feydeau, Georges
Fichte, Johann Gottlieb
　　1762-1814 .... **NCLC 62**
　　See also DLB 90
Ficino, Marsilio 1433-1499 .... **LC 12, 152**
　　See also LMFS 1
Fiedeler, Hans
　　See Doeblin, Alfred
Fiedler, Leslie A(aron) 1917-2003 ..... **CLC 4,**
　　13, 24
　　See also AMWS 13; CA 9-12R, 212; CANR
　　　7, 63; CN 1, 2, 3, 4, 5, 6; DLB 28, 67;
　　　EWL 3; MAL 5; MTCW 1, 2; RGAL 4;
　　　TUS
Field, Andrew 1938- .... **CLC 44**
　　See also CA 97-100; CANR 25
Field, Eugene 1850-1895 .... **NCLC 3**
　　See also DLB 23, 42, 140; DLBD 13; MAI-
　　　CYA 1, 2; RGAL 4; SATA 16
Field, Gans T.
　　See Wellman, Manly Wade
Field, Michael 1915-1971 .... **TCLC 43**
　　See also CA 29-32R
Fielding, Helen 1958- .... **CLC 146, 217**
　　See also AAYA 65; CA 172; CANR 127;
　　　DLB 231; MTFW 2005
Fielding, Henry 1707-1754 .... **LC 1, 46, 85,**
　　151, 154; WLC 2
　　See also BRW 3; BRWR 1; CDBLB 1660-
　　　1789; DA; DA3; DAB; DAC; DAM
　　　DRAM, MST, NOV; DLB 39, 84, 101;
　　　NFS 18, 32; RGEL 2; TEA; WLIT 3
Fielding, Sarah 1710-1768 .... **LC 1, 44**
　　See also DLB 39; RGEL 2; TEA
Fields, W. C. 1880-1946 .... **TCLC 80**
　　See also DLB 44
Fierstein, Harvey 1954- .... **CLC 33**
　　See also CA 123, 129; CAD; CD 5, 6;
　　　CPW; DA3; DAM DRAM, POP; DFS 6;
　　　DLB 266; GLL; MAL 5
Fierstein, Harvey Forbes
　　See Fierstein, Harvey
Figes, Eva 1932- .... **CLC 31**
　　See also CA 53-56; CANR 4, 44, 83, 207;
　　　CN 2, 3, 4, 5, 6, 7; DLB 14, 271; FW;
　　　RGHL
Filippo, Eduardo de
　　See de Filippo, Eduardo
Finch, Anne 1661-1720 ..... **LC 3, 137; PC 21**
　　See also BRWS 9; DLB 95; PFS 30
Finch, Robert (Duer Claydon)
　　1900-1995 .... **CLC 18**
　　See also CA 57-60; CANR 9, 24, 49; CP 1,
　　　2, 3, 4, 5, 6; DLB 88
Findley, Timothy 1930-2002 ..... **CLC 27, 102**
　　See also AMWS 20; CA 25-28R, 206;
　　　CANR 12, 42, 69, 109; CCA 1; CN 4, 5,
　　　6, 7; DAC; DAM MST; DLB 53; FANT;
　　　RHW
Fink, William
　　See Mencken, H. L.
Firbank, Louis 1942- .... **CLC 21**
　　See also CA 117
Firbank, (Arthur Annesley) Ronald
　　1886-1926 .... **TCLC 1**
　　See also BRWS 2; CA 104, 177; DLB 36;
　　　EWL 3; RGEL 2
Firdaosi
　　See Ferdowsi, Abu'l Qasem
Firdausi
　　See Ferdowsi, Abu'l Qasem
Firdavsi, Abulqosimi
　　See Ferdowsi, Abu'l Qasem

Firdavsii, Abulqosim
See Ferdowsi, Abu'l Qasem

Firdawsi, Abu al-Qasim
See Ferdowsi, Abu'l Qasem

Firdosi
See Ferdowsi, Abu'l Qasem

Firdousi
See Ferdowsi, Abu'l Qasem

Firdousi, Abu'l-Qasim
See Ferdowsi, Abu'l Qasem

Firdovsi, A.
See Ferdowsi, Abu'l Qasem

Firdovsi, Abulgasim
See Ferdowsi, Abu'l Qasem

Firdusi
See Ferdowsi, Abu'l Qasem

Fish, Stanley 1938- .... **CLC 142**
See also CA 112, 132; CANR 90; DLB 67

Fish, Stanley E.
See Fish, Stanley

Fish, Stanley Eugene
See Fish, Stanley

Fisher, Dorothy (Frances) Canfield
1879-1958 .... **TCLC 87**
See also CA 114, 136; CANR 80; CLR 71;
CWRI 5; DLB 9, 102, 284; MAICYA 1,
2; MAL 5; YABC 1

Fisher, M(ary) F(rances) K(ennedy)
1908-1992 .... **CLC 76, 87**
See also AMWS 17; CA 77-80, 138; CANR
44; MTCW 2

Fisher, Roy 1930- .... **CLC 25**
See also CA 81-84; CAAS 10; CANR 16;
CP 1, 2, 3, 4, 5, 6, 7; DLB 40

Fisher, Rudolph 1897-1934 ...... **BLC 1:2; HR
1:2; SSC 25; TCLC 11**
See also BW 1, 3; CA 107, 124; CANR 80;
DAM MULT; DLB 51, 102

Fisher, Vardis (Alvero) 1895-1968 .... **CLC 7;
TCLC 140**
See also CA 5-8R, 25-28R; CANR 68; DLB
9, 206; MAL 5; RGAL 4; TCWW 1, 2

Fiske, Tarleton
See Bloch, Robert (Albert)

Fitch, Clarke
See Sinclair, Upton

Fitch, John IV
See Cormier, Robert

Fitzgerald, Captain Hugh
See Baum, L. Frank

FitzGerald, Edward 1809-1883 ...... **NCLC 9,
153; PC 79**
See also BRW 4; DLB 32; RGEL 2

Fitzgerald, F. Scott 1896-1940 ...... **SSC 6, 31,
75; TCLC 1, 6, 14, 28, 55, 157; WLC 2**
See also AAYA 24; AITN 1; AMW; AMWC
2; AMWR 1; BPFB 1; CA 110, 123;
CDALB 1917-1929; DA; DA3; DAB;
DAC; DAM MST, NOV; DLB 4, 9, 86,
219, 273; DLBD 1, 15, 16; DLBY 1981,
1996; EWL 3; EXPN; EXPS; LAIT 3;
MAL 5; MTCW 1, 2; MTFW 2005; NFS
2, 19, 20; RGAL 4; RGSF 2; SSFS 4, 15,
21, 25; TUS

Fitzgerald, Francis Scott Key
See Fitzgerald, F. Scott

Fitzgerald, Penelope 1916-2000 . **CLC 19, 51,
61, 143**
See also BRWS 5; CA 85-88, 190; CAAS
10; CANR 56, 86, 131; CN 3, 4, 5, 6, 7;
DLB 14, 194, 326; EWL 3; MTCW 2;
MTFW 2005

Fitzgerald, Robert (Stuart)
1910-1985 .... **CLC 39**
See also CA 1-4R, 114; CANR 1; CP 1, 2,
3, 4; DLBY 1980; MAL 5

FitzGerald, Robert D(avid)
1902-1987 .... **CLC 19**
See also CA 17-20R; CP 1, 2, 3, 4; DLB
260; RGEL 2

Fitzgerald, Zelda (Sayre)
1900-1948 .... **TCLC 52**
See also AMWS 9; CA 117, 126; DLBY
1984

Flanagan, Thomas (James Bonner)
1923-2002 .... **CLC 25, 52**
See also CA 108, 206; CANR 55; CN 3, 4,
5, 6, 7; DLBY 1980; INT CA-108; MTCW
1; RHW; TCLE 1:1

Flashman, Harry Paget
See Fraser, George MacDonald

Flaubert, Gustave 1821-1880 .... **NCLC 2, 10,
19, 62, 66, 135, 179, 185; SSC 11, 60;
WLC 2**
See also DA; DA3; DAB; DAC; DAM
MST, NOV; DLB 119, 301; EW 7; EXPS;
GFL 1789 to the Present; LAIT 2; LMFS
1; NFS 14; RGSF 2; RGWL 2, 3; SSFS
6; TWA

Flavius Josephus
See Josephus, Flavius

Flecker, Herman Elroy
See Flecker, (Herman) James Elroy

Flecker, (Herman) James Elroy
1884-1915 .... **TCLC 43**
See also CA 109, 150; DLB 10, 19; RGEL
2

Fleming, Ian 1908-1964 ... **CLC 3, 30; TCLC
193**
See also AAYA 26; BPFB 1; BRWS 14; CA
5-8R; CANR 59; CDBLB 1945-1960;
CMW 4; CPW; DA3; DAM POP; DLB
87, 201; MSW; MTCW 1, 2; MTFW
2005; RGEL 2; SATA 9; TEA; YAW

Fleming, Ian Lancaster
See Fleming, Ian

Fleming, Thomas 1927- .... **CLC 37**
See also CA 5-8R; CANR 10, 102, 155,
197; INT CANR-10; SATA 8

Fleming, Thomas James
See Fleming, Thomas

Fletcher, John 1579-1625 . **DC 6; LC 33, 151**
See also BRW 2; CDBLB Before 1660;
DLB 58; RGEL 2; TEA

Fletcher, John Gould 1886-1950 .... **TCLC 35**
See also CA 107, 167; DLB 4, 45; LMFS
2; MAL 5; RGAL 4

Fleur, Paul
See Pohl, Frederik

Flieg, Helmut
See Heym, Stefan

Flooglebuckle, Al
See Spiegelman, Art

Flying Officer X
See Bates, H(erbert) E(rnest)

Fo, Dario 1926- .... **CLC 32, 109, 227; DC 10**
See also CA 116, 128; CANR 68, 114, 134,
164; CWW 2; DA3; DAM DRAM; DFS
23; DLB 330; DLBY 1997; EWL 3;
MTCW 1, 2; MTFW 2005; WLIT 7

Foden, Giles 1967- .... **CLC 231**
See also CA 240; DLB 267; NFS 15

Fogarty, Jonathan Titulescu Esq.
See Farrell, James T(homas)

Follett, Ken 1949- .... **CLC 18**
See also AAYA 6, 50; BEST 89:4; BPFB 1;
CA 81-84; CANR 13, 33, 54, 102, 156,
197; CMW 4; CPW; DA3; DAM NOV,
POP; DLB 87; DLBY 1981; INT CANR-
33; LNFS 3; MTCW 1

Follett, Kenneth Martin
See Follett, Ken

Fondane, Benjamin 1898-1944 ..... **TCLC 159**

Fontane, Theodor 1819-1898 . **NCLC 26, 163**
See also CDWLB 2; DLB 129; EW 6;
RGWL 2, 3; TWA

Fonte, Moderata 1555-1592 .... **LC 118**

Fontenelle, Bernard Le Bovier de
1657-1757 .... **LC 140**
See also DLB 268, 313; GFL Beginnings to
1789

Fontenot, Chester CLC 65

Fonvizin, Denis Ivanovich
1744(?)-1792 .... **LC 81**
See also DLB 150; RGWL 2, 3

Foote, Albert Horton
See Foote, Horton

Foote, Horton 1916-2009 .... **CLC 51, 91**
See also AAYA 82; CA 73-76, 284; CAD;
CANR 34, 51, 110; CD 5, 6; CSW; DA3;
DAM DRAM; DFS 20; DLB 26, 266;
EWL 3; INT CANR-34; MTFW 2005

Foote, Mary Hallock 1847-1938 .. **TCLC 108**
See also DLB 186, 188, 202, 221; TCWW
2

Foote, Samuel 1721-1777 .... **LC 106**
See also DLB 89; RGEL 2

Foote, Shelby 1916-2005 .... **CLC 75, 224**
See also AAYA 40; CA 5-8R, 240; CANR
3, 45, 74, 131; CN 1, 2, 3, 4, 5, 6, 7;
CPW; CSW; DA3; DAM NOV, POP;
DLB 2, 17; MAL 5; MTCW 2; MTFW
2005; RHW

Forbes, Cosmo
See Lewton, Val

Forbes, Esther 1891-1967 .... **CLC 12**
See also AAYA 17; BYA 2; CA 13-14, 25-
28R; CAP 1; CLR 27, 147; DLB 22;
JRDA; MAICYA 1, 2; RHW; SATA 2,
100; YAW

Forche, Carolyn 1950- .. **CLC 25, 83, 86; PC
10**
See also CA 109, 117; CANR 50, 74, 138;
CP 4, 5, 6, 7; CWP; DA3; DAM POET;
DLB 5, 193; INT CA-117; MAL 5;
MTCW 2; MTFW 2005; PFS 18; RGAL
4

Forche, Carolyn Louise
See Forche, Carolyn

Ford, Elbur
See Hibbert, Eleanor Alice Burford

Ford, Ford Madox 1873-1939 ... **TCLC 1, 15,
39, 57, 172**
See also BRW 6; CA 104, 132; CANR 74;
CDBLB 1914-1945; DA3; DAM NOV;
DLB 34, 98, 162; EWL 3; MTCW 1, 2;
NFS 28; RGEL 2; RHW; TEA

Ford, Helen
See Garner, Helen

Ford, Henry 1863-1947 .... **TCLC 73**
See also CA 115, 148

Ford, Jack
See Ford, John

Ford, John 1586-1639 .... **DC 8; LC 68, 153**
See also BRW 2; CDBLB Before 1660;
DA3; DAM DRAM; DFS 7; DLB 58;
IDTP; RGEL 2

Ford, John 1895-1973 .... **CLC 16**
See also AAYA 75; CA 187, 45-48

Ford, Richard 1944- ... **CLC 46, 99, 205, 277**
See also AMWS 5; CA 69-72; CANR 11,
47, 86, 128, 164; CN 5, 6, 7; CSW; DLB
227; EWL 3; MAL 5; MTCW 2; MTFW
2005; NFS 25; RGAL 4; RGSF 2

Ford, Webster
See Masters, Edgar Lee

Foreman, Richard 1937- .... **CLC 50**
See also CA 65-68; CAD; CANR 32, 63,
143; CD 5, 6

Forester, C. S. 1899-1966 ..... **CLC 35; TCLC 152**
See also CA 73-76, 25-28R; CANR 83; DLB 191; RGEL 2; RHW; SATA 13

Forester, Cecil Scott
See Forester, C. S.

Forez
See Mauriac, Francois (Charles)

Forman, James
See Forman, James D.

Forman, James D. 1932-2009 .... **CLC 21**
See also AAYA 17; CA 9-12R; CANR 4, 19, 42; JRDA; MAICYA 1, 2; SATA 8, 70; YAW

Forman, James Douglas
See Forman, James D.

Forman, Milos 1932- .... **CLC 164**
See also AAYA 63; CA 109

Fornes, Maria Irene 1930- .... **CLC 39, 61, 187; DC 10; HLCS 1**
See also CA 25-28R; CAD; CANR 28, 81; CD 5, 6; CWD; DFS 25; DLB 7, 341; HW 1, 2; INT CANR-28; LLW; MAL 5; MTCW 1; RGAL 4

Forrest, Leon (Richard)
1937-1997 .... **BLCS; CLC 4**
See also AFAW 2; BW 2; CA 89-92, 162; CAAS 7; CANR 25, 52, 87; CN 4, 5, 6; DLB 33

Forster, E. M. 1879-1970 .. **CLC 1, 2, 3, 4, 9, 10, 13, 15, 22, 45, 77; SSC 27, 96; TCLC 125; WLC 2**
See also AAYA 2, 37; BRW 6; BRWR 2; BYA 12; CA 13-14, 25-28R; CANR 45; CAP 1; CDBLB 1914-1945; DA; DA3; DAB; DAC; DAM MST, NOV; DLB 34, 98, 162, 178, 195; DLBD 10; EWL 3; EXPN; LAIT 3; LMFS 1; MTCW 1, 2; MTFW 2005; NCFS 1; NFS 3, 10, 11; RGEL 2; RGSF 2; SATA 57; SUFW 1; TEA; WLIT 4

Forster, Edward Morgan
See Forster, E. M.

Forster, John 1812-1876 .... **NCLC 11**
See also DLB 144, 184

Forster, Margaret 1938- .... **CLC 149**
See also CA 133; CANR 62, 115, 175; CN 4, 5, 6, 7; DLB 155, 271

Forsyth, Frederick 1938- .... **CLC 2, 5, 36**
See also BEST 89:4; CA 85-88; CANR 38, 62, 115, 137, 183; CMW 4; CN 3, 4, 5, 6, 7; CPW; DAM NOV, POP; DLB 87; MTCW 1, 2; MTFW 2005

Fort, Paul
See Stockton, Francis Richard

Forten, Charlotte
See Grimke, Charlotte L. Forten

Forten, Charlotte L. 1837-1914
See Grimke, Charlotte L. Forten

Fortinbras
See Grieg, (Johan) Nordahl (Brun)

Foscolo, Ugo 1778-1827 .... **NCLC 8, 97**
See also EW 5; WLIT 7

Fosse, Bob 1927-1987 .... **CLC 20**
See also AAYA 82; CA 110, 123

Fosse, Robert L.
See Fosse, Bob

Foster, Hannah Webster
1758-1840 .... **NCLC 99**
See also DLB 37, 200; RGAL 4

Foster, Stephen Collins
1826-1864 .... **NCLC 26**
See also RGAL 4

Foucault, Michel 1926-1984 . **CLC 31, 34, 69**
See also CA 105, 113; CANR 34; DLB 242; EW 13; EWL 3; GFL 1789 to the Present; GLL 1; LMFS 2; MTCW 1, 2; TWA

Fouque, Friedrich (Heinrich Karl) de la Motte 1777-1843 .... **NCLC 2**
See also DLB 90; RGWL 2, 3; SUFW 1

Fourier, Charles 1772-1837 .... **NCLC 51**

Fournier, Henri-Alban 1886-1914 ... **TCLC 6**
See also CA 104, 179; DLB 65; EWL 3; GFL 1789 to the Present; RGWL 2, 3

Fournier, Pierre 1916-1997 .... **CLC 11**
See also CA 89-92; CANR 16, 40; EWL 3; RGHL

Fowles, John 1926-2005 .... **CLC 1, 2, 3, 4, 6, 9, 10, 15, 33, 87, 287; SSC 33, 128**
See also BPFB 1; BRWS 1; CA 5-8R, 245; CANR 25, 71, 103; CDBLB 1960 to Present; CN 1, 2, 3, 4, 5, 6, 7; DA3; DAB; DAC; DAM MST; DLB 14, 139, 207; EWL 3; HGG; MTCW 1, 2; MTFW 2005; NFS 21; RGEL 2; RHW; SATA 22; SATA-Obit 171; TEA; WLIT 4

Fowles, John Robert
See Fowles, John

Fox, Norma Diane
See Mazer, Norma Fox

Fox, Paula 1923- .... **CLC 2, 8, 121**
See also AAYA 3, 37; BYA 3, 8; CA 73-76; CANR 20, 36, 62, 105, 200; CLR 1, 44, 96; DLB 52; JRDA; MAICYA 1, 2; MTCW 1; NFS 12; SATA 17, 60, 120, 167; WYA; YAW

Fox, William Price, Jr.
See Fox, William Price

Fox, William Price 1926- .... **CLC 22**
See also CA 17-20R; CAAS 19; CANR 11, 142, 189; CSW; DLB 2; DLBY 1981

Foxe, John 1517(?)-1587 .... **LC 14, 166**
See also DLB 132

Frame, Janet 1924-2004 ...... **CLC 2, 3, 6, 22, 66, 96, 237; SSC 29, 127**
See also CA 1-4R, 224; CANR 2, 36, 76, 135; CN 1, 2, 3, 4, 5, 6, 7; CP 2, 3, 4; CWP; EWL 3; MTCW 1,2; RGEL 2; RGSF 2; SATA 119; TWA

France, Anatole 1844-1924 .... **TCLC 9**
See also CA 106, 127; DA3; DAM NOV; DLB 123, 330; EWL 3; GFL 1789 to the Present; MTCW 1, 2; RGWL 2, 3; SUFW 1; TWA

Francis, Claude .... **CLC 50**
See also CA 192

Francis, Dick 1920-2010 . **CLC 2, 22, 42, 102**
See also AAYA 5, 21; BEST 89:3; BPFB 1; CA 5-8R; CANR 9, 42, 68, 100, 141, 179; CDBLB 1960 to Present; CMW 4; CN 2, 3, 4, 5, 6; DA3; DAM POP; DLB 87; INT CANR-9; MSW; MTCW 1, 2; MTFW 2005

Francis, Paula Marie
See Allen, Paula Gunn

Francis, Richard Stanley
See Francis, Dick

Francis, Robert (Churchill)
1901-1987 .... **CLC 15; PC 34**
See also AMWS 9; CA 1-4R, 123; CANR 1; CP 1, 2, 3, 4; EXPP; PFS 12; TCLE 1:1

Francis, Lord Jeffrey
See Jeffrey, Francis

Franco, Veronica 1546-1591 .... **LC 171**
See also WLIT 7

Frank, Anne 1929-1945 ... **TCLC 17; WLC 2**
See also AAYA 12; BYA 1; CA 113, 133; CANR 68; CLR 101; DA; DA3; DAB; DAC; DAM MST; LAIT 4; MAICYA 2; MAICYAS 1; MTCW 1, 2; MTFW 2005; NCFS 2; RGHL; SATA 87; SATA-Brief 42; WYA; YAW

Frank, Annelies Marie
See Frank, Anne

Frank, Bruno 1887-1945 .... **TCLC 81**
See also CA 189; DLB 118; EWL 3

Frank, Elizabeth 1945- .... **CLC 39**
See also CA 121, 126; CANR 78, 150; INT CA-126

Frankl, Viktor E(mil) 1905-1997 ...... **CLC 93**
See also CA 65-68, 161; RGHL

Franklin, Benjamin
See Hasek, Jaroslav

Franklin, Benjamin 1706-1790 .. **LC 25, 134; WLCS**
See also AMW; CDALB 1640-1865; DA; DA3; DAB; DAC; DAM MST; DLB 24, 43, 73, 183; LAIT 1; RGAL 4; TUS

Franklin, Madeleine
See L'Engle, Madeleine

Franklin, Madeleine L'Engle
See L'Engle, Madeleine

Franklin, Madeleine L'Engle Camp
See L'Engle, Madeleine

Franklin, (Stella Maria Sarah) Miles (Lampe) 1879-1954 .... **TCLC 7**
See also CA 104, 164; DLB 230; FW; MTCW 2; RGEL 2; TWA

Franzen, Jonathan 1959- .... **CLC 202**
See also AAYA 65; AMWS 20; CA 129; CANR 105, 166

Fraser, Antonia 1932- .... **CLC 32, 107**
See also AAYA 57; CA 85-88; CANR 44, 65, 119, 164; CMW; DLB 276; MTCW 1, 2; MTFW 2005; SATA-Brief 32

Fraser, George MacDonald
1925-2008 .... **CLC 7**
See also AAYA 48; CA 45-48, 180, 268; CAAE 180; CANR 2, 48, 74, 192; DLB 352; MTCW 2; RHW

Fraser, Sylvia 1935- .... **CLC 64**
See also CA 45-48; CANR 1, 16, 60; CCA 1

Frater Perdurabo
See Crowley, Edward Alexander

Frayn, Michael 1933- .... **CLC 3, 7, 31, 47, 176; DC 27**
See also AAYA 69; BRWC 2; BRWS 7; CA 5-8R; CANR 30, 69, 114, 133, 166; CBD; CD 5, 6; CN 1, 2, 3, 4, 5, 6, 7; DAM DRAM, NOV; DFS 22; DLB 13, 14, 194, 245; FANT; MTCW 1, 2; MTFW 2005; SFW 4

Fraze, Candida 1945- .... **CLC 50**
See also CA 126

Fraze, Candida Merrill
See Fraze, Candida

Frazer, Andrew
See Marlowe, Stephen

Frazer, J(ames) G(eorge)
1854-1941 .... **TCLC 32**
See also BRWS 3; CA 118; NCFS 5

Frazer, Robert Caine
See Creasey, John

Frazer, Sir James George
See Frazer, J(ames) G(eorge)

Frazier, Charles 1950- .... **CLC 109, 224**
See also AAYA 34; CA 161; CANR 126, 170; CSW; DLB 292; MTFW 2005; NFS 25

Frazier, Charles R.
See Frazier, Charles

Frazier, Charles Robinson
See Frazier, Charles

Frazier, Ian 1951- .... **CLC 46**
See also CA 130; CANR 54, 93, 193

Frederic, Harold 1856-1898 ... **NCLC 10, 175**
See also AMW; DLB 12, 23; DLBD 13; MAL 5; NFS 22; RGAL 4

Frederick, John
See Faust, Frederick

Frederick the Great 1712-1786 .... **LC 14**

Fredro, Aleksander 1793-1876 .... **NCLC 8**

Freeling, Nicolas 1927-2003 .... **CLC 38**
See also CA 49-52, 218; CAAS 12; CANR 1, 17, 50, 84; CMW 4; CN 1, 2, 3, 4, 5, 6; DLB 87

Freeman, Douglas Southall
1886-1953 .... **TCLC 11**
See also CA 109, 195; DLB 17; DLBD 17

Freeman, Judith 1946- .... **CLC 55**
See also CA 148; CANR 120, 179; DLB 256

Freeman, Mary E(leanor) Wilkins
1852-1930 .... **SSC 1, 47, 113; TCLC 9**
See also CA 106, 177; DLB 12, 78, 221; EXPS; FW; HGG; MBL; RGAL 4; RGSF 2; SSFS 4, 8, 26; SUFW 1; TUS

Freeman, R(ichard) Austin
1862-1943 .... **TCLC 21**
See also CA 113; CANR 84; CMW 4; DLB 70

French, Albert 1943- .... **CLC 86**
See also BW 3; CA 167

French, Antonia
See Kureishi, Hanif

French, Marilyn 1929-2009 . **CLC 10, 18, 60, 177**
See also BPFB 1; CA 69-72, 286; CANR 3, 31, 134, 163; CN 5, 6, 7; CPW; DAM DRAM, NOV, POP; FL 1:5; FW; INT CANR-31; MTCW 1, 2; MTFW 2005

French, Paul
See Asimov, Isaac

Freneau, Philip Morin 1752-1832 .. **NCLC 1, 111**
See also AMWS 2; DLB 37, 43; RGAL 4

Freud, Sigmund 1856-1939 .... **TCLC 52**
See also CA 115, 133; CANR 69; DLB 296; EW 8; EWL 3; LATS 1:1; MTCW 1, 2; MTFW 2005; NCFS 3; TWA

Freytag, Gustav 1816-1895 .... **NCLC 109**
See also DLB 129

Friedan, Betty 1921-2006 .... **CLC 74**
See also CA 65-68, 248; CANR 18, 45, 74; DLB 246; FW; MTCW 1, 2; MTFW 2005; NCFS 5

Friedan, Betty Naomi
See Friedan, Betty

Friedlander, Saul 1932- .... **CLC 90**
See also CA 117, 130; CANR 72; RGHL

Friedman, B(ernard) H(arper)
1926- .... **CLC 7**
See also CA 1-4R; CANR 3, 48

Friedman, Bruce Jay 1930- ...... **CLC 3, 5, 56**
See also CA 9-12R; CAD; CANR 25, 52, 101; CD 5, 6; CN 1, 2, 3, 4, 5, 6, 7; DLB 2, 28, 244; INT CANR-25; MAL 5; SSFS 18

Friel, Brian 1929- .. **CLC 5, 42, 59, 115, 253; DC 8; SSC 76**
See also BRWS 5; CA 21-24R; CANR 33, 69, 131; CBD; CD 5, 6; DFS 11; DLB 13, 319; EWL 3; MTCW 1; RGEL 2; TEA

Friis-Baastad, Babbis Ellinor
1921-1970 .... **CLC 12**
See also CA 17-20R, 134; SATA 7

Frisch, Max 1911-1991 ...... **CLC 3, 9, 14, 18, 32, 44; TCLC 121**
See also CA 85-88, 134; CANR 32, 74; CD-WLB 2; DAM DRAM, NOV; DFS 25; DLB 69, 124; EW 13; EWL 3; MTCW 1, 2; MTFW 2005; RGHL; RGWL 2, 3

Froehlich, Peter
See Gay, Peter

Fromentin, Eugene (Samuel Auguste)
1820-1876 .... **NCLC 10, 125**
See also DLB 123; GFL 1789 to the Present

Frost, Frederick
See Faust, Frederick

Frost, Robert 1874-1963 . **CLC 1, 3, 4, 9, 10, 13, 15, 26, 34, 44; PC 1, 39, 71; TCLC 236; WLC 2**
See also AAYA 21; AMW; AMWR 1; CA 89-92; CANR 33; CDALB 1917-1929; CLR 67; DA; DA3; DAB; DAC; DAM MST, POET; DLB 54, 284, 342; DLBD 7; EWL 3; EXPP; MAL 5; MTCW 1, 2; MTFW 2005; PAB; PFS 1, 2, 3, 4, 5, 6, 7, 10, 13, 32, 35; RGAL 4; SATA 14; TUS; WP; WYA

Frost, Robert Lee
See Frost, Robert

Froude, James Anthony
1818-1894 .... **NCLC 43**
See also DLB 18, 57, 144

Froy, Herald
See Waterhouse, Keith

Fry, Christopher 1907-2005 .. **CLC 2, 10, 14; DC 36**
See also BRWS 3; CA 17-20R, 240; CAAS 23; CANR 9, 30, 74, 132; CBD; CD 5, 6; CP 1, 2, 3, 4, 5, 6, 7; DAM DRAM; DLB 13; EWL 3; MTCW 1, 2; MTFW 2005; RGEL 2; SATA 66; TEA

Frye, (Herman) Northrop
1912-1991 .... **CLC 24, 70; TCLC 165**
See also CA 5-8R, 133; CANR 8, 37; DLB 67, 68, 246; EWL 3; MTCW 1, 2; MTFW 2005; RGAL 4; TWA

Fuchs, Daniel 1909-1993 .... **CLC 8, 22**
See also CA 81-84, 142; CAAS 5; CANR 40; CN 1, 2, 3, 4, 5; DLB 9, 26, 28; DLBY 1993; MAL 5

Fuchs, Daniel 1934- .... **CLC 34**
See also CA 37-40R; CANR 14, 48

Fuentes, Carlos 1928- .. **CLC 3, 8, 10, 13, 22, 41, 60, 113, 288; HLC 1; SSC 24, 125; WLC 2**
See also AAYA 4, 45; AITN 2; BPFB 1; CA 69-72; CANR 10, 32, 68, 104, 138, 197; CDWLB 3; CWW 2; DA; DA3; DAB; DAC; DAM MST, MULT, NOV; DLB 113; DNFS 2; EWL 3; HW 1, 2; LAIT 3; LATS 1:2; LAW; LAWS 1; LMFS 2; MTCW 1, 2; MTFW 2005; NFS 8; RGSF 2; RGWL 2, 3; TWA; WLIT 1

Fuentes, Gregorio Lopez y
See Lopez y Fuentes, Gregorio

Fuentes Macias, Carlos Manuel
See Fuentes, Carlos

Fuertes, Gloria 1918-1998 .... **PC 27**
See also CA 178, 180; DLB 108; HW 2; SATA 115

Fugard, Athol 1932- .... **CLC 5, 9, 14, 25, 40, 80, 211; DC 3**
See also AAYA 17; AFW; BRWS 15; CA 85-88; CANR 32, 54, 118; CD 5, 6; DAM DRAM; DFS 3, 6, 10, 24; DLB 225; DNFS 1, 2; EWL 3; LATS 1:2; MTCW 1; MTFW 2005; RGEL 2; WLIT 2

Fugard, Harold Athol
See Fugard, Athol

Fugard, Sheila 1932- .... **CLC 48**
See also CA 125

Fujiwara no Teika 1162-1241 .... **CMLC 73**
See also DLB 203

Fukuyama, Francis 1952- .... **CLC 131**
See also CA 140; CANR 72, 125, 170

Fuller, Charles (H.), (Jr.) 1939- ..... **BLC 1:2; CLC 25; DC 1**
See also BW 2; CA 108, 112; CAD; CANR 87; CD 5, 6; DAM DRAM, MULT; DFS 8; DLB 38, 266; EWL 3; INT CA-112; MAL 5; MTCW 1

Fuller, Henry Blake 1857-1929 .... **TCLC 103**
See also CA 108, 177; DLB 12; RGAL 4

Fuller, John (Leopold) 1937- .... **CLC 62**
See also CA 21-24R; CANR 9, 44; CP 1, 2, 3, 4, 5, 6, 7; DLB 40

Fuller, Margaret 1810-1850 ...... **NCLC 5, 50, 211**
See also AMWS 2; CDALB 1640-1865; DLB 1, 59, 73, 183, 223, 239; FW; LMFS 1; SATA 25

Fuller, Roy (Broadbent) 1912-1991 ... **CLC 4, 28**
See also BRWS 7; CA 5-8R, 135; CAAS 10; CANR 53, 83; CN 1, 2, 3, 4, 5; CP 1, 2, 3, 4, 5; CWRI 5; DLB 15, 20; EWL 3; RGEL 2; SATA 87

Fuller, Sarah Margaret
See Fuller, Margaret

Fuller, Thomas 1608-1661 .... **LC 111**
See also DLB 151

Fulton, Alice 1952- .... **CLC 52**
See also CA 116; CANR 57, 88, 200; CP 5, 6, 7; CWP; DLB 193; PFS 25

Fundi
See Baraka, Amiri

Furey, Michael
See Ward, Arthur Henry Sarsfield

Furphy, Joseph 1843-1912 .... **TCLC 25**
See also CA 163; DLB 230; EWL 3; RGEL 2

Furst, Alan 1941- .... **CLC 255**
See also CA 69-72; CANR 12, 34, 59, 102, 159, 193; DLB 350; DLBY 01

Fuson, Robert H(enderson) 1927- .... **CLC 70**
See also CA 89-92; CANR 103

Fussell, Paul 1924- .... **CLC 74**
See also BEST 90:1; CA 17-20R; CANR 8, 21, 35, 69, 135; INT CANR-21; MTCW 1, 2; MTFW 2005

Futabatei, Shimei 1864-1909 .... **TCLC 44**
See also CA 162; DLB 180; MJW

Futabatei Shimei
See Futabatei, Shimei

Futrelle, Jacques 1875-1912 .... **TCLC 19**
See also CA 113, 155; CMW 4

GAB
See Russell, George William

Gaberman, Judie Angell
See Angell, Judie

Gaboriau, Emile 1835-1873 .... **NCLC 14**
See also CMW 4; MSW

Gadda, Carlo Emilio 1893-1973 ...... **CLC 11; TCLC 144**
See also CA 89-92; DLB 177; EWL 3; WLIT 7

Gaddis, William 1922-1998 ... **CLC 1, 3, 6, 8, 10, 19, 43, 86**
See also AMWS 4; BPFB 1; CA 17-20R, 172; CANR 21, 48, 148; CN 1, 2, 3, 4, 5, 6; DLB 2, 278; EWL 3; MAL 5; MTCW 1, 2; MTFW 2005; RGAL 4

Gage, Walter
See Inge, William (Motter)

Gaiman, Neil 1960- .... **CLC 195**
See also AAYA 19, 42, 82; CA 133; CANR 81, 129, 188; CLR 109; DLB 261; HGG; MTFW 2005; SATA 85, 146, 197; SFW 4; SUFW 2

Gaiman, Neil Richard
See Gaiman, Neil

Gaines, Ernest J. 1933- ..... **BLC 1:2; CLC 3, 11, 18, 86, 181; SSC 68, 137**
See also AAYA 18; AFAW 1, 2; AITN 1; BPFB 2; BW 2, 3; BYA 6; CA 9-12R; CANR 6, 24, 42, 75, 126; CDALB 1968-1988; CLR 62; CN 1, 2, 3, 4, 5, 6, 7; CSW; DA3; DAM MULT; DLB 2, 33, 152; DLBY 1980; EWL 3; EXPN; LAIT 5; LATS 1:2; MAL 5; MTCW 1, 2; MTFW 2005; NFS 5, 7, 16; RGAL 4; RGSF 2; RHW; SATA 86; SSFS 5; YAW

Gaines, Ernest James
See Gaines, Ernest J.

Gaitskill, Mary 1954- .... **CLC 69**
See also CA 128; CANR 61, 152, 208; DLB
244; TCLE 1:1
Gaitskill, Mary Lawrence
See Gaitskill, Mary
Gaius Suetonius Tranquillus
See Suetonius
Galdos, Benito Perez
See Perez Galdos, Benito
Gale, Zona 1874-1938 .... **DC 30; TCLC 7**
See also CA 105, 153; CANR 84; DAM
DRAM; DFS 17; DLB 9, 78, 228; RGAL
4
Galeano, Eduardo 1940- ... **CLC 72; HLCS 1**
See also CA 29-32R; CANR 13, 32, 100,
163; HW 1
Galeano, Eduardo Hughes
See Galeano, Eduardo
Galiano, Juan Valera y Alcala
See Valera y Alcala-Galiano, Juan
Galilei, Galileo 1564-1642 .... **LC 45**
Gallagher, Tess 1943- .... **CLC 18, 63; PC 9**
See also CA 106; CP 3, 4, 5, 6, 7; CWP;
DAM POET; DLB 120, 212, 244; PFS 16
Gallant, Mavis 1922- ..... **CLC 7, 18, 38, 172,
288; SSC 5, 78**
See also CA 69-72; CANR 29, 69, 117;
CCA 1; CN 1, 2, 3, 4, 5, 6, 7; DAC; DAM
MST; DLB 53; EWL 3; MTCW 1, 2;
MTFW 2005; RGEL 2; RGSF 2
Gallant, Roy A(rthur) 1924- .... **CLC 17**
See also CA 5-8R; CANR 4, 29, 54, 117;
CLR 30; MAICYA 1, 2; SATA 4, 68, 110
Gallico, Paul 1897-1976 .... **CLC 2**
See also AITN 1; CA 5-8R; 69-72; CANR
23; CN 1, 2; DLB 9, 171; FANT; MAI-
CYA 1, 2; SATA 13
Gallico, Paul William
See Gallico, Paul
Gallo, Max Louis 1932- .... **CLC 95**
See also CA 85-88
Gallois, Lucien
See Desnos, Robert
Gallup, Ralph
See Whitemore, Hugh (John)
Galsworthy, John 1867-1933 .... **SSC 22;
TCLC 1, 45; WLC 2**
See also BRW 6; CA 104, 141; CANR 75;
CDBLB 1890-1914; DA; DA3; DAB;
DAC; DAM DRAM, MST, NOV; DLB
10, 34, 98, 162, 330; DLBD 16; EWL 3;
MTCW 2; RGEL 2; SSFS 3; TEA
Galt, John 1779-1839 .... **NCLC 1, 110**
See also DLB 99, 116, 159; RGEL 2; RGSF
2
Galvin, James 1951- .... **CLC 38**
See also CA 108; CANR 26
Gamboa, Federico 1864-1939 .... **TCLC 36**
See also CA 167; HW 2; LAW
Gandhi, M. K.
See Gandhi, Mohandas Karamchand
Gandhi, Mahatma
See Gandhi, Mohandas Karamchand
Gandhi, Mohandas Karamchand
1869-1948 .... **TCLC 59**
See also CA 121, 132; DA3; DAM MULT;
DLB 323; MTCW 1, 2
Gann, Ernest Kellogg 1910-1991 ..... **CLC 23**
See also AITN 1; BPFB 2; CA 1-4R, 136;
CANR 1, 83; RHW
Gao Xingjian
See Xingjian, Gao
Garber, Eric
See Holleran, Andrew
Garber, Esther
See Lee, Tanith

Garcia, Cristina 1958- .... **CLC 76**
See also AMWS 11; CA 141; CANR 73,
130, 172; CN 7; DLB 292; DNFS 1; EWL
3; HW 2; LLW; MTFW 2005; SATA 208
Garcia Lorca, Federico 1898-1936 ...... **DC 2;
HLC 2; PC 3; TCLC 1, 7, 49, 181,
197; WLC 2**
See also AAYA 46; CA 104, 131; CANR
81; DA; DA3; DAB; DAC; DAM DRAM,
MST, MULT, POET; DFS 4; DLB 108;
EW 11; EWL 3; HW 1, 2; LATS 1:2;
MTCW 1, 2; MTFW 2005; PFS 20, 31;
RGWL 2, 3; TWA; WP
Garcia Marquez, Gabriel 1928- .... **CLC 2, 3,
8, 10, 15, 27, 47, 55, 68, 170, 254; HLC
1; SSC 8, 83; WLC 3**
See also AAYA 3, 33; BEST 89:1, 90:4;
BPFB 2; BYA 12, 16; CA 33-36R; CANR
10, 28, 50, 75, 82, 128, 204; CDWLB 3;
CPW; CWW 2; DA; DA3; DAB; DAC;
DAM MST, MULT, NOV, POP; DLB 113,
330; DNFS 1, 2; EWL 3; EXPN; EXPS;
HW 1, 2; LAIT 2; LATS 1:2; LAW;
LAWS 1; LMFS 2; MTCW 1, 2; MTFW
2005; NCFS 3; NFS 1, 5, 10; RGSF 2;
RGWL 2, 3; SSFS 1, 6, 16, 21; TWA;
WLIT 1
Garcia Marquez, Gabriel Jose
See Garcia Marquez, Gabriel
Garcia Marquez, Gabriel Jose
See Garcia Marquez, Gabriel
Garcilaso de la Vega, El Inca
1539-1616 .... **HLCS 1; LC 127**
See also DLB 318; LAW
Gard, Janice
See Latham, Jean Lee
Gard, Roger Martin du
See Martin du Gard, Roger
Gardam, Jane 1928- .... **CLC 43**
See also CA 49-52; CANR 2, 18, 33, 54,
106, 167, 206; CLR 12; DLB 14, 161,
231; MAICYA 1, 2; MTCW 1; SAAS 9;
SATA 39, 76, 130; SATA-Brief 28; YAW
Gardam, Jane Mary
See Gardam, Jane
Gardens, S. S.
See Snodgrass, W. D.
Gardner, Herb(ert George)
1934-2003 .... **CLC 44**
See also CA 149, 220; CAD; CANR 119;
CD 5, 6; DFS 18, 20
Gardner, John, Jr. 1933-1982 ... **CLC 2, 3, 5,
7, 8, 10, 18, 28, 34; SSC 7; TCLC 195**
See also AAYA 45; AITN 1; AMWS 6;
BPFB 2; CA 65-68, 107; CANR 33, 73;
CDALBS; CN 2, 3; CPW; DA3; DAM
NOV, POP; DLB 2; DLBY 1982; EWL 3;
FANT; LATS 1:2; MAL 5; MTCW 1, 2;
MTFW 2005; NFS 3; RGAL 4; RGSF 2;
SATA 40; SATA-Obit 31; SSFS 8
Gardner, John 1926-2007 .... **CLC 30**
See also CA 103, 263; CANR 15, 69, 127,
183; CMW 4; CPW; DAM POP; MTCW
1
Gardner, John Champlin, Jr.
See Gardner, John, Jr.
Gardner, John Edmund
See Gardner, John
Gardner, Miriam
See Bradley, Marion Zimmer
Gardner, Noel
See Kuttner, Henry
Gardons, S.S.
See Snodgrass, W. D.
Garfield, Leon 1921-1996 .... **CLC 12**
See also AAYA 8, 69; BYA 1, 3; CA 17-
20R, 152; CANR 38, 41, 78; CLR 21;
DLB 161; JRDA; MAICYA 1, 2; MAIC-
YAS 1; SATA 1, 32, 76; SATA-Obit 90;
TEA; WYA; YAW

Garland, (Hannibal) Hamlin
1860-1940 .... **SSC 18, 117; TCLC 3**
See also CA 104; DLB 12, 71, 78, 186;
MAL 5; RGAL 4; RGSF 2; TCWW 1, 2
Garneau, (Hector de) Saint-Denys
1912-1943 .... **TCLC 13**
See also CA 111; DLB 88
Garner, Alan 1934- .... **CLC 17**
See also AAYA 18; BYA 3, 5; CA 73-76,
178; CAAE 178; CANR 15, 64, 134; CLR
20, 130; CPW; DAB; DAM POP; DLB
161, 261; FANT; MAICYA 1, 2; MTCW
1, 2; MTFW 2005; SATA 18, 69; SATA-
Essay 108; SUFW 1, 2; YAW
Garner, Helen 1942- .... **SSC 135**
See also CA 124, 127; CANR 71, 206; CN
4, 5, 6, 7; DLB 325; GLL 2; RGSF 2
Garner, Hugh 1913-1979 .... **CLC 13**
See also CA 69-72; CANR 31; CCA 1; CN
1, 2; DLB 68
Garnett, David 1892-1981 .... **CLC 3**
See also CA 5-8R, 103; CANR 17, 79; CN
1, 2; DLB 34; FANT; MTCW 2; RGEL 2;
SFW 4; SUFW 1
Garnier, Robert c. 1545-1590 .... **LC 119**
See also DLB 327; GFL Beginnings to 1789
Garrett, George 1929-2008 ... **CLC 3, 11, 51;
SSC 30**
See also AMWS 7; BPFB 2; CA 1-4R, 202,
272; CAAE 202; CAAS 5; CANR 1, 42,
67, 109, 199; CN 1, 2, 3, 4, 5, 6, 7; CP 1,
2, 3, 4, 5, 6, 7; CSW; DLB 2, 5, 130, 152;
DLBY 1983
Garrett, George P.
See Garrett, George
Garrett, George Palmer
See Garrett, George
Garrett, George Palmer, Jr.
See Garrett, George
Garrick, David 1717-1779 .... **LC 15, 156**
See also DAM DRAM; DLB 84, 213;
RGEL 2
Garrigue, Jean 1914-1972 .... **CLC 2, 8**
See also CA 5-8R, 37-40R; CANR 20; CP
1; MAL 5
Garrison, Frederick
See Sinclair, Upton
Garrison, William Lloyd
1805-1879 .... **NCLC 149**
See also CDALB 1640-1865; DLB 1, 43,
235
Garro, Elena 1920(?)-1998 .. **HLCS 1; TCLC
153**
See also CA 131, 169; CWW 2; DLB 145;
EWL 3; HW 1; LAWS 1; WLIT 1
Garth, Will
See Hamilton, Edmond; Kuttner, Henry
Garvey, Marcus (Moziah, Jr.)
1887-1940 ..... **BLC 1:2; HR 1:2; TCLC
41**
See also BW 1; CA 120, 124; CANR 79;
DAM MULT; DLB 345
Gary, Romain
See Kacew, Romain
Gascar, Pierre
See Fournier, Pierre
Gascoigne, George 1539-1577 .... **LC 108**
See also DLB 136; RGEL 2
Gascoyne, David (Emery)
1916-2001 .... **CLC 45**
See also CA 65-68, 200; CANR 10, 28, 54;
CP 1, 2, 3, 4, 5, 6, 7; DLB 20; MTCW 1;
RGEL 2
Gaskell, Elizabeth 1810-1865 ... **NCLC 5, 70,
97, 137, 214; SSC 25, 97**
See also AAYA 80; BRW 5; BRWR 3; CD-
BLB 1832-1890; DAB; DAM MST; DLB
21, 144, 159; RGEL 2; RGSF 2; TEA

Greve, Felix Paul (Berthold Friedrich)
1879-1948 .... **TCLC 4**
See also CA 104, 141, 175; CANR 79; DAC; DAM MST; DLB 92; RGEL 2; TCWW 1, 2

Greville, Fulke 1554-1628 .... **LC 79**
See also BRWS 11; DLB 62, 172; RGEL 2

Grey, Lady Jane 1537-1554 .... **LC 93**
See also DLB 132

Grey, Zane 1872-1939 .... **TCLC 6**
See also BPFB 2; CA 104, 132; DA3; DAM POP; DLB 9, 212; MTCW 1, 2; MTFW 2005; RGAL 4; TCWW 1, 2; TUS

Griboedov, Aleksandr Sergeevich
1795(?)-1829 .... **NCLC 129**
See also DLB 205; RGWL 2, 3

Grieg, (Johan) Nordahl (Brun)
1902-1943 .... **TCLC 10**
See also CA 107, 189; EWL 3

Grieve, C. M. 1892-1978 ... **CLC 2, 4, 11, 19, 63; PC 9**
See also BRWS 12; CA 5-8R; 85-88; CANR 33, 107; CDBLB 1945-1960; CP 1, 2; DAM POET; DLB 20; EWL 3; MTCW 1; RGEL 2

Grieve, Christopher Murray
See Grieve, C. M.

Griffin, Gerald 1803-1840 .... **NCLC 7**
See also DLB 159; RGEL 2

Griffin, John Howard 1920-1980 ..... **CLC 68**
See also AITN 1; CA 1-4R, 101; CANR 2

Griffin, Peter 1942- .... **CLC 39**
See also CA 136

Griffith, David Lewelyn Wark
See Griffith, D.W.

Griffith, D.W. 1875(?)-1948 .... **TCLC 68**
See also AAYA 78; CA 119, 150; CANR 80

Griffith, Lawrence
See Griffith, D.W.

Griffiths, Trevor 1935- .... **CLC 13, 52**
See also CA 97-100; CANR 45; CBD; CD 5, 6; DLB 13, 245

Griggs, Sutton (Elbert)
1872-1930 .... **TCLC 77**
See also CA 123, 186; DLB 50

Grigson, Geoffrey (Edward Harvey)
1905-1985 .... **CLC 7, 39**
See also CA 25-28R, 118; CANR 20, 33; CP 1, 2, 3, 4; DLB 27; MTCW 1, 2

Grile, Dod
See Bierce, Ambrose

Grillparzer, Franz 1791-1872 .... **DC 14; NCLC 1, 102; SSC 37**
See also CDWLB 2; DLB 133; EW 5; RGWL 2, 3; TWA

Grimble, Reverend Charles James
See Eliot, T. S.

Grimke, Angelina Emily Weld
See Grimke, Angelina Weld

Grimke, Angelina Weld 1880-1958 ... **DC 38; HR 1:2**
See also BW 1; CA 124; DAM POET; DLB 50, 54; FW

Grimke, Charlotte L. Forten
1837(?)-1914 .... **BLC 1:2; TCLC 16**
See also BW 1; CA 117, 124; DAM MULT, POET; DLB 50, 239

Grimke, Charlotte Lottie Forten
See Grimke, Charlotte L. Forten

Grimm, Jacob Ludwig Karl
1785-1863 .... **NCLC 3, 77; SSC 36, 88**
See also CLR 112; DLB 90; MAICYA 1, 2; RGSF 2; RGWL 2, 3; SATA 22; WCH

Grimm, Wilhelm Karl 1786-1859 .. **NCLC 3, 77; SSC 36**
See also CDWLB 2; CLR 112; DLB 90; MAICYA 1, 2; RGSF 2; RGWL 2, 3; SATA 22; WCH

Grimm and Grim
See Grimm, Jacob Ludwig Karl; Grimm, Wilhelm Karl

Grimm Brothers
See Grimm, Jacob Ludwig Karl; Grimm, Wilhelm Karl

Grimmelshausen, Hans Jakob Christoffel von
See Grimmelshausen, Johann Jakob Christoffel von

Grimmelshausen, Johann Jakob Christoffel von 1621-1676 .... **LC 6**
See also CDWLB 2; DLB 168; RGWL 2, 3

Grindel, Eugene 1895-1952 .... **PC 38; TCLC 7, 41**
See also CA 104, 193; EWL 3; GFL 1789 to the Present; LMFS 2; RGWL 2, 3

Grisham, John 1955- .... **CLC 84, 273**
See also AAYA 14, 47; BPFB 2; CA 138; CANR 47, 69, 114, 133; CMW 4; CN 6, 7; CPW; CSW; DA3; DAM POP; LNFS 1; MSW; MTCW 2; MTFW 2005

Grosseteste, Robert 1175(?)-1253 . **CMLC 62**
See also DLB 115

Grossman, David 1954- .... **CLC 67, 231**
See also CA 138; CANR 114, 175; CWW 2; DLB 299; EWL 3; RGHL; WLIT 6

Grossman, Vasilii Semenovich
See Grossman, Vasily

Grossman, Vasily 1905-1964 .... **CLC 41**
See also CA 124, 130; DLB 272; MTCW 1; RGHL

Grossman, Vasily Semenovich
See Grossman, Vasily

Grove, Frederick Philip
See Greve, Felix Paul (Berthold Friedrich)

Grubb
See Crumb, R.

Grumbach, Doris 1918- .... **CLC 13, 22, 64**
See also CA 5-8R; CAAS 2; CANR 9, 42, 70, 127; CN 6, 7; INT CANR-9; MTCW 2; MTFW 2005

Grundtvig, Nikolai Frederik Severin
1783-1872 .... **NCLC 1, 158**
See also DLB 300

Grunge
See Crumb, R.

Grunwald, Lisa 1959- .... **CLC 44**
See also CA 120; CANR 148

Gryphius, Andreas 1616-1664 .... **LC 89**
See also CDWLB 2; DLB 164; RGWL 2, 3

Guare, John 1938- .... **CLC 8, 14, 29, 67; DC 20**
See also CA 73-76; CAD; CANR 21, 69, 118; CD 5, 6; DAM DRAM; DFS 8, 13; DLB 7, 249; EWL 3; MAL 5; MTCW 1, 2; RGAL 4

Guarini, Battista 1538-1612 .... **LC 102**
See also DLB 339

Gubar, Susan 1944- .... **CLC 145**
See also CA 108; CANR 45, 70, 139, 179; FW; MTCW 1; RGAL 4

Gubar, Susan David
See Gubar, Susan

Gudjonsson, Halldor Kiljan
1902-1998 .... **CLC 25**
See also CA 103, 164; CWW 2; DLB 293, 331; EW 12; EWL 3; RGWL 2, 3

Guedes, Vincente
See Pessoa, Fernando

Guenter, Erich
See Eich, Gunter

Guest, Barbara 1920-2006 ... **CLC 34; PC 55**
See also BG 1:2; CA 25-28R, 248; CANR 11, 44, 84; CP 1, 2, 3, 4, 5, 6, 7; CWP; DLB 5, 193

Guest, Edgar A(lbert) 1881-1959 ... **TCLC 95**
See also CA 112, 168

Guest, Judith 1936- .... **CLC 8, 30**
See also AAYA 7, 66; CA 77-80; CANR 15, 75, 138; DA3; DAM NOV, POP; EXPN; INT CANR-15; LAIT 5; MTCW 1, 2; MTFW 2005; NFS 1, 33

Guest, Judith Ann
See Guest, Judith

Guevara, Che
See Guevara (Serna), Ernesto

Guevara (Serna), Ernesto
1928-1967 .... **CLC 87; HLC 1**
See also CA 127, 111; CANR 56; DAM MULT; HW 1

Guicciardini, Francesco 1483-1540 ..... **LC 49**

Guido delle Colonne c. 1215-c. 1290 .... **CMLC 90**

Guild, Nicholas M. 1944- .... **CLC 33**
See also CA 93-96

Guillemin, Jacques
See Sartre, Jean-Paul

Guillen, Jorge 1893-1984 . **CLC 11; HLCS 1; PC 35; TCLC 233**
See also CA 89-92, 112; DAM MULT, POET; DLB 108; EWL 3; HW 1; RGWL 2, 3

Guillen, Nicolas 1902-1989 ... **BLC 1:2; CLC 48, 79; HLC 1; PC 23**
See also BW 2; CA 116, 125, 129; CANR 84; DAM MST, MULT, POET; DLB 283; EWL 3; HW 1; LAW; RGWL 2, 3; WP

Guillen, Nicolas Cristobal
See Guillen, Nicolas

Guillen y Alvarez, Jorge
See Guillen, Jorge

Guillevic, (Eugene) 1907-1997 .... **CLC 33**
See also CA 93-96; CWW 2

Guillois
See Desnos, Robert

Guillois, Valentin
See Desnos, Robert

Guimaraes Rosa, Joao 1908-1967 ... **CLC 23; HLCS 1**
See also CA 175; 89-92; DLB 113, 307; EWL 3; LAW; RGSF 2; RGWL 2, 3; WLIT 1

Guiney, Louise Imogen
1861-1920 .... **TCLC 41**
See also CA 160; DLB 54; RGAL 4

Guinizelli, Guido c. 1230-1276 ...... **CMLC 49**
See also WLIT 7

Guinizzelli, Guido
See Guinizelli, Guido

Guiraldes, Ricardo (Guillermo)
1886-1927 .... **TCLC 39**
See also CA 131; EWL 3; HW 1; LAW; MTCW 1

Guma, Alex La
See La Guma, Alex

Gumilev, Nikolai (Stepanovich)
1886-1921 .... **TCLC 60**
See also CA 165; DLB 295; EWL 3

Gumilyov, Nikolay Stepanovich
See Gumilev, Nikolai (Stepanovich)

Gump, P. Q.
See Card, Orson Scott

Gunesekera, Romesh 1954- .... **CLC 91**
See also BRWS 10; CA 159; CANR 140, 172; CN 6, 7; DLB 267, 323

Gunn, Bill
See Gunn, William Harrison

Gunn, Thom 1929-2004 ..... **CLC 3, 6, 18, 32, 81; PC 26**
See also BRWR 3; BRWS 4; CA 17-20R, 227; CANR 9, 33, 116; CDBLB 1960 to Present; CP 1, 2, 3, 4, 5, 6, 7; DAM POET; DLB 27; INT CANR-33; MTCW 1; PFS 9; RGEL 2

Harrison, Tony 1937- .... **CLC 43, 129**
See also BRWS 5; CA 65-68; CANR 44, 98; CBD; CD 5, 6; CP 2, 3, 4, 5, 6, 7; DLB 40, 245; MTCW 1; RGEL 2

Harriss, Will(ard Irvin) 1922- .... **CLC 34**
See also CA 111

Hart, Ellis
See Ellison, Harlan

Hart, Josephine 1942(?)- .... **CLC 70**
See also CA 138; CANR 70, 149; CPW; DAM POP

Hart, Moss 1904-1961 .... **CLC 66**
See also CA 109; 89-92; CANR 84; DAM DRAM; DFS 1; DLB 7, 266; RGAL 4

Harte, Bret 1836(?)-1902 .. **SSC 8, 59; TCLC 1, 25; WLC 3**
See also AMWS 2; CA 104, 140; CANR 80; CDALB 1865-1917; DA; DA3; DAC; DAM MST; DLB 12, 64, 74, 79, 186; EXPS; LAIT 2; RGAL 4; RGSF 2; SATA 26; SSFS 3; TUS

Harte, Francis Brett
See Harte, Bret

Hartley, L(eslie) P(oles) 1895-1972 ... **CLC 2, 22; SSC 125**
See also BRWS 7; CA 45-48, 37-40R; CANR 33; CN 1; DLB 15, 139; EWL 3; HGG; MTCW 1, 2; MTFW 2005; RGEL 2; RGSF 2; SUFW 1

Hartman, Geoffrey H. 1929- .... **CLC 27**
See also CA 117, 125; CANR 79; DLB 67

Hartmann, Sadakichi 1869-1944 ... **TCLC 73**
See also CA 157; DLB 54

Hartmann von Aue c. 1170-c. 1210 .... **CMLC 15**
See also CDWLB 2; DLB 138; RGWL 2, 3

Hartog, Jan de
See de Hartog, Jan

Haruf, Kent 1943- .... **CLC 34**
See also AAYA 44; CA 149; CANR 91, 131

Harvey, Caroline
See Trollope, Joanna

Harvey, Gabriel 1550(?)-1631 .... **LC 88**
See also DLB 167, 213, 281

Harvey, Jack
See Rankin, Ian

Harwood, Ronald 1934- .... **CLC 32**
See also CA 1-4R; CANR 4, 55, 150; CBD; CD 5, 6; DAM DRAM, MST; DLB 13

Hasegawa Tatsunosuke
See Futabatei, Shimei

Hasek, Jaroslav 1883-1923 ... **SSC 69; TCLC 4**
See also CA 104, 129; CDWLB 4; DLB 215; EW 9; EWL 3; MTCW 1, 2; RGSF 2; RGWL 2, 3

Hasek, Jaroslav Matej Frantisek
See Hasek, Jaroslav

Hass, Robert 1941- ...... **CLC 18, 39, 99, 287; PC 16**
See also AMWS 6; CA 111; CANR 30, 50, 71, 187; CP 3, 4, 5, 6, 7; DLB 105, 206; EWL 3; MAL 5; MTFW 2005; RGAL 4; SATA 94; TCLE 1:1

Hassler, Jon 1933-2008 .... **CLC 263**
See also CA 73-76, 270; CANR 21, 80, 161; CN 6, 7; INT CANR-21; SATA 19; SATA-Obit 191

Hassler, Jon Francis
See Hassler, Jon

Hastings, Hudson
See Kuttner, Henry

Hastings, Selina CLC 44
See also CA 257

Hastings, Selina Shirley
See Hastings, Selina

Hastings, Victor
See Disch, Thomas M.

Hathorne, John 1641-1717 .... **LC 38**

Hatteras, Amelia
See Mencken, H. L.

Hatteras, Owen
See Mencken, H. L.; Nathan, George Jean

Hauff, Wilhelm 1802-1827 .... **NCLC 185**
See also CLR 155; DLB 90; SUFW 1

Hauptmann, Gerhart 1862-1946 .... **DC 34; SSC 37; TCLC 4**
See also CA 104, 153; CDWLB 2; DAM DRAM; DLB 66, 118, 330; EW 8; EWL 3; RGSF 2; RGWL 2, 3; TWA

Hauptmann, Gerhart Johann Robert
See Hauptmann, Gerhart

Havel, Vaclav 1936- ..... **CLC 25, 58, 65, 123; DC 6**
See also CA 104; CANR 36, 63, 124, 175; CDWLB 4; CWW 2; DA3; DAM DRAM; DFS 10; DLB 232; EWL 3; LMFS 2; MTCW 1, 2; MTFW 2005; RGWL 3

Haviaras, Stratis
See Chaviaras, Strates

Hawes, Stephen 1475(?)-1529(?) .... **LC 17**
See also DLB 132; RGEL 2

Hawkes, John 1925-1998 .. **CLC 1, 2, 3, 4, 7, 9, 14, 15, 27, 49**
See also BPFB 2; CA 1-4R, 167; CANR 2, 47, 64; CN 1, 2, 3, 4, 5, 6; DLB 2, 7, 227; DLBY 1980, 1998; EWL 3; MAL 5; MTCW 1, 2; MTFW 2005; RGAL 4

Hawking, S. W.
See Hawking, Stephen W.

Hawking, Stephen W. 1942- ..... **CLC 63, 105**
See also AAYA 13; BEST 89:1; CA 126, 129; CANR 48, 115; CPW; DA3; MTCW 2; MTFW 2005

Hawking, Stephen William
See Hawking, Stephen W.

Hawkins, Anthony Hope
See Hope, Anthony

Hawthorne, Julian 1846-1934 .... **TCLC 25**
See also CA 165; HGG

Hawthorne, Nathaniel 1804-1864 ... **NCLC 2, 10, 17, 23, 39, 79, 95, 158, 171, 191, 226; SSC 3, 29, 39, 89, 130; WLC 3**
See also AAYA 18; AMW; AMWC 1; AMWR 1; BPFB 2; BYA 3; CDALB 1640-1865; CLR 103; DA; DA3; DAB; DAC; DAM MST, NOV; DLB 1, 74, 183, 223, 269; EXPN; EXPS; GL 2; HGG; LAIT 1; NFS 1, 20; RGAL 4; RGSF 2; SSFS 1, 7, 11, 15, 30; SUFW 1; TUS; WCH; YABC 2

Hawthorne, Sophia Peabody 1809-1871 .... **NCLC 150**
See also DLB 183, 239

Haxton, Josephine Ayres
See Douglas, Ellen

Hayaseca y Eizaguirre, Jorge
See Echegaray (y Eizaguirre), Jose (Maria Waldo)

Hayashi, Fumiko 1904-1951 .... **TCLC 27**
See also CA 161; DLB 180; EWL 3

Hayashi Fumiko
See Hayashi, Fumiko

Haycraft, Anna 1932-2005 .... **CLC 40**
See also CA 122, 237; CANR 90, 141; CN 4, 5, 6; DLB 194; MTCW 2; MTFW 2005

Haycraft, Anna Margaret
See Haycraft, Anna

Hayden, Robert
See Hayden, Robert Earl

Hayden, Robert E.
See Hayden, Robert Earl

Hayden, Robert Earl 1913-1980 .... **BLC 1:2; CLC 5, 9, 14, 37; PC 6**
See also AFAW 1, 2; AMWS 2; BW 1, 3; CA 69-72; 97-100; CABS 2; CANR 24, 75, 82; CDALB 1941-1968; CP 1, 2, 3; DA; DAC; DAM MST, MULT, POET; DLB 5, 76; EWL 3; EXPP; MAL 5; MTCW 1, 2; PFS 1, 31; RGAL 4; SATA 19; SATA-Obit 26; WP

Haydon, Benjamin Robert 1786-1846 .... **NCLC 146**
See also DLB 110

Hayek, F(riedrich) A(ugust von) 1899-1992 .... **TCLC 109**
See also CA 93-96, 137; CANR 20; MTCW 1, 2

Hayford, J(oseph) E(phraim) Casely
See Casely-Hayford, J(oseph) E(phraim)

Hayman, Ronald 1932- .... **CLC 44**
See also CA 25-28R; CANR 18, 50, 88; CD 5, 6; DLB 155

Hayne, Paul Hamilton 1830-1886 . **NCLC 94**
See also DLB 3, 64, 79, 248; RGAL 4

Hays, Mary 1760-1843 .... **NCLC 114**
See also DLB 142, 158; RGEL 2

Haywood, Eliza (Fowler) 1693(?)-1756 .... **LC 1, 44, 177**
See also BRWS 12; DLB 39; RGEL 2

Hazlitt, William 1778-1830 ...... **NCLC 29, 82**
See also BRW 4; DLB 110, 158; RGEL 2; TEA

Hazzard, Shirley 1931- .... **CLC 18, 218**
See also CA 9-12R; CANR 4, 70, 127; CN 1, 2, 3, 4, 5, 6, 7; DLB 289; DLBY 1982; MTCW 1

Head, Bessie 1937-1986 . **BLC 1:2, 2:2; CLC 25, 67; SSC 52**
See also AFW; BW 2, 3; CA 29-32R, 119; CANR 25, 82; CDWLB 3; CN 1, 2, 3, 4; DA3; DAM MULT; DLB 117, 225; EWL 3; EXPS; FL 1:6; FW; MTCW 1, 2; MTFW 2005; NFS 31; RGSF 2; SSFS 5, 13, 30; WLIT 2; WWE 1

Headley, Elizabeth
See Harrison, Elizabeth (Allen) Cavanna

Headon, (Nicky) Topper 1956(?)- ..... **CLC 30**

Heaney, Seamus 1939- . **CLC 5, 7, 14, 25, 37, 74, 91, 171, 225; PC 18, 100; WLCS**
See also AAYA 61; BRWR 1; BRWS 2; CA 85-88; CANR 25, 48, 75, 91, 128, 184; CDBLB 1960 to Present; CP 1, 2, 3, 4, 5, 6, 7; DA3; DAB; DAM POET; DLB 40, 330; DLBY 1995; EWL 3; EXPP; MTCW 1, 2; MTFW 2005; PAB; PFS 2, 5, 8, 17, 30; RGEL 2; TEA; WLIT 4

Heaney, Seamus Justin
See Heaney, Seamus

Hearn, Lafcadio 1850-1904 .... **TCLC 9**
See also AAYA 79; CA 105, 166; DLB 12, 78, 189; HGG; MAL 5; RGAL 4

Hearn, Patricio Lafcadio Tessima Carlos
See Hearn, Lafcadio

Hearne, Samuel 1745-1792 .... **LC 95**
See also DLB 99

Hearne, Vicki 1946-2001 .... **CLC 56**
See also CA 139, 201

Hearon, Shelby 1931- .... **CLC 63**
See also AITN 2; AMWS 8; CA 25-28R; CAAS 11; CANR 18, 48, 103, 146; CSW

Heat-Moon, William Least 1939- ..... **CLC 29**
See also AAYA 9, 66; ANW; CA 115, 119; CANR 47, 89, 206; CPW; INT CA-119

Hebbel, Friedrich 1813-1863 . **DC 21; NCLC 43**
See also CDWLB 2; DAM DRAM; DLB 129; EW 6; RGWL 2, 3

Hebert, Anne 1916-2000 . **CLC 4, 13, 29, 246**
See also CA 85-88, 187; CANR 69, 126; CCA 1; CWP; CWW 2; DA3; DAC; DAM MST, POET; DLB 68; EWL 3; GFL 1789 to the Present; MTCW 1, 2; MTFW 2005; PFS 20

Hecht, Anthony (Evan) 1923-2004 .... **CLC 8, 13, 19; PC 70**
See also AMWS 10; CA 9-12R, 232; CANR 6, 108; CP 1, 2, 3, 4, 5, 6, 7; DAM POET; DLB 5, 169; EWL 3; PFS 6; WP

Hecht, Ben 1894-1964 ..... **CLC 8; TCLC 101**
See also CA 85-88; DFS 9; DLB 7, 9, 25, 26, 28, 86; FANT; IDFW 3, 4; RGAL 4

Hedayat, Sadeq 1903-1951 . **SSC 131; TCLC 21**
See also CA 120; EWL 3; RGSF 2

Hegel, Georg Wilhelm Friedrich 1770-1831 .... **NCLC 46, 151**
See also DLB 90; TWA

Heidegger, Martin 1889-1976 .... **CLC 24**
See also CA 81-84; 65-68; CANR 34; DLB 296; MTCW 1, 2; MTFW 2005

Heidenstam, (Carl Gustaf) Verner von 1859-1940 .... **TCLC 5**
See also CA 104; DLB 330

Heidi Louise
See Erdrich, Louise

Heifner, Jack 1946- .... **CLC 11**
See also CA 105; CANR 47

Heijermans, Herman 1864-1924 .... **TCLC 24**
See also CA 123; EWL 3

Heilbrun, Carolyn G. 1926-2003 ..... **CLC 25, 173**
See also BPFB 1; CA 45-48, 220; CANR 1, 28, 58, 94; CMW; CPW; DLB 306; FW; MSW

Heilbrun, Carolyn Gold
See Heilbrun, Carolyn G.

Hein, Christoph 1944- .... **CLC 154**
See also CA 158; CANR 108; CDWLB 2; CWW 2; DLB 124

Heine, Heinrich 1797-1856 .... **NCLC 4, 54, 147; PC 25**
See also CDWLB 2; DLB 90; EW 5; RGWL 2, 3; TWA

Heinemann, Larry 1944- .... **CLC 50**
See also CA 110; CAAS 21; CANR 31, 81, 156; DLBD 9; INT CANR-31

Heinemann, Larry Curtiss
See Heinemann, Larry

Heiney, Donald (William) 1921-1993 . **CLC 9**
See also CA 1-4R, 142; CANR 3, 58; FANT

Heinlein, Robert A. 1907-1988 .. **CLC 1, 3, 8, 14, 26, 55; SSC 55**
See also AAYA 17; BPFB 2; BYA 4, 13; CA 1-4R, 125; CANR 1, 20, 53; CLR 75; CN 1, 2, 3, 4; CPW; DA3; DAM POP; DLB 8; EXPS; JRDA; LAIT 5; LMFS 2; MAICYA 1, 2; MTCW 1, 2; MTFW 2005; RGAL 4; SATA 9, 69; SATA-Obit 56; SCFW 1, 2; SFW 4; SSFS 7; YAW

Hejinian, Lyn 1941- .... **PC 108**
See also CA 153; CANR 85; CP 4, 5, 6, 7; CWP; DLB 165; PFS 27; RGAL 4

Held, Peter
See Vance, Jack

Heldris of Cornwall fl. 13th cent.
- .... **CMLC 97**

Helforth, John
See Doolittle, Hilda

Heliodorus fl. 3rd cent. - .... **CMLC 52**
See also WLIT 8

Hellenhofferu, Vojtech Kapristian z
See Hasek, Jaroslav

Heller, Joseph 1923-1999 . **CLC 1, 3, 5, 8, 11, 36, 63; TCLC 131, 151; WLC 3**
See also AAYA 24; AITN 1; AMWS 4; BPFB 2; BYA 1; CA 5-8R, 187; CABS 1; CANR 8, 42, 66, 126; CN 1, 2, 3, 4, 5, 6; CPW; DA; DA3; DAB; DAC; DAM MST, NOV, POP; DLB 2, 28, 227; DLBY 1980, 2002; EWL 3; EXPN; INT CANR-8; LAIT 4; MAL 5; MTCW 1, 2; MTFW 2005; NFS 1; RGAL 4; TUS; YAW

Hellman, Lillian 1905-1984 . **CLC 2, 4, 8, 14, 18, 34, 44, 52; DC 1; TCLC 119**
See also AAYA 47; AITN 1, 2; AMWS 1; CA 13-16R, 112; CAD; CANR 33; CWD; DA3; DAM DRAM; DFS 1, 3, 14; DLB 7, 228; DLBY 1984; EWL 3; FL 1:6; FW; LAIT 3; MAL 5; MBL; MTCW 1, 2; MTFW 2005; RGAL 4; TUS

Hellman, Lillian Florence
See Hellman, Lillian

Heloise c. 1095-c. 1164 .... **CMLC 122**

Helprin, Mark 1947- .... **CLC 7, 10, 22, 32**
See also CA 81-84; CANR 47, 64, 124; CDALBS; CN 7; CPW; DA3; DAM NOV, POP; DLB 335; DLBY 1985; FANT; MAL 5; MTCW 1, 2; MTFW 2005; SSFS 25; SUFW 2

Helvetius, Claude-Adrien 1715-1771 .. **LC 26**
See also DLB 313

Helyar, Jane Penelope Josephine 1933- .... **CLC 17**
See also CA 21-24R; CANR 10, 26; CWRI 5; SAAS 2; SATA 5; SATA-Essay 138

Hemans, Felicia 1793-1835 ...... **NCLC 29, 71**
See also DLB 96; RGEL 2

Hemingway, Ernest 1899-1961 .. **CLC 1, 3, 6, 8, 10, 13, 19, 30, 34, 39, 41, 44, 50, 61, 80; SSC 1, 25, 36, 40, 63, 117, 137; TCLC 115, 203; WLC 3**
See also AAYA 19; AMW; AMWC 1; AMWR 1; BPFB 2; BYA 2, 3, 13, 15; CA 77-80; CANR 34; CDALB 1917-1929; DA; DA3; DAB; DAC; DAM MST, NOV; DLB 4, 9, 102, 210, 308, 316, 330; DLBD 1, 15, 16; DLBY 1981, 1987, 1996, 1998; EWL 3; EXPN; EXPS; LAIT 3, 4; LATS 1:1; MAL 5; MTCW 1, 2; MTFW 2005; NFS 1, 5, 6, 14; RGAL 4; RGSF 2; SSFS 17; TUS; WYA

Hemingway, Ernest Miller
See Hemingway, Ernest

Hempel, Amy 1951- .... **CLC 39**
See also CA 118, 137; CANR 70, 166; DA3; DLB 218; EXPS; MTCW 2; MTFW 2005; SSFS 2

Henderson, F. C.
See Mencken, H. L.

Henderson, Mary
See Mavor, Osborne Henry

Henderson, Sylvia
See Ashton-Warner, Sylvia (Constance)

Henderson, Zenna (Chlarson) 1917-1983 .... **SSC 29**
See also CA 1-4R, 133; CANR 1, 84; DLB 8; SATA 5; SFW 4

Henkin, Joshua 1964- .... **CLC 119**
See also CA 161; CANR 186; DLB 350

Henley, Beth 1952- ... **CLC 23, 255; DC 6, 14**
See also AAYA 70; CA 107; CABS 3; CAD; CANR 32, 73, 140; CD 5, 6; CSW; CWD; DA3; DAM DRAM, MST; DFS 2, 21, 26; DLBY 1986; FW; MTCW 1, 2; MTFW 2005

Henley, Elizabeth Becker
See Henley, Beth

Henley, William Ernest 1849-1903 .. **TCLC 8**
See also CA 105, 234; DLB 19; RGEL 2

Hennissart, Martha 1929- .... **CLC 2**
See also BPFB 2; CA 85-88; CANR 64; CMW 4; DLB 306

Henry VIII 1491-1547 .... **LC 10**
See also DLB 132

Henry, O. 1862-1910 . **SSC 5, 49, 117; TCLC 1, 19; WLC 3**
See also AAYA 41; AMWS 2; CA 104, 131; CDALB 1865-1917; DA; DA3; DAB; DAC; DAM MST; DLB 12, 78, 79; EXPS; MAL 5; MTCW 1, 2; MTFW 2005; RGAL 4; RGSF 2; SSFS 2, 18, 27, 31; TCWW 1, 2; TUS; YABC 2

Henry, Oliver
See Henry, O.

Henry, Patrick 1736-1799 .... **LC 25**
See also LAIT 1

Henryson, Robert 1430(?)-1506(?) ..... **LC 20, 110; PC 65**
See also BRWS 7; DLB 146; RGEL 2

Henschke, Alfred
See Klabund

Henson, Lance 1944- .... **NNAL**
See also CA 146; DLB 175

Hentoff, Nat(han Irving) 1925- .... **CLC 26**
See also AAYA 4, 42; BYA 6; CA 1-4R; CAAS 6; CANR 5, 25, 77, 114; CLR 1, 52; DLB 345; INT CANR-25; JRDA; MAICYA 1, 2; SATA 42, 69, 133; SATA-Brief 27; WYA; YAW

Heppenstall, (John) Rayner 1911-1981 .... **CLC 10**
See also CA 1-4R, 103; CANR 29; CN 1, 2; CP 1, 2, 3; EWL 3

Heraclitus c. 540B.C.-c. 450B.C. ... **CMLC 22**
See also DLB 176

Herbert, Edward 1583-1648 .... **LC 177**
See also DLB 121, 151, 252; RGEL 2

Herbert, Frank 1920-1986 ... **CLC 12, 23, 35, 44, 85**
See also AAYA 21; BPFB 2; BYA 4, 14; CA 53-56, 118; CANR 5, 43; CDALBS; CPW; DAM POP; DLB 8; INT CANR-5; LAIT 5; MTCW 1, 2; MTFW 2005; NFS 17, 31; SATA 9, 37; SATA-Obit 47; SCFW 1, 2; SFW 4; YAW

Herbert, George 1593-1633 . **LC 24, 121; PC 4**
See also BRW 2; BRWR 2; CDBLB Before 1660; DAB; DAM POET; DLB 126; EXPP; PFS 25; RGEL 2; TEA; WP

Herbert, Zbigniew 1924-1998 ..... **CLC 9, 43; PC 50; TCLC 168**
See also CA 89-92, 169; CANR 36, 74, 177; CDWLB 4; CWW 2; DAM POET; DLB 232; EWL 3; MTCW 1; PFS 22

Herbert of Cherbury, Lord
See Herbert, Edward

Herbst, Josephine (Frey) 1897-1969 .... **CLC 34; TCLC 243**
See also CA 5-8R, 25-28R; DLB 9

Herder, Johann Gottfried von 1744-1803 .... **NCLC 8, 186**
See also DLB 97; EW 4; TWA

Heredia, Jose Maria 1803-1839 ...... **HLCS 2; NCLC 209**
See also LAW

Hergesheimer, Joseph 1880-1954 ... **TCLC 11**
See also CA 109, 194; DLB 102, 9; RGAL 4

Herlihy, James Leo 1927-1993 .... **CLC 6**
See also CA 1-4R, 143; CAD; CANR 2; CN 1, 2, 3, 4, 5

Herman, William
See Bierce, Ambrose

Hermogenes fl. c. 175- .... **CMLC 6**

Hernandez, Jose 1834-1886 .... **NCLC 17**
See also LAW; RGWL 2, 3; WLIT 1

Herodotus c. 484B.C.-c. 420B.C. .. **CMLC 17**
See also AW 1; CDWLB 1; DLB 176; RGWL 2, 3; TWA; WLIT 8

Herr, Michael 1940(?)- .... **CLC 231**
See also CA 89-92; CANR 68, 142; DLB 185; MTCW 1

Herrick, Robert 1591-1674 .. **LC 13, 145; PC 9**
See also BRW 2; BRWC 2; DA; DAB; DAC; DAM MST, POP; DLB 126; EXPP; PFS 13, 29; RGAL 4; RGEL 2; TEA; WP

Herring, Guilles
See Somerville, Edith Oenone

Hitler, Adolf 1889-1945 .... **TCLC 53**
See also CA 117, 147

Hoagland, Edward (Morley) 1932- .. **CLC 28**
See also ANW; CA 1-4R; CANR 2, 31, 57, 107; CN 1, 2, 3, 4, 5, 6, 7; DLB 6; SATA 51; TCWW 2

Hoban, Russell 1925- .... **CLC 7, 25**
See also BPFB 2; CA 5-8R; CANR 23, 37, 66, 114, 138; CLR 3, 69, 139; CN 4, 5, 6, 7; CWRI 5; DAM NOV; DLB 52; FANT; MAICYA 1, 2; MTCW 1, 2; MTFW 2005; SATA 1, 40, 78, 136; SFW 4; SUFW 2; TCLE 1:1

Hobbes, Thomas 1588-1679 .... **LC 36, 142**
See also DLB 151, 252, 281; RGEL 2

Hobbs, Perry
See Blackmur, R(ichard) P(almer)

Hobson, Laura Z(ametkin)
1900-1986 .... **CLC 7, 25**
See also BPFB 2; CA 17-20R, 118; CANR 55; CN 1, 2, 3, 4; DLB 28; SATA 52

Hoccleve, Thomas c. 1368-c. 1437 ...... **LC 75**
See also DLB 146; RGEL 2

Hoch, Edward D. 1930-2008 .... **SSC 119**
See also CA 29-32R; CANR 11, 27, 51, 97; CMW 4; DLB 306; SFW 4

Hoch, Edward Dentinger
See Hoch, Edward D.

Hochhuth, Rolf 1931- .... **CLC 4, 11, 18**
See also CA 5-8R; CANR 33, 75, 136; CWW 2; DAM DRAM; DLB 124; EWL 3; MTCW 1, 2; MTFW 2005; RGHL

Hochman, Sandra 1936- .... **CLC 3, 8**
See also CA 5-8R; CP 1, 2, 3, 4, 5; DLB 5

Hochwaelder, Fritz 1911-1986 .... **CLC 36**
See also CA 29-32R, 120; CANR 42; DAM DRAM; EWL 3; MTCW 1; RGWL 2, 3

Hochwalder, Fritz
See Hochwaelder, Fritz

Hocking, Mary 1921- .... **CLC 13**
See also CA 101; CANR 18, 40

Hocking, Mary Eunice
See Hocking, Mary

Hodge, Merle 1944- .... **BLC 2:2**
See also EWL 3

Hodgins, Jack 1938- .... **CLC 23; SSC 132**
See also CA 93-96; CN 4, 5, 6, 7; DLB 60

Hodgson, William Hope
1877(?)-1918 .... **TCLC 13**
See also CA 111, 164; CMW 4; DLB 70, 153, 156, 178; HGG; MTCW 2; SFW 4; SUFW 1

Hoeg, Peter
See Hoeg, Peter

Hoeg, Peter 1957- .... **CLC 95, 156**
See also CA 151; CANR 75, 202; CMW 4; DA3; DLB 214; EWL 3; MTCW 2; MTFW 2005; NFS 17; RGWL 3; SSFS 18

Hoffman, Alice 1952- .... **CLC 51**
See also AAYA 37; AMWS 10; CA 77-80; CANR 34, 66, 100, 138, 170; CN 4, 5, 6, 7; CPW; DAM NOV; DLB 292; MAL 5; MTCW 1, 2; MTFW 2005; TCLE 1:1

Hoffman, Daniel (Gerard) 1923- . **CLC 6, 13, 23**
See also CA 1-4R; CANR 4, 142; CP 1, 2, 3, 4, 5, 6, 7; DLB 5; TCLE 1:1

Hoffman, Eva 1945- .... **CLC 182**
See also AMWS 16; CA 132; CANR 146, 209

Hoffman, Stanley 1944- .... **CLC 5**
See also CA 77-80

Hoffman, William 1925-2009 .... **CLC 141**
See also AMWS 18; CA 21-24R; CANR 9, 103; CSW; DLB 234; TCLE 1:1

Hoffman, William M.
See Hoffman, William M(oses)

Hoffman, William M(oses) 1939- ..... **CLC 40**
See also CA 57-60; CAD; CANR 11, 71; CD 5, 6

Hoffmann, E(rnst) T(heodor) A(madeus)
1776-1822 ..... **NCLC 2, 183; SSC 13, 92**
See also CDWLB 2; CLR 133; DLB 90; EW 5; GL 2; RGSF 2; RGWL 2, 3; SATA 27; SUFW 1; WCH

Hofmann, Gert 1931-1993 .... **CLC 54**
See also CA 128; CANR 145; EWL 3; RGHL

Hofmannsthal, Hugo von 1874-1929 ... **DC 4; TCLC 11**
See also CA 106, 153; CDWLB 2; DAM DRAM; DFS 17; DLB 81, 118; EW 9; EWL 3; RGWL 2, 3

Hogan, Linda 1947- .... **CLC 73, 290; NNAL; PC 35**
See also AMWS 4; ANW; BYA 12; CA 120, 226; CAAE 226; CANR 45, 73, 129, 196; CWP; DAM MULT; DLB 175; SATA 132; TCWW 2

Hogarth, Charles
See Creasey, John

Hogarth, Emmett
See Polonsky, Abraham (Lincoln)

Hogarth, William 1697-1764 .... **LC 112**
See also AAYA 56

Hogg, James 1770-1835 .. **NCLC 4, 109; SSC 130**
See also BRWS 10; DLB 93, 116, 159; GL 2; HGG; RGEL 2; SUFW 1

Holbach, Paul-Henri Thiry
1723-1789 .... **LC 14**
See also DLB 313

Holberg, Ludvig 1684-1754 .... **LC 6**
See also DLB 300; RGWL 2, 3

Holbrook, John
See Vance, Jack

Holcroft, Thomas 1745-1809 .... **NCLC 85**
See also DLB 39, 89, 158; RGEL 2

Holden, Ursula 1921- .... **CLC 18**
See also CA 101; CAAS 8; CANR 22

Holderlin, (Johann Christian) Friedrich
1770-1843 .... **NCLC 16, 187; PC 4**
See also CDWLB 2; DLB 90; EW 5; RGWL 2, 3

Holdstock, Robert 1948-2009 .... **CLC 39**
See also CA 131; CANR 81, 207; DLB 261; FANT; HGG; SFW 4; SUFW 2

Holdstock, Robert P.
See Holdstock, Robert

Holinshed, Raphael fl. 1580- .... **LC 69**
See also DLB 167; RGEL 2

Holland, Isabelle (Christian)
1920-2002 .... **CLC 21**
See also AAYA 11, 64; CA 21-24R, 205; CAAE 181; CANR 10, 25, 47; CLR 57; CWRI 5; JRDA; LAIT 4; MAICYA 1, 2; SATA 8, 70; SATA-Essay 103; SATA-Obit 132; WYA

Holland, Marcus
See Caldwell, (Janet Miriam) Taylor (Holland)

Hollander, John 1929- .... **CLC 2, 5, 8, 14**
See also CA 1-4R; CANR 1, 52, 136; CP 1, 2, 3, 4, 5, 6, 7; DLB 5; MAL 5; SATA 13

Hollander, Paul
See Silverberg, Robert

Holleran, Andrew 1943(?)- .... **CLC 38**
See also CA 144; CANR 89, 162; GLL 1

Holley, Marietta 1836(?)-1926 .... **TCLC 99**
See also CA 118; DLB 11; FL 1:3

Hollinghurst, Alan 1954- .... **CLC 55, 91**
See also BRWS 10; CA 114; CN 5, 6, 7; DLB 207, 326; GLL 1

Hollis, Jim
See Summers, Hollis (Spurgeon, Jr.)

Holly, Buddy 1936-1959 .... **TCLC 65**
See also CA 213

Holmes, Gordon
See Shiel, M. P.

Holmes, John
See Souster, (Holmes) Raymond

Holmes, John Clellon 1926-1988 ...... **CLC 56**
See also BG 1:2; CA 9-12R, 125; CANR 4; CN 1, 2, 3, 4; DLB 16, 237

Holmes, Oliver Wendell, Jr.
1841-1935 .... **TCLC 77**
See also CA 114, 186

Holmes, Oliver Wendell
1809-1894 .... **NCLC 14, 81; PC 71**
See also AMWS 1; CDALB 1640-1865; DLB 1, 189, 235; EXPP; PFS 24; RGAL 4; SATA 34

Holmes, Raymond
See Souster, (Holmes) Raymond

Holt, Samuel
See Westlake, Donald E.

Holt, Victoria
See Hibbert, Eleanor Alice Burford

Holub, Miroslav 1923-1998 .... **CLC 4**
See also CA 21-24R, 169; CANR 10; CD-WLB 4; CWW 2; DLB 232; EWL 3; RGWL 3

Holz, Detlev
See Benjamin, Walter

Homer c. 8th cent. B.C.- ..... **CMLC 1, 16, 61, 121; PC 23; WLCS**
See also AW 1; CDWLB 1; DA; DA3; DAB; DAC; DAM MST, POET; DLB 176; EFS 1; LAIT 1; LMFS 1; RGWL 2, 3; TWA; WLIT 8; WP

Hong, Maxine Ting Ting
See Kingston, Maxine Hong

Hongo, Garrett Kaoru 1951- .... **PC 23**
See also CA 133; CAAS 22; CP 5, 6, 7; DLB 120, 312; EWL 3; EXPP; PFS 25, 33; RGAL 4

Honig, Edwin 1919- .... **CLC 33**
See also CA 5-8R; CAAS 8; CANR 4, 45, 144; CP 1, 2, 3, 4, 5, 6, 7; DLB 5

Hood, Hugh (John Blagdon) 1928- . **CLC 15, 28, 273; SSC 42**
See also CA 49-52; CAAS 17; CANR 1, 33, 87; CN 1, 2, 3, 4, 5, 6, 7; DLB 53; RGSF 2

Hood, Thomas 1799-1845 . **NCLC 16; PC 93**
See also BRW 4; DLB 96; RGEL 2

Hooker, (Peter) Jeremy 1941- .... **CLC 43**
See also CA 77-80; CANR 22; CP 2, 3, 4, 5, 6, 7; DLB 40

Hooker, Richard 1554-1600 .... **LC 95**
See also BRW 1; DLB 132; RGEL 2

Hooker, Thomas 1586-1647 .... **LC 137**
See also DLB 24

hooks, bell 1952(?)- .... **BLCS; CLC 94**
See also BW 2; CA 143; CANR 87, 126; DLB 246; MTCW 2; MTFW 2005; SATA 115, 170

Hooper, Johnson Jones
1815-1862 .... **NCLC 177**
See also DLB 3, 11, 248; RGAL 4

Hope, A(lec) D(erwent) 1907-2000 .... **CLC 3, 51; PC 56**
See also BRWS 7; CA 21-24R, 188; CANR 33, 74; CP 1, 2, 3, 4, 5; DLB 289; EWL 3; MTCW 1, 2; MTFW 2005; PFS 8; RGEL 2

Hope, Anthony 1863-1933 .... **TCLC 83**
See also CA 157; DLB 153, 156; RGEL 2; RHW

Hope, Brian
See Creasey, John

Hope, Christopher 1944- .... **CLC 52**
See also AFW; CA 106; CANR 47, 101, 177; CN 4, 5, 6, 7; DLB 225; SATA 62

Hope, Christopher David Tully
See Hope, Christopher

Hopkins, Gerard Manley
1844-1889 .... **NCLC 17, 189; PC 15; WLC 3**
See also BRW 5; BRWR 2; CDBLB 1890-1914; DA; DA3; DAB; DAC; DAM MST, POET; DLB 35, 57; EXPP; PAB; PFS 26; RGEL 2; TEA; WP

Hopkins, John (Richard) 1931-1998 .. **CLC 4**
See also CA 85-88, 169; CBD; CD 5, 6

Hopkins, Pauline Elizabeth
1859-1930 .... **BLC 1:2; TCLC 28**
See also AFAW 2; BW 2, 3; CA 141; CANR 82; DAM MULT; DLB 50

Hopkinson, Francis 1737-1791 .... **LC 25**
See also DLB 31; RGAL 4

Hopley, George
See Hopley-Woolrich, Cornell George

Hopley-Woolrich, Cornell George
1903-1968 .... **CLC 77**
See also CA 13-14; CANR 58, 156; CAP 1; CMW 4; DLB 226; MSW; MTCW 2

Horace 65B.C.-8B.C. . **CMLC 39, 125; PC 46**
See also AW 2; CDWLB 1; DLB 211; RGWL 2, 3; WLIT 8

Horatio
See Proust, Marcel

Horgan, Paul (George Vincent
O'Shaughnessy) 1903-1995 .. **CLC 9, 53**
See also BPFB 2; CA 13-16R, 147; CANR 9, 35; CN 1, 2, 3, 4, 5; DAM NOV; DLB 102, 212; DLBY 1985; INT CANR-9; MTCW 1, 2; MTFW 2005; SATA 13; SATA-Obit 84; TCWW 1, 2

Horkheimer, Max 1895-1973 .... **TCLC 132**
See also CA 216, 41-44R; DLB 296

Horn, Peter
See Kuttner, Henry

Hornby, Nicholas Peter John
See Hornby, Nick

Hornby, Nick 1957(?)- .... **CLC 243**
See also AAYA 74; BRWS 15; CA 151; CANR 104, 151, 191; CN 7; DLB 207, 352

Horne, Frank 1899-1974 .... **HR 1:2**
See also BW 1; CA 125; 53-56; DLB 51; WP

Horne, Richard Henry Hengist
1802(?)-1884 .... **NCLC 127**
See also DLB 32; SATA 29

Hornem, Horace Esq.
See Lord Byron

Horne Tooke, John 1736-1812 ..... **NCLC 195**

Horney, Karen (Clementine Theodore
Danielsen) 1885-1952 .... **TCLC 71**
See also CA 114, 165; DLB 246; FW

Hornung, E(rnest) W(illiam)
1866-1921 .... **TCLC 59**
See also CA 108, 160; CMW 4; DLB 70

Horovitz, Israel 1939- .... **CLC 56**
See also CA 33-36R; CAD; CANR 46, 59; CD 5, 6; DAM DRAM; DLB 7, 341; MAL 5

Horton, George Moses
1797(?)-1883(?) .... **NCLC 87**
See also DLB 50

Horvath, odon von 1901-1938
See von Horvath, Odon
See also EWL 3

Horvath, Oedoen von -1938
See von Horvath, Odon

Horwitz, Julius 1920-1986 .... **CLC 14**
See also CA 9-12R, 119; CANR 12

Horwitz, Ronald
See Harwood, Ronald

Hospital, Janette Turner 1942- .... **CLC 42, 145**
See also CA 108; CANR 48, 166, 200; CN 5, 6, 7; DLB 325; DLBY 2002; RGSF 2

Hosseini, Khaled 1965- .... **CLC 254**
See also CA 225; LNFS 1, 3; SATA 156

Hostos, E. M. de
See Hostos (y Bonilla), Eugenio Maria de

Hostos, Eugenio M. de
See Hostos (y Bonilla), Eugenio Maria de

Hostos, Eugenio Maria
See Hostos (y Bonilla), Eugenio Maria de

Hostos (y Bonilla), Eugenio Maria de
1839-1903 .... **TCLC 24**
See also CA 123, 131; HW 1

Houdini
See Lovecraft, H. P.

Houellebecq, Michel 1958- .... **CLC 179**
See also CA 185; CANR 140; MTFW 2005

Hougan, Carolyn 1943-2007 .... **CLC 34**
See also CA 139, 257

Household, Geoffrey (Edward West)
1900-1988 .... **CLC 11**
See also CA 77-80, 126; CANR 58; CMW 4; CN 1, 2, 3, 4; DLB 87; SATA 14; SATA-Obit 59

Housman, A. E. 1859-1936 . **PC 2, 43; TCLC 1, 10; WLCS**
See also AAYA 66; BRW 6; CA 104, 125; DA; DA3; DAB; DAC; DAM MST, POET; DLB 19, 284; EWL 3; EXPP; MTCW 1, 2; MTFW 2005; PAB; PFS 4, 7; RGEL 2; TEA; WP

Housman, Alfred Edward
See Housman, A. E.

Housman, Laurence 1865-1959 .... **TCLC 7**
See also CA 106, 155; DLB 10; FANT; RGEL 2; SATA 25

Houston, Jeanne Wakatsuki 1934- .... **AAL**
See also AAYA 49; CA 103, 232; CAAE 232; CAAS 16; CANR 29, 123, 167; LAIT 4; SATA 78, 168; SATA-Essay 168

Hove, Chenjerai 1956- .... **BLC 2:2**
See also CP 7

Howard, Elizabeth Jane 1923- ..... **CLC 7, 29**
See also BRWS 11; CA 5-8R; CANR 8, 62, 146; CN 1, 2, 3, 4, 5, 6, 7

Howard, Maureen 1930- .... **CLC 5, 14, 46, 151**
See also CA 53-56; CANR 31, 75, 140; CN 4, 5, 6, 7; DLBY 1983; INT CANR-31; MTCW 1, 2; MTFW 2005

Howard, Richard 1929- .... **CLC 7, 10, 47**
See also AITN 1; CA 85-88; CANR 25, 80, 154; CP 1, 2, 3, 4, 5, 6, 7; DLB 5; INT CANR-25; MAL 5

Howard, Robert E 1906-1936 .... **TCLC 8**
See also AAYA 80; BPFB 2; BYA 5; CA 105, 157; CANR 155; FANT; SUFW 1; TCWW 1, 2

Howard, Robert Ervin
See Howard, Robert E

Howard, Warren F.
See Pohl, Frederik

Howe, Fanny 1940- .... **CLC 47**
See also CA 117, 187; CAAE 187; CAAS 27; CANR 70, 116, 184; CP 6, 7; CWP; SATA-Brief 52

Howe, Fanny Quincy
See Howe, Fanny

Howe, Irving 1920-1993 .... **CLC 85**
See also AMWS 6; CA 9-12R, 141; CANR 21, 50; DLB 67; EWL 3; MAL 5; MTCW 1, 2; MTFW 2005

Howe, Julia Ward 1819-1910 . **PC 81; TCLC 21**
See also CA 117, 191; DLB 1, 189, 235; FW

Howe, Susan 1937- .... **CLC 72, 152; PC 54**
See also AMWS 4; CA 160; CANR 209; CP 5, 6, 7; CWP; DLB 120; FW; RGAL 4

Howe, Tina 1937- .... **CLC 48**
See also CA 109; CAD; CANR 125; CD 5, 6; CWD; DLB 341

Howell, James 1594(?)-1666 .... **LC 13**
See also DLB 151

Howells, W. D.
See Howells, William Dean

Howells, William D.
See Howells, William Dean

Howells, William Dean 1837-1920 ... **SSC 36; TCLC 7, 17, 41**
See also AMW; CA 104, 134; CDALB 1865-1917; DLB 12, 64, 74, 79, 189; LMFS 1; MAL 5; MTCW 2; RGAL 4; TUS

Howes, Barbara 1914-1996 .... **CLC 15**
See also CA 9-12R, 151; CAAS 3; CANR 53; CP 1, 2, 3, 4, 5, 6; SATA 5; TCLE 1:1

Hrabal, Bohumil 1914-1997 ...... **CLC 13, 67; TCLC 155**
See also CA 106, 156; CAAS 12; CANR 57; CWW 2; DLB 232; EWL 3; RGSF 2

Hrabanus Maurus 776(?)-856 .... **CMLC 78**
See also DLB 148

Hroswitha of Gandersheim
See Hrotsvit of Gandersheim

Hrotsvit of Gandersheim c. 935-c.
1000 .... **CMLC 29, 123**
See also DLB 148

Hsi, Chu 1130-1200 .... **CMLC 42**

Hsun, Lu
See Shu-Jen, Chou

Hubbard, L. Ron 1911-1986 .... **CLC 43**
See also AAYA 64; CA 77-80, 118; CANR 52; CPW; DA3; DAM POP; FANT; MTCW 2; MTFW 2005; SFW 4

Hubbard, Lafayette Ronald
See Hubbard, L. Ron

Huch, Ricarda (Octavia)
1864-1947 .... **TCLC 13**
See also CA 111, 189; DLB 66; EWL 3

Huddle, David 1942- .... **CLC 49**
See also CA 57-60, 261; CAAS 20; CANR 89; DLB 130

Hudson, Jeffery
See Crichton, Michael

Hudson, Jeffrey
See Crichton, Michael

Hudson, W(illiam) H(enry)
1841-1922 .... **TCLC 29**
See also CA 115, 190; DLB 98, 153, 174; RGEL 2; SATA 35

Hueffer, Ford Madox
See Ford, Ford Madox

Hughart, Barry 1934- .... **CLC 39**
See also CA 137; FANT; SFW 4; SUFW 2

Hughes, Colin
See Creasey, John

Hughes, David (John) 1930-2005 ..... **CLC 48**
See also CA 116, 129, 238; CN 4, 5, 6, 7; DLB 14

Hughes, Edward James
See Hughes, Ted

Hughes, James Langston
See Hughes, Langston

Hughes, Langston 1902-1967 .... **BLC 1:2; CLC 1, 5, 10, 15, 35, 44, 108; DC 3; HR 1:2; PC 1, 53; SSC 6, 90; WLC 3**
See also AAYA 12; AFAW 1, 2; AMWR 1; AMWS 1; BW 1, 3; CA 1-4R, 25-28R; CANR 1, 34, 82; CDALB 1929-1941; CLR 17; DA; DA3; DAB; DAC; DAM DRAM, MST, MULT, POET; DFS 6, 18; DLB 4, 7, 48, 51, 86, 228, 315; EWL 3; EXPP; EXPS; JRDA; LAIT 3; LMFS 2;

MAICYA 1, 2; MAL 5; MTCW 1, 2; MTFW 2005; NFS 21; PAB; PFS 1, 3, 6, 10, 15, 30; RGAL 4; RGSF 2; SATA 4, 33; SSFS 4, 7, 29; TUS; WCH; WP; YAW

Hughes, Richard (Arthur Warren)
1900-1976 .... **CLC 1, 11; TCLC 204**
See also CA 5-8R; 65-68; CANR 4; CN 1, 2; DAM NOV; DLB 15, 161; EWL 3; MTCW 1; RGEL 2; SATA 8; SATA-Obit 25

Hughes, Ted 1930-1998 . **CLC 2, 4, 9, 14, 37, 119; PC 7, 89**
See also BRWC 2; BRWR 2; BRWS 1; CA 1-4R, 171; CANR 1, 33, 66, 108; CLR 3, 131; CP 1, 2, 3, 4, 5, 6; DA3; DAB; DAC; DAM MST, POET; DLB 40, 161; EWL 3; EXPP; MAICYA 1, 2; MTCW 1, 2; MTFW 2005; PAB; PFS 4, 19, 32; RGEL 2; SATA 49; SATA-Brief 27; SATA-Obit 107; TEA; YAW

Hughes, Thomas 1822-1896 .... **NCLC 207**
See also BYA 3; DLB 18, 163; LAIT 2; RGEL 2; SATA 31

Hugo, Richard
See Huch, Ricarda (Octavia)

Hugo, Richard F(ranklin)
1923-1982 .... **CLC 6, 18, 32; PC 68**
See also AMWS 6; CA 49-52, 108; CANR 3; CP 1, 2, 3; DAM POET; DLB 5, 206; EWL 3; MAL 5; PFS 17; RGAL 4

Hugo, Victor 1802-1885 ..... **DC 38; NCLC 3, 10, 21, 161, 189; PC 17; WLC 3**
See also AAYA 28; DA; DA3; DAB; DAC; DAM DRAM, MST, NOV, POET; DLB 119, 192, 217; EFS 2; EW 6; EXPN; GFL 1789 to the Present; LAIT 1, 2; NFS 5, 20; RGWL 2, 3; SATA 47; TWA

Hugo, Victor Marie
See Hugo, Victor

Huidobro, Vicente
See Huidobro Fernandez, Vicente Garcia

Huidobro Fernandez, Vicente Garcia
1893-1948 .... **TCLC 31**
See also CA 131; DLB 283; EWL 3; HW 1; LAW

Hulme, Keri 1947- .... **CLC 39, 130**
See also CA 125; CANR 69; CN 4, 5, 6, 7; CP 6, 7; CWP; DLB 326; EWL 3; FW; INT CA-125; NFS 24

Hulme, T(homas) E(rnest)
1883-1917 .... **TCLC 21**
See also BRWS 6; CA 117, 203; DLB 19

Humboldt, Alexander von
1769-1859 .... **NCLC 170**
See also DLB 90

Humboldt, Wilhelm von
1767-1835 .... **NCLC 134**
See also DLB 90

Hume, David 1711-1776 .. **LC 7, 56, 156, 157**
See also BRWS 3; DLB 104, 252, 336; LMFS 1; TEA

Humphrey, William 1924-1997 .... **CLC 45**
See also AMWS 9; CA 77-80, 160; CANR 68; CN 1, 2, 3, 4, 5, 6; CSW; DLB 6, 212, 234, 278; TCWW 1, 2

Humphreys, Emyr Owen 1919- .... **CLC 47**
See also CA 5-8R; CANR 3, 24; CN 1, 2, 3, 4, 5, 6, 7; DLB 15

Humphreys, Josephine 1945- ..... **CLC 34, 57**
See also CA 121, 127; CANR 97; CSW; DLB 292; INT CA-127

Huneker, James Gibbons
1860-1921 .... **TCLC 65**
See also CA 193; DLB 71; RGAL 4

Hungerford, Hesba Fay
See Brinsmead, H(esba) F(ay)

Hungerford, Pixie
See Brinsmead, H(esba) F(ay)

Hunt, E. Howard 1918-2007 .... **CLC 3**
See also AITN 1; CA 45-48, 256; CANR 2, 47, 103, 160; CMW 4

Hunt, Everette Howard, Jr.
See Hunt, E. Howard

Hunt, Francesca
See Holland, Isabelle (Christian)

Hunt, Howard
See Hunt, E. Howard

Hunt, Kyle
See Creasey, John

Hunt, (James Henry) Leigh
1784-1859 .... **NCLC 1, 70; PC 73**
See also DAM POET; DLB 96, 110, 144; RGEL 2; TEA

Hunt, Marsha 1946- .... **CLC 70**
See also BW 2, 3; CA 143; CANR 79

Hunt, Violet 1866(?)-1942 .... **TCLC 53**
See also CA 184; DLB 162, 197

Hunter, E. Waldo
See Sturgeon, Theodore (Hamilton)

Hunter, Evan 1926-2005 .... **CLC 11, 31**
See also AAYA 39; BPFB 2; CA 5-8R, 241; CANR 5, 38, 62, 97, 149; CMW 4; CN 1, 2, 3, 4, 5, 6, 7; CPW; DAM POP; DLB 306; DLBY 1982; INT CANR-5; MSW; MTCW 1; SATA 25; SATA-Obit 167; SFW 4

Hunter, Kristin
See Lattany, Kristin Hunter

Hunter, Mary
See Austin, Mary Hunter

Hunter, Mollie 1922- .... **CLC 21**
See also AAYA 13, 71; BYA 6; CANR 37, 78; CLR 25; DLB 161; JRDA; MAICYA 1, 2; SAAS 7; SATA 2, 54, 106, 139; SATA-Essay 139; WYA; YAW

Hunter, Robert (?)-1734 .... **LC 7**

Hurston, Zora Neale 1891-1960 ..... **BLC 1:2; CLC 7, 30, 61; DC 12; HR 1:2; SSC 4, 80; TCLC 121, 131; WLCS**
See also AAYA 15, 71; AFAW 1, 2; AMWS 6; BW 1, 3; BYA 12; CA 85-88; CANR 61; CDALBS; DA; DA3; DAC; DAM MST, MULT, NOV; DFS 6; DLB 51, 86; EWL 3; EXPN; EXPS; FL 1:6; FW; LAIT 3; LATS 1:1; LMFS 2; MAL 5; MBL; MTCW 1, 2; MTFW 2005; NFS 3; RGAL 4; RGSF 2; SSFS 1, 6, 11, 19, 21; TUS; YAW

Husserl, E. G.
See Husserl, Edmund (Gustav Albrecht)

Husserl, Edmund (Gustav Albrecht)
1859-1938 .... **TCLC 100**
See also CA 116, 133; DLB 296

Huston, John (Marcellus)
1906-1987 .... **CLC 20**
See also CA 73-76, 123; CANR 34; DLB 26

Hustvedt, Siri 1955- .... **CLC 76**
See also CA 137; CANR 149, 191

Hutcheson, Francis 1694-1746 .... **LC 157**
See also DLB 252

Hutchinson, Lucy 1620-1675 .... **LC 149**

Hutten, Ulrich von 1488-1523 .... **LC 16**
See also DLB 179

Huxley, Aldous 1894-1963 . **CLC 1, 3, 4, 5, 8, 11, 18, 35, 79; SSC 39; WLC 3**
See also AAYA 11; BPFB 2; BRW 7; CA 85-88; CANR 44, 99; CDBLB 1914-1945; CLR 151; DA; DA3; DAB; DAC; DAM MST, NOV; DLB 36, 100, 162, 195, 255; EWL 3; EXPN; LAIT 5; LMFS 2; MTCW 1, 2; MTFW 2005; NFS 6; RGEL 2; SATA 63; SCFW 1, 2; SFW 4; TEA; YAW

Huxley, Aldous Leonard
See Huxley, Aldous

Huxley, T(homas) H(enry)
1825-1895 .... **NCLC 67**
See also DLB 57; TEA

Huygens, Constantijn 1596-1687 .... **LC 114**
See also RGWL 2, 3

Huysmans, Joris-Karl 1848-1907 ... **TCLC 7, 69, 212**
See also CA 104, 165; DLB 123; EW 7; GFL 1789 to the Present; LMFS 2; RGWL 2, 3

Hwang, David Henry 1957- .... **CLC 55, 196; DC 4, 23**
See also CA 127, 132; CAD; CANR 76, 124; CD 5, 6; DA3; DAM DRAM; DFS 11, 18; DLB 212, 228, 312; INT CA-132; MAL 5; MTCW 2; MTFW 2005; RGAL 4

Hyatt, Daniel
See James, Daniel (Lewis)

Hyde, Anthony 1946- .... **CLC 42**
See also CA 136; CCA 1

Hyde, Margaret O. 1917- .... **CLC 21**
See also CA 1-4R; CANR 1, 36, 137, 181; CLR 23; JRDA; MAICYA 1, 2; SAAS 8; SATA 1, 42, 76, 139

Hyde, Margaret Oldroyd
See Hyde, Margaret O.

Hynes, James 1956(?)- .... **CLC 65**
See also CA 164; CANR 105

Hypatia c. 370-415 .... **CMLC 35**

Ian, Janis 1951- .... **CLC 21**
See also CA 105, 187; CANR 206

Ibanez, Vicente Blasco
See Blasco Ibanez, Vicente

Ibarbourou, Juana de
1895(?)-1979 .... **HLCS 2**
See also DLB 290; HW 1; LAW

Ibarguengoitia, Jorge 1928-1983 ..... **CLC 37; TCLC 148**
See also CA 124, 113; EWL 3; HW 1

Ibn Arabi 1165-1240 .... **CMLC 105**

Ibn Battuta, Abu Abdalla
1304-1368(?) .... **CMLC 57**
See also WLIT 2

Ibn Hazm 994-1064 .... **CMLC 64**

Ibn Zaydun 1003-1070 .... **CMLC 89**

Ibsen, Henrik 1828-1906 .... **DC 2, 30; TCLC 2, 8, 16, 37, 52; WLC 3**
See also AAYA 46; CA 104, 141; DA; DA3; DAB; DAC; DAM DRAM, MST; DFS 1, 6, 8, 10, 11, 15, 16, 25; DLB 354; EW 7; LAIT 2; LATS 1:1; MTFW 2005; RGWL 2, 3

Ibsen, Henrik Johan
See Ibsen, Henrik

Ibuse, Masuji 1898-1993 .... **CLC 22**
See also CA 127, 141; CWW 2; DLB 180; EWL 3; MJW; RGWL 3

Ibuse Masuji
See Ibuse, Masuji

Ichikawa, Kon 1915-2008 .... **CLC 20**
See also CA 121, 269

Ichiyo, Higuchi 1872-1896 .... **NCLC 49**
See also MJW

Idle, Eric 1943- .... **CLC 21**
See also CA 116; CANR 35, 91, 148; DLB 352

Idris, Yusuf 1927-1991 ... **SSC 74; TCLC 232**
See also AFW; DLB 346; EWL 3; RGSF 2, 3; RGWL 3; WLIT 2

Ignatieff, Michael 1947- .... **CLC 236**
See also CA 144; CANR 88, 156; CN 6, 7; DLB 267

Ignatieff, Michael Grant
See Ignatieff, Michael

Jakes, John William
  See Jakes, John
James I 1394-1437 .... **LC 20**
  See also RGEL 2
James, Alice 1848-1892 .... **NCLC 206**
  See also DLB 221
James, Andrew
  See Kirkup, James
James, C(yril) L(ionel) R(obert)
  1901-1989 .... **BLCS; CLC 33**
  See also BW 2; CA 117, 125, 128; CANR
  62; CN 1, 2, 3, 4; DLB 125; MTCW 1
James, Daniel (Lewis) 1911-1988 ..... **CLC 33**
  See also CA 174, 125; DLB 122
James, Dynely
  See Mayne, William
James, Henry Sr. 1811-1882 .... **NCLC 53**
James, Henry 1843-1916 .... **SSC 8, 32, 47,**
  108; TCLC 2, 11, 24, 40, 47, 64, 171;
  WLC 3
  See also AAYA 84; AMW; AMWC 1;
  AMWR 1; BPFB 2; BRW 6; CA 104, 132;
  CDALB 1865-1917; DA; DA3; DAB;
  DAC; DAM MST, NOV; DLB 12, 71, 74,
  189; DLBD 13; EWL 3; EXPS; GL 2;
  HGG; LAIT 2; MAL 5; MTCW 1, 2;
  MTFW 2005; NFS 12, 16, 19, 32; RGAL
  4; RGEL 2; RGSF 2; SSFS 9; SUFW 1;
  TUS
James, M. R.
  See James, Montague
James, Mary
  See Meaker, Marijane
James, Montague 1862-1936 ...... **SSC 16, 93;**
  TCLC 6
  See also CA 104, 203; DLB 156, 201;
  HGG; RGEL 2; RGSF 2; SUFW 1
James, Montague Rhodes
  See James, Montague
James, P. D. 1920- .... **CLC 18, 46, 122, 226**
  See also BEST 90:2; BPFB 2; BRWS 4;
  CA 21-24R; CANR 17, 43, 65, 112, 201;
  CDBLB 1960 to Present; CMW 4; CN 4,
  5, 6, 7; CPW; DA3; DAM POP; DLB 87,
  276; DLBD 17; MSW; MTCW 1, 2;
  MTFW 2005; TEA
James, Philip
  See Moorcock, Michael
James, Samuel
  See Stephens, James
James, Seumas
  See Stephens, James
James, Stephen
  See Stephens, James
James, T. F.
  See Fleming, Thomas
James, William 1842-1910 .... **TCLC 15, 32**
  See also AMW; CA 109, 193; DLB 270,
  284; MAL 5; NCFS 5; RGAL 4
Jameson, Anna 1794-1860 .... **NCLC 43**
  See also DLB 99, 166
Jameson, Fredric 1934- .... **CLC 142**
  See also CA 196; CANR 169; DLB 67;
  LMFS 2
Jameson, Fredric R.
  See Jameson, Fredric
James VI of Scotland 1566-1625 .... **LC 109**
  See also DLB 151, 172
Jami, Nur al-Din 'Abd al-Rahman
  1414-1492 .... **LC 9**
Jammes, Francis 1868-1938 .... **TCLC 75**
  See also CA 198; EWL 3; GFL 1789 to the
  Present
Jandl, Ernst 1925-2000 .... **CLC 34**
  See also CA 200; EWL 3
Janowitz, Tama 1957- .... **CLC 43, 145**
  See also CA 106; CANR 52, 89, 129; CN
  5, 6, 7; CPW; DAM POP; DLB 292;
  MTFW 2005

Jansson, Tove (Marika) 1914-2001 ... **SSC 96**
  See also CA 17-20R, 196; CANR 38, 118;
  CLR 2, 125; CWW 2; DLB 257; EWL 3;
  MAICYA 1, 2; RGSF 2; SATA 3, 41
Japrisot, Sebastien 1931-
  See Rossi, Jean-Baptiste
Jarrell, Randall 1914-1965 .... **CLC 1, 2, 6, 9,**
  13, 49; PC 41; TCLC 177
  See also AMW; BYA 5; CA 5-8R, 25-28R;
  CABS 2; CANR 6, 34; CDALB 1941-
  1968; CLR 6, 111; CWRI 5; DAM POET;
  DLB 48, 52; EWL 3; EXPP; MAICYA 1,
  2; MAL 5; MTCW 1, 2; PAB; PFS 2, 31;
  RGAL 4; SATA 7
Jarry, Alfred 1873-1907 .... **SSC 20; TCLC 2,**
  14, 147
  See also CA 104, 153; DA3; DAM DRAM;
  DFS 8; DLB 192, 258; EW 9; EWL 3;
  GFL 1789 to the Present; RGWL 2, 3;
  TWA
Jarvis, E.K.
  See Ellison, Harlan; Silverberg, Robert
Jawien, Andrzej
  See John Paul II, Pope
Jaynes, Roderick
  See Coen, Ethan
Jeake, Samuel, Jr.
  See Aiken, Conrad
Jean-Louis
  See Kerouac, Jack
Jean Paul 1763-1825 .... **NCLC 7**
Jefferies, (John) Richard
  1848-1887 .... **NCLC 47**
  See also BRWS 5; DLB 98, 141; RGEL 2;
  SATA 16; SFW 4
Jeffers, John Robinson
  See Jeffers, Robinson
Jeffers, Robinson 1887-1962 .... **CLC 2, 3, 11,**
  15, 54; PC 17; WLC 3
  See also AMWS 2; CA 85-88; CANR 35;
  CDALB 1917-1929; DA; DAC; DAM
  MST, POET; DLB 45, 212, 342; EWL 3;
  MAL 5; MTCW 1, 2; MTFW 2005; PAB;
  PFS 3, 4; RGAL 4
Jefferson, Janet
  See Mencken, H. L.
Jefferson, Thomas 1743-1826 . **NCLC 11, 103**
  See also AAYA 54; ANW; CDALB 1640-
  1865; DA3; DLB 31, 183; LAIT 1; RGAL
  4
Jeffrey, Francis 1773-1850 .... **NCLC 33**
  See also DLB 107
Jelakowitch, Ivan
  See Heijermans, Herman
Jelinek, Elfriede 1946- .... **CLC 169**
  See also AAYA 68; CA 154; CANR 169;
  DLB 85, 330; FW
Jellicoe, (Patricia) Ann 1927- .... **CLC 27**
  See also CA 85-88; CBD; CD 5, 6; CWD;
  CWRI 5; DLB 13, 233; FW
Jelloun, Tahar ben
  See Ben Jelloun, Tahar
Jemyma
  See Holley, Marietta
Jen, Gish 1955- .... **AAL; CLC 70, 198, 260**
  See also AMWC 2; CA 135; CANR 89,
  130; CN 7; DLB 312; NFS 30
Jen, Lillian
  See Jen, Gish
Jenkins, (John) Robin 1912- .... **CLC 52**
  See also CA 1-4R; CANR 1, 135; CN 1, 2,
  3, 4, 5, 6, 7; DLB 14, 271
Jennings, Elizabeth (Joan)
  1926-2001 .... **CLC 5, 14, 131**
  See also BRWS 5; CA 61-64, 200; CAAS
  5; CANR 8, 39, 66, 127; CP 1, 2, 3, 4, 5,
  6, 7; CWP; DLB 27; EWL 3; MTCW 1;
  SATA 66

Jennings, Waylon 1937-2002 .... **CLC 21**
Jensen, Johannes V(ilhelm)
  1873-1950 .... **TCLC 41**
  See also CA 170; DLB 214, 330; EWL 3;
  RGWL 3
Jensen, Laura 1948- .... **CLC 37**
  See also CA 103
Jensen, Laura Linnea
  See Jensen, Laura
Jensen, Wilhelm 1837-1911 .... **SSC 140**
Jerome, Saint 345-420 .... **CMLC 30**
  See also RGWL 3
Jerome, Jerome K(lapka)
  1859-1927 .... **TCLC 23**
  See also CA 119, 177; DLB 10, 34, 135;
  RGEL 2
Jerrold, Douglas William
  1803-1857 .... **NCLC 2**
  See also DLB 158, 159, 344; RGEL 2
Jewett, Sarah Orne 1849-1909 ..... **SSC 6, 44,**
  110, 138; TCLC 1, 22
  See also AAYA 76; AMW; AMWC 2;
  AMWR 2; CA 108, 127; CANR 71; DLB
  12, 74, 221; EXPS; FL 1:3; FW; MAL 5;
  MBL; NFS 15; RGAL 4; RGSF 2; SATA
  15; SSFS 4
Jewett, Theodora Sarah Orne
  See Jewett, Sarah Orne
Jewsbury, Geraldine (Endsor)
  1812-1880 .... **NCLC 22**
  See also DLB 21
Jhabvala, Ruth Prawer 1927- . **CLC 4, 8, 29,**
  94, 138, 284; SSC 91
  See also BRWS 5; CA 1-4R; CANR 2, 29,
  51, 74, 91, 128; CN 1, 2, 3, 4, 5, 6, 7;
  DAB; DAM NOV; DLB 139, 194, 323,
  326; EWL 3; IDFW 3, 4; INT CANR-29;
  MTCW 1, 2; MTFW 2005; RGSF 2;
  RGWL 2; RHW; TEA
Jibran, Kahlil
  See Gibran, Kahlil
Jibran, Khalil
  See Gibran, Kahlil
Jiles, Paulette 1943- .... **CLC 13, 58**
  See also CA 101; CANR 70, 124, 170; CP
  5; CWP
Jimenez, Juan Ramon 1881-1958 ..... **HLC 1;**
  PC 7; TCLC 4, 183
  See also CA 104, 131; CANR 74; DAM
  MULT, POET; DLB 134, 330; EW 9;
  EWL 3; HW 1; MTCW 1, 2; MTFW
  2005; RGWL 2, 3
Jimenez, Ramon
  See Jimenez, Juan Ramon
Jimenez Mantecon, Juan
  See Jimenez, Juan Ramon
Jimenez Mantecon, Juan Ramon
  See Jimenez, Juan Ramon
Jin, Ba 1904-2005 .... **CLC 18**
  See Cantu, Robert Clark
  See also CA 105, 244; CWW 2; DLB 328;
  EWL 3
Jin, Ha
  See Jin, Xuefei
Jin, Xuefei 1956- .... **CLC 109, 262**
  See also AMWS 18; CA 152; CANR 91,
  130, 184; DLB 244, 292; MTFW 2005;
  NFS 25; SSFS 17
Jin Ha
  See Jin, Xuefei
Jodelle, Etienne 1532-1573 .... **LC 119**
  See also DLB 327; GFL Beginnings to 1789
Joel, Billy
  See Joel, William Martin
Joel, William Martin 1949- .... **CLC 26**
  See also CA 108
John, St.
  See John of Damascus, St.

Jorgenson, Ivar
See Silverberg, Robert
Joseph, George Ghevarughese CLC 70
Josephson, Mary
See O'Doherty, Brian
Josephus, Flavius c. 37-100 ..... CMLC 13, 93
See also AW 2; DLB 176; WLIT 8
Josh
See Twain, Mark
Josiah Allen's Wife
See Holley, Marietta
Josipovici, Gabriel 1940- ...... CLC 6, 43, 153
See also CA 37-40R, 224; CAAE 224;
CAAS 8; CANR 47, 84; CN 3, 4, 5, 6, 7;
DLB 14, 319
Josipovici, Gabriel David
See Josipovici, Gabriel
Joubert, Joseph 1754-1824 .... NCLC 9
Jouve, Pierre Jean 1887-1976 .... CLC 47
See also CA 252; 65-68; DLB 258; EWL 3
Jovine, Francesco 1902-1950 .... TCLC 79
See also DLB 264; EWL 3
Joyaux, Julia
See Kristeva, Julia
Joyce, James 1882-1941 .... DC 16; PC 22;
SSC 3, 26, 44, 64, 118, 122; TCLC 3, 8,
16, 35, 52, 159; WLC 3
See also AAYA 42; BRW 7; BRWC 1;
BRWR 3; BYA 11, 13; CA 104, 126; CD-
BLB 1914-1945; DA; DA3; DAB; DAC;
DAM MST, NOV, POET; DLB 10, 19,
36, 162, 247; EWL 3; EXPN; EXPS;
LAIT 3; LMFS 1, 2; MTCW 1, 2; MTFW
2005; NFS 7, 26; RGSF 2; SSFS 1, 19;
TEA; WLIT 4
Joyce, James Augustine Aloysius
See Joyce, James
Jozsef, Attila 1905-1937 .... TCLC 22
See also CA 116, 230; CDWLB 4; DLB
215; EWL 3
Juana Ines de la Cruz, Sor
1651(?)-1695 ... HLCS 1; LC 5, 136; PC
24
See also DLB 305; FW; LAW; RGWL 2, 3;
WLIT 1
Juana Inez de La Cruz, Sor
See Juana Ines de la Cruz, Sor
Juan Manuel, Don 1282-1348 .... CMLC 88
Judd, Cyril
See Kornbluth, C(yril) M.; Pohl, Frederik
Juenger, Ernst 1895-1998 .... CLC 125
See also CA 101, 167; CANR 21, 47, 106;
CDWLB 2; DLB 56; EWL 3; RGWL 2, 3
Julian of Norwich 1342(?)-1416(?) . LC 6, 52
See also BRWS 12; DLB 146; LMFS 1
Julius Caesar 100B.C.-44B.C. .... CMLC 47
See also AW 1; CDWLB 1; DLB 211;
RGWL 2, 3; WLIT 8
Jung, Patricia B.
See Hope, Christopher
Junger, Ernst
See Juenger, Ernst
Junger, Sebastian 1962- .... CLC 109
See also AAYA 28; CA 165; CANR 130,
171; MTFW 2005
Juniper, Alex
See Hospital, Janette Turner
Junius
See Luxemburg, Rosa
Junzaburo, Nishiwaki
See Nishiwaki, Junzaburo
Just, Ward 1935- .... CLC 4, 27
See also CA 25-28R; CANR 32, 87; CN 6,
7; DLB 335; INT CANR-32
Just, Ward Swift
See Just, Ward

Justice, Donald 1925-2004 ... CLC 6, 19, 102;
PC 64
See also AMWS 7; CA 5-8R, 230; CANR
26, 54, 74, 121, 122, 169; CP 1, 2, 3, 4,
5, 6, 7; CSW; DAM POET; DLBY 1983;
EWL 3; INT CANR-26; MAL 5; MTCW
2; PFS 14; TCLE 1:1
Justice, Donald Rodney
See Justice, Donald
Juvenal c. 55-c. 127 .... CMLC 8, 115
See also AW 2; CDWLB 1; DLB 211;
RGWL 2, 3; WLIT 8
Juvenis
See Bourne, Randolph S(illiman)
K., Alice
See Knapp, Caroline
Kabakov, Sasha CLC 59
Kabir 1398(?)-1448(?) .... LC 109; PC 56
See also RGWL 2, 3
Kacew, Romain 1914-1980 .... CLC 25
See also CA 108, 102; DLB 83, 299; RGHL
Kacew, Roman
See Kacew, Romain
Kadare, Ismail 1936- .... CLC 52, 190
See also CA 161; CANR 165; DLB 353;
EWL 3; RGWL 3
Kadohata, Cynthia 1956(?)- ..... CLC 59, 122
See also AAYA 71; CA 140; CANR 124,
205; CLR 121; LNFS 1; SATA 155, 180
Kadohata, Cynthia L.
See Kadohata, Cynthia
Kafka, Franz 1883-1924 ... SSC 5, 29, 35, 60,
128; TCLC 2, 6, 13, 29, 47, 53, 112,
179; WLC 3
See also AAYA 31; BPFB 2; CA 105, 126;
CDWLB 2; DA; DA3; DAB; DAC; DAM
MST, NOV; DLB 81; EW 9; EWL 3;
EXPS; LATS 1:1; LMFS 2; MTCW 1, 2;
MTFW 2005; NFS 7, 34; RGSF 2; RGWL
2, 3; SFW 4; SSFS 3, 7, 12; TWA
Kafu
See Nagai, Kafu
Kahanovitch, Pinchas
See Der Nister
Kahanovitsch, Pinkhes
See Der Nister
Kahanovitsh, Pinkhes
See Der Nister
Kahn, Roger 1927- .... CLC 30
See also CA 25-28R; CANR 44, 69, 152;
DLB 171; SATA 37
Kain, Saul
See Sassoon, Siegfried
Kaiser, Georg 1878-1945 .... TCLC 9, 220
See also CA 106, 190; CDWLB 2; DLB
124; EWL 3; LMFS 2; RGWL 2, 3
Kaledin, Sergei CLC 59
Kaletski, Alexander 1946- .... CLC 39
See also CA 118, 143
Kalidasa fl. c. 400-455 .... CMLC 9; PC 22
See also RGWL 2, 3
Kallman, Chester (Simon)
1921-1975 .... CLC 2
See also CA 45-48; 53-56; CANR 3; CP 1,
2
Kaminsky, Melvin CLC 12, 217
See Brooks, Mel
See also AAYA 13, 48; DLB 26
Kaminsky, Stuart
See Kaminsky, Stuart M.
Kaminsky, Stuart M. 1934-2009 ...... CLC 59
See also CA 73-76, 292; CANR 29, 53, 89,
161, 190; CMW 4
Kaminsky, Stuart Melvin
See Kaminsky, Stuart M.
Kamo no Chomei 1153(?)-1216 .... CMLC 66
See also DLB 203

Kamo no Nagaakira
See Kamo no Chomei
Kandinsky, Wassily 1866-1944 .... TCLC 92
See also AAYA 64; CA 118, 155
Kane, Francis
See Robbins, Harold
Kane, Paul
See Simon, Paul
Kane, Sarah 1971-1999 .... DC 31
See also BRWS 8; CA 190; CD 5, 6; DLB
310
Kanin, Garson 1912-1999 .... CLC 22
See also AITN 1; CA 5-8R, 177; CAD;
CANR 7, 78; DLB 7; IDFW 3, 4
Kaniuk, Yoram 1930- .... CLC 19
See also CA 134; DLB 299; RGHL
Kant, Immanuel 1724-1804 ..... NCLC 27, 67
See also DLB 94
Kantor, MacKinlay 1904-1977 .... CLC 7
See also CA 61-64; 73-76; CANR 60, 63;
CN 1, 2; DLB 9, 102; MAL 5; MTCW 2;
RHW; TCWW 1, 2
Kanze Motokiyo
See Zeami
Kaplan, David Michael 1946- .... CLC 50
See also CA 187
Kaplan, James 1951- .... CLC 59
See also CA 135; CANR 121
Karadzic, Vuk Stefanovic
1787-1864 .... NCLC 115
See also CDWLB 4; DLB 147
Karageorge, Michael
See Anderson, Poul
Karamzin, Nikolai Mikhailovich
1766-1826 .... NCLC 3, 173
See also DLB 150; RGSF 2
Karapanou, Margarita 1946- .... CLC 13
See also CA 101
Karinthy, Frigyes 1887-1938 .... TCLC 47
See also CA 170; DLB 215; EWL 3
Karl, Frederick R(obert)
1927-2004 .... CLC 34
See also CA 5-8R, 226; CANR 3, 44, 143
Karr, Mary 1955- .... CLC 188
See also AMWS 11; CA 151; CANR 100,
191; MTFW 2005; NCFS 5
Kastel, Warren
See Silverberg, Robert
Kataev, Evgeny Petrovich
1903-1942 .... TCLC 21
See also CA 120; DLB 272
Kataphusin
See Ruskin, John
Katz, Steve 1935- .... CLC 47
See also CA 25-28R; CAAS 14, 64; CANR
12; CN 4, 5, 6, 7; DLBY 1983
Kauffman, Janet 1945- .... CLC 42
See also CA 117; CANR 43, 84; DLB 218;
DLBY 1986
Kaufman, Bob (Garnell)
1925-1986 .... CLC 49; PC 74
See also BG 1:3; BW 1; CA 41-44R, 118;
CANR 22; CP 1; DLB 16, 41
Kaufman, George S. 1889-1961 ...... CLC 38;
DC 17
See also CA 108; 93-96; DAM DRAM;
DFS 1, 10; DLB 7; INT CA-108; MTCW
2; MTFW 2005; RGAL 4; TUS
Kaufman, Moises 1963- .... DC 26
See also CA 211; DFS 22; MTFW 2005
Kaufman, Sue
See Barondess, Sue K.
Kavafis, Konstantinos Petrov
See Cavafy, Constantine
Kavan, Anna 1901-1968 .... CLC 5, 13, 82
See also BRWS 7; CA 5-8R; CANR 6, 57;
DLB 255; MTCW 1; RGEL 2; SFW 4

Author Index

Kristofferson, Kris 1936- .... **CLC 26**
  See also CA 104
Krizanc, John 1956- .... **CLC 57**
  See also CA 187
Krleza, Miroslav 1893-1981 .... **CLC 8, 114**
  See also CA 97-100, 105; CANR 50; CD-
  WLB 4; DLB 147; EW 11; RGWL 2, 3
Kroetsch, Robert (Paul) 1927- .... **CLC 5, 23,**
  57, 132, 286
  See also CA 17-20R; CANR 8, 38; CCA 1;
  CN 2, 3, 4, 5, 6, 7; CP 6, 7; DAC; DAM
  POET; DLB 53; MTCW 1
Kroetz, Franz
  See Kroetz, Franz Xaver
Kroetz, Franz Xaver 1946- .... **CLC 41**
  See also CA 130; CANR 142; CWW 2;
  EWL 3
Kroker, Arthur (W.) 1945- .... **CLC 77**
  See also CA 161
Kroniuk, Lisa
  See Berton, Pierre (Francis de Marigny)
Kropotkin, Peter 1842-1921 .... **TCLC 36**
  See also CA 119, 219; DLB 277
Kropotkin, Peter Aleksieevich
  See Kropotkin, Peter
Kropotkin, Petr Alekseevich
  See Kropotkin, Peter
Krotkov, Yuri 1917-1981 .... **CLC 19**
  See also CA 102
Krumb
  See Crumb, R.
Krumgold, Joseph (Quincy)
  1908-1980 .... **CLC 12**
  See also BYA 1, 2; CA 9-12R, 101; CANR
  7; MAICYA 1, 2; SATA 1, 48; SATA-Obit
  23; YAW
Krumwitz
  See Crumb, R.
Krutch, Joseph Wood 1893-1970 ..... **CLC 24**
  See also ANW; CA 1-4R, 25-28R; CANR
  4; DLB 63, 206, 275
Krutzch, Gus
  See Eliot, T. S.
Krylov, Ivan Andreevich
  1768(?)-1844 .... **NCLC 1**
  See also DLB 150
Kubin, Alfred (Leopold Isidor)
  1877-1959 .... **TCLC 23**
  See also CA 112, 149; CANR 104; DLB 81
Kubrick, Stanley 1928-1999 .... **CLC 16;**
  TCLC 112
  See also AAYA 30; CA 81-84, 177; CANR
  33; DLB 26
Kueng, Hans
  See Kung, Hans
Kumin, Maxine 1925- .... **CLC 5, 13, 28, 164;**
  PC 15
  See also AITN 2; AMWS 4; ANW; CA
  1-4R, 271; CAAE 271; CAAS 8; CANR
  1, 21, 69, 115, 140; CP 2, 3, 4, 5, 6, 7;
  CWP; DA3; DAM POET; DLB 5; EWL
  3; EXPP; MTCW 1, 2; MTFW 2005;
  PAB; PFS 18; SATA 12
Kumin, Maxine Winokur
  See Kumin, Maxine
Kundera, Milan 1929- . **CLC 4, 9, 19, 32, 68,**
  115, 135, 234; SSC 24
  See also AAYA 2, 62; BPFB 2; CA 85-88;
  CANR 19, 52, 74, 144; CDWLB 4; CWW
  2; DA3; DAM NOV; DLB 232; EW 13;
  EWL 3; MTCW 1, 2; MTFW 2005; NFS
  18, 27; RGSF 2; RGWL 3; SSFS 10
Kunene, Mazisi 1930-2006 .... **CLC 85**
  See also BW 1, 3; CA 125, 252; CANR 81;
  CP 1, 6, 7; DLB 117
Kunene, Mazisi Raymond
  See Kunene, Mazisi
Kunene, Mazisi Raymond Fakazi Mngoni
  See Kunene, Mazisi

Kung, Hans
  See Kung, Hans
Kung, Hans 1928- .... **CLC 130**
  See also CA 53-56; CANR 66, 134; MTCW
  1, 2; MTFW 2005
Kunikida, Tetsuo
  See Kunikida Doppo
Kunikida Doppo 1869(?)-1908 .... **TCLC 99**
  See also DLB 180; EWL 3
Kunikida Tetsuo
  See Kunikida Doppo
Kunitz, Stanley 1905-2006 ..... **CLC 6, 11, 14,**
  148, 293; PC 19
  See also AMWS 3; CA 41-44R, 250; CANR
  26, 57, 98; CP 1, 2, 3, 4, 5, 6, 7; DA3;
  DLB 48; INT CANR-26; MAL 5; MTCW
  1, 2; MTFW 2005; PFS 11; RGAL 4
Kunitz, Stanley Jasspon
  See Kunitz, Stanley
Kunze, Reiner 1933- .... **CLC 10**
  See also CA 93-96; CWW 2; DLB 75; EWL
  3
Kuprin, Aleksander Ivanovich
  1870-1938 .... **TCLC 5**
  See also CA 104, 182; DLB 295; EWL 3
Kuprin, Aleksandr Ivanovich
  See Kuprin, Aleksander Ivanovich
Kuprin, Alexandr Ivanovich
  See Kuprin, Aleksander Ivanovich
Kureishi, Hanif 1954- ...... **CLC 64, 135, 284;**
  DC 26
  See also BRWS 11; CA 139; CANR 113,
  197; CBD; CD 5, 6; CN 6, 7; DLB 194,
  245, 352; GLL 2; IDFW 4; WLIT 4;
  WWE 1
Kurosawa, Akira 1910-1998 ..... **CLC 16, 119**
  See also AAYA 11, 64; CA 101, 170; CANR
  46; DAM MULT
Kushner, Tony 1956- .... **CLC 81, 203; DC 10**
  See also AAYA 61; AMWS 9; CA 144;
  CAD; CANR 74, 130; CD 5, 6; DA3;
  DAM DRAM; DFS 5; DLB 228; EWL 3;
  GLL 1; LAIT 5; MAL 5; MTCW 2;
  MTFW 2005; RGAL 4; RGHL; SATA 160
Kuttner, Henry 1915-1958 .... **TCLC 10**
  See also CA 107, 157; DLB 8; FANT;
  SCFW 1, 2; SFW 4
Kutty, Madhavi
  See Das, Kamala
Kuzma, Greg 1944- .... **CLC 7**
  See also CA 33-36R; CANR 70
Kuzmin, Mikhail (Alekseevich)
  1872(?)-1936 .... **TCLC 40**
  See also CA 170; DLB 295; EWL 3
Kyd, Thomas 1558-1594 .. **DC 3; LC 22, 125**
  See also BRW 1; DAM DRAM; DFS 21;
  DLB 62; IDTP; LMFS 1; RGEL 2; TEA;
  WLIT 3
Kyprianos, Iossif
  See Samarakis, Antonis
L. S.
  See Stephen, Sir Leslie
Labe, Louise 1521-1566 .... **LC 120**
  See also DLB 327
Labrunie, Gerard
  See Nerval, Gerard de
La Bruyere, Jean de 1645-1696 .. **LC 17, 168**
  See also DLB 268; EW 3; GFL Beginnings
  to 1789
LaBute, Neil 1963- .... **CLC 225**
  See also CA 240
Lacan, Jacques (Marie Emile)
  1901-1981 .... **CLC 75**
  See also CA 121, 104; DLB 296; EWL 3;
  TWA
Laclos, Pierre-Ambroise Francois
  1741-1803 .... **NCLC 4, 87**
  See also DLB 313; EW 4; GFL Beginnings
  to 1789; RGWL 2, 3

La Colere, Francois
  See Aragon, Louis
Lacolere, Francois
  See Aragon, Louis
Lactantius c. 250-c. 325 .... **CMLC 118**
La Deshabilleuse
  See Simenon, Georges
Lady Gregory
  See Gregory, Lady Isabella Augusta (Persse)
Lady of Quality, A
  See Bagnold, Enid
La Fayette, Marie-(Madelaine Pioche de la
  Vergne) 1634-1693 .... **LC 2, 144**
  See also DLB 268; GFL Beginnings to
  1789; RGWL 2, 3
Lafayette, Marie-Madeleine
  See La Fayette, Marie-(Madelaine Pioche
  de la Vergne)
Lafayette, Rene
  See Hubbard, L. Ron
La Flesche, Francis 1857(?)-1932 ...... **NNAL**
  See also CA 144; CANR 83; DLB 175
La Fontaine, Jean de 1621-1695 . **LC 50, 184**
  See also DLB 268; EW 3; GFL Beginnings
  to 1789; MAICYA 1, 2; RGWL 2, 3;
  SATA 18
LaForet, Carmen 1921-2004 .... **CLC 219**
  See also CA 246; CWW 2; DLB 322; EWL
  3
LaForet Diaz, Carmen
  See LaForet, Carmen
Laforgue, Jules 1860-1887 .... **NCLC 5, 53,**
  221; PC 14; SSC 20
  See also DLB 217; EW 7; GFL 1789 to the
  Present; RGWL 2, 3
Lagerkvist, Paer 1891-1974 ... **CLC 7, 10, 13,**
  54; SSC 12; TCLC 144
  See also CA 85-88, 49-52; DA3; DAM
  DRAM, NOV; DLB 259, 331; EW 10;
  EWL 3; MTCW 1, 2; MTFW 2005; RGSF
  2; RGWL 2, 3; TWA
Lagerkvist, Paer Fabian
  See Lagerkvist, Paer
Lagerkvist, Par
  See Lagerkvist, Paer
Lagerloef, Selma
  See Lagerlof, Selma
Lagerloef, Selma Ottiliana Lovisa
  See Lagerlof, Selma
Lagerlof, Selma 1858-1940 .... **TCLC 4, 36**
  See also CA 108, 188; CLR 7; DLB 259,
  331; MTCW 2; RGWL 2, 3; SATA 15;
  SSFS 18
Lagerlof, Selma Ottiliana Lovisa
  See Lagerlof, Selma
La Guma, Alex 1925-1985 .. **BLCS; CLC 19;**
  TCLC 140
  See also AFW; BW 1, 3; CA 49-52, 118;
  CANR 25, 81; CDWLB 3; CN 1, 2, 3;
  CP 1; DAM NOV; DLB 117, 225; EWL
  3; MTCW 1, 2; MTFW 2005; WLIT 2;
  WWE 1
La Guma, Justin Alexander
  See La Guma, Alex
Lahiri, Jhumpa 1967- .... **CLC 282; SSC 96**
  See also AAYA 56; CA 193; CANR 134,
  184; DLB 323; MTFW 2005; NFS 31;
  SSFS 19, 27
Laidlaw, A. K.
  See Grieve, C. M.
Lainez, Manuel Mujica
  See Mujica Lainez, Manuel
Laing, R(onald) D(avid) 1927-1989 . **CLC 95**
  See also CA 107, 129; CANR 34; MTCW 1
Laishley, Alex
  See Booth, Martin

Levine, Philip 1928- .. **CLC 2, 4, 5, 9, 14, 33, 118; PC 22**
See also AMWS 5; CA 9-12R; CANR 9, 37, 52, 116, 156; CP 1, 2, 3, 4, 5, 6, 7; DAM POET; DLB 5; EWL 3; MAL 5; PFS 8

Levinson, Deirdre 1931- .... **CLC 49**
See also CA 73-76; CANR 70

Levi-Strauss, Claude 1908-2008 .... **CLC 38**
See also CA 1-4R; CANR 6, 32, 57; DLB 242; EWL 3; GFL 1789 to the Present; MTCW 1, 2; TWA

Levitin, Sonia 1934- .... **CLC 17**
See also AAYA 13, 48; CA 29-32R; CANR 14, 32, 79, 182; CLR 53; JRDA; MAI-CYA 1, 2; SAAS 2; SATA 4, 68, 119, 131, 192; SATA-Essay 131; YAW

Levon, O. U.
See Kesey, Ken

Levy, Amy 1861-1889 .... **NCLC 59, 203**
See also DLB 156, 240

Lewees, John
See Stockton, Francis Richard

Lewes, George Henry 1817-1878 .. **NCLC 25, 215**
See also DLB 55, 144

Lewis, Alun 1915-1944 .... **SSC 40; TCLC 3**
See also BRW 7; CA 104, 188; DLB 20, 162; PAB; RGEL 2

Lewis, C. Day
See Day Lewis, C.

Lewis, C. S. 1898-1963 .. **CLC 1, 3, 6, 14, 27, 124; WLC 4**
See also AAYA 3, 39; BPFB 2; BRWS 3; BYA 15, 16; CA 81-84; CANR 33, 71, 132; CDBLB 1945-1960; CLR 3, 27, 109; CWRI 5; DA; DA3; DAB; DAC; DAM MST, NOV, POP; DLB 15, 100, 160, 255; EWL 3; FANT; JRDA; LMFS 2; MAI-CYA 1, 2; MTCW 1, 2; MTFW 2005; NFS 24; RGEL 2; SATA 13, 100; SCFW 1, 2; SFW 4; SUFW 1; TEA; WCH; WYA; YAW

Lewis, Cecil Day
See Day Lewis, C.

Lewis, Clive Staples
See Lewis, C. S.

Lewis, Harry Sinclair
See Lewis, Sinclair

Lewis, Janet 1899-1998 .... **CLC 41**
See also CA 9-12R, 172; CANR 29, 63; CAP 1; CN 1, 2, 3, 4, 5, 6; DLBY 1987; RHW; TCWW 2

Lewis, Matthew Gregory 1775-1818 .... **NCLC 11, 62**
See also DLB 39, 158, 178; GL 3; HGG; LMFS 1; RGEL 2; SUFW

Lewis, Sinclair 1885-1951 ... **TCLC 4, 13, 23, 39, 215; WLC 4**
See also AMW; AMWC 1; BPFB 2; CA 104, 133; CANR 132; CDALB 1917-1929; DA; DA3; DAB; DAC; DAM MST, NOV; DLB 9, 102, 284, 331; DLBD 1; EWL 3; LAIT 3; MAL 5; MTCW 1, 2; MTFW 2005; NFS 15, 19, 22, 34; RGAL 4; TUS

Lewis, (Percy) Wyndham 1884(?)-1957 . **SSC 34; TCLC 2, 9, 104, 216**
See also AAYA 77; BRW 7; CA 104, 157; DLB 15; EWL 3; FANT; MTCW 2; MTFW 2005; RGEL 2

Lewisohn, Ludwig 1883-1955 .... **TCLC 19**
See also CA 107, 203; DLB 4, 9, 28, 102; MAL 5

Lewton, Val 1904-1951 .... **TCLC 76**
See also CA 199; IDFW 3, 4

Leyner, Mark 1956- .... **CLC 92**
See also CA 110; CANR 28, 53; DA3; DLB 292; MTCW 2; MTFW 2005

Leyton, E.K.
See Campbell, Ramsey

Lezama Lima, Jose 1910-1976 .... **CLC 4, 10, 101; HLCS 2**
See also CA 77-80; CANR 71; DAM MULT; DLB 113, 283; EWL 3; HW 1, 2; LAW; RGWL 2, 3

L'Heureux, John (Clarke) 1934- ...... **CLC 52**
See also CA 13-16R; CANR 23, 45, 88; CP 1, 2, 3, 4; DLB 244

Li, Fei-kan
See Jin, Ba

Li Ch'ing-chao 1081(?)-1141(?) .... **CMLC 71**

Lichtenberg, Georg Christoph 1742-1799 .... **LC 162**
See also DLB 94

Liddell, C. H.
See Kuttner, Henry

Lie, Jonas (Lauritz Idemil) 1833-1908(?) .... **TCLC 5**
See also CA 115

Lieber, Joel 1937-1971 .... **CLC 6**
See also CA 73-76, 29-32R

Lieber, Stanley Martin
See Lee, Stan

Lieberman, Laurence (James) 1935- .... **CLC 4, 36**
See also CA 17-20R; CANR 8, 36, 89; CP 1, 2, 3, 4, 5, 6, 7

Lieh Tzu fl. 7th cent. B.C.-5th cent. B.C. .... **CMLC 27**

Lieksman, Anders
See Haavikko, Paavo Juhani

Lifton, Robert Jay 1926- .... **CLC 67**
See also CA 17-20R; CANR 27, 78, 161; INT CANR-27; SATA 66

Lightfoot, Gordon 1938- .... **CLC 26**
See also CA 109, 242

Lightfoot, Gordon Meredith
See Lightfoot, Gordon

Lightman, Alan P. 1948- .... **CLC 81**
See also CA 141; CANR 63, 105, 138, 178; MTFW 2005; NFS 29

Lightman, Alan Paige
See Lightman, Alan P.

Ligotti, Thomas 1953- .... **CLC 44; SSC 16**
See also CA 123; CANR 49, 135; HGG; SUFW 2

Ligotti, Thomas Robert
See Ligotti, Thomas

Li Ho 791-817 .... **PC 13**

Li Ju-chen c. 1763-c. 1830 .... **NCLC 137**

Liking, Werewere 1950- .... **BLC 2:2**
See also CA 293; EWL 3

Lilar, Francoise
See Mallet-Joris, Francoise

Liliencron, Detlev
See Liliencron, Detlev von

Liliencron, Detlev von 1844-1909 .. **TCLC 18**
See also CA 117

Liliencron, Friedrich Adolf Axel Detlev von
See Liliencron, Detlev von

Liliencron, Friedrich Detlev von
See Liliencron, Detlev von

Lille, Alain de
See Alain de Lille

Lillo, George 1691-1739 .... **LC 131**
See also DLB 84; RGEL 2

Lilly, William 1602-1681 .... **LC 27**

Lima, Jose Lezama
See Lezama Lima, Jose

Lima Barreto, Afonso Henrique de 1881-1922 .... **TCLC 23**
See also CA 117, 181; DLB 307; LAW

Lima Barreto, Afonso Henriques de
See Lima Barreto, Afonso Henrique de

Limonov, Eduard
See Limonov, Edward

Limonov, Edward 1944- .... **CLC 67**
See also CA 137; DLB 317

Lin, Frank
See Atherton, Gertrude (Franklin Horn)

Lin, Yutang 1895-1976 .... **TCLC 149**
See also CA 45-48; 65-68; CANR 2; RGAL 4

Lincoln, Abraham 1809-1865 .... **NCLC 18, 201**
See also LAIT 2

Lincoln, Geoffrey
See Mortimer, John

Lind, Jakov 1927-2007 ... **CLC 1, 2, 4, 27, 82**
See also CA 9-12R, 257; CAAS 4; CANR 7; DLB 299; EWL 3; RGHL

Lindbergh, Anne Morrow 1906-2001 .... **CLC 82**
See also BPFB 2; CA 17-20R, 193; CANR 16, 73; DAM NOV; MTCW 1, 2; MTFW 2005; SATA 33; SATA-Obit 125; TUS

Lindbergh, Anne Spencer Morrow
See Lindbergh, Anne Morrow

Lindholm, Anna Margaret
See Haycraft, Anna

Lindsay, David 1878(?)-1945 .... **TCLC 15**
See also CA 113, 187; DLB 255; FANT; SFW 4; SUFW 1

Lindsay, Nicholas Vachel
See Lindsay, Vachel

Lindsay, Vachel 1879-1931 ..... **PC 23; TCLC 17; WLC 4**
See also AMWS 1; CA 114, 135; CANR 79; CDALB 1865-1917; DA; DA3; DAC; DAM MST, POET; DLB 54; EWL 3; EXPP; MAL 5; RGAL 4; SATA 40; WP

Linke-Poot
See Doeblin, Alfred

Linney, Romulus 1930- .... **CLC 51**
See also CA 1-4R; CAD; CANR 40, 44, 79; CD 5, 6; CSW; RGAL 4

Linton, Eliza Lynn 1822-1898 .... **NCLC 41**
See also DLB 18

Li Po 701-763 .... **CMLC 2, 86; PC 29**
See also PFS 20; WP

Lippard, George 1822-1854 .... **NCLC 198**
See also DLB 202

Lipsius, Justus 1547-1606 .... **LC 16**

Lipsyte, Robert 1938- .... **CLC 21**
See also AAYA 7, 45; CA 17-20R; CANR 8, 57, 146, 189; CLR 23, 76; DA; DAC; DAM MST, NOV; JRDA; LAIT 5; MAI-CYA 1, 2; NFS 35; SATA 5, 68, 113, 161, 198; WYA; YAW

Lipsyte, Robert Michael
See Lipsyte, Robert

Lish, Gordon 1934- .... **CLC 45; SSC 18**
See also CA 113, 117; CANR 79, 151; DLB 130; INT CA-117

Lish, Gordon Jay
See Lish, Gordon

Lispector, Clarice 1925(?)-1977 .... **CLC 43; HLCS 2; SSC 34, 96**
See also CA 139, 116; CANR 71; CDWLB 3; DLB 113, 307; DNFS 1; EWL 3; FW; HW 2; LAW; RGSF 2; RGWL 2, 3; WLIT 1

Liszt, Franz 1811-1886 .... **NCLC 199**

Littell, Robert 1935(?)- .... **CLC 42**
See also CA 109, 112; CANR 64, 115, 162; CMW 4

Little, Malcolm
See Malcolm X

Littlewit, Humphrey Gent.
See Lovecraft, H. P.

Litwos
See Sienkiewicz, Henryk (Adam Alexander Pius)

Liu, E. 1857-1909 .... **TCLC 15**
See also CA 115, 190; DLB 328

Lively, Penelope 1933- .... **CLC 32, 50**
See also BPFB 2; CA 41-44R; CANR 29, 67, 79, 131, 172; CLR 7; CN 5, 6, 7; CWRI 5; DAM NOV; DLB 14, 161, 207, 326; FANT; JRDA; MAICYA 1, 2; MTCW 1, 2; MTFW 2005; SATA 7, 60, 101, 164; TEA

Lively, Penelope Margaret
See Lively, Penelope

Livesay, Dorothy (Kathleen)
1909-1996 .... **CLC 4, 15, 79**
See also AITN 2; CA 25-28R; CAAS 8; CANR 36, 67; CP 1, 2, 3, 4, 5; DAC; DAM MST, POET; DLB 68; FW; MTCW 1; RGEL 2; TWA

Livius Andronicus c. 284B.C.-c.
204B.C. .... **CMLC 102**

Livy c. 59B.C.-c. 12 .... **CMLC 11**
See also AW 2; CDWLB 1; DLB 211; RGWL 2, 3; WLIT 8

Li Yaotang
See Jin, Ba

Li-Young, Lee
See Lee, Li-Young

Lizardi, Jose Joaquin Fernandez de
1776-1827 .... **NCLC 30**
See also LAW

Llewellyn, Richard
See Llewellyn Lloyd, Richard Dafydd Vivian

Llewellyn Lloyd, Richard Dafydd Vivian
1906-1983 .... **CLC 7, 80**
See also CA 53-56, 111; CANR 7, 71; DLB 15; NFS 30; SATA 11; SATA-Obit 37

Llosa, Jorge Mario Pedro Vargas
See Vargas Llosa, Mario

Llosa, Mario Vargas
See Vargas Llosa, Mario

Lloyd, Manda
See Mander, (Mary) Jane

Lloyd Webber, Andrew 1948- .... **CLC 21**
See also AAYA 1, 38; CA 116, 149; DAM DRAM; DFS 7; SATA 56

Llull, Ramon c. 1235-c. 1316 .... **CMLC 12, 114**

Lobb, Ebenezer
See Upward, Allen

Lochhead, Liz 1947- .... **CLC 286**
See also CA 81-84; CANR 79; CBD; CD 5, 6; CP 2, 3, 4, 5, 6, 7; CWD; CWP; DLB 310

Locke, Alain Leroy 1885-1954 .... **BLCS; HR 1:3; TCLC 43**
See also AMWS 14; BW 1, 3; CA 106, 124; CANR 79; DLB 51; LMFS 2; MAL 5; RGAL 4

Locke, John 1632-1704 .... **LC 7, 35, 135**
See also DLB 31, 101, 213, 252; RGEL 2; WLIT 3

Locke-Elliott, Sumner
See Elliott, Sumner Locke

Lockhart, John Gibson 1794-1854 .. **NCLC 6**
See also DLB 110, 116, 144

Lockridge, Ross (Franklin), Jr.
1914-1948 .... **TCLC 111**
See also CA 108, 145; CANR 79; DLB 143; DLBY 1980; MAL 5; RGAL 4; RHW

Lockwood, Robert
See Johnson, Robert

Lodge, David 1935- .... **CLC 36, 141, 293**
See also BEST 90:1; BRWS 4; CA 17-20R; CANR 19, 53, 92, 139, 197; CN 1, 2, 3, 4, 5, 6, 7; CPW; DAM POP; DLB 14, 194; EWL 3; INT CANR-19; MTCW 1, 2; MTFW 2005

Lodge, David John
See Lodge, David

Lodge, Thomas 1558-1625 .... **LC 41**
See also DLB 172; RGEL 2

Loewinsohn, Ron(ald William)
1937- .... **CLC 52**
See also CA 25-28R; CANR 71; CP 1, 2, 3, 4

Logan, Jake
See Smith, Martin Cruz

Logan, John (Burton) 1923-1987 .... **CLC 5**
See also CA 77-80, 124; CANR 45; CP 1, 2, 3, 4; DLB 5

Lo-Johansson, (Karl) Ivar
1901-1990 .... **TCLC 216**
See also CA 102, 131; CANR 20, 79, 137; DLB 259; EWL 3; RGWL 2, 3

Lo Kuan-chung 1330(?)-1400(?) .... **LC 12**

Lomax, Pearl
See Cleage, Pearl

Lomax, Pearl Cleage
See Cleage, Pearl

Lombard, Nap
See Johnson, Pamela Hansford

Lombard, Peter 1100(?)-1160(?) ... **CMLC 72**

Lombino, Salvatore
See Hunter, Evan

London, Jack 1876-1916 .... **SSC 4, 49, 133; TCLC 9, 15, 39; WLC 4**
See also AAYA 13, 75; AITN 2; AMW; BPFB 2; BYA 4, 13; CA 110, 119; CANR 73; CDALB 1865-1917; CLR 108; DA; DA3; DAB; DAC; DAM MST, NOV; DLB 8, 12, 78, 212; EWL 3; EXPS; JRDA; LAIT 3; MAICYA 1, 2,; MAL 5; MTCW 1, 2; MTFW 2005; NFS 8, 19, 35; RGAL 4; RGSF 2; SATA 18; SFW 4; SSFS 7; TCWW 1, 2; TUS; WYA; YAW

London, John Griffith
See London, Jack

Long, Emmett
See Leonard, Elmore

Longbaugh, Harry
See Goldman, William

Longfellow, Henry Wadsworth
1807-1882 .... **NCLC 2, 45, 101, 103; PC 30; WLCS**
See also AMW; AMWR 2; CDALB 1640-1865; CLR 99; DA; DA3; DAB; DAC; DAM MST, POET; DLB 1, 59, 235; EXPP; PAB; PFS 2, 7, 17, 31; RGAL 4; SATA 19; TUS; WP

Longinus c. 1st cent. - .... **CMLC 27**
See also AW 2; DLB 176

Longley, Michael 1939- .... **CLC 29**
See also BRWS 8; CA 102; CP 1, 2, 3, 4, 5, 6, 7; DLB 40

Longstreet, Augustus Baldwin
1790-1870 .... **NCLC 159**
See also DLB 3, 11, 74, 248; RGAL 4

Longus fl. c. 2nd cent. - .... **CMLC 7**

Longway, A. Hugh
See Lang, Andrew

Lonnbohm, Armas Eino Leopold
See Lonnbohm, Armas Eino Leopold

Lonnbohm, Armas Eino Leopold
1878-1926 .... **TCLC 24**
See also CA 123; EWL 3

Lonnrot, Elias 1802-1884 .... **NCLC 53**
See also EFS 1

Lonsdale, Roger CLC 65

Lopate, Phillip 1943- .... **CLC 29**
See also CA 97-100; CANR 88, 157, 196; DLBY 1980; INT CA-97-100

Lopez, Barry 1945- .... **CLC 70**
See also AAYA 9, 63; ANW; CA 65-68; CANR 7, 23, 47, 68, 92; DLB 256, 275, 335; INT CANR-7, CANR-23; MTCW 1; RGAL 4; SATA 67

Lopez, Barry Holstun
See Lopez, Barry

Lopez de Mendoza, Inigo
See Santillana, Inigo Lopez de Mendoza, Marques de

Lopez Portillo (y Pacheco), Jose
1920-2004 .... **CLC 46**
See also CA 129, 224; HW 1

Lopez y Fuentes, Gregorio
1897(?)-1966 .... **CLC 32**
See also CA 131; EWL 3; HW 1

Lorca, Federico Garcia
See Garcia Lorca, Federico

Lord, Audre
See Lorde, Audre

Lord, Bette Bao 1938- .... **AAL; CLC 23**
See also BEST 90:3; BPFB 2; CA 107; CANR 41, 79; CLR 151; INT CA-107; SATA 58

Lord Auch
See Bataille, Georges

Lord Brooke
See Greville, Fulke

Lord Byron 1788-1824 .... **DC 24; NCLC 2, 12, 109, 149; PC 16, 95; WLC 1**
See also AAYA 64; BRW 4; BRWC 2; CD-BLB 1789-1832; DA; DA3; DAB; DAC; DAM MST, POET; DLB 96, 110; EXPP; LMFS 1; PAB; PFS 1, 14, 29, 35; RGEL 2; TEA; WLIT 3; WP

Lord Dunsany
See Dunsany, Edward John Moreton Drax Plunkett

Lorde, Audre 1934-1992 .... **BLC 1:2, 2:2; CLC 18, 71; PC 12; TCLC 173**
See also AFAW 1, 2; BW 1, 3; CA 25-28R, 142; CANR 16, 26, 46, 82; CP 2, 3, 4, 5; DA3; DAM MULT, POET; DLB 41; EWL 3; FW; GLL 1; MAL 5; MTCW 1, 2; MTFW 2005; PFS 16, 32; RGAL 4

Lorde, Audre Geraldine
See Lorde, Audre

Lord Houghton
See Milnes, Richard Monckton

Lord Jeffrey
See Jeffrey, Francis

Loreaux, Nichol CLC 65

Lorenzo, Heberto Padilla
See Padilla (Lorenzo), Heberto

Loris
See Hofmannsthal, Hugo von

Loti, Pierre
See Viaud, Julien

Lottie
See Grimke, Charlotte L. Forten

Lou, Henri
See Andreas-Salome, Lou

Louie, David Wong 1954- .... **CLC 70**
See also CA 139; CANR 120

Louis, Adrian C. NNAL
See also CA 223

Louis, Father M.
See Merton, Thomas

Louise, Heidi
See Erdrich, Louise

Lovecraft, H. P. 1890-1937 .... **SSC 3, 52; TCLC 4, 22**
See also AAYA 14; BPFB 2; CA 104, 133; CANR 106; DA3; DAM POP; HGG; MTCW 1, 2; MTFW 2005; RGAL 4; SCFW 1, 2; SFW 4; SUFW

Lovecraft, Howard Phillips
See Lovecraft, H. P.

Lovelace, Earl 1935- .... **CLC 51; SSC 141**
See also BW 2; CA 77-80; CANR 41, 72, 114; CD 5, 6; CDWLB 3; CN 1, 2, 3, 4, 5, 6, 7; DLB 125; EWL 3; MTCW 1

Lovelace, Richard 1618-1658 ..... **LC 24, 158; PC 69**
See also BRW 2; DLB 131; EXPP; PAB; PFS 32, 34; RGEL 2

Markfield, Wallace (Arthur)
1926-2002 .... **CLC 8**
See also CA 69-72, 208; CAAS 3; CN 1, 2, 3, 4, 5, 6, 7; DLB 2, 28; DLBY 2002

Markham, Edwin 1852-1940 .... **TCLC 47**
See also CA 160; DLB 54, 186; MAL 5; RGAL 4

Markham, Robert
See Amis, Kingsley

Marks, J.
See Highwater, Jamake (Mamake)

Marks-Highwater, J.
See Highwater, Jamake (Mamake)

Markson, David M. 1927-2010 .... **CLC 67**
See also AMWS 17; CA 49-52; CANR 1, 91, 158; CN 5, 6

Markson, David Merrill
See Markson, David M.

Marlatt, Daphne (Buckle) 1942- .... **CLC 168**
See also CA 25-28R; CANR 17, 39; CN 6, 7; CP 4, 5, 6, 7; CWP; DLB 60; FW

Marley, Bob
See Marley, Robert Nesta

Marley, Robert Nesta 1945-1981 ...... **CLC 17**
See also CA 107, 103

Marlowe, Christopher 1564-1593 . **DC 1; LC 22, 47, 117; PC 57; WLC 4**
See also BRW 1; BRWR 1; CDBLB Before 1660; DA; DA3; DAB; DAC; DAM DRAM, MST; DFS 1, 5, 13, 21; DLB 62; EXPP; LMFS 1; PFS 22; RGEL 2; TEA; WLIT 3

Marlowe, Stephen 1928-2008 .... **CLC 70**
See also CA 13-16R, 269; CANR 6, 55; CMW 4; SFW 4

Marmion, Shakerley 1603-1639 .... **LC 89**
See also DLB 58; RGEL 2

Marmontel, Jean-Francois 1723-1799 .. **LC 2**
See also DLB 314

Maron, Monika 1941- .... **CLC 165**
See also CA 201

Marot, Clement c. 1496-1544 .... **LC 133**
See also DLB 327; GFL Beginnings to 1789

Marquand, John P(hillips)
1893-1960 .... **CLC 2, 10**
See also AMW; BPFB 2; CA 85-88; CANR 73; CMW 4; DLB 9, 102; EWL 3; MAL 5; MTCW 2; RGAL 4

Marques, Rene 1919-1979 .. **CLC 96; HLC 2**
See also CA 97-100; 85-88; CANR 78; DAM MULT; DLB 305; EWL 3; HW 1, 2; LAW; RGSF 2

Marquez, Gabriel Garcia
See Garcia Marquez, Gabriel

Marquez, Gabriel Garcia
See Garcia Marquez, Gabriel

Marquis, Don(ald Robert Perry)
1878-1937 .... **TCLC 7**
See also CA 104, 166; DLB 11, 25; MAL 5; RGAL 4

Marquis de Sade
See Sade, Donatien Alphonse Francois

Marric, J. J.
See Creasey, John

Marryat, Frederick 1792-1848 .... **NCLC 3**
See also DLB 21, 163; RGEL 2; WCH

Marsden, James
See Creasey, John

Marsh, Edith Ngaio
See Marsh, Ngaio

Marsh, Edward 1872-1953 .... **TCLC 99**

Marsh, Ngaio 1895-1982 .... **CLC 7, 53**
See also CA 9-12R; CANR 6, 58; CMW 4; CN 1, 2, 3; CPW; DAM POP; DLB 77; MSW; MTCW 1, 2; RGEL 2; TEA

Marshall, Alan
See Westlake, Donald E.

Marshall, Allen
See Westlake, Donald E.

Marshall, Garry 1934- .... **CLC 17**
See also AAYA 3; CA 111; SATA 60

Marshall, Paule 1929- .... **BLC 1:3, 2:3; CLC 27, 72, 253; SSC 3**
See also AFAW 1, 2; AMWS 11; BPFB 2; BW 2, 3; CA 77-80; CANR 25, 73, 129, 209; CN 1, 2, 3, 4, 5, 6, 7; DA3; DAM MULT; DLB 33, 157, 227; EWL 3; LATS 1:2; MAL 5; MTCW 1, 2; MTFW 2005; RGAL 4; SSFS 15

Marshallik
See Zangwill, Israel

Marsilius of Inghen c.
1340-1396 .... **CMLC 106**

Marsten, Richard
See Hunter, Evan

Marston, John 1576-1634 ...... **DC 37; LC 33, 172**
See also BRW 2; DAM DRAM; DLB 58, 172; RGEL 2

Martel, Yann 1963- .... **CLC 192**
See also AAYA 67; CA 146; CANR 114; DLB 326, 334; LNFS 2; MTFW 2005; NFS 27

Martens, Adolphe-Adhemar
See Ghelderode, Michel de

Martha, Henry
See Harris, Mark

Marti, Jose 1853-1895 ..... **HLC 2; NCLC 63; PC 76**
See also DAM MULT; DLB 290; HW 2; LAW; RGWL 2, 3; WLIT 1

Martial c. 40-c. 104 .... **CMLC 35; PC 10**
See also AW 2; CDWLB 1; DLB 211; RGWL 2, 3

Martin, Ken
See Hubbard, L. Ron

Martin, Richard
See Creasey, John

Martin, Steve 1945- .... **CLC 30, 217**
See also AAYA 53; CA 97-100; CANR 30, 100, 140, 195; DFS 19; MTCW 1; MTFW 2005

Martin, Valerie 1948- .... **CLC 89**
See also BEST 90:2; CA 85-88; CANR 49, 89, 165, 200

Martin, Violet Florence 1862-1915 .. **SSC 56; TCLC 51**

Martin, Webber
See Silverberg, Robert

Martindale, Patrick Victor
See White, Patrick

Martin du Gard, Roger
1881-1958 .... **TCLC 24**
See also CA 118; CANR 94; DLB 65, 331; EWL 3; GFL 1789 to the Present; RGWL 2, 3

Martineau, Harriet 1802-1876 ...... **NCLC 26, 137**
See also BRWS 15; DLB 21, 55, 159, 163, 166, 190; FW; RGEL 2; YABC 2

Martines, Julia
See O'Faolain, Julia

Martinez, Enrique Gonzalez
See Gonzalez Martinez, Enrique

Martinez, Jacinto Benavente y
See Benavente, Jacinto

Martinez de la Rosa, Francisco de Paula
1787-1862 .... **NCLC 102**
See also TWA

Martinez Ruiz, Jose 1873-1967 .... **CLC 11**
See also CA 93-96; DLB 322; EW 3; EWL 3; HW 1

Martinez Sierra, Gregorio
See Martinez Sierra, Maria

Martinez Sierra, Gregorio
1881-1947 .... **TCLC 6**
See also CA 115; EWL 3

Martinez Sierra, Maria 1874-1974 .. **TCLC 6**
See also CA 250, 115; EWL 3

Martinsen, Martin
See Follett, Ken

Martinson, Harry (Edmund)
1904-1978 .... **CLC 14**
See also CA 77-80; CANR 34, 130; DLB 259, 331; EWL 3

Marti y Perez, Jose Julian
See Marti, Jose

Martyn, Edward 1859-1923 .... **TCLC 131**
See also CA 179; DLB 10; RGEL 2

Marut, Ret
See Traven, B.

Marut, Robert
See Traven, B.

Marvell, Andrew 1621-1678 ... **LC 4, 43, 179; PC 10, 86; WLC 4**
See also BRW 2; BRWR 2; CDBLB 1660-1789; DA; DAB; DAC; DAM MST, POET; DLB 131; EXPP; PFS 5; RGEL 2; TEA; WP

Marx, Karl 1818-1883 .... **NCLC 17, 114**
See also DLB 129; LATS 1:1; TWA

Marx, Karl Heinrich
See Marx, Karl

Masaoka, Shiki -1902
See Masaoka, Tsunenori

Masaoka, Tsunenori 1867-1902 ..... **TCLC 18**
See also CA 117, 191; EWL 3; RGWL 3; TWA

Masaoka Shiki
See Masaoka, Tsunenori

Masefield, John (Edward)
1878-1967 .... **CLC 11, 47; PC 78**
See also CA 19-20, 25-28R; CANR 33; CAP 2; CDBLB 1890-1914; DAM POET; DLB 10, 19, 153, 160; EWL 3; EXPP; FANT; MTCW 1, 2; PFS 5; RGEL 2; SATA 19

Maso, Carole 1955(?)- .... **CLC 44**
See also CA 170; CANR 148; CN 7; GLL 2; RGAL 4

Mason, Bobbie Ann 1940- ... **CLC 28, 43, 82, 154; SSC 4, 101**
See also AAYA 5, 42; AMWS 8; BPFB 2; CA 53-56; CANR 11, 31, 58, 83, 125, 169; CDALBS; CN 5, 6, 7; CSW; DA3; DLB 173; DLBY 1987; EWL 3; EXPS; INT CANR-31; MAL 5; MTCW 1, 2; MTFW 2005; NFS 4; RGAL 4; RGSF 2; SSFS 3, 8, 20; TCLE 1:2; YAW

Mason, Ernst
See Pohl, Frederik

Mason, Hunni B.
See Sternheim, (William Adolf) Carl

Mason, Lee W.
See Malzberg, Barry N(athaniel)

Mason, Nick 1945- .... **CLC 35**

Mason, Tally
See Derleth, August (William)

Mass, Anna **CLC 59**

Mass, William
See Gibson, William

Massinger, Philip 1583-1640 .. **DC 39; LC 70**
See also BRWS 11; DLB 58; RGEL 2

Master Lao
See Lao Tzu

Masters, Edgar Lee 1868-1950 ...... **PC 1, 36; TCLC 2, 25; WLCS**
See also AMWS 1; CA 104, 133; CDALB 1865-1917; DA; DAC; DAM MST, POET; DLB 54; EWL 3; EXPP; MAL 5; MTCW 1, 2; MTFW 2005; RGAL 4; TUS; WP

Masters, Hilary 1928- .... **CLC 48**
　　See also CA 25-28R, 217; CAAE 217;
　　CANR 13, 47, 97, 171; CN 6, 7; DLB
　　244
Masters, Hilary Thomas
　　See Masters, Hilary
Mastrosimone, William 1947- .... **CLC 36**
　　See also CA 186; CAD; CD 5, 6
Mathe, Albert
　　See Camus, Albert
Mather, Cotton 1663-1728 .... **LC 38**
　　See also AMWS 2; CDALB 1640-1865;
　　DLB 24, 30, 140; RGAL 4; TUS
Mather, Increase 1639-1723 .... **LC 38, 161**
　　See also DLB 24
Mathers, Marshall
　　See Eminem
Mathers, Marshall Bruce
　　See Eminem
Matheson, Richard 1926- .... **CLC 37, 267**
　　See also AAYA 31; CA 97-100; CANR 88,
　　99; DLB 8, 44; HGG; INT CA-97-100;
　　SCFW 1, 2; SFW 4; SUFW 2
Matheson, Richard Burton
　　See Matheson, Richard
Mathews, Harry 1930- .... **CLC 6, 52**
　　See also CA 21-24R; CAAS 6; CANR 18,
　　40, 98, 160; CN 5, 6, 7
Mathews, John Joseph 1894-1979 .. **CLC 84;**
　　NNAL
　　See also CA 19-20, 142; CANR 45; CAP 2;
　　DAM MULT; DLB 175; TCWW 1, 2
Mathias, Roland 1915-2007 .... **CLC 45**
　　See also CA 97-100, 263; CANR 19, 41;
　　CP 1, 2, 3, 4, 5, 6, 7; DLB 27
Mathias, Roland Glyn
　　See Mathias, Roland
Matsuo Basho 1644(?)-1694 ...... **LC 62; PC 3**
　　See also DAM POET; PFS 2, 7, 18; RGWL
　　2, 3; WP
Mattheson, Rodney
　　See Creasey, John
Matthew, James
　　See Barrie, J. M.
Matthew of Vendome c. 1130-c.
　　1200 .... **CMLC 99**
　　See also DLB 208
Matthews, (James) Brander
　　1852-1929 .... **TCLC 95**
　　See also CA 181; DLB 71, 78; DLBD 13
Matthews, Greg 1949- .... **CLC 45**
　　See also CA 135
Matthews, William (Procter III)
　　1942-1997 .... **CLC 40**
　　See also AMWS 9; CA 29-32R, 162; CAAS
　　18; CANR 12, 57; CP 2, 3, 4, 5, 6; DLB
　　5
Matthias, John (Edward) 1941- .... **CLC 9**
　　See also CA 33-36R; CANR 56; CP 4, 5, 6,
　　7
Matthiessen, F(rancis) O(tto)
　　1902-1950 .... **TCLC 100**
　　See also CA 185; DLB 63; MAL 5
Matthiessen, Peter 1927- ... **CLC 5, 7, 11, 32,**
　　64, 245
　　See also AAYA 6, 40; AMWS 5; ANW;
　　BEST 90:4; BPFB 2; CA 9-12R; CANR
　　21, 50, 73, 100, 138; CN 1, 2, 3, 4, 5, 6,
　　7; DA3; DAM NOV; DLB 6, 173, 275;
　　MAL 5; MTCW 1, 2; MTFW 2005; SATA
　　27
Maturin, Charles Robert
　　1780(?)-1824 .... **NCLC 6, 169**
　　See also BRWS 8; DLB 178; GL 3; HGG;
　　LMFS 1; RGEL 2; SUFW
Matute (Ausejo), Ana Maria 1925- .. **CLC 11**
　　See also CA 89-92; CANR 129; CWW 2;
　　DLB 322; EWL 3; MTCW 1; RGSF 2

Maugham, W. S.
　　See Maugham, W. Somerset
Maugham, W. Somerset 1874-1965 ... **CLC 1,**
　　11, 15, 67, 93; SSC 8, 94; TCLC 208;
　　WLC 4
　　See also AAYA 55; BPFB 2; BRW 6; CA
　　5-8R, 25-28R; CANR 40, 127; CDBLB
　　1914-1945; CMW 4; DA; DA3; DAB;
　　DAC; DAM DRAM, MST, NOV; DFS
　　22; DLB 10, 36, 77, 100, 162, 195; EWL
　　3; LAIT 3; MTCW 1, 2; MTFW 2005;
　　NFS 23, 35; RGEL 2; RGSF 2; SATA 54;
　　SSFS 17
Maugham, William S.
　　See Maugham, W. Somerset
Maugham, William Somerset
　　See Maugham, W. Somerset
Maupassant, Guy de 1850-1893 ..... **NCLC 1,**
　　42, 83; SSC 1, 64, 132; WLC 4
　　See also BYA 14; DA; DA3; DAB; DAC;
　　DAM MST; DLB 123; EW 7; EXPS; GFL
　　1789 to the Present; LAIT 2; LMFS 1;
　　RGSF 2; RGWL 2, 3; SSFS 4, 21, 28, 31;
　　SUFW; TWA
Maupassant, Henri Rene Albert Guy de
　　See Maupassant, Guy de
Maupin, Armistead 1944- .... **CLC 95**
　　See also CA 125, 130; CANR 58, 101, 183;
　　CPW; DA3; DAM POP; DLB 278; GLL
　　1; INT CA-130; MTCW 2; MTFW 2005
Maupin, Armistead Jones, Jr.
　　See Maupin, Armistead
Maurhut, Richard
　　See Traven, B.
Mauriac, Claude 1914-1996 .... **CLC 9**
　　See also CA 89-92, 152; CWW 2; DLB 83;
　　EWL 3; GFL 1789 to the Present
Mauriac, Francois (Charles)
　　1885-1970 .... **CLC 4, 9, 56; SSC 24**
　　See also CA 25-28; CAP 2; DLB 65, 331;
　　EW 10; EWL 3; GFL 1789 to the Present;
　　MTCW 1, 2; MTFW 2005; RGWL 2, 3;
　　TWA
Mavor, Osborne Henry 1888-1951 .. **TCLC 3**
　　See also CA 104; DLB 10; EWL 3
Maxwell, Glyn 1962- .... **CLC 238**
　　See also CA 154; CANR 88, 183; CP 6, 7;
　　PFS 23
Maxwell, William (Keepers, Jr.)
　　1908-2000 .... **CLC 19**
　　See also AMWS 8; CA 93-96, 189; CANR
　　54, 95; CN 1, 2, 3, 4, 5, 6, 7; DLB 218,
　　278; DLBY 1980; INT CA-93-96; MAL
　　5; SATA-Obit 128
May, Elaine 1932- .... **CLC 16**
　　See also CA 124, 142; CAD; CWD; DLB
　　44
Mayakovski, Vladimir 1893-1930 ... **TCLC 4,**
　　18
　　See also CA 104, 158; EW 11; EWL 3;
　　IDTP; MTCW 2; MTFW 2005; RGWL 2,
　　3; SFW 4; TWA; WP
Mayakovski, Vladimir Vladimirovich
　　See Mayakovski, Vladimir
Mayakovsky, Vladimir
　　See Mayakovski, Vladimir
Mayhew, Henry 1812-1887 .... **NCLC 31**
　　See also BRWS 16; DLB 18, 55, 190
Mayle, Peter 1939(?)- .... **CLC 89**
　　See also CA 139; CANR 64, 109, 168
Maynard, Joyce 1953- .... **CLC 23**
　　See also CA 111, 129; CANR 64, 169
Mayne, William 1928-2010 .... **CLC 12**
　　See also AAYA 20; CA 9-12R; CANR 37,
　　80, 100; CLR 25, 123; FANT; JRDA;
　　MAICYA 1, 2; MAICYAS 1; SAAS 11;
　　SATA 6, 68, 122; SUFW 2; YAW
Mayne, William James Carter
　　See Mayne, William

Mayo, Jim
　　See L'Amour, Louis
Maysles, Albert 1926- .... **CLC 16**
　　See also CA 29-32R
Maysles, David 1932-1987 .... **CLC 16**
　　See also CA 191
Mazer, Norma Fox 1931-2009 .... **CLC 26**
　　See also AAYA 5, 36; BYA 1, 8; CA 69-72,
　　292; CANR 12, 32, 66, 129, 189; CLR
　　23; JRDA; MAICYA 1, 2; SAAS 1; SATA
　　24, 67, 105, 168, 198; WYA; YAW
Mazzini, Guiseppe 1805-1872 .... **NCLC 34**
McAlmon, Robert (Menzies)
　　1895-1956 .... **TCLC 97**
　　See also CA 107, 168; DLB 4, 45; DLBD
　　15; GLL 1
McAuley, James Phillip 1917-1976 .. **CLC 45**
　　See also CA 97-100; CP 1, 2; DLB 260;
　　RGEL 2
McBain, Ed
　　See Hunter, Evan
McBrien, William 1930- .... **CLC 44**
　　See also CA 107; CANR 90
McBrien, William Augustine
　　See McBrien, William
McCabe, Pat
　　See McCabe, Patrick
McCabe, Patrick 1955- .... **CLC 133**
　　See also BRWS 9; CA 130; CANR 50, 90,
　　168, 202; CN 6, 7; DLB 194
McCaffrey, Anne 1926- .... **CLC 17**
　　See also AAYA 6, 34; AITN 2; BEST 89:2;
　　BPFB 2; BYA 5; CA 25-28R, 227; CAAE
　　227; CANR 15, 35, 55, 96, 169; CLR 49,
　　130; CPW; DA3; DAM NOV, POP; DLB
　　8; JRDA; MAICYA 1, 2; MTCW 1, 2;
　　MTFW 2005; SAAS 11; SATA 8, 70, 116,
　　152; SATA-Essay 152; SFW 4; SUFW 2;
　　WYA; YAW
McCaffrey, Anne Inez
　　See McCaffrey, Anne
McCall, Nathan 1955(?)- .... **CLC 86**
　　See also AAYA 59; BW 3; CA 146; CANR
　　88, 186
McCall Smith, Alexander
　　See Smith, Alexander McCall
McCann, Arthur
　　See Campbell, John W(ood, Jr.)
McCann, Edson
　　See Pohl, Frederik
McCarthy, Charles
　　See McCarthy, Cormac
McCarthy, Charles, Jr.
　　See McCarthy, Cormac
McCarthy, Cormac 1933- .... **CLC 4, 57, 101,**
　　204, 295
　　See also AAYA 41; AMWS 8; BPFB 2; CA
　　13-16R; CANR 10, 42, 69, 101, 161, 171;
　　CN 6, 7; CPW; CSW; DA3; DAM POP;
　　DLB 6, 143, 256; EWL 3; LATS 1:2;
　　LNFS 3; MAL 5; MTCW 2; MTFW 2005;
　　TCLE 1:2; TCWW 2
McCarthy, Mary 1912-1989 ...... **CLC 1, 3, 5,**
　　14, 24, 39, 59; SSC 24
　　See also AMW; BPFB 2; CA 5-8R, 129;
　　CANR 16, 50, 64; CN 1, 2, 3, 4; DA3;
　　DLB 2; DLBY 1981; EWL 3; FW; INT
　　CANR-16; MAL 5; MBL; MTCW 1, 2;
　　MTFW 2005; RGAL 4; TUS
McCarthy, Mary Therese
　　See McCarthy, Mary
McCartney, James Paul
　　See McCartney, Paul
McCartney, Paul 1942- .... **CLC 12, 35**
　　See also CA 146; CANR 111
McCauley, Stephen 1955- .... **CLC 50**
　　See also CA 141
McClaren, Peter CLC 70

Mda, Zakes 1948- .... **BLC 2:3; CLC 262**
    See also BRWS 15; CA 205; CANR 151,
    185; CD 5, 6; DLB 225
Mda, Zanemvula
    See Mda, Zakes
Mda, Zanemvula Kizito Gatyeni
    See Mda, Zakes
Mead, George Herbert 1863-1931 . **TCLC 89**
    See also CA 212; DLB 270
Mead, Margaret 1901-1978 .... **CLC 37**
    See also AITN 1; CA 1-4R; 81-84; CANR
    4; DA3; FW; MTCW 1, 2; SATA-Obit 20
Meaker, M. J.
    See Meaker, Marijane
Meaker, Marijane 1927- .... **CLC 12, 35**
    See also AAYA 2, 23, 82; BYA 1, 7, 8; CA
    107; CANR 37, 63, 145, 180; CLR 29;
    GLL 2; INT CA-107; JRDA; MAICYA 1,
    2; MAICYAS 1; MTCW 1; SAAS 1;
    SATA 20, 61, 99, 160; SATA-Essay 111;
    WYA; YAW
Meaker, Marijane Agnes
    See Meaker, Marijane
Mechthild von Magdeburg c. 1207-c.
    1282 .... **CMLC 91**
    See also DLB 138
Medoff, Mark (Howard) 1940- .... **CLC 6, 23**
    See also AITN 1; CA 53-56; CAD; CANR
    5; CD 5, 6; DAM DRAM; DFS 4; DLB
    7; INT CANR-5
Medvedev, P. N.
    See Bakhtin, Mikhail Mikhailovich
Meged, Aharon
    See Megged, Aharon
Meged, Aron
    See Megged, Aharon
Megged, Aharon 1920- .... **CLC 9**
    See also CA 49-52; CAAS 13; CANR 1,
    140; EWL 3; RGHL
Mehta, Deepa 1950- .... **CLC 208**
Mehta, Gita 1943- .... **CLC 179**
    See also CA 225; CN 7; DNFS 2
Mehta, Ved 1934- .... **CLC 37**
    See also CA 1-4R, 212; CAAE 212; CANR
    2, 23, 69; DLB 323; MTCW 1; MTFW
    2005
Melanchthon, Philipp 1497-1560 .... **LC 90**
    See also DLB 179
Melanter
    See Blackmore, R(ichard) D(oddridge)
Meleager c. 140B.C.-c. 70B.C. ...... **CMLC 53**
Melies, Georges 1861-1938 .... **TCLC 81**
Melikow, Loris
    See Hofmannsthal, Hugo von
Melmoth, Sebastian
    See Wilde, Oscar
Melo Neto, Joao Cabral de
    See Cabral de Melo Neto, Joao
Meltzer, Milton 1915-2009 .... **CLC 26**
    See also AAYA 8, 45; BYA 2, 6; CA 13-
    16R, 290; CANR 38, 92, 107, 192; CLR
    13; DLB 61; JRDA; MAICYA 1, 2; SAAS
    1; SATA 1, 50, 80, 128, 201; SATA-Essay
    124; WYA; YAW
Melville, Herman 1819-1891 ..... **NCLC 3, 12,
    29, 45, 49, 91, 93, 123, 157, 181, 193,
    221; PC 82; SSC 1, 17, 46, 95, 141;
    WLC 4**
    See also AAYA 25; AMW; AMWR 1;
    CDALB 1640-1865; DA; DA3; DAB;
    DAC; DAM MST, NOV; DLB 3, 74, 250,
    254, 349; EXPN; EXPS; GL 3; LAIT 1,
    2; NFS 7, 9, 32; RGAL 4; RGSF 2; SATA
    59; SSFS 3; TUS
Members, Mark
    See Powell, Anthony
Membreno, Alejandro CLC 59
Menand, Louis 1952- .... **CLC 208**
    See also CA 200

Menander c. 342B.C.-c. 293B.C. .... **CMLC 9,
    51, 101; DC 3**
    See also AW 1; CDWLB 1; DAM DRAM;
    DLB 176; LMFS 1; RGWL 2, 3
Menchu, Rigoberta 1959- .. **CLC 160; HLCS
    2**
    See also CA 175; CANR 135; DNFS 1;
    WLIT 1
Mencken, H. L. 1880-1956 .... **TCLC 13, 18**
    See also AMW; CA 105, 125; CDALB
    1917-1929; DLB 11, 29, 63, 137, 222;
    EWL 3; MAL 5; MTCW 1, 2; MTFW
    2005; NCFS 4; RGAL 4; TUS
Mencken, Henry Louis
    See Mencken, H. L.
Mendelsohn, Jane 1965- .... **CLC 99**
    See also CA 154; CANR 94
Mendelssohn, Moses 1729-1786 .... **LC 142**
    See also DLB 97
Mendoza, Inigo Lopez de
    See Santillana, Inigo Lopez de Mendoza,
    Marques de
Menton, Francisco de
    See Chin, Frank
Mercer, David 1928-1980 .... **CLC 5**
    See also CA 9-12R, 102; CANR 23; CBD;
    DAM DRAM; DLB 13, 310; MTCW 1;
    RGEL 2
Merchant, Paul
    See Ellison, Harlan
Meredith, George 1828-1909 .. **PC 60; TCLC
    17, 43**
    See also CA 117, 153; CANR 80; CDBLB
    1832-1890; DAM POET; DLB 18, 35, 57,
    159; RGEL 2; TEA
Meredith, William 1919-2007 ...... **CLC 4, 13,
    22, 55; PC 28**
    See also CA 9-12R, 260; CAAS 14; CANR
    6, 40, 129; CP 1, 2, 3, 4, 5, 6, 7; DAM
    POET; DLB 5; MAL 5
Meredith, William Morris
    See Meredith, William
Merezhkovsky, Dmitrii Sergeevich
    See Merezhkovsky, Dmitry Sergeyevich
Merezhkovsky, Dmitry Sergeevich
    See Merezhkovsky, Dmitry Sergeyevich
Merezhkovsky, Dmitry Sergeyevich
    1865-1941 .... **TCLC 29**
    See also CA 169; DLB 295; EWL 3
Merezhkovsky, Zinaida
    See Gippius, Zinaida
Merimee, Prosper 1803-1870 . **DC 33; NCLC
    6, 65; SSC 7, 77**
    See also DLB 119, 192; EW 6; EXPS; GFL
    1789 to the Present; RGSF 2; RGWL 2,
    3; SSFS 8; SUFW
Merkin, Daphne 1954- .... **CLC 44**
    See also CA 123
Merleau-Ponty, Maurice
    1908-1961 .... **TCLC 156**
    See also CA 114; 89-92; DLB 296; GFL
    1789 to the Present
Merlin, Arthur
    See Blish, James
Mernissi, Fatima 1940- .... **CLC 171**
    See also CA 152; DLB 346; FW
Merrill, James 1926-1995 ...... **CLC 2, 3, 6, 8,
    13, 18, 34, 91; PC 28; TCLC 173**
    See also AMWS 3; CA 13-16R, 147; CANR
    10, 49, 63, 108; CP 1, 2, 3, 4; DA3; DAM
    POET; DLB 5, 165; DLBY 1985; EWL 3;
    INT CANR-10; MAL 5; MTCW 1, 2;
    MTFW 2005; PAB; PFS 23; RGAL 4
Merrill, James Ingram
    See Merrill, James
Merriman, Alex
    See Silverberg, Robert

Merriman, Brian 1747-1805 .... **NCLC 70**
Merritt, E. B.
    See Waddington, Miriam
Merton, Thomas 1915-1968 ..... **CLC 1, 3, 11,
    34, 83; PC 10**
    See also AAYA 61; AMWS 8; CA 5-8R;
    25-28R; CANR 22, 53, 111, 131; DA3;
    DLB 48; DLBY 1981; MAL 5; MTCW 1,
    2; MTFW 2005
Merton, Thomas James
    See Merton, Thomas
Merwin, William Stanley
    See Merwin, W.S.
Merwin, W.S. 1927- ..... **CLC 1, 2, 3, 5, 8, 13,
    18, 45, 88; PC 45**
    See also AMWS 3; CA 13-16R; CANR 15,
    51, 112, 140; CP 1, 2, 3, 4, 5, 6, 7; DA3;
    DAM POET; DLB 5, 169, 342; EWL 3;
    INT CANR-15; MAL 5; MTCW 1, 2;
    MTFW 2005; PAB; PFS 5, 15; RGAL 4
Metastasio, Pietro 1698-1782 .... **LC 115**
    See also RGWL 2, 3
Metcalf, John 1938- .... **CLC 37; SSC 43**
    See also CA 113; CN 4, 5, 6, 7; DLB 60;
    RGSF 2; TWA
Metcalf, Suzanne
    See Baum, L. Frank
Mew, Charlotte (Mary) 1870-1928 .. **PC 107;
    TCLC 8**
    See also CA 105, 189; DLB 19, 135; RGEL
    2
Mewshaw, Michael 1943- .... **CLC 9**
    See also CA 53-56; CANR 7, 47, 147;
    DLBY 1980
Meyer, Conrad Ferdinand
    1825-1898 .... **NCLC 81; SSC 30**
    See also DLB 129; EW; RGWL 2, 3
Meyer, Gustav 1868-1932 .... **TCLC 21**
    See also CA 117, 190; DLB 81; EWL 3
Meyer, June
    See Jordan, June
Meyer, Lynn
    See Slavitt, David R.
Meyer, Stephenie 1973- .... **CLC 280**
    See also AAYA 77; CA 253; CANR 192;
    CLR 142; SATA 193
Meyer-Meyrink, Gustav
    See Meyer, Gustav
Meyers, Jeffrey 1939- .... **CLC 39**
    See also CA 73-76, 186; CAAE 186; CANR
    54, 102, 159; DLB 111
**Meynell, Alice (Christina Gertrude
    Thompson)** 1847-1922 .... **TCLC 6;
    PC-112**
    See also CA 104, 177; DLB 19, 98; RGEL
    2
Meyrink, Gustav
    See Meyer, Gustav
Mhlophe, Gcina 1960- .... **BLC 2:3**
Michaels, Leonard 1933-2003 ..... **CLC 6, 25;
    SSC 16**
    See also AMWS 16; CA 61-64, 216; CANR
    21, 62, 119, 179; CN 3, 45, 6, 7; DLB
    130; MTCW 1; TCLE 1:2
Michaux, Henri 1899-1984 .... **CLC 8, 19**
    See also CA 85-88, 114; DLB 258; EWL 3;
    GFL 1789 to the Present; RGWL 2, 3
Micheaux, Oscar (Devereaux)
    1884-1951 .... **TCLC 76**
    See also BW 3; CA 174; DLB 50; TCWW
    2
Michelangelo 1475-1564 .... **LC 12**
    See also AAYA 43
Michelet, Jules 1798-1874 ...... **NCLC 31, 218**
    See also EW 5; GFL 1789 to the Present
Michels, Robert 1876-1936 .... **TCLC 88**
    See also CA 212

Mitchell, W(illiam) O(rmond)
1914-1998 .... **CLC 25**
See also CA 77-80, 165; CANR 15, 43; CN
1, 2, 3, 4, 5, 6; DAC; DAM MST; DLB
88; TCLE 1:2

Mitchell, William (Lendrum)
1879-1936 .... **TCLC 81**
See also CA 213

Mitford, Mary Russell 1787-1855 ... **NCLC 4**
See also DLB 110, 116; RGEL 2

Mitford, Nancy 1904-1973 .... **CLC 44**
See also BRWS 10; CA 9-12R; CN 1; DLB
191; RGEL 2

Miyamoto, (Chujo) Yuriko
1899-1951 .... **TCLC 37**
See also CA 170, 174; DLB 180

Miyamoto Yuriko
See Miyamoto, (Chujo) Yuriko

Miyazawa, Kenji 1896-1933 .... **TCLC 76**
See also CA 157; EWL 3; RGWL 3

Miyazawa Kenji
See Miyazawa, Kenji

Mizoguchi, Kenji 1898-1956 .... **TCLC 72**
See also CA 167

Mo, Timothy (Peter) 1950- .... **CLC 46, 134**
See also CA 117; CANR 128; CN 5, 6, 7;
DLB 194; MTCW 1; WLIT 4; WWE 1

Mo, Yan
See Yan, Mo

Moberg, Carl Arthur
See Moberg, Vilhelm

Moberg, Vilhelm 1898-1973 .... **TCLC 224**
See also CA 97-100, 45-48; CANR 135;
DLB 259; EW 11; EWL 3

Modarressi, Taghi (M.) 1931-1997 ... **CLC 44**
See also CA 121, 134; INT CA-134

Modiano, Patrick (Jean) 1945- .... **CLC 18, 218**
See also CA 85-88; CANR 17, 40, 115;
CWW 2; DLB 83, 299; EWL 3; RGHL

Mofolo, Thomas 1875(?)-1948 .... **BLC 1:3; TCLC 22**
See also AFW; CA 121, 153; CANR 83;
DAM MULT; DLB 225; EWL 3; MTCW
2; MTFW 2005; WLIT 2

Mofolo, Thomas Mokopu
See Mofolo, Thomas

Mohr, Nicholasa 1938- .... **CLC 12; HLC 2**
See also AAYA 8, 46; CA 49-52; CANR 1,
32, 64; CLR 22; DAM MULT; DLB 145;
HW 1, 2; JRDA; LAIT 5; LLW; MAICYA
2; MAICYAS 1; RGAL 4; SAAS 8; SATA
8, 97; SATA-Essay 113; WYA; YAW

Moi, Toril 1953- .... **CLC 172**
See also CA 154; CANR 102; FW

Mojtabai, A(nn) G(race) 1938- ..... **CLC 5, 9, 15, 29**
See also CA 85-88; CANR 88

Moliere 1622-1673 ..... **DC 13; LC 10, 28, 64, 125, 127; WLC 4**
See also DA; DA3; DAB; DAC; DAM
DRAM, MST; DFS 13, 18, 20; DLB 268;
EW 3; GFL Beginnings to 1789; LATS
1:1; RGWL 2, 3; TWA

Molin, Charles
See Mayne, William

Molina, Antonio Munoz 1956- .... **CLC 289**
See also DLB 322

Molnar, Ferenc 1878-1952 .... **TCLC 20**
See also CA 109, 153; CANR 83; CDWLB
4; DAM DRAM; DLB 215; EWL 3;
RGWL 2, 3

Momaday, N. Scott 1934- ...... **CLC 2, 19, 85, 95, 160; NNAL; PC 25; WLCS**
See also AAYA 11, 64; AMWS 4; ANW;
BPFB 2; BYA 12; CA 25-28R; CANR 14,
34, 68, 134; CDALBS; CN 2, 3, 4, 5, 6,
7; CPW; DA; DA3; DAB; DAC; DAM
MST, MULT, NOV, POP; DLB 143, 175,

256; EWL 3; EXPP; INT CANR-14;
LAIT 4; LATS 1:2; MAL 5; MTCW 1, 2;
MTFW 2005; NFS 10; PFS 2, 11; RGAL
4; SATA 48; SATA-Brief 30; TCWW 1,
2; WP; YAW

Momaday, Navarre Scott
See Momaday, N. Scott

Momala, Ville i
See Moberg, Vilhelm

Monette, Paul 1945-1995 .... **CLC 82**
See also AMWS 10; CA 139, 147; CN 6;
DLB 350; GLL 1

Monroe, Harriet 1860-1936 .... **TCLC 12**
See also CA 109, 204; DLB 54, 91

Monroe, Lyle
See Heinlein, Robert A.

Montagu, Elizabeth 1720-1800 .... **NCLC 7, 117**
See also DLB 356; FW

Montagu, Mary (Pierrepont) Wortley
1689-1762 .... **LC 9, 57; PC 16**
See also DLB 95, 101; FL 1:1; RGEL 2

Montagu, W. H.
See Coleridge, Samuel Taylor

Montague, John (Patrick) 1929- ..... **CLC 13, 46; PC 106**
See also BRWS 15; CA 9-12R; CANR 9,
69, 121; CP 1, 2, 3, 4, 5, 6, 7; DLB 40;
EWL 3; MTCW 1; PFS 12; RGEL 2;
TCLE 1:2

Montaigne, Michel de 1533-1592 .... **LC 8, 105; WLC 4**
See also DA; DAB; DAC; DAM MST;
DLB 327; EW 2; GFL Beginnings to
1789; LMFS 1; RGWL 2, 3; TWA

Montaigne, Michel Eyquem de
See Montaigne, Michel de

Montale, Eugenio 1896-1981 ... **CLC 7, 9, 18; PC 13**
See also CA 17-20R, 104; CANR 30; DLB
114, 331; EW 11; EWL 3; MTCW 1; PFS
22; RGWL 2, 3; TWA; WLIT 7

Montesquieu, Charles-Louis de Secondat
1689-1755 .... **LC 7, 69**
See also DLB 314; EW 3; GFL Beginnings
to 1789; TWA

Montessori, Maria 1870-1952 ...... **TCLC 103**
See also CA 115, 147

Montgomery, Bruce 1921(?)-1978 .... **CLC 22**
See also CA 179, 104; CMW 4; DLB 87;
MSW

Montgomery, L. M. 1874-1942 ..... **TCLC 51, 140**
See also AAYA 12; BYA 1; CA 108, 137;
CLR 8, 91, 145; DA3; DAC; DAM MST;
DLB 92; DLBD 14; JRDA; MAICYA 1,
2; MTCW 2; MTFW 2005; RGEL 2;
SATA 100; TWA; WCH; WYA; YABC 1

Montgomery, Lucy Maud
See Montgomery, L. M.

Montgomery, Marion, Jr. 1925- .... **CLC 7**
See also AITN 1; CA 1-4R; CANR 3, 48,
162; CSW; DLB 6

Montgomery, Marion H. 1925-
See Montgomery, Marion, Jr.

Montgomery, Max
See Davenport, Guy (Mattison, Jr.)

Montgomery, Robert Bruce
See Montgomery, Bruce

Montherlant, Henry de 1896-1972 .... **CLC 8, 19**
See also CA 85-88, 37-40R; DAM DRAM;
DLB 72, 321; EW 11; EWL 3; GFL 1789
to the Present; MTCW 1

Montherlant, Henry Milon de
See Montherlant, Henry de

Monty Python
See Chapman, Graham; Cleese, John
(Marwood); Gilliam, Terry; Idle, Eric;
Jones, Terence Graham Parry; Palin,
Michael

Moodie, Susanna (Strickland)
1803-1885 .... **NCLC 14, 113**
See also DLB 99

Moody, Hiram
See Moody, Rick

Moody, Hiram F. III
See Moody, Rick

Moody, Minerva
See Alcott, Louisa May

Moody, Rick 1961- .... **CLC 147**
See also CA 138; CANR 64, 112, 179;
MTFW 2005

Moody, William Vaughan
1869-1910 .... **TCLC 105**
See also CA 110, 178; DLB 7, 54; MAL 5;
RGAL 4

Mooney, Edward 1951- .... **CLC 25**
See also CA 130

Mooney, Ted
See Mooney, Edward

Moorcock, Michael 1939- ...... **CLC 5, 27, 58, 236**
See also AAYA 26; CA 45-48; CAAS 5;
CANR 2, 17, 38, 64, 122, 203; CN 5, 6,
7; DLB 14, 231, 261, 319; FANT; MTCW
1, 2; MTFW 2005; SATA 93, 166; SCFW
1, 2; SFW 4; SUFW 1, 2

Moorcock, Michael John
See Moorcock, Michael

Moorcock, Michael John
See Moorcock, Michael

Moore, Al
See Moore, Alan

Moore, Alan 1953- .... **CLC 230**
See also AAYA 51; CA 204; CANR 138,
184; DLB 261; MTFW 2005; SFW 4

Moore, Alice Ruth
See Nelson, Alice Ruth Moore Dunbar

Moore, Brian 1921-1999 ... **CLC 1, 3, 5, 7, 8, 19, 32, 90**
See also BRWS 9; CA 1-4R, 174; CANR 1,
25, 42, 63; CCA 1; CN 1, 2, 3, 4, 5, 6;
DAB; DAC; DAM MST; DLB 251; EWL
3; FANT; MTCW 1, 2; MTFW 2005;
RGEL 2

Moore, Edward
See Muir, Edwin

Moore, G. E. 1873-1958 .... **TCLC 89**
See also DLB 262

Moore, George Augustus
1852-1933 .... **SSC 19, 134; TCLC 7**
See also BRW 6; CA 104, 177; DLB 10,
18, 57, 135; EWL 3; RGEL 2; RGSF 2

Moore, Lorrie 1957- ..... **CLC 39, 45, 68, 165**
See also AMWS 10; CA 116; CANR 39,
83, 139; CN 5, 6, 7; DLB 234; MTFW
2005; SSFS 19

Moore, Marianne 1887-1972 . **CLC 1, 2, 4, 8, 10, 13, 19, 47; PC 4, 49; WLCS**
See also AMW; CA 1-4R, 33-36R; CANR
3, 61; CDALB 1929-1941; CP 1; DA;
DA3; DAB; DAC; DAM MST, POET;
DLB 45; DLBD 7; EWL 3; EXPP; FL 1:6;
MAL 5; MBL; MTCW 1, 2; MTFW 2005;
PAB; PFS 14, 17; RGAL 4; SATA 20;
TUS; WP

Moore, Marianne Craig
See Moore, Marianne

Moore, Marie Lorena
See Moore, Lorrie

Moore, Michael 1954- .... **CLC 218**
See also AAYA 53; CA 166; CANR 150

Moore, Thomas 1779-1852 .... **NCLC 6, 110**
See also DLB 96, 144; RGEL 2

Moorhouse, Frank 1938- .... **SSC 40**
  See also CA 118; CANR 92; CN 3, 4, 5, 6,
  7; DLB 289; RGSF 2

Mootoo, Shani 1958(?)- .... **CLC 294**
  See also CA 174; CANR 156

Mora, Pat 1942- .... **HLC 2**
  See also AMWS 13; CA 129; CANR 57,
  81, 112, 171; CLR 58; DAM MULT; DLB
  209; HW 1, 2; LLW; MAICYA 2; MTFW
  2005; PFS 33, 35; SATA 92, 134, 186

Moraga, Cherrie 1952- ... **CLC 126, 250; DC
  22**
  See also CA 131; CANR 66, 154; DAM
  MULT; DLB 82, 249; FW; GLL 1; HW 1,
  2; LLW

Moran, J.L.
  See Whitaker, Rod

Morand, Paul 1888-1976 .... **CLC 41; SSC 22**
  See also CA 184; 69-72; DLB 65; EWL 3

Morante, Elsa 1918-1985 .... **CLC 8, 47**
  See also CA 85-88, 117; CANR 35; DLB
  177; EWL 3; MTCW 1, 2; MTFW 2005;
  RGHL; RGWL 2, 3; WLIT 7

Moravia, Alberto
  See Pincherle, Alberto

Morck, Paul
  See Rolvaag, O.E.

More, Hannah 1745-1833 ...... **NCLC 27, 141**
  See also DLB 107, 109, 116, 158; RGEL 2

More, Henry 1614-1687 .... **LC 9**
  See also DLB 126, 252

More, Sir Thomas 1478(?)-1535 ... **LC 10, 32,
  140**
  See also BRWC 1; BRWS 7; DLB 136, 281;
  LMFS 1; NFS 29; RGEL 2; TEA

Moreas, Jean
  See Papadiamantopoulos, Johannes

Moreton, Andrew Esq.
  See Defoe, Daniel

Moreton, Lee
  See Boucicault, Dion

Morgan, Berry 1919-2002 .... **CLC 6**
  See also CA 49-52, 208; DLB 6

Morgan, Claire
  See Highsmith, Patricia

Morgan, Edwin 1920- .... **CLC 31**
  See also BRWS 9; CA 5-8R; CANR 3, 43,
  90; CP 1, 2, 3, 4, 5, 6, 7; DLB 27

Morgan, Edwin George
  See Morgan, Edwin

Morgan, (George) Frederick
  1922-2004 .... **CLC 23**
  See also CA 17-20R, 224; CANR 21, 144;
  CP 2, 3, 4, 5, 6, 7

Morgan, Harriet
  See Mencken, H. L.

Morgan, Jane
  See Cooper, James Fenimore

Morgan, Janet 1945- .... **CLC 39**
  See also CA 65-68

Morgan, Lady 1776(?)-1859 .... **NCLC 29**
  See also DLB 116, 158; RGEL 2

Morgan, Robin (Evonne) 1941- .... **CLC 2**
  See also CA 69-72; CANR 29, 68; FW;
  GLL 1; MTCW 1; SATA 80

Morgan, Scott
  See Kuttner, Henry

Morgan, Seth 1949(?)-1990 .... **CLC 65**
  See also CA 185, 132

**Morgenstern, Christian (Otto Josef
  Wolfgang)** 1871-1914 .... **TCLC 8**
  See also CA 105, 191; EWL 3

Morgenstern, S.
  See Goldman, William

Mori, Rintaro
  See Mori Ogai

Mori, Toshio 1910-1980 ... **AAL; SSC 83, 123**
  See also CA 116, 244; DLB 312; RGSF 2

Moricz, Zsigmond 1879-1942 .... **TCLC 33**
  See also CA 165; DLB 215; EWL 3

Morike, Eduard (Friedrich)
  1804-1875 .... **NCLC 10, 201**
  See also DLB 133; RGWL 2, 3

Morin, Jean-Paul
  See Whitaker, Rod

Mori Ogai 1862-1922 .... **TCLC 14**
  See also CA 110, 164; DLB 180; EWL 3;
  MJW; RGWL 3; TWA

Moritz, Karl Philipp 1756-1793 .... **LC 2, 162**
  See also DLB 94

Morland, Peter Henry
  See Faust, Frederick

Morley, Christopher (Darlington)
  1890-1957 .... **TCLC 87**
  See also CA 112, 213; DLB 9; MAL 5;
  RGAL 4

Morren, Theophil
  See Hofmannsthal, Hugo von

Morris, Bill 1952- .... **CLC 76**
  See also CA 225

Morris, Julian
  See West, Morris L(anglo)

Morris, Steveland Judkins (?)-
  See Wonder, Stevie

Morris, William 1834-1896 ..... **NCLC 4, 233;
  PC 55**
  See also BRW 5; CDBLB 1832-1890; DLB
  18, 35, 57, 156, 178, 184; FANT; RGEL
  2; SFW 4; SUFW

Morris, Wright (Marion) 1910-1998 . **CLC 1,
  3, 7, 18, 37; TCLC 107**
  See also AMW; CA 9-12R, 167; CANR 21,
  81; CN 1, 2, 3, 4, 5, 6; DLB 2, 206, 218;
  DLBY 1981; EWL 3; MAL 5; MTCW 1,
  2; MTFW 2005; RGAL 4; TCWW 1, 2

Morrison, Arthur 1863-1945 .... **SSC 40;
  TCLC 72**
  See also CA 120, 157; CMW 4; DLB 70,
  135, 197; RGEL 2

Morrison, Chloe Anthony Wofford
  See Morrison, Toni

Morrison, James Douglas
  1943-1971 .... **CLC 17**
  See also CA 73-76; CANR 40

Morrison, Jim
  See Morrison, James Douglas

Morrison, John Gordon 1904-1998 ... **SSC 93**
  See also CA 103; CANR 92; DLB 260

Morrison, Toni 1931- . **BLC 1:3, 2:3; CLC 4,
  10, 22, 55, 81, 87, 173, 194; SSC 126;
  WLC 4**
  See also AAYA 1, 22, 61; AFAW 1, 2;
  AMWC 1; AMWS 3; BPFB 2; BW 2, 3;
  CA 29-32R; CANR 27, 42, 67, 113, 124,
  204; CDALB 1968-1988; CLR 99; CN 3,
  4, 5, 6, 7; CPW; DA; DA3; DAB; DAC;
  DAM MST, MULT, NOV, POP; DLB 6,
  33, 143, 331; DLBY 1981; EWL 3;
  EXPN; FL 1:6; FW; GL 3; LAIT 2, 4;
  LATS 1:2; LMFS 2; MAL 5; MBL;
  MTCW 1, 2; MTFW 2005; NFS 1, 6, 8,
  14; RGAL 4; RHW; SATA 57, 144; SSFS
  5; TCLE 1:2; TUS; YAW

Morrison, Van 1945- .... **CLC 21**
  See also CA 116, 168

Morrissy, Mary 1957- .... **CLC 99**
  See also CA 205; DLB 267

Mortimer, John 1923-2009 .... **CLC 28, 43**
  See Morton, Kate
  See also CA 13-16R, 282; CANR 21, 69,
  109, 172; CBD; CD 5, 6; CDBLB 1960
  to Present; CMW 4; CN 5, 6, 7; CPW;
  DA3; DAM DRAM, POP; DLB 13, 245,
  271; INT CANR-21; MSW; MTCW 1, 2;
  MTFW 2005; RGEL 2

Mortimer, John C.
  See Mortimer, John

Mortimer, John Clifford
  See Mortimer, John

Mortimer, Penelope (Ruth)
  1918-1999 .... **CLC 5**
  See also CA 57-60, 187; CANR 45, 88; CN
  1, 2, 3, 4, 5, 6

Mortimer, Sir John
  See Mortimer, John

Morton, Anthony
  See Creasey, John

Morton, Thomas 1579(?)-1647(?) .... **LC 72**
  See also DLB 24; RGEL 2

Mosca, Gaetano 1858-1941 .... **TCLC 75**

Moses, Daniel David 1952- .... **NNAL**
  See also CA 186; CANR 160; DLB 334

Mosher, Howard Frank 1943- .... **CLC 62**
  See also CA 139; CANR 65, 115, 181

Mosley, Nicholas 1923- .... **CLC 43, 70**
  See also CA 69-72; CANR 41, 60, 108, 158;
  CN 1, 2, 3, 4, 5, 6, 7; DLB 14, 207

Mosley, Walter 1952- ... **BLCS; CLC 97, 184,
  278**
  See also AAYA 57; AMWS 13; BPFB 2;
  BW 2; CA 142; CANR 57, 92, 136, 172,
  201; CMW 4; CN 7; CPW; DA3; DAM
  MULT, POP; DLB 306; MSW; MTCW 2;
  MTFW 2005

Moss, Howard 1922-1987 . **CLC 7, 14, 45, 50**
  See also CA 1-4R, 123; CANR 1, 44; CP 1,
  2, 3, 4; DAM POET; DLB 5

Mossgiel, Rab
  See Burns, Robert

Motion, Andrew 1952- .... **CLC 47**
  See also BRWS 7; CA 146; CANR 90, 142;
  CP 4, 5, 6, 7; DLB 40; MTFW 2005

Motion, Andrew Peter
  See Motion, Andrew

Motley, Willard (Francis)
  1909-1965 .... **CLC 18**
  See also AMWS 17; BW 1; CA 117, 106;
  CANR 88; DLB 76, 143

Motoori, Norinaga 1730-1801 .... **NCLC 45**

Mott, Michael (Charles Alston)
  1930- .... **CLC 15, 34**
  See also CA 5-8R; CAAS 7; CANR 7, 29

Moulsworth, Martha 1577-1646 .... **LC 168**

Mountain Wolf Woman 1884-1960 . **CLC 92;
  NNAL**
  See also CA 144; CANR 90

Moure, Erin 1955- .... **CLC 88**
  See also CA 113; CP 5, 6, 7; CWP; DLB
  60

Mourning Dove 1885(?)-1936 .... **NNAL**
  See also CA 144; CANR 90; DAM MULT;
  DLB 175, 221

Mowat, Farley 1921- .... **CLC 26**
  See also AAYA 1, 50; BYA 2; CA 1-4R;
  CANR 4, 24, 42, 68, 108; CLR 20; CPW;
  DAC; DAM MST; DLB 68; INT CANR-
  24; JRDA; MAICYA 1, 2; MTCW 1, 2;
  MTFW 2005; SATA 3, 55; YAW

Mowat, Farley McGill
  See Mowat, Farley

Mowatt, Anna Cora 1819-1870 ..... **NCLC 74**
  See also RGAL 4

Moye, Guan
  See Yan, Mo

Mo Yen
  See Yan, Mo

Moyers, Bill 1934- .... **CLC 74**
  See also AITN 2; CA 61-64; CANR 31, 52,
  148

Mphahlele, Es'kia 1919-2008 .... **BLC 1:3;
  CLC 25, 133, 280**
  See also AFW; BW 2, 3; CA 81-84, 278;
  CANR 26, 76; CDWLB 3; CN 4, 5, 6;
  DA3; DAM MULT; DLB 125, 225; EWL
  3; MTCW 2; MTFW 2005; RGSF 2;
  SATA 119; SATA-Obit 198; SSFS 11

Nicolas, F. R. E.
　See Freeling, Nicolas
Niedecker, Lorine 1903-1970 ..... **CLC 10, 42; PC 42**
　See also CA 25-28; CAP 2; DAM POET; DLB 48
Nietzsche, Friedrich 1844-1900 ..... **TCLC 10, 18, 55**
　See also CA 107, 121; CDWLB 2; DLB 129; EW 7; RGWL 2, 3; TWA
Nietzsche, Friedrich Wilhelm
　See Nietzsche, Friedrich
Nievo, Ippolito 1831-1861 .... **NCLC 22**
Nightingale, Anne Redmon 1943- .... **CLC 22**
　See also CA 103; DLBY 1986
Nightingale, Florence 1820-1910 ... **TCLC 85**
　See also CA 188; DLB 166
Nijo Yoshimoto 1320-1388 .... **CMLC 49**
　See also DLB 203
Nik. T. O.
　See Annensky, Innokenty (Fyodorovich)
Nin, Anais 1903-1977 ..... **CLC 1, 4, 8, 11, 14, 60, 127; SSC 10; TCLC 224**
　See also AITN 2; AMWS 10; BPFB 2; CA 13-16R; 69-72; CANR 22, 53; CN 1, 2; DAM NOV, POP; DLB 2, 4, 152; EWL 3; GLL 2; MAL 5; MBL; MTCW 1, 2; MTFW 2005; RGAL 4; RGSF 2
Nisbet, Robert A(lexander)
　1913-1996 .... **TCLC 117**
　See also CA 25-28R, 153; CANR 17; INT CANR-17
Nishida, Kitaro 1870-1945 .... **TCLC 83**
Nishiwaki, Junzaburo 1894-1982 .... **PC 15**
　See also CA 194, 107; EWL 3; MJW; RGWL 3
Nissenson, Hugh 1933- .... **CLC 4, 9**
　See also CA 17-20R; CANR 27, 108, 151; CN 5, 6; DLB 28, 335
Nister, Der
　See Der Nister
Niven, Larry 1938- .... **CLC 8**
　See also AAYA 27; BPFB 2; BYA 10; CA 21-24R, 207; CAAE 207; CAAS 12; CANR 14, 44, 66, 113, 155, 206; CPW; DAM POP; DLB 8; MTCW 1, 2; SATA 95, 171; SCFW 1, 2; SFW 4
Niven, Laurence Van Cott
　See Niven, Larry
Niven, Laurence VanCott
　See Niven, Larry
Nixon, Agnes Eckhardt 1927- .... **CLC 21**
　See also CA 110
Nizan, Paul 1905-1940 .... **TCLC 40**
　See also CA 161; DLB 72; EWL 3; GFL 1789 to the Present
Nkosi, Lewis 1936- .... **BLC 1:3; CLC 45**
　See also BW 1, 3; CA 65-68; CANR 27, 81; CBD; CD 5, 6; DAM MULT; DLB 157, 225; WWE 1
Nodier, (Jean) Charles (Emmanuel)
　1780-1844 .... **NCLC 19**
　See also DLB 119; GFL 1789 to the Present
Noguchi, Yone 1875-1947 .... **TCLC 80**
Nolan, Brian
　See O Nuallain, Brian
Nolan, Christopher 1965-2009 .... **CLC 58**
　See also CA 111, 283; CANR 88
Nolan, Christopher John
　See Nolan, Christopher
Noon, Jeff 1957- .... **CLC 91**
　See also CA 148; CANR 83; DLB 267; SFW 4
Norden, Charles
　See Durrell, Lawrence
Nordhoff, Charles Bernard
　1887-1947 .... **TCLC 23**
　See also CA 108, 211; DLB 9; LAIT 1; RHW 1; SATA 23

Norfolk, Lawrence 1963- .... **CLC 76**
　See also CA 144; CANR 85; CN 6, 7; DLB 267
Norman, Marsha (Williams) 1947- . **CLC 28, 186; DC 8**
　See also CA 105; CABS 3; CAD; CANR 41, 131; CD 5, 6; CSW; CWD; DAM DRAM; DFS 2; DLB 266; DLBY 1984; FW; MAL 5
Normyx
　See Douglas, (George) Norman
Norris, Benjamin Franklin, Jr.
　See Norris, Frank
Norris, Frank 1870-1902 ...... **SSC 28; TCLC 24, 155, 211**
　See also AAYA 57; AMW; AMWC 2; BPFB 2; CA 110, 160; CDALB 1865-1917; DLB 12, 71, 186; LMFS 2; MAL 5; NFS 12; RGAL 4; TCWW 1, 2; TUS
Norris, Kathleen 1947- .... **CLC 248**
　See also CA 160; CANR 113, 199
Norris, Leslie 1921-2006 .... **CLC 14**
　See also CA 11-12, 251; CANR 14, 117; CAP 1; CP 1, 2, 3, 4, 5, 6, 7; DLB 27, 256
North, Andrew
　See Norton, Andre
North, Anthony
　See Koontz, Dean
North, Captain George
　See Stevenson, Robert Louis
North, Captain George
　See Stevenson, Robert Louis
North, Milou
　See Erdrich, Louise
Northrup, B. A.
　See Hubbard, L. Ron
North Staffs
　See Hulme, T(homas) E(rnest)
Northup, Solomon 1808-1863 ...... **NCLC 105**
Norton, Alice Mary
　See Norton, Andre
Norton, Andre 1912-2005 .... **CLC 12**
　See also AAYA 83; BPFB 2; BYA 4, 10, 12; CA 1-4R, 237; CANR 2, 31, 68, 108, 149; CLR 50; DLB 8, 52; JRDA; MAICYA 1, 2; MTCW 1; SATA 1, 43, 91; SUFW 1, 2; YAW
Norton, Caroline 1808-1877 .. **NCLC 47, 205**
　See also DLB 21, 159, 199
Norway, Nevil Shute
　See Shute, Nevil
Norwid, Cyprian Kamil
　1821-1883 .... **NCLC 17**
　See also RGWL 3
Nosille, Nabrah
　See Ellison, Harlan
Nossack, Hans Erich 1901-1977 .... **CLC 6**
　See also CA 93-96; 85-88; CANR 156; DLB 69; EWL 3
Nostradamus 1503-1566 .... **LC 27**
Nosu, Chuji
　See Ozu, Yasujiro
Notenburg, Eleanora (Genrikhovna) von
　See Guro, Elena (Genrikhovna)
Nova, Craig 1945- .... **CLC 7, 31**
　See also CA 45-48; CANR 2, 53, 127
Novak, Joseph
　See Kosinski, Jerzy
Novalis 1772-1801 .... **NCLC 13, 178**
　See also CDWLB 2; DLB 90; EW 5; RGWL 2, 3
Novick, Peter 1934- .... **CLC 164**
　See also CA 188
Novis, Emile
　See Weil, Simone

Nowlan, Alden (Albert) 1933-1983 ... **CLC 15**
　See also CA 9-12R; CANR 5; CP 1, 2, 3; DAC; DAM MST; DLB 53; PFS 12
Noyes, Alfred 1880-1958 ...... **PC 27; TCLC 7**
　See also CA 104, 188; DLB 20; EXPP; FANT; PFS 4; RGEL 2
Nugent, Richard Bruce
　1906(?)-1987 .... **HR 1:3**
　See also BW 1; CA 125; CANR 198; DLB 51; GLL 2
Nunez, Elizabeth 1944- .... **BLC 2:3**
　See also CA 223
Nunn, Kem .... **CLC 34**
　See also CA 159; CANR 204
Nussbaum, Martha Craven 1947- .. **CLC 203**
　See also CA 134; CANR 102, 176
Nwapa, Flora (Nwanzuruaha)
　1931-1993 .... **BLCS; CLC 133**
　See also BW 2; CA 143; CANR 83; CD-WLB 3; CWRI 5; DLB 125; EWL 3; WLIT 2
Nye, Robert 1939- .... **CLC 13, 42**
　See also BRWS 10; CA 33-36R; CANR 29, 67, 107; CN 1, 2, 3, 4, 5, 6, 7; CP 1, 2, 3, 4, 5, 6, 7; CWRI 5; DAM NOV; DLB 14, 271; FANT; HGG; MTCW 1; RHW; SATA 6
Nyro, Laura 1947-1997 .... **CLC 17**
　See also CA 194
O. Henry
　See Henry, O.
Oates, Joyce Carol 1938- .. **CLC 1, 2, 3, 6, 9, 11, 15, 19, 33, 52, 108, 134, 228; SSC 6, 70, 121; WLC 4**
　See also AAYA 15, 52; AITN 1; AMWS 2; BEST 89:2; BPFB 2; BYA 11; CA 5-8R; CANR 25, 45, 74, 113, 129, 165; CDALB 1968-1988; CN 1, 2, 3, 4, 5, 6, 7; CP 5, 6, 7; CPW; CWP; DA; DA3; DAB; DAC; DAM MST, NOV, POP; DLB 2, 5, 130; DLBY 1981; EWL 3; EXPS; FL 1:6; FW; GL 3; HGG; INT CANR-25; LAIT 4; MAL 5; MBL; MTCW 1, 2; MTFW 2005; NFS 8, 24; RGAL 4; RGSF 2; SATA 159; SSFS 1, 8, 17; SUFW 2; TUS
O'Brian, E. G.
　See Clarke, Arthur C.
O'Brian, Patrick 1914-2000 .... **CLC 152**
　See also AAYA 55; BRWS 12; CA 144, 187; CANR 74, 201; CPW; MTCW 2; MTFW 2005; RHW
O'Brien, Darcy 1939-1998 .... **CLC 11**
　See also CA 21-24R, 167; CANR 8, 59
O'Brien, Edna 1932- ..... **CLC 3, 5, 8, 13, 36, 65, 116, 237; SSC 10, 77**
　See also BRWS 5; CA 1-4R; CANR 6, 41, 65, 102, 169; CDBLB 1960 to Present; CN 1, 2, 3, 4, 5, 6, 7; DA3; DAM NOV; DLB 14, 231, 319; EWL 3; FW; MTCW 1, 2; MTFW 2005; RGSF 2; WLIT 4
O'Brien, E.G.
　See Clarke, Arthur C.
O'Brien, Fitz-James 1828-1862 ..... **NCLC 21**
　See also DLB 74; RGAL 4; SUFW
O'Brien, Flann
　See O Nuallain, Brian
O'Brien, Richard 1942- .... **CLC 17**
　See also CA 124
O'Brien, Tim 1946- .... **CLC 7, 19, 40, 103, 211; SSC 74, 123**
　See also AAYA 16; AMWS 5; CA 85-88; CANR 40, 58, 133; CDALBS; CN 5, 6, 7; CPW; DA3; DAM POP; DLB 152; DLBD 9; DLBY 1980; LATS 1:2; MAL 5; MTCW 2; MTFW 2005; RGAL 4; SSFS 5, 15, 29; TCLE 1:2
O'Brien, William Timothy
　See O'Brien, Tim

Obstfelder, Sigbjorn 1866-1900 ..... **TCLC 23**
See also CA 123; DLB 354

O'Casey, Brenda
See Haycraft, Anna

O'Casey, Sean 1880-1964 .... **CLC 1, 5, 9, 11, 15, 88; DC 12; WLCS**
See also BRW 7; CA 89-92; CANR 62; CBD; CDBLB 1914-1945; DA3; DAB; DAC; DAM DRAM, MST; DFS 19; DLB 10; EWL 3; MTCW 1, 2; MTFW 2005; RGEL 2; TEA; WLIT 4

O'Cathasaigh, Sean
See O'Casey, Sean

Occom, Samson 1723-1792 .... **LC 60; NNAL**
See also DLB 175

Occomy, Marita (Odette) Bonner 1899(?)-1971 ..... **HR 1:2; PC 72; TCLC 179**
See also BW 2; CA 142; DFS 13; DLB 51, 228

Ochs, Phil(ip David) 1940-1976 .... **CLC 17**
See also CA 185; 65-68

O'Connor, Edwin (Greene) 1918-1968 .... **CLC 14**
See also CA 93-96, 25-28R; MAL 5

O'Connor, Flannery 1925-1964 ..... **CLC 1, 2, 3, 6, 10, 13, 15, 21, 66, 104; SSC 1, 23, 61, 82, 111; TCLC 132; WLC 4**
See also AAYA 7; AMW; AMWR 2; BPFB 3; BYA 16; CA 1-4R; CANR 3, 41; CDALB 1941-1968; DA; DA3; DAB; DAC; DAM MST, NOV; DLB 2, 152; DLBD 12; DLBY 1980; EWL 3; EXPS; LAIT 5; MAL 5; MBL; MTCW 1, 2; MTFW 2005; NFS 3, 21; RGAL 4; RGSF 2; SSFS 2, 7, 10, 19; TUS

O'Connor, Frank 1903-1966
See O'Donovan, Michael Francis

O'Connor, Mary Flannery
See O'Connor, Flannery

O'Dell, Scott 1898-1989 .... **CLC 30**
See also AAYA 3, 44; BPFB 3; BYA 1, 2, 3, 5; CA 61-64, 129; CANR 12, 30, 112; CLR 1, 16, 126; DLB 52; JRDA; MAICYA 1, 2; SATA 12, 60, 134; WYA; YAW

Odets, Clifford 1906-1963 ..... **CLC 2, 28, 98; DC 6; TCLC 244**
See also AMWS 2; CA 85-88; CAD; CANR 62; DAM DRAM; DFS 3, 17, 20; DLB 7, 26, 341; EWL 3; MAL 5; MTCW 1, 2; MTFW 2005; RGAL 4; TUS

O'Doherty, Brian 1928- .... **CLC 76**
See also CA 105; CANR 108

O'Donnell, K. M.
See Malzberg, Barry N(athaniel)

O'Donnell, Lawrence
See Kuttner, Henry

O'Donovan, Michael Francis 1903-1966 .... **CLC 14, 23; SSC 5, 109**
See also BRWS 14; CA 93-96; CANR 84; DLB 162; EWL 3; RGSF 2; SSFS 5

Oe, Kenzaburo 1935- .. **CLC 10, 36, 86, 187; SSC 20**
See also CA 97-100; CANR 36, 50, 74, 126; CWW 2; DA3; DAM NOV; DLB 182, 331; DLBY 1994; EWL 3; LATS 1:2; MJW; MTCW 1, 2; MTFW 2005; RGSF 2; RGWL 2, 3

Oe Kenzaburo
See Oe, Kenzaburo

O'Faolain, Julia 1932- .... **CLC 6, 19, 47, 108**
See also CA 81-84; CAAS 2; CANR 12, 61; CN 2, 3, 4, 5, 6, 7; DLB 14, 231, 319; FW; MTCW 1; RHW

O'Faolain, Sean 1900-1991 ...... **CLC 1, 7, 14, 32, 70; SSC 13; TCLC 143**
See also CA 61-64, 134; CANR 12, 66; CN 1, 2, 3, 4; DLB 15, 162; MTCW 1, 2; MTFW 2005; RGEL 2; RGSF 2

O'Flaherty, Liam 1896-1984 .... **CLC 5, 34; SSC 6, 116**
See also CA 101, 113; CANR 35; CN 1, 2, 3; DLB 36, 162; DLBY 1984; MTCW 1, 2; MTFW 2005; RGEL 2; RGSF 2; SSFS 5, 20

Ogai
See Mori Ogai

Ogilvy, Gavin
See Barrie, J. M.

O'Grady, Standish (James) 1846-1928 .... **TCLC 5**
See also CA 104, 157

O'Grady, Timothy 1951- .... **CLC 59**
See also CA 138

O'Hara, Frank 1926-1966 .... **CLC 2, 5, 13, 78; PC 45**
See also CA 9-12R, 25-28R; CANR 33; DA3; DAM POET; DLB 5, 16, 193; EWL 3; MAL 5; MTCW 1, 2; MTFW 2005; PFS 8, 12, 34; RGAL 4; WP

O'Hara, John 1905-1970 . **CLC 1, 2, 3, 6, 11, 42; SSC 15**
See also AMW; BPFB 3; CA 5-8R, 25-28R; CANR 31, 60; CDALB 1929-1941; DAM NOV; DLB 9, 86, 324; DLBD 2; EWL 3; MAL 5; MTCW 1, 2; MTFW 2005; NFS 11; RGAL 4; RGSF 2

O'Hara, John Henry
See O'Hara, John

O'Hehir, Diana 1929- .... **CLC 41**
See also CA 245; CANR 177

O'Hehir, Diana F.
See O'Hehir, Diana

Ohiyesa
See Eastman, Charles A(lexander)

Okada, John 1923-1971 .... **AAL**
See also BYA 14; CA 212; DLB 312; NFS 25

O'Kelly, Seamus 1881(?)-1918 .... **SSC 136**

Okigbo, Christopher 1930-1967 ..... **BLC 1:3; CLC 25, 84; PC 7; TCLC 171**
See also AFW; BW 1, 3; CA 77-80; CANR 74; CDWLB 3; DAM MULT, POET; DLB 125; EWL 3; MTCW 1, 2; MTFW 2005; RGEL 2

Okigbo, Christopher Ifenayichukwu
See Okigbo, Christopher

Okri, Ben 1959- .... **BLC 2:3; CLC 87, 223; SSC 127**
See also AFW; BRWS 5; BW 2, 3; CA 130, 138; CANR 65, 128; CN 5, 6, 7; DLB 157, 231, 319, 326; EWL 3; INT CA-138; MTCW 2; MTFW 2005; RGSF 2; SSFS 20; WLIT 2; WWE 1

Old Boy
See Hughes, Thomas

Olds, Sharon 1942- .. **CLC 32, 39, 85; PC 22**
See also AMWS 10; CA 101; CANR 18, 41, 66, 98, 135; CP 5, 6, 7; CPW; CWP; DAM POET; DLB 120; MAL 5; MTCW 2; MTFW 2005; PFS 17

Oldstyle, Jonathan
See Irving, Washington

Olesha, Iurii
See Olesha, Yuri (Karlovich)

Olesha, Iurii Karlovich
See Olesha, Yuri (Karlovich)

Olesha, Yuri (Karlovich) 1899-1960 . **CLC 8; SSC 69; TCLC 136**
See also CA 85-88; DLB 272; EW 11; EWL 3; RGWL 2, 3

Olesha, Yury Karlovich
See Olesha, Yuri (Karlovich)

Oliphant, Mrs.
See Oliphant, Margaret (Oliphant Wilson)

Oliphant, Laurence 1829(?)-1888 .. **NCLC 47**
See also DLB 18, 166

Oliphant, Margaret (Oliphant Wilson) 1828-1897 ... **NCLC 11, 61, 221; SSC 25**
See also BRWS 10; DLB 18, 159, 190; HGG; RGEL 2; RGSF 2; SUFW

Oliver, Mary 1935- ... **CLC 19, 34, 98; PC 75**
See also AMWS 7; CA 21-24R; CANR 9, 43, 84, 92, 138; CP 4, 5, 6, 7; CWP; DLB 5, 193, 342; EWL 3; MTFW 2005; PFS 15, 31

Olivi, Peter 1248-1298 .... **CMLC 114**

Olivier, Laurence (Kerr) 1907-1989 . **CLC 20**
See also CA 111, 150, 129

O.L.S.
See Russell, George William

Olsen, Tillie 1912-2007 .... **CLC 4, 13, 114; SSC 11, 103**
See also AAYA 51; AMWS 13; BYA 11; CA 1-4R, 256; CANR 1, 43, 74, 132; CDALBS; CN 2, 3, 4, 5, 6, 7; DA; DA3; DAB; DAC; DAM MST; DLB 28, 206; DLBY 1980; EWL 3; EXPS; FW; MAL 5; MTCW 1, 2; MTFW 2005; RGAL 4; RGSF 2; SSFS 1; TCLE 1:2; TCWW 2; TUS

Olson, Charles 1910-1970 . **CLC 1, 2, 5, 6, 9, 11, 29; PC 19**
See also AMWS 2; CA 13-16, 25-28R; CABS 2; CANR 35, 61; CAP 1; CP 1; DAM POET; DLB 5, 16, 193; EWL 3; MAL 5; MTCW 1, 2; RGAL 4; WP

Olson, Charles John
See Olson, Charles

Olson, Merle Theodore
See Olson, Toby

Olson, Toby 1937- .... **CLC 28**
See also CA 65-68; CAAS 11; CANR 9, 31, 84, 175; CP 3, 4, 5, 6, 7

Olyesha, Yuri
See Olesha, Yuri (Karlovich)

Olympiodorus of Thebes c. 375-c. 430 .... **CMLC 59**

Omar Khayyam
See Khayyam, Omar

Ondaatje, Michael 1943- ..... **CLC 14, 29, 51, 76, 180, 258; PC 28**
See also AAYA 66; CA 77-80; CANR 42, 74, 109, 133, 172; CN 5, 6, 7; CP 1, 2, 3, 4, 5, 6, 7; DA3; DAB; DAC; DAM MST; DLB 60, 323, 326; EWL 3; LATS 1:2; LMFS 2; MTCW 2; MTFW 2005; NFS 23; PFS 8, 19; TCLE 1:2; TWA; WWE 1

Ondaatje, Philip Michael
See Ondaatje, Michael

Oneal, Elizabeth 1934- .... **CLC 30**
See also AAYA 5, 41; BYA 13; CA 106; CANR 28, 84; CLR 13; JRDA; MAICYA 1, 2; SATA 30, 82; WYA; YAW

Oneal, Zibby
See Oneal, Elizabeth

O'Neill, Eugene 1888-1953 ..... **DC 20; TCLC 1, 6, 27, 49, 225; WLC 4**
See also AAYA 54; AITN 1; AMW; AMWC 1; CA 110, 132; CAD; CANR 131; CDALB 1929-1941; DA; DA3; DAB; DAC; DAM DRAM, MST; DFS 2, 4, 5, 6, 9, 11, 12, 16, 20, 26, 27; DLB 7, 331; EWL 3; LAIT 3; LMFS 2; MAL 5; MTCW 1, 2; MTFW 2005; RGAL 4; TUS

O'Neill, Eugene Gladstone
See O'Neill, Eugene

Onetti, Juan Carlos 1909-1994 ... **CLC 7, 10; HLCS 2; SSC 23; TCLC 131**
See also CA 85-88, 145; CANR 32, 63; CDWLB 3; CWW 2; DAM MULT, NOV; DLB 113; EWL 3; HW 1, 2; LAW; MTCW 1, 2; MTFW 2005; RGSF 2

O'Nolan, Brian
See O Nuallain, Brian

O Nuallain, Brian 1911-1966 .... **CLC 1, 4, 5, 7, 10, 47**
    See also BRWS 2; CA 21-22, 25-28R; CAP 2; DLB 231; EWL 3; FANT; RGEL 2; TEA
Ophuls, Max
    See Ophuls, Max
Ophuls, Max 1902-1957 .... **TCLC 79**
    See also CA 113
Opie, Amelia 1769-1853 .... **NCLC 65**
    See also DLB 116, 159; RGEL 2
Oppen, George 1908-1984 ..... **CLC 7, 13, 34; PC 35; TCLC 107**
    See also CA 13-16R, 113; CANR 8, 82; CP 1, 2, 3; DLB 5, 165
Oppenheim, E(dward) Phillips
    1866-1946 .... **TCLC 45**
    See also CA 111, 202; CMW 4; DLB 70
Oppenheimer, Max
    See Ophuls, Max
Opuls, Max
    See Ophuls, Max
Orage, A(lfred) R(ichard)
    1873-1934 .... **TCLC 157**
    See also CA 122
Origen c. 185-c. 254 .... **CMLC 19**
Orlovitz, Gil 1918-1973 .... **CLC 22**
    See also CA 77-80, 45-48; CN 1; CP 1, 2; DLB 2, 5
Orosius c. 385-c. 420 .... **CMLC 100**
O'Rourke, Patrick Jake
    See O'Rourke, P.J.
O'Rourke, P.J. 1947- .... **CLC 209**
    See also CA 77-80; CANR 13, 41, 67, 111, 155; CPW; DAM POP; DLB 185
Orris
    See Ingelow, Jean
Ortega y Gasset, Jose 1883-1955 ...... **HLC 2; TCLC 9**
    See also CA 106, 130; DAM MULT; EW 9; EWL 3; HW 1, 2; MTCW 1, 2; MTFW 2005
Ortese, Anna Maria 1914-1998 .... **CLC 89**
    See also DLB 177; EWL 3
Ortiz, Simon
    See Ortiz, Simon J.
Ortiz, Simon J. 1941- . **CLC 45, 208; NNAL; PC 17**
    See also AMWS 4; CA 134; CANR 69, 118, 164; CP 3, 4, 5, 6, 7; DAM MULT, POET; DLB 120, 175, 256, 342; EXPP; MAL 5; PFS 4, 16; RGAL 4; SSFS 22; TCWW 2
Ortiz, Simon Joseph
    See Ortiz, Simon J.
Orton, Joe
    See Orton, John Kingsley
Orton, John Kingsley 1933-1967 .... **CLC 4, 13, 43; DC 3; TCLC 157**
    See also BRWS 5; CA 85-88; CANR 35, 66; CBD; CDBLB 1960 to Present; DAM DRAM; DFS 3, 6; DLB 13, 310; GLL 1; MTCW 1, 2; MTFW 2005; RGEL 2; TEA; WLIT 4
Orwell, George 1903-1950 .... **SSC 68; TCLC 2, 6, 15, 31, 51, 123, 128, 129; WLC 4**
    See also BPFB 3; BRW 7; BYA 5; CA 104, 132; CDBLB 1945-1960; CLR 68; DA; DA3; DAB; DAC; DAM MST, NOV; DLB 15, 98, 195, 255; EWL 3; EXPN; LAIT 4, 5; LATS 1:1; MTCW 1, 2; MTFW 2005; NFS 3, 7; RGEL 2; SATA 29; SCFW 1, 2; SFW 4; SSFS 4; TEA; WLIT 4; YAW X
Osborne, David
    See Silverberg, Robert
Osborne, Dorothy 1627-1695 .... **LC 141**
Osborne, George
    See Silverberg, Robert

Osborne, John 1929-1994 .... **CLC 1, 2, 5, 11, 45; DC 38; TCLC 153; WLC 4**
    See also BRWS 1; CA 13-16R, 147; CANR 21, 56; CBD; CDBLB 1945-1960; DA; DAB; DAC; DAM DRAM, MST; DFS 4, 19, 24; DLB 13; EWL 3; MTCW 1, 2; MTFW 2005; RGEL 2
Osborne, Lawrence 1958- .... **CLC 50**
    See also CA 189; CANR 152
Osbourne, Lloyd 1868-1947 .... **TCLC 93**
Osceola
    See Blixen, Karen
Osgood, Frances Sargent
    1811-1850 .... **NCLC 141**
    See also DLB 250
Oshima, Nagisa 1932- .... **CLC 20**
    See also CA 116, 121; CANR 78
Oskison, John Milton
    1874-1947 .... **NNAL; TCLC 35**
    See also CA 144; CANR 84; DAM MULT; DLB 175
Ossoli, Sarah Margaret
    See Fuller, Margaret
Ossoli, Sarah Margaret Fuller
    See Fuller, Margaret
Ostriker, Alicia 1937- .... **CLC 132**
    See also CA 25-28R; CAAS 24; CANR 10, 30, 62, 99, 167; CWP; DLB 120; EXPP; PFS 19, 26
Ostriker, Alicia Suskin
    See Ostriker, Alicia
Ostrovsky, Aleksandr Nikolaevich
    See Ostrovsky, Alexander
Ostrovsky, Alexander 1823-1886 .. **NCLC 30, 57**
    See also DLB 277
Osundare, Niyi 1947- .... **BLC 2:3**
    See also AFW; BW 3; CA 176; CDWLB 3; CP 7; DLB 157
Otero, Blas de 1916-1979 .... **CLC 11**
    See also CA 89-92; DLB 134; EWL 3
O'Trigger, Sir Lucius
    See Horne, Richard Henry Hengist
Otto, Rudolf 1869-1937 .... **TCLC 85**
Otto, Whitney 1955- .... **CLC 70**
    See also CA 140; CANR 120
Otway, Thomas 1652-1685 .. **DC 24; LC 106, 170**
    See also DAM DRAM; DLB 80; RGEL 2
Ouida
    See De La Ramee, Marie Louise
Ouologuem, Yambo 1940- .... **CLC 146, 293**
    See also CA 111, 176
Ousmane, Sembene 1923-2007 .... **BLC 1:3, 2:3; CLC 66**
    See also AFW; BW 1, 3; CA 117, 125, 261; CANR 81; CWW 2; EWL 3; MTCW 1; WLIT 2
Ovid 43B.C.-17 .... **CMLC 7, 108; PC 2**
    See also AW 2; CDWLB 1; DA3; DAM POET; DLB 211; PFS 22; RGWL 2, 3; WLIT 8; WP
Owen, Hugh
    See Faust, Frederick
Owen, Wilfred (Edward Salter)
    1893-1918 ..... **PC 19, 102; TCLC 5, 27; WLC 4**
    See also BRW 6; CA 104, 141; CDBLB 1914-1945; DA; DAB; DAC; DAM MST, POET; DLB 20; EWL 3; EXPP; MTCW 2; MTFW 2005; PFS 10; RGEL 2; WLIT 4
Owens, Louis (Dean) 1948-2002 .... **NNAL**
    See also CA 137, 179, 207; CAAE 179; CAAS 24; CANR 71
Owens, Rochelle 1936- .... **CLC 8**
    See also CA 17-20R; CAAS 2; CAD; CANR 39; CD 5, 6; CP 1, 2, 3, 4, 5, 6, 7; CWD; CWP

Oz, Amos 1939- ...... **CLC 5, 8, 11, 27, 33, 54; SSC 66**
    See also AAYA 84; CA 53-56; CANR 27, 47, 65, 113, 138, 175; CWW 2; DAM NOV; EWL 3; MTCW 1, 2; MTFW 2005; RGHL; RGSF 2; RGWL 3; WLIT 6
Ozick, Cynthia 1928- . **CLC 3, 7, 28, 62, 155, 262; SSC 15, 60, 123**
    See also AMWS 5; BEST 90:1; CA 17-20R; CANR 23, 58, 116, 160, 187; CN 3, 4, 5, 6, 7; CPW; DA3; DAM NOV, POP; DLB 28, 152, 299; DLBY 1982; EWL 3; EXPS; INT CANR-23; MAL 5; MTCW 1, 2; MTFW 2005; RGAL 4; RGHL; RGSF 2; SSFS 3, 12, 22
Ozu, Yasujiro 1903-1963 .... **CLC 16**
    See also CA 112
Pabst, G. W. 1885-1967 .... **TCLC 127**
Pacheco, C.
    See Pessoa, Fernando
Pacheco, Jose Emilio 1939- .... **HLC 2**
    See also CA 111, 131; CANR 65; CWW 2; DAM MULT; DLB 290; EWL 3; HW 1, 2; RGSF 2
Pa Chin
    See Jin, Ba
Pack, Robert 1929- .... **CLC 13**
    See also CA 1-4R; CANR 3, 44, 82; CP 1, 2, 3, 4, 5, 6, 7; DLB 5; SATA 118
Packer, Vin
    See Meaker, Marijane
Padgett, Lewis
    See Kuttner, Henry
Padilla (Lorenzo), Heberto
    1932-2000 .... **CLC 38**
    See also AITN 1; CA 123, 131, 189; CWW 2; EWL 3; HW 1
Paerdurabo, Frater
    See Crowley, Edward Alexander
Page, James Patrick 1944- .... **CLC 12**
    See also CA 204
Page, Jimmy 1944-
    See Page, James Patrick
Page, Louise 1955- .... **CLC 40**
    See also CA 140; CANR 76; CBD; CD 5, 6; CWD; DLB 233
Page, Patricia Kathleen
    See Page, P.K.
Page, P.K. 1916-2010 .... **CLC 7, 18; PC 12**
    See also CA 53-56; CANR 4, 22, 65; CCA 1; CP 1, 2, 3, 4, 5, 6, 7; DAC; DAM MST; DLB 68; MTCW 1; RGEL 2
Page, Stanton
    See Fuller, Henry Blake
Page, Thomas Nelson 1853-1922 .... **SSC 23**
    See also CA 118, 177; DLB 12, 78; DLBD 13; RGAL 4
Pagels, Elaine
    See Pagels, Elaine Hiesey
Pagels, Elaine Hiesey 1943- .... **CLC 104**
    See also CA 45-48; CANR 2, 24, 51, 151; FW; NCFS 4
Paget, Violet 1856-1935 .. **SSC 33, 98; TCLC 5**
    See also CA 104, 166; DLB 57, 153, 156, 174, 178; GLL 1; HGG; SUFW 1
Paget-Lowe, Henry
    See Lovecraft, H. P.
Paglia, Camille 1947- .... **CLC 68**
    See also CA 140; CANR 72, 139; CPW; FW; GLL 2; MTCW 2; MTFW 2005
Pagnol, Marcel (Paul)
    1895-1974 .... **TCLC 208**
    See also CA 128, 49-52; DLB 321; EWL 3; GFL 1789 to the Present; MTCW 1; RGWL 2, 3
Paige, Richard
    See Koontz, Dean

Paton Walsh, Jill 1937- .... **CLC 35**
See also AAYA 11, 47; BYA 1, 8; CA 262;
CAAE 262; CANR 38, 83, 158; CLR 2,
6, 128; DLB 161; JRDA; MAICYA 1, 2;
SAAS 3; SATA 4, 72, 109, 190; SATA-
Essay 190; WYA; YAW

Patsauq, Markoosie 1942- .... **NNAL**
See also CA 101; CLR 23; CWRI 5; DAM
MULT

Patterson, (Horace) Orlando (Lloyd)
1940- .... **BLCS**
See also BW 1; CA 65-68; CANR 27, 84;
CN 1, 2, 3, 4, 5, 6

Patton, George S(mith), Jr.
1885-1945 .... **TCLC 79**
See also CA 189

Paulding, James Kirke 1778-1860 ... **NCLC 2**
See also DLB 3, 59, 74, 250; RGAL 4

Paulin, Thomas Neilson
See Paulin, Tom

Paulin, Tom 1949- .... **CLC 37, 177**
See also CA 123, 128; CANR 98; CP 3, 4,
5, 6, 7; DLB 40

Pausanias c. 1st cent. - .... **CMLC 36**

Paustovsky, Konstantin (Georgievich)
1892-1968 .... **CLC 40**
See also CA 93-96, 25-28R; DLB 272;
EWL 3

Pavese, Cesare 1908-1950 .... **PC 13; SSC 19;**
TCLC 3, 240
See also CA 104, 169; DLB 128, 177; EW
12; EWL 3; PFS 20; RGSF 2; RGWL 2,
3; TWA; WLIT 7

Pavic, Milorad 1929-2009 .... **CLC 60**
See also CA 136; CDWLB 4; CWW 2; DLB
181; EWL 3; RGWL 3

Pavlov, Ivan Petrovich 1849-1936 . **TCLC 91**
See also CA 118, 180

Pavlova, Karolina Karlovna
1807-1893 .... **NCLC 138**
See also DLB 205

Payne, Alan
See Jakes, John

Payne, Rachel Ann
See Jakes, John

Paz, Gil
See Lugones, Leopoldo

Paz, Octavio 1914-1998 . **CLC 3, 4, 6, 10, 19,**
51, 65, 119; HLC 2; PC 1, 48; TCLC
211; WLC 4
See also AAYA 50; CA 73-76, 165; CANR
32, 65, 104; CWW 2; DA; DA3; DAB;
DAC; DAM MST, MULT, POET; DLB
290, 331; DLBY 1990, 1998; DNFS 1;
EWL 3; HW 1, 2; LAW; LAWS 1; MTCW
1, 2; MTFW 2005; PFS 18, 30; RGWL 2,
3; SSFS 13; TWA; WLIT 1

p'Bitek, Okot 1931-1982 . **BLC 1:3; CLC 96;**
TCLC 149
See also AFW; BW 2, 3; CA 124, 107;
CANR 82; CP 1, 2, 3; DAM MULT; DLB
125; EWL 3; MTCW 1, 2; MTFW 2005;
RGEL 2; WLIT 2

Peabody, Elizabeth Palmer
1804-1894 .... **NCLC 169**
See also DLB 1, 223

Peacham, Henry 1578-1644(?) .... **LC 119**
See also DLB 151

Peacock, Molly 1947- .... **CLC 60**
See also CA 103, 262; CAAE 262; CAAS
21; CANR 52, 84; CP 5, 6, 7; CWP; DLB
120, 282

Peacock, Thomas Love
1785-1866 .... **NCLC 22; PC 87**
See also BRW 4; DLB 96, 116; RGEL 2;
RGSF 2

Peake, Mervyn 1911-1968 .... **CLC 7, 54**
See also CA 5-8R, 25-28R; CANR 3; DLB
15, 160, 255; FANT; MTCW 1; RGEL 2;
SATA 23; SFW 4

Pearce, Ann Philippa
See Pearce, Philippa

Pearce, Philippa 1920-2006 .... **CLC 21**
See also BYA 5; CA 5-8R, 255; CANR 4,
109; CLR 9; CWRI 5; DLB 161; FANT;
MAICYA 1; SATA 1, 67, 129; SATA-Obit
179

Pearl, Eric
See Elman, Richard (Martin)

Pearson, Jean Mary
See Gardam, Jane

Pearson, Thomas Reid
See Pearson, T.R.

Pearson, T.R. 1956- .... **CLC 39**
See also CA 120, 130; CANR 97, 147, 185;
CSW; INT CA-130

Peck, Dale 1967- .... **CLC 81**
See also CA 146; CANR 72, 127, 180; GLL
2

Peck, John (Frederick) 1941- .... **CLC 3**
See also CA 49-52; CANR 3, 100; CP 4, 5,
6, 7

Peck, Richard 1934- .... **CLC 21**
See also AAYA 1, 24; BYA 1, 6, 8, 11; CA
85-88; CANR 19, 38, 129, 178; CLR 15,
142; INT CANR-19; JRDA; MAICYA 1,
2; SAAS 2; SATA 18, 55, 97, 110, 158,
190; SATA-Essay 110; WYA; YAW

Peck, Richard Wayne
See Peck, Richard

Peck, Robert Newton 1928- .... **CLC 17**
See also AAYA 3, 43; BYA 1, 6; CA 81-84,
182; CAAE 182; CANR 31, 63, 127; CLR
45; DA; DAC; DAM MST; JRDA; LAIT
3; MAICYA 1, 2; NFS 29; SAAS 1; SATA
21, 62, 111, 156; SATA-Essay 108; WYA;
YAW

Peckinpah, David Samuel
See Peckinpah, Sam

Peckinpah, Sam 1925-1984 .... **CLC 20**
See also CA 109, 114; CANR 82

Pedersen, Knut 1859-1952 .. **TCLC 2, 14, 49,**
151, 203
See also AAYA 79; CA 104, 119; CANR
63; DLB 297, 330; EW 8; EWL 8; MTCW
1, 2; RGWL 2, 3

Peele, George 1556-1596 .... **DC 27; LC 115**
See also BRW 1; DLB 62, 167; RGEL 2

Peeslake, Gaffer
See Durrell, Lawrence

Peguy, Charles (Pierre)
1873-1914 .... **TCLC 10**
See also CA 107, 193; DLB 258; EWL 3;
GFL 1789 to the Present

Peirce, Charles Sanders
1839-1914 .... **TCLC 81**
See also CA 194; DLB 270

Pelagius c. 350-c. 418 .... **CMLC 118**

Pelecanos, George P. 1957- .... **CLC 236**
See also CA 138; CANR 122, 165, 194;
DLB 306

Pelevin, Victor 1962- .... **CLC 238**
See also CA 154; CANR 88, 159, 197; DLB
285

Pelevin, Viktor Olegovich
See Pelevin, Victor

Pellicer, Carlos 1897(?)-1977 .... **HLCS 2**
See also CA 153, 69-72; DLB 290; EWL 3;
HW 1

Pena, Ramon del Valle y
See Valle-Inclan, Ramon del

Pendennis, Arthur Esquir
See Thackeray, William Makepeace

Penn, Arthur
See Matthews, (James) Brander

Penn, William 1644-1718 .... **LC 25**
See also DLB 24

PEPECE
See Prado (Calvo), Pedro

Pepys, Samuel 1633-1703 ... **LC 11, 58; WLC**
4
See also BRW 2; CDBLB 1660-1789; DA;
DA3; DAB; DAC; DAM MST; DLB 101,
213; NCFS 4; RGEL 2; TEA; WLIT 3

Percy, Thomas 1729-1811 .... **NCLC 95**
See also DLB 104

Percy, Walker 1916-1990 .... **CLC 2, 3, 6, 8,**
14, 18, 47, 65
See also AMWS 3; BPFB 3; CA 1-4R, 131;
CANR 1, 23, 64; CN 1, 2, 3, 4; CPW;
CSW; DA3; DAM NOV, POP; DLB 2;
DLBY 1980, 1990; EWL 3; MAL 5;
MTCW 1, 2; MTFW 2005; RGAL 4; TUS

Percy, William Alexander
1885-1942 .... **TCLC 84**
See also CA 163; MTCW 2

Perdurabo, Frater
See Crowley, Edward Alexander

Perec, Georges 1936-1982 .... **CLC 56, 116**
See also CA 141; DLB 83, 299; EWL 3;
GFL 1789 to the Present; RGHL; RGWL
3

Pereda (y Sanchez de Porrua), Jose Maria
de 1833-1906 .... **TCLC 16**
See also CA 117

Pereda y Porrua, Jose Maria de
See Pereda (y Sanchez de Porrua), Jose
Maria de

Peregoy, George Weems
See Mencken, H. L.

Perelman, S(idney) J(oseph)
1904-1979 .. **CLC 3, 5, 9, 15, 23, 44, 49;**
SSC 32
See also AAYA 79; AITN 1, 2; BPFB 3;
CA 73-76, 89-92; CANR 18; DAM
DRAM; DLB 11, 44; MTCW 1, 2; MTFW
2005; RGAL 4

Peret, Benjamin 1899-1959 .... **PC 33; TCLC**
20
See also CA 117, 186; GFL 1789 to the
Present

Perets, Yitskhok Leybush
See Peretz, Isaac Loeb

Peretz, Isaac Leib (?)-
See Peretz, Isaac Loeb

Peretz, Isaac Loeb 1851-1915 .... **SSC 26;**
TCLC 16
See Peretz, Isaac Leib
See also CA 109, 201; DLB 333

Peretz, Yitzkhok Leibush
See Peretz, Isaac Loeb

Perez Galdos, Benito 1843-1920 ..... **HLCS 2;**
TCLC 27
See also CA 125, 153; EW 7; EWL 3; HW
1; RGWL 2, 3

Peri Rossi, Cristina 1941- .. **CLC 156; HLCS**
2
See also CA 131; CANR 59, 81; CWW 2;
DLB 145, 290; EWL 3; HW 1, 2

Perlata
See Peret, Benjamin

Perloff, Marjorie G(abrielle)
1931- .... **CLC 137**
See also CA 57-60; CANR 7, 22, 49, 104

Perrault, Charles 1628-1703 .... **LC 2, 56**
See also BYA 4; CLR 79, 134; DLB 268;
GFL Beginnings to 1789; MAICYA 1, 2;
RGWL 2, 3; SATA 25; WCH

Perrotta, Tom 1961- .... **CLC 266**
See also CA 162; CANR 99, 155, 197

Perry, Anne 1938- .... **CLC 126**
See also CA 101; CANR 22, 50, 84, 150,
177; CMW 4; CN 6, 7; CPW; DLB 276

Postl, Carl
See Sealsfield, Charles

Postman, Neil 1931(?)-2003 .... **CLC 244**
See also CA 102, 221

Potocki, Jan 1761-1815 .... **NCLC 229**

Potok, Chaim 1929-2002 ... **CLC 2, 7, 14, 26, 112**
See also AAYA 15, 50; AITN 1, 2; BPFB 3; BYA 1; CA 17-20R, 208; CANR 19, 35, 64, 98; CLR 92; CN 4, 5, 6; DA3; DAM NOV; DLB 28, 152; EXPN; INT CANR-19; LAIT 4; MTCW 1, 2; MTFW 2005; NFS 4, 34; RGHL; SATA 33, 106; SATA-Obit 134; TUS; YAW

Potok, Herbert Harold
See Potok, Chaim

Potok, Herman Harold
See Potok, Chaim

Potter, Dennis (Christopher George)
1935-1994 .... **CLC 58, 86, 123**
See also BRWS 10; CA 107, 145; CANR 33, 61; CBD; DLB 233; MTCW 1

Pound, Ezra 1885-1972 . **CLC 1, 2, 3, 4, 5, 7, 10, 13, 18, 34, 48, 50, 112; PC 4, 95; WLC 5**
See also AAYA 47; AMW; AMWR 1; CA 5-8R, 37-40R; CANR 40; CDALB 1917-1929; CP 1; DA; DA3; DAB; DAC; DAM MST, POET; DLB 4, 45, 63; DLBD 15; EFS 2; EWL 3; EXPP; LMFS 2; MAL 5; MTCW 1, 2; MTFW 2005; PAB; PFS 2, 8, 16; RGAL 4; TUS; WP

Pound, Ezra Weston Loomis
See Pound, Ezra

Povod, Reinaldo 1959-1994 .... **CLC 44**
See also CA 136, 146; CANR 83

Powell, Adam Clayton, Jr.
1908-1972 .... **BLC 1:3; CLC 89**
See also BW 1, 3; CA 102, 33-36R; CANR 86; DAM MULT; DLB 345

Powell, Anthony 1905-2000 ... **CLC 1, 3, 7, 9, 10, 31**
See also BRW 7; CA 1-4R, 189; CANR 1, 32, 62, 107; CDBLB 1945-1960; CN 1, 2, 3, 4, 5, 6; DLB 15; EWL 3; MTCW 1, 2; MTFW 2005; RGEL 2; TEA

Powell, Dawn 1896(?)-1965 .... **CLC 66**
See also CA 5-8R; CANR 121; DLBY 1997

Powell, Padgett 1952- .... **CLC 34**
See also CA 126; CANR 63, 101; CSW; DLB 234; DLBY 01; SSFS 25

Power, Susan 1961- .... **CLC 91**
See also BYA 14; CA 160; CANR 135; NFS 11

Powers, J(ames) F(arl) 1917-1999 ..... **CLC 1, 4, 8, 57; SSC 4**
See also CA 1-4R, 181; CANR 2, 61; CN 1, 2, 3, 4, 5, 6; DLB 130; MTCW 1; RGAL 4; RGSF 2

Powers, John
See Powers, John R.

Powers, John R. 1945- .... **CLC 66**
See also CA 69-72

Powers, Richard 1957- .... **CLC 93, 292**
See also AMWS 9; BPFB 3; CA 148; CANR 80, 180; CN 6, 7; DLB 350; MTFW 2005; TCLE 1:2

Powers, Richard S.
See Powers, Richard

Pownall, David 1938- .... **CLC 10**
See also CA 89-92, 180; CAAS 18; CANR 49, 101; CBD; CD 5, 6; CN 4, 5, 6, 7; DLB 14

Powys, John Cowper 1872-1963 ... **CLC 7, 9, 15, 46, 125**
See also CA 85-88; CANR 106; DLB 15, 255; EWL 3; FANT; MTCW 1, 2; MTFW 2005; RGEL 2; SUFW

Powys, T(heodore) F(rancis)
1875-1953 .... **TCLC 9**
See also BRWS 8; CA 106, 189; DLB 36, 162; EWL 3; FANT; RGEL 2; SUFW

Pozzo, Modesta
See Fonte, Moderata

Prado (Calvo), Pedro 1886-1952 ... **TCLC 75**
See also CA 131; DLB 283; HW 1; LAW

Prager, Emily 1952- .... **CLC 56**
See also CA 204

Pratchett, Terence David John
See Pratchett, Terry

Pratchett, Terry 1948- .... **CLC 197**
See also AAYA 19, 54; BPFB 3; CA 143; CANR 87, 126, 170; CLR 64; CN 6, 7; CPW; CWRI 5; FANT; MTFW 2005; SATA 82, 139, 185; SFW 4; SUFW 2

Pratolini, Vasco 1913-1991 .... **TCLC 124**
See also CA 211; DLB 177; EWL 3; RGWL 2, 3

Pratt, E(dwin) J(ohn) 1883(?)-1964 . **CLC 19**
See also CA 141, 93-96; CANR 77; DAC; DAM POET; DLB 92; EWL 3; RGEL 2; TWA

Premacanda
See Srivastava, Dhanpat Rai

Premchand
See Srivastava, Dhanpat Rai

Prem Chand, Munshi
See Srivastava, Dhanpat Rai

Premchand, Munshi
See Srivastava, Dhanpat Rai

Prescott, William Hickling
1796-1859 .... **NCLC 163**
See also DLB 1, 30, 59, 235

Preseren, France 1800-1849 .... **NCLC 127**
See also CDWLB 4; DLB 147

Preussler, Otfried 1923- .... **CLC 17**
See also CA 77-80; SATA 24

Prevert, Jacques 1900-1977 .... **CLC 15**
See also CA 77-80, 69-72; CANR 29, 61, 207; DLB 258; EWL 3; GFL 1789 to the Present; IDFW 3, 4; MTCW 1; RGWL 2, 3; SATA-Obit 30

Prevert, Jacques Henri Marie
See Prevert, Jacques

Prevost, (Antoine Francois)
1697-1763 .... **LC 1, 174**
See also DLB 314; EW 4; GFL Beginnings to 1789; RGWL 2, 3

Price, Edward Reynolds
See Price, Reynolds

Price, Reynolds 1933- ... **CLC 3, 6, 13, 43, 50, 63, 212; SSC 22**
See also AMWS 6; CA 1-4R; CANR 1, 37, 57, 87, 128, 177; CN 1, 2, 3, 4, 5, 6, 7; CSW; DAM NOV; DLB 2, 218, 278; EWL 3; INT CANR-37; MAL 5; MTFW 2005; NFS 18

Price, Richard 1949- .... **CLC 6, 12**
See also CA 49-52; CANR 3, 147, 190; CN 7; DLBY 1981

Prichard, Katharine Susannah
1883-1969 .... **CLC 46**
See also CA 11-12; CANR 33; CAP 1; DLB 260; MTCW 1; RGEL 2; RGSF 2; SATA 66

Priestley, J(ohn) B(oynton)
1894-1984 .... **CLC 2, 5, 9, 34**
See also BRW 7; CA 9-12R, 113; CANR 33; CDBLB 1914-1945; CN 1, 2, 3; DA3; DAM DRAM, NOV; DLB 10, 34, 77, 100, 139; DLBY 1984; EWL 3; MTCW 1, 2; MTFW 2005; RGEL 2; SFW 4

Prince 1958- .... **CLC 35**
See also CA 213

Prince, F(rank) T(empleton)
1912-2003 .... **CLC 22**
See also CA 101, 219; CANR 43, 79; CP 1, 2, 3, 4, 5, 6, 7; DLB 20

Prince Kropotkin
See Kropotkin, Peter

Prior, Matthew 1664-1721 ...... **LC 4; PC 102**
See also DLB 95; RGEL 2

Prishvin, Mikhail 1873-1954 .... **TCLC 75**
See also DLB 272; EWL 3 !**

Prishvin, Mikhail Mikhailovich
See Prishvin, Mikhail

Pritchard, William H(arrison)
1932- .... **CLC 34**
See also CA 65-68; CANR 23, 95; DLB 111

Pritchett, V(ictor) S(awdon)
1900-1997 .. **CLC 5, 13, 15, 41; SSC 14, 126**
See also BPFB 3; BRWS 3; CA 61-64, 157; CANR 31, 63; CN 1, 2, 3, 4, 5, 6; DA3; DAM NOV; DLB 15, 139; EWL 3; MTCW 1, 2; MTFW 2005; RGEL 2; RGSF 2; TEA

Private 19022
See Manning, Frederic

Probst, Mark 1925- .... **CLC 59**
See also CA 130

Procaccino, Michael
See Cristofer, Michael

Proclus c. 412-c. 485 .... **CMLC 81**

Prokosch, Frederic 1908-1989 ...... **CLC 4, 48**
See also CA 73-76, 128; CANR 82; CN 1, 2, 3, 4; CP 1, 2, 3, 4; DLB 48; MTCW 2

Propertius, Sextus c. 50B.C.-c. 16B.C. .... **CMLC 32**
See also AW 2; CDWLB 1; DLB 211; RGWL 2, 3; WLIT 8

Prophet, The
See Dreiser, Theodore

Prose, Francine 1947- .... **CLC 45, 231**
See also AMWS 16; CA 109, 112; CANR 46, 95, 132, 175; DLB 234; MTFW 2005; SATA 101, 149, 198

Protagoras c. 490B.C.-420B.C. ...... **CMLC 85**
See also DLB 176

Proudhon
See Cunha, Euclides (Rodrigues Pimenta) da

Proulx, Annie 1935- . **CLC 81, 158, 250; SSC 128**
See also AAYA 81; AMWS 7; BPFB 3; CA 145; CANR 65, 110, 206; CN 6, 7; CPW 1; DA3; DAM POP; DLB 335, 350; MAL 5; MTCW 2; MTFW 2005; SSFS 18, 23

Proulx, E. Annie
See Proulx, Annie

Proulx, Edna Annie
See Proulx, Annie

Proust, Marcel 1871-1922 ..... **SSC 75; TCLC 7, 13, 33, 220; WLC 5**
See also AAYA 58; BPFB 3; CA 104, 120; CANR 110; DA; DA3; DAB; DAC; DAM MST, NOV; DLB 65; EW 8; EWL 3; GFL 1789 to the Present; MTCW 1, 2; MTFW 2005; RGWL 2, 3; TWA

Proust, Valentin-Louis-George-Eugene Marcel
See Proust, Marcel

Prowler, Harley
See Masters, Edgar Lee

Prudentius, Aurelius Clemens 348-c. 405 .... **CMLC 78**
See also EW 1; RGWL 2, 3

Prudhomme, Rene Francois Armand
See Sully Prudhomme, Rene-Francois-Armand

Prus, Boleslaw 1845-1912 .... **TCLC 48**
See also RGWL 2, 3

Prynne, William 1600-1669 .... **LC 148**

Prynne, Xavier
  See Hardwick, Elizabeth

Pryor, Aaron Richard
  See Pryor, Richard

Pryor, Richard 1940-2005 .... **CLC 26**
  See also CA 122, 152, 246

Pryor, Richard Franklin Lenox Thomas
  See Pryor, Richard

Przybyszewski, Stanislaw
  1868-1927 .... **TCLC 36**
  See also CA 160; DLB 66; EWL 3

Pseudo-Dionysius the Areopagite fl. c. 5th
  cent. - .... **CMLC 89**
  See also DLB 115

Pteleon
  See Grieve, C. M.

Puckett, Lute
  See Masters, Edgar Lee

Puig, Manuel 1932-1990 .... **CLC 3, 5, 10, 28,
  65, 133; HLC 2; TCLC 227**
  See also BPFB 3; CA 45-48; CANR 2, 32,
  63; CDWLB 3; DA3; DAM MULT; DLB
  113; DNFS 1; EWL 3; GLL 1; HW 1, 2;
  LAW; MTCW 1, 2; MTFW 2005; RGWL
  2, 3; TWA; WLIT 1

Pulitzer, Joseph 1847-1911 .... **TCLC 76**
  See also CA 114; DLB 23

Pullman, Philip 1946- .... **CLC 245**
  See also AAYA 15, 41; BRWS 13; BYA 8,
  13; CA 127; CANR 50, 77, 105, 134, 190;
  CLR 20, 62, 84; JRDA; MAICYA 1, 2;
  MAICYAS 1; MTFW 2005; SAAS 17;
  SATA 65, 103, 150, 198; SUFW 2; WYAS
  1; YAW

Purchas, Samuel 1577(?)-1626 .... **LC 70**
  See also DLB 151

Purdy, A(lfred) W(ellington)
  1918-2000 .... **CLC 3, 6, 14, 50**
  See also CA 81-84, 189; CAAS 17; CANR
  42, 66; CP 1, 2, 3, 4, 5, 6, 7; DAC; DAM
  MST, POET; DLB 88; PFS 5; RGEL 2

Purdy, James 1914-2009 .... **CLC 2, 4, 10, 28,
  52, 286**
  See also AMWS 7; CA 33-36R, 284; CAAS
  1; CANR 19, 51, 132; CN 1, 2, 3, 4, 5, 6,
  7; DLB 2, 218; EWL 3; INT CANR-19;
  MAL 5; MTCW 1; RGAL 4

Purdy, James Amos
  See Purdy, James

Purdy, James Otis
  See Purdy, James

Pure, Simon
  See Swinnerton, Frank Arthur

Pushkin, Aleksandr Sergeevich
  See Pushkin, Alexander

Pushkin, Alexander 1799-1837 . **NCLC 3, 27,
  83; PC 10; SSC 27, 55, 99; WLC 5**
  See also DA; DA3; DAB; DAC; DAM
  DRAM, MST, POET; DLB 205; EW 5;
  EXPS; PFS 28, 34; RGSF 2; RGWL 2, 3;
  SATA 61; SSFS 9; TWA

Pushkin, Alexander Sergeyevich
  See Pushkin, Alexander

P'u Sung-ling 1640-1715 .... **LC 49; SSC 31**

Putnam, Arthur Lee
  See Alger, Horatio, Jr.

Puttenham, George 1529(?)-1590 ...... **LC 116**
  See also DLB 281

Puzo, Mario 1920-1999 .... **CLC 1, 2, 6, 36,
  107**
  See also BPFB 3; CA 65-68, 185; CANR 4,
  42, 65, 99, 131; CN 1, 2, 3, 4, 5, 6; CPW;
  DA3; DAM NOV, POP; DLB 6; MTCW
  1, 2; MTFW 2005; NFS 16; RGAL 4

Pygge, Edward
  See Barnes, Julian

Pyle, Ernest Taylor
  See Pyle, Ernie

Pyle, Ernie 1900-1945 .... **TCLC 75**
  See also CA 115, 160; DLB 29; MTCW 2

Pyle, Howard 1853-1911 .... **TCLC 81**
  See also AAYA 57; BYA 2, 4; CA 109, 137;
  CLR 22, 117; DLB 42, 188; DLBD 13;
  LAIT 1; MAICYA 1, 2; SATA 16, 100;
  WCH; YAW

Pym, Barbara (Mary Crampton)
  1913-1980 .... **CLC 13, 19, 37, 111**
  See also BPFB 3; BRWS 2; CA 13-14, 97-
  100; CANR 13, 34; CAP 1; DLB 14, 207;
  DLBY 1987; EWL 3; MTCW 1, 2; MTFW
  2005; RGEL 2; TEA

Pynchon, Thomas 1937- .. **CLC 2, 3, 6, 9, 11,
  18, 33, 62, 72, 123, 192, 213; SSC 14,
  84; WLC 5**
  See also AMWS 2; BEST 90:2; BPFB 3;
  CA 17-20R; CANR 22, 46, 73, 142, 198;
  CN 1, 2, 3, 4, 5, 6, 7; CPW 1; DA; DA3;
  DAB; DAC; DAM MST, NOV, POP;
  DLB 2, 173; EWL 3; MAL 5; MTCW 1,
  2; MTFW 2005; NFS 23; RGAL 4; SFW
  4; TCLE 1:2; TUS

Pynchon, Thomas Ruggels, Jr.
  See Pynchon, Thomas

Pynchon, Thomas Ruggles
  See Pynchon, Thomas

Pythagoras c. 582B.C.-c. 507B.C. . **CMLC 22**
  See also DLB 176

Q
  See Quiller-Couch, Sir Arthur (Thomas)

Qian, Chongzhu
  See Ch'ien, Chung-shu

Qian, Sima 145B.C.-c. 89B.C. .... **CMLC 72**

Qian Zhongshu
  See Ch'ien, Chung-shu

Qroll
  See Dagerman, Stig (Halvard)

Quarles, Francis 1592-1644 .... **LC 117**
  See also DLB 126; RGEL 2

Quarrington, Paul 1953-2010 .... **CLC 65**
  See also CA 129; CANR 62, 95

Quarrington, Paul Lewis
  See Quarrington, Paul

Quasimodo, Salvatore 1901-1968 .... **CLC 10;
  PC 47**
  See also CA 13-16, 25-28R; CAP 1; DLB
  114, 332; EW 12; EWL 3; MTCW 1;
  RGWL 2, 3

Quatermass, Martin
  See Carpenter, John

Quay, Stephen 1947- .... **CLC 95**
  See also CA 189

Quay, Timothy 1947- .... **CLC 95**
  See also CA 189

Queen, Ellery
  See Dannay, Frederic; Hoch, Edward D.;
  Lee, Manfred B.; Marlowe, Stephen; Stur-
  geon, Theodore (Hamilton); Vance, Jack

Queneau, Raymond 1903-1976 ..... **CLC 2, 5,
  10, 42; TCLC 233**
  See also CA 77-80, 69-72; CANR 32; DLB
  72, 258; EW 12; EWL 3; GFL 1789 to
  the Present; MTCW 1, 2; RGWL 2, 3

Quevedo, Francisco de 1580-1645 ...... **LC 23,
  160**

Quiller-Couch, Sir Arthur (Thomas)
  1863-1944 .... **TCLC 53**
  See also CA 118, 166; DLB 135, 153, 190;
  HGG; RGEL 2; SUFW 1

Quin, Ann 1936-1973 .... **CLC 6**
  See also CA 9-12R, 45-48; CANR 148; CN
  1; DLB 14, 231

Quin, Ann Marie
  See Quin, Ann

Quincey, Thomas de
  See De Quincey, Thomas

Quindlen, Anna 1953- .... **CLC 191**
  See also AAYA 35; AMWS 17; CA 138;
  CANR 73, 126; DA3; DLB 292; MTCW
  2; MTFW 2005

Quinn, Martin
  See Smith, Martin Cruz

Quinn, Peter 1947- .... **CLC 91**
  See also CA 197; CANR 147

Quinn, Peter A.
  See Quinn, Peter

Quinn, Simon
  See Smith, Martin Cruz

Quintana, Leroy V. 1944- ...... **HLC 2; PC 36**
  See also CA 131; CANR 65, 139; DAM
  MULT; DLB 82; HW 1, 2

Quintilian c. 40-c. 100 .... **CMLC 77**
  See also AW 2; DLB 211; RGWL 2, 3

Quiroga, Horacio (Sylvestre)
  1878-1937 ... **HLC 2; SSC 89; TCLC 20**
  See also CA 117, 131; DAM MULT; EWL
  3; HW 1; LAW; MTCW 1; RGSF 2;
  WLIT 1

Quoirez, Francoise 1935-2004 ... **CLC 3, 6, 9,
  17, 36**
  See also CA 49-52, 231; CANR 6, 39, 73;
  CWW 2; DLB 83; EWL 3; GFL 1789 to
  the Present; MTCW 1, 2; MTFW 2005;
  TWA

Raabe, Wilhelm (Karl) 1831-1910 . **TCLC 45**
  See also CA 167; DLB 129

Rabe, David (William) 1940- .. **CLC 4, 8, 33,
  200; DC 16**
  See also CA 85-88; CABS 3; CAD; CANR
  59, 129; CD 5, 6; DAM DRAM; DFS 3,
  8, 13; DLB 7, 228; EWL 3; MAL 5

Rabelais, Francois 1494-1553 .... **LC 5, 60;
  WLC 5**
  See also DA; DAB; DAC; DAM MST;
  DLB 327; EW 2; GFL Beginnings to
  1789; LMFS 1; RGWL 2, 3; TWA

Rabi'a al-'Adawiyya c. 717-c.
  801 .... **CMLC 83**
  See also DLB 311

Rabinovitch, Sholem 1859-1916 .... **SSC 33,
  125; TCLC 1, 35**
  See also CA 104; DLB 333; TWA

Rabinovitsh, Sholem Yankev
  See Rabinovitch, Sholem

Rabinowitz, Sholem Yakov
  See Rabinovitch, Sholem

Rabinowitz, Solomon
  See Rabinovitch, Sholem

Rabinyan, Dorit 1972- .... **CLC 119**
  See also CA 170; CANR 147

Rachilde
  See Vallette, Marguerite Eymery; Vallette,
  Marguerite Eymery

Racine, Jean 1639-1699 .. **DC 32; LC 28, 113**
  See also DA3; DAB; DAM MST; DLB 268;
  EW 3; GFL Beginnings to 1789; LMFS
  1; RGWL 2, 3; TWA

Radcliffe, Ann 1764-1823 .. **NCLC 6, 55, 106,
  223**
  See also BRWR 3; DLB 39, 178; GL 3;
  HGG; LMFS 1; RGEL 2; SUFW; WLIT
  3

Radclyffe-Hall, Marguerite
  See Hall, Radclyffe

Radiguet, Raymond 1903-1923 ...... **TCLC 29**
  See also CA 162; DLB 65; EWL 3; GFL
  1789 to the Present; RGWL 2, 3

Radishchev, Aleksandr Nikolaevich
  1749-1802 .... **NCLC 190**
  See also DLB 150

Radishchev, Alexander
  See Radishchev, Aleksandr Nikolaevich

Radnoti, Miklos 1909-1944 .... **TCLC 16**
  See also CA 118, 212; CDWLB 4; DLB
  215; EWL 3; RGHL; RGWL 2, 3

Reiner, Max
  See Caldwell, (Janet Miriam) Taylor (Holland)
Reis, Ricardo
  See Pessoa, Fernando
Reizenstein, Elmer Leopold
  See Rice, Elmer (Leopold)
Remark, Erich Paul
  See Remarque, Erich Maria
Remarque, Erich Maria 1898-1970 . **CLC 21**
  See also AAYA 27; BPFB 3; CA 77-80, 29-32R; CDWLB 2; DA; DA3; DAB; DAC; DAM MST, NOV; DLB 56; EWL 3; EXPN; LAIT 3; MTCW 1, 2; MTFW 2005; NFS 4; RGHL; RGWL 2, 3
Remington, Frederic S(ackrider)
  1861-1909 .... **TCLC 89**
  See also CA 108, 169; DLB 12, 186, 188; SATA 41; TCWW 2
Remizov, A.
  See Remizov, Aleksei (Mikhailovich)
Remizov, A. M.
  See Remizov, Aleksei (Mikhailovich)
Remizov, Aleksei (Mikhailovich)
  1877-1957 .... **TCLC 27**
  See also CA 125, 133; DLB 295; EWL 3
Remizov, Alexey Mikhaylovich
  See Remizov, Aleksei (Mikhailovich)
Renan, Joseph Ernest 1823-1892 . **NCLC 26, 145**
  See also GFL 1789 to the Present
Renard, Jules(-Pierre) 1864-1910 .. **TCLC 17**
  See also CA 117, 202; GFL 1789 to the Present
Renart, Jean fl. 13th cent. - .... **CMLC 83**
Renault, Mary 1905-1983 .... **CLC 3, 11, 17**
  See also BPFB 3; BYA 2; CA 81-84, 111; CANR 74; CN 1, 2, 3; DA3; DLBY 1983; EWL 3; GLL 1; LAIT 1; MTCW 2; MTFW 2005; RGEL 2; RHW; SATA 23; SATA-Obit 36; TEA
Rendell, Ruth
  See Rendell, Ruth
Rendell, Ruth 1930- ...... **CLC 28, 48, 50, 295**
  See also BEST 90:4; BPFB 3; BRWS 9; CA 109; CANR 32, 52, 74, 127, 162, 190; CN 5, 6, 7; CPW; DAM POP; DLB 87, 276; INT CANR-32; MSW; MTCW 1, 2; MTFW 2005
Rendell, Ruth Barbara
  See Rendell, Ruth
Renoir, Jean 1894-1979 .... **CLC 20**
  See also CA 129, 85-88
Rensie, Willis
  See Eisner, Will
Resnais, Alain 1922- .... **CLC 16**
Revard, Carter 1931- .... **NNAL**
  See also CA 144; CANR 81, 153; PFS 5
Reverdy, Pierre 1889-1960 .... **CLC 53**
  See also CA 97-100, 89-92; DLB 258; EWL 3; GFL 1789 to the Present
Reverend Mandju
  See Su, Chien
Rexroth, Kenneth 1905-1982 .... **CLC 1, 2, 6, 11, 22, 49, 112; PC 20, 95**
  See also BG 1:3; CA 5-8R, 107; CANR 14, 34, 63; CDALB 1941-1968; CP 1, 2, 3; DAM POET; DLB 16, 48, 165, 212; DLBY 1982; EWL 3; INT CANR-14; MAL 5; MTCW 1, 2; MTFW 2005; RGAL 4
Reyes, Alfonso 1889-1959 .... **HLCS 2; TCLC 33**
  See also CA 131; EWL 3; HW 1; LAW
Reyes y Basoalto, Ricardo Eliecer Neftali
  See Neruda, Pablo
Reymont, Wladyslaw (Stanislaw)
  1868(?)-1925 .... **TCLC 5**
  See also CA 104; DLB 332; EWL 3

Reynolds, John Hamilton
  1794-1852 .... **NCLC 146**
  See also DLB 96
Reynolds, Jonathan 1942- .... **CLC 6, 38**
  See also CA 65-68; CANR 28, 176
Reynolds, Joshua 1723-1792 .... **LC 15**
  See also DLB 104
Reynolds, Michael S(hane)
  1937-2000 .... **CLC 44**
  See also CA 65-68, 189; CANR 9, 89, 97
Reza, Yasmina 1959- .... **DC 34**
  See also AAYA 69; CA 171; CANR 145; DFS 19; DLB 321
Reznikoff, Charles 1894-1976 .... **CLC 9**
  See also AMWS 14; CA 33-36, 61-64; CAP 2; CP 1, 2; DLB 28, 45; RGHL; WP
Rezzori, Gregor von
  See Rezzori d'Arezzo, Gregor von
Rezzori d'Arezzo, Gregor von
  1914-1998 .... **CLC 25**
  See also CA 122, 136, 167
Rhine, Richard
  See Silverstein, Alvin; Silverstein, Virginia B.
Rhodes, Eugene Manlove
  1869-1934 .... **TCLC 53**
  See also CA 198; DLB 256; TCWW 1, 2
R'hoone, Lord
  See Balzac, Honore de
Rhys, Jean 1890-1979 .... **CLC 2, 4, 6, 14, 19, 51, 124; SSC 21, 76**
  See also BRWS 2; CA 25-28R, 85-88; CANR 35, 62; CDBLB 1945-1960; CD-WLB 3; CN 1, 2; DA3; DAM NOV; DLB 36, 117, 162; DNFS 2; EWL 3; LATS 1:1; MTCW 1, 2; MTFW 2005; NFS 19; RGEL 2; RGSF 2; RHW; TEA; WWE 1
Ribeiro, Darcy 1922-1997 .... **CLC 34**
  See also CA 33-36R, 156; EWL 3
Ribeiro, Joao Ubaldo (Osorio Pimentel)
  1941- .... **CLC 10, 67**
  See also CA 81-84; CWW 2; EWL 3
Ribman, Ronald (Burt) 1932- .... **CLC 7**
  See also CA 21-24R; CAD; CANR 46, 80; CD 5, 6
Ricci, Nino 1959- .... **CLC 70**
  See also CA 137; CANR 130; CCA 1
Ricci, Nino Pio
  See Ricci, Nino
Rice, Anne 1941- .... **CLC 41, 128**
  See also AAYA 9, 53; AMWS 7; BEST 89:2; BPFB 3; CA 65-68; CANR 12, 36, 53, 74, 100, 133, 190; CN 6, 7; CPW; CSW; DA3; DAM POP; DLB 292; GL 3; GLL 2; HGG; MTCW 2; MTFW 2005; SUFW 2; YAW
Rice, Elmer (Leopold) 1892-1967 ...... **CLC 7, 49; TCLC 221**
  See also CA 21-22, 25-28R; CAP 2; DAM DRAM; DFS 12; DLB 4, 7; EWL 3; IDTP; MAL 5; MTCW 1, 2; RGAL 4
Rice, Tim 1944- .... **CLC 21**
  See also CA 103; CANR 46; DFS 7
Rice, Timothy Miles Bindon
  See Rice, Tim
Rich, Adrienne 1929- ..... **CLC 3, 6, 7, 11, 18, 36, 73, 76, 125; PC 5**
  See also AAYA 69; AMWR 2; AMWS 1; CA 9-12R; CANR 20, 53, 74, 128, 199; CDALBS; CP 1, 2, 3, 4, 5, 6, 7; CSW; CWP; DA3; DAM POET; DLB 5, 67; EWL 3; EXPP; FL 1:6; FW; MAL 5; MBL; MTCW 1, 2; MTFW 2005; PAB; PFS 15, 29; RGAL 4; RGHL; WP
Rich, Adrienne Cecile
  See Rich, Adrienne
Rich, Barbara
  See Graves, Robert

Rich, Robert
  See Trumbo, Dalton
Richard, Keith
  See Richards, Keith
Richards, David Adams 1950- .... **CLC 59**
  See also CA 93-96; CANR 60, 110, 156; CN 7; DAC; DLB 53; TCLE 1:2
Richards, I(vor) A(rmstrong)
  1893-1979 .... **CLC 14, 24**
  See also BRWS 2; CA 41-44R, 89-92; CANR 34, 74; CP 1, 2; DLB 27; EWL 3; MTCW 2; RGEL 2
Richards, Keith 1943- .... **CLC 17**
  See also CA 107; CANR 77
Richardson, Anne
  See Roiphe, Anne
Richardson, Dorothy Miller
  1873-1957 .... **TCLC 3, 203**
  See also BRWS 13; CA 104, 192; DLB 36; EWL 3; FW; RGEL 2
Richardson, Ethel Florence Lindesay
  1870-1946 .... **TCLC 4**
  See also CA 105, 190; DLB 197, 230; EWL 3; RGEL 2; RGSF 2; RHW
Richardson, Henrietta
  See Richardson, Ethel Florence Lindesay
Richardson, Henry Handel
  See Richardson, Ethel Florence Lindesay
Richardson, John 1796-1852 .... **NCLC 55**
  See also CCA 1; DAC; DLB 99
Richardson, Samuel 1689-1761 ...... **LC 1, 44, 138; WLC 5**
  See also BRW 3; CDBLB 1660-1789; DA; DAB; DAC; DAM MST, NOV; DLB 39; RGEL 2; TEA; WLIT 3
Richardson, Willis 1889-1977 .... **HR 1:3**
  See also BW 1; CA 124; DLB 51; SATA 60
Richardson Robertson, Ethel Florence Lindesay
  See Richardson, Ethel Florence Lindesay
Richler, Mordecai 1931-2001 .... **CLC 3, 5, 9, 13, 18, 46, 70, 185, 271**
  See also AITN 1; CA 65-68, 201; CANR 31, 62, 111; CCA 1; CLR 17; CN 1, 2, 3, 4, 5, 7; CWRI 5; DAC; DAM MST, NOV; DLB 53; EWL 3; MAICYA 1, 2; MTCW 1, 2; MTFW 2005; RGEL 2; RGHL; SATA 44, 98; SATA-Brief 27; TWA
Richter, Conrad (Michael)
  1890-1968 .... **CLC 30**
  See also AAYA 21; AMWS 18; BYA 2; CA 5-8R, 25-28R; CANR 23; DLB 9, 212; LAIT 1; MAL 5; MTCW 1, 2; MTFW 2005; RGAL 4; SATA 3; TCWW 1, 2; TUS; YAW
Ricostranza, Tom
  See Ellis, Trey
Riddell, Charlotte 1832-1906 .... **TCLC 40**
  See also CA 165; DLB 156; HGG; SUFW
Riddell, Mrs. J. H.
  See Riddell, Charlotte
Ridge, John Rollin 1827-1867 ...... **NCLC 82; NNAL**
  See also CA 144; DAM MULT; DLB 175
Ridgeway, Jason
  See Marlowe, Stephen
Ridgway, Keith 1965- .... **CLC 119**
  See also CA 172; CANR 144
Riding, Laura
  See Jackson, Laura
Riefenstahl, Berta Helene Amalia
  1902-2003 .... **CLC 16, 190**
  See also CA 108, 220
Riefenstahl, Leni
  See Riefenstahl, Berta Helene Amalia
Riffe, Ernest
  See Bergman, Ingmar
Riffe, Ernest Ingmar
  See Bergman, Ingmar

Riggs, (Rolla) Lynn
1899-1954 .... **NNAL; TCLC 56**
See also CA 144; DAM MULT; DLB 175

Riis, Jacob A(ugust) 1849-1914 ..... **TCLC 80**
See also CA 113, 168; DLB 23

Rikki
See Ducornet, Erica

Riley, James Whitcomb 1849-1916 .... **PC 48;**
TCLC 51
See also CA 118, 137; DAM POET; MAI-
CYA 1, 2; RGAL 4; SATA 17

Riley, Tex
See Creasey, John

Rilke, Rainer Maria 1875-1926 .... **PC 2;**
TCLC 1, 6, 19, 195
See also CA 104, 132; CANR 62, 99; CD-
WLB 2; DA3; DAM POET; DLB 81; EW
9; EWL 3; MTCW 1, 2; MTFW 2005;
PFS 19, 27; RGWL 2, 3; TWA; WP

Rimbaud, Arthur 1854-1891 ..... **NCLC 4, 35,**
82, 227; PC 3, 57; WLC 5
See also DA; DA3; DAB; DAC; DAM
MST, POET; DLB 217; EW 7; GFL 1789
to the Present; LMFS 2; PFS 28; RGWL
2, 3; TWA; WP

Rimbaud, Jean Nicholas Arthur
See Rimbaud, Arthur

Rinehart, Mary Roberts
1876-1958 .... **TCLC 52**
See also BPFB 3; CA 108, 166; RGAL 4;
RHW

Ringmaster, The
See Mencken, H. L.

Ringwood, Gwen(dolyn Margaret) Pharis
1910-1984 .... **CLC 48**
See also CA 148, 112; DLB 88

Rio, Michel 1945(?)- .... **CLC 43**
See also CA 201

Rios, Alberto 1952- .... **PC 57**
See also AAYA 66; AMWS 4; CA 113;
CANR 34, 79, 137; CP 6, 7; DLB 122;
HW 2; MTFW 2005; PFS 11

Rios, Alberto Alvaro
See Rios, Alberto

Ritsos, Giannes
See Ritsos, Yannis

Ritsos, Yannis 1909-1990 .... **CLC 6, 13, 31**
See also CA 77-80, 133; CANR 39, 61; EW
12; EWL 3; MTCW 1; RGWL 2, 3

Ritter, Erika 1948(?)- .... **CLC 52**
See also CD 5, 6; CWD

Rivera, Jose Eustasio 1889-1928 ... **TCLC 35**
See also CA 162; EWL 3; HW 1, 2; LAW

Rivera, Tomas 1935-1984 .... **HLCS 2**
See also CA 49-52; CANR 32; DLB 82;
HW 1; LLW; RGAL 4; SSFS 15; TCWW
2; WLIT 1

Rivers, Conrad Kent 1933-1968 .... **CLC 1**
See also BW 1; CA 85-88; DLB 41

Rivers, Elfrida
See Bradley, Marion Zimmer

Riverside, John
See Heinlein, Robert A.

Rizal, Jose 1861-1896 .... **NCLC 27**
See also DLB 348

Roa Bastos, Augusto 1917-2005 ...... **CLC 45;**
HLC 2
See also CA 131, 238; CWW 2; DAM
MULT; DLB 113; EWL 3; HW 1; LAW;
RGSF 2; WLIT 1

Roa Bastos, Augusto Jose Antonio
See Roa Bastos, Augusto

Robbe-Grillet, Alain 1922-2008 ..... **CLC 1, 2,**
4, 6, 8, 10, 14, 43, 128, 287
See also BPFB 3; CA 9-12R, 269; CANR
33, 65, 115; CWW 2; DLB 83; EW 13;
EWL 3; GFL 1789 to the Present; IDFW
3, 4; MTCW 1, 2; MTFW 2005; RGWL
2, 3; SSFS 15

Robbins, Harold 1916-1997 .... **CLC 5**
See also BPFB 3; CA 73-76, 162; CANR
26, 54, 112, 156; DA3; DAM NOV;
MTCW 1, 2

Robbins, Thomas Eugene 1936- . **CLC 9, 32,**
64
See also AAYA 32; AMWS 10; BEST 90:3;
BPFB 3; CA 81-84; CANR 29, 59, 95,
139; CN 3, 4, 5, 6, 7; CPW; CSW; DA3;
DAM NOV, POP; DLBY 1980; MTCW
1, 2; MTFW 2005

Robbins, Tom
See Robbins, Thomas Eugene

Robbins, Trina 1938- .... **CLC 21**
See also AAYA 61; CA 128; CANR 152

Robert de Boron fl. 12th cent. - .... **CMLC 94**

Roberts, Charles G(eorge) D(ouglas)
1860-1943 .... **SSC 91; TCLC 8**
See also CA 105, 188; CLR 33; CWRI 5;
DLB 92; RGEL 2; RGSF 2; SATA 88;
SATA-Brief 29

Roberts, Elizabeth Madox
1886-1941 .... **TCLC 68**
See also CA 111, 166; CLR 100; CWRI 5;
DLB 9, 54, 102; RGAL 4; RHW; SATA
33; SATA-Brief 27; TCWW 2; WCH

Roberts, Kate 1891-1985 .... **CLC 15**
See also CA 107, 116; DLB 319

Roberts, Keith (John Kingston)
1935-2000 .... **CLC 14**
See also BRWS 10; CA 25-28R; CANR 46;
DLB 261; SFW 4

Roberts, Kenneth (Lewis)
1885-1957 .... **TCLC 23**
See also CA 109, 199; DLB 9; MAL 5;
RGAL 4; RHW

Roberts, Michele 1949- .... **CLC 48, 178**
See also BRWS 15; CA 115; CANR 58,
120, 164, 200; CN 6, 7; DLB 231; FW

Roberts, Michele Brigitte
See Roberts, Michele

Robertson, Ellis
See Ellison, Harlan; Silverberg, Robert

Robertson, Thomas William
1829-1871 .... **NCLC 35**
See also DAM DRAM; DLB 344; RGEL 2

Robertson, Tom
See Robertson, Thomas William

Robeson, Kenneth
See Dent, Lester

Robinson, Edwin Arlington
1869-1935 .... **PC 1, 35; TCLC 5, 101**
See also AAYA 72; AMW; CA 104, 133;
CDALB 1865-1917; DA; DAC; DAM
MST, POET; DLB 54; EWL 3; EXPP;
MAL 5; MTCW 1, 2; MTFW 2005; PAB;
PFS 4, 35; RGAL 4; WP

Robinson, Henry Crabb
1775-1867 .... **NCLC 15**
See also DLB 107

Robinson, Jill 1936- .... **CLC 10**
See also CA 102; CANR 120; INT CA-102

Robinson, Kim Stanley 1952- ... **CLC 34, 248**
See also AAYA 26; CA 126; CANR 113,
139, 173; CN 6, 7; MTFW 2005; SATA
109; SCFW 2; SFW 4

Robinson, Lloyd
See Silverberg, Robert

Robinson, Marilynne 1943- ..... **CLC 25, 180,**
276
See also AAYA 69; CA 116; CANR 80, 140,
192; CN 4, 5, 6, 7; DLB 206, 350; MTFW
2005; NFS 24

Robinson, Mary 1758-1800 .... **NCLC 142**
See also BRWS 13; DLB 158; FW

Robinson, Smokey
See Robinson, William, Jr.

Robinson, William, Jr. 1940- .... **CLC 21**
See also CA 116

Robison, Mary 1949- .... **CLC 42, 98**
See also CA 113, 116; CANR 87, 206; CN
4, 5, 6, 7; DLB 130; INT CA-116; RGSF
2

Roches, Catherine des 1542-1587 ...... **LC 117**
See also DLB 327

Rochester
See Wilmot, John

Rod, Edouard 1857-1910 .... **TCLC 52**

Roddenberry, Eugene Wesley
1921-1991 .... **CLC 17**
See also AAYA 5; CA 110, 135; CANR 37;
SATA 45; SATA-Obit 69

Roddenberry, Gene
See Roddenberry, Eugene Wesley

Rodgers, Mary 1931- .... **CLC 12**
See also BYA 5; CA 49-52; CANR 8, 55,
90; CLR 20; CWRI 5; INT CANR-8;
JRDA; MAICYA 1, 2; SATA 8, 130

Rodgers, W(illiam) R(obert)
1909-1969 .... **CLC 7**
See also CA 85-88; DLB 20; RGEL 2

Rodman, Eric
See Silverberg, Robert

Rodman, Howard 1920(?)-1985 .... **CLC 65**
See also CA 118

Rodman, Maia
See Wojciechowska, Maia (Teresa)

Rodo, Jose Enrique 1871(?)-1917 .... **HLCS 2**
See also CA 178; EWL 3; HW 2; LAW

Rodolph, Utto
See Ouologuem, Yambo

Rodriguez, Claudio 1934-1999 .... **CLC 10**
See also CA 188; DLB 134

Rodriguez, Richard 1944- .... **CLC 155; HLC**
2
See also AMWS 14; CA 110; CANR 66,
116; DAM MULT; DLB 82, 256; HW 1,
2; LAIT 5; LLW; MTFW 2005; NCFS 3;
WLIT 1

Roethke, Theodore 1908-1963 ... **CLC 1, 3, 8,**
11, 19, 46, 101; PC 15
See also AMW; CA 81-84; CABS 2;
CDALB 1941-1968; DA3; DAM POET;
DLB 5, 206; EWL 3; EXPP; MAL 5;
MTCW 1, 2; PAB; PFS 3, 34; RGAL 4;
WP

Roethke, Theodore Huebner
See Roethke, Theodore

Rogers, Carl R(ansom)
1902-1987 .... **TCLC 125**
See also CA 1-4R, 121; CANR 1, 18;
MTCW 1

Rogers, Samuel 1763-1855 .... **NCLC 69**
See also DLB 93; RGEL 2

Rogers, Thomas 1927-2007 .... **CLC 57**
See also CA 89-92, 259; CANR 163; INT
CA-89-92

Rogers, Thomas Hunton
See Rogers, Thomas

Rogers, Will(iam Penn Adair)
1879-1935 .... **NNAL; TCLC 8, 71**
See also CA 105, 144; DA3; DAM MULT;
DLB 11; MTCW 2

Rogin, Gilbert 1929- .... **CLC 18**
See also CA 65-68; CANR 15

Rohan, Koda
See Koda Shigeyuki

Rohlfs, Anna Katharine Green
See Green, Anna Katharine

Rohmer, Eric 1920-2010 .... **CLC 16**
See also CA 110

Rohmer, Sax
See Ward, Arthur Henry Sarsfield

Roiphe, Anne 1935- .... **CLC 3, 9**
See also CA 89-92; CANR 45, 73, 138, 170;
DLBY 1980; INT CA-89-92

Roiphe, Anne Richardson
See Roiphe, Anne

Rojas, Fernando de 1475-1541 ... **HLCS 1, 2;
LC 23, 169**
See also DLB 286; RGWL 2, 3

Rojas, Gonzalo 1917- .... **HLCS 2**
See also CA 178; HW 2; LAWS 1

Rolaag, Ole Edvart
See Rolvaag, O.E.

Roland (de la Platiere), Marie-Jeanne
1754-1793 .... **LC 98**
See also DLB 314

**Rolfe, Frederick (William Serafino Austin
Lewis Mary)** 1860-1913 .... **TCLC 12**
See also CA 107, 210; DLB 34, 156; GLL
1; RGEL 2

Rolland, Romain 1866-1944 .... **TCLC 23**
See also CA 118, 197; DLB 65, 284, 332;
EWL 3; GFL 1789 to the Present; RGWL
2, 3

Rolle, Richard c. 1300-c. 1349 ...... **CMLC 21**
See also DLB 146; LMFS 1; RGEL 2

Rolvaag, O.E.
See Rolvaag, O.E.

Rolvaag, O.E.
See Rolvaag, O.E.

Rolvaag, O.E. 1876-1931 .... **TCLC 17, 207**
See also AAYA 75; CA 117, 171; DLB 9,
212; MAL 5; NFS 5; RGAL 4; TCWW 1,
2

Romain Arnaud, Saint
See Aragon, Louis

Romains, Jules 1885-1972 .... **CLC 7**
See also CA 85-88; CANR 34; DLB 65,
321; EWL 3; GFL 1789 to the Present;
MTCW 1

Romero, Jose Ruben 1890-1952 .... **TCLC 14**
See also CA 114, 131; EWL 3; HW 1; LAW

Ronsard, Pierre de 1524-1585 . **LC 6, 54; PC
11, 105**
See also DLB 327; EW 2; GFL Beginnings
to 1789; RGWL 2, 3; TWA

Rooke, Leon 1934- .... **CLC 25, 34**
See also CA 25-28R; CANR 23, 53; CCA
1; CPW; DAM POP

Roosevelt, Franklin Delano
1882-1945 .... **TCLC 93**
See also CA 116, 173; LAIT 3

Roosevelt, Theodore 1858-1919 ..... **TCLC 69**
See also CA 115, 170; DLB 47, 186, 275

Roper, Margaret c. 1505-1544 .... **LC 147**

Roper, William 1498-1578 .... **LC 10**

Roquelaure, A. N.
See Rice, Anne

Rosa, Joao Guimaraes 1908-1967
See Guimaraes Rosa, Joao

Rose, Wendy 1948- . **CLC 85; NNAL; PC 13**
See also CA 53-56; CANR 5, 51; CWP;
DAM MULT; DLB 175; PFS 13; RGAL
4; SATA 12

Rosen, R.D. 1949- .... **CLC 39**
See also CA 77-80; CANR 62, 120, 175;
CMW 4; INT CANR-30

Rosen, Richard
See Rosen, R.D.

Rosen, Richard Dean
See Rosen, R.D.

Rosenberg, Isaac 1890-1918 .... **TCLC 12**
See also BRW 6; CA 107, 188; DLB 20,
216; EWL 3; PAB; RGEL 2

Rosenblatt, Joe
See Rosenblatt, Joseph

Rosenblatt, Joseph 1933- .... **CLC 15**
See also CA 89-92; CP 3, 4, 5, 6, 7; INT
CA-89-92

Rosenfeld, Samuel
See Tzara, Tristan

Rosenstock, Sami
See Tzara, Tristan

Rosenstock, Samuel
See Tzara, Tristan

Rosenthal, M(acha) L(ouis)
1917-1996 .... **CLC 28**
See also CA 1-4R, 152; CAAS 6; CANR 4,
51; CP 1, 2, 3, 4, 5, 6; DLB 5; SATA 59

Ross, Barnaby
See Dannay, Frederic; Lee, Manfred B.

Ross, Bernard L.
See Follett, Ken

Ross, J. H.
See Lawrence, T. E.

Ross, John Hume
See Lawrence, T. E.

Ross, Martin 1862-1915
See Martin, Violet Florence
See also DLB 135; GLL 2; RGEL 2; RGSF
2

Ross, (James) Sinclair 1908-1996 ... **CLC 13;
SSC 24**
See also CA 73-76; CANR 81; CN 1, 2, 3,
4, 5, 6; DAC; DAM MST; DLB 88;
RGEL 2; RGSF 2; TCWW 1, 2

Rossetti, Christina 1830-1894 ... **NCLC 2, 50,
66, 186; PC 7; WLC 5**
See also AAYA 51; BRW 5; BRWR 3; BYA
4; CLR 115; DA; DA3; DAB; DAC;
DAM MST, POET; DLB 35, 163, 240;
EXPP; FL 1:3; LATS 1:1; MAICYA 1;
PFS 10, 14, 27, 34; RGEL 2; SATA 20;
TEA; WCH

Rossetti, Christina Georgina
See Rossetti, Christina

Rossetti, Dante Gabriel 1828-1882 . **NCLC 4,
77; PC 44; WLC 5**
See also AAYA 51; BRW 5; CDBLB 1832-
1890; DA; DAB; DAC; DAM MST,
POET; DLB 35; EXPP; RGEL 2; TEA

Rossi, Cristina Peri
See Peri Rossi, Cristina

Rossi, Jean-Baptiste 1931-2003 .... **CLC 90**
See also CA 201, 215; CMW 4; NFS 18

Rossner, Judith 1935-2005 .... **CLC 6, 9, 29**
See also AITN 2; BEST 90:3; BPFB 3; CA
17-20R; CANR 18, 51, 73; CN 4, 5,
6, 7; DLB 6; INT CANR-18; MAL 5;
MTCW 1, 2; MTFW 2005

Rossner, Judith Perelman
See Rossner, Judith

Rostand, Edmond 1868-1918 . **DC 10; TCLC
6, 37**
See also CA 104, 126; DA; DA3; DAB;
DAC; DAM DRAM, MST; DFS 1; DLB
192; LAIT 1; MTCW 1; RGWL 2, 3;
TWA

Rostand, Edmond Eugene Alexis
See Rostand, Edmond

Roth, Henry 1906-1995 ... **CLC 2, 6, 11, 104;
SSC 134**
See also AMWS 9; CA 11-12, 149; CANR
38, 63; CAP 1; CN 1, 2, 3, 4, 5, 6; DA3;
DLB 28; EWL 3; MAL 5; MTCW 1, 2;
MTFW 2005; RGAL 4

Roth, (Moses) Joseph 1894-1939 ... **TCLC 33**
See also CA 160; DLB 85; EWL 3; RGWL
2, 3

Roth, Philip 1933- ... **CLC 1, 2, 3, 4, 6, 9, 15,
22, 31, 47, 66, 86, 119, 201; SSC 26,
102; WLC 5**
See also AAYA 67; AMWR 2; AMWS 3;
BEST 90:3; BPFB 3; CA 1-4R; CANR 1,
22, 36, 55, 89, 132, 170; CDALB 1968-
1988; CN 3, 4, 5, 6, 7; CPW 1; DA; DA3;
DAB; DAC; DAM MST, NOV, POP;
DLB 2, 28, 173; DLBY 1982; EWL 3;
MAL 5; MTCW 1, 2; MTFW 2005; NFS
25; RGAL 4; RGHL; RGSF 2; SSFS 12,
18; TUS

Roth, Philip Milton
See Roth, Philip

Rothenberg, Jerome 1931- .... **CLC 6, 57**
See also CA 45-48; CANR 1, 106; CP 1, 2,
3, 4, 5, 6, 7; DLB 5, 193

Rotter, Pat CLC 65

Roumain, Jacques 1907-1944 .... **BLC 1:3;
TCLC 19**
See also BW 1; CA 117, 125; DAM MULT;
EWL 3

Roumain, Jacques Jean Baptiste
See Roumain, Jacques

Rourke, Constance Mayfield
1885-1941 .... **TCLC 12**
See also CA 107, 200; MAL 5; YABC 1

Rousseau, Jean-Baptiste 1671-1741 ...... **LC 9**

Rousseau, Jean-Jacques 1712-1778 .... **LC 14,
36, 122; WLC 5**
See also DA; DA3; DAB; DAC; DAM
MST; DLB 314; EW 4; GFL Beginnings
to 1789; LMFS 1; RGWL 2, 3; TWA

Roussel, Raymond 1877-1933 .... **TCLC 20**
See also CA 117, 201; EWL 3; GFL 1789
to the Present

Rovit, Earl (Herbert) 1927- .... **CLC 7**
See also CA 5-8R; CANR 12

Rowe, Elizabeth Singer 1674-1737 ..... **LC 44**
See also DLB 39, 95

Rowe, Nicholas 1674-1718 .... **LC 8**
See also DLB 84; RGEL 2

Rowlandson, Mary 1637(?)-1678 .... **LC 66**
See also DLB 24, 200; RGAL 4

Rowley, Ames Dorrance
See Lovecraft, H. P.

Rowley, William 1585(?)-1626 ... **LC 100, 123**
See also DFS 22; DLB 58; RGEL 2

Rowling, J.K. 1965- .... **CLC 137, 217**
See also AAYA 34, 82; BRWS 16; BYA 11,
13, 14; CA 173; CANR 128, 157; CLR
66, 80, 112; LNFS 1, 2, 3; MAICYA 2;
MTFW 2005; SATA 109, 174; SUFW 2

Rowling, Joanne Kathleen
See Rowling, J.K.

Rowson, Susanna Haswell
1762(?)-1824 .... **NCLC 5, 69, 182**
See also AMWS 15; DLB 37, 200; RGAL 4

Roy, Arundhati 1960(?)- .... **CLC 109, 210**
See also CA 163; CANR 90, 126; CN 7;
DLB 323, 326; DLBY 1997; EWL 3;
LATS 1:2; MTFW 2005; NFS 22; WWE
1

Roy, Gabrielle 1909-1983 .... **CLC 10, 14**
See also CA 53-56, 110; CANR 5, 61; CCA
1; DAB; DAC; DAM MST; DLB 68;
EWL 3; MTCW 1; RGWL 2, 3; SATA
104; TCLE 1:2

Royko, Mike 1932-1997 .... **CLC 109**
See also CA 89-92, 157; CANR 26, 111;
CPW

Rozanov, Vasilii Vasil'evich
See Rozanov, Vassili

Rozanov, Vasily Vasilyevich
See Rozanov, Vassili

Rozanov, Vassili 1856-1919 .... **TCLC 104**
See also DLB 295; EWL 3

Rozewicz, Tadeusz 1921- ...... **CLC 9, 23, 139**
See also CA 108; CANR 36, 66; CWW 2;
DA3; DAM POET; DLB 232; EWL 3;
MTCW 1, 2; MTFW 2005; RGHL;
RGWL 3

Ruark, Gibbons 1941- .... **CLC 3**
See also CA 33-36R; CAAS 23; CANR 14,
31, 57; DLB 120

Rubens, Bernice (Ruth) 1923-2004 . **CLC 19,
31**
See also CA 25-28R, 232; CANR 33, 65,
128; CN 1, 2, 3, 4, 5, 6, 7; DLB 14, 207,
326; MTCW 1

Rubin, Harold
See Robbins, Harold

to the Present; LMFS 2; MTCW 1, 2;
MTFW 2005; NFS 21; RGHL; RGSF 2;
RGWL 2, 3; SSFS 9; TWA

Sassoon, Siegfried 1886-1967 .. **CLC 36, 130;
PC 12**
See also BRW 6; CA 104, 25-28R; CANR
36; DAB; DAM MST, NOV, POET; DLB
20, 191; DLBD 18; EWL 3; MTCW 1, 2;
MTFW 2005; PAB; PFS 28; RGEL 2;
TEA

Sassoon, Siegfried Lorraine
See Sassoon, Siegfried

Satterfield, Charles
See Pohl, Frederik

Satyremont
See Peret, Benjamin

Saul, John III
See Saul, John

Saul, John 1942- .... **CLC 46**
See also AAYA 10, 62; CA 81-
84; CANR 16, 40, 81, 176; CPW; DAM
NOV, POP; HGG; SATA 98

Saul, John W.
See Saul, John

Saul, John W. III
See Saul, John

Saul, John Woodruff III
See Saul, John

Saunders, Caleb
See Heinlein, Robert A.

Saura (Atares), Carlos 1932-1998 .... **CLC 20**
See also CA 114, 131; CANR 79; HW 1

Sauser, Frederic Louis
See Sauser-Hall, Frederic

Sauser-Hall, Frederic 1887-1961 ..... **CLC 18,
106**
See also CA 102, 93-96; CANR 36, 62;
DLB 258; EWL 3; GFL 1789 to the
Present; MTCW 1; WP

Saussure, Ferdinand de
1857-1913 .... **TCLC 49**
See also DLB 242

Savage, Catharine
See Brosman, Catharine Savage

Savage, Richard 1697(?)-1743 .... **LC 96**
See also DLB 95; RGEL 2

Savage, Thomas 1915-2003 .... **CLC 40**
See also CA 126, 132, 218; CAAS 15; CN
6, 7; INT CA-132; SATA-Obit 147;
TCWW 2

Savan, Glenn 1953-2003 .... **CLC 50**
See also CA 225

Savonarola, Girolamo 1452-1498 ...... **LC 152**
See also LMFS 1

Sax, Robert
See Johnson, Robert

Saxo Grammaticus c. 1150-c.
1222 .... **CMLC 58**

Saxton, Robert
See Johnson, Robert

Sayers, Dorothy L(eigh) 1893-1957 . **SSC 71;
TCLC 2, 15, 237**
See also BPFB 3; BRWS 3; CA 104, 119;
CANR 60; CDBLB 1914-1945; CMW 4;
DAM POP; DLB 10, 36, 77, 100; MSW;
MTCW 1, 2; MTFW 2005; RGEL 2;
SSFS 12; TEA

Sayers, Valerie 1952- .... **CLC 50, 122**
See also CA 134; CANR 61; CSW

Sayles, John (Thomas) 1950- .... **CLC 7, 10,
14, 198**
See also CA 57-60; CANR 41, 84; DLB 44

Scamander, Newt
See Rowling, J.K.

Scammell, Michael 1935- .... **CLC 34**
See also CA 156

Scannel, John Vernon
See Scannell, Vernon

Scannell, Vernon 1922-2007 .... **CLC 49**
See also CA 5-8R, 266; CANR 8, 24, 57,
143; CN 1, 2; CP 1, 2, 3, 4, 5, 6, 7; CWRI
5; DLB 27; SATA 59; SATA-Obit 188

Scarlett, Susan
See Streatfeild, Noel

Scarron 1847-1910
See Mikszath, Kalman

Scarron, Paul 1610-1660 .... **LC 116**
See also GFL Beginnings to 1789; RGWL
2, 3

Sceve, Maurice c. 1500-c. 1564 . **LC 180; PC
111**
See also DLB 327; GFL Beginnings to 1789

Schaeffer, Susan Fromberg 1941- ..... **CLC 6,
11, 22**
See also CA 49-52; CANR 18, 65, 160; CN
4, 5, 6, 7; DLB 28, 299; MTCW 1, 2;
MTFW 2005; SATA 22

Schama, Simon 1945- .... **CLC 150**
See also BEST 89:4; CA 105; CANR 39,
91, 168, 207

Schama, Simon Michael
See Schama, Simon

Schary, Jill
See Robinson, Jill

Schell, Jonathan 1943- .... **CLC 35**
See also CA 73-76; CANR 12, 117, 187

Schelling, Friedrich Wilhelm Joseph von
1775-1854 .... **NCLC 30**
See also DLB 90

Scherer, Jean-Marie Maurice
See Rohmer, Eric

Schevill, James (Erwin) 1920- .... **CLC 7**
See also CA 5-8R; CAAS 12; CAD; CD 5,
6; CP 1, 2, 3, 4, 5

Schiller, Friedrich von 1759-1805 ...... **DC 12;
NCLC 39, 69, 166**
See also CDWLB 2; DAM DRAM; DLB
94; EW 5; RGWL 2, 3; TWA

Schisgal, Murray (Joseph) 1926- .... **CLC 6**
See also CA 21-24R; CAD; CANR 48, 86;
CD 5, 6; MAL 5

Schlee, Ann 1934- .... **CLC 35**
See also CA 101; CANR 29, 88; SATA 44;
SATA-Brief 36

Schlegel, August Wilhelm von
1767-1845 .... **NCLC 15, 142**
See also DLB 94; RGWL 2, 3

Schlegel, Friedrich 1772-1829 .... **NCLC 45,
226**
See also DLB 90; EW 5; RGWL 2, 3; TWA

Schlegel, Johann Elias (von)
1719(?)-1749 .... **LC 5**

Schleiermacher, Friedrich
1768-1834 .... **NCLC 107**
See also DLB 90

Schlesinger, Arthur M., Jr.
1917-2007 .... **CLC 84**
See Schlesinger, Arthur Meier
See also AITN 1; CA 1-4R, 257; CANR 1,
28, 58, 105, 187; DLB 17; INT CANR-
28; MTCW 1, 2; SATA 61; SATA-Obit
181

Schlink, Bernhard 1944- .... **CLC 174**
See also CA 163; CANR 116, 175; RGHL

Schmidt, Arno (Otto) 1914-1979 ...... **CLC 56**
See also CA 128, 109; DLB 69; EWL 3

Schmitz, Aron Hector 1861-1928 ..... **SSC 25;
TCLC 2, 35, 244**
See also CA 104, 122; DLB 264; EW 8;
EWL 3; MTCW 1; RGWL 2, 3; WLIT 7

Schnackenberg, Gjertrud 1953- ...... **CLC 40;
PC 45**
See also AMWS 15; CA 116; CANR 100;
CP 5, 6, 7; CWP; DLB 120, 282; PFS 13,
25

Schnackenberg, Gjertrud Cecelia
See Schnackenberg, Gjertrud

Schneider, Leonard Alfred
1925-1966 .... **CLC 21**
See also CA 89-92

Schnitzler, Arthur 1862-1931 ..... **DC 17; SSC
15, 61; TCLC 4**
See also CA 104; CDWLB 2; DLB 81, 118;
EW 8; EWL 3; RGSF 2; RGWL 2, 3

Schoenberg, Arnold Franz Walter
1874-1951 .... **TCLC 75**
See also CA 109, 188

Schonberg, Arnold
See Schoenberg, Arnold Franz Walter

Schopenhauer, Arthur 1788-1860 . **NCLC 51,
157**
See also DLB 90; EW 5

Schor, Sandra (M.) 1932(?)-1990 ..... **CLC 65**
See also CA 132

Schorer, Mark 1908-1977 .... **CLC 9**
See also CA 5-8R, 73-76; CANR 7; CN 1,
2; DLB 103

Schrader, Paul (Joseph) 1946- . **CLC 26, 212**
See also CA 37-40R; CANR 41; DLB 44

Schreber, Daniel 1842-1911 .... **TCLC 123**

Schreiner, Olive 1855-1920 ...... **TCLC 9, 235**
See also AFW; BRWS 2; CA 105, 154;
DLB 18, 156, 190, 225; EWL 3; FW;
RGEL 2; TWA; WLIT 2; WWE 1

Schreiner, Olive Emilie Albertina
See Schreiner, Olive

Schulberg, Budd 1914-2009 .... **CLC 7, 48**
See also AMWS 18; BPFB 3; CA 25-28R,
289; CANR 19, 87, 178; CN 1, 2, 3, 4, 5,
6, 7; DLB 6, 26, 28; DLBY 1981, 2001;
MAL 5

Schulberg, Budd Wilson
See Schulberg, Budd

Schulberg, Seymour Wilson
See Schulberg, Budd

Schulman, Arnold
See Trumbo, Dalton

Schulz, Bruno 1892-1942 .. **SSC 13; TCLC 5,
51**
See also CA 115, 123; CANR 86; CDWLB
4; DLB 215; EWL 3; MTCW 2; MTFW
2005; RGSF 2; RGWL 2, 3

Schulz, Charles M. 1922-2000 .... **CLC 12**
See also AAYA 39; CA 9-12R, 187; CANR
6, 132; INT CANR-6; MTFW 2005;
SATA 10; SATA-Obit 118

Schulz, Charles Monroe
See Schulz, Charles M.

Schumacher, E(rnst) F(riedrich)
1911-1977 .... **CLC 80**
See also CA 81-84, 73-76; CANR 34, 85

Schumann, Robert 1810-1856 ...... **NCLC 143**

Schuyler, George Samuel 1895-1977 . **HR 1:3**
See also BW 2; CA 81-84, 73-76; CANR
42; DLB 29, 51

Schuyler, James Marcus 1923-1991 .. **CLC 5,
23; PC 88**
See also CA 101, 134; CP 1, 2, 3, 4, 5;
DAM POET; DLB 5, 169; EWL 3; INT
CA-101; MAL 5; WP

Schwartz, Delmore (David)
1913-1966 . **CLC 2, 4, 10, 45, 87; PC 8;
SSC 105**
See also AMWS 2; CA 17-18, 25-28R;
CANR 35; CAP 2; DLB 28, 48; EWL 3;
MAL 5; MTCW 1, 2; MTFW 2005; PAB;
RGAL 4; TUS

Schwartz, Ernst
See Ozu, Yasujiro

Schwartz, John Burnham 1965- .... **CLC 59**
See also CA 132; CANR 116, 188

Schwartz, Lynne Sharon 1939- .... **CLC 31**
See also CA 103; CANR 44, 89, 160; DLB
218; MTCW 2; MTFW 2005

Schwartz, Muriel A.
See Eliot, T. S.

Schwarz-Bart, Andre 1928-2006 .... **CLC 2, 4**
See also CA 89-92, 253; CANR 109; DLB 299; RGHL

Schwarz-Bart, Simone 1938- . **BLCS; CLC 7**
See also BW 2; CA 97-100; CANR 117; EWL 3

Schwerner, Armand 1927-1999 .... **PC 42**
See also CA 9-12R, 179; CANR 50, 85; CP 2, 3, 4, 5, 6; DLB 165

Schwitters, Kurt (Hermann Edward Karl Julius) 1887-1948 .... **TCLC 95**
See also CA 158

Schwob, Marcel (Mayer Andre) 1867-1905 .... **TCLC 20**
See also CA 117, 168; DLB 123; GFL 1789 to the Present

Sciascia, Leonardo 1921-1989 .. **CLC 8, 9, 41**
See also CA 85-88, 130; CANR 35; DLB 177; EWL 3; MTCW 1; RGWL 2, 3

Scoppettone, Sandra 1936- .... **CLC 26**
See also AAYA 11, 65; BYA 8; CA 5-8R; CANR 41, 73, 157; GLL 1; MAICYA 2; MAICYAS 1; SATA 9, 92; WYA; YAW

Scorsese, Martin 1942- .... **CLC 20, 89, 207**
See also AAYA 38; CA 110, 114; CANR 46, 85

Scotland, Jay
See Jakes, John

Scott, Duncan Campbell 1862-1947 .... **TCLC 6**
See also CA 104, 153; DAC; DLB 92; RGEL 2

Scott, Evelyn 1893-1963 .... **CLC 43**
See also CA 104, 112; CANR 64; DLB 9, 48; RHW

Scott, F(rancis) R(eginald) 1899-1985 .... **CLC 22**
See also CA 101, 114; CANR 87; CP 1, 2, 3, 4; DLB 88; INT CA-101; RGEL 2

Scott, Frank
See Scott, F(rancis) R(eginald)

Scott, Joan
See Scott, Joan Wallach

Scott, Joan W.
See Scott, Joan Wallach

Scott, Joan Wallach 1941- .... **CLC 65**
See also CA 293

Scott, Joanna 1960- .... **CLC 50**
See also AMWS 17; CA 126; CANR 53, 92, 168

Scott, Joanna Jeanne
See Scott, Joanna

Scott, Paul (Mark) 1920-1978 ...... **CLC 9, 60**
See also BRWS 1; CA 81-84, 77-80; CANR 33; CN 1, 2; DLB 14, 207, 326; EWL 3; MTCW 1; RGEL 2; RHW; WWE 1

Scott, Ridley 1937- .... **CLC 183**
See also AAYA 13, 43

Scott, Sarah 1723-1795 .... **LC 44**
See also DLB 39

Scott, Sir Walter 1771-1832 .... **NCLC 15, 69, 110, 209; PC 13; SSC 32; WLC 5**
See also AAYA 22; BRW 4; BYA 2; CD-BLB 1789-1832; CLR 154; DA; DAB; DAC; DAM MST, NOV, POET; DLB 93, 107, 116, 144, 159; GL 3; LAIT 1; NFS 31; RGEL 2; RGSF 2; SSFS 10; SUFW 1; TEA; WLIT 3; YABC 2

Scribe, Augustin Eugene
See Scribe, (Augustin) Eugene

Scribe, (Augustin) Eugene 1791-1861 . **DC 5; NCLC 16**
See also DAM DRAM; DLB 192; GFL 1789 to the Present; RGWL 2, 3

Scrum, R.
See Crumb, R.

Scudery, Georges de 1601-1667 .... **LC 75**
See also GFL Beginnings to 1789

Scudery, Madeleine de 1607-1701 .. **LC 2, 58**
See also DLB 268; GFL Beginnings to 1789

Scum
See Crumb, R.

Scumbag, Little Bobby
See Crumb, R.

Seabrook, John
See Hubbard, L. Ron

Seacole, Mary Jane Grant 1805-1881 .... **NCLC 147**
See also DLB 166

Sealsfield, Charles 1793-1864 .... **NCLC 233**
See also DLB 133, 186

Sealy, I(rwin) Allan 1951- .... **CLC 55**
See also CA 136; CN 6, 7

Search, Alexander
See Pessoa, Fernando

Seare, Nicholas
See Whitaker, Rod

Sebald, W(infried) G(eorg) 1944-2001 .... **CLC 194, 296**
See also BRWS 8; CA 159, 202; CANR 98; MTFW 2005; RGHL

Sebastian, Lee
See Silverberg, Robert

Sebastian Owl
See Thompson, Hunter S.

Sebestyen, Igen
See Sebestyen, Ouida

Sebestyen, Ouida 1924- .... **CLC 30**
See also AAYA 8; BYA 7; CA 107; CANR 40, 114; CLR 17; JRDA; MAICYA 1, 2; SAAS 10; SATA 39, 140; WYA; YAW

Sebold, Alice 1963- .... **CLC 193**
See also AAYA 56; CA 203; CANR 181; LNFS 1; MTFW 2005

Second Duke of Buckingham
See Villiers, George

Secundus, H. Scriblerus
See Fielding, Henry

Sedges, John
See Buck, Pearl S.

Sedgwick, Catharine Maria 1789-1867 .... **NCLC 19, 98**
See also DLB 1, 74, 183, 239, 243, 254; FL 1:3; RGAL 4

Sedley, Sir Charles 1639-1701 .... **LC 168**
See also BRW 2; DLB 131; RGEL 2

Sedulius Scottus 9th cent. -c. 874 .. **CMLC 86**

Seebohm, Victoria
See Glendinning, Victoria

Seelye, John (Douglas) 1931- .... **CLC 7**
See also CA 97-100; CANR 70; INT CA-97-100; TCWW 1, 2

Seferiades, Giorgos Stylianou
See Seferis, George

Seferis, George 1900-1971 .... **CLC 5, 11; TCLC 213**
See also CA 5-8R, 33-36R; CANR 5, 36; DLB 332; EW 12; EWL 3; MTCW 1; RGWL 2, 3

Segal, Erich 1937-2010 .... **CLC 3, 10**
See also BEST 89:1; BPFB 3; CA 25-28R; CANR 20, 36, 65, 113; CPW; DAM POP; DLBY 1986; INT CANR-20; MTCW 1

Segal, Erich Wolf
See Segal, Erich

Seger, Bob 1945- .... **CLC 35**

Seghers
See Radvanyi, Netty

Seghers, Anna
See Radvanyi, Netty

Seidel, Frederick 1936- .... **CLC 18**
See also CA 13-16R; CANR 8, 99, 180; CP 1, 2, 3, 4, 5, 6, 7; DLBY 1984

Seidel, Frederick Lewis
See Seidel, Frederick

Seifert, Jaroslav 1901-1986 . **CLC 34, 44, 93; PC 47**
See also CA 127; CDWLB 4; DLB 215, 332; EWL 3; MTCW 1, 2

Sei Shonagon c. 966-1017(?) ..... **CMLC 6, 89**

Sejour, Victor 1817-1874 .... **DC 10**
See also DLB 50

Sejour Marcou et Ferrand, Juan Victor
See Sejour, Victor

Selby, Hubert, Jr. 1928-2004 ..... **CLC 1, 2, 4, 8; SSC 20**
See also CA 13-16R, 226; CANR 33, 85; CN 1, 2, 3, 4, 5, 6, 7; DLB 2, 227; MAL 5

Self, Will 1961- .... **CLC 282**
See also BRWS 5; CA 143; CANR 83, 126, 171, 201; CN 6, 7; DLB 207

Self, William
See Self, Will

Self, William Woodward
See Self, Will

Selzer, Richard 1928- .... **CLC 74**
See also CA 65-68; CANR 14, 106, 204

Sembene, Ousmane
See Ousmane, Sembene

Senancour, Etienne Pivert de 1770-1846 .... **NCLC 16**
See also DLB 119; GFL 1789 to the Present

Sender, Ramon (Jose) 1902-1982 ...... **CLC 8; HLC 2; TCLC 136**
See also CA 5-8R, 105; CANR 8; DAM MULT; DLB 322; EWL 3; HW 1; MTCW 1; RGWL 2, 3

Seneca, Lucius Annaeus c. 4B.C.-c. 65 .... **CMLC 6, 107; DC 5**
See also AW 2; CDWLB 1; DAM DRAM; DLB 211; RGWL 2, 3; TWA; WLIT 8

Seneca the Younger
See Seneca, Lucius Annaeus

Senghor, Leopold Sedar 1906-2001 .. **BLC 1:3; CLC 54, 130; PC 25**
See also AFW; BW 2; CA 116, 125, 203; CANR 47, 74, 134; CWW 2; DAM MULT, POET; DNFS 2; EWL 3; GFL 1789 to the Present; MTCW 1, 2; MTFW 2005; TWA

Senior, Olive (Marjorie) 1941- .... **SSC 78**
See also BW 3; CA 154; CANR 86, 126; CN 6; CP 6, 7; CWP; DLB 157; EWL 3; RGSF 2

Senna, Danzy 1970- .... **CLC 119**
See also CA 169; CANR 130, 184

Sepheriades, Georgios
See Seferis, George

Serling, (Edward) Rod(man) 1924-1975 .... **CLC 30**
See also AAYA 14; AITN 1; CA 162, 57-60; DLB 26; SFW 4

Serna, Ramon Gomez de la
See Gomez de la Serna, Ramon

Serpieres
See Guillevic, (Eugene)

Service, Robert
See Service, Robert W.

Service, Robert W. 1874(?)-1958 .... **PC 70; TCLC 15; WLC 5**
See also BYA 4; CA 115, 140; CANR 84; DA; DAB; DAC; DAM MST, POET; DLB 92; PFS 10; RGEL 2; SATA 20

Service, Robert William
See Service, Robert W.

Servius c. 370-c. 431 .... **CMLC 120**

Seth, Vikram 1952- .... **CLC 43, 90, 277**
See also BRWS 10; CA 121, 127; CANR 50, 74, 131; CN 6, 7; CP 5, 6, 7; DA3; DAM MULT; DLB 120, 271, 282, 323; EWL 3; INT CA-127; MTCW 2; MTFW 2005; WWE 1

Sherwood, Frances 1940- .... **CLC 81**
See also CA 146, 220; CAAE 220; CANR 158

Sherwood, Robert E(mmet) 1896-1955 .... **DC 36; TCLC 3**
See also CA 104, 153; CANR 86; DAM DRAM; DFS 11, 15, 17; DLB 7, 26, 249; IDFW 3, 4; MAL 5; RGAL 4

Shestov, Lev 1866-1938 .... **TCLC 56**

Shevchenko, Taras 1814-1861 .... **NCLC 54**

Shiel, M. P. 1865-1947 .... **TCLC 8**
See also CA 106, 160; DLB 153; HGG; MTCW 2; MTFW 2005; SCFW 1, 2; SFW 4; SUFW

Shiel, Matthew Phipps
See Shiel, M. P.

Shields, Carol 1935-2003 . **CLC 91, 113, 193; SSC 126**
See also AMWS 7; CA 81-84, 218; CANR 51, 74, 98, 133; CCA 1; CN 6, 7; CPW; DA3; DAC; DLB 334, 350; MTCW 2; MTFW 2005; NFS 23

Shields, David 1956- .... **CLC 97**
See also CA 124; CANR 48, 99, 112, 157

Shields, David Jonathan
See Shields, David

Shiga, Naoya 1883-1971 .... **CLC 33; SSC 23; TCLC 172**
See also CA 101, 33-36R; DLB 180; EWL 3; MJW; RGWL 3

Shiga Naoya
See Shiga, Naoya

Shilts, Randy 1951-1994 .... **CLC 85**
See also AAYA 19; CA 115, 127, 144; CANR 45; DA3; GLL 1; INT CA-127; MTCW 2; MTFW 2005

Shimazaki, Haruki 1872-1943 .... **TCLC 5**
See also CA 105, 134; CANR 84; DLB 180; EWL 3; MJW; RGWL 3

Shimazaki Toson
See Shimazaki, Haruki

Shirley, James 1596-1666 .... **DC 25; LC 96**
See also DLB 58; RGEL 2

Shirley Hastings, Selina
See Hastings, Selina

Sholem Aleykhem
See Rabinovitch, Sholem

Sholokhov, Mikhail 1905-1984 ..... **CLC 7, 15**
See also CA 101, 112; DLB 272, 332; EWL 3; MTCW 1, 2; MTFW 2005; RGWL 2, 3; SATA-Obit 36

Sholokhov, Mikhail Aleksandrovich
See Sholokhov, Mikhail

Sholom Aleichem 1859-1916
See Rabinovitch, Sholem

Shone, Patric
See Hanley, James

Showalter, Elaine 1941- .... **CLC 169**
See also CA 57-60; CANR 58, 106, 208; DLB 67; FW; GLL 2

Shreve, Susan
See Shreve, Susan Richards

Shreve, Susan Richards 1939- .... **CLC 23**
See also CA 49-52; CAAS 5; CANR 5, 38, 69, 100, 159, 199; MAICYA 1, 2; SATA 46, 95, 152; SATA-Brief 41

Shue, Larry 1946-1985 .... **CLC 52**
See also CA 145, 117; DAM DRAM; DFS 7

Shu-Jen, Chou 1881-1936 . **SSC 20; TCLC 3**
See also CA 104; EWL 3

Shulman, Alix Kates 1932- .... **CLC 2, 10**
See also CA 29-32R; CANR 43, 199; FW; SATA 7

Shuster, Joe 1914-1992 .... **CLC 21**
See also AAYA 50

Shute, Nevil 1899-1960 .... **CLC 30**
See also BPFB 3; CA 102, 93-96; CANR 85; DLB 255; MTCW 2; NFS 9; RHW 4; SFW 4

Shuttle, Penelope (Diane) 1947- .... **CLC 7**
See also CA 93-96; CANR 39, 84, 92, 108; CP 3, 4, 5, 6, 7; CWP; DLB 14, 40

Shvarts, Elena 1948-2010 .... **PC 50**
See also CA 147

Sidhwa, Bapsi 1939-
See Sidhwa, Bapsy (N.)

Sidhwa, Bapsy (N.) 1938- .... **CLC 168**
See also CA 108; CANR 25, 57; CN 6, 7; DLB 323; FW

Sidney, Mary 1561-1621 .... **LC 19, 39, 182**
See also DLB 167

Sidney, Sir Philip 1554-1586 .... **LC 19, 39, 131; PC 32**
See also BRW 1; BRWR 2; CDBLB Before 1660; DA; DA3; DAB; DAC; DAM MST, POET; DLB 167; EXPP; PAB; PFS 30; RGEL 2; TEA; WP

Sidney Herbert, Mary
See Sidney, Mary

Siegel, Jerome 1914-1996 .... **CLC 21**
See also AAYA 50; CA 116, 169, 151

Siegel, Jerry
See Siegel, Jerome

Sienkiewicz, Henryk (Adam Alexander Pius) 1846-1916 .... **TCLC 3**
See also CA 104, 134; CANR 84; DLB 332; EWL 3; RGSF 2; RGWL 2, 3

Sierra, Gregorio Martinez
See Martinez Sierra, Gregorio

Sierra, Maria de la O'LeJarraga Martinez
See Martinez Sierra, Maria

Sigal, Clancy 1926- .... **CLC 7**
See also CA 1-4R; CANR 85, 184; CN 1, 2, 3, 4, 5, 6, 7

Siger of Brabant 1240(?)-1284(?) . **CMLC 69**
See also DLB 115

Sigourney, Lydia H.
See Sigourney, Lydia Howard
See also DLB 73, 183

Sigourney, Lydia Howard 1791-1865 .... **NCLC 21, 87**
See Sigourney, Lydia H.
See also DLB 1, 42, 239, 243

Sigourney, Lydia Howard Huntley
See Sigourney, Lydia Howard

Sigourney, Lydia Huntley
See Sigourney, Lydia Howard

Siguenza y Gongora, Carlos de 1645-1700 .... **HLCS 2; LC 8**
See also LAW

Sigurjonsson, Johann
See Sigurjonsson, Johann

Sigurjonsson, Johann 1880-1919 ... **TCLC 27**
See also CA 170; DLB 293; EWL 3

Sikelianos, Angelos 1884-1951 .... **PC 29; TCLC 39**
See also EWL 3; RGWL 2, 3

Silkin, Jon 1930-1997 .... **CLC 2, 6, 43**
See also CA 5-8R; CAAS 5; CANR 89; CP 1, 2, 3, 4, 5, 6; DLB 27

Silko, Leslie 1948- ...... **CLC 23, 74, 114, 211; NNAL; SSC 37, 66; WLCS**
See also AAYA 14; AMWS 4; ANW; BYA 12; CA 115, 122; CANR 45, 65, 118; CN 4, 5, 6, 7; CP 4, 5, 6, 7; CPW 1; CWP; DA; DA3; DAC; DAM MST, MULT, POP; DLB 143, 175, 256, 275; EWL 3; EXPP; EXPS; LAIT 4; MAL 5; MTCW 2; MTFW 2005; NFS 4; PFS 9, 16; RGAL 4; RGSF 2; SSFS 4, 8, 10, 11; TCWW 1, 2

Silko, Leslie Marmon
See Silko, Leslie

Sillanpaa, Frans Eemil 1888-1964 ... **CLC 19**
See also CA 129, 93-96; DLB 332; EWL 3; MTCW 1

Sillitoe, Alan 1928-2010 . **CLC 1, 3, 6, 10, 19, 57, 148**
See also AITN 1; BRWS 5; CA 9-12R, 191; CAAE 191; CAAS 2; CANR 8, 26, 55, 139; CDBLB 1960 to Present; CN 1, 2, 3, 4, 5, 6; CP 1, 2, 3, 4, 5; DLB 14, 139; EWL 3; MTCW 1, 2; MTFW 2005; RGEL 2; RGSF 2; SATA 61

Silone, Ignazio 1900-1978 .... **CLC 4**
See also CA 25-28, 81-84; CANR 34; CAP 2; DLB 264; EW 12; EWL 3; MTCW 1; RGSF 2; RGWL 2, 3

Silone, Ignazione
See Silone, Ignazio

Siluriensis, Leolinus
See Jones, Arthur Llewellyn

Silver, Joan Micklin 1935- .... **CLC 20**
See also CA 114, 121; INT CA-121

Silver, Nicholas
See Faust, Frederick

Silverberg, Robert 1935- .... **CLC 7, 140**
See also AAYA 24; BPFB 3; BYA 7, 9; CA 1-4R, 186; CAAE 186; CAAS 3; CANR 1, 20, 36, 85, 140, 175; CLR 59; CN 6, 7; CPW; DAM POP; DLB 8; INT CANR-20; MAICYA 1, 2; MTCW 1, 2; MTFW 2005; SATA 13, 91; SATA-Essay 104; SCFW 1, 2; SFW 4; SUFW 2

Silverstein, Alvin 1933- .... **CLC 17**
See also CA 49-52; CANR 2; CLR 25; JRDA; MAICYA 1, 2; SATA 8, 69, 124

Silverstein, Shel 1932-1999 .... **PC 49**
See also AAYA 40; BW 3; CA 107, 179; CANR 47, 74, 81; CLR 5, 96; CWRI 5; JRDA; MAICYA 1, 2; MTCW 2; MTFW 2005; SATA 33, 92; SATA-Brief 27; SATA-Obit 116

Silverstein, Sheldon Allan
See Silverstein, Shel

Silverstein, Virginia B. 1937- .... **CLC 17**
See also CA 49-52; CANR 2; CLR 25; JRDA; MAICYA 1, 2; SATA 8, 69, 124

Silverstein, Virginia Barbara Opshelor
See Silverstein, Virginia B.

Sim, Georges
See Simenon, Georges

Simak, Clifford D(onald) 1904-1988 . **CLC 1, 55**
See also CA 1-4R, 125; CANR 1, 35; DLB 8; MTCW 1; SATA-Obit 56; SCFW 1, 2; SFW 4

Simenon, Georges 1903-1989 .... **CLC 1, 2, 3, 8, 18, 47**
See also BPFB 3; CA 85-88, 129; CANR 35; CMW 4; DA3; DAM POP; DLB 72; DLBY 1989; EW 12; EWL 3; GFL 1789 to the Present; MSW; MTCW 1, 2; MTFW 2005; RGWL 2, 3

Simenon, Georges Jacques Christian
See Simenon, Georges

Simic, Charles 1938- .... **CLC 6, 9, 22, 49, 68, 130, 256; PC 69**
See also AAYA 78; AMWS 8; CA 29-32R; CAAS 4; CANR 12, 33, 52, 61, 96, 140; CP 2, 3, 4, 5, 6, 7; DA3; DAM POET; DLB 105; MAL 5; MTCW 2; MTFW 2005; PFS 7, 33; RGAL 4; WP

Simmel, Georg 1858-1918 .... **TCLC 64**
See also CA 157; DLB 296

Simmons, Charles (Paul) 1924- .... **CLC 57**
See also CA 89-92; INT CA-89-92

Simmons, Dan 1948- .... **CLC 44**
See also AAYA 16, 54; CA 138; CANR 53, 81, 126, 174, 204; CPW; DAM POP; HGG; SUFW 2

Smith, David (Jeddie) 1942- .... **CLC 22, 42**
  See also CA 49-52; CAAS 7; CANR 1, 59, 120; CP 3, 4, 5, 6, 7; CSW; DAM POET; DLB 5

Smith, Iain Crichton 1928-1998 .... **CLC 64**
  See also BRWS 9; CA 21-24R, 171; CN 1, 2, 3, 4, 5, 6; CP 1, 2, 3, 4, 5, 6; DLB 40, 139, 319, 352; RGSF 2

Smith, John 1580(?)-1631 .... **LC 9**
  See also DLB 24, 30; TUS

Smith, Johnston
  See Crane, Stephen

Smith, Joseph, Jr. 1805-1844 .... **NCLC 53**

Smith, Kevin 1970- .... **CLC 223**
  See also AAYA 37; CA 166; CANR 131, 201

Smith, Lee 1944- .... **CLC 25, 73, 258; SSC 142**
  See also CA 114, 119; CANR 46, 118, 173; CN 7; CSW; DLB 143; DLBY 1983; EWL 3; INT CA-119; RGAL 4

Smith, Martin
  See Smith, Martin Cruz

Smith, Martin Cruz 1942- .. **CLC 25; NNAL**
  See Smith, Martin Cruz
  See also BEST 89:4; BPFB 3; CA 85-88; CANR 6, 23, 43, 65, 119, 184; CMW 4; CPW; DAM MULT, POP; HGG; INT CANR-23; MTCW 2; MTFW 2005; RGAL 4

Smith, Patti 1946- .... **CLC 12**
  See also CA 93-96; CANR 63, 168

Smith, Pauline (Urmson)
  1882-1959 .... **TCLC 25**
  See also DLB 225; EWL 3

Smith, R. Alexander McCall
  See Smith, Alexander McCall

Smith, Rosamond
  See Oates, Joyce Carol

Smith, Seba 1792-1868 .... **NCLC 187**
  See also DLB 1, 11, 243

Smith, Sheila Kaye
  See Kaye-Smith, Sheila

Smith, Stevie 1902-1971 .... **CLC 3, 8, 25, 44; PC 12**
  See also BRWR 3; BRWS 2; CA 17-18, 29-32R; CANR 35; CAP 2; CP 1; DAM POET; DLB 20; EWL 3; MTCW 1, 2; PAB; PFS 3; RGEL 2; TEA

Smith, Wilbur 1933- .... **CLC 33**
  See also CA 13-16R; CANR 7, 46, 66, 134, 180; CPW; MTCW 1, 2; MTFW 2005

Smith, Wilbur Addison
  See Smith, Wilbur

Smith, William Jay 1918- .... **CLC 6**
  See also AMWS 13; CA 5-8R; CANR 44, 106; CP 1, 2, 3, 4, 5, 6, 7; CSW; CWRI 5; DLB 5; MAICYA 1, 2; SAAS 22; SATA 2, 68, 154; SATA-Essay 154; TCLE 1:2

Smith, Woodrow Wilson
  See Kuttner, Henry

Smith, Zadie 1975- .... **CLC 158**
  See also AAYA 50; CA 193; CANR 204; DLB 347; MTFW 2005

Smolenskin, Peretz 1842-1885 .... **NCLC 30**

Smollett, Tobias (George) 1721-1771 ... **LC 2, 46**
  See also BRW 3; CDBLB 1660-1789; DLB 39, 104; RGEL 2; TEA

Snodgrass, Quentin Curtius
  See Twain, Mark

Snodgrass, Thomas Jefferson
  See Twain, Mark

Snodgrass, W. D. 1926-2009 .... **CLC 2, 6, 10, 18, 68; PC 74**
  See also AMWS 6; CA 1-4R, 282; CANR 6, 36, 65, 85, 185; CP 1, 2, 3, 4, 5, 6, 7; DAM POET; DLB 5; MAL 5; MTCW 1, 2; MTFW 2005; PFS 29; RGAL 4; TCLE 1:2

Snodgrass, W. de Witt
  See Snodgrass, W. D.

Snodgrass, William de Witt
  See Snodgrass, W. D.

Snodgrass, William De Witt
  See Snodgrass, W. D.

Snorri Sturluson 1179-1241 .... **CMLC 56**
  See also RGWL 2, 3

Snow, C(harles) P(ercy) 1905-1980 ... **CLC 1, 4, 6, 9, 13, 19**
  See also BRW 7; CA 5-8R, 101; CANR 28; CDBLB 1945-1960; CN 1, 2; DAM NOV; DLB 15, 77; DLBD 17; EWL 3; MTCW 1, 2; MTFW 2005; RGEL 2; TEA

Snow, Frances Compton
  See Adams, Henry

Snyder, Gary 1930- . **CLC 1, 2, 5, 9, 32, 120; PC 21**
  See also AAYA 72; AMWS 8; ANW; BG 1:3; CA 17-20R; CANR 30, 60, 125; CP 1, 2, 3, 4, 5, 6, 7; DA3; DAM POET; DLB 5, 16, 165, 212, 237, 275, 342; EWL 3; MAL 5; MTCW 2; MTFW 2005; PFS 9, 19; RGAL 4; WP

Snyder, Gary Sherman
  See Snyder, Gary

Snyder, Zilpha Keatley 1927- .... **CLC 17**
  See also AAYA 15; BYA 1; CA 9-12R, 252; CAAE 252; CANR 38, 202; CLR 31, 121; JRDA; MAICYA 1, 2; SAAS 2; SATA 1, 28, 75, 110, 163; SATA-Essay 112, 163; YAW

Soares, Bernardo
  See Pessoa, Fernando

Sobh, A.
  See Shamlu, Ahmad

Sobh, Alef
  See Shamlu, Ahmad

Sobol, Joshua 1939- .... **CLC 60**
  See also CA 200; CWW 2; RGHL

Sobol, Yehoshua 1939-
  See Sobol, Joshua

Socrates 470B.C.-399B.C. .... **CMLC 27**

Soderberg, Hjalmar 1869-1941 ...... **TCLC 39**
  See also DLB 259; EWL 3; RGSF 2

Soderbergh, Steven 1963- .... **CLC 154**
  See also AAYA 43; CA 243

Soderbergh, Steven Andrew
  See Soderbergh, Steven

Sodergran, Edith 1892-1923 .... **TCLC 31**
  See also CA 202; DLB 259; EW 11; EWL 3; RGWL 2, 3

Soedergran, Edith Irene
  See Sodergran, Edith

Softly, Edgar
  See Lovecraft, H. P.

Softly, Edward
  See Lovecraft, H. P.

Sokolov, Alexander V. 1943- .... **CLC 59**
  See also CA 73-76; CWW 2; DLB 285; EWL 3; RGWL 2, 3

Sokolov, Alexander Vsevolodovich
  See Sokolov, Alexander V.

Sokolov, Raymond 1941- .... **CLC 7**
  See also CA 85-88

Sokolov, Sasha
  See Sokolov, Alexander V.

Solo, Jay
  See Ellison, Harlan

Sologub, Fedor
  See Teternikov, Fyodor Kuzmich

Sologub, Feodor
  See Teternikov, Fyodor Kuzmich

Sologub, Fyodor
  See Teternikov, Fyodor Kuzmich

Solomons, Ikey Esquir
  See Thackeray, William Makepeace

Solomos, Dionysios 1798-1857 .... **NCLC 15**

Solwoska, Mara
  See French, Marilyn

Solzhenitsyn, Aleksandr 1918-2008 ... **CLC 1, 2, 4, 7, 9, 10, 18, 26, 34, 78, 134, 235; SSC 32, 105; WLC 5**
  See also AAYA 49; AITN 1; BPFB 3; CA 69-72; CANR 40, 65, 116; CWW 2; DA; DA3; DAB; DAC; DAM MST, NOV; DLB 302, 332; EW 13; EWL 3; EXPS; LAIT 4; MTCW 1, 2; MTFW 2005; NFS 6; RGSF 2; RGWL 2, 3; SSFS 9; TWA

Solzhenitsyn, Aleksandr I.
  See Solzhenitsyn, Aleksandr

Solzhenitsyn, Aleksandr Isayevich
  See Solzhenitsyn, Aleksandr

Somers, Jane
  See Lessing, Doris

Somerville, Edith Oenone
  1858-1949 .... **SSC 56; TCLC 51**
  See also CA 196; DLB 135; RGEL 2; RGSF 2

Somerville & Ross
  See Martin, Violet Florence; Somerville, Edith Oenone

Sommer, Scott 1951- .... **CLC 25**
  See also CA 106

Sommers, Christina Hoff 1950- ...... **CLC 197**
  See also CA 153; CANR 95

Sondheim, Stephen 1930- .. **CLC 30, 39, 147; DC 22**
  See also AAYA 11, 66; CA 103; CANR 47, 67, 125; DAM DRAM; DFS 25, 27; LAIT 4

Sondheim, Stephen Joshua
  See Sondheim, Stephen

Sone, Monica 1919- .... **AAL**
  See also DLB 312

Song, Cathy 1955- .... **AAL; PC 21**
  See also CA 154; CANR 118; CWP; DLB 169, 312; EXPP; FW; PFS 5

Sontag, Susan 1933-2004 ... **CLC 1, 2, 10, 13, 31, 105, 195, 277**
  See also AMWS 3; CA 17-20R, 234; CANR 25, 51, 74, 97, 184; CN 1, 2, 3, 4, 5, 6, 7; CPW; DA3; DAM POP; DLB 2, 67; EWL 3; MAL 5; MBL; MTCW 1, 2; MTFW 2005; RGAL 4; RHW; SSFS 10

Sophocles 496(?)B.C.-406(?)B.C. .... **CMLC 2, 47, 51, 86; DC 1; WLCS**
  See also AW 1; CDWLB 1; DA; DA3; DAB; DAC; DAM DRAM, MST; DFS 1, 4, 8, 24; DLB 176; LAIT 1; LATS 1:1; LMFS 1; RGWL 2, 3; TWA; WLIT 8

Sordello 1189-1269 .... **CMLC 15**

Sorel, Georges 1847-1922 .... **TCLC 91**
  See also CA 118, 188

Sorel, Julia
  See Drexler, Rosalyn

Sorokin, Vladimir .... **CLC 59**
  See also CA 258; DLB 285

Sorokin, Vladimir Georgievich
  See Sorokin, Vladimir

Sorrentino, Gilbert 1929-2006 .... **CLC 3, 7, 14, 22, 40, 247**
  See also CA 77-80, 250; CANR 14, 33, 115, 157; CN 3, 4, 5, 6, 7; CP 1, 2, 3, 4, 5, 6, 7; DLB 5, 173; DLBY 1980; INT CANR-14

Soseki
  See Natsume, Soseki

Stapledon, (William) Olaf
1886-1950 .... **TCLC 22**
See also CA 111, 162; DLB 15, 255; SCFW
1, 2; SFW 4

Starbuck, George (Edwin)
1931-1996 .... **CLC 53**
See also CA 21-24R, 153; CANR 23; CP 1,
2, 3, 4, 5, 6; DAM POET

Stark, Richard
See Westlake, Donald E.

Statius c. 45-c. 96 .... **CMLC 91**
See also AW 2; DLB 211

Staunton, Schuyler
See Baum, L. Frank

Stead, Christina (Ellen) 1902-1983 ... **CLC 2,**
5, 8, 32, 80; TCLC 244
See also BRWS 4; CA 13-16R, 109; CANR
33, 40; CN 1, 2, 3; DLB 260; EWL 3;
FW; MTCW 1, 2; MTFW 2005; NFS 27;
RGEL 2; RGSF 2; WWE 1

Stead, Robert J(ames) C(ampbell)
1880-1959 .... **TCLC 225**
See also CA 186; DLB 92; TCWW 1, 2

Stead, William Thomas
1849-1912 .... **TCLC 48**
See also BRWS 13; CA 167

Stebnitsky, M.
See Leskov, Nikolai (Semyonovich)

Steele, Richard 1672-1729 ... **LC 18, 156, 159**
See also BRW 3; CDBLB 1660-1789; DLB
84, 101; RGEL 2; WLIT 3

Steele, Timothy (Reid) 1948- .... **CLC 45**
See also CA 93-96; CANR 16, 50, 92; CP
5, 6, 7; DLB 120, 282

Steffens, (Joseph) Lincoln
1866-1936 .... **TCLC 20**
See also CA 117, 198; DLB 303; MAL 5

Stegner, Wallace 1909-1993 ... **CLC 9, 49, 81;**
SSC 27
See also AITN 1; AMWS 4; ANW; BEST
90:3; BPFB 3; CA 1-4R, 141; CAAS 9;
CANR 1, 21, 46; CN 1, 2, 3, 4, 5; DAM
NOV; DLB 9, 206, 275; DLBY 1993;
EWL 3; MAL 5; MTCW 1, 2; MTFW
2005; RGAL 4; TCWW 1, 2; TUS

Stegner, Wallace Earle
See Stegner, Wallace

Stein, Gertrude 1874-1946 .... **DC 19; PC 18;**
SSC 42, 105; TCLC 1, 6, 28, 48; WLC
5
See also AAYA 64; AMW; AMWC 2; CA
104, 132; CANR 108; CDALB 1917-
1929; DA; DA3; DAB; DAC; DAM MST,
NOV, POET; DLB 4, 54, 86, 228; DLBD
15; EWL 3; EXPS; FL 1:6; GLL 1; MAL
5; MBL; MTCW 1, 2; MTFW 2005;
NCFS 4; NFS 27; RGAL 4; RGSF 2;
SSFS 5; TUS; WP

Steinbeck, John 1902-1968 .. **CLC 1, 5, 9, 13,**
21, 34, 45, 75, 124; SSC 11, 37, 77, 135;
TCLC 135; WLC 5
See also AAYA 12; AMW; BPFB 3; BYA 2,
3, 13; CA 1-4R, 25-28R; CANR 1, 35;
CDALB 1929-1941; DA; DA3; DAB;
DAC; DAM DRAM, MST, NOV; DLB 7,
9, 212, 275, 309, 332; DLBD 2; EWL 3;
EXPS; LAIT 3; MAL 5; MTCW 1, 2;
MTFW 2005; NFS 1, 5, 7, 17, 19, 28, 34;
RGAL 4; RGSF 2; RHW; SATA 9; SSFS
3, 6, 22; TCWW 1, 2; TUS; WYA; YAW

Steinbeck, John Ernst
See Steinbeck, John

Steinem, Gloria 1934- .... **CLC 63**
See also CA 53-56; CANR 28, 51, 139;
DLB 246; FL 1:1; FW; MTCW 1, 2;
MTFW 2005

Steiner, George 1929- .... **CLC 24, 221**
See also CA 73-76; CANR 31, 67, 108;
DAM NOV; DLB 67, 299; EWL 3;
MTCW 1, 2; MTFW 2005; RGHL; SATA
62

Steiner, K. Leslie
See Delany, Samuel R., Jr.

Steiner, Rudolf 1861-1925 .... **TCLC 13**
See also CA 107

Stendhal 1783-1842 .... **NCLC 23, 46, 178;**
SSC 27; WLC 5
See also DA; DA3; DAB; DAC; DAM
MST, NOV; DLB 119; EW 5; GFL 1789
to the Present; RGWL 2, 3; TWA

Stephen, Adeline Virginia
See Woolf, Virginia

Stephen, Sir Leslie 1832-1904 .... **TCLC 23**
See also BRW 5; CA 123; DLB 57, 144,
190

Stephen, Sir Leslie
See Stephen, Sir Leslie

Stephen, Virginia
See Woolf, Virginia

Stephens, James 1882(?)-1950 .... **SSC 50;**
TCLC 4
See also CA 104, 192; DLB 19, 153, 162;
EWL 3; FANT; RGEL 2; SUFW

Stephens, Reed
See Donaldson, Stephen R.

Stephenson, Neal 1959- .... **CLC 220**
See also AAYA 38; CA 122; CANR 88, 138,
195; CN 7; MTFW 2005; SFW 4

Steptoe, Lydia
See Barnes, Djuna

Sterchi, Beat 1949- .... **CLC 65**
See also CA 203

Sterling, Brett
See Bradbury, Ray; Hamilton, Edmond

Sterling, Bruce 1954- .... **CLC 72**
See also AAYA 78; CA 119; CANR 44, 135,
184; CN 7; MTFW 2005; SCFW 2; SFW
4

Sterling, George 1869-1926 .... **TCLC 20**
See also CA 117, 165; DLB 54

Stern, Gerald 1925- .... **CLC 40, 100**
See also AMWS 9; CA 81-84; CANR 28,
94, 206; CP 3, 4, 5, 6, 7; DLB 105; PFS
26; RGAL 4

Stern, Richard (Gustave) 1928- ... **CLC 4, 39**
See also CA 1-4R; CANR 1, 25, 52, 120;
CN 1, 2, 3, 4, 5, 6, 7; DLB 218; DLBY
1987; INT CANR-25

Sternberg, Josef von 1894-1969 .... **CLC 20**
See also CA 81-84

Sterne, Laurence 1713-1768 .. **LC 2, 48, 156;**
WLC 5
See also BRW 3; BRWC 1; CDBLB 1660-
1789; DA; DAB; DAC; DAM MST, NOV;
DLB 39; RGEL 2; TEA

Sternheim, (William Adolf) Carl
1878-1942 .... **TCLC 8, 223**
See also CA 105, 193; DLB 56, 118; EWL
3; IDTP; RGWL 2, 3

Stetson, Charlotte Perkins
See Gilman, Charlotte Perkins

Stevens, Margaret Dean
See Aldrich, Bess Streeter

Stevens, Mark 1951- .... **CLC 34**
See also CA 122

Stevens, R. L.
See Hoch, Edward D.

Stevens, Wallace 1879-1955 .... **PC 6, 110;**
TCLC 3, 12, 45; WLC 5
See also AMW; AMWR 1; CA 104, 124;
CANR 181; CDALB 1929-1941; DA;
DA3; DAB; DAC; DAM MST, POET;
DLB 54, 342; EWL 3; EXPP; MAL 5;
MTCW 1, 2; PAB; PFS 13, 16, 35; RGAL
4; TUS; WP

Stevenson, Anne (Katharine) 1933- .. **CLC 7,**
33
See also BRWS 6; CA 17-20R; CAAS 9;
CANR 9, 33, 123; CP 3, 4, 5, 6, 7; CWP;
DLB 40; MTCW 1; RHW

Stevenson, Robert Louis
1850-1894 ...... **NCLC 5, 14, 63, 193; PC**
84; SSC 11, 51, 126; WLC 5
See also AAYA 24; BPFB 3; BRW 5;
BRWC 1; BRWR 1; BYA 1, 2, 4, 13; CD-
BLB 1890-1914; CLR 10, 11, 107; DA;
DA3; DAB; DAC; DAM MST, NOV;
DLB 18, 57, 141, 156, 174; DLBD 13;
GL 3; HGG; JRDA; LAIT 1, 3; MAICYA
1, 2; NFS 11, 20, 33; RGEL 2; RGSF 2;
SATA 100; SUFW; TEA; WCH; WLIT 4;
WYA; YABC 2; YAW

Stevenson, Robert Louis Balfour
See Stevenson, Robert Louis

Stewart, J(ohn) I(nnes) M(ackintosh)
1906-1994 .... **CLC 7, 14, 32**
See also CA 85-88, 147; CAAS 3; CANR
47; CMW 4; CN 1, 2, 3, 4, 5; DLB 276;
MSW; MTCW 1, 2

Stewart, Mary (Florence Elinor)
1916- .... **CLC 7, 35, 117**
See also AAYA 29, 73; BPFB 3; CA 1-4R;
CANR 1, 59, 130; CMW 4; CPW; DAB;
FANT; RHW; SATA 12; YAW

Stewart, Mary Rainbow
See Stewart, Mary (Florence Elinor)

Stewart, Will
See Williamson, John Stewart

Stifle, June
See Campbell, Maria

Stifter, Adalbert 1805-1868 ... **NCLC 41, 198;**
SSC 28
See also CDWLB 2; DLB 133; RGSF 2;
RGWL 2, 3

Still, James 1906-2001 .... **CLC 49**
See also CA 65-68, 195; CAAS 17; CANR
10, 26; CSW; DLB 9; DLBY 01; SATA
29; SATA-Obit 127

Sting 1951- .... **CLC 26**
See also CA 167

Stirling, Arthur
See Sinclair, Upton

Stitt, Milan 1941-2009 .... **CLC 29**
See also CA 69-72, 284

Stitt, Milan William
See Stitt, Milan

Stockton, Francis Richard
1834-1902 .... **TCLC 47**
See also AAYA 68; BYA 4, 13; CA 108,
137; DLB 42, 74; DLBD 13; EXPS; MAI-
CYA 1, 2; SATA 44; SATA-Brief 32; SFW
4; SSFS 3; SUFW; WCH

Stockton, Frank R.
See Stockton, Francis Richard

Stoddard, Charles
See Kuttner, Henry

Stoker, Abraham
See Stoker, Bram

Stoker, Bram 1847-1912 ... **SSC 62; TCLC 8,**
144; WLC 6
See also AAYA 23; BPFB 3; BRWS 3; BYA
5; CA 105, 150; CDBLB 1890-1914; DA;
DA3; DAB; DAC; DAM MST, NOV;
DLB 304; GL 3; HGG; LATS 1:1; MTFW
2005; NFS 18; RGEL 2; SATA 29; SUFW;
TEA; WLIT 4

Stolz, Mary 1920-2006 .... **CLC 12**
See also AAYA 8, 73; AITN 1; CA 5-8R,
255; CANR 13, 41, 112; JRDA; MAICYA
1, 2; SAAS 3; SATA 10, 71, 133; SATA-
Obit 180; YAW

Stolz, Mary Slattery
See Stolz, Mary

Stone, Irving 1903-1989 .... **CLC 7**
See also AITN 1; BPFB 3; CA 1-4R, 129;
CAAS 3; CANR 1, 23; CN 1, 2, 3, 4;
CPW; DA3; DAM POP; INT CANR-23;
MTCW 1, 2; MTFW 2005; RHW; SATA
3; SATA-Obit 64

Sun Tzu c. 400B.C.-c. 320B.C. ...... **CMLC 56**
Surayya, Kamala
   See Das, Kamala
Surayya Kamala
   See Das, Kamala
Surdas c. 1478-c. 1583 .... **LC 163**
   See also RGWL 2, 3
Surrey, Henry Howard 1517-1574 ... **LC 121;**
   PC 59
   See also BRW 1; RGEL 2
Surtees, Robert Smith 1805-1864 .. **NCLC 14**
   See also DLB 21; RGEL 2
Susann, Jacqueline 1921-1974 .... **CLC 3**
   See also AITN 1; BPFB 3; CA 65-68, 53-
   56; MTCW 1, 2
Su Shi
   See Su Shih
Su Shih 1036-1101 .... **CMLC 15**
   See also RGWL 2, 3
Suskind, Patrick 1949- .... **CLC 44, 182**
   See also BPFB 3; CA 145; CWW 2
Suso, Heinrich c. 1295-1366 .... **CMLC 87**
Sutcliff, Rosemary 1920-1992 .... **CLC 26**
   See also AAYA 10; BRWS 16; BYA 1, 4;
   CA 5-8R, 139; CANR 37; CLR 1, 37,
   138; CPW; DAB; DAC; DAM MST, POP;
   JRDA; LATS 1:1; MAICYA 1, 2; MAIC-
   YAS 1; RHW; SATA 6, 44, 78; SATA-
   Obit 73; WYA; YAW
Sutherland, Efua (Theodora Morgue)
   1924-1996 .... **BLC 2:3**
   See also AFW; BW 1; CA 105; CWD; DLB
   117; EWL 3; IDTP; SATA 25
Sutro, Alfred 1863-1933 .... **TCLC 6**
   See also CA 105, 185; DLB 10; RGEL 2
Sutton, Henry
   See Slavitt, David R.
Su Yuan-ying
   See Su, Chien
Su Yuean-ying
   See Su, Chien
Suzuki, D. T.
   See Suzuki, Daisetz Teitaro
Suzuki, Daisetz T.
   See Suzuki, Daisetz Teitaro
Suzuki, Daisetz Teitaro
   1870-1966 .... **TCLC 109**
   See also CA 121, 111; MTCW 1, 2; MTFW
   2005
Suzuki, Teitaro
   See Suzuki, Daisetz Teitaro
Svareff, Count Vladimir
   See Crowley, Edward Alexander
Svevo, Italo
   See Schmitz, Aron Hector
Swados, Elizabeth 1951- .... **CLC 12**
   See also CA 97-100; CANR 49, 163; INT
   CA-97-100
Swados, Elizabeth A.
   See Swados, Elizabeth
Swados, Harvey 1920-1972 .... **CLC 5**
   See also CA 5-8R, 37-40R; CANR 6; CN
   1; DLB 2, 335; MAL 5
Swados, Liz
   See Swados, Elizabeth
Swan, Gladys 1934- .... **CLC 69**
   See also CA 101; CANR 17, 39; TCLE 1:2
Swanson, Logan
   See Matheson, Richard
Swarthout, Glendon (Fred)
   1918-1992 .... **CLC 35**
   See also AAYA 55; CA 1-4R, 139; CANR
   1, 47; CN 1, 2, 3, 4, 5; LAIT 5; NFS 29;
   SATA 26; TCWW 1, 2; YAW
Swedenborg, Emanuel 1688-1772 ..... **LC 105**
Sweet, Sarah C.
   See Jewett, Sarah Orne

Swenson, May 1919-1989 ...... **CLC 4, 14, 61,**
   106; PC 14
   See also AMWS 4; CA 5-8R, 130; CANR
   36, 61, 131; CP 1, 2, 3, 4; DA; DAB;
   DAC; DAM MST, POET; DLB 5; EXPP;
   GLL 2; MAL 5; MTCW 1, 2; MTFW
   2005; PFS 16, 30; SATA 15; WP
Swift, Augustus
   See Lovecraft, H. P.
Swift, Graham 1949- .... **CLC 41, 88, 233**
   See also BRWC 2; BRWS 5; CA 117, 122;
   CANR 46, 71, 128, 181; CN 4, 5, 6, 7;
   DLB 194, 326; MTCW 2; MTFW 2005;
   NFS 18; RGSF 2
Swift, Jonathan 1667-1745 ..... **LC 1, 42, 101;**
   PC 9; WLC 6
   See also AAYA 41; BRW 3; BRWC 1;
   BRWR 1; BYA 5, 14; CDBLB 1660-1789;
   CLR 53; DA; DA3; DAB; DAC; DAM
   MST, NOV, POET; DLB 39, 95, 101;
   EXPN; LAIT 1; NFS 6; PFS 27; RGEL 2;
   SATA 19; TEA; WCH; WLIT 3
Swinburne, Algernon Charles
   1837-1909 ... **PC 24; TCLC 8, 36; WLC**
   6
   See also BRW 5; CA 105, 140; CDBLB
   1832-1890; DA; DA3; DAB; DAC; DAM
   MST, POET; DLB 35, 57; PAB; RGEL 2;
   TEA
Swinfen, Ann CLC 34
   See also CA 202
Swinnerton, Frank (Arthur)
   1884-1982 .... **CLC 31**
   See also CA 202, 108; CN 1, 2, 3; DLB 34
Swinnerton, Frank Arthur
   1884-1982 .... **CLC 31**
   See also CA 108; DLB 34
Swithen, John
   See King, Stephen
Sylvia
   See Ashton-Warner, Sylvia (Constance)
Symmes, Robert Edward
   See Duncan, Robert
Symonds, John Addington
   1840-1893 .... **NCLC 34**
   See also BRWS 14; DLB 57, 144
Symons, Arthur 1865-1945 ..... **TCLC 11, 243**
   See also BRWS 14; CA 107, 189; DLB 19,
   57, 149; RGEL 2
Symons, Julian (Gustave)
   1912-1994 .... **CLC 2, 14, 32**
   See also CA 49-52, 147; CAAS 3; CANR
   3, 33, 59; CMW 4; CN 1, 2, 3, 4, 5; CP 1,
   3, 4; DLB 87, 155; DLBY 1992; MSW;
   MTCW 1
Synge, Edmund John Millington
   See Synge, John Millington
Synge, J. M.
   See Synge, John Millington
Synge, John Millington 1871-1909 ...... **DC 2;**
   TCLC 6, 37
   See also BRW 6; BRWR 1; CA 104, 141;
   CDBLB 1890-1914; DAM DRAM; DFS
   18; DLB 10, 19; EWL 3; RGEL 2; TEA;
   WLIT 4
Syruc, J.
   See Milosz, Czeslaw
Szirtes, George 1948- .... **CLC 46; PC 51**
   See also CA 109; CANR 27, 61, 117; CP 4,
   5, 6, 7
Szymborska, Wislawa 1923- ... **CLC 99, 190;**
   PC 44
   See also AAYA 76; CA 154; CANR 91, 133,
   181; CDWLB 4; CWP; CWW 2; DA3;
   DLB 232, 332; DLBY 1996; EWL 3;
   MTCW 2; MTFW 2005; PFS 15, 27, 31,
   34; RGHL; RGWL 3
T. O., Nik
   See Annensky, Innokenty (Fyodorovich)

Tabori, George 1914-2007 .... **CLC 19**
   See also CA 49-52, 262; CANR 4, 69;
   CBD; CD 5, 6; DLB 245; RGHL
Tacitus c. 55-c. 117 .... **CMLC 56**
   See also AW 2; CDWLB 1; DLB 211;
   RGWL 2, 3; WLIT 8
Tadjo, Veronique 1955- .... **BLC 2:3**
   See also EWL 3
Tagore, Rabindranath 1861-1941 .... **PC 8;**
   SSC 48; TCLC 3, 53
   See also CA 104, 120; DA3; DAM DRAM,
   POET; DFS 26; DLB 323, 332; EWL 3;
   MTCW 1, 2; MTFW 2005; PFS 18; RGEL
   2; RGSF 2; RGWL 2, 3; TWA
Taine, Hippolyte Adolphe
   1828-1893 .... **NCLC 15**
   See also EW 7; GFL 1789 to the Present
Talayesva, Don C. 1890-(?) .... **NNAL**
Talese, Gay 1932- .... **CLC 37, 232**
   See also AITN 1; AMWS 17; CA 1-4R;
   CANR 9, 58, 137, 177; DLB 185; INT
   CANR-9; MTCW 1, 2; MTFW 2005
Tallent, Elizabeth 1954- .... **CLC 45**
   See also CA 117; CANR 72; DLB 130
Tallmountain, Mary 1918-1997 .... **NNAL**
   See also CA 146, 161; DLB 193
Tally, Ted 1952- .... **CLC 42**
   See also CA 120, 124; CAD; CANR 125;
   CD 5, 6; INT CA-124
Talvik, Heiti 1904-1947 .... **TCLC 87**
   See also EWL 3
Tamayo y Baus, Manuel
   1829-1898 .... **NCLC 1**
Tammsaare, A(nton) H(ansen)
   1878-1940 .... **TCLC 27**
   See also CA 164; CDWLB 4; DLB 220;
   EWL 3
Tam'si, Tchicaya U
   See Tchicaya, Gerald Felix
Tan, Amy 1952- ..... **AAL; CLC 59, 120, 151,**
   257
   See also AAYA 9, 48; AMWS 10; BEST
   89:3; BPFB 3; CA 136; CANR 54, 105,
   132; CDALBS; CN 6, 7; CPW 1; DA3;
   DAM MULT, NOV, POP; DLB 173, 312;
   EXPN; FL 1:6; FW; LAIT 3, 5; MAL 5;
   MTCW 2; MTFW 2005; NFS 1, 13, 16,
   31, 35; RGAL 4; SATA 75; SSFS 9; YAW
Tan, Amy Ruth
   See Tan, Amy
Tandem, Carl Felix
   See Spitteler, Carl
Tandem, Felix
   See Spitteler, Carl
Tania B.
   See Blixen, Karen
Tanizaki, Jun'ichiro 1886-1965 ... **CLC 8, 14,**
   28; SSC 21
   See also CA 93-96, 25-28R; DLB 180;
   EWL 3; MJW; MTCW 2; MTFW 2005;
   RGSF 2; RGWL 2
Tanizaki Jun'ichiro
   See Tanizaki, Jun'ichiro
Tannen, Deborah 1945- .... **CLC 206**
   See also CA 118; CANR 95
Tannen, Deborah Frances
   See Tannen, Deborah
Tanner, William
   See Amis, Kingsley
Tante, Dilly
   See Kunitz, Stanley
Tao Lao
   See Storni, Alfonsina
Tapahonso, Luci 1953- .... **NNAL; PC 65**
   See also CA 145; CANR 72, 127; DLB 175
Tarantino, Quentin 1963- .... **CLC 125, 230**
   See also AAYA 58; CA 171; CANR 125
Tarantino, Quentin Jerome
   See Tarantino, Quentin

Tomlin, Mary Jane
See Tomlin, Lily

Tomlin, Mary Jean
See Tomlin, Lily

Tomline, F. Latour
See Gilbert, W(illiam) S(chwenck)

Tomlinson, (Alfred) Charles 1927- .... **CLC 2, 4, 6, 13, 45; PC 17**
See also CA 5-8R; CANR 33; CP 1, 2, 3, 4, 5, 6, 7; DAM POET; DLB 40; TCLE 1:2

Tomlinson, H(enry) M(ajor)
1873-1958 .... **TCLC 71**
See also CA 118, 161; DLB 36, 100, 195

Tomlinson, Mary Jane
See Tomlin, Lily

Tonna, Charlotte Elizabeth
1790-1846 .... **NCLC 135**
See also DLB 163

Tonson, Jacob fl. 1655(?)-1736 .... **LC 86**
See also DLB 170

Toole, John Kennedy 1937-1969 ..... **CLC 19, 64**
See also BPFB 3; CA 104; DLBY 1981; MTCW 2; MTFW 2005

Toomer, Eugene
See Toomer, Jean

Toomer, Eugene Pinchback
See Toomer, Jean

Toomer, Jean 1894-1967 ... **BLC 1:3; CLC 1, 4, 13, 22; HR 1:3; PC 7; SSC 1, 45, 138; TCLC 172; WLCS**
See also AFAW 1, 2; AMWS 3, 9; BW 1; CA 85-88; CDALB 1917-1929; DA3; DAM MULT; DLB 45, 51; EWL 3; EXPP; EXPS; LMFS 2; MAL 5; MTCW 1, 2; MTFW 2005; NFS 11; PFS 31; RGAL 4; RGSF 2; SSFS 5

Toomer, Nathan Jean
See Toomer, Jean

Toomer, Nathan Pinchback
See Toomer, Jean

Torley, Luke
See Blish, James

Tornimparte, Alessandra
See Ginzburg, Natalia

Torre, Raoul della
See Mencken, H. L.

Torrence, Ridgely 1874-1950 .... **TCLC 97**
See also DLB 54, 249; MAL 5

Torrey, E. Fuller 1937- .... **CLC 34**
See also CA 119; CANR 71, 158

Torrey, Edwin Fuller
See Torrey, E. Fuller

Torsvan, Ben Traven
See Traven, B.

Torsvan, Benno Traven
See Traven, B.

Torsvan, Berick Traven
See Traven, B.

Torsvan, Berwick Traven
See Traven, B.

Torsvan, Bruno Traven
See Traven, B.

Torsvan, Traven
See Traven, B.

Toson
See Shimazaki, Haruki

Tourneur, Cyril 1575(?)-1626 ...... **LC 66, 181**
See also BRW 2; DAM DRAM; DLB 58; RGEL 2

Tournier, Michel 1924- .... **CLC 6, 23, 36, 95, 249; SSC 88**
See also CA 49-52; CANR 3, 36, 74, 149; CWW 2; DLB 83; EWL 3; GFL 1789 to the Present; MTCW 1, 2; SATA 23

Tournier, Michel Edouard
See Tournier, Michel

Tournimparte, Alessandra
See Ginzburg, Natalia

Towers, Ivar
See Kornbluth, C(yril) M.

Towne, Robert (Burton) 1936(?)- ..... **CLC 87**
See also CA 108; DLB 44; IDFW 3, 4

Townsend, Sue 1946- .... **CLC 61**
See also AAYA 28; CA 119, 127; CANR 65, 107, 202; CBD; CD 5, 6; CPW; CWD; DAB; DAC; DAM MST; DLB 271, 352; INT CA-127; SATA 55, 93; SATA-Brief 48; YAW

Townsend, Susan Lilian
See Townsend, Sue

Townshend, Pete
See Townshend, Peter

Townshend, Peter 1945- .... **CLC 17, 42**
See also CA 107

Townshend, Peter Dennis Blandford
See Townshend, Peter

Tozzi, Federigo 1883-1920 .... **TCLC 31**
See also CA 160; CANR 110; DLB 264; EWL 3; WLIT 7

Trafford, F. G.
See Riddell, Charlotte

Traherne, Thomas 1637(?)-1674 .. **LC 99; PC 70**
See also BRW 2; BRWS 11; DLB 131; PAB; RGEL 2

Traill, Catharine Parr 1802-1899 .. **NCLC 31**
See also DLB 99

Trakl, Georg 1887-1914 ...... **PC 20; TCLC 5, 239**
See also CA 104, 165; EW 10; EWL 3; LMFS 2; MTCW 2; RGWL 2, 3

Trambley, Estela Portillo
See Portillo Trambley, Estela

Tranquilli, Secondino
See Silone, Ignazio

Transtroemer, Tomas Gosta
See Transtromer, Tomas

Transtromer, Tomas 1931- .... **CLC 52, 65**
See also CA 117, 129; CAAS 17; CANR 115, 172; CWW 2; DAM POET; DLB 257; EWL 3; PFS 21

Transtromer, Tomas Goesta
See Transtromer, Tomas

Transtromer, Tomas Gosta
See Transtromer, Tomas

Transtromer, Tomas Gosta
See Transtromer, Tomas

Traven, B. 1882(?)-1969 .... **CLC 8, 11**
See also CA 19-20, 25-28R; CAP 2; DLB 9, 56; EWL 3; MTCW 1; RGAL 4

Trediakovsky, Vasilii Kirillovich
1703-1769 .... **LC 68**
See also DLB 150

Treitel, Jonathan 1959- .... **CLC 70**
See also CA 210; DLB 267

Trelawny, Edward John
1792-1881 .... **NCLC 85**
See also DLB 110, 116, 144

Tremain, Rose 1943- .... **CLC 42**
See also CA 97-100; CANR 44, 95, 186; CN 4, 5, 6, 7; DLB 14, 271; RGSF 2; RHW

Tremblay, Michel 1942- .... **CLC 29, 102, 225**
See also CA 116, 128; CCA 1; CWW 2; DAC; DAM MST; DLB 60; EWL 3; GLL 1; MTCW 1, 2; MTFW 2005

Trevanian
See Whitaker, Rod

Trevisa, John c. 1342-c. 1402 .... **LC 139**
See also BRWS 9; DLB 146

Trevor, Frances
See Teasdale, Sara

Trevor, Glen
See Hilton, James

Trevor, William 1928- ... **CLC 1, 2, 3, 4, 5, 6, 7; SSC 21, 58**
See also BRWS 4; CA 9-12R; CANR 4, 37, 55, 76, 102, 139, 195; CBD; CD 5, 6; DAM NOV; DLB 14, 139; EWL 3; INT CANR-37; LATS 1:2; MTCW 1, 2; MTFW 2005; RGEL 2; RGSF 2; SSFS 10; TCLE 1:2; TEA

Triana, Jose 1931(?)- .... **DC 39**
See also CA 131; DLB 305; EWL 3; HW 1; LAW

Trifonov, Iurii (Valentinovich)
See Trifonov, Yuri (Valentinovich)

Trifonov, Yuri (Valentinovich)
1925-1981 .... **CLC 45**
See also CA 126, 103; DLB 302; EWL 3; MTCW 1; RGWL 2, 3

Trifonov, Yury Valentinovich
See Trifonov, Yuri (Valentinovich)

Trilling, Diana (Rubin) 1905-1996 . **CLC 129**
See also CA 5-8R, 154; CANR 10, 46; INT CANR-10; MTCW 1, 2

Trilling, Lionel 1905-1975 ..... **CLC 9, 11, 24; SSC 75**
See also AMWS 3; CA 9-12R, 61-64; CANR 10, 105; CN 1, 2; DLB 28, 63; EWL 3; INT CANR-10; MAL 5; MTCW 1, 2; RGAL 4; TUS

Trimball, W. H.
See Mencken, H. L.

Tristan
See Gomez de la Serna, Ramon

Tristram
See Housman, A. E.

Trogdon, William
See Heat-Moon, William Least

Trogdon, William Lewis
See Heat-Moon, William Least

Trogdon, William Lewis
See Heat-Moon, William Least

Trollope, Anthony 1815-1882 .... **NCLC 6, 33, 101, 215; SSC 28, 133; WLC 6**
See also BRW 5; CDBLB 1832-1890; DA; DA3; DAB; DAC; DAM MST, NOV; DLB 21, 57, 159; RGEL 2; RGSF 2; SATA 22

Trollope, Frances 1779-1863 .... **NCLC 30**
See also DLB 21, 166

Trollope, Joanna 1943- .... **CLC 186**
See also CA 101; CANR 58, 95, 149, 191; CN 7; CPW; DLB 207; RHW

Trotsky, Leon 1879-1940 .... **TCLC 22**
See also CA 118, 167

Trotter, Catharine 1679-1749 .... **LC 8, 165**
See also BRWS 16; DLB 84, 252

Trotter, Wilfred 1872-1939 .... **TCLC 97**

Troupe, Quincy 1943- .... **BLC 2:3**
See also BW 2; CA 113, 124; CANR 43, 90, 126; DLB 41

Trout, Kilgore
See Farmer, Philip Jose

Trow, George William Swift
See Trow, George W.S.

Trow, George W.S. 1943-2006 .... **CLC 52**
See also CA 126, 255; CANR 91

Troyat, Henri 1911-2007 .... **CLC 23**
See also CA 45-48, 258; CANR 2, 33, 67, 117; GFL 1789 to the Present; MTCW 1

Trudeau, Garretson Beekman
See Trudeau, G.B.

Trudeau, Garry
See Trudeau, G.B.

Trudeau, Garry B.
See Trudeau, G.B.

Trudeau, G.B. 1948- .... **CLC 12**
See also AAYA 10, 60; AITN 2; CA 81-84; CANR 31; SATA 35, 168

Truffaut, Francois 1932-1984 ... **CLC 20, 101**
   See also AAYA 84; CA 81-84, 113; CANR
   34
Trumbo, Dalton 1905-1976 .... **CLC 19**
   See also CA 21-24R, 69-72; CANR 10; CN
   1, 2; DLB 26; IDFW 3, 4; YAW
Trumbull, John 1750-1831 .... **NCLC 30**
   See also DLB 31; RGAL 4
Trundlett, Helen B.
   See Eliot, T. S.
Truth, Sojourner 1797(?)-1883 ...... **NCLC 94**
   See also DLB 239; FW; LAIT 2
Tryon, Thomas 1926-1991 .... **CLC 3, 11**
   See also AITN 1; BPFB 3; CA 29-32R, 135;
   CANR 32, 77; CPW; DA3; DAM POP;
   HGG; MTCW 1
Tryon, Tom
   See Tryon, Thomas
Ts'ao Hsueh-ch'in 1715(?)-1763 .... **LC 1**
Tsurayuki Ed. fl. 10th cent. - .... **PC 73**
Tsvetaeva, Marina 1892-1941 . **PC 14; TCLC
   7, 35**
   See also CA 104, 128; CANR 73; DLB 295;
   EW 11; MTCW 1, 2; PFS 29; RGWL 2, 3
Tsvetaeva Efron, Marina Ivanovna
   See Tsvetaeva, Marina
Tuck, Lily 1938- .... **CLC 70**
   See also AAYA 74; CA 139; CANR 90, 192
Tuckerman, Frederick Goddard
   1821-1873 .... **PC 85**
   See also DLB 243; RGAL 4
Tu Fu 712-770 .... **PC 9**
   See also DAM MULT; PFS 32; RGWL 2,
   3; TWA; WP
Tulsidas, Gosvami 1532(?)-1623 .... **LC 158**
   See also RGWL 2, 3
Tunis, John R(oberts) 1889-1975 ..... **CLC 12**
   See also BYA 1; CA 61-64; CANR 62; DLB
   22, 171; JRDA; MAICYA 1, 2; SATA 37;
   SATA-Brief 30; YAW
Tuohy, Frank
   See Tuohy, John Francis
Tuohy, John Francis 1925- .... **CLC 37**
   See also CA 5-8R, 178; CANR 3, 47; CN
   1, 2, 3, 4, 5, 6, 7; DLB 14, 139
Turco, Lewis 1934- .... **CLC 11, 63**
   See also CA 13-16R; CAAS 22; CANR 24,
   51, 185; CP 1, 2, 3, 4, 5, 6, 7; DLBY
   1984; TCLE 1:2
Turco, Lewis Putnam
   See Turco, Lewis
Turgenev, Ivan 1818-1883 . **DC 7; NCLC 21,
   37, 122; SSC 7, 57; WLC 6**
   See also AAYA 58; DA; DAB; DAC; DAM
   MST, NOV; DFS 6; DLB 238, 284; EW
   6; LATS 1:1; NFS 16; RGSF 2; RGWL 2,
   3; TWA
Turgenev, Ivan Sergeevich
   See Turgenev, Ivan
Turgot, Anne-Robert-Jacques
   1727-1781 .... **LC 26**
   See also DLB 314
Turner, Frederick 1943- .... **CLC 48**
   See also CA 73-76, 227; CAAE 227; CAAS
   10; CANR 12, 30, 56; DLB 40, 282
Turton, James
   See Crace, Jim
Tutu, Desmond M(pilo) 1931- .... **BLC 1:3;
   CLC 80**
   See also BW 1, 3; CA 125; CANR 67, 81;
   DAM MULT
Tutuola, Amos 1920-1997 .... **BLC 1:3, 2:3;
   CLC 5, 14, 29; TCLC 188**
   See also AAYA 76; AFW; BW 2, 3; CA
   9-12R, 159; CANR 27, 66; CDWLB 3;
   CN 1, 2, 3, 4, 5, 6; DA3; DAM MULT;
   DLB 125; DNFS 2; EWL 3; MTCW 1, 2;
   MTFW 2005; RGEL 2; WLIT 2

Twain, Mark 1835-1910 ... **SSC 6, 26, 34, 87,
   119; TCLC 6, 12, 19, 36, 48, 59, 161,
   185; WLC 6**
   See also AAYA 20; AMW; AMWC 1; BPFB
   3; BYA 2, 3, 11, 14; CA 104, 135; CDALB
   1865-1917; CLR 58, 60, 66, 156; DA;
   DA3; DAB; DAC; DAM MST, NOV;
   DLB 12, 23, 64, 74, 186, 189, 11, 343;
   EXPN; EXPS; JRDA; LAIT 2; LMFS 1;
   MAICYA 1, 2; MAL 5; NCFS 4; NFS 1,
   6; RGAL 4; RGSF 2; SATA 100; SFW 4;
   SSFS 1, 7, 16, 21, 27; SUFW; TUS;
   WCH; WYA; YABC 2; YAW
Twohill, Maggie
   See Angell, Judie
Tyler, Anne 1941- . **CLC 7, 11, 18, 28, 44, 59,
   103, 205, 265**
   See also AAYA 18, 60; AMWS 4; BEST
   89:1; BPFB 3; BYA 12; CA 9-12R; CANR
   11, 33, 53, 109, 132, 168; CDALBS; CN
   1, 2, 3, 4, 5, 6, 7; CPW; CSW; DAM
   NOV, POP; DLB 6, 143; DLBY 1982;
   EWL 3; EXPN; LATS 1:2; MAL 5; MBL;
   MTCW 1, 2; MTFW 2005; NFS 2, 7, 10;
   RGAL 4; SATA 7, 90, 173; SSFS 1, 31;
   TCLE 1:2; TUS; YAW
Tyler, Royall 1757-1826 .... **NCLC 3**
   See also DLB 37; RGAL 4
Tynan, Katharine 1861-1931 ... **TCLC 3, 217**
   See also CA 104, 167; DLB 153, 240; FW
Tyndale, William c. 1484-1536 .... **LC 103**
   See also DLB 132
Tyutchev, Fyodor 1803-1873 .... **NCLC 34**
Tzara, Tristan 1896-1963 .... **CLC 47; PC 27;
   TCLC 168**
   See also CA 153, 89-92; DAM POET; EWL
   3; MTCW 2
Uc de Saint Circ c. 1190B.C.-13th cent.
   B.C. .... **CMLC 102**
Uchida, Yoshiko 1921-1992 .... **AAL**
   See also AAYA 16; BYA 2, 3; CA 13-16R,
   139; CANR 6, 22, 47, 61; CDALBS; CLR
   6, 56; CWRI 5; DLB 312; JRDA; MAI-
   CYA 1, 2; MTCW 1, 2; MTFW 2005;
   NFS 26; SAAS 1; SATA 1, 53; SATA-Obit
   72; SSFS 31
Udall, Nicholas 1504-1556 .... **LC 84**
   See also DLB 62; RGEL 2
Ueda Akinari 1734-1809 .... **NCLC 131**
Uhry, Alfred 1936- .... **CLC 55; DC 28**
   See also CA 127, 133; CAD; CANR 112;
   CD 5, 6; CSW; DA3; DAM DRAM, POP;
   DFS 11, 15; INT CA-133; MTFW 2005
Ulf, Haerved
   See Strindberg, August
Ulf, Harved
   See Strindberg, August
Ulibarri, Sabine R(eyes)
   1919-2003 .... **CLC 83; HLCS 2**
   See also CA 131, 214; CANR 81; DAM
   MULT; DLB 82; HW 1, 2; RGSF 2
Ulyanov, V. I.
   See Lenin
Ulyanov, Vladimir Ilyich
   See Lenin
Ulyanov-Lenin
   See Lenin
Unamuno, Miguel de 1864-1936 .... **HLC 2;
   SSC 11, 69; TCLC 2, 9, 148, 237**
   See also CA 104, 131; CANR 81; DAM
   MULT, NOV; DLB 108, 322; EW 8; EWL
   3; HW 1, 2; MTCW 1, 2; MTFW 2005;
   RGSF 2; RGWL 2, 3; SSFS 20; TWA
Unamuno y Jugo, Miguel de
   See Unamuno, Miguel de
Uncle Shelby
   See Silverstein, Shel
Undercliffe, Errol
   See Campbell, Ramsey

Underwood, Miles
   See Glassco, John
Undset, Sigrid 1882-1949 .... **TCLC 3, 197;
   WLC 6**
   See also AAYA 77; CA 104, 129; DA; DA3;
   DAB; DAC; DAM MST, NOV; DLB 293,
   332; EW 9; EWL 3; FW; MTCW 1, 2;
   MTFW 2005; RGWL 2, 3
Ungaretti, Giuseppe 1888-1970 ... **CLC 7, 11,
   15; PC 57; TCLC 200**
   See also CA 19-20, 25-28R; CAP 2; DLB
   114; EW 10; EWL 3; PFS 20; RGWL 2,
   3; WLIT 7
Unger, Douglas 1952- .... **CLC 34**
   See also CA 130; CANR 94, 155
Unsworth, Barry 1930- .... **CLC 76, 127**
   See also BRWS 7; CA 25-28R; CANR 30,
   54, 125, 171, 202; CN 6, 7; DLB 194,
   326
Unsworth, Barry Forster
   See Unsworth, Barry
Updike, John 1932-2009 .... **CLC 1, 2, 3, 5, 7,
   9, 13, 15, 23, 34, 43, 70, 139, 214, 278;
   PC 90; SSC 13, 27, 103; WLC 6**
   See also AAYA 36; AMW; AMWC 1;
   AMWR 1; BPFB 3; BYA 12; CA 1-4R,
   282; CABS 1; CANR 4, 33, 51, 94, 133,
   197; CDALB 1968-1988; CN 1, 2, 3, 4,
   5, 6, 7; CP 1, 2, 3, 4, 5, 6, 7; CPW 1;
   DA; DA3; DAB; DAC; DAM MST, NOV,
   POET, POP; DLB 2, 5, 143, 218, 227;
   DLBD 3; DLBY 1980, 1982, 1997; EWL
   3; EXPP; HGG; MAL 5; MTCW 1, 2;
   MTFW 2005; NFS 12, 24; RGAL 4;
   RGSF 2; SSFS 3, 19; TUS
Updike, John Hoyer
   See Updike, John
Upshaw, Margaret Mitchell
   See Mitchell, Margaret
Upton, Mark
   See Sanders, Lawrence
Upward, Allen 1863-1926 .... **TCLC 85**
   See also CA 117, 187; DLB 36
Urdang, Constance (Henriette)
   1922-1996 .... **CLC 47**
   See also CA 21-24R; CANR 9, 24; CP 1, 2,
   3, 4, 5, 6; CWP
Urfe, Honore d' 1567(?)-1625 .... **LC 132**
   See also DLB 268; GFL Beginnings to
   1789; RGWL 2, 3
Uriel, Henry
   See Faust, Frederick
Uris, Leon 1924-2003 .... **CLC 7, 32**
   See also AITN 1, 2; AMWS 20; BEST 89:2;
   BPFB 3; CA 1-4R, 217; CANR 1, 40, 65,
   123; CN 1, 2, 3, 4, 5, 6; CPW 1; DA3;
   DAM NOV, POP; MTCW 1, 2; MTFW
   2005; RGHL; SATA 49; SATA-Obit 146
Urista, Alberto 1947- .... **HLCS 1; PC 34**
   See also CA 45-48R; CANR 2, 32; DLB
   82; HW 1; LLW
Urista Heredia, Alberto Baltazar
   See Urista, Alberto
Urmuz
   See Codrescu, Andrei
Urquhart, Guy
   See McAlmon, Robert (Menzies)
Urquhart, Jane 1949- .... **CLC 90, 242**
   See also CA 113; CANR 32, 68, 116, 157;
   CCA 1; DAC; DLB 334
Usigli, Rodolfo 1905-1979 .... **HLCS 1**
   See also CA 131; DLB 305; EWL 3; HW 1;
   LAW
Usk, Thomas (?)-1388 .... **CMLC 76**
   See also DLB 146

Ustinov, Peter (Alexander)
1921-2004 .... **CLC 1**
See also AITN 1; CA 13-16R, 225; CANR
25, 51; CBD; CD 5, 6; DLB 13; MTCW
2

U Tam'si, Gerald Felix Tchicaya
See Tchicaya, Gerald Felix

U Tam'si, Tchicaya
See Tchicaya, Gerald Felix

Vachss, Andrew 1942- .... **CLC 106**
See also CA 118, 214; CAAE 214; CANR
44, 95, 153, 197; CMW 4

Vachss, Andrew H.
See Vachss, Andrew

Vachss, Andrew Henry
See Vachss, Andrew

Vaculik, Ludvik 1926- .... **CLC 7**
See also CA 53-56; CANR 72; CWW 2;
DLB 232; EWL 3

Vaihinger, Hans 1852-1933 .... **TCLC 71**
See also CA 116, 166

Valdez, Luis (Miguel) 1940- ..... **CLC 84; DC
10; HLC 2**
See also CA 101; CAD; CANR 32, 81; CD
5, 6; DAM MULT; DFS 5; DLB 122;
EWL 3; HW 1; LAIT 4; LLW

Valenzuela, Luisa 1938- .... **CLC 31, 104;
HLCS 2; SSC 14, 82**
See also CA 101; CANR 32, 65, 123; CD-
WLB 3; CWW 2; DAM MULT; DLB 113;
EWL 3; FW; HW 1, 2; LAW; RGSF 2;
RGWL 3; SSFS 29

Valera y Alcala-Galiano, Juan
1824-1905 .... **TCLC 10**
See also CA 106

Valerius Maximus CMLC 64
See also DLB 211

Valery, Ambroise Paul Toussaint Jules
See Valery, Paul

Valery, Paul 1871-1945 ... **PC 9; TCLC 4, 15,
231**
See also CA 104, 122; DA3; DAM POET;
DLB 258; EW 8; EWL 3; GFL 1789 to
the Present; MTCW 1, 2; MTFW 2005;
RGWL 2, 3; TWA

Valle-Inclan, Ramon del 1866-1936 .. **HLC 2;
TCLC 5, 228**
See also CA 106, 153; CANR 80; DAM
MULT; DLB 134, 322; EW 8; EWL 3;
HW 2; RGSF 2; RGWL 2, 3

Valle-Inclan, Ramon Maria del
See Valle-Inclan, Ramon del

Vallejo, Antonio Buero
See Buero Vallejo, Antonio

Vallejo, Cesar 1892-1938 ... **HLC 2; TCLC 3,
56**
See also CA 105, 153; DAM MULT; DLB
290; EWL 3; HW 1; LAW; PFS 26;
RGWL 2, 3

Vallejo, Cesar Abraham
See Vallejo, Cesar

Valles, Jules 1832-1885 .... **NCLC 71**
See also DLB 123; GFL 1789 to the Present

Vallette, Marguerite Eymery
1860-1953 .... **TCLC 67**
See also CA 182; DLB 123, 192; EWL 3

Valle Y Pena, Ramon del
See Valle-Inclan, Ramon del

Van Ash, Cay 1918-1994 .... **CLC 34**
See also CA 220

Vanbrugh, Sir John 1664-1726 ... **DC 40; LC
21**
See also BRW 2; DAM DRAM; DLB 80;
IDTP; RGEL 2

Van Campen, Karl
See Campbell, John W(ood, Jr.)

Vance, Gerald
See Silverberg, Robert

Vance, Jack 1916- .... **CLC 35**
See also CA 29-32R; CANR 17, 65, 154;
CMW 4; DLB 8; FANT; MTCW 1; SCFW
1, 2; SFW 4; SUFW 1, 2

Vance, John Holbrook
See Vance, Jack

**Van Den Bogarde, Derek Jules Gaspard
Ulric Niven** 1921-1999 .... **CLC 14**
See also CA 77-80, 179; DLB 14

Vandenburgh, Jane CLC 59
See also CA 168; CANR 208

Vanderhaeghe, Guy 1951- .... **CLC 41**
See also BPFB 3; CA 113; CANR 72, 145;
CN 7; DLB 334

van der Post, Laurens (Jan)
1906-1996 .... **CLC 5**
See also AFW; CA 5-8R, 155; CANR 35;
CN 1, 2, 3, 4, 5, 6; DLB 204; RGEL 2

van de Wetering, Janwillem
1931-2008 .... **CLC 47**
See also CA 49-52, 274; CANR 4, 62, 90;
CMW 4

Van Dine, S. S.
See Wright, Willard Huntington

Van Doren, Carl (Clinton)
1885-1950 .... **TCLC 18**
See also CA 111, 168

Van Doren, Mark 1894-1972 .... **CLC 6, 10**
See also CA 1-4R, 37-40R; CANR 3; CN
1; CP 1; DLB 45, 284, 335; MAL 5;
MTCW 1, 2; RGAL 4

Van Druten, John (William)
1901-1957 .... **TCLC 2**
See also CA 104, 161; DLB 10; MAL 5;
RGAL 4

Van Duyn, Mona 1921-2004 .... **CLC 3, 7, 63,
116**
See also CA 9-12R, 234; CANR 7, 38, 60,
116; CP 1, 2, 3, 4, 5, 6, 7; CWP; DAM
POET; DLB 5; MAL 5; MTFW 2005;
PFS 20

Van Dyne, Edith
See Baum, L. Frank

van Herk, Aritha 1954- .... **CLC 249**
See also CA 101; CANR 94; DLB 334

van Itallie, Jean-Claude 1936- .... **CLC 3**
See also CA 45-48; CAAS 2; CAD; CANR
1, 48; CD 5, 6; DLB 7

Van Loot, Cornelius Obenchain
See Roberts, Kenneth (Lewis)

van Ostaijen, Paul 1896-1928 .... **TCLC 33**
See also CA 163

Van Peebles, Melvin 1932- .... **CLC 2, 20**
See also BW 2, 3; CA 85-88; CANR 27,
67, 82; DAM MULT

van Schendel, Arthur(-Francois-Emile)
1874-1946 .... **TCLC 56**
See also EWL 3

Van See, John
See Vance, Jack

Vansittart, Peter 1920-2008 .... **CLC 42**
See also CA 1-4R, 278; CANR 3, 49, 90;
CN 4, 5, 6, 7; RHW

Van Vechten, Carl 1880-1964 ... **CLC 33; HR
1:3**
See also AMWS 2; CA 183, 89-92; DLB 4,
9, 51; RGAL 4

van Vogt, A(lfred) E(lton) 1912-2000 . **CLC 1**
See also BPFB 3; BYA 13, 14; CA 21-24R,
190; CANR 28; DLB 8, 251; SATA 14;
SATA-Obit 124; SCFW 1, 2; SFW 4

Vara, Madeleine
See Jackson, Laura

Varda, Agnes 1928- .... **CLC 16**
See also CA 116, 122

Vargas Llosa, Jorge Mario Pedro
See Vargas Llosa, Mario

Vargas Llosa, Mario 1936- .. **CLC 3, 6, 9, 10,
15, 31, 42, 85, 181; HLC 2**
See also BPFB 3; CA 73-76; CANR 18, 32,
42, 67, 116, 140, 173; CDWLB 3; CWW
2; DA; DA3; DAB; DAC; DAM MST,
MULT, NOV; DLB 145; DNFS 2; EWL
3; HW 1, 2; LAIT 5; LATS 1:2; LAW;
LAWS 1; MTCW 1, 2; MTFW 2005;
RGWL 2, 3; SSFS 14; TWA; WLIT 1

Varnhagen von Ense, Rahel
1771-1833 .... **NCLC 130**
See also DLB 90

Vasari, Giorgio 1511-1574 .... **LC 114**

Vasilikos, Vasiles
See Vassilikos, Vassilis

Vasiliu, Gheorghe
See Bacovia, George

Vassa, Gustavus
See Equiano, Olaudah

Vassilikos, Vassilis 1933- .... **CLC 4, 8**
See also CA 81-84; CANR 75, 149; EWL 3

Vaughan, Henry 1621-1695 .... **LC 27; PC 81**
See also BRW 2; DLB 131; PAB; RGEL 2

Vaughn, Stephanie CLC 62

Vazov, Ivan (Minchov) 1850-1921 . **TCLC 25**
See also CA 121, 167; CDWLB 4; DLB 147

Veblen, Thorstein B(unde)
1857-1929 .... **TCLC 31**
See also AMWS 1; CA 115, 165; DLB 246;
MAL 5

Vega, Lope de 1562-1635 ... **HLCS 2; LC 23,
119**
See also EW 2; RGWL 2, 3

Veldeke, Heinrich von c. 1145-c.
1190 .... **CMLC 85**

Vendler, Helen 1933- .... **CLC 138**
See also CA 41-44R; CANR 25, 72, 136,
190; MTCW 1, 2; MTFW 2005

Vendler, Helen Hennessy
See Vendler, Helen

Venison, Alfred
See Pound, Ezra

Ventsel, Elena Sergeevna
1907-2002 .... **CLC 59**
See also CA 154; CWW 2; DLB 302

Venttsel', Elena Sergeevna
See Ventsel, Elena Sergeevna

Verdi, Marie de
See Mencken, H. L.

Verdu, Matilde
See Cela, Camilo Jose

Verga, Giovanni (Carmelo)
1840-1922 ..... **SSC 21, 87; TCLC 3, 227**
See also CA 104, 123; CANR 101; EW 7;
EWL 3; RGSF 2; RGWL 2, 3; WLIT 7

Vergil 70B.C.-19B.C. .. **CMLC 9, 40, 101; PC
12; WLCS**
See also AW 2; CDWLB 1; DA; DA3;
DAB; DAC; DAM MST, POET; DLB
211; EFS 1; LAIT 1; LMFS 1; RGWL 2,
3; WLIT 8; WP

Vergil, Polydore c. 1470-1555 .... **LC 108**
See also DLB 132

Verhaeren, Emile (Adolphe Gustave)
1855-1916 .... **TCLC 12**
See also CA 109; EWL 3; GFL 1789 to the
Present

Verlaine, Paul 1844-1896 .. **NCLC 2, 51, 230;
PC 2, 32**
See also DAM POET; DLB 217; EW 7;
GFL 1789 to the Present; LMFS 2; RGWL
2, 3; TWA

Verlaine, Paul Marie
See Verlaine, Paul

Verne, Jules 1828-1905 .... **TCLC 6, 52**
See also AAYA 16; BYA 4; CA 110, 131;
CLR 88; DA3; DLB 123; GFL 1789 to
the Present; JRDA; LAIT 2; LMFS 2;
MAICYA 1, 2; MTFW 2005; NFS 30, 34;
RGWL 2, 3; SATA 21; SCFW 1, 2; SFW
4; TWA; WCH

Verne, Jules Gabriel
See Verne, Jules

Verus, Marcus Annius
See Aurelius, Marcus

Very, Jones 1813-1880 .... **NCLC 9; PC 86**
See also DLB 1, 243; RGAL 4

Very, Rev. C.
See Crowley, Edward Alexander

Vesaas, Tarjei 1897-1970 .... **CLC 48**
See also CA 190, 29-32R; DLB 297; EW
11; EWL 3; RGWL 3

Vialis, Gaston
See Simenon, Georges

Vian, Boris 1920-1959(?) .... **TCLC 9**
See also CA 106, 164; CANR 111; DLB
72, 321; EWL 3; GFL 1789 to the Present;
MTCW 2; RGWL 2, 3

Viator, Vacuus
See Hughes, Thomas

Viaud, Julien 1850-1923 .... **TCLC 11, 239**
See also CA 107; DLB 123; GFL 1789 to
the Present

Viaud, Louis Marie Julien
See Viaud, Julien

Vicar, Henry
See Felsen, Henry Gregor

Vicente, Gil 1465-c. 1536 .... **LC 99**
See also DLB 318; IDTP; RGWL 2, 3

Vicker, Angus
See Felsen, Henry Gregor

Vico, Giambattista
See Vico, Giovanni Battista

Vico, Giovanni Battista 1668-1744 .... **LC 138**
See also EW 3; WLIT 7

Vidal, Eugene Luther Gore
See Vidal, Gore

Vidal, Gore 1925- ...... **CLC 2, 4, 6, 8, 10, 22,
33, 72, 142, 289**
See also AAYA 64; AITN 1; AMWS 4;
BEST 90:2; BPFB 3; CA 5-8R; CAD;
CANR 13, 45, 65, 100, 132, 167; CD 5,
6; CDALBS; CN 1, 2, 3, 4, 5, 6, 7; CPW;
DA3; DAM NOV, POP; DFS 2; DLB 6,
152; EWL 3; GLL 1; INT CANR-13;
MAL 5; MTCW 1, 2; MTFW 2005;
RGAL 4; RHW; TUS

Viereck, Peter 1916-2006 .... **CLC 4; PC 27**
See also CA 1-4R, 250; CANR 1, 47; CP 1,
2, 3, 4, 5, 6, 7; DLB 5; MAL 5; PFS 9,
14

Viereck, Peter Robert Edwin
See Viereck, Peter

Vigny, Alfred de 1797-1863 .... **NCLC 7, 102;
PC 26**
See also DAM POET; DLB 119, 192, 217;
EW 5; GFL 1789 to the Present; RGWL
2, 3

Vigny, Alfred Victor de
See Vigny, Alfred de

Vilakazi, Benedict Wallet
1906-1947 .... **TCLC 37**
See also CA 168

Vile, Curt
See Moore, Alan

Villa, Jose Garcia 1914-1997 ... **AAL; PC 22;
TCLC 176**
See also CA 25-28R; CANR 12, 118; CP 1,
2, 3, 4; DLB 312; EWL 3; EXPP

Villard, Oswald Garrison
1872-1949 .... **TCLC 160**
See also CA 113, 162; DLB 25, 91

Villarreal, Jose Antonio 1924- .... **HLC 2**
See also CA 133; CANR 93; DAM MULT;
DLB 82; HW 1; LAIT 4; RGAL 4

Villaurrutia, Xavier 1903-1950 ...... **TCLC 80**
See also CA 192; EWL 3; HW 1; LAW

Villaverde, Cirilo 1812-1894 .... **NCLC 121**
See also LAW

Villehardouin, Geoffroi de
1150(?)-1218(?) .... **CMLC 38**

Villiers, George 1628-1687 .... **LC 107**
See also DLB 80; RGEL 2

**Villiers de l'Isle Adam, Jean Marie Mathias
Philippe Auguste** 1838-1889 ... **NCLC 3;
SSC 14**
See also DLB 123, 192; GFL 1789 to the
Present; RGSF 2

Villon, Francois 1431-1463(?) .... **LC 62, 166;
PC 13**
See also DLB 208; EW 2; RGWL 2, 3;
TWA

Vine, Barbara
See Rendell, Ruth

Vinge, Joan (Carol) D(ennison)
1948- .... **CLC 30; SSC 24**
See also AAYA 32; BPFB 3; CA 93-96;
CANR 72; SATA 36, 113; SFW 4; YAW

Viola, Herman J(oseph) 1938- .... **CLC 70**
See also CA 61-64; CANR 8, 23, 48, 91;
SATA 126

Violis, G.
See Simenon, Georges

Viramontes, Helena Maria 1954- .... **HLCS 2**
See also CA 159; CANR 182; CLR 285;
DLB 122, 350; HW 2; LLW

Virgil
See Vergil

Visconti, Luchino 1906-1976 .... **CLC 16**
See also CA 81-84, 65-68; CANR 39

Vitry, Jacques de
See Jacques de Vitry

Vittorini, Elio 1908-1966 .... **CLC 6, 9, 14**
See also CA 133, 25-28R; DLB 264; EW
12; EWL 3; RGWL 2, 3

Vivekananda, Swami 1863-1902 .... **TCLC 88**

Vives, Juan Luis 1493-1540 .... **LC 170**
See also DLB 318

Vizenor, Gerald Robert 1934- .... **CLC 103,
263; NNAL**
See also CA 13-16R, 205; CAAE 205;
CAAS 22; CANR 5, 21, 44, 67; DAM
MULT; DLB 175, 227; MTCW 2; MTFW
2005; TCWW 2

Vizinczey, Stephen 1933- .... **CLC 40**
See also CA 128; CCA 1; INT CA-128

Vliet, R(ussell) G(ordon)
1929-1984 .... **CLC 22**
See also CA 37-40R, 112; CANR 18; CP 2,
3

Vogau, Boris Andreevich
See Vogau, Boris Andreyevich

Vogau, Boris Andreyevich
1894-1938 .... **SSC 48; TCLC 23**
See also CA 123, 218; DLB 272; EWL 3;
RGSF 2; RGWL 2, 3

Vogel, Paula A. 1951- .. **CLC 76, 290; DC 19**
See also CA 108; CAD; CANR 119, 140;
CD 5, 6; CWD; DFS 14; DLB 341;
MTFW 2005; RGAL 4

Vogel, Paula Anne
See Vogel, Paula A.

Voigt, Cynthia 1942- .... **CLC 30**
See also AAYA 3, 30; BYA 1, 3, 6, 7, 8;
CA 106; CANR 18, 37, 40, 94, 145; CLR
13, 48, 141; INT CANR-18; JRDA; LAIT
5; MAICYA 1, 2; MAICYAS 1; MTFW
2005; SATA 48, 79, 116, 160; SATA-Brief
33; WYA; YAW

Voigt, Ellen Bryant 1943- .... **CLC 54**
See also CA 69-72; CANR 11, 29, 55, 115,
171; CP 5, 6, 7; CSW; CWP; DLB 120;
PFS 23, 33

Voinovich, Vladimir 1932- .. **CLC 10, 49, 147**
See also CA 81-84; CAAS 12; CANR 33,
67, 150; CWW 2; DLB 302; MTCW 1

Voinovich, Vladimir Nikolaevich
See Voinovich, Vladimir

Vollmann, William T. 1959- ...... **CLC 89, 227**
See also AMWS 17; CA 134; CANR 67,
116, 185; CN 7; CPW; DA3; DAM NOV,
POP; DLB 350; MTCW 2; MTFW 2005

Voloshinov, V. N.
See Bakhtin, Mikhail Mikhailovich

Voltaire 1694-1778 .. **LC 14, 79, 110; SSC 12,
112; WLC 6**
See also BYA 13; DA; DA3; DAB; DAC;
DAM DRAM, MST; DLB 314; EW 4;
GFL Beginnings to 1789; LATS 1:1;
LMFS 1; NFS 7; RGWL 2, 3; TWA

von Aschendrof, Baron Ignatz
See Ford, Ford Madox

von Chamisso, Adelbert
See Chamisso, Adelbert von

von Daeniken, Erich 1935- .... **CLC 30**
See also AITN 1; CA 37-40R; CANR 17,
44

von Daniken, Erich
See von Daeniken, Erich

von Eschenbach, Wolfram c. 1170-c.
1220 .... **CMLC 5**
See also CDWLB 2; DLB 138; EW 1;
RGWL 2, 3

von Hartmann, Eduard
1842-1906 .... **TCLC 96**

von Hayek, Friedrich August
See Hayek, F(riedrich) A(ugust von)

von Heidenstam, (Carl Gustaf) Verner
See Heidenstam, (Carl Gustaf) Verner von

von Heyse, Paul (Johann Ludwig)
See Heyse, Paul (Johann Ludwig von)

von Hofmannsthal, Hugo
See Hofmannsthal, Hugo von

von Horvath, Odon
See von Horvath, Odon

von Horvath, Odon
See von Horvath, Odon

von Horvath, Odon 1901-1938 .... **TCLC 45**
See also CA 118, 184, 194; DLB 85, 124;
RGWL 2, 3

von Horvath, Oedoen
See von Horvath, Odon

von Kleist, Heinrich
See Kleist, Heinrich von

Vonnegut, Kurt, Jr.
See Vonnegut, Kurt

Vonnegut, Kurt 1922-2007 .... **CLC 1, 2, 3, 4,
5, 8, 12, 22, 40, 60, 111, 212, 254; SSC
8; WLC 6**
See also AAYA 6, 44; AITN 1; AMWS 2;
BEST 90:4; BPFB 3; BYA 3, 14; CA
1-4R, 259; CANR 1, 25, 49, 75, 92, 207;
CDALB 1968-1988; CN 1, 2, 3, 4, 5, 6,
7; CPW 1; DA; DA3; DAB; DAC; DAM
MST, NOV, POP; DLB 2, 8, 152; DLBD
3; DLBY 1980; EWL 3; EXPN; EXPS;
LAIT 4; LMFS 2; MAL 5; MTCW 1, 2;
MTFW 2005; NFS 3, 28; RGAL 4;
SCFW; SFW 4; SSFS 5; TUS; YAW

Von Rachen, Kurt
See Hubbard, L. Ron

von Sternberg, Josef
See Sternberg, Josef von

Vorster, Gordon 1924- .... **CLC 34**
See also CA 133

Vosce, Trudie
See Ozick, Cynthia

Witkiewicz, Stanislaw Ignacy
1885-1939 .... **TCLC 8, 237**
See also CA 105, 162; CDWLB 4; DLB
215; EW 10; EWL 3; RGWL 2, 3; SFW 4

Wittgenstein, Ludwig (Josef Johann)
1889-1951 .... **TCLC 59**
See also CA 113, 164; DLB 262; MTCW 2

Wittig, Monique 1935-2003 .... **CLC 22**
See also CA 116, 135, 212; CANR 143;
CWW 2; DLB 83; EWL 3; FW; GLL 1

Wittlin, Jozef 1896-1976 .... **CLC 25**
See also CA 49-52, 65-68; CANR 3; EWL
3

Wodehouse, P. G. 1881-1975 ..... **CLC 1, 2, 5,
10, 22; SSC 2, 115; TCLC 108**
See also AAYA 65; AITN 2; BRWS 3; CA
45-48, 57-60; CANR 3, 33; CDBLB
1914-1945; CN 1, 2; CPW 1; DA3; DAB;
DAC; DAM NOV; DLB 34, 162, 352;
EWL 3; MTCW 1, 2; MTFW 2005; RGEL
2; RGSF 2; SATA 22; SSFS 10

Wodehouse, Pelham Grenville
See Wodehouse, P. G.

Woiwode, L.
See Woiwode, Larry

Woiwode, Larry 1941- .... **CLC 6, 10**
See also CA 73-76; CANR 16, 94, 192; CN
3, 4, 5, 6, 7; DLB 6; INT CANR-16

Woiwode, Larry Alfred
See Woiwode, Larry

Wojciechowska, Maia (Teresa)
1927-2002 .... **CLC 26**
See also AAYA 8, 46; BYA 3; CA 9-12R,
183, 209; CAAE 183; CANR 4, 41; CLR
1; JRDA; MAICYA 1, 2; SAAS 1; SATA
1, 28, 83; SATA-Essay 104; SATA-Obit
134; YAW

Wojtyla, Karol (Jozef)
See John Paul II, Pope

Wojtyla, Karol (Josef)
See John Paul II, Pope

Wolf, Christa 1929- ...... **CLC 14, 29, 58, 150,
261**
See also CA 85-88; CANR 45, 123; CD-
WLB 2; CWW 2; DLB 75; EWL 3; FW;
MTCW 1; RGWL 2, 3; SSFS 14

Wolf, Naomi 1962- .... **CLC 157**
See also CA 141; CANR 110; FW; MTFW
2005

Wolfe, Gene 1931- .... **CLC 25**
See also AAYA 35; CA 57-60; CAAS 9;
CANR 6, 32, 60, 152, 197; CPW; DAM
POP; DLB 8; FANT; MTCW 2; MTFW
2005; SATA 118, 165; SCFW 2; SFW 4;
SUFW 2

Wolfe, Gene Rodman
See Wolfe, Gene

Wolfe, George C. 1954- .... **BLCS; CLC 49**
See also CA 149; CAD; CD 5, 6

Wolfe, Thomas 1900-1938 .... **SSC 33, 113;
TCLC 4, 13, 29, 61; WLC 6**
See also AMW; BPFB 3; CA 104, 132;
CANR 102; CDALB 1929-1941; DA;
DA3; DAB; DAC; DAM MST, NOV;
DLB 9, 102, 229; DLBD 2, 16; DLBY
1985, 1997; EWL 3; MAL 5; MTCW 1,
2; NFS 18; RGAL 4; SSFS 18; TUS

Wolfe, Thomas Clayton
See Wolfe, Thomas

Wolfe, Thomas Kennerly
See Wolfe, Tom, Jr.

Wolfe, Tom, Jr. 1931- .... **CLC 1, 2, 9, 15, 35,
51, 147**
See also AAYA 8, 67; AITN 2; AMWS 3;
BEST 89:1; BPFB 3; CA 13-16R; CANR
9, 33, 70, 104; CN 5, 6, 7; CPW; CSW;
DA3; DAM POP; DLB 152, 185 185;
EWL 3; INT CANR-9; LAIT 5; MTCW
1, 2; MTFW 2005; RGAL 4; TUS

Wolff, Geoffrey 1937- .... **CLC 41**
See also CA 29-32R; CANR 29, 43, 78, 154

Wolff, Geoffrey Ansell
See Wolff, Geoffrey

Wolff, Sonia
See Levitin, Sonia

Wolff, Tobias 1945- .... **CLC 39, 64, 172; SSC
63, 136**
See also AAYA 16; AMWS 7; BEST 90:2;
BYA 12; CA 114, 117; CAAS 22; CANR
54, 76, 96, 192; CN 5, 6, 7; CSW; DA3;
DLB 130; EWL 3; INT CA-117; MTCW
2; MTFW 2005; RGAL 4; RGSF 2; SSFS
4, 11

Wolff, Tobias Jonathan Ansell
See Wolff, Tobias

Wolitzer, Hilma 1930- .... **CLC 17**
See also CA 65-68; CANR 18, 40, 172; INT
CANR-18; SATA 31; YAW

Wollstonecraft, Mary 1759-1797 .... **LC 5, 50,
90, 147**
See also BRWS 3; CDBLB 1789-1832;
DLB 39, 104, 158, 252; FL 1:1; FW;
LAIT 1; RGEL 2; TEA; WLIT 3

Wonder, Stevie 1950- .... **CLC 12**
See also CA 111

Wong, Jade Snow 1922-2006 .... **CLC 17**
See also CA 109, 249; CANR 91; SATA
112; SATA-Obit 175

Wood, Ellen Price
See Wood, Mrs. Henry

Wood, Mrs. Henry 1814-1887 ...... **NCLC 178**
See also CMW 4; DLB 18; SUFW

Wood, James 1965- .... **CLC 238**
See also CA 235

Woodberry, George Edward
1855-1930 .... **TCLC 73**
See also CA 165; DLB 71, 103

Woodcott, Keith
See Brunner, John (Kilian Houston)

Woodruff, Robert W.
See Mencken, H. L.

Woodward, Bob 1943- .... **CLC 240**
See also CA 69-72; CANR 31, 67, 107, 176;
MTCW 1

Woodward, Robert Upshur
See Woodward, Bob

Woolf, Adeline Virginia
See Woolf, Virginia

Woolf, Virginia 1882-1941 .... **SSC 7, 79;
TCLC 1, 5, 20, 43, 56, 101, 123, 128;
WLC 6**
See also AAYA 44; BPFB 3; BRW 7;
BRWC 2; BRWR 1; CA 104, 130; CANR
64, 132; CDBLB 1914-1945; DA; DA3;
DAB; DAC; DAM MST, NOV; DLB 36,
100, 162; DLBD 10; EWL 3; EXPS; FL
1:6; FW; LAIT 3; LATS 1:1; LMFS 2;
MTCW 1, 2; MTFW 2005; NCFS 2; NFS
8, 12, 28; RGEL 2; RGSF 2; SSFS 4, 12;
TEA; WLIT 4

Woollcott, Alexander (Humphreys)
1887-1943 .... **TCLC 5**
See also CA 105, 161; DLB 29

Woolman, John 1720-1772 .... **LC 155**
See also DLB 31

Woolrich, Cornell
See Hopley-Woolrich, Cornell George

Woolson, Constance Fenimore
1840-1894 .... **NCLC 82; SSC 90**
See also DLB 12, 74, 189, 221; RGAL 4

Wordsworth, Dorothy 1771-1855 . **NCLC 25,
138**
See also DLB 107

Wordsworth, William 1770-1850 .. **NCLC 12,
38, 111, 166, 206; PC 4, 67; WLC 6**
See also AAYA 70; BRW 4; BRWC 1; CD-
BLB 1789-1832; DA; DA3; DAB; DAC;
DAM MST, POET; DLB 93, 107; EXPP;
LATS 1:1; LMFS 1; PAB; PFS 2, 33;
RGEL 2; TEA; WLIT 3; WP

Wotton, Sir Henry 1568-1639 .... **LC 68**
See also DLB 121; RGEL 2

Wouk, Herman 1915- .... **CLC 1, 9, 38**
See also BPFB 2, 3; CA 5-8R; CANR 6,
33, 67, 146; CDALBS; CN 1, 2, 3, 4, 5,
6; CPW; DA3; DAM NOV, POP; DLBY
1982; INT CANR-6; LAIT 4; MAL 5;
MTCW 1, 2; MTFW 2005; NFS 7; TUS

Wright, Charles 1932-2008 ... **BLC 1:3; CLC
49**
See also BW 1; CA 9-12R, 278; CANR 26;
CN 1, 2, 3, 4, 5, 6, 7; DAM MULT,
POET; DLB 33

Wright, Charles 1935- ... **CLC 6, 13, 28, 119,
146**
See also AMWS 5; CA 29-32R; CAAS 7;
CANR 23, 36, 62, 88, 135, 180; CP 3, 4,
5, 6, 7; DLB 165; DLBY 1982; EWL 3;
MTCW 1, 2; MTFW 2005; PFS 10, 35

Wright, Charles Penzel, Jr.
See Wright, Charles

Wright, Charles Stevenson
See Wright, Charles

Wright, Frances 1795-1852 .... **NCLC 74**
See also DLB 73

Wright, Frank Lloyd 1867-1959 .... **TCLC 95**
See also AAYA 33; CA 174

Wright, Harold Bell 1872-1944 .... **TCLC 183**
See also BPFB 3; CA 110; DLB 9; TCWW
2

Wright, Jack R.
See Harris, Mark

Wright, James (Arlington)
1927-1980 .... **CLC 3, 5, 10, 28; PC 36**
See also AITN 2; AMWS 3; CA 49-52, 97-
100; CANR 4, 34, 64; CDALBS; CP 1, 2;
DAM POET; DLB 5, 169, 342; EWL 3;
EXPP; MAL 5; MTCW 1, 2; MTFW
2005; PFS 7, 8; RGAL 4; TUS; WP

Wright, Judith 1915-2000 ... **CLC 11, 53; PC
14**
See also CA 13-16R, 188; CANR 31, 76,
93; CP 1, 2, 3, 4, 5, 6, 7; CWP; DLB 260;
EWL 3; MTCW 1, 2; MTFW 2005; PFS
8; RGEL 2; SATA 14; SATA-Obit 121

Wright, Judith Arundell
See Wright, Judith

Wright, L(aurali) R. 1939- .... **CLC 44**
See also CA 138; CMW 4

Wright, Richard 1908-1960 .. **BLC 1:3; CLC
1, 3, 4, 9, 14, 21, 48, 74; SSC 2, 109;
TCLC 136, 180; WLC 6**
See also AAYA 5, 42; AFAW 1, 2; AMW;
BPFB 3; BW 1; BYA 2; CA 108; CANR
64; CDALB 1929-1941; DA; DA3; DAB;
DAC; DAM MST, MULT, NOV; DLB 76,
102; DLBD 2; EWL 3; EXPN; LAIT 3,
4; MAL 5; MTCW 1, 2; MTFW 2005;
NCFS 1; NFS 1, 7; RGAL 4; RGSF 2;
SSFS 3, 9, 15, 20; TUS; YAW

Wright, Richard B. 1937- .... **CLC 6**
See also CA 85-88; CANR 120; DLB 53

Wright, Richard Bruce
See Wright, Richard B.

Wright, Richard Nathaniel
See Wright, Richard

Wright, Rick 1945- .... **CLC 35**

Wright, Rowland
See Wells, Carolyn

Wright, Stephen 1946- .... **CLC 33**
See also CA 237; DLB 350

Literary Criticism Series
Cumulative Topic Index

This index lists all topic entries in Gale's *Children's Literature Review* (CLR), *Classical and Medieval Literature Criticism* (CMLC), *Contemporary Literary Criticism* (CLC), *Drama Criticism* (DC), *Literature Criticism from 1400 to 1800* (LC), *Nineteenth-Century Literature Criticism* (NCLC), *Short Story Criticism* (SSC), and *Twentieth-Century Literary Criticism* (TCLC). The index also lists topic entries in the Gale Critical Companion Collection, which includes the following publications: *The Beat Generation* (BG), *Feminism in Literature* (FL), *Gothic Literature* (GL), and *Harlem Renaissance* (HR).

LITERARY CRITICISM SERIES

TCLC Cumulative Nationality Index

AMERICAN

Abbey, Edward **160**
Acker, Kathy **191**
Adams, Andy **56**
Adams, Brooks **80**
Adams, Henry (Brooks) **4, 52**
Addams, Jane **76**
Agee, James (Rufus) **1, 19, 180**
Aldrich, Bess (Genevra) Streeter **125**
Allen, Fred **87**
Anderson, Maxwell **2, 144**
Anderson, Sherwood **1, 10, 24, 123**
Anthony, Susan B(rownell) **84**
Arendt, Hannah **193**
Arnow, Harriette **196**
Atherton, Gertrude (Franklin Horn) **2**
Auden, W(ystan) H(ugh) **223**
Austin, Mary (Hunter) **25**
Baker, Ray Stannard **47**
Baker, Carlos (Heard) **119**
Baldwin, James **229**
Bambara, Toni Cade **116**
Barnes, Djuna **212**
Barry, Philip **11**
Baum, L(yman) Frank **7, 132**
Beard, Charles A(ustin) **15**
Becker, Carl (Lotus) **63**
Belasco, David **3**
Bell, James Madison **43**
Benchley, Robert (Charles) **1, 55**
Benedict, Ruth (Fulton) **60**
Benét, Stephen Vincent **7**
Benét, William Rose **28**
Bettelheim, Bruno **143**
Bierce, Ambrose (Gwinett) **1, 7, 44**
Biggers, Earl Derr **65**
Bishop, Elizabeth **121**
Bishop, John Peale **103**
Black Elk **33**
Boas, Franz **56**
Bodenheim, Maxwell **44**
Bok, Edward W. **101**
Bonner, Marita **179**
Bourne, Randolph S(illiman) **16**
Bowles, Paul **209**
Boyd, James **115**
Boyd, Thomas (Alexander) **111**
Bradford, Gamaliel **36**
Brautigan, Richard **133**
Brennan, Christopher John **17**
Brennan, Maeve **124**
Brodkey, Harold (Roy) **123**
Brodsky, Joseph **219**
Bromfield, Louis (Brucker) **11**
Broun, Heywood **104**
Bryan, William Jennings **99**
Burroughs, Edgar Rice **2, 32**
Burroughs, William S(eward) **121**
Cabell, James Branch **6**
Cable, George Washington **4**
Cahan, Abraham **71**
Caldwell, Erskine (Preston) **117**

Campbell, Joseph **140**
Capote, Truman **164**
Cardozo, Benjamin N(athan) **65**
Carnegie, Dale **53**
Cather, Willa (Sibert) **1, 11, 31, 99, 132, 152**
Chambers, Robert W(illiam) **41**
Chambers, (David) Whittaker **129**
Chandler, Raymond (Thornton) **1, 7, 179**
Chapman, John Jay **7**
Chase, Mary Ellen **124**
Chesnutt, Charles W(addell) **5, 39**
Childress, Alice **116**
Chopin, Katherine **5, 14, 127, 199**
Cobb, Irvin S(hrewsbury) **77**
Coffin, Robert P(eter) Tristram **95**
Cohan, George M(ichael) **60**
Comstock, Anthony **13**
Cotter, Joseph Seamon Sr. **28**
Cram, Ralph Adams **45**
Crane, (Harold) Hart **2, 5, 80**
Crane, Stephen (Townley) **11, 17, 32, 216**
Crawford, F(rancis) Marion **10**
Crothers, Rachel **19**
Cullen, Countée **4, 37, 220**
Cummings, E. E. **137**
Dahlberg, Edward **208**
Darrow, Clarence (Seward) **81**
Davis, Rebecca (Blaine) Harding **6**
Davis, Richard Harding **24**
Day, Clarence (Shepard Jr.) **25**
Dent, Lester **72**
De Voto, Bernard (Augustine) **29**
Dewey, John **95**
Dickey, James **151**
Dixon, Thomas, Jr. **163**
di Donato, Pietro **159**
Dreiser, Theodore (Herman Albert) **10, 18, 35, 83**
Du Bois, W. E. B. **169**
Dulles, John Foster **72**
Dunbar, Paul Laurence **2, 12**
Duncan, Isadora **68**
Dunne, Finley Peter **28**
Eastman, Charles A(lexander) **55**
Eddy, Mary (Ann Morse) Baker **71**
Einstein, Albert **65**
Eliot, T.S. **236**
Erskine, John **84**
Farrell, James T. **228**
Faulkner, William **141**
Faust, Frederick (Schiller) **49**
Fenollosa, Ernest (Francisco) **91**
Fields, W. C. **80**
Fisher, Dorothy (Frances) Canfield **87**
Fisher, Rudolph **11**
Fisher, Vardis **140**
Fitzgerald, F(rancis) Scott (Key) **1, 6, 14, 28, 55, 157**
Fitzgerald, Zelda (Sayre) **52**
Fletcher, John Gould **35**
Foote, Mary Hallock **108**
Ford, Henry **73**
Forten, Charlotte L. **16**

Freeman, Douglas Southall **11**
Freeman, Mary E(leanor) Wilkins **9**
Frost, Robert **236**
Fuller, Henry Blake **103**
Futrelle, Jacques **19**
Gale, Zona **7**
Gardner, John **195**
Garland, (Hannibal) Hamlin **3**
Gibran, Kahlil **1, 9, 205**
Gilman, Charlotte (Anna) Perkins (Stetson) **9, 37, 117, 201**
Ginsberg, Allen **120**
Glasgow, Ellen (Anderson Gholson) **2, 7, 239**
Glaspell, Susan **55, 175**
Goldman, Emma **13**
Gordon, Caroline **241**
Green, Anna Katharine **63**
Grey, Zane **6**
Griffith, D(avid Lewelyn) W(ark) **68**
Griggs, Sutton (Elbert) **77**
Guest, Edgar A(lbert) **95**
Guiney, Louise Imogen **41**
Haley, Alex **147**
Hall, James Norman **23**
Hammett, Dashiell **187**
Handy, W(illiam) C(hristopher) **97**
Hansberry, Lorraine **192**
Harper, Frances Ellen Watkins **14, 217**
Harris, Joel Chandler **2**
Harte, (Francis) Bret(t) **1, 25**
Hartmann, Sadakichi **73**
Hatteras, Owen **18**
Hawthorne, Julian **25**
Hearn, (Patricio) Lafcadio (Tessima Carlos) **9**
Hecht, Ben **101**
Heller, Joseph **131, 151**
Hellman, Lillian (Florence) **119**
Hemingway, Ernest (Miller) **115, 203**
Henry, O. **1, 19**
Hergesheimer, Joseph **11**
Heyward, (Edwin) DuBose **59**
Higginson, Thomas Wentworth **36**
Himes, Chester **139**
Holley, Marietta **99**
Holly, Buddy **65**
Holmes, Oliver Wendell Jr. **77**
Hopkins, Pauline Elizabeth **28**
Horney, Karen (Clementine Theodore Danielsen) **71**
Howard, Robert E(rvin) **8**
Howe, Julia Ward **21**
Howells, William Dean **7, 17, 41**
Huneker, James Gibbons **65**
Hurston, Zora Neale **121, 131**
Ince, Thomas H. **89**
Isherwood, Christopher **227**
Jackson, Shirley **187**
James, Henry **2, 11, 24, 40, 47, 64, 171**
James, William **15, 32**
Jarrell, Randall **177**
Jewett, (Theodora) Sarah Orne **1, 22**
Johnson, James Weldon **3, 19, 175**

Nationality Index

TCLC-244 Title Index